ANTI-TERRORISM AND CRIMINAL ENFORCEMENT

Fourth Edition

■ ■ ■

By

Norman Abrams

Distinguished Professor of Law Emeritus
University of California, Los Angeles

AMERICAN CASEBOOK SERIES®

WEST®
A Thomson Reuters business

Mat #41097744

THIS BOOK IS DEDICATED
TO
HANNA AND SAM
AND
NAOMI AND BRIAN

PREFACE TO THE FOURTH EDITION

This new edition is a major revamping of the casebook, in order to make it a more effective teaching tool. The book has been reorganized, streamlined, shortened and reflects a dominant theme throughout: It highlights differences in the criminal law/procedure rules applied in civilian terrorism cases and those used in ordinary crime matters as well as in military commission processes. The book is now divided into two main parts; the first deals with enforcement issues in a civilian mode; the second, using military process. Some chapters have been omitted and new chapters added. Treatment of materials from the earlier editions has in many instances been modified to emphasize the dominant theme.

The chapter dealing with Anti-terrorism Legislative Packages, for example, has not been retained. While this chapter provided a useful historical perspective on the development of U.S. terrorism statutory law pre-and post-9/11, in the current edition, it would be a digression from the main theme of the book. Further, while this material provided useful background for the students, it did not lend itself to effective use in classroom teaching. For faculty who wish to make it available to their students, permission is hereby granted to adopters of the 4th edition to reproduce copies of Chapter 2 in the 3rd edition for use in the classroom.[1]

The separate chapter dealing with Bases for Expansive Executive Authority has also been omitted; material from that chapter is reflected at other points in the book. It was thought better to deal with the government's claims of expansive authority in the specific contexts in which they were raised, for example, the Department of Justice white paper supporting the executive branch's Terrorist Surveillance Program (TSP) (which included electronic eavesdropping by the NSA on conversations between persons in the U.S. and abroad). Further, the decision not to retain the chapter is supported by the fact that the more expansive claims of presidential authority by the Bush administration have been replaced by the Obama administration's seeming exclusive reliance on the Authorization to Use Military Force (AUMF) joint resolution passed by the Congress and the laws of war.

Chapters have been added that involve devoting more material to certain subjects than was reflected in earlier editions. Thus, a separate chapter has been added that highlights the government's methods for obtaining documents, records and other physical materials in terrorism investigations through search warrants (secretly issued and enforced) and through national security letters (the equivalent of an administrative subpoena). While there was material on these topics in previous editions, the treatment in this edition

---

1. If you wish to reproduce this chapter for your students and a copy of the third edition is not available to you, please contact the author, Norman Abrams, at abrams@law.ucla.edu is more focused, extensive and elevated in significance through placement in a separate chapter. Similarly, the subject of targeted killing is now treated in a separate chapter in the military mode portion of the book.

As mentioned above, the dominant theme of the book is to highlight the differences between terrorism enforcement and ordinary crime enforcement as well as between civilian and military terrorism enforcement. Thus in Part One, at the outset, terrorism legislation is addressed generally, with special attention to the definitions and uses of the terrorism concept as well as to what factors make particular crimes into terrorism offenses. The focus then shifts to the frequently-prosecuted and unique material support terrorism offenses. Part One then continues with various investigative methods typically used by the government in terrorism cases and the special rules that are applicable, comparing them, along the way, with ordinary crime investigative authority. Thus, a series of chapters cover proactive surveillance[2] (e.g. involving investigation in public assemblages or through publicly available sources), electronic surveillance, obtaining records and documents through search or subpoena, and obtaining information through interrogation, irregular[3] rendition (transferring persons apprehended abroad to the U.S. or a foreign country without legal process) and detaining individuals through the use of material witness authority or authority over aliens. Part One concludes with an examination of the classified information issues that frequently arise in civilian terrorism trials; in Part Two, the same subject is addressed in the military commission setting.

The second Part of the book contains four chapters: The first two deal with detention in military custody (the issues on this subject are diverse and complex), military commissions and the rules of procedure and evidence applicable therein and the crimes subject to prosecution before the commissions. Consideration of military commission rules of procedure and evidence provides an opportunity to compare them with the rules applied in civilian terrorism trials, and the materials are designed to facilitate such comparisons.

The last two chapters in this Part (the final Epilogue chapter stands by itself) deal with the difficult issues relating to targeted killing (essentially, another military mode method of dealing with terrorists), and the use of U.S. military forces on the domestic front and the Posse Comitatus Act.

While the book is designed primarily for use in teaching a specialized two or three unit advanced substantive and procedure criminal law course or seminar, the opportunity is also taken, wherever appropriate, to place the materials in the national setting of larger issues relating to enforcement against terrorism. Thus, for example, the materials include extended Notes dealing with topics such as the Obama Administration's Anti-terrorism Policies; Civil Suits challenging the Government's Enforcement Practices; and the Controversy surrounding the Proposed Closing of the Guantanamo Bay Facility. The book also includes some material on criminal charges brought by

---

   2. In the previous edition, this was termed "Political Surveillance."

   3. In the previous edition, this was termed "Extraordinary Rendition."

foreign governments against U.S. agents for irregular renditions perpetrated on foreign soil without permission from the foreign government.

The book consists of text, notes and questions, cases and statutory and administrative materials. Wherever practicable, original materials are utilized. In a few instances, some important statutes, for example, the Foreign Intelligence Surveillance Acts, the Classified Information Procedures Act and the Military Commissions Act are reproduced, somewhat edited, but nevertheless in quite lengthy form. This represents an author's judgment call: there are three principal options in presenting such material—1) reproduce it in the text in extenso; 2) edit the statutes severely; 3) place the extensive statutory material in an appendix, possibly with severely edited versions in the main text. The first option was chosen because the students benefit from seeing all or most of the statutory context. While the third option makes the same material available to the students, it is believed that the back and forth required between the main text and the appendix material is not conducive to efficient class discussion.

Finally, as would be expected, this new edition has been updated to include the latest Supreme Court and federal court cases, for example, review of the conviction of a lawyer for violating the material support in-aid-of-terrorist-activity statute (United States v. Stewart, 2009); a challenge to the constitutionality of the material support of-a-foreign-terrorist-organization statute (Holder v. Humanitarian Law Project, 2010); standing to challenge the constitutionality of a provision of the FISA Amendments Act of 2008 authorizing government electronic surveillance targeting non-US persons outside the United States in order to gather foreign intelligence (Amnesty International USA v. Clapper, 2011); the right of persons detained at Guantanamo to obtain habeas corpus (Boumediene v. Bush, 2008) and the right of detainees at Bagram Air Force Base in Afghanistan to obtain habeas corpus (Al–Maqaleh v. Gates, 2010); the right of an alleged wrongfully-detained material witness to obtain redress from high government officials (Ashcroft v. al-Kidd, 2011) and the standing of the father of a person targeted-to-be-killed to obtain due process for his son (Al–Aulaqi v. Obama, 2010). It also contains the latest terrorism-related statutes, for example, the FISA Amendments Act of 2008 and the Military Commissions Act of 2009; as well as Executive Orders issued by President Obama, for example, on Ensuring Lawful Interrogations, 2009, and on Periodic Review of Persons Detained at Guantanamo, 2011; and recently-promulgated internal governmental (unclassified) guidelines, for example, the FBI's Domestic Investigations and Operations Guide, 2008, and the FBI interrogation guidelines regarding Miranda warnings, 2010 (which only came to public attention in March, 2011).

I hope that those who use the book, both students and faculty, find it as fascinating a subject matter as I do. Comments are welcomed from those who use the book in their classes.

NORMAN ABRAMS

August 2011

Preface to the Third Edition

There is so much that is new in the content and organization of this book that it is fair to describe it as much more than simply an updating of the previous edition.

Thus, for example, chapters have been added or expanded in significant ways:

- A new chapter on Extraordinary Rendition and Interrogation/ Torture has been added, and the materials on those topics have been significantly expanded from the earlier edition.
- Government Secrecy has been elevated to chapter-level status and partnered in a single chapter with the Classified Information Procedures Act material.
- The Foreign Intelligence Surveillance Act chapter has been expanded through the addition of substantial material on the NSA eavesdropping and data mining controversies and through partnering it with the U.S. Agents Acting Abroad section.
- The coverage of the chapter that introduces the subject of the scope of Executive Authority has been expanded to include National Security and Inherent Presidential power as possible bases for the exercise of such authority.
- Most of the chapters have been expanded from what they were in the previous edition:
- The chapter on Enemy Combatant detentions has grown the most—by more than one third—reflecting the vast new material that has appeared since the previous edition. That chapter also now includes an in-depth treatment of the Padilla and al-Marri cases.
- Overall, the entire book has expanded by almost one third, reflecting the fact that new case law has been handed down in every subfield of anti-terrorism law, many new issues have arisen, much new scholarly literature has been published and numerous new statutes have been enacted.

There also has been some reorganization of the book:

- The Classified Information Procedures Act material dealing with the handling of such information in ordinary criminal trials, for example, has been moved forward in the book (from chapter 9 to chapter 6) so that it comes before, not after, the material on detention, deportation proceedings, the Combatant Status Review Tribunals, Administrative Review Tribunals and trials before Military Commissions. This move makes it possible for students to be able to compare the handling of classified information in ordinary federal criminal trials with the handling of such material in various kinds of terrorism-related adjudicatory proceedings.

- The Foreign Intelligence Surveillance Act chapter has been moved (from chapter 10 to chapter 7) so that it no longer follows but rather precedes the chapters dealing with detention and the various kinds of adjudicative special terrorism-related proceedings. Appearing just before the new chapter on Extraordinary Rendition and Interrogation/Torture, these two chapters together provide substantial coverage of the principal kinds of governmental enforcement practices utilized in pursuing and investigating terrorists.

While some material has been compressed and treated more briefly than in the previous edition—otherwise the size of the book would have gotten out of hand—the book contains a great many new cases. Examples include, in chapter 6, United States v. Paracha, a case similar to the final Moussaoui court of appeals case; in chapter 7, United States v. Ning Wen which addresses the issues raised by the significant purpose formula under FISA; in connection with the NSA controversy, American Civil Liberties Union v. National Security Agency, which, inter alia, addresses the meaning of the legal formula of "electronic surveillance" under FISA; in chapter 8, El-Masri v. United States, a civil suit by an alleged victim of extraordinary rendition; in chapter 9, civil law suits after-the-fact challenging 1) a material witness detention, Al-Kidd v. Gonzales and 2) immigration law detentions, Iqbal v. Hasty; in chapter 10, Bismullah v. Gates, dealing with the scope of what should be provided as the record on appeal from a CSRT hearing (petition for certiorari to the Supreme Court pending); also the court of appeals decision in Boumediene v. Bush, testing the congressional withdrawal of habeas jurisdiction in alien enemy combatant/detention cases (currently pending before the Supreme Court); also the various decisions in the Jose Padilla case, including the court of appeals decision in Padilla v. Hanft and the Supreme Court's disposition of Padilla's petition for certiorari; and finally, the court of appeals panel decision in al-Marri v. Wright (awaiting decision in en banc rehearing); and in chapter 11, the Supreme Court's decision in Hamdan v. Rumsfeld.

The book also contains significant new legislative or quasi-legislative materials excerpted or described, including the Protect America Act, the RESTORE Act legislative bill, the Detainee Treatment Act, the Military Commissions Act and the Manual for Military Commissions.

The terrorism-related legal literature has also been growing at a rapid rate, and an effort has been made in certain areas to provide citations and, at appropriate junctures, new excerpted material. In addition, the book includes some key statements made by government officials—for example, the President's and the Secretary of State's public statements regarding Extraordinary Rendition. Also included are excerpts, at relevant points, from the then-Attorney General-nominee Michael Mukasey's responses to questions regarding executive authority and the torture/waterboarding controversy.

As noted in the Preface to First Edition, this volume is appropriately viewed as a specialized federal criminal law casebook, containing unique substantive criminal law and criminal procedure/criminal law administration materials that arise out of a rapidly growing, and enormously important politically and socially relevant area of the law. It is intended primarily for use in a two unit advanced course to be taught in the second or third year of law school, but the book has expanded so much in coverage that it can easily now be used to teach a three unit course. It can also be used to teach a seminar, though the book has been designed primarily for being taught in a course on Anti-terrorism Law. An abridged version of the book is also available that can be used to supplement the first year Criminal Law course or to teach a seminar or a course or seminar at the undergraduate level.

NORMAN ABRAMS

May, 2008

Preface to the Second Edition

This new edition contains literally dozens of new cases and important items that have become available in the 22 months since the first edition appeared: The field continues to develop with extraordinary speed.

The organization and chapter development from the first edition—the book is divided into three principal parts—continues to make both logical and pedagogical sense, and the same choices regarding coverage, in the main, have been retained. In the natural evolution of the subject, some topics have been added or expanded. For example, the very limited amount of material in the first edition on the subject of torture and interrogation has been increased. Similarly, the availability of extensive new material on enemy combatant status now warrants treatment of that subject in a separate chapter of its own rather than as one section in a chapter dealing with other bases for extended detention.

New material has been added to every chapter in the book, and new cases in a majority of them. Some of the chapters have been substantially redone, while changes in others involve the addition of substantial new materials, including entirely new cases or the substitution of the decisions of higher courts for opinions contained in the first edition.

Without attempting to describe all of the many changes in book, here are some of the highlights:

In Chapter 2, which describes the major legislative packages dealing with terrorism enacted by the Congress, special attention is now focused on the most controversial features of the USA PATRIOT Act, which have garnered special attention from the media and civil liberties groups. Most of the controversial provisions of the Act have sunset clauses, and the issue of whether to continue them will be under consideration in the Congress at least through the remainder of 2005.

Some cases have been added to Chapter 3, which in the first edition was restricted to statutes defining terrorist offenses. Perhaps most note-worthy is the inclusion of terrorism hoax cases which, in the absence of a terrorism hoax statute, had been prosecuted under the weapons of mass destruction statute. A new hoax offense, added by the Intellligence Reform and Terrorism Prevention Act of 2004 to the panoply of federal terrorism statutes, is also reproduced in this chapter.

Chapter 4 dealing with the material support offenses has been substantially recast and expanded, and now includes coverage of 18 U.S.C. § 2339A as well as § 2339B. The Lynne Stewart prosecution, United States v. Sattar, is used as a centerpiece in the chapter.

Chapter 5 now includes some substantial law review excerpts dealing with alternatives to the Bush Administration's emphasis on the legal notion that we are "at war" and heavy reliance on the President's role as Commander-in-chief and military authority.

Chapter 6 contains new case materials dealing with goverment's use of the material witness statute and alien status to detain individuals for extended periods and highlights the question whether the government's authority in terrorism cases to detain people is broader than in other contexts.

Chapter 7 contains the new cases dealing with the authority of the military branch of the government to detain individuals as enemy combatants, including the Supreme Court decisions and the district court decisions dealing with the Guantanamo detainees as well as Padilla v. Hanft, the Padilla case, begun again in South Carolina in the wake of the Supreme Court's decision in the original case. It also now includes important material on torture and background memoranda relating to the enemy combatant versus POW issue.

Added to Chapter 8 are materials relating to the substantive crimes charged in the military commission proceedings now in process and Hamdan v. Rumsfeld, the first judicial decision arising out of those proceedings.

The focus in Chapter 9 has been broadened to take account of approaches to dealing with the treatment of classified information in judicial proceedings in addition to the Classified Information Procedures Act. Case law development since the first edition highlights and invites comparative assessment of different approaches to the problem of classified information.

Some material has been added to Chapter 10 that sharpens the focus on the use of FISA warrant authority in terrorism cases. Finally, some new case and law review material have been added to Chapters 11 and 12, which deal with political surveillance and the use of the military in domestic law enforcement, and Chapter 13, which deals with actions of U.S. agents abroad, now also includes material on legal issues relating to the use of torture in interrogations.

The pace of change in this fascinating field means, of course, that Supplements and new editions will be forthcoming on a regular basis, with short time lags between them. I hope soon also to have established a website for making available the most current materials.

NORMAN ABRAMS

April, 2005

PREFACE TO THE FIRST EDITION

The occasion for the writing of this casebook was my teaching of a Seminar on Anti-terrorism and the Law in the Fall, 2002, after being largely away from law teaching (while serving in the campus administration) for a ten year period. Once I launched into the preparation of materials for the Seminar, it did not take long to realize that the importance and intrinsic interest of the topics and the nature of the available materials make this not only an excellent subject for a course or a seminar but also an ideal candidate for casebook treatment. When I began, while I appreciated the societal importance of the subject matter, I did not realize how extraordinarily active this area of the law would become over the short span of six months, and I certainly underestimated how exciting the materials would turn out to be, when viewed against the backdrop of traditional casebook subjects.

The casebook is intended primarily for use in a two unit advanced course to be taught in the second or third year. The book can also be used in connection with a seminar on the subject of anti-terrorism enforcement. In my own teaching of the Seminar, I used less than one half of the materials, which at the time were in preliminary draft form, for the first half of the semester (the students made oral presentations in the second half). Of course, there are a variety of ways to teach a seminar, and the choice of approach will dictate how much of the book you will want to use in that context. Finally, for those who might wish to supplement the first year Criminal Law course with a substantial segment devoted to anti-terrorism criminal enforcement, assignment of selections from the book offers, I believe, a rich menu of materials from which to choose. The book may also be used at the undergraduate level for either a course or a seminar.

The casebook can be viewed as a kind of specialized federal criminal law work. It is, of course, that and much more. While the title of the book is <u>Anti-terrorism and Criminal Enforcement</u>, the book develops and plays off of the tension between a criminal or law enforcement approach, on the one hand, and a wartime, military and intelligence basis, on the other. While the starting point is criminal enforcement—this is not a treatment that uses constitutional or international law or governmental relations issues as its raison—there is no way to avoid addressing these latter issues along the way. Further, the book is not restricted to a treatment of substantive criminal law issues, although it certainly includes them; nor is it restricted to process and procedure and issues of criminal enforcement administration, although it also addresses such matters. An effort has been made to adopt an approach that brings together all of these different emphases in a coherent, integrated package.

The book is divided into three principal Parts which provide the organizing basis for the development and ordering of the material. The first Part provides an overview and emphasizes criminal law-related legislation dealing with the terrorism problem. The second Part focuses on detention and adjudication-related issues, while the third Part looks at issues raised by the techniques of investigation and information-gathering used in anti-terrorism criminal enforcement.

While the selection of topics is largely defined by the subject matter, some difficult choices had to be made—for example, what kinds of investigatory and enforcement techniques to include? A case can surely be made for the inclusion of some topics that do not appear in the book—*e.g.*, profiling, interrogation rules, asset freezing, and civil suits against terrorism-supporting states. A preference not to allow the book to become too large meant that such subjects could not be included. Generally, in determining coverage, topics were chosen that were not likely to be treated in depth in other courses in the curriculum and that were directly related to criminal enforcement or a substitute for such enforcement—*e.g.*, extended detention of suspected persons.

Many of the current or recent prosecutions of terrorism cases are mentioned throughout these materials. Because it is a good idea to give students the flavor of official documents connected to such cases, copies of some documents connected to some of the most prominent prosecutions are included in an Appendix. Instructors, of course, may wish to assign this material and use it as a basis for analysis and discussion.

An effort was made to keep track of the relevant major criminal enforcement developments in the field of anti-terrorism in the year and a half since September 11. This is, of course, an extraordinarily active legal field, with developments occurring almost weekly through new judicial decisions, executive or administrative initiatives and new legislation or legislative proposals, plus enforcement activities in the field. Undoubtedly, even while this book is being published, new developments will be occurring. It will be up to the individual instructor to keep an eye out and supplement the casebook materials as needed, until those new developments can be included in a Supplement or subsequent edition.

NORMAN ABRAMS

January, 2003

ACKNOWLEDGMENTS

I wish to thank R. James Suzano, UCLA Law 2013 for his able research assistance in gathering materials used in this volume. I am also grateful to Rob Arnay and Hillary Bryn Stakem, both UCLA Law 2012, for their careful proofreading of the text; and to Scott Dewey, UCLA Law Library, for his excellent assistance in the final proofing process. Finally, I want to express my continuing great appreciation to Tal Grietzer, UCLA Law School, for his technical wizardry and all-round aid in the preparation of this volume.

I would also like to thank the following individuals and organizations for the permission each has granted to reprint excerpts from their publications.

Floyd Abrams, *The First Amendment and the War Against Terrorism*, 5 U. PA. J. CONST. L. 1 (2002) Copyright © (2002) By the University of Pennsylvania Journal of Constitutional Law. Reprinted by permission.

Norman Abrams, *Developments in US Anti-terrorism Law, Checks and Balances Undermined*, 4 J. INT'L CRIM. JUST. 1117 (2006) Copyright © (2006) By the Journal of International Criminal Justice . Reprinted by permission.

Norman Abrams, *The Material Support Terrorism Offenses: Perspectives Derived from the (Early) Model Penal Code*, 1 J. NAT'L SECURITY L. & POL'Y 5, 9–11 (2005) Copyright © (2005) By the Journal of National Security Law & Policy. Reprinted by permission.

An Amnesty International Report, *USA: Below the Radar: Secret Flights to Torture and 'Disappearance'*, AI INDEX: AMR 51/051/2006 AMNESTY INTERNATIONAL 5 APRIL 2006, Copyright © (2006) By Amnesty International. Reprinted by permission.

Kenneth Anderson, *What To Do With Bin Laden and Al Qaeda Terrorists?: A Qualified Defense of Military Commissions and United States Policy on Detainees At Guantanamo Bay Naval Base*, 25 HARV. J.L. & PUB POL'Y 591 (2002) Copyright © (2002) By the Harvard Journal of Law & Public Policy. Reprinted by permission.

Phillip Carter, *Why Can the Army Help Cops Catch the D.C. Sniper?*, SLATE, Oct. 17, 2002 Copyright © (2002) By Slate Magazine. Reprinted by permission.

Erwin Chemerinsky *Losing Liberties: Applying a Foreign Intelligence Model to Domestic Law Enforcement*, 51 UCLA L. REV. 1619 (2004) Copyright © 2004 By the Regents of the University of California. Reprinted by permission.

David Cole, *The Priority of Morality: the Emergency Constitution's Blind Spot*, 113 YALE L.J. 1753 (2004) Copyright © 2004 By the Yale Law Journal Company. Reprinted by permission.

Ashley J. Craw, *A Call to Arms: Civil Disorder Following Hurricane , Katrina Warrants Attack on The Posse Comitatus Act*, 14 GEO. MASON L. REV. 829 (2007) Copyright © (2007) By the George Mason Law Review. Reprinted by permission.

Major Kirk L. Davies, *The Imposition of Martial Law In The United States*, 49 A.F. L. REV. 67 (2000) Copyright © 2000 By the Air Force Judge Advocate General School. Reprinted by permission.

Christina Deconcini & Kareem Shora, Panel Discussion, *Perversities and Prospects: Whither Immigration Enforcement and Detention in the Anti–Terrorism Aftermath?*, 9 GEO. J. ON POVERTY L. & POL'Y 1 (2002) Reprinted with permission of the publisher, Georgetown Journal on Poverty Law & Policy © 2002.

Alan M. Dershowitz, *The Torture Warrant: A Response to Professor Strauss*, 48 N.Y.L. SCH. L.REV. 275 (2003) Copyright © 2003 By the New York Law School Law Review. Reprinted by permission.

Christian M. De Vos, *Mind, the Gap: Purpose, Pain, and the Difference between Torture and Inhuman Treatment*, 14 No. 2 HUM. RTS. BRIEF 4 (2007) Copyright © (2007) By the Human Rights Brief. Reprinted by permission.

John T. Elliff, *The Attorney General's Guidelines for FBI Investigations*, 69 CORNELL L. REV. 785 (1984) Copyright © (1984) BY the Cornell Law Review. Reprinted by permission.

FEDERALIST SOCIETY, WHITE PAPER ON THE USA PATRIOT ACT OF 2001: CRIMINAL PROCEDURE SECTIONS (2001) Copyright © (2001) By the Federalist Society. Reprinted by permission.

George P. Fletcher, *On the Crimes Subject to Prosecution in Military Commissions* , J. INT'L CRIM. JUST. 39 (2007) Copyright © (2007) By the Journal of International Criminal Justice . Reprinted by permission.

George P. Fletcher, *War Crimes Proceedings in Iraq? The Bush Administration's Dilemma*, April 4, 2003, at http://writ.news.findlaw.com/commentary/20030404_fletcher.html Copyright © 2003 By FindLaw. Reprinted by permission.

Matthew Carlton Hammond, Note, *The Posse Comitatus Act: A Principle in Need of Renewal*, 75 WASH. U. L.Q. 953 (1997) Copyright © (1997) By the Washington University Law Quarterly. Reprinted by permission.

Harold Hongju Koh, *The Case Against Military Commissions*, 96 AM. J. INT'L L. 337)2002) Reproduced with permission from 96 AJIL 337 (2002), © The American Society of International Law.

Laurie L. Levenson, *Detention, Material Witnesses and the War on Terrorism*, 35 LOY. L.A. L. REV. 1217 (2002) Copyright © (2002) By the Loyola of Los Angeles Law Review. Reprinted by permission.

David M. Park, Note, *Re-Examining the Attorney General's Guidelines for FBI Investigations of Domestic Groups*, 39 ARIZ. L. REV. 769 (1997) Copyright © (1997) by the Arizona Board of Regents. Reprinted by permission.

Heidee Stoller, Tahlia Townsend, Rashad Hussain, and Marcia Yablon, *Developments in Law and Policy: The Costs of Post–9/11 National Security Strategy*, 22 YALE L. & POL'Y REV. 197 (2004) Copyright © 2004 By the Yale Law & Policy Review. Reprinted by permission.

Brian Z. Tamanaha, *A Critical Review of the Classified Information Procedures Act*, 13 AM. J. CRIM. L. 277 (1987) Copyright © (1987) By the American Journal of Criminal Law. Reprinted by permission.

Elllen C. Yaroshefsky, *The Slow Erosion of the Adversary System: Article III Courts, FISA, CIPA and Ethical Dilemmas*, 5 CARDOZO PUB. L. POL'Y & ETHICS J. 203 (2006) Copyright © (2006) By the author and Cardozo Public Law, Policy, and Ethics Journal. Reprinted by permission.

SUMMARY OF CONTENTS

Page

PREFACE TO THE FOURTH EDITION — v
PREFACE TO THE THIRD EDITION — ix
PREFACE TO THE SECOND EDITION — xiii
PREFACE TO THE FIRST EDITION — xv
ACKNOWLEDGMENTS — xvii
TABLE OF CASES — xxxiii
TABLE OF STATUTES — xxxvii

Chapter 1. Overview — 1

PART 1.   IN A CIVILIAN MODE

Chapter 2.   Definitions of Terrorism; Terrorism Statutes — 8
A. Introduction — 8
B. Terrorism: Definitions and Definitional Approaches — 22
C. Selected Terrorism Statutes — 33
D. International Terrorism Prosecutions Since 9/11 — 53

Chapter 3.   Providing Material Support for Use in Terrorist Offenses or Material Support to a Foreign Terrorist Organization: 18 U.S.C. § 2339A, § 2339B — 57
A. Introduction—18 U.S.C. § 2339A and § 2339B — 57
B. The Many Uses of the "Personnel" Term in the Material Support Listing — 63
C. Mens Rea Issues Under §§ 2339A and 2339B: Knowledge or Specific Intent — 81
D. The Humanitarian Law Project Decision, § 2339B: "Training" and "Expert Advice or Assistance," "Service," "Personnel"; Specific Intent; Constitutional Issues—Vagueness and First Amendment — 87
E. Administrative Designation as a "Foreign Terrorist Organization" for Purposes of § 2339B; Hearing Procedure and Judicial Review Under 8 U.S.C. § 1189 — 101

Chapter 4.   Proactive Surveillance — 127
A. Introduction — 127
B. Relevant Federal Executive Order and Guidelines — 130
C. Litigating Issues Raised by Proactive Surveillance — 141

Chapter 5.   Electronic Surveillance — 160
A. The Foreign Intelligence Surveillance Act (FISA) and Electronic Surveillance Within the United States — 161

Page

B. The Terrorist Surveillance Program (TSP) Controversy and Electronic Surveillance Abroad ----- 200
C. Post–TSP Legislation Dealing With Electronic Surveillance With Links to Persons Abroad and in the U.S. ----- 215

Chapter 6. Searches and Administrative Subpoenas ----- **246**
A. Introduction ----- 246
B. Searches Within the United States ----- 247
C. U.S. Agents Acting Abroad—Fourth Amendment and Related Issues ----- 260
D. Administrative and Judicial Subpoenas to Obtain Records, Documents, etc.—National Security Letters and Section 215 (50 U.S.C. § 1861) Orders ----- 277

Chapter 7. Interrogation and Irregular Rendition ----- **306**
A. Introduction ----- 306
B. Obtaining Terrorism–Related Information Through Interrogation ----- 307
C. Irregular Rendition ----- 353

Chapter 8. Material Witness and Immigration Detention ----- **399**
A. Introduction ----- 399
B. Material Witness Detention ----- 401
C. Detention of Aliens ----- 427

Chapter 9. Classified Information in Civilian Terrorism Trials ----- **467**
A. Introduction—The Classified Information Procedures Act ----- 467
B. The Classified Information Procedures Act ----- 469
C. Adjudging the Adequacy of Substitutions for Classified Information ----- 475
D. Classified Information and the Right of Confrontation ----- 481
E. Classified Information and the Right to Compulsory Process of Witnesses ----- 492
F. Security Clearance for Counsel ----- 511

PART 2. IN A MILITARY MODE

Chapter 10. Detention in Military Custody ----- **528**
A. Introduction ----- 528
B. Legal Basis for Extended Military Detention; Process Due Detainees ----- 528
C. Process Due Detainees at Guantanamo; Disposition of Guantanamo and the Remaining Detainees ----- 554
D. Military Custody for Persons Arrested in the United States— Citizen and Non–Citizen: The Jose Padilla and Ali Saleh Kahlah Al–Marri Cases ----- 622

Chapter 11. Military Commissions ----- **641**
A. Legal Authority ----- 641
B. Selected Military Commission Evidentiary Rules ----- 689
C. The Provisions of the MCA of 2009 ----- 694
D. Summary Review of the History of the Post–9/11 Military Commissions Trials ----- 726
E. The Choice Between Military and Civilian Custody and Military Commission and Civilian Prosecution ----- 730
F. Literature Regarding Military Commissions ----- 732

Page

Chapter 12. Targeted Killing --- **734**
A. Introduction--- 734
B. Executive Orders -- 735
C. Policy Issues --- 735
D. The Al–Aulaqi Case-- 739

Chapter 13. Using the Military in Domestic Law Enforcement --- **745**
A. Introduction--- 745
B. Interpretation and Application of the Posse Comitatus Act -------------- 749
C. Exceptions to the Posse Comitatus Rule? More Extensive Use of the
    Military in Emergencies and for Other Purposes? ---------------------- 761

Chapter 14. Epilogue --- **770**

Index--- 775

TABLE OF CONTENTS

	Page
PREFACE TO THE FOURTH EDITION	v
PREFACE TO THE THIRD EDITION	ix
PREFACE TO THE SECOND EDITION	xiii
PREFACE TO THE FIRST EDITION	xv
ACKNOWLEDGMENTS	xvii
TABLE OF CASES	xxxiii
TABLE OF STATUTES	xxxvii

Chapter 1. Overview **1**
   Note on the Obama Administration's Anti–Terrorism Policies and Related
     Actions 3
   The Content of Specific Chapters 4

PART 1. IN A CIVILIAN MODE

Chapter 2. Definitions of Terrorism; Terrorism Statutes **8**
A. Introduction 8
   1. Coverage of the Chapter 8
   2. Contexts in Which Terrorism and Definitions of Terrorism May
      Be Used 8
     United States v. Yousef 9
B. Terrorism: Definitions and Definitional Approaches 22
   1. In General 22
   2. Statutory Definitions of Terrorism 24
   3. Policy Definitions of Terrorism and Enforcement Policy; Listing
      of Terrorist Organizations 27
     a. The State Department 27
     b. The Department of Justice 30
     c. The Federal Bureau of Investigation 30
   4. Definitions of Terrorism: What Difference Does It Make? 31
     a. A Critique of One Definition 31
     b. Selected Problems in Applying the Definitions 32
C. Selected Terrorism Statutes 33
   United States v. Yousef 35
   Note on Other Terrorism–Related Offenses 52
D. International Terrorism Prosecutions Since 9/11 53

**Chapter 3. Providing Material Support for Use in Terrorist
     Offenses or Material Support to a Foreign Terrorist Or-
     ganization: 18 U.S.C. § 2339A, § 2339B** **57**
A. Introduction—18 U.S.C. § 2339A and § 2339B 57
   1. Inchoate Offense Aspect 57
   2. Comparison With Complicity 58

Page

A. Introduction—18 U.S.C. § 2339A and § 2339B—Continued
  3. Adaptability 59
  4. The Coverage of This Chapter 60
  5. The Current Statutes: § 2339A and § 2339B 60
  6. A Bit of History: Issues of Statutory Interpretation and Legislative Amendments 62
B. The Many Uses of the "Personnel" Term in the Material Support Listing 63
  United States v. Abu–Jihaad 63
  United States v. Stewart 68
C. Mens Rea Issues Under §§ 2339A and 2339B: Knowledge or Specific Intent 81
D. The Humanitarian Law Project Decision, § 2339B: "Training" and "Expert Advice or Assistance," "Service," "Personnel"; Specific Intent; Constitutional Issues—Vagueness and First Amendment ... 87
  Holder v. Humanitarian Law Project 87
E. Administrative Designation as a "Foreign Terrorist Organization" for Purposes of § 2339B; Hearing Procedure and Judicial Review Under 8 U.S.C. § 1189 101
  1. The Statutory Scheme 101
  2. Judicial Review by the Affected Organization of the Secretary's Designation 107
    People's Mojahedin Organization of Iran v. U.S. Department of State 107
  3. Can the FTO Designation Be Challenged in a Criminal Prosecution for a Violation of § 2339B? 120
    United States v. Afshari 121

Chapter 4. Proactive Surveillance **127**
A. Introduction 127
  Note on Civil Suits Challenging the Legality of Government Enforcement Practices in Investigating and Apprehending Suspected Terrorists 127
B. Relevant Federal Executive Order and Guidelines 130
C. Litigating Issues Raised by Proactive Surveillance 141
  1. Proactive Surveillance by the U.S. Military 141
    Laird v. Tatum 141
  2. Proactive Surveillance by a City Police Department and the FBI ... 147
    Alliance to End Repression v. City of Chicago 147
    Dinler v. City of New York 158

Chapter 5. Electronic Surveillance **160**
A. The Foreign Intelligence Surveillance Act (FISA) and Electronic Surveillance Within the United States 161
  1. Introduction 161
  2. The FISA Statute 162
  3. Comparing Surveillance Under FISA and Under 18 U.S.C. § 2510 et seq. 176
    a. The Probable Cause Requirement 176
      Note on Probable Cause under FISA 176
    b. Duration of the Intercept; Time Period Within Which Target Must Be Notified About the Interception 179

Page

A. The Foreign Intelligence Surveillance Act (FISA) and Electronic Surveillance Within the United States—Continued

   c. Other Comparisons Between the FISA and 18 U.S.C. § 2518 Surveillances 179

   d. Statistical Comparison of FISA and Title III Electronic Surveillances 179

   4. Another Perspective on the Relationship Between FISA Electronic Surveillance and Ordinary Crime Surveillance: The Multiple Purpose Issue 181

      a. Background–History and the Relevant Statutory Provisions 181

      b. Applying the Significant Purpose Formula 185
      United States v. Ning Wen 185

   5. Criminal Prosecution Using FISA–Derived Material 191
      United States v. Duggan 191

B. The Terrorist Surveillance Program (TSP) Controversy and Electronic Surveillance Abroad 200

   1. Background 200

   2. A Perspective on the TSP From Within the Government 203
      Unclassified Report on President's Surveillance Program 203

   3. Materials Bearing on the Legality of the TSP 205

   4. Litigation Involving the NSA'S TSP Program 214

C. Post–TSP Legislation Dealing With Electronic Surveillance With Links to Persons Abroad and in the U.S. 215
   Amnesty International, USA v. Clapper 237

Chapter 6. Searches and Administrative Subpoenas **246**
A. Introduction 246
B. Searches Within the United States 247

   1. Introduction 247

   2. Title 50, U.S.C. § 1821 et seq. 248

   3. Federal Rules of Criminal Procedure 255

   4. Title 18 Provision Supplementing Federal Rules of Criminal Procedure 258

C. U.S. Agents Acting Abroad—Fourth Amendment and Related Issues 260

   1. Introduction 260

   2. Searches Abroad—Premises of a Non–U.S. Person; U.S. Person Search by Non–U.S. Agents 260
      United States v. Verdugo–Urquidez 261

   3. Search Abroad of the Premises of a U.S. Person by U.S. Agents; Foreign Intelligence Purpose 270
      In re Terrorist Bombings of U.S. Embassies in East Africa—United States v. Odeh 270

D. Administrative and Judicial Subpoenas to Obtain Records, Documents, etc.—National Security Letters and Section 215 (50 U.S.C. § 1861) Orders 277

   1. Introduction 277

   2. Authority to Issue National Security Letters 278

   3. Judicial Review of NSL's 280

   4. The Library Provision—Section 215 (50 U.S.C. § 1861) 281

   5. Authority to Issue Administrative Subpoenas in Drug–Related Investigations 284
      Doe v. Mukasey 288

Page

Chapter 7.   Interrogation and Irregular Rendition ---------------- **306**
A. Introduction --- 306
B. Obtaining Terrorism–Related Information Through Interrogation ----- 307
   1. The Torture Controversy -------------------------------------- 307
     a. Background --- 307
     b. Memoranda and Statements of Officials in the Bush Administration Regarding the Legality of Various Methods of Interrogation -- 309
     c. A Comment on the Approach That Distinguishes Torture From Cruel, Inhuman or Degrading Treatment --------------- 313
     d. Literature --- 316
     e. The Ticking Bomb Debate ------------------------------- 316
     f. The Army Field Manual Interrogation Provisions ---------- 317
   2. The Obama Executive Order Adopting the AFM Guidelines -------- 319
   3. Legal Issues Arising Out of the Interrogation of Terrorist Suspects --- 325
     a. The Admissibility in Criminal Prosecutions in U.S. District Courts of Confessions Obtained Abroad ------------------- 325
       In re Terrorist Bombings of U.S. Embassies in East Africa—United States v. Odeh -------------------------------------- 326
     b. Invocation of the Public Safety Exception to the Miranda Warning/Waiver Requirements in Terrorism and Terrorism/Intelligence Contexts ------------------------------ 339
     c. Coerced Confessions and Terrorism Intelligence ------------ 343
       United States v. Abu Ali ------------------------------- 344
C. Irregular Rendition -- 353
   1. Introduction -- 353
   2. Kidnapping in Lieu of Extradition; Extradition Treaties -------- 356
     United States v. Alvarez–Machain ------------------------- 356
   3. Acknowledgment by the U.S. Government of Transfers of Persons, Interrogations and "Black Sites" ------------------------- 368
   4. Lawsuits Brought by Alleged Victims of Irregular Rendition -------- 371
     Arar v. Ashcroft --- 371
   5. Criminal Charges by Foreign Governments Against U.S. Agents Who Allegedly Perpetrated Irregular Rendition Transfers -------- 392
   6. An Unofficial, Nongovernmental Report About the Practice of Irregular Rendition -- 393
   7. Irregular Rendition literature -------------------------------- 398

Chapter 8.   Material Witness and Immigration Detention --------- **399**
A. Introduction --- 399
B. Material Witness Detention -- 401
   1. Introduction -- 401
   2. Direct Challenge to Material Witness Detention ---------------- 403
     United States v. Awadallah ------------------------------- 403
   3. Civil Lawsuit Alleging Illegal Detention as a Material Witness ----- 416
     Ashcroft v. al–Kidd -------------------------------------- 416
     al–Kidd v. Ashcroft -------------------------------------- 421
C. Detention of Aliens -- 427
   1. Introduction -- 427
   2. Post 9/11/01 Detentions and Removals Based on Immigration Law Violations --- 428

Page

C. Detention of Aliens—Continued
    a. The Use of Authority to Detain Aliens in Violation of the Immigration Laws as an Aid to Terrorism Investigation and as a Form of Preventive Detention ----- 428
    b. Must Deportation Hearings Be Open to the Public and the Press? ----- 429
        Haddad v. Ashcroft ----- 433
        Detroit Free Press v. Ashcroft ----- 438
        Haddad v. Ashcroft ----- 439
    c. Is Indefinite, Open–Ended Detention Possible in Connection With Efforts to Remove an Individual From the United States? ----- 440
        Zadvydas v. Davis ----- 440
    d. Civil Suits by Aliens of Middle Eastern Origin Seeking Redress for Post–9/11 Detentions ----- 450
        Ashcroft v. Iqbal ----- 450
    e. Statutory Detention and Removal Provisions Directed Specifically Toward Terrorists Under the USA PATRIOT Act and Other Immigration Law Provisions ----- 457

Chapter 9. Classified Information in Civilian Terrorism Trials ----- 467
A. Introduction—The Classified Information Procedures Act ----- 467
B. The Classified Information Procedures Act ----- 469
C. Adjudging the Adequacy of Substitutions for Classified Information ----- 475
    United States v. Rezaq ----- 475
D. Classified Information and the Right of Confrontation ----- 481
    United States v. Abu Ali ----- 481
E. Classified Information and the Right to Compulsory Process of Witnesses ----- 492
    United States v. Moussaoui ----- 492
F. Security Clearance for Counsel ----- 511
    United States v. Bin Laden ----- 513

PART 2. IN A MILITARY MODE

Chapter 10. Detention in Military Custody ----- 528
A. Introduction ----- 528
B. Legal Basis for Extended Military Detention; Process Due Detainees ----- 528
    1. The AUMF ----- 528
    2. The Military Order Issued by the President ----- 529
    3. Hamdi and Its Aftermath ----- 537
        Hamdi v. Rumsfeld ----- 537
C. Process Due Detainees at Guantanamo; Disposition of Guantanamo and the Remaining Detainees ----- 554
    1. Do the Detainees Have Habeas Corpus Rights in U.S. Courts? ----- 554
        Boumediene v. Bush ----- 554
        Al–Maqaleh v. Gates ----- 577
        Maqaleh v. Gates ----- 585
    2. Post–Boumediene Habeas Corpus Reviews ----- 586
        Bensayah v. Obama ----- 586
    3. Military Administrative Process for Determining the Status of Detainees ----- 599
        a. Evolution of the Military Administrative Process ----- 599
        b. The Obama Administration Policy ----- 607

Page

C. Process Due Detainees at Guantanamo; Disposition of Guantanamo and the Remaining Detainees—Continued
Note on the Controversy Surrounding the Proposed Closure of the Guantanamo Bay Facility and Where to Prosecute Gitmo Detainees; Where to detain and prosecute new apprehended detainees 619
D. Military Custody for Persons Arrested in the United States— Citizen and Non–Citizen: The Jose Padilla and Ali Saleh Kahlah Al–Marri Cases 622
  1. The Saga of Jose Padilla 622
    Padilla v. Hanft 622
    Note on Strategic Considerations in the Civilian Criminal Prosecution of Jose Padilla 634
    Padilla v. Hanft 632
    United States v. Padilla 635
  2. Ali Saleh Kahlah Al–Marri 639

Chapter 11. Military Commissions **641**
A. Legal Authority 641
  1. The Quirin Case 641
    Ex Parte Quirin 641
  2. The President's Military Order Redux 652
  3. Relevant Military Jurisdiction and Procedure Statutes 657
  4. Authority to Establish Military Commissions—The Hamdan Case 658
    Hamdan v. Rumsfeld 658
  5. The Response to Hamdan—Congressional Enactment of the Military Commissions Act of 2006, and Later, the Military Commissions Act of 2009 688
B. Selected Military Commission Evidentiary Rules 689
  1. Search and Seizure–Exclusionary Rule 690
  2. Miranda Warnings 690
  3. Confessions 691
  4. Hearsay 692
  5. Classified Information 693
C. The Provisions of the MCA of 2009 694
D. Summary Review of the History of the Post–9/11 Military Commissions Trials 726
E. The Choice Between Military and Civilian Custody and Military Commission and Civilian Prosecution 730
F. Literature Regarding Military Commissions 732

Chapter 12. Targeted Killing **734**
A. Introduction 734
B. Executive Orders 735
C. Policy Issues 735
D. The Al–Aulaqi Case 739
  Nasser Al–Aulaqi v. Obama 739

Chapter 13. Using the Military in Domestic Law Enforcement **745**
A. Introduction 745
B. Interpretation and Application of the Posse Comitatus Act 749
  United States v. Yunis 749

Page

C. Exceptions to the Posse Comitatus Rule? More Extensive Use of the Military in Emergencies and for Other Purposes? ---------------------- 761

Chapter 14. Epilogue --- **770**

INDEX-- 775

TABLE OF CASES

The principal cases are in bold type. Cases cited or discussed in the text are in roman type. References are to pages. Cases cited in principal cases and within other quoted materials are not included.

Abdah v. Obama, 708 F.Supp.2d 9 (D.D.C. 2010), 596

Abdi, United States v., 498 F.Supp.2d 1048 (S.D.Ohio 2007), 522

Abu Ali, United States v., 528 F.3d 210 (4th Cir.2008), 337, **344, 481**

Abu–Ali, United States v., Cr. No. 05–53 (E.D. Va. 2005), 215

Abu–Jihaad, United States v., 630 F.3d 102 (2nd Cir.2010), 67, 190, 199

Abu–Jihaad, United States v., 600 F.Supp.2d 362 (D.Conn.2009), **63**

Adamo Wrecking Co. v. United States, 434 U.S. 275, 98 S.Ct. 566, 54 L.Ed.2d 538 (1978), 125

Afshari, United States v., 392 F.3d 1031 (9th Cir.2004), **121**

Al–Arian, United States v., 308 F.Supp.2d 1322 (M.D.Fla.2004), 83

Al–Arian, United States v., 267 F.Supp.2d 1258 (M.D.Fla.2003), 521

Al–Aulaqi v. Obama, 727 F.Supp.2d 1 (D.D.C.2010), **739**

al Bahlul, United States v., ___ F.Supp.2d ___, 2011 WL 4916373 (USCMCR 2011), 728

Al–Bihani v. Obama, 590 F.3d 866, 389 U.S.App.D.C. 26 (D.C.Cir.2010), 595

Aldawsari, United States v., 2011 WL 668355 (N.D.Tex.2011), 41

Al–Haramain Islamic Foundation, Inc. v. Bush, 507 F.3d 1190 (9th Cir.2007), 215

Al–Haramain Islamic Foundation, Inc. v. George W. Bush, National Security Agency, 2010 WL 5663950 (N.D.Cal.2010), 214

Al–Kidd v. Ashcroft, 2007 WL 2786867 (9th Cir.2007), **421**

Al–Kidd v. Gonzales, 2006 WL 5429570 (D.Idaho 2006), 421

Alliance To End Repression v. City of Chicago, 2009 WL 2015154 (7th Cir.2009), 156

Alliance To End Repression v. City of Chicago, 356 F.3d 767 (7th Cir.2004), 156

Alliance to End Repression v. City of Chicago, 237 F.3d 799 (7th Cir.2001), **147**

All Matters Submitted to Foreign Intelligence Surveillance Court, In re, 218 F.Supp.2d 611 (Foreign Intel.Surv.Ct.2002), 199

Al Maqaleh v. Gates, 605 F.3d 84, 390 U.S.App.D.C. 352 (D.C.Cir.2010), **577**

al–Marri v. Pucciarelli, 534 F.3d 213 (4th Cir. 2008), 639

al–Marri v. Spagone, ___ U.S. ___, 129 S.Ct. 1545, 173 L.Ed.2d 671 (2009), 639

Al–Timimi, United States v., No. 05–4761 (4th Cir. 2006), 215

Alvarez–Machain, United States v., 504 U.S. 655, 112 S.Ct. 2188, 119 L.Ed.2d 441 (1992), 355, **356**

American Civil Liberties Union v. City of Chicago, 2009 WL 2409907 (N.D.Ill.2009), 156

American Civil Liberties Union v. National Sec. Agency, 493 F.3d 644 (6th Cir.2007), 200, 211

American Civil Liberties Union v. National Sec. Agency, 438 F.Supp.2d 754 (E.D.Mich. 2006), 202

American Civil Liberties Union v. United States Dept. of Justice, 321 F.Supp.2d 24 (D.D.C.2004), 286

American Civil Liberties Union of Illinois v. City of Chicago, 2008 WL 4450304 (N.D.Ill. 2008), 156

Amnesty Intern. USA v. Clapper, 638 F.3d 118 (2nd Cir.2011), **237**

Application of (see name of party)

Arar v. Ashcroft, 585 F.3d 559 (2nd Cir. 2009), 365, **371**

Armed Forces in the Field, 1956 WL 54807 (U.S. Treaty 1956), 320

Ashcroft v. al–Kidd, ___ U.S. ___, 131 S.Ct. 2074, 179 L.Ed.2d 1149 (2011), **416**

Ashcroft v. Iqbal, 556 U.S. 662, 129 S.Ct. 1937, 173 L.Ed.2d 868 (2009), **450**

Awad v. Obama, 608 F.3d 1, 391 U.S.App.D.C. 79 (D.C.Cir.2010), 595

Awadallah, United States v., 349 F.3d 42 (2nd Cir.2003), 401, **403**

Barhoumi v. Obama, 609 F.3d 416, 391 U.S.App.D.C. 207 (D.C.Cir.2010), 595

Barona, United States v., 56 F.3d 1087 (9th Cir.1995), 267

Benkahla, United States v., 437 F.Supp.2d 541 (E.D.Va.2006), 199

Bensayah v. Obama, 610 F.3d 718, 391 U.S.App.D.C. 333 (D.C.Cir.2010), **586**

Bin Laden, United States v., 58 F.Supp.2d 113 (S.D.N.Y.1999), **513**

Biton v. Palestinian Interim Self–Government Authority, 310 F.Supp.2d 172 (D.D.C.2004), 53

Boumediene v. Bush, 553 U.S. 723, 128 S.Ct. 2229, 171 L.Ed.2d 41 (2008), **554**

Bridgewater, United States v., 175 F.Supp.2d 141 (D.Puerto Rico 2001), 367

Center for Nat. Sec. Studies v. United States Dept. of Justice, 331 F.3d 918, 356 U.S.App. D.C. 333 (D.C.Cir.2003), 401

Center For Nat. Sec. Studies v. United States Dept. of Justice, 215 F.Supp.2d 94 (D.D.C. 2002), 414

Chan Hok Shek, United States v., 2010 WL 4694448 (D.Mass.2010), 337

Clark v. Martinez, 543 U.S. 371, 125 S.Ct. 716, 160 L.Ed.2d 734 (2005), 448

Detroit Free Press v. Ashcroft, 2002 WL 31317398 (E.D.Mich.2002), **438**

Detroit Free Press v. Ashcroft, 303 F.3d 681 (6th Cir.2002), 429

Dinler v. City of New York, 607 F.3d 923 (2nd Cir.2010), **158**

Directives Pursuant to Section 105B of Foreign Intelligence Surveillance Act, In re, 551 F.3d 1004 (Foreign Int.Surv.Ct.Rev.2008), 245

Doe v. Holder, 703 F.Supp.2d 313 (S.D.N.Y. 2010), 300

Doe v. Mukasey, 549 F.3d 861 (2nd Cir.2008), **288**

Donovan v. Spadea, 757 F.2d 74 (3rd Cir.1985), 278

Duggan, United States v., 743 F.2d 59 (2nd Cir.1984), **191**

El–Masri v. United States, 479 F.3d 296 (4th Cir.2007), 382

Ex parte (see name of party)

Fernandez, United States v., 913 F.2d 148 (4th Cir.1990), 479

Frank, United States v., 599 F.3d 1221 (11th Cir.2010), 337

Ghailani, United States v., 761 F.Supp.2d 167 (S.D.N.Y.2011), 620

Gilbert v. United States, 165 F.3d 470 (6th Cir.1999), 756

Goba, United States v., 2007 WL 4404977 (W.D.N.Y.2007), 79

Goba, United States v., 220 F.Supp.2d 182 (W.D.N.Y.2002), 79

Graham, United States v., 275 F.3d 490 (6th Cir.2001), 20

Guantanamo Bay, Detainee Litigation, In re, Misc. No. 08–442 (TFH), 535

Haddad v. Ashcroft, 2003 WL 22220524 (6th Cir.2003), **439**

Haddad v. Ashcroft, 221 F.Supp.2d 799 (E.D.Mich.2002), **433**

Hamdan v. Rumsfeld, 548 U.S. 557, 126 S.Ct. 2749, 165 L.Ed.2d 723 (2006), **658**

Hamdi v. Rumsfeld, 542 U.S. 507, 124 S.Ct. 2633, 159 L.Ed.2d 578 (2004), **537**

Handschu v. Special Services Div., 2008 WL 515695 (S.D.N.Y.2008), 156

Handschu v. Special Services Div., 288 F.Supp.2d 411 (S.D.N.Y.2003), 156

Handschu v. Special Services Div., 288 F.Supp.2d 404 (S.D.N.Y.2003), 156

Handschu v. Special Services Div., 273 F.Supp.2d 327 (S.D.N.Y.2003), 156

Handschu v. Special Services Division, 2007 WL 1711775 (S.D.N.Y.2007), 156

Hassoun, United States v., 2007 WL 1068127 (S.D.Fla.2007), 199

Haynes v. Washington, 373 U.S. 503, 83 S.Ct. 1336, 10 L.Ed.2d 513 (1963), 343

Heller, United States v., 625 F.2d 594 (5th Cir.1980), 337

Hepting v. AT & T Corp., 439 F.Supp.2d 974 (N.D.Cal.2006), 201, 202

Holder v. Humanitarian Law Project, ___ U.S. ___, 130 S.Ct. 2705, 177 L.Ed.2d 355 (2010), **87**

Holy Land Foundation for Relief and Development, United States v., 2007 WL 2011319 (N.D.Tex.2007), 199

Holy Land Foundation for Relief and Development, United States v., 2007 WL 1498813 (N.D.Tex.2007), 85

Humanitarian Law Project v. Reno, 9 F.Supp.2d 1176 (C.D.Cal.1998), 87

Imam, United States v., 10–Cr–00019–RJD, Doc. 53 (filed E.D.N.Y. 7/7/10), 48

In re (see name of party)

Jayyousi, United States v., 657 F.3d 1085 (11th Cir.2011), 639

Karake, United States v., 443 F.Supp.2d 8 (D.D.C.2006), 352

Kasi v. Angelone, 300 F.3d 487 (4th Cir.2002), 368

Khalil, United States v., 214 F.3d 111 (2nd Cir.2000), 339

Laird v. Tatum, 408 U.S. 1, 92 S.Ct. 2318, 33 L.Ed.2d 154 (1972), **141, 745**

Leyra v. Denno, 347 U.S. 556, 74 S.Ct. 716, 98 L.Ed. 948 (1954), 344

Lynumn v. Illinois, 372 U.S. 528, 83 S.Ct. 917, 9 L.Ed.2d 922 (1963), 343

Mapp v. Ohio, 367 U.S. 643, 81 S.Ct. 1684, 6 L.Ed.2d 1081 (1961), 266

Maqaleh v. Gates, 2011 WL 666883 (D.D.C. 2011), **585**

Marzook, United States v., 435 F.Supp.2d 778 (N.D.Ill.2006), 199, 259

Material Witness Warrant, In re Application of, 213 F.Supp.2d 287 (S.D.N.Y.2002), 401, 414, 415

Mohamed v. Jeppesen Dataplan, Inc., 614 F.3d 1070 (9th Cir.2010), 385

Moussaoui, United States v., 591 F.3d 263 (4th Cir.2010), 510

Moussaoui, United States v., 382 F.3d 453 (4th Cir.2004), **492**

National Council of Resistance of Iran v. Department of State, 373 F.3d 152, 362 U.S.App.D.C. 143 (D.C.Cir.2004), 119

National Council of Resistance of Iran v. Department of State, 251 F.3d 192, 346 U.S.App.D.C. 131 (D.C.Cir.2001), 114

National Sec. Agency Telecommunications Records Litigation, In re, 700 F.Supp.2d 1182 (N.D.Cal.2010), 214

New York v. Quarles, 467 U.S. 649, 104 S.Ct. 2626, 81 L.Ed.2d 550 (1984), 339

Nicholson, United States v., 955 F.Supp. 588 (E.D.Va.1997), 199

Ning Wen, United States v., 477 F.3d 896 (7th Cir.2007), **185**

North Jersey Media Group, Inc. v. Ashcroft, 308 F.3d 198 (3rd Cir.2002), 429

Oakley, United States v., 2007 WL 4118298 (E.D.Tenn.2007), 523

Odah, Al v. United States, 559 F.3d 539, 385 U.S.App.D.C. 110 (D.C.Cir.2009), 598

Padilla v. Hanft, 547 U.S. 1062, 126 S.Ct. 1649, 164 L.Ed.2d 409 (2006), **632**

Padilla v. Hanft, 423 F.3d 386 (4th Cir.2005), **622**

Padilla, United States v., 2007 WL 1079090 (S.D.Fla.2007), **635**

Paracha, United States v., 2006 WL 12768 (S.D.N.Y.2006), 510

Pelton, United States v., 835 F.2d 1067 (4th Cir.1987), 199

People's Mojahedin Organization of Iran v. United States Dept. of State, 182 F.3d 17, 337 U.S.App.D.C. 106 (D.C.Cir.1999), 114

People's Mojahedin Organization of Iran v. United States Dept. of State, 613 F.3d 220, 392 U.S.App.D.C. 55 (D.C.Cir. 2010), **107**

Peterson, United States v., 812 F.2d 486 (9th Cir.1987), 268

Quirin, Ex parte, 317 U.S. 1, 63 S.Ct. 2, 87 L.Ed. 3 (1942), 551, **641,** 657

Rasul v. Bush, 542 U.S. 466, 124 S.Ct. 2686, 159 L.Ed.2d 548 (2004), 552, 554

Reynolds, United States v., 381 F.3d 404 (5th Cir.2004), 40

Rezaq, United States v., 134 F.3d 1121, 328 U.S.App.D.C. 297 (D.C.Cir.1998), **475**

Richmond Newspapers, Inc. v. Virginia, 448 U.S. 555, 100 S.Ct. 2814, 65 L.Ed.2d 973 (1980), 429

Rogers v. Richmond, 365 U.S. 534, 81 S.Ct. 735, 5 L.Ed.2d 760 (1961), 343

Rosenthal, United States v., 793 F.2d 1214 (11th Cir.1986), 266

Rumsfeld v. Padilla, 542 U.S. 426, 124 S.Ct. 2711, 159 L.Ed.2d 513 (2004), 552

Salahi v. Obama, 710 F.Supp.2d 1 (D.D.C. 2010), 595

Salerno, United States v., 481 U.S. 739, 107 S.Ct. 2095, 95 L.Ed.2d 697 (1987), 400

Salim, United States v., 287 F.Supp.2d 250 (S.D.N.Y.2003), 47

Sarkissian, United States v., 841 F.2d 959 (9th Cir.1988), 199

Sattar, United States v., 314 F.Supp.2d 279 (S.D.N.Y.2004), 67

Sealed Case, In re, 310 F.3d 717 (Foreign Int. Surv.Ct.Rev.2002), 181, 186, 199

Securities and Exchange Commission v. Dresser Industries, Inc., 628 F.2d 1368, 202 U.S.App.D.C. 345 (D.C.Cir.1980), 278

Smith ex rel. Smith v. Islamic Emirate of Afghanistan, 262 F.Supp.2d 217 (S.D.N.Y. 2003), 53

Sosa v. Alvarez–Machain, 542 U.S. 692, 124 S.Ct. 2739, 159 L.Ed.2d 718 (2004), 368

Spano v. New York, 360 U.S. 315, 79 S.Ct. 1202, 3 L.Ed.2d 1265 (1959), 344

Stewart, United States v., 590 F.3d 93 (2nd Cir.2009), **68**

Taylor, United States v., 2003 WL 22073040 (S.D.N.Y.2003), 40

Terrorist Bombings of United States Embassies in East Africa–United States v. Odeh, In re, 552 F.3d 157 (2nd Cir.2008), **270**

Terrorist Bombings of United States Embassies in East Africa, In re, 552 F.3d 177 (2nd Cir.2008), **326**

Terry v. Ohio, 392 U.S. 1, 88 S.Ct. 1868, 20 L.Ed.2d 889 (1968), 459

Thurston, United States v., 2007 WL 1500176 (D.Or.2007), 17

Toscanino, United States v., 500 F.2d 267 (2nd Cir.1974), 365

United States v. _____ (see opposing party)

U.S. Dist. Court for Eastern Dist. of Mich., Southern Division, United States v., 407 U.S. 297, 92 S.Ct. 2125, 32 L.Ed.2d 752 (1972), 162

Verdugo–Urquidez, United States v., 494 U.S. 259, 110 S.Ct. 1056, 108 L.Ed.2d 222 (1990), **261**

Watts v. Indiana, 338 U.S. 49, 69 S.Ct. 1347, 93 L.Ed. 1801 (1949), 553

Yakus v. United States, 321 U.S. 414, 64 S.Ct. 660, 88 L.Ed. 834 (1944), 124

Youngstown Sheet & Tube Co. v. Sawyer, 343 U.S. 579, 72 S.Ct. 863, 96 L.Ed. 1153 (1952), 535

Yousef, United States v., 327 F.3d 56 (2nd Cir.2003), **9, 35**

Yunis, United States v., 924 F.2d 1086, 288 U.S.App.D.C. 129 (D.C.Cir.1991), 355, 749

Yunis, United States v., 681 F.Supp. 891 (D.D.C.1988), **749**

Zadvydas v. Davis, 533 U.S. 678, 121 S.Ct. 2491, 150 L.Ed.2d 653 (2001), **440**

TABLE OF STATUTES

UNITED STATES

UNITED STATES CONSTITUTION

Art.	This Work Page
I, § 8	728

Amend.	
5	309
8	309
14	309

UNITED STATES CODE ANNOTATED

8 U.S.C.A.—Aliens and Nationality

Sec.	This Work Page
1182	24
1182	25
1189	101
1189	107
1189	117
1189	118
1226(a)(2)	460
1226a	448
1226a	457
1226a	459
1226a	461
1226a	466
1226a(a)(2)	459
1226a(a)(3)	459
1226a(a)(6)	448
1227	459
1227	460
1227	461
1227	465
1531—1537	459
1531—1534	460
1531	461
1532	462
1533	462
1534	464

10 U.S.C.A.—Armed Forces

Sec.	This Work Page
331	746
333	766
333	767
371—382	749
821	657
836	657

UNITED STATES CODE ANNOTATED

10 U.S.C.A.—Armed Forces

Sec.	This Work Page
948a	694
948b	695
948c	696
948d	696
948j	696
948k	697
948m	698
948r	691
948r	692
948r	699
949a	700
949c	703
949d	704
949j	705
949m	707
950f	717
950g	718

12 U.S.C.A.—Banks and Banking

Sec.	This Work Page
2414(a)(5)	277

15 U.S.C.A.—Commerce and Trade

Sec.	This Work Page
1681u	277
1681v	277

18 U.S.C.A.—Crimes and Criminal Procedure

Sec.	This Work Page
Ch. 113	34
Ch. 113B	33
Ch. 113B	53
175c	52
793(d)	67
844	40
844(e)	40
956	33
956	37
956	38
956	48
1038	40
1038	41
1993	52

UNITED STATES CODE ANNOTATED
18 U.S.C.A.—Crimes and Criminal Procedure

Sec.	This Work Page
2331	24
2331	25
2331	53
2332	34
2332	37
2332	38
2332	40
2332	48
2332a(A)(2)(A)	41
2332(d)	34
2332(d)	35
2332(d)	37
2332(d)	47
2332a	23
2332a	38
2332a	39
2332a	40
2332a	41
2332a	46
2332a	48
2332a	52
2332a(a)	40
2332a(b)	40
2332b	23
2332b	41
2332b	45
2332b	46
2332b	47
2332b	49
2332b(g)(1)	45
2332b(g)(5)	46
2332b(g)(5)	47
2332d	52
2332e	52
2332f	23
2332f	48
2332f	51
2332f	52
2332f(b)	51
2332g	52
2332h	52
2333	53
2339	23
2339A(b)	62
2339D	79
2339A	23
2339A	24
2339A	41
2339A	57
2339A	58
2339A	60
2339A	62
2339A	63
2339A	79
2339A	81
2339A	83
2339B	23
2339B	48
2339B	57
2339B	58
2339B	60

UNITED STATES CODE ANNOTATED
18 U.S.C.A.—Crimes and Criminal Procedure

Sec.	This Work Page
2339B	61
2339B	62
2339B	63
2339B	79
2339B	80
2339B	81
2339B	83
2339B	84
2339B	85
2339B	87
2339B	101
2339B	120
2340	307
2340	308
2340A	307
2340A	308
2340A	311
2510—2522	162
2510 et seq.	161
2510 et seq.	176
2511	210
2511(2)(f)	209
2511(3)	162
2517	182
2518	176
2518	178
2518	179
2705	258
2709	277
2709	278
2709	284
2709	287
2709	288
2709(f)	287
3103	258
3103a	258
3103a	259
3142	402
3142	414
3142(e)	400
3144	401
3144	402
3144	414
3511	278
3511	280
3511	284
3511	287
3511	288
4001(a)	552

18 U.S.C.A.App.—Crimes and Criminal Procedure

Sec.	This Work Page
1	469
1—16	469
2	469
3	469
4	470
5	470

UNITED STATES CODE ANNOTATED

18 U.S.C.A.App.—Crimes and Criminal Procedure

Sec.	This Work Page
6	471
7	473
8	473
9	474
10	474
12	474

21 U.S.C.A.—Food and Drugs

Sec.	This Work Page
876—877	278
876—877	287

22 U.S.C.A.—Foreign Relations and Intercourse

Sec.	This Work Page
2291	269
2291(c)	269
2656f	24
2656f	26

26 U.S.C.A.—Internal Revenue Code

Sec.	This Work Page
7602	278

50 U.S.C.A.—War and National Defense

Sec.	This Work Page
403–5d	182
436	277
1801	32
1801	162
1801	163
1801	177
1801	178
1801	210
1801et seq.	247
1801(a)(4)	176
1801(b)(1)(C)	176
1801(b)(1)(C)	178
1801(b)(2)(C)	176
1801(f)	209
1802	168
1803	163
1803	169
1804	170
1804	184
1804(a)(3)	179
1804(a)(7)(B)	184
1805	172
1805	176
1805	179
1805(f)	269
1806	181
1806	183

UNITED STATES CODE ANNOTATED

50 U.S.C.A.—War and National Defense

Sec.	This Work Page
1806(a)	181
1806(b)	181
1821—1825	247
1821	248
1822	249
1822—1825	277
1823	250
1823—1824	259
1824	252
1825	254
1861	277
1861	278
1861	288
1861	300
1861(2)	284
1881	215
1881a	216
1881a	237
1881b	222
1881b	237
1881c	226
1881c	237
1881e	229
1885a	229
1885b	231

STATUTES AT LARGE

Year	This Work Page
1980, P.L. 96–456	469
1980, P.L. 96–456	511
2002, P.L. 107–296	747

POPULAR NAME ACTS

CLASSIFIED INFORMATION PROCEDURE ACT

Sec.	This Work Page
4	480
6	480
6(a)	480
6(c)(2)	480
6(e)(1)	479

HOMELAND SECURITY ACT

Sec.	This Work Page
876	278
876	284
876	747
877	285
886	747
886	748

INSIDER TRADING ACT

Sec.	This Work Page
6952	400

MILITARY COMMISSIONS ACT OF 2009

Sec.	This Work Page
948(a)(7)	536
948i	696
949a(b)(3)(A)	690
949a(b)(3)(B)	691
949a(b)(3)(D) et. seq.	692
949k	706
949l	707
949o	708
949p–1	709
949p–1 through p–7	693
949p–2	709
949p–3	710
949p–4	710
949p–6	712
949p–7	716
950q	720
950r	720
950s	720
950t	720

MILITARY MARINE ACT

Sec.	This Work Page
950p	719

OMNIBUS DIPLOMATIC SECURITY AND ANTITERRORISM ACT

Sec.	This Work Page
2332	22

PATRIOT ACT

Sec.	This Work Page
104	747
215	246
215	277
215	278
215	281
215	285
215	286

PATRIOT ACT

Sec.	This Work Page
215	287
215	288

2012 NATIONAL DEFENSE AUTHORIZATION ACT

Sec.	This Work Page
1031	536
1040	690
1253	536

USA PATRIOT ACT

Sec.	This Work Page
416	130
880	130
1514	130

FEDERAL RULES OF CRIMINAL PROCEDURE

Rule	This Work Page
41	255
41	259
46	401
46	402
46	414

EXECUTIVE ORDERS

No.	This Work Page
11905	735
12333	735

CODE OF FEDERAL REGULATIONS

Tit.	This Work Page
32, § 213.10(a)(7)	756

FEDERAL REGISTER

Vol.	This Work Page
41, p. 7703	735
46, p. 59941	735
66, p. 57833	530
66, p. 57833	653

ANTI-TERRORISM AND CRIMINAL ENFORCEMENT

Fourth Edition

CHAPTER 1

OVERVIEW

■ ■ ■

The materials in this casebook focus on the U.S. Government's efforts to prevent and punish terrorism, that is, anti-terrorism. Why a book and a course on anti-terrorism? Is it simply another criminal law and procedure casebook targeted at a particular kind of criminal activity? Although that is an apt general description, the book (and the course) are much more than that. Especially since September 11, 2001, the executive branch of the U.S. government has claimed authority to exercise investigative, detention and prosecutorial authority, as well as several extraordinary remedies in relation to terrorism that extends much beyond the governmental powers used against ordinary crime. Congress has generally supported the executive branch's approach by enacting legislation broadening governmental authority, especially in terrorism cases. And the courts, generally, though with some exceptions, have sustained executive branch and congressional legal positions. A study of the law of anti-terrorism thus entails a detailed examination of an expansive application of governmental power regarding criminal law and procedure issues involving terrorists, with special attention paid to the respective roles of the three branches of government.

More specifically, an important way in which the government has claimed the authority to act expansively in regard to terrorism is through the use of military authority and process. Accordingly, the materials in this casebook are divided into two basic Parts: Part 2 is devoted to the military approach in enforcement against terrorism which triggers a complex and significant set of legal issues, while Part 1 covers the exercise of non-military and civilian authority in this area of the law. Even in Part 1, however, our study focuses on the ways in which non-military enforcement rules relating to terrorists and those suspected of terrorism differ from civilian criminal enforcement against ordinary crime.

Thus, in Part 1, we shall examine specific legal areas (e.g. the government's use of electronic surveillance against terrorism) in which the executive has made expansive claims of presidential authority, the sources of which are variously described as "to protect the national security," or "inherent presidential authority," or authority derived from

1

the President's status as Commander-in-chief (a claim which, of course, might have been treated in the military approach reflected in Part 2). These various claims of enhanced presidential authority to address terrorism have been made in specific legal areas, and we address them in the book in the context of the legal areas in which the claims have been made.

On the civilian side, too, rules different from those used in ordinary criminal cases are being used in terrorism matters, without invoking claims of expansive executive authority. Congress, for example, has enacted substantive offenses (the material support offenses) aimed at terrorism that break new conceptual ground, and thus far these offenses have not been copied in ordinary crimes. Similarly, Congress has enacted some statutes which give the FBI authority in terrorism matters that the agency does not otherwise possess. Also, as a constitutional matter, there are some existing terrorism exceptions to otherwise applicable constitutional rules and still other exceptions that might be extended to terrorism cases. An example is the FBI's promulgation of special rules regarding Miranda warnings in terrorism interrogations, which have yet to be tested in the courts.

Finally, some existing procedures, for example, relating to material witnesses and aliens, in the post–9/11 environment were used more extensively in terrorism matters than would otherwise have been normal. All of these different expansive uses of the civilian criminal legal system are addressed in Part 1 of the casebook.

The military rules in Part 2 are, of course, mostly different from civilian criminal process. To be studied are, for example: the relevant source(s) of the military's authority to act in this area, use of military detention authority in various contexts, abroad and in this country, against aliens and against U.S. citizens; the sources and details of the substantive criminal law in trials before military commissions; and the rules of procedure and evidence applied in such proceedings

While the civil-military line is the basic boundary in the organization of the book, it is not an ironclad line; some materials located in one Part might have placed in the other, and the use of the distinction sometimes fails to come to grips with the gradations in the authority being exercised. The basic and overall approach of the book, applicable to both Parts, is to examine the nature of, and extent to which criminal enforcement against terrorism in the 21st century differs from ordinary criminal enforcement.

Of course, this overall approach calls for some familiarity, on the part of students, with the substantive law and rules governing enforcement practices applied in ordinary criminal cases. Since the book is designed for an advanced course, it is assumed that students will have previously taken the usually-required basic first year course in criminal law; this is helpful. Because special rules and approaches are often being used in terrorism cases, it is also helpful, but not a prerequisite, if students have previously taken a course in constitutional criminal procedure. While it is obviously not possible to cover in this course all of the rules and legal doctrines used in ordinary criminal enforcement, in selected contexts—for example, in comparing the electronic surveillance rules applicable in terrorism cases and those applied for ordinary crimes—the latter rules are described in summary fashion.

While the book emphasizes the law being applied in terrorism cases, both civilian and military, and lends itself to hardnosed legal analysis, it is also desirable to pay attention to the impact of the 9/11 trauma, relevant background considerations, developments over time, political context and the significance of the shift from the administration of President Bush to President Obama. An effort is made in the book to encourage reference to such matters.

Indeed, the two most momentous events relating to enforcement against terrorism that have occurred since September 11, 2001, may have been the advent of a new President with a new administration in 2009, and the killing of Osama Bin Laden in the spring of 2011. Both events might have been expected to effect major changes in how terrorism is addressed by the federal government. Thus far, little has changed in the wake of the two occurrences (it may be too soon to tell whether Bin Laden's death will lead to any changes in the U.S. approach, but as of this writing, it seems doubtful).

There is, of course, an overriding, powerful theme reflected in questions explored in different contexts in this volume, sometimes made explicit, sometimes not—whether the particular governmental steps under consideration are necessary to maintain our security and to what extent will those steps take away from us elements of our traditional civil liberties and cause a change in the nature of our society. The purpose of this book is to make available through original and secondary sources and analytical and discussion text and questions the raw material for addressing this theme in an informed, balanced way—presenting, to the extent possible, relevant information on both sides of the many issues, hopefully without prejudgment or bias.

NOTE ON THE OBAMA ADMINISTRATION'S ANTI-TERRORISM POLICIES AND RELATED ACTIONS

It was anticipated that when Barack Obama became President in January, 2009, there would be dramatic changes in the policies and actions of the administration in regard to anti-terrorism enforcement. Potentially, the entire approach to anti-terrorism enforcement, including the use of military tribunals, designation of persons as "enemy combatants" and the like, could have changed. As it turned out, certain changes have been announced or implemented while in many instances, the same or similar policies have continued to be applied. By way of introduction to our general subject, this Note gives an overview of many of the changes that have been made as well as the areas in which policies similar to those of the previous administration have been continued. The reader may wish to refer back to this Note, in connection with various topics mentioned here, when addressing the materials in the casebook.

At the outset, almost immediately after the Inauguration, the Obama administration moved quickly to take certain actions. A 120 day suspension of trials before the military commissions was requested. It was announced that the so-called "black sites," long-term secret detention locations in foreign countries where terrorist suspects apprehended abroad were detained and interrogated, presumably by the CIA, would be closed. The President took a step to act on his campaign promise to close the Guantanamo Bay Naval Station detention facility, by announcing that it would be closed, as soon as practicable, and not later then one year hence. Administration officials indicated that waterboarding was torture, a position that members of the Bush Administration had declined to take; the President also signed an order prohibiting the use of interrogation techniques not authorized under the standards detailed in the Army Field Manual.

Ali Saleh Kahlah al-Marri, the second person arrested in the United States to be declared an "enemy combatant" and shifted to military custody, was switched back to civilian custody for prosecution in a civilian court. A Department of Justice press release indicated that the detainees at Guantanamo would no longer be designated as "enemy combatants." And Secretary of State Clinton told the press that the administration was no longer using the phrase "war on terror."

In March, the Department of Justice released a series of legal opinions which between 2001 and 2002 had been written to provide legal advice on presidential authority, the detention and trial of individuals detained as "enemy combatants" and related matters. In April, four memoranda dealing with the legality of interrogation techniques authorized for use by the CIA were also released.

All of the foregoing actions can be viewed as involving modifications of the Bush administration's policy and approach in dealing with terrorism. But there were also actions that adhered, in the main, to the Bush approach. In March, for example, the Department of Justice filed a memorandum in court in which the government claimed a broad authority to detain the men being held in Guantanamo, basing it on the Authorization to Use Military Force joint resolution by Congress and on the laws of war. In the Jeppesen Dataplan case, infra p. 385, (involving a civil suit against an airline for providing airplanes for the government's rendition program), the government sought dismissal of the suit on the ground of the state secrets privilege—a position that the Bush administration had taken in a number of lawsuits against the government or its agents. And President Obama early in his term signed an executive order authorizing the continued "rendition" of persons suspected of terrorism to foreign countries for interrogation.

The Obama administration also adhered to the previous administration's position arguing that habeas corpus was not available to detainees at the U.S. airbase in Bagram, Afghanistan. Similarly, just as President Bush did, President Obama has continued the controversial practice of using signing statements to announce that the government will not enforce specific provisions of new legislation that are believed to be unconstitutional. President Bush engaged in this practice very frequently and in regard to terrorism-related legislation. President Obama indicated he would use this practice sparingly and not without first consulting with the Attorney General.

The administration engaged in a review of the cases of the approximately 245 detainees still remaining in Guantanamo and decided that many of them could be released, that some could be prosecuted in federal court, but that, significantly, the prosecution of some would continue to be in military commission trials. The administration indicated that it would propose some amendments of the rules of evidence and procedures provided for in the Military Commission Act, enacted at the behest of the Bush administration. In this connection, there were indications that there would be a few detainees who could not be prosecuted (presumably either because the evidence against them had been obtained by torture or was too sensitive to be used in court), and the administration was working on legislation to authorize their indefinite detention, again a substantive position taken by the Bush administration. Subsequently, however, the Obama administration issued an executive order on this subject rather than seeking legislative authorization.

The Obama administration moved to release many of the remaining Guantanamo detainees, in aid of its intended closing of the facility, but encountered difficulties in getting other countries to take them and resistance in the Congress to releasing any into the United States. Moreover, with respect to those who will continue to be incarcerated, there was strong congressional resistance to using U.S. prisons, the objections taking the form of "not in my state." Among other moves, a provision was attached to the National Defense Appropriations Bill for Fiscal 2011 and also for Fiscal 2012 that would continue to bar any appropriations until the administration submitted a plan to the Congress for dealing with the detainees after Guantanamo is closed.

Overall, commentators and the media have noted that the substantive differences between Bush administration policies and Obama administration policies are not as great as might have been expected. The main difference seems to be in the underlying claims of authority: Bush claimed inherent authority as Commander-in-chief as one of the principal grounds for his exercise of specific powers. Obama is much more inclined to look to legislative authorization and to seek such authority from the Congress when necessary. See Charles Savage, To Critics New Policy on Terror Looks Old, NY Times, July 2, 2009, A11; Peter Baker, A "Surgical Approach" to Policy and Its Pitfalls, NY Times, May 22, 2009, A1.

The Content of Specific Chapters

The book is about terrorism and begins in Part 1 with a) a consideration of the definition(s) of terrorism and how the concept is used in the legal system, and b) a general overview of anti-terrorism legislation (ch. 2). It then provides an opportunity to examine in depth two conceptually-new crimes in the federal criminal code, which are now being frequently used in terrorism prosecutions (ch. 3). It also focuses on the use in anti-terrorism enforcement of special approaches, e.g. proactive surveillance by both civilian and military investigative agencies (ch. 4), and special rules governing electronic surveillance (ch. 5); search authority and the use of administrative subpoenas to obtain records (ch. 6); interrogation and extraordinary rendition (ch. 7); and the use of the material witness statute and authority over aliens [which are instances of non-special rules that have been specially used] (ch. 8), and courtroom procedures for dealing with classified information that are frequently at issue in terrorism cases (ch. 9).

On the military side in Part 2, the book examines the use of military custody as a basis for long-term detention, with reference mainly to the detainees at the Guantanamo Bay, Cuba, detention facility but also the use of that status for two individuals who had been apprehended within the United States (ch. 10); studies the operational aspects of the military commissions, including the substantive law of crimes and rules of evidence applied in such proceedings (ch. 11); discusses the issues involved in the practice of targeted killing (ch. 12); and then finishes the Part 2 portion of the book with an examination of the general legal framework governing the use of the military in domestic law enforcement (ch.13), which, in part, harks back to chapter 4. The book concludes with an Epilogue chapter (ch. 14).

PART 1

IN A CIVILIAN MODE

∎ ∎ ∎

CHAPTER 2

DEFINITIONS OF TERRORISM; TERRORISM STATUTES

■ ■ ■

A. INTRODUCTION

1. COVERAGE OF THE CHAPTER

The purpose of this chapter is to provide an introduction to the idea of terrorism, how it is used in the legal system, and how it is defined and used in varying statutory contexts. Specifically, we review contexts in which the concept of terrorism and definitions of terrorism are legally relevant; survey various definitions of terrorism and definitional approaches used in various sources, e.g., in statutes and federal agency policies; examine a number of federal terrorism statutes of various types; and reproduce a portion of a federal report on international terrorism prosecutions since September 11, 2001.

2. CONTEXTS IN WHICH TERRORISM AND DEFINITIONS OF TERRORISM MAY BE USED

What is terrorism? What acts warrant calling the perpetrator a terrorist? Is the concept of terrorism defined by the kind of conduct engaged in or by the goals of the person engaged in the conduct, or by some other factors? Definitions vary, and there are many different contexts, both legal and non-legal, in which the concepts of terrorism or terrorist may be used. We may speculate that the definition of terrorism may differ depending on the purpose for formulating the definition, or the use to which the concept of terrorism is being put. Is there a core concept of terrorism that should be utilized no matter what legal issue is in question? The purpose of this chapter is first to identify some of the different legal contexts in which the concept of terrorism may be relevant, and second to examine some approaches to defining terrorism, especially those found in the U.S. legal system, and issues that arise around them, and finally, to briefly review how the concept of terrorism is treated in those federal statutes that can reasonably be viewed as describing crimes of terrorism.

The reasons for formulating a legal definition of terrorism vary. For example, the concept of terrorism may be incorporated into the mens rea of an offense as a measure of its seriousness, or even as an element of the actus reus of the offense indicating the type of conduct that is prohibited. Or the fact that an offense involves terrorism may be relied upon as a sentence enhancing factor under the federal Sentencing Guidelines.

Further, terrorism may be used as a concept in keeping crime statistics and as a measure of the danger level in the country. It is also used as a basis for organizing sections in criminal enforcement and prosecutorial offices, and it could, conceivably, be used as a basis for determining domestic jurisdiction over certain types of criminality committed in an international setting.

UNITED STATES v. YOUSEF

327 F.3d 56 (2d Cir. 2003)

JOHN M. WALKER, JR.; RALPH K. WINTER; JOSE A. CABRANES, JUDGES:

Defendants-appellants Ramzi Yousef, Eyad Ismoil, and Abdul Hakim Murad appeal from judgments of conviction entered in the United States District Court for the Southern District of New York (Kevin Thomas Duffy, *Judge*) on April 13, June 2, and June 15, 1998, respectively. Judge Duffy presided over two separate jury trials. In the first trial, Yousef, Murad, and Wali Khan Amin Shah were tried on charges relating to a conspiracy to bomb United States commercial airliners in Southeast Asia. In the second trial, Yousef and Ismoil were tried for their involvement in the February 1993 bombing of the World Trade Center in New York City.

. . .

A year and a half after the World Trade Center bombing, Yousef entered Manila, the capital of the Philippines, under an assumed name. By September 1994, Yousef had devised a plan to attack United States airliners. According to the plan, five individuals would place bombs aboard twelve United States-flag aircraft that served routes in Southeast Asia. The conspirators would board an airliner in Southeast Asia, assemble a bomb on the plane, and then exit the plane during its first layover. As the planes continued on toward their next destinations, the time-bombs would detonate. Eleven of the twelve flights targeted were ultimately destined for cities in the United States.

Yousef and his co-conspirators performed several tests in preparation for the airline bombings. In December 1994, Yousef and Wali Khan Amin Shah placed one of the bombs they had constructed in a Manila movie theater. The bomb exploded, injuring several patrons of the theater. Ten days later, Yousef planted another test bomb under a passenger's seat during the first leg of a Philippine Airlines flight from Manila to Japan. Yousef disembarked from the plane during the stopover and then made his way back to Manila. During the second leg of the flight, the bomb exploded, killing one passenger, a Japanese national, and injuring others.

The plot to bomb the United States-flag airliners was uncovered in January 1995, only two weeks before the conspirators intended to carry it out. . . . Yousef fled the country, but was captured in Pakistan the next month.

. . .

The trial of Yousef, Murad, and Shah on the airline bombing charges began on May 29, 1996 and ended on September 5, 1996, when the jury found all three defendants guilty on all counts. . . .

Yousef was sentenced for both convictions on January 8, 1998. . . . For the airline bombing convictions, Yousef was sentenced principally to a term of life imprisonment, to be served consecutively to his 240 year sentence for the World Trade Center bombing.

. . .

In Count Fifteen, the defendants were charged with violating 18 U.S.C. § 2332(b) and (d) by conspiring to kill United States nationals while they were located outside of the United States. In Count Sixteen, the defendants were charged with violating 18 U.S.C. § 2332a by conspiring to use a weapon of mass destruction outside the United States against United States nationals.

. . .

The defendants were charged in Counts Seventeen and Eighteen with violating 18 U.S.C. §§ 924(c) and 2 by using and carrying a destructive device during and in connection with a violent crime. The violent crime underlying Count Seventeen was the conspiracy to bomb aircraft charged in Count Twelve. In Count Eighteen, the underlying violent crime was the conspiracy to kill United States nationals charged in Count Fifteen.

. . .

In Count Nineteen, Yousef alone was charged with violating 18 U.S.C. § 32(b)(3) for placing a bomb on a civil aircraft registered in another country. Specifically, Yousef was charged with planting a bomb on board a Philippine Airlines flight traveling from the Philippines to Japan on December 11, 1994. The aircraft was a civil aircraft registered in the Philippines.

There is no dispute that Congress intended § 32(b) to apply to attacks on non-United States-flag aircraft. The statute applies expressly to placing a bomb on aircraft registered in other countries while in flight, no matter where the attack is committed, and provides for jurisdiction over such extraterritorial crimes whenever, *inter alia*, "an offender is afterwards found in the United States." 18 U.S.C. § 32(b).

Yousef argues that he was wrongly charged in Count Nineteen because he was brought here against his will when Pakistan transferred him to United States custody for prosecution on charges relating to the World

Trade Center bombing and, therefore, he was not "found in the United States" within the meaning of § 32(b)....

Upon examining the persuasive interpretation by other courts of an identical jurisdictional provision in a related statute, *see* United States v. Rezaq, 328 U.S. App. D.C. 297, 134 F.3d 1121, 1130–32, 1143 (D.C. Cir. 1998); United States v. Yunis, 288 U.S. App. D.C. 129, 924 F.2d 1086, 1092 (D.C. Cir. 1991), as well as the purpose and plain language of 18 U.S.C. § 32(b), we hold that Yousef was "found in the United States" within the meaning of § 32(b).

. . .

On appeal, Yousef challenges the District Court's jurisdiction over Counts Twelve through Nineteen of the indictment by arguing that customary international law does not provide a basis for jurisdiction over these counts and that United States law is subordinate to customary international law and therefore cannot provide a basis for jurisdiction.[4] He particularly contests the District Court's conclusion that customary international law permits the United States to prosecute him under the so-called universality principle for the bombing of Philippine Airlines Flight 434 charged in Count Nineteen. Yousef claims that, absent a universally agreed-upon definition of "terrorism" and an international consensus that terrorism is a subject matter over which universal jurisdiction may be exercised, the United States cannot rest jurisdiction over him for this "terrorist" act *either* on the universality principle or on any United States positive law, which, he claims, necessarily is subordinate to customary international law.

Yousef's arguments fail. First, irrespective of whether customary international law provides a basis for jurisdiction over Yousef for Counts Twelve through Nineteen, United States law provides a separate and complete basis for jurisdiction over each of these counts and, contrary to Yousef's assertions, United States law is not subordinate to customary international law or necessarily subordinate to treaty-based international law and, in fact, may conflict with both. Further contrary to Yousef's claims, customary international law *does* provide a substantial basis for jurisdiction by the United States over each of these counts, although not (as the District Court held) under the universality principle.

---

4. Customary international law is comprised of those practices and customs that States view as obligatory and that are engaged in or otherwise acceded to by a preponderance of States in a uniform and consistent fashion. ... Customary international law recognizes five bases on which a State may exercise criminal jurisdiction over a citizen or non-citizen for acts committed outside of the prosecuting State. These five well-recognized bases of criminal jurisdiction are: (1) the "objective territorial principle," which provides for jurisdiction over conduct committed outside a State's borders that has, or is intended to have, a substantial effect within its territory; (2) the "nationality principle," which provides for jurisdiction over extraterritorial acts committed by a State's own citizen; (3) the "protective principle," which provides for jurisdiction over acts committed outside the State that harm the State's interests; (4) the "passive personality principle," which provides for jurisdiction over acts that harm a State's citizens abroad; and (5) the "universality principle," which provides for jurisdiction over extraterritorial acts by a citizen or non-citizen that are so heinous as to be universally condemned by all civilized nations....

While the District Court correctly held that jurisdiction was proper over each count, and we affirm the substance of its rulings in full, we hold that the District Court erred in partially grounding its exercise of jurisdiction over Count Nineteen—the bombing of Philippine Airlines Flight 434 while en route from Manila, the Philippines, via Cebu, to Japan on the universality principle.

We conclude, instead, that jurisdiction over Count Nineteen was proper, first, under domestic law, 18 U.S.C. § 32; second, under the *aut dedere aut punire* ("extradite or prosecute") jurisdiction created by the Montreal Convention, as implemented in 18 U.S.C. § 32 (destruction of aircraft) and 49 U.S.C. § 46502 (aircraft piracy); and third, under the *protective* principle of the customary international law of criminal jurisdiction.

1. Bases of Jurisdiction over the Counts Charged

a. Relationship between Domestic and International Law in Yousef's Prosecution

Jurisdiction over Yousef on Counts Twelve through Nineteen was based on 18 U.S.C. § 32. Yousef argues that this statute cannot give rise to jurisdiction because his prosecution thereunder conflicts with established principles of customary international law. Yousef's argument fails because, while customary international law may inform the judgment of our courts in an appropriate case, it cannot alter or constrain the making of law by the political branches of the government as ordained by the Constitution.

. . .

It has long been established that customary international law is part of the law of the United States to the limited extent that "where there is *no treaty*, and *no controlling executive or legislative act or judicial decision*, resort must be had to the customs and usages of civilized nations."

While it is permissible for United States law to conflict with customary international law, where legislation is susceptible to multiple interpretations, the interpretation that does not conflict with "the law of nations" is preferred. . . .

. . .

3. Jurisdiction over Count Nineteen

a. The District Court's Holding and Yousef's Challenges on Appeal

Count Nineteen, the bombing of Philippine Airlines Flight 434, appears to present a less straightforward jurisdictional issue because the airplane that was bombed was not a United States-flag aircraft, it was flying between two destinations outside of the United States, and there is no evidence that any United States citizens were aboard the flight or were targets of the bombing. The District Court nevertheless concluded that jurisdiction over Yousef for the offenses charged in Count Nineteen was proper, *inter alia*, under the principle of "universal jurisdiction."

Yousef makes a two-part argument on appeal challenging the District Court's holding with respect to the Court's jurisdiction over Count Nineteen. First, he claims that the District Court erred in holding that the universality principle provides jurisdiction over Count Nineteen. He bases this claim on the argument that, if his placing the bomb on the Philippine Airlines plane constituted terrorism, then jurisdiction under the universality principle is improper because terrorism is not universally condemned by the community of States and, therefore, is not subject to universal jurisdiction under customary international law. Second, he argues that because customary international law does not provide for the punishment of terrorist acts under the universality principle, such failure precludes or invalidates United States laws that provide for the prosecution of such acts that occur extraterritorially.

. . .

We hold that the District Court erred as a matter of law in relying upon the universality principle as a basis for jurisdiction over the acts charged in Count Nineteen and further hold that customary international law currently does not provide for the prosecution of "terrorist" acts under the universality principle, in part due to the failure of States to achieve anything like consensus on the definition of terrorism. However, . . . we hold that Yousef's conduct charged in Count Nineteen-regardless of whether it is termed "terrorist"-constitutes the core conduct proscribed by the Montreal Convention and its implementing legislation. Accordingly, Yousef's prosecution and conviction on this Count is both consistent with and required by the United States' treaty obligations and domestic laws. We therefore reject Yousef's claim that jurisdiction over Count Nineteen was lacking and affirm the substance of the District Court's ruling.

i. The District Court's Opinion

In holding that it could exercise universal jurisdiction over Yousef for Count Nineteen, the District Court stated:

The issue of exercising extraterritorial jurisdiction over a criminal prosecution based on universal jurisdiction was also discussed in United States v. Yunis, [288 U.S. App. D.C. 129, 924 F.2d 1086 (D.C. Cir. 1991)]. . . .

The *Yunis* court did not decide that universal jurisdiction was insufficient as the sole basis for jurisdiction under the Antihijacking Act. . . .

Endorsing the exercise of universal jurisdiction in the prosecution of an aircraft-related crime, the [Yunis] court stated that "aircraft hijacking may well be one of the few crimes so clearly condemned under the law of nations that states may assert universal jurisdiction to bring offenders to justice, even when the state has no territorial connection to the hijacking and its citizens are not involved."

The court in *Yunis* cited to the Restatement (Third) of the Foreign Relations Law to support exercise of universal jurisdiction in a criminal prosecution related to crimes involving aircraft. Section 404 [of the Restatement (Third)] states, "[a] state has jurisdiction to define and prescribe punishment for certain offenses recognized by the community of nations as of universal concern, such as piracy, slave trade, attacks on or hijacking of aircraft, genocide, war crimes, and perhaps certain acts of terrorism, even where none of the other bases of jurisdiction indicated in § 402 is present." Restatement (Third) § 404 (1987).

Yousef, 927 F. Supp. at 681

The District Court then added:

> The disregard for human life which would accompany the placing of a bomb aboard an airplane with the intent for that bomb to explode while the airplane is in flight and fully occupied with people, or otherwise sabotaging that plane, is at least as heinous a crime of international concern as hijacking a plane.

> . . .

> The District Court erred in holding that the universality principle provides a basis for jurisdiction over Yousef for the acts charged in Count Nineteen because the universality principle permits jurisdiction over only a limited set of crimes that cannot be expanded judicially, . . .

> . . .

The universality principle permits a State to prosecute an offender of any nationality for an offense committed outside of that State and without contacts to that State, but only for the few, near-unique offenses uniformly recognized by the "civilized nations" as an offense against the "Law of Nations." The strictly limited set of crimes subject to universal jurisdiction cannot be expanded by drawing an analogy between some new crime such as placing a bomb on board an airplane and universal jurisdiction's traditional subjects. . . .

The class of crimes subject to universal jurisdiction traditionally included only piracy. . . . In modern times, the class of crimes over which States can exercise universal jurisdiction has been extended to include war crimes and acts identified after the Second World War as "crimes against humanity."

> . . .

Universal jurisdiction over violations of the laws of war was not suggested until the Second World War. . . . Following the Second World War, the United States and other nations recognized "war crimes"[5] and

---

5. The Charter of the International Military Tribunal, which tried war criminals of the Second World War, defined "war crimes" as:

violations of the laws or customs of war . . . including, but not . . . limited to, murder, ill-treatment or deportation to slave labor or for any other purpose of civilian population of or in occupied territory, murder or ill-treatment of prisoners of war or persons on the seas, killing of "crimes against humanity," including "genocide,"[6] as crimes for which international law permits the exercise of universal jurisdiction.

. . .

The historical restriction of universal jurisdiction to piracy, war crimes, and crimes against humanity demonstrates that universal jurisdiction arises under customary international law only where crimes (1) are universally condemned by the community of nations, and (2) by their nature occur either outside of a State or where there is no State capable of punishing, or competent to punish, the crime (as in a time of war).

Unlike those offenses supporting universal jurisdiction under customary international law—that is, piracy, war crimes, and crimes against humanity—that now have fairly precise definitions and that have achieved universal condemnation, "terrorism" is a term as loosely deployed as it is powerfully charged. Judge Harry T. Edwards of the District of Columbia Circuit stated eighteen years ago in Tel–Oren v. Libyan Arab Republic, 233 U.S. App. D.C. 384, 726 F.2d 774 (D.C. Cir. 1984), that "while this nation unequivocally condemns all terrorist acts, that sentiment is not universal. Indeed, the nations of the world are so divisively split on the legitimacy of such aggression as to make it impossible to pinpoint an area of harmony or consensus." Id. at 795 (Edwards, J., concurring).

. . .

We regrettably are no closer now than eighteen years ago to an international consensus on the definition of terrorism or even its proscription;[7] the mere existence of the phrase "state-sponsored terrorism" proves the absence of agreement on basic terms among a large number of States that terrorism violates public international law. Moreover, there continues

---

hostages, plunder of public or private property, wanton destruction of cities, towns, or villages, or devastation not justified by military necessity[.]

6. The Charter describes "crimes against humanity" as:

murder, extermination, enslavement, deportation, and other inhumane acts committed against any civilian population, before or during the war, or persecutions on political, racial, or religious grounds in execution of or in connection with any crime within the jurisdiction of the Tribunal, whether or not in violation of domestic law of the country where perpetrated.

The Charter of the International Military Tribunal, Art. 6(c), *in* 1 Trial of the Major War Criminals before the International Military Tribunal 11 (1947).

7. For example, each side of the Israeli–Palestinian conflict charges the other with "terrorism," sentiments echoed by their allies. *See, e.g.,* Todd S. Purdum, *What Do You Mean, 'Terrorist'?*, N.Y. Times, Apr. 7, 2002, Week in Review, at 1 ("If Israel sees its military campaign in the West Bank as a justifiable echo of Mr. Bush's assault on Al Qaeda, Palestinians claim affinity with the American colonists' revolt against an occupying power."). The Organization of the Islamic Conference met in Kuala Lumpur, Malaysia, in April 2002, to define terrorism; the host of the conference, Malaysian Prime Minister Mahathir Mohamad, proposed a definition of terrorism as "all attacks on civilians"; the conference's final declaration, however, stated that terrorism consists only of attacks on civilians perpetrated by non-Palestinians, stating that the Conference " 'rejects any attempt to link terrorism to the struggle of the Palestinian people in the exercise of their inalienable right to establish their independent state.' " *Id.* (quoting statements by Mohamad and contained in the conference's final declaration). Sentiments at the conference were far from uniform, however: The deputy foreign minister of Bosnia–Herzegovina stated that "if a person kills or harms a civilian . . . he is a terrorist" irrespective of the "race or religion" of the perpetrator and the victims. *Terrorism Issue Splits Muslim Conferees*, Chi. Trib., April 2, 2002, at 10 (quoting statements of Bosnian–Herzegovinian delegate to conference).

to be strenuous disagreement among States about what actions do or do not constitute terrorism, nor have we shaken ourselves free of the cliche that "one man's terrorist is another man's freedom fighter."[8]

. . .

While it is true, as Yousef asserts, that the District Court erred in concluding that the universality principle conferred jurisdiction over the crimes charged in Count Nineteen, Yousef's claim that principles of customary international law constrain Congress's power to enact laws that proscribe extraterritorial conduct is simply wrong.

. . .

Although the government is not required to prove that its prosecution of Yousef comported with any of the customary international law bases of criminal jurisdiction, we note that, in fact, Yousef's prosecution by the United States *is* consistent with the "protective principle" of international law. The protective (or "security") principle permits a State to assume jurisdiction over non-nationals for acts done abroad that affect the security of the State. . . .

The stated purpose of Yousef's plot to destroy United States commercial aircraft was to influence United States foreign policy, the making of which clearly constitutes a "governmental function." The bombing of the

---

8. Confusion on the definition of "terrorism" abounds. *See, e.g.*, Craig S. Smith, *Debate Over Iraq Raises Fears of a Shrinking Role for NATO*, N.Y. Times, Jan. 26, 2003, at L 26 (quoting Celeste A. Wallander, senior fellow at the Center for Strategic and International Studies, as stating that even among members of the North Atlantic Treaty Alliance ("NATO") there is no consensus "on how to define transnational terrorism").

Terrorism is defined variously by the perpetrators' motives, methods, targets, and victims. Motive-based definitions suffer from confusion because of the attempt to carve out an exception for assertedly legitimate armed struggle in pursuit of self-determination. For example, under one of the various United Nations resolutions addressing terrorism, armed and violent acts do not constitute "terrorism" if committed by peoples seeking self-determination in opposition to a violently enforced occupation. *See, e.g.*, Declaration on Principles of International Law Concerning Friendly Relations Among Co-operating States in Accordance with the Charter of the United Nations, Oct. 24, 1970, G.A. Res. 2625, 25 U.N. GAOR Supp. (No. 28) at 21, U.N. Doc. A/8028 (1971), reprinted in 9 I.L.M. 1292 (1970). This attempt to distinguish "terrorists" from "freedom fighters" potentially could legitimate as non-terrorist certain groups nearly universally recognized as terrorist, including the Irish Republican Army, Hezbollah, and Hamas. . . .

By contrast, the European Convention on the Suppression of Terrorism defines terrorism solely based on the methods of violence the perpetrator employs, and explicitly removes political judgment of the acts by defining most violent acts as "non-political" (regardless of the perpetrator's claimed motive). European Convention on the Suppression of Terrorism, Nov. 10, 1976, Europ. T.S. No. 90. Thus, in Article I, the Convention defines as terrorism any offenses, *inter alia*, "involving the use of a bomb, grenade, rocket, automatic firearm, or letter or parcel bomb if this use endangers persons," a definition that may fail to circumscribe the offense adequately.

The Arab Convention on the Suppression of Terrorism (Cairo, Apr. 22, 1998), *reprinted in* International Instruments Related to the Prevention and Suppression of International Terrorism, 152–73 (United Nations 2001), while condemning terrorism, takes a uniquely restrictive approach to defining it, stating that offenses committed against the interests of Arab states are "terrorist offenses," while offenses committed elsewhere or against other peoples or interests are not. *Id.* at Art. I.3 (defining "terrorist offence" as any of several defined violent actions that occur "in any of the Contracting States, or against their nationals, property or interests"). The Convention further defines as legitimate (non-terrorist) "all cases of struggle by whatever means, including armed struggle," unless such struggles "prejudice the territorial integrity of any Arab State." *Id.* at Art. II(a).

. . .

Philippine Airlines flight at issue in Count Nineteen, which killed one Japanese national and maimed another, was merely a test-run that Yousef executed to ensure that the tactics and devices the conspirators planned to use on United States aircraft operated properly.

Documentation stored on Yousef's laptop computer and adduced at trial demonstrates that the Philippine Airlines bombing constituted part of the co-conspirators' plan to detonate numerous bombs on United States-flag aircraft.

.   .   .

QUESTIONS AND NOTES

1.   How many different bases for the exercise of U.S. legal authority to prosecute conduct perpetrated abroad are discussed in Yousef? How many of these, in turn, are propositions regarding U.S. law? How many reflect principles of international law?

2.   Suppose that the Congress were to enact a statute that purported to establish U.S. authority to prosecute an act of terrorism perpetrated against any country and perpetrated anywhere in the world. Would it comply with principles of international law?

3.   Suppose a U.S. navy vessel stops a ship (sailing under a foreign flag) on the high seas (headed for, let us say, Portugal), and in their search for drugs, discover an illicit nuclear weapon. Is there jurisdiction under U.S. law to prosecute those on the ship who are in possession and control of this bomb? If not, should there be? Consider after you have reviewed the offenses described in this section of the casebook whether the conduct involved runs afoul of any of these offenses. (Note, of course, the difference between the question of whether there is jurisdiction and whether the conduct involved is prohibited by a provision of the federal criminal code.)

4.   A number of the terrorism-related crimes in Title 18, U.S.C. that are set forth, infra, in this chapter of the casebook contain detailed jurisdictional provisions for dealing with criminal conduct engaged in outside of the United States. Consider which category of jurisdiction described in Yousef supports each particular jurisdictional base in these statutes.

5.   The Yousef court concluded that there is no basis under the notion of universal jurisdiction for prosecuting airplane hijacking or blowing up a passenger airplane because there is no international consensus on what constitutes terrorism. Do you think this conclusion is sound? What kind of arguments might be formulated in response? What are the differences between piracy and terrorism that warrant applying the universality principle for the former and not the latter?

6.   A legal context in which "terrorist" acts may be legally significant is the "terrorism" enhancement factor under the federal Sentencing Guidelines. See United States v. Thurston, 2007 WL 1500176 (D.Ore. 2007):

> The court is asked to decide whether the sentencing enhancement for terrorism under § 3A1.4 of the United States Sentencing Guidelines applies to the defendants in the above-captioned cases, based on their

convictions for conspiracy to commit arson and destruction of an energy facility of the United States and for the predicate offenses of arson, attempted arson, and destruction of an energy facility.

. . .

At the outset, it is important to clarify the court's role in this proceeding. The issue the court must decide is not whether the defendants are "terrorists" as the word commonly is used and understood in today's political and cultural climate.

. . .

Additionally, contrary to many defendants' assertions, the court is not entering into uncharted waters. As discussed in this opinion, the terrorism enhancement has been applied in several cases where the offenses of conviction caused only property damage. While the number of decisions may not be significant, these cases provide the court with considerable guidance.

. . .

Pursuant to negotiated plea agreements, all defendants have pled guilty to one count of conspiracy to commit arson and the destruction of an energy facility in violation of 18 U.S.C. § 371. In addition to conspiracy, defendants Tubbs, Gerlach, Meyerhoff, McGowan, Savoie, Tankersley, Block, Zacher, and Paul pled guilty to numerous counts of arson and attempted arson of property used in or affecting interstate commerce in violation of 18 U.S.C. § 844(i). Defendants Tubbs and Thurston also pled guilty to arson of federal government property in violation of 18 U.S.C. § 844(f)(1), and defendants Gerlach and Meyerhoff pled guilty to the destruction of an energy facility in violation of 18 U.S.C. § 1366(a). Defendants' convictions are based on the following undisputed facts, as admitted by defendants in their plea agreements and as set forth in the Presentence Investigation Report and the government's sentencing memorandum.

Beginning in October 1996 and continuing through October 2001, defendants and other individuals formed a conspiracy to damage or destroy private and government property. Specifically, defendants conspired to commit a series of arson and other offenses on behalf of the Animal Liberation Front (ALF) and the Earth Liberation Front (ELF). The conspirators targeted federal government agencies and private parties they believed responsible for degradation of the environment, tree harvesting, and cruel treatment of animals. Eventually, the targets of arson expanded to include entities involved in genetic research.

. . .

By 2001, the conspirators had committed numerous acts of arson or attempted arson and destroyed a high voltage electrical tower across five different states. The offenses included: arson of the Dutch Girl Dairy in Eugene, Oregon in December 1995; arson and attempted arson of the United States Forest Service (USFS) Ranger Station in Detroit, Oregon in October 1996; arson of the USFS Ranger Station in Oakridge, Oregon in October 1996; arson of Cavel West Meat Packing Plant in Redmond,

Oregon in July 1997; arson of the Bureau of Land Management (BLM) Wild Horse Corrals near Burns, Oregon in November 1997; arson of the United States Department of Agriculture Animal Plan Health Inspection Service and Animal Damage Control Facility in Olympia, Washington in June 1998;.... These actions damaged or destroyed numerous buildings and vehicles, causing tens of millions of dollars in damages.

After the arson offenses, the conspirators often sent "communiques" attributing responsibility for the particular arson to ELF or ALF and explaining the motivation for the offense. For example, a communique on behalf of ALF described the Cavel West arson in detail and accepted responsibility for destroying the "horse murdering plant." Similarly, following the fire at Childers Meat Company, a communique declared that "[a]s long as companies continue to operate and profit off of Mother Earth and Her sentient animal beings, the Animal Liberation Front will continue to target these operations and their insurance companies until they are all out of business." After the Litchfield BLM Wild Horse Corral arson, a communique was released opposing the asserted BLM policy of "round[ing] up thousands of wild horses and burros to clear public land for grazing cattle" and warning of future actions: "In the name of all that is wild we will continue to target industries and organizations that seek to profit by destroying the earth."

. . .

Defendants next argue that their convictions under 18 U.S.C. §§ 844(f)(1), 844(i), and 1366(a) cannot support imposition of the terrorism enhancement, because none of their offenses created a substantial risk of harm. Defendants contend that Congress did not intend that the enhancement apply to offenses that caused only property damage but did not cause injury or death.

. . .

However, this court is bound by the canons of statutory construction, and I find that resolution of this issue begins and ends with the plain language of the statute and Sentencing Guidelines.... Second, the definition of "federal crime of terrorism" does not import the element of "substantial risk of serious bodily injury" included in 18 U.S.C. § 2332b(a)(1)(A). Instead, Congress defined a "federal crimes of terrorism" as the commission of specific offenses along with the intent or desire to influence, affect, or retaliate against government conduct.

. . .

I find that a "federal crime of terrorism" under § 2332b(g)(5) does not require a substantial risk of injury.

. . .

Defendants argue that the government cannot establish the necessary motivational element to support the terrorism enhancement, because their offenses were calculated merely to gain and generate publicity rather than to influence, affect, or retaliate against government conduct. Additionally, with respect to the arson of private property, defendants maintain that they targeted those businesses with the intent to influence or affect the conduct of private parties rather than the conduct of government. . . .

The government responds that the court must look at the totality of the circumstances surrounding each arson to determine whether each offense was calculated to influence, affect, or retaliate against government conduct.

As stated during argument, the court cannot determine conclusively whether the offenses were intended to influence, affect, or retaliate against government conduct until relevant evidence is presented at the defendants' sentencing hearings. At the same time, defendants point is well taken; the definition of "federal crime of terrorism" explicitly requires an intent "to influence or affect the *conduct of government* by intimidation or coercion, or to retaliate against *government conduct.*" 18 U.S.C. § 2332b(g)(5)(A) (emphasis added). Thus, the government must establish that the defendants targeted government conduct rather than the conduct of private individuals or corporations.

     . . .

7. Apart from the particular statute at issue in the Thurston case, should the concept of terrorism be restricted to acts targeting the government, or should it also include violence directed against private individuals or corporations?

8. Prior to the sentencing in the *Thurston* case, supra, Caroline Paul, the sister of one of the defendants, wrote an op-ed piece in the Los Angeles Times in which she argued that this was the first time terrorism sentencing enhancements were claimed when the defendants took affirmative steps to make certain that no one would be hurt. While conceding that egregious property damage was caused, she contended that it was "still just property damage." She also stated, "Could it really be true that the most powerful country in the world feels 'coerced' by a bunch of bunny huggers? Is the . . . leader of this nation being bullied by vegans?"

LA Times, May 24, 2007, latimes.com/news/opinion/la-oe-paul 24 May. Apart from the matter of statutory construction, should the notion of terrorism, or at least terrorism used as a basis for sentencing enhancement, be restricted to violent acts that cause injury to persons?

9. Most of the terrorism cases addressed in this volume involve international terrorism. Is there any reason to restrict our focus to the international sphere? The Thurston case illustrates what may be termed domestic terrorism. As we shall see in the next section, both domestic and international terrorism are defined under federal law. For another example of a sentencing enhancement case involving domestic terrorism, see United States v. Graham, 275 F.3d 490 (6th Cir. 2001):

Graham and Huggett were members of a militia group called the Michigan Militia Wolverines in the early years of their marijuana cultivation business. Huggett testified that, at some point after 1995, Graham and others were expelled from the Wolverines because they were advocating violence against the government. In the summer of 1996, those individuals who had left the Wolverines formed a new militia group called the "North American Militia" ("NAM"). The purpose of the militia group was to prepare for a "war" with the government and ultimately to overthrow the government. NAM members advocated an offensive "first strike" against the government, out of fear that the government was planning an attack against them. The war was sometimes referred to as an "Armageddon." ... Various dates for attack were selected, beginning with June 7, 1997, although each date was subsequently postponed by Carter.

Undercover Bureau of Alcohol, Tobacco, and Firearms ("ATF") Agent Robert Stumpenhaus infiltrated NAM sometime in April 1997. Agent Stumpenhaus testified at trial that he participated in over ten meetings at Speed's and at the mall with various members of NAM. Stumpenhaus and other witnesses who testified at trial reported that among their activities, NAM collected and stockpiled weapons; held target practice and conducted paramilitary training; selected various federal and state "hard" and "soft" targets; and plotted strategy for their war. Stumpenhaus reported that Carter's strategy was to attack certain targets in Calhoun County, Michigan, and the surrounding area, create chaos, and then attempt to "hold on" for three to five days while militias in other parts of the country would rise up against the government. In preparation for their war, NAM members participated in training activities, such as going on "bivouacs;" learning "close quarters battle;" and securing a building with weapons and emptying the building of people and weapons.

Under Carter's direction, each member of the militia was assigned to a three-person "cell" which was responsible for "taking out" various "hard" and "soft" targets in a certain geographical region. Among the "hard" targets selected for attack were: (1) the intersection of Interstate 94 and U.S. Route 131 near Kalamazoo, Michigan; (2) power facilities; (3) fuel depots and gas stations; and (4) communication facilities such as a TV station in Kalamazoo, Michigan. Also mentioned as a site for attack was the nearby Fort Custer Army National Guard Post. NAM's goal was to cut off transportation, electricity, gas, and communication to the area. Among the "soft" targets identified were federal prosecutors, judges, and other federal officials as well as Senator Carl Levin of Michigan and other members of Congress. . . .

. . .

. . . . The district court concluded that Graham and his co-conspirators intended to influence and intimidate federal officers in the performance of their duties; that they conspired to possess machine guns and other weapons; and that they discussed plans to attack their targets with the weapons they had acquired, all in furtherance of the conspiracy.

Based on our review of the record, we cannot say that the district court's findings of fact are clearly erroneous.

B. TERRORISM: DEFINITIONS AND DEFINITIONAL APPROACHES

1. IN GENERAL

Definitions of terrorism that are relevant to the federal criminal enforcement process can be found in various sources. The most important source for our purposes is statutory: Some statutes that would probably be described as aimed at terrorist activities contain specific definitions of terrorism; some do not. The feature that arguably makes a crime terrorism may be contained in the elements of the offense even though there is no specific definition of terrorism in the statute. Some non-criminal statutes also contain definitions of terrorism, and these may be incorporated by reference into criminal enforcement contexts. Further, definitions of the concept also can be found in federal administrative regulations and administrative policy, formal or informal, as articulated by various government agencies. In the United States, both at the federal level and in the states, in the criminal enforcement context, different statutory definitions of the term "terrorism" may be found, but the definitions tend to fall into typical patterns and within certain parameters.

As was noted in United States v. Yousef, supra, in other countries and on the international level, questions of what constitutes "terrorism" and what definition should be used are often controversial and embroiled in varying political outlooks and ideological concerns. See generally Gabriel Soll, Terrorism: The Known Element No One Can Define, 11 Willamette J. Int'l L. & Disp. Resol. 123 (2004); Yonah Alexander, Terrorism in the Twenty-first Century: Threats and Responses, 12 DePaul Bus.L.J. 59 (2004), and see generally, Yonah Alexander & Edgar H. Brenner, Legal Aspects of Terrorism in the United States (2000).

The most common approach in our federal criminal system relies on a general definition in the form of something like, "a purpose to coerce a government to do something or to retaliate against a government." While there are variations in the exact terms used in these general definitions, these differences tend to be matters of degree and detail. Review the statutes that contain formulations using such an approach in section C., infra, as well as the material below in this section that also use this kind of approach and see how many variations you can identify. Is there anything which commends one variation in preference to others?

A second approach is one which contains a general definition but combines it with a list of statutory offenses, with the combination of the two being the marker for terrorism. See, e.g., 18 U.S.C. § 2332b, infra, p. 41.

A third variation simply uses a list of offenses that are deemed terrorism-related offenses. Differences among the approaches that use a listing of offenses turn on which offenses are listed. Compare, e.g., § 2339A, infra, p. 60 with § 2332b, infra, p. 41.

A fourth type is one which does not use a definition as such. If the offense is viewed as terrorism, it flows from the nature of the harmful conduct engaged in. Illustrative are §§ 2332a, infra, p. 38 and § 2332f, infra, p. 48, offenses involving the use of weapons of mass destruction and bombing of public facilities, respectively.

A fifth category is one which arguably uses a surrogate concept for the concept of terrorism—for example, the transcending national boundaries formula found in § 2332b, infra, p. 41.

Finally, in administrative policy formulations relating to terrorist activity, one finds formulations that tend to be less analytically tight and may combine elements of several of the categories described above as well as others. Of course, some of the administrative formulations simply cross-reference to and rely upon one of the statutory definitions.

Is it a matter of happenstance that there are so many different statutory approaches to the concept and definition of terrorism? Or is the explanation to be found in some notion of the purpose or relevance of treating an offense as one of terrorism? Examine these materials with a view to determining how many different purposes or uses for the definition of terrorism (or related concepts) you can find.

In a number of instances, criminal or crime-related statutes refer to and incorporate by reference a definition of terrorism used in another area of the law, for example, the immigration laws. See, e.g., § 2339B.

Not only definitions of terrorism simpliciter are found in these materials. Other terrorism-related concepts are also used, for example, "terrorist activity"; "terrorist organization"; and, as previously mentioned, "international terrorism" and "domestic terrorism." Issues similar to those involving the definition of terrorism also arise regarding the use of these variations.

In connection with the definitions that are borrowed, the determination of whether a phrase such as "terrorist organization" applies to a particular group or entity may be initially made in an administrative proceeding rather than in the course of the judicial proceedings in which it is later used. In effect, not only the definition but also the procedures for applying the definition may be borrowed from another area of the law. In Chapter 3, special issues raised by this type of approach are examined.

Over the course of the past two or three decades, many new statutes have been enacted defining new terrorism crimes: a number of these have broken new ground. Most of these statutes can be found in Title 18 of the Federal Criminal Code. Our main focus in this chapter is on the various criminal statutory definitions of terrorism and on those Title 18 offenses that are specifically aimed at terrorism. Of course, prosecutions of individuals for terrorism-related conduct are also frequently based on crimes that are not inherently crimes of terrorism, that is, they can be committed in non-terrorism as well as terrorism contexts. It is the context that moves such offenses into the terrorism arena. A list of the types of offenses that have been utilized in some of the terrorism cases prosecuted over the past several years covers a broad range of federal offenses. See infra, section D, p. 53.

The incidence of prosecutions for terrorism-related conduct has been growing significantly in recent years, but viewed as part of the total nationwide or total federal criminal caseload, terrorism cases continue to be a very small proportion of these totals. Of course, a single terrorism crime, successfully completed, can cause catastrophic destruction and loss of life. We cannot be certain whether the relatively low incidence of prosecutions reflects the fact that there are not a great many people planning acts of terrorism, or that the law enforcement authorities have only been able to apprehend and build cases to prosecute against a few while there may be many more "out there" planning terrorist incidents. We shall learn more about these issues with the passage of time.

In section C., infra, a selection of statutes that can reasonably be described as defining terrorist crimes is examined. A number of these statutes have unusual features that warrant attention and are addressed through a series of questions and hypothetical fact situations. Section D reproduces excerpts from a federal report on terrorism prosecutions.

In chapter 3, infra, we shall examine in much more depth the case law interpreting and applying two of the more heavily used of these anti-terrorism offenses, the material support statutes, 18 U.S.C. §§ 2339A and 2339B.

2. STATUTORY DEFINITIONS OF TERRORISM

Perhaps the most significant of these statutes for our purposes is § 2331, in Title 18, U.S.C. This provision defines the terms "international terrorism" and "domestic terrorism" as those words are used in the legislative chapter that contains most of the general terrorism statutes found in the federal criminal code. A number of these offenses are discussed in section C., infra. Consider, among the offenses treated in section C, how many of them use the terms international or domestic terrorism.

A definitional provision found in the Immigration and Nationality Act, § 1182, Title 8, U.S.C., sets forth the terrorism-related grounds for excluding aliens from the United States. This provision is also used, however, through incorporation by reference in certain federal criminal terrorism statutes.

The main purpose of the definition of terrorism in section 2656f, Title 22, U.S.C., is to provide a definition that can be used as the basis for the State Department's annual report on the terrorist threat worldwide. This definition is also incorporated by reference into some criminal enforcement contexts.

18 U.S.C. § 2331. Definitions

As used in this chapter—

(1) the term "international terrorism" means activities that

(A) involve violent acts or acts dangerous to human life that are a violation of the criminal laws of the United States or of any State, or that would be a criminal violation if committed within the jurisdiction of the United States or of any State;

(B) appear to be intended—

(i) to intimidate or coerce a civilian population;

(ii) to influence the policy of a government by intimidation or coercion; or

(iii) to affect the conduct of a government by mass destruction, assassination, or kidnapping; and

(C) occur primarily outside the territorial jurisdiction of the United States, or transcend national boundaries in terms of the means by which they are accomplished, the persons they appear intended to intimidate or coerce, or the locale in which their perpetrators operate or seek asylum;

. . .

(5) the term "domestic terrorism" means activities that—

(A) involve acts dangerous to human life that are a violation of the criminal laws of the United States or of any State;

(B) appear to be intended

(i) to intimidate or coerce a civilian population;

(ii) to influence the policy of a government by intimidation or coercion; or

(iii) to affect the conduct of a government by mass destruction, assassination, or kidnapping; and

(C) occur primarily within the territorial jurisdiction of the United States.

8 U.S.C. § 1182

8 U.S.C. § 1182 is a lengthy section which, inter alia, sets forth grounds on which aliens may be ruled to be inadmissible to the United States. Among its many provisions are those which determine that a person who engages in terrorist activities is inadmissible to the U.S. In that connection § 1182 contains a definition of "terrorist activity."

(a)

3.

B.

(iii) Terrorist activity defined.

As used in this Act, the term "terrorist activity" means any activity which is unlawful under the laws of the place where it is committed (or which, if it had been committed in the United States, would be unlawful under the laws of the United States or any State) and which involves any of the following:

(I) The highjacking or sabotage of any conveyance (including an aircraft, vessel, or vehicle).

(II) The seizing or detaining, and threatening to kill, injure, or continue to detain, another individual in order to compel a third person (including a governmental organization) to do or abstain from doing any act as an explicit or implicit condition for the release of the individual seized or detained.

(III) A violent attack upon an internationally protected person (as defined in section 1116(b)(4) of title 18, United States Code) or upon the liberty of such a person.

(IV) An assassination.

(V) The use of any

(a) biological agent, chemical agent, or nuclear weapon or device, or

(b) explosive, firearm, or other weapon or dangerous device (other than for mere personal monetary gain), with intent to endanger, directly or indirectly, the safety of one or more individuals or to cause substantial damage to property.

(VI) A threat, attempt, or conspiracy to do any of the foregoing.

. . .

22 U.S.C. § 2656f. Annual country reports on terrorism

(a) Requirement of annual country reports on terrorism

The Secretary of State shall transmit to the Speaker of the House of Representatives and the Committee on Foreign Relations of the Senate, by April 30 of each year, a full and complete report providing—

(1) detailed assessments with respect to each foreign country

(A) in which acts of international terrorism occurred which were, in the opinion of the Secretary, of major significance;

. . .

(2) all relevant information about the activities during the preceding year of any terrorist group, and any umbrella group under which such terrorist group falls, known to be responsible for the kidnapping or death of an American citizen during the preceding five years, any terrorist group known to be financed by countries about which Congress was notified during the preceding year pursuant to section 2405(j) of the Appendix to Title 50, and any other known international terrorist group which the Secretary determines should be the subject of such report;

. . .

(d) Definitions

As used in this section

(1) the term "international terrorism" means terrorism involving citizens or the territory of more than 1 country;

(2) the term "terrorism" means premeditated, politically motivated violence perpetrated against noncombatant targets by subnational groups or clandestine agents; and

(3) the term "terrorist group" means any group practicing, or which has significant subgroups which practice, international terrorism.

Do you think it might be feasible to incorporate definitions of all of the relevant terms into a single definition section that could be used for all of these different contexts?

3. POLICY DEFINITIONS OF TERRORISM AND ENFORCEMENT POLICY; LISTING OF TERRORIST ORGANIZATIONS

Many government departments have responsibilities relating to anti-terrorism efforts, and a number of these have some role in criminal enforcement in aid of anti-terrorism efforts. Coordination and communication among these agencies is now the responsibility of the Homeland Security Department. At this point, we examine enforcement policy statements relating to the anti-terrorism efforts of several different agencies, the State Department, the Department of Justice and the Federal Bureau of Investigation.

a. The State Department

Department of State, Patterns of Global Terrorism 2001 (released May 21, 2002):

The US Government (USG) has established four primary counter-terrorism "lists" to serve as tools in the fight against terrorism: The State Sponsors of Terrorism, Foreign Terrorist Organizations (FTO), Executive Order 13224, and the Terrorist Exclusion (TEL) list. Each list has its individual mechanisms, but they all serve to prevent terrorism, punish terrorists and their supporters, and pressure changes in the behavior of designated states and groups.

Because these lists are a means to fight terrorism, rather than an end in themselves, they are not designed or intended to be immutable. The USG encourages states and organizations to take the necessary actions to get out of the terrorism business. The bar for a state or group being removed from a USG terrorism list is and must be high— it must end all involvement in any facet of terrorism, including passive support, and satisfy all USG counterterrorism concerns.

State Sponsors of Terrorism

The Secretary of State is authorized to designate a government as a "State Sponsor of Terrorism" if that government "has repeatedly provided support for acts of international terrorism." United States law requires the imposition of various sanctions on a state so designated. . . . Currently, there are seven countries on the list: Cuba, Iran, Iraq,[1] Libya,[2] North Korea, Sudan, and Syria.

Foreign Terrorist Organizations (FTOs)

The Secretary of State is authorized to designate as FTOs groups that conduct international terrorism and threaten the interests of the United States. Designation allows the USG to block designees' assets in US financial institutions; criminalizes witting provision of material support to designated groups; and allows the USG to block visas for members of FTOs without having to show that the individual was involved in specific terrorist activities. FTO designation also sends a strong signal that any group that engages in terrorism regardless of its purported goals will be condemned and penalized for its actions.

Executive Order 13224 Terrorist Financing

President Bush signed Executive Order 13224 on 23 September 2001, to give the USG a strong tool for eliminating the financial supporters and networks of terrorism. EO 13224 enables the USG to block designees' assets in any financial institution in the United States or held by any US person. . . . At the end of 2001, EO 13224 designations allowed the USG, as well as Coalition partners acting in concert, to block tens of millions of dollars intended to bankroll the murderous activities of al-Qaida and other terrorist groups.

Comprehensive List of Terrorists and Groups Identified Under Executive Order 13224

Executive Order 13224, signed by President Bush on September 23, 2001, blocks the assets of organizations and individuals linked to terrorism. There are more than a hundred such groups, entities, and individuals covered by the Executive Order. [The original list was

---

1. Iraq is no longer listed as a state sponsor of terrorism.

2. Libya's designation as a state sponsor of terrorism was rescinded on June 30, 2003.

promulgated on September 23, 2001 and updated periodically since then. A brief sampling of names on the list is reproduced below.]

Original Annex: September 23, 2001

al-Qaida/Islamic Army*

Abu Sayyaf Group*

Armed Islamic Group (GIA)*

Harakat ul-Mujahidin (HUM)*

al-Jihad (Egyptian Islamic Jihad)*

Asbat al-Ansar*

Libyan Islamic Fighting Group (Al Jama'a al-Islamiyyah al-Mu-qatilah bi-Libya)

Designated on 2 November 2001

Abu Nidal organization (ANO)

al-Gama'a al-Islamiyya (Islamic Group)

HAMAS (Islamic Resistance Movement)

Hizballah (Party of God)

Kahane Chai (Kach)

Kurdistan Workers' Party (PKK)

Liberation Tigers of Tamil Eelam (LTTE)

Mujahedin-e Khalq Organization (MEK)

National Liberation Army (ELN)

Palestine Islamic Jihad (PIJ)

Palestine Liberation Front (PLF)

Popular Front for the Liberation of Palestine (PFLP)

Popular Front for the Liberation of Palestine–General Command (PFLP–GC)

Real IRA

Revolutionary Armed Forces of Colombia (FARC)

Revolutionary Nuclei (possible successor to ELA)

Shining Path (Sendero Luminoso, SL)

United Self–Defense Forces of Colombia (AUC)

Designated on 4 December 2001

Holy Land Foundation

Beit El–Mal Holdings

al-Aqsa Islamic Bank

Patriot USA Act: Terrorist Exclusion List

President Bush on 26 October 2001, signed into law a comprehensive counterterrorism bill (Public Law 107–56, also known as USA PATRIOT). The new law strengthened enforcement tools and made improvements to the last major terrorism bill, the Antiterrorism and Effective Death Penalty Act of 1996. The Patriot USA Act also created a Terrorist Exclusion List (TEL) with immigration consequences for groups named therein. Designation on the TEL allows the USG to exclude or deport aliens who provide material assistance to, or solicit for a designated organization.

Statement on the Designation of 39 Organizations on the USA PA-TRIOT Act's "Terrorist Exclusion List" (Press Statement, Philip T. Reeker, Deputy Spokesman, Washington, DC.)

To further protect the safety of the United States and its citizens, Secretary of State Colin L. Powell, in consultation with the Attorney General, on 5 December designated 39 groups as Terrorist Exclusion List (TEL) organizations under section 212 of the Immigration and Nationality Act, as amended by the new USA PATRIOT Act. By designating these groups, the Secretary has strengthened the United States' ability to exclude supporters of terrorism from the country or to deport them.

b. The Department of Justice

The Department of Justice has traditionally had as one of its enforcement priorities Terrorism and Counter–Intelligence. The following excerpt is taken from Department of Justice, The Attorney General's Guidelines on General Crimes, Racketeering Enterprise and Terrorism Enterprise Investigations (2002):

. . .

A terrorism enterprise investigation may be initiated when facts or circumstances reasonably indicate that two or more persons are engaged in an enterprise for the purpose of: (1) furthering political or social goals wholly or in part through activities that involve force or violence and a federal crime, (2) engaging in terrorism as defined in 18 U.S.C. 2331(1) or (5) that involves a federal crime, or (3) committing any offense described in 18 U.S.C. 2332b(G)(5)(B). . . .

As with the other types of full investigations authorized by these Guidelines, any lawful investigative technique may be used in terrorism enterprise investigations, including the development of sources and informants and undercover activities and operation. The "reasonable indication" standard for commencing a terrorism enterprise investigation is the same as that for general crimes and racketeering enterprise investigations. . . . [I]t is substantially lower than probable cause.

c. The Federal Bureau of Investigation

Policies and procedures applied by the FBI can be found, for example, in the Code of Federal Regulations, the Attorney General Guidelines, supra, in documents such as Department of Justice, Federal Bureau of Investigation, Counterterrorism Threat Assessment and Warning Unit, Counterterrorism Division, Terrorism in the United States (1999), and in The Attorney General Guidelines for FBI Foreign Intelligence Collection and Foreign Counterintellligence Investigations.

Department of Justice, Federal Bureau of Investigation, Counterterrorism Threat Assessment and Warning Unit, Counterterrorism Division, Terrorism in the United States (1999):

> Domestic terrorism investigations are conducted in accordance with The Attorney General Guidelines on General Crimes, Racketeering Enterprises, and Domestic Security/Terrorism Investigations....
>
> International terrorism investigations are conducted in accordance with The Attorney General Guidelines for FBI Foreign Intelligence Collection and Foreign Counterintelligence Investigations. These guidelines set the predication level and limits for investigating U.S. persons or foreign nationals in the United States who are targeting national security interests on behalf of a foreign power.
>
> Although various Executive Orders, Presidential Decision Directives, and congressional statutes address the issue of terrorism, there is no single federal law specifically making terrorism a crime. Terrorists are arrested and convicted under existing criminal statutes....
>
> There is no single, universally accepted definition of terrorism. Terrorism is defined in the Code of Federal Regulations as "... the unlawful use of force and violence against persons or property to intimidate or coerce a government, the civilian population, or any segment thereof, in furtherance of political or social objectives." (28 C.F.R. Section 0.85)
>
> The FBI further describes terrorism as either domestic or international, depending on the origin, base, and objectives of terrorists.

4. DEFINITIONS OF TERRORISM: WHAT DIFFERENCE DOES IT MAKE?

a. A Critique of One Definition

Erwin Chemerinsky, Losing Liberties: Applying a Foreign Intelligence Model to Domestic Law Enforcement, 51 UCLA L. Rev. 1619, 1623–1624 (2004):

> Section 802 of the Patriot Act provides a definition of "domestic terrorism," which is the predicate for the application of many provisions of the law. The term is defined as activities occurring primarily within the territorial jurisdiction of the United States and involving acts dangerous to human life that are a violation of the criminal laws of the United States or any state and that appear to be intended to either "intimidate or coerce a civilian population," "influence the

policy of a government by intimidation or coercion," or "affect the conduct of a government by mass destruction, assassination or kidnaping."

This is an incredibly broad definition. Many lawful protests might be seen as trying to coerce or intimidate government or civilian populations. If they are large enough, they might even be seen as dangerous to human life. An antiwar protest rally where windows are intentionally broken in a federal building could be prosecuted as terrorist activity. Most crimes, from assault to robbery to rape to kidnapping to extortion, are intended to coerce. The result is that the broad powers granted to the government by the Patriot Act are not limited to what common understanding would define as terrorism.

b. Selected Problems in Applying the Definitions

1. On July 4, 2002, an Egyptian citizen who was living in Irvine, California but had recently returned from a visit to Egypt pulled a gun at the El Al counter at Los Angeles International Airport, started shooting and killed two people and wounded others before he himself was killed by a security guard. The FBI investigated and, as reported in public statements, concluded it was not a terrorist act. Several newspaper articles discussed the issue. See, e.g. Joe Mathews & Henry Weinstein, A Matter for Debate: Was This a Terrorist Attack? Semantics: To the Israelis, It Seems Clear That It Was. But U.S. Government Officials, from the White House to the FBI, Take a More Cautious Approach, L.A. Times, July 6, 2002 at A17; Greg Kirkorian, LAX Shooter Motivated by Personal Woes, Probe Finds; Investigation: Federal Agents Say Egyptian Man Acted Alone When He Opened Fire at El Al Counter on July 4, L.A. Times, Sept. 5, 2002 at Metro section 1. According to newspaper reports quoting government officials, the man acted alone, had no connection to any political organizations and was depressed by personal problems. Do you think that under the definition of terrorism that is applied by the FBI, supra, it arguably was anyway a terrorist act? Under any of the other definitions of terrorism presented in these materials, supra? What difference does it make whether the FBI treats it as a terrorist act or not? Does it make a difference in the way the crime is treated statistically? Might it affect the crimes with which the perpetrator could have been charged if he had survived?

2. The Foreign Intelligence Surveillance Act, discussed in Chapter 5, infra, provides authority for electronic surveillance to obtain foreign intelligence information relating to "... international terrorism by a foreign power or agent of a foreign power." Surveillances under the Act need not comply with the usual Fourth Amendment standards. The Definitions section of the Act (50 U.S.C. § 1801) uses the same definition of "international terrorism" used by the FBI, section B. 3. c., supra. Additionally under the Act, the definition of "foreign power" includes the following: "... a group engaged in international terrorism ..."; "... a foreign-based political organization...." Suppose that members of a

South American drug cartel who are involved in the international drug trade plan to kill a senior U.S. official working in their country in retaliation for a successful "drug bust" by the U.S. Navy on one of their vessels on the high seas. Is this activity subject to surveillance under the FISA statute?

3. A terrorism statute enacted by the Virginia legislature in 2002 provides the death penalty for killings committed with "the intent to intimidate or coerce a civilian population or influence the policy, conduct or activities of the government ... through intimidation or coercion." This statute was used to prosecute John Lee Malvo and John Allen Muhammad, who were accused as snipers who terrorized the Washington D.C. area and made demands for a 10 million dollar ransom. Do you think that the actions of the snipers constituted terrorism, as a general proposition? Under the Virginia statute? Does this mean that any one who engages in an extended crime spree in Virginia might be subject to being prosecuted under the state's terrorism statute?

C. SELECTED TERRORISM STATUTES

Many of the general federal anti-terrorism criminal statutes in Chapter 113B of Title 18, plus a few other relevant statutes, are treated in this section. Questions and Notes that follow the provisions, and a few judicial decisions applying them, can be used as a guide to issues of interpretation under these statutory provisions.

Title 18. United States Code

CHAPTER 45

Foreign Relations

§ 956. Conspiracy to kill, kidnap, maim, or injure persons or damage property in a foreign country

(a)(1) Whoever, within the jurisdiction of the United States, conspires with one or more other persons, regardless of where such other person or persons are located, to commit at any place outside the United States an act that would constitute the offense of murder, kidnapping, or maiming if committed in the special maritime and territorial jurisdiction of the United States shall, if any of the conspirators commits an act within the jurisdiction of the United States to effect any object of the conspiracy, be punished as provided in subsection (a)(2).

(2) The punishment for an offense under subsection (a)(1) of this section is—

(A) imprisonment for any term of years or for life if the offense is conspiracy to murder or kidnap; and

(B) imprisonment for not more than 35 years if the offense is conspiracy to maim.

(b) Whoever, within the jurisdiction of the United States, conspires with one or more persons, regardless of where such other person or persons are located, to damage or destroy specific property situated within a foreign country and belonging to a foreign government or to any political subdivision thereof with which the United States is at peace, or any railroad, canal, bridge, airport, airfield, or other public utility, public conveyance, or public structure, or any religious, educational, or cultural property so situated, shall, if any of the conspirators commits an act within the jurisdiction of the United States to effect any object of the conspiracy, be imprisoned not more than 25 years.

QUESTIONS AND NOTES

Is section 956 a terrorism statute? If it is not, should it be made into one by adding to it a provision such as is found in section 2332(d), the next statute in this series? Examples of the use of this section include prosecutions of persons who planned to travel to Somalia to join a extremist terrorist organization there, Al Shabaab and fight in furtherance of establishing an Islamist state that accords with its extremist ideology. See, e.g., U.S. v. Alessa, Information (D. N.J. Mar. 3, 2011). The statute was also used in United States v. Stewart, infra, ch. 3, at p. 68 and the civilian prosecution of Jose Padilla, discussed in ch. 10, at p. 622.

Chapter 113, Terrorism
§ 2332. Criminal penalties

(a) **Homicide.** Whoever kills a national of the United States, while such national is outside the United States, shall

(1) if the killing is murder (as defined in section 1111(a)), be fined under this title, punished by death or imprisonment for any term of years or for life, or both;

(2) if the killing is a voluntary manslaughter as defined in section 1112(a) of this title, be fined under this title or imprisoned not more than ten years, or both; and

(3) if the killing is an involuntary manslaughter as defined in section 1112(a) of this title, be fined under this title or imprisoned not more than three years, or both.

(b) **Attempt or conspiracy with respect to homicide.**— Whoever outside the United States attempts to kill, or engages in a conspiracy to kill, a national of the United States shall

(1) in the case of an attempt to commit a killing that is a murder as defined in this chapter, be fined under this title or imprisoned not more than 20 years, or both; and

(2) in the case of a conspiracy by two or more persons to commit a killing that is a murder as defined in section 1111(a) of this title, if one or more of such persons do any overt act to effect

the object of the conspiracy, be fined under this title or imprisoned for any term of years or for life, or both so fined and so imprisoned.

(c) Other conduct. Whoever outside the United States engages in physical violence

(1) with intent to cause serious bodily injury to a national of the United States; or

(2) with the result that serious bodily injury is caused to a national of the United States;

shall be fined under this title or imprisoned not more than ten years, or both.

(d) Limitation on prosecution. No prosecution for any offense described in this section shall be undertaken by the United States except on written certification of the Attorney General or the highest ranking subordinate of the Attorney General with responsibility for criminal prosecutions that, in the judgment of the certifying official, such offense was intended to coerce, intimidate, or retaliate against a government or a civilian population.

———

The following case, a different portion of which was reproduced supra, p. 9, involves application of subsection (d) of § 2332, which is a rather unusual provision in the federal criminal code.

UNITED STATES v. YOUSEF

327 F.3d 56 (2d Cir.2003), cert. den. 540 U.S. 933 (2003)

[The facts and international criminal jurisdiction issues in the case are reproduced supra, p. 9]

. . .

II.　Conviction of Yousef Under 18 U.S.C. § 2332

Yousef argues that we should overturn his conviction on Count Fifteen because 18 U.S.C. § 2332 unconstitutionally delegates legislative power to the Attorney General of the United States. Alternatively, he contends that his conviction should be overturned because the District Court failed to charge the jury that it had to find intent to retaliate against the United States and its citizens as an element of the crime charged in Count Fifteen.

In Count Fifteen, Yousef and his co-defendants were charged with conspiring to kill United States nationals outside the United States in violation of 18 U.S.C. § 2332(b) and (d).

Under 18 U.S.C. § 2332(a) it is a crime to "kill . . . a national of the United States, while such national is outside the United States." Section

2332(b) prohibits any person outside the United States from "engaging in a conspiracy to kill . . . a national of the United States." Section 2332(d) is entitled "Limitation on prosecution" and provides:

> No prosecution for any offense described in this section shall be undertaken by the United States except on written certification of the Attorney General or the highest ranking subordinate of the Attorney General with responsibility for criminal prosecutions that, in the judgment of the certifying official, such offense was intended to coerce, intimidate, or retaliate against a government or a civilian population.

A. Prosecutorial Discretion Under Section 2332(d)

Yousef argues that § 2332 is an unconstitutional delegation of legislative authority, because the statute authorizes the Attorney General to define what conduct constitutes an offense.

Section 2332 does not represent an unconstitutional delegation of power to the Attorney General. Indeed, § 2332(d) does not delegate any legislative power to the Attorney General. Rather, it merely sets limits on how the Attorney General can exercise his discretion to prosecute. . . . Section 2332(d) limits the Justice Department's prosecution of crimes under § 2332 to those crimes in which the defendant intended to target the Government or civilian population of the United States. Exercise of such prosecutorial discretion involves no rulemaking power on the part of the Executive Branch and, therefore, cannot constitute delegation of legislative power to the Attorney General—let alone an unlawful delegation of such power.

Even if § 2332(d) did represent a delegation of legislative power to the Attorney General, such a delegation would not be unconstitutional. It has long been the rule that Congress may delegate some of its legislative powers to the Executive Branch, so long as that delegation is made "under the limitation of a prescribed standard."

. . .

Subsection (d) provides a clearly intelligible principle to which the Attorney General must adhere-namely, to prosecute only those cases where the intent of the offense was to coerce, intimidate, or retaliate against the Government or civilian population of the United States. In sum, § 2332 does not unconstitutionally delegate legislative power to the Attorney General.

Nor does 2332 unconstitutionally remove an element of the offense from the jury. Although a criminal defendant has the right to a jury determination of every element of the crime, *see* Apprendi v. New Jersey, 530 U.S. 466, 477, 147 L. Ed. 2d 435, 120 S. Ct. 2348 (2000), an analysis of the text and structure of § 2332 demonstrates that subsection (d) does not comprise an element of the offenses proscribed by § 2332. First, subsection (d) follows three self-contained subsections each of which defines the elements of a distinct offense. *See* 18 U.S.C. § 2332(a)–(d). In particular, each subsection of (a) through (c) imposes an attendant level of intent, and none of these subsections makes reference to § 2332(d). Second, subsection (d) is expressly designated as a "limit on prosecution" rather than as an element of the offenses set forth in § 2332. We conclude, therefore, that the District Court did not err by failing to charge an intent to retaliate against the United States Government or its citizens. Even if the Court had erred in this regard, any error would have been harmless, given the overwhelming evidence that the defendants specifically intended the aircraft bombings to serve as retaliation against the United States Government and its citizens for United States foreign policy.

. . .

QUESTIONS AND NOTES

1. Is § 2332, Title 18, United States Code, a terrorism offense? What substantive criminal conduct is covered by this offense? Note that neither the word terrorism nor any of its variants appears in § 2332. If § 2332 is perceived as a terrorism offense, what practical or legal function does the concept of terrorism serve in this context?

2. Yousef is one of the only cases involving a challenge to subsection (d) of § 2332. Note that subsection (d) establishes a fact determination procedure to be conducted in the office of the Attorney General that is separate from the trial. For a discussion of the special issues posed by this provision, see Norman Abrams, Exploring Limits on the Use of Administrative Agencies in the Felony Criminal Process, 33 Israel L. Rev. 539, 542–556 (1999). Also see Brandon S. Chabner, Comment: The Omnibus Diplomatic Security and Antiterrorism Act of 1986: Prescribing and Enforcing U.S. Law Against Terrorist Violence Overseas, 37 UCLA L. Rev. 985 (1990). Would it have been appropriate to include a similar provision in 18 U.S.C. § 956, supra, p. 33.

3. Does the Attorney General's certification procedure in section (d) address the question of whether the act was done with a terrorism purpose? Does the Attorney General's certification relate to an element of the offense? In the Congress, the Conference Committee Report for this legislation stated that the issue involved in the Attorney General's certification is not an element of the offense. If it were, would the procedure be constitutional? Consult Abrams, op. cit. supra note 2: ". . . it . . . would seem to be the type of factor that would normally be an element of the offense, that is, it addresses the purpose with which the act was done." What might be the reason(s) why the determination of whether the conduct was engaged in with the indicated purpose was not included as one of the elements of the offense?

4. Is the matter as to which the Attorney General makes a certification jurisdictional? If it is jurisdictional, is the procedure constitutional? See Andreas F. Lowenfeld, U.S. Enforcement Abroad: The Constitution and International Law, 83 Am. J. Int'l L. 880, 891 (1989). Also see Note: Extraterritorial Jurisdiction over Acts of Terrorism Committed Abroad: Omnibus Diplomatic Security and Antiterrorism Act of 1986, 72 Cornell L. Rev. 549, 599 (1987).

5. In determining whether to initiate prosecution in an ordinary criminal case, the prosecutor makes a judgment whether the conduct involved is sufficient to constitute the offense. Is the Attorney General's certification procedure different from the usual prosecutorial determination to prosecute? Sometimes there is pre-existing policy promulgated by the prosecutor to govern the exercise of his/her discretion whether to prosecute, and the prosecutorial decision whether to prosecute takes such policy into account. Is the Attorney General's certification similar? The same? Consult generally, Norman Abrams, Internal Policy: Guiding the Exercise of Prosecutorial Discretion, 19 UCLA L.Rev. 1 (1971).

6. The Yousef court rejected the constitutional challenge to § 2332 based on the nondelegation doctrine. Is there any other legal ground on which § 2332 or its application might be challenged?

7. In March, 2011, 14 defendants who had been seized on the high seas near the coast of Africa were indicted in the Eastern District of Virginia, for piracy (18 U.S.C. § 1651), conspiracy to commit kidnapping (18 U.S.C. § 1201), possessing, using, a firearm in furtherance of a crime of violence (18 U.S.C. § 924), based on their seizing of an American yacht and holding four U.S. citizens as hostages and demanding ransom. The accused in the end killed the four hostages. The defendants were not indicted for a violation of 18 U.S.C. § 2332. Could they have been charged with a violation of that statute? For the indictment, see Case 2:11–cr–00034–MSD–DEM DOC. 3 (filed March 3, 2011, E.D. Va. Norfolk Div).

2. 18 U.S.C. § 2332a. Use of certain weapons of mass destruction

§ 2332a. Use of weapons of mass destruction

(a) Offense against a national of the United States or within the United States.—A person who, without lawful authority, uses, threatens, or attempts or conspires to use, a weapon of mass destruction—

(1) against a national of the United States while such national is outside of the United States;

(2) against any person or property within the United States, and

(A) the mail or any facility of interstate or foreign commerce is used in furtherance of the offense;

(B) such property is used in interstate or foreign commerce or in an activity that affects interstate or foreign commerce;

(C) any perpetrator travels in or causes another to travel in interstate or foreign commerce in furtherance of the offense; or

(D) the offense, or the results of the offense, affect interstate or foreign commerce, or, in the case of a threat, attempt, or conspiracy, would have affected interstate or foreign commerce;

(3) against any property that is owned, leased or used by the United States or by any department or agency of the United States, whether the property is within or outside of the United States; or

(4) against any property within the United States that is owned, leased, or used by a foreign government,

shall be imprisoned for any term of years or for life, and if death results, shall be punished by death or imprisoned for any term of years or for life.

(b) Offense by national of the United States outside of the United States.—Any national of the United States who, without lawful authority, uses, or threatens, attempts, or conspires to use, a weapon of mass destruction outside of the United States shall be imprisoned for any term of years or for life, and if death results, shall be punished by death, or by imprisonment for any term of years or for life.

(c) Definitions.—For purposes of this section—

(1) the term "national of the United States" has the meaning given in section 101(a)(22) of the Immigration and Nationality Act (8 U.S.C. 1101(a)(22));

(2) the term "weapon of mass destruction" means—

(A) any destructive device as defined in section 921 of this title;

(B) any weapon that is designed or intended to cause death or serious bodily injury through the release, dissemination, or impact of toxic or poisonous chemicals, or their precursors;

(C) any weapon involving a biological agent, toxin, or vector (as those terms are defined in section 178 of this title); or

(D) any weapon that is designed to release radiation or radioactivity at a level dangerous to human life; and

(3) the term "property" includes all real and personal property.

Questions and Notes

1. Is § 2332a a terrorism offense? Note that this provision also does not include the word terrorism or any of its variants, nor does it otherwise contain a definition of the concept of terrorism. Is it nevertheless a terrorism offense? In other words, should any use of a weapon of mass destruction (as that concept is defined in this provision) be deemed to amount to a crime of

terrorism? If you conclude that it is a terrorism offense, what definition or concept of terrorism are you applying?

2. Note the different bases for federal criminal jurisdiction that are listed in this provision—e.g. offense against a U.S. national outside of the U.S. Compare these jurisdictional bases with the basis used in § 2332, supra.

3. Does it seem odd to you that jurisdiction over an offense involving the killing or injury of a person within the United States may require that interstate or foreign commerce be affected while the killing or injuring of U.S. nationals abroad simpliciter is a sufficient jurisdictional basis?

4. Are there other jurisdictional bases that might have been utilized in § 2332a? How far should U.S. criminal jurisdiction extend with respect to the use of weapons of mass destruction? Can you think of other categories of conduct that should be covered?

5. Note that §§ 2332a(a) and 2332a(b) both contain the clause, "without lawful authority." What kind of situations might be covered by the "without lawful authority" language?

6. Arguing that the defendant had "threatened" to use a weapon of mass destruction, anthrax, the government used § 2332a as the basis for prosecuting a flurry of terrorist hoax incidents that occurred after the September 11, 2001 terrorist attacks. Various issues of interpretation arose as to whether § 2332a applied to the facts in these cases. For example, if the "threatening" language referred to the fact that anthrax was in the building, was this a "threat to use" anthrax within the meaning of the statute? See United States v. Taylor, 2003 WL 22073040 (S.D.N.Y.) (Held: No). Is it necessary that the "threat" refer to future action? Suppose the defendant had said, "I have just dumped anthrax in your air conditioner." See United States v. Reynolds, 381 F.3d 404 (5th Cir. 2004) (Held: Yes, there is a basis for criminal liability under 2332a). Must there be a present capacity to carry out the threat?

7. Do you think that § 2332a was intended to cover hoax situations, even those involving threats relating to weapons of mass destruction? Note the penalty provided for a violation of § 2332a, "any term of years or life." How would you interpret the threat provision to exclude coverage of hoaxes? Arguably, the government used § 2332a to prosecute such cases because it had no other basis for prosecution in cases like the anthrax threats, and the hoaxes were becoming a serious problem for law enforcement.

8. In December, 2004, Zameer Mohamed pleaded guilty to a federal charge of using a telephone to communicate false information about an explosive attack. LA Times, Dec. 22, 2004, p. B6. Mohamed was charged under 18 U.S.C. § 844, which, inter alia, covers transporting explosives and damaging property by means of fire or explosives and in § 844(e) covers making threats to use fire or explosives, knowing the same to be false, but until 2004, there was no federal provision on the books comparable to § 844(e) relating to a biological weapon like anthrax.

9. On December 17, 2004, § 1038 of Title 18 was added to the United States Code by the Intelligence Reform and Terrorism Prevention Act of 2004, which made criminal engaging "in any conduct with intent to convey false or

misleading information under circumstances where such information may reasonably be believed and where such information indicates that an activity has taken, is taking, or will take place that would constitute a violation of"— [§ 1038 here lists various prohibitory statutes dealing with biological weapons, chemical weapons, nuclear devices, explosives, etc.]. § 1038 provides for a five year penalty for the basic crime with higher maxima if any one is injured or killed as a result of the conduct.

10. The enactment of § 1038 filled a gap in federal law by attempting to address in a comprehensive way the problem of hoaxes relating to threatened terrorist activity. A question that remains after enactment of § 1038 involves the fate of decisions that pre–§ 1038 had upheld the extension of section 2332a to fill a gap in federal law and to cover hoax situations. In future hoax situations, should federal prosecutors be able to charge under both § 1038 and § 2332a? This is an example of a recurring pattern in federal criminal law: A statutory offense is interpreted expansively to fill a gap in the coverage of the law (and possibly would not have been so interpreted had there not been such a gap), and later Congress enacts a specific statute to cover the situation. The case law establishing the original expansive interpretation remains on the books. It has usually been held that prosecutors can then charge under both statutes. For some examples of this recurring pattern, see Norman Abrams, Sara Sun Beale and Susan Riva Klein, Federal Criminal Law and Its Enforcement, at Notes 1–2, 205–207 (5th ed. 2010).

11. See United States v. Aldawsari, 2011 WL 668355 (N.D. Tex. 2011). Defendant purchased the ingredients for making an improvised explosive device (IED), and did research on the internet in aid of his plan to prepare such device and use it in some place where crowds were gathered. He was charged with an attempted violation of 18 U.S.C. § 2332a(a)(2)(A). The evidence did not reveal that anyone else was involved. Revisit this case when you study Ch. 3, infra, and consider whether Aldawsari might also have been charged with a violation of 18 U.S.C. § 2339A.

3. 18 U.S.C. § 2332b. Acts of terrorism transcending national boundaries

§ 2332b. Acts of terrorism transcending national boundaries

(a) Prohibited acts.

(1) Offenses.—Whoever, involving conduct transcending national boundaries and in a circumstance described in subsection (b)—

(A) kills, kidnaps, maims, commits an assault resulting in serious bodily injury, or assaults with a dangerous weapon any person within the United States; or

(B) creates a substantial risk of serious bodily injury to any other person by destroying or damaging any structure, conveyance, or other real or personal property within the United States or by attempting or conspiring to destroy or damage any structure, conveyance, or other real or personal property within the United States;

in violation of the laws of any State, or the United States, shall be punished as prescribed in subsection (c).

(2) Treatment of threats, attempts and conspiracies.— Whoever threatens to commit an offense under paragraph (1), or attempts or conspires to do so, shall be punished under subsection (c).

(b) Jurisdictional bases.

(1) Circumstances.—The circumstances referred to in subsection (a) are

(A) the mail or any facility of interstate or foreign commerce is used in furtherance of the offense;

(B) the offense obstructs, delays, or affects interstate or foreign commerce, or would have so obstructed, delayed, or affected interstate or foreign commerce if the offense had been consummated;

(C) the victim, or intended victim, is the United States Government, a member of the uniformed services, or any official, officer, employee, or agent of the legislative, executive, or judicial branches, or of any department or agency, of the United States;

(D) the structure, conveyance, or other real or personal property is, in whole or in part, owned, possessed, or leased to the United States, or any department or agency of the United States;

(E) the offense is committed in the territorial sea (including the airspace above and the seabed and subsoil below, and artificial islands and fixed structures erected thereon) of the United States; or

(F) the offense is committed within the special maritime and territorial jurisdiction of the United States.

(2) Co-conspirators and accessories after the fact.— Jurisdiction shall exist over all principals and co-conspirators of an offense under this section, and accessories after the fact to any offense under this section, if at least one of the circumstances described in subparagraphs (A) through (F) of paragraph (1) is applicable to at least one offender.

(c) Penalties.

(1) Penalties.—Whoever violates this section shall be punished

(A) for a killing, or if death results to any person from any other conduct prohibited by this section, by death, or by imprisonment for any term of years or for life;

(B) for kidnapping, by imprisonment for any term of years or for life;

(C) for maiming, by imprisonment for not more than 35 years;

(D) for assault with a dangerous weapon or assault resulting in serious bodily injury, by imprisonment for not more than 30 years;

(E) for destroying or damaging any structure, conveyance, or other real or personal property, by imprisonment for not more than 25 years;

(F) for attempting or conspiring to commit an offense, for any term of years up to the maximum punishment that would have applied had the offense been completed; and

(G) for threatening to commit an offense under this section, by imprisonment for not more than 10 years.

(2) Consecutive sentence.—Notwithstanding any other provision of law, the court shall not place on probation any person convicted of a violation of this section; nor shall the term of imprisonment imposed under this section run concurrently with any other term of imprisonment.

(d) Proof requirements.—The following shall apply to prosecutions under this section:

(1) Knowledge.—The prosecution is not required to prove knowledge by any defendant of a jurisdictional base alleged in the indictment.

(2) State law.—In a prosecution under this section that is based upon the adoption of State law, only the elements of the offense under State law, and not any provisions pertaining to criminal procedure or evidence, are adopted.

(e) Extraterritorial jurisdiction.—There is extraterritorial Federal jurisdiction—

(1) over any offense under subsection (a), including any threat, attempt, or conspiracy to commit such offense; and

(2) over conduct which, under section 3 [(b)(2)], renders any person an accessory after the fact to an offense under subsection (a).

(f) Investigative authority.—In addition to any other investigative authority with respect to violations of this title, the Attorney General shall have primary investigative responsibility for all Federal crimes of terrorism, and any violation of section 351(e), 844(e), 844(f)(1), 956(b), 1361, 1366(b), 1366(c), 1751(e), 2152, or 2156 of this title, and the Secretary of the Treasury shall assist the Attorney General at the request of the Attorney General. Nothing in this section shall be construed to interfere with the authority of the United States Secret Service under section 3056.

(g) Definitions.—As used in this section—

(1) the term "conduct transcending national boundaries" means conduct occurring outside of the United States in addition to the conduct occurring in the United States;

(2) the term "facility of interstate or foreign commerce" has the meaning given that term in section 1958(b)(2);

(3) the term "serious bodily injury" has the meaning given that term in section 1365(g)(3);

(4) the term "territorial sea of the United States" means all waters extending seaward to 12 nautical miles from the baselines of the United States, determined in accordance with international law; and

(5) the term "Federal crime of terrorism" means an offense that—

(A) is calculated to influence or affect the conduct of government by intimidation or coercion, or to retaliate against government conduct; and

(B) is a violation of

(i) section 32 (relating to destruction of aircraft or aircraft facilities), 37 (relating to violence at international airports), 81 (relating to arson within special maritime and territorial jurisdiction), 175 or 175b (relating to biological weapons), 229 (relating to chemical weapons), subsection (a), (b), (c), or (d) of section 351 (relating to congressional, cabinet, and Supreme Court assassination and kidnaping), 831 (relating to nuclear materials), 842(m) or (n) (relating to plastic explosives), 844(f)(2) or (3) (relating to arson and bombing of Government property risking or causing death), 844(i) (relating to arson and bombing of property used in interstate commerce), 930(c) (relating to killing or attempted killing during an attack on a Federal facility with a dangerous weapon), 956(a)(1) (relating to conspiracy to murder, kidnap, or maim persons abroad), 1030(a)(1) (relating to protection of computers), 1030(a)(5)(A)(i) resulting in damage as defined in 1030(a)(5)(B)(ii) through (v) (relating to protection of computers), 1114 (relating to killing or attempted killing of officers and employees of the United States), 1116 (relating to murder or manslaughter of foreign officials, official guests, or internationally protected persons), 1203 (relating to hostage taking), 1362 (relating to destruction of communication lines, stations, or systems), 1363 (relating to injury to buildings or property within special maritime and territorial jurisdiction of the United States), 1366(a) (relating to destruction of an energy facility), 1751(a), (b), (c), or (d) (relating to Presidential and Presidential staff assassination and kidnaping), 1992 (relating to wrecking trains), 1993 (relating to terrorist attacks and other acts of violence against mass transportation systems), 2155 (relating to destruction of national defense materials, premises, or utilities), 2280 (relating to violence against maritime navigation), 2281 (relating to violence against maritime fixed platforms), 2332 (relating to certain homicides and other violence against United States nationals occurring outside of the United States), 2332a (relating to use of weapons of mass destruction), 2332b (relating to acts of terrorism transcending national boundaries), 2339 (relating to harboring terrorists), 2339A (relating to providing material support to terrorists), 2339B (relating to providing material support to terrorist organizations), or 2340A (relating to torture) of this title;

> **(ii)** section 236 (relating to sabotage of nuclear facilities or fuel) of the Atomic Energy Act of 1954 (*42 U.S.C. 2284*); or

> **(iii)** section 46502 (relating to aircraft piracy), the second sentence of section 46504 (relating to assault on a flight crew with a dangerous weapon), section 46505(b)(3) or (c) (relating to explosive or incendiary devices, or endangerment of human life by means of weapons, on aircraft), section 46506 if homicide or attempted homicide is involved (relating to application of certain criminal laws to acts on aircraft), or section 60123(b) (relating to destruction of interstate gas or hazardous liquid pipeline facility) of title 49.

QUESTIONS AND NOTES

1. § 2332b is a complex statute that requires careful attention to its many clauses.

What is the substantive scope of § 2332b? Through the breadth of the conduct covered and the number of different jurisdictional bases provided, the substantive scope of § 2332b initially appears to be extremely broad. Note, however, the limiting concept for the offense to be committed: the crime must involve conduct transcending national boundaries. See subsec. (g)(1) for the definition of this phrase.

2. Do you think that, without invoking any of the specific jurisdictional language listed in subsection (b), there might have been a basis for federal jurisdiction over conduct that occurs both outside and inside of the United States and that results in the commission of conduct prohibited under the

federal criminal code or under state law? Is there a jurisdictional basis under principles of international law for the U.S. to prosecute such conduct? See United States v. Yousef, supra, p. 9.

3.   The jurisdictional bases listed in subsection (b) are, of course, standard commerce power, use of the mails and federal interest jurisdictional bases. Section 2332a, discussed supra, p. 39, contains a much shorter list of jurisdictional bases in its provisions. In 2332a, should the drafters have used the same bases that are used in 2332b?

4.   The caption of § 2332b refers to "acts of terrorism transcending national boundaries." Does any other language in § 2332b define "acts of terrorism?" Examine the substantive provisions of the section very carefully. Is there any place in the statute where the concept of terrorism or one of the definitions of terrorism is inserted in or is part of a provision describing a substantive violation of this section?

5.   The substantive offenses created by this section involve violent conduct such as killing, kidnapping, maiming and assault. § 2332b, however, contains no requirement that this conduct be committed with a terrorist purpose. Recall the caption of this section that refers to "acts of terrorism." Is there any language in this statute that would require that the killings or kidnappings, etc. that otherwise violate this provision must involve terrorism, however one defines terrorism?

6.   As noted supra, this section does require that the conduct involved "transcend national boundaries." The definition of that phrase refers to conduct both outside and inside the boundaries of the United States. Is the fact, for example, that a killing involved conduct that transcended national boundaries a fact that makes it terrorism? Can you conjure up a fact situation that fits that description that would in your judgment be fairly denoted as a crime of terrorism? Can you conjure up other situations that would involve the indicated violent crime and involve conduct that transcended national boundaries that could not fairly be described as a crime involving terrorism? How adequate is the concept of "transcending national boundaries" as a marker for terrorism?

7.   Note that the phrase "Federal crime of terrorism" appears in subsection (f) and is defined in subsec. (g)(5). Do you think that this phrase is intended to have the same meaning as "acts of terrorism" used in the caption to this section?

8.   What does subsection (f) tell us about the function of the concept of "Federal crimes of terrorism" as used in this section? Does that function have anything to do with the substantive offenses created by this section? Does "Federal crimes of terrorism" appear anywhere else in this section (that is, apart from the definitional provision in (g)(5))? If the answer is no, is it fair to conclude therefore that the federal crime of terrorism defined in this section has no connection, or very little connection, to the substantive offense(s) created by this section?

9.   In United States v. Thurston, supra, p. 17, note 6, we saw one function of the definition of "Federal crime of terrorism" found in § 2332b(g)(5); it is used as a sentencing enhancement factor under the

Federal Sentencing Guidelines, by virtue of a provision of the Guidelines that refers to § 2332b(g)(5).

10.   United States v. Salim, 287 F. Supp. 2d 250 (S.D.N.Y. 2003) contains a description of the legislative history of the sentencing guideline, § 3A1.4, that refers to the definition of federal crime of terrorism in § 2332b(g)(5) and also the legislative history of § 2332b(g)(5).

That history may be summarized as follows: The legislation originally contained (as a precondition to initiating a prosecution under the section) a provision requiring certification by the Attorney General that the conduct involved a "transcending of national boundaries" activity and that it involved conduct with a terrorism-type purpose. In a subsequent version of the legislation, this certification provision was then changed to require certification that a federal crime of terrorism was involved (as that phrase is defined in this section). In this last-mentioned version of the statute, the concept of a federal crime of terrorism was also used as a basis for describing the investigative authority of the Attorney General. Then in the final version of the bill that became § 2332b, the certification provision was removed from the section and the investigative authority provision was left as the only clause in 2332b in which the federal crime of terrorism definition still played a role. Meanwhile, the "transcending national boundaries" language which had also been contained in an earlier version of the certification provision was shifted from that provision to become one of the elements of the offense.

Contrast the treatment in the final version of the bill of the "transcending national boundaries" concept with that of the language, "federal crime of terrorism."

This legislative history reveals that § 2332b originally contained a certification provision similar to the one we previously considered in § 2332(d), supra, p. 35. If this certification provision had remained in the final bill, the concept and definition of federal crime of terrorism would have limited the scope of application of § 2332b, albeit not as an element of the offense but rather through an administrative factfinding determination in each case by the Attorney General. However, with the removal of the certification provision from the bill that became law, there was nothing in the specific language of § 2332b that restricted its application to terrorism contexts—either through a required element of the offense or through a determination by the chief prosecutor in the federal criminal system. And so § 2332b was left without any clear marker of terrorism attached to its substantive provisions.

For what reasons, might the Attorney General/certification provision have been removed by the Conference Committee from the bill that became law? Do you think that the legislators realized the effect of this removal on the scope of application of § 2332b?

How likely it is that prosecutions under § 2332b will occur in non-terrorism contexts? How would you expect prosecutors to use § 2332b? Would you anticipate that they would only invoke the section in cases that could reasonably be characterized as involving terrorism? If you were a prosecutor, what might lead you to conclude that the statute should only be used in terrorism cases? Would you feel that you were legally restricted to so use the statute? Or would this simply involve prosecutors exercising their discretion to limit the application of the section to terrorism contexts? In other words, how would this be different, if it would be different, from the Attorney General's certification if the certification provision had been retained in the statute?

11. Section 2332b has been utilized in some prominent terrorism prosecutions, including the persons convicted of the bombing of two U.S. embassies in Africa, and in the charges brought against Zacarias Moussaoui. See infra, p. 492 et seq.

A terrorism investigation widely reported in the press resulted in an indictment filed in New York against a number of defendants including Najibullah Zazi. The case illustrates how a number of different terrorism offenses may be combined in a single indictment. It included a charge under § 2332b as well as under § 956 (see supra, p. 33), § 2332a (see supra, p. 38), and under two sections treated in ch. 3 infra, § 2339B (providing material support to a foreign terrorist organization) and § 2339D (receiving military training from a foreign terrorist organization). See United States v. Imam, 10–Cr–00019–RJD, Doc. 53 (filed E.D.N.Y. 7/7/10).

12. It is noteworthy that in none of the "terrorism" offenses that we have examined so far is the standard type of definition of terrorism, e.g., "with intent to coerce, intimidate or retaliate against a government", etc. incorporated as an element of the offense. In § 2332, this kind of language is incorporated into the certification procedure. Section 2332a, which describes an offense which by its nature may be seen as involving terrorism, does not contain such a provision, and § 2332b in its final form contains as a term of the statute what at most can be viewed as a weak surrogate, transcending national boundaries, instead of the standard definition. Are we beginning to see a pattern here, and if so, what is it, and what might account for it?

4.   18 U.S.C. § 2332f. Bombing of places of public use, etc.

18 U.S.C. § 2332f. Bombing of places of public use, government facilities, public transportation systems and infrastructure facilities

(a) Offenses.

(1) In general. Whoever unlawfully delivers, places, discharges, or detonates an explosive or other lethal device in, into, or against a place of public use, a state or government facility, a public transportation system, or an infrastructure facility—

(A) with the intent to cause death or serious bodily injury, or

(B) with the intent to cause extensive destruction of such a place, facility, or system, where such destruction results in or is likely to result in major economic loss,

shall be punished as prescribed in subsection (c).

(2) Attempts and conspiracies. Whoever attempts or conspires to commit an offense under paragraph (1) shall be punished as prescribed in subsection (c).

(b) Jurisdiction. There is jurisdiction over the offenses in subsection (a) if—

(1) the offense takes place in the United States and

(A) the offense is committed against another state or a government facility of such state, including its embassy or other diplomatic or consular premises of that state;

(B) the offense is committed in an attempt to compel another state or the United States to do or abstain from doing any act;

(C) at the time the offense is committed, it is committed

(i) on board a vessel flying the flag of another state;

(ii) on board an aircraft which is registered under the laws of another state; or

(iii) on board an aircraft which is operated by the government of another state;

(D) a perpetrator is found outside the United States;

(E) a perpetrator is a national of another state or a stateless person; or

(F) a victim is a national of another state or a stateless person;

(2) the offense takes place outside the United States and

(A) a perpetrator is a national of the United States or is a stateless person whose habitual residence is in the United States;

(B) a victim is a national of the United States;

(C) a perpetrator is found in the United States;

(D) the offense is committed in an attempt to compel the United States to do or abstain from doing any act;

(E) the offense is committed against a state or government facility of the United States, including an embassy or other diplomatic or consular premises of the United States;

(F) the offense is committed on board a vessel flying the flag of the United States or an aircraft which is registered under the laws of the United States at the time the offense is committed; or

(G) the offense is committed on board an aircraft which is operated by the United States.

(c) Penalties. Whoever violates this section shall be punished as provided under section 2332a(a) of this title.

(d) Exemptions to Jurisdiction. This section does not apply to

(1) the activities of armed forces during an armed conflict, as those terms are understood under the law of war, which are governed by that law,

(2) activities undertaken by military forces of a state in the exercise of their official duties; or

(3) offenses committed within the United States, where the alleged offender and the victims are United States citizens and the alleged offender is found in the United States, or where jurisdiction is predicated solely on the nationality of the victims or the alleged offender and the offense has no substantial effect on interstate or foreign commerce.

(e) Definitions. As used in this section, the term

(1) 'serious bodily injury' has the meaning given that term in section 1365(g)(3) of this title;

(2) 'national of the United States' has the meaning given that term in section 101(a)(22) of the Immigration and Nationality Act *(8 U.S.C. 1101*(a)(22));

(3) 'state or government facility' includes any permanent or temporary facility or conveyance that is used or occupied by representatives of a state, members of Government, the legislature or the judiciary or by officials or employees of a state or any other public authority or entity or by employees or officials of an intergovernmental organization in connection with their official duties;

(4) 'intergovernmental organization' includes international organization (as defined in section 1116(b)(5) of this title);

(5) 'infrastructure facility' means any publicly or privately owned facility providing or distributing services for the benefit of the public, such as water, sewage, energy, fuel, or communications;

(6) 'place of public use' means those parts of any building, land, street, waterway, or other location that are accessible or open to members of the public, whether continuously, periodically, or occasionally, and encompasses any commercial, business, cultural, historical, educational, religious, governmental, entertainment, recreational, or similar place that is so accessible or open to the public;

(7) 'public transportation system' means all facilities, conveyances, and instrumentalities, whether publicly or privately owned, that are used in or for publicly available services for the transportation of persons or cargo;

(8) 'explosive' has the meaning given in section 844(j) of this title insofar that it is designed, or has the capability, to cause death, serious bodily injury, or substantial material damage;

(9) 'other lethal device' means any weapon or device that is designed or has the capability to cause death, serious bodily injury, or substantial damage to property through the release, dissemination, or impact of toxic chemicals, biological agents, or toxins (as those terms are defined in section 178 of this title) or radiation or radioactive material;

(10) 'military forces of a state' means the armed forces of a state which are organized, trained, and equipped under its internal law for the primary purpose of national defense or security, and persons acting in support of those armed forces who are under their formal command, control, and responsibility;

(11) 'armed conflict' does not include internal disturbances and tensions, such as riots, isolated and sporadic acts of violence, and other acts of a similar nature; and

(12) 'state' has the same meaning as that term has under international law, and includes all political subdivisions thereof.

. . .

QUESTIONS AND NOTES

1. Does section 2332f describe a crime of "terrorism"? A crime of "international terrorism"? If so, what feature(s) of the offense make(s) it such? What definition of terrorism are you using?

2. The jurisdictional provisions in § 2332f(b) are complex and warrant careful study. It may be helpful in working your way through these provisions to consider the following questions:

a. If the offense takes place in the United States, is each of the factors contained in (b)(1)A, B, C, D, E, and F, an independent basis for jurisdiction? If so, does this mean that if, let us say, a bombing of a subway station occurs in Chicago, and a perpetrator is apprehended in Canada, there is jurisdiction to prosecute him under § 2332f?

b. Similarly, in the case of the type of bombing described in a., if the perpetrator is found in Chicago and he or she is a national of a foreign country, is there jurisdiction?

c. If in the Oklahoma City bombing perpetrated by Timothy McVeigh, one of the victims of the bombing was a tourist from Mexico, would there be jurisdiction to prosecute McVeigh under this statute? If none of the victims was a foreign person, would there be any possible basis for finding jurisdiction under this section?

d. If a bombing of the London Underground occurs, and a perpetrator, who is a member of al Qaeda, is found in New York City, would there be jurisdiction to prosecute him under this provision? Would it make any difference if the perpetrator is a U.S. citizen, or not?

3. Refer back to the various international law theories of a basis for exercise of jurisdiction to prosecute described in United States v. Yousef, supra, p. 11. How many of these theories undergird the various jurisdictional

provisions of § 2332f? More specifically, if there is jurisdiction to prosecute the offender described in note 2d., supra, even if he is not a U.S. citizen, what theory of international jurisdiction might be invoked in support? Would it be relevant that an International Convention for the Suppression of Terrorist Bombing (to which the U.S. is a signatory) went into effect in May, 2001 and that it deals with the subject of terrorist bombing of public transportation systems? What would you want to know about the provisions of this Convention?

4.   Note the Exemptions to Jurisdiction provision in subsection (d).

a.   Would members of Al Qaeda who engage in acts covered by subsection (a) be exempted from criminal liability under this section by subsection (d)(1)? Would members of the Taliban who in military actions in Afghanistan bombed a bridge be exempted under (d)(1) or (2)? What about actions of our own military in Afghanistan?

b.   No other provision of sec. 2332f, apart from the last clause of (d)(3) provides for jurisdiction based on effect on interstate or foreign commerce. Does the last clause of (d)(3) turn effect on interstate or foreign commerce into one of the jurisdictional bases for this offense?

5.   For a related offense that deals with terrorist attacks against mass transportation systems, see 18 U.S.C. § 1993.

NOTE ON OTHER TERRORISM-RELATED OFFENSES

18 U.S.C. § 2332e authorizes the Attorney General to request military assistance in matters involving the enforcement of § 2332a relating to weapons of mass destruction. For discussion of issues relating to the use of the military in domestic law enforcement contexts, see Chapter 13, infra.

Three additional offenses aimed at specific kinds of catastrophic offenses were enacted as part of the Intelligence Reform and Terrorism Prevention Act signed into law in December, 2004: a) 18 U.S.C. § 2332g (prohibition against producing, acquiring, transferring, using, possessing, threatening to use, etc. missile systems designed to destroy aircraft); b) 18 U.S.C. § 2332h (prohibition against producing, acquiring, transferring, using, possessing, threatening to use, etc., radiological dispersal devices, that is, any weapon that is designed or intended to release radiation or radioactivity at a level dangerous to human life); and c) 18 U.S.C. § 175c (prohibition against producing, engineering, synthesizing, acquiring, transferring using, possessing and threatening to use, variola virus [a virus that can cause human smallpox]).

A major approach taken by the federal government in its enforcement efforts is also to utilize legislation which targets specific types of activities that support terrorism. Thus, 18 U.S.C. § 2332d is part of a package of provisions aimed at cutting off financial support for terrorist organizations and terrorist activity. In this instance, the criminal provision is aimed at discouraging countries that support terrorist organizations from doing so. The method of discouragement is to penalize such countries by prohibiting U.S. persons from doing business with them. This in turn is one of a series of measures designed to economically isolate such countries. The method is indirect, and the ultimate target is remote. How effective do you think such measures are likely to be? Consult generally, Stephen C. Warnecke, Note, A Preemptive Strike: Using RICO and the AEDPA to Attack the Financial Strength of International Terrorist Organizations, 78 B.U. L. Rev. 177 (1998).

A very different kind of enforcement approach is reflected in Title 18, U.S.C. § 2333, a provision that is unusual because it does not establish a crime but rather provides a civil remedy. Section 2333 creates a cause of action for a treble damage suit for any person injured in their person or property by an act of international terrorism. Section 2333 is mentioned here even though it provides a civil remedy while the rest of the materials in this volume emphasize criminal enforcement because it provides a useful comparison to make. Query: Why should the civil remedy be limited to acts of "international terrorism?" Recall that "international terrorism" is defined for purposes of chapter 113B, Title 18, in section 2331, which was reproduced supra, p. 25. For some examples of suits filed under § 2333, see Smith v. Islamic Emirate of Afghanistan, 262 F. Supp. 2d 217 (S.D.N.Y. 2003); Biton v. Palestinian Interim Self–Government Authority, 310 F. Supp. 2d 172 (D.D.C. 2004).

D. INTERNATIONAL TERRORISM PROSECUTIONS SINCE 9/11

NOTE

Reproduced following this Note is an introduction to a report on international terrorism and terrorism-related conviction statistics from 9/11 through March 18, 2010, prepared by the Counterterrorism Section of the National Security Division of the Department of Justice. These statistics reflect prosecutions of terrorism and terrorism-related cases in the federal civilian court system. The accompanying chart, not reproduced here, can be found at http://www.fas.org/irp/agency/doj/doj032610–stats.pdf. Also see Letter from the Assistant Attorney General, available at http://www.justice.gov/cjs/docs/terrorism-crimes-letter.html.

The question of whether persons accused of terrorism should be handled in the civilian courts or in military commission proceedings has generated much controversy since 9/11. For the most part, persons apprehended in the United States have been dealt with in the civilian system, although there have been exceptions. For the most part, at least until recently, persons apprehended abroad have been handled in the military system, although, again, there have been exceptions. Attorney General Holder's announcement in the fall, 2009 that it was planned to prosecute in civilian proceedings a handful of the persons detained in military custody at Guantanamo, including some directly involved in the planning that led to the 9/11 terrorist attacks, served to escalate the controversy about the choice between civilian and military trials; it became a political issue. While the Attorney General has not backed down from his announced choice of a civilian forum for some of the detainees, as a result of the controversy, he did decide to shift the prosecutions of the handful of persons accused of plotting the 9/11 attacks back to the military commission process.

The fact that a large number of terrorism cases have been successfully prosecuted in the federal courts while only a few such cases have been brought to closure in the military commission system has been advanced as an argument in support of civilian handling of such cases. Accordingly, the statistics detailed below are part of the background for consideration of this issue, which is a recurring question throughout the book. We return to it in Part 2 of the volume.

Note that the report adopts a distinction between what are termed Category I and Category II cases. Category I cases involve violations of federal statutes that directly relate to international terrorism. These statutes coincide to a large degree with the statutes that were treated or described in section C., supra.

INTRODUCTION TO NATIONAL SECURITY DIVISION STATISTICS ON UNSEALED INTERNATIONAL TERRORISM AND TERRORISM–RELATED CONVICTIONS

The National Security Division's International Terrorism and Terrorism–Related Statistics Chart tracks convictions resulting from international terrorism investigations conducted since September 11, 2001, including investigations of terrorist acts planned or committed outside the territorial jurisdiction of the United States over which Federal criminal jurisdiction exists and those within the United States involving international terrorists and terrorist groups. Convictions listed on the chart involve the use of a variety of Federal criminal statutes available to prevent, disrupt, and punish international terrorism and related criminal activity. The convictions are the product of the Department's aggressive, consistent, and coordinated national enforcement effort with respect to international terrorism that was undertaken after the September 11, 2001 terrorist attacks.

Criminal cases arising from international terrorism investigations are divided into two categories, according to the requisite level of coordination and monitoring required by the Counterterrorism Section of the National Security Division (or its predecessor section in the Criminal Division). This coordination and monitoring exists in response to the expanded Federal criminal jurisdiction over and importance of international terrorism matters and the need to ensure coherent, consistent, and effective Federal prosecutions related to such matters. Typically, multiple defendants in a case are classified in the same category.

Category I cases involve violations of federal statutes that are directly related to international terrorism and that are utilized regularly in international terrorism matters. These statutes prohibit, for example, terrorist acts abroad against United States nationals, the use of weapons of mass destruction, conspiracy to murder persons overseas, providing material support to terrorists or foreign terrorist organizations, receiving military style training from foreign terrorist organizations, and bombings of public places or government facilities. A complete list of Category I offenses is found in Appendix A.

Category II cases include defendants charged with violating a variety of other statutes where the investigation involved an identified link to international terrorism. These Category II cases include offenses such as those involving fraud, immigration, firearms, drugs, false statements, perjury, and obstruction of justice, as well as general conspiracy charges under 18 U.S.C. § 371. Prosecuting terror-related targets using Category II offenses and others is often an effective method—and sometimes the only available method—of deterring and disrupting potential terrorist planning and support activities. This approach underscores the wide variety of tools available in the U.S. criminal justice system for disrupting terror activity. Examples of Category II offenses are listed in Appendix B, and examples of Category II cases are described in Appendix C to illustrate the kinds of connections to international terrorism that are not apparent from the nature of the offenses of conviction themselves. [ed. Appendices B and C are not reproduced here.]

The chart includes the defendant's name, district, charging date, charges brought, classification category, conviction date and conviction charges. If a convicted defendant has been sentenced, the relevant date and sentence imposed is included. The chart is constantly being updated with new convictions, but currently includes only unsealed convictions from September 11, 2001 to March 18, 2010. The chart does not include defendants whose convictions remain under seal, nor does it include defendants who have been charged with a terrorism or terrorism-related offense but have not been convicted either at trial or by guilty plea. This chart does not include convictions related solely to domestic terrorism. Note that the chart maintained by the National Security Division is distinct from statistics maintained by the Bureau of Prisons to track inmates with terrorist connections. The chart lists more than 150 defendants classified in Category I and more than 240 defendants classified in Category II.

The chart is organized by conviction date, with the most recent convictions first. The earliest defendants included on the chart were identified and detained in the course of the nationwide investigation conducted after September 11, 2001, and were subsequently charged with a criminal offense. Since then, additional defendants have been added who, at the time of charging, appeared to have a connection to international terrorism, even if they were not charged with a terrorism offense. The decision to add defendants to the chart is made on a case-by-case basis by career prosecutors in the National Security Division's Counterterrorism Section, whose primary responsibility is investigating and prosecuting international and domestic terrorism cases to prevent and disrupt acts of terrorism anywhere in the world that impact on significant United States interests and persons.

Appendix A

Category I Offenses Aircraft Sabotage (18 U.S.C. § 32)

Animal Enterprise Terrorism (18 U.S.C. § 43) Crimes Against Internationally Protected Persons (18 U.S.C. §§ 112, 878, 1116, 1201(a)(4)) Use of Biological, Nuclear, Chemical or Other Weapons of Mass Destruction (18 U.S.C. §§ 175, 175b, 229, 831, 2332a)

Production, Transfer, or Possession of Variola Virus (Smallpox) (18 U.S.C. § 175c)

Participation in Nuclear and WMD Threats to the United States (18 U.S.C. § 832) Conspiracy Within the United States to Murder, Kidnap, or Maim Persons or to Damage Certain Property Overseas (18 U.S.C. § 956)

Hostage Taking (18 U.S.C. § 1203) Terrorist Attacks Against Mass Transportation Systems (18 U.S.C. § 1993) Terrorist Acts Abroad Against United States Nationals (18 U.S.C. § 2332) Terrorism Transcending National Boundaries (18 U.S.C. § 2332b)

Bombings of places of public use, Government facilities, public transportation systems and infrastructure facilities (18 U.S.C. § 2332f)

Missile Systems designed to Destroy Aircraft (18 U.S.C. § 2332g) Production, Transfer, or Possession of Radiological Dispersal Devices (18 U.S.C. § 2332h) Harboring Terrorists (18 U.S.C. § 2339) Providing Material Support to Terrorists (18 U.S.C. § 2339A) Providing Material Support to Designated Terrorist Organizations (18 U.S.C. § 2339B) Prohibition Against Financing of Terrorism (18 U.S.C. § 2339C) Receiving Military–Type Training from an FTO (18 U.S.C. § 2339D) Narco–Terrorism (21 U.S.C. § 1010A) Sabotage of Nuclear Facilities or Fuel (42 U.S.C. § 2284) Aircraft Piracy (49 U.S.C. § 46502)

Violations of IEEPA (50 U.S.C. § 1705(b)) involving E.O. 12947 (Terrorists Who Threaten to Disrupt the Middle East Peace Process); E.O. 13224 (Blocking Property and Prohibiting Transactions With Persons Who Commit, Threaten to Commit, or Support Terrorism or Global Terrorism List); and E.O. 13129 (Blocking Property and Prohibiting Transactions With the Taliban).

CHAPTER 3

PROVIDING MATERIAL SUPPORT FOR USE IN TERRORIST OFFENSES OR MATERIAL SUPPORT TO A FOREIGN TERRORIST ORGANIZATION: 18 U.S.C. § 2339A, § 2339B

■ ■ ■

A.   INTRODUCTION—18 U.S.C. § 2339A AND § 2339B

The materials in the previous chapter highlight the fact that many different statutory offenses can be used in prosecuting conduct relating to terrorism, and that in many instances, more than one terrorism offense may be chargeable. In this chapter, we focus on just two anti-terrorism crimes—18 U.S.C. § 2339A (providing material support in aid of terrorist offenses) and § 2339B (providing material support to a foreign terrorist organization)—which are being charged in the post–9/11 period, and especially in the past several years, more frequently than any other terrorism offenses.

1.   INCHOATE OFFENSE ASPECT

It is noteworthy that most of the cases prosecuted under 2339A and 2339B do not directly involve violent actions themselves but rather conduct early in the chronology of events that lead up to violence—for example, training in the use of explosives, or providing funds that support terrorist activities or the terrorist organization, or providing personnel, namely, oneself, to assist in the activities of the terrorist organization. The material support offenses thus are frequently being used to prosecute preparatory or precursor conduct. The use of these offenses as a basis for prosecution has enabled the government to spread its criminal enforcement net widely and intervene, nip in the bud, and then prosecute and convict individuals on their way to becoming terrorists or those who by their support increase the likelihood that the terrorists will succeed. In many instances, these offenses are also being used to add to the number of offenses charged: most terrorism-related conduct that is otherwise criminal involves conduct that provides support either to the commission of terrorism offenses or to terrorist organizational activities.

Is this type of strategy aimed at precursor conduct a good strategy for the government to pursue? Is there any downside associated with adopting this kind of strategy? Until these offenses were enacted, the two offense categories most frequently used to prosecute inchoate or preparatory conduct were attempts and conspiracy. As you progress through these materials, consider whether and how the material support offenses are similar to, or different from, attempts and conspiracy charges. See generally, Robert M. Chesney, Beyond Conspiracy? Anticipatory Prosecution and the Challenge of Unaffiliated Terrorism, 80 S. Cal. L. Rev. 425 (2007).

2. COMPARISON WITH COMPLICITY

These offenses share certain special characteristics: they are doctrinally innovative. See Norman Abrams, The Material Support Terrorism Offenses: Perspectives Derived from the (Early) Model Penal Code, 1 J. Nat'l Sec. L. & Pol'y 5, 9–11 (2005) where § 2339A and § 2339B are described as follows:

> ... Both offenses are, in essence, specialized forms of a kind of complicity crime. Typically we define as a substantive offense conduct that involves direct commission of a harm. Normally, under modern criminal law, complicity liability is derivative from a substantive offense and is not itself defined as a separate substantive crime, though it is, of course, a basis for making a person liable for the substantive offense. Thus, a person who aids and abets others who commit a bank robbery is liable for the bank robbery, as if he or she had directly committed the robbery. Stating the matter more formally, in addition to holding criminally liable the direct perpetrators of such offenses (primary party liability), we can also hold individuals liable as accomplices to the commission of the substantive offense if they aided or abetted the commission of the offense....

> Sections 2339A and 2339B are different from traditional forms of complicity liability insofar as each makes the provision of material support to the commission of offenses (directly in the case of 2339A or more indirectly in the case of 2339B), itself an independent substantive offense, with its own penalty, rather than a form of secondary liability to a substantive offense. Moreover, each is a serious offense, with a maximum penalty of 15 years or possible life imprisonment if death of a person results....

> Second, unlike traditional complicity, which uses a general phrase such as "aid or abet" to describe the kind of conduct that can be a basis for secondary liability, material support is defined in the statute by a listing of categories of specific kinds of conduct.... [T]his

categorical approach to defining the actus reus of the material support offenses is a central and significant feature of these new crimes.

Third, unlike traditional complicity liability which applies to all offenses, each of these offenses is limited to terrorism-related contexts by a general description or specification of the offenses, the provision of material support for which, leads to criminal liability. As previously mentioned, under 2339A, a list of terrorism offenses is set forth as the possible object of the material support that triggers liability. A special feature of 2339B is the fact that the direct object of the support is not terrorism offenses themselves but rather a "terrorist organization," that is, an organization that engages in terrorist crimes.

Fourth, viewing 2339A and 2339B as forms of complicity that have been converted into substantive offenses, we should take note of the fact that unlike the basis for traditional complicity liability, under these sections, it is not required that the substantive offense for which the "accomplice" has provided "aid" must have itself have been committed.

Finally, perhaps the most important feature of these complicity-like crimes is the fact that 2339B requires knowledge and 2339A, at a minimum, requires knowledge as the requisite mens rea. Though the knowledge requirement for 2339A is more specific than for 2339B insofar as it relates to a specific offense or offenses, neither requires the kind of mens rea that most court require for complicity—a mens rea of purpose.

3. ADAPTABILITY

Both of these offenses are adaptable to an endless variety of uses. For example, providing financial assistance in aid of the listed federal offenses is covered as well as financial assistance to a foreign terrorist organization. As we shall see, however, all kinds of other aid in support of the listed offenses or provided to an FTO are also within these statutes. And some of the items listed as "material support" have been interpreted in such a way that they cover a host of other kinds of aid to or participation in terrorist activities or the activities of an FTO. The result is that these statutes cover an extraordinary range of different kinds of acts and activities. This is not to say that this is necessarily a bad result; it is, however, a fact worth taking note of, and suggests that we should pay attention to this aspect of these statutes as we move through this chapter.

The adaptability of these statutes also has another consequence. It makes it possible to apply the statutes to conduct that, at a minimum, resembles facially innocent conduct, and at a maximum raises serious first amendment issues, when such conduct is criminalized. We shall have occasion in this chapter to address these kinds of issues and concerns.

4. THE COVERAGE OF THIS CHAPTER

These two statutory offenses have been used frequently by prosecutors in the post–9/11 period. Numerous issues of statutory interpretation have been adjudicated, and, as a result, the statutes have been amended. We describe a bit of this history and then examine how prosecutors have used the "personnel" term in the listing of material support as a way to expand the application of the concept of material support.

We also review the requisite mens rea elements under the two statutes: Is purpose or specific intent required, or is knowledge sufficient? We then study the recent Supreme Court decision, Humanitarian Law Project v. Holder, which deals with application of several of the terms that can amount to providing material support, namely "expert assistance" and "training," in a prosecution under § 2339B; the HLP decision also addresses the specific intent issue and deals with the first amendment and vagueness questions raised by the plaintiffs in a pre-enforcement context.

And finally, we examine the procedural issues that surround the administrative determination by the Secretary of State that a particular organization is a foreign terrorist organization and direct judicial review of the Secretary's decision, as well as the legal questions that arise from the statutory preclusion of consideration of the validity of the FTO designation in a criminal prosecution under § 2339B.

5. THE CURRENT STATUTES: § 2339A AND § 2339B

2339A. Providing material support to terrorists

(a) **Offense.**—Whoever provides material support or resources or conceals or disguises the nature, location, source, or ownership of material support or resources, knowing or intending that they are to be used in preparation for, or in carrying out, a violation of section 32, 37, 81, 175, 229, 351, 831, 842(m) or (n), 844(f) or (i), 930(c), 956, 1114, 1116, 1203, 1361, 1362, 1363, 1366, 1751, 1992, 2155, 2156, 2280, 2281, 2332, 2332a, 2332b, 2332f, or 2340A of this title, section 236 of the Atomic Energy Act of 1954 (42 U.S.C. 2284), section 46502 or 60123(b) of title 49, or any offense listed in section 2332b(g)(5)(B) (except for sections 2339A and 2339B) or in preparation for, or in carrying out, the concealment of an escape from the commission of any such violation, or attempts or conspires to do such an act, shall be fined under this title, imprisoned not more than 15 years, or both, and, if the death of any person results, shall be imprisoned for any term of years or for life. A violation of this section may be prosecuted in any Federal judicial district in which the underlying offense was committed, or in any other Federal judicial district as provided by law.

(b) **Definitions.**—As used in this section—

(1) the term "material support or resources" means any property, tangible or intangible, or service, including currency or monetary instruments or financial securities, financial services, lodging, training, expert advice or assistance, safehouses, false documentation or identification, communications equipment, facilities, weapons, lethal substances, explosives, personnel (1 or more individuals who may be or include oneself), and transportation, except medicine or religious materials;

(2) the term "training" means instruction or teaching designed to impart a specific skill, as opposed to general knowledge; and

(3) the term "expert advice or assistance" means advice or assistance derived from scientific, technical or other specialized knowledge.

2339B. Providing material support or resources to designated foreign terrorist organizations

(a) Prohibited activities.—

(1) **Unlawful conduct.**—Whoever knowingly provides material support or resources to a foreign terrorist organization, or attempts or conspires to do so, shall be fined under this title or imprisoned not more than 15 years, or both, and, if the death of any person results, shall be imprisoned for any term of years or for life. To violate this paragraph, a person must have knowledge that the organization is a designated terrorist organization (as defined in subsection (g)(6)), that the organization has engaged or engages in terrorist activity (as defined in section 212(a)(3)(B) of the Immigration and Nationality Act), or that the organization has engaged or engages in terrorism (as defined in section 140(d)(2) of the Foreign Relations Authorization Act, Fiscal Years 1988 and 1989).

. . .

(g) Definitions.—As used in this section—

. . .

(4) the term "material support or resources" has the same meaning given that term in section 2339A (including the definitions of "training" and "expert advice or assistance" in that section);

. . .

(6) the term "terrorist organization" means an organization designated as a terrorist organization under section 219 of the Immigration and Nationality Act.

(h) Provision of personnel.—No person may be prosecuted under this section in connection with the term "personnel" unless that person has knowingly provided, attempted to provide, or conspired to provide a foreign terrorist organization with 1 or more individuals (who may be or include himself) to work under that terrorist organization's direction or control or to organize, manage, supervise, or otherwise direct the operation of that organization. Individuals who act entirely independently of the foreign terrorist organization to advance its goals or objectives shall not be considered to be working under the foreign terrorist organization's direction and control.

(i) **Rule of construction.**—Nothing in this section shall be construed or applied so as to abridge the exercise of rights guaranteed under the First Amendment to the Constitution of the United States.

(j) **Exception.**—No person may be prosecuted under this section in connection with the term "personnel", "training", or "expert advice or assistance" if the provision of that material support or resources to a foreign terrorist organization was approved by the Secretary of State with the concurrence of the Attorney General. The Secretary of State may not approve the provision of any material support that may be used to carry out terrorist activity (as defined in section 212(a)(3)(B)(iii) of the Immigration and Nationality Act).

6. A BIT OF HISTORY: ISSUES OF STATUTORY INTERPRETATION AND LEGISLATIVE AMENDMENTS

The crimes defined in § 2339A and § 2339B differ in a number of respects, but they both use the concept of material support which is defined in § 2339A(b) for purposes of § 2339A, and this definition is also incorporated by reference into § 2339B by virtue of subsection (g)(4) of § 2339B.

The majority of the statutory interpretation issues that have arisen under § 2339A and § 2339B have involved construing the specific terms listed under the "material support and resources" subsection. Most of the decisions interpreting the two statutes have been handed down since September 11, 2001; most of the prosecutions under the material support statutes have been brought during this period.

In 2004, a number of judicial decisions interpreting these terms triggered a legislative response that culminated in the Intelligence Reform and Terrorism Protection Act of 2004 (IRTPA), which included language that amended both § 2339A and § 2339B. The current version of these statutory provisions, reproduced supra, includes these IRTPA amendments. To fully understand the purpose and context of the amendments, however, it is useful to review both the original statutory language as well as the judicial interpretations that led to them.

In some instances, absent a familiarity with the relevant earlier judicial decision(s), the IRTPA amendments appear to be very odd and to introduce into the statute rather awkward language. In many instances, the language of the specific amendment incorporates into statutory form and in effect confirms a prior judicial interpretation. In a very few instances, the statutory amendment represents a congressional choice between two conflicting judicial decisions. What might be the purpose(s) of a legislative amendment that simply incorporates into the statute a prior judicial construction of a statutory term where there is no conflict in the case law?

The pre-IRPTA language defined "material support and resources" in § 2339A as follows:

§ 2339A.　Providing material support to terrorists

. . .

(b) Definition.—In this section, the term "material support or resources" means currency or monetary instruments or financial securities, financial services, lodging, training, expert advice or assistance, safehouses, false documentation or identification, communications equipment, facilities, weapons, lethal substances, explosives, personnel, transportation, and other physical assets, except medicine or religious materials.

The language contained in the current version of § 2339B in subsec. (a)(1), describing the kind of knowledge required and in subsec. (h) relating to the provision of personnel was added by IRTPA and was not contained in the pre–2004 version of the statute. The parenthetical clause defining personnel, "(1 or more individuals who may be or include oneself)," was also added to § 2339A in 2004 in the subsection defining "material support."

B.　THE MANY USES OF THE "PERSONNEL" TERM IN THE MATERIAL SUPPORT LISTING

UNITED STATES v. ABU–JIHAAD

600 F. Supp. 2d 362 (D. Conn. 2009)

MEMORANDUM OF DECISION

MARK R. KRAVITZ, DISTRICT JUDGE.

Following a six-day trial in March 2008, a jury convicted Defendant Hassan Abu–Jihaad on two charges: (1) disclosing national defense information to those not entitled to receive it in violation of 18 U.S.C. § 793(d); and (2) providing material support to terrorists in violation of 18 U.S.C. § 2339A and § 2. The Government alleged that in 2001, while Mr. Abu–Jihaad was serving as a U.S. Navy Signalman aboard the destroyer, the *U.S.S. Benfold,* he disclosed classified information regarding the movement of the Fifth Fleet Battle Group, which included the aircraft carrier, the *U.S.S. Constellation,* to individuals in London associated with Azzam Publications, an organization that the Government alleged supported violent Islamic jihad. According to the Government, Mr. Abu–Jihaad knew or intended that the information he disclosed would be used to kill United States nationals. By its verdict, the jury agreed with the Government's assertions. Mr. Abu–Jihaad now moves for judgment of acquittal. . . .

> [Ed. After stating the facts at length and assessing the evidence, Judge Kravitz denied the motion for judgment of acquittal on the charge under 18 U.S.C § 793(d). Subsequently the defendant was sentenced to 10 years imprisonment on this charge. The judge then proceeded to consider the charge under § 2339A. He first concluded that the government's theory that the defendant had provided material support by providing "physical assets" was not sustainable.

> Note that the government's case was entirely circumstantial; the prosecutor had presented no direct evidence that the defendant had provided the battle group information to Azzam Publications. The information was found on a computer floppy disk in 2006 and only circumstantially linked to the defendant. The government's theory was that the defendant had provided the battle group information in the spring of 2001 prior to the sailing of the battle group. One of the items of evidence contributing to the circumstantial case was an email sent by the defendant to Azzam in which the defendant praised the earlier bombing of the navy vessel, the U.S.S. Cole, as a "martyrdom operation," and derided the United States as an "infidel" and "Kuffar nation." The judge also stated, "It is also fair to read his e-mail as giving thanks to the 'mujahideen' as 'american enemies' and as the 'true champions and soldiers of Allah.' "

> The opinion then proceeded to address the question of whether the defendant had provided "personnel" within the meaning of "material support" under § 2339A.]

. . . As to "personnel," the Government argued to the jury-and the jury accepted-that by providing national defense information to Azzam, Mr. Abu–Jihaad had provided himself as "personnel." Mr. Abu–Jihaad's conviction for providing personnel presents a much closer question than the conviction for providing physical assets. . . . The task is made all the more difficult because the Second Circuit has not yet ruled on the scope of the term "personnel" in that statute, Congress amended the definition of "personnel" in § 2339B but not in § 2339A, and the case law that does exist is not entirely consistent.

Notably, all of the legislative history states that the new language added to § 2339B in 2004 was only a clarification of the definition of personnel and not a substantive change. . . .

. . . [A]s an initial matter, the Court must decide whether the amended definition of "personnel" in § 2339B applies to § 2339A as well, for even the Government concedes that if the amended definition in § 2339B applies to § 2339A, the evidence is wanting. Though the legislative history describes the definition of "personnel" in § 2339B as a mere clarification, the fact that Congress chose not to apply the more detailed definition to

§ 2339A causes the Court to believe that the definition Congress provided for § 2339B should not apply to § 2339A. . . . The Court must presume that Congress was aware that the definition of "personnel" was relevant to both sections, but chose to include the more detailed definition in one section and not the other. This presumption is even stronger because Congress changed the definition of "personnel" in § 2339A by adding "1 or more individuals who may be or include oneself" at the same time it added the more detailed definition of "personnel" to § 2339B. Nor is there any indication in the legislative history that Congress intended the § 2339B definition to apply to § 2339A.

Therefore, the Court is left with the language of § 2339A, which does not define either the word "provide" or "personnel." The Supreme Court has repeatedly explained that "[w]hen a word is not defined by statute, we normally construe it in accord with its ordinary or natural meaning." Ordinarily, the term "provide" means to make available, to furnish, and to arrange for, supply, or transfer, see Random House Webster's Unabridged Dictionary (2001), and that is what the Court told the jury (without objection). . . . Furthermore, . . ., there is no reason to suppose from the language of the statute that "provides" is limited to a physical transfer or delivery of personnel:

> [S]tatutory terms are to be interpreted in their context in light of their placement and purpose in the statutory scheme. A defendant would reasonably be providing material support or resources by making these items or services available with the requisite knowledge or intent. Limiting the definition of "provides" to the physical transfer of an asset would result in a strained and untenable reading of the statute. Thus, there is no basis to limit the meaning of "provides . . . personnel" to the physical transfer of personnel, and not to include making personnel available—which is in accord with the ordinary and natural use of the term "provide," and which is consistent with its placement in the statute and the purpose of proscribing the provision of resources to be used for a prohibited purpose.

Likewise, the term "personnel" is also not defined in § 2339A. The plain meaning of that term includes "a body of persons employed by or active in an organization, service or place of work." See Random House Webster's Unabridged Dictionary (2001). In the context of § 2339A, it seems apparent that the term refers to those individuals who are provided or made available to prepare for or carry out the crimes prohibited by the statute. The individual need not be an "employee" or "quasi-employee," but there must be some form of coordination, joint action, or understanding. Entirely independent action is not sufficient to qualify as being at least "active in" an organization as required by the definition of personnel. Therefore, one who makes resources in the form of individuals (including himself) available, or furnishes individuals (including himself), for the purpose of actively preparing for or carrying out the crimes prohibited by the statute through some form of coordinated action is guilty of violating § 2339A. See, e.g., United States v. Marzook, 383

F.Supp.2d 1056, 1064 (N.D.Ill.2005) (holding that the term "personnel" includes recruiting others to join Hamas).

. . .

Thus, the Court applies the definition of providing personnel as stated above. . . . The difficulty of applying that definition to the facts of this case arises from the Government's theory of guilt, which was that by disclosing national defense information to Azzam, Mr. Abu–Jihaad was, in effect, making himself available to terrorists for the purpose of killing U.S. nationals. That is, by providing information alone to Azzam-an act that was not directly prohibited by § 2339A–Mr. Abu–Jihaad provided personnel—that is, Mr. Abu–Jihaad himself—to Azzam, knowing that he or his assistance would be used to prepare for, or carry out, the killing of U.S. nationals.

That theory of guilt puts a strain on the language of the statute. For if the Government's argument were accepted, an individual who provided a terrorist organization with, say, weapons—perhaps by selling them at market price—would also be deemed to have provided the organization with personnel—namely, the gun dealer himself. Of course, one can imagine situations where an individual makes both himself and others available to terrorist organizations and also provides the organizations with weapons, money, or other tangible resources. But that is not invariably the case. That is, merely providing an organization with a resource, even a prohibited resource, is not necessarily the same thing as providing personnel to prepare for or carry out the prohibited purposes of the statute through some form of coordinated or joint action. For if that were the case, then much of the definition of "material support or resources" would be entirely redundant; providing weapons, explosives, or anything else on the list would also automatically constitute the provision of personnel as well.

To be sure, context and facts matter. Yet, it is context and facts that are entirely missing in this case. For we do not know how Mr. Abu–Jihaad conveyed the defense information to Azzam or what arrangements, if any, they had with each other. It could well be that Mr. Abu–Jihaad asked Azzam how he could help in supporting jihad, they told him to send defense information about the movements of the battlegroup so terrorists could attack the battlegroup, and Mr. Abu–Jihaad did as requested. In those circumstances, the Court would have little difficulty concluding that Mr. Abu–Jihaad had volunteered himself as personnel, acting in coordination with Azzam to kill U.S. nationals. On the other hand, perhaps Mr. Abu–Jihaad on a whim simply sent defense information to Azzam on one occasion, not knowing if Azzam wanted it and without any pre-disclosure or post-disclosure communication with Azzam about the information. In those circumstances, he surely provided defense information to someone not entitled to receive it, as the Court has previously found, but it would be linguistically odd to describe that lone, voluntary act as making personnel available to Azzam. . . .

The Government recognizes this gap in the evidence and seeks to get around it by pointing to a general request by Azzam to its readership in November 2000, in which it sought aid for the Taliban by requesting money, gas masks, or battlefield medical services. Of course, Azzam also exhorted its readers to assist in violent jihad. But to build a quid pro quo or understanding from these generalized requests for assistance is more than the evidence will bear, even taking all reasonable inferences in the light most favorable to the Government. In short, the evidence showed beyond a reasonable doubt that Mr. Abu–Jihaad provided classified defense information to Azzam. He may also have made himself available to assist Azzam in violent jihad. However, we simply do not know that from the evidence presented, even viewing the evidence in the light most favorable to the Government. Therefore, the Court will grant the Motion for Judgment of Acquittal on the material support charge under 18 U.S.C. § 2339A.

QUESTIONS AND NOTES

1. The defendant, Abu–Jihaad, in the principal case above appealed his conviction under 18 U.S.C. § 793(d); the Second Circuit affirmed. United States v. Abu–Jihaad, 630 F.3d 102 (2d Cir. 2010). The judgment of acquittal on the 18 U.S.C. § 2339A charge was not reviewed or commented upon by the appellate court. Between the district court decision in Abu–Jihaad and the court of appeals decision, a different panel of the Circuit handed down the decision in United States v. Stewart which is reproduced below.

2. *United States v. Stewart*, reproduced following this Note, is the opinion of the Second Circuit on appeal from the district court's decision in *United States v. Sattar*, 314 F. Supp. 2d 279 (S.D.N.Y. 2004). The district court case involved a prosecution of a lawyer who, while visiting her client in prison, assisted the translator to communicate messages to the prisoner's alleged co-conspirators outside the prison and herself made statements to the press that communicated messages from the prisoner. The facts are further detailed in the court of appeals opinion below. The trial judge in *Sattar* had dismissed two counts of the original indictment as unconstitutionally vague; the government amended the indictment, and the second time around, the district court upheld the indictment against the same claim, stating:

> Counts One and Two of the original indictment charged that Sattar, Stewart, and Yousry conspired to violate 18 U.S.C. § 2339B and committed a substantive violation of that statute by, among other means, providing themselves as "personnel" to a designated FTO and by providing "communications equipment" to an FTO by using their own telephones to further the goals of an FTO. . . .

> The Court dismissed Counts One and Two of the original indictment as unconstitutionally vague as applied to the conduct alleged in those counts. Concerning the "provision" of "communications equipment," the Court held that "by criminalizing the mere use of phones and other means of communication the statute provides neither notice nor standards for its application such that it is unconstitutionally vague as

applied." The Court further concluded that by prohibiting the "provision" of "personnel," including oneself, to a "foreign terrorist organization," § 2339B could conceivably apply to someone engaging in advocacy on behalf of such an organization, conduct protected by the First Amendment. The Court noted that mere membership in an organization could not be prohibited without a requirement that the Government prove the defendants' specific intent to further the FTO's unlawful ends, ... but the statute provided no means to distinguish providing oneself to an organization from mere membership in the organization.

The S1 Indictment,[1] on the other hand, which charges a violation of 18 U.S.C. § 2339A rather than § 2339B, no longer charges Stewart and Yousry with providing themselves as personnel to an FTO, but rather with providing and conspiring to provide personnel—by making Sheikh Abdel Rahman, not themselves, available as a co-conspirator—to the conspiracy alleged in Count Two, namely the conspiracy to kill and kidnap persons in a foreign country. It also charges them with concealing and disguising the nature, location, and source of that personnel by disguising that Sheikh Abdel Rahman was a co-conspirator. These actions were allegedly done with the knowledge and intent that such personnel was to be used in preparation for, or in carrying out, the conspiracy to kill and kidnap persons in a foreign country. This is the heightened specific intent required by § 2339A.

Following a jury verdict convicting her of a number of offenses, Steward appealed to the United States Court of Appeals for the Second Circuit.

UNITED STATES v. STEWART

590 F.3d 93 (2d Cir. 2009)

Before: WALKER, CALABRESI, and SACK, CIRCUIT JUDGES.

[JUDGE CALABRESI concurred, and also filed a separate concurring opinion. JUDGE WALKER concurred in part and dissented in part in a separate opinion.]

SACK, CIRCUIT JUDGE:

Defendants Lynne Stewart, Mohammed Yousry, and Ahmed Abdel Sattar appeal from judgments of conviction of the United States District Court for the Southern District of New York for various crimes arising from their contacts with and behavior relating to government restrictions on communications and other contacts with Sheikh Omar Ahmad Ali Abdel Rahman. Rahman is serving a life sentence in a maximum security prison for terrorism-related crimes of seditious conspiracy, solicitation of murder, solicitation of an attack on American military installations, conspiracy to murder, and a conspiracy to bomb. He is subject to "Special Administrative Measures" ("SAMs") restricting his ability to communicate with persons outside of the prison in which he is incarcerated so as to prevent him from continuing to lead terrorist organizations and their members. The government cross-appeals from the defendants' sentences.

---

1. Ed. That is, the superseding indictment now before the court.

We would be remiss if we did not, at the outset, commend the district court for its thoroughness, thoughtfulness, and effectiveness in the conduct of these unusually lengthy, difficult, and sensitive proceedings. Much of what follows simply reports what it did and tracks what it said.

We affirm the judgments of conviction. We also affirm the sentences of Yousry and Sattar. We remand the case, however, with respect to the sentence of Stewart, and also with respect to the sentences of Yousry and Sattar in light of the resentencing of Stewart.

In particular, we affirm the judgments as to each defendant's conviction of conspiring to defraud the United States, in violation of 18 U.S.C. § 371, by violating SAMs imposed upon Abdel Rahman. Contrary to the defendants' arguments, the evidence is sufficient to sustain these convictions. Moreover, we reject both Stewart's argument that, as a lawyer, she was not bound by the SAMs, and her belated argument collaterally attacking their constitutionality.

We affirm as to Sattar's conviction of conspiring to murder persons in a foreign country in violation of 18 U.S.C. § 956, and his conviction of soliciting persons to commit crimes of violence-viz., murder and conspiracy to commit murder-in violation of 18 U.S.C. § 373. We conclude that the evidence is sufficient to sustain these convictions, especially in light of testimony establishing that Sattar attempted to undermine a unilateral cease-fire by an Egyptian terrorist organization and to draft a *fatwa* calling for, *inter alia,* the killing of "Jews and Crusaders."

We affirm as to Stewart's and Yousry's convictions of providing and concealing material support to the conspiracy to murder persons in a foreign country in violation of 18 U.S.C. § 2339A and 18 U.S.C. § 2, and of conspiring to provide and conceal such support in violation of 18 U.S.C. § 371. We conclude that the charges were valid-that 18 U.S.C. § 2339A is neither unconstitutionally vague as applied nor a "logical absurdity," as Stewart asserts-and that the evidence was sufficient to sustain the convictions. We also reject Stewart's claims that her purported attempt to serve as a "zealous advocate" for her client provides her with immunity from the convictions.

Finally, we affirm Stewart's convictions for knowingly and willfully making false statements in violation of 18 U.S.C. § 1001 when she affirmed that she intended to, and would, abide by the SAMs. In light of her repeated and flagrant violation of the SAMs, a reasonable factfinder could conclude that Stewart's representations that she intended to and would abide by the SAMs were knowingly false when made.

We reject the remaining challenges to the convictions. . . .

. . .

We also affirm the sentences of Sattar and Yousry. We conclude that the district court committed neither procedural error in calculating the applicable Guidelines ranges, nor substantive error in varying from those ranges pursuant to its consideration of the factors set forth in 18 U.S.C. § 3553(a)....

We cannot affirm Stewart's sentence on the basis of the record before us. Because the district court declined to find whether Stewart committed perjury at trial, we cannot conclude that the mitigating factors found to support her sentence can reasonably bear the weight assigned to them. This is so particularly in light of the seriousness of her criminal conduct, her responsibilities as a member of the bar, and her role as counsel for Abdel Rahman. We therefore remand the cause to the district court for further consideration of her sentence, in light of, among other things, the charges of perjury against her and of any other matter it deems necessary or advisable, and direct the court to revoke Stewart's and Yousry's bail pending appeal and to order them to surrender to the United States Marshal to begin serving their sentences forthwith.

. . .

[Ed. note: The district court had sentenced the defendant Sattar to a 288–month term of incarceration to be followed by a five-year term of supervised release and a $300 special assessment; Stewart was sentenced to a 28–month term of incarceration to be followed by a two-year term of supervised release and a $500 special assessment; and Yousry was sentenced to a 20–month term of incarceration to be followed by a two-year term of supervised release and a $300 special assessment.]

The transcript of the trials in the cases on appeal runs in excess of thirteen thousand pages. The district court issued nine opinions and a wide variety of orders addressing issues presented during the course of the proceedings. The filings in this Court reflect the massiveness of the record. We therefore describe the proceedings in the district court and the relevant facts only in the detail we think necessary to explain our decision. In reviewing the conviction, we set forth the facts, as we must, in the light most favorable to the government.

. . .

In October 1995, Sheikh Omar Ahmad Ali Abdel Rahman was convicted of a variety of terrorism-related crimes in the United States District Court for the Southern District of New York. According to the government's evidence at his trial,

Abdel Rahman, a blind Islamic scholar and cleric, was the leader of [a] seditious conspiracy, the purpose of which was "jihad," in the sense of a struggle against the enemies of Islam. Indicative of this purpose, in a speech to his followers Abdel Rahman instructed that they were to "do jihad with the sword, with the cannon, with the grenades, with the missile ... against God's enemies." Abdel Rahman's role in the conspiracy was generally limited to overall supervision and direction of the membership, as he made efforts to remain a level above the details of individual operations. However, as a cleric and the group's leader, Abdel Rahman was entitled to dispense fatwas, religious opinions on the holiness of an act, to members of the group sanctioning proposed courses of conduct and advising them whether the acts would be in furtherance of jihad.

. . .

Following his conviction and appeal therefrom, Abdel Rahman's legal team focused on two goals: improving his conditions of confinement, and obtaining his transfer from prison in the United States to Egypt.

. . .

Federal regulations provide that the Bureau of Prisons may implement SAMs, [ed. "Special Administrative Measures"] '[u]pon direction of the Attorney General,' when 'reasonably necessary to protect persons against the risk of death or serious bodily injury.' The Bureau of Prisons, following Abdel Rahman's remand to its custody in August 1997, imposed severely restrictive SAMs upon him. They were designed to prevent him from directing or facilitating yet more violent acts of terrorism from his prison cell. The SAMs have been renewed, and sometimes modified, every 120 days since they were first imposed.

The May 11, 1998, SAMs applicable to Abdel Rahman "prohibited [him] from having contact with . . . others (except as noted in this document) that could foreseeably result in [his] communicating information (sending or receiving) that could circumvent the SAM intent of significantly limiting [his] ability to communicate (send or receive) terrorist information." To enforce this general prohibition, the measures regulated Abdel Rahman's telephone contacts, and his visitors' visits. The measures limited his telephone contacts solely to his attorneys of record and his wife, and prevented matters discussed in those calls from being "divulged in any manner to any third party." The measures required the screening of all his outgoing and incoming non-legal mail, and prohibited him from "talk[ing] with, or otherwise communicat[ing] with, any representative of the news media," including "through [his] attorney(s)/staff, or otherwise," The measures also provided for the monitoring of all non-legal visits. On the condition that his attorneys would not divulge any information to third parties, Abdel Rahman was permitted to communicate with his legal team by telephone, with fewer restrictions than with other persons. Members of this legal team included lawyers Ramsey Clark, Abdeen Jabara, Lawrence Schilling, and defendant Lynne Stewart.

. . .

Stewart repeatedly executed such statements. On May 1, 1998, she signed a document entitled "Attorney Affirmation," in which she affirmed, under penalty of perjury, the truth of specified statements regarding the then-applicable SAMs: that she had read the May 11, 1998, version of the SAMs; that she "underst[ood] the restrictions contained in that document and agree[d] to abide by its terms"; that during her visits to Abdel Rahman she would "employ only cleared translators/interpreters and [would] not leave [any] translator/interpreter alone with inmate Abdel Rahman"; and that she would "only be accompanied by translators for the purpose of communicating with inmate Abdel Rahman concerning legal matters." Affirmation of Lynne Stewart, May 1, 1998. Stewart also affirmed that neither she nor any member of her office would "forward any mail received from inmate Abdel Rahman to a third person" nor would she "use [her] meetings, correspondence or phone calls with Abdel Rahman to pass messages between third parties (including, but not limited to, the media) and Abdel Rahman." On May 16, 2000, and again on May 7, 2001, Stewart signed similar affirmations under penalty of perjury, again affirming that she had read the most recent versions of the SAMs, and that she would not use her contact with Abdel Rahman to pass messages between him and third parties, including members of the media. Affirmation of Lynne Stewart, May 16, 2000; Affirmation of Lynne Stewart, May 7, 2001.

Defendant Mohammed Yousry, a middle-aged New York University graduate student who served as one of the legal team's translators had also been, in that capacity, a member of Abdel Rahman's trial team. As a translator, Yousry was permitted to read to Abdel Rahman, who is blind, and to take dictation from him.

Various members of the team, including Stewart and Yousry, also maintained contact with defendant Ahmed Abdel Sattar, who had served as a paralegal during Abdel Rahman's trial. The evidence established that Sattar was in continual contact with various members of al-Gama'a abroad.

. . .

Sometime in 1997, more than three years after Abdel Rahman was taken into federal custody, a faction of al-Gama'a declared a unilateral "cease-fire," i.e., a halting of violent operations, in Egypt. When the cease-fire was first announced, Abdel Rahman was understood to support it.

In November 1997, despite the cease-fire, a group associated with al-Gama'a attacked, killed, and mutilated the bodies of more than sixty tourists, guides, and guards at the Hatshepsut Temple in Luxor, Egypt. Rifa'i Taha Musa ("Taha")—a military leader of al-Gama'a, a follower of Abdel Rahman, and an unindicted co-conspirator herein—was involved in the incident. Alaa Abdul Raziq Atia ("Atia"), later a leader of al-Gama'a's military wing in Egypt, was also involved in the killings. Al–Gama'a later claimed responsibility for the attack and demanded Abdel Rahman's release from prison in the United States.

. . .

At about this time, defendant Sattar was in contact with members of al-Gama'a, who were divided over their support for what remained of the cease-fire. Pro-cease-fire and anti-cease-fire factions developed, and members of the organization wanted Abdel Rahman to take a position on the matter. To that end, several wrote messages addressed to Abdel Rahman, which they sent to Sattar for delivery to Abdel Rahman. Sattar gave the messages to Stewart and Yousry, who surreptitiously brought the messages with them to Abdel Rahman during a subsequent visit in May 2000.

Yousry read the messages to Abdel Rahman during the visit, and Abdel Rahman dictated to Yousry responses to some of them. Yousry and Stewart then smuggled the responses out ... among their legal papers, and sent them to Sattar. As directed by Abdel Rahman, Sattar informed various members of al-Gama'a that Abdel Rahman was willing to reconsider the effectiveness of the cease-fire and had rejected the associated idea that al-Gama'a should form a political party in Egypt.

News of Abdel Rahman's purported position spread. But some members of the media in the Middle East expressed skepticism about the veracity of Sattar's representations, questioning whether they in fact came from Abdel Rahman or whether Sattar had fabricated them himself. To refute those reports, Sattar and Yousry asked one of Abdel Rahman's lawyers, former United States Attorney General Ramsey Clark, to tell a reporter for an Arabic-language newspaper that Abdel Rahman opposed al-Gama'a's formation of a political party. Clark, they thought, would be perceived as more authoritative than Sattar. Clark eventually agreed to talk to the reporter. He told the reporter that "[t]he Sheikh has said he believes that the formation of a new political party to engage in politics in Egypt at this time is ... not correct and should not be done."

. . .

Taha sent ... [a] message to Sattar to be relayed to Abdel Rahman urging Abdel Rahman to support the termination of the cease-fire and noting that Taha and his associates needed a "powerful word" from Abdel Rahman to achieve this goal. Taha told Sattar that such support from Abdel Rahman would "strengthen me among the brothers." Sattar agreed to send the message to Abdel Rahman and prepared a letter to Abdel Rahman for that purpose. In mid-September 1999, Clark and Yousry surreptitiously took the letter, along with newspaper articles relating to the killing of Kidwani in Egypt, with them during a visit to Abdel Rahman in FMC Rochester. Yousry read the letter and newspaper clippings aloud to Abdel Rahman. From these documents, Abdel Rahman first learned of Kidwani's death.

Abdel Rahman dictated a letter to Yousry in response.

> To those against whom war is made, permission is given to fight, because they are wronged (oppressed)—and verily God is most powerful for their aid.... The latest thing published in the newspapers was about the Egyptian regime's killing of four members of the Group. This is ... enough proof that the Egyptian regime does not have the intention to interact with this peaceful Initiative [i.e., the cease-fire] which aims at unification. I therefore demand that my brothers, the sons of [al-Gama'a] do a comprehensive review of the Initiative and its results. I also demand that they consider themselves absolved from it.

Sattar expected Clark to make a public statement to similar effect, but Clark declined to do so.

On February 18 and 19, 2000, Yousry and Abdeen Jabara, an Arabic-speaking lawyer and member of Abdel Rahman's legal team, visited Abdel Rahman. . . . They brought with them another letter which included another message from Taha, again asking for Abdel Rahman's support for ending the ceasefire. But Jabara would not permit Abdel Rahman to dictate a letter to Yousry in response. And, notwithstanding pressure from Sattar and Taha, Jabara, like Clark before him, refused to issue any public statement regarding Abdel Rahman's position on the matter.

. . .

On May 18, 2000, Stewart met with Sattar, who gave her more letters for Abdel Rahman, including another message from Taha yet again seeking Abdel Rahman's approval of an end to the cease-fire. Taha asked Abdel Rahman to take a "more forceful position" regarding the end of the cease-fire and to "dictate some points we can announce in a press conference with Lynne."

On May 19 and 20, 2000, Stewart and Yousry visited Abdel Rahman, taking Sattar's most recent letters with them, including the letter containing the message from Taha. Unbeknownst to them, the government, pursuant to a warrant, videotaped the meetings. Yousry told Abdel Rahman that Abu Sayyaf—an Islamic terrorist group in the Philippines—had taken hostages to be used in bargaining for the release of Abdel Rahman and others. When Yousry explained to Stewart that he was "telling the Sheikh about the Abu Sayyaf group in the Philippines" and how "they took hostages," Stewart replied, "Good for them."

From the beginning of the visit, Stewart was aware of the prison guards' presence. For example, she asked Yousry, "Do they usually sit like this and watch us?" And during this meeting, Stewart and Yousry took overt steps to ensure that the nature of their communication with Abdel Rahman would be concealed from the prison guards. As she suggested to Yousry, they "should give them [i.e., the guards] something to watch.". When the guards were standing close to the window of the conference room in which Abdel Rahman, Stewart, and Yousry, were meeting Yousry told Stewart to "look at me and talk a little bit because they are watching us closely." While Yousry read the message to Abdel Rahman, Stewart uttered a meaningless series of phrases to Yousry so that it would appear to an observer as though she was taking part in a three-way conversation: "I am talking to you about . . . him going to have a, uh, chocolate eh . . . heart attack here. . . . Why don't you stop a minute now. And say to him that, you know, 'You understood what we are saying.' " As Stewart spoke, Yousry said to Abdel Rahman, "I don't know, Sir, they are standing very close by the glass. . . . Lynne says, when they look, you look at me a little, talk, then look at the Sheikh."

Stewart continued to talk while Yousry read aloud Taha's statement in Sattar's letter. Yousry explained to Abdel Rahman that "Lynne just says anything, [laughing] Sir." Stewart remarked, "I can get an academy award for it."

    . . .

Stewart and Yousry also took evasive action when a guard appeared to take interest in their conversation. At one point, while Yousry was conversing with Abdel Rahman, Stewart touched Yousry's hand and said "Why don't you stop there and we'll talk a minute urn, the, uh. . . . Ahmed's youngest son needs glasses, did you know that?". Yousry then explained to Abdel Rahman, "Lynne says, stop a little because they are by the glass." Id. Not long afterwards, Stewart tapped with the pen on the paper in front of Yousry and told him to "continue reading this 'cause this is setting up the organizational system around his conditions." Yousry continued reading. Stewart then made a series of statements unrelated to the substance of the conversation between Yousry and Abdel Rahman. Yousry kept Abdel Rahman informed of what Yousry and Stewart were doing, noting that "Lynne continues to eh, she's watching them, she's watching them," to which Abdel Rahman replied, "[v]ery good, very good." After Yousry finished reading Taha's message to Abdel Rahman, he returned it to a notebook that he had brought with him and with which he left.

    . . .

Meanwhile, Stewart and Yousry continued to engage in what Stewart later called "[c]overing noises," and other tactics designed to obscure the nature of what they were doing. . . .

At the end of the visit, Stewart and Yousry took the Yousry-transcribed responses from Abdel Rahman with them from the prison, and later gave them to Sattar. Sattar then passed them along to Taha and another member of al-Gama'a. Sattar also spoke to various members of al-Gama'a, informing them that Abdel Rahman would have "no objection" to a return to violence.

At about this time, Sattar told members of al-Gama'a that Stewart would be making a public statement about Abdel Rahman's views on the cease-fire. Sattar and Stewart first discussed what Stewart would say to the press. Then, on June 13, 2000, Sattar and Stewart spoke to Esmat Salaheddin, a Reuters reporter based in Cairo. Stewart told Salaheddin that Rahman "is withdrawing his support for the ceasefire that currently exists." She explained that Abdel Rahman had made the statement from prison two weeks before.

The next day, other Middle Eastern press outlets carried the news that Abdel Rahman had withdrawn his support for the cease-fire. Many noted that for the cease-fire to hold, Abdel Rahman's support was essential.

On June 20, 2000, Stewart participated in a telephone conference with Abdel Rahman. She then sent another statement on Abdel Rahman's behalf via facsimile to Salaheddin, the Reuters reporter in Cairo. The telecopy said, "Everything said in the previous statements is correct" and quoted Abdel Rahman as saying, "I do withdraw my support to the [cease-fire] initiative." Statement for Release, Abdel Rahman, June 20, 2000. Following Stewart's statements on Abdel Rahman's behalf, several members of al-Gama'a began preparations to engage anew in acts of violence.

On October 4, 2000, Sattar and Taha completed a fatwa on Abdel Rahman's behalf, imitating his style, "mandating the killing of the Israelis everywhere" and "the killing [of] the Jews wherever they are and wherever they are found." Sattar sent the fatwa to, among others, Atia, who had in the meantime become the military leader of al-Gama'a. Upon receiving the message, Atia began preparing for an attack. But, on October 19, 2000, before Atia could act, the Egyptian authorities raided his hideout, killing him and killing or arresting other al-Gama'a members.

. . .

The dissemination of some of the speech introduced at trial might be viewed as nothing more than the expression of views on the broad political situation in Egypt. For example, in reaffirming that he was withdrawing his support for the cease-fire, Abdel Rahman said that he had "expressed [his] opinion and left the matters to [his] brothers to examine it and study it." Statement for Release, Abdel Rahman, June 20, 2000.

But a reasonable jury could have found, in light of Abdel Rahman's role as "spiritual" leader of al-Gama'a, that his messages were ultimately intended to sway al-Gama'a members to end the cease-fire, and by implication to commit criminal acts of violence. Abdel Rahman's statements were therefore not an expression of opinion, but a call to arms.

The evidence establishes, moreover, more than a one-way broadcast of Abdel Rahman's views. Abdel Rahman's comments were made in direct response to solicitations of his views from other al-Gama'a members who were seeking to effect an end to the cease-fire and to resume violence. In light of the information available to Abdel Rahman at the time, a reasonable jury could have read his statements as tailored to and necessary for al-Gama'a's operations and increased use of violence. Viewed through this lens, Abdel Rahman's statements were not materially different in substance from a crime boss making decisions about his criminal enterprise from prison and ordering a "hit."

. . . Stewart and Yousry argue that the prosecution did not prove the requisite mental state to sustain their convictions. They contend that they were not aware of the existence of the conspiracy charged in Count Two and therefore could not have intended to aid it.

These arguments are unavailing. From the evidence at trial, a reasonable factfinder could have concluded that Stewart and Yousry knew (1) that an active group of people within al-Gama'a including, most notably, Taha, sought to commit violent crimes but were hindered by the cease-fire and by those members of al-Gama'a who sought to adhere to it; (2) that the support of Abdel Rahman—a key leader of the group—was critical to the continued maintenance of the cease-fire; and (3) that, in light of the letters and messages from Taha and Sattar that Yousry read to Abdel Rahman in prison, Abdel Rahman's particular opinion regarding the cease-fire—and not the view of any other person—would be dispositive on the question of whether al-Gama'a members would continue to abide by the cease-fire. A reasonable factfinder could thus have concluded that Yousry and Stewart actively and intentionally facilitated communications between Abdel Rahman and al-Gama'a, in part by engaging in various ruses during the course of their visits to Abdel Rahman, and thereby effectively delivered Abdel Rahman's order to commit violence. Stewart also did so by reaffirming to the press Abdel Rahman's stated withdrawal of support for the cease-fire, thereby dispelling any notion that the message came not from Abdel Rahman himself, but was instead fabricated by members of the pro-violence faction of al-Gama'a.

. . .

The initial charges raised the possibility, moreover, that under the government's reading of the statute, "a lawyer, acting as an agent of her client, an alleged leader of an FTO, could [be] subject to criminal prosecution as a 'quasi-employee.'" As we shall see, the charges in the superseding indictment do not pose this risk.

A statute is unconstitutionally vague as applied "if it fails to provide people of ordinary intelligence a reasonable opportunity to understand what conduct it prohibits" or "if it authorizes or even encourages arbitrary and discriminatory enforcement." As a general matter, scienter requirements may "ameliorate[ ]" concerns of improper notice.

We are satisfied that section 2339A's knowledge-or-intent formulation saves the statute from being unconstitutionally vague as applied here. Unlike the application of section 2339B proposed in the initial indictment, the superseding indictment required the jury to find that the defendants knew or intended the criminal uses to which the conspiracy would put the material support they provided, thereby eliminating concerns about inadequate notice. In other words, if Stewart and Yousry knew that their actions provided material support to a conspiracy to end the cease-fire and thereby unloose deadly acts of terrorism by al-Gama'a and others, then they were on notice that what they were doing was prohibited by a statute that criminalizes the provision of material support "knowing or intending that [such support is] to be used in preparation for, or in carrying out," criminal actions. 18 U.S.C. § 2339A.

Stewart and Yousry argue nonetheless that several statutory terms, such as "personnel," are unconstitutionally vague as applied to them. They note that "personnel," undefined at the relevant time, applies equally to sections 2339A and 2339B, *compare id.* § 2339A(b)(1) (2000) *with id.* § 2339B(g)(4) (2000). They point out that the district court held this term to be unconstitutionally vague in *Sattar I.*

We agree, however, with the district court's conclusion that "[t]he meaning of 'personnel' is clear in the context of § 2339A when applied to personnel who are to be used in preparation for, or in carrying out, specific crimes." By applying, in the first indictment, the prohibition against providing "personnel" to the conspiracy to a circumstance in which the defendants provided themselves, the government created a situation in which the defendants could be punished for, in effect, providing themselves to speak out in support of the program or principles of a foreign terrorist organization, an activity protected by the First Amendment. The more limited charge that they knowingly or intentionally provided Abdel Rahman (as "personnel"), whose voice of command or words of approbation were a means by which al-Gama'a members could prepare for, or carry out, terrorist acts in Egypt, does not carry the same risk with its corresponding constitutional implications.

In addition, the heightened scienter requirement in section 2339A constrains prosecutorial discretion, and ameliorates concerns of arbitrary and discriminatory enforcement. Similar scienter requirements have saved other statutes from void-for-vagueness challenges

. . .

[After a detailed analysis of the application of the Sentencing Guidelines to the defendants, Judge Sack concluded with the following:]

A district court's failure to find particular facts will in no way impede our review in some, perhaps in most, situations; this, however, is not one of them. Especially in light of the absence of a finding that Stewart did not commit perjury at trial or otherwise obstruct justice, we think it preferable not to determine whether her sentence was substantively reasonable.

We therefore remand this matter to the district court for resentencing, in the course of which we direct the court to determine the issue of perjury and if it finds such perjury, to resentence Stewart so as to reflect that finding. The district court should also consider whether Stewart's conduct as a lawyer triggers the special-skill/abuse-of-trust enhancement under the Guidelines, and reconsider the extent to which Stewart's status as a lawyer affects the appropriate sentence. Finally, the district court should further consider the overall question whether the sentence to be given is appropriate in view of the magnitude of the offense, which the court itself has explicitly recognized. Although we do not preclude the district court's election to continue to impose a non-Guidelines sentence, we do require that such a sentence, selected after the reconsideration we have directed, begin with the terrorism enhancement and take that enhancement into account. We have serious doubts that the sentence given was reasonable, but think it appropriate to hear from the district court further before deciding the issue.

. . .

Although we find no procedural or substantive error in connection with the sentencing of Sattar and Yousry, we nonetheless remand their cases, too. We conclude that, inasmuch as the interrelationship among the sentences of the co-defendants is a principal consideration as to a proper sentence of Stewart, the district court should have the ability, if not the obligation, to resentence them as well.

After the district court completes the resentencing, jurisdiction may be restored to this Court by letter from any party, and the Office of the Clerk of this Court shall set an expeditious briefing schedule and refer the matter to this panel for further review.

[Ed. On remand from the circuit panel's decision, supra, on July, 15, 2010, the trial judge resentenced Ms. Stewart and imposed a ten year term of imprisonment. In support of the revised sentence, the judge cited statements she was reported to have made after the first sentence was imposed which he said showed remorselessness; he also cited the fact that she had commit perjury in her testimony.]

QUESTIONS AND NOTES

1. Suppose the second circuit opinion in Stewart had been decided before the trial court's acquittal decision in Abu–Jihaad. Would the judge in the latter case have been less likely to acquit on the 2339A charge? Is the trial judge's judgment of acquittal on the § 2339A charge in Abu–Jihaad inconsistent with the second circuit panel opinion in Stewart?

2. Suppose Abdel Rahman had himself been able to communicate directly with his co-conspirators in Egypt. Would he have been guilty of a violation of § 2339A on a theory that he provided personnel, himself, to them. Is that different from what Abu–Jihaad did? What are the differences, if any?

3. At one point in his opinion, the trial judge in Abu–Jihaad suggests that an expansive reading of the personnel term could make the rest of the terms in the material support superfluous. Do you agree? Are there any other terms in the definition of material support that have a similar potential?

4. What does it mean to "provide ... training?" Note the new language added to the statute in 2004 defined "training" and "expert knowledge," which, pre–2004, were not defined in the statute.

5. In a number of instances, individuals, having traveled abroad from the U.S., for example, to Afghanistan, to receive military training to prepare them allegedly to engage in terrorist activities, were prosecuted under § 2339B on the theory that they provided "personnel," namely, themselves to a FTO. See, e.g., United States v. Goba, 220 F. Supp. 2d 182 (W.D.N.Y.2002). See also United States v. Goba, 2007 WL 4404977 (W.D.N.Y. 2007), reducing Goba's sentence for providing substantial assistance to the government.

6. In 2004, as part of IRTPA, a new offense was added to Title 18, U.S.C. § 2339D, receiving military-type training from a foreign terrorist organization. That section provides:

§ 2339D. Receiving military-type training from a foreign terrorist organization

(a) **Offense.**—Whoever knowingly receives military-type training from or on behalf of any organization designated at the time of the training by the Secretary of State under section 219(a)(1) of the Immigration and Nationality Act as a foreign terrorist organization shall be fined under this title or imprisoned for ten years, or both. To violate this subsection, a person must have knowledge that the organization is a designated terrorist organization (as defined in subsection (c)(4)), that the organization has engaged or engages in terrorist activity (as defined in section 212 of the Immigration and Nationality Act), or that the organization has engaged or engages in terrorism (as defined in section 140(d)(2) of the Foreign Relations Authorization Act, Fiscal Years 1988 and 1989).

(b) **Extraterritorial jurisdiction**.—There is extraterritorial Federal jurisdiction over an offense under this section. There is jurisdiction over an offense under subsection (a) if—

(1) an offender is a national of the United States (as defined in 101(a)(22) of the Immigration and Nationality Act) or an alien lawfully admitted for permanent residence in the United States (as defined in section 101(a)(20) of the Immigration and Nationality Act);

(2) an offender is a stateless person whose habitual residence is in the United States;

(3) after the conduct required for the offense occurs an offender is brought into or found in the United States, even if the conduct required for the offense occurs outside the United States;

(4) the offense occurs in whole or in part within the United States;

(5) the offense occurs in or affects interstate or foreign commerce; or

(6) an offender aids or abets any person over whom jurisdiction exists under this paragraph in committing an offense under subsection (a) or conspires with any person over whom jurisdiction exists under this paragraph to commit an offense under subsection (a).

(c) Definitions.—As used in this section—

(1) the term "military-type training" includes training in means or methods that can cause death or serious bodily injury, destroy or damage property, or disrupt services to critical infrastructure, or training on the use, storage, production, or assembly of any explosive, firearm or other weapon, including any weapon of mass destruction (as defined in section 2232a(c)(2));

. . .

Accordingly, individuals who receive military training provided by a foreign terrorist organization, assuming the necessary mens rea is present, are now subject to prosecution under the new offense. Will they also continue to be subject to prosecution for such conduct under § 2339B, so that now they will have committed two offenses rather than just one? If so, this would be another example of a recurring pattern in federal criminal law—prosecution of newly-occurring criminal conduct under a general statute, and Congress then enacts a new statute targeted at the conduct.

7. Given the breadth of coverage of what can constitute "material support" under § 2339A and § 2339B, which has been achieved through the original legislation, subsequent judicial interpretations and legislative amendments, is there any type of support or aid to terrorist offenses or to foreign terrorist organizations that is not likely to be treated as "material support?" Given the apparent open-endedness of the definitional list, is the list really needed? Given the present status of the definition of "material support," would it not be simpler to make the offense, "Whoever provides material support . . . ," or "Whoever provides aid . . . ," or even, "Whoever aids and abets . . . ," without any specific listing of different kinds of support? What is the legal consequence of retaining the list or of eliminating it?

C. MENS REA ISSUES UNDER §§ 2339A AND 2339B: KNOWLEDGE OR SPECIFIC INTENT

QUESTIONS AND NOTES

1. § 2339A contains a mens rea element of "knowing or intending" that the material support being provided is to be used in the commission of specified offenses, while § 2339B contains a mens rea of "knowingly" providing material support to a foreign terrorist organization. Accordingly, both provisions establish knowledge as the requisite mens rea. Neither statute *requires* a mens rea of purpose or intent. Note that the circuit court in Stewart, supra, referred to the heightened scienter under 2339A. Recall the point made in the Introduction to this Chapter, that traditional complicity has been interpreted by the majority of courts to require a mens rea of purpose or the equivalent.

2. In Abrams' article on the material support offenses, op. cit. supra, p. 58, he offered the following explanation for why the specific categories of material support may have been listed in the statute:

> To appreciate why the statutory definition may have been drafted in the form of specific categories of support, we need to return to basic principles of accessorial liability, beginning with some quotations from an early draft of the Model Penal Code. In discussing the mens rea for complicity proposed in Tentative Draft No. 1 of the Code, the Comment stated:

>> "The issue is whether knowingly facilitating the commission of a crime ought to be sufficient for complicity, absent a true purpose to advance the criminal end. . . .

>> "The problem has had most attention in the federal courts where there is division of opinion as to the criterion that measures liability. The Second Circuit, speaking through Judge Learned Hand, has taken the position that the traditional definitions of complicity (aiding, abetting . . .) . . . carry an implication of purposive attitude towards it."

In this early Draft of the Model Penal Code, Professor Herbert Wechsler, the Reporter for the Code, rejected the idea that purposive aid should be an absolute prerequisite for complicity liability, instead concluding:

"... [W]hen a true purpose to further the crime is lacking, the draft requires that the accessorial behavior substantially facilitate commission of the crime ... This qualification provides a basis for discrimination that should satisfy the common sense of justice."

In other words, something less than purpose, i.e. knowledge, can suffice where the aid that is provided is substantial in assisting the commission of the crime. Wechsler's innovative approach to complicity in Tentative Draft No. 1 of the Model Penal Code was not, however, accepted by the Council of the American Law Institute. Instead, the traditional approach was retained, that is, for complicity there must be a purpose to promote or facilitate the commission of the crime.

This bit of Model Penal Code history helps to put into perspective and provides us with a possible explanation for the approach taken by the drafters of §§ 2339A and 2339B. They wanted to broaden the reach of the statute since proving purpose might prove difficult in some cases where the imposition of liability might nevertheless be warranted. But a statute that simply made knowing aid a basis for serious criminal liability would be likely to meet opposition on the ground that it extended liability too far, encompassing, for example (as the same Comment to the Model Penal Code noted), the "minor employee" or "the vendor who supplies materials readily available upon the market." So it is arguable that what the drafters did—whether or not they had this in mind—was to adopt what was in fact a version of the original MPC complicity draft, basing liability on knowledge plus "substantial facilitation," but with a special twist. Rather than adopt a general formula of substantial aid or facilitation, they opted for a categorical approach to the aid/facilitation concept. On this view, "material support" is the rough equivalent of substantial facilitation but rather than use that general phrase, the concept is defined and delimited by a series of specific categories, namely, currency ... lodging, training, expert advice or assistance, ... etc.

3. Are you persuaded by Abrams' explanation for why the material support offenses may have been constructed in this way? What criticisms of the theory can be offered?

4. As you read through this chapter, consider how the Abrams theory fits with the constructions that the courts have given to the specific terms in the categorical list defining material support? If the courts had agreed with Abrams' explanation, should they have interpreted these terms differently?

5. What are likely to be the practical consequences of the choices that the courts appear to have made in interpreting the specific terms in the categorical list defining material support? Does this choice represent sound law enforcement policy in dealing with terrorism?

6. Taking into account the constructions given to the material support listing and the requisite mentes reae for the two material support offenses,

how does the sweep of liability under these offenses compare with liability for similar conduct based on the crime of conspiracy? See Abrams, op.cit. supra, p. 58 at 29–30.

7. While the statutory language in § 2339A and § 2339B seems clearly to make a mens rea of knowledge sufficient, some courts have considered the question of whether a mens rea for § 2339B of more than knowledge is constitutionally required.

8. In United States v. Al–Arian, 308 F. Supp. 2d 1322 (M.D. Fla. 2004), the district judge read a specific intent element into § 2339B, stating:

> . . . [T]he statute could likewise punish other innocent conduct, such as where a person in New York City (where the United Nations is located) gave a FTO member a ride from the airport to the United Nations before the member petitioned the United Nations. Such conduct could be punished as providing "transportation" to a FTO under Section 2339B. The end result . . . is to render a substantial portion of Section 2339B unconstitutionally vague.
>
> But, it is not necessary to do such serious damage to the statute. . . . This Court concludes that it is more consistent with Congress's intent, which was to prohibit material support from FTOs to the "fullest possible basis," to imply a *mens rea* requirement to the "material support" element of Section 2339B(a)(1). Therefore, this Court concludes that to convict a defendant under Section 2339B(a)(1) the government must prove beyond a reasonable doubt that the defendant knew that: (a) the organization was a FTO or had committed unlawful activities that caused it to be so designated; and (b) what he was furnishing was "material support." To avoid Fifth Amendment personal guilt problems, this Court concludes that the government must show more than a defendant knew something was within a category of "material support" in order to meet (b). In order to meet (b), the government must show that the defendant knew (had a specific intent) that the support would further the illegal activities of a FTO.
>
> This Court does not believe this burden is that great in the typical case. Often, such an intent will be easily inferred. For example, a jury could infer a specific intent to further the illegal activities of a FTO when a defendant knowingly provides weapons, explosives, or lethal substances to an organization that he knows is a FTO because of the nature of the support. Likewise, a jury could infer a specific intent when a defendant knows that the organization continues to commit illegal acts and the defendant provides funds to that organization knowing that money is fungible and, once received, the donee can use the funds for any purpose it chooses. That is, by its nature, money carries an inherent danger for furthering the illegal aims of an organization. Congress said as much when it found that FTOs were "so tainted by their criminal conduct that any contribution to such an organization facilitates that conduct."
>
> This opinion in no way creates a safe harbor for terrorists or their supporters to try and avoid prosecution through utilization of shell "charitable organizations" or by directing money through the memo line

of a check towards lawful activities.[1] This Court believes that a jury can quickly peer through such facades when appropriate. This is especially true if other facts indicate a defendant's true intent, like where defendants or conspirators utilize codes or unusual transaction practices to transfer funds. Instead, this Court's holding works to avoid potential constitutional problems and fully accomplish congressional intent.

9.   In a subsequent opinion, 329 F. Supp. 2d 1294 (M.D. Fla. 2004), the district court judge in Al–Arian further elaborated on his interpretation of the statute to require specific intent:

> The government first argues that it was unnecessary for this Court to interpret Section 2339B(a)(1) as implying a specific intent requirement in order to satisfy the due process requirements of personal guilt.... This Court disagrees, however, that *Scales* and its progeny require any different result than this Court reached in its prior order. Indeed, the very language utilized by the Supreme Court in *Scales* raised the serious constitutional concerns that this Court recognized in its prior order.

> The bottom line of the government's argument is that in its opinion due process personal guilt problems only arise in membership statutes and Section 2339B is not a membership statute. The government relies heavily on the fact that the Smith Act, the act under review in *Scales,* was a membership statute. Indeed, this Court does not quarrel with the government that the Supreme Court in *Scales* held that "[m]embership, without more, in an organization engaged in illegal advocacy" is insufficient to justify individual criminal liability. *Scales* is not so narrowly worded, however, to be limited to just membership statutes. The Supreme Court's opening sentence in its Fifth Amendment section states a much broader principle that is expressly not limited to membership statutes. In that section, the Court stated:

>> In our jurisprudence guilt is personal, and when imposition of punishment on a status *or on conduct* can only be justified by reference to the relationship of that status *or conduct* to other concededly criminal activity ... that relationship must be sufficiently substantial to satisfy the concept of personal guilt in order to withstand attack under the Due Process Clause of the Fifth Amendment.

367 U.S. at 224–25, 81 S.Ct. 1469 (emphasis added).

10.   The 2004 amendments of § 2339B occurred after the opinions in the Al–Arian case, supra, were handed down, but before the trial of Al–Arian was completed. In instructions to the jury, the district court judge included a specific intent requirement, consistent with the opinion reproduced supra. Al–Arian was found not guilty on eight counts, and the jury failed to reach agreement on nine counts. Three of the not guilty verdicts involved § 2339B charges, but on the charge of conspiring to violate § 2339B, they failed to agree. Do you think that including a specific intent element in the jury instruction may have contributed to the jury verdict in the case? Are you

---

1.   For example, a donation to a suicide bomber's family given with the intent to encourage others to engage in such activities or support such activities would satisfy this specific intent requirement.

persuaded by the judge's comment regarding the no-safe harbor-for-terrorists in the last paragraph of the Al–Arian opinion, supra?

11. Sami Al–Arian was not retried on the counts upon which the jury had disagreed. Instead, a settlement was reached with the government under the terms of which he pleaded guilty, was sentenced to a time-limited sentence and agreed to be deported at the end of serving the sentence. Press Release, Office of the U.S.Attorney, Middle Dist. of Fla., April 17, 2006.

Specifically, Al–Arian was sentenced to 57 months in prison but was given credit for time already served which left a balance of 19 months. Subsequent to his release, he was subpoenaed in March, 2008, to testify before a federal grand jury in Virginia regarding an alleged "Muslim terror triangle" located in Northern Virginia. Al–Arian refused to testify. Accordingly, he was charged with criminal contempt in June, 2008 and in September, 2008, he was released on bond, subject to house arrest. An issue in the case is whether requiring him to testify in the Virginia inquiry is precluded by the plea agreement in the Florida prosecution. The judge had scheduled a hearing in the matter in April, 2009, but the hearing was postponed. The matter is pending.

12. The specific intent issue under § 2339B issue appears to have been definitively resolved by subsequent decision of the Supreme Court. See Humanitarian Law Project v. Holder, reproduced in the next subsection.

13. See United States v. Holy Land Foundation for Relief and Development, 2007 WL 1498813 (N.D. Tex. 2007):

> The defendants argue that counts 1–12 do not charge an offense under 18 U.S.C. § 2339B because those paragraphs accuse them of supporting organizations operated by or for Hamas but do not allege that the defendants supported Hamas directly. Section 2339B proscribes the knowing provision of "material support or resources to a foreign terrorist organization" as well as attempting or conspiring to provide such support if the person providing the support knows that the organization (1) is a "designated terrorist organization" that (2) has engaged or engages in "terrorist activity" or that (3) has engaged or engages in "terrorism," as those terms are defined by relevant statutes. 28 U.S.C. § 2339B(a)(1).
>
> Count one of the superseding indictment, in relevant part, charges the defendants with providing "material support and resources to the designated Foreign Terrorist Organization HAMAS by raising funds in the United States and elsewhere, and sending those funds to organizations and programs in the West Bank and Gaza, and elsewhere, which operated on behalf of, or under the control of, HAMAS." Similarly, counts two through twelve of the superseding indictment charge the defendants with knowingly providing or attempting to provide support to HAMAS by giving money to specific organizations "which operated on behalf of, or under the control of, HAMAS." The defendants contend this is insufficient because they did not give money directly to Hamas, and "[n]othing in the language of the statute proscribes providing material support to an organization 'acting on behalf of, or under the control of'" a foreign terrorist organization. Defendant's Motion at 10. The court disagrees.

The indictment charges the defendants with knowingly giving money to Hamas by giving it to organizations operated by and for Hamas. The defendants essentially ask this court to hold that it is lawful to support a terrorist organization as long as the money is funneled through a subsidiary or affiliate that has not been independently designated as a terrorist organization. Such a ruling would completely eviscerate the statute by allowing anyone intelligent enough to launder donations to clandestinely give financial support to terrorist organizations without legal consequences. If the defendants intended that the organizations to whom they gave money should pass the money to Hamas—as the indictment alleges—then they violated the clear language of 28 U.S.C. § 2339B.

The defendants next contend that if their donations to alleged subsidiaries of Hamas violated the statute, then § 2339B is unconstitutional because "[n]othing in the language of the statute gives a person of common intelligence notice that he or she may be found guilty of violating that statute by providing humanitarian aid through organizations alleged (although not designated) to be associated with" a foreign terrorist organization. The defendants give insufficient credit to people of "common intelligence." It requires no extraordinary acumen to realize that funneling money to an organization operated by or on behalf of a specially designated terrorist organization with the intent that the money be passed on to the designated terrorist group would, at the very least, constitute an attempt to provide support or resources to the terrorist organization in contravention of § 2339B. The statute would be unconstitutional in its application to the defendants only if it sought to punish them for innocently giving money to organizations which they later learned were affiliated with Hamas. However, if the government is unable to prove that the defendants knew the groups to whom they gave money were affiliated with Hamas when they provided support, then the defendants cannot be found guilty under the terms of the statute. *See* 18 U.S.C. § 2339B(a)(1). Accordingly, § 2339B is not unconstitutional as applied to the defendants, and the defendants' motion to dismiss counts one through twelve of the superseding indictment is denied.

14.   Did the court in the Holy Land Foundation opinion, supra, note 13, read into the statute a specific intent requirement?

15.   The government's proof in the Holy Land Foundation prosecution, supra, note 13, was aimed at showing that zakat committees in the West Bank and Gaza to which the individual defendants and the Holy Land Foundation donated money were linked to and controlled by Hamas, an organization that had been officially designated as a foreign terrorist organization, and that the defendants knew this. The government's proof of the linkages between Hamas and the zakat committees was mainly based on the testimony of a former Israeli intelligence agent who was presented as an expert witness on the subject. He testified in a closed courtroom and was only identified by a first name. In the end, the jury failed to reach agreement on most of the charges (acquitting on a few), and the judge declared a mistrial. The government indicated that it would retry the case. See The Dallas Morning News, Inc., 2007–10–22.

16. The Holy Land Foundation case was retried. On November 24, 2008, the Holy Land Foundation and five of its officials and organizers were found guilty on 108 separate counts, including providing material support to a designated foreign terrorist organization, money laundering, tax fraud and various conspiracy counts. The jury also concluded that the Foundation should forfeit 12.4 million dollars related to money laundering counts on which convictions were obtained. In the second trial, the prosecution had dropped 29 counts against two of the defendants, called some new witnesses and simplified the evidence presented to the jury. In May, 2009, the five individual defendants were sentenced: the two founding members of the organization were each sentenced to 65 years in prison; another defendant was sentenced to 20 years, and two others to 15 years each. See LA Times, Nov. 25, 2008, A12, and NY Times, May 28, 2009, A19.

D. THE HUMANITARIAN LAW PROJECT DECISION, § 2339B: "TRAINING" AND "EXPERT ADVICE OR ASSISTANCE," "SERVICE," "PERSONNEL"; SPECIFIC INTENT; CONSTITUTIONAL ISSUES—VAGUENESS AND FIRST AMENDMENT

The Supreme Court's decision in Holder v. Humanitarian Law Project was the culmination of a lengthy series of decisions in the lower courts[2] over a 12 year period, addressing, in a pre-enforcement context, a series of constitutional and statutory interpretation issues raised by 18 U.S.C. § 2339B. It was the first time that the Supreme Court had occasion to address the material support statutes.

HOLDER v. HUMANITARIAN LAW PROJECT

130 S.Ct. 2705 (2010)

[ROBERTS, C. J., delivered the opinion of the Court, in which STEVENS, SCALIA, KENNEDY, THOMAS, and ALITO, JJ., joined. BREYER, J., filed a dissenting opinion, in which GINSBURG and SOTOMAYOR, JJ., joined.]

CHIEF JUSTICE ROBERTS delivered the opinion of the Court.

Congress has prohibited the provision of "material support or resources" to certain foreign organizations that engage in terrorist activity. 18 U.S.C. § 2339B(a)(1). That prohibition is based on a finding that the specified organizations "are so tainted by their criminal conduct that any

---

2. The trial judge in the Abu–Jihaad case had listed the various Humanitarian Law Project decisions as follows: *Humanitarian Law Project v. Reno,* 9 F.Supp.2d 1176 (C.D.Cal.1998), *aff'd,* 205 F.3d 1130 (9th Cir.2000), *on subsequent appeal sub nom. Humanitarian Law Project v. U.S. Dep't of Justice,* 352 F.3d 382 (9th Cir.2003), *reh. en banc granted,* 382 F.3d 1154 (9th Cir.2004), *judgment vacated,* 393 F.3d 902 (9th Cir.2004), *on remand sub nom. Humanitarian Law Project v. Gonzales,* 380 F.Supp.2d 1134 (C.D.Cal.2005), *aff'd sub nom. Humanitarian Law Project v. Mukasey,* 509 F.3d 1122 (9th Cir.2007).

contribution to such an organization facilitates that conduct." Antiterrorism and Effective Death Penalty Act of 1996 (AEDPA), § 301(a)(7), 110 Stat. 1247, note following 18 U.S.C. § 2339B (Findings and Purpose). The plaintiffs in this litigation seek to provide support to two such organizations. Plaintiffs claim that they seek to facilitate only the lawful, nonviolent purposes of those groups, and that applying the material-support law to prevent them from doing so violates the Constitution. In particular, they claim that the statute is too vague, in violation of the Fifth Amendment, and that it infringes their rights to freedom of speech and association, in violation of the First Amendment. We conclude that the material-support statute is constitutional as applied to the particular activities plaintiffs have told us they wish to pursue. We do not, however, address the resolution of more difficult cases that may arise under the statute in the future.

This litigation concerns 18 U.S.C. § 2339B, which makes it a federal crime to "knowingly provid[e] material support or resources to a foreign terrorist organization." Congress has amended the definition of "material support or resources" periodically, but at present it is defined as follows:

> "[T]he term 'material support or resources' means any property, tangible or intangible, or service, including currency or monetary instruments or financial securities, financial services, lodging, training, expert advice or assistance, safehouses, false documentation or identification, communications equipment, facilities, weapons, lethal substances, explosives, personnel (1 or more individuals who may be or include oneself), and transportation, except medicine or religious materials." § 2339A(b)(1); see also § 2339B(g)(4).

The authority to designate an entity a "foreign terrorist organization" rests with the Secretary of State. 8 U.S.C. §§ 1189(a)(1), (d)(4)....

In 1997, the Secretary of State designated 30 groups as foreign terrorist organizations. See 62 Fed. Reg. 52650. Two of those groups are the Kurdistan Workers' Party (also known as the Partiya Karkeran Kurdistan, or PKK) and the Liberation Tigers of Tamil Eelam (LTTE). The PKK is an organization founded in 1974 with the aim of establishing an independent Kurdish state in southeastern Turkey. *Humanitarian Law Project v. Reno*, 9 F. Supp. 2d 1176, 1180–1181 (CD Cal. 1998). The LTTE is an organization founded in 1976 for the purpose of creating an independent Tamil state in Sri Lanka. 9 F. Supp. 2d, at 1182; Brief for Government 6. The District Court in this action found that the PKK and the LTTE engage in political and humanitarian activities. See 9 F. Supp. 2d, at 1180–1182. The Government has presented evidence that both groups have also committed numerous terrorist attacks, some of which have harmed American citizens. The LTTE sought judicial review of its designation as a foreign terrorist organization; the D. C. Circuit upheld that designation. See *People's Mojahedin Organization of Iran v. Dept. of State*, 182 F. 3d 17, 18–19, 25 (1999). The PKK did not challenge its designation.

Plaintiffs in this litigation are two U. S. citizens and six domestic organizations: the Humanitarian Law Project (HLP) (a human rights organization with consultative status to the United Nations); Ralph Fertig (the HLP's president, and a retired administrative law judge); Nagalingam Jeyalingam (a Tamil physician, born in Sri Lanka and a naturalized U. S. citizen); and five nonprofit groups dedicated to the interests of persons of Tamil descent. . . .

As relevant here, plaintiffs claimed that the material-support statute was unconstitutional on two grounds: First, it violated their freedom of speech and freedom of association under the First Amendment, because it criminalized their provision of material support to the PKK and the LTTE, without requiring the Government to prove that plaintiffs had a specific intent to further the unlawful ends of those organizations. Second, plaintiffs argued that the statute was unconstitutionally vague.

. . .

[Ed.: The Court here described the complicated path of the litigation in this case whereby the matter traveled up and down between the district court and the Ninth Circuit several times. In the meantime, the IRTPA statute's amendments of the material support statutes had been enacted, and ultimately, the relevant current terms of that statute were applied to the issues being litigated, first by the district court, then by the U.S. Court of Appeals. After describing the path of the litigation, the Court continued.]

In IRTPA, Congress clarified the mental state necessary to violate § 2339B, requiring knowledge of the foreign group's designation as a terrorist organization or the group's commission of terrorist acts. § 2339B(a)(1). Congress also added the term "service" to the definition of "material support or resources," § 2339A(b)(1), and defined "training" to mean "instruction or teaching designed to impart a specific skill, as opposed to general knowledge," § 2339A(b)(2). It also defined "expert advice or assistance" to mean "advice or assistance derived from scientific, technical or other specialized knowledge." § 2339A(b)(3). Finally, IRTPA clarified the scope of the term "personnel" by providing:

> "No person may be prosecuted under [§ 2339B] in connection with the term 'personnel' unless that person has knowingly provided, attempted to provide, or conspired to provide a foreign terrorist organization with 1 or more individuals (who may be or include himself) to work under that terrorist organization's direction or control or to organize, manage, supervise, or otherwise direct the operation of that organization. Individuals who act entirely independently of the foreign terrorist organization to advance its goals or objectives shall not be considered to be working under the foreign terrorist organization's direction and control." § 2339B(h).

. . .

Given the complicated 12–year history of this litigation, we pause to clarify the questions before us. Plaintiffs challenge § 2339B's prohibition on four types of material support—"training," "expert advice or assistance," "service," and "personnel." They raise three constitutional claims. First, plaintiffs claim that § 2339B violates the Due Process Clause of the Fifth Amendment because these four statutory terms are impermissibly vague. Second, plaintiffs claim that § 2339B violates their freedom of speech under the First Amendment. Third, plaintiffs claim that § 2339B violates their First Amendment freedom of association.

Plaintiffs do not challenge the above statutory terms in all their applications. Rather, plaintiffs claim that § 2339B is invalid to the extent it prohibits them from engaging in certain specified activities. With respect to the HLP and Judge Fertig, those activities are: (1) "train[ing] members of [the] PKK on how to use humanitarian and international law to peacefully resolve disputes"; (2) "engag[ing] in political advocacy on behalf of Kurds who live in Turkey"; and (3) "teach[ing] PKK members how to petition various representative bodies such as the United Nations for relief." With respect to the other plaintiffs, those activities are: (1) "train[ing] members of [the] LTTE to present claims for tsunami-related aid to mediators and international bodies"; (2) "offer[ing] their legal expertise in negotiating peace agreements between the LTTE and the Sri Lankan government"; and (3) "engag[ing] in political advocacy on behalf of Tamils who live in Sri Lanka."

. . .

One last point. Plaintiffs seek preenforcement review of a criminal statute. Before addressing the merits, we must be sure that this is a justiciable case or controversy under Article III. We conclude that it is: Plaintiffs face "a credible threat of prosecution" and "should not be required to await and undergo a criminal prosecution as the sole means of seeking relief."

. . .

Plaintiffs claim, as a threshold matter, that we should affirm the Court of Appeals without reaching any issues of constitutional law. They contend that we should interpret the material-support statute, when applied to speech, to require proof that a defendant intended to further a foreign terrorist organization's illegal activities. That interpretation, they say, would end the litigation because plaintiffs' proposed activities consist of speech, but plaintiffs do not intend to further unlawful conduct by the PKK or the LTTE.

We reject plaintiffs' interpretation of § 2339B because it is inconsistent with the text of the statute. Section 2339B(a)(1) prohibits "knowingly" providing material support. It then specifically describes the type of knowledge that is required: "To violate this paragraph, a person must have knowledge that the organization is a designated terrorist organization . . . , that the organization has engaged or engages in terrorist activity . . . , or that the organization has engaged or engages in terrorism. . . ."

Congress plainly spoke to the necessary mental state for a violation of § 2339B, and it chose knowledge about the organization's connection to terrorism, not specific intent to further the organization's terrorist activities.

. . .

Finally, plaintiffs give the game away when they argue that a specific intent requirement should apply only when the material-support statute applies to speech. There is no basis whatever in the text of § 2339B to read the same provisions in that statute as requiring intent in some circumstances but not others. It is therefore clear that plaintiffs are asking us not to interpret § 2339B, but to revise it. "Although this Court will often strain to construe legislation so as to save it against constitutional attack, it must not and will not carry this to the point of perverting the purpose of a statute." *Scales v. United States*, 367 U.S. 203, 211 (1961).

Scales is the case on which plaintiffs most heavily rely, but it is readily distinguishable. That case involved the Smith Act, which prohibited membership in a group advocating the violent overthrow of the government. The Court held that a person could not be convicted under the statute unless he had knowledge of the group's illegal advocacy and a specific intent to bring about violent overthrow. This action is different: Section 2339B does not criminalize mere membership in a designated foreign terrorist organization. It instead prohibits providing "material support" to such a group. Nothing about *Scales* suggests the need for a specific intent requirement in such a case. The Court in *Scales*, moreover, relied on both statutory text and precedent that had interpreted closely related provisions of the Smith Act to require specific intent. Plaintiffs point to nothing similar here.

We cannot avoid the constitutional issues in this litigation through plaintiffs' proposed interpretation of § 2339B.

. . .

We turn to the question whether the material-support statute, as applied to plaintiffs, is impermissibly vague under the Due Process Clause of the Fifth Amendment. "A conviction fails to comport with due process if the statute under which it is obtained fails to provide a person of ordinary intelligence fair notice of what is prohibited, or is so standardless that it authorizes or encourages seriously discriminatory enforcement." *United States v. Williams*, 553 U. S. 285, 304 (2008). We consider whether a statute is vague as applied to the particular facts at issue, ... We have said that when a statute "interferes with the right of free speech or of association, a more stringent vagueness test should apply." "But 'perfect clarity and precise guidance have never been required even of regulations that restrict expressive activity.' " *Williams, supra*, at 304.

. . .

Under a proper analysis, plaintiffs' claims of vagueness lack merit. Plaintiffs do not argue that the material-support statute grants too much enforcement discretion to the Government. We therefore address only whether the statute "provide[s] a person of ordinary intelligence fair notice of what is prohibited."

As a general matter, the statutory terms at issue here are quite different from the sorts of terms that we have previously declared to be vague. We have in the past "struck down statutes that tied criminal culpability to whether the defendant's conduct was 'annoying' or 'indecent'—wholly subjective judgments without statutory definitions, narrowing context, or settled legal meanings." [S]ee also *Papachristou v. Jacksonville*, 405 U.S. 156, n.1 (1972) (holding vague an ordinance that punished "vagrants," defined to include "rogues and vagabonds," "persons who use juggling," and "common night walkers" (internal quotation marks omitted)). Applying the statutory terms in this action—"training," "expert advice or assistance," "service," and "personnel"—does not require similarly untethered, subjective judgments.

Congress also took care to add narrowing definitions to the material-support statute over time. These definitions increased the clarity of the statute's terms. . . .

Of course, the scope of the material-support statute may not be clear in every application. But the dispositive point here is that the statutory terms are clear in their application to plaintiffs' proposed conduct, which means that plaintiffs' vagueness challenge must fail. Even assuming that a heightened standard applies because the material-support statute potentially implicates speech, the statutory terms are not vague as applied to plaintiffs. . . .

Most of the activities in which plaintiffs seek to engage readily fall within the scope of the terms "training" and "expert advice or assistance." Plaintiffs want to "train members of [the] PKK on how to use humanitarian and international law to peacefully resolve disputes," and "teach PKK members how to petition various representative bodies such as the United Nations for relief." A person of ordinary intelligence would understand that instruction on resolving disputes through international law falls within the statute's definition of "training" because it imparts a "specific skill," not "general knowledge." § 2339A(b)(2). Plaintiffs' activities also fall comfortably within the scope of "expert advice or assistance": A reasonable person would recognize that teaching the PKK how to petition for humanitarian relief before the United Nations involves advice derived from, as the statute puts it, "specialized knowledge." § 2339A(b)(3). In fact, plaintiffs themselves have repeatedly used the terms "training" and "expert advice" throughout this litigation to describe their own proposed activities, demonstrating that these common terms readily and naturally cover plaintiffs' conduct.

Plaintiffs respond by pointing to hypothetical situations designed to test the limits of "training" and "expert advice or assistance." They argue that the statutory definitions of these terms use words of degree—like "specific," "general," and "specialized"—and that it is difficult to apply those definitions in particular cases. . . .

Whatever force these arguments might have in the abstract, they are beside the point here. . . .

Plaintiffs also contend that they want to engage in "political advocacy" on behalf of Kurds living in Turkey and Tamils living in Sri Lanka. They are concerned that such advocacy might be regarded as "material support" in the form of providing "personnel" or "service[s]," and assert that the statute is unconstitutionally vague because they cannot tell.

As for "personnel," Congress enacted a limiting definition in IRTPA that answers plaintiffs' vagueness concerns. Providing material support that constitutes "personnel" is defined as knowingly providing a person "to work under that terrorist organization's direction or control or to organize, manage, supervise, or otherwise direct the operation of that organization." § 2339B(h). The statute makes clear that "personnel" does not cover *independent* advocacy: "Individuals who act entirely independently of the foreign terrorist organization to advance its goals or objectives shall not be considered to be working under the foreign terrorist organization's direction and control."

"[S]ervice" similarly refers to concerted activity, not independent advocacy. See Webster's Third New International Dictionary 2075 (1993) (defining "service" to mean "the performance of work commanded or paid for by another: a servant's duty: attendance on a superior"; or "an act done for the benefit or at the command of another"). Context confirms that ordinary meaning here. The statute prohibits providing a service "*to* a foreign terrorist organization." § 2339B(a)(1) (emphasis added). The use of the word "to" indicates a connection between the service and the foreign group. We think a person of ordinary intelligence would understand that independently advocating for a cause is different from providing a service to a group that is advocating for that cause.

. . . The other types of material support listed in the statute, including "lodging," "weapons," "explosives," and "transportation," § 2339A(b)(1), are not forms of support that could be provided independently of a foreign terrorist organization. We interpret "service" along the same lines. Thus, any independent advocacy in which plaintiffs wish to engage is not prohibited by § 2339B. On the other hand, a person of ordinary intelligence would understand the term "service" to cover advocacy performed in coordination with, or at the direction of, a foreign terrorist organization.

Plaintiffs argue that this construction of the statute poses difficult questions of exactly how much direction or coordination is necessary for an activity to constitute a "service." . . . Plaintiffs have not provided any specific articulation of the degree to which *they* seek to coordinate their advocacy with the PKK and the LTTE. They have instead described the form of their intended advocacy only in the most general terms. . . .

Deciding whether activities described at such a level of generality would constitute prohibited "service[s]" under the statute would require "sheer speculation"—which means that plaintiffs cannot prevail in their preenforcement challenge. It is apparent with respect to these claims that "gradations of fact or charge would make a difference as to criminal liability," and so "adjudication of the reach and constitutionality of [the statute] must await a concrete fact situation."

. . .

We next consider whether the material-support statute, as applied to plaintiffs, violates the freedom of speech guaranteed by the First Amendment. . . .

For its part, the Government takes the foregoing too far, claiming that the only thing truly at issue in this litigation is conduct, not speech. . .

The Government is wrong that the only thing actually at issue in this litigation is conduct, . . .

Plaintiffs want to speak to the PKK and the LTTE, and whether they may do so under § 2339B depends on what they say. If plaintiffs' speech to those groups imparts a "specific skill" or communicates advice derived from "specialized knowledge"—for example, training on the use of international law or advice on petitioning the United Nations—then it is barred. On the other hand, plaintiffs' speech is not barred if it imparts only general or unspecialized knowledge.

. . .

The First Amendment issue before us is more refined than either plaintiffs or the Government would have it. It is not whether the Government may prohibit pure political speech, or may prohibit material support in the form of conduct. It is instead whether the Government may prohibit what plaintiffs want to do—provide material support to the PKK and LTTE in the form of speech.

Everyone agrees that the Government's interest in combating terrorism is an urgent objective of the highest order. Plaintiffs' complaint is that the ban on material support, applied to what they wish to do, is not "necessary to further that interest." The objective of combating terrorism does not justify prohibiting their speech, plaintiffs argue, because their support will advance only the legitimate activities of the designated terrorist organizations, not their terrorism. *Id.*, at 51–52.

Whether foreign terrorist organizations meaningfully segregate support of their legitimate activities from support of terrorism is an empirical question. When it enacted § 2339B in 1996, Congress made specific findings regarding the serious threat posed by international terrorism. One of those findings explicitly rejects plaintiffs' contention that their support would not further the terrorist activities of the PKK and LTTE: "[F]oreign organizations that engage in terrorist activity are so tainted by their criminal conduct that *any contribution to such an organization facilitates that conduct.*"

Plaintiffs argue that the reference to "any contribution" in this finding meant only monetary support. There is no reason to read the finding to be so limited, particularly because Congress expressly prohibited so much more than monetary support in § 2339B. Congress's use of the term "contribution" is best read to reflect a determination that any form of material support furnished "to" a foreign terrorist organization should be barred, which is precisely what the material-support statute does. Indeed, when Congress enacted § 2339B, Congress simultaneously removed an exception that had existed in § 2339A(a) (1994 ed.) for the provision of material support in the form of "humanitarian assistance to persons not directly involved in" terrorist activity. AEDPA § 323, 110 Stat. 1255; 205 F. 3d, at 1136. That repeal demonstrates that Congress considered and rejected the view that ostensibly peaceful aid would have no harmful effects.

We are convinced that Congress was justified in rejecting that view. The PKK and the LTTE are deadly groups. "The PKK's insurgency has claimed more than 22,000 lives." Declaration of Kenneth R. McKune, App. 128, ¶ 5. The LTTE has engaged in extensive suicide bombings and political assassinations, including killings of the Sri Lankan President, Security Minister, and Deputy Defense Minister. *Id.*, at 130–132; Brief for Government 6–7. "...

Material support meant to "promot[e] peaceable, lawful conduct," can further terrorism by foreign groups in multiple ways. "Material support" is a valuable resource by definition. Such support frees up other resources within the organization that may be put to violent ends. It also importantly helps lend legitimacy to foreign terrorist groups—legitimacy that makes it easier for those groups to persist, to recruit members, and to raise funds—all of which facilitate more terrorist attacks. "Terrorist organizations do not maintain *organizational* 'firewalls' that would prevent or deter ... sharing and commingling of support and benefits." McKune Affidavit, App. 135, ¶ 11. "[I]nvestigators have revealed how terrorist groups systematically conceal their activities behind charitable, social, and political fronts." M. Levitt, Hamas: Politics, Charity, and Terrorism in the Service of Jihad 2–3 (2006). "Indeed, some designated foreign terrorist organizations use social and political components to recruit personnel to carry out terrorist operations, and to provide support to criminal terrorists and their families in aid of such operations." McKune Affidavit, App. 135, ¶ 11; Levitt, *supra*, at 2 ("Muddying the waters between its political activism, good works, and terrorist attacks, Hamas is able to use its overt political and charitable organizations as a financial and logistical support network for its terrorist operations").

Money is fungible, and "[w]hen foreign terrorist organizations that have a dual structure raise funds, they highlight the civilian and humanitarian ends to which such moneys could be put." McKune Affidavit, App.

134, ¶ 9. But "there is reason to believe that foreign terrorist organizations do not maintain legitimate *financial* firewalls between those funds raised for civil, nonviolent activities, and those ultimately used to support violent, terrorist operations." *Id.*, at 135, ¶ 12. . . . There is evidence that the PKK and the LTTE, in particular, have not "respected the line between humanitarian and violent activities." McKune Affidavit, App. 135, ¶ 13 (discussing PKK); see *id.*, at 134 (LTTE).

The dissent argues that there is "no natural stopping place" for the proposition that aiding a foreign terrorist organization's lawful activity promotes the terrorist organization as a whole. But Congress has settled on just such a natural stopping place: The statute reaches only material support coordinated with or under the direction of a designated foreign terrorist organization. Independent advocacy that might be viewed as promoting the group's legitimacy is not covered.

Providing foreign terrorist groups with material support in any form also furthers terrorism by straining the United States' relationships with its allies and undermining cooperative efforts between nations to prevent terrorist attacks. We see no reason to question Congress's finding that "international cooperation is required for an effective response to terrorism, as demonstrated by the numerous multilateral conventions in force providing universal prosecutive jurisdiction over persons involved in a variety of terrorist acts, including hostage taking, murder of an internationally protected person, and aircraft piracy and sabotage." . . .

For example, the Republic of Turkey—a fellow member of NATO—is defending itself against a violent insurgency waged by the PKK. That nation and our other allies would react sharply to Americans furnishing material support to foreign groups like the PKK, and would hardly be mollified by the explanation that the support was meant only to further those groups' "legitimate" activities. From Turkey's perspective, there likely are no such activities. . . .

. . .

In analyzing whether it is possible in practice to distinguish material support for a foreign terrorist group's violent activities and its nonviolent activities, we do not rely exclusively on our own inferences drawn from the record evidence. We have before us an affidavit stating the Executive Branch's conclusion on that question. The State Department informs us that "[t]he experience and analysis of the U.S. government agencies charged with combating terrorism strongly suppor[t]" Congress's finding that all contributions to foreign terrorist organizations further their terrorism. McKune Affidavit, App. 133, ¶ 8. . . .

That evaluation of the facts by the Executive, like Congress's assessment, is entitled to deference. This litigation implicates sensitive and weighty interests of national security and foreign affairs. The PKK and the LTTE have committed terrorist acts against American citizens abroad, and the material-support statute addresses acute foreign policy concerns involving relationships with our Nation's allies. . . . It is vital in this context "not to substitute . . . our own evaluation of evidence for a reasonable evaluation by the Legislative Branch."

Our precedents, old and new, make clear that concerns of national security and foreign relations do not warrant abdication of the judicial role. We do not defer to the Government's reading of the First Amendment, even when such interests are at stake. We are one with the dissent that the Government's "authority and expertise in these matters do not automatically trump the Court's own obligation to secure the protection that the Constitution grants to individuals." But when it comes to collecting evidence and drawing factual inferences in this area, "the lack of competence on the part of the courts is marked," and respect for the Government's conclusions is appropriate.

One reason for that respect is that national security and foreign policy concerns arise in connection with efforts to confront evolving threats in an area where information can be difficult to obtain and the impact of certain conduct difficult to assess. The dissent slights these real constraints in demanding hard proof—with "detail," "specific facts," and "specific evidence"—that plaintiffs' proposed activities will support terrorist attacks. That would be a dangerous requirement. In this context, conclusions must often be based on informed judgment rather than concrete evidence, and that reality affects what we may reasonably insist on from the Government. The material-support statute is, on its face, a preventive measure—it criminalizes not terrorist attacks themselves, but aid that makes the attacks more likely to occur. The Government, when seeking to prevent imminent harms in the context of international affairs and national security, is not required to conclusively link all the pieces in the puzzle before we grant weight to its empirical conclusions. . . .

. . . In this litigation, . . . Congress and the Executive are uniquely positioned to make principled distinctions between activities that will further terrorist conduct and undermine United States foreign policy, and those that will not.

At bottom, plaintiffs simply disagree with the considered judgment of Congress and the Executive that providing material support to a designated foreign terrorist organization—even seemingly benign support—bolsters the terrorist activities of that organization. That judgment, however, is entitled to significant weight, and we have persuasive evidence before us to sustain it. Given the sensitive interests in national security and foreign affairs at stake, the political branches have adequately substantiated their determination that, to serve the Government's interest in preventing terrorism, it was necessary to prohibit providing material support in the form of training, expert advice, personnel, and services to foreign terrorist groups, even if the supporters meant to promote only the groups' nonviolent ends.

. . .

. . . [T]he dissent fails to address the real dangers at stake. It instead considers only the possible benefits of plaintiffs' proposed activities in the abstract. The dissent seems unwilling to entertain the prospect that training and advising a designated foreign terrorist organization on how to take advantage of international entities might benefit that organization in a way that facilitates its terrorist activities. In the dissent's world, such training is all to the good. Congress and the Executive, however, have concluded that we live in a different world: one in which the designated foreign terrorist organizations "are so tainted by their criminal conduct that any contribution to such an organization facilitates that conduct."

. . .

All this is not to say that any future applications of the material-support statute to speech or advocacy will survive First Amendment scrutiny. It is also not to say that any other statute relating to speech and terrorism would satisfy the First Amendment. In particular, we in no way suggest that a regulation of independent speech would pass constitutional muster, even if the Government were to show that such speech benefits foreign terrorist organizations. We also do not suggest that Congress could extend the same prohibition on material support at issue here to domestic organizations. We simply hold that, in prohibiting the particular forms of support that plaintiffs seek to provide to foreign terrorist groups, § 2339B does not violate the freedom of speech.

. . .

The judgment of the United States Court of Appeals for the Ninth Circuit is affirmed in part and reversed in part, and the cases are remanded for further proceedings consistent with this opinion.

JUSTICE BREYER, with whom JUSTICES GINSBURG and SOTOMAYOR join, dissenting.

Like the Court, and substantially for the reasons it gives, I do not think this statute is unconstitutionally vague. But I cannot agree with the Court's conclusion that the Constitution permits the Government to prosecute the plaintiffs criminally for engaging in coordinated teaching and advocacy furthering the designated organizations' lawful political objectives. In my view, the Government has not met its burden of showing that an interpretation of the statute that would prohibit this speech- and association-related activity serves the Government's compelling interest in combating terrorism. And I would interpret the statute as normally placing activity of this kind outside its scope.

. . .

. . . Consider the cases involving the protection the First Amendment offered those who joined the Communist Party intending only to further its peaceful activities. In those cases, this Court took account of congressional findings that the Communist Party not only advocated theoretically but also sought to put into practice the overthrow of our Government through force and violence. The Court had previously accepted Congress' determinations that the American Communist Party was a "Communist action organization" which (1) acted under the "control, direction, and discipline" of the world Communist movement, a movement that sought to employ "espionage, sabotage, terrorism, and any other means deemed necessary, to establish a Communist totalitarian dictatorship," and (2) "endeavor[ed]" to bring about "the overthrow of existing governments by . . . force if necessary." *Communist Party of United States v. Subversive Activities Control Bd.*, 367 U.S. 1, 5–6 (1961) (internal quotation marks omitted).

Nonetheless, the Court held that the First Amendment protected an American's right to belong to that party—despite whatever "legitimating" effect membership might have had—as long as the person did not share the party's unlawful purposes. See, *e.g., De Jonge*, 299 U.S. 353; *Scales*, 367 U.S., at 228–230; *Elfbrandt v. Russell*, 384 U.S. 11, 17 (1966); *Keyishian v. Board of Regents of Univ. of State of N.Y.*, 385 U.S. 589, 605–610 (1967); *Robel*, 389 U.S. 258 (holding that national security interests did not justify overbroad criminal prohibition on members of Communist-affiliated organizations working in any defense-related facility. . . .

Nor can the Government overcome these considerations simply by narrowing the covered activities to those that involve *coordinated*, rather than *independent,* advocacy. Conversations, discussions, or logistical arrangements might well prove necessary to carry out the speech-related activities here at issue (just as conversations and discussions are a necessary part of *membership* in any organization). The Government does not distinguish this kind of "coordination" from any other. I am not aware of any form of words that might be used to describe "coordination" that would not, at a minimum, seriously chill not only the kind of activities the plaintiffs raise before us, but also the "independent advocacy" the Government purports to permit. And, as for the Government's willingness to distinguish *independent* advocacy from *coordinated* advocacy, the former is *more* likely, not *less* likely, to confer legitimacy than the latter. Thus, other things being equal, the distinction "coordination" makes is arbitrary in respect to furthering the statute's purposes. And a rule of law that finds the "legitimacy" argument adequate in respect to the latter would have a hard time distinguishing a statute that sought to attack the former.

     . . .

In my own view, the majority's arguments stretch the concept of "fungibility" beyond constitutional limits. . . .

Moreover, the risk that those who are taught will put otherwise innocent speech or knowledge to bad use is omnipresent, at least where that risk rests on little more than (even informed) speculation. Hence to accept this kind of argument without more and to apply it to the teaching of a subject such as international human rights law is to adopt a rule of law that, contrary to the Constitution's text and First Amendment precedent, would automatically forbid the teaching of any subject in a case where national security interests conflict with the First Amendment. The

Constitution does not allow all such conflicts to be decided in the Government's favor.

The majority, as I have said, cannot limit the scope of its arguments through its claim that the plaintiffs remain free to engage in the protected activity *as long as it is not "coordinated."* That is because there is no practical way to organize classes for a group (say, wishing to learn about human rights law) without *"coordination."* Nor can the majority limit the scope of its argument by pointing to some special limiting circumstance present here. That is because the only evidence the majority offers to support its general claim consists of a single reference to a book about terrorism, which the Government did not mention, and which apparently says no more than that at one time the PKK suspended its armed struggle and then returned to it.

Second, the majority discusses the plaintiffs' proposal to " 'teach PKK members how to petition various representative bodies such as the United Nations *for relief.'* " The majority's only argument with respect to this proposal is that the relief obtained "could readily include monetary aid," which the PKK might use to buy guns. The majority misunderstands the word "relief." In *this* context, as the record makes clear, the word "relief" does not refer to "money." It refers to recognition under the Geneva Conventions. . . .

Throughout, the majority emphasizes that it would defer strongly to Congress' "informed judgment." But here, there is no evidence that Congress has made such a judgment regarding the specific activities at issue in these cases. See *infra*, at 20–21. In any event, "whenever the fundamental rights of free speech and assembly are alleged to have been invaded, it must remain open [for judicial determination] whether there actually did exist at the time a clear danger; whether the danger, if any, was imminent; and whether the evil apprehended was one so substantial as to justify the stringent restriction interposed by the legislature." . . .

I concede that the Government's expertise in foreign affairs may warrant deference in respect to many matters, *e.g.*, our relations with Turkey. But it remains for this Court to decide whether the Government has shown that such an interest justifies criminalizing speech activity otherwise protected by the First Amendment. And the fact that other nations may like us less for granting that protection cannot in and of itself carry the day.

Finally, I would reemphasize that neither the Government nor the majority points to any specific facts that show that the speech-related activities before us are fungible in some *special way* or confer some *special* legitimacy upon the PKK. Rather, their arguments in this respect are general and speculative. Those arguments would apply to virtually all speech-related support for a dual-purpose group's peaceful activities (irrespective of whether the speech-related activity is coordinated). Both First Amendment logic and First Amendment case law prevent us from "sacrific[ing] First Amendment protections for so speculative a gain."

. . .

For the reasons I have set forth, I believe application of the statute as the Government interprets it would gravely and without adequate justification injure interests of the kind the First Amendment protects. Thus, there is "a serious doubt" as to the statute's constitutionality. . . .

I believe that a construction that would avoid the constitutional problem is "fairly possible." In particular, I would read the statute as criminalizing First–Amendment-protected pure speech and association only when the defendant knows or intends that those activities will assist the organization's unlawful terrorist actions. Under this reading, the Government would have to show, at a minimum, that such defendants provided support that they knew was significantly likely to help the organization pursue its unlawful terrorist aims. . . .

E.   ADMINISTRATIVE DESIGNATION AS A "FOREIGN TERRORIST ORGANIZATION" FOR PURPOSES OF § 2339B; HEARING PROCEDURE AND JUDICIAL REVIEW UNDER 8 U.S.C. § 1189

As we have seen in the previous subsections of this chapter, § 2339B makes it a crime to knowingly provide material support to a foreign terrorist organization. Subsection (g)(6) of § 2339B refers to a "terrorist organization" designated under section 219 of the Immigration and Nationality Act, i.e. 8 U.S.C. § 1189 as amended by the Intelligence Reform and Terrorism Prevention Act of 2004. Pertinent portions of the 2004 version of § 1189 are reproduced below.

1.   THE STATUTORY SCHEME

§ 1189.   Designation of foreign terrorist organizations

(a) Designation

(1) In general

The Secretary is authorized to designate an organization as a foreign terrorist organization in accordance with this subsection if the Secretary finds that—

(A) the organization is a foreign organization;

(B) the organization engages in terrorist activity (as defined in section 1182(a)(3)(B) of this title or terrorism (as defined in section 2656f(d)(2) of Title 22), or retains the capability and intent to engage in terrorist activity or terrorism; and

(C) the terrorist activity or terrorism of the organization threatens the security of United States nationals or the national security of the United States.

(2) Procedure

    (A) Notice

        (i) To congressional leaders

Seven days before making a designation under this subsection, the Secretary shall, by classified communication, notify the Speaker and Minority Leader of the House of Representatives, the President pro tempore, Majority Leader, and Minority Leader of the Senate, and the members of the relevant committees of the House of Representatives and the Senate, in writing, of the intent to designate an organization under this subsection, together with the findings made under paragraph (1) with respect to that organization, and the factual basis therefor.

        (ii) Publication in Federal Register

The Secretary shall publish the designation in the Federal Register seven days after providing the notification under clause (i).

    (B) Effect of designation

        (i) For purposes of section 2339B of Title 18, a designation under this subsection shall take effect upon publication under subparagraph (A)(ii).

        (ii) Any designation under this subsection shall cease to have effect upon an Act of Congress disapproving such designation.

    (C) Freezing of assets

Upon notification under paragraph (2)(A)(i), the Secretary of the Treasury may require United States financial institutions possessing or controlling any assets of any foreign organization included in the notification to block all financial transactions involving those assets until further directive from either the Secretary of the Treasury, Act of Congress, or order of court.

(3) Record

    (A) In general

In making a designation under this subsection, the Secretary shall create an administrative record.

    (B) Classified information

The Secretary may consider classified information in making a designation under this subsection. Classified information shall not be subject to disclosure for such time as it remains classified, except that such information may be disclosed to a court ex parte and in camera for purposes of judicial review under subsection (c) of this section.

(4) Period of designation

(A) In general

A designation under this subsection shall be effective for all purposes until revoked under paragraph (5) or (6) or set aside pursuant to subsection (c) of this section.

(B) Review of designation upon petition

(i) In general

The Secretary shall review the designation of a foreign terrorist organization under the procedures set forth in clauses (iii) and (iv) if the designated organization files a petition for revocation within the petition period described in clause (ii).

(ii) Petition period

For purposes of clause (i)—

(I) if the designated organization has not previously filed a petition for revocation under this subparagraph, the petition period begins 2 years after the date on which the designation was made; or

(II) if the designated organization has previously filed a petition for revocation under this subparagraph, the petition period begins 2 years after the date of the determination made under clause (iv) on that petition.

(iii) Procedures

Any foreign terrorist organization that submits a petition for revocation under this subparagraph must provide evidence in that petition that the relevant circumstances described in paragraph (1) are sufficiently different from the circumstances that were the basis for the designation such that a revocation with respect to the organization is warranted.

(iv) Determination

(I) In general

Not later than 180 days after receiving a petition for revocation submitted under this subparagraph, the Secretary shall make a determination as to such revocation.

(II) Classified information

The Secretary may consider classified information in making a determination in response to a petition for revocation. Classified information shall not be subject to disclosure for such time as it remains classified, except that such information may be disclosed to a court ex parte and in camera for purposes of judicial review under subsection (c) of this section.

(III) Publication of determination

A determination made by the Secretary under this clause shall be published in the Federal Register.

(IV) Procedures

Any revocation by the Secretary shall be made in accordance with paragraph (6).

(C) Other review of designation

(i) In general

If in a 5–year period no review has taken place under subparagraph (B), the Secretary shall review the designation of the foreign terrorist organization in order to determine whether such designation should be revoked pursuant to paragraph (6).

(ii) Procedures

If a review does not take place pursuant to subparagraph (B) in response to a petition for revocation that is filed in accordance with that subparagraph, then the review shall be conducted pursuant to procedures established by the Secretary. The results of such review and the applicable procedures shall not be reviewable in any court.

(iii) Publication of results of review

The Secretary shall publish any determination made pursuant to this subparagraph in the Federal Register.

(5) Revocation by Act of Congress

The Congress, by an Act of Congress, may block or revoke a designation made under paragraph (1).

(6) Revocation based on change in circumstances

(A) In general

The Secretary may revoke a designation made under paragraph (1) at any time, and shall revoke a designation upon completion of a review conducted pursuant to subparagraphs (B) and (C) of paragraph (4) if the Secretary finds that—

(i) the circumstances that were the basis for the designation have changed in such a manner as to warrant revocation; or

(ii) the national security of the United States warrants a revocation.

(B) Procedure

The procedural requirements of paragraphs (2) and (3) shall apply to a revocation under this paragraph. Any revocation shall take effect on the date specified in the revocation or upon publication in the Federal Register if no effective date is specified.

(7) Effect of revocation

The revocation of a designation under paragraph (5) or (6) shall not affect any action or proceeding based on conduct committed prior to the effective date of such revocation.

(8) Use of designation in trial or hearing

If a designation under this subsection has become effective under paragraph (2)(B) a defendant in a criminal action or an alien in a removal proceeding shall not be permitted to raise any question concerning the validity of the issuance of such designation as a defense or an objection at any trial or hearing.

(b) Amendments to a designation

(1) In general

The Secretary may amend a designation under this subsection if the Secretary finds that the organization has changed its name, adopted a new alias, dissolved and then reconstituted itself under a different name or names, or merged with another organization.

(2) Procedure

Amendments made to a designation in accordance with paragraph (1) shall be effective upon publication in the Federal Register. Subparagraphs (B) and (C) of subsection (a)(2) of this section shall apply to an amended designation upon such publication. Paragraphs (2)(A)(i), (4), (5), (6), (7), and (8) of subsection (a) of this section shall also apply to an amended designation.

(3) Administrative record

The administrative record shall be corrected to include the amendments as well as any additional relevant information that supports those amendments.

(4) Classified information

The Secretary may consider classified information in amending a designation in accordance with this subsection. Classified information shall not be subject to disclosure for such time as it remains classified, except that such information may be disclosed to a court ex parte and in camera for purposes of judicial review under subsection (c) of this section.

(c) Judicial review of designation

(1) In general

Not later than 30 days after publication in the Federal Register of a designation, an amended designation, or a determination in response to a petition for revocation, the designated organization may seek judicial review in the United States Court of Appeals for the District of Columbia Circuit.

(2) Basis of review

Review under this subsection shall be based solely upon the administrative record, except that the Government may submit, for ex parte and in camera review, classified information used in making the designation, amended designation, or determination in response to a petition for revocation.

(3) Scope of review

The Court shall hold unlawful and set aside a designation, amended designation, or determination in response to a petition for revocation the court finds to be—

    (A) arbitrary, capricious, an abuse of discretion, or otherwise not in accordance with law;

    (B) contrary to constitutional right, power, privilege, or immunity;

    (C) in excess of statutory jurisdiction, authority, or limitation, or short of statutory right;

    (D) lacking substantial support in the administrative record taken as a whole or in classified information submitted to the court under paragraph (2), or

    (E) not in accord with the procedures required by law.

(4) Judicial review invoked

The pendency of an action for judicial review of a designation, amended designation, or determination in response to a petition for revocation shall not affect the application of this section, unless the court issues a final order setting aside the designation, amended designation, or determination in response to a petition for revocation.

(d) Definitions

As used in this section—

. . . Secretary means Secretary of State, in consultation with the Secretary of the Treasury and the Attorney General.

QUESTIONS AND NOTES

1. Prior to the 2004 amendment of § 1189, the statute provided that designation as a foreign terrorist organization was for a two year period which could be renewed if the Secretary initiated a new designation action. Thus the pre–2004 process required a new proceeding every two years if the designation was to continue. Instead, as can be seen from the statutory scheme supra, the 2004 amendment made the designation continuing subject to a) a revocation proceeding initiated by the designated organization, which could only be considered if two years had passed since the previous consideration; and b) a review every five years if the designation had not been reviewed during the intervening period. The effect of the amendment, of course, was to cut down considerably on the number of proceedings under § 1189.

2. Note that § 1189 deals with the subject of revocation before describing the procedures and standards for judicial review of a designation. Note also that under the statute, only the designated organization can seek judicial review. Finally, take note of subsec. (a)8 which bars collateral attack on the designation by the defendant in a criminal case. Issues raised by this provision are considered below in subsec. 3.

3. All of the case law involving direct judicial review of a designation as a foreign terrorist organization, somewhat oddly, is contained in a series of cases involving the same organization, the National Council of Resistance of Iran (aka) People's Mojahedin Organization of Iran). The most recent decision in this series was handed down on July, 16, 2010 by the U.S. Court of Appeals for the District of Columbia.

2. JUDICIAL REVIEW BY THE AFFECTED ORGANIZATION OF THE SECRETARY'S DESIGNATION

PEOPLE'S MOJAHEDIN ORGANIZATION OF IRAN v. U.S. DEPARTMENT OF STATE

613 F.3d 220 (D.C. Cir. 2010)

Before HENDERSON and TATEL, CIRCUIT JUDGES, and WILLIAMS, SENIOR CIRCUIT JUDGE.

PER CURIAM:

This case is the fifth in a series of related actions challenging the United States Secretary of State's designation of the Mojahedin-e Khalq Organization (MEK) and its aliases as a Foreign Terrorist Organization (FTO). The MEK, also called the People's Mojahedin Organization of Iran (PMOI), has challenged its FTO status before this court three times. *See People's Mojahedin Org. of Iran v. U.S. Dep't of State*, 182 F.3d 17, 18–19 (D.C.Cir.1999) *(PMOI I); Nat'l Council of Resistance of Iran v. Dep't of State*, 251 F.3d 192, 195–96 (D.C.Cir.2001) *(NCRI I); People's Mojahedin Org. of Iran v. U.S. Dep't of State*, 327 F.3d 1238, 1239 (D.C.Cir.2003) *(PMOI I)*. The National Council of Resistance of Iran (NCRI), which the

United States Department of State (State) considers an alias or alter ego of the PMOI, has challenged its FTO status twice—once with the PMOI and once on its own. *See NCRI I,* 251 F.3d at 197; *Nat'l Council of Resistance of Iran v. Dep't of State,* 373 F.3d 152, 154 (D.C.Cir.2004) (*NCRI II*). In *NCRI I,* the court remanded the petition to the Secretary to provide certain due process protections to the PMOI and the NCRI. *See* 251 F.3d at 209. In the other three cases, including both petitions for review following remand in *NCRI I,* the court denied the petitioners' challenges.

On July 15, 2008, citing a change in its circumstances, the PMOI petitioned State and its Secretary for revocation of the PMOI's FTO designation. After assembling a record comprised of materials submitted by both the PMOI and the U.S. intelligence community, including classified information, the Secretary rejected the PMOI's petition on January 12, 2009. *See* In the Matter of the Review of the Designation of Mujahedin-e Khalq Organization (MEK), and All Designated Aliases, as a Foreign Terrorist Organization, 74 Fed.Reg. 1273, 1273–74 (Jan. 12, 2009). The PMOI now seeks review of the Secretary's decision. We conclude that the Secretary failed to accord the PMOI the due process protections outlined in our previous decisions and therefore remand.

. . .

This action began in July 2008, when the PMOI filed a petition for revocation of its 2003 Redesignation. The PMOI argued that the 2003 Redesignation should be revoked because of its dramatically changed circumstances since the Secretary's and this court's last reviews. It submitted evidence to the Secretary of its changed circumstances, asserting that, since its initial FTO designation in 1997, it had: ceased its military campaign against the Iranian regime and renounced violence in 2001; voluntarily handed over its arms to U.S. forces in Iraq and cooperated with U.S. officials at Camp Ashraf (where all of its members operating in Iraq are consolidated) in 2003; shared intelligence with the U.S. government regarding Iran's nuclear program; in 2004 obtained "protected person" status under the Fourth Geneva Convention for all PMOI members at Camp Ashraf based on the U.S. investigators' conclusions that none was a combatant or had committed a crime under any U.S. laws; disbanded its military units and disarmed the PMOI members at Ashraf, all of whom signed a document rejecting violence and terror; and obtained delisting as a terrorist organization from the United Kingdom (the Proscribed Organisations Appeal Commission and the Court of Appeal) in 2008 and from the European Union (the European Court of First Instance) in 2009. The PMOI also thrice supplemented its petition with additional information and letters in support from members of the U.S. Congress, members of the UK and European parliaments and retired members of the U.S. military, among others.

After reviewing an administrative record consisting of both classified and unclassified information, the Secretary denied the PMOI's petition and published its denial in the Federal Register on January 12, 2009. *See* 74 Fed.Reg. at 1273–74. She also provided the PMOI with a heavily redacted 20–page administrative summary of State's review of the record, which summary referred to 33 exhibits, many of which were also heavily or entirely redacted. *See* Admin. Summ. (Jan. 8, 2009) (Unclassified Version); Revised Admin. Summ. (Apr. 24, 2009) (Unclassified Version). The Secretary's determination was based on the administrative record, "supporting exhibits and supplemental filings by the MEK in support of the Petition, as well as information from a variety of sources, including the U.S. Intelligence Community." Revised Admin. Summ. 2. She wrote that "in considering the evidence as a whole, the MEK has not shown that the relevant circumstances are sufficiently different from the circumstances that were the basis for the 2003 re-designation," and that "[a]s a consequence, the MEK continues to be a foreign organization that engages in terrorist activity . . . or terrorism . . . or retains the capability and intent to" do so. *Id.; see* 74 Fed.Reg. at 1273–74. Nevertheless she also noted:

> In light of the evidence submitted by the MEK that it has renounced terrorism and the uncertainty surrounding the MEK presence in Iraq, the continued designation of the MEK should be re-examined by the Secretary of State in the next two years even if the MEK does not file a petition for revocation.

Revised Admin. Summ. 20. Although the Secretary informed the PMOI of her decision the day before it was published in the Federal Register, she did not provide the organization any unclassified material on which she intended to rely. *See* Resp'ts' Br. 20 (*after* denying revocation petition "[t]he State Department . . . provided to the PMOI an unclassified summary of the evidence in the record and the agency's analysis of the issues").

The PMOI filed a timely petition for review on February 11, 2009 under 8 U.S.C. § 1189(c). It asks us to vacate the Secretary's decision and remand with instructions to revoke its FTO designation based on a lack of substantial support in the record. Alternatively, the PMOI asks us to vacate its designation on the ground that the Secretary did not comply with the due process requirements set forth in our earlier decisions by failing to provide it with advance notice of her proposed action and the unclassified record on which she intended to rely, as well as by failing to provide it with any access to the classified record.

State submitted its classified administrative record on March 30, 2009 for ex parte and in camera review under 8 U.S.C. § 1189(c)(2); it subsequently filed a redacted, unclassified version in August 2009. In filing the latter document, State noted that it intended to file additional documents as soon as its declassification review was finished. It later supplemented the record with newly declassified material twice—once on September 8, 2009, the day the PMOI's opening brief was due, and again on October 27, 2009, about two weeks before the PMOI's reply brief due date.

Ordinarily, we would be required to decide whether to set aside the Secretary's denial of the PMOI's revocation petition on the ground that her conclusion that the PMOI "engages in terrorist activity ... or terrorism ... or retains the capability and intent to engage in terrorist activity or terrorism," Revised Admin. Summ. 2–3, "lack[s] substantial support in the administrative record taken as a whole or in classified information submitted to the court." 8 U.S.C. § 1189(c)(3)(D).

Here, however, we need not determine the adequacy of the record because, as the PMOI argues, our review "is not sufficient to supply the otherwise absent due process protection" of notice to the designated organization and an opportunity for a meaningful hearing. *NCRI I,* 251 F.3d at 208 (designated organization entitled to "opportunity to be heard 'at a meaningful time and in a meaningful manner'" (quoting *Mathews v. Eldridge,* 424 U.S. 319, 333, 96 S.Ct. 893, 47 L.Ed.2d 18 (1976))). In other words, even were we to agree with State that the record is sufficient, we cannot uphold the designation absent the procedural safeguards required by our precedent. Specifically, our cases require the Secretary to notify the PMOI of the unclassified material "upon which [s]he propose[d] to rely" and to allow the PMOI "the opportunity to present, at least in written form, such evidence as [it] may be able to produce to rebut the administrative record or otherwise negate the proposition that" it is an FTO. *NCRI I,* 251 F.3d at 209.

This did not happen here. The PMOI was notified of the Secretary's decision and permitted access to the unclassified portion of the record only *after* the decision was final. And even though the PMOI was given the opportunity to include in the record its own evidence supporting delisting, it had no opportunity to rebut the unclassified portion of the record the Secretary was compiling—an omission, the PMOI argues, that deprived it of the due process protections detailed in our previous decisions. *See* Pet'r's Br. 23 ("[T]he Secretary's decision is procedurally infirm because PMOI was given no opportunity to rebut the administrative record....").

State does not deny that the Secretary failed to provide the type of notice specified in *NCRI I.* But it argues that she complied with our precedent well enough in light of the statutory scheme as altered by the 2004 AEDPA amendments and the "flexible" nature of due process. Arg. Tr. 22:18–21; *see NCRI I,* 251 F.3d at 205 (quoting *Morrissey v. Brewer,* 408 U.S. 471, 481, 92 S.Ct. 2593, 33 L.Ed.2d 484 (1972)). Within that framework, State argues, the Secretary provided the PMOI with all of the process constitutionally due by informally meeting with the PMOI in October 2008 (at the PMOI's request), by allowing the PMOI to supplement the administrative record with evidence of its own and by sharing unclassified material with the PMOI (but not before her denial of the revocation petition). *See* Resp'ts' Br. 18, 44–45 (citing *PMOI II,* 327 F.3d at 1242; *NCRI I,* 251 F.3d at 208–09) (PMOI received "notice along with the opportunity to be effectively heard" and "nothing more is required by this Court"). State also urges that, even if the Secretary should have turned over the unclassified portion of the record before its January 2009 decision, her failure to do so was harmless.

We disagree on both counts. Nothing in the 2004 amendments provides a basis for relaxing the due process requirements we outlined for the redesignation decision at issue in *NCRI I*. Although phrased slightly differently, the Secretary's fundamental inquiry is the same for both redesignation under the old statute and revocation under the new. *Compare* 8 U.S.C. § 1189(a)(4)(B) (2003) (redesignation appropriate if "relevant circumstances" initially warranting designation "still exist") *with id.* § 1189(a)(6) (revocation appropriate if "circumstances that were the basis for the designation have changed in such a manner as to warrant revocation"). So, too, is our standard of review the same under both versions of the statute whether we review a "designation," a "redesignation" or a "petition for revocation." *See id.* § 1189(c)(3). And while the amended version of the statute puts the burden on an FTO to "provide evidence" of changed circumstances, *see id.* § 1189(a)(4)(B)(iii), the Secretary must still compile a record supporting the continued designation, *see id.* § 1189(a)(6)(B). In short, we have held due process requires that the PMOI be notified of the unclassified material on which the Secretary proposes to rely and an opportunity to respond to that material *before* its redesignation; nothing in the amended statute suggests that this protection is any less necessary in the revocation context.

Nor do we find the Secretary's failure to provide the required notice and unclassified material in advance of her decision harmless because the information at the "heart" of the Secretary's decision is classified and could not have been shared in any event. State's characterization notwithstanding, at argument it acknowledged that the Secretary's decision was based not on "just the classified information" but rather "on the record as a whole." Arg. Tr. 31:24–32:1–7; *see* Suppl. Admin. R. 19 ("In considering the body of evidence as a whole, intelligence and national security experts conclude that the MEK has not demonstrated that the circumstances that were the basis for the original designation have changed in such a manner as to warrant revocation."). Hence, State asks us to assume that nothing the PMOI would have offered—not even evidence refuting whatever *unclassified* material the Secretary may have relied on—could have changed her mind. We explicitly rejected this argument in *NCRI I. See* 251 F.3d at 209 ("We have no reason to presume that the petitioners in this particular case could have offered evidence which might have either changed the Secretary's mind or affected the adequacy of the record[, but] ... without the due process protections which we have outlined, we cannot presume the contrary either."). Far from *assuming* that the classified record obviated further review, we held that our limited role "is not sufficient to supply the otherwise absent due process protection."

To illustrate, during the briefing in this case, the Secretary twice supplemented the unclassified record with formerly classified materials. These disclosures include the statement that PMOI members planned suicide attacks in Karbala. Because it learned of this information only after it petitioned for judicial review, the PMOI attempts to distinguish and discredit it for the first time before us. *See* Pet'r's Reply Br. 21 (calling allegations "so manifestly implausible that they earned no mention in the Government's brief"). Citing *PMOI I,* 182 F.3d at 19, 25, State argues that the Secretary may consider "sources named and unnamed, the accuracy of which we have no way of evaluating," and that we cannot make any "judgment whatsoever regarding whether the material before the Secretary is or is not true." Nevertheless, to the extent we defer to the Secretary's fact-finding process, we have done so with the understanding that the Secretary has adhered to the procedural safeguards of the due process clause, *see NCRI I,* 251 F.3d at 209, and afforded the designated organization a fair opportunity to respond to the unclassified record.

At oral argument, State suggested that the PMOI, now in possession of the unclassified portions of the record (including the newly declassified material), may go back to the Secretary and provide evidence to rebut it. *See* Arg. Tr. 26:19–20. We think a better approach is the one the then-Secretary took after remand in *NCRI I,* when, apparently faced with a similar time crunch, he made a designation that was to be reevaluated once he fully reviewed the supplemented record. *See NCRI II,* 373 F.3d at 155 ("At that time, the State Department assured NCRI that although 'the present situation . . . requires continued designation of [NCRI] as an alias of MEK for now,' upon the completion of review of NCRI's submissions, 'the Secretary will make a *de novo* determination in light of the entire record, including the material you have submitted.' " (quoting Letter of Ambassador Francis X. Taylor, Coordinator for Counterterrorism, U.S. Dep't of State, at 1 (Oct. 5, 2001))).

Our reluctance to accept State's "no harm, no foul" theory is greater in light of the fact that we are unsure what material the Secretary in fact relied on or to what portion of 8 U.S.C. § 1189(a)(1)(B) she found it relevant. While "it is emphatically not our province to second-guess the Secretary's judgment as to which affidavits to credit and upon whose conclusions to rely," the Congress has required us to determine "whether the 'support' marshaled for the Secretary's designation was 'substantial.' " *NCRI II,* 373 F.3d at 159 (quoting 8 U.S.C. § 1889A(b)(3)(D)). Some of the reports included in the Secretary's analysis on their face express reservations about the accuracy of the information contained therein. *See, e.g.,* Suppl. Admin. R., MEK–11 (describing "possible plans to attack [the] international zone in Baghdad" but conceding that "the ultimate sources of the information was [sic] unknown and as such, their access, veracity, and motivations were unknown"). Similarly, while including reports about the Karbala suicide attack plot described above, the Secretary did not indicate whether she accepted or discredited the reports and we do not know whether the PMOI can rebut the reports.

In other instances, the Secretary cited a source that it seemed to regard as credible but did not indicate to what part of the statute the source's information was relevant. For example, her analysis described a federal grand jury indictment alleging that MEK has engaged in fraud in fundraising operations and she faulted the PMOI for failing to discuss its finances in its submission to the Secretary. Suppl. Admin. R. 11. It is unclear, however, whether the Secretary believes that fundraising under false pretenses is direct evidence of terrorist activity or instead bears on the PMOI's "capability" to engage in terrorist activity in the future or its "intent" to do so. 8 U.S.C. § 1189(a)(1)(B). While we will not substitute our judgement for that of the Secretary in deciding which sources are credible, we must determine whether the record before her provides "a sufficient basis for a reasonable person to conclude" that the statutory requirements have been met. *Kahane Chai,* 466 F.3d at 129 (citing *PMOI I,* 182 F.3d at 25). Without knowing whether, or how, the Secretary evaluated the record material, we are unable to do so.

As we noted in *NCRI I,* "[w]e recognize that a strict and immediate application of the principles of law which we have set forth herein could be taken to require a revocation of the designation[ ] before us[, but] . . . we also recognize the realities of the foreign policy and national security concerns asserted by the Secretary in support of th[e] designation." 251 F.3d at 209. We thus leave the designation in place but remand with instructions to the Secretary to provide the PMOI the opportunity to review and rebut the unclassified portions of the record on which she relied. In so doing, we emphasize two things:

First, as earlier explained, the Secretary should indicate in her administrative summary which sources she regards as sufficiently credible that she relies on them; and she should explain to which part of section 1 189(a)(1)(B) the information she relies on relates. Second, although the Secretary must give the PMOI an opportunity to rebut the unclassified material on which she relies, AEDPA does not allow access to the classified record as it makes clear that classified material "shall not be subject to disclosure for such time as it remains classified, except that such information may be disclosed to a court ex parte and in camera for purposes of judicial review." 8 U.S.C. § 1189(a)(4)(B)(iv)(II); *see id.* § 1189(c)(2) (providing for court's "ex parte and in camera review" of "classified information used in making the designation"). Our cases under AEDPA have suggested that this procedure can satisfy due process requirements, at least where the Secretary has not relied critically on classified material and the unclassified material provided to the FTO is sufficient to justify the designation. *See NCRI II,* 373 F.3d at 159–60; *PMOI II,* 327 F.3d at 1243 ("We already decided in [*NCRI I*] that due process required the disclosure of *only* the unclassified portions of the administrative record.") (emphasis in original); *NCRI I,* 251 F.3d at 202, 208–09 ("We acknowledge that in reviewing the whole record, we have included the classified material[, but] . . . we will not and cannot disclose the contents of the record," which "is within the privilege and prerogative of the executive"); . . . . We note, however, that none of the AEDPA cases decides whether an administrative decision relying critically on undisclosed classified material would comport with due process because in none was the classified record essential to uphold an FTO designation. But they do indicate that, for the purpose of today's remand, affording PMOI an opportunity to review and rebut the unclassified portions of the record, coupled with the Secretary's assurance that she has evaluated the material—and the sources therefor—that she relied on to make her decision, may be sufficient to provide the requisite due process.

For the reasons set forth above, the Secretary's denial of the People's Mojahedin of Iran's petition for revocation of its 2003 designation as a foreign terrorist organization is remanded to the Secretary for further proceedings consistent with this opinion.

[KAREN LECRAFT HENDERSON, CIRCUIT JUDGE, wrote a concurring opinion.]

QUESTIONS AND NOTES

1. In the first of the PMOI cases, People's Mojahedin Organization of Iran v. United States Department of State, 182 F.3d 17 (D.C. Cir. 1999), cert. denied 529 U.S. 1104 (2000), the court concluded that the organization could not raise due process claims:

> From all that appears, the LTTE and the Mek have no presence in the United States. Their status as foreign is uncontested.... A foreign entity without property or presence in this country has no constitutional rights, under the due process clause or otherwise. "Aliens receive constitutional protections [only] when they have come within the territory of the United States and developed substantial connections with this country." United States v. Verdugo–Urquidez, 494 U.S. 259, 271, 110 S.Ct. 1056, 108 L.Ed.2d 222 (1990). No one would suppose that a foreign nation had a due process right to notice and a hearing before the Executive imposed an embargo on it for the purpose of coercing a change in policy.

> Whatever rights the LTTE and the MEK enjoy in regard to these cases are therefore statutory rights only. Because Congress so allowed, the LTTE and the MEK are entitled to contest their designations on the grounds set forth in § 1189(b)(3). Under the statute, they may for instance seek our judgment about whether the Secretary followed statutory procedures, or whether she made the requisite findings, or whether the record she assembled substantially supports her findings.

2. As indicated in the principal case, in the second case in the series, National Council of Resistance of Iran v. Department of State, 251 F.3d 192 (D.C. Cir. 2001), the court concluded that the organization had a presence in the U.S. sufficient to give it due process protection and proceeded to spell out what due process required in this context:

> . . .

> The government admits that the record before us reflects that the NCRI "has an overt presence within the National Press Building in Washington, D.C.," and further recognizes that the NCRI claims an interest in a small bank account.

> . . .

In any event, we are not undertaking to determine, as a general matter, how "substantial" an alien's connections with this country must be to merit the protections of the Due Process Clause or any other part of the Constitution. Rather, we have reviewed the entire record including the classified information and determine that NCRI can rightly lay claim to having come within the territory of the United States and developed substantial connections with this country. We acknowledge that in reviewing the whole record, we have included the classified material. As we noted above and in People's Mojahedin, we will not and cannot disclose the contents of the record. We note further that the PMOI has made little serious assertion of an independent presence in the United States. Unfortunately for the cause of the Secretary, the PMOI does not need one. Insofar as PMOI's claimed presence is concerned, the United States is now hoist with its own petard. The Secretary concluded in her designation, which we upheld for the reasons set forth above, that the NCRI and the PMOI are one. The NCRI is present in the United States. If A is B, and B is present, then A is present also.

. . .

We . . . proceed to consider whether the PMOI and NCRI have been deprived of a constitutional right.

. . .

The government rightly reminds us that the Supreme Court established in Mathews v. Eldridge and indeed even before that decision, that identification of the specific dictates of due process generally requires consideration of three distinct factors: first, the private interests that will be affected by the official action; second, the risk of an erroneous deprivation of such interest of the procedure used, and the probable value, if any, of additional or substitute procedural safeguards; and finally, the government's interest, including the function involved and the fiscal and administrative burdens that the additional or substitute procedural requirements would entail.

. . .

The Secretary reviews the three elements of the balancing inquiry . . . to conclude that "the balancing tips decidedly in favor of the government and justifies postponing review until after the Secretary's designation." However, while we acknowledge that the factors set forth, being drawn as they are from the Supreme Court case, are necessarily the right ones, we must note that the government has made little effort to tie the factors to the question of "when" as opposed to "what" due process is to be afforded.

. . .

As to the third . . . factor—"the government's interest, including the function involved in the fiscal and administrative burdens that the additional or substitute procedural requirement would entail,"—the Secretary rightly reminds us that "no governmental interest is more compelling than the security of the nation." It is on this very point that the Secretary most clearly has failed to distinguish between the what of the

Due Process Clause and the when. Certainly the United States enjoys a privilege in classified information affecting national security so strong that even a criminal defendant to whose defense such information is relevant cannot pierce that privilege absent a specific showing of materiality. As we will discuss further infra, that strong interest of the government clearly affects the nature—the "what" of the due process which must be afforded petitioners. It is not immediately apparent how that affects the "when" of the process—that is, whether due process may be effectively provided post-deprivation as opposed to pre-deprivation.

... It is simply not the case, however, that the Secretary has shown how affording the organizations whatever due process they are due before their designation as foreign terrorist organizations and the resulting deprivation of right would interfere with the Secretary's duty to carry out foreign policy.

To oversimplify, assume the Secretary gives notice to one of the entities that:

> We are considering designating you as a foreign terrorist organization, and in addition to classified information, we will be using the following summarized administrative record. You have the right to come forward with any other evidence you may have that you are not a foreign terrorist organization.

It is not immediately apparent how the foreign policy goals of the government in general and the Secretary in particular would be inherently impaired by that notice. It is particularly difficult to discern how such a notice could interfere with the Secretary's legitimate goals were it presented to an entity such as the PMOI concerning its redesignation. We recognize, as we have recognized before, that items of classified information which do not appear dangerous or perhaps even important to judges might "make all too much sense to a foreign counterintelligence specialist who could learn much about this nation's intelligence-gathering capabilities from what these documents revealed about sources and methods." We extend that recognition to the possibility that alerting a previously undesignated organization to the impending designation as a foreign terrorist organization might work harm to this county's foreign policy goals in ways that the court would not immediately perceive. We therefore wish to make plain that we do not foreclose the possibility of the Secretary, in an appropriate case, demonstrating the necessity of withholding all notice and all opportunity to present evidence until the designation is already made. The difficulty with that in the present case is that the Secretary has made no attempt at such a showing.

We therefore hold that the Secretary must afford the limited due process available to the putative foreign terrorist organization prior to the deprivation worked by designating that entity as such with its attendant consequences, unless he can make a showing of particularized need.

. . .

To make plain ..., those procedures which have been held to satisfy the Due Process Clause have "included notice of the action sought," along with the opportunity to effectively be heard. This, we hold, is what the Constitution requires of the Secretary in designating organizations as foreign terrorist organizations under the statute. The Secretary must afford to the entities under consideration notice that the designation is impending. Upon an adequate showing to the court, the Secretary may provide this notice after the designation where earlier notification would impinge upon the security and other foreign policy goals of the United States.

The notice must include the action sought, but need not disclose the classified information to be presented in camera and ex parte to the court under the statute. This is within the privilege and prerogative of the executive, and we do not intend to compel a breach in the security which that branch is charged to protect. However, the Secretary has shown no reason not to offer the designated entities notice of the administrative record which will in any event be filed publicly, at the very latest at the time of the court's review. We therefore require that as soon as the Secretary has reached a tentative determination that the designation is impending, the Secretary must provide notice of those unclassified items upon which he proposes to rely to the entity to be designated. There must then be some compliance with the hearing requirement of due process jurisprudence—that is, the opportunity to be heard at a meaningful time and in a meaningful manner recognized.... We do not suggest "that a hearing closely approximating a judicial trial is necessary." We do, however, require that the Secretary afford to entities considered for imminent designation the opportunity to present, at least in written form, such evidence as those entities may be able to produce to rebut the administrative record or otherwise negate the proposition that they are foreign terrorist organizations.

3. In the National Council case, supra, note 2, the court did not find that the government's argument (the foreign policy and national security nature of the evidence) for dispensing with pre-deprivation notice and opportunity to present evidence was supported by an adequate showing, while recognizing that such a showing possibly could be made in an appropriate case. What other kinds of factors, other than foreign policy and national security concerns, might support dispensing with pre-deprivation process? Consult Designation of Foreign Terrorist Organizations under the AEDPA: The National Council Court Erred in Requiring Pre-designation Process, 2002 B.Y.U. L. Rev. 675 (2002).

4. The court in National Council, supra note 2, ordered as a remedy that "the petitioners be afforded the opportunity to file responses to the nonclassified evidence against them, to file evidence in support of their allegations that they are not terrorist organizations, and that they be afforded an opportunity to be meaningfully heard by the Secretary upon the relevant findings." In the National Council case, there was both classified and nonclassified evidence in the administrative record. Suppose that the record consisted only of classified evidence. (The language of § 1189 does not appear to preclude such a possibility.) How meaningfully would the due process right granted by the

National Council court be in such a context? Is it arguable that the most important due process protection needed by an affected organization is adequate judicial review of the Secretary's finding?

5.   Section 1189 provides that classified information may be considered in deciding whether to designate an organization as a foreign terrorist organization. It does not apply the provisions of the Classified Information Procedures Act, which by its terms applies in criminal prosecutions. CIPA, which is treated in chapter 9, infra, provides that where classified information is involved, an effort should be made to provide a substitute, for example, a summary that does not disclose the confidential information, and if such efforts fail, the judge may dismiss the prosecution. Would it be appropriate or desirable to apply the CIPA in § 1189 proceedings?

6.   What would you have advised the Secretary of State to do in the wake of the decision in the National Council case, supra note 2? Seek review in the Supreme Court? Provide to the organizations involved in National Council the procedural protections ordered by the court? Provide such procedural protections in all subsequent designation cases? Go back and reopen all previous designation cases and provide the prescribed procedural protections? Seek an amendment of § 1189 to codify by statute the procedural requirements prescribed by the court in National Council?

7.   In the aftermath of the National Council case, we inquired by telephone and fax to the State Department in two different offices as to how the Department was responding to the National Council court's decision. One State Department official, in reply to a question, indicated that they did not plan to amend § 1189 procedures as a result of the National Council decision and expressed concern about notifying terrorist groups about their designation and thus allowing them to hide their assets. Query, is the concern about the possibility that assets will be hidden a sufficient reason to provide only post-designation hearings? Should the National Council court have considered this concern in its opinion?

A more formal response was received from the Office of Legal Adviser, Law Enforcement and Intelligence, in response to a faxed inquiry:

> Your facsimile ... was referred to me. You asked whether the Secretary of State is implementing or plans to implement the procedures outlined by the court in National Council ..., in other cases of designating a foreign terrorist organization.

> Without waiving its right to challenge the correctness of the decision of the court in National Council ..., the State Department has implemented such procedures where applicable. The D.C. Circuit's ruling in National Council ... made clear, however, that the threshold question is first whether a foreign entity is present within the United States and has sufficient connections with this country to bring it within our constitutional framework. If the necessary quantum of presence and connections is missing, entities can claim no rights under the Due Process Clause. Thus, where foreign entities do not have sufficient connections with the United States such that the provisions of the Constitution could be applied to them, notice and hearings and similar procedures are not

provided. See, e.g., 32 County Sovereignty Comm. v. Department of State, 292 F.3d 797, 799 (D.C. Cir. 2002).

8. What kind of presence in the U.S. is needed in order to qualify for due process protection? In the 32 County case, cited, supra note 7, the court stated: "[T]he affidavits petitioners submitted . . . demonstrate only that some of their American 'members' personally rented post office boxes and utilized a bank account to transmit funds and information to . . . [the organization] in Ireland. The affidavits do not aver that . . . [the organization] possessed any controlling interest in property located within the United States, nor do they demonstrate any other form of presence here."

9. Are there practical problems in providing notice and other procedural opportunities to the kind of organizations that are likely to be designated as foreign terrorist organizations? Consider the type of organizations that are already listed, supra, pp. 28–30. First, all of these organizations are by definition foreign; second, many of them are also secretive and hidden. It is as if the government were obligated to provide notice to the Mafia. How does one go about it?

It is not happenstance that in the history of the designation process, only three organizations have sought judicial review of the designation and one of those was the alter ego of the second.

10. As referred to in note 7, supra, an additional issue considered in some of the NCRI–MEK series of cases is whether one organization was the alter ego of the other. The issue was litigated most fully in National Council of Resistance v. Department of State, 373 F.3d 152 (D.C. Cir. 2004):

> . . . NCRI submitted voluminous materials that purported to demonstrate that it was sufficiently independent of MEK that it could not be considered an alias of that organization. . . .
>
> . . .
>
> NCRI's primary argument is that the Secretary's conclusion that NCRI is an alias of MEK lacks substantial support in the administrative record. NCRI insists that it is an umbrella organization of Iranian dissident persons and groups of which MEK is only a single member, no more powerful than any other. In addressing this contention, we begin with our earlier holding in this action. In *NCRI*, we concluded—based on the record then presented to us—that the Secretary's designation of NCRI as an alias of MEK "does not lack substantial support and . . . is neither arbitrary, capricious, nor otherwise not in accordance with law." Athough that decision is obviously not determinative of the question before us today—we are now reviewing a record that has since been supplemented both by the Government and NCRI—its holding must nevertheless inform our decision here. Logically, NCRI's challenge can succeed only if the new record materials establish its independence from MEK so that we can no longer affirm that "the Secretary, on the face of things, had enough information before [him] to come to the conclusion" that NCRI is an alias of MEK. Having reviewed the supplemented administrative record as a whole and the classified information appended to it, we conclude that NCRI has not met this burden.

To explain our decision, we must first review what it means—in the very particular context of AEDPA—for one organization to be an alias of another.

. . .

Just as it is silly to suppose "that Congress empowered the Secretary to designate a terrorist organization . . . only for such periods of time as it took such organization to give itself a new name, and then let it happily resume the same status it would have enjoyed had it never been designated," so too it is implausible to think that Congress permitted the Secretary to designate an FTO to cut off its support in and from the United States, but did not authorize the Secretary to prevent that FTO from marshaling all the same support via juridically separate agents subject to its control. For instance, under NCRI's conception, the Government could designate XYZ organization as an FTO in an effort to block United States support to that organization, but could not, without a separate FTO designation, ban the transfer of material support to XYZ's fundraising affiliate, FTO Fundraiser, Inc. The crabbed view of alias status advanced by NCRI is at war not only with the antiterrorism objective of AEDPA, but common sense as well.

We need not plumb all the complexities of agency law to determine when an agent, under AEDPA, is the alias of its principal. It is sufficient for our purposes to note that the requisite relationship for alias status is established at least when one organization so dominates and controls another that the latter can no longer be considered meaningfully independent from the former. . . .

We thus frame our inquiry here as whether "the Secretary, on the face of things, had enough information before [him] to come to the conclusion" that NCRI was dominated and controlled by MEK. Based on our review of the entire administrative record and the classified materials appended thereto, we find that the Secretary did have an adequate basis for his conclusion. While our determination is buttressed by classified information provided to us on an *ex parte* and *in camera* basis—the contents of which we cannot discuss—the voluminous unclassified materials contained in the administrative record by themselves and by a comfortable margin provide sufficient support for the Secretary's conclusion, given the standard of review. . . .

3. CAN THE FTO DESIGNATION BE CHALLENGED IN A CRIMINAL PROSECUTION FOR A VIOLATION OF § 2339B?

The National Council and PMOI cases, discussed in the previous subsection, all involved direct judicial review of the Secretary's decision to designate the plaintiff organization as a foreign terrorist organization. Issues relating to the designation can also arise in a criminal prosecution of an individual or institution charged with having provided material support to a designated FTO under 18 U.S.C. § 2339B.

UNITED STATES v. AFSHARI

392 F.3d 1031 (9th Cir. 2004)

Defendants bring the instant Motion on various grounds, arguing that a portion of the Antiterrorism and Effective Death Penalty Act of 1996 (the "AEDPA")—to wit, 8 U.S.C. § 1189(a)(8)—can be read to authorize the judicial examination of its constitutionality. Further, Defendants argue that, if such review is precluded, 8 U.S.C. § 1189 ("Section 1189") must be held to be unconstitutional under the U.S. Constitution's separation of powers principles articulated in Article III, the First and Sixth Amendments, and the Due Process Clause of the Fifth Amendment. The relevant portion of Section 1189 states, in pertinent part: If an organization has been designated to be a Foreign Terrorist Organization ("FTO") under paragraph (2)(B) of Section 1189, "a defendant in a criminal action or an alien in a removal proceeding shall not be permitted to raise any question concerning the validity of the issuance of such designation as a defense or an objection at any trial or hearing." 8 U.S.C. § 1189(a)(8). The Court addresses each of Defendants' arguments in turn.

. . .

The issues raised by Defendants are not novel and, indeed, many have been raised and addressed by our sister courts. The U.S. Government indicted the Defendants in March 2001 based upon the Secretary of State's designations of the Mujahedin-e Khalq ("MEK") as an FTO. . . .

As explained below, the issues raised by Defendants in the instant motion constitute an attempt to re-litigate a significant number of issues which, while admittedly complex and have already been adjudicated by both the Ninth Circuit and the D.C. Circuit.

. . .

Defendants' first argue that Section 1198 should be construed so as to authorize review of the validity of the MEK's designation as an FTO. In so arguing, Defendants state the long-held principle of statutory construction that "every reasonable construction must be resorted to in order to save a statute from unconstitutionality." Yet, rather than reading Section 1189 to bar review of constitutional claims (an admittedly unconstitutional construction), this Court finds that the AEDPA is subject to constitutional challenge, as it was in *Afshari*. [Ed. United States v. Afshari, 392 F.3d 1031 (9th Cir. 2004).]

. . . [T]he Court finds that 1189(a)(8) is subject to judicial review for constitutionality, yet this does not significantly impact the Court's decision with respect to the issues raised in the instant Motion as the both the Ninth Circuit and the D.C. Circuit have already addressed the constitutionality of Section 1189(a)(8).

. . .

Defendants' next argue that this Court should construe Section 1189(a)(8) to preserve judicial authority to examine the validity of the designation in this case. More specifically, Defendants contend that they should be permitted to argue that the MEK does not meet the criteria for designation as a terrorist organization, rather than arguing that the designation as a whole was invalid (a point which the D.C. Circuit has already ruled upon). That is a distinction without a difference as both the plain text of Section 1189 and the D.C. Circuit's holding in *NCRI* make plain that a criminal defendant may not raise *"any question* concerning the validity of the issuance of" an FTO designation. 8 U.S.C. 1189(a)(8). Further, in *NCRI* the Ninth Circuit upheld the constitutional validity of Congress' decision to permit challenges to FTO designations only where brought by the FTO itself, as opposed to a challenge brought by an individual. *Afshari,* 426 F.3d at 1154–58 (citing 8 U.S.C. § 1189(c) ["Not later than 30 days after publication in the Federal Register of a designation, an amended designation, or a determination in response to a petition for revocation, the designated organization may seek judicial review in the United States Court of Appeals for the District of Columbia Circuit."]). In so holding, the Ninth Circuit explained that this congressional restriction "avoids the awkwardness of criminalizing material support for a designated organization in some circuits but not others, as varying decisions in the different regional circuits might."

For the foregoing reasons, the Court finds that Section 1189(a)(8) does not permit Defendants to challenge the validity of the MEK's designation as an FTO. In so holding the Court is mindful of the deeply troubling fact that many FTO designations may be completely immune from challenge because no individual may ever challenge the designation and, as a practical matter, most organizations may not be able to challenge the designation on their behalf—even if it is unconstitutional. However, principles of vertical stare decisis prevent this Court from altering the holdings of either the 9th Circuit or the D.C. Circuit.

. . .

Defendants next argue that the *Afshari* Court did not consider the possibility that Section 1189 violates separation of powers principles under Article III insofar as it prohibits a defendant in a criminal proceeding from attacking the validity of the underlying relevant FTO designation. However, while the *Afshari* Court may *arguably* be said to have refrained from expressly considering this issue, it certainly implicitly considered this issue in reaching its opinion, stating, *inter alia:*

The district court found that it was a facially unconstitutional restriction on judicial review of the designation for Congress to assign such review exclusively to the D.C. Circuit. We reject that position. Many administrative determinations are reviewable only by petition to the correct circuit court, bypassing the district court, and that procedure has generally been accepted. Many are reviewable only in the D.C. Circuit, or the Federal Circuit, and those restrictions have also been generally accepted. The congressional restriction does not interfere with the opportunity for judicial review, *as the MEK's extensive litigation history shows*.... Congress clearly chose to delegate policymaking authority to the President and Department of State with respect to designation of terrorist organizations, and to keep such policymaking authority out of the hands of United States Attorneys and juries....

Stated differently, the *Afshari* Court resolved this issue under the political question doctrine, which requires Article III courts to refrain from adjudicating certain political issues. Moreover, the *Afshari* Court was not presented with a case in which the FTO at issue had not exercised its option, under Section 1189, to challenge its designation as an FTO—nor are we. Indeed, this grave issue is not yet ripe for adjudication, as it is not presently before us. Instead, as stated earlier, we are presented with a situation in which the MEK received judicial review of its designation as an FTO whereas the individual defendants at issue did not. While this issue is constitutionally troubling, it was addressed by the *Afshari* Court, which faced the extraordinarily difficult task of balancing the efficiencies and expertise of the Secretary of State in classifying an entity as an FTO against values at the very heart of our judicial system as to the separation of powers, as expressed within Article III.

Even assuming *arguendo* that the *Afshari* Court had not already addressed the issue before us today, Defendants would have a difficult time making an impenetrable Article III separation of powers claim due to the fact that the jurisprudence regarding the necessity of judicial review of agency determinations is extraordinarily complicated and confused....

Additionally, as the Government points out in its opposition papers, the theory put forth by the Defendants in the Instant Motion presents substantial obstacles to effective jurisprudence in the area of national security concerns. For example, under Defendants' reasoning, no criminal prosecution could proceed under 18 U.S.C. § 2332d(a), which prohibits the knowing engagement in financial transactions with foreign supporters of terrorism, without a finding by a jury that the foreign state at issue had engaged in act(s) constituting the support of terrorism. One struggles to envisage how a jury could undertake such an endeavor. And yet, as eluded to earlier, the Court is mindful of the fact that Article III, § 1 not only preserves litigants their interest in an impartial and independent federal adjudication of claims within the judicial power of the United States, but also serve as "an inseparable element of the constitutional system of checks and balances." Moreover, although "an absolute construction of Article III is not possible in this area of 'frequently arcane distinctions and confusing precedents,'" the danger of Congress or the Executive encroaching on Article III judicial powers is at its highest in a criminal prosecution.

Notwithstanding this Court's profound concerns with the separation of powers principles implicated in the instant case, it is mindful and respectful of the general political question doctrine, particularly as it was applied to the instant case in *Afshari*. In *Afshari*, the Ninth Circuit explicitly noted:

The sometimes subtle analysis of a foreign organization's political program to determine whether it is indeed a terrorist threat to the United States is particularly within the expertise of the State Department and the Executive Branch. Juries could not make reliable determinations without extensive foreign policy education and the disclosure of classified materials. Nor is it appropriate for a jury in a criminal case to make foreign policy decisions for the United States. Leaving the determination of whether a group is a 'foreign terrorist organization' to the Executive Branch, coupled with the procedural protections and judicial review afforded by the statute, is both a reasonable and a constitutional way to make such determinations. The Constitution does not forbid Congress from requiring individuals, whether they agree with the Executive Branch determination or not, to refrain from furnishing material assistance to designated terrorist organizations during the period of designation.

For the foregoing reasons, Defendants' request for an independent examination of the MEK's designation as an FTO, upon this Court's own record, must be denied.

. . .

Defendants finally argue that Section 1189's bar to judicial examination by this Court of the FTO designation violates due process. Defendants contend that even thought the Ninth Circuit rejected their due process argument in *Afshari*, 426 F.3d at 1155–59, the court failed to address the line of Supreme Court precedent based on *Yakus v. United States*, 321 U.S. 414, 64 S.Ct. 660, 88 L.Ed. 834 (1944). However, Defendants provide this Court with no authority suggesting that it can overrule an appellate decision because the appellate court failed to discuss a particular Supreme Court precedent. As a result, the Court finds that Defendants' due process argument is foreclosed.

For the foregoing reasons, Defendants' Motion is denied.

Questions and Notes

1. Afshari holds that it is constitutionally permissible to bar a criminal defendant from raising as a defense at his trial on a charge of providing material support to an FTO that the FTO designation was not well-founded. This amounts to a decision that it is permissible to preclude a criminal defendant from raising as a defense the validity of a designation that provides one of the elements of the charge against him. Consider in this connection the following case:

In Yakus v. United States, 321 U.S. 414 (1944), during World War II, the Emergency Price Control Act provided for review of a price regulation through a procedure for protest and review in the Emergency Court of Appeals. The applicable statute was interpreted to bar the defendant from attacking the validity of the price regulation in a criminal prosecution for violation of the regulation. The Supreme Court upheld the Act as applied against a constitutional due process challenge. Chief Justice Stone for the majority wrote:

"[W]e are pointed to no principle of law or provision of the Constitution ... which precludes the practice, ... of splitting the trial for violation of an administrative regulation by committing the determination of the issue of its validity to the agency which created it, and the issue of the violation to a court which is given jurisdiction to punish violations. Such a requirement presents no novel constitutional issue...."

In dissent, Justice Rutledge wrote:

"The effect is to segregate out of the trial proper issues, whether of law or fact relating to the validity of the law for violation of which the defendants are charged, and to leave to the criminal court only the determination of whether a violation of the regulation as written actually took place.... On facts material to the validity of the regulation the persons charged are deprived of a full trial in the state or district where the crime occurs."

2. Also see Adamo Wrecking Co. v. United States, 434 U.S. 275 (1978), which involved the Clean Air Act under which the Administrator of the Environmental Protection Agency was authorized to promulgate emission standards for "hazardous air pollutants." Knowing violation of an emission standard was punishable as a crime under the Act. The Act provided for judicial review of an emission standard within 30 days after promulgation and provided that the action of the Administrator was not otherwise subject to review in civil or criminal proceedings for enforcement. Adamo Wrecking was charged criminally with having knowingly violated an emission standard and tried to defend on the ground that that the purported emission standard in the matter was not an emission standard within the meaning of the Act. A majority of the Court ruled that such a defense could be raised by a criminal defendant. Justice Powell, concurring, said the following:

"If the constitutional validity of sec. 307(b) of the Clean Air Act had been raised by the petitioner, I think it would have merited serious consideration ... The Act ... is similar to the preclusion provisions of the Emergency Price Control Act before the Court in Yakus, and petitioner may have thought the decision in that case effectively foreclosed a due process challenge in the present case. Although I express no considered judgment, I think Yakus is at least arguably distinguishable. The statute there came before the Court during World War II, and it can be viewed as a valid exercise of the war powers of Congress ..."

Justice Powell also stated:

"The 30 day limitation on judicial review imposed by the Clean Air Act would offer precariously little time for many affected persons even if some adequate method of notice were afforded. It also is totally unrealistic to assume that more than a fraction of the persons and entities affected by a regulation—especially small contractors scattered across the country—would have knowledge of its promulgation or familiarity with or access to the Federal Register.''

3. Justice Powell in Adamo Wrecking mentioned the fact that Yakus may be explained as having been a decision made in wartime and as an exercise of the war powers of Congress. Consider in connection with the issues raised in this section the implications of the view that we are at war against terrorism.

CHAPTER 4

PROACTIVE SURVEILLANCE

■ ■ ■

A. INTRODUCTION

NOTE ON CIVIL SUITS CHALLENGING THE LEGALITY OF GOVERNMENT ENFORCEMENT PRACTICES IN INVESTIGATING AND APPREHENDING SUSPECTED TERRORISTS

It may be worthwhile at this point in the materials to take a step back and take a broader view of the pattern of recent case law developments in the government's enforcement efforts against terrorism. Chapters 4, 5, 6, 7, and 8 in the casebook contain materials which describe investigation practices engaged in by the government during the Bush administration, and which, to some extent, have continued under the Obama administration.

More recently, as revealed by these materials, there have been a series of civil lawsuits brought by persons who have alleged that they were injured by one or more of the government investigatory practices described in these chapters. While this is a book about criminal enforcement, these civil suits have had the potential to test the legality of these various criminal investigatory practices and thus are relevant to our subject matter. The government, however, has consistently responded to these civil lawsuits by invoking various legal doctrines, which, when their applicability has been upheld, have had the effect of blocking judicial consideration of the merits of the constitutional and statutory claims asserted by the civil plaintiffs.

Thus, for example, in the *El Masri* case (casebook, p. 382), the government invoked, inter alia, the state secrets doctrine. In *Arar* (see p. 371) limitations on *Bivens* as a basis for recovery were relied upon. In *Jeppesen Dataplan* (see p. 385), the application of the state secrets doctrine again was at issue. In *al-Kidd* (see p. 416), the doctrines of absolute and qualified immunity of high government officials were utilized. In *Ashcroft v. Iqba* (p. 450) the adequacy of the pleading of facts was a basis for the Supreme Court's decision.

For the most part, the government has been successful at the court of appeals level in its efforts to block consideration of the merits of these claims. When it has lost at that level in a three judge panel decision, it typically has sought a rehearing en banc. See, e.g., *Jeppesen Dataplan*, supra. If denied the en banc rehearing, it has sought certiorari review by the Supreme Court. See, e.g. *al-Kidd,* supra. Generally, thus far, the Supreme Court in its granting and denying of petitions for certiorari in these cases, has allowed the government effectively to block consideration of the issues on the merits. See, e.g. the denial of certiorari in *Arar.* The continuation of this pattern is further tested by whether the Court grants the certiorari petition in cases where the government has lost at the court of appeals level, as it did in *Iqbal.* The *al-Kidd* petition where the Court granted certiorari and then reversed the decision below is the most recent illustration of this pattern.

What may also be of special interest regarding these cases is that the pattern and legal strategy of seeking to block consideration of the merits of plaintiffs' claims through invocation of various legal doctrines which began under the Bush administration has continued under President Obama. While the Obama administration, in some instances, has adopted policies designed to eliminate some of the most extreme investigative practices engaged in under the administration of President Bush, the reluctance to have the practices under Bush or Obama subjected to judicial review on the merits remains unchanged. Compare, generally, Norman Abrams, Developments in U.S. Anti-terrorism Law, Checks and Balances Undermined, 4 *J.Internat. C.J.* 1117 (2006).

In this chapter and the succeeding chapters in this Part, we address issues raised by the enforcement methods used by the government in terrorism matters—to acquire information, apprehend and transfer persons suspected of terrorism, and some specific issues often raised in civilian terrorism trials not addressed under the heading of acquiring information. Specifically, these chapters address the seeking-to-acquire-terrorism-related-information through methods involving proactive surveillance, electronic surveillance, searches and administrative subpoenas, interrogation and rendition, as well as through the use of the material witness statute and authority in regard to aliens. Specific issues that often arise in civilian terrorism trials relating to the use of classified information are also considered in this Part.

We shall be attentive to the major controversies, triggered by expansive use of governmental authority, which have arisen in a number of these acquisition-of-information arenas: for example, the TSP controversy in the electronic surveillance arena; the fracas surrounding the use of the "library" provision and national security letters; the national anguish over the use of torture in interrogation; and the litigation surrounding the practice of extraordinary rendition of persons suspected of being terrorists.

We shall also examine some of the common rules and standards issues that arise in connection with each of the different methods used by the government to acquire terrorism-related information, comparing them with the rules and standards applied in ordinary criminal matters, as well as with each other: for example, the factual basis on which government agents can lawfully act; whether it makes a difference that the government "intrusion" occurs abroad; the extent to which secrecy applies to the government action, at the time, and afterward; and the extent to which special exigency triggers even more enlarged powers.

By proactive surveillance is meant surveillance and inquiries by the investigating arms of the federal government where agents make use of public or general sources of information and gather information in public venues. Such surveillance and investigation is aimed at uncovering criminal behavior or leads thereto in contexts where there is not a quantum of specific evidence akin to that which normally underlies criminal investigation. The basic inquiry is whether and to what extent there are limitations on this type of activity by law enforcement agencies, specifically the FBI, that flow from internal policies and rules, statutes or the Constitution.

There is a wide range of law enforcement activities that fall under this heading. The main focus here will be on surveillance activities such as sending undercover agents into public meetings or to join organizations, both political and other kinds, or sending agents into mosques, churches and synagogues and other places of public gathering, and surfing the net and other public information sources, all with a view to gathering information regarding possible criminal behavior. Are there government policies that authorize or control, restrict or prohibit such activities? Must the government have a specific quantum of evidence regarding suspected terrorism-related activities involving, for example, a political organization or a mosque, synagogue or church before sending an agent undercover to participate in the organization or attend services at the suspected site? Are there restrictions on what the government agents can do in these contexts?

Proactive surveillance by federal government agents usually increases significantly during wartime or during periods of social unrest or upheaval. Such surveillance during periods of stress becomes a sensitive area in which there are legitimate concerns about civil liberties, and there is a need to strike the proper balance between security and civil liberty. While there may be a perceived need for more proactive governmental investigative activity during such periods, there is also a concern about the chilling effect of government's intrusion into the arena of political and religious discourse and possible trenching on First Amendment freedoms.

The FBI is the principal agency that engages in these types of investigatory activities, and the internal rules and guidelines governing permissible FBI activities of this type are of special interest. Guidelines governing FBI surveillance and investigatory activities have been issued and revised over the years by various Attorneys General, and we examine closely the latest version of such guidelines. The permissibility and lawfulness of such surveillance is itself an important legal and policy issue.

There have been periods, for example, the late 1960's, when the FBI engaged in activities that went much beyond possibly permissible and lawful surveillance and inquiries and that involved some clear-cut abuses. Subsequent Attorney General Guidelines not only defined the lines for permissible political surveillance but were aimed at prohibiting abusive activities.

In addition to regulation of this area by guidelines, Congress, on occasion, has granted authority to gather certain kinds of information that may come under the general heading of proactive surveillance as it is used in this Chapter. Thus, section 416 of the USA PATRIOT Act authorizes the Attorney General to fully implement the existing foreign-student monitoring program, and broadens the coverage of existing law to include all students at any institution of higher education or vocational school.

There are also provisions in the Homeland Security Act that are aimed at allaying concerns about too much proactive surveillance. Section 880 of the Act prohibits implementation of the TIPS program by which citizens with regular routes that brought them into contact with people were encouraged to report possible terrorism-related activities. Section 1514 of the same Act precludes the Homeland Security Act from being interpreted to authorize a national identification system or card. Proactive surveillance and inquiry activities, of course, may touch on constitutionally protected interests.

In subsection B of this chapter, we examine relevant excerpts from the current Attorney General Guidelines and study features of the FBI Domestic Investigations and Operations Guidelines which implement the AG Guidelines, both of which govern the proactive surveillance practices of the FBI. In subsection C, we discuss a couple of examples of efforts to litigate issues raised by proactive surveillance practices of law enforcement agencies, with special attention to Laird v. Tatum.

B. RELEVANT FEDERAL EXECUTIVE ORDER AND GUIDELINES

There are three primary sources that currently govern the engaging by the FBI in what we have termed "proactive surveillance." In 1981, President Reagan promulgated Executive Order 12333, which, though having since been amended in regard to our subject in certain technical respects, is still operative 30 years later. E.O. 12333 prohibited intelligence agents from joining or participating in any organization in the United States without disclosing the person's intelligence affiliation to officials of the organization "except in accordance with procedures established... and approved by the Attorney General after consultation with the Director" of National Intelligence. Authorization for such participation is to be given "only if it is essential to achieving lawful purposes as determined by the head of the relevant agency." With certain limited exceptions, no such participation may be undertaken "for the purpose of influencing the activity of the organization or its members."

In September, 2008, toward the end of the Bush administration, Attorney General Mukasey issued The Attorney General's Guidelines for Domestic FBI Operations. These Guidelines consolidated and replaced various sets of guidelines issued by previous attorneys general over a period of many years.

In December, 2008, the FBI promulgated internally its Domestic Investigations and Operations Guide (DIOG) which is a very detailed implementation of the Attorney General Mukasey Guidelines. It is noteworthy that the DIOG only became publicly available in September 2009 as a result of a Freedom of Information request, but then only in a heavily redacted version that states, throughout, that the provisions contained in the now publicly-available document are unclassified and "for official use only." The DIOG states that it "applies to all investigative activities and intelligence collection activities conducted by the FBI within the United States or outside the territories of all countries. This policy document does not apply to investigative and intelligence collection activities of the FBI in foreign countries; those are governed by The Attorney General's Guidelines for Extraterritorial FBI Operations." The purpose is to "standardize policy so that criminal, national security, and foreign intelligence investigative activities are consistently and uniformly accomplished whenever possible . . . ."

We reproduce below excerpts from both the Attorney General's Guidelines and summarize relevant features of the DIOG. We emphasize, however, that the limited selection of provisions of the DIOG that are referred to here are taken from a very detailed document, over 300 pages long. It is difficult to communicate the full flavor of the document with this limited description.

As you examine the material bearing on these documents, consider such questions as the following: What factual basis must an FBI agent have, in connection with an inquiry in aid of trying to prevent terrorism, to surf the web for information, examine public records, attend religious services at a mosque, church or synagogue without disclosing his or her identity, join an organization without notifying the head of the organization that he/she is an FBI agent engaged in an assessment, etc.? To what extent can an agent take into account race or ethnicity in making decisions about any of the foregoing activities? How long may the agent keep in the files a record of the information obtained through any of the foregoing activities?

Excerpts from The Attorney General's Guidelines for Domestic FBI Operations (2008)

1.

. . .

C.

. . .

4.   Undisclosed Participation in Organizations

Undisclosed participation in organizations in activities under these Guidelines shall be conducted in accordance with FBI policy approved by the Attorney General.

. . .

II. Investigations and Intelligence Gathering

. . .

This Part authorizes different levels of information gathering activity, which afford the FBI flexibility, under appropriate standards and procedures, to adapt the methods utilized and the information sought to the nature of the matter under investigation and the character of the information supporting the need for investigation.

Assessments, authorized by Subpart A of this Part, require an authorized purpose but not any particular factual predication. For example, to carry out its central mission of preventing the commission of terrorist acts against the United States and its people, the FBI must proactively draw on available sources of information to identify terrorist threats and activities. It cannot be content to wait for leads to come in through the actions of others, but rather must be vigilant in detecting terrorist activities to the full extent permitted by law, with an eye towards early intervention and prevention of acts of terrorism before they occur. . . . The proactive investigative authority conveyed in assessments is designed for, and may be utilized by, the FBI in the discharge of these responsibilities. . . .

. . . [A]sessments may be undertaken proactively with such objectives as detecting criminal activities; obtaining information on individuals, groups, or organizations of possible investigative interest, either because they may be involved in criminal or national security-threatening activities or because they may be targeted for attack or victimization by such activities; and identifying and assessing individuals who may have value as human sources. For example, assessment activities may involve proactively surfing the Internet to find publicly accessible websites and services through which recruitment by terrorist organizations and promotion of terrorist crimes is openly taking place. . . .

The methods authorized in assessments are generally those of relatively low intrusiveness, such as obtaining publicly available information, checking government records, and requesting information from members of the public. These Guidelines do not impose supervisory approval requirements in assessments, given the types of techniques that are authorized at this stage (e.g., perusing the Internet for publicly available information). However, FBI policy will prescribe supervisory approval requirements for certain assessments, considering such matters as the purpose of the assessment and the methods being utilized.

Beyond the proactive information gathering functions described above, assessments may be used when allegations or other information concerning crimes or threats to the national security is received or obtained, and the matter can be checked out or resolved through the relatively non-intrusive methods authorized in assessments. The checking of investigative leads in this manner can avoid the need to proceed to more formal levels of investigative activity, if the results of an assessment indicate that further investigation is not warranted.

Subpart B of this Part authorizes a second level of investigative activity, predicated investigations. The purposes or objectives of predicated investigations are essentially the same as those of assessments, but predication as provided in these Guidelines is needed—generally, allegations, reports, facts or circumstances indicative of possible criminal or national security threatening activity, or the potential for acquiring information responsive to foreign intelligence requirements—and supervisory approval must be obtained, to initiate predicated investigations. Corresponding to the stronger predication and approval requirements, all lawful methods may be used in predicated investigations. A classified directive provides further specification concerning circumstances supporting certain predicated investigations. . . .

Salient features of the FBI's Domestic Investigations and Operations Guide (DIOG) (2008).

In the wake of the promulgation of the Attorney General's Guidelines in September, 2008, the FBI issued its first-ever Domestic and Operations Guide (DIOGA) in December, 2008. The document was intended to be internal and confidential, though a redacted version, marked Unclassified and For Official Use Only was made public through a Freedom of Information request. The 300+ page document is essentially a single comprehensive set of internal guidelines for domestic matters, updated, had previously been set forth in a series of different sets of guideline documents. The DIOG contains many provisions and statements that are relevant to the subject of this chapter.

For example, the DIOG indicates that if religious practitioners are involved in, or religious facilities are used for, activities that are properly the subject of FBI investigative or intelligence collection activities, the religious aspect of their activities does not immunize them from investigation. The DIOG emphasizes that such investigations must be properly documented. Similarly, the DIOG indicates that if investigative experience and reliable intelligence reveal that members of a terrorist group are known to commonly possess a combination of religion-based characteristics such as the group leader stating that acts of terrorism are based in religious doctrine, it is rational and lawful to consider such a combination in gathering intelligence about the group.

The DIOG also indicates that DOJ guidance and FBI policy permit the FBI to identify locations of concentrated ethnic communities if these locations will reasonably aid the analysis of potential threats and vulnerabilities.

The DIOG makes clear that the investigative method used should balance the level of intrusion against investigative requirements. This type of balancing test is particularly important when the information sought involves clearly-established constitutional, statutory, or evidentiary right (such as obtaining information from religious, or academic institutions or public fora where First Amendment rights are being exercised), but is to be applied in all circumstances to ensure that the least intrusive alternative feasible is being utilized.

The DIOG (and the Attorney General Guidelines) authorize as a type of investigative activity "assessments" which do not require a particular factual-predication but do require an authorized purpose. Although no particular factual predication is required, the basis of an assessment cannot be arbitrary or groundless speculation, nor can an assessment be based solely on the exercise of First Amendment protected activities or on the race, ethnicity, national origin or religion of the subject. Although difficult to define, no particular factual predication, is less than information or allegation required for the initiation of a preliminary investigation. FBI employees who conduct assessments are responsible for assuring that assessments are not pursued for frivolous or improper purposes.

The DIOG states that detecting and interrupting criminal activities at their early stages, and preventing crimes from occurring in the first place is preferable to allowing criminal plots to come to fruition. Hence, assessments may also be undertaken proactively with such objectives as obtaining information on individuals, groups or organizations of possible investigative interest.

The DIOG lists categories of assessments and requirements applicable to each activity, e.g. whether approval is a requirement, duration requirements and review at the end of specified periods. While this much of the approach taken in the DIOG can be discerned, the content and substance of the specific categories and the related requirements are revealed in the document only to a limited extent because of heavy redactions.

The DIOG lists investigative methods that may be used in assessments and predicated investigations: Obtaining publicly available information, for example, does not require supervisory approval except as to information that is gathered at a religious service. Publicly available information is information that is published or broadcast for public consumption, available on request to the public, accessible online or otherwise to the public, available to the public by subscription or purchase, available at a meeting open to the public, obtainable by visiting any place or attending an event that is open to the public; or available to be seen or heard by any casual observer not involving unconsented intrusion into private places.

A second method involves engaging in observation or surveillance not requiring a court order where the surveillance does not infringe on a reasonable expectation of privacy and trespass is not required, that is, where the surveillance consists of deliberate observation of persons, places or events, on a limited or continuous basis, in a public or semi-public (e.g., commercial business open to the public) setting.

Other methods include accessing FBI and Department of Justice records and examining records maintained by other federal or governmental entities; using online services and resources; interviewing or requesting information from members of the public and private entities; accepting information voluntarily provided by governmental or private entities; and using and recruiting human sources in conformity with relevant governmental policies.

The DIOG also contains guidelines regarding the retention and maintenance of records with the basic standard being whether the information is relevant to the FBI's law enforcement or national security activity. If an assessment results in no sufficient basis to justify further investigation of the individual or group, the records to be retained must be clearly annotated to that effect.

QUESTIONS AND NOTES

1.　The ACLU criticized the Mukasey Guidelines and the DIOG on the ground, among others, that "[u]nder the new 'assessment' authority, FBI agents can investigate anyone they choose, so long as they claim they are acting to prevent crime, protect national security, or collect foreign intelligence, with absolutely no requirement of a factual connection between their authorizing purpose and the conduct of the individuals they are investigating." Is this an accurate characterization of the basis on which an FBI agent can initiate an assessment?

2.　Consider the following Letter to the Editor in response to an article in the Los Angeles Time regarding the operation of the 2008 Attorney General Guidelines. Does it respond to the concern articulated by the ACLU— see note 1, supra? Does it describe aspects of the Guidelines and DIOG that are likely to make them more protective of civil liberties interests than previous versions? See, e.g., note 6 below.

To the Editor:

"*F.B.I. Casts Wide Net Under Relaxed Rules for Terror Inquiries, Data Show*" (news article, March 27) suggests that in late 2008, new guidelines created a relaxed standard for certain investigative activity and implies that the "relaxed" standard led to a substantial increase in assessments. In fact, the F.B.I. has long engaged in the prompt and limited checking of leads.

The 2008 Attorney General guidelines and the F.B.I.'s Domestic Investigations and Operations Guide did specify clearly for the first time how and where leads being assessed must be documented—whether the lead concerns a criminal or a national security threat. As noted in the article, previously this sort of assessment activity was not tracked.

The new guidelines and policies, together with information technology and new record-keeping systems, now allow the F.B.I. to track investigative activity at every level, including assessments, and to ascertain how many develop sufficient information to warrant the opening of an investigation.

The assessment, with its limited investigative techniques, is a valuable tool to ensure that we can "connect the dots" between disparate pieces of information to keep the country safe while still respecting the civil liberty and privacy rights of every American.

VALERIE CAPRONI

General Counsel

Federal Bureau of Investigation

Washington, March 29, 2011

3. Under a prior version of the Attorney General Guidelines, "threat assessments" were conducted "to investigate or collect information relating to threats to the national security, including information on individuals, groups, and organizations of possible investigative interests, and information concerning possible targets of international terrorism, espionage, foreign computer intrusion, or other threats to the national security." How do assessments under the 2008 Guidelines differ?

4. On July 28, 2010, newspapers reported on instances of cheating by FBI agents being tested on understanding of the Guidelines, and the story became an occasion for criticisms of the authority that the Guidelines gave, for example, to enter mosques and otherwise focus investigations on members of religious groups. See Associated Press story, July 28, 2010, http://www.law.com/jsp/article.jsp?id=1202463982395.

The notion of FBI agents cheating on tests that probed their knowledge of the Guidelines, of course, seems bizarre. What might account for it? Consider in this connection the length and detail in the DIOG, and also take into account the fact that the provisions dealing with justification and file reviews are exceedingly complex.

5. Attorney General Ashcroft revised the then-existing Guidelines in 2002. Brief excerpts from the Ashcroft Guidelines are reproduced below. Compare these provisions with the 2008 Mukasey Guidelines.

Excerpts from the Ashcroft Attorney General Guidelines, As revised May 30, 2002

VI.   Counterterrorism Activities and Other Authorization

. . .

A.   Counterterrorism Activities

     1.   Information Systems

The FBI is authorized to operate and participate in identification, tracking, and information systems for the purpose of identifying and locating terrorists,.... Systems within the scope of this paragraph may draw on and retain pertinent information from any source permitted by law, including information derived from past or ongoing investigative activities; other information collected or provided by governmental entities such as foreign intelligence information and lookout list information, publicly available information, whether obtained directly or through services or resources (whether nonprofit or commercial) that compile or analyze such information; and information voluntarily provided by private entities. . . .

2. Visiting Public Places and Events

For the purpose of detecting or preventing terrorist activities, the FBI is authorized to visit any place and attend any event that is open to the public, on the same terms and conditions as members of the public generally. No information obtained from such visits shall be retained unless it relates to potential criminal or terrorist activity.

A. Other Authorizations

. . . [T]he authorized law enforcement activities of the FBI include carrying out and retaining information resulting from the following activities:

1. General Topical Research

The FBI is authorized to carry out general topical research, including conducting online searches and accessing online sites and forums as a part of such research on the same terms and conditions as members of the public generally. . . . It does not include online searches for information by individuals' names or other individual identifiers, except where such searches are incidental to topical research, such as searching to locate writings on a topic by searching under the names of the authors who write on the topic, or searching by name of a party to a case in conducting legal research.

. . .

B. Protection of Privacy and Other Limitations

1. General Limitations

The law enforcement activities authorized by this Part do not include maintaining files on individuals solely for the purpose of monitoring activities protected by the First Amendment or the lawful exercise of any other rights secured by the Constitution or laws of the United States.

. . .

6. Some of the earlier history of the Attorney General Guidelines is recounted in the following two articles.

John T. Elliff, The Attorney General's Guidelines for FBI Investigations, 69 Cornell L. Rev. 785 (1984):

On March 7, 1983, Attorney General William French Smith issued new guidelines for FBI investigations in the areas of domestic security, racketeering enterprise, and general crimes. They replaced previous guidelines for FBI domestic security investigations issued in 1976 by Attorney General Edward H. Levi and guidelines for FBI racketeering enterprise and general crimes investigations issued in 1980 by Attorney General Benjamin R. Civiletti.

. . .

. . .

Before the Levi guidelines, the FBI Intelligence Division conducted internal security investigations of "subversive activities," as well as foreign counterintelligence investigations of hostile intelligence agents and international terrorists. Although internal security investigations sometimes led to criminal prosecutions for acts of violence, their scope and purposes were broader. Through the mid–1970s, FBI internal security investigations emphasized collection of extensive political intelligence on organizations and individuals espousing revolutionary, racist, or otherwise "extremist" ideological viewpoints. Before World War II, President Roosevelt asked FBI Director J. Edgar Hoover to gather intelligence about the domestic political influence of communist and fascist groups, and subsequent presidents maintained this assignment. Congress reinforced the FBI's internal security mandate with legislation such as the Smith Act of 1940 and the Voorhis Act, which punished those who advocated violent overthrow of the government, and the Internal Security Act of 1950, which required registration of Communist groups and their members and provided for detention of "dangerous" individuals in a national emergency.

During the 1960s the FBI widened the scope of its internal security investigations to include investigations of the civil rights and antiwar movements. These investigations were aimed at gathering information on Communist or "extremist" influence in the groups and acquiring advance knowledge of any disruptive demonstrations or acts of violence. The FBI went beyond investigation and employed so-called COINTELPRO operations to disrupt groups and discredit or harass individuals. When Attorney General William Saxbe released a public report on COINTELPRO in 1974, he described some of these tactics as "abhorrent in a free society."

The Levi guidelines and accompanying administrative reforms abandoned the FBI's previous internal security policies. . . . The FBI Intelligence Division devoted its attention to investigating hostile foreign intelligence operations, including Soviet efforts to influence domestic politics through the Communist Party and its front organizations.

. . .

David M. Park, Note: Re–Examining the Attorney General's Guidelines for FBI Investigations of Domestic Groups, 39 Ariz. L. Rev. 769 (1997).

When a massive fertilizer bomb destroyed the Alfred P. Murrah building in Oklahoma City on April 19, 1995, Americans found themselves confronted with a new threat to their security: domestic terrorist groups. . . .

In the aftermath of the bombing, lawmakers began searching for proactive solutions to prevent further acts of terrorism by domestic groups. The Federal Bureau of Investigation, the nation's primary criminal investigative agency, was an important focal point in this initial search for solutions. Several politicians suggested the possibility of increasing the FBI's investigative powers. They proposed that a broadening of the FBI Guidelines, a set of rules the Bureau adopted to govern its methods of investigation, could help prevent future attacks. The idea of expanding the Guidelines, however, died a quick death. Virtually all the FBI's top officials, including Director Louis Freeh, Attorney General Janet Reno, and Deputy Attorney General Jamie Gorelick, agreed that the current Guidelines already provided the FBI with enough power to investigate terrorist groups. They concluded an alteration of the Guidelines was unnecessary. Instead, Freeh, Reno and Gorelick announced the FBI would now begin to interpret the current version more expansively.

This announcement was not well received by civil libertarians. Many civil rights activists felt FBI activity within the current "narrow" interpretation of the Guidelines was already too invasive and certainly did not want to see these practices expanded. Activists questioned the value gained by increased FBI investigations when weighed against the loss of freedom that would surely accompany any increase in the Bureau's activities. The FBI's history of harassing non-violent political groups was another point of contention among civil rights watchdogs. Any alteration that would give the FBI greater ability to investigate domestic groups would be met with great suspicion. Additionally, civil libertarians suggested that any changes in the Guidelines or investigative procedures that granted the FBI greater authority could be constitutionally challenged.

. . .

In the wake of the Oklahoma City bombing, the FBI announced its solution to help prevent acts of domestic terrorism. Rather than ask to be granted more power, FBI officials chose to use more of the power they had already been granted by interpreting their Guidelines (the current Smith version) more expansively. In the past, the FBI had been reluctant to begin investigations of groups that advocated violence to achieve social or political objectives, unless it anticipated an imminent violation of federal law. The fact that the group may have had the ability to carry out its violent objectives was irrelevant, as long as there was no indication of an "imminent violation."

According to current Director Louis Freeh, the more expansive interpretation would now allow the FBI to begin an investigation of a group advocating violence to achieve social or political objectives somewhere short of an imminent violation of federal law, if it was apparent the group had the ability to carry out its objectives. Such a group would now fall within the Guidelines' "reasonable indication" requirement to begin an investigation.

While this appears to be a reasonable interpretation of the Guidelines, it has caused some concern among civil libertarians, who believe that such an expansive reading will lead to an impermissible infringement upon constitutional rights. They challenge this reading of the Guidelines on two grounds: the First Amendment rights of free expression and free assembly, and the Fourth Amendment protections against illegal searches and seizures.

7. Floyd Abrams, The First Amendment and the War Against Terrorism, 5 U. Pa. J. Const. L. 1, 6 (2002).

> Let me pose another question, one that I answer the same way. It is whether FBI agents should be permitted to attend public meetings of a political or religious nature for the purpose of reporting upon what is said there. When it did so in the 1950s and 1960s, some of the worst abuses of the regime of J. Edgar Hoover occurred. The "chill" on speech was real; Hoover intended just that and achieved just that. It was a civil liberties disaster. After Hoover died, new guidelines, drafted by former Attorneys General Edward Levi and William French Smith, were adopted, effectively barring FBI agents from doing so in most circumstances. Those limits were hailed by civil libertarians—and they should have been. A quarter of a century has now passed, however, and we now face new risks. Shall we now permit, as Attorney General Ashcroft has determined, FBI surveillance of such events? If the Bureau believes that public statements made in a particular mosque, say, may be of assistance in preventing future acts of terrorism, but it is short of proof sufficient to demonstrate the likelihood of criminal behavior, should surveillance of the event be permitted? I think so. Yet when we make that trade-off, we obviously risk the very governmental overreaching and misconduct that tends to accompany any broadening of governmental powers. I have thus far cited examples that fall in the area in which I would be most inclined to give the government some greater powers. It is what we might characterize as the area of prevention of terrorism rather than punishment of it. Obviously, these areas intersect; punishment is, after all, supposed to prevent as well as to punish. But the more we move away from the surveillance mold and into that of how we treat individuals that we have already apprehended, the less willing I think we should be to move even incrementally away from the rules that have historically governed the way we treat people we have apprehended and we believe have committed grievous wrongs.

8. What kind of concerns might a civil libertarian have about the new guidelines? Maintaining files on people? The chilling effect of never knowing who in an organization is a government agent? The possibility that permitting fishing expeditions may lead to worse abuses?

9. What can the government gain from having agents join political organizations or visit places of worship? Is this a good investment of resources from a prevention or enforcement perspective?

10. The DIOG characterizes applicable constitutional law principles governing free speech, religious freedom and freedom of assembly issues and includes some discussion of Supreme Court cases, including Laird v. Tatum, reproduced below.

C. LITIGATING ISSUES RAISED BY PROACTIVE SURVEILLANCE

1. PROACTIVE SURVEILLANCE BY THE U.S. MILITARY

LAIRD v. TATUM

408 U.S. 1 (1972)

BURGER, C. J., delivered the opinion of the Court, in which WHITE, BLACK-MUN, POWELL, and REHNQUIST, JJ., joined. DOUGLAS, J., filed a dissenting opinion in which MARSHALL, J., joined. BRENNAN, J., filed a dissenting opinion in which STEWART and MARSHALL, JJ., joined.

MR. CHIEF JUSTICE BURGER delivered the opinion of the Court.

Respondents brought this class action in the District Court seeking declaratory and injunctive relief on their claim that their rights were being invaded by the Department of the Army's alleged "surveillance of lawful and peaceful civilian political activity." The petitioners in response described the activity as "gathering by lawful means . . . [and] maintaining and using in their intelligence activities . . . information relating to potential or actual civil disturbances [or] street demonstrations." . . . On the basis of the pleadings, the affidavits before the court, and the oral arguments advanced at the hearing, the District Court granted petitioners' motion to dismiss, holding that there was no justiciable claim for relief.

On appeal, a divided Court of Appeals reversed and ordered the case remanded for further proceedings. We granted certiorari to consider whether, as the Court of Appeals held, respondents presented a justiciable controversy in complaining of a "chilling" effect on the exercise of their First Amendment rights where such effect is allegedly caused, not by any "specific action of the Army against them, [but] only [by] the existence and operation of the intelligence gathering and distributing system, which is confined to the Army and related civilian investigative agencies." We reverse.

(1)

There is in the record a considerable amount of background information regarding the activities of which respondents complained; this information is set out primarily in the affidavits that were filed by the parties in connection with the District Court's consideration of respondents' motion for a preliminary injunction and petitioners' motion to dismiss. A brief review of that information is helpful to an understanding of the issues.

The President is authorized by 10 U. S. C. § 331 to make use of the armed forces to quell insurrection and other domestic violence if and when the conditions described in that section obtain within one of the States. Pursuant to those provisions, President Johnson ordered federal troops to assist local authorities at the time of the civil disorders in Detroit, Michigan, in the summer of 1967 and during the disturbances that followed the assassination of Dr. Martin Luther King. Prior to the Detroit disorders, the Army had a general contingency plan for providing such assistance to local authorities, but the 1967 experience led Army authorities to believe that more attention should be given to such preparatory planning. The data-gathering system here involved is said to have been established in connection with the development of more detailed and specific contingency planning designed to permit the Army, when called upon to assist local authorities, to be able to respond effectively with a minimum of force. As the Court of Appeals observed,

> "In performing this type [of] function the Army is essentially a police force or the back-up of a local police force. To quell disturbances or to prevent further disturbances the Army needs the same tools and, most importantly, the same information to which local police forces have access. Since the Army is sent into territory almost invariably unfamiliar to most soldiers and their commanders, their need for information is likely to be greater than that of the hometown policeman."

No logical argument can be made for compelling the military to use *blind* force. When force is employed it should be intelligently directed, and this depends upon having reliable information—in time. As Chief Justice John Marshall said of [General George] Washington, 'A general must be governed by his intelligence and must regulate his measures by his information. It is his duty to obtain correct information....' So we take it as undeniable that the military, *i.e.*, the Army, need a certain amount of information in order to perform their constitutional and statutory missions.

    . . .

The system put into operation as a result of the Army's 1967 experience consisted essentially of the collection of information about public activities that were thought to have at least some potential for civil disorder, the reporting of that information to Army Intelligence headquarters at Fort Holabird, Maryland, the dissemination of these reports from headquarters to major Army posts around the country, and the storage of the reported information in a computer data bank located at Fort Holabird. The information itself was collected by a variety of means, but it is significant that the principal sources of information were the news media and publications in general circulation. Some of the information came from Army Intelligence agents who attended meetings that were open to the public and who wrote field reports describing the meetings, giving such data as the name of the sponsoring organization, the identity of speakers, the approximate number of persons in attendance, and an indication of whether any disorder occurred. And still other information was provided to the Army by civilian law enforcement agencies.

The material filed by the Government in the District Court reveals that Army Intelligence has field offices in various parts of the country; these offices are staffed in the aggregate with approximately 1,000 agents, 94% of whose time is devoted to the organization's principal mission, which is unrelated to the domestic surveillance system here involved.

By early 1970 Congress became concerned with the scope of the Army's domestic surveillance system; hearings on the matter were held before the Subcommittee on Constitutional Rights of the Senate Committee on the Judiciary. Meanwhile, the Army, in the course of a review of the system, ordered a significant reduction in its scope. For example, information referred to in the complaint as the "blacklist" and the records in the computer data bank at Fort Holabird were found unnecessary and were destroyed, along with other related records. One copy of all the material relevant to the instant suit was retained, however, because of the pendency of this litigation.

. . .

In briefs for petitioners filed with this Court, the Solicitor General has called our attention to certain directives issued by the Army and the Department of Defense subsequent to the District Court's dismissal of the action; these directives indicate that the Army's review of the needs of its domestic intelligence activities has indeed been a continuing one and that those activities have since been significantly reduced.

The District Court held a combined hearing on respondents' motion for a preliminary injunction and petitioners' motion for dismissal and thereafter announced its holding that respondents had failed to state a claim upon which relief could be granted. It was the view of the District Court that respondents failed to allege any action on the part of the Army that was unlawful in itself and further failed to allege any injury or any realistic threats to their rights growing out of the Army's actions.

In reversing, the Court of Appeals noted that respondents "have some difficulty in establishing visible injury":

> "[They] freely admit that they complain of no specific action of the Army against them. . . . There is no evidence of illegal or unlawful surveillance activities. We are not cited to any clandestine intrusion by a military agent. So far as is yet shown, the information gathered is nothing more than a good newspaper reporter would be able to gather by attendance at public meetings and the clipping of articles from publications available on any newsstand."

The court took note of petitioners' argument "that nothing [detrimental to respondents] has been done, that nothing is contemplated to be done, and even if some action by the Army against [respondents] were possibly foreseeable, such would not present a presently justiciable controversy." With respect to this argument, the Court of Appeals had this to say:

> "This position of the [petitioners] does not accord full measure to the rather unique argument advanced by appellants [respondents]. While [respondents] do indeed argue that in the future it is possible that information relating to matters far beyond the responsibilities of the military may be misused by the military to the detriment of these civilian [respondents], yet [respondents] do not attempt to establish this as a definitely foreseeable event, or to base their complaint on this ground. Rather, [respondents] contend that the *present existence of this system* of gathering and distributing information, allegedly far beyond the mission requirements of the Army, constitutes an impermissible burden on [respondents] and other persons similarly situated which exercises a *present inhibiting effect* on their full expression and utilization of their First Amendment rights . . ."

Our examination of the record satisfies us that the Court of Appeals properly identified the issue presented, namely, whether the jurisdiction of a federal court may be invoked by a complainant who alleges that the exercise of his First Amendment rights is being chilled by the mere existence, without more, of a governmental investigative and data-gathering activity that is alleged to be broader in scope than is reasonably necessary for the accomplishment of a valid governmental purpose. We conclude, however, that, having properly identified the issue, the Court of Appeals decided that issue incorrectly.

In recent years this Court has found in a number of cases that constitutional violations may arise from the deterrent, or "chilling," effect of governmental regulations that fall short of a direct prohibition against the exercise of First Amendment rights. In none of these cases, however, did the chilling effect arise merely from the individual's knowledge that a governmental agency was engaged in certain activities or from the individual's concomitant fear that, armed with the fruits of those activities, the agency might in the future take some *other* and additional action detrimental to that individual. Rather, in each of these cases, the challenged exercise of governmental power was regulatory, proscriptive, or compulsory in nature, and the complainant was either presently or prospectively subject to the regulations, proscriptions, or compulsions that he was challenging.

The respondents do not meet this test; their claim, simply stated, is that they disagree with the judgments made by the Executive Branch with respect to the type and amount of information the Army needs and that the very existence of the Army's data-gathering system produces a constitutionally impermissible chilling effect upon the exercise of their First Amendment rights. That alleged "chilling" effect may perhaps be seen as arising from respondents' very perception of the system as inappropriate to the Army's role under our form of government, or as arising from respondents' beliefs that it is inherently dangerous for the military to be concerned with activities in the civilian sector, or as arising from respondents' less generalized yet speculative apprehensiveness that the Army may at some future date misuse the information in some way that would cause direct harm to respondents. Allegations of a subjective "chill" are not an adequate substitute for a claim of specific present objective harm or a threat of specific future harm; "the federal courts established pursuant to Article III of the Constitution do not render advisory opinions." *United Public Workers v. Mitchell*, 330 U.S. 75, 89 (1947).

Stripped to its essentials, what respondents appear to be seeking is a broad-scale investigation, conducted by themselves as private parties armed with the subpoena power of a federal district court and the power of cross-examination, to probe into the Army's intelligence gathering activities, with the district court determining at the conclusion of that investigation the extent to which those activities may or may not be appropriate to the Army's mission. The following excerpt from the opinion of the Court of Appeals suggests the broad sweep implicit in its holding:

> . . .

> "[I]n the judgment of the civilian head of the Army not everything being done in the operation of this intelligence system was necessary to the performance of the military mission. *If the Secretary of the Army can formulate and implement such judgment based on facts within his Departmental knowledge, the United States District Court can hear evidence, ascertain the facts, and decide what, if any, further restrictions on the complained-of activities are called for* to confine the military to their legitimate sphere of activity and to protect [respondents'] allegedly infringed constitutional rights." 144 U.S.App.D.C., at 83, 444 F.2d, at 958. (Emphasis added.)

Carried to its logical end, this approach would have the federal courts as virtually continuing monitors of the wisdom and soundness of Executive action; such a role is appropriate for the Congress acting through its committees and the "power of the purse"; it is not the role of the judiciary, absent actual present or immediately threatened injury resulting from unlawful governmental action.

We, of course, intimate no view with respect to the propriety or desirability, from a policy standpoint, of the challenged activities of the Department of the Army; our conclusion is a narrow one, namely, that on this record the respondents have not presented a case for resolution by the courts.

MR. JUSTICE DOUGLAS joined by MR. JUSTICE MARSHALL, dissenting.

> . . .

II

The claim that respondents have no standing to challenge the Army's surveillance of them and the other members of the class they seek to represent is too transparent for serious argument. The surveillance of the

Army over the civilian sector-a part of society hitherto immune from its control-is a serious charge. It is alleged that the Army maintains files on the membership, ideology, programs, and practices of virtually every activist political group in the country, including groups such as the Southern Christian Leadership Conference, Clergy and Laymen United Against the War in Vietnam, the American Civil Liberties Union, Women's Strike for Peace, and the National Association for the Advancement of Colored People. The Army uses undercover agents to infiltrate these civilian groups and to reach into confidential files of students and other groups. The Army moves as a secret group among civilian audiences, using cameras and electronic ears for surveillance. The data it collects are distributed to civilian officials in state, federal, and local governments and to each military intelligence unit and troop command under the Army's jurisdiction (both here and abroad); and these data are stored in one or more data banks.

Those are the allegations; and the charge is that the purpose and effect of the system of surveillance is to harass and intimidate the respondents and to deter them from exercising their rights of political expression, protest, and dissent 'by invading their privacy, damaging their reputations, adversely affecting their employment and their opportunities for employment, and in other ways.' Their fear is that 'permanent reports of their activities will be maintained in the Army's data bank, and their 'profiles' will appear in the so-called 'Blaklist' and that all of this information will be released to numerous federal and state agencies upon request.'

. . .

One need not wait to sue until he loses his job or until his reputation is defamed. To withhold standing to sue until that time arrives would in practical effect immunize from judicial scrutiny all surveillance activities, regardless of their misuse and their deterrent effect. . . .

The present controversy is not a remote, imaginary conflict. Respondents were targets of the Army's surveillance. First, the surveillance was not casual but massive and comprehensive. Second, the intelligence reports were regularly and widely circulated and were exchanged with reports of the FBI, state and municipal police departments, and the CIA. Third, the Army's surveillance was not collecting material in public records but staking out teams of agents, infiltrating undercover agents, creating command posts inside meetings, posing as press photographers and newsmen, posing as TV newsmen, posing as students, and shadowing public figures.

Finally, we know from the hearings conducted by Senator Ervin that the Army has misused or abused its reporting functions. Thus, Senator Ervin concluded that reports of the Army have been 'taken from the Intelligence Command's highly inaccurate civil disturbance teletype and filed in Army dossiers on persons who have held, or were being considered for, security clearances, thus contaminating what are supposed to be investigative reports with unverified gossip and rumor. This practice directly jeopardized the employment and employment opportunities of persons seeking sensitive positions with the federal government or defense industry.'

Surveillance of civilians is none of the Army's constitutional business and Congress has not undertaken to entrust it with any such function. The fact that since this litigation started the Army's surveillance may have been cut back is not an end of the matter. Whether there has been an actual cutback or whether the announcements are merely a ruse can be determined only after a hearing in the District Court. We are advised by an amicus curiae brief filed by a group of former Army Intelligence Agents that Army surveillance of civilians is rooted in secret programs of long standing.

. . .

This case involves a cancer in our body politic. It is a measure of the disease which afflicts us. Army surveillance, like Army regimentation, is at war with the principles of the First Amendment. Those who already walk submissively will say there is no cause for alarm. But submissiveness is not our heritage. The First Amendment was designed to allow rebellion to remain as our heritage. The Constitution was designed to keep government off the backs of the people. The Bill of Rights was added to keep the precincts of belief and expression, of the press, of political and social activities free from surveillance. The Bill of Rights was designed to keep agents of government and official eavesdroppers away from assemblies of people. The aim was to allow men to be free and independent and to assert their rights against government. There can be no influence more paralyzing of that objective than Army surveillance. When an intelligence officer looks over every noncomformist's shoulder in the library, or walks invisibly by his side in a picket line, or infiltrates his club, the America once extolled as the voice of liberty heard around the world no longer is cast in the image which Jefferson and Madison designed. . . .

2. PROACTIVE SURVEILLANCE BY A CITY POLICE DEPARTMENT AND THE FBI

ALLIANCE TO END REPRESSION v. CITY OF CHICAGO

237 F.3d 799 (7th Cir.2001)

POSNER, CIRCUIT JUDGE.

More than a quarter of a century ago a number of individuals and organizations brought suit under 42 U.S.C. § 1983 against the United States and the City of Chicago, claiming that the FBI's Chicago office and the Chicago Police Department's intelligence division were violating the plaintiffs' First Amendment rights by overly intrusive and improperly motivated investigations of alleged subversive activities. In 1981, before a trial could be held, the defendants agreed to a consent decree, which was approved by then district judge Getzendanner the following year, imposing detailed and onerous restrictions on the defendants' powers of investigation. 561 F.Supp. 537 (N.D.Ill.1982). The City has now asked the district court to modify the decree to make the restrictions that it places on the City less onerous. Fed. R. Civ. P. 60(b)(5). The district court has refused, and the City has appealed, pointing out that the decree is so strict that Judge Getzendanner said she would not have awarded the plaintiffs such draconian relief (but for the defendants' acquiescence) even if they had proved all the allegations of their complaint in a trial. 561 F.Supp. at 551.

The City argues that it has been in compliance with the decree throughout the almost two decades in which the decree has been in force and it points out that during this period the Supreme Court and this court have become ever more emphatic that the federal judiciary must endeavor to return the control of local governmental activities to local government at the earliest possible opportunity compatible with achievement of the objectives of the decree that transferred that control to the federal courts. The City also argues that the culture of local law enforcement and the character of the threats to public safety by ideologically motivated criminals have so far changed as to make much of the decree obsolete and points out that the Supreme Court has adopted a more flexible standard for the modification of decrees entered in institutional reform litigation than the Swift standard of yore. Although the federal government has not joined the City in seeking to modify the decree, the provisions applicable to the FBI are different and were interpreted by us in an earlier phase of this litigation to impose far lighter restrictions on FBI investigations than the district court had interpreted the decree to impose. *Alliance to End Repression v. City of Chicago,* 742 F.2d 1007 (7th Cir.1984) (en banc).

The core of the decree, which the City does not seek to modify, forbids investigations intended to interfere with or deter the exercise of the freedom of expression that the First Amendment protects, and requires the City to commission independent periodic audits of the City's compliance with the decree. The effect of these provisions is to add the threat of civil and criminal contempt to the usual sanctions for infringing civil rights and, through the requirement of the audits, to make it easier to detect such infringements. These are substantial enhancements of the ordinary deterrent effect of constitutional law. *Id.* at 1014–15. They annex swift and severe sanctions to the ordinary tort remedies (mainly 42 U.S.C. § 1983) for violations of that law.

The periphery of the decree, which the City considers insufficiently protective of the public safety and wishes to have lanced, comprises a dizzying array of highly specific restrictions on investigations of potential terrorists and other politically or ideologically motivated criminals. Investigations "directed toward First Amendment conduct," a defined term referring to any investigation likely to involve the collection of information about protected activity or the investigation of anyone engaged in such activity, may be conducted only for the purpose of obtaining evidence of past, present, or impending criminal conduct and only if the Chicago police already have a reasonable suspicion of such conduct. Unless "unavoidably necessary to the investigation of a reasonably suspected crime," the police may not collect information about the political group to which the target of an investigation belongs or about other members of the group or people attending the group's meetings. The investigation must terminate as soon as reasonable suspicion of criminal conduct is dispelled and upon termination all information protected by the First Amendment must be purged from the investigatory file. An investigation may not be conducted on the basis of mere advocacy of violent conduct (what the decree terms "ideological rhetoric"); only a "brief preliminary inquiry" is permitted on that basis and it must cease unless it generates a reasonable suspicion of criminal conduct. Use of undercover informants is strictly limited along with the gathering of information at rallies or other public assemblies of advocates of violence and other political extremists. There is more to the decree, and some qualifications and other nuances that we have omitted, but our summary gives the flavor.

From the 1920s to the 1970s the intelligence division of the Chicago Police Department contained a unit nicknamed the "Red Squad" which spied on, infiltrated, and harassed a wide variety of political groups that included but were not limited to left-and right-wing extremists. Most of the groups, including most of the politically extreme groups, were not only lawful, and engaged in expressive activities protected by the First Amendment, but also harmless. The motives of the Red Squad were largely political and ideological, though they included a legitimate concern with genuine threats to public order. Demonstrations against U.S. participation in the Vietnam War that climaxed in the disruption of the Democratic National Convention in Chicago in 1968, race riots in Chicago and other major cities in the same period, and the contemporaneous criminal activities of the Black Panthers, the Weathermen, and Puerto Rican separatists, all against a backdrop of acute racial and Cold War tensions, political assassinations (notably of President Kennedy, Senator Robert Kennedy, and Martin Luther King, Jr.), and communist subversion, fueled a widespread belief in the need for zealous police activity directed against political militants.

The era in which the Red Squad flourished is history, along with the Red Squad itself. The instabilities of that era have largely disappeared. Fear of communist subversion, so strong a motivator of constitutional infringements in those days, has disappeared along with the Soviet Union and the Cold War. Legal controls over the police, legal sanctions for the infringement of constitutional rights, have multiplied. The culture that created and nourished the Red Squad has evaporated. The consent decree has done its job. To this the plaintiffs reply mainly by pointing us to accusations that during the 1996 Democratic National Convention, the first to be held in Chicago since the disaster of 1968, some Chicago police officers, fearing a repetition, reverted to the old ways and harassed demonstrators. But that was at worst a temporally limited, an isolated, and very much a situation-specific lapse; in its ad hoc, unorganized, and episodic character it resembled not at all the activities of the Red Squad, which were organized, systematic, and protracted.

Mere compliance with a decree over a period of years, the plaintiffs argue, does not in itself justify the lifting of the decree.

The City in any event is asking only that the decree be modified, not that it be abrogated; and its grounds for modification go beyond a mere history of compliance. The City wants flexibility to meet new threats to the safety of Chicago's citizens. In the heyday of the Red Squad, law enforcers from J. Edgar Hoover's FBI on down to the local level in Chicago focused to an unhealthy degree on political dissidents, whose primary activity was advocacy though it sometimes spilled over into violence. Today the concern, prudent and not paranoid, is with ideologically motivated terrorism. The City does not want to resurrect the Red Squad. It wants to be able to keep tabs on incipient terrorist groups. New groups of political extremists, believers in and advocates of violence, form daily around the world. If one forms in or migrates to Chicago, the decree renders the police helpless to do anything to protect the public against the day when the group decides to commit a terrorist act. Until the group goes beyond the advocacy of violence and begins preparatory actions that might create reasonable suspicion of imminent criminal activity, the hands of the police are tied. And if the police have been forbidden to investigate until then, if the investigation cannot begin until the group is well on its way toward the commission of terrorist acts, the investigation may come too late to prevent the acts or to identify the perpetrators. If police get wind that a group of people have begun meeting and discussing the desirability of committing acts of violence in pursuit of an ideological agenda, a due regard for the public safety counsels allowing the police department to monitor the statements of the group's members, to build a file, perhaps to plant an undercover agent.

All this the First Amendment permits (unless the motives of the police are improper or the methods forbidden by the Fourth Amendment or other provisions of federal or state law, see *Alliance to End Repression v. City of Chicago, supra,* 742 F.2d at 1014–15, and cases cited there), but the decree forbids. The decree impedes efforts by the police to cope with the problems of today because earlier generations of police coped improperly with the problems of yesterday. Because of what the Red Squad did many years ago, today's Chicago police are fated unless the decree is modified to labor indefinitely under severe handicaps that other American police are free from. First Amendment rights are secure. But under the decree as written and interpreted, the public safety is insecure and the prerogatives of local government scorned. To continue federal judicial micromanagement of local investigations of domestic and international terrorist activities in Chicago is to undermine the federal system and to trifle with the public safety. Every consideration favors modification; the City has made a compelling case for the modification that it seeks.

Modification is not abrogation. The modified decree will leave the Chicago police under considerably greater constraints than the police forces of other cities. A violation of the constitutional rights of any person whom the Chicago police investigate will be a violation of the decree and not just of the Constitution itself and so will invite summary punishment by the exercise of the contempt power, while the requirement of outside audits will make it more difficult for the Chicago police than for their counterparts in the other big cities to commit constitutional violations undetected.

The judgment of the district court is reversed and the case remanded with instructions to make the modifications in the consent decree that the City has requested.

QUESTIONS AND NOTES

1. The original consent decree settlement in the Alliance to End Repression case contained the following provisions:

3.4. The parties agree that the following general principles apply to FBI activities relating to the domestic activities of United States persons:

(a) The FBI, in conducting domestic security investigations and inquiries, shall be concerned only with conduct and only such conduct as is forbidden by a criminal law of the United States, or by a state criminal law when authorized by federal statute. The FBI shall not conduct an investigation solely on the basis of activities protected by the First Amendment of the Constitution of the United States, or on the lawful exercise of any right secured by the Constitution or laws of the United States.

(b) The FBI, in investigating United States persons, shall not employ any technique designed to impair their lawful and constitutionally protected political conduct or to defame the character or reputation of a United States person.

(c) The FBI shall conduct its investigations with minimal intrusion consistent with the need to collect information or evidence in a timely and effective manner, and shall conduct investigations in a manner reasonably designed to minimize unnecessary collection and recording of information about the lawful exercise of First Amendment rights.

3.5. In return for the release of all claims, as more fully set forth in Paragraph 3.8, below, the Attorney General and the Director of the FBI, on behalf of themselves, their successors, and their subordinates, agree that:

(a) Any electronic surveillance activities in the City of Chicago shall be in accordance with the Constitution and applicable federal statutes, including 18 U.S.C. §§ 2510–20 (1976) and 50 U.S.C. §§ 1801–11 (Supp. II 1978).

(b) They shall not conduct in the City of Chicago any warrantless unconsented physical searches in domestic security investigations, any unlawful unconsented physical searches of premises or property of U.S. persons in foreign intelligence collection or foreign counterintelligence investigations, any unlawful entries that constitute searches under the Fourth Amendment, or any unlawful disruption or harassment of the lawful activities of any United States person. Nothing in this subsection shall prohibit a warrantless search in circumstances in which a warrant is not required to conduct a search for law enforcement purposes. As used in this subsection the term "unconsented physical searches" does not apply to a search for the purpose of placing, maintaining, or removing authorized electronic surveillance devices or conducting surveys in connection therewith; or to the receipt by the FBI of information, property or materials furnished by individuals acting on their own initiative, without direction or request by the FBI, regardless of the manner of acquisition.

(c) Any of the following investigative activities in domestic security investigations or in foreign intelligence collection or foreign counterintelligence investigations concerning U.S. persons shall comply with all applicable federal statutes, Presidential Executive Orders, written Departmental or Bureau regulations, guidelines and other procedures established in accordance with such statutes or Executive Orders, including but not limited to the procedures and instructions listed in para. 2.1 above. The statutes, Executive Orders, regulations, guidelines and procedures referred to in the preceding sentence are those in effect on the effective date of this Joint Stipulation.

(1) Physical or photographic surveillance of any U.S. person in the City of Chicago not employed by the Department of Justice.

(2) Participation in any organization in the City of Chicago by FBI personnel or informants or assets without disclosing their intelligence affiliation to appropriate officials in the organization; and

(3) The acquisition, dissemination and storage of information about U.S. persons in the City of Chicago not employed by the Department of Justice.

3.6. Any provision of Paragraph 3.5 shall be superseded by:

(a) Any future federal statute or Presidential Executive Order specifically authorizing or directing the Attorney General or the Director of the FBI, or their subordinates, to utilize any investigative techniques described in Paragraph 3.5, or

(b) Any future written Departmental or Bureau regulation, guideline or other procedure relating to the use of the investigative techniques described in Paragraph 3.5, which is established in accordance with and is consistent with such statute or Presidential Executive Order, or

(c) Any future or amended written Departmental or Bureau regulation, guideline or other procedure relating to the use of the investigative techniques described in Paragraph 3.5(c), which is established in accordance with and is consistent with an existing statute or Presidential Executive Order or pursuant to the Attorney General's supervisory responsibilities to manage and direct the activities of the Department of Justice,

Provided, that future or amended written Departmental or Bureau regulations, guidelines or other procedures, or conduct relating to the use of investigative techniques described in Paragraph 3.5 shall be in accordance with the principles stated in Paragraph 3.4, and the applicable provisions of federal statutes and the United States Constitution.

2. Are the provisions of the consent decree, reproduced in note 1, above, consistent with the Mukasey Guidelines and the DIOG or do they impose greater restrictions than do those guidelines?

3. Is a different balance or tone struck in the Mukasey Guidelines than in the police practices that led to the consent decree? Consider: In 1984, several years after the consent decree was entered in the Alliance to End Repression case, the district judge issued an order, 561 F.Supp. 575 (N.D.Ill. 1983), enjoining the FBI from applying a provision of new Attorney General Guidelines on the ground that it was inconsistent with the consent decree:

> For the reasons stated, defendants are hereby permanently enjoined from implementing within the City of Chicago the following provision found in the Attorney General's Guidelines on General Crimes, Racketeering Enterprises and Domestic Security/Terrorism Investigations promulgated March 7, 1983:

> When, however, statements advocate criminal activity ... an investigation under these Guidelines may be warranted unless it is apparent, from the circumstances or the context in which the statements are made, that there is no prospect of harm.

4. In another one of the many opinions in this 30 year odyssey of litigation, Judge Posner reversed the district judge's ruling described in note 3 above, 742 F.2d 1007 (7th Cir.1984), stating:

> We understand the plaintiffs' concern with the repressive effect of prolonged and intrusive investigations of inoffensive groups and individuals. But their concern does not require that paragraph 3.4(a) be interpreted to protect organizations *with violent aims* from such investigations. The organizations that the decree sought to protect, organizations such as the ACLU and the NAACP, do not go around making threats to commit violent acts, and are not the acorns from which grow such trees as the FALN, the Posse Comitatus, the White Knights of the Ku Klux Klan, the Black Liberation Army, the New World Liberation Front, the Republic of New Africa, the Weather Underground, the Jewish Armed Resistance, Omega 9, and other menacing groups. ... Nor should the plaintiffs worry that unless Judge Getzendanner's injunction stands, overzealous government officials will interpret "statements advocat[ing] criminal activity" in the sentence she enjoined in the Smith Guidelines so broadly as to embrace the harmless statements of people whose politics the officials happen to dislike. That would be a reckless interpretation, especially since the Guidelines do not authorize the FBI to base a domestic security/terrorist investigation on the advocacy of *non*-violent crimes such as draft resistance—advocacy that might conceivably if improbably be imputed to an organization like the ACLU by hostile law-enforcement officers. It still would not be an organization that advocated political or

social change through violence; passive resistance and civil disobedience are nonviolent.

But if despite all this some law enforcers do misread the Smith Guidelines as authorizing them to resume the abuses that led to this lawsuit in the first place, they will, of course, be violating the consent decree. Whether intelligently or stupidly interpreted the Smith Guidelines confer no immunities and do not supersede the decree (except for the dispensation in ¶ 3.6, not in issue here, that permits new guidelines to supersede parts of ¶ 3.5, which relate to the techniques rather than purposes of investigations). Those who follow them are not thereby raised above the law; and the plaintiffs' lawyers are busy monitoring compliance with the decree to make sure the new guidelines do not result in investigations that violate the decree.

Moreover, the sentence the district court enjoined is not the only sentence in the Smith Guidelines that defines the scope of FBI domestic security investigations. It says that an investigation "may be warranted," but does not explain when it *would* be warranted. For that you must go elsewhere in the Guidelines—to the provision that states:

> A domestic security/terrorism investigation may be initiated when the facts or circumstances reasonably indicate that two or more persons are engaged in an enterprise for the purpose of furthering political or social goals wholly or in part through activities that involve force or violence and a violation of the criminal laws of the United States.... In determining whether an investigation should be conducted, the FBI shall consider all of the circumstances including (1) the magnitude of the threatened harm; (2) the likelihood it will occur; (3) the immediacy of the threat; and (4) the danger to privacy and free expression posed by an investigation.

Thus, before the FBI can be authorized to investigate, it is required to assess the magnitude, likelihood, and imminence of the threatened harm from the activities to be investigated (and as is evident from the first sentence in the quoted passage, the harm must be of a type that the government is entitled to prevent though its criminal laws). Having been directed by the Guidelines to make such an assessment, the FBI is not free to ignore the results.

The Smith Guidelines, like the Levi Guidelines before them, are nationwide in their intended application. We doubt that any neutral observer would think it appropriate that the FBI should be governed by other than a uniform national set of investigatory standards—that it should operate under one set of constraints everywhere but Chicago, and under another and tighter set in Chicago, so that this city can become a sanctuary for nascent terrorist organizations. To some extent the FBI is unavoidably under a tighter rein in Chicago than elsewhere, because of the consent decree, which applies only to Chicago. But there is no reason to magnify the disparity by looking for conflict between two sets of general language—the general principles of the decree and the general principles of the Smith Guidelines. Should they conflict in practice there will be time to force revision of the Guidelines. It would be different if the

Guidelines and the decree were completely irreconcilable on their face. They are not.

. . .

A due regard for the separation of powers, the flexibility of equity, the ambiguity of the decree, the generality of the new Justice Department guidelines, the sensitivity and importance of the subject matter, and the limitations of judicial competence argues against precipitating a premature confrontation between the judicial and executive branches in a setting where inevitably some people will say, with pardonable exaggeration, that the federal judiciary is playing fast and loose with the public safety. Fine-tuning investigative guidelines is the responsibility of the executive branch, not us. Our duty is to enforce the decree. Any actual as distinct from purely verbal threat to compliance with the decree lies in the future; we decline to anticipate that the Justice Department will so interpret the new FBI guidelines as to violate the district court's decree.

We do not depreciate the abuses of police power that led to the decree—abuses that were part of a national pattern that included such grotesque incidents as the following: after Martin Luther King was "named 'Man of the Year' by *Time* magazine, the FBI decided to 'take him off' his pedestal,' [']reduce him completely in influence,' and select and promote its own candidate to 'assume the role of the leadership of the Negro people.' " . . . These abuses ought not be forgotten. But neither do we want to emulate the Bourbon kings, of whom it was said that they learned nothing and forgot nothing. The abuses that gave rise to this suit ended a decade ago, and much has changed since then, including the management of the Bureau, whose present director is a former federal circuit judge, and the amount of supervision of the FBI by the Attorney General, which, as the issuance of published guidelines suggests, is greater than it used to be. Also, although the number of bombings and other violent acts by domestic terrorist organizations has not risen over this period, public concern with domestic terrorism has risen—which is understandable considering the continued rise in international terrorism and the increasing lethality of the weapons available to terrorists. . . . By reading the critical sentence in the decree as prohibiting improperly *motivated* investigations (other parts of the decree, not in issue in this appeal, prohibit improper investigative techniques), we can reconcile the decree and the new guidelines, maintain a proper separation of powers, yet protect the First Amendment rights of the plaintiffs and the other class members.

. . . If the consent decree will bear an alternative interpretation it ought to be given one.

The order of the district court is reversed with directions to dissolve the injunction.

5. In still another incarnation of the Alliance to End Repression litigation, Judge Posner denied a claim by the class representatives of the plaintiffs in the case for more than $1 million in attorney fees for services rendered between 1994 and 2001: for services rendered in two proceedings for contempt of the original decree which failed and for opposing the modification of the

decree, which opposition also failed; and for efforts to monitor the City's compliance with the decree. Alliance to End Repression v. City of Chicago, 356 F.3d 767 (7th Cir.2004).

6. The modified consent decree at issue in the Alliance to End Repression v. City of Chicago line of cases was finally dissolved with the consent of the parties, some 35 years after the litigation began. See Alliance To End Repression v. City of Chicago, 328 F.Appx. 339, 2009 WL 2015154 (7th Cir.). Also see ACLU v. City of Chicago, 2008 WL 4450304 (N.D. Ill.) (not reported in F.Supp. 2d). But litigation growing out of the modified consent decree has continued, even after the dissolution of the decree, involving lawsuits alleging violation of the decree while it was still in force. *See ACLU v. City of Chicago,* 2009 WL 2409907 (N.D.Ill.).

7. Lawsuits similar to the one that led to the Chicago consent decree have been litigated in other cities. For example, in New York City, a suit similar to that involved in the Chicago series of cases has also been litigated. The city sought to be able to conduct undercover investigations of political groups where there is no evidence of criminality. In 1971, a settlement had been reached as the outcome of a lawsuit filed by the Black Panther Party, which provided that the police must obtain approval from a three person panel if they wish to conduct undercover investigations of political groups. Much later, the city sued to remove the requirement that they must first obtain permission from the panel. (Judge Charles Haight agreed to a request by the City of New York and New York Police Department to modify various restrictions on political surveillance, but he left in place a three member oversight board that can investigate specific complaints). Benjamin Weiser, Rules Eased for Surveillance of New York Groups, N.Y.Times.com, February 12, 2003.

Subsequently, in two decisions, Judge Haight modified the existing guidelines as requested by the City Police Department. See Handschu v. Special Services Division, 273 F. Supp. 2d 327 (S.D.N.Y. 2003) and 288 F. Supp. 2d 404 (S.D. N.Y. 2003). Several months later, however, he handed down the following decision in which he criticized the NYPD for the way in which a police inspector questioned persons arrested at a rally protesting the U.S. invasion of Iraq, and as a result he modestly strengthened the consent decree. See Handschu v. Special Services Division, 288 F. Supp. 2d 411 (S.D.N.Y. 2003). Subsequent litigation in the matter revolved around an underlying substantive question—whether a purpose to investigate political activity or a police purpose was involved when the police photographed or videotaped a demonstration and whether the police conduct violated NYPD Guidelines or the Constitution. See Handschu v. Special Services Division, 2008 WL 515695 (S.D.N.Y.) (not reported in F.Supp. 2d).

See also Handschu v. Special Services Division, 2007 WL 1711775 (S.D.N.Y.2007) in which Judge Haight concluded a long opinion with the following:

> ... [V]iolations of Modified *Handschu* and the NYPD Guidelines must rise to a constitutional level for contempt of this Court to issue. In general injunctive relief is also available only if there is a constitutional violation; however, if it were shown that the NYPD had adopted a policy

that disregards the NYPD Guidelines, the Court may exercise its continuing equitable powers in granting appropriate injunctive relief. The NYPD Guidelines only apply where the police have the purpose of investigating political activity.

In the same case, Judge Haight also opined in footnote 19:

> . . . [E]ven if the purpose of investigating political activity operates in conjunction with a permissible operational objective listed in the Order, the NYPD Guidelines are triggered and their procedures must be followed. If, for instance, an officer wished to videotape a demonstration for the purpose of deterring terrorism, he would still need to follow the procedures of the NYPD Guidelines if he also possessed the purpose of collecting information or evidence about political activity as a means of achieving his counter-terrorism goal. Merely having a counter-terrorism purpose does not get him out from under the yoke of the Guidelines where they apply. To the extent that the Note to Order 47 has not been interpreted in this fashion, but rather to suggest that the presence of a non-investigative purpose excuses the officer from application to the Intelligence Division, it would be misinforming officers about their obligations.

8. On October 30, 2007, the Los Angeles Police Department announced a plan to map Muslim communities in Los Angeles in order to understand the Muslim community and deepen the engagement between LAPD and Muslim citizens. The commanding officer of LAPD's Counter–Terrorism Bureau indicated that the mapping was intended to lay out the geographic locations of the many different Muslim population groups around Los Angeles and take a deeper look at their history, demographics, language, culture, ethnic breakdown, socio-economic status and social interactions. The goal was to identify communities within the larger Muslim community that might be "susceptible to violent, ideologically-based extremism." The LAPD would then use an information-based approach in connection with its outreach efforts to identify community problems and find possible solutions. See LA Times online edition, November 10, 2007. Would such a mapping of Muslim communities be permissible under the DIOG and the Mukasey Guidelines?

The proposed mapping created a strong negative reaction in the Muslim community and civil liberties groups and within two weeks after being announced, the planned mapping program was shelved, while the LAPD stated that it would continue with its outreach efforts. See MSNBC on line: US News, Crime and Courts, November 15, 2007.

9. In October, 2007, officials from several local police departments around the country, including, New York City, Kansas City, Miami–Dade and Los Angeles, testified before the Homeland Security Committee of the U.S. Senate (Joe Lieberman, Conn., Chair) reporting about programs they had begun, to address and counter terrorism. For example, the Kansas City Police Department reported that its police officers are being taught about Islamic culture, concepts of Jihad, and cultivating resources in the community to assist them in identifying indications of terrorist activity.

10. In August, 2007, the New York City Police Department issued a 90 page report from its Intelligence Division entitled, "Radicalization in the

West: The Home-grown Threat," analyzing what was described as a trend of radicalization that motivated unremarkable residents or citizens to become terrorism perpetrators. The report concluded that intervention at as early a point as possible was necessary to break the radicalization pattern. For a critique of the N.Y. report see the Capital Cloak blog, August 16, 2007, /o-be-wise.blogspot.com/2007/08/nypd-shoots-own-foot-with-terror-report.html.

11.   Are the local police activities described in notes 8–10, supra, appropriate activities for the police to undertake? A threat to civil liberties? Likely to be effective approaches for police departments to take in trying to deter and prevent terrorism?

12.   Litigation regarding police handling of demonstrations continues in New York City. One of the latest rounds revolves around a discovery motion in a suit brought against the City by demonstrators.

DINLER v. CITY OF NEW YORK

607 F.3d 923 (2d Cir. 2010)

The question presented is whether we should issue a writ of mandamus to overturn an order of the United States District Court for the Southern District of New York (Richard J. Sullivan, *Judge*) granting a motion to compel the production of certain sensitive intelligence reports prepared by undercover officers of the New York City Police Department ("NYPD"). In answering that question, we are called upon to examine the circumstances in which the so-called "law enforcement privilege" must yield to the needs of a party seeking discovery in a civil action.

Plaintiffs-respondents . . . are protesters and other persons who were arrested, detained, and fingerprinted after demonstrating at the 2004 Republican National Convention ("RNC") in New York City. They brought the underlying suits under 42 U.S.C. § 1983 and state law claiming that their arrest and treatment at the hands of the NYPD violated the United States Constitution and New York law.

During pretrial discovery proceedings, plaintiffs brought a motion to compel the City to produce roughly 1800 pages of confidential reports created by undercover NYPD officers who were investigating potential security threats in the months before the RNC. (Using the NYPD's parlance, we refer to these 1800 pages of reports as the "Field Reports" or simply the "Reports.") The City opposed the motion to compel by asserting, among other things, that the documents were protected from disclosure by the law enforcement privilege.

Magistrate Judge James C. Francis IV, . . . granted plaintiffs' motion to compel. The City filed objections to that decision with Judge Sullivan, and Judge Sullivan affirmed Magistrate Judge Francis's order in its entirety.

. . .

. . . [W]e hold as follows:

(a) The City has met its burden of showing that the law enforcement privilege applies to the Field Reports because the Reports, even as redacted by the District Court, contain detailed information about the NYPD's undercover "law enforcement techniques and procedures."

(b) Plaintiffs do not have a "compelling need" for the Field Reports because the Reports do not contradict, undermine, or otherwise cast doubt upon the End User Reports-the documents upon which the City will rely in defending its arrest and fingerprinting procedures.

(c) Because plaintiffs do not have a "compelling need," they have not overcome the "strong presumption" against lifting the law enforcement privilege.

(5) The City's right to a writ of mandamus is "clear and indisputable" because the District Court committed three errors that amounted to a "clear abuse of discretion," if not a "judicial usurpation of power."

(a) The District Court indisputably committed legal error when it failed to apply a strong presumption against lifting the law enforcement privilege.

(b) The District Court indisputably committed legal error when it failed to require that plaintiffs show a compelling need for the Field Reports.

(c) The District Court indisputably made a clearly erroneous assessment of the evidence when it found that plaintiffs' need for the Field Reports outweighed the public's interest in maintaining the integrity of the NYPD's undercover operations and the safety of NYPD officers.

For the foregoing reasons, despite the admirable care of the District Court in dealing with these sensitive and complex questions, we grant the City's petition for a writ of mandamus; we vacate the December 10, 2009 order of the District Court; and we instruct the District Court to deny plaintiffs' motion to compel the production of the Field Reports.

CHAPTER 5

ELECTRONIC SURVEILLANCE

■ ■ ■

Among the numerous ways in which the federal government is making use of its limited resources in enforcement efforts against terrorism, electronic surveillance has loomed large. Obtaining judicial approval for electronic surveillance directed against ordinary crime requires that the agents have information roughly equivalent to that which would be required were they seeking judicial approval of a search warrant. In such instances, they already would be directing their efforts against an individual or individuals with probable cause to believe that a crime had been committed and the individual(s) in question had committed it.

The basis for obtaining judicial approval of electronic surveillance directed against terrorism is different; we examine the differences in this chapter. For present purposes, it is sufficient to note that the terrorism electronic surveillance "warrant" gives government agencies authority to seek terrorism intelligence, that is, information that will help to prevent future terrorism offenses and may not require focused evidence of specific criminality like a traditional search warrant. Because less is required than for a search warrant, it is also useful to compare the basis on which government agents can seek approval for terrorism-related electronic surveillance with the basis on which the FBI can engage in the type of proactive inquiries, surveillance or participating in public meetings, attending mosques, etc., discussed in the previous chapter. Judicial approval for terrorism-related electronic surveillance may be viewed as lying somewhere in between the basis for traditional search warrants and the aforementioned proactive FBI inquiries.

Much of the terrorism-related electronic surveillance engaged in by the government is conducted by the FBI under the judicial approval process established by the Foreign Intelligence Surveillance Act (FISA). FISA as originally enacted was intended to deal with electronic surveillances conducted within the United States. Additionally, however, it was known that various kinds of electronic surveillance were conducted by the National Security Agency (NSA) abroad, without obtaining judicial approval under FISA, or otherwise. While we only have limited information about FISA surveillances, we know even less about NSA eavesdropping, which is very highly classified. The general assumption, however, has been that the NSA is conducting its national security-related electronic surveillance outside of the United States.

In 2005, the New York Times reported that, without obtaining judicial approval under the FISA statute or otherwise, the NSA had been conducting terrorism-related electronic surveillance of conversations between persons in the U.S. and persons abroad, later determined to be under a program authorized by the President—the Terrorism Surveillance Program (TSP). A controversy developed in the wake of this disclosure that was played out in the Congress, in the media and among scholars and which eventually led to the enactment of the FISA Amendments Act of 2008.

The organization of the materials in this chapter reflects the foregoing description and history. Subsection A, the lengthiest part, deals in detail with the FISA, largely as it applies within the United States, and the various issues and comparisons that it engenders. Subsection B treats the TSP controversy as well as some other broad-gauge electronic surveillance programs that became known during the same period and also includes materials relating to the Bush administration's claims of presidential authority for these various programs. Subsection C reproduces the 2008 FISA Amendments Act, and addresses the issues that are raised by this statute.

A. THE FOREIGN INTELLIGENCE SURVEILLANCE ACT (FISA) AND ELECTRONIC SURVEILLANCE WITHIN THE UNITED STATES

1. INTRODUCTION

Electronic surveillance of private conversations and physical searches of private premises by government agents in the United States must comply with the requirements of the Fourth Amendment. In the federal system, electronic surveillance taking place as part of an ordinary criminal investigation must also comply with relevant federal statutes. The statutory requirements establishing a warrant procedure for this type of electronic surveillance are set down in Title III of the Omnibus Crime Control and Safe Streets Act of 1968, codified at 18 U.S.C § 2510 et seq.

Ten years later, In 1978, the Foreign Intelligence Surveillance Act was enacted: It gave the Attorney General a broad power to authorize, without court order, electronic surveillance to acquire foreign intelligence information if it is directed solely at communications exclusively between or among foreign powers. However, if the surveillance is directed at agents of foreign powers or is likely to acquire the contents of foreign intelligence communications involving a United States person (defined as a U.S. citizen or a permanent resident alien), the FISA established a procedure for obtaining approval by a special secret court. This warrant-type approval procedure involves the application of standards that differ from those provided in Title III, supra.

It may be useful here to pause for a moment and back up, to provide a bit of the history and background to the FISA. Until 1968, there was no federal legislation on the books providing a judicial authorization procedure for electronic surveillance by federal agents. However, beginning probably with the presidency of Franklin D. Roosevelt, some electronic surveillance without court approval was conducted by government agents under the authority of the Executive Branch, that is, the President, in aid of "national security." With the enactment of the FISA statute in 1978, it was thought that there was no longer a need for such warrantless national security electronic surveillance within the United States (apart from that which was specifically authorized under FISA).

Beginning with the Kennedy administration in the early 1960's, Congress each year had considered legislative bills proposing a judicial authorization procedure for electronic surveillance based on a probable cause standard, modeled generally after the procedure and standards used to obtain warrants for physical searches. Finally, in 1968, legislation on this subject was enacted. 18 U.S.C. §§ 2510–2522 established a judicial approval procedure for electronic surveillance in the investigation of ordinary crimes. In one of those provisions, § 2511(3), it was provided that nothing in this statute "shall limit the constitutional power of the President" to protect the national security of the United States.

Subsequently, the Supreme Court in United States v. United States District Court, 407 U.S. 297 (1972), ruled: that the government lacked the power to conduct electronic surveillance without judicial approval in "domestic security" cases; that Congress could establish standards governing electronic surveillance in such cases; and that these could differ from those applied in ordinary crime cases. The Court expressly did not rule, however, whether the government could engage in surveillance of foreign governments or their agents without judicial approval.

Six years later in 1978, enactment of the FISA established procedures and standards for judicial authorization of electronic surveillance by government agents to obtain foreign intelligence information. Viewed against this historical backdrop, rather than expanding federal authority, the FISA can be seen as a statute that reined in the Executive Branch, regulating a kind of electronic eavesdropping that previously had been, on occasion, authorized by the President and had been uncontrolled by the judiciary. Viewed, however, from a different perspective—the kind of authority applied in ordinary criminal cases under Title III—the standards for authorizing electronic eavesdropping under FISA do expand federal eavesdropping authority.

2. THE FISA STATUTE

The FISA statute is found at 50 U.S.C. § 1801 et seq. Section 1803 provides for appointment by the Chief Justice of a court of eleven district judges to hear ex parte applications by the government and to approve orders for foreign intelligence electronic surveillance anywhere in the

United States. Section 1803 also provides for appointment of a three-judge court to review denials of applications made under the Act and for review of the decisions of that court through a petition for a writ of certiorari to the Supreme Court. The proceedings of the FISA court and the FISA reviewing court are held in secret, and the opinions of these courts are normally not published. The main provisions of the FISA statute are reproduced below.

§ 1801. Definitions

As used in this subchapter:

(a) "Foreign power" means—

(1) a foreign government or any component thereof, whether or not recognized by the United States;

(2) a faction of a foreign nation or nations, not substantially composed of United States persons;

(3) an entity that is openly acknowledged by a foreign government or governments to be directed and controlled by such foreign government or governments;

(4) a group engaged in international terrorism or activities in preparation therefor;

(5) a foreign-based political organization, not substantially composed of United States persons;

(6) an entity that is directed and controlled by a foreign government or governments; or

(7) an entity not substantially composed of United States persons that is engaged in the international proliferation of weapons of mass destruction.

(b) "Agent of a foreign power" means—

(1) any person other than a United States person, who—

(A) acts in the United States as an officer or employee of a foreign power, or as a member of a foreign power as defined in subsection (a)(4) of this section;

(B) acts for or on behalf of a foreign power which engages in clandestine intelligence activities in the United States contrary to the interests of the United States, when the circumstances of such person's presence in the United States indicate that such person may engage in such activities in the United States, or when such person knowingly aids or abets any person in the conduct of such activities or knowingly conspires with any person to engage in such activities;

(C) engages in international terrorism or activities in preparation therefore;

(D) engages in the international proliferation of weapons of mass destruction, or activities in preparation therefor; or

(E) engages in the international proliferation of weapons of mass destruction, or activities in preparation therefor for or on behalf of a foreign power; or

(2) any person who—

(A) knowingly engages in clandestine intelligence gathering activities for or on behalf of a foreign power, which activities involve or may involve a violation of the criminal statutes of the United States;

(B) pursuant to the direction of an intelligence service or network of a foreign power, knowingly engages in any other clandestine intelligence activities for or on behalf of such foreign power, which activities involve or are about to involve a violation of the criminal statutes of the United States;

(C) knowingly engages in sabotage or international terrorism, or activities that are in preparation therefor, for or on behalf of a foreign power;

(D) knowingly enters the United States under a false or fraudulent identity for or on behalf of a foreign power or, while in the United States, knowingly assumes a false or fraudulent identity for or on behalf of a foreign power; or

(E) knowingly aids or abets any person in the conduct of activities described in subparagraph (A), (B), or (C) or knowingly conspires with any person to engage in activities described in subparagraph (A), (B), or (C).

(c) "International terrorism" means activities that—

(1) involve violent acts or acts dangerous to human life that are a violation of the criminal laws of the United States or of any State, or that would be a criminal violation if committed within the jurisdiction of the United States or any State;

(2) appear to be intended—

(A) to intimidate or coerce a civilian population;

(B) to influence the policy of a government by intimidation or coercion; or

(C) to affect the conduct of a government by assassination or kidnapping; and

(3) occur totally outside the United States, or transcend national boundaries in terms of the means by which they are accomplished, the persons they appear intended to coerce or intimidate, or the locale in which their perpetrators operate or seek asylum.

(d) "Sabotage" means activities that involve a violation of chapter 105 of Title 18, or that would involve such a violation if committed against the United States.

(e) "Foreign intelligence information" means—

(1) information that relates to, and if concerning a United States person is necessary to, the ability of the United States to protect against—

(A) actual or potential attack or other grave hostile acts of a foreign power or an agent of a foreign power;

(B) sabotage, international terrorism, or the international proliferation of weapons of mass destruction by a foreign power or an agent of a foreign power; or

(C) clandestine intelligence activities by an intelligence service or network of a foreign power or by an agent of a foreign power; or

(2) information with respect to a foreign power or foreign territory that relates to, and if concerning a United States person is necessary to—

(A) the national defense or the security of the United States; or

(B) the conduct of the foreign affairs of the United States.

(f) "Electronic surveillance" means—

(1) the acquisition by an electronic, mechanical, or other surveillance device of the contents of any wire or radio communication sent by or intended to be received by a particular, known United States person who is in the United States, if the contents are acquired by intentionally targeting that United States person, under circumstances in which a person has a reasonable expectation of privacy and a warrant would be required for law enforcement purposes;

(2) the acquisition by an electronic, mechanical, or other surveillance device of the contents of any wire communication to or from a person in the United States, without the consent of any party thereto, if such acquisition occurs in the United States, but does not include the acquisition of those communications of computer trespassers that would be permissible under section 2511(2)(i) of Title 18;

(3) the intentional acquisition by an electronic, mechanical, or other surveillance device of the contents of any radio communication, under circumstances in which a person has a reasonable expectation of privacy and a warrant would be required for law

enforcement purposes, and if both the sender and all intended recipients are located within the United States; or

(4) the installation or use of an electronic, mechanical, or other surveillance device in the United States for monitoring to acquire information, other than from a wire or radio communication, under circumstances in which a person has a reasonable expectation of privacy and a warrant would be required for law enforcement purposes.

(g) "Attorney General" means the Attorney General of the United States (or Acting Attorney General), the Deputy Attorney General, or, upon the designation of the Attorney General, the Assistant Attorney General designated as the Assistant Attorney General for National Security under section 507A of title 28, United States Code.

(h) "Minimization procedures", with respect to electronic surveillance, means—

(1) specific procedures, which shall be adopted by the Attorney General, that are reasonably designed in light of the purpose and technique of the particular surveillance, to minimize the acquisition and retention, and prohibit the dissemination, of nonpublicly available information concerning unconsenting United States persons consistent with the need of the United States to obtain, produce, and disseminate foreign intelligence information;

(2) procedures that require that nonpublicly available information, which is not foreign intelligence information, as defined in subsection (e)(1) of this section, shall not be disseminated in a manner that identifies any United States person, without such person's consent, unless such person's identity is necessary to understand foreign intelligence information or assess its importance;

(3) notwithstanding paragraphs (1) and (2), procedures that allow for the retention and dissemination of information that is evidence of a crime which has been, is being, or is about to be committed and that is to be retained or disseminated for law enforcement purposes; and

(4) notwithstanding paragraphs (1), (2), and (3), with respect to any electronic surveillance approved pursuant to section 1802(a) of this title, procedures that require that no contents of any communication to which a United States person is a party shall be disclosed, disseminated, or used for any purpose or retained for longer than 72 hours unless a court order under section 1805 of this title is obtained or unless the Attorney General determines that the information indicates a threat of death or serious bodily harm to any person.

(i) "United States person" means a citizen of the United States, an alien lawfully admitted for permanent residence (as defined in section 1101(a)(20) of Title 8), an unincorporated association a substantial number of members of which are citizens of the United States or aliens lawfully admitted for permanent residence, or a corporation which is incorporated in the United States, but does not include a corporation or an association which is a foreign power, as defined in subsection (a)(1), (2), or (3) of this section.

(j) "United States", when used in a geographic sense, means all areas under the territorial sovereignty of the United States and the Trust Territory of the Pacific Islands.

(k) "Aggrieved person" means a person who is the target of an electronic surveillance or any other person whose communications or activities were subject to electronic surveillance.

(l) "Wire communication" means any communication while it is being carried by a wire, cable, or other like connection furnished or operated by any person engaged as a common carrier in providing or operating such facilities for the transmission of interstate or foreign communications.

(m) "Person" means any individual, including any officer or employee of the Federal Government, or any group, entity, association, corporation, or foreign power.

(n) "Contents", when used with respect to a communication, includes any information concerning the identity of the parties to such communication or the existence, substance, purport, or meaning of that communication.

(o) "State" means any State of the United States, the District of Columbia, the Commonwealth of Puerto Rico, the Trust Territory of the Pacific Islands, and any territory or possession of the United States.

(p) "Weapon of mass destruction" means—

    (1) any explosive, incendiary, or poison gas device that is designed, intended, or has the capability to cause a mass casualty incident;

    (2) any weapon that is designed, intended, or has the capability to cause death or serious bodily injury to a significant number of persons through the release, dissemination, or impact of toxic or poisonous chemicals or their precursors;

    (3) any weapon involving a biological agent, toxin, or vector (as such terms are defined in section 178 of Title 18) that is designed, intended, or has the capability to cause death, illness, or serious bodily injury to a significant number of persons; or

    (4) any weapon that is designed, intended, or has the capability to release radiation or radioactivity causing death, illness, or serious bodily injury to a significant number of persons.

§ 1802. Electronic surveillance authorization without court order; certification by Attorney General; reports to Congressional committees; transmittal under seal; duties and compensation of communication common carrier; applications; jurisdiction of court

(a)(1) Notwithstanding any other law, the President, through the Attorney General, may authorize electronic surveillance without a court order under this subchapter to acquire foreign intelligence information for periods of up to one year if the Attorney General certifies in writing under oath that—

    (A) the electronic surveillance is solely directed at—

        (i) the acquisition of the contents of communications transmitted by means of communications used exclusively between or among foreign powers, as defined in section 1801(a)(1), (2), or (3) of this title; or

        (ii) the acquisition of technical intelligence, other than the spoken communications of individuals, from property or premises under the open and exclusive control of a foreign power, as defined in section 1801(a)(1), (2), or (3) of this title;

    (B) there is no substantial likelihood that the surveillance will acquire the contents of any communication to which a United States person is a party; and

    (C) the proposed minimization procedures with respect to such surveillance meet the definition of minimization procedures under section 1801(h) of this title; and if the Attorney General reports such minimization procedures and any changes thereto to the House Permanent Select Committee on Intelligence and the Senate Select Committee on Intelligence at least thirty days prior to their effective date, unless the Attorney General determines immediate action is required and notifies the committees immediately of such minimization procedures and the reason for their becoming effective immediately.

(2) An electronic surveillance authorized by this subsection may be conducted only in accordance with the Attorney General's certification and the minimization procedures adopted by him. The Attorney General shall assess compliance with such procedures and shall report such assessments to the House Permanent Select Committee on Intelligence and the Senate Select Committee on Intelligence under the provisions of section 1808(a) of this title.

(3) The Attorney General shall immediately transmit under seal to the court established under section 1803(a) of this title a copy of his certification. Such certification shall be maintained under security measures established by the Chief Justice with the concurrence of the Attorney General, in consultation with the Director of Central Intelligence, and shall remain sealed unless—

(A) an application for a court order with respect to the surveillance is made under sections 1801(h)(4) and 1804 of this title; or

(B) the certification is necessary to determine the legality of the surveillance under section 1806(f) of this title.

(4) With respect to electronic surveillance authorized by this subsection, the Attorney General may direct a specified communication common carrier to—

(A) furnish all information, facilities, or technical assistance necessary to accomplish the electronic surveillance in such a manner as will protect its secrecy and produce a minimum of interference with the services that such carrier is providing its customers; and

(B) maintain under security procedures approved by the Attorney General and the Director of Central Intelligence any records concerning the surveillance or the aid furnished which such carrier wishes to retain.

The Government shall compensate, at the prevailing rate, such carrier for furnishing such aid.

(b) Applications for a court order under this subchapter are authorized if the President has, by written authorization, empowered the [Attorney] General to approve applications to the court having jurisdiction under section 1803 of this title, and a judge to whom an application is made may, notwithstanding any other law, grant an order, in conformity with section 1805 of this title, approving electronic surveillance of a foreign power or an agent of a foreign power for the purpose of obtaining foreign intelligence information, except that the court shall not have jurisdiction to grant any order approving electronic surveillance directed solely as described in paragraph (1)(A) of subsection (a) of this section unless such surveillance may involve the acquisition of communications of any United States person.

§ 1803. Designation of judges

(a) Court to hear applications and grant orders; record of denial; transmittal to court of review.

The Chief Justice of the United States shall publicly designate 11 district court judges from seven of the United States judicial circuits of whom no fewer than 3 shall reside within 20 miles of the District of Columbia who shall constitute a court which shall have jurisdiction to hear applications for and grant orders approving electronic surveillance anywhere within the United States under the procedures set forth in this Act, except that no judge designated under this subsection shall hear the same application for electronic surveillance under this Act which has been denied previously by another judge designated under this subsection. If any judge so designated denies an application for an order authorizing electronic surveillance under this Act, such judge shall provide immediately for the record a written statement of each reason for his decision and, on motion of the United States, the record shall be transmitted, under seal, to the court of review established in subsection (b).

(b) Court of review; record, transmittal to Supreme Court.

The Chief Justice shall publicly designate three judges, one of whom shall be publicly designated as the presiding judge, from the United States district courts or courts of appeals who together shall comprise a court of review which shall have jurisdiction to review the denial of any application made under this Act. If such court determines that the application was properly denied, the court shall immediately provide for the record a written statement of each reason for its decision and, on petition of the United States for a writ of certiorari, the record shall be transmitted under seal to the Supreme Court, which shall have jurisdiction to review such decision.

(c) Expeditious conduct of proceedings; security measures for maintenance of records.

Proceedings under this Act shall be conducted as expeditiously as possible. The record of proceedings under this Act, including applications made and orders granted, shall be maintained under security measures established by the Chief Justice in consultation with the Attorney General and the Director of Central Intelligence.

(d) Tenure.

Each judge designated under this section shall so serve for a maximum of seven years and shall not be eligible for redesignation, except that the judges first designated under subsection (a) shall be designated for terms of from one to seven years so that one term expires each year, and that judges first designated under subsection (b) shall be designated for terms of three, five, and seven years.

§ 1804. Applications for court orders

(a) Submission by Federal officer; approval of Attorney General; contents.

Each application for an order approving electronic surveillance under this subchapter shall be made by a Federal officer in writing upon oath or affirmation to a judge having jurisdiction under section 1803 of this title. Each application shall require the approval of the Attorney General based upon his finding that it satisfies the criteria and requirements of such application as set forth in this subchapter. It shall include—

(1) the identity of the Federal officer making the application;

(2) the authority conferred on the Attorney General by the President of the United States and the approval of the Attorney General to make the application;

(3) the identity, if known, or a description of the target of the electronic surveillance;

(4) a statement of the facts and circumstances relied upon by the applicant to justify his belief that—

(A) the target of the electronic surveillance is a foreign power or an agent of a foreign power; and

(B) each of the facilities or places at which the electronic surveillance is directed is being used, or is about to be used, by a foreign power or an agent of a foreign power;

(5) a statement of the proposed minimization procedures;

(6) a detailed description of the nature of the information sought and the type of communications or activities to be subjected to the surveillance;

(7) a certification or certifications by the Assistant to the President for National Security Affairs or an executive branch official or officials designated by the President from among those executive officers employed in the area of national security or defense and appointed by the President with the advice and consent of the Senate—

(A) that the certifying official deems the information sought to be foreign intelligence information;

(B) that a significant purpose of the surveillance is to obtain foreign intelligence information;

(C) that such information cannot reasonably be obtained by normal investigative techniques;

(D) that designates the type of foreign intelligence information being sought according to the categories described in section 1801(e) of this title; and

(E) including a statement of the basis for the certification that—

(i) the information sought is the type of foreign intelligence information designated; and

(ii) such information cannot reasonably be obtained by normal investigative techniques;

(8) a statement of the means by which the surveillance will be effected and a statement whether physical entry is required to effect the surveillance;

(9) a statement of the facts concerning all previous applications that have been made to any judge under this subchapter involving any of the persons, facilities, or places specified in the application, and the action taken on each previous application;

(10) a statement of the period of time for which the electronic surveillance is required to be maintained, and if the nature of

the intelligence gathering is such that the approval of the use of electronic surveillance under this subchapter should not automatically terminate when the described type of information has first been obtained, a description of facts supporting the belief that additional information of the same type will be obtained thereafter; and

(11) whenever more than one electronic, mechanical or other surveillance device is to be used with respect to a particular proposed electronic surveillance, the coverage of the devices involved and what minimization procedures apply to information acquired by each device.

(b) Exclusion of certain information respecting foreign power targets.

Whenever the target of the electronic surveillance is a foreign power, as defined in section 1801(a)(1), (2), or (3) of this title, and each of the facilities or places at which the surveillance is directed is owned, leased, or exclusively used by that foreign power, the application need not contain the information required by paragraphs (6), (7)(E), (8), and (11) of subsection (a) of this section, but shall state whether physical entry is required to effect the surveillance and shall contain such information about the surveillance techniques and communications or other information concerning United States persons likely to be obtained as may be necessary to assess the proposed minimization procedures.

. . .

§ 1805. Issuance of order

(a) Necessary findings.

Upon an application made pursuant to section 1804 of this title, the judge shall enter an ex parte order as requested or as modified approving the electronic surveillance if he finds that—

(1) the President has authorized the Attorney General to approve applications for electronic surveillance for foreign intelligence information;

(2) the application has been made by a Federal officer and approved by the Attorney General;

(3) on the basis of the facts submitted by the applicant there is probable cause to believe that—

(A) the target of the electronic surveillance is a foreign power or an agent of a foreign power: Provided, That no United States person may be considered a foreign power or an agent of a foreign power solely upon the basis of activities protected by the first amendment to the Constitution of the United States; and

(B) each of the facilities or places at which the electronic surveillance is directed is being used, or is about to be used, by a foreign power or an agent of a foreign power;

(4) the proposed minimization procedures meet the definition of minimization procedures under section 1801(h) of this title;

. . .

(b) Determination of probable cause

In determining whether or not probable cause exists for purposes of an order under subsection (a)(3), a judge may consider past activities of the target, as well as facts and circumstances relating to current or future activities of the target.

. . .

(e) Duration of order; extensions; review of circumstances under which information was acquired, retained or disseminated.

(1) An order issued under this section may approve an electronic surveillance for the period necessary to achieve its purpose, or for ninety days, whichever is less, except that

(A) an order under this section shall approve an electronic surveillance targeted against a foreign power, as defined in section 1801(a)(1), (2), or (3) of this title, for the period specified in the application or for one year, whichever is less, and

(B) an order under this chapter for a surveillance targeted against an agent of a foreign power, as defined in section 1801(b)(1)(A) of this title may be for the period specified in the application or for 120 days, whichever is less.

(2) Extensions of an order issued under this subchapter may be granted on the same basis as an original order upon an application for an extension and new findings made in the same manner as required for an original order, except that

(A) an extension of an order under this chapter for a surveillance targeted against a foreign power, as defined in section 1801(a)(5) or (6) of this title, or against a foreign power as defined in section 1801(a)(4) of this title that is not a United States person, may be for a period not to exceed one year if the judge finds probable cause to believe that no communication of any individual United States person will be acquired during the period, and

(B) an extension of an order under this chapter for a surveillance targeted against an agent of a foreign power as defined in section 1801(b)(1)(A) of this title may be for a period not to exceed 1 year.

(3) At or before the end of the period of time for which electronic surveillance is approved by an order or an extension, the judge may assess compliance with the minimization procedures by reviewing the circumstances under which information concerning United States persons was acquired, retained, or disseminated.

(f) Emergency orders.

Notwithstanding any other provision of this subchapter, when the Attorney General reasonably determines that—

(1) an emergency situation exists with respect to the employment of electronic surveillance to obtain foreign intelligence information before an order authorizing such surveillance can with due diligence be obtained; and

(2) the factual basis for issuance of an order under this subchapter to approve such surveillance exists; he may authorize the emergency employment of electronic surveillance if a judge having jurisdiction under section 1803 of this title is informed by the Attorney General or his designee at the time of such authorization that the decision has been made to employ emergency electronic surveillance and if an application in accordance with this subchapter is made to that judge as soon as practicable, but not more than 72 hours after the Attorney General authorizes such surveillance. If the Attorney General authorizes such emergency employment of electronic surveillance, he shall require that the minimization procedures required by this subchapter for the issuance of a judicial order be followed. . . .

QUESTIONS AND NOTES

1. A good description of the origins of the FISA statute and how it functions is contained in the following excerpt from a Statement for the Record, given by J. Michael McConnell, Director of National Intelligence before the U.S. Senate Judiciary Committee on September 25, 2007:

The Foreign Intelligence Surveillance Act, or FISA, is the nation's statute for conducting electronic surveillance and physical search for foreign intelligence purposes. FISA was passed in 1978, and was carefully crafted to balance the nation's need to collect foreign intelligence information with the protection of civil liberties and privacy rights. I find it helpful to remember that while today's political climate is charged with a significant degree of alarm about activities of the Executive Branch going unchecked, the late 1970's were even more intensely charged by extensively documented Government abuses. We must be ever mindful that FISA was passed in the era of Watergate and in the aftermath of the Church and Pike investigations, and therefore this foundational law has an important legacy of protecting the rights of Americans. Changes we make to this law must honor that legacy to protect Americans, both in their privacy and against foreign threats.

FISA is a complex statute, but in short it does several things. The 1978 law provided for the creation of a special court, the Foreign Intelligence Surveillance Court, which is comprised of federal district court judges who have been selected by the Chief Justice to serve. The Court's members devote a considerable amount of time and effort, over a term of seven years, serving the nation in this capacity, while at the same time fulfilling their district court responsibilities. We are grateful for their service.

The original 1978 FISA provided for Court approval of electronic surveillance operations against foreign powers and agents of foreign powers, within the United States. Congress crafted the law specifically to exclude the Intelligence Community's surveillance operations against targets outside the United States, including where those targets were in communication with Americans, so long as the U.S. side of that communication was not the real target.

FISA has a number of substantial requirements, several of which I will highlight here. A detailed application must be made by an Intelligence Community agency, such as the Federal Bureau of Investigation (FBI), through the Department of Justice, to the FISA Court. The application must be approved by the Attorney General, and certified by another high ranking national security official, such as the FBI Director. The applications that are prepared for presentation to the FISA Court contain extensive information. For example, an application that targets an agent of an international terrorist group might include detailed facts describing the target of the surveillance, the target's activities, the terrorist network in which the target is believed to be acting on behalf of, and investigative results or other intelligence information that would be relevant to the Court's findings. These applications are carefully prepared, subject to multiple layers of review for legal and factual sufficiency, and often resemble finished intelligence products.

Once the Government files its application with the Court, a judge reads the application, conducts a hearing as appropriate, and makes a number of findings, including that there is probable cause that the target of the surveillance is a foreign power or an agent of a foreign power, and that the facilities that will be targeted are used or about to be used by the target. If the judge does not find that the application meets the requirements of the statute, the judge can either request additional information from the government, or deny the application. These extensive findings, including the requirement of probable cause, are intended to apply to persons inside the United States.

It is my steadfast belief that the balance struck by Congress in 1978 was not only elegant, it was the right balance: it safeguarded privacy protection and civil liberties for those inside the United States by requiring Court approval for conducting electronic surveillance within the country, while specifically allowing the Intelligence Community to collect foreign intelligence against foreign intelligence targets located overseas. I believe that balance is the correct one, and I look forward to working with you to maintaining that balance to protect our citizens as we continue our dialogue to achieve lasting FISA modernization.

2. How does probable cause under FISA compare with traditional probable cause applied under search warrant procedures? The issues involved in this comparison are addressed in the next subsection.

3. The FISA statute was amended in December, 2004 by language contained in the Intelligence Reform and Terrorism Prevention Act of 2004, adding § 1801(b)(1)(C). What is the effect of this amendment on the scope of authority that the FBI has to invoke FISA in terrorism investigations? Consider in this connection also how § 1801(a)(4) and § 1801(b)(2)(C) relate to the new provision. Does the new provision broaden the FBI's FISA terrorism authority to any significant extent?

3. COMPARING SURVEILLANCE UNDER FISA AND UNDER 18 U.S.C. § 2510 ET SEQ.

An important issue relating to FISA surveillances is how far they permit the government to depart from the "normal" Title III judicial approval requirements (18 U.S.C. § 2510 et seq.). In this connection, a detailed comparison of the probable cause, duration and informing-the-target requirements, as well as other features of both categories of surveillances is useful.

a. The Probable Cause Requirement

a) Before an order approving electronic surveillance can be issued under 18 U.S.C. § 2518, the judge must find that there is probable cause for belief that an individual is committing, has committed, or is about to commit a particular offense. There must also be probable cause for belief that particular communications concerning that offense will be obtained and that the facilities are being or are about to be used in connection with the commission of the offense.

b) Under FISA, there is also a probable cause requirement, but on its face it does not require probable cause as to the commission of a crime. Rather under 50 U.S.C. § 1805, there must be probable cause that the target is a foreign power or the agent of a foreign power.

NOTE ON PROBABLE CAUSE UNDER *FISA*

1. **Links to criminality.** The issue of the extent to which the probable cause specified under 1805 relates to criminality is somewhat more complicated than at first appears. True, it relates to whether the target is a foreign power or agent of a foreign power, but how are those terms defined? Foreign power is defined to include foreign governments or government-like or-related entities. No mention of criminality here, but a foreign government can hardly claim the benefit of the probable cause requirement of the Fourth Amendment. The definition of foreign power also includes: a group engaged in international terrorism or in activities in preparation therefor. Insofar as the

probable cause is that the target is such a group, the probable cause would seem to refer to a criminal behavior component.

Suppose the probable cause relates to *"an agent* of a foreign power." How is that phrase defined? Does it include a criminal conduct component? The definition of agent of a foreign power found in section 1801 is repeated below. It is a multi-part definition that one needs to work one's way through.

§ 1801. Definitions

. . .

(b) "Agent of a foreign power" means—

(1) any person other than a United States person, who—

(A) acts in the United States as an officer or employee of a foreign power, or as a member of a foreign power as defined in subsection (a)(4) of this section;

(B) acts for or on behalf of a foreign power which engages in clandestine intelligence activities in the United States contrary to the interests of the United States, when the circumstances of such person's presence in the United States indicate that such person may engage in such activities in the United States, or when such person knowingly aids or abets any person in the conduct of such activities or knowingly conspires with any person to engage in such activities;

(C) engages in international terrorism or activities in preparation therefore; or

(2) any person who—

(A) knowingly engages in clandestine intelligence gathering activities for or on behalf of a foreign power, which activities involve or may involve a violation of the criminal statutes of the United States;

(B) pursuant to the direction of an intelligence service or network of a foreign power, knowingly engages in any other clandestine intelligence activities for or on behalf of such foreign power, which activities involve or are about to involve a violation of the criminal statutes of the United States;

(C) knowingly engages in sabotage or international terrorism, or activities that are in preparation therefor, for or on behalf of a foreign power;

(D) knowingly enters the United States under a false or fraudulent identity for or on behalf of a foreign power or, while in the United States, knowingly assumes a false or fraudulent identity for or on behalf of a foreign power; or

(E) knowingly aids or abets any person in the conduct of activities described in subparagraph (A), (B), or (C) or knowingly conspires with any person to engage in activities described in subparagraph (A), (B), or (C).

Given this definition, it would seem that the phrase, "probable cause that a person is an agent of a foreign power," always requires some type of criminal conduct unless the person is so denoted because he/she is an officer or employee of a foreign power. If the person is not so labeled because an officer or employee of a foreign power, it does requires that the agent has engaged in, or be connected to some kind of criminal conduct, namely, engaging in clandestine intelligence activities that are a violation of criminal statutes or engaging in international terrorism, or having engaged in some form of identity theft.

With the December, 2004 amendment of § 1801(b)(1)(C), probable cause that an individual "engages in international terrorism or activities in preparation therefore" will suffice. While under the new language, the probable cause may relate to the conduct of an individual rather than a group, it still requires probable cause relating to terrorist activity or preparations therefore—again, it would seem to require some measure of criminal activity-related behavior. How does it compare with the probable-cause-that-an-individual-is-committing-a-crime formula under 18 U.S.C § 2518? Section 2518 requires a specific offense and, arguably some element of temporal immediacy. Is there more of a criminal conduct element in the FISA probable cause determination than initially appeared? Is it, however, less than what is required under § 2518? Section 1801 requires criminality but does not require the identification of specific statutory offenses. Overall, it seems phrased in a more general way, but it is not, as is generally thought, divorced from a connection to criminality—except where a foreign power, in the traditional sense, or one of its officers or employees, is the target.

2. **Limitation on the scope of the listening.** The scope of the electronic surveillance under § 2518 is delimited by the notion that there must be probable cause for a belief that particular communications concerning the offense will be obtained and that the facilities are being or are about to be used in connection with the commission of the offense. Under FISA, the scope is delimited differently. Rather the information sought must be "foreign intelligence information," which is defined as follows:

(e) "Foreign intelligence information" means—

(1) information that relates to, and if concerning a United States person is necessary to, the ability of the United States to protect against—

(A) actual or potential attack or other grave hostile acts of a foreign power or an agent of a foreign power;

(B) sabotage or international terrorism by a foreign power or an agent of a foreign power; or

(C) clandestine intelligence activities by an intelligence service or network of a foreign power or by an agent of a foreign power; or

(2) information with respect to a foreign power or foreign territory that relates to, and if concerning a United States person is necessary to—

(A) the national defense or the security of the United States; or

(B) the conduct of the foreign affairs of the United States.

The scope limitation under FISA is generally broader than under § 2518, and insofar as one of the definitions uses as a reference point "the national defense or security of the United States," or "the conduct of the foreign affairs of the United States" it is much, much broader.

b. Duration of the Intercept; Time Period Within Which Target Must Be Notified About the Interception

a) Under 18 U.S.C. § 2518, the duration of the interception is limited to 30 days. Extensions can be granted by the judge but for not more than another 30 days per extension. Not later than 90 days after the period of the interception is terminated, the person named in the order approving the interception and such other parties to intercepted communications as the judge in his discretion determines, are to be provided information about the interception.

b) Under the FISA, section 1805, the duration of the interception may be 90 days or 120 days, or in some circumstances as much as one year, and extensions may be for the period originally authorized or in certain cases for one year. Significantly, in what is perhaps the most important difference between the two categories of electronic eavesdropping, there is no requirement under the FISA that the persons whose communications have been intercepted be notified subsequently about the interception.

c. Other Comparisons Between the FISA and 18 U.S.C. § 2518 Surveillances

The FISA permits surveillance under some circumstances even though the target has not been identified, 50 U.S.C. § 1804(a)(3), which would seem inconsistent with the Fourth Amendment requirement that the place to be searched and the person and things to be seized be described with particularity. Minimization procedures under the FISA should also be compared with those required under Title III. Also, under the FISA, if the case ripens into a criminal prosecution, the application and orders may be reviewed by the district judge in camera and ex parte, without giving the surveilled party access to them. The Attorney General also has authority under 50 U.S.C. § 1805 to issue surveillance orders in "emergency situations."

d. Statistical Comparison of FISA and Title III Electronic Surveillances

Since it first went into operation in 1979, there have been more than 14,000 applications for judicial approval of FISA surveillances. Until 2003, reportedly, no FISA application for judicial approval of a surveillance had been denied in the almost 25 year history of the Act although some had been modified. The actual number of applications between 1978 and 1995 averaged more than 500 each year. Since 1995, as reported in annual letters from the Attorney General to the Administrative Office of the Courts and to the Speaker of the House, there has been a gradual increase in the annual numbers: in 1995, 697; 1996, 839; 1997, 749; 1998, 796; 1999, 886; 2000, 1005; 2001, 932; 2002, 1228.

The letter for 2003, dated April 20, 2004, reported a significant spike in the number of applications, 1727. These include those applications for approval of searches which were solely electronic, solely physical or a combination of both electronic surveillance and physical search. For the first time, too, the report indicated that the FISA court had turned down some applications, four in all, but as a result of modification and resubmission, the court approved a total of 1724 applications. The letter also reported that the court had made substantial modifications in 79 applications.

In 2004, the number crept up to 1758 with the court approving a total of 1754. But then in 2005, the number of applications presented jumped again by more than 300 to 2074, with 2072 approved. And these numbers held steady in 2006 with 2181 applications submitted and 2176 approved; one application was reported to have been rejected in 2006. In a letter, dated May 14, 2009, sent to the chairs of the Senate and House Judiciary and Intelligence Committees, the Department of Justice reported that in calendar 2008, 2083 requests for foreign intelligence electronic and/or physical searches were approved; also during that period, the court turned down one request and modified two others.

At first, the foregoing numbers seem truly extraordinary—in the year, 2000, for example, an average of almost 3 applications a day and in 2003, the number jumps to almost 5 a day. And in 2006, to almost 6 a day! Can there really be so much foreign intelligence surveillance going on? These numbers are tempered somewhat, however, when one realizes that the numbers include both initial applications and applications for extensions. There is thus a kind of double counting if one is trying to determine how many surveillances are ongoing (as opposed to how many judicial determinations have occurred). Nevertheless, the numbers are quite large.

What is the comparable number of Title III federal wiretaps? Between 1995 and 2005 the number of federal wiretaps authorized ranged from 479 to 730, averaging about 567 per year. Through, 2005, the two highest authorization years were 2004 (730) and 2005 (625). Extensions are reported separately; for example, there were 601 in 1991 and 1008 in 2001.

Only the foregoing type of FISA statistics are reported publicly. More extensive reports are made only to the congressional Intelligence Committees. In the period leading up to the enactment of the Intelligence Reform and Terrorism Prevention Act of 2004, a bill was introduced that would have required more information to be disclosed publicly. What came out of Congress, however, was legislation (sec. 6002 of the Intelligence Reform and Terrorism Prevention Act of 2004) that imposed more detailed reporting obligations on the Attorney General, but only in reports to the Intelligence Committees and Judiciary Committees of the two Houses of Congress.

4. ANOTHER PERSPECTIVE ON THE RELATIONSHIP BETWEEN FISA ELECTRONIC SURVEILLANCE AND ORDINARY CRIME SURVEILLANCE: THE MULTIPLE PURPOSE ISSUE

a. Background–History and the Relevant Statutory Provisions

Because the FISA modifies the "normal" Fourth Amendment requirements, one way to limit its impact on privacy interests would be to restrict its use to the obtaining of "foreign intelligence information." Indeed, the original notion behind the Executive Branch's conducting electronic surveillance for foreign intelligence purposes without judicial authorization may have been that intelligence gathering can be done entirely separate and insulated from criminal investigation and prosecution. The notion may have been that the gathering of foreign intelligence usefully can serve many purposes that are not dependent on, or involve criminal prosecution—e.g., it can, for example: a) inform foreign policy; b) be used on occasion to expel foreign diplomats engaged in intelligence work; and c) help to protect the national security through the forestalling of plots directed against the United States.

Whatever the original conception may have been, in the early implementation of the FISA, a distinction was drawn between gathering information for intelligence purposes and gathering it for use by law enforcement for prosecution purposes (see the recounting of this history in In re Sealed Case, 310 F.3d 717 (F.I.S.Ct.Rev. 2002)). In the statute itself, however, no hard lines were drawn. The specific language of the FISA did not bar the use by law enforcement personnel of information gathered for foreign intelligence purposes; indeed it seemed to contemplate such use, but it did single out such use for special treatment and generally did not seem to encourage it. For example, see the FISA provisions as originally enacted, 50 U.S.C. § 1806(a) and (b).

§ 1806. Use of information

(a) Compliance with minimization procedures; privileged communications; lawful purposes

Information acquired from an electronic surveillance conducted pursuant to this subchapter concerning any United States person may be used and disclosed by Federal officers and employees without the consent of the United States person only in accordance with the minimization procedures required by this subchapter. No otherwise privileged communication obtained in accordance with, or in violation of, the provisions of this subchapter shall lose its privileged character. No information acquired from an electronic surveillance pursuant to this subchapter may be used or disclosed by Federal officers or employees except for lawful purposes.

(b) Statement for disclosure

No information acquired pursuant to this subchapter shall be disclosed for law enforcement purposes unless such disclosure is accompanied by a statement that such information, or any information derived therefrom, may only be used in a criminal proceeding with the advance authorization of the Attorney General.

Provisions incorporated into the FISA post–9/11 by the USA PATRIOT Act (Public Law 107–56, 115 Stat. 272) and the Homeland Security Act (Public Law 107–296, 116 Stat. 2135) appear to have been aimed at shifting the emphasis from the discouraging of use of the information for a different purpose. These amendments appear to encourage the sharing of information between foreign intelligence personnel and law enforcement personnel. Issues of statutory interpretation are presented, however. How far do the new provisions in the FISA, added to by the USA PATRIOT Act, go in permitting the intermixing of the foreign intelligence and law enforcement functions? The USA PATRIOT Act added language that authorized the sharing by foreign intelligence personnel from their side, 50 U.S.C. § 403–5d (note the phrase "obtained as part of a criminal investigation,"), and similarly sharing by law enforcement personnel from their side, 18 U.S.C. § 2517.

TITLE 50, UNITED STATES CODE (WAR AND NATIONAL DEFENSE)

§ 403–5d. Foreign intelligence information

(1) In general

Notwithstanding any other provision of law, it shall be lawful for foreign intelligence or counterintelligence (as defined in section 401a of this title) or foreign intelligence information obtained as part of a criminal investigation to be disclosed to any Federal law enforcement, intelligence, protective, immigration, national defense, or national security official in order to assist the official receiving that information in the performance of his official duties. Any Federal official who receives information pursuant to this provision may use that information only as necessary in the conduct of that person's official duties subject to any limitations on the unauthorized disclosure of such information.

. . .

TITLE 18, UNITED STATES CODE (CRIMES AND CRIMINAL PROCEDURE)

§ 2517. Authorization for disclosure and use of intercepted wire, oral, or electronic communications

(6) Any investigative or law enforcement officer, or attorney for the Government, who by any means authorized by this chapter, has obtained knowledge of the contents of any wire, oral, or electronic communication, or evidence derived therefrom, may disclose such contents to any other Federal law enforcement, intelligence, protective, immigration, national defense, or national security official to the extent that such contents include foreign intelligence or counterintelligence (as defined in section 3 of the National Security Act of 1947 (50 U.S.C. 401a)), or foreign intelligence information (as defined in subsection (19) of section 2510 of this title), to assist the official who is to receive that information in the performance of his official duties. Any Federal official who receives information pursuant to this provision may use that information only as necessary in the conduct of that person's official duties subject to any limitations on the unauthorized disclosure of such information.

The issues here go beyond the sharing of information, however. Ultimately the question is whether it should be permissible to undertake a foreign intelligence-type surveillance that also has a law enforcement, that is, a criminal prosecution, purpose; and whether it should be permissible to have such investigations led by law enforcement rather than foreign intelligence personnel? Those who favor these types of undertakings see no harm in them and argue that otherwise law enforcement is frustrated in their efforts to deal with terrorists and terrorist activity, and government intelligence personnel are not able to do their job properly. Those who oppose it argue that permitting the use of foreign intelligence surveillance, with its watered-down standards, secrecy and lack of protection for the U.S. person, is a way to get around the requirements of the Fourth Amendment; that it will lead to abuses whereby a foreign intelligence purpose will be inappropriately used to obtain judicial authorization to eavesdrop or search; and that ultimately, it establishes a slippery slope leading to the undermining of Fourth Amendment protections.

In addition to the sharing provisions quoted above, there are two other amendments added by the USA PATRIOT Act that are highly relevant to this subject. The Act added section (k) to § 1806, quoted above. Section (k) provides:

§ 1806. Use of information

. . .

(k) Consultation with Federal law enforcement officer

(1) Federal officers who conduct electronic surveillance to acquire foreign intelligence information under this title may consult with Federal law enforcement officers to coordinate efforts to investigate or protect against

(A) actual or potential attack or other grave hostile acts of a foreign power or an agent of a foreign power;

(B) sabotage or international terrorism by a foreign power or an agent of a foreign power; or

(C) clandestine intelligence activities by an intelligence service or network of a foreign power or by an agent of a foreign power.

(2) Coordination authorized under paragraph (1) shall not preclude the certification required by section 1104(a)(7)(B) of this title or the entry of an order under section 1105 of this title.

In addition, an amendment was made in 50 U.S.C. § 1804(a)(7)(B).

§ 1804. Applications for court orders

(a) Submission by Federal officer; approval of Attorney General; contents

Each application for an order approving electronic surveillance under this subchapter shall be made by a Federal officer in writing upon oath or affirmation to a judge having jurisdiction under section 1803 of this title. Each application shall require the approval of the Attorney General based upon his finding that it satisfies the criteria and requirements of such application as set forth in this subchapter. It shall include—

. . .

(7) a certification . . .

(A) that the certifying official deems the information sought to be foreign intelligence information;

(B) that a significant purpose of the surveillance is to obtain foreign intelligence information;

(C) that such information cannot reasonably be obtained by normal investigative techniques;

. . .

Previously (a)(7)(B) of 50 U.S.C. § 1804 had provided that the obtaining of foreign intelligence information be "the purpose of the surveillance." That previous formulation had been interpreted to mean that the "primary purpose" of the surveillance must have been to obtain foreign intelligence information. The history of the evolution of that interpretation is set forth in the In re Sealed case.

Did changing the language from "the purpose," i.e. from the primary purpose, to "a significant purpose," open the door to a contention that the primary purpose of the surveillance could be a law enforcement purpose, provided only that foreign intelligence information gathering was also a significant purpose of the eavesdropping?

Further, does the language of section (k)(1) added to § 1806, as reproduced above, support the undertaking of a coordinated foreign intelligence and criminal investigation?

b. Applying the Significant Purpose Formula

UNITED STATES v. NING WEN
477 F.3d 896 (7th Cir. 2007)

Before EASTERBROOK, CHIEF JUDGE, and BAUER and EVANS, CIRCUIT JUDGES.

EASTERBROOK, CHIEF JUDGE.

A jury found Ning Wen guilty of violating the export-control laws by providing militarily useful technology to the People's Republic of China without the required license. He has been sentenced to 60 months' imprisonment. His only argument on appeal is that the district court should have suppressed evidence derived from a wiretap approved under the Foreign Intelligence Surveillance Act. After reviewing the materials *in camera,* the judge concluded that the intercept order was amply justified and denied this motion.

As enacted in 1978, FISA applied to interceptions the "primary purpose" of which was foreign intelligence; as amended in 2001 by the USA PATRIOT Act, the statute applies to interceptions that have international intelligence as a "significant purpose". 50 U.S.C. § 1804(a)(7)(B). The Foreign Intelligence Surveillance Court of Review has concluded that the amended statute allows domestic use of intercepted evidence as long as a "significant" international objective is in view at the intercept's inception. *Sealed Case,* 310 F.3d 717 (F.I.S.Ct.Rev.2002). Wen asks us to disagree with that decision and hold that evidence gathered under FISA cannot be used in domestic criminal investigations or prosecutions, even when the "domestic" crime is linked to international espionage, once that international investigation has "fizzled out" (Wen's phrase) and the investigation of domestic crime necessarily assumes primary significance.

The statutory question under the current version of the Act is whether acquiring international intelligence is a "significant purpose" of the intercept. The intercept's "primary" purpose may or may not be pertinent to the fourth amendment (we discuss that subject below) but is not pertinent to the validity of the intercept under the statute. Like the district court, we have reviewed the affidavits *in camera* and conclude that the statutory standards for an intercept order have been satisfied. There is no basis for suppression under FISA itself. 50 U.S.C. § 1806(e), (g).

The fourth amendment does not supply a better footing for exclusion. FISA requires each intercept to be authorized by a warrant from a federal district judge. See 50 U.S.C. § 1803(a).

. . .

The only plausible constitutional objection to the warrant actually issued would be that FISA uses a definition of "probable cause" that does not depend on whether a domestic crime has been committed. Under 50 U.S.C. § 1805(a)(3), an order may be based on probable cause to believe that the target is an agent of a foreign power and that the conversations to be intercepted concern the agent's dealings with that foreign power; the judge need not find probable cause to believe that the foreign agent probably is violating the law of this nation (although this may be implied by the findings that FISA does require).

Yet we know from the administrative-search cases that the "probable cause" of which the fourth amendment speaks is not necessarily probable cause to believe that any law is being violated. The Court held in *Camara v. Municipal Court,* 387 U.S. 523, 87 S.Ct. 1727, 18 L.Ed.2d 930 (1967), and *See v. Seattle,* 387 U.S. 541, 87 S.Ct. 1741, 18 L.Ed.2d 930 (1967), that municipal officials may not barge into homes or businesses to look for violations of the housing code; they must have warrants, which may issue on probable cause to believe that the city has adopted a reasonable system of inspections and is not targeting citizens for irregular or malicious reasons.

These principles carry over to FISA. Probable cause to believe that a foreign agent is communicating with his controllers outside our borders makes an interception reasonable. If, while conducting this surveillance, agents discover evidence of a domestic crime, they may use it to prosecute for that offense. That the agents may have known that they were likely to hear evidence of domestic crime does not make the interception less reasonable than if they were ignorant of this possibility. ... In *Horton v. California,* 496 U.S. 128, 110 S.Ct. 2301, 110 L.Ed.2d 112 (1990), the Court held that evidence in plain view may be seized without a warrant even though the police expected to find it. Likewise evidence of a domestic crime, acquired during an intercept that is reasonable because it concerns traffic between a foreign state and one of its agents in the United States, may be used in a domestic prosecution whether or not the agents expected to learn about the domestic offense. It is enough that the intercept be adequately justified without regard to the possibility that evidence of domestic offenses will turn up. Interception of Wen's conversations was adequately justified under FISA's terms, so there is no constitutional obstacle to using evidence of any domestic crimes he committed. AF-FIRMED.

QUESTIONS AND NOTES

1. Excerpts from the opinion in a published decision of the Foreign Intelligence Court of Review identify various issues that can arise in applying the significant purpose formula. See In re Sealed Case, 310 F.3d 717 (F.I.S.Ct. Rev. 2002):

> No committee reports accompanied the Patriot Act but the floor statements make congressional intent quite apparent. The Senate Judiciary Committee Chairman Senator Leahy acknowledged that "[p]rotection against these foreign-based threats by any lawful means is within the scope of the definition of 'foreign intelligence information,' and the use of FISA to gather evidence for the enforcement of these laws was contemplated in the enactment of FISA." 147 Cong. Rec. S11004 (Oct. 25, 2001).

"This bill ... break[s] down traditional barriers between law enforcement and foreign intelligence. This is not done just to combat international terrorism, but for any criminal investigation that overlaps a broad definition of 'foreign intelligence.' " 147 Cong. Rec. S10992 (Oct. 25, 2001) (statement of Sen. Leahy). And Senator Feinstein, a "strong support[er]," was also explicit.

> The ultimate objective was to make it easier to collect foreign intelligence information under the Foreign Intelligence Surveillance Act, FISA. Under current law, authorities can proceed with surveillance under FISA only if the primary purpose of the investigation is to collect foreign intelligence.

> But in today's world things are not so simple. In many cases, surveillance will have two key goals—the gathering of foreign intelligence, and the gathering of evidence for a criminal prosecution. Determining which purpose is the "primary" purpose of the investigation can be difficult, and will only become more so as we coordinate our intelligence and law enforcement efforts in the war against terror.

> Rather than forcing law enforcement to decide which purpose is primary—law enforcement or foreign intelligence gathering, this bill strikes a new balance. It will now require that a "significant" purpose of the investigation must be foreign intelligence gathering to proceed with surveillance under FISA. The effect of this provision will be to make it easier for law enforcement to obtain a FISA search or surveillance warrant for those cases where the subject of the surveillance is both a potential source of valuable intelligence and the potential target of a criminal prosecution. Many of the individuals involved in supporting the September 11 attacks may well fall into both of these categories.

147 Cong. Rec. S10591 (Oct. 11, 2001).

. . .

... [T]he Patriot Act amendments clearly disapprove the primary purpose test. And as a matter of straightforward logic, if a FISA application can be granted even if "foreign intelligence" is only a significant—not a primary—purpose, another purpose can be primary. One other legitimate purpose that could exist is to prosecute a target for a foreign intelligence crime....

That leaves us with something of an analytic conundrum. On the one hand, Congress did not amend the definition of foreign intelligence information which, we have explained, includes evidence of foreign intelligence crimes. On the other hand, Congress accepted the dichotomy between foreign intelligence and law enforcement by adopting the significant purpose test. Nevertheless, it is our task to do our best to read the statute to honor congressional intent. The better reading, it seems to us, excludes from the purpose of gaining foreign intelligence information a sole objective of criminal prosecution. We therefore reject the government's argument to the contrary. Yet this may not make much practical difference. Because, as the government points out, when it commences an electronic surveillance of a foreign agent, typically it will not have decided whether to prosecute the agent (whatever may be the subjective intent of the investigators or lawyers who initiate an investigation). So long as the government entertains a realistic option of dealing with the agent other than through criminal prosecution, it satisfies the significant purpose test.

The important point is—and here we agree with the government—the Patriot Act amendment, by using the word "significant," eliminated any justification for the FISA court to balance the relative weight the government places on criminal prosecution as compared to other counter-intelligence responses. If the certification of the application's purpose articulates a broader objective than criminal prosecution—such as stopping an ongoing conspiracy—and includes other potential non-prosecutorial responses, the government meets the statutory test. Of course, if the court concluded that the government's sole objective was merely to gain evidence of past criminal conduct—even foreign intelligence crimes—to punish the agent rather than halt ongoing espionage or terrorist activity, the application should be denied.

The government claims that even prosecutions of non-foreign intelligence crimes are consistent with a purpose of gaining foreign intelligence information so long as the government's objective is to stop espionage or terrorism by putting an agent of a foreign power in prison. That interpretation transgresses the original FISA. It will be recalled that Congress intended ... to prevent the government from targeting a foreign agent when its "true purpose" was to gain non-foreign intelligence information—such as evidence of ordinary crimes or scandals. (If the government inadvertently came upon evidence of ordinary crimes, FISA provided for the transmission of that evidence to the proper authority. 50 U.S.C. § 1801(h)(3).) It can be argued, however, that by providing that an application is to be granted if the government has only a "significant purpose" of gaining foreign intelligence information, the Patriot Act allows the government to have a primary objective of prosecuting an agent for a non-foreign intelligence crime. Yet we think that would be an anomalous reading of the amendment. For we see not the slightest indication that Congress meant to give that power to the Executive Branch. Accordingly, the manifestation of such a purpose, it seems to us, would continue to disqualify an application. That is not to deny that ordinary crimes might be inextricably intertwined with foreign intelligence crimes. For example, if a group of international terrorists were to engage in bank robberies in order to finance the manufacture of a bomb, evidence of the bank robbery should be treated just as evidence of the terrorist act itself. But the FISA process cannot be used as a device to investigate wholly unrelated ordinary crimes.

One final point; we think the government's purpose as set forth in a section 1804(a)(7)(B) certification is to be judged by the national security official's articulation and not by a FISA court inquiry into the origins of an investigation nor an examination of the personnel involved. It is up to the Director of the FBI, who typically certifies, to determine the government's national security purpose, as approved by the Attorney General or Deputy Attorney General. This is not a standard whose application the FISA court legitimately reviews by seeking to inquire into which Justice Department officials were instigators of an investigation. All Justice Department officers—including those in the FBI—are under the control of the Attorney General. If he wishes a particular investigation to be run by an officer of any division, that is his prerogative. There is nothing in FISA or the Patriot Act that suggests otherwise. That means, perforce, if the FISA court has reason to doubt that the government has any real non-prosecutorial purpose in seeking foreign intelligence information it can demand further inquiry into the certifying officer's purpose—or perhaps even the Attorney General's or Deputy Attorney General's reasons for approval. The important point is that the relevant purpose is that of those senior officials in the Executive Branch who have the responsibility of appraising the government's national security needs.

2.　Reportedly, government investigations of terrorist activity was energized by the decision in the In re Sealed case, supra; that prior to that decision, federal prosecutors had assumed that FISA information was off limits in criminal cases. See Glenn R. Simpson and Jess Bravin, New Powers Fuel Legal Assault on Suspected Terror Supporters, Wall Street Journal, Jan. 21, 2003.

3.　In an investigation of a suspected terrorist cell, the FBI obtains a FISA search warrant to search the homes of the cell members and also obtains judicial approval for electronic surveillance of these same individuals. Clearly the FBI wishes to prevent any planned terrorist attacks. But if they get evidence of planning of these attacks, they will wish also to prosecute these individuals. At some point law enforcement personnel and prosecutors concerned with prosecution will need to be brought into the picture. Does it make sense, did it ever make sense to try to build a wall between intelligence and law enforcement personnel in the context of this kind of scenario?

4.　a. The FBI has information that members of a motorcycle gang involved in illegal drug trafficking who have been under law enforcement investigation have been in touch with foreign agents who the Bureau believes are plotting a terrorist action. The FBI believes that the foreign agents are exploring the possibility of importing drugs, selling them to the motorcycle gang and using the profits to help finance the terrorist plot. The Justice Department wishes to obtain judicial approval under FISA for electronic surveillance and physical searches directed against members of the motorcycle gang as well as the foreign agents. Should the FISA court approve an order authorizing the surveillance?

b.　The FBI has been investigating a drug ring. It learns that there is a new member of the ring who in the past has had ties to al Qaeda. It requests an order under FISA approving electronic surveillance of all members of the ring. What result?

c.　A member of a terrorist group now defunct has slipped into the United States surreptitiously. The FBI wishes to obtain a judicial order under FISA to listen in to his telephone conversations. Their purpose is: a) to determine whether he is currently planning any terrorist activity; and b) to gather evidence about a past terrorist bomb planting in which they believe he was involved. What result?

5. What does the court of review opinion in In re Sealed Case, supra note 1, have to say, if anything about the propriety of a sharing of information between personnel with a law enforcement-prosecution mission and those with a foreign intelligence mission during the course of an investigation?

6. As we learned in ch. 2, persons charged with terrorism crimes are often also charged with non-terrorism crimes. What bearing does that fact have on the In re Sealed Case's observations? Sometimes, where, for one reason or another, terrorism crimes cannot be proved against a person suspected of being a terrorist, the government will prosecute the individual for non-terrorism crimes which he has committed. Is that practice inconsistent with the court's dicta in In re Sealed Case? How would you reconcile the court's statements with the practice of prosecuting for non-terrorism crimes in order to put a suspected terrorist in prison?

7. The Second Circuit addressed the constitutionality of the significant purpose limitation under the Fourth Amendment. United States v. Abu–Jihaad, 630 F.3d 102 (2d Cir.2010):

> ... [T]he Fourth Amendment warrant requirement demands a showing of probable cause reasonable to the purpose being pursued. Thus, identification of purpose is necessary to assess the reasonableness of the probable cause standards at issue. Where multiple purposes are significant to an investigation, however, the Fourth Amendment does not require the government to identify a primary purpose or limit its ability to secure a warrant to satisfaction of the standards for that purpose. Rather, the government may secure a warrant under the probable cause standards applicable to any purpose that it pursues in good faith. Thus, we identify no constitutional defects in FISA's certification requirement of "a significant" rather than a primary "purpose ... to obtain foreign intelligence information."

8. The FISA Court of Review also concluded as reasonable under the Fourth Amendment the Patriot Act's substitution of "a significant purpose" for the talismanic phrase "primary purpose." *In re Sealed Case*, 310 F.3d at 742–45.

9. The In re Sealed Case, supra, triggered much law review commentary, most of it expressing concern about the watering down of Fourth Amendment protections that would result from the PATRIOT Act amendments of the FISA statute and the FISA Review Court's decision in the matter. See, e.g., George P. Varghese, A Sense of Purpose: The Role of Law Enforcement in Foreign Intelligence Surveillance, 152 U.Pa. L.Rev. 385 (2003); Nola K. Breglio, Note: Leaving FISA Behind: The Need to Return to Warrantless Foreign Intelligence Surveillance, 113 Yale L.J. 179 (2003); David Hardin, The Fuss Over Two Small Words: The Unconstitutionality of the USA PATRIOT Act Amendments to FISA Under the Fourth Amendment, 71 Geo. Wash.L.Rev. 291 (2003); John E. Branch III, Statutory Misinterpretation: The Foreign Intelligence Court of Review's Interpretation of the "Signif-

icant Purpose" Requirement of the Foreign Intelligence Surveillance Act, 81 N.C.L.Rev. 2075 (2003).

5. CRIMINAL PROSECUTION USING FISA–DERIVED MATERIAL

UNITED STATES v. DUGGAN

743 F.2d 59 (2d Cir. 1984)

KEARSE, CIRCUIT JUDGE:

The principal issues raised in this appeal by alleged agents of the Provisional Irish Republican Army ("PIRA") concern the constitutionality and proper application of the Foreign Intelligence Surveillance Act ("FISA" or the "Act"), 50 U.S.C. §§ 1801–1811 (Supp. V 1981). Defendants Andrew Duggan, Eamon Meehan, Gabriel Megahey, and Colm Mcehan appeal from judgments of conviction entered in the United States District Court for the Eastern District of New York, after a jury trial before Charles P. Sifton, *Judge*. Duggan, Megahey, and Eamon Meehan were convicted of (a) unlicensed exportation of items on the United States Munitions List, in violation of 22 U.S.C. § 2778(b)(2) (1982) (count 2); (b) transportation of explosives in interstate commerce without a license, in violation of 18 U.S.C. § 842(a)(3)(A) (1982) (count 3); (c) transportation of explosives in interstate commerce knowing that the explosives would be used to kill, injure, or intimidate individuals, in violation of 18 U.S.C. § 844(d) (1982) (count 4); (d) transportation in interstate commerce of firearms with their serial numbers removed, in violation of 18 U.S.C. § 922(k) (1982) (count 5); (e) delivery to a common carrier of a shipment containing firearms without giving notice to the carrier of the contents of the shipment, in violation of 18 U.S.C. § 922(e) (1982) (count 6); (f) conspiracy to violate both 26 U.S.C. § 5861(d) (1982), which proscribes possession of unregistered destructive devices, and the statutes listed in counts 3 through 6, in violation of 18 U.S.C. § 371 (1982) (count 1). Colm Meehan was acquitted on the two counts involving interstate transportation of explosives (counts 3 and 4) and was convicted on all other counts. The Meehans were also convicted of possessing guns while illegal aliens, in violation of 18 U.S.C. app. § 1202(a)(5) (1982) (count 7).

On appeal, all of the defendants contend principally (1) that the district court erred in refusing to suppress evidence obtained through a wiretap pursuant to FISA on the grounds that (a) FISA is unconstitutionally broad and violates the probable cause requirement of the Fourth Amendment, and (b) the government failed to comply with FISA's prerequisites for wire surveillance; . . . .

. . . In general the evidence, presented largely through the testimony of Hanratty, videotapes of meetings between PIRA members and undercover law enforcement agents, and tape recordings of telephone conversations involving Megahey, showed defendants as part of a network of men working clandestinely on behalf of PIRA to acquire explosives, weapons, ammunition, and remote-controlled detonation devices in the United States to be exported to Northern Ireland for use in terrorist activities. Megahey, an Irish national who sought political asylum in the United States, was the leader and financier of PIRA operations in the United States. Duggan, an American citizen, was Megahey's assistant in contacting sellers of electronic equipment to be used in remote-controlled bombs and other sophisticated weaponry. Eamon Meehan, under the direction of Megahey, gathered and stored firearms and explosives; Eamon and his brother Colm—both aliens living illegally in the United States—secreted these materials in a shipment of goods bound for Northern Ireland.

. . .

1.　The Pretrial Motion to Suppress the FISA Materials

On July 27, 1982, pursuant to the provisions of FISA, 50 U.S.C. § 1806(b), the Acting Attorney General of the United States, Edward C. Schmults, authorized the use at trial of tape recordings and information obtained pursuant to the FISA surveillance of the activities of the defendants. Shortly thereafter, pursuant to 50 U.S.C. § 1806(c), the government notified the court and the defendants of its intention to introduce evidence from the FISA surveillance at trial. In the following months, the government provided the defendants with copies of all tape recordings, transcripts, surveillance logs, and pen register tapes of all telephone conversations resulting from the surveillance.

Defendants moved to suppress the fruits of the FISA surveillance on a variety of grounds. They contended that FISA surveillance violates a target's First, Fourth, and Fifth Amendment rights because it is too broad; violates the doctrine of separation of powers because it requires the courts to decide political questions; and denies due process and equal protection to aliens. In addition, defendants contended that the requirements set forth in FISA had not been met because an insufficient basis had been provided for the issuance of the surveillance order and because the government had failed to comply with FISA's "minimization" requirements. They also contended that FISA had been improperly used simply to obtain evidence of criminal activity rather than to protect the national security. Defendants asked the court to hold an evidentiary hearing to determine these issues.

The government in turn moved to have the trial court determine the propriety of the electronic surveillance on an *ex parte, in camera* basis pursuant to 50 U.S.C. § 1806(f). In support of this application, the government filed an Affidavit and Claim of Privilege of Acting Attorney General Schmults. The affidavit stated that the FISA applications contained sensitive information concerning United States intelligence sources and methods and other information relating to the efforts of the United States to combat international terrorism. It certified that public disclosure or an adversary hearing with respect to this information would harm the national security of the United States. An additional affidavit of the Acting Attorney General, submitted to the district court *in camera,* set forth in greater detail the facts upon which the claim of privilege was based. After reviewing all of these materials, Judge Sifton rejected all of defendants' FISA arguments on their merits in a thorough opinion *sub nom. United States v. Megahey,* 553 F.Supp. 1180 (E.D.N.Y.1982) ("*Megahey*"), ...

2. The Posttrial FISA Motion

Following their convictions, defendants asserted new challenges to FISA, to wit, (1) that the surveillance was unlawful because Duggan had not been named as a target, and (2) that the trial evidence revealed that the court had been misled as to the basis for the issuance of the FISA order. The court rejected the first contention on the grounds that it was untimely raised and that there was no requirement that the government name more than one target of the surveillance. The court rejected defendants' second contention after reviewing the public and *in camera* documents and determining that it had not in fact been misled.

. . .

Defendants mount two types of challenge with regard to FISA. First, they contend that the Act is unconstitutional on several grounds. In addition, they contend that even if FISA is not unconstitutional, its requirements were not met in this case.

A. The Constitutionality of FISA

Defendants contend that FISA is unconstitutional principally on the grounds that (1) it is so broad as to deprive certain persons of due process of law, (2) it violates the probable cause requirement of the Fourth Amendment, and (3) it deprives nonresident aliens of the equal protection of the law. We find no merit in these contentions.

1. The Scope of the Act

Defendants argue that FISA is impermissibly broad in several respects. The sections of the Act relied upon by the defendants to show that the Act is impermissibly broad are simply irrelevant to this case. The sections and definitions plainly applicable to Megahey are explicit, unequivocal, and clearly defined.

Nor are we impressed by defendants' argument that insofar as § 1801(e)(2) defines foreign intelligence information as information that "relates to ... (A) the national defense or the security of the United States; or (B) the conduct of the foreign affairs of the United States" it is impermissibly vague. Section 1801(e)(1)(B) defines foreign intelligence information as "information that relates to ... the ability of the United States to protect against ... international terrorism by a foreign power or an agent of a foreign power." Given the information provided by Hanratty, the government plainly had a basis under this section for describing the information sought by surveillance of Megahey, self-proclaimed leader of an international terrorist group, as foreign intelligence information.

Thus, even if we thought § 1801(e)(2)'s concepts of national defense, national security, or conduct of foreign affairs to be vague, which we do not, we would find therein no basis for reversing the convictions of these defendants, whose circumstances were governed by an entirely different definition.

2.   The Probable Cause Requirement of the Fourth Amendment

The Fourth Amendment provides that "no warrants shall issue, but upon probable cause...." Defendants argue principally (1) that the Amendment applies to all proposed surveillances, including those in national security cases, and (2) that even if there were an exception for national security matters, it would not apply to terrorism cases where the objects of the terrorism are entirely outside of the United States. We reject these contentions.

Prior to the enactment of FISA, virtually every court that had addressed the issue had concluded that the President had the inherent power to conduct warrantless electronic surveillance to collect foreign intelligence information, and that such surveillances constituted an exception to the warrant requirement of the Fourth Amendment ...

In *Keith,* the government argued that Title III of the Omnibus Crime Control and Safe Streets Act, 18 U.S.C. §§ 2510 *et seq.* ("Title III"), recognized the constitutional authority of the President to conduct domestic security surveillances without a warrant. The Court rejected this argument, noting that the legislative history made clear that Title III was not intended to legislate with respect to national security surveillances. The Court went on to hold that a warrant was required in *Keith* under the Fourth Amendment; but the implication of its discussion was that the warrant requirement is flexible and that different standards may be compatible with the Fourth Amendment in light of the different purposes and practical considerations of domestic national security surveillances. 407 U.S. at 321–24, 92 S.Ct. at 2138–40. Thus, the Court observed that domestic security surveillance may involve different policy and practical considerations from the surveillance of "ordinary crime." The gathering of security intelligence is often long range and involves the interrelation of various sources and types of information. The exact targets of such surveillance may be more difficult to identify than in surveillance operations against many types of crime specified in Title III. Often, too, the emphasis of domestic intelligence gathering is on the prevention of unlawful activity or the enhancement of the Government's preparedness for some possible future crisis or emergency. Thus, the focus of domestic surveillance may be less precise than that directed against more conventional types of crime.... Different standards [for surveillance involving domestic security] may be compatible with the Fourth Amendment if they are reasonable both in relation to the legitimate need of Government for intelligence information and the protected rights of our citizens. For the warrant application may vary according to the governmental interest to be enforced and the nature of citizen rights deserving protection.

Against this background, Congress passed FISA to settle what it believed to be the unresolved question of the applicability of the Fourth Amendment warrant requirement to electronic surveillance for foreign intelligence purposes, and to "remove any doubt as to the lawfulness of such surveillance." H.R.Rep. 1283, pt. I, 95th Cong., 2d Sess. 25 (1978) ("House Report"). FISA reflects both Congress's "legislative judgment" that the court orders and other procedural safeguards laid out in the Act "are necessary to insure that electronic surveillance by the U.S. Government within this country conforms to the fundamental principles of the fourth amendment," S.Rep. No. 701, 95th Cong., 2d Sess. 13, *reprinted in* 1978 U.S.Code Cong. & Ad.News 3973, 3982 ("Senate Report 95–701"), and its attempt to fashion a "secure framework by which the Executive Branch may conduct legitimate electronic surveillance for foreign intelligence purposes within the context of this Nation's commitment to privacy and individual rights." S.Rep. No. 604, 95th Cong., 1st Sess. 15, *reprinted in* 1978 U.S.Code Cong. & Ad.News 3904, 3916 ("Senate Report 95–604"). In constructing this framework, Congress gave close scrutiny to departures from those Fourth Amendment doctrines applicable in the criminal-investigation context in order to ensure that the procedures established in [FISA] are reasonable in relation to legitimate foreign counterintelligence requirements and the protected rights of individuals. Their reasonableness depends, in part, upon an assessment of the difficulties of investigating activities planned, directed, and supported from abroad by foreign intelligence services and foreign-based terrorist groups. The differences between ordinary criminal investigations to gather evidence of specific crimes and foreign counterintelligence investigations to uncover and monitor clandestine activities have been taken into account. Other factors include the international responsibilities of the United States, the duties of the Federal Government to the States in matters involving foreign terrorism, and the need to maintain the secrecy of lawful counterintelligence sources and methods.

We regard the procedures fashioned in FISA as a constitutionally adequate balancing of the individual's Fourth Amendment rights against the nation's need to obtain foreign intelligence information. The governmental concerns are detailed in the passages quoted above from *Keith* and the legislative history of FISA, and those concerns make reasonable the adoption of prerequisites to surveillance that are less stringent than those precedent to the issuance of a warrant for a criminal investigation. Against this background, the Act requires that the FISA Judge find probable cause to believe that the target is a foreign power or an agent of a foreign power, and that the place at which the electronic surveillance is to be directed is being used or is about to be used by a foreign power or an agent of a foreign power; and it requires him to find that the application meets the requirements of the Act. These requirements make it reasonable to dispense with a requirement that the FISA Judge find probable cause to believe that surveillance will in fact lead to the gathering of foreign intelligence information. Further, if the target is a United States person, the Act requires the FISA Judge to determine that the executive branch's certifications pursuant to § 1804(a)(7) are not clearly erroneous in light of the application as a whole, and to find that the application properly proposes, as required by § 1801(h), to minimize the intrusion upon the target's privacy.

We conclude that these requirements provide an appropriate balance between the individual's interest in privacy and the government's need to obtain foreign intelligence information, and that FISA does not violate the probable cause requirement of the Fourth Amendment.

Nor is there any merit to defendants' contention that the national security interests of the United States are not implicated by acts of terrorism directed wholly outside the United States. The government points out that if other nations were to harbor terrorists and give them safe haven for staging terrorist activities against the United States, United States national security would be threatened. As a reciprocal matter, the United States cannot afford to give safe haven to terrorists who seek to carry out raids against other nations. Thus, international terrorism conducted from the United States, no matter where it is directed, may well have a substantial effect on United States national security and foreign policy.

. . .

B.   Compliance with the Requirements of FISA

Defendants contend that, even if FISA is constitutional, the evidence derived from the wiretap should have been suppressed because the provisions of FISA were not complied with, in that (1) the surveillance was conducted as part of a criminal investigation, rather than a national security investigation; (2) the district court erred in failing to disclose the information contained in the FISA applications and orders; and (3) Duggan, although allegedly a "target" of the FISA surveillance, was not so named in the FISA applications. We reject each of these contentions.

. . .

The Alleged Use of FISA Surveillance to Conduct a Criminal Investigation

Defendants contend that the surveillance of Megahey's telephone was not authorized by FISA because the information was sought as part of a criminal investigation. We see no grounds for concluding that the requirements of FISA were not met.

FISA permits federal officials to obtain orders authorizing electronics surveillance "for the purpose of obtaining foreign intelligence information." 50 U.S.C. § 1802(b). The requirement that foreign intelligence information be the primary objective of the surveillance is plain not only from the language of § 1802(b) but also from the requirements in § 1804 as to what the application must contain. The application must contain a certification by a designated official of the executive branch that the purpose of the surveillance is to acquire foreign intelligence information, and the certification must set forth the basis for the certifying official's belief that the information sought is the type of foreign intelligence information described. *Id.* § 1804(a)(7).

Once this certification is made, however, it is, under FISA, subjected to only minimal scrutiny by the courts. Congress deemed it a sufficient check in this regard to require the FISA Judge (1) to find probable cause to believe that the target of the requested surveillance is an agent of a foreign power; (2) to find that the application is complete and in proper form; and (3) when the target is a United States person, to find that the certifications are not "clearly erroneous." The FISA Judge, in reviewing the application, is not to second-guess the executive branch official's certification that the objective of the surveillance is foreign intelligence information. Further, Congress intended that, when a person affected by a FISA surveillance challenges the FISA Court's order, a reviewing court is to have no greater authority to second-guess the executive branch's certifications than has the FISA Judge. [I]n determining the legality of a surveillance . . . the trial judge . . . [is] not to make determinations which the issuing judge is not authorized to make. Where the bill specifies the scope or nature of judicial review in the consideration of an application, any review under these subsections is similarly constrained. For example, when reviewing the certifications required by [§ 1804(a)(7)], unless there is a prima facie showing of a fraudulent statement by a certifying officer, procedural regularity is the only determination to be made if a non-U.S. person is the target. . . .

We see no basis for any suggestion in the present case that the application to the FISA Court did not meet the statutory requirement for certifying that the information sought was foreign intelligence information. At the time of the FISA application, the executive branch was aware that PIRA was an international terrorist organization and that Megahey played a leadership role in PIRA activities. In such circumstances, the foreign intelligence value of a FISA wiretap on Megahey's telephone would be plain: he would likely be a prime source of information relating to PIRA membership, goals, methods, and operations. The publicly filed government affidavits in this case make clear that the FISA surveillance was instituted as part of an investigation of international terrorism. Moreover, we have reviewed the *in camera* submissions to the FISA Judge, and we agree with the district court's finding that "the purpose of the surveillance in this case, both initially and throughout, was to secure foreign intelligence information and was not, as [the] defendants assert, directed towards criminal investigation or the institution of a criminal prosecution." *Megahey,* 553 F.Supp. at 1190.

Finally, we emphasize that otherwise valid FISA surveillance is not tainted simply because the government can anticipate that the fruits of such surveillance may later be used, as allowed by § 1806(b), as evidence in a criminal trial. Congress recognized that in many cases the concerns of the government with respect to foreign intelligence will overlap those with respect to law enforcement. Thus, one Senate Report noted that [i]ntelligence and criminal law enforcement tend to merge in [the area of foreign counterintelligence investigations]. . . .

. . .

In sum, FISA authorizes surveillance for the purpose of obtaining foreign intelligence information; the information possessed about Megahey involved international terrorism; and the fact that domestic law enforcement concerns may also have been implicated did not eliminate the government's ability to obtain a valid FISA order.

2.   The District Court's Refusal to Disclose the Substance of the FISA Applications

Defendant's contention that the district court erred in refusing to disclose the substance of the affidavits and certifications that accompanied the FISA applications need not detain us long. Section 1806(f) of FISA provides for *in camera, ex parte* review of the documents where the Attorney General has filed an affidavit stating that disclosure of the FISA applications and orders would harm the national security of the United States . . .

We see no error in Judge Sifton's determination that disclosure was not necessary for an accurate determination of the legality of the surveillance of Megahey. Defendants have made no showing of misrepresented facts; they do not argue that Megahey was not clearly identified as a target. They have made no other presentation warranting disclosure. Under the circumstances, Judge Sifton did not abuse his discretion.

3.   The Failure to Name Duggan as a Target of the Surveillance

Defendants contend that the fruits of the FISA surveillance should be suppressed because Duggan was not named as a target of the surveillance. The import of this argument is, apparently, that because Duggan is a United States person, the preconditions to granting an FISA order allowing surveillance of Duggan would have been more stringent than they were for surveillance of Megahey, a nonresident alien. Defendants' motion to suppress the evidence on this ground was properly denied by the district court on the grounds that it was untimely and lacked merit.

. . .

Defendants were thus twice put on notice prior to trial that Duggan had not been named as a target and they could have advanced the Duggan-omission argument in timely fashion. Their failure to do so constituted a waiver.

If defendants' argument as to the omission of Duggan had not been waived, we would reject it on its merits. The identification requirement imposed by FISA is only that an application for surveillance identify the "target of the electronic surveillance." 50 U.S.C. § 1804(a)(3)....

. . .

The judgments of conviction are affirmed. The mandate shall issue forthwith.

QUESTIONS AND NOTES

1.　Duggan is an early case in which a criminal prosecution involving the use of FISA-derived material reached the federal district courts and courts of appeal. See also United States v. Nicholson, 955 F.Supp. 588 (E.D.Va.1997); United States v. Pelton, 835 F.2d 1067 (4th Cir.1987); United States v. Sarkissian, 841 F.2d 959 (9th Cir. 1988). Post–9/11, there has been an increase in the number of prosecutions in which issues growing out of the results of a FISA-authorized investigation have been raised. See, for example, United States v. Holy Land Foundation for Relief and Development, 2007 WL 2011319 (N.D.Tex. 2007); United States v. Hassoun, 2007 WL 1068127 (S.D.Fla. 2007); United States v. Benkahla, 437 F.Supp.2d 541 (E.D.Va. 2006); United States v. Marzook, 435 F.Supp.2d 778 (N.D.Ill.2006), although in some of these cases, the FISA surveillance occurred pre–9/11. See, for example, the Marzook case, supra. We have seen the Holy Land Foundation case previously, supra, p. 85, and the Hassoun case, supra, is the same case in which Jose Padilla, whose saga will be treated in detail infra, chapter 10, was one of the defendants. See also United States v. Abu–Jihaad, 630 F.3d 102 (2d Cir. 2010).

2.　FISA proceedings are secret and ex parte. They are conducted by the special FISA court, not in a regular courtroom but in a special room through "a series of doors and secret codes." Jonathan Turley, A Shot Across the Bow From the Darkness, LA Times, August 26, 2002, B9. Accordingly, we rarely get a glimpse of the court, with neither the public nor the suspected person(s) being present or normally having access to published materials arising out of the proceedings. When criminal prosecutions relating to the FISA matter do occur, however, they provide a limited window into the earlier-occurring FISA proceedings. Duggan and similar cases provide such a window and also give a valuable perspective on how the FISA process and issues relating thereto are viewed by judges not directly involved in the FISA judicial approval process. They help us to understand how the FISA process works, and they are a vehicle for addressing the constitutional issues raised by that process.

3.　A more direct view into the FISA court process was provided in 2002 when two opinions, one from the FISA lower court and one from the FISA court of review were made public; this was a very unusual event. See In re All Matters Submitted to the Foreign Intelligence Surveillance Court ("In re FISC"), 218 F.Supp.2d 611 (Foreign Intel.Surv.Ct.2002) and In re Sealed Case, 310 F.3d 717 (F.I.S.Ct.Rev.2002), an excerpt from which was reproduced in note 1, supra, p. 186.

B. THE TERRORIST SURVEILLANCE PROGRAM (TSP) CONTROVERSY AND ELECTRONIC SURVEILLANCE ABROAD

1. BACKGROUND

Sometime after September 11, 2001, President Bush approved a secret Terrorist Surveillance Program that authorized the National Security Agency (NSA) to electronically eavesdrop, without obtaining judicial approval, on international communications into and out of the United States between persons linked to al Qaeda or related terrorist organizations. The existence of the program was first disclosed in the New York Times in December 2005. Details and specifics of the TSP have not been publicly disclosed but its existence has been confirmed by the administration. See ACLU v. National Security Agency, 493 F.3d 644 (6th Cir.2007):

> Sometime after the September 11, 2001, terrorist attacks, President Bush authorized the NSA to begin a counter-terrorism operation that has come to be known as the Terrorist Surveillance Program ("TSP"). Although the specifics remain undisclosed, it has been publicly acknowledged that the TSP includes the interception (i.e., wiretapping), without warrants, of telephone and email communications where one party to the communication is located outside the United States and the NSA has "a reasonable basis to conclude that one party to the communication is a member of al Qaeda, affiliated with al Qaeda, or a member of an organization affiliated with al Qaeda, or working in support of al Qaeda." *See* Press Briefing by Att'y Gen. Alberto Gonzales and Gen. Michael Hayden, Principal Deputy Dir. for Nat'l Intelligence (Dec. 19, 2005), *available at* http://www.whitehouse.gov/news/releases/2005/12/print/20051219–1.html (last visited July 2, 2007).[1]

---

1. [footnote by the court] In *Hepting v. AT & T Corp.,* the District Court for the Northern District of California collected and documented certain publicly available information, which provides some background and context for the present case:

"The *New York Times* disclosed the [TSP] on December 16, 2005. (James Risen and Eric Lichtlau, *Bush Lets U.S. Spy on Callers Without Courts,* The New York Times (Dec. 16, 2005)). The following day, President George W Bush confirmed the existence of a 'terrorist surveillance program' in his weekly radio address:

'In the weeks following the [September 11, 2001] terrorist attacks on our Nation, I authorized the National Security Agency, consistent with U.S. law and the Constitution, to intercept the international communications of people with known links to Al Qaeda and related terrorist organizations. Before we intercept these communications, the Government must have information that establishes a clear link to these terrorist networks.'

"[Transcript] *available at* http://www.whitehouse.gov/news/releases/2005/12/print/20051217.html (last visited July 19, 2006). The President also described the mechanism by which the program is authorized and reviewed:

'The activities I authorized are reviewed approximately every 45 days. Each review is based on a fresh intelligence assessment of terrorist threats to the continuity of our Government and the threat of catastrophic damage to our homeland. During each assessment, previous activities under the authorization are reviewed. The review includes approval by our Nation's top legal officials, including the Attorney General and the Counsel to the President. I have

In May, 2006, USA Today reported the existence of a second NSA program alleging that three major communications companies, BellSouth Corp., Verizon Communications Inc. and AT & T had provided millions of telephone calling records to the NSA and that the Agency used these databases not to listen in or record conversations but rather to analyze calling patterns in an effort to detect terrorist activity—a type of data mining. A fourth company, Qwest Communications International, Inc. was reported to have declined to participate in the program. Officials at BellSouth and Verizon subsequently denied providing any customer telephone records to the government. AT & T and the government neither confirmed nor denied the USA Today report.

Subsequently, and over the course of the next two years, activities occurred on a number of fronts growing out of these disclosures. In January, 2006, the Department of Justice issued a lengthy legal memorandum, referred to as a White Paper, defending the legality of the electronic surveillance conducted under the TSP.

A number of senators and representatives made public statements about the TSP, and congressional committees conducted hearings on the program and its legality, often expressing frustration about not being able to obtain sufficient information about the Program's details. See, e.g., Department of Justice Responses to the House Judiciary Committee Minority Members Joint Questions Regarding the NSA Terrorist Surveillance Program, March 24, 2006, available at http://fas.org/irp/agency/doj/fisa/doj032406.pdf. In this document, the majority of the DOJ's responses to the congressional questions declined to disclose the requested information, noting the "classified and sensitive" nature of the Program.

---

reauthorized this program more than 30 times since the September the 11th attacks, and I intend to do so for as long as our Nation faces a continuing threat from Al Qaeda and related groups.

'The NSA's activities under this authorization are thoroughly reviewed by the Justice Department and NSA's top legal officials, including NSA's General Counsel and Inspector General. Leaders in Congress have been briefed more than a dozen times on this authorization and the activities conducted under it. Intelligence officials involved in this activity also receive extensive training to ensure they perform their duties consistent with the letter and intent of the authorization.'

"Id.

"Attorney General Alberto Gonzales subsequently confirmed that this program intercepts 'contents of communications where ... one party to the communication is outside the United States' and the government has 'a reasonable basis to conclude that one party to the communication is a member of al Qaeda, affiliated with al Qaeda, or a member of an organization affiliated with al Qaeda, or working in support of al Qaeda.' [Press Briefing] *available at* http://www.whitehouse.gov/news/releases/2005/12/print/20051219–1.html (last visited July 19, 2005). The Attorney General also noted, 'This [program] is not about wiretapping everyone. This is a very concentrated, very limited program focused at gaining information about our enemy.' *Id.* at 5. The President has also made a public statement, of which the court takes judicial notice, that the government's 'international activities strictly target al Qaeda and their known affiliates,' 'the government does not listen to domestic phone calls without court approval' and the government is 'not mining or trolling through the personal lives of millions of innocent Americans.' The White House, President Bush Discusses NSA Surveillance Program (May 11, 2006), [*available at*] http://www.whitehouse.gov/news/releases/2006/05/20060511–1.html (last visited July 19, 2005)."

Hepting v. AT & T Corp., 439 F.Supp.2d 974, 986–87 (N.D.Cal.2006).

Lawsuits seeking to enjoin the TSP and otherwise seeking redress were filed. For an example of one such case where the district judge ruled that the Program was unconstitutional, see ACLU v. National Security Agency, 438 F.Supp.2d 754 (E.D.Mich. 2006). Subsequently, the administration reversed course to a limited extent; it had earlier rejected proposals that the TSP surveillances be brought to the FISA court for approval, but as described in ACLU v. National Security Agency, 493 F.3d 644, n. 4 (6th Cir.2007), the administration for the first time brought the FISA court into the TSP picture:

> On January 10, 2007, "a Judge of the Foreign Intelligence Surveillance Court issued orders authorizing the government to target for collection international communications into or out of the United States where there is probable cause to believe that one of the communicants is a member or agent of al Qaeda or an associated terrorist organization." Letter from Att'y Gen. Alberto Gonzales to Chair. of the Comm. on the Judiciary Patrick Leahy (Jan. 17, 2007), *available at* http://graphics8.nytimes.com/packages/pdf/politics/ 20060117gonzalesLetter. pdf (last visited July 2, 2007). According to a letter written by the Attorney General, "any electronic surveillance that was occurring as part of the [TSP] will now be conducted subject to the approval of the Foreign Intelligence Surveillance Court."

The district court order in the ACLU v. NSA case, supra, was appealed, and in July, 2007, the Sixth Circuit reversed, finding that the plaintiffs did not have standing.

Lawsuits were also filed based on the alleged data mining. AT & T customers sued AT & T alleging constitutional and statutory violations and seeking damages and injunctive and declaratory relief. See, e.g., Hepting v. AT & T Corp., 439 F.Supp. 2d 974 (N.D.Cal.2006). Meanwhile, defendants throughout the country in terrorist prosecutions and in other types of cases, too, sought disclosure from the government as to whether they had been eavesdropped upon under the TSP, hoping to prove that was the case and that the eavesdropping was illegal and somehow tainted their prosecution.

Reportedly in the spring or summer of 2007, the FISA court, now newly having undertaken some kind of review of the TSP surveillances, handed down a decision that presented a problem for the government in operating the TSP program. Although the relevant judicial decision(s) was [were] secret and not published, statements by government officials indicated that the legal problem was created by the fact that what had been considered to be purely international electronic surveillances (i.e. between two parties outside of the United States), sometimes involved the communication traveling through a communications switching station within the U.S. To address this type of issue and to harden up the legal foundation for the TSP program, the administration sought new legislation toward the very end of the congressional session in the summer of 2007.

In August, 2007, Congress enacted the Protect America Act, PL 110–55, designed to address the legal problems of the TSP program. However, it was a temporary fix. The congressional action was rushed, and many of the legislators wanted to return to the subject and legislate on the subject more carefully. Accordingly, it was provided in the Act that it would sunset after 180 days, i.e., on January 31, 2008. In the next few months, there was a great amount of activity in both houses of the Congress regarding the content of the legislation that would replace the Protect America Act. A major point of controversy was whether the final legislation would contain a provision granting immunity from civil liability to the telephone companies that had cooperated with the government's TSP program. Finally, in July, 2008, the new legislation to address these issues, titled the FISA Amendments Act of 2008, was passed and signed into law. The provisions of this Act are reproduced, and issues relating to it are treated in subsection C of this chapter, infra.

2. A PERSPECTIVE ON THE TSP FROM WITHIN THE GOVERNMENT

On July 10, 2009, a report was issued titled, Unclassified Report on President's Surveillance Program. The Report had been prepared by the Inspectors General of the CIA, DOD, DOJ, NSA, and the Office of the DNI [ed. Director of National Intelligence–ODNI] and can be found at: www. fas.org/irp/eprint/psp.pdf. Excerpts from the Report are reproduced below. It appears from these excerpts that the President authorized surveillance activities that extended beyond the TSP program. The exact nature of these activities remains highly classified. The entire report merits examination.

UNCLASSIFIED REPORT ON PRESIDENT'S SURVEILLANCE PROGRAM

. . .

Shortly thereafter, the President authorized the NSA to undertake a number of new, highly classified intelligence activities. All of these activities were authorized in a single Presidential Authorization that was periodically reauthorized.

The specific intelligence activities that were permitted by the Presidential Authorizations remain highly classified, except that beginning in December 2005 the President and other Administration officials acknowledged that these activities included the interception without a court order of certain international communications where there is "a reasonable basis to conclude that one party to the communication is a member of al-Qa'ida, affiliated with al-Qa'ida, or a member of an organization affiliated with al-Qa'ida." The President and other Administration officials referred to this publicly disclosed activity as the "Terrorist Surveillance Program," a convention we follow in this unclassified report. We refer to other intelligence activities authorized under the Presidential Authorizations as the "Other Intelligence Activities." The specific details of the Other Intelligence Activities remain highly classified, although the Attorney General publicly acknowledged the existence of such activities in August 2007. Together, the Terrorist Surveillance Program and the Other Intelligence Activities comprise the PSP.

. . .

CONCLUSION

Pursuant to the FISA Amendments Act of 2008, the Inspectors General [ed. IGs] of the DOJ, DoD, ODNI, NSA, and CIA conducted reviews of the PSP. In this report, the classified report, and the accompanying individual reports of the participating IGs, we describe how, following the terrorist attacks of September 11, 2001, the President directed that the NSA's signals intelligence collection capabilities be used to detect and prevent acts of terrorism within the United States.

Pursuant to this authority the NSA conducted new intelligence activities, including the collection of the content of communications into and out of the United States, where one party to the communication was reasonably believed to be a member of al-Qa'ida or its affiliates. The NSA analyzed this information for dissemination as leads to the IC[ed. Intelligence Community], principally to the CIA and the FBI. As described in the IG reports, the scope of this collection authority changed over the course of the PSP.

The IG reports describe the role of each of the participating agencies in the PSP, including the NSA's management and oversight of the collection and analysis process, the CIA's and FBI's use of the PSP-derived intelligence in their counterterrorism efforts, the ODNI's involvement in the program by providing periodic threat assessments and using the program intelligence to produce analytical products, and DOJ's role in analyzing and certifying the legality of the PSP. With the exception of the NSA, the DoD had limited involvement in the PSP.

The IG reports also describe the conflicting views surrounding the legality of aspects of the PSP during 2004, the confrontation between officials from DOJ and the White House about the legal basis for parts of the program, as well as the resolution of that conflict. The ensuing transition of the PSP from presidential authority to statutory authority under FISA is also described in the IG reports.

The IGs also examined the impact of PSP information on counterterrorism efforts. Many senior IC officials believe that the PSP filled a gap in intelligence collection thought to exist under the FISA statute shortly after the al-Qa'ida terrorist attacks against the United States. Others within the IC, including FBI agents, CIA analysts and officers, and other officials had difficulty evaluating the precise contribution of the PSP to counterterrorism efforts because it was most often viewed as one source among many available analytic and intelligence-gathering tools in these efforts. The IG reports describe several examples of how PSP-derived information factored into specific investigations and operations.

Finally, the collection activities pursued under the PSP, and under FISA following the PSP's transition to that authority, involved unprecedented collection activities. We believe the retention and use by IC organizations of information collected under the PSP and FISA should be carefully monitored.

3. MATERIALS BEARING ON THE LEGALITY OF THE TSP

Sometime after the eruption of the controversy regarding the TSP program, the Department of Justice issued a memorandum, a so-called White Paper, justifying the legality of the program. Excerpts from this memorandum are reproduced below.

Washington, D.C. 20530

January 19, 2006

LEGAL AUTHORITIES SUPPORTING THE ACTIVITIES OF THE NATIONAL SECURITY AGENCY DESCRIBED BY THE PRESIDENT

As the President has explained, since shortly after the attacks of September 11, 2001, he has authorized the National Security Agency ("NSA") to intercept international communications into and out of the United States of persons linked to al Qaeda or related terrorist organizations. The purpose of these intercepts is to establish an early warning system to detect and prevent another catastrophic terrorist attack on the United States. This paper addresses, in an unclassified form, the legal basis for the NSA activities described by the President ("NSA activities").

SUMMARY

. . .

The NSA activities are supported by the President's well-recognized inherent constitutional authority as Commander in Chief and sole organ for the Nation in foreign affairs to conduct warrantless surveillance of enemy forces for intelligence purposes to detect and disrupt armed attacks on the United States. The President has the chief responsibility under the Constitution to protect America from attack, and the Constitution gives the President the authority necessary to fulfill that solemn responsibility. The President has made clear that he will exercise all authority available to him, consistent with the Constitution, to protect the people of the United States.

In the specific context of the current armed conflict with al Qaeda and related terrorist organizations, Congress by statute has confirmed and supplemented the President's recognized authority under Article II of the Constitution to conduct such warrantless surveillance to prevent further catastrophic attacks on the homeland. In its first legislative response to the terrorist attacks of September 11th, Congress authorized the President to "use all necessary and appropriate force against those nations, organizations, or persons he determines planned, authorized, committed, or aided the terrorist attacks" of September 11th in order to prevent "any future acts of international terrorism against the United States." Authorization for Use of Military Force, Pub. L. No. 107–40, § 2(a), 115 Stat. 224, 224 (Sept. 18, 2001) (reported as a note to 50 U.S.C.A. § 1541) ("AUMF"). History conclusively demonstrates that warrantless communications intelligence targeted at the enemy in time of armed conflict is a traditional and fundamental incident of the use of military force authorized by the AUMF. The Supreme Court's interpretation of the AUMF in *Hamdi v. Rumsfeld*, 542 U.S. 507 (2004), confirms that Congress in the AUMF gave its express approval to the military conflict against al Qaeda and its allies and thereby to the President's use of all traditional and accepted incidents of force in this current military conflict— including warrantless electronic surveillance to intercept enemy communications both at home and abroad. This understanding of the AUMF demonstrates Congress's support for the President's authority to protect the Nation and, at the same time, adheres to Justice O'Connor's admonition that "a state of war is not a blank check for the President," *Hamdi*, 542 U.S. at 536 (plurality opinion), particularly in view of the narrow scope of the NSA activities.

The AUMF places the President at the zenith of his powers in authorizing the NSA activities. Under the tripartite framework set forth by Justice Jackson in *Youngstown Sheet & Tube Co. v. Sawyer*, 343 U.S. 579, 635–38 (1952) (Jackson, J., concurring), Presidential authority is analyzed to determine whether the President is acting in accordance with congressional authorization (category I), whether he acts in the absence of a grant or denial of authority by Congress (category II), or whether he uses his own authority under the Constitution to take actions incompatible with congressional measures (category III). Because of the broad authorization provided in the AUMF, the President's action here falls within category I of Justice Jackson's framework. Accordingly, the President's power in authorizing the NSA activities is at its height because he acted "pursuant to an express or implied authorization of Congress," and his power "includes all that he possesses in his own right plus all that Congress can delegate." *Id.* at 635.

The NSA activities are consistent with the preexisting statutory framework generally applicable to the interception of communications in the United States—the Foreign Intelligence Surveillance Act ("FISA"), as amended, 50 U.S.C. §§ 1801–1862 (2000 & Supp. II 2002), and relevant related provisions in chapter 119 of title 18.1

Although FISA generally requires judicial approval of electronic surveillance, FISA also contemplates that Congress may authorize such surveillance by a statute other than FISA. See 50 U.S.C. § 1809(a) (prohibiting any person from intentionally "engag[ing] ... in electronic surveillance under color of law except as authorized by statute"). The AUMF, as construed by the Supreme Court in *Hamdi* and as confirmed by the history and tradition of armed conflict, is just such a statute. Accordingly, electronic surveillance conducted by the President pursuant to the AUMF, including the NSA activities, is fully consistent with FISA and falls within category I of Justice Jackson's framework.

Even if there were ambiguity about whether FISA, read together with the AUMF, permits the President to authorize the NSA activities, the canon of constitutional avoidance requires reading these statutes in harmony to overcome any restrictions in FISA and Title III, at least as they might otherwise apply to the congressionally authorized armed conflict with al Qaeda. Indeed, were FISA and Title III interpreted to impede the President's ability to use the traditional tool of electronic surveillance to detect and prevent future attacks by a declared enemy that has already struck at the homeland and is engaged in ongoing operations against the United States, the constitutionality of FISA, as applied to that situation, would be called into very serious doubt. In fact, if this difficult constitutional question had to be addressed, FISA would be unconstitutional as applied to this narrow context. Importantly, the FISA Court of Review itself recognized just three years ago that the President retains constitutional authority to conduct foreign surveillance apart from the FISA framework, and the President is certainly entitled, at a minimum, to rely on that judicial interpretation of the Constitution and FISA.

Finally, the NSA activities fully comply with the requirements of the Fourth Amendment. The interception of communications described by the President falls within a well-established exception to the warrant requirement and satisfies the Fourth Amendment's fundamental requirement of reasonableness. The NSA activities are thus constitutionally permissible and fully protective of civil liberties....

QUESTIONS AND NOTES

1. How many different arguments in support of the TSP program are articulated in the DOJ summary of the arguments made in the White Paper?

2. Fourteen scholars and former government officials joined in writing a letter dated January 9, 2007, to the Senate Judiciary Committee responding to the arguments made in the DOJ White Paper, characterizing the Justice Department's legal defense of the TSP program as failing "to identify any plausible legal authority for ... [the] surveillance [program]." The letter contended:

"[T]he AUMF cannot reasonably be construed to implicitly authorize warrantless electronic surveillance in the United States during wartime, where Congress has expressly and specifically addressed that precise questions in FISA and limited any such warrantless surveillance to the first fifteen days of war."

Regarding the DOJ claim of "inherent" presidential authority, the letter responded,

"Congress indisputably has authority to regulate electronic surveillance within the United States as it has done in FISA. Where Congress has so regulated, the President can act in contravention of statute only if his authority is *exclusive*, and not subject to the check of statutory regulation."

Further, the letter argued,

Moreover, to construe the AUMF as the DOJ suggests would itself raise serious constitutional questions under the Fourth Amendment. The Supreme Court has never upheld warrantless wiretapping within the United States. Accordingly, the principle that statutes should be construed to avoid serious constitutional questions provides an additional reason for concluding that the AUMF does not authorize the President's actions. . . ."

A Response to the Justice Department from Law Professors and Former Government Officials, January 9, 2007. See also Elizabeth B. Bazan & Jennifer K. Elsea, Congressional Research Memorandum, Presidential Authority to Conduct Warrantless Electronic Surveillance to Gather Foreign Intelligence Information, January 5, 2006.

Who has the better of the argument?

3. Many of the critics of the TSP program argued that using FISA procedures would not have disadvantaged the TSP program electronic surveillance and would ensure judicial oversight of the surveillances in the program, where the surveillance impacted on the domestic end of a communication. Of course, the critics did not have very specific information about the TSP program. Among the issues addressed in the Department of Justice Responses to the House Judiciary Committee Minority Members Joint Questions Regarding the NSA Terrorist Surveillance Program, March 24, 2006, the DOJ said the following,

Among the advantages offered by the Terrorist Surveillance Program compared to FISA is *who* makes the probable cause determination and how many layers of review must occur before surveillance begins. Under the Terrorist Surveillance Program, professional intelligence officers, who are experts on al Qaeda and its tactics (including its use of communication systems), with appropriate and rigorous oversight, make the decisions about which international communications should be intercepted. . . .

By contrast, pursuing "prior judicial review by the FISA court" requires significantly more time. . . . [T]he Government must assemble a voluminous application, obtain the approval of the Attorney General himself and senior administrative national security officials, submit the materials to the court and await its decision. . . . [A]s a practical matter, it is necessary for NSA intelligence officers, NSA lawyers, Justice Department lawyers, and the Attorney General to review a matter before even emergency surveillance would begin....

4. Footnotes 5 and 6 in the White Paper, and a related comment in the Department of Justice's Responses to the House Judiciary Committee's Oversight Questions regarding the NSA Terrorist Surveillance Program, taken together with 18 U.S.C. § 2511(2)(f) and 50 U.S.C. § 1801(f), all of which are reproduced below, add still another potential issue to the mix in any examination of the legality of the NSA TSP program.

    a.   Footnote 5 in the DOJ White Paper:

    5.   To avoid revealing details about the operation of the program, it is assumed for purposes of this paper that the activities described by the President constitute "electronic surveillance," as defined by FISA, 50 U.S.C. § 1801(f).

    b.   Footnote 6 in the DOJ White Paper:

    6.   FISA's legislative history reveals that these provisions were intended to exclude certain intelligence activities conducted by the National Security Agency from the coverage of FISA. According to the report of the Senate Judiciary Committee on FISA, "this provision [ed. referencing what became the first part of section 2511(2)(f)] is designed to make clear that the legislation does not deal with international signals intelligence activities as currently engaged in by the National Security Agency and electronic surveillance conducted outside the United States." S. Rep. No. 95–604, at 64 (1978), *reprinted* in 1978 U.S.C.C.A.N. 3904, 3965. The legislative history also makes clear that the definition of "electronic surveillance" was crafted for the same reason. *See id.* at 33–34, 1978 U.S.C.C.A.N. at 3934–36. FISA thereby "adopts the view expressed by the Attorney General during the hearings that enacting statutory controls to regulate the National Security Agency and the surveillance of Americans abroad raises problems best left to separate legislation." *Id.* at 64, 1978 U.S.C.C.A.N. at 3965. Such legislation placing limitations on traditional NSA activities was drafted, but never passed. *See* National Intelligence Reorganization and Reform Act of 1978: Hearings Before the Senate Select Committee on Intelligence, 95th Cong., 2d Sess. 999–1007 (1978) (text of unenacted legislation). And Congress understood that the NSA surveillance that it intended categorically to exclude from FISA could include the monitoring of international communications into or out of the United States of U.S. citizens. The report specifically referred to the Church Committee report for its description of the NSA's activities, S. Rep. No. 95–604, at 64 n.63, 1978 U.S.C.C.A.N. at 3965–66 n.63, which stated that "the NSA intercepts messages passing over international lines of communication, some of which have one terminal within the United States. Traveling over these lines of communication, especially those with one terminal in the United States, are messages of Americans...." S. Rep. 94–755, at Book II, 308 (1976). Congress's understanding in the legislative history of FISA that such communications could be intercepted outside FISA procedures is notable.

c. Excerpt from the DOJ Responses to the House Judiciary Committee's Oversight Questions . . .:

. . . [W]e note that the Department's legal analysis [viz. the White Paper] assumes, solely for purposes of that analysis, that the targeted interception of international communications authorized under the Terrorist Surveillance Program would constitute "electronic surveillance" as defined by FISA. As noted in our January 19 paper [viz. the White Paper], we cannot confirm whether that is actually the case without disclosing sensitive classified information.

d. 18 U.S.C. § 2511(2)(f):

§ 2511. Interception and disclosure of wire, oral, or electronic communications prohibited

. . .

(2)

. . .

(f) Nothing contained in this chapter or chapter 121 or 206 of this title, or section 705 of the Communications Act of 1934, shall be deemed to affect the acquisition by the United States Government of foreign intelligence information from international or foreign communications, or foreign intelligence activities conducted in accordance with otherwise applicable Federal law involving a foreign electronic communications system, utilizing a means other than electronic surveillance as defined in section 101 of the Foreign Intelligence Surveillance Act of 1978, and procedures in this chapter or chapter 121 and the Foreign Intelligence Surveillance Act of 1978 shall be the exclusive means by which electronic surveillance, as defined in section 101 of such Act, and the interception of domestic wire, oral, and electronic communications may be conducted.

e. 50 U.S.C. § 1801(f) [§ 1801 is section 101 of the FISA statute—referred to in § 2511(2)(f) in note d. above].

50 U.S.C. § 1801

. . .

(f) "Electronic surveillance" means—

(1) the acquisition by an electronic, mechanical, or other surveillance device of the contents of any wire or radio communication sent by or intended to be received by a particular, known United States person who is in the United States, if the contents are acquired by intentionally targeting that United States person, under circumstances in which a person has a reasonable expectation of privacy and a warrant would be required for law enforcement purposes;

(2) the acquisition by an electronic, mechanical, or other surveillance device of the contents of any wire communication to or from a person in the United States, without the consent of any party thereto, if such acquisition occurs in the United States, but does not include the acquisition of those communications of computer tres-

passers that would be permissible under section 2511(2)(i) of Title 18;

(3) the intentional acquisition by an electronic, mechanical, or other surveillance device of the contents of any radio communication, under circumstances in which a person has a reasonable expectation of privacy and a warrant would be required for law enforcement purposes, and if both the sender and all intended recipients are located within the United States; or

(4) the installation or use of an electronic, mechanical, or other surveillance device in the United States for monitoring to acquire information, other than from a wire or radio communication, under circumstances in which a person has a reasonable expectation of privacy and a warrant would be required for law enforcement purposes.

5.   What is the significance of the materials contained in note 4, supra, especially the material defining "electronic surveillance"? What is the significance of the fact that the DOJ has declined to affirm definitively whether the TSP program involves "electronic surveillance"? Do you infer from that fact that the conduct of the TSP does involve electronic surveillance? Or do you draw the contrary inference? How might it be possible that the controversial aspect of the TSP does not involve "electronic surveillance"? If the TSP does not involve "electronic surveillance," what would be the legal implications of that fact?

6.   Some of the issues suggested by the materials in note 4, supra, were commented upon in American Civil Liberties Union v. National Security Agency, 493 F.3d 644 (6th Cir.2007), cert. denied, 552 U.S. 1179 (2008):

BATCHELDER, J., delivered the judgment of the court. GIBBONS, J. delivered a separate opinion concurring in the judgment only. GILMAN, J. delivered a separate dissenting opinion.

Alice M. Batchelder, Circuit Judge.

. . .

The plaintiffs in this action include journalists, academics, and lawyers who regularly communicate with individuals located overseas, who the plaintiffs believe are the types of people the NSA suspects of being al Qaeda terrorists, affiliates, or supporters, and are therefore likely to be monitored under the TSP [Terrorist Surveillance Program]. From this suspicion, and the limited factual foundation in this case, the plaintiffs allege that they have a "well founded belief" that their communications are being tapped. According to the plaintiffs, the NSA's operation of the TSP—and the possibility of warrantless surveillance—subjects them to conditions that constitute an irreparable harm.

. . .

2.   Title III

Title III of the Omnibus Crime Control and Safe Streets Act of 1968 ("Title III"), 18 U.S.C. §§ 2510–22, generally regulates the government's interception of wire, oral, and electronic communications. The first relevant question is whether Title III applies to the type of surveillance conducted by the NSA under the TSP, considering Title III's express limitations.

> Nothing contained in this [statute (i.e., Title III)] ... shall be deemed to affect [1] the acquisition by the United States Government of foreign intelligence information from international or foreign communications, or [2] foreign intelligence activities conducted in accordance with otherwise applicable Federal law involving a foreign electronic communications system, utilizing a means other than electronic surveillance as defined in section 101 of the Foreign Intelligence Surveillance Act of 1978, and [3] procedures in this [statute (i.e., Title III)] ... and the Foreign Intelligence Surveillance Act of 1978 shall be the exclusive means by which electronic surveillance, as defined in section 101 of such Act, and the interception of domestic wire, oral, and electronic communications may be conducted.

18 U.S.C. § 2511(2)(f).

When this statutory language is parsed into its three individual clauses, its limitations become clear. The first clause disclaims Title III applicability generally—acknowledging that Title III does not apply to "the acquisition by the United States Government of foreign intelligence information from international or foreign communications." The second clause disclaims Title III applicability specifically—recognizing that Title III does not govern "foreign intelligence activities conducted in accordance with otherwise applicable Federal law involving a foreign electronic communications system, utilizing a means other than electronic surveillance as defined in [FISA]." The final clause, which is known as the "exclusivity provision," recognizes the respective roles of Title III and FISA, by stating that the "procedures in [Title III] and [FISA] shall be the exclusive means by which electronic surveillance, as defined in section 101 of [FISA] and the interception of domestic wire, oral, and electronic communications may be conducted."

The first clause of § 2511(2)(f)—stating that Title III does not govern the acquisition of "foreign intelligence information from international or foreign communications"—expressly disclaims application of Title III to surveillance activities of the type at issue in the present case. The NSA monitors international communications for the purpose of acquiring foreign intelligence about terrorist organizations; this type of surveillance falls squarely under the disclaimer found in the first clause of § 2511(2)(f). By its own terms, then, Title III does not apply to the conduct of which the plaintiffs complain.

. . .

Because the first clause of § 2511(2)(f) expressly disclaims Title III's application to this case, it is unnecessary to construe the second and third clauses. But, it is worth acknowledging that these two clauses raise complex legal issues which cannot be resolved on the present record. The second clause explains that Title III does not apply if four factors are all satisfied: (1) the defendant is engaged in "foreign intelligence activities"; (2) the defendant is acting "in accordance with otherwise applicable Federal law"; (3) the defendant's surveillance involves a "foreign electronic communications system"; and (4) the defendant utilizes "a means other than electronic surveillance" as defined in FISA. These factors raise a host of intricate issues, such as whether the NSA's wiretapping actually involves "electronic surveillance" as defined in FISA, and whether the NSA is acting in accordance with federal law, such as the Authorization for Use of Military Force ("AUMF"), Pub.L. 107–40, § 2, 115 Stat. 224 (2001). Some of these issues involve sophisticated legal questions or complex factual questions. But, resolving these issues is unnecessary because the first clause of § 2511(2)(f) conclusively disclaims Title III's application.

It is likewise unnecessary, at this point, to delve into the numerous issues raised by the third clause, i.e., the exclusivity provision. The exclusivity provision differs from the first two clauses of § 2511(2)(f), in that it does not merely disclaim Title III's application. Instead, it states that Title III and FISA shall be the "exclusive means" by which particular types of surveillance may occur, thus prescribing the separate roles of Title III and FISA, rather than the application of Title III alone. The plaintiffs assert a statutory cause of action for the NSA's alleged violation of the exclusivity provision, which I address separately.... It is, therefore, unnecessary to dissect the exclusivity provision at this point in the analysis.

Because the first clause of § 2511(2)(f) states that Title III does not apply to the internationally focused surveillance activities challenged in this case, the plaintiffs have not asserted a viable cause of action under Title III.

3. FISA

The Foreign Intelligence Surveillance Act of 1978 ("FISA"), 50 U.S.C. § 1801 *et seq.*,—as the separate and distinct counterpart to Title III—governs the interception of electronic communications involving foreign intelligence information. *See* 50 U.S.C. § 1802(a)(1). FISA is fraught with detailed statutory definitions and is expressly limited, by its own terms, to situations in which the President has authorized "electronic surveillance," as defined in 50 U.S.C. § 1801(f), for the purposes of acquiring "foreign intelligence information," as defined in 50 U.S.C. § 1801(e).

First, the surveillance in question must acquire "foreign intelligence information," which includes "information that relates to ... the ability of the United States to protect against ... international terrorism." 50 U.S.C. § 1801(e)(1)(B). In the present case, the NSA intercepts communications in which it has a *"reasonable basis* to conclude that one party to the communication is a member of al Qaeda, affiliated with al Qaeda, or a member of an organization affiliated with al Qaeda, or working in support of al Qaeda." *See* Press Briefing by Att'y Gen. Alberto Gonzales and Gen. Michael Hayden, Principal Deputy Dir. for Nat'l Intelligence (Dec. 19,

2005), *available at* http://www.whitehouse.gov/news/releases/2005/12/print/20051219–1.html (last visited July 2, 2007) (emphasis added). The proclaimed purpose is to prevent future terrorist attacks, *see id.* ("This is a very concentrated, very limited program focused at gaining information about our enemy."), and thus the NSA's conduct satisfies this statutory requirement.

Next, the interception must occur by "electronic surveillance." According to the plaintiffs, the government's admission that it intercepts telephone and email communications—which involve electronic media and are generally considered, in common parlance, forms of electronic communications—is tantamount to admitting that the NSA engaged in "electronic surveillance" for purposes of FISA. This argument fails upon recognition that "electronic surveillance" has a very particular, detailed meaning under FISA—a legal definition that requires careful consideration of numerous factors such as the types of communications acquired, the location of the parties to the acquired communications, the location where the acquisition occurred, the location of any surveillance, device, and the reasonableness of the parties' expectation of privacy. *See* 50 U.S.C. § 1801(f). The plaintiffs have not shown, and cannot show, that the NSA's surveillance activities include the sort of conduct that would satisfy FISA's definition of "electronic surveillance," and the present record does not demonstrate that the NSA's conduct falls within FISA's definitions.

4. LITIGATION INVOLVING THE NSA'S TSP PROGRAM

The TSP program essentially ended in 2007, but the disclosures regarding the program led to a number of lawsuits seeking to determine whether particular individuals had been surveilled and testing the legality of the program. Generally such legal efforts were stymied: the government, as it did in other areas of enforcement practices, challenged the standing of the plaintiffs, invoked the states secrets privilege, and generally declined to disclose on national security grounds whether particular individuals had been eavesdropped upon without a warrant under the program. A few U.S. court of appeals and a number of district courts addressed the issues in these cases. In one instance, a district judge did reach the merits, mainly based on inadvertent and advertent disclosures by the government that indicated that electronic surveillance of the plaintiffs had taken place. Because there was no evidence that a FISA warrant had been obtained, the court concluded that the surveillance was unlawful. In re National Security Agency Telecommunications Records Litigation, 700 F. Supp. 2d 1182 (N.D. Cal. 2010). After extensive litigation, the court granted the plaintiffs' motion for summary judgment. Subsequently, a verdict/settlement ensued, sub nom. Al–Haramain Islamic Foundation v. Bush, 2010 WL 5663950, in which the government was ordered to pay more than two million dollars, most of which went for attorneys' fees. Also see Al–Haramain Islamic Foundation v. Bush, 507 F.3d 1190 (9th Cir. 2007) for an earlier stage in this litigation.

As noted, civil plaintiffs and criminal defendants have made motions to order the government to disclose whether any warrantless electronic surveillance had been directed against them. In one such case, the court of appeals vacated an appeal and remanded the case to allow the district court to entertain a motion to disclose any unauthorized electronic surveillance. United States v. Al–Timimi, No. 05–4761 (4th Cir. 2006). On November 21, 2007, the New York Times reported that following the issuance of the order in the Al–Timimi case in April 2006, the issue was "bogged down" in the trial court for 18 months during which intelligence officials made a series of classified appearances before the court; neither the defense lawyers nor the trial prosecutors were allowed to be present. The New York Times story reported that the trial judge told the prosecution that she wanted the government to arrange to give both the trial prosecutors and defense lawyers clearance to review the classified material in the case, and the judge indicated that she was prepared to order a new trial if the problem was not resolved. The story indicated that to obtain the necessary clearances relating to the NSA program might require action by the President since he "personally handled the decisions on issuing clearances for the NSA eavesdropping program." NY Times, Nov. 21, 2007, A18. See also United States v. Abu Ali, Cr. No. 05–53 (E.D. Va. 2005).

C. POST–TSP LEGISLATION DEALING WITH ELECTRONIC SURVEILLANCE WITH LINKS TO PERSONS ABROAD AND IN THE U.S.

The Protect America Act, hurriedly enacted in 2007 as a stopgap measure, lapsed in February, 2008. Subsequently, after difficult negotiations, the FISA Amendments Act, which is reproduced below, was enacted in July, 2008.

FISA Amendments Act of 2008

50 U.S.C.

TITLE I—FOREIGN INTELLIGENCE SURVEILLANCE

§ 1881. Definitions

(a) In general

The terms "agent of a foreign power", "Attorney General", "contents", "electronic surveillance", "foreign intelligence information", "foreign power", "person", "United States", and "United States person" have the meanings given such terms in section 1801 of this title, except as specifically provided in this subchapter.

. . .

§ 1881a. Procedures for targeting certain persons outside the United States other than United States persons

(a) Authorization

Notwithstanding any other provision of law, upon the issuance of an order in accordance with subsection (i)(3) or a determination under subsection (c)(2), the Attorney General and the Director of National Intelligence may authorize jointly, for a period of up to 1 year from the effective date of the authorization, the targeting of persons reasonably believed to be located outside the United States to acquire foreign intelligence information.

(b) Limitations

An acquisition authorized under subsection (a)—

    (1) may not intentionally target any person known at the time of acquisition to be located in the United States;

    (2) may not intentionally target a person reasonably believed to be located outside the United States if the purpose of such acquisition is to target a particular, known person reasonably believed to be in the United States;

    (3) may not intentionally target a United States person reasonably believed to be located outside the United States;

    (4) may not intentionally acquire any communication as to which the sender and all intended recipients are known at the time of the acquisition to be located in the United States; and

    (5) shall be conducted in a manner consistent with the fourth amendment to the Constitution of the United States.

(c) Conduct of acquisition

    (1) In general

An acquisition authorized under subsection (a) shall be conducted only in accordance with—

        (A) the targeting and minimization procedures adopted in accordance with subsections (d) and (e); and

        (B) upon submission of a certification in accordance with subsection (g), such certification.

    (2) Determination

A determination under this paragraph and for purposes of subsection (a) is a determination by the Attorney General and the Director of National Intelligence that exigent circumstances exist because, without immediate implementation of an authorization under subsection (a), intelligence important to the national security of the United States may be lost or not timely acquired and time does not permit the issuance of an order pursuant to subsection (i)(3) prior to the implementation of such authorization.

(3) Timing of determination

The Attorney General and the Director of National Intelligence may make the determination under paragraph (2)—

    (A) before the submission of a certification in accordance with subsection (g); or

    (B) by amending a certification pursuant to subsection (i)(1)(C) at any time during which judicial review under subsection (i) of such certification is pending.

(4) Construction

Nothing in subchapter I of this chapter shall be construed to require an application for a court order under such subchapter I of this chapter for an acquisition that is targeted in accordance with this section at a person reasonably believed to be located outside the United States.

(d) Targeting procedures

    (1) Requirement to adopt

The Attorney General, in consultation with the Director of National Intelligence, shall adopt targeting procedures that are reasonably designed to—

    (A) ensure that any acquisition authorized under subsection (a) is limited to targeting persons reasonably believed to be located outside the United States; and

    (B) prevent the intentional acquisition of any communication as to which the sender and all intended recipients are known at the time of the acquisition to be located in the United States.

    (2) Judicial review

The procedures adopted in accordance with paragraph (1) shall be subject to judicial review pursuant to subsection (i).

(e) Minimization procedures

    (1) Requirement to adopt

The Attorney General, in consultation with the Director of National Intelligence, shall adopt minimization procedures that meet the definition of minimization procedures under section 1801(h) or 1821(4) of this title, as appropriate, for acquisitions authorized under subsection (a).

    (2) Judicial review

The minimization procedures adopted in accordance with paragraph (1) shall be subject to judicial review pursuant to subsection (i).

(f) Guidelines for compliance with limitations

    (1) Requirement to adopt

The Attorney General, in consultation with the Director of National Intelligence, shall adopt guidelines to ensure—

    (A) compliance with the limitations in subsection (b); and

    (B) that an application for a court order is filed as required by this chapter.

(2) Submission of guidelines

The Attorney General shall provide the guidelines adopted in accordance with paragraph (1) to—

    (A) the congressional intelligence committees;

    (B) the Committees on the Judiciary of the Senate and the House of Representatives; and

    (C) the Foreign Intelligence Surveillance Court.

(g) Certification

    (1) In general

        (A) Requirement

        Subject to subparagraph (B), prior to the implementation of an authorization under subsection (a), the Attorney General and the Director of National Intelligence shall provide to the Foreign Intelligence Surveillance Court a written certification and any supporting affidavit, under oath and under seal, in accordance with this subsection.

        (B) Exception

        If the Attorney General and the Director of National Intelligence make a determination under subsection (c)(2) and time does not permit the submission of a certification under this subsection prior to the implementation of an authorization under subsection (a), the Attorney General and the Director of National Intelligence shall submit to the Court a certification for such authorization as soon as practicable but in no event later than 7 days after such determination is made.

    (2) Requirements

    A certification made under this subsection shall—

        (A) attest that—

            (i) there are procedures in place that have been approved, have been submitted for approval, or will be submitted with the certification for approval by the Foreign Intelligence Surveillance Court that are reasonably designed to—

                (I) ensure that an acquisition authorized under subsection (a) is limited to targeting persons reasonably believed to be located outside the United States; and

    (II) prevent the intentional acquisition of any communication as to which the sender and all intended recipients are known at the time of the acquisition to be located in the United States;

  (ii) the minimization procedures to be used with respect to such acquisition—

    (I) meet the definition of minimization procedures under section 1801(h) or 1821(4) of this title, as appropriate; and

    (II) have been approved, have been submitted for approval, or will be submitted with the certification for approval by the Foreign Intelligence Surveillance Court;

  (iii) guidelines have been adopted in accordance with subsection (f) to ensure compliance with the limitations in subsection (b) and to ensure that an application for a court order is filed as required by this chapter;

  (iv) the procedures and guidelines referred to in clauses (i), (ii), and (iii) are consistent with the requirements of the fourth amendment to the Constitution of the United States;

  (v) a significant purpose of the acquisition is to obtain foreign intelligence information;

  (vi) the acquisition involves obtaining foreign intelligence information from or with the assistance of an electronic communication service provider; and

  (vii) the acquisition complies with the limitations in subsection (b);

(B) include the procedures adopted in accordance with subsections (d) and (e);

(C) be supported, as appropriate, by the affidavit of any appropriate official in the area of national security who is—

  (i) appointed by the President, by and with the advice and consent of the Senate; or

  (ii) the head of an element of the intelligence community;

. . .

A certification made under this subsection is not required to identify the specific facilities, places, premises, or property at which an acquisition authorized under subsection (a) will be directed or conducted.

. . .

(6) Review

A certification submitted in accordance with this subsection shall be subject to judicial review pursuant to subsection (i).

(h) Directives and judicial review of directives

(1) Authority

With respect to an acquisition authorized under subsection (a), the Attorney General and the Director of National Intelligence may direct, in writing, an electronic communication service provider to—

> **(A)** immediately provide the Government with all information, facilities, or assistance necessary to accomplish the acquisition in a manner that will protect the secrecy of the acquisition and produce a minimum of interference with the services that such electronic communication service provider is providing to the target of the acquisition; and

> **(B)** maintain under security procedures approved by the Attorney General and the Director of National Intelligence any records concerning the acquisition or the aid furnished that such electronic communication service provider wishes to maintain.

(2) Compensation

The Government shall compensate, at the prevailing rate, an electronic communication service provider for providing information, facilities, or assistance in accordance with a directive issued pursuant to paragraph (1).

(3) Release from liability

No cause of action shall lie in any court against any electronic communication service provider for providing any information, facilities, or assistance in accordance with a directive issued pursuant to paragraph (1).

. . .

> (A) Order to compel

> If an electronic communication service provider fails to comply with a directive issued pursuant to paragraph (1), the Attorney General may file a petition for an order to compel the electronic communication service provider to comply with the directive with the Foreign Intelligence Surveillance Court, which shall have jurisdiction to review such petition.

. . .

> (C) Procedures for review

> A judge considering a petition filed under subparagraph (A) shall, not later than 30 days after being assigned such

petition, issue an order requiring the electronic communication service provider to comply with the directive or any part of it, as issued or as modified, if the judge finds that the directive meets the requirements of this section and is otherwise lawful. The judge shall provide a written statement for the record of the reasons for a determination under this paragraph.

(D) Contempt of Court

Failure to obey an order issued under this paragraph may be punished by the Court as contempt of court.

. . .

(6) Appeal

(A) Appeal to the Court of Review

The Government or an electronic communication service provider receiving a directive issued pursuant to paragraph (1) may file a petition with the Foreign Intelligence Surveillance Court of Review for review of a decision issued pursuant to paragraph (4) or (5). The Court of Review shall have jurisdiction to consider such petition and shall provide a written statement for the record of the reasons for a decision under this subparagraph.

(B) Certiorari to the Supreme Court

The Government or an electronic communication service provider receiving a directive issued pursuant to paragraph (1) may file a petition for a writ of certiorari for review of a decision of the Court of Review issued under subparagraph (A). The record for such review shall be transmitted under seal to the Supreme Court of the United States, which shall have jurisdiction to review such decision.

(i) Judicial review of certifications and procedures

(1) In general

(A) Review by the Foreign Intelligence Surveillance Court

The Foreign Intelligence Surveillance Court shall have jurisdiction to review a certification submitted in accordance with subsection (g) and the targeting and minimization procedures adopted in accordance with subsections (d) and (e), and amendments to such certification or such procedures.

. . .

(2) Review

The Court shall review the following:

(A) Certification

A certification submitted in accordance with subsection (g) to determine whether the certification contains all the required elements.

(B) Targeting procedures

The targeting procedures adopted in accordance with subsection (d) to assess whether the procedures are reasonably designed to—

(i) ensure that an acquisition authorized under subsection (a) is limited to targeting persons reasonably believed to be located outside the United States; and

(ii) prevent the intentional acquisition of any communication as to which the sender and all intended recipients are known at the time of the acquisition to be located in the United States.

(C) Minimization procedures

The minimization procedures adopted in accordance with subsection (e) to assess whether such procedures meet the definition of minimization procedures under section 1801(h) or section 1821(4) of this title, as appropriate.

(3) Orders

(A) Approval

If the Court finds that a certification submitted in accordance with subsection (g) contains all the required elements and that the targeting and minimization procedures adopted in accordance with subsections (d) and (e) are consistent with the requirements of those subsections and with the fourth amendment to the Constitution of the United States, the Court shall enter an order approving the certification and the use, or continued use in the case of an acquisition authorized pursuant to a determination under subsection (c)(2), of the procedures for the acquisition.

. . .

The Foreign Intelligence Surveillance Court shall maintain a record of a proceeding under this section, including petitions, appeals, orders, and statements of reasons for a decision, under security measures adopted by the Chief Justice of the United States, in consultation with the Attorney General and the Director of National Intelligence.

. . .

§ 1881b. Certain acquisitions inside the United States targeting United States persons outside the United States

(a) Jurisdiction of the Foreign Intelligence Surveillance Court

(1) In general

The Foreign Intelligence Surveillance Court shall have jurisdiction to review an application and to enter an order approving the targeting of a United States person reasonably believed to be located outside the United States to acquire foreign intelligence information, if the acquisition constitutes electronic surveillance or the acquisition of stored electronic communications or stored electronic data that requires an order under this chapter, and such acquisition is conducted within the United States.

(2) Limitation

If a United States person targeted under this subsection is reasonably believed to be located in the United States during the effective period of an order issued pursuant to subsection (c), an acquisition targeting such United States person under this section shall cease unless the targeted United States person is again reasonably believed to be located outside the United States while an order issued pursuant to subsection (c) is in effect. Nothing in this section shall be construed to limit the authority of the Government to seek an order or authorization under, or otherwise engage in any activity that is authorized under, any other subchapter of this chapter.

(b) Application

(1) In general

Each application for an order under this section shall be made by a Federal officer in writing upon oath or affirmation to a judge having jurisdiction under subsection (a)(1). Each application shall require the approval of the Attorney General based upon the Attorney General's finding that it satisfies the criteria and requirements of such application, as set forth in this section, and shall include—

    (A) the identity of the Federal officer making the application;

    (B) the identity, if known, or a description of the United States person who is the target of the acquisition;

    (C) a statement of the facts and circumstances relied upon to justify the applicant's belief that the United States person who is the target of the acquisition is—

        (i) a person reasonably believed to be located outside the United States; and

        (ii) a foreign power, an agent of a foreign power, or an officer or employee of a foreign power;

    (D) a statement of proposed minimization procedures that meet the definition of minimization procedures under section 1801(h) or 1821(4) of this title, as appropriate;

(E) a description of the nature of the information sought and the type of communications or activities to be subjected to acquisition;

(F) a certification made by the Attorney General or an official specified in section 1804(a)(6) of this title that—

(i) the certifying official deems the information sought to be foreign intelligence information;

(ii) a significant purpose of the acquisition is to obtain foreign intelligence information;

(iii) such information cannot reasonably be obtained by normal investigative techniques;

(iv) designates the type of foreign intelligence information being sought according to the categories described in section 1801(e) of this title; and

(v) includes a statement of the basis for the certification that—

(I) the information sought is the type of foreign intelligence information designated; and

(II) such information cannot reasonably be obtained by normal investigative techniques;

(G) a summary statement of the means by which the acquisition will be conducted and whether physical entry is required to effect the acquisition;

(H) the identity of any electronic communication service provider necessary to effect the acquisition, provided that the application is not required to identify the specific facilities, places, premises, or property at which the acquisition authorized under this section will be directed or conducted;

(I) a statement of the facts concerning any previous applications that have been made to any judge of the Foreign Intelligence Surveillance Court involving the United States person specified in the application and the action taken on each previous application; and

(J) a statement of the period of time for which the acquisition is required to be maintained, provided that such period of time shall not exceed 90 days per application.

. . .

(6) Duration

An order approved under this subsection shall be effective for a period not to exceed 90 days and such order may be renewed for additional 90–day periods upon submission of renewal applications meeting the requirements of subsection (b).

(7) Compliance

At or prior to the end of the period of time for which an acquisition is approved by an order or extension under this section, the judge may assess compliance with the minimization procedures referred to in paragraph (1)(C) by reviewing the circumstances under which information concerning United States persons was acquired, retained, or disseminated.

(d) Emergency authorization

(1) Authority for emergency authorization

Notwithstanding any other provision of this chapter, if the Attorney General reasonably determines that—

(A) an emergency situation exists with respect to the acquisition of foreign intelligence information for which an order may be obtained under subsection (c) before an order authorizing such acquisition can with due diligence be obtained, and

(B) the factual basis for issuance of an order under this subsection to approve such acquisition exists,

the Attorney General may authorize such acquisition if a judge having jurisdiction under subsection (a)(1) is informed by the Attorney General, or a designee of the Attorney General, at the time of such authorization that the decision has been made to conduct such acquisition and if an application in accordance with this section is made to a judge of the Foreign Intelligence Surveillance Court as soon as practicable, but not more than 7 days after the Attorney General authorizes such acquisition.

(2) Minimization procedures

If the Attorney General authorizes an acquisition under paragraph (1), the Attorney General shall require that the minimization procedures referred to in subsection (c)(1)(C) for the issuance of a judicial order be followed.

(3) Termination of emergency authorization

In the absence of a judicial order approving an acquisition under paragraph (1), such acquisition shall terminate when the information sought is obtained, when the application for the order is denied, or after the expiration of 7 days from the time of authorization by the Attorney General, whichever is earliest.

(4) Use of information

If an application for approval submitted pursuant to paragraph (1) is denied, or in any other case where the acquisition is terminated and no order is issued approving the acquisition, no information obtained or evidence derived from such acquisition, except under circumstances in which the target of the acquisition is determined not to be a United States person, shall be received in evidence or otherwise disclosed in any trial, hearing, or other proceeding in or before any court, grand jury, department, office, agency, regulatory body, legislative committee, or other authority of the United States, a State, or political subdivision thereof, and no information concerning any United States person acquired from such acquisition shall subsequently be used or disclosed in any other manner by Federal officers or employees without the consent of such person, except with the approval of the Attorney General if the information indicates a threat of death or serious bodily harm to any person.

(e) Release from liability

No cause of action shall lie in any court against any electronic communication service provider for providing any information, facilities, or assistance in accordance with an order or request for emergency assistance issued pursuant to subsection (c) or (d), respectively.

(f) Appeal

(1) Appeal to the Foreign Intelligence Surveillance Court of Review

The Government may file a petition with the Foreign Intelligence Surveillance Court of Review for review of an order issued pursuant to subsection (c). The Court of Review shall have jurisdiction to consider such petition and shall provide a written statement for the record of the reasons for a decision under this paragraph.

(2) Certiorari to the Supreme Court

The Government may file a petition for a writ of certiorari for review of a decision of the Court of Review issued under paragraph (1). The record for such review shall be transmitted under seal to the Supreme Court of the United States, which shall have jurisdiction to review such decision.

(g) Construction

Except as provided in this section, nothing in this chapter shall be construed to require an application for a court order for an acquisition that is targeted in accordance with this section at a United States person reasonably believed to be located outside the United States.

§ 1881c. Other acquisitions targeting United States persons outside the United States

(a) Jurisdiction and scope

(1) Jurisdiction

The Foreign Intelligence Surveillance Court shall have jurisdiction to enter an order pursuant to subsection (c).

(2) Scope

No element of the intelligence community may intentionally target, for the purpose of acquiring foreign intelligence information, a United States person reasonably believed to be located outside the United States under circumstances in which the targeted United States person has a reasonable expectation of privacy and a warrant would be required if the acquisition were conducted inside the United States for law enforcement purposes, unless a judge of the Foreign Intelligence Surveillance Court has entered an order with respect to such targeted United States person or the Attorney General has authorized an emergency acquisition pursuant to subsection (c) or (d), respectively, or any other provision of this chapter.

(3) Limitations

(A) Moving or misidentified targets

If a United States person targeted under this subsection is reasonably believed to be located in the United States during the effective period of an order issued pursuant to subsection (c), an acquisition targeting such United States person under this section shall cease unless the targeted United States person is again reasonably believed to be located outside the United States during the effective period of such order.

(B) Applicability

If an acquisition for foreign intelligence purposes is to be conducted inside the United States and could be authorized under section 1881b of this title, the acquisition may only be conducted if authorized under section 1881b of this title or in accordance with another provision of this chapter other than this section.

(C) Construction

Nothing in this paragraph shall be construed to limit the authority of the Government to seek an order or authorization under, or otherwise engage in any activity that is authorized under, any other subchapter of this chapter.

(b) Application

Each application for an order under this section shall be made by a Federal officer in writing upon oath or affirmation to a judge having jurisdiction under subsection (a)(1). Each application shall require the approval of the Attorney General based upon the Attorney General's finding that it satisfies the criteria and requirements of such application as set forth in this section and shall include—

(1) the identity of the Federal officer making the application;

(2) the identity, if known, or a description of the specific United States person who is the target of the acquisition;

(3) a statement of the facts and circumstances relied upon to justify the applicant's belief that the United States person who is the target of the acquisition is—

(A) a person reasonably believed to be located outside the United States; and

(B) a foreign power, an agent of a foreign power, or an officer or employee of a foreign power;

(4) a statement of proposed minimization procedures that meet the definition of minimization procedures under section 1801(h) or 1821(4) of this title, as appropriate;

(5) a certification made by the Attorney General, an official specified in section 1804(a)(6) of this title, or the head of an element of the intelligence community that—

(A) the certifying official deems the information sought to be foreign intelligence information; and

(B) a significant purpose of the acquisition is to obtain foreign intelligence information;

(6) a statement of the facts concerning any previous applications that have been made to any judge of the Foreign Intelligence Surveillance Court involving the United States person specified in the application and the action taken on each previous application; and

(7) a statement of the period of time for which the acquisition is required to be maintained, provided that such period of time shall not exceed 90 days per application.

(c) Order

(1) Findings

Upon an application made pursuant to subsection (b), the Foreign Intelligence Surveillance Court shall enter an ex parte order as requested or as modified by the Court if the Court finds that—

(A) the application has been made by a Federal officer and approved by the Attorney General;

(B) on the basis of the facts submitted by the applicant, for the United States person who is the target of the acquisition, there is probable cause to believe that the target is—

(i) a person reasonably believed to be located outside the United States; and

(ii) a foreign power, an agent of a foreign power, or an officer or employee of a foreign power;

(C) the proposed minimization procedures, with respect to their dissemination provisions, meet the definition of minimization procedures under section 1801(h) or 1821(4) of this title, as appropriate; and

(D) the application that has been filed contains all statements and certifications required by subsection (b) and the certification provided under subsection (b)(5) is not clearly erroneous on the basis of the information furnished under subsection (b).

(2) Probable cause

In determining whether or not probable cause exists for purposes of paragraph (1)(B), a judge having jurisdiction under subsection (a)(1) may consider past activities of the target and facts and circumstances relating to current or future activities of the target. No United States person may be considered a foreign power, agent of a foreign power, or officer or employee of a foreign power solely upon the basis of activities protected by the first amendment to the Constitution of the United States.

An order under this paragraph shall be effective for a period not to exceed 90 days and such order may be renewed for additional 90–day periods upon submission of renewal applications meeting the requirements of subsection (b).

. . .

§ 1881e. Use of information acquired under this subchapter

(a) Information acquired under section 1881a of this title

Information acquired from an acquisition conducted under section 1881a of this title shall be deemed to be information acquired from an electronic surveillance pursuant to subchapter I of this chapter for purposes of section 1806 of this title, except for the purposes of subsection (j) of such section.

(b) Information acquired under section 1881b of this title

Information acquired from an acquisition conducted under section 1881b of this title shall be deemed to be information acquired from an electronic surveillance pursuant to subchapter I of this chapter for purposes of section 1806 of this title.

. . .

§ 1885a. Procedures for implementing statutory defenses

(a) Requirement for certification

Notwithstanding any other provision of law, a civil action may not lie or be maintained in a Federal or State court against any person for providing assistance to an element of the intelligence community, and shall be promptly dismissed, if the Attorney General certifies to the district court of the United States in which such action is pending that—

(1) any assistance by that person was provided pursuant to an order of the court established under section 1803(a) of this title directing such assistance;

(2) any assistance by that person was provided pursuant to a certification in writing under section 2511(2)(a)(ii)(B) or 2709(b) of Title 18;

(3) any assistance by that person was provided pursuant to a directive under section 1802(a)(4), 1805b(e), or 1881a(h) of this title directing such assistance;

(4) in the case of a covered civil action, the assistance alleged to have been provided by the electronic communication service provider was—

(A) in connection with an intelligence activity involving communications that was—

(i) authorized by the President during the period beginning on September 11, 2001, and ending on January 17, 2007; and

(ii) designed to detect or prevent a terrorist attack, or activities in preparation for a terrorist attack, against the United States; and

(B) the subject of a written request or directive, or a series of written requests or directives, from the Attorney General or the head of an element of the intelligence community (or the deputy of such person) to the electronic communication service provider indicating that the activity was—

(i) authorized by the President; and

(ii) determined to be lawful; or

(5) the person did not provide the alleged assistance.

(b) Judicial review

(1) Review of certifications

A certification under subsection (a) shall be given effect unless the court finds that such certification is not supported by substantial evidence provided to the court pursuant to this section.

(2) Supplemental materials

In its review of a certification under subsection (a), the court may examine the court order, certification, written request, or directive described in subsection (a) and any relevant court order, certification, written request, or directive submitted pursuant to subsection (d).

(c) Limitations on disclosure

If the Attorney General files a declaration under section 1746 of Title 28, that disclosure of a certification made pursuant to subsection (a) or the supplemental materials provided pursuant to subsection (b) or (d) would harm the national security of the United States, the court shall—

(1) review such certification and the supplemental materials in camera and ex parte; and

(2) limit any public disclosure concerning such certification and the supplemental materials, including any public order following such in camera and ex parte review, to a statement as to whether the case is dismissed and a description of the legal standards that govern the order, without disclosing the paragraph of subsection (a) that is the basis for the certification.

(d) Role of the parties

Any plaintiff or defendant in a civil action may submit any relevant court order, certification, written request, or directive to the district court referred to in subsection (a) for review and shall be permitted to participate in the briefing or argument of any legal issue in a judicial proceeding conducted pursuant to this section, but only to the extent that such participation does not require the disclosure of classified information to such party. To the extent that classified information is relevant to the proceeding or would be revealed in the determination of an issue, the court shall review such information in camera and ex parte, and shall issue any part of the court's written order that would reveal classified information in camera and ex parte and maintain such part under seal.

. . .

§ 1885b. Preemption

(a) In general

No State shall have authority to—

(1) conduct an investigation into an electronic communication service provider's alleged assistance to an element of the intelligence community;

(2) require through regulation or any other means the disclosure of information about an electronic communication service provider's alleged assistance to an element of the intelligence community;

(3) impose any administrative sanction on an electronic communication service provider for assistance to an element of the intelligence community; or

(4) commence or maintain a civil action or other proceeding to enforce a requirement that an electronic communication service provider disclose information concerning alleged assistance to an element of the intelligence community.

(b) Suits by the United States

The United States may bring suit to enforce the provisions of this section.

(c) Jurisdiction

The district courts of the United States shall have jurisdiction over any civil action brought by the United States to enforce the provisions of this section.

(d) Application

This section shall apply to any investigation, action, or proceeding that is pending on or commenced after July 10, 2008.

QUESTIONS AND NOTES

1. On September 25, 2007, the Director of National Intelligence, J. Michael McConnell, testified before the U.S. Senate Judiciary Committee regarding the Protect America Act, what purposes it served and what additional changes in the legislation were needed. Portions of his testimony help to explain some of the government's concerns that led to the enactment of particular provisions of the FISA Amendments Act:

Good morning Chairman Leahy, Ranking Member Specter, and Members of the Committee:

Thank you for inviting me to appear here today in my capacity as head of the United States Intelligence Community (IC). I appreciate this opportunity. . . .

Before I begin, I need to note that some of the specifics that support my testimony cannot be discussed in open session. . . . I will be as open as I can, but such discussion comes with degrees of risk. This is because open discussion of specific foreign intelligence collection capabilities could cause us to lose those very same capabilities. Therefore, on certain specific issues, I am happy to discuss matters further with Members in a classified setting.

. . .

I learned that our collection using the authorities provided by FISA were instrumental in protecting the nation from foreign security threats, but that, due to changes in technology, the law was actually preventing us from collecting additional foreign intelligence information needed to provide insight, understanding and warning about threats to Americans.

And so I turned to my colleagues in the Intelligence Community to ask what we could do to fix this problem, and I learned that a number of intelligence professionals had been working on this issue for some time already. In fact, over a year ago, in July 2006, the Director of the National Security Agency (NSA), Lieutenant General Keith Alexander, and the Director of the Central Intelligence Agency (CIA), General Mike Hayden, testified before this Committee regarding proposals that were being considered to update FISA.

. . .

Technology Changed

FISA's definition of electronic surveillance, prior to the Protect America Act and as passed in 1978, has not kept pace with technology. Let me explain what I mean by that. FISA was enacted before cell phones, before e-mail, and before the Internet was a tool used by hundreds of millions of people worldwide every day. When the law was passed in 1978, almost all local calls were on a wire and almost all international communications were in the air, known as "wireless" communications. Therefore, FISA was written to distinguish between collection on a wire and collection out of the air.

Now, in the age of modern telecommunications, the situation is completely reversed; most international communications are on a wire and local calls are in the air. Communications technology has evolved in ways that have had unfortunate consequences under FISA. Communications that, in 1978, would have been transmitted via radio or satellite, are now transmitted principally via fiber optic cables. While Congress in 1978 specifically excluded from FISA's scope radio and satellite communications, certain "in wire" or fiber optic cable transmissions fell under FISA's definition of electronic surveillance. Congress' intent on this issue is clearly stated in the legislative history:

> "the legislation does not deal with international signals intelligence activities as currently engaged in by the National Security Agency and electronic surveillance conducted outside the United States."

Thus, technological changes have brought within FISA's scope communications that the 1978 Congress did not intend to be covered.

Similarly, FISA originally placed a premium on the location of the collection. Legislators in 1978 could not have been expected to predict an integrated global communications grid that makes geography an increasingly irrelevant factor. Today a single communication can transit the world even if the two people communicating are only a few miles apart.

And yet, simply because our law has not kept pace with our technology, communications intended to be excluded from FISA, were included. This has real consequences to our men and women in the IC working to protect the nation from foreign threats.

For these reasons, prior to Congress passing the Protect America Act last month, in a significant number of cases, IC agencies were required to make a showing of probable cause in order to target for surveillance the communications of a foreign intelligence target located overseas. Then, they needed to explain that probable cause finding in documentation, and obtain approval of the FISA Court to collect against a foreign terrorist located in a foreign country. Frequently, although not always, that person's communications were with another foreign person located overseas. In such cases, prior to the Protect America Act, FISA's requirement to obtain a court order, based on a showing of probable cause, slowed, and in some cases prevented altogether, the Government's ability to collect foreign intelligence information, without serving any substantial privacy or civil liberties interests.

National Security Threats

. . .

What Does the Protect America Act Do?

The Protect America Act, passed by Congress and signed into law by the President on August 5, 2007, has already made the nation safer by allowing the Intelligence Community to close existing gaps in our foreign intelligence collection.

First, it clarified that the definition of electronic surveillance under FISA should not be construed to encompass surveillance directed at a person reasonably believed to be located outside the United States. This provision is at the heart of this legislation: its effect is that the IC must no longer obtain court approval when the target of the acquisition is a foreign intelligence target located outside the United States.

. . .

Second, the Act provides that the FISA Court has a role in determining that the procedures used by the IC to determine that the target is outside the United States are reasonable. Specifically, the Attorney General must submit to the FISA Court the procedures we use to make that determination.

Third, the Act provides a mechanism by which communications providers can be compelled to cooperate. The Act allows the Attorney General and DNI to direct communications providers to provide information, facilities and assistance necessary to acquire information when targeting foreign intelligence targets located outside the United States.

Fourth, the Act provides liability protection for private parties who assist the IC, when complying with a lawful directive issued pursuant to the Protect America Act.

And fifth, and importantly, FISA, as amended by the Protect America Act, continues to require that we obtain a court order to conduct electronic surveillance or physical search when targeting persons located in the United States.

By passing this law, Congress gave the IC the ability to close critical intelligence gaps. When I talk about a gap, what I mean is foreign intelligence information that we should have been collecting, that we were not collecting. We were not collecting this important foreign intelligence information because, due solely to changes in technology, FISA would have required that we obtain court orders to conduct electronic surveillance of foreign intelligence targets located outside the United States. This is not what Congress originally intended. These items:

- removing targets located outside the United States from the definition of electronic surveillance;

- providing for Court review of the procedures by which we determine that the acquisition concerns persons located outside the United States;

- providing a means to compel the assistance of the private sector;

- liability protection; and

- the continued requirement of a court order to target those within the United States,

are the pillars of the Protect America Act, and I look forward to working with Members of both parties to make these provisions permanent.

Common Misperceptions About the Protect America Act

In the public debate over the course of the last month since Congress passed the Act, I have heard a number of incorrect interpretations of the Protect America Act. The Department of Justice has sent a letter to this Committee explaining these incorrect interpretations.

To clarify, we are not using the Protect America Act to change the manner in which we conduct electronic surveillance or physical search of Americans abroad. The IC has operated for nearly 30 years under section 2.5 of Executive Order 12333, which provides that the Attorney General must make an individualized finding that there is probable cause to believe that an American abroad is an agent of a foreign power, before the IC may conduct electronic surveillance or physical search of that person. These determinations are reviewed for legal sufficiency by the same group of career attorneys within the Department of Justice who prepare FISA applications. We have not, nor do we intend to change our practice in that respect. Executive Order 12333 and this practice has been in place since 1981.

. . .

For example, some have advocated for a proposal that would exclude only "foreign-to-foreign" communications from FISA's scope. I have, and will continue to, oppose any proposal that takes this approach for the following reason: it will not correct the problem our intelligence operators have faced. Eliminating from FISA's scope communications between foreign persons outside the United States will not meet our needs in two ways:

First, it would not unburden us from obtaining Court approval for communications obtained from foreign intelligence targets abroad. This is because an analyst cannot know, in many cases, prior to requesting legal authority to target a particular foreign intelligence target abroad, with whom that person will communicate. This is not a matter of legality, or even solely of technology, but merely of common sense. If the statute were amended to carve out communications between foreigners from requiring Court approval, the IC would still, in many cases and in an abundance of caution, have to seek a Court order anyway, because an analyst would not be able to demonstrate, with certainty, that the communications that would be collected would be exclusively between persons located outside the United States.

Second, one of the most important and useful pieces of intelligence we could obtain is a communication from a foreign terrorist outside the United States to a previously unknown "sleeper" or coconspirator inside the United States. Therefore, we need to have agility, speed and focus in collecting the communications of foreign intelligence targets outside the United States who may communicate with a "sleeper" or coconspirator who is inside the United States.

Moreover, such a limitation is unnecessary to protect the legitimate privacy rights of persons inside the United States. Under the Protect America Act, we have well established mechanisms for properly handling communications of U.S. persons that may be collected incidentally. These procedures, referred to as minimization procedures, have been used by the IC for decades. Our analytic workforce has been extensively trained on using minimization procedures to adequately protect U.S. person information from being inappropriately disseminated.

The minimization procedures that Intelligence Community agencies follow are Attorney General approved guidelines issued pursuant to Executive Order 12333. These minimization procedures apply to the acquisition, retention and dissemination of U.S. person information. These procedures have proven over time to be both a reliable and practical method of ensuring the constitutional reasonableness of IC's collection activities.

In considering our proposal to permanently remove foreign intelligence targets located outside the United States from FISA's court approval requirements, I understand that there is concern that we would use the authorities granted by the Protect America Act to effectively target a person in the United States, by simply saying that we are targeting a foreigner located outside the United States. This is what has been referred to as "reverse targeting."

Let me be clear on how I view reverse targeting: it is unlawful. Again, we believe the appropriate focus for whether court approval should be required, is who the target is, and where the target is located. If the target of the surveillance is a person inside the United States, then we seek FISA Court approval for that collection. Similarly, if the target of the surveillance is a U.S. person outside the United States, then we obtain Attorney General approval under Executive Order 12333, as has been our practice for decades. If the target is a foreign person located overseas, consistent with FISA today, the IC should not be required to obtain a warrant.

Moreover, for operational reasons, the Intelligence Community has little incentive to engage in reverse targeting. If a foreign intelligence target who poses a threat is located within the United States, then we would want to investigate that person more fully. In this case, reverse targeting would be an ineffective technique for protecting against the activities of a foreign intelligence target located inside the United States. In order to conduct electronic surveillance or physical search operations against a person in the United States, the FBI, which would conduct the investigation, would seek FISA Court approval for techniques that, in a law enforcement context, would require a warrant.

. . .

Mr. Chairman, this concludes my remarks.

———————

2. Note that the central distinction that appears to have been applied prior to 2007 was between surveillances that are conducted abroad of persons who are abroad, on the one hand, and surveillances that are conducted in the U.S., on the other, and the initial controversy that arose, when the TSP was disclosed, concerned surveillances where the international and domestic were both involved. How did the FISA Amendments Act change the perspective? What is the primary focus, the main organizing principle under the FAA? What is the difference in scope of application of 1881a on the one hand, and 1881b on the other hand? How do the sections differ with respect to authorization requirements?

3. Is there a judicial approval requirement under 1881a as well as under 1881b? Are they the same?

4. How do 1881b and 1881c differ? Do they both require a court order in order to lawfully engage in the type of electronic surveillance involved? Do they both apply to the targeting of a U.S. person abroad? Are both of these sections needed? How are they different, if they are different? To what extent is the distinction between them tied to the definition of "electronic surveillance"?

5. Suppose a non-U.S. person abroad is targeted and electronically overheard with proper authorization (which section is applicable?), and that person calls someone in the United States? Can the government lawfully continue to listen in to the conversation? Does it make any difference whether the person at the U.S. end of the conversation was a U.S. person, or not?

6. Recall what was deemed controversial under the TSP program. Does the FAA authorize what was deemed by many to have been unlawful under the TSP program?

7. Overall, does the FAA handle the subject of electronic surveillance abroad in a reasonable manner? Would you draw the lines any differently? Is the FAA constitutional?

AMNESTY INTERNATIONAL, USA v. CLAPPER

638 F.3d 118 (2d Cir. 2011)

Gerard E. Lynch, *Circuit Judge*:

Attorneys, journalists, and labor, legal, media, and human rights organizations brought this action facially challenging the constitutionality of Section 702 of the Foreign Intelligence Surveillance Act of 1978 ("FISA"), which was added to FISA by Section 101(a)(2) of the FISA Amendments Act of 2008 (the "FAA"), and codified at *50 U.S.C. § 1881a*.

Section 702 creates new procedures for authorizing government electronic surveillance targeting non-United States persons outside the United States for purposes of collecting foreign intelligence. The plaintiffs complain that the procedures violate the *Fourth Amendment*, the *First Amendment*, Article III of the Constitution, and the principle of separation of powers because they "allow[] the executive branch sweeping and virtually unregulated authority to monitor the international communications . . . of law-abiding U.S. citizens and residents."

The merits of the plaintiffs' claims are not before us. The *only* issue presented by this appeal is whether the plaintiffs are legally in a position to assert these claims in a federal court, not whether the claims are to any degree valid. Their merit is an issue for another court on another day. The district court (Koeltl, J.) granted the government summary judgment because it found that the plaintiffs lacked standing. On appeal, the plaintiffs argue that they have standing because the FAA's new procedures 1 cause them to fear that their communications will be monitored, and thus force them to undertake costly and burdensome measures to protect the confidentiality of international communications necessary to carrying out their jobs. Because standing may be based on a reasonable fear of future injury and costs incurred to avoid that injury, and the plaintiffs have established that they have a reasonable fear of injury and have incurred costs to avoid it, we agree that they have standing. We therefore reverse the district court's judgment.

. . .

C. Comparison of Pre-and Post–FAA Surveillance Authorization Procedures

The plaintiffs highlight two differences between the pre-and post-FAA surveillance authorization procedures. First, whereas under the preexisting FISA scheme the government had to submit an individualized application for surveillance identifying the particular target, facility, type of information sought, and procedures to be used, under the FAA, the government need not submit a similarly individualized application—it need not identify the particular target or facility to be monitored. Compare *50 U.S.C. § 1805(c)(1)*, with id. *§ 1881a(d)(1), 1881a(g)(4)*. Second, whereas under the preexisting FISA scheme the FISC had to find probable cause to believe both that the surveillance target is a "foreign power" or agent thereof and that the facilities to be monitored were being used or about to be used by a foreign power or its agent, under the FAA the FISC no longer needs to make any probable-cause determination at all. Instead, the FISC simply verifies that the government has made the proper certifications. In practice, these new authorization procedures mean that surveillance orders can be significantly broader under the FAA than they previously could have been. Prior to the FAA, surveillance orders could only authorize the government to monitor specific individuals or facilities. Under the FAA, by contrast, the plaintiffs allege that an acquisition order could seek, for example, "[a]ll telephone and e-mail communications to and from countries of foreign policy interest—for example, Russia, Venezuela, or Israel—including communications made to and from U.S. citizens and residents." Moreover, the specific showing of probable cause previously required, and the requirement of judicial review of that showing, have been eliminated. The government has not directly challenged this characterization.

An additional distinction concerns who monitors compliance with statutory limitations on the surveillance procedures. The preexisting FISA scheme allowed ongoing judicial review by the FISC. Id. § 1805(d)(3). But under the FAA, the judiciary may not monitor compliance on an ongoing basis; the FISC may review the minimization procedures only prospectively, when the government seeks its initial surveillance authorization. Rather, the executive—namely the AG and DNI—bears the responsibility of monitoring ongoing compliance, and although the FISC receives the executive's reports, it cannot rely on them to alter or revoke its previous surveillance authorizations.

. . .

The plaintiffs are attorneys and human rights, labor, legal, and media organizations whose work requires international communications with individuals they believe the government will likely monitor under the FAA. 9 The plaintiffs sued the DNI, the AG, and the Director of the National Security Agency ("NSA") in their official capacities (collectively, "the government").

. . . On July 10, 2008, the same day Congress enacted the FAA, the plaintiffs filed their complaint alleging that the FAA "allows the executive branch sweeping and virtually unregulated authority to monitor the international communications . . . of law-abiding U.S. citizens and residents." The plaintiffs alleged that they feared that under the FAA the government would intercept their sensitive international communications that were necessary to carrying out their jobs, and that they therefore had to take costly and burdensome measures to protect the confidentiality of those communications. They sought declaratory and injunctive relief, alleging that the FAA facially violates the *Fourth Amendment*, the *First Amendment*, Article III of the Constitution, and the principle of separation of powers.

. . .

The district court found the plaintiffs' fear of future surveillance too speculative to confer standing. It stated:

> The plaintiffs have failed to establish standing to challenge the constitutionality of the FAA on the basis of their fear of surveillance. The plaintiffs can only demonstrate an abstract fear that their communications will be monitored under the FAA. The FAA creates a framework within which intervening federal officials may apply for approval from the FISC to authorize surveillance targeting non-United States persons located outside the United States to acquire

foreign intelligence information. The FAA sets forth the requirements that an application to obtain a surveillance order from the FISC must satisfy. Contrary to the characterization of the statute in the plaintiffs' motion papers, the FAA itself does not authorize the surveillance of the plaintiffs' communications. Indeed, the FAA neither authorizes surveillance nor identifies on its face a class of persons that includes the plaintiffs. Rather the FAA authorizes specified federal officials to seek a surveillance order from the FISC. That order cannot target the plaintiffs and whether an order will be sought that affects the plaintiffs' rights, and whether such an order would be granted by the FISC, is completely speculative.

. . .

To arrive at this conclusion, the district court relied on three lines of cases. First, the court looked to cases where plaintiffs have sought standing to challenge electronic surveillance schemes, namely *United Presbyterian Church in the U.S.A. v. Reagan, 738 F.2d 1375, 238 U.S. App. D.C. 229 (D.C. Cir. 1984)*, and *ACLU v. NSA, 493 F.3d 644 (6th Cir. 2007)*. Both of these cases rejected the plaintiffs' standing arguments, which were based on their fear of future injuries, because the plaintiffs' respective fears were too speculative. The district court found those cases apposite and persuasive. See *Amnesty Int'l, 646 F. Supp. 2d at 645–47*.

Second, the court examined " 'physical surveillance cases' where the Supreme Court reached the merits of challenges to laws or policies authorizing drug or alcohol testing for specific classes of persons, without requiring that the plaintiffs had actually submitted to such testing before bringing such challenges." *Id. at 647–48*. The district court held that those cases have "no application to this case, where the plaintiffs are not required to do anything or to submit to anything, and where there is no showing that the Government has authorized any action against [a class of persons including] the plaintiffs." *Id. at 648*.

Finally, the district court examined standing cases outside the surveillance context, and said those cases:

> stand for the proposition that a plaintiff may challenge a specific law or regulation before it is enforced against the plaintiff if the plaintiff is subject to that law or regulation and has a well-founded fear that it will be so enforced. The plaintiffs in this case have made no showing that they are subject to any specific law or regulation that they seek to challenge. The FAA does not require that the plaintiffs do anything or refrain from doing anything such that they might have a well-founded fear that the Government would take action against them for failing to abide by the statute. Moreover, the FAA does not authorize surveillance of the plaintiffs' communications and the plaintiffs have made no showing that the Government has sought any such surveillance pursuant to the general framework set forth in the statute or that such surveillance has been authorized.

Id. at 649.

. . .

As for the plaintiffs' economic and professional costs, the court found that those injuries are "not truly independent of the [plaintiffs'] first basis" for standing, because those costs "flow directly from the plaintiffs' fear of surveillance." *Id. at 653.* The court said that "[t]o allow the plaintiffs to bring this action on the basis of such costs would essentially be to accept a repackaged version of the first failed basis for standing." Id. Moreover, the court held that "because the plaintiffs have failed to show that they are subject to the FAA and that they face a threat of harm from its enforcement, the chilling of their speech that they attribute to the statute is actually the result of their purely subjective fear of surveillance."

. . .

On appeal, the plaintiffs reassert that they have suffered two types of injuries. First, they claim that they fear that the government will intercept their sensitive international communications, because the FAA "plainly authorizes the acquisition of [their] international communications," and their communications are "likely to be monitored under it." Second, they claim that anticipation of this future injury also inflicts a present injury "by compelling them to take costly and burdensome measures to protect the confidentiality of their international communications" and by compromising their "ability to locate witnesses, cultivate sources, gather information, communicate confidential information to their clients, and to engage in other legitimate and constitutionally protected communications."

The district court and the parties have focused on whether the plaintiffs' asserted injuries satisfy the injury-in-fact component of the standing inquiry. Although they are correct that the plaintiffs' first asserted injury—the possibility of being monitored in the future—raises a question of injury in fact, because probabilistic injuries constitute injuries in fact only when they reach a certain threshold of likelihood, see *City of Los Angeles v. Lyons, 461 U.S. 95, 107 n.8, 103 S. Ct. 1660, 75 L. Ed. 2d 675 (1983),* the plaintiffs' second asserted injury alleges the most mundane of injuries in fact: the expenditure of funds. The plaintiffs' declarations, which, as discussed above, we must accept as true, establish that they have already incurred professional and economic costs to avoid interception. Having accepted the truthfulness of the plaintiffs' declarations for purposes of the summary judgment motion, the government cannot now dispute whether the plaintiffs genuinely fear being intercepted, or whether the plaintiffs have actually incurred the costs they claim to have incurred. Thus, we have little doubt that the plaintiffs have satisfied the injury-in-fact requirement.

As to the second asserted injury—their present-injury theory—that the plaintiffs have demonstrated injuries in fact is not sufficient in itself to establish standing. The plaintiffs must also prove that the injuries are caused by the challenged statute and that a favorable judgment would redress them. The government's challenge to the plaintiffs' standing based on their incurred professional and economic costs focuses on whether there is a "causal connection between [the plaintiffs'] injury and the [legislation] complained of." *Lujan, 504 U.S. at 560.* The causal chain can be broken where a plaintiff's self-inflicted injury results from his "unreasonable decision . . . to bring about a harm that he knew to be avoidable." *St. Pierre v. Dyer, 208 F.3d 394, 403 (2d Cir. 2000).* However, standing is not defeated merely because the plaintiff has in some sense contributed to his own injury. . . . Standing is defeated only if it is concluded that the injury is so completely due to the plaintiff's own fault as to break the causal chain." 13A Charles Alan Wright, Arthur R. Miller & Edward H. Cooper, Federal Practice and Procedure § 3531.5, at 361–62 (3d ed. 2008) (footnotes omitted).

If the plaintiffs can show that it was not unreasonable for them to incur costs out of fear that the government will intercept their communications under the FAA, then the measures they took to avoid interception can support standing. If the possibility of interception is remote or fanciful, however, their present-injury theory fails because the plaintiffs would have no reasonable basis for fearing interception under the FAA, and they cannot bootstrap their way into standing by unreasonably incurring costs to avoid a merely speculative or highly unlikely potential harm.

. . .

Here, the plaintiffs' actions were "fairly traceable" to the FAA. Because, as we shall explain, the plaintiffs' fears were reasonable even under the stringent reasonableness standards found in *future-injury* cases, and because the plaintiffs incurred these professional and economic costs as a direct result of that reasonable fear, their present injuries in fact clearly satisfy the requirements for standing. We therefore need not and do not decide whether the degree of likelihood necessary to establish a causal relationship between an actual present injury and the challenged governmental action is as stringent as that necessary for a potential harm in itself to confer standing. However, the line of future-injury standing cases provides a helpful framework for analyzing the plaintiffs' present-injury arguments. Those cases bolster our conclusion that the professional and economic harms the plaintiffs suffered here were fairly traceable to the FAA, and were not the result of an "unreasonable decision" on their part "to bring about a harm that [they] knew to be avoidable." *St. Pierre, 208 F.3d at 403.*

. . .

The government argues that the plaintiffs can obtain standing only by showing either that they have been monitored or that it is "effectively certain" that they will be monitored. The plaintiffs fall short of this standard, according to the government, because they "simply speculate that they will be subjected to governmental action taken pursuant to [the FAA]."

But the government overstates the standard for determining when a present injury linked to a contingent future injury can support standing. The plaintiffs have demonstrated that they suffered present injuries in fact—concrete economic and professional harms—that are fairly traceable to the FAA and redressable by a favorable judgment. The plaintiffs need not show that they have been or certainly will be monitored. Indeed, even in cases where plaintiffs allege an injury based solely on prospective government action, they need only show a "realistic danger" of "direct injury," they allege a prospective injury to *First Amendment* rights, they must show only " 'an actual and well-founded fear' " of injury.

. . .

The plaintiffs have established that they suffered *present* injuries in fact—economic and professional harms—stemming from a reasonable fear of *future* harmful government conduct. They have asserted that the FAA permits broad monitoring through mass surveillance orders that authorize the government to collect thousands or millions of communications, including communications between the plaintiffs and their overseas contacts. The FAA is susceptible to such an interpretation, and the government has not controverted this interpretation or offered a more compelling one.

. . .

Furthermore, the plaintiffs have good reason to believe that their communications, in particular, will fall within the scope of the broad surveillance that they can assume the government will conduct. The plaintiffs testify that in order to carry out their jobs they must regularly communicate by telephone and e-mail with precisely the sorts of individuals that the government will most likely seek to monitor—i.e., individuals "the U.S. government believes or believed to be associated with terrorist organizations," "political and human rights activists who oppose governments that are supported economically or militarily by the U.S. government," and "people located in geographic areas that are a special focus of the U.S. government's counterterrorism or diplomatic efforts." The plaintiffs' assessment that these individuals are likely targets of FAA surveillance is reasonable, and the government has not disputed that assertion.

On these facts, it is reasonably likely that the plaintiffs' communications will be monitored under the FAA. The instant plaintiffs' fears of surveillance are by no means based on "mere conjecture," delusional fantasy, or unfounded speculation. *Baur, 352 F.3d at 636* (to establish standing, a plaintiff "must allege that he faces a direct risk of harm which rises above mere conjecture"). Their fears are fairly traceable to the FAA because they are based on a reasonable interpretation of the challenged statute and a realistic understanding of the world. Conferring standing on these plaintiffs is not tantamount to conferring standing on "any or all citizens who no more than assert that certain practices of law enforcement offices are unconstitutional." *Lyons, 461 U.S. at 111*. Most law abiding citizens have no occasion to communicate with suspected terrorists; relatively few Americans have occasion to engage in international communications relevant to "foreign intelligence." These plaintiffs however, have successfully demonstrated that their legitimate professions make it quite likely that their communications will be intercepted if the government—as seems inevitable—exercises the authority granted by the FAA.

. . .

Empirical evidence supports this expectation: in 2008, the government sought 2,082 surveillance orders, and the FISC approved 2,081 of them. We do not know how many of these applications, if any, came after the FAA was enacted on July 10, 2008. At the very least, though, the evidence does not show that the FISC actually rejects a significant number of applications for FAA surveillance orders. Without a stronger showing that the FISC interposes a significant intervening step, we cannot find that the mere existence of this intervening step prevents the plaintiffs from obtaining standing to challenge the FAA.

. . .

Since it is reasonable for the plaintiffs to seek to avoid being monitored, we must consider whether the particular measures they took were reasonable. They were. In some instances the plaintiffs did not communicate certain information they otherwise would have communicated by e-mail or telephone; and in other instances they incurred the costly burdens of traveling to communicate or to obtain that information in person rather than electronically. These are not overreactions to the FAA; they are appropriate measures that a reasonably prudent person who plausibly anticipates that his conversations are likely to be monitored, and who finds it important to avoid such monitoring, would take to avoid being overheard. The plaintiffs have therefore established that those injuries are linked to the statute they challenge.

In sum, the FAA has put the plaintiffs in a lose-lose situation: either they can continue to communicate sensitive information electronically and bear a substantial risk of being monitored under a statute they allege to be unconstitutional, or they can incur financial and professional costs to avoid being monitored. Either way, the FAA directly affects them.

. . .

CONCLUSION

The plaintiffs' uncontroverted testimony that they fear their sensitive international electronic communications being monitored and that they have taken costly measures to avoid being monitored—because we deem that fear and those actions to be reasonable in the circumstances of this case—establishes injuries in fact that we find are causally linked to the allegedly unconstitutional FAA. We therefore find that plaintiffs have standing to challenge the constitutionality of the FAA in federal court.

QUESTIONS AND NOTES

1. The Clapper case, supra, was a decision only on the standing issue and did not reach the merits of the plaintiffs' constitutional claims. Given the court's decision that granted the plaintiffs' standing, what should the government now do? Seek en banc rehearing; seek review by the Supreme Court; or go to trial on the merits? Note that the Supreme Court has been generally supportive of the government's posture in these cases, typically denying certiorari when the government has won in the court below and granting it where the government has lost. See Note, pp. 127–128 supra. What can the government lose by going to trial on the merits? In such a trial, what issues would be before the court?

2. A decision by the United States Foreign Intelligence Surveillance Court of Review, In re: Directives [Redacted Text] Pursuant to Section 105B of the Foreign Intelligence Surveillance Act, 551 F.3d 1004 (FISA Ct. Rev. 2008), addressed constitutional issues raised by the Protect America Act. (Some of the certifications and directives under the Act's provisions continued in effect after the statute had lapsed so the case was not mooted.) Although the PAA is a different statute from the FISA Amendments Act, some of the issues are similar to those posed under the FAA. Accordingly, the case is a relevant authority on some of the constitutional issues posed by the FAA.

3. The FISA Amendments Act of 2008 has been the subject of a significant literature.

See Jessica LoConte, The FISA Amendments Act of 2008: Protecting Americans By Monitoring International Communications: Is it Reasonable? 6 Pace Int'l L. Rev. Online Companion 1; William C. Banks, Ten Questions: Responses to the Ten questions: Is the FISA Amendments Act of 2008 Good Policy? Is it Constitutional? 35 Wm. Mitchell L. Rev. 5007 (2009); Nate Olsen, Congress and the Court: Retroactive Immunity in the FISA Amendments Act and the Problem of United States v. Klein, 2009 Utah L. Rev. 1353 (2009); Jonathan D. Forgang, "The Right of the People": The NSA, The FISA Amendments Act of 2008, and Foreign Intelligence Surveillance of Americans Overseas, 78 Fordham L. Rev. 217 (2009); Elizabeth Johnson, Surveillance and Privacy Under the Obama Administration: The Foreign Intelligence Surveillance Act of 1978 Amendments Act of 2008 and the Attorney General's Guidelines for Domestic FBI Operations, 5 ISJLP 419 (2010); Zachary Keller, Big Brother's Little Helpers: Telecommunication Immunity and the FISA Amendment Act of 2008, 70 Ohio St. L.J. 1215 (2009); Stephanie Cooper Blum, What Really is at Stake with the FISA Amendments Act of 2008 and Ideas for Future Surveillance Reform, 18 B.U. Pub. Int. L.J. 269 (2009); Recent Legislation: Electronic Surveillance–Congress Grants Telecommunications Companies Retroactive Immunity from Civil Suits for Complying with NSA Terrorist Surveillance Program.–FISA Amendments Act of 2008, Pub, L, No, 110–261, 122 Stat. 2346, 122 Harv. L. Rev. 1271 (2009); William C. Banks, Programmatic Surveillance and FISA: Of Needles in Haystacks, 88 Tex. L. Rev. 1633 (2010).

CHAPTER 6

SEARCHES AND ADMINISTRATIVE SUBPOENAS

■ ■ ■

A. INTRODUCTION

In this chapter, we examine the different legal tools and the applicable doctrines used by the government in terrorism cases to obtain physical items or information in the form of records, documents, books and information, including computerized records, from persons who are targets of an investigation and from others who are in possession of records, as well as other tangible things that have some connection to an investigation.

There are two basic types of legal tools addressed in this chapter, 1) search warrants and 2) subpoenas and subpoena-like demands or orders. Authorization for and the applicable standards and rules for, foreign intelligence search warrants for searches in the United States are contained in the Foreign Intelligence Surveillance Act (FISA); statutory provisions dealing with physical searches were added to the FISA statute in 1994—see subsection B below. The standards and rules applicable to such warrants should be compared with the warrants issued in ordinary criminal cases. The applicable law for searches abroad, both generally and in foreign intelligence cases—whether, for example, search warrants are required in such cases, is the subject of inquiry in subsection C, infra. Consider, for example, whether a search warrant equivalent to the type of provisions contained in the FISA Amendments Act of 2008 (discussed in ch. 5, supra) is needed for searches involving an international feature.

The topic addressed in section D, infra, is the use of administrative subpoenas—called national security letters to obtain records, documents, etc. useful in a terrorism investigation. Specifically, in this subsection the legal aspects of national security letters are addressed; to be compared with the so-called "library" provision, orders under section 215 of the USA PATRIOT Act (now 50 U.S.C. 1861), which must be issued by a judge. Both of these legal tools are also compared with administrative and judicially-authorized subpoenas used in other areas of criminal enforcement.

The chapter also provides an opportunity to compare search warrants and subpoenas, specifically administrative subpoenas, as ways of obtaining records, documents and other kinds of evidence in aid of an investigation. There are, of course, obvious differences generally between searches pursuant to a warrant and obtaining information through the use of subpoenas, and this chapter highlights the specific differences in connection with their use in terrorism-related investigations.

To cite just a few of the obvious comparisons, search warrants do not require any voluntary action on the part of the owner of the premises to be searched. Subpoenas require the person to whom the order is directed to produce the described material. Search warrants are more often than not directed against a target of the investigation. Subpoenas may be directed against either the investigatory target or a third party possessor of records, information, etc. In the case of subpoenas used in terrorism investigations, they are almost always directed against third parties. Search warrants must be approved by a judicial officer based on a specific factual finding, probable cause relating to evidence of a crime, etc. in ordinary criminal cases, and for terrorism cases, the type of finding specified in the FISA. Administrative subpoenas are issued by an executive branch official, and the necessary factual premise varies but most often it is "relevant to an investigation," a lesser standard than any form of probable cause.

B.   SEARCHES WITHIN THE UNITED STATES

1.   INTRODUCTION

Sections 1821–1825, Title 50, U.S.C. establish the authority to issue search warrants for foreign intelligence information. The standards and rules roughly parallel those governing electronic surveillance to obtain foreign intelligence, 50 U.S.C. §§ 1801 et seq., and which were treated in ch. 5 supra. Differences between the electronic surveillance and physical search provisions generally reflect differences between physical searches and electronic surveillance. In addressing the search warrant provisions in this chapter, it is assumed that the reader has previously studied chapter 5 so that it is not necessary again to review here the definitions previously treated in that chapter, e.g. the definitions of foreign power, and agent of a foreign power which apply equally to electronic surveillance and physical search warrants.

Excerpts from the search warrant provisions are reproduced below, followed by a series of questions regarding their scope and application. Because a requirement of secrecy generally attaches to the approval process for, and execution of these warrants, there is little publicly available law on this subject. Even the type of limited information that has thus far become public in regard to FISA electronic surveillance (see ch. 5) has thus far generally not surfaced with respect to the FISA search warrant process. For comparison purposes, Rule 41, Federal Rules of

Criminal Procedure and 18 U.S.C. § 3103a which govern the issuance of search warrants in ordinary criminal cases, are also reproduced here.

2.   TITLE 50, U.S.C.

§ 1821.   Definitions

As used in this subchapter:

. . .

(4) "Minimization procedures" with respect to physical search, means—

(A) specific procedures, which shall be adopted by the Attorney General, that are reasonably designed in light of the purposes and technique of the particular physical search, to minimize the acquisition and retention, and prohibit the dissemination, of nonpublicly available information concerning unconsenting United States persons consistent with the need of the United States to obtain, produce, and disseminate foreign intelligence information;

(B) procedures that require that nonpublicly available information, which is not foreign intelligence information, as defined in section 1801(e)(1) of this title, shall not be disseminated in a manner that identifies any United States person, without such person's consent, unless such person's identity is necessary to understand such foreign intelligence information or assess its importance;

(C) notwithstanding subparagraphs (A) and (B), procedures that allow for the retention and dissemination of information that is evidence of a crime which has been, is being, or is about to be committed and that is to be retained or disseminated for law enforcement purposes; and

(D) notwithstanding subparagraphs (A), (B), and (C), with respect to any physical search approved pursuant to section 1822(a) of this title, procedures that require that no information, material, or property of a United States person shall be disclosed, disseminated, or used for any purpose or retained for longer than 72 hours unless a court order under section 1824 of this title is obtained or unless the Attorney General determines that the information indicates a threat of death or serious bodily harm to any person.

(5) "Physical search" means any physical intrusion within the United States into premises or property (including examination of the interior of property by technical means) that is intended to result in a seizure, reproduction, inspection, or alteration of information, material, or property, under circumstances in which a person has a reasonable expectation of privacy and a warrant would be required for law enforcement purposes, but does not include (A) "electronic surveillance", as defined in section 1801(f) of this title, or (B) the acquisition by the United States Government of foreign intelligence information from international or foreign communications, or foreign intelligence activities conducted in accordance with otherwise applicable Federal law involving a foreign electronic communications system, utilizing a means other than electronic surveillance as defined in section 1801(f) of this title.

§ 1822. Authorization of physical searches for foreign intelligence purposes

(a) Presidential authorization

(1) Notwithstanding any other provision of law, the President, acting through the Attorney General, may authorize physical searches without a court order under this subchapter to acquire foreign intelligence information for periods of up to one year if—

(A) the Attorney General certifies in writing under oath that—

(i) the physical search is solely directed at premises, information, material, or property used exclusively by, or under the open and exclusive control of, a foreign power or powers (as defined in section 1801(a)(1), (2), or (3) of this title);

(ii) there is no substantial likelihood that the physical search will involve the premises, information, material, or property of a United States person; and

(iii) the proposed minimization procedures with respect to such physical search meet the definition of minimization procedures under paragraphs (1) through (4) of section 1821(4) of this title; and

. . .

(2) A physical search authorized by this subsection may be conducted only in accordance with the certification and minimization procedures adopted by the Attorney General. The Attorney General shall assess compliance with such procedures and shall report such assessments to the Permanent Select Committee on Intelligence of the House of Representatives and the Select Committee on Intelligence of the Senate under the provisions of section 1826 of this title.

. . .

(4)(A) With respect to physical searches authorized by this subsection, the Attorney General may direct a specified landlord, custodian, or other specified person to—

(i) furnish all information, facilities, or assistance necessary to accomplish the physical search in such a manner as will protect its secrecy and produce a minimum of interference with the services that such landlord, custodian, or other person is providing the target of the physical search; and

(ii) maintain under security procedures approved by the Attorney General and the Director of National Intelligence any records concerning the search or the aid furnished that such person wishes to retain.

(B) The Government shall compensate, at the prevailing rate, such landlord, custodian, or other person for furnishing such aid.

(b) Application for order; authorization

Applications for a court order under this subchapter are authorized if the President has, by written authorization, empowered the Attorney General to approve applications to the Foreign Intelligence Surveillance Court. Notwithstanding any other provision of law, a judge of the court to whom application is made may grant an order in accordance with section 1824 of this title approving a physical search in the United States of the premises, property, information, or material of a foreign power or an agent of a foreign power for the purpose of collecting foreign intelligence information.

. . .

(d) Court of review; record; transmittal to Supreme Court

The court of review established under section 1803(b) of this title shall have jurisdiction to review the denial of any application made under this subchapter.

. . .

§ 1823. Application for order

(a) Submission by Federal officer; approval of Attorney General; contents

Each application for an order approving a physical search under this subchapter shall be made by a Federal officer in writing upon oath or affirmation to a judge of the Foreign Intelligence Surveillance Court. Each application shall require the approval of the Attorney General based upon the Attorney General's finding that it satisfies the criteria and requirements for such application as set forth in this subchapter. Each application shall include—

(1) the identity of the Federal officer making the application;

(2) the identity, if known, or a description of the target of the search, and a description of the premises or property to be searched and of the information, material, or property to be seized, reproduced, or altered;

(3) a statement of the facts and circumstances relied upon by the applicant to justify the applicant's belief that—

(A) the target of the physical search is a foreign power or an agent of a foreign power;

(B) the premises or property to be searched contains foreign intelligence information; and

(C) the premises or property to be searched is or is about to be owned, used, possessed by, or is in transit to or from a foreign power or an agent of a foreign power;

(4) a statement of the proposed minimization procedures;

(5) a statement of the nature of the foreign intelligence sought and the manner in which the physical search is to be conducted;

(6) a certification or certifications by the Assistant to the President for National Security Affairs, [ed. other specified officials] . . .

(A) that the certifying official deems the information sought to be foreign intelligence information;

(B) that a significant purpose of the search is to obtain foreign intelligence information;

(C) that such information cannot reasonably be obtained by normal investigative techniques;

(D) that designates the type of foreign intelligence information being sought according to the categories described in section 1801(e) of this title; and

. . .

(7) where the physical search involves a search of the residence of a United States person, the Attorney General shall state what investigative techniques have previously been utilized to obtain the foreign intelligence information concerned and the degree to which these techniques resulted in acquiring such information; and

(8) a statement of the facts concerning all previous applications that have been made to any judge under this subchapter involving any of the persons, premises, or property specified in the application, and the action taken on each previous application.

. . .

(d) Personal review by Attorney General

(1)(A) Upon written request of the Director of the Federal Bureau of Investigation, the Secretary of Defense, the Secretary of State, the Director of National Intelligence, or the Director of the Central Intelligence Agency, the Attorney General shall personally review under subsection (a) of this section an application under that subsection for a target described in section 1801(b)(2) of this title.

. . .

§ 1824. Issuance of order

. . .

(b) Determination of probable cause

In determining whether or not probable cause exists for purposes of an order under subsection (a)(2) of this section, a judge may consider past activities of the target, as well as facts and circumstances relating to current or future activities of the target.

(c) Specifications and directions of orders

An order approving a physical search under this section shall—

    (1) specify—

        (A) the identity, if known, or a description of the target of the physical search;

        (B) the nature and location of each of the premises or property to be searched;

        (C) the type of information, material, or property to be seized, altered, or reproduced;

        (D) a statement of the manner in which the physical search is to be conducted and, whenever more than one physical search is authorized under the order, the authorized scope of each search and what minimization procedures shall apply to the information acquired by each search; and

        (E) the period of time during which physical searches are approved; and

    (2) direct—

        (A) that the minimization procedures be followed;

        . . .;

    and

        (E) that the Federal officer conducting the physical search promptly report to the court the circumstances and results of the physical search.

(d) Duration of order; extensions; assessment of compliance

    (1) An order issued under this section may approve a physical search for the period necessary to achieve its purpose, or for 90 days, whichever is less, except that (A) an order under this section shall approve a physical search targeted against a foreign power, as defined in paragraph (1), (2), or (3) of section 1801(a) of this title, for the period specified in the application or for one year, whichever is less, and (B) an order under this section for a physical search targeted against an agent of a foreign power who is not a United States person may be for the period specified in the application or for 120 days, whichever is less.

(2) Extensions of an order issued under this subchapter may be granted on the same basis as the original order upon an application for an extension and new findings made in the same manner as required for the original order, except that an extension of an order under this chapter for a physical search targeted against a foreign power, as defined in paragraph (5), (6), or (7) of section 1801(a) of this title, or against a foreign power, as defined in section 1801(a)(4) of this title, that is not a United States person, or against an agent of a foreign power who is not a United States person, may be for a period not to exceed one year if the judge finds probable cause to believe that no property of any individual United States person will be acquired during the period.

(3) At or before the end of the period of time for which a physical search is approved by an order or an extension, or at any time after a physical search is carried out, the judge may assess compliance with the minimization procedures by reviewing the circumstances under which information concerning United States persons was acquired, retained, or disseminated.

(e)(1) Notwithstanding any other provision of this subchapter, the Attorney General may authorize the emergency employment of a physical search if the Attorney General—

    (A) reasonably determines that an emergency situation exists with respect to the employment of a physical search to obtain foreign intelligence information before an order authorizing such physical search can with due diligence be obtained;

    (B) reasonably determines that the factual basis for issuance of an order under this subchapter to approve such physical search exists;

    (C) informs, either personally or through a designee, a judge of the Foreign Intelligence Surveillance Court at the time of such authorization that the decision has been made to employ an emergency physical search; and

    (D) makes an application in accordance with this subchapter to a judge of the Foreign Intelligence Surveillance Court as soon as practicable, but not more than 7 days after the Attorney General authorizes such physical search.

(2) If the Attorney General authorizes the emergency employment of a physical search under paragraph (1), the Attorney

General shall require that the minimization procedures required by this subchapter for the issuance of a judicial order be followed.

(3) In the absence of a judicial order approving such physical search, the physical search shall terminate when the information sought is obtained, when the application for the order is denied, or after the expiration of 7 days from the time of authorization by the Attorney General, whichever is earliest.

(4) A denial of the application made under this subsection may be reviewed as provided in section 1803 of this title.

(5) In the event that such application for approval is denied, or in any other case where the physical search is terminated and no order is issued approving the physical search, no information obtained or evidence derived from such physical search shall be received in evidence or otherwise disclosed in any trial, hearing, or other proceeding in or before any court, grand jury, department, office, agency, regulatory body, legislative committee, or other authority of the United States, a State, or political subdivision thereof, and no information concerning any United States person acquired from such physical search shall subsequently be used or disclosed in any other manner by Federal officers or employees without the consent of such person, except with the approval of the Attorney General if the information indicates a threat of death or serious bodily harm to any person.

. . .

§ 1825. Use of information

. . .

(b) Notice of search and identification of property seized, altered, or reproduced

Where a physical search authorized and conducted pursuant to section 1824 of this title involves the residence of a United States person, and, at any time after the search the Attorney General determines there is no national security interest in continuing to maintain the secrecy of the search, the Attorney General shall provide notice to the United States person whose residence was searched of the fact of the search conducted pursuant to this chapter and shall identify any property of such person seized, altered, or reproduced during such search.

. . .

(f) Motion to suppress

(1) Any person against whom evidence obtained or derived from a physical search to which he is an aggrieved person is to be, or has been, introduced or otherwise used or disclosed in any trial, hearing, or other proceeding in or before any court, department, officer, agency, regulatory body, or other authority of the

United States, a State, or a political subdivision thereof, may move to suppress the evidence obtained or derived from such search on the grounds that—

    (A) the information was unlawfully acquired; or

    (B) the physical search was not made in conformity with an order of authorization or approval.

(2) Such a motion shall be made before the trial, hearing, or other proceeding unless there was no opportunity to make such a motion or the person was not aware of the grounds of the motion.

(g) In camera and ex parte review by district court

. . .

(j) Notification of emergency execution of physical search; contents; postponement, suspension, or elimination

(1) If an emergency execution of a physical search is authorized under section 1824(d) of this title and a subsequent order approving the search is not obtained, the judge shall cause to be served on any United States person named in the application and on such other United States persons subject to the search as the judge may determine in his discretion it is in the interests of justice to serve, notice of—

    (A) the fact of the application;

    (B) the period of the search; and

    (C) the fact that during the period information was or was not obtained.

(2) On an ex parte showing of good cause to the judge, the serving of the notice required by this subsection may be postponed or suspended for a period not to exceed 90 days. Thereafter, on a further ex parte showing of good cause, the court shall forego ordering the serving of the notice required under this subsection.

. . .

3. FEDERAL RULES OF CRIMINAL PROCEDURE

Rule 41. Search and Seizure

(a) Scope and Definitions.

. . .

    (2) Definitions. The following definitions apply under this rule:

        (A) "Property" includes documents, books, papers, any other tangible objects, and information.

        (B) "Daytime" means the hours between 6:00 a.m. and 10:00 p.m. according to local time.

    (C) "Federal law enforcement officer" means a government agent (other than an attorney for the government) who is engaged in enforcing the criminal laws and is within any category of officers authorized by the Attorney General to request a search warrant.

    (D) "Domestic terrorism" and "international terrorism" have the meanings set out in 18 U.S.C. § 2331.

. . .

(b) Authority to Issue a Warrant. At the request of a federal law enforcement officer or an attorney for the government:

    (1) a magistrate judge with authority in the district—or if none is reasonably available, a judge of a state court of record in the district—has authority to issue a warrant to search for and seize a person or property located within the district;

. . .

    (3) a magistrate judge—in an investigation of domestic terrorism or international terrorism—with authority in any district in which activities related to the terrorism may have occurred has authority to issue a warrant for a person or property within or outside that district;

. . .

(c) Persons or Property Subject to Search or Seizure. A warrant may be issued for any of the following:

    (1) evidence of a crime;

    (2) contraband, fruits of crime, or other items illegally possessed;

    (3) property designed for use, intended for use, or used in committing a crime; or

    (4) a person to be arrested or a person who is unlawfully restrained.

(d) Obtaining a Warrant.

    (1) In General. After receiving an affidavit or other information, a magistrate judge—or if authorized by Rule 41(b), a judge of a state court of record—must issue the warrant if there is probable cause to search for and seize a person or property or to install and use a tracking device.

. . .

(e) Issuing the Warrant.

    (1) In General. The magistrate judge or a judge of a state court of record must issue the warrant to an officer authorized to execute it.

    (2) Contents of the Warrant.

(A) Warrant to Search for and Seize a Person or Property.... the warrant must identify the person or property to be searched, identify any person or property to be seized, and designate the magistrate judge to whom it must be returned. The warrant must command the officer to:

(i) execute the warrant within a specified time no longer than 14 days;

(ii) execute the warrant during the daytime, unless the judge for good cause expressly authorizes execution at another time; and

(iii) return the warrant to the magistrate judge designated in the warrant.

. . .

(f) Executing and Returning the Warrant.

(1) Warrant to Search for and Seize a Person or Property.

(A) Noting the Time. The officer executing the warrant must enter on it the exact date and time it was executed.

(B) Inventory. An officer present during the execution of the warrant must prepare and verify an inventory of any property seized. The officer must do so in the presence of another officer and the person from whom, or from whose premises, the property was taken. If either one is not present, the officer must prepare and verify the inventory in the presence of at least one other credible person....

(C) Receipt. The officer executing the warrant must give a copy of the warrant and a receipt for the property taken to the person from whom, or from whose premises, the property was taken or leave a copy of the warrant and receipt at the place where the officer took the property.

(D) Return. The officer executing the warrant must promptly return it—together with a copy of the inventory— to the magistrate judge designated on the warrant. The judge must, on request, give a copy of the inventory to the person from whom, or from whose premises, the property was taken and to the applicant for the warrant.

. . .

(3) Delayed Notice. Upon the government's request, a magistrate judge—or if authorized by Rule 41(b), a judge of a state court of record—may delay any notice required by this rule if the delay is authorized by statute.

(g) Motion to Return Property. A person aggrieved by an unlawful search and seizure of property or by the deprivation of property may move for the property's return. The motion must be filed in the district where the property was seized. The court must receive evidence on any factual issue necessary to decide the motion. If it grants the motion, the court must return the property to the movant, but may impose reasonable conditions to protect access to the property and its use in later proceedings.

(h) Motion to Suppress. A defendant may move to suppress evidence in the court where the trial will occur, as Rule 12 provides.

4. TITLE 18 PROVISION SUPPLEMENTING FEDERAL RULES OF CRIMINAL PROCEDURE

18 U.S.C.

§ 3103a. Additional grounds for issuing warrant

(a) In general.—In addition to the grounds for issuing a warrant in section 3103[1] of this title, a warrant may be issued to search for and seize any property that constitutes evidence of a criminal offense in violation of the laws of the United States.

(b) Delay.—With respect to the issuance of any warrant or court order under this section, or any other rule of law, to search for and seize any property or material that constitutes evidence of a criminal offense in violation of the laws of the United States, any notice required, or that may be required, to be given may be delayed if—

(1) the court finds reasonable cause to believe that providing immediate notification of the execution of the warrant may have an adverse result (as defined in section 2705,[2] except if the adverse results consist only of unduly delaying a trial);

. . .

and

(3) the warrant provides for the giving of such notice within a reasonable period not to exceed 30 days after the date of its execution, or on a later date certain if the facts of the case justify a longer period of delay.

(c) Extensions of delay.—Any period of delay authorized by this section may be extended by the court for good cause shown, subject to the condition that extensions should only be granted upon an updated showing of the need for further delay and that each additional delay should be limited to periods of 90 days or less, unless the facts of the case justify a longer period of delay.

. . .

---

1. 18 U.S.C. § 3103 is Rule 41(b), Fed.R.Cr.P., supra, p 256.
2. 18 U.S.C. § 2705 contains the following definition of "adverse result":
   (2) An adverse result . . . is—
   (A) endangering the life or physical safety of an individual;
   (B) flight from prosecution;
   (C) destruction of or tampering with evidence;
   (D) intimidation of potential witnesses; or
   (E) otherwise seriously jeopardizing an investigation or unduly delaying a trial.

Questions and Notes

1. FISA was amended in 1994 to authorize physical searches to obtain foreign intelligence under the same general criteria that applied to electronic surveillance. See United States v. Marzook, 435 F.Supp.2d 778 (N.D.Ill.2006):

> As originally drafted, FISA did not provide a protocol for obtaining permission to conduct physical searches to obtain foreign intelligence. In 1994, however, Congress amended FISA to encompass physical searches conducted for foreign intelligence purposes. Pub.L. 103–359 §§ 301–09 (1994). In essence, the government bears the same burden as that for obtaining electronic surveillance. A federal officer seeking approval of a physical search under FISA must submit an application to a FISA court.

2. How does the probable cause required for a physical search under §§ 1823–24 compare with the probable cause for a search warrant for ordinary crimes?

3. In what ways other than the probable cause element do the requirements or applicable rules for foreign intelligence physical searches differ from ordinary crime search warrants? What would you describe as the most salient difference?

4. Under what circumstances, must the fact of a foreign intelligence search and what was obtained be disclosed to the person whose premises were searched? Is there a specified time limit within which such disclosure must be made? Compare the same issues under Rule 41, F.R.Cr.P and 18 U.S.C. § 3103a.

5. Is there an oddity and concern with respect to applying the same type of secrecy requirements to physical searches that are applicable to electronic surveillance "searches"? Consider, for example, the manner in which a secret foreign intelligence physical search must be conducted, leaving no trace of the fact of the search? How secret can the search be if objects are seized in the course of the search? On the other hand, suppose the purpose of the search is to gain access to the target's computer and copy information from its hard drive.

6. Are the search warrant provisions under §§ 1823–24 applicable outside the United States? Is there a geographic limitation provision in the statute? Which provision?

7. Suppose a physical search of the premises of a United States person is conducted outside of the United States. Do the physical search provisions of the FISA have any application? If not, what rules apply? See subsection C, infra.

8. What bearing does the fact that the premises or privacy of a United States person would be violated by the physical search to be undertaken? Does this mean that a warrant cannot be obtained under the provisions of the FISA?

9. Under what circumstances can a foreign intelligence search be conducted without a warrant? What conditions and requirements are applicable to such searches?

C. U.S. AGENTS ACTING ABROAD—FOURTH AMENDMENT AND RELATED ISSUES

1. INTRODUCTION

The TSP electronic surveillance controversy that was the subject of discussion in chapter 5, which led to the enactment of the provisions of the FISA Amendments Act of 2008, involved electronic surveillance of communcations between persons located outside and inside of the United States. In particular cases, it may have also involved United States persons. In chapter 5, in the context of such electronic surveillance, much of the focus of the materials is on the application of the relevant statutes. In this subsection, we primarily study whether fourth amendment protections apply to physical searches (and electronic surveillance) that take place entirely outside of the United States, but we also address other related issues. Some of the discussion harks back to, and is relevant to issues touched upon in chapter 5.

The basic questions are, how far do U.S. constitutional protections extend? Should the extension of the reach of U.S. criminal laws carry with it application of rights protected by the U.S. Constitution? Are U.S. agents limited by the Constitution in the actions they can engage in while abroad to the same extent as in the territorial United States? Or are our agents freer to engage in actions abroad that would not be lawful if done here? Further, what kinds of factors bear on what our agents can or cannot lawfully (i.e. lawful under U.S. law) do? Does it matter whether they are working in cooperation with official personnel of the host country and/or complying with the laws of the host country? Are there limits imposed by international law that bear on these issues?

Accordingly, in this section, we address questions growing out of various kinds of actions by U.S. agents, usually FBI or CIA, acting in foreign lands. The kinds of actions by U.S. agents that are examined in this section include investigation and information-gathering of various kinds—e.g., electronic surveillance, and search and arrest. See generally, Ronald J. Sievert, War on Terrorism or Global Law Enforcement Operation?, 78 Notre Dame L.Rev. 307 (2003). Related topics are addressed in chapter 7, infra, namely the interrogation of terrorism suspects abroad and rendition, that is, transfer of persons seized abroad to another country or to a prison facility in a U.S. jurisdiction.

2. SEARCHES ABROAD—PREMISES OF A NON–U.S. PERSON; U.S. PERSON SEARCH BY NON–U.S. AGENTS

The Supreme Court addressed some of the issues raised by searches conducted abroad by U.S. agents in the following case.

UNITED STATES v. VERDUGO–URQUIDEZ

494 U.S. 259 (1990)

[CHIEF JUSTICE REHNQUIST delivered the opinion of the Court, in which WHITE, O'CONNOR, SCALIA, and KENNEDY, JJ., joined. JUSTICE KENNEDY filed a concurring opinion; JUSTICE STEVENS filed an opinion concurring in the judgment; JUSTICE BRENNAN filed a dissenting opinion, in which JUSTICE MARSHALL joined; JUSTICE BLACKMUN filed a dissenting opinion.]

CHIEF JUSTICE REHNQUIST delivered the Opinion of the Court:

The question presented by this case is whether the Fourth Amendment applies to the search and seizure by United States agents of property that is owned by a nonresident alien and located in a foreign country. We hold that it does not.

Respondent Rene Martin Verdugo–Urquidez is a citizen and resident of Mexico. He is believed by the United States Drug Enforcement Agency (DEA) to be one of the leaders of a large and violent organization in Mexico that smuggles narcotics into the United States. Based on a complaint charging respondent with various narcotics-related offenses, the Government obtained a warrant for his arrest on August 3, 1985. In January 1986, Mexican police officers, after discussions with United States marshals, apprehended Verdugo–Urquidez in Mexico and transported him to the United States Border Patrol station in Calexico, California. There, United States marshals arrested respondent and eventually moved him to a correctional center in San Diego, California, where he remains incarcerated pending trial.

Following respondent's arrest, Terry Bowen, a DEA agent assigned to the Calexico DEA office, decided to arrange for searches of Verdugo–Urquidez's Mexican residences located in Mexicali and San Felipe. Bowen believed that the searches would reveal evidence related to respondent's alleged narcotics trafficking activities and his involvement in the kidnaping and torture-murder of DEA Special Agent Enrique Camarena Salazar (for which respondent subsequently has been convicted in a separate prosecution. See *United States v. Verdugo–Urquidez*, No. CR–87–422–ER (C.D. Cal., Nov. 22, 1988)). Bowen telephoned Walter White, the Assistant Special Agent in charge of the DEA office in Mexico City, and asked him to seek authorization for the search from the Director General of the Mexican Federal Judicial Police (MFJP). After several attempts to reach high ranking Mexican officials, White eventually contacted the Director General, who authorized the searches and promised the cooperation of Mexican authorities. Thereafter, DEA agents working in concert with officers of the MFJP searched respondent's properties in Mexicali and San Felipe and seized certain documents. In particular, the search of the Mexicali residence uncovered a tally sheet, which the Government believes reflects the quantities of marijuana smuggled by Verdugo–Urquidez into the United States.

. . .

Before analyzing the scope of the Fourth Amendment, we think it significant to note that it operates in a different manner than the Fifth Amendment, which is not at issue in this case. The privilege against self-incrimination guaranteed by the Fifth Amendment is a fundamental trial right of criminal defendants. Although conduct by law enforcement officials prior to trial may ultimately impair that right, a constitutional violation occurs only at trial. The Fourth Amendment functions differently. It prohibits "unreasonable searches and seizures" whether or not the evidence is sought to be used in a criminal trial, and a violation of the Amendment is "fully accomplished" at the time of an unreasonable governmental intrusion. For purposes of this case, therefore, if there were a constitutional violation, it occurred solely in Mexico. Whether evidence obtained from respondent's Mexican residences should be excluded at trial in the United States is a remedial question separate from the existence *vel non* of the constitutional violation.

The Fourth Amendment provides:

> "The right of the people to be secure in their persons, houses, papers, and effects, against unreasonable searches and seizures, shall not be violated. . . ."

That text, by contrast with the Fifth and Sixth Amendments, extends its reach only to "the people." Contrary to the suggestion of *amici curiae* that the Framers used this phrase "simply to avoid [an] awkward rhetorical redundancy," "the people" seems to have been a term of art employed in select parts of the Constitution. The Preamble declares that the Constitution is ordained and established by "the People of the United States." The Second Amendment protects "the right of the people to keep and bear Arms," and the Ninth and Tenth Amendments provide that certain rights and powers are retained by and reserved to "the people." See also U.S. Const., Amdt. 1 ("Congress shall make no law . . . abridging . . . *the right of the people* peaceably to assemble") (emphasis added); Art. I, § 2, cl. 1 ("The House of Representatives shall be composed of Members chosen every second Year *by the People of the several States*") (emphasis added). While this textual exegesis is by no means conclusive, it suggests that "the people" protected by the Fourth Amendment, and by the First and Second Amendments, and to whom rights and powers are reserved in the Ninth and Tenth Amendments, refers to a class of persons who are part of a national community or who have otherwise developed sufficient connection with this country to be considered part of that community. . . . The language of these Amendments contrasts with the words "person" and "accused" used in the Fifth and Sixth Amendments regulating procedure in criminal cases.

. . .

The available historical data show . . . that the purpose of the Fourth Amendment was to protect the people of the United States against arbitrary action by their own Government; it was never suggested that the provision was intended to restrain the actions of the Federal Government against aliens outside of the United States territory.

. . .

Justice Stevens' concurrence in the judgment takes the view that even though the search took place in Mexico, it is nonetheless governed by the requirements of the Fourth Amendment because respondent was "lawfully present in the United States . . . even though he was brought and held here against his will." But this sort of presence—lawful but involuntary—is not of the sort to indicate any substantial connection with our country. The extent to which respondent might claim the protection of the Fourth Amendment if the duration of his stay in the United States were to be prolonged—by a prison sentence, for example—we need not decide. When the search of his house in Mexico took place, he had been present in the United States for only a matter of days. We do not think the applicability of the Fourth Amendment to the search of premises in Mexico should turn on the fortuitous circumstance of whether the custodian of its nonresident alien owner had or had not transported him to the United States at the time the search was made.

. . .

Not only are history and case law against respondent, but as pointed out in *Johnson v. Eisentrager*, 339 U.S. 763 (1950), the result of accepting his claim would have significant and deleterious consequences for the United States in conducting activities beyond its boundaries. The rule adopted by the Court of Appeals would apply not only to law enforcement operations abroad, but also to other foreign policy operations which might result in "searches or seizures." The United States frequently employs armed forces outside this country—over 200 times in our history—for the protection of American citizens or national security. Congressional Research Service, Instances of Use of United States Armed Forces Abroad, 1798–1989 (E. Collier ed. 1989). Application of the Fourth Amendment to those circumstances could significantly disrupt the ability of the political branches to respond to foreign situations involving our national interest. Were respondent to prevail, aliens with no attachment to this country might well bring actions for damages to remedy claimed violations of the Fourth Amendment in foreign countries or in international waters. See *Bivens v. Six Unknown Federal Narcotics Agents*, 403 U.S. 388 (1971); cf. *Tennessee v. Garner*, 471 U.S. 1 (1985); *Graham v. Connor*, 490 U.S. 386 (1989). Perhaps a *Bivens* action might be unavailable in some or all of these situations due to " 'special factors counselling hesitation,' " but the Government would still be faced with case-by-case adjudications concerning the availability of such an action. And even were *Bivens* deemed wholly inapplicable in cases of foreign activity, that would not obviate the problems attending the application of the Fourth Amendment abroad to aliens. The Members of the Executive and Legislative Branches are sworn to uphold the Constitution, and they presumably desire to follow its commands. But the Court of Appeals' global view of its applicability would plunge them into a sea of uncertainty as to what might be reasonable in the way of searches and seizures conducted abroad. Indeed, the Court of Appeals held that absent exigent circumstances, United States agents could not effect a "search or seizure" for law enforcement purposes in a foreign country without first obtaining a warrant—which would be a dead letter outside the United States—from a magistrate in this country. Even if no warrant were required, American agents would have to articulate specific facts giving them probable cause to undertake a search or seizure if they wished to comply with the Fourth Amendment as conceived by the Court of Appeals.

We think that the text of the Fourth Amendment, its history, and our cases discussing the application of the Constitution to aliens and extraterritorially require rejection of respondent's claim. At the time of the search, he was a citizen and resident of Mexico with no voluntary attachment to the United States, and the place searched was located in Mexico. Under these circumstances, the Fourth Amendment has no application.

For better or for worse, we live in a world of nation-states in which our Government must be able to "function effectively in the company of sovereign nations." Some who violate our laws may live outside our borders under a regime quite different from that which obtains in this country. Situations threatening to important American interests may arise halfway around the globe, situations which in the view of the political branches of our Government require an American response with armed force. If there are to be restrictions on searches and seizures which occur incident to such American action, they must be imposed by the political branches through diplomatic understanding, treaty, or legislation.

The judgment of the Court of Appeals is accordingly

Reversed.

JUSTICE KENNEDY, concurring.

I agree that no violation of the Fourth Amendment has occurred and that we must reverse the judgment of the Court of Appeals. Although some explanation of my views is appropriate given the difficulties of this case, I do not believe they depart in fundamental respects from the opinion of the Court, which I join.

. . .

The question before us then becomes what constitutional standards apply when the Government acts, in reference to an alien, within its sphere of foreign operations. . . .

The conditions and considerations of this case would make adherence to the Fourth Amendment's warrant requirement impracticable and anomalous. . . . [T]he Constitution does not require United States agents to obtain a warrant when searching the foreign home of a nonresident alien. If the search had occurred in a residence within the United States, I have little doubt that the full protections of the Fourth Amendment would apply. But that is not this case. The absence of local judges or magistrates available to issue warrants, the differing and perhaps unascertainable conceptions of reasonableness and privacy that prevail abroad, and the need to cooperate with foreign officials all indicate that the Fourth Amendment's warrant requirement should not apply in Mexico as it does in this country. For this reason, in addition to the other persuasive justifications stated by the Court, I agree that no violation of the Fourth Amendment has occurred in the case before us. The rights of a citizen, as to whom the United States has continuing obligations, are not presented by this case.

I do not mean to imply, and the Court has not decided, that persons in the position of the respondent have no constitutional protection. The United States is prosecuting a foreign national in a court established under Article III, and all of the trial proceedings are governed by the Constitution. All would agree, for instance, that the dictates of the Due Process Clause of the Fifth Amendment protect the defendant.... Nothing approaching a violation of due process has occurred in this case.

JUSTICE STEVENS, concurring in the judgment.

... I do agree, however, with the Government's submission that the search conducted by the United States agents with the approval and cooperation of the Mexican authorities was not "unreasonable" as that term is used in the first Clause of the Amendment. I do not believe the Warrant Clause has any application to searches of noncitizens' homes in foreign jurisdictions because American magistrates have no power to authorize such searches. I therefore concur in the Court's judgment.

[JUSTICES BRENNAN, BLACKMUN and MARSHALL dissented.]

QUESTIONS AND NOTES

1. U.S. agents may be involved in electronic surveillance or a physical search outside of the United States in any of a number of different factual contexts. The U.S. agents may be active participants, either acting alone or in collaboration with local police agents, or the action may be conducted by the foreign police acting on their own.

The objects of the surveillance or search may be foreign citizens or nationals or U.S. citizens or permanent residents of the United States, or persons with some other degree of connection to the U.S. The surveillance or search may comply with the law of the foreign jurisdiction or not.

The main question that has been raised, as in the principal case, is the extent to which U.S. constitutional limitations may be applicable. The constitutional limits on police conduct embodied in the Fourth Amendment have not been held to apply to the conduct of foreign police officials acting abroad; such officials are not bound by U.S. constitutional standards. The courts of appeal that have considered the question have held that the Fourth Amendment applies to searches and unconsented-to electronic surveillances conducted abroad by U.S. government agents against U.S. citizens. See Justice Brennan dissenting in Verdugo–Urquidez (omitted in the portion of the case reproduced above).

Suppose that an electronic surveillance or a search that would be illegal under U.S. law is conducted by a foreign police official on foreign soil against a U.S. citizen and then the evidence thus obtained is turned over to FBI agents for use in a U.S. prosecution. What would you expect to be the result?

The cases have held that in this situation the U.S. agents can use the evidence and introduce it at the defendant's U.S. trial. This situation is called the "international silver platter doctrine"—the evidence is received by the U.S. agents "on a silver platter." A similar doctrine was applied regarding parallel interactions between state and federal police officials in the United States prior to the decision in Mapp v. Ohio, 367 U.S. 643 (1961).

However, if the participation of U.S. agents in the activity is so substantial as to convert the activity into a joint venture with the foreign officials, constitutional standards are applied and the evidence will be excluded at trial if those standards are violated.

A number of U.S. courts of appeal have considered joint venture issues. *See, e.g.,* United States v. Rosenthal, 793 F.2d 1214 (11th Cir. 1986):

Rosenthal contends that due to Fourth Amendment violations the trial court erred in failing to grant his motion to suppress monitored telephone conversations from his home in Colombia and evidence seized from his residence after his arrest. We disagree.

From September 10, 1983, until September 27, 1983, Rosenthal's residential telephone was monitored by the Colombian law enforcement officials as authorized by a Colombian Magistrate. Rosenthal was arrested on September 27, 1983, pursuant to an expulsion order issued by Colombian authorities. After the arrest, Rosenthal's residence was searched by Colombian National Police. Present at the search was Lt. Betancur, the Chief of the Anti–Drug Corps of the Colombian National Police, eight or nine D.A.S. (Colombian Immigration) Agents and four American federal agents. The Colombians were interested in arresting Rosenthal, expelling him from the country and searching his house for information regarding an assassination attempt on the Colombian Minister of Justice. Evidence obtained by foreign police officers from searches carried out in their own countries is generally admissible in American courts regardless of whether the search complied with the Fourth Amendment. The reasoning usually tendered in support of this limitation is the doubtful deterrent effect on foreign police practices that will follow from a punitive exclusion of the evidence in question by an American court. There are two exceptions to the general rule. The first, which is not applicable here, provides for exclusion of the evidence if the conduct of the foreign officers shocks the conscience of the American court. The second exception, which Rosenthal argues is applicable here, provides that if American law enforcement officials substantially participate in the foreign search, or if the foreign authorities actually conducting the search were acting as agents for their American counterparts, the exclusionary rule can be invoked. Here, testimony indicates that the decision to arrest Rosenthal was made by Lt. Betancur. The day before the arrest American and Colombian agents met at the DEA office where the American agents were apprised of the specific plans for the arrest and advised of the Colombians' plans to search Rosenthal's residence. At the request of the Colombian National Police, the American agents were present when the residence was searched but testimony indicates that all evidence was seized by the Colombian officials.

Fourth Amendment rights are generally inapplicable to an action by a foreign sovereign in its own territory in enforcing its own laws, even though American officials are present and cooperate in some degree. *Government of Canal Zone v. Sierra*, 594 F.2d 60 (5th Cir. 1979). In *Stonehill v. United States*, 405 F.2d 738 (9th Cir. 1968), the Ninth Circuit held that before the Fourth Amendment applies, the participation of federal agents must be so substantial so as to convert the search into a joint venture.

Judge Tidwell, after having heard the evidence, in applying the same to the law, determined that the American officers' participation in the search did not constitute a joint venture. He determined this from the facts. He ultimately concluded that the search was legal. This was a mixed question of law and fact. We find that his determination of the facts was not clearly erroneous and his application to the law was not in error. The search being not violative of the Fourth Amendment rendered the evidence further admissible.

Compare United States v. Barona, 56 F.3d 1087 (9th Cir. 1995) with the Rosenthal case:

It is not clear, therefore, that Villabona or the other non-citizen defendants in this case are entitled to receive any Fourth Amendment protection whatsoever. Any entitlement that they may have to invoke the Fourth Amendment in the context of an *extraterritorial* search is by no means clear. We could hold, therefore, that Barona, Martinez, and Villabona have failed to demonstrate that, at the time of the extraterritorial search, they were "People of the United States" entitled to receive the "full panoply of rights guaranteed by our Constitution." We choose, however, not to reach the question because even if they were entitled to invoke the Fourth Amendment, their effort would be unsuccessful.

Bennett, Harris, and McCarver are all United States citizens, and thus can invoke the protection of the Fourth Amendment generally. Our cases establishing the exception as to when the Fourth Amendment can be invoked in an extraterritorial search control our analysis.

First, the district court did not clearly err in finding that the four Danish wiretaps at issue were "joint ventures." In [United States v.] *Peterson,* we gave weight to the fact that the DEA "was involved daily in translating and decoding intercepted transmissions as well as advising the [foreign] authorities of their relevance." 812 F.2d at 490. Similarly here, the "American Embassy" was interested in the movement of Villabona and Bennett, American agents requested the wiretaps, information obtained was immediately forwarded to them, and throughout the surveillance a Spanish to English interpreter was provided by the United States.

Because there was a joint venture, we must decide whether the search was reasonable. In determining whether the search was reasonable, we must first consult the law of the relevant foreign countries.

. . .

. . . After carefully reviewing the record, we are satisfied that Danish law was followed.

. . .

A fifth wiretap occurred in Milan, Italy. On December 9, 1987, Villabona and Bennett arrived in Milan from Copenhagen. The day before, the Danish police notified a United States special agent of this planned trip. He, in turn, telephoned a United States special agent in Milan and requested physical surveillance. The latter agent contacted Major Rabiti of the Guardia Di Finanza and requested a watch on Villabona and Bennett. Rabiti obtained authorization to wiretap their hotel room.

The district court found that this wiretap was not the product of a joint venture between United States and Italian authorities. That a United States agent told Rabiti about Villabona and Bennett did not create a "joint venture" between the United States and Italy regarding this wiretap. . . . We hold that the district court did not clearly err when it found no joint investigation surrounding the Milan wiretap, and, therefore, that Fourth Amendment principles do not apply. Because the wiretap was conducted by foreign officials without substantial United States involvement, the results are admissible.

In summary, the finding that the Milan wiretap was not a joint venture is not clearly erroneous. The finding that the Danish wiretaps were conducted pursuant to a joint venture is also not clearly erroneous, but Danish law was complied with for each Danish wiretap. None of the evidence from the wiretaps is therefore subject to exclusion under the Fourth Amendment.

2.   How much contact with the U.S. must an alien have in order to be afforded Fourth Amendment protection against searches or electronic surveillance on foreign soil by U.S agents? Do the opinions in the principal case provide an answer to this question?

3.   Because the result in these cases often turns on the fact that the defendant did not have sufficient connections with the United States, or the degree of participation of the U.S. agents was insufficient to make them joint venturers with the foreign police, the courts rarely have needed to address the question of what the applicable substantive Fourth Amendment standards are in such cases. Dissenting in the principal case, Justice Brennan argued that the same Fourth Amendment standards applicable in a domestic context should be applied in the foreign context, but the issue was not addressed by the full Court. In United States v. Peterson, 812 F.2d 486 (9th Cir. 1987), Judge Kennedy (now Justice Kennedy) stated that the law of the foreign country must be consulted as part of the determination of whether the search or surveillance was reasonable. *See also* United States v. Barona, *supra*, on the same issue.

4. Problems

a. Suppose that U.S. agents are held to have been in a joint venture with foreign police in conducting a search against a U.S. citizen on foreign soil, and therefore Fourth Amendment standards are applicable. Suppose, too, that Judge Kennedy's opinion in the Peterson case, supra, is deemed part of the controlling authority. What result if the law of the foreign jurisdiction was not followed, but the U.S. agents acting in good faith relied on assurances by their foreign counterparts that the foreign law was being followed?

b. Suppose that there were not such assurances provided, but the suspect was suspected of being a terrorist within the meaning of FISA and the U.S. agents had enough information to have obtained a FISA warrant, but being abroad, it was not feasible to do so? See 50 U.S.C. § 1805(f), supra, p. 174. Regarding the physical search issue, see § 1821(5), supra, p. 248.

5. In connection with the issues discussed above, one should also take into account the fact that the United States has mutual legal assistance treaties (MLAT's) with other countries. These treaties have helped to facilitate the U.S.'s ability to obtain evidence from abroad. The MLAT's regulate such matters as searches and electronic surveillances, obtaining documents, freezing assets and maintaining evidence. The MLAT's are a fairly new development, having been first entered into in the 1970's. The United States has now entered into more than 40 such bilateral agreements.

For example, the U.S. entered into a MLAT with Mexico in 1991. The treaty requires both countries to "tak[e] all appropriate measures that they have legal authority to take" to provide mutual assistance to the other in criminal matters, including executing requests for searches and seizures. It is also provided that nothing in the Treaty "empowers one party's authorities to undertake, in the territorial jurisdiction of the other, the exercise and performance of the functions or authority exclusively entrusted to the authorities of that other party by its national laws or regulations." *See* Eric Bentley, Jr., Toward an International Fourth Amendment: Rethinking Searches and Seizures Abroad after Verdugo–Urquidez, 27 Vand. J. Transnat'l L. 329 (1994). *See also* Ethan A. Nadelmann, The Role of the United States in the International Enforcement of Criminal Law, 31 Harv. Int'l L. J. 37, 62–63 (1990). DEA guidelines provide that: "DEA representatives will not engage or participate in unilateral investigative operations or other activities outside the scope of the formal or informal agreement developed between the United States and the host government unless these activities have express and explicit approval of a responsible host government official." Quoted in the Brief for the United States, United States v. Verdugo–Urquidez at 26, n. 25.

6. Account should also be taken of the so-called Mansfield Amendment which is set forth in 22 U.S.C. § 2291(c):

§ 2291. Policy, general authorities, coordination, foreign police actions, definitions, and other provisions

. . .

(c) Participation in foreign police actions

(1) Prohibition on effecting an arrest

No officer or employee of the United States may directly effect an arrest in any foreign country as part of any foreign police action with respect to narcotics control efforts, notwithstanding any other provision of law.

(2) Participation in arrest actions

Paragraph (1) does not prohibit an officer or employee of the United States, with the approval of the United States chief of mission, from being present when foreign officers are effecting an arrest or from assisting foreign officers who are effecting an arrest.

(3) Exception for exigent, threatening circumstances

Paragraph (1) does not prohibit an officer or employee from taking direct action to protect life or safety if exigent circumstances arise which are unanticipated and which pose an immediate threat to United States officers or employees, officers or employees of a foreign government, or members of the public.

(4) Exception for maritime law enforcement

With the agreement of a foreign country, paragraph (1) does not apply with respect to maritime law enforcement operations in the territorial sea or archipelagic waters of that country.

(5) Interrogations

No officer or employee of the United States may interrogate or be present during the interrogation of any United States person arrested in any foreign country with respect to narcotics control efforts without the written consent of such person.

(6) Exception for Status of Forces arrangements

This subsection does not apply to the activities of the United States Armed Forces in carrying out their responsibilities under applicable Status of Forces arrangements.

7.   The Mansfield Amendment only applies in narcotics cases. Of course, terrorism cases may sometimes have a narcotics feature where the terrorists engage in narcotics activities to raise funds. International narcotics operations may sometimes also qualify under the definitions of terrorism.

3.   SEARCH ABROAD OF THE PREMISES OF A U.S. PERSON BY U.S. AGENTS; FOREIGN INTELLIGENCE PURPOSE

IN RE TERRORIST BOMBINGS OF U.S. EMBASSIES IN EAST AFRICA—UNITED STATES v. ODEH

552 F.3d 157 (2d Cir. 2008), cert. denied 130 S.Ct. 1050 (2010)

Before: FEINBERG, NEWMAN, and CABRANES, CIRCUIT JUDGES.

JOSÉ A. CABRANES, CIRCUIT JUDGE:

Defendant-appellant Wadih El–Hage, a citizen of the United States, challenges his conviction in the United States District Court for the

Southern District of New York (LEONARD B. SAND, Judge) on numerous charges arising from his involvement in the August 7, 1998 bombings of the American Embassies in Nairobi, Kenya and Dar es Salaam, Tanzania (the "August 7 bombings"). In this opinion we consider El–Hage's challenge to the District Court's denial of his motion to suppress evidence obtained by the government from an August 1997 search of his residence in Nairobi, Kenya and electronic surveillance of telephone lines—land-based and cellular-conducted in Kenya between August 1996 and August 1997....

El–Hage contends that the District Court erred by (1) recognizing a foreign intelligence exception to the Fourth Amendment's warrant requirement, (2) concluding that the search of El–Hage's home and surveillance of his telephone lines qualified for inclusion in that exception, and (3) resolving El–Hage's motion on the basis of an ex parte review of classified materials, without affording El–Hage's counsel access to those materials or holding a suppression hearing. Because we hold that the Fourth Amendment's requirement of reasonableness—and not the Warrant Clause—governs extraterritorial searches of U.S. citizens and that the searches challenged on this appeal were reasonable, we find no error in the District Court's denial of El–Hage's suppression motion. In addition, the District Court's ex parte, in camera evaluation of evidence submitted by the government in opposition to El–Hage's suppression motion was appropriate in light of national security considerations that argued in favor of maintaining the confidentiality of that evidence. El–Hage's Fourth Amendment challenge to his conviction is therefore without merit.

American intelligence became aware of al Qaeda's presence in Kenya by mid–1996 and identified five telephone numbers used by suspected al Qaeda associates. From August 1996 through August 1997, American intelligence officials monitored these telephone lines, including two El–Hage used: a phone line in the building where El–Hage lived and his cell phone. The Attorney General of the United States then authorized intelligence operatives to target El–Hage in particular. This authorization, first issued on April 4, 1997, was renewed in July 1997. Working with Kenyan authorities, U.S. officials searched El–Hage's home in Nairobi on August 21, 1997, pursuant to a document shown to El–Hage's wife that was "identified as a Kenyan warrant authorizing a search for 'stolen property.'" ... El–Hage was not present during the search of his home. It is uncontested that the agents did not apply for or obtain a warrant from a U.S. court.

El–Hage filed a pretrial motion pursuant to the Fourth Amendment for the suppression of (1) evidence seized during the August 1997 search of his home in Nairobi and the fruits thereof; (2) evidence obtained through electronic surveillance of four telephone lines, including the telephone for his Nairobi residence and his Kenyan cellular phone, conducted between August 1996 and August 1997; ... The government opposed El–Hage's motion on the ground that the Fourth Amendment's warrant requirement is inapplicable to overseas searches conducted for the purpose of gathering foreign intelligence. It also asserted that the need for an evidentiary hearing probing the basis for the Kenyan searches was outweighed by the need to maintain the confidentiality of the underlying intelligence. . . .

As a preliminary matter, we address El–Hage's objection to the District Court's resolution of his suppression motion on the basis of an in camera, ex parte review of evidence submitted by the government. El–Hage argues strenuously that without an evidentiary hearing the District Court could not properly evaluate the merits of his motion. Specifically, El–Hage contends that had he been permitted access to those materials and given an opportunity to be heard with regard to them, he would have argued that (1) the majority of the intercepted communications were unrelated to national security, (2) the government failed to limit (or "minimize") its surveillance of irrelevant communications, (3) the search of his Kenyan home was pursuant to a criminal investigation and not part of an effort to gather foreign intelligence, and (4) the surveillance was not conducted in "good faith on any level." . . . We disagree. In light of the limited factual inquiry into evidence of consequence to national security that was necessary to resolve El–Hage's motion and because the legal issues were "thoroughly briefed by the parties,", we see no error—much less an abuse of discretion-in the District Court's decision to review in camera the government's ex parte submissions.

. . .

In order to determine whether El–Hage's suppression motion was properly denied by the District Court, we must first determine whether and to what extent the Fourth Amendment's safeguards apply to overseas searches involving U.S. citizens. In United States v. Toscanino, a case involving a Fourth Amendment challenge to overseas wiretapping of a non-U.S. citizen, we observed that it was "well settled" that "the Bill of Rights has extraterritorial application to the conduct abroad of federal agents directed against United States citizens"; see also United States v. Verdugo–Urquidez, 494 U.S. 259, 283 n. 7, 110 S.Ct. 1056, 108 L.Ed.2d 222 (1990) (Brennan, J., dissenting) (recognizing "the rule, accepted by every Court of Appeals to have considered the question, that the Fourth Amendment applies to searches conducted by the United States Government against United States citizens abroad"); . . . Nevertheless, we have not yet determined the specific question of the applicability of the Fourth Amendment's Warrant Clause to overseas searches. Faced with that question now, we hold that the Fourth Amendment's warrant requirement does not govern searches conducted abroad by U.S. agents; such searches of U.S. citizens need only satisfy the Fourth Amendment's requirement of reasonableness.

. . .

The question of whether a warrant is required for overseas searches of U.S. citizens has not been decided by the Supreme Court, by our Court, or, as far as we are able to determine, by any of our sister circuits. While never addressing the question directly, the Supreme Court provided some guidance on the issue in United States v. Verdugo–Urquidez, ... With respect to the applicability of the Warrant Clause abroad, the Court expressed doubt that the clause governed any overseas searches conducted by U.S. agents, explaining that warrants issued to conduct overseas searches "would be a dead letter outside the United States." Elaborating on this observation in a concurring opinion, Justice Kennedy concluded:

> The absence of local judges or magistrates available to issue warrants, the differing and perhaps unascertainable conceptions of reasonableness and privacy that prevail abroad, and the need to cooperate with foreign officials all indicate that the Fourth Amendment's warrant requirement should not apply in Mexico as it does in this country.

These observations and the following reasons weigh against imposing a warrant requirement on overseas searches.

First, there is nothing in our history or our precedents suggesting that U.S. officials must first obtain a warrant before conducting an overseas search. El–Hage has pointed to no authority—and we are aware of none—directly supporting the proposition that warrants are necessary for searches conducted abroad by U.S. law enforcement officers or local agents acting in collaboration with them; nor has El–Hage identified any instances in our history where a foreign search was conducted pursuant to an American search warrant. This dearth of authority is not surprising in light of the history of the Fourth Amendment and its Warrant Clause as well as the history of international affairs....

. . .

While we cannot say that the practices of foreign governments have any bearing on the constitutionality of a similar practice by our government, we find it notable that El–Hage has not pointed to any instance in which another country imposed any comparable requirements on its own law enforcement officers.

The interest served by the warrant requirement in having a "neutral and detached magistrate" evaluate the reasonableness of a search is, in part, based on separation of powers concerns—namely, the need to interpose a judicial officer between the zealous police officer ferreting out crime and the subject of the search ... These interests are lessened in the circumstances presented here for two reasons. First, a domestic judicial officer's ability to determine the reasonableness of a search is diminished where the search occurs on foreign soil. Second, the acknowledged wide discretion afforded the executive branch in foreign affairs ought to be respected in these circumstances.

A warrant serves a further purpose in limiting the scope of the search to places described with particularity or "the persons or things to be seized" in the warrant. U.S. Const. amend. IV. In the instant case, we are satisfied that the scope of the searches at issue was not unreasonable.

Second, nothing in the history of the foreign relations of the United States would require that U.S. officials obtain warrants from foreign magistrates before conducting searches overseas or, indeed, to suppose that all other states have search and investigation rules akin to our own.

. . . The American procedure of issuing search warrants on a showing of probable cause simply does not extend throughout the globe and, pursuant to the Supreme Court's instructions, the Constitution does not condition our government's investigative powers on the practices of foreign legal regimes "quite different from that which obtains in this country."

Third, if U.S. judicial officers were to issue search warrants intended to have extraterritorial effect, such warrants would have dubious legal significance, if any, in a foreign nation. . . .

Fourth and finally, it is by no means clear that U.S. judicial officers could be authorized to issue warrants for overseas searches, . . . , although we need not resolve that issue here.

For these reasons, we hold that the Fourth Amendment's Warrant Clause has no extraterritorial application and that foreign searches of U.S. citizens conducted by U.S. agents are subject only to the Fourth Amendment's requirement of reasonableness.

The District Court's recognition of an exception to the warrant requirement for foreign intelligence searches finds support in the pre-FISA law of other circuits. See United States v. Truong Dinh Hung, 629 F.2d 908, 913 (4th Cir.1980); United States v. Buck, 548 F.2d 871, 875 (9th Cir.1977); United States v. Butenko, 494 F.2d 593, 605 (3d Cir.1974); United States v. Brown, 484 F.2d 418, 426 (5th Cir.1973). We decline to adopt this view, however, because the exception requires an inquiry into whether the "primary purpose" of the search is foreign intelligence collection. This distinction between a "primary purpose" and other purposes is inapt.

. . .

To determine whether a search is reasonable under the Fourth Amendment, we examine the "totality of the circumstances" to balance "on the one hand, the degree to which it intrudes upon an individual's privacy and, on the other, the degree to which it is needed for the promotion of legitimate governmental interests." [W]e conclude that the searches' intrusion on El–Hage's privacy was outweighed by the government's manifest need to monitor his activities as *an operative of al Qaeda because of the extreme threat al Qaeda presented, and continues to present, to national security. In light of these circumstances, the Kenyan searches were reasonable, notwithstanding El–Hage's objections, and therefore not prohibited by the Fourth Amendment.

. . .

... U.S. intelligence officers became aware of al Qaeda's presence in Kenya in the spring of 1996. At about that time, they identified five telephone lines used by suspected al Qaeda associates, one of which was located in the same building as El–Hage's Nairobi home; another was a cellular phone used by El–Hage. After these telephone lines had been monitored for several months, the Attorney General of the United States authorized surveillance specifically targeting El–Hage. That authorization was renewed four months later, and, one month after that, U.S. agents searched El–Hage's home in Nairobi. This sequence of events is indicative of a disciplined approach to gathering indisputably vital intelligence on the activities of a foreign terrorist organization. U.S. agents did not breach the privacy of El–Hage's home on a whim or on the basis of an unsubstantiated tip; rather, they monitored telephonic communications involving him for nearly a year and conducted surveillance of his activities for five months before concluding that it was necessary to search his home. In light of these findings of fact, which El–Hage has not contested as clearly erroneous, we conclude that the search, while undoubtedly intrusive on El–Hage's privacy, was restrained in execution and narrow in focus.

Balanced against this restrained and limited intrusion on El–Hage's privacy, we have the government's manifest need to investigate possible threats to national security.... The government had evidence establishing that El–Hage was working with al Qaeda in Kenya. On the basis of these findings of fact, we agree with the District Court that, at the time of the search of El–Hage's home, the government had a powerful need to gather additional intelligence on al Qaeda's activities in Kenya, which it had linked to El–Hage.

Balancing the search's limited intrusion on El–Hage's privacy against the manifest need of the government to monitor the activities of al Qaeda, which had been connected to El–Hage through a year of surveillance, we hold that the search of El–Hage's Nairobi residence was reasonable under the Fourth Amendment.

. . .

It cannot be denied that El–Hage suffered, while abroad, a significant invasion of privacy by virtue of the government's year-long surveillance of his telephonic communications.... For its part, the government does not contradict El–Hage's claims that the surveillance was broad and loosely "minimized." Instead, the government sets forth a variety of reasons justifying the breadth of the surveillance. These justifications, regardless of their merit, do not lessen the intrusion El–Hage suffered while abroad, and we accord this intrusion substantial weight in our balancing analysis.

Turning to the government's interest, we encounter again the self-evident need to investigate threats to national security presented by foreign terrorist organizations. When U.S. intelligence learned that five telephone lines were being used by suspected al Qaeda operatives, the need to monitor communications traveling on those lines was paramount, and we are loath to discount—much less disparage—the government's decision to do so.

Our balancing of these compelling, and competing, interests turns on whether the scope of the intrusion here was justified by the government's surveillance needs. We conclude that it was, for at least the following four reasons.

First, complex, wide-ranging, and decentralized organizations, such as al Qaeda, warrant sustained and intense monitoring in order to understand their features and identify their members. . . . Second, foreign intelligence gathering of the sort considered here must delve into the superficially mundane because it is not always readily apparent what information is relevant. . . .

Third, members of covert terrorist organizations, as with other sophisticated criminal enterprises, often communicate in code, or at least through ambiguous language.

. . . Fourth, because the monitored conversations were conducted in foreign languages, the task of determining relevance and identifying coded language was further complicated. . . .

Because the surveillance of suspected al Qaeda operatives must be sustained and thorough in order to be effective, we cannot conclude that the scope of the government's electronic surveillance was overbroad. While the intrusion on El–Hage's privacy was great, the need for the government to so intrude was even greater. Accordingly, the electronic surveillance, like the search of El–Hage's Nairobi residence, was reasonable under the Fourth Amendment.

In sum, because the searches at issue in this appeal were reasonable, they comport with the applicable requirement of the Fourth Amendment and, therefore, El–Hage's motion to suppress the evidence resulting from those searches was properly denied by the District Court.

. . .

Questions and Notes

1. The materials in this subsection, address generally the issues raised in searches involving U.S. agents that take place abroad. Odeh adds to the mix the fact that the search occurred abroad in connection with a matter involving national security/forcign intelligence concerns. Does that fact change the applicable conclusions?

2. The Odeh case involved both physical searches and electronic surveillance. The government appeared to have had a purpose to obtain foreign intelligence information. Does the FISA statute as originally enacted have any relevance to the Odeh case? If the FISA Amendments Act of 2008 had been in force at the time of the Odeh events, would it have been relevant to the Odeh case?

3. In resolving the issue in the case, did the court in Odeh take into account the foreign intelligence goal of the search? How did it deal with it in

its opinion? Did the court give any weight to the fact that there were foreign intelligence/national security issues in the case? Stating the matter differently, how did the government argue the relevance of the foreign intelligence purpose of the investigation? Was the government's argument too narrow?

4. As we saw in the previous subsection of this chapter, there is no statute dealing with physical searches abroad comparable to §§ 1822–25, which deals with the topic on the domestic front. Would it be useful to enact a statute that deals with physical searches by U.S. agents of the premises of U.S. persons abroad?

5. Given the fact that the court in Odeh applied a standard of reasonableness under the Fourth Amendment and declined to apply the warrant clause, and that the Supreme Court denied certiorari in the matter, does it make sense to bring a warrant requirement back into such cases through enactment of a new statute?

6. See generally, Bombed Away: How The Second Circuit Destroyed Fourth Amendment Rights Of U.S. Citizens Abroad, 2010 B.Y.U. L. Rev. 719 (2010); Streaming The International Silver Platter Doctrine: Coordinating Transnational Law Enforcement In The Age Of Global Terrorism And Technology, 49 Colum. J. Transnat'l L. 411 (2011); Corey M. Then, Note, Searches and Seizures of Americans Abroad: Re–Examining the Fourth Amendment's Warrant Clause and the Foreign Intelligence Exception Five Years After United States v. Bin Laden, 55 Duke L.J. 1059 (2006).

D. ADMINISTRATIVE AND JUDICIAL SUBPOENAS TO OBTAIN RECORDS, DOCUMENTS, ETC.—NATIONAL SECURITY LETTERS AND SECTION 215 (50 U.S.C. § 1861) ORDERS

1. INTRODUCTION

As indicated in the Introduction to this chapter, the government can obtain records, documents and other tangibles through a search warrant process or through the issuance of what amounts to a subpoena directing a person or institution to produce specified materials in their possession. In the field of foreign intelligence or international terrorism, National Security Letters or section 215 orders (often called the "library provision" because of concerns that it would be frequently used to obtain library records of patrons) can be utilized to obtain records, documents and other kinds of information, usually from third party holders. NSL letters are used very frequently for this purpose; section 215 has not been used very often. Authority to issue National Security Letters in order to seek different kinds of records is authorized under a number of different statutes, see 18 U.S.C. § 2709 (electronic subscriber information); 12 U.S.C. § 3414(a)(5) (financial records); 15 U.S.C. § 1681u (credit history); 15 U.S.C. § 1681v (full credit reports); 50 U.S.C. § 436 (information concerning investigation of improper disclosure of classified information).

Section 215 is codified at 50 U.S.C. § 1861. To issue an order under this provision, which can be used to demand the production of any tangible things (including books, papers, records, etc.), approval must be obtained from a judge of the Foreign Intelligence Surveillance Court or a special designated U.S. Magistrate. In general form, section 215 is a type of judicially approved subpoena duces tecum.

In general form, National Security Letters amount to administrative subpoenas which are widely utilized elsewhere in the legal system and, in some instances, in relation to, or in direct aid of criminal investigation. Note that the designated purpose of NSL subpoenas is not criminal enforcement, but rather to obtain foreign intelligence information, especially regarding terrorism. Federal agencies which have administrative subpoena authority include: the Drug Enforcement Agency, see 21 U.S.C. § 876; the IRS, see 26 U.S.C. § 7602; the SEC, see SEC v. Dresser Industries, 628 F. 2d 1368 (D.C. Cir. 1980); the Labor Management Reporting and Disclosure Act, see Donovan v. Spadea, 757 F.2d 74 (3d Cir. 1985).

NSL and section 215 are somewhat controversial. The question is whether they are truly simply another kind of administrative or judicially-approved subpoena, or whether they have some features that make them unique and involve a significant expansion of governmental powers. In order to be able to make the appropriate comparisons of the significance of the NSL's and section 215, we reproduce below: a) the most frequently used NSL authorization statute, 18 U.S.C. § 2709 as well as b) the provisions governing judicial review for the several different NSL statutes, 18 U.S.C § 3511; c) the Section 215 statute (50 U.S.C § 1861); and d) by way of illustration and for purposes of comparison, an administrative subpoena available in a non-terrorism legal setting—provisions governing the issuance of administrative subpoenas used in drug enforcement investigations, 21 U.S.C. § 876–877.

2. AUTHORITY TO ISSUE NATIONAL SECURITY LETTERS

18 U.S.C. § 2709

(a) **Duty to provide.** A wire or electronic communication service provider shall comply with a request for subscriber information and toll billing records information, or electronic communication transactional records in its custody or possession made by the Director of the Federal Bureau of Investigation under subsection (b) of this section.

(b) **Required Certification.** The Director of the Federal Bureau of Investigation, or his designee in a position not lower than Deputy Assistant Director at Bureau headquarters or a Special Agent in Charge in a Bureau field office designated by the Director, may—

(1) request the name, address, length of service, and local and long distance toll billing records of a person or entity if the

Director (or his designee) certifies in writing to the wire or electronic communication service provider to which the request is made that the name, address, length of service, and toll billing records sought are relevant to an authorized investigation to protect against international terrorism or clandestine intelligence activities, provided that such an investigation of a United States person is not conducted solely on the basis of activities protected by the first amendment to the Constitution of the United States; and

. . .

(c) Prohibition of certain disclosure.—

(1) If the Director of the Federal Bureau of Investigation, or his designee . . . certifies that otherwise there may result a danger to the national security of the United States, interference with a criminal, counterterrorism, or counterintelligence investigation, interference with diplomatic relations, or danger to the life or physical safety of any person, no wire or electronic communications service provider, or officer, employee, or agent thereof, shall disclose to any person (other than those to whom such disclosure is necessary to comply with the request or an attorney to obtain legal advice or legal assistance with respect to the request) that the Federal Bureau of Investigation has sought or obtained access to information or records under this section.

. . .

(3) Any recipient disclosing to those persons necessary to comply with the request or to an attorney to obtain legal advice or legal assistance with respect to the request shall inform such person of any applicable nondisclosure requirement. Any person who receives a disclosure under this subsection shall be subject to the same prohibitions on disclosure under paragraph (1).

(4) At the request of the Director of the Federal Bureau of Investigation or the designee of the Director, any person making or intending to make a disclosure under this section shall identify to the Director or such designee the person to whom such disclosure will be made or to whom such disclosure was made prior to the request, except that nothing in this section shall require a person to inform the Director or such designee of the identity of an attorney to whom disclosure was made or will be made to obtain legal advice or legal assistance with respect to the request under subsection (a).

. . .

(f) Libraries.—A library (as that term is defined in section 213(1) of the Library Services and Technology Act (20 U.S.C. 9122(1))), the services of which include access to the Internet, books, journals, magazines, newspapers, or other similar forms of communication in print or digitally by patrons for their use, review, examination, or circulation, is not a wire or electronic communication service provider for purposes of this section, unless the library is providing the services defined in section 2510(15) ("electronic communication service") of this title.

3. JUDICIAL REVIEW OF NSL'S

18 U.S.C. § 3511. Judicial review of requests for information

(a) The recipient of a request for records, a report, or other information under section 2709(b) of this title, section 626(a) or (b) or 627(a) of the Fair Credit Reporting Act, section 1114(a)(5)(A) of the Right to Financial Privacy Act, or section 802(a) of the National Security Act of 1947 may, in the United States district court for the district in which that person or entity does business or resides, petition for an order modifying or setting aside the request. The court may modify or set aside the request if compliance would be unreasonable, oppressive, or otherwise unlawful.

(b)

. . .

(2) If the petition is filed within one year of the request for records, a report, or other information under section 2709(b) of this title, section 626(a) or (b) or 627(a) of the Fair Credit Reporting Act, section 1114(a)(5)(A) of the Right to Financial Privacy Act, or section 802(a) of the National Security Act of 1947, the court may modify or set aside such a nondisclosure requirement if it finds that there is no reason to believe that disclosure may endanger the national security of the United States, interfere with a criminal, counterterrorism, or counterintelligence investigation, interfere with diplomatic relations, or endanger the life or physical safety of any person. If, at the time of the petition, the Attorney General, Deputy Attorney General, an Assistant Attorney General, or the Director of the Federal Bureau of Investigation, or in the case of a request by a department, agency, or instrumentality of the Federal Government other than the Department of Justice, the head or deputy head of such department, agency, or instrumentality, certifies that disclosure may endanger the national security of the United States or interfere with diplomatic relations, such certification shall be treated as conclusive unless the court finds that the certification was made in bad faith.

(3) If the petition is filed one year or more after the request for records, a report, or other information under section 2709(b) of this title, section 626(a) or (b) or 627(a) of the Fair Credit Reporting Act, section 1114(a)(5)(A) of the Right to Financial Privacy Act, or section 802(a) of the National Security Act of

1947, the Attorney General, Deputy Attorney General, an Assistant Attorney General, or the Director of the Federal Bureau of Investigation, or his designee . . . or in the case of a request by a department, agency, or instrumentality of the Federal Government other than the Federal Bureau of Investigation, the head or deputy head of such department, agency, or instrumentality, within ninety days of the filing of the petition, shall either terminate the nondisclosure requirement or re-certify that disclosure may result in a danger to the national security of the United States, interference with a criminal, counterterrorism, or counterintelligence investigation, interference with diplomatic relations, or danger to the life or physical safety of any person. In the event of re-certification, the court may modify or set aside such a nondisclosure requirement if it finds that there is no reason to believe that disclosure may endanger the national security of the United States, interfere with a criminal, counterterrorism, or counterintelligence investigation, interfere with diplomatic relations, or endanger the life or physical safety of any person. If the recertification that disclosure may endanger the national security of the United States or interfere with diplomatic relations is made by the Attorney General, Deputy Attorney General, an Assistant Attorney General, or the Director of the Federal Bureau of Investigation, such certification shall be treated as conclusive unless the court finds that the recertification was made in bad faith. If the court denies a petition for an order modifying or setting aside a nondisclosure requirement under this paragraph, the recipient shall be precluded for a period of one year from filing another petition to modify or set aside such nondisclosure requirement.

. . .

(e) In all proceedings under this section, the court shall, upon request of the government, review ex parte and in camera any government submission or portions thereof, which may include classified information.

4.　THE LIBRARY PROVISION—SECTION 215 (50 U.S.C. § 1861)

50 U.S.C. § 1861

(a)(1) Subject to paragraph (3), the Director of the Federal Bureau of Investigation or a designee of the Director (whose rank shall be no lower than Assistant Special Agent in Charge) may make an application for an order requiring the production of any tangible things (including books, records, papers, documents, and other items) for an investigation to obtain foreign intelligence information not concerning a United States person or to protect against international terrorism or clandestine intelligence activities, provided that such investigation of a United States person is not conducted solely upon the basis of activities protected by the first amendment to the Constitution.

(2) An investigation conducted under this section shall

(A) be conducted under guidelines approved by the Attorney General under Executive Order 12333 (or a successor order); and

(B) not be conducted of a United States person solely upon the basis of activities protected by the first amendment to the Constitution of the United States.

(3) In the case of an application for an order requiring the production of library circulation records, library patron lists, book sales records, book customer lists, firearms sales records, tax return records, educational records, or medical records containing information that would identify a person, the Director of the Federal Bureau of Investigation may delegate the authority to make such application to either the Deputy Director of the Federal Bureau of Investigation or the Executive Assistant Director for National Security (or any successor position). The Deputy Director or the Executive Assistant Director may not further delegate such authority.

(b) Each application under this section

(1) shall be made to—

(A) a judge of the court established by section 1803(a) of this title; or

(B) a United States Magistrate Judge under chapter 43 of Title 28, who is publicly designated by the Chief Justice of the United States to have the power to hear applications and grant orders for the production of tangible things under this section on behalf of a judge of that court; and

(2) shall include—

(A) a statement of facts showing that there are reasonable grounds to believe that the tangible things sought are relevant to an authorized investigation (other than a threat assessment) conducted in accordance with subsection (a)(2) of this section to obtain foreign intelligence information not concerning a United States person or to protect against international terrorism or clandestine intelligence activities, such things being presumptively relevant to an authorized investigation if the applicant shows in the statement of the facts that they pertain to—

(i) a foreign power or an agent of a foreign power;

(ii) the activities of a suspected agent of a foreign power who is the subject of such authorized investigation; or

(iii) an individual in contact with, or known to, a suspected agent of a foreign power who is the subject of such authorized investigation; and

(B) an enumeration of the minimization procedures adopted by the Attorney General under subsection (g) of this section that are applicable to the retention and dissemination by the Federal Bureau of Investigation of any tangible things to be made available to the Federal Bureau of Investigation based on the order requested in such application.

(c)(1) Upon an application made pursuant to this section, if the judge finds that the application meets the requirements of subsections (a) and (b) of this section, the judge shall enter an ex parte order as requested, or as modified, approving the release of tangible things. Such order shall direct that minimization procedures adopted pursuant to subsection (g) of this section be followed.

(2) An order under this subsection—

(A) shall describe the tangible things that are ordered to be produced with sufficient particularity to permit them to be fairly identified;

(B) shall include the date on which the tangible things must be provided, which shall allow a reasonable period of time within which the tangible things can be assembled and made available;

(C) shall provide clear and conspicuous notice of the principles and procedures described in subsection (d) of this section;

(D) may only require the production of a tangible thing if such thing can be obtained with a subpoena duces tecum issued by a court of the United States in aid of a grand jury investigation or with any other order issued by a court of the United States directing the production of records or tangible things; and

(E) shall not disclose that such order is issued for purposes of an investigation described in subsection (a) of this section.

(d)(1) No person shall disclose to any other person that the Federal bureau of investigation has sought or obtained tangible things pursuant to an order under this section, other than to

(A) those persons to whom disclosure is necessary to comply with such order;

(B) an attorney to obtain legal advice or assistance with respect to the production of things in response to the order; or

(C) other persons as permitted by the Director of the Federal Bureau of Investigation or the designee of the Director.

(2)(A) A person to whom disclosure is made pursuant to paragraph (1) shall be subject to the nondisclosure requirements applicable to a person to whom an order is directed under this section in the same manner as such person.

(B) Any person who discloses to a person described in subparagraph (A), (B), or (C) of paragraph (1) that the Federal Bureau of Investigation has sought or obtained tangible things pursuant to an order under this section shall notify such person of the nondisclosure requirements of this subsection.

. . .

(e) A person who, in good faith, produces tangible things under an order pursuant to this section shall not be liable to any other person for such production. Such production shall not be deemed to constitute a waiver of any privilege in any other proceeding or context.

. . .

[Ed. Subsection (2) of § 1861, omitted here, contains provisions dealing with standards for judicial review of a § 1861 order that are very similar to those contained in § 3511, reproduced supra, which provides for judicial review of a § 2709 order and similar orders under other NSL provisions.]

5. AUTHORITY TO ISSUE ADMINISTRATIVE SUBPOENAS IN DRUG–RELATED INVESTIGATIONS

§ 876. Subpenas

(a) Authorization of use by Attorney General

In any investigation relating to his functions under this subchapter with respect to controlled substances, listed chemicals, tableting machines, or encapsulating machines, the Attorney General may subpena witnesses, compel the attendance and testimony of witnesses, and require the production of any records (including books, papers, documents, and other tangible things which constitute or contain evidence) which the Attorney General finds relevant or material to the investigation. The attendance of witnesses and the production of records may be required from any place in any State or in any territory or other place subject to the jurisdiction of the United States at any designated place of hearing; except that a witness shall not be required to appear at any hearing more than 500 miles distant from the place where he was served with a subpena. Witnesses summoned under this section shall be paid the same fees and mileage that are paid witnesses in the courts of the United States.

. . .

§ 877. Judicial review

All final determinations, findings, and conclusions of the Attorney General under this subchapter shall be final and conclusive decisions of the matters involved, except that any person aggrieved by a final decision of the Attorney General may obtain review of the decision in the United States Court of Appeals for the District of Columbia or for the circuit in which his principal place of business is located upon petition filed with the court and delivered to the Attorney General within thirty days after notice of the decision. Findings of fact by the Attorney General, if supported by substantial evidence, shall be conclusive.

QUESTIONS AND NOTES

1. In the aftermath of 9/11, the USA PATRIOT Act was enacted, and it soon became a center of controversy and a lightning rod for criticism. Among the targets of special criticism was the so-called "library" provision, section 215. In an article in the Wall Street Journal, Nov. 12, 2004, a former Congressman, Bob Barr, who sat on the Judiciary Committee when the PATRIOT Act was passed, expressed the view that section 215 (the seizure of tangible things, such as library records) was one of the provisions representing the "most significant problems." Barr's criticism of section 215 was that it expanded the category of what could be seized under FISA authority from business records to "any tangible thing" from any third party record holder and lowered the applicable standard of facts based on which an order could be issued from "specific and articulable facts" to "relevant" to an investigation. Professor (now Dean) Chemerinsky was another strong critic:

> . . . One of the most troubling and controversial provisions of the Act is section 215, which provides the Director of the FBI broad authority to obtain records "to protect against international terrorism or clandestine intelligence activities." This allows the FISA Court to issue orders for "production of any tangible things (including books, records, papers, documents, and other items)." When such information is provided, "no person shall disclose to any other person . . . that the [FBI] has sought or obtained tangible things under this section." . . .

Under this provision the government has broad access to records about a person. For example, the government can obtain from libraries a list of the books that a person has borrowed. No probable cause or even reasonable suspicion is required. Nor must the government meet the usual Fourth Amendment requirement to list with specification what is sought; the Act authorizes orders for "production of any tangible thing."

A library, or other institution, ordered to produce the information cannot disclose to the person that the request has been made. Erwin Chemerinsky, Losing Liberties: Applying a Foreign Intelligence Model to Domestic Law Enforcement, 51 UCLA L. Rev. 1619, 1623–1628 (2004).

2. There was an oddity in the criticism insofar as it seemed to focus primarily on the government's invoking section 215 to obtain information from libraries when in fact the provision itself applied much more broadly and there was little evidence of its widespread use against libraries. A series of news articles in the Los Angeles Times, the New York Times and the Washington Post between March and July, 2003, disclosed the following reported information:

> Associations of libraries, booksellers and writers announced a drive to collect a million signatures in support of bills in Congress to amend [section 215].... One report indicated that 25,000 signatures had been collected already.

> More than 200 cities and towns passed nonbinding resolutions in opposition to it.

It is hard to account for this widespread reaction to a provision which did not especially target libraries and had hardly been used.

3. After declining over a period of time to reveal how many times section 215 had been used on the ground that the information was classified, and in speeches decrying the attacks on section 215 as "baseless hysteria," in September 2003, Attorney General Ashcroft indicated that he would declassify the information, and subsequently in a speech he stated that section 215 had never been used. LA Times, Sept. 19, 2003, p. A30.

4. In response to a district court decision, ACLU v. U.S. Department of Justice, 321 F.Supp. 2d 24 (D.D.C. 2004), the government turned over a large number of documents (the first batch consisted of 338 pages, many of them with names or other information blacked out). One of those documents revealed that approximately a month after the Attorney General had stated that section 215 had not been used, there was a request for approval of the use of the provision from an office of the FBI. Wash. Post, June 18, 2004, p. A11. It was also reported that in the fall, 2003, seven out of almost 600 public and private libraries surveyed reported that they had received requests for information about patrons or circulation records from the FBI while 14 libraries declined to answer some of the survey questions because they were afraid that providing the information would violate the law. Boston Globe, March 9, 2004, p. E5.

5. In July, 2004, an amendment was added to a spending bill in the House of Representatives that would have amended section 215 and prohibited funds from being made available to make an application for an order requiring the production of library circulation records, library patron lists, library internet records, book sales records and book customer lists. The amendment failed on a vote of 210 to 210. During this period, while the Administration was engaged in a vigorous lobbying effort to defeat the bill, the Justice Department sent a letter reporting that "a member of a terrorist group closely affiliated with Al Qaeda used Internet services provided by a

public library" at least twice in recent months. NY Times, July 9, 2004, p. A16.

6. In 2006, libraries were expressly excluded from the coverage of the national security letter provision. See 18 U.S.C § 2709(f), supra. Prior to that time there was a question about whether libraries were covered by that section, and at least in some cases, the section was invoked to obtain information from libraries. Prior to the 2006 amendment, if you were an FBI agent seeking information from a library, which provision would you be more likely to use, section 215 or 2709?

7. To answer the question whether the NSL's and section 215 expand government authority beyond what is appropriate, it is useful to compare the NSL's and section 215 orders with each other and with another kind of administrative subpoena (in this instance, administrative subpoena authority in drug investigations), in regard to the following: a) the purpose of the issuance of the subpoena or summons; b) the factual basis or standard on which the government can act to acquire books, records, documents, etc.; c) the scope of the different legal authorizations—how broad are the categories of tangible things that can be seized or demanded; d) whether the specific person involved is the target of the investigation or a third party; e) whether judicial approval must be obtained prior to the government action; f) whether an obligation of secrecy applies to the particular government action, and the nature and extent of that obligation; and g) whether the order to produce requested material is subject to judicial review and the standard of review.

8. From a comparison of the relevant provisions, it should be apparent that the NSL and section 215 statutory authority do not differ significantly from the drug investigation subpoena authority with regard to the factual basis or standard on which the request or order can be issued, that is, the drug provision is a precedent from another investigatory area for using a "relevant to an investigation" standard. Stating the matter differently, why should the government be able to obtain records, etc. in a drug investigation by applying a relevant to an investigation standard and not be able to use a similar standard in a terrorism investigation? Recall, however, that Congressman Barr and Professor Chemerinsky were critical of the relevant to an investigation standard. Are there reasons why arguably a higher standard should be applicable in a terrorism investigation than in a drug enforcement matter? Are there contrary arguments that can be offered?

9. There do not seem to be significant differences between provisions of the drug investigation subpoena provision and §§ 2709 and 215 with regard to the scope of the authorization and the fact of whether the request or order is subject to judicial review (though there are significant differences with respect to the substantive limits on judicial review). The most striking difference between § 876–877, on the one hand, and §§ 2709, 3511 and 215, on the other hand, is that there is no provision providing for secrecy in connection with drug investigation subpoenas issued under §§ 876 and 877, whereas the secrecy provisions under §§ 2709, 215 and 3511 are elaborate, complex and substantial. In this connection, consider the following two notes.

10. One of the drafters of the PATRIOT Act, Professor Viet Dinh of Georgetown University's law school and formerly an Assistant Attorney

General, was reported to have said: "There is this weird never-neverland, where the ACLU is insisting on an illogically broad reading. . . . Section 215 in and of itself is not objectionable. The thing that makes it objectionable to people is the automatic confidentiality provision." Boston Globe, March 9, 2004, p. E5. Professor Philip B. Heymann of the Harvard Law School was reported to have said, "In the area of access to records, there are always two concerns. One is that the government will use the information for the wrong purpose, particularly a political one. The other concern is . . . people are going to be inhibited in their activities. They will fear that the dirty book they take out will become a government record." N.Y.Times, February 26, 2004, p. A18.

11.   Regarding the criticisms of section 215, consider Professor Dinh's point that the real problem with 215 is the automatic confidentiality provision—that is, that persons who provide an individual's records to the government are prohibited from informing him/her. Is the secrecy mandated by the Act justified? At the time Professor Dinh made his comments, the confidentiality requirement was essentially absolute. Subsequently, in 2006, section 215 (as well as 2709 plus 3511) were amended into their present form, establishing provisions for judicial review by the recipient of the NSL request or 215 order and also providing a standard for continuation of the obligation of secrecy. Is 215 (as well as 2709) more acceptable now, or is the practical effect of these new provisions to enable the government still to continue the obligation of confidentiality indefinitely?

Consider the material in the next note. Is this an instance where the government's desire for secrecy, while perhaps useful and necessary in their enforcement efforts, may also make the government's enforcement program and policies more controversial and less acceptable to the public than they deserve to be? The government's penchant for secrecy and its desire to avoid judicial review of the merits of many of its controversial actions are a recurring theme in these materials.

12.   Recall Professor Heymann's point that people are inhibited in their activities by a fear that the government will keep a record of what they do. In connection with this concern, does it matter whether the provision is in fact being utilized? On the other hand, might the government make an argument that a) the evidence that a provision like section 215 has not been extensively used supports the contention that the government is not going to abuse this provision, and b) *the government needs a provision like this, so that it is available to be used when an appropriate context arises?*

13.   Assess the nondisclosure provisions in § 1861. How would you revise them, if at all? Is the provision for judicial review in § 3511 adequate?

DOE v. MUKASEY

549 F.3d 861 (2d Cir. 2008)

Before: NEWMAN, CALABRESI, and SOTOMAYOR, CIRCUIT JUDGES.

JON O. NEWMAN, CIRCUIT JUDGE:

This appeal concerns challenges to the constitutionality of statutes regulating the issuance by the Federal Bureau of Investigation ("FBI") of a type of administrative subpoena generally known as a National Security Letter ("NSL") to electronic communication service providers ("ECSPs"). *See* 18 U.S.C. §§ 2709, 3511 (collectively "the NSL statutes"). ECSPs are typically telephone companies or Internet service providers. An NSL, in the context of this appeal, is a request for information about specified persons or entities who are subscribers to an ECSP and about their telephone or Internet activity. Primarily at issue on this appeal are challenges to the provisions (1) prohibiting the recipient from disclosing the fact that an NSL has been received, *see* 18 U.S.C. § 2709(c), and (2) structuring judicial review of the nondisclosure requirement, *see id.* § 3511(b).

These challenges arise on an appeal by the United States from the September 7, 2007, judgment of the District Court for the Southern District of New York (Victor Marrero, District Judge), enjoining FBI officials from (1) issuing NSLs under section 2709, (2) enforcing the nondisclosure requirement of subsection 2709(c), and (3) enforcing the provisions for judicial review of the nondisclosure requirement contained in subsection 3511(b). *See Doe v. Gonzales,* 500 F.Supp.2d 379 (S.D.N.Y. 2007) ("*Doe II*"). The District Court ruled that subsections 2709(c) and 3511(b) are unconstitutional on First Amendment and separation-of-powers grounds, and that subsection 2709(c) could not be severed from section 2709.

We agree that the challenged statutes do not comply with the First Amendment, although not to the extent determined by the District Court, and we also conclude that the relief ordered by the District Court is too broad. We therefore affirm in part, reverse in part, and remand for further proceedings.

Background

The parties. The Plaintiffs–Appellees are an Internet service provider (John Doe, Inc.), the provider's former president (John Doe), the American Civil Liberties Union ("ACLU"), and the American Civil Liberties Union Foundation ("ACLUF"). The Defendants–Appellants are the Attorney General, the Director of the FBI, and the General Counsel of the FBI, all sued in their official capacities.

The NSL. In February 2004, the FBI delivered the NSL at issue in this litigation to John Doe, Inc. The letter directed John Doe, Inc., "to provide the [FBI] the names, addresses, lengths of service and electronic communication transactional records, to include [other information] (not to include message content and/or subject fields) for [a specific] email address." The letter certified that the information sought was relevant to an investigation against international terrorism or clandestine intelligence activities and advised John Doe, Inc., that the law "prohibit[ed] any officer, employee or agent" of the company from "disclosing to any person that the FBI has sought or obtained access to information or records" pursuant to the NSL provisions. The letter also asked that John Doe provide the relevant information personally to a designated FBI office.

. . .

Discussion

The validity of the NSL issued to John Doe, Inc., is no longer at issue because the Government has withdrawn it, but the prohibition on disclosing receipt of the NSL remains. We therefore consider only the Government's challenges to the District Court's rulings with respect to the nondisclosure requirement, although to the extent that the nondisclosure requirement encounters valid constitutional objections, we will consider the provisions authorizing the issuance of NSLs in connection with the issue of severance.

I.   Applicable Principles

The First Amendment principles relevant to the District Court's rulings are well established, although their application to the statutory provisions at issue requires careful consideration. A judicial order "forbidding certain communications when issued in advance of the time that such communications are to occur" is generally regarded as a "prior restraint," and is "the most serious and the least tolerable infringement on First Amendment rights," "Any prior restraint on expression comes to [a court] with a heavy presumption against its constitutional validity," and "carries a heavy burden of showing justification," *id.* A content-based restriction is subject to review under the standard of strict scrutiny, requiring a showing that the restriction is "narrowly tailored to promote a compelling Government interest."

. . .

The national security context in which NSLs are authorized imposes on courts a significant obligation to defer to judgments of Executive Branch officials. "[C]ourts traditionally have been reluctant to intrude upon the authority of the Executive in . . . national security affairs," and the Supreme Court has acknowledged that terrorism might provide the basis for arguments "for heightened deference to the judgments of the political branches with respect to matters of national security," *Zadvydas v. Davis,* 533 U.S. 678, 696, 121 S.Ct. 2491, 150 L.Ed.2d 653 (2001).

. . . It is well established that courts should resolve ambiguities in statutes in a manner that avoids substantial constitutional issues.

Less clear is the authority of courts to revise a statute to overcome a constitutional defect. Of course, it is the province of the Legislative Branch to legislate. But in limited circumstances the Supreme Court has undertaken to fill in a statutory gap arising from the invalidation of a portion of a statute. . . .

. . .

Closely related to the issue of whether a court should revise a statute to avoid or overcome a constitutional defect is the issue of whether to sever the unconstitutional portion of a statute or invalidate an entire statute or even an entire statutory scheme. In general, the choice, as stated by the Supreme Court, depends on whether "the legislature [would] have preferred what is left of its statute to no statute at all." ...

   . . .

II.   The Parties' Contentions

With these principles in mind, we turn to the parties' basic contentions. From the Plaintiffs' standpoint, the nondisclosure requirement of subsection 2709(c) is a straightforward content-based prior restraint that must be tested against all the substantive and procedural limitations applicable to such an impairment of expression. In their view, the nondisclosure requirement is content-based because it proscribes disclosure of the entire category of speech concerning the fact and details of the issuance of an NSL, and it is a prior restraint in the literal sense that it is imposed before an NSL recipient has an opportunity to speak. From these premises, the Plaintiffs conclude that subsection 2709(c) is unconstitutional under strict scrutiny review because it prohibits disclosure in circumstances not narrowly tailored to a compelling governmental interest and operates as a licensing scheme without the procedural requirement of placing on the Government the burden of initiating judicial review and sustaining a burden of proof. The Plaintiffs also challenge subsection 3511(b) on the grounds that (1) the judicial review provisions do not require the Government to initiate judicial review and to sustain a burden of proof and (2) certification of certain risks by senior governmental officials is entitled to a conclusive presumption (absent bad faith). These aspects of subsection 3511(b) are alleged to violate First Amendment procedural standards and the separation of powers.

The Government responds that, to whatever extent the nondisclosure requirement can be considered a content-based prior restraint, it is subject to less rigorous scrutiny than that imposed on more typical First Amendment claimants who wish to speak or parade in public places, distribute literature, or exhibit movies. The Government points out that the nondisclosure requirement arises not to suppress a pre-existing desire to speak, but only as a result of governmental interaction with an NSL recipient. In the Government's view, the nondisclosure requirement survives a First Amendment challenge on the same rationale that has permitted secrecy requirements to be imposed on witnesses before grand juries, and judicial misconduct proceedings, and on a person or entity that acquired sensitive material through pretrial discovery

III.   The Interpretation of the NSL Statutes

In assessing these contentions, we need to interpret the nondisclosure requirements before ruling on their constitutionality. [S]ubsection 2709(c) specifies what senior FBI officials must certify to trigger the nondisclosure requirement, and subsection 3511(b) specifies, in similar but not identical language, what a district court must find in order to modify or set aside such a requirement. Senior FBI officials must certify that in the absence of a nondisclosure requirement "there may result a danger to the national security of the United States, interference with a criminal, counterterrorism, or counterintelligence investigation, interference with diplomatic relations, or danger to the life or physical safety of any person." 18 U.S.C. § 2709(c)(1). Upon challenge by an NSL recipient, a district court may modify or set aside a nondisclosure requirement "if it finds that there is no reason to believe that disclosure may endanger the national security of the United States, interfere with a criminal, counterterrorism, or counterintelligence investigation, interfere with diplomatic relations, or endanger the life or physical safety of any person." *Id.* § 3511(b)(2).

These provisions present three issues for interpretation: (1) what is the scope of the enumerated harms? (2) what justifies a nondisclosure requirement? and (3) which side has the burden of proof?

The enumerated harms. The first issue concerns the scope of the language identifying the enumerated harms. It is the risk of these harms that senior FBI officials must certify in order to impose the nondisclosure requirement. These harms are "danger to the national security of the United States, interference with a criminal, counterterrorism, or counterintelligence investigation, interference with diplomatic relations, or danger to the life or physical safety of any person." 18 U.S.C. § 2709(c)(1). The last phrase is particularly troublesome. It could extend the Government's power to impose secrecy to a broad range of information relevant to such matters as ordinary tortious conduct, based on the risk of "danger to the physical safety of any person." A secrecy requirement of such broad scope would present highly problematic First Amendment issues. However, this potential reach of the nondisclosure requirement can be reined in if all the enumerated harms are keyed to the same standard that governs information sought by an NSL, *i.e.*, "relevant to an authorized investigation to protect against international terrorism or clandestine intelligence activities." *Id.* § 2709(b)(1), (2).

At oral argument, the Government wisely urged us to avoid this problem by construing the scope of the enumerated harms in light of the purposes for which an NSL is issued. We readily accept that view of the nondisclosure requirement, thereby at least narrowing, though not eliminating, the First Amendment issues. Thus, we will adjudicate the constitutionality of the nondisclosure requirement in subsection 2709(c) by construing this requirement to apply only when senior FBI officials certify that disclosure may result in an enumerated harm that is related to "an authorized investigation to protect against international terrorism or clandestine intelligence activities."

The required showing. The second issue concerns what must be shown to maintain a nondisclosure requirement upon judicial review. A district court, considering a challenge filed within one year of the issuance of an NSL, is authorized to modify or set aside a nondisclosure requirement "if it finds that there is no reason to believe that disclosure may" risk one of the enumerated harms. 18 U.S.C. § 3511(b)(2). At oral argument, the Government took the position that "reason" in the quoted phrase means "good reason." We accept this common-sense understanding of subsection 3511(b)(2). We take a similar view of the identical language in subsection 3511(b)(3), governing a challenge filed more than one year after the issuance of an NSL.

Moreover, a reason will not qualify as "good" if it surmounts only a standard of frivolousness. We understand the statutory requirement of a finding that an enumerated harm "may result" to mean more than a conceivable possibility. The upholding of nondisclosure does not require the certainty, or even the imminence of, an enumerated harm, but some reasonable likelihood must be shown. The Government acknowledges that "while the 'reason to believe' standard in subsection 3511(b) unquestionably contemplates a deferential standard of review, in no way does it foreclose a court from evaluating the reasonableness of the FBI's judgments."

The burden of proof. The third issue concerns the burden of proof applicable to the finding contemplated by subsection 3511(b)(2). Does this provision mean that, in order to have a district court modify or set aside a nondisclosure requirement, an ECSP must persuade a court that there is no good reason to believe that disclosure may risk one of the enumerated harms, or that, in order to maintain a nondisclosure requirement, the Government must persuade a court that there is a good reason to believe that disclosure may risk one of the enumerated harms? As the Government acknowledged at oral argument, subsection 3511(b) is silent as to the burden of proof. The Government also acknowledged at oral argument that these provisions should be understood to place on the Government the burden to persuade a district court that there is a good reason to believe that disclosure may risk one of the enumerated harms, and that a district court, in order to maintain a nondisclosure order, must find that such a good reason exists. This avoids requiring a district court, in order to modify or set aside a nondisclosure order, to find a negative, *i.e.*, that no good reason exists to believe that disclosure may risk one of the enumerated harms.

Under the principles outlined above, we are satisfied that we may accept the Government's concessions on all three matters of statutory interpretation without trenching on Congress's prerogative to legislate. We will therefore construe subsection 2709(c)(1) to mean that the enumerated harms must be related to "an authorized investigation to protect against international terrorism or clandestine intelligence activities," 18 U.S.C. § 2709(b)(1), (2), and construe subsections 3511(b)(2) and (3) to place on the Government the burden to persuade a district court that there is a good reason to believe that disclosure may result in one of the enumerated harms, and to mean that a district court, in order to maintain a nondisclosure order, must find that such a good reason exists.

IV. Constitutionality of the NSL Statutes

(a) *Basic approach.* Turning to the First Amendment issues with respect to the NSL statutes as thus construed, we believe that the proper path to decision lies between the broad positions asserted by the parties. Although the nondisclosure requirement is in some sense a prior restraint, as urged by the Plaintiffs, it is not a typical example of such a restriction for it is not a restraint imposed on those who customarily wish to exercise rights of free expression, such as speakers in public fora, distributors of literature, or exhibitors of movies. And although the nondisclosure requirement is triggered by the content of a category of information, that category, consisting of the fact of receipt of an NSL and some related details, is far more limited than the broad categories of information that have been at issue with respect to typical content-based restrictions.

On the other hand, we do not accept the Government's contentions that the nondisclosure requirement can be considered to satisfy First Amendment standards based on analogies to secrecy rules applicable to grand juries, judicial misconduct proceedings, and certain interactions between individuals and governmental entities. The justification for grand jury secrecy inheres in the nature of the proceeding. . . .

Although these interests do not warrant a prohibition on disclosure of a witness's own testimony after the term of the grand jury has ended, they generally suffice to maintain grand jury secrecy against First Amendment claims to divulge information a witness obtained through participation in the grand jury process. Unlike the grand jury proceeding, as to which interests in secrecy arise from the nature of the proceeding, the nondisclosure requirement of subsection 2709(c) is imposed at the demand of the Executive Branch under circumstances where secrecy might or might not be warranted, depending on the circumstances alleged to justify such secrecy.

The Government's analogy to permissible limitations on disclosures in connection with judicial misconduct proceedings also fails to justify the nondisclosure requirement of subsection 2709(c). . . .

The Government's analogy to certain interactions between an individual and governmental entities is also unavailing. The Government seeks to enlist cases involving classification of former CIA employees' information as top secret, and a prohibition on disclosure of information obtained by a litigant through court-ordered discovery. We fail to appreciate the analogy between the individuals or the entity seeking disclosure in those cases and John Doe, Inc., who had no interaction with the Government until the Government imposed its nondisclosure requirement upon it.

The nondisclosure requirement of subsection 2709(c) is not a typical prior restraint or a typical content-based restriction warranting the most rigorous First Amendment scrutiny. On the other hand, the Government's analogies to nondisclosure prohibitions in other contexts do not persuade us to use a significantly diminished standard of review. In any event, John Doe, Inc., has been restrained from publicly expressing a category of information, albeit a narrow one, and that information is relevant to intended criticism of a governmental activity . . .

The panel is not in agreement as to whether, in this context, we should examine subsection 2709(c) under a standard of traditional strict scrutiny or under a standard that, in view of the context, is not quite as "exacting" a form of strict scrutiny. Ultimately, this disagreement has no bearing on our disposition because, as we discuss below, the only two limitations on NSL procedures required by First Amendment procedural standards would be required under either degree of scrutiny. We note that, for purposes of the litigation in this Court, the Government has conceded that strict scrutiny is the applicable standard.

(b) *Strict scrutiny.* Under strict scrutiny review, the Government must demonstrate that the nondisclosure requirement is "narrowly tailored to promote a compelling Government interest," and that there are no "less restrictive alternatives [that] would be at least as effective in achieving the legitimate purpose that the statute was enacted to serve." Since "[i]t is obvious and unarguable that no governmental interest is more compelling than the security of the Nation," the principal strict scrutiny issue turns on whether the narrow tailoring requirement is met, and this issue, as the District Court observed, essentially concerns the process by which the nondisclosure requirement is imposed and tested.

With subsections 2709(c) and 3511(b) interpreted as set forth above, two aspects of that process remain principally at issue: the absence of a requirement that the Government initiate judicial review of the lawfulness of a nondisclosure requirement and the degree of deference a district court is obliged to accord to the certification of senior governmental officials in ordering nondisclosure.

(i) *Absence of requirement that the Government initiate judicial review.* The Plaintiffs alleged, and the District Court agreed, that the third *Freedman* procedural requirement applies to the NSL statutes, requiring the Government to initiate judicial review of its imposition of a nondisclosure requirement. *See Freedman,* 380 U.S. at 58–59, 85 S.Ct. 734.

The Government advances several arguments why the third *Freedman* safeguard should not apply to judicial review of the nondisclosure requirement. First, the Government contends that it would be unduly burdened if it had to initiate a lawsuit to enforce the nondisclosure requirement in the more than 40,000 NSL requests that were issued in 2005 alone, according to the 2007 report of the Inspector General of the Department of Justice ("OIG Report"). Related to this argument is the point, advanced in the Government's brief to distinguish *Freedman,* that "there is no reason to believe that most recipients of NSLs wish to disclose that fact to anyone."

Instead of determining whether, as the Government contends, a burden of initiating litigation can prevent application of the third *Freedman* procedural safeguard, we consider an available means of minimizing that burden, use of which would substantially avoid the Government's argument. The Government could inform each NSL recipient that it should give the Government prompt notice, perhaps within ten days, in the event that the recipient wishes to contest the nondisclosure requirement. Upon receipt of such notice, the Government could be accorded a limited time, perhaps 30 days, to initiate a judicial review proceeding to maintain the nondisclosure requirement, and the proceeding would have to be concluded within a prescribed time, perhaps 60 days. In accordance with the first and second *Freedman* safeguards, the NSL could inform the recipient that the nondisclosure requirement would remain in effect during the entire interval of the recipient's decision whether to contest the nondisclosure requirement, the Government's prompt application to a court, and the court's prompt adjudication on the merits. *See Freedman,* 380 U.S. at 58, 85 S.Ct. 734. The NSL could also inform the recipient that the nondisclosure requirement would remain in effect if the recipient declines to give the Government notice of an intent to challenge the requirement or, upon a challenge, if the Government prevails in court. If the Government is correct that very few NSL recipients have any interest in challenging the nondisclosure requirement (perhaps no more than three have done so thus far), this "reciprocal notice procedure" would nearly eliminate the Government's burden to initiate litigation (with a corresponding minimal burden on NSL recipients to defend numerous lawsuits). Thus, the Government's litigating burden can be substantially minimized, and the resulting slight burden is not a reason for precluding application of the third *Freedman* safeguard.

. . .

We acknowledge, however, that the nondisclosure requirement of subsection 2709(c) is not facially a licensing scheme of the sort at issue in *Freedman.* Unlike an exhibitor of movies, John Doe, Inc., did not intend to speak and was not subject to any administrative restraint on speaking prior to the Government's issuance of an NSL. Nevertheless, once the NSL arrived, John Doe, Inc., did wish to speak publicly about it and was prohibited from doing so by an administrative order. *Freedman*'s third requirement cannot be disregarded simply because subsection 2709(c) does not impose a traditional licensing scheme.

The availability of a minimally burdensome reciprocal notice procedure for governmental initiation of judicial review and the inadequacy of the Government's attempts to avoid the third *Freedman* safeguard persuade us that this safeguard, normally required where strict scrutiny applies, must be observed. Therefore, in the absence of Government-initiated judicial review, subsection 3511(b) is not narrowly tailored to conform to First Amendment procedural standards. We conclude, as did the District Court, that subsection 3511(b) does not survive either traditional strict scrutiny or a slightly less exacting measure of such scrutiny.

(ii) *Deference to administrative discretion.* The Plaintiffs contended, and the District Court agreed, that the judicial review contemplated by subsection 3511(b) authorizes a degree of deference to the Executive Branch that is inconsistent with First Amendment standards. Although acknowledging that "national security is a compelling interest justifying nondisclosure in certain situations," the District Court faulted the review provision in several respects. First, the Court stated that the statute "requires the court to blindly credit a finding that there 'may' be a reason—potentially any conceivable and not patently frivolous reason—for it to believe disclosure will result in a certain harm." Our construction of the statute, however, avoids that concern. As indicated above, we interpret subsection 3511(b) to place on the Government the burden to show a "good" reason to believe that disclosure may result in an enumerated harm, *i.e.,* a harm related to "an authorized investigation to protect against international terrorism or clandestine intelligence activities," and to place on a district court an obligation to make the "may result" finding only after consideration, albeit deferential, of the Government's explanation concerning the risk of an enumerated harm.

Assessing the Government's showing of a good reason to believe that an enumerated harm may result will present a district court with a delicate task. While the court will normally defer to the Government's considered assessment of *why* disclosure in a particular case may result in an enumerated harm related to such grave matters as international terrorism or clandestine intelligence activities, it cannot, consistent with strict scrutiny standards, uphold a nondisclosure requirement on a conclusory assurance that such a likelihood exists. In this case, the director of the FBI certified that "the disclosure of the NSL itself or its contents may endanger the national security of the United States." To accept that conclusion without requiring some elaboration would "cast Article III judges in the role of petty functionaries, persons required to enter as a court judgment an executive officer's decision, but stripped of capacity to evaluate independently whether the executive's decision is correct."

In showing why disclosure would risk an enumerated harm, the Government must at least indicate the nature of the apprehended harm and provide a court with some basis to assure itself (based on *in camera* presentations where appropriate) that the link between disclosure and risk of harm is substantial. As the Government acknowledges, "Nothing in [subs]ection 3511(b) would require a district court to confine judicial review to the FBI's necessarily unelaborated public statement about the need for nondisclosure. The provisions in [subs]ections 3511(d) and (e) for *ex parte* and *in camera* review provide a ready mechanism for the FBI to provide a more complete explanation of its reasoning, and the court is free to elicit such an explanation as part of the review process."

We have every confidence that district judges can discharge their review responsibility with faithfulness to First Amendment considerations and without intruding on the prerogative of the Executive Branch to exercise its judgment on matters of national security. Such a judgment is not to be second-guessed, but a court must receive some indication that the judgment has been soundly reached. . . .

. . . A demonstration of a reasonable likelihood of potential harm, related to international terrorism or clandestine intelligence activities, will virtually always outweigh the First Amendment interest in speaking about such a limited and particularized occurrence as the receipt of an NSL and will suffice to maintain the secrecy of the fact of such receipt.

. . .

There is not meaningful judicial review of the decision of the Executive Branch to prohibit speech if the position of the Executive Branch that speech would be harmful is "conclusive" on a reviewing court, absent only a demonstration of bad faith. To accept deference to that extraordinary degree would be to reduce strict scrutiny to no scrutiny, save only in the rarest of situations where bad faith could be shown. Under either traditional strict scrutiny or a less exacting application of that standard, some demonstration from the Executive Branch of the need for secrecy is required in order to conform the nondisclosure requirement to First Amendment standards. The fiat of a governmental official, though senior in rank and doubtless honorable in the execution of official duties, cannot displace the judicial obligation to enforce constitutional requirements. "Under no circumstances should the Judiciary become the handmaiden of the Executive."

V.   Remedy

To recapitulate our conclusions, we (1) construe subsection 2709(c) to permit a nondisclosure requirement only when senior FBI officials certify that disclosure may result in an enumerated harm that is related to "an authorized investigation to protect against international terrorism or clandestine intelligence activities," (2) construe subsections 3511(b)(2) and (b)(3) to place on the Government the burden to show that a good reason exists to expect that disclosure of receipt of an NSL will risk an enumerated harm, (3) construe subsections 3511(b)(2) and (b)(3) to mean that the Government satisfies its burden when it makes an adequate demonstration as to why disclosure in a particular case may result in an enumerated harm, (4) rule that subsections 2709(c) and 3511(b) are unconstitutional to the extent that they impose a nondisclosure requirement without placing on the Government the burden of initiating judicial review of that requirement, and (5) rule that subsections 3511(b)(2) and (b)(3) are unconstitutional to the extent that, upon such review, a governmental official's certification that disclosure may endanger the national security of the United States or interfere with diplomatic relations is treated as conclusive.

... We are satisfied ... that, once the Government has initiated judicial review and prevailed on the merits, limiting an NSL recipient to annual opportunities thereafter to terminate the nondisclosure requirement does not violate First Amendment procedural requirements. The information subject to nondisclosure is extremely limited, and, once the need for secrecy—avoiding risk of harm related to international terrorism—has been shown, that need is not likely to dissipate soon.

In those instances where an NSL recipient gives notice of an intent to challenge the disclosure requirement, the Government would have several options for completing the reciprocal notice procedure by commencing such review. First, it is arguable that the Government can adapt the authority now set forth in subsection 3511(c) for the purpose of initiating judicial review. That provision authorizes the Attorney General to "invoke the aid of any [relevant] district court" in the event of "a failure to comply with a request for ... information made to any person or entity under section 2709(b)" or other provisions authorizing NSLs. 18 U.S.C. § 3511(c). Since an NSL includes both a request for information and a direction not to disclose that the FBI has sought or obtained information, an NSL recipient's timely notice of intent to disclose, furnished in response to notice in an NSL of an opportunity to contest the nondisclosure requirement, can perhaps be considered the functional equivalent of the "failure to comply" contemplated by subsection 3511(c). Second, the Government might be able to identify some other statutory authority to invoke the equitable power of a district court to prevent a disclosure that the Government can demonstrate would risk harm to national security. Third, and as a last resort, the Government could seek explicit congressional authorization to initiate judicial review of a nondisclosure requirement that a recipient wishes to challenge. We leave it to the Government to consider how to discharge its obligation to initiate judicial review.

... Although the conclusive presumption clause of subsections 3511(b)(2) and (b)(3) must be stricken, we invalidate subsection 2709(c) and the remainder of subsection 3511(b) only to the extent that they fail to provide for Government-initiated judicial review. The Government can respond to this partial invalidation ruling by using the suggested reciprocal notice procedure. With this procedure in place, subsections 2709(c) and 3511(b) would survive First Amendment challenge.

. . .

We have no doubt that if Congress had understood that First Amendment considerations required the Government to initiate judicial review of a nondisclosure requirement and precluded a conclusive certification by the Attorney General, it would have wanted the remainder of the NSL statutes to remain in force. Congress would surely have wanted the Government to retain the authority to issue NSLs even if all aspects of the nondisclosure requirement of subsection 2709(c) and the judicial review provisions of section 3511(b) had been invalidated. As the Government points out, even without a nondisclosure requirement, it can protect the national interest by issuing NSLs only where it expects compliance with a request for secrecy to be honored. *A fortiori,* authority to issue NSLs should be preserved in view of the limiting constructions and limited invalidations we have ordered. We therefore sever the conclusive presumption language of subsection 3511(b) and leave intact the remainder of subsection 3511(b) and the entirety of section 2709 (with Government-initiated judicial review required). As a result of this ruling, we modify the District Court's injunction by limiting it to enjoining FBI officials from enforcing the nondisclosure requirement of section 2709(c) in the absence of Government-initiated judicial review.

There remains for consideration the issue of the procedure to be followed with respect to judicial review of the nondisclosure requirement with respect to the NSL issued to John Doe, Inc. Although we have ruled that the Government is obliged to initiate judicial review of a nondisclosure requirement, it would be pointless to dismiss the pending litigation and direct the Government to start anew. With judicial review already initiated in the District Court and the constitutionality of the disclosure requirement salvaged by the statutory interpretations and partial invalidations we have ordered, the sounder course is to remand so that the Government may have an opportunity to sustain its burden of proof and satisfy the constitutional standards we have outlined for maintaining the disclosure requirement. *See* 28 U.S.C. § 2106.

Conclusion

Accordingly, for all the foregoing reasons, subsections 2709(c) and 3511(b) are construed in conformity with this opinion and partially invalidated only to the extent set forth in this opinion, the injunction is modified as set forth in this opinion, and the judgment of the District Court is affirmed in part, reversed in part, and remanded for further proceedings consistent with this opinion.

QUESTIONS AND NOTES

1. For the disposition of the principal case, supra, on remand, see Doe v. Holder, 703 F.Supp. 2d 313 (S.D.N.Y.2010).

2. In May, 2009, the Department of Justice reported that during the calendar year, 2008, the FBI made 24,744 national security letter requests for information involving 7225 individuals. In addition, the Foreign Intelligence Surveillance Act Court approved all 13 requests by the government to access business records under 50 U.S.C. § 1861. See Letter from Assistant Attorney General Ron Weich to the Chairs of the Judiciary and Intelligence Committees, dated May, 14, 2009. Of the NSL requests, nearly 5,000 were for "corrective NSLs," issued to support oral requests for information made under exigent circumstances to telecommunications providers. Thus approximately 20,000 original NSL's were issued in 2008. Note that corrective NSLs requests may have been counted differently in previous years.

3. In 2007, the Inspector General of the Department of Justice had issued a highly critical report regarding the FBI's use of NSL's, reporting that between 2003 and 2005 more than 140,000 NSL's were issued, far more than reported in the annual reports. An unclassified version of the OIG Report, formally titled "A Review of the Federal Bureau of Investigation's Use of National Security Letters," is available at <http://www.usdoj.gov/oig/special/s 0703b/final.pdf>, last visited Oct. 20, 2008. An unclassified version of a follow-up 2008 OIG Report, formally titled "A Review of the FBI's Use of National Security Letters: Assessment of Corrective Actions and Examination of NSL Usage in 2006," is available at <http://www.usdoj.gov/oig/special/s 0803b/final.pdf>, last visited Oct. 20, 2008. As a result of these and other criticisms in the Inspector General's report, a new system of tracking and documenting NSL's was instituted which was first used in 2008. See 2009 WL 1522926, 77 USLW 2726 (2009).

4. In 2010, the General Counsel of the FBI testified before a subcommittee of the House Judiciary Committee regarding the aftermath and follow-up of the 2007 Inspector General's report. Excerpts from this testimony appear below:

Testimony of Valerie E. Caproni, General Counsel, FBI, before the Subcommittee on the Constitution, Civil Rights and Civil Liberties, House Judiciary Committee, April 14, 2010

. . .

Exigent Letters

In 2007, the OIG found that one unit at FBI Headquarters had issued over 700 exigent letters requesting toll billing records for various telephone numbers. All of the letters stated that there were exigent circumstances but did not describe the exigency. In fact, sometimes there was no emergency. Although ECPA's emergency disclosure provision found at 18 U.S.C. § 2702(c)(4) (discussed in more detail below) does not require the FBI to provide any legal process to obtain records voluntarily from a telephone company in order to respond to a qualifying emergency, many of the letters stated that federal grand jury subpoenas had been requested for the records. In fact, no such request for grand jury subpoenas had been made, and no one intended that such a request would be made. Similarly, other exigent letters promised NSLs, which—though also legally unnecessary if there is a qualifying emergency—the agents and analysts, in fact, intended would be sent. Unfortunately, the FBI did not keep adequate records reflecting the nature of the emergencies, the telephone numbers for which records were sought, and whether the promised future process—whether legally required or not—was ever actually issued.

It should be emphasized, however, that exigent letters were not—and were never intended to be—NSLs. Rather, they appear to have been a sort of "place-holder," born out of a misunderstanding of the import of the USA Patriot Act's amendments to ECPA. For reasons lost in the fog of history—but no doubt partially the result of the intense pace of activity in the months following the 9/11 attacks—the FBI did not adequately educate our workforce that Congress had provided a clear mechanism to obtain records in emergency situations. Although guidance was eventually provided in August 2005, the employees who had been using exigent letters for several years simply did not recognize the applicability of that guidance to their situation. In its most recent report on the issue, the OIG confirmed what the FBI acknowledged to Congress and the public in 2007: Exigent letters were sometimes used when there was no emergency and the FBI had inadequate internal controls to ensure that the promised legal process was provided. The 2010 report confirmed that these practices resulted in the FBI requesting telephone toll billing records associated with approximately 4,400 telephone numbers between 2003 and 2006.

In response to the OIG's 2007 report, in March 2007 the FBI formally barred the use of exigent letters to obtain telephone records and established detailed policies for obtaining toll billing records during an emergency situation. Since that time, employees who need to obtain

ECPA-protected records on an emergency basis must do so in accordance with 18 U.S.C. § 2702. Section 2702(c)(4), which permits a carrier to provide information regarding its customers to the government "if the provider, in good faith, believes that an emergency involving danger of death or serious physical injury to any person requires disclosure without delay of information relating to the emergency." In addition to providing guidance on Section 2702 itself, we established approval and documentation requirements for requests made under this provision. As promised by Director Mueller and me in our testimony following the OIG's first report and by me in repeated briefings of congressional staff, beginning in 2007, the FBI commenced an effort to ensure that we retained only exigent letter-related telephone records for which we had a lawful basis. To that end, we dedicated significant resources to researching all of the numbers that appeared on known exigent letters and on the so-called "blanket NSLs" (discussed in more detail below). The reconciliation project team conducted a complete review, even though the disclosure of approximately half of the records at issue was not forbidden by ECPA and/or was connected to a clear emergency situation. The reconciliation project team used a conservative approach: they initially retained records for which already-existing legal process (usually an NSL or grand jury subpoena) was located. If no legal process was found, then new "corrective" NSLs were issued where ECPA allowed us to do so (i.e., the national security investigation to which the telephone records were relevant was still pending). In fact, we located or issued legal process for the overwhelming majority of the 4,400 telephone numbers. If we found no previously existing legal process and we could not legally issue new process (e.g., the case to which the records were relevant had since been closed), we would only then consider whether emergency circumstances existed at the time we requested the records. As to that group of telephone numbers, if we could not conclude that there had, in fact, been an emergency that would have qualified under section 2702, we purged the telephone records from our files and databases. These actions were fully briefed to the FBI's congressional oversight committees last year, and we appreciate the finding of the OIG that our "approach to determine which records to retain and which to purge was reasonable" (Report at 276). We are currently developing an automated system—similar in concept to the NSL system that we have briefed and demonstrated to your staffs -to generate and document emergency disclosure requests pursuant to Section 2702. Our experience with the NSL system is that it has greatly reduced non-substantive errors in NSLs, and we believe that an automated Section 2702 system would do the same. I would now like to address a few specific matters raised by the OIG's 2010 report.

Blanket NSLs The OIG's 2010 report discusses in detail 11 so-called "blanket NSLs." These blanket NSLs were not discussed with an FBI attorney prior to their preparation nor reviewed by an FBI attorney prior to their issuance. We continue to believe—as we briefed this committee in 2007—that the blanket NSLs were a good-faith but ill-conceived attempt by the Counterterrorism Division to address the backlog of numbers for which the FBI believed it had unfulfilled obligations to provide legal process as they had promised through exigent letters. The common problem with all of the blanket NSLs was that there was no electronic communication (EC) prepared describing how the information sought by the NSL was relevant to a national security investigation. Under FBI policy, such ECs are required for all NSLs. Because there was no EC, there was no documentation that connected the telephone numbers listed on the blanket NSLs to specific, pending national security investigations. As discussed above, following the 2007 report, the FBI examined each telephone number included on a blanket NSLs to determine whether there was a legal basis to retain any records obtained for the number. If we could not confirm a legal basis for retention, we purged any records we had for the number.

As noted, none of the blanket NSLs was reviewed by an FBI attorney. In March 2007, the FBI changed its policy to require attorney approval before an NSL may be issued. That policy requirement is enforced through the NSL system that automatically routes all NSLs though an attorney prior to issuance.

Other Informal Requests In addition to exigent letters and blanket NSLs, the 2010 report discusses other informal means by which the FBI Headquarters unit obtained information regarding telephone numbers. "Quick peeks" and "sneak peeks" are the terms used in the report to describe an FBI employee asking a telephone company employee to determine whether records for a telephone number existed, not what those records actually contained.

In a similar type of request, FBI employees would ask whether there was "calling activity" associated with a particular number (i.e., whether the particular telephone number was being used). Such information was conveyed to the FBI for 39 telephone numbers.

As the OIG noted, the mere existence of records or the fact that there is calling activity associated with a particular telephone number is protected by ECPA. Accordingly, we made clear in March 2007 that no telephone records may be acquired in advance of legal process, unless there is an emergency situation under Section 2702 and the emergency request procedures are followed. In addition, our Domestic Investigation Operational Guidelines (DIOG), which compiled all FBI operational policy into one document, provides an exclusive list of acceptable methods for obtaining telephone toll records.

Reporter Records The OIG's 2010 report describes three situations in which the FBI might have come into contact with protected telephone toll information of reporters. In fact, in only one case were any reporter's toll records actually provided to the FBI, and that occurred over five years ago. In that one instance, neither the substantive case agent nor any member of the investigative or prosecutorial team was aware that records had been obtained, and the FBI made no use of them. Furthermore, the only FBI employees who ever accessed the records were the analyst who initially uploaded them to our telephone records databases and an analyst involved in the exigent letter reconciliation project described above. When we learned in 2008 that we had such records, we purged them from our telephone records databases.

Although we did not use the records, Department of Justice (DOJ) regulations require attorney general approval before the issuance of grand jury subpoenas seeking toll billing records of members of the media. While no grand jury subpoena was issued in this instance, such legal process would have been the appropriate way, if at all, to obtain the records at issue given the nature of the investigation. Accordingly, when we learned that we had reporters' toll records without advance attorney general approval, we notified the reporters that their toll records had been obtained, and the Director personally called the editors of the newspapers to apologize.

Although this appears to have been an isolated incident, we issued guidance in 2008 making clear the requirements for obtaining toll records of members of the media. The DIOG similarly discusses the steps required to seek such records.

. . .

OLC Opinion

The OIG's 2010 report discusses a January 8, 2010 opinion issued by the Department of Justice's Office of Legal Counsel (OLC), which concluded that ECPA does not forbid electronic communications service providers, in certain circumstances, from disclosing certain call detail records to the FBI on a voluntary basis without legal process or a qualifying emergency under Section 2702. Many members of Congress have asked questions about this OLC opinion, which is classified. It is my understanding that this opinion has been shared with our oversight committees, including this committee, at the appropriate security level. Because of the classified nature of the OLC opinion, I cannot address it in this forum, but am available to discuss it in a secure setting. I can, however, state that the OLC opinion did not in any way factor into the FBI's flawed practice of using exigent letters between 2003 and 2006 nor did it affect in any way the records-retention decisions made by the FBI as part of the reconciliation project discussed above.

Accountability

The 2010 report notes that the OIG provided its findings to the Department of Justice's Public Integrity Section. The Public Integrity Section declined prosecution of any individuals relating to the exigent letters matter. Now that the OIG's report is complete, the FBI's Office of Professional Responsibility will have an opportunity to review the OIG's findings and determine whether any discipline of any employee is appropriate.

Conclusion

Finally, the FBI appreciates the 2010 report's recognition that FBI employees involved in this matter were attempting to advance legitimate FBI investigations, and that FBI personnel "typically requested the telephone records to pursue [their] critical counterterrorism mission" (Report at 214).

This does not excuse our failure to have in place appropriate internal controls, but it places the practices of that one FBI Headquarters unit in context: "Some of the exigent letters and other improper practices [described] in this report were used to obtain telephone records that the FBI used to evaluate some of the most serious terrorist threats posed to the United States in the last few years"

These employees were and many remain on the front lines of our fight against terrorists. At the same time, as Director Mueller has repeatedly acknowledged, we can only achieve our mission of keeping the country safe if we are trusted by all.

CHAPTER 7

INTERROGATION AND IRREGULAR RENDITION

■ ■ ■

A. INTRODUCTION

This chapter deals, first, with issues relating to the interrogation of terrorist suspects and second, the practice, adopted under the Bush administration and, apparently continuing under the Obama administration, of seizing suspected individuals abroad, whether on an active battlefield or not, and transferring them, without legal process, to another often-distant location. This practice has been variously labeled "extraordinary rendition," or "irregular rendition," and we use the latter terminology here.

Both of these topics could have been placed in Part 2 since they sometimes involve, to one extent or another, the use of the military arm of the government. In effect, they lie astride the border between civilian and military process. We have chosen to treat them here, but we shall come briefly back to the subject in Part 2 when we address rules of admissibility in military commission trials.

The interrogation of terrorism suspects is first addressed through a discussion of the torture controversy, that is, the issues that arose out of the use of extreme methods of interrogation under the Bush administration in the wake of the 9/11 attacks. As one of his first acts after taking office, President Obama issued an Executive Order that effectively prohibited the use of the interrogation techniques that had triggered the torture controversy, by requiring that the interrogation rules set forth in the Army Field Manual, as revised in 2006, be followed. We examine these rules and in subsequent subsections in this chapter, canvass a number of different rules relating to interrogation, including, for example, whether Miranda warning are required for interrogations that take place abroad; the extent to which these requirements vary depending on the degree of participation of U.S. agents in conducting the interrogation; application of the Quarles "public safety" exception to the Miranda warning/waiver requirements in a terrorism context; the promulgation of new FBI interrogation guidelines in reliance on the Quarles doctrine; how, assuming prosecution in a federal civilian court, the court will apply constitutional coerced confession doctrine, or stating the issue another way, how the AFM interrogation rules comport with that doctrine; and finally, the standards applied by U.S. courts where a confession is obtained by non-U.S. agents, using allegedly coercive interrogation techniques.

In subsection C of this chapter, we address the subject of extraordinary, that is, irregular rendition. Other methods of transfer of individuals from one country to another, such as extradition, are first addressed. Government policies and opinions bearing on the legal issues and remedies available when persons are taken against their will from one country to another are reviewed. Case law involving lawsuits against the government, government officials and private companies that allegedly assisted in implementing irregular rendition is presented for discussion, as is a description of foreign prosecution of U.S. officials and agents for having engaged in irregular rendition in the foreign territory. Some material is presented on the important question, what is the policy of the Obama administration regarding irregular rendition, although this material by no means provides a definitive answer.

B. OBTAINING TERRORISM–RELATED INFORMATION THROUGH INTERROGATION

1. THE TORTURE CONTROVERSY

a. Background

In 2003 and 2004, reports and pictures of abusive treatment of prisoners in Iraq and reports of some abuse of prisoners in Guantanamo and abusive interrogation of individuals who had been transferred to foreign countries through extraordinary rendition made headlines and stirred up enormous controversy and soul-searching. There was a question whether abusive treatment had been authorized, condoned or fostered by actions or statements of the administration. Questions also arose as to the legality of using extreme methods of interrogation.

The United States is a party to the Convention against Torture and Other Cruel, Inhuman and Degrading Treatment or Punishment. The Convention which went into force with respect to the United States on November 20, 1994 is implemented by federal statute in 18 U.S.C. §§ 2340 and 2340A. The signing and ratifying of the Convention against Torture is subject to a number of reservations and understandings. Thus, the Senate's advice and consent is subject to the following understanding:

> The United States understands that, in order to constitute torture, an act must be specifically intended to inflict severe physical or mental pain or suffering and that mental pain or suffering refers to prolonged mental harm caused by or resulting from: (1) the intentional infliction or threatened infliction of severe physical pain or suffer-

ing; (2) the administration or application, or threatened administration or application, of mind-altering substances or other procedures calculated to disrupt profoundly the senses or the personality; (3) the threat of imminent death; or (4) the threat that another person will imminently be subjected to death, severe physical pain or suffering, or the administration or application of mind-altering substances or other procedures calculated to disrupt profoundly the senses or personality.

The definition of torture contained in this understanding largely tracks the definition of torture adopted by the Congress in 18 U.S.C § 2340, below. Are there any differences between the two definitions?

§ 2340.   As used in this chapter—

(1) "torture" means an act committed by a person acting under the color of law specifically intended to inflict severe physical or mental pain or suffering (other than pain or suffering incidental to lawful sanctions) upon another person within his custody or physical control;

(2) "severe mental pain or suffering" means the prolonged mental harm caused by or resulting from—

(A) the intentional infliction or threatened infliction of severe physical pain or suffering;

(B) the administration or application, or threatened administration or application, of mind-altering substances or other procedures calculated to disrupt profoundly the senses or the personality;

(C) the threat of imminent death; or

(D) the threat that another person will imminently be subjected to death, severe physical pain or suffering, or the administration or application of mind-altering substances or other procedures calculated to disrupt profoundly the senses or personality; and

(3) "United States" means the several States of the United States, the District of Columbia, and the commonwealths, territories, and possessions of the United States.

§ 2340A.   Torture

(a) Offense.—Whoever outside the United States commits or attempts to commit torture shall be fined under this title or imprisoned not more than 20 years, or both, and if death results to any person from conduct prohibited by this subsection, shall be punished by death or imprisoned for any term of years or for life.

(b) Jurisdiction.—There is jurisdiction over the activity prohibited in subsection (a) if—

(1) the alleged offender is a national of the United States; or

(2) the alleged offender is present in the United States, irrespective of the nationality of the victim or alleged offender.

(c) Conspiracy.—A person who conspires to commit an offense under this section shall be subject to the same penalties (other than the penalty of death) as the penalties prescribed for the offense, the commission of which was the object of the conspiracy.

Further, the Convention not only bans torture but also prohibits "cruel, inhuman or degrading treatment or punishment." With respect to this latter prohibition, the Senate's advice and consent is subject to the following reservation: That the United States considers itself bound by the obligation under Article 16 to prevent "cruel, inhuman or degrading treatment or punishment," only insofar as the term "cruel, inhuman or degrading treatment or punishment" means the cruel, unusual and inhumane treatment or punishment prohibited by the Fifth, Eighth, and/or Fourteenth Amendments to the Constitution of the United States.

Whereas in the wake of the ratification of the Convention, the U.S. in 1994, enacted statutory provisions criminalizing torture, legislation prohibiting cruel, inhuman or degrading treatment by U.S. officials was not passed until 2005, and this statute is not in the form of a criminal provision.

As it turned out, a distinction between torture, on the one hand, and cruel, inhuman, or degrading treatment, on the other hand, became a key element in the legal strategy of the Bush administration relating to the use of extreme methods of interrogation in the wake of the 9/11 attacks.

b. Memoranda and Statements of Officials in the Bush Administration Regarding the Legality of Various Methods of Interrogation

Beginning in early fall, 2002, within the Bush administration, the treatment of the prisoners seized in Afghanistan and in Iraq and what techniques could be used in interrogating them were the subject of a series of high level memoranda in the Departments of Justice and Defense:

1) In a memorandum dated August 1, 2002 (sometimes referred to as the Bybee memorandum), the Office of Legal Counsel in the Department of Justice responded to a request from Alberto R. Gonzales, then Counsel to the President and later, Attorney General, to comment on the standards of conduct under the Convention Against Torture. Pertinent conclusions in this memorandum included the following:

> We conclude that for an act to constitute torture as defined in Section 2340, it must inflict pain that is difficult to endure. Physical pain amounting to torture must be equivalent in intensity to the pain accompanying serious physical injury, such as organ failure, impairment of bodily function, or even death. For purely mental pain or suffering to amount to torture under Section 2340, it must result in significant psychological harm of significant duration, e.g., lasting for months or even years. We

conclude that the mental harm also must result from one of the predicate acts listed in the statute, namely: threats of imminent death; threats of infliction of the kind of pain that would amount to physical torture; infliction of such physical pain as a means of psychological torture; use of drugs or other procedures designed to deeply disrupt the senses, or fundamentally alter an individual's personality; or threatening to do any of these things to a third party.... We conclude that the statute, taken as a whole makes plain that it prohibits only extreme acts.

2) In the Department of Defense, an October 11, 2002 Legal Brief on Proposed Counter–Resistance Strategies stated: "To ensure the security of the United States and its Allies, more aggressive interrogation techniques than the ones presently used, such as the methods proposed in the attached recommendation, may be required in order to obtain information from detainees that are resisting interrogation efforts and are suspected of having significant information essential to national security." The brief went on to discuss the legal issues relating to interrogation techniques under international and domestic law and characterized the legality of certain techniques as follows:

> With regard to Category II methods, the use of stress positions such as the proposed standing for four hours, the use of isolation for up to thirty days, and interrogating the detainee in an environment other than the standard interrogation booth are all legally permissible so long as no severe physical pain is inflicted and prolonged mental harm intended, and because there is a legitimate governmental objective in obtaining the information necessary....

> The deprivation of light and auditory stimuli, the placement of a hood over the detainee's head during transportation and questioning, and the use of 20 hour interrogations are all legally permissible so long as there is an important governmental objective....

> With respect to the Category III advanced counter-resistance strategies, the use of scenarios designed to convince the detainee that death or severely painful consequences are imminent is not illegal for the same aforementioned reasons that there is a compelling governmental interest and it is not done intentionally to cause prolonged harm. However, caution should be utilized with this technique because the torture statute specifically mentions making death threats as an example of inflicting mental pain and suffering. Exposure to cold weather or water is permissible with appropriate medical monitoring. The use of a wet towel to induce the misperception of suffocation would be permissible if not done with the specific intent to cause prolonged mental harm, and absent medical evidence that it would....

3) In an action memo, dated November 27, 2002, from William J. Haynes II, General Counsel of the Defense Department to the Secretary of Defense, it was recommended that only Category I and II techniques be used to aid in interrogating detainees at Guantanamo Bay, with the addition of one of the techniques in the more aggressive Category III, namely, "use of mild, non-injurious physical contact such as grabbing, poking in the chest with the finger, and light pushing." The recommendation was approved by Secretary Rumsfeld on December 2, 2002, but he also attached a handwritten note that stated: "However, I stand for 8–10 hours a day. Why is standing limited to 4 hours?"

4) On January 15, 2003, Secretary of Defense Rumsfeld sent a memo rescinding the approval of Category I and II techniques (along with the thumb poking Category III technique). The memo also indicated that specific requests to use Category I or II techniques should be forwarded to him, that humane treatment of detainees should continue regardless of the techniques used, and that an attached memo to the General Counsel was setting in motion a study to be completed in 15 days.

5) In a Draft Pentagon Working Group Report on Detainee Interrogations in the Global War on Terrorism, dated March 6, 2003, originally revealed in an exclusive story by Wall Street Journal reporter Jesse Bravin, it was stated that "the Torture Convention prohibits torture only as defined in the U.S. Understanding, and prohibits "cruel, inhuman, and degrading treatment and punishment" only to the extent of the U.S. Reservation relating to the U.S. Constitution." The Report also extensively discussed the fact that criminal liability could not be imposed under § 2340A, absent specific intent to inflict severe pain.

6) On December 30, 2004, a memorandum was made public that had been sent earlier from the Acting Assistant Attorney General for the Office of Legal Counsel to Deputy Attorney General James B. Comey. It included the following statements:

> Torture is abhorrent both to American law and values and to international norms. . . .

> Questions have since been raised, both by this Office and by others, about the appropriateness and relevance of the non-statutory discussion in the August 2002 Memorandum [Ed. See 1) above], and also about various aspects of the statutory analysis, in particular the statement that "severe" pain under the statute was limited to pain "equivalent in intensity to the pain accompanying serious physical injury, such as organ failure, impairment of bodily function, or even death." . . .

> This Memorandum supersedes the August 2002 Memorandum in its entirety. Because the discussion in that memorandum concerning the President's Commander-in-Chief power and the potential defenses to liability was—and remains—unnecessary, it has been eliminated from the analysis that follows. Consideration of the bounds of any such authority would be inconsistent with

the President's unequivocal directive that United States personnel not engage in torture.

7) As indicated in 6) above, the President had issued a directive that U.S. personnel not engage in torture. Of course, the application of the prohibition depended on how torture was to be defined.

8) Subsequently, on April 16, 2009, the Department of Justice officially released four legal memoranda prepared in 2002 and in 2005, directed to John Rizzo, General Counsel of the CIA. These memoranda were designed to provide legal advice to the CIA with regard to the use of various interrogation techniques in questioning high value al Qaeda detainees. Each of the memoranda examined the use of specific techniques—the memos went into excruciating detail on a variety of different techniques (reaching conclusions such as, e.g., "The waterboard does not ... inflict 'severe pain or suffering,'" Bybee Memo to Rizzo, Aug. 1, 2002).

In fact, there had been earlier leaks or release of other memoranda including perhaps the most controversial, the so-called Bybee Memorandum, which has been described in 1) above.

The official release of these four memoranda, all at once, ignited a storm of controversy in the media that continued for some time.—about extremely harsh interrogation practices under the Bush administration and the lawyers and other officials involved in approving and authorizing them. Much attention focused on the practice of waterboarding—inducing in the person being interrogated a sense of drowning and suffocation by pouring water over the nose and mouth when in a reclined position. Information was disclosed that waterboarding had been used to obtain information from three of the "high value" detainees and that this technique had been used on some of them a great many times. Earlier reports in 2007, however, had indicated that the Director of the CIA had in the previous year taken waterboarding off the list of techniques approved for use. See http://blogs.abcnews.com/theblotter/2007/09/cia-bans-water-.html.

There was strong criticism of the legal analyses in these memoranda by a number of legal scholars, and there were calls by some human rights advocates for criminal prosecution of the authors of the memoranda. Reportedly, John Yoo, currently a law professor at UC, Berkeley was the principal author of the Bybee memoranda. Jay S. Bybee, his superior in the Office of Legal Counsel is now a federal circuit court judge.

President Obama announced that the interrogators who relied on these legal opinions would not be investigated or prosecuted if they had stayed within the parameters of the legal advice in the memoranda. He indicated that the Justice Department would make the decisions on whether others should be prosecuted, but his comments emphasized that we should be looking forward.

The targets of the investigation have not been without their defenders who suggested that the authors were acting in good faith under intense pressure in the post–9/11 climate and that the Bybee memorandum caused no long-term legal damage because it was withdrawn and redrafted.

c. A Comment on the Approach That Distinguishes Torture From Cruel, Inhuman or Degrading Treatment

For a comment on the distinction between torture and cruel, inhuman or degrading treatment, see Christian M. De Vos, Mind, the Gap: Purpose, Pain, and the Difference between Torture and Inhuman Treatment, 14 No. 2 Hum. Rts. Brief 4 (2007):

> Condemnation of torture is universal and its prohibition forms not only part of customary international law, but has joined that narrow category of crimes so egregious as to demand universal criminal jurisdiction. Yet despite the considerable progress made towards outlawing torture, there is a frequent and growing tendency to circumvent the law against it by drawing ever finer distinctions between its depravities and the "lesser" acts of what is commonly known as cruel, inhuman, or degrading treatment (CIDT), which is also prohibited but not criminalized as extensively as torture. Perhaps most emblematic of such circumvention has been the Bush administration's policies toward torture and inhuman treatment in the wake of its putative "War on Terror," which this article adopts as its case study. In so doing, it examines how the now infamous torture memos produced by the Department of Justice's Office of Legal Counsel exploited the "gap" between torture and CIDT by focusing almost exclusively on the severity of treatment and the degree of pain suffered.... it ignores important jurisprudential developments emphasizing the principal distinction between the two. Even more troubling, however, is the perverted effect this approach has had on debates over torture itself, making it too often the centerpiece of discussion at the cost of "lesser," but more common abuses, such as CIDT.
>
>   . . .
>
> A new assault on the legal regime prohibiting torture and inhuman treatment began shortly after September 11, 2001, when the "United States and an increasing number of other governments ... adopted a legal position which, while acknowledging the absolute nature of the prohibition on torture, [put] the absolute nature of the prohibition on CIDT in question." Most emblematic of this attempt was the authoring of a 2002 Department of Justice memorandum (Bybee Memo) by the Office of Legal Counsel for Alberto Gonzales, then Counsel to President Bush and now U.S. Attorney General. Principally authored by Deputy Assistant Attorney General John Yoo, the Bybee Memo provided a detailed legal analysis of Section 2340 of the United States Criminal Code, which was implemented as part of U.S. obligations to criminalize torture after ratifying CAT [Conven-

tion against Torture] in 1992. Section 2340A makes it a criminal offense for any persons outside of the U.S. to commit (or attempt to commit) an act of torture, while § 2340, tracking the language of Article 1 of CAT, defines such an act as one "committed by a person acting under the color of law specifically intended to inflict severe physical or mental pain or suffering (other than pain or suffering that is incidental to lawful sanctions) upon another person within his custody or physical control." Significantly, the statutes do not criminalize inhuman treatment. Rather, it was the U.S. position prior to ratifying CAT that the "vagueness of the phrase [cruel, inhuman, and degrading] could not be construed to bar acts not prohibited by the U.S. Constitution." As a result, the government declared that it only considered itself bound by the obligation to prevent CIDT "insofar as the term ... means the cruel, unusual, and inhumane treatment or punishment prohibited by the Fifth, Eighth, and/or Fourteenth Amendments."

While there is much to criticize in the Bybee Memo, especially noteworthy is the extremely high threshold for torture it set forth, defined as:

> [I]ntense pain or suffering of the kind that is equivalent to the pain that would be associated with serious physical injury so severe that death, organ failure, or permanent damage resulting in a loss of significant body function will likely result.

Additionally, with respect to psychological torture, the memo opined that:

> Severe mental pain requires suffering not just at the moment of infliction but it also requires lasting psychological harm, such as seen in mental disorders like post-traumatic stress disorder ... Because the acts inflicting torture are extreme, there is a significant range of acts that might constitute cruel, inhuman, or degrading treatment or punishment but fail to rise to the level of torture.

Essentially, the Bybee Memo stood for the proposition that the "key statutory phrase in the definition of torture" is whether it causes severe pain or suffering.

This rationale, in turn, served as the legal basis for the now infamous interrogation techniques applied to suspected terrorists at the Guantanamo Bay facilities and, undoubtedly, in Afghanistan and Iraq as well. Indeed, by December 2002, former Defense Secretary Donald Rumsfeld had authorized the use of aggressive interrogation techniques (a menu of nineteen "counter-resistance techniques," in the administration's parlance) that tested the very limits of the Bybee Memo, including the use of stress positions for up to four hours, interrogations for up to twenty hours, solitary detention for up to thirty days, forced grooming, removal of all comfort items (including the Koran and toilet paper), hooding, the removal of clothing, forced shaving of facial hair, auditory/environmental manipulation, and "mild non-injurious physical contact."

The extent of the abuse perpetuated by these techniques is still unknown, but will certainly continue to be scrutinized.... Indeed, the findings of the U.S. government itself underscore the primacy the Bybee Memo attached to severity as a means of distinguishing between torture and inhuman treatment. An official investigation into the case of Mohammed al-Qahtani, suspected of being the "20th hijacker" in the September 11th attacks, is illustrative. In response to concerns raised by FBI agents as to the interrogation techniques used on al-Qahtani, military investigators began reviewing his case and found that:

> [D]etainee No. 063 was forced to wear a bra. He had a thong placed on his head. He was massaged by a female interrogator who straddled him like a lap dancer. He was told that his mother and sisters were whores. He was told that other detainees knew he was gay. He was forced to dance with a male interrogator. He was strip-searched in front of women. He was led on a leash and forced to perform dog tricks. He was doused with water. He was prevented from praying. He was forced to watch as an interrogator squatted over the Koran.

In July 2005, the Army's internal investigation determined that Major General Geoffrey Miller—then commander of the detention facilities at Guantanamo (and later Iraq's Abu Ghraib prison)—had failed to adequately monitor the interrogation of al-Qahtani but determined that "technically, no torture occurred." Similarly, then Secretary of Defense Donald Rumsfeld stated prior to the Army's investigation, "My impression is that what has been charged thus far is abuse, which I believe technically is different from torture ... I don't know if ... it is correct to say ... that torture has taken place, or that there's been a conviction for torture. And therefore I'm not going to address the torture word."

It took two years and the public horror of Abu Ghraib for the Bybee Memo, which only came to light after being leaked to the press, to be formally withdrawn and replaced with a new memorandum prepared by Acting Assistant Attorney General Daniel Levin (Levin Memo). The Levin Memo asserts that it "supersedes the August 2002 Memorandum in its entirety" and repudiates some of the more extreme aspects of the Bybee Memo's interpretation of torture. Unfortunately, however, it retains the Bybee Memo's core distinction between torture and CIDT, i.e., that the decisive criterion for distinguishing between the two is the severity of pain or suffering inflicted on a victim. The memo notes, in part, that "[d]rawing distinctions among gradations of pain (for example, severe, mild, moderate, substantial, extreme, intense, excruciating, or agonizing) is obviously not an easy task" but such distinctions nevertheless form the heart of its analysis. Notably, this approach remains significantly out of step with international law and the later jurisprudence of both the European Court and the Committee against Torture.

Note that an effort was made to draw a sharp legal distinction between torture and cruel, inhuman or degrading treatment with the enactment of the Military Commissions Act of 2006. The relevant provisions are discussed infra, chapter 11.

d. Literature

The reports of torture in Iraq and Guantanamo and the government memoranda on the subject triggered a significant amount of discussion and debate in the law journals. See, e.g., John Alan Cohan, *Torture and the Necessity Doctrine*, 41 Val. U. L. Rev. 1587 (2007); Henry Shue, *Torture in Dreamland: Disposing of the Ticking Time Bomb*, 37 Case W. Res. J. Int'l L. 231 (2005); M. Cherif Bassiouni, *The Institutionalization of Torture under the Bush Administration*, 37 Case W. Res. J. Int'l L. 389 (2005); John Duberstein, *Excluding Torture: a Comparison of the British and American Approaches to Evidence Obtained by Third Party Torture*, 32 N.C.J. Int'l L. & Com. Reg. 159 (2006); John Radsan, *A Better Model for Interrogating High–Level Terrorists*, 79 Temp. L. Rev. 1227 (2006); American Civil Liberties Union [ACLU], Enduring Abuse: Torture and Cruel Treatment by the United States at Home and Abroad (2006), *available at* http://www.aclu.org/safefree/torture/torture_report.pdf. Also see Marcy Strauss, Torture, 48 N.Y.L. Sch. L.Rev. 201 (2003) and Alan M. Dershowitz, The Torture Warrant: A Response to Professor Strauss, 48 N.Y.L. Sch. L.Rev. 275 (2003).

e. The Ticking Bomb Debate

Consider the following views. What factors need to be taken into account or need to be known in choosing among them?

> 1) "I am generally against torture as a *normative* matter, and I would like to see its use minimized.... I think that if we ever confronted an actual case of imminent mass terrorism that could be prevented by the infliction of torture, we would use torture (even lethal torture)....
>
> "... I pose the issue as follows: If torture is in fact being and/or would in fact be used in an actual ticking bomb mass terrorism case, would it be normatively better or worse to have such torture regulated by some kind of warrant...." See Alan M. Dershowitz, The Torture Warrant: A Response to Professor Strauss, 48 N.Y. L. Sch. L.Rev. 275 (2003).
>
> 2) "Dershowitz believes that the occasions for the use of torture should be regularized—by requiring a judicial warrant.... But he overlooks an argument for leaving such things to executive discretion. If rules are promulgated permitting torture in defined circumstances, some officials are bound to want to explore the outer bounds of the

rules. Better to leave in place the formal and customary prohibitions, but with the understanding that that they will not be enforced in extreme circumstances." Richard A. Posner, The Best Offense, The New Republic, Sept. 2, 2002, 28, quoted in Dershowitz, op. cit. supra note 5 at 279.

3) "We would articulate the Posner approach somewhat differently and with a slightly different rationale. Better to leave in place the customary prohibitions which make torture a crime, thus warning the police that if they torture they are opening themselves up to criminal penalties. Despite that warning, in the most extreme emergency, the police are highly likely to disregard the warning and do what they think is necessary, taking the risk of criminal sanctions later. This approach helps to ensure that the narrowest possible interpretation will be given to the emergency that leads the police to engage in torture, that is, where the police instinct for self-preservation overcomes their fear of criminal sanctions that might be imposed subsequently." Norman Abrams, Terrorism Prosecutions in Federal Court: Exceptions to Constitutional Evidence Rules and the Development of a Cabined Exception for Coerced Confessions, UCLA School of Law Research Paper No. 11–14 (2011) at n. 94.

f. The Army Field Manual Interrogation Provisions

After much discussion within and without the Department of Defense, including consideration of having two sets of standards for military interrogations, one classified and one unclassified, in September 2006, a revised Army Field Manual on Interrogation, FM 2–22.3 (FM 34–52), was issued. Inter alia, this Manual serves as the sole set of standards and rules governing the interrogation of prisoners by the military. The Manual contains provisions prohibiting certain interrogation techniques and permitting others. Illustrative provisions are set forth below.

> **5–74.** All captured or detained personnel, regardless of status, shall be treated humanely, and in accordance with the Detainee Treatment Act of 2005 and DOD Directive 2310.1E, "Department of Defense Detainee Program," and no person in the custody or under the control of DOD, regardless of nationality or physical location, shall be subject to torture or cruel, inhuman, or degrading treatment or punishment, in accordance with and as defined in US law. . . .
>
> Use of torture is not only illegal but also it is a poor technique that yields unreliable results, may damage subsequent collection efforts, and can induce the source to say what he thinks the HUMINT collector wants to hear. Use of torture can also have many possible negative consequences at national and international levels.
>
> All prisoners and detainees, regardless of status, will be treated humanely. Cruel, inhuman and degrading treatment is prohibited. The Detainee Treatment Act of 2005 defines "cruel,

inhuman or degrading treatment" as the cruel unusual, and inhumane treatment or punishment prohibited by the Fifth, Eighth, and Fourteenth Amendments to the U.S. Constitution. This definition refers to an extensive body of law developed by the courts of the United States to determine when, under various circumstances, treatment of individuals would be inconsistent with American constitutional standards related to concepts of dignity, civilization, humanity, decency and fundamental fairness. All DOD procedures for treatment of prisoners and detainees have been reviewed and are consistent with these standards, as well as our obligations under international law as interpreted by the United States.

. . .

The following actions will not be approved and cannot be condoned in any circumstances: forcing an individual to perform or simulate sexual acts or to pose in a sexual manner; exposing an individual to outrageously lewd and sexually provocative behavior; intentionally damaging or destroying an individual's religious articles.

5–75. If used in conjunction with intelligence interrogations, prohibited actions include, but are not limited to—

> Forcing the detainee to be naked, perform sexual acts, or pose in a sexual manner.
>
> Placing hoods or sacks over the head of a detainee; using duct tape over the eyes.
>
> Applying beatings, electric shock, burns, or other forms of physical pain.
>
> "Waterboarding."
>
> Using military working dogs.
>
> Inducing hypothermia or heat injury.
>
> Conducting mock executions.
>
> Depriving the detainee of necessary food, water, or medical care.

. . .

CAUTION: Although no single comprehensive source defines impermissible coercion, certain acts are clearly prohibited. Certain prohibited physical coercion may be obvious, such as physically abusing the subject of the screening or interrogation. Other forms of impermissible coercion may be more subtle, and may include threats to turn the individual over to others to be abused; subjecting the individual to impermissible humiliating or degrading treatment; implying harm to the individual or his property. Other prohibited actions include implying a deprivation of applicable protections guaranteed by law because of a failure to cooperate; threatening to separate parents from their children; or forcing a protected person to guide US forces in a dangerous area. Where there is doubt, you should consult your supervisor or servicing judge advocate.

Many standard interrogation techniques not involving physical means are permitted under the AFM with few limitations. Thus the AFM authorizes: playing on the emotions of the detainee—love, hate, fear; offering incentives to provide information; exploiting the detainees weak self-esteem and ego strength; offering to protect the detainee from things he fears; impressing on him the futility of resisting or inducing the idea that the interrogator knows everything.

Distinguishing between acceptable and unacceptable practices under the AFM relating to religion illustrates the sometimes difficult line drawing that may need to be done regarding acceptable interrogation practices. Thus, the AFM states:

> Although it is acceptable to use religion in all interrogation approaches, even to express doubts about a religion, an interrogator is not permitted to denigrate a religion's symbols (for example, a Koran, prayer rug, icon, or religious statue) or violate a religion's tenets, except where appropriate for health, safety, and security reasons.

Under the AFM, many forms of deception are permissible. An interrogator may:

> use ruses of war to build rapport with interrogation sources, and this may include posing or "passing himself off" as someone other than a military interrogator [or an interrogator from another country].

But the AFM does impose some specific restrictions on deceptions. The interrogator must not pose as—

> A doctor, medic, or any other type of medical personnel.

> Any member of the International Committee of the Red Cross (ICRC) or its affiliates. Such a ruse is a violation of US treaty obligations.

> A chaplain or clergyman.

> A journalist.

> A member of the US Congress.[3]

2. THE OBAMA EXECUTIVE ORDER ADOPTING THE AFM GUIDELINES

On January 22, 2009, a turning point was arguably reached, the use of extreme interrogation methods in terrorism investigations was prohibit-

---

3. U.S. Dep't of the Army, Field Manual 2–22.3, *Human Intelligence Collector Operations* (Sept. 2006).

ed, and an effort was made to leave the torture controversy behind (although still to be argued about and still alive for those who wished that individuals should be prosecuted or the facts pursued before a kind of truth commission). On that date, newly inaugurated President Obama signed the following Executive Order:

EXECUTIVE ORDER—ENSURING LAWFUL INTERROGATIONS

By the authority vested in me by the Constitution and the laws of the United States of America, in order to improve the effectiveness of human intelligence gathering, to promote the safe, lawful, and humane treatment of individuals in United States custody and of United States personnel who are detained in armed conflicts, to ensure compliance with the treaty obligations of the United States, including the Geneva Conventions, and to take care that the laws of the United States are faithfully executed, I hereby order as follows:

Section 1. Revocation. Executive Order 13440 of July 20, 2007, is revoked. All executive directives, orders, and regulations inconsistent with this order, including but not limited to those issued to or by the Central Intelligence Agency (CIA) from September 11, 2001, to January 20, 2009, concerning detention or the interrogation of detained individuals, are revoked to the extent of their inconsistency with this order. Heads of departments and agencies shall take all necessary steps to ensure that all directives, orders, and regulations of their respective departments or agencies are consistent with this order. Upon request, the Attorney General shall provide guidance about which directives, orders, and regulations are inconsistent with this order.

Sec. 2.   Definitions. As used in this order:

. . .

(c) "Common Article 3" means Article 3 of each of the Geneva Conventions.

(d) "Convention Against Torture" means the Convention Against Torture and Other Cruel, Inhuman or Degrading Treatment or Punishment, December 10, 1984, 1465 U.N.T.S. 85, S. Treaty Doc. No. 100–20 (1988).

(e) "Geneva Conventions" means:

(i) the Convention for the Amelioration of the Condition of the Wounded and Sick in Armed Forces in the Field, August 12, 1949 (6 UST 3114);

(ii) the Convention for the Amelioration of the Condition of Wounded, Sick and Shipwrecked Members of Armed Forces at Sea, August 12, 1949 (6 UST 3217);

(iii) the Convention Relative to the Treatment of Prisoners of War, August 12, 1949 (6 UST 3316); and

(iv) the Convention Relative to the Protection of Civilian Persons in Time of War, August 12, 1949 (6 UST 3516).

(f) "Treated humanely," "violence to life and person," "murder of all kinds," "mutilation," "cruel treatment," "torture," "outrages upon personal dignity," and "humiliating and degrading treatment" refer to, and have the same meaning as, those same terms in Common Article 3.

(g) The terms "detention facilities" and "detention facility" in section 4(a) of this order do not refer to facilities used only to hold people on a short-term, transitory basis.

Sec. 3. Standards and Practices for Interrogation of Individuals in the Custody or Control of the United States in Armed Conflicts.

(a) Common Article 3 Standards as a Minimum Baseline. Consistent with the requirements of the Federal torture statute, 18 U.S.C. 2340 2340A, section 1003 of the Detainee Treatment Act of 2005, 42 U.S.C. 2000dd, the Convention Against Torture, Common Article 3, and other laws regulating the treatment and interrogation of individuals detained in any armed conflict, such persons shall in all circumstances be treated humanely and shall not be subjected to violence to life and person (including murder of all kinds, mutilation, cruel treatment, and torture), nor to outrages upon personal dignity (including humiliating and degrading treatment), whenever such individuals are in the custody or under the effective control of an officer, employee, or other agent of the United States Government or detained within a facility owned, operated, or controlled by a department or agency of the United States.

(b) Interrogation Techniques and Interrogation–Related Treatment. Effective immediately, an individual in the custody or under the effective control of an officer, employee, or other agent of the United States Government, or detained within a facility owned, operated, or controlled by a department or agency of the United States, in any armed conflict, shall not be subjected to any interrogation technique or approach, or any treatment related to interrogation, that is not authorized by and listed in Army Field Manual 2 22.3 (Manual). Interrogation techniques, approaches, and treatments described in the Manual shall be implemented strictly in accord with the principles, processes, conditions, and limitations the Manual prescribes. Where processes required by the Manual, such as a requirement of approval by specified Department of Defense officials, are inapposite to a department or an agency other than the Department of Defense, such a department or agency shall use processes that are substantially equivalent to the processes the Manual prescribes for the Department of Defense. Nothing in this section shall preclude the Federal Bureau of Investigation, or other Federal law enforcement agencies, from continuing to use authorized, non-coercive techniques of interrogation that are designed to elicit voluntary statements and do not involve the use of force, threats, or promises.

(c) Interpretations of Common Article 3 and the Army Field Manual. From this day forward, unless the Attorney General with appropriate consultation provides further guidance, officers, employees, and other agents of the United States Government may, in conducting interrogations, act in reliance upon Army Field Manual 2 22.3, but may not, in conducting interrogations, rely upon any interpretation of the law governing interrogation—including interpretations of Federal criminal laws, the Convention Against Torture, Common Article 3, Army Field Manual 2 22.3, and its predecessor document, Army Field Manual 34 52 issued by the Department of Justice between September 11, 2001, and January 20, 2009.

Sec. 4. Prohibition of Certain Detention Facilities, and Red Cross Access to Detained Individuals.

(a) CIA Detention. The CIA shall close as expeditiously as possible any detention facilities that it currently operates and shall not operate any such detention facility in the future.

(b) International Committee of the Red Cross Access to Detained Individuals. All departments and agencies of the Federal Government shall provide the International Committee of the Red Cross with notification of, and timely access to, any individual detained in any armed conflict in the custody or under the effective control of an officer, employee, or other agent of the United States Government or detained within a facility owned, operated, or controlled by a department or agency of the United States Government, consistent with Department of Defense regulations and policies.

Sec. 5. Special Interagency Task Force on Interrogation and Transfer Policies.

(a) Establishment of Special Interagency Task Force. There shall be established a Special Task Force on Interrogation and Transfer Policies (Special Task Force) to review interrogation and transfer policies.

. . .

Subsequently, Attorney General Holder issued the following statement:

Washington, D.C. August 24, 2009

WASHINGTON—Attorney General Eric Holder today announced that the Special Task Force on Interrogations and Transfer Policies, which was created pursuant to Executive Order 13491 on Jan. 22, 2009, has proposed that the Obama Administration establish a specialized interrogation group to bring together officials from law enforcement, the U.S. Intelligence Community, and the Department of Defense to conduct interrogations in a manner that will strengthen national security consistent with the rule of law.

The Task Force also made policy recommendations with respect to scenarios in which the United States moves or facilitates the movement of a person from one country to another or from U.S. custody to the custody of another country to ensure that U.S. practices in such transfers comply with U.S. law, policy and international obligations and do not result in the transfer of individuals to face torture.

"The new policies proposed by the Task Force will allow us to draw the best personnel from across the government to conduct interrogations that will yield valuable intelligence and strengthen our national security," said Attorney General Holder. "There is no tension between strengthening our national security and meeting our commitment to the rule of law, and these new policies will accomplish both."

Interrogations

After extensively consulting with representatives of the Armed Forces, the relevant agencies in the Intelligence Community, and some of the nation's most experienced and skilled interrogators, the Task Force concluded that the Army Field Manual provides appropriate guidance on interrogation for military interrogators and that no additional or different guidance was necessary for other agencies. These conclusions rested on the Task Force's unanimous assessment, including that of the Intelligence Community, that the practices and techniques identified by the Army Field Manual or currently used by law enforcement provide adequate and effective means of conducting interrogations.

The Task Force concluded, however, that the United States could improve its ability to interrogate the most dangerous terrorists by forming a specialized interrogation group, or High–Value Detainee Interrogation Group (HIG), that would bring together the most effective and experienced interrogators and support personnel from across the Intelligence Community, the Department of Defense and law enforcement. The creation of the HIG would build upon a proposal developed by the Intelligence Science Board.

To accomplish that goal, the Task Force recommended that the HIG should coordinate the deployment of mobile teams of experienced interrogators, analysts, subject matter experts and linguists to conduct interrogations of high-value terrorists if the United States obtains the ability to interrogate them. The primary goal of this elite interrogation group would be gathering intelligence to prevent terrorist attacks and otherwise to protect national security. Advance planning and interagency coordination prior to interrogations would also allow the United States, where appropriate, to preserve the option of gathering information to be used in potential criminal investigations and prosecutions.

The Task Force recommended that the specialized interrogation group be administratively housed within the Federal Bureau of Investigation, with its principal function being intelligence gathering, rather than law enforcement. Moreover, the Task Force recommended that the group be subject to policy guidance and oversight coordinated by the National Security Council.

The Task Force also recommended that this specialized interrogation group develop a set of best practices and disseminate these for training purposes among agencies that conduct interrogations. In addition, the Task Force recommended that a scientific research program for interrogation be established to study the comparative effectiveness of interrogation approaches and techniques, with the goal of identifying the existing techniques that are most effective and developing new lawful techniques to improve intelligence interrogations.

. . . [Ed. additional excerpts from Attorney General Holder's report regarding the Task Force recommendations on Transfer (i.e. irregular rendition) are presented infra, p. 391.]

QUESTIONS AND NOTES

1. Problems: Consider whether the AFM interrogation provisions must be followed in connection with the interrogations of the following individuals.

     a. In 2011, a member of al Qaeda is apprehended on an international air flight with a bomb in his possession which he managed to smuggle past the security inspection. He is transferred to a U.S. aircraft carrier on the high seas and interrogated there.

     b. Same case as a., but the individual is brought to New York City and interrogated by FBI agents.

     c. A small group of al Qaeda sympathizers who are legal residents of the United States are apprehended by the FBI and interrogated in New York City. There is evidence that they have been planning to plant a series of bombs in the New York subway in retaliation for the killing of Osama Bin Laden by U.S. forces.

     d. Same case as c. except that the members of the group have no connection or association with al Qaeda. They are Muslims who believe that the U.S. government has been attacking Muslims worldwide, and they plan to plant bombs in the New York subway as a form of retaliation.

2. The adoption of the Army Field Manual interrogation guidelines in 2006 and the issuance in 2009 of the Executive Order quoted above, shifted the ground rules for the interrogation of terror suspects by establishing a list of prohibited as well as permitted techniques and methods of interrogation. As a result of the torture controversy, most of the attention of scholars and others had been on extreme methods of interrogation, but the change in

approach now enabled a focus on ground rules for interrogation at the other end of the spectrum: what kinds of techniques are permissible?

3.   In 2009, the Attorney General announced that five of the terrorist leaders detained in military custody at Guantanamo Bay would be prosecuted in a federal court in New York City rather than in military commission proceedings and that in the future some detainees would be tried before military commissions and some in federal court. The Attorney General's announcement triggered a great deal of criticism and opposition in the Congress—mainly from those who thought that these high value detainees should be prosecuted in military commission proceedings rather than in federal court—and, after a lengthy period, he backed away from his previous announcement and indicated that these particular defendants would be prosecuted before military commissions. Meanwhile, however, the government went ahead with one prosecution of a relatively minor Guantanamo detainee in the federal court in New York City, and in July, 2011, announced that another detainee seized abroad would also be prosecuted in NYC.

4.   Adopting the Army Field Manual interrogation rules while, at the same time, beginning to prosecute detainees from Guantanamo and others seized abroad in federal court poses the question whether interrogation statements obtained using the AFM interrogation rules meet constitutional standards of admissibility applied in the civilian courts. Issues raised by this question are addressed infra in this chapter. Further, additional interrogation issues triggered by the many different factual variations that arise in practice merit examination.

Most people have assumed that the evidentiary rules, including the interrogation rules, applied in military commissions would be more favorable to the prosecution than those applicable in federal court. Indeed, this assumed difference is one of the reasons why many people in the Congress have preferred military rather than civilian prosecution. The question of how the military commission rules of evidentiary admissibility compare with civilian federal court rules is explored further in chapter 11, infra.

3.   LEGAL ISSUES ARISING OUT OF THE INTERROGATION OF TERRORIST SUSPECTS

a.   The Admissibility in Criminal Prosecutions in U.S. District Courts of Confessions Obtained Abroad

Can a non-resident alien with no connection to the U.S. who was interrogated abroad by U.S. agents or with the participation of U.S. agents claim the benefit of Fifth Amendment protections in a federal criminal prosecution in this country? Consider the following case:

IN RE TERRORIST BOMBINGS OF U.S. EMBASSIES IN EAST AFRICA—UNITED STATES v. ODEH

552 F.3d 177 (2d Cir. 2008), certiorari denied, Odeh v. United States, 129 S.Ct. 2765

Before: FEINBERG, NEWMAN, and CABRANES, CIRCUIT JUDGES.

JOSÉ A. CABRANES, CIRCUIT JUDGE:

Defendants-appellants Mohamed Rashed Daoud Al–'Owhali and Mohamed Sadeek Odeh challenge their convictions in the United States District Court for the Southern District of New York (Leonard B. Sand, Judge) on numerous charges arising from their involvement in the August 7, 1998 bombings of the American Embassies in Nairobi, Kenya and Dar es Salaam, Tanzania (the "August 7 bombings"). In this opinion we consider their challenges to the District Court's rulings that denied, for the most part, their respective motions to suppress statements each of them made overseas to U.S. and non-U.S. officials. . . .

Al–'Owhali and Odeh contend that neither the "Advice of Rights" form ("AOR") that they received nor the subsequent oral warnings of an Assistant United States Attorney ("AUSA") satisfied Miranda v. Arizona. In addition, Al–'Owhali asserts that the conditions of his confinement made his statements involuntary and therefore inadmissible under the Fifth Amendment. . . .

As explained in greater detail below, all of these claims lack merit. The AUSA's oral warnings fulfilled, and the AOR substantially complied with, the government's obligations, insofar as it had any, under Miranda, and the admission of Al–'Owhali's and Odeh's statements did not otherwise run afoul of the Fifth Amendment.

A. Factual Overview

1. Al–'Owhali

Al–'Owhali was detained on August 12, 1998 by Kenyan authorities in "an arrest [that] was valid under Kenyan law." United States v. Bin Laden, 132 F.Supp.2d 168, 173 (S.D.N.Y.2001). Within one hour of his arrest, Al–'Owhali was transported to Kenyan police headquarters in Nairobi and interrogated by two members of the Joint Terrorist Task Force-an FBI Special Agent and a New York City police detective-operating out of New York City and two officers of Kenya's national police. The New York police detective presented Al–'Owhali with an Advice of Rights form often used by U.S. law enforcement when operating overseas. The AOR, written in English, read in its entirety as follows:

We are representatives of the United States Government. Under our laws, you have certain rights. Before we ask you any questions, we want to be sure that you understand those rights.

You do not have to speak to us or answer any questions. Even if you have already spoken to the Kenyan authorities, you do not have to speak to us now.

If you do speak with us, anything that you say may be used against you in a court in the United States or elsewhere.

In the United States, you would have the right to talk to a lawyer to get advice before we ask you any questions and you could have a lawyer with you during questioning. In the United States, if you could not afford a lawyer, one would be appointed for you, if you wish, before any questioning.

Because we are not in the United States, we cannot ensure that you will have a lawyer appointed for you before any questioning.

If you decide to speak with us now, without a lawyer present, you will still have the right to stop answering questions at any time.

You should also understand that if you decide not to speak with us, that fact cannot be used as evidence against you in a court in the United States.

I have read this statement of my rights and I understand what my rights are. I am willing to make a statement and answer questions. I do not want a lawyer at this time. I understand and know what I am doing. No promises or threats have been made to me and no pressure or coercion of any kind has been used against me.

Al–'Owhali told the American law enforcement agents that he could not read English and had a limited understanding of spoken English. Accordingly, the police detective "read the AOR aloud in English, going slowly and checking for visual signs of comprehension. Al–'Owhali appeared to [the detective to] understand, replied that he understood when asked, and signed his alias at the bottom of the AOR in Arabic when requested to do so." A one-hour interrogation ensued, in which Al–'Owhali responded in "broken English."

Finding their ability to communicate with Al–'Owhali limited by the end of that hour, the agents decided to continue Al–'Owhali's interrogation with the assistance of an interpreter. The special agent began this interview by reading the AOR in English, which the interpreter translated into Arabic. *Id.* Al–'Owhali stated that he "understood that the warning was the same one as from the morning session," "understood his rights as described therein," and "agreed to answer questions." Al–'Owhali was then interviewed for about three hours and, thereafter, was questioned on eight other days:[4] At the start of each of the interviews on August 13, 14, 17 and 21, the agents showed Al–'Owhali the signed AOR, asked whether he remembered his rights, and whether he would continue to answer their questions. Al–'Owhali consented on each occasion. Until August 21, he denied any involvement in the embassy bombings.

During the August 21 interview, the U.S. agents described the inculpatory evidence they had gathered on Al–'Owhali, and "[a]fter acknowledging that the agents 'knew everything,' Al–'Owhali said that he would

---

4. The interviews lasted between two and four hours, with the exception of the interviews on August 22 and August 25, which lasted seven and nine hours respectively.

tell the truth about his involvement in the bombing if he could be tried in the United States." He explained that the reason he wanted to stand trial in the United States was "because the United States was his enemy, not Kenya."

. . .

2. Odeh

On August 7, 1998, Pakistani immigration officials detained Odeh, following his arrival at the Karachi airport on a flight from Kenya, on the ground that he used a false passport. . . . he as held in Pakistani custody until August 14, during which time he was interrogated by Pakistani officials. *Id.* On August 14, Odeh was transported to Nairobi, Kenya, and transferred from Pakistani custody to Kenyan custody. The next day, he was interrogated by two special agents of the FBI, an AUSA, and three Kenyan police officers. Odeh communicated with his interrogators, without difficulty, entirely in English. The U.S. officials explained to Odeh that whether or not he spoke with Pakistani authorities during his detention in Karachi had no bearing on his decision to speak to them. "Thereafter, when Odeh raised the issue of his admissions to the Pakistani authorities, he was told that the Americans did not know or care about what had transpired in Pakistan." One of the FBI special agents read Odeh an AOR similar in all material respects to the one read to Al–'Owhali. . . .

. . .

As the FBI special agent read the AOR, Odeh asked about the availability of a lawyer but did not specifically request one. After further discussion of the AOR and Odeh's willingness to speak to U.S. officials, the interview temporarily ceased so that the AUSA could investigate whether Kenyan counsel was available to Odeh.

Believing that Odeh lacked financial resources, the AUSA inquired into the availability of appointed-but not privately retained-Kenyan counsel. A "high-ranking" Kenyan law enforcement officer informed the AUSA that under Kenyan law, appointed counsel was not provided at the investigative stage and it was their "practice to continue questioning a person who requests an appointed attorney." The AUSA informed Odeh of what he had learned from the Kenyan police officer, verified that Odeh had not already retained an attorney, and then orally informed him of his rights under Miranda:

Odeh was told that he had the right to remain silent and that invocation of the right to silence could not be used against him in court. He was also told that if he did speak to the American officials, statements that he made could be used against him. With respect to the right to counsel, AUSA [redacted] told Odeh that he was entitled to have an attorney present and to have an attorney appointed if he could not afford one. However, AUSA [redacted] informed Odeh that no American attorney was currently available to represent him in Kenya. AUSA [redacted] emphasized that Odeh was "the boss" with respect to answering questions without an attorney present.

The AUSA explained that Odeh could (1) exercise his right to remain silent; (2) invoke his right to have an attorney present, in which case the Americans would leave the room and he could then decide whether or not to speak with the Kenyan police; or (3) speak to both the American and Kenyan authorities without the presence of an attorney. Odeh suggested a fourth possibility: "speaking with the American officials outside the presence of the Kenyans." While the U.S. and Kenyan authorities were investigating the viability of Odeh's proposal, Odeh changed his mind and decided to speak to both the U.S. and Kenyan officials. Odeh then signed the AOR. Odeh never stated a desire to hire an attorney, and "[i]n fact, he asked the officials what would happen if he subsequently decided that he did not want to speak without a lawyer present." In response, the AUSA "informed him that he always had the right to stop talking with the American officials."

After signing the AOR on August 15, Odeh was interviewed for about seven hours. During the interrogation the next day, the AUSA again informed Odeh that he had the right to the presence of an attorney at the interview, even though no American attorney was available, and that if Odeh wanted an attorney, the Americans would not interrogate him. Odeh expressed his willingness to answer questions and did not request an attorney, but he did make inquiries into the status of property confiscated upon his arrest. Odeh was interrogated on a daily basis from approximately 9:00 a.m. to 6:00 p.m. until he was taken to the United States on August 27, 1998. During these sessions, "Odeh admitted that he was a member of al Qaeda but denied any participation in (or foreknowledge of) the embassy bombings." When Odeh was transferred to American custody on August 27, he was given the standard Miranda warnings.

B. Al-'Owhali's and Odeh's Challenges to the Denial of their Motions to Suppress Inculpatory Statements

. . .

2. The Applicability of the Fifth Amendment and Miranda to the Admission at Trial of Inculpatory Statements Made in Foreign Custody to U.S. Agents

Like the District Court, we conclude that the admissibility at trial of statements made to U.S. agents by foreign nationals held in foreign custody is governed by the Fifth Amendment. Indeed, the government does not argue otherwise. Although we need not decide whether we agree with the District Court as to all aspects of its ruling on the Fifth Amendment and Miranda, it suffices to hold, as described in greater detail below, that insofar as Miranda might apply to interrogations conducted overseas, that decision is satisfied when a U.S. agent informs a foreign detainee of his rights under the U.S. Constitution when questioned overseas.

We note that U.S. agents acting overseas need not become experts in foreign criminal procedure in order to comply with Miranda; nor need they advocate for the appointment of local counsel on a foreign suspect's behalf. While doing so may provide additional grounds for finding that any statements obtained in the course of interrogations were made voluntarily, it is not required by either the Fifth Amendment or Miranda. If the suspect chooses to make a knowing and voluntary waiver of his rights after a warning adapted to the circumstances of questioning overseas and chooses to speak with a U.S. agent, then neither the Fifth Amendment nor Miranda will bar the admission of his statement at trial.

... While a violation of the Fourth Amendment's prohibition of unreasonable searches and seizures occurs at the time of the search or seizure, regardless of whether unlawfully obtained evidence is ever offered at trial, a violation of the Fifth Amendment's right against self-incrimination occurs only when a compelled statement is offered at trial against the defendant ... For this reason, it naturally follows that, regardless of the origin—i.e., domestic or foreign-of a statement, it cannot be admitted at trial in the United States if the statement was "compelled." Similarly, it does not matter whether the defendant is a U.S. citizen or a foreign national: "no person" tried in the civilian courts of the United States can be compelled "to be a witness against himself."

. . .

Accordingly, we hold that foreign nationals interrogated overseas but tried in the civilian courts of the United States are protected by the Fifth Amendment's self-incrimination clause.

. . .

Having determined that the Fifth Amendment right against self-incrimination governs the admissibility at trial of statements made overseas, we turn to the related question of Miranda's applicability to overseas interrogations conducted by U.S. agents. The Supreme Court has not ruled on this particular question, but it has held that the framework established by "Miranda ... govern[s] the admissibility of statements made during custodial interrogation in both state and federal courts." Dickerson v. United States, 530 U.S. 428, 432, 120 S.Ct. 2326, 147 L.Ed.2d 405 (2000). Proceeding on the assumption that the Miranda framework generally governs the admissibility of statements obtained overseas by U.S. agents, we conclude that the application of that framework to overseas interrogations may differ from its domestic application, depending on local circumstances, in keeping with the context-specific nature of the Miranda rule.

In Dickerson, the Supreme Court explained that the Miranda "warning/waiver" framework arose from the risk "that the coercion inherent in custodial interrogation blurs the line between voluntary and involuntary statements, and thus heightens the risk that an individual will not be 'accorded his privilege under the Fifth Amendment ... not to be compelled to incriminate himself.'"... In response, the Court set forth "constitutional guidelines" conditioning the admissibility of statements obtained in custodial interrogations on whether a suspect had been warned that he:

"has the right to remain silent, that anything he says can be used against him in a court of law, that he has the right to the presence of an attorney, and that if he cannot afford an attorney one will be appointed for him prior to any questioning if he so desires."

Undergirding these guidelines are two objectives: "trustworthiness and deterrence." ... Thus, courts suppress un-warned statements, even those that may otherwise be voluntary and trustworthy, in order to deter future misconduct by law enforcement agents.

Recognizing that the threat of suppression in U.S. courts for failure to comply with Miranda holds little sway over foreign authorities, we have declined to suppress un-warned statements obtained overseas by foreign officials.... Instead of applying Miranda in such cases, we have required that "[w]henever a court is asked to rule upon the admissibility of a statement made to a foreign police officer, the court must consider the totality of the circumstances to determine whether the statement was voluntary. If the court finds the statement involuntary, it must exclude this because of its inherent unreliability."

When U.S. law enforcement agents or officials are involved in overseas interrogation, however, the deterrence rationale retains its force. In such circumstances, the twin goals of ensuring trustworthiness and deterring misconduct might compel the application of Miranda. We suggested as much in Yousef, 327 F.3d at 56. In Yousef, we observed that "statements taken by foreign police in the absence of Miranda warnings are admissible if voluntary," subject to two exceptions. One of these exceptions—the so-called "joint venture doctrine"—appears to have been "implicitly adopted" by our Court, even though we have "failed to define its precise contours."[5] Pursuant to this exception, "statements elicited during overseas interrogation by foreign police in the absence of Miranda warnings must be suppressed whenever United States law enforcement agents actively participate in questioning conducted by foreign authorities."....
In light of these precedents, we proceed on the assumption that the Miranda "warning/waiver" framework generally governs the admissibility in our domestic courts of custodial statements obtained by U.S. officials from individuals during their detention under the authority of foreign governments.[6]

---

5. The other exception noted by the Yousef Court pertains to "statements obtained under circumstances that 'shock the judicial conscience.'"

6. Our recognition that Miranda might apply to foreign detainees held overseas should in no way impair the ability of the U.S. government to gather foreign intelligence. First, Miranda's "public safety" exception, see New York v. Quarles, 467 U.S. 649, 104 S.Ct. 2626, 81 L.Ed.2d 550 (1984), would likely apply overseas with no less force than it does domestically. When exigent circumstances compel an un-warned interrogation in order to protect the public, Miranda would not impair the government's ability to obtain that information. Second, we emphasize that the Miranda framework governs only the admission of custodial statements at U.S. trials. Insofar as

Even if we were to conclude, rather than assume, that Miranda applies to overseas interrogations involving U.S. agents, that would not mean that U.S. agents must recite verbatim the familiar Miranda warnings to those detained in foreign lands.

. . .

As . . . decisions demonstrate, where Miranda has been applied to overseas interrogations by U.S. agents, it has been so applied in a flexible fashion to accommodate the exigencies of local conditions. This context-specific approach is wholly consistent with our reading of the Supreme Court decisions construing the Miranda framework, and we now apply that approach to the facts of this case.[7]

. . .

In cases where a suspect has no entitlement to counsel under the law of the foreign land, it would be misleading to inform him falsely that he was guaranteed the presence or appointment of an attorney—and Miranda does not require the provision of false assurances.

The warning at issue here was candid: It explained the rights provided by the U.S. Constitution, while recognizing that, because defendants were detained outside the United States, U.S. law did not govern the terms of their detention or interrogation. Rather than indicating that defendants had no right to appointed counsel, the AOR stated that defendants may have to look to local law for the effectuation of those rights. Indeed, the facts presented by Odeh's case bear this out. Upon hearing the AOR's warnings, Odeh did not assume that counsel was unavailable; instead, he inquired whether counsel was available under Kenyan law. For these reasons, we do not equate the language of the AOR with a statement that counsel was unavailable. Instead, we read that language as a candid acknowledgment of the possible disparity between rights established by the U.S. Constitution, on the one hand, and the availability of counsel and entitlement to the assistance of counsel under the law of the detaining authority, on the other.

The District Court compensated for this potential disparity between U.S. constitutional rights and the rights that obtain overseas by requiring U.S. agents to study local criminal procedure and urge local officials to provide suspects with counsel, if requested, so as to "replicate" the rights that they would have in the United States. We do not agree that Miranda requires such efforts.

. . . In other words, Miranda requires government agents to be the conduits of information to detained suspects—both as to (1) their rights under the U.S. Constitution to the presence and appointment of counsel at

U.S. agents do not seek to introduce statements obtained through overseas custodial interrogations at U.S. trials, Miranda's strictures would not apply.

7. Because we conclude that, assuming they apply, the strictures of Miranda were satisfied in this case, we leave for another day the question of whether the Miranda "warning/waiver" framework governs the admissibility of statements obtained by U.S. agents in the course of custodial interrogations conducted overseas.

custodial interrogations and (2) the procedures through which they might be able to vindicate those rights under local law. It does not compel the police to serve as advocates for detainees before local authorities, endeavoring to expand the rights and privileges available under local law. This is not to say that if, after being informed of his Miranda rights, a detainee insists on the immediate appointment of counsel as a condition of making a statement, the U.S. officials are barred from attempting to expedite the provision of counsel. Quite the contrary; doing so is perfectly consistent with Miranda, but it is not required.

Because compliance with Miranda does not require law enforcement to advocate on behalf of suspects detained in the United States, we see no basis for adopting a different rule for detainees held overseas by foreign powers. It is true that the rights of foreign detainees to the presence and appointment of counsel will depend on foreign law, but, as noted above, Miranda does not require the provision of legal services. It requires only that, until legal services are either provided or waived, no interrogation take place. At the request of foreign detainees or on their own initiative, U.S. agents are free to describe the procedures by which attorneys are made available in foreign countries, so long as they make an honest, good faith effort to provide accurate information. Foreign detainees may, of course, insist that they receive local counsel or U.S. counsel as a condition of making a statement. In response, U.S. agents may, in their discretion, appeal to local authorities to appoint counsel or even obtain U.S. counsel for them. Alternatively, foreign detainees may determine that, in light of the difficulty of obtaining or unavailability of counsel under local law, it is in their best interests to waive their right to counsel and make a statement to U.S. agents.

We are aware that, as defendants urge, foreign detainees may run the risk of refusing to speak to U.S. officials only to find themselves forced to speak to their foreign jailors. This would be so, however, even if U.S. agents made efforts to secure counsel on their behalf and those efforts proved fruitless. The risk of being forced to speak to their foreign jailors would also exist, moreover, if U.S. agents were not involved at all. Of course, statements obtained under these circumstances could not be admitted in a U.S. trial if the situation indicated that the statements were made involuntarily.

Our decision not to impose additional duties on U.S. agents operating overseas is animated, in part, by our recognition that it is only through the cooperation of local authorities that U.S. agents obtain access to foreign detainees. We have no desire to strain that spirit of cooperation by compelling U.S. agents to press foreign governments for the provision of legal rights not recognized by their criminal justice systems.

. . .

Although we do not find the advice of rights concerning counsel as deficient as did the District Court, we think the wording that was used created a needless risk of misunderstanding by stating, albeit accurately, what the right to counsel would have been had the interrogation occurred in the United States. An advice of rights should state only what rights are available, not what rights would be available if circumstances were different. This does not mean that U.S. agents need to determine what rights are in fact available under local law. All they need to say is that counsel rights depend on local law, and that U.S. agents will afford the accused whatever rights are available under local law. Thus, an AOR used hereafter might usefully advise as to counsel rights in the following language:

Whether you can retain a lawyer, or have a lawyer appointed for you, and whether you can consult with a lawyer and have a lawyer present during questioning are matters that depend on local law, and we cannot advise you on such matters. If local authorities permit you to obtain counsel (retained or appointed) and to consult with a lawyer at this time, you may attempt to obtain and consult with an attorney before speaking with us. Similarly, if local authorities permit you to have a lawyer present during questioning by local authorities, your lawyer may attend any questioning by us.

For these reasons, we conclude that the AOR substantially complied with whatever Miranda requirements were applicable, but we need not rule definitively on the matter because of the adequacy of the subsequent oral warning, and because the error, if any, in excluding the statements obtained prior to the oral warning benefitted defendants and was therefore harmless.

. . .

c.   Defendants' Waiver of their Miranda Rights and their Subsequent Statements

Al-'Owhali and Odeh contend that the conditions of their confinement made their Miranda waivers and subsequent statements involuntary. Al-'Owhali urges that his "secret and relentless interrogation . . . over a ten day period of incommunicado and solitary confinement in a Kenyan prison" renders all of the statements he made during his incarceration, including his Miranda waiver, involuntary. According to Al-'Owhali, his "only chance to escape this prolonged isolation and interrogation, and to have an attorney to consult, was to confess his involvement in the bombing, which would enable him to go to America, where he would have an attorney." Similarly, Odeh argues that his "choice was not really between remaining silent or talking, but between talking to the Kenyans alone or talking to them and the Americans." The circumstances in which he made this choice were "disturbing," in his view, because he agreed to make a statement only after having been left alone with Kenyan police officers, whom he accuses of having a "reputation . . . for torture." With respect to whether the waiver was knowing under the Miranda framework, Odeh argues that it was not because he did not "underst[and] that he had the option of delaying the interrogation for even a day or two in order to obtain counsel" and "was not provided with the option of speaking with the Jordanian consulate, or the chance to consult with his wife."

. . .

We "will affirm a district court's conclusion that a defendant knowingly and voluntarily waived his constitutional rights if any reasonable view of the evidence supports it." . . . [A]s the Supreme Court has observed, "cases in which a defendant can make a colorable argument that a self-incriminating statement was 'compelled' despite the fact that the law enforcement authorities adhered to the dictates of Miranda are rare."

i. The Miranda Waivers

. . . We . . . conclude that the Miranda waivers of Al–'Owhali and Odeh were executed voluntarily.

Turning to the question of whether the waivers were executed knowingly, we observe that only Odeh challenges the District Court's ruling on this score. The District Court found:

Odeh told the Americans that he was comfortable speaking English and that he would ask clarifying questions if he did not understand his rights or anything else the agents said. At no time did Odeh indicate that he was experiencing comprehension problems during the interview sessions. Furthermore, AUSA [redacted] explained to Odeh his Miranda rights with a tremendous degree of conscientiousness, precision, and detail. Odeh himself asked AUSA [redacted] a number of follow-up questions concerning his rights, thereby revealing Odeh's grasp of the salient issues. Because Odeh fully appreciated the fact that he was the "boss" as to whether he would accede to questioning by Americans, we find Odeh's waiver to be knowing and intelligent.

. . .

We therefore conclude that both Al–'Owhali and Odeh knowingly and voluntarily executed valid Miranda waivers.

ii. The Voluntariness of the Statements

We now consider the question of whether the circumstances of Al–'Owhali and Odeh's confinement rendered their statements involuntary. In order to do so, "we must examine the totality of the circumstances. Specifically, these circumstances include 1) the accused's characteristics, 2) the conditions of the interrogation, and 3) the conduct of the police."

. . . [T]he District Court found that Al–'Owhali had a basic understanding of spoken English, received two years of university-level education, and was familiar with political and world events. With respect to the conditions of his confinement, the District Court found that Al–'Owhali was held in "incommunicado detention" for fourteen days, at first in a ten-by-eleven foot cell and then in an eight-by-eight foot cell, and during this time, he received medical attention "as needed." The District Court noted "[a] photograph of Al–'Owhali in his cell, taken at some point during his U.S. interrogation in Kenya, show[ing] him smiling and striking a triumphant pose." The District Court described the interrogation sessions, which were "intermittent and reasonable in duration," as follows:

Al–'Owhali was never in handcuffs during any of his interviews in Kenya. All interviews were held in a library-like room fitted with tables and chairs. Frequent breaks were taken to allow Al–'Owhali to use the restroom, pray, and eat. Prayer breaks lasted for about 15 minutes. Bottled water was provided upon request; food was often provided by the agents. No threats were made by the U.S. agents, nor were any promises made.

The District Court also took note of the "evidence that Al–'Owhali regarded his sessions with [an FBI agent] as a cat-and-mouse game between trained professionals."

We have no reason to doubt the District Court's conclusion that Al–'Owhali was "a well-educated and intelligent individual ... [whose] demeanor before the Americans was one indicative of confidence, not of intimidation." Likewise, there is no evidence in the record suggesting that the conduct of Al–'Owhali's interrogators was oppressive; quite the contrary: they permitted breaks, provided food and water, limited the duration of the sessions, and never placed him in restraints. Indeed, Al–'Owhali does not appear to argue otherwise, as his challenge to the voluntariness of his statements centers primarily on the circumstances of his incommunicado detention in Kenya. The District Court found the conditions of his confinement, "although non-ideal ... far from oppressive." *Id.* Al–'Owhali argues, however, that the length of time he was held in detention imposed "terrible psychological and coercive pressures" on him. Al–'Owhali

Without minimizing in any way the potentially coercive effects of incommunicado detention lasting for fourteen days, we must consider this fact as only one data point—albeit a significant one—in our totality-of-the-circumstances analysis.[8] ... Weighing against the potentially coercive circumstances of Al–'Owhali's confinement are the District Court's careful findings of fact regarding Al–'Owhali's personal characteristics (his education, his knowledge of English and current events, and his demeanor) and the restrained conduct of his interrogators (who never resorted to threats, promises, or coercion to obtain information from him, and who informed him of his rights from the very beginning). In addition, we must consider the District Court's conclusion that—

what truly motivated Al–'Owhali to inculpate himself was his own overriding desire that he be tried in the United States. As he declared to the U.S. agents interviewing him, it was the United States which was his enemy, not Kenya. Particularly significant is the fact that the suggestion that he be tried in America was initiated entirely by Al–'Owhali. And

---

8. As noted earlier, incommunicado detention describes detention without contact with the outside world and is not to be confused with solitary confinement.

when Al–'Owhali was dissatisfied by the less-than-firm assurances offered . . ., he demanded that AUSA [redacted] do better.

Taking into account the totality of the circumstances, as we must, we cannot conclude that, because Al–'Owhali was detained incommunicado for fourteen days, the statements he made after waiving his Miranda rights were involuntary. . . .

Odeh does not argue explicitly that his post-warning statements were made involuntarily . . . The only question that concerns us in this regard is whether, unlike Al–'Owhali, Odeh's fourteen-day incommunicado detention rendered involuntary his post-warning statements. We conclude that it did not.

. . . [W]e conclude that, in light of the District Court's findings regarding Odeh's personal characteristics, the absence of oppressive interrogation methods, and his decision to speak with U.S. officials immediately upon encountering them, Odeh's post-warning statements cannot be attributed to the coercive effects of his incommunicado detention.

. . . To summarize, we hold:

(1) The inculpatory statements of Al–'Owhali and Odeh that were obtained overseas by U.S. agents were properly admitted at trial because (a) the oral warnings of the federal prosecutor satisfied, and the "Advice of Rights" form signed by defendants substantially complied with, the government's obligations, insofar as it had any, under Miranda v. Arizona, and (b) the statements were not obtained involuntarily from defendants in violation of the Fifth Amendment;

. . .

For these reasons, and for those set forth in In re Terrorist Bombings of U.S. Embassies in East Africa, 552 F.3d 93 (2d Cir.2008), the judgments of conviction entered by the District Court against Al–'Owhali and Odeh are affirmed in all respects.

QUESTIONS AND NOTES

1. Not all the case law agrees with the doctrine in the principal case. See, for example, the summary of authorities in United States v. Chan Hok Shek, 2010 WL 4694448 (D.Mass):

Neither the Supreme Court nor the First Circuit has considered whether the *Fifth Amendment's Miranda* requirements apply to interrogations of aliens conducted by U.S. agents on foreign soil. At least one federal appeals court has directly addressed this question and concluded that the privilege does apply.[4] *See In re Terrorist Bombings of U.S.*

---

4. Several circuits have addressed interrogations of *U.S. citizens* abroad by U.S. agents and have found that those statements are entitled to the *Fifth Amendment* privilege. *See, e.g., United States v. Frank, 599 F.3d 1221, 1228–29 (11th Cir. 2010)* (following *United States v. Heller, 625 F.2d 594, 596–98 (5th Cir. 1980)); United States v. Abu Ali, 528 F.3d 210, 227–28 (4th Cir. 2008)* (Wilkinson, Motz, Traxler, JJ.) (following *Heller*). These cases did not specifically address the

Embassies in E. Africa, 552 F.3d 177, 199 (2d Cir. 2008) (noting that a violation of the *Fifth Amendment's* privilege against self-incrimination takes place when the unlawfully obtained statement is offered at trial, not at the point at which the statement was elicited, and, therefore, no foreign defendant "tried in the civilian courts of the United States can be compelled to be a witness against himself"); *see also United States v. Heller*, 625 F.2d 594, 599 (5th Cir. 1980) (Kravitch, J.) (noting that "if American officials participated in the foreign search or interrogation, or if the foreign authorities were acting as agents for their American counterparts, the exclusionary rule should be invoked"). However, other circuits have held that "non-resident aliens who have insufficient contacts with the United States are not entitled to *Fifth Amendment* protections." *See, e.g., Jifry v. FAA*, 370 F.3d 1174, 1182, 361 U.S. App. D.C. 450 (D.C. Cir. 2004); *see also People's Mojahedin Org. of Iran v. U.S. Dep't of State*, 182 F.3d 17, 22, 337 U.S. App. D.C. 106 (D.C. Cir. 1999) ("A foreign entity without property or presence in this country has no constitutional rights, under the *due process clause* or otherwise."). It is therefore unclear whether the *Fifth Amendment's* privilege against self-incrimination attaches when U.S. agents question a foreign national and non-U.S. resident outside of U.S. territory. However, while I view the analysis in *In re Terrorist Bombings* as compelling, I need not reach that issue here in order to rule on the motion to suppress because Chan was not "in custody" and, therefore, the agents were not obligated to give him *Miranda* warnings.

2. Recall the rules applied in a search and seizure context abroad as described in the material in chapter 6, supra. Should the fifth amendment interrogation rules be different? Does the Odeh's analysis follow from the fact where there is a factual basis for a fifth amendment violation it does not actually legally occur until the statements involved are offered into evidence in a trial in the U.S.? Must there be a legal basis for the claim that the police conduct at the earlier point in time violated applicable constitutional standards? Is there such, if the person involved was not entitled to the protection of the U.S. Constitution? Note that the Odeh court did not actually decide the fifth amendment issue but only "assumed" that conclusion for purposes of its analysis.

3. See footnote 6 in Odeh supra. It is one of the first times that a court recognized the possible application of the "public safety" exception to the Miranda warning/waiver requirements in a terrorism/intelligence context. We address the relevant issues in subsection b, infra. In subsection c., we then consider the applicable rules regarding coerced statements.

4. See generally, Mark A. Godsey, The New Frontier of Constitutional Confession Law—The International Arena: Exploring the Admissibility of Confessions Taken by U.S. Investigators from Non–Americans Abroad, 91 Geo. L.J. 851 (2003); Adam Shedd, The Fifth Amendment Privilege Against Self–Incrimination—Does It Exist Extra-territorially? 77 Tul.L.Rev. 767 (2003).

---

question whether the nationality and/or residency of the person being questioned is determinative of whether the *Fifth Amendment* applies to interrogations conducted overseas.

b. Invocation of the Public Safety Exception to the Miranda Warning/Waiver Requirements in Terrorism and Terrorism/Intelligence Contexts

1) The Quarles decision—*In New York v. Quarles,* 467 U.S. 649 (1984), a majority of the Supreme Court carved out a public safety exception to the *Miranda* requirements in a situation where there was immediate need for the police to learn where the suspect had gotten rid of a gun. The police, having apprehended the suspect in a supermarket, asked him, without giving him Miranda warnings, where the gun was (the suspect was wearing an empty shoulder holster), and the suspect responded, "The gun is over there." The Court ruled that the suspect's statement was admissible because of "concern for public safety."

2) Application of the public safety exception in a terrorism case—The exception was applied in a terrorism case in United States v. Khalil, 214 F.3d 111 (2d Cir. 2000), but the fact situation, arguably, involved the same type of immediate exigency as was involved in Quarles itself:

> The officers peeked into the black bag and saw wiring. Technicians thereafter examined the bag's contents; they found pipe bombs, observed that a switch on one of the bombs had been flipped, and were concerned that the bomb would explode before they could disarm it. Other officers went to the hospital and questioned Abu Mezer that morning as to how many bombs there were, how many switches were on each bomb, which wires should be cut to disarm the bombs, and whether there were any timers. Abu Mezer answered all of these questions, stating that he had made five bombs, that they contained gunpowder, and that each would explode when its four switches were flipped. Abu Mezer was also asked whether he had planned to kill himself in the explosion, to which he responded simply, " 'Poof.' "...

> . . .

> [T]he [trial] court ruled that the "public safety" exception,... made interrogation permissible without *Miranda* warnings. Abu Mezer challenges that ruling only insofar as the court failed to suppress his response to the question whether he had intended to kill himself in detonating the bombs, his response having been simply, "Poof." He contends that that question was unrelated to the matter of public safety. We are inclined to disagree, given that Abu Mezer's vision as to whether or not he would survive his attempt to detonate the bomb had the potential for shedding light on the bomb's stability.

3) The FBI Guidelines—The public safety exception has been relied upon for an extension beyond the kind of immediate exigency situations involved in Quarles and Khalil. Specifically, in March 2011, the New York Times reported about an FBI internal memorandum, dated October, 2010, setting forth guidelines for interrogation of operational terrorists within the United States which, arguably, extends the exception beyond immediately-exigent circumstances.

Apart from the footnote dictum in Odeh, approving application of the exception to terrorism/intelligence situations, the courts have not yet definitively ruled on the issue thereby posed. Meanwhile there has been support for this kind of extension, but the support is not unanimous. See, e.g., Amos N. Guiora, Relearning Lessons of History: Miranda and Counterterrorism, 71 La.L.Rev. 1147 (2011). Cf. Norman Abrams, Terrorism Prosecutions in Federal Court: Exceptions to Constitutional Evidence Rules and the Development of a Cabined Exception for Coerced Confessions, UCLA School of Law Research Paper No. 11–14 (2011). Rep. Adam Schiff introduced a bill titled, Questioning of Terrorism Suspects Act of 2010, H.R. 5934, 111th Cong. (2010) which expresses "the 'sense of Congress'" that the Quarles "public safety" exception to Miranda permits "unwarned interrogation of terrorism suspects for as long as is necessary to protect the public from pending or planned attacks when a significant purpose of the interrogation is to gather intelligence and not solely to elicit testimonial evidence."

The FBI guidelines

U.S. Department of Justice

Federal Bureau of Investigation

October 21, 2010

Custodial Interrogation for Public Safety and Intelligence–Gathering Purposes of Operational Terrorists Inside the United States

Identifying and apprehending suspected terrorists, interrogating them to obtain intelligence about terrorist activities and impending terrorist attacks, and lawfully detaining them so that they do not pose a continuing threat to our communities are critical to protecting the American people. The Department of Justice and the FBI believe that we can maximize our ability to accomplish these objectives by continuing to adhere to FBI policy regarding the use of Miranda warnings for custodial interrogation of operational terrorists [2] who are arrested inside the United States:

1. If applicable, agents should ask any and all questions that are reasonably prompted by an immediate concern for the safety of the public or the arresting agents without advising the arrestee of his Miranda rights. [3]

2. After all applicable public safety questions have been exhausted, agents should advise the arrestee of his Miranda rights and seek a waiver of those rights before any further interrogation occurs, absent exceptional circumstances described below.

3. There may be exceptional cases in which, although all relevant public safety questions have been asked, agents nonetheless conclude that continued unwarned interrogation is necessary to collect valuable and timely intelligence not related to any immediate threat, and that the government's interest in obtaining this intelligence outweighs the disadvantages of proceeding with unwarned

interrogation. [4] In these instances, agents should seek SAC approval to proceed with unwarned interrogation after the public safety questioning is concluded. Whenever feasible, the SAC will consult with FBI–HQ (including OGC) and Department of Justice attorneys before granting approval. Presentment of an arrestee may not be delayed simply to continue the interrogation, unless the defendant has timely waived prompt presentment.

The determination whether particular unwarned questions are justified on public safety grounds must always be made on a case-by-case basis based on all the facts and circumstances. In light of the magnitude and complexity of the threat often posed by terrorist organizations, particularly international terrorist organizations, and the nature of their attacks, the circumstances surrounding an arrest of an operational terrorist may warrant significantly more extensive public safety interrogation without Miranda warnings than would be permissible in an ordinary criminal case. Depending on the facts, such interrogation might include, for example, questions about possible impending or coordinated terrorist attacks; the location, nature, and threat posed by weapons that might post an imminent danger to the public; and the identities, locations, and activities or intentions of accomplices who may be plotting additional imminent attacks.

As noted above, if there is time to consult with FBI–HQ (including OGC) and Department of Justice attorneys regarding the interrogation strategy to be followed prior to reading the defendant his Miranda rights, the field office should endeavor to do so. Nevertheless, the agents on the scene who are interacting with the arrestee are in the best position to assess what questions are necessary to secure their safety and the safety of the public, and how long the post-arrest interview can practically be delayed while interrogation strategy is being discussed.

[1]　This guidance applies only to arrestees who have not been indicted and who are not known to be represented by an attorney. For policy on interrogation of indicted defendants, see Legal Handbook for Special Agents (LHBSA) Section 7–3.2 For policy on contact with represented persons, see LHBSA Sections 7–4.1 and 8–3.2.2.

[2]　For these purposes, an operational terrorist is an arrestee who is reasonably believed to be either a high-level member of an international terrorist group; or an operative who has personally conducted or attempted to conduct a terrorist operation that involved risk to life; or an individual knowledgeable about operational details of a pending terrorist operation.

[3]　The Supreme Court held in New York v. Quarles, 467 U.S. 649 (1984), that if law enforcement officials engage in custodial interrogation of an individual that is "reasonably prompted by a concern for the public safety," any statements the individual provides in the course of such interrogation shall not be inadmissible in any

criminal proceeding on the basis that the warnings described in Miranda v. Arizona 384 U.S. 436 (1966), were not provided. The court noted that this exception to the Miranda rule is a narrow one and that "in each case it will be circumscribed by the [public safety] exigency which justifies it." 467 U.S. at 657.

[4] The Supreme Court has strongly suggested that an arrestee's Fifth Amendment right against self-incrimination is not violated at the time a statement is taken without Miranda warnings, but instead may be violated only if and when the government introduces an unwarned statement in a criminal proceeding against the defendant. See Chavez v. Martinez, 538 U.S. 760, 769 (2003) (plurality op.); id. at 789 (Kennedy, J., concurring in part and dissenting in part); cf. also id. at 778–79 (Souter, J., concurring in the judgment); see also United States v. Patane, 542 U.S. 630, 641 (2004) (plurality opinion) ("[V]iolations [of the Fifth Amendment right against self-incrimination] occur, if at all, only upon the admission of unwarned statements into evidence at trial."); United States v. Verdugo–Urquidez, 494 U.S. 259, 264 (1990) ("[A] violation [of the Fifth Amendment right against self-incrimination] occurs only at trial.")

QUESTIONS AND NOTES

1. Illustrative of the kind of public safety matters that warrant proceeding with unwarned interrogation are described in the guidelines as concerns about—

possible impending or coordinated terrorist attacks; the location, nature, and threat posed by weapons that might post an imminent danger to the public; and the identities, locations, and activities or intentions of accomplices who may be plotting additional imminent attacks.

Is it fair to describe information about such matters as terrorism intelligence?

2. The guidelines suggest that sometimes it may be appropriate to continue with unwarned interrogation even after there is no longer a public safety justification, that is, where—

agents ... conclude that continued unwarned interrogation is necessary to collect valuable and timely intelligence not related to any immediate threat, and that the government's interest in obtaining this intelligence outweighs the disadvantages of proceeding with unwarned interrogation.

a. How does the terrorism intelligence that involves a public safety justification differ from the terrorism intelligence that lacks such justification?

b. Referring to the last-quoted statement, what are "the disadvantages of proceeding with unwarned interrogation" that may be outweighed by "the government's interest in obtaining this intelligence"? What kind of disadvantages may be involved here?

c. Explain the consequences of proceeding with unwarned interrogation after the public safety justification no longer is applicable.

d. Assume that FBI agents interrogate a suspected operational terrorist in a situation where they are trying to gain intelligence about possible imminent terrorist attacks, and then continue with a wide-ranging inquiry to gain broader information about the terrorist network. The interrogation results in a lengthy transcript of the terrorist's responses to questions. What criterion should the court use to determine which statements in the transcript should be admissible in the criminal prosecution of the terrorist in federal court?

c. Coerced Confessions and Terrorism Intelligence

1) Since Miranda v. Arizona was decided in 1966, the U.S. Supreme Court has handed down very few coerced confession decisions, whereas prior to Miranda, Court decided many such cases. See, e.g., the following statement quoted by the Odeh court, suggesting an explanation for the fall-off in coerced confession decisions:

> ... [A]s the Supreme Court has observed, "cases in which a defendant can make a colorable argument that a self-incriminating statement was 'compelled' despite the fact that the law enforcement authorities adhered to the dictates of Miranda are rare."

Rather the focus where Miranda warnings have been given and the suspect waives and responds to questions tends to be on a different voluntariness issue, whether the waiver was voluntary. The very fact of the warnings and waiver makes it more difficult for the suspect to succeed with a claim of coercion.

Of course, if in future terrorism/intelligence interrogations, Miranda warnings (and consequent waivers) are not going to be given, or are not given early in the interrogation in reliance on exigent circumstances under the FBI guidelines, supra, the insulating effect of the Miranda warnings will not be present. In such cases, it will be as if we are thrust back into a pre-Miranda period where the focus is once more likely to be on whether the statements obtained are coerced within the meaning of the applicable constitutional principles.

2) In a series of decisions that preceded the Miranda decision in the decade of the 1950's and early 60's, the Supreme Court increasingly had found coercion in situations that did not involve physical brutality or the use of extreme methods of questioning. Thus, for example, the Supreme Court took into account: whether the confession was obtained by threats, for example, to prosecute a loved one, or to take away the custody of the suspect's children[9]; the fact that the police refused to allow the suspect to call his wife until he gave a statement[10]; whether some forms of deception were used, for example, a false friend technique where the police officer, a

---

9. See, e.g., Lynumn v. Illinois, 372 U.S. 528 (1963). Also see Rogers v. Richmond, 365 U.S. 534 (1961).

10. See Haynes v. Washington, 373 U.S. 503 (1963).

childhood friend of the suspect, told him that his calling him got him in trouble and put his job at risk[11]; and where the interrogator concealed the fact that he was a psychiatrist, leading the suspect to believe he was an ordinary physician who was there to treat his sinus condition.[12]

3) Recall the interrogation rules set forth in the Army Field Manual, supra, p. 317, especially the guidelines for interrogation methods that are permitted. How do the AFM methods compare with the police techniques described in the previous paragraph which the Supreme Court has held contributed to the determination that the confessions thereby obtained were coerced? Will use of the AFM-approved interrogation methods comply with constitutional coerced confession standards applied by the federal courts? For a proposal suggesting recognition of a public safety/intelligence exception to coerced confession doctrine, along the lines of the Quarles exception to the Miranda requirements, see Norman Abrams, Terrorism Prosecutions in Federal Court: Exceptions to Constitutional Evidence Rules and the Development of a Cabined Exception for Coerced Confessions, UCLA School of Law Research Paper No. 11–14 (2011).

UNITED STATES v. ABU ALI

528 F.3d 210 (4th Cir. 2008)

[Affirmed in part, reversed in part, and remanded by published opinion. JUDGE WILKINSON, JUDGE MOTZ, and JUDGE TRAXLER wrote a joint opinion in this case. JUDGE WILKINSON and JUDGE TRAXLER join the opinion in its entirety. JUDGE MOTZ joins the opinion with the exception of footnote 5 and Section VII [ed. not reproduced here], as to which she has written a dissenting statement and opinion.]

WILKINSON, MOTZ, and TRAXLER, CIRCUIT JUDGES:

Ahmed Omar Abu Ali was convicted by a jury of nine criminal counts arising from his affiliation with an al-Qaeda terrorist cell located in Medina, Saudi Arabia, and its plans to carry out a number of terrorist acts in this country. He was sentenced by the district court to 360 months imprisonment and 360 months of supervised release following imprisonment. Abu Ali appeals his convictions and the government cross-appeals his sentence. For the following reasons, we affirm the conviction, but we vacate and remand for purposes of resentencing.

Unlike some others suspected of terrorist acts and designs upon the United States, Abu Ali was formally charged and tried according to the customary processes of the criminal justice system. Persons of good will may disagree over the precise extent to which the formal criminal justice process must be utilized when those suspected of participation in terrorist cells and networks are involved. There should be no disagreement, however, that the criminal justice system does retain an important place in the ongoing effort to deter and punish terrorist acts without the sacrifice of

---

11.   See Spano v. New York, 360 U.S. 315 (1959).

12.   See Leyra v. Denno, 347 U.S. 556 (1954).

American constitutional norms and bedrock values. As will be apparent herein, the criminal justice system is not without those attributes of adaptation that will permit it to function in the post–9/11 world. These adaptations, however, need not and must not come at the expense of the requirement that an accused receive a fundamentally fair trial. In this case, we are satisfied that Abu Ali received a fair trial, though not a perfect one, and that the criminal justice system performed those functions which the Constitution envisioned for it. The three of us unanimously express our conviction that this is so in this opinion, which we have jointly authored.

Some differences do exist, however, among the panel members. Judge Wilkinson and Judge Traxler join in the opinion in its entirety. Judge Motz dissents (in footnote 6) from the majority's holding that the interrogation of Abu Ali on June 15, 2003, did not constitute a joint venture between law enforcement officers of Saudi Arabia and those of the United States. Judge Motz likewise dissents from Section VII of the panel's opinion, which directs that the case be remanded to the district court for the purposes of resentencing.

I.

A.

Abu Ali is an American citizen. He was born in Texas and raised in Falls Church, Virginia by his mother and father, the latter of whom was employed at the Royal Embassy of Saudi Arabia in Washington, D.C. After graduating from the Saudi Islamic Academy in Virginia, Abu Ali studied for one semester at the University of Maryland and then enrolled in the Institute in Virginia to study Islamic Sciences.

In September 2002, at the age of 21, Abu Ali left his home in Falls Church, Virginia and traveled to Saudi Arabia to study at the Islamic University in Medina. Within a few months of his arrival in Medina, Abu Ali contacted Moeith al-Qahtani ("al-Qahtani"). Abu Ali and al-Qahtani had become friends two years earlier when Abu Ali attended an Islamic summer study session in Saudi Arabia and, upon his return to Saudi Arabia, Abu Ali renewed the friendship. The two "often talked about jihad" and, in November 2002, al-Qahtani introduced Abu Ali to Sultan Jubran Sultan al-Qahtani ("Sultan Jubran"), who was also known by the name of "Ali." Sultan Jubran had been a mujahid soldier during the United States bombing of Tora Bora in Afghanistan (a major battle between al-Qaeda/Taliban forces and United States forces during the Afghanistan invasion) and, when introduced to Abu Ali, was second-in-command of an al-Qaeda cell in Medina. Abu Ali "accepted and liked the idea" of meeting the "mujahid brother." After their introduction, he and Sultan Jubran also talked "about the virtues of jihad" and exchanged cell phone numbers to keep in touch.

In the ensuing months, Abu Ali and Sultan Jubran continued their discussions.... Shortly thereafter, Sultan Jubran did contact Abu Ali and the two men met again in Jiddah, Saudi Arabia, which is just to the south of Medina. At this meeting, Sultan Jubran urged Abu Ali to engage in jihad against America. According to Abu Ali, Sultan Jubran "told me that they had something to do" and "asked [me] to be ready to join them in working against America." Abu Ali "immediately accepted, because of my hatred of the [United States] for what I felt was its support of Israel against the Palestinian people, and because I was originally from Jerusalem."

Later, Sultan Jubran advised Abu Ali that Abu Ali would soon be meeting "the person in charge of the organization." According to Abu Ali, Sultan Jubran "explained to me that I was one of them now, and that I could speak in the name of al-Qaeda." A few days later, Sultan Jubran arranged a meeting between himself, Abu Ali, and Ali Abd alRahman al-Faq'asi al-Ghamdi ("al-Faq'asi"), the leader or "brother in charge" of the al-Qaeda terrorist cell in Medina, who was also known by the name of "Adil."

Abu Ali and al-Faq'asi met a number of times thereafter to discuss the Medina cell's plans for jihad. More specifically, al-Faq'asi advised Abu Ali that an assignment was planned inside the United States and the two men discussed and considered a number of alternatives for terrorist attacks within the United States. According to Abu Ali, al-Faq'asi "presented me with two ideas, based on the fact that I was a [United States] citizen and that I had not engaged in jihad before." "The first idea was to carry out a major operation that he would arrange." The second was "that I would go to the [United States], settle down, find work, lead a normal life, blend into American society and marry a Christian," which would allow him to "plan successive operations inside the [United States] for which . . . al-Faq'asi would send individuals to carry out." In other words, Abu Ali, who was a United States citizen able to return at will and move freely about in the country, would marry a Christian woman, live an overtly normal life to deflect attention, establish a sleeper cell within this country, and prepare for operation instructions and additional operatives to assist.

After this introduction to al-Faq'asi, Abu Ali "became directly connected" to the leader of the cell and "stopped seeing or hearing from Sultan" Jubran. However, he "continued to meet . . . al-Faq'asi in various places" and "discuss [ed] how to carry out the assignment in the [United States]." According to Abu Ali, he met with al-Faq'asi on six separate occasions to plan such terrorist operations within the United States. In the course of these meetings, Abu Ali suggested assassinations or kidnappings of members of the United States Senate, the United States Army, and the Bush Administration, a plan to rescue the prisoners at Guantanamo Bay, and plans to blow up American warplanes on United States bases and at United States ports, similar to the USS Cole operation. Al–Faq'asi suggested an operation similar to the 9/11 bombings, but which would originate in planes departing from Britain or Australia for Canada in order to circumvent the requirements of a United States visa to enter the country, and plans to assassinate President Bush. With regard to the presidential assassination, Abu Ali suggested two possibilities: an assassination plot involving at least three snipers to fire upon the President while in public or a martyr operation conducted while the President was out greeting the public.

In the course of these plans and discussions, Al–Faq'asi requested that Abu Ali move out of the dormitory where he lived and advised Abu Ali that a "suitable residence" would be found where he "could be trained on manufacturing explosives, information gathering, and forgery." Abu Ali went with al-Faq'asi to live in a villa in the al-Iskan neighborhood in Medina for training. Using the name "Ashraf," Abu Ali was trained by a man called "Ahmad" on how to assemble and disassemble the Kalashnikov machine gun, five of which were located in the villa along with ammunition. . . .

In addition to training, the al-Faq'asi Medina cell provided Abu Ali with finances and equipment. He was given money to buy a laptop computer, a cell phone, and books, as well as written materials on security and methods of concealment. He was also given a USB memory chip that included a clip taken during the bombing of Afghanistan which contained the voices of American pilots, and tasked with translating the recording into Arabic.

. . .

. . . [O]n May 12, 2003, al-Qaeda carried out a number of suicide bombings in Riyadh, killing approximately 34 people including 9 Americans. That night, Abu Ali and the other cell members performed guard duty at the cell's safehouses. After the bombings, Abu Ali and a number of the others moved to a second villa in an al-Iskan neighborhood where they stayed for three days, although Abu Ali did not spend the night in the villa with the others. According to Abu Ali, the villa contained "a dimly-lit room that contained wires and cell phones, . . . machine guns, ammunition, a pistol and a hand grenade." Later, the group moved back to the farm, where Abu Ali continued his training in explosives and forgery. He received lessons from Majid (Mohammad Salem al-Ghamdi) on forging and removing seals, altering photos, and removing visas, and received lessons from al-Faq'asi on explosives, making explosives, and compounds. Another man, Umar al-Hakmi, provided lessons on fuses and wiring.

On May 26 and 27, 2003, authorities with the Saudi Mabahith received orders to raid several suspected terrorist safe houses in Medina, including the safe house in the Al–Azhari villa where Abu Ali had received training. Among the evidence retrieved during the search of one safe house was an English translation of an American pilot's radio transmission and a paper with Abu Ali's additional alias names of "Hani" and "Hanimohawk" written on it. The authorities also recovered a number of automatic rifles and guns, ammunition, fertilizer, hand grenades, cell phones which were being converted to explosives, as well as computers, cameras, walkie-talkies, and laminating equipment for identification cards. A number of members of the al-Faq'asi terrorist cell were arrested during the raids, including al-Ghamdi, who had trained Abu Ali, and Sheikh Nasser, who had given Abu Ali the blessing for the presidential assassination. Al–Faq'asi and Sultan Jubran, disguised in women's clothing, escaped.

During subsequent questioning by the Saudi authorities, al-Ghamdi informed the Mabahith that one of their members was a student at the University of Medina of either American or European background who went by the alias "Reda" or "Ashraf." Further investigative efforts resulted in the photo identification of Abu Ali as the American or European member of the cell.

On June 8, 2003, Abu Ali was arrested by the Mabahith at the Islamic University in Medina and his dormitory room was searched. Among the items found there were a GPS device, jihad literature, a walkie talkie, a United States passport, a Jordanian passport and identification card, a Nokia cellular telephone, a telephone notebook containing al-Qahtani's name, and literature on jihad. Abu Ali was then flown from Medina to Riyadh, where he was interrogated by the Mabahith. Although he initially denied involvement with the al-Faq'asi cell, he confessed when the Mabahith officers addressed him with his alias names of "Reda" and "Ashraf." Specifically, Abu Ali confessed to his affiliation with al-Qaeda and, in particular, the Medina cell headed by al-Faq'asi. According to Abu Ali, he joined the al-Qaeda cell "to prepare and train for an operation inside the [United States]," including an "intention to prepare and train to kill the [United States] President." In addition to written confessions, the Mabahith obtained a videotaped confession in which Abu Ali admitted his affiliation with the Medina cell and its plans to conduct terrorist operations within the United States, including the plan to assassinate President Bush and to destroy airliners destined to this country.

Following Abu Ali's arrest by the Saudi authorities, the FBI was notified of his suspected involvement in the al-Qaeda cell in Saudi Arabia and advised that the cell was planning on conducting terrorism operations in the United States. Although the FBI requested access to Abu Ali, the Mabahith denied the request. On June 15, 2003, the Mabahith allowed the FBI to supply proposed questions, but later rejected the list and the breadth of the inquiry sought. Ultimately, the Mabahith only agreed to ask Abu Ali six of those questions and to allow the FBI officers to observe his responses through a one-way mirror. Abu Ali was asked whether he was tasked to assassinate the President (as had been reported by the Mabahith to the FBI), when he arrived in Saudi Arabia, whether he knew of any planned terrorist attacks against American, Saudi, or Western interests, whether he was recruited by any terrorist organization, whether he had used false passports, and the nature of his father's position in the Embassy. Other than consular contact, the United States was denied all access to Abu Ali until September of 2003.

In the meantime, on June 16, 2003, the FBI obtained and executed a search warrant at Abu Ali's home in Virginia. Among the items found there, the agents discovered a printout of the buddy list of email addresses from MSN Hotmail account Ahmedabuali@hotmail.com, which contained an address of abumuslim99@hotmail.com for al-Qahtani, an address book containing the name of al-Qahtani, a two-page article praising the 9/11 attacks in this country, a handguns magazine addressed to Abu Ali which contained a feature article on methods for the concealed carrying of handguns, and an email message from an unknown individual to Abu Ali discussing opportunities for Muslim fighters in the conflict between Muslim rebels and Russians in Chechnya.

B.

On February 3, 2005, a federal grand jury returned an indictment against Abu Ali. The Saudi officials surrendered Abu Ali to United States authorities and he was flown back to the United States on February 21, 2005 ... In the superseding indictment, Abu Ali was charged with the following offenses: Conspiracy to Provide Material Support and Resources to a Designated Foreign Terrorist Organization (al-Qaeda), in violation of 18 U.S.C.A. § 2339B (Count 1); Providing Material Support and Resources to a Designated Foreign Terrorist Organization (al-Qaeda), in violation of 18 U.S.C.A. § 2339B (Count 2); Conspiracy to Provide Material Support to Terrorists, in violation of 18 U.S.C.A. § 2339A (Count 3); Providing Material Support to Terrorists, in violation of 18 U.S.C.A. § 2339A (Count 4); Contribution of Services to al-Qaeda, in violation of 50 U.S.C.A. § 1705(b), 31 C.F.R. § 595.204 (Count 5); Receipt of Funds and Services from al-Qaeda, 50 U.S.C.A. § 1705(b), 31 C.F.R. § 595.204 (Count 6); Conspiracy to Assassinate the President of the United States, 18 U.S.C. § 1751 (Count 7); Conspiracy to Commit Aircraft Piracy, 49 U.S.C.A. § 46502(a)(2) (Count 8); and Conspiracy to Destroy Aircraft, 18 U.S.C.A. § 32(b)(4) (Count 9).

On November 22, 2005, Abu Ali was convicted of all charges. He was subsequently sentenced to 360 months imprisonment to be followed by a term of 360 months of supervised release. Abu Ali appeals his convictions and his sentence on a number of grounds and the government cross-appeals the sentence.

. . .

Abu Ali next claims that all of his statements and confessions while in Saudi custody should have been suppressed as involuntary. The district court rejected this argument, finding that the government had "demonstrated by a 'preponderance of the evidence' that any incriminating statements" made by Abu Ali while in Saudi custody in June and July, 2003, were "voluntary" and so admissible at trial.

When *Miranda* warnings are unnecessary, as in the case of an interrogation by foreign officials, we assess the voluntariness of a defendant's statements by asking whether the confession is "the product of an essentially free and unconstrained choice by its maker." If it is, "it may be used against him." But, if the defendant's "will has been overborne and his capacity for self-determination critically impaired, the use of his confession offends due process." The government acknowledges that "[t]he crucial inquiry is whether [Abu Ali's] will has been 'overborne,'" and maintains that it was not; Abu Ali, of course, contends that it was.

In evaluating whether a defendant's will has been overborne, courts must assess the totality of the circumstances, taking into account characteristics of the accused, and details of the interrogation ...: "the youth of the accused, his lack of education, or his low intelligence, the lack of any advice to the accused of his constitutional rights, the length of detention, the repeated and prolonged nature of the questioning, and the use of physical punishment such as the deprivation of food or sleep." We review a trial court's legal conclusion as to the voluntariness of an accused's statements *de novo,* but its "findings of fact on the circumstances surrounding the confession" for clear error. We particularly defer to a district court's credibility determinations, for "it is the role of the district court to observe witnesses and weigh their credibility during a pre-trial motion to suppress."

In this case, after hearing nearly fourteen days of testimony, the court issued a 113–page opinion describing and analyzing the testimony of over 20 witnesses, including Abu Ali, his Saudi captors, FBI agents, and American consular officials who met with Abu Ali during his detention in Saudi Arabia, as well as psychiatrists, other doctors, and nurses. The court evaluated the demeanor and testimony of these witnesses, and then made extensive findings of fact as to the credibility of the witnesses, including Abu Ali, and the conditions of Abu Ali's confinement and interrogation. We need only briefly summarize these factual findings here.

Initially, the court properly recognized that "torture, and evidence obtained thereby, have no place in the American system of justice." But, based on its evaluations of "the credibility of the witnesses," and "the quality of the evidence presented," the district court found itself "left with lingering questions concerning the credibility of Mr. Abu Ali and his claim that he was tortured," The court credited the testimony of the Saudi Arresting Officer and the Lieutenant Colonel (the Warden at the Medina detention facility where Abu Ali was held for two days following his arrest) that no Saudi official used coercive interrogation techniques on Abu Ali. The court found that the Lieutenant Colonel's testimony that Abu Ali was never abused was believable while Abu Ali's contrary testimony "raise[d] questions that bear on the defendant's credibility."

In addition, the court relied on the testimony of two other Saudi officials, the Brigadier General and the Captain, that the interrogation of Abu Ali in Riyadh "was conducted in the absence of threats or torture." The court found "implausible" Abu Ali's "claim about having been whipped" during the early period of his detention because several Saudi and American witnesses who observed him during this period reported behavior "that do[es] not coincide with how a recently beaten person would behave." Moreover, the court found that "[s]ome aspects" of Abu Ali's testimony "just do not flow logically," and observed that "during his testimony, there were times where Mr. Abu Ali seemed to deflect the question," Finally, the court considered, but found deficiencies in, the testimony of Abu Ali's medical experts who supported his torture claim, crediting instead the testimony of the government's experts that Abu Ali showed no physical or psychological signs of mistreatment.

The district court largely rested its legal conclusion that Abu Ali's statements were voluntary on its factual findings concerning his claims of torture and abuse. Our thorough review of the record provides no basis for finding clear error in any of those findings. This, however, does not end our inquiry. We must evaluate the voluntariness of Abu Ali's confessions *de novo,* looking to the totality of the circumstances to determine whether his will was "overborne."

In making this evaluation, we consider that Abu Ali was not provided the legal protections—including prompt presentment and Miranda warnings—that the Constitution requires be provided to suspects by United States law enforcement officers. Saudi Arabia is a sovereign nation with its own legal system, and the failure to provide Abu Ali these protections does not, in and of itself, require exclusion of the statements Abu Ali made in Saudi custody. At the same time, we do consider the absence of these protections as one factor in the totality of circumstances in evaluating whether Abu Ali made his statements voluntarily.

In making this voluntariness determination, we also look to the district court's factual findings as to Abu Ali's personal characteristics, and the conditions of his confinement. The court noted that Abu Ali "is an intelligent, well-educated man with a rich and graphic vocabulary," and found him "intelligent, capable, and articulate." It is undisputed that Abu Ali attended school in Saudi Arabia, and he does not allege any religious, cultural, or linguistic difficulties in dealing with his Saudi interrogators. Indeed, he responded to his interrogators' questions in Arabic, and the district court found that the Saudi officers provided him with a prayer rug and Koran among other accommodations. For these reasons, Abu Ali's personal characteristics did not render him particularly susceptible to coercion or pressure.

In addition, the district court rejected Abu Ali's testimony that the Saudis subjected him to coercive conditions of confinement. Instead, the court found believable the testimony of Saudi officers that they confined Abu Ali under reasonable conditions, including provision of three meals a day, and a cell with a bed, blanket and pillow. The court further found believable Saudi testimony that Saudi authorities did not question Abu Ali during his initial detention in Medina, and noted that Abu Ali's own description of the Riyadh interrogation suggested that he was not questioned in Medina.

Saudi authorities did question Abu Ali after transporting him to Riyadh on June 10, 2003. But, the district court credited their testimony that "Abu Ali was granted breaks, access to food, water, a bathroom, and refreshments during breaks in questioning," and that they did not attempt to deprive him of sleep. The court further found believable testimony from Saudi authorities that during just the second session of questioning, on June 11th, Abu Ali "began his lengthy and detailed confession." Abu Ali's extensive written responses to questions, beginning June 11, 2003—his second day in Riyadh—support this finding. Although the questioning of Abu Ali lasted many days, that he began to confess in great detail on just the second day of interrogation indicates that his will was not overborne by prolonged questioning.

After consideration of all of the evidence and the extensive factual findings made by the district court, we conclude that Abu Ali's statements were voluntary. Abu Ali was intelligent, articulate, and comfortable with the language and culture of the country in which he was detained and questioned. The district court found, based upon copious record evidence, that he was not tortured, abused, threatened, held in cruel conditions, or subjected to coercive interrogations. On the basis of the totality of these circumstances, we conclude that Abu Ali's statements were "the product of an essentially free and unconstrained choice."

QUESTIONS AND NOTES

1. Abu Ali, the defendant in the principal case, was not given Miranda warnings by his Saudi interrogators. The court ruled that this failure was not a violation of his rights, but that if U.S. agents had been joint venturers with the Saudis in the interrogation, the failure to give Miranda warnings would have violated his rights. A majority of the panel, in a portion not reproduced here, concluded that on the facts there was no joint venture between the U.S. agents and the Saudis in conducting the interrogation. Do you agree with this conclusion? What facts bear on the issue?

2. The issue presented in the excerpt from the principal case reproduced here is whether Abu Ali's confession to the Saudi interrogators was coerced. If it was, the confession would have been inadmissible. What standard does the court apply in determining whether his confession was coerced? Did the court apply the same standard of voluntariness that it would have applied to an interrogation conducted by U.S. agents? Should it be the same standard? Compare footnote 5 in the Odeh case, supra.

3. Compare with Abu Ali, the decision in United States v. Karake, 443 F.Supp.2d 8 (D.D.C. 2006). Rwandan nationals and members of the Liberation Army of Rwanda (ALIR), were charged with murder, conspiracy to commit murder, and using a firearm during a crime of violence in connection with the killings of two United States tourists in Uganda. In a motion to suppress hearing the district court held that the defendants, statements were inadmissible: the statements to Rwandan officials were involuntary; the taint of the earlier involuntary statements was not attenuated in connection with the

statements made by the defendants to U.S. officials; and any waiver of Miranda rights was not voluntary.

Except for Nyaminani's two earliest statements, all of the statements at issue were made while defendants were housed at what the Rwandans have referred to as a military "barracks," known as Kami, located outside the Rwandan capital of Kigali. Kami Camp, approximately 200 acres in size, houses between 90 and 120 Rwandan soldiers. According to Captain Alex Kibingo, who was in charge of Kami during the relevant time period, the camp was used to store military equipment such as uniforms, guns and bullets. Kami also served as a detention center for Rwandan soldiers who were subject to disciplinary action and captured ALIR soldiers prior to their transport to repatriation camps in Rwanda's Ruhengeri province. Most, but not all, of the statements obtained by Rwandan officials out of the presence of Americans were taken at Kami by Kibingo. Defendants were transported from Kami to the Rwandan National Police Headquarters at Kacyiru ("Police Headquarters" or "Kacyiru") for all of the interrogations in which American investigators participated.

. . .

While the Court has thoroughly explained its reasons for rejecting Kibingo's testimony and for its finding that defendants' statements were the product of coercion, there is one further observation that convinces the Court of the correctness of its credibility determinations and its ultimate finding of involuntariness. Over the course of the defendants' detention at Kami, an unmistakable pattern continually repeated itself. Each defendant initially denied his involvement at Bwindi, but was then held incommunicado at Kami until Kibingo extracted statements that he believed were wanted either by his superiors or the Americans and were needed in order to solve the murders, close the investigation, or support a prosecution. With the exception of Nyaminani, the Rwandans did not even inform the U.S. investigators that they had a suspect in custody until they were informed that a defendant had confessed, and each initial confession was obtained only by Kibingo while no one else was present. He would then deliver the information to his superiors who, in turn, several days later, would contact Kayumba, at which point Bachmann would conduct an interrogation. If the defendant provided less information than was expected, as happened with respect to each defendant, he was returned to Kami and subjected to further interrogation and mistreatment. Only after Kibingo announced to the Rwandans that he had obtained further information, was the defendant returned to the Americans for more questioning.

C. IRREGULAR RENDITION

1. INTRODUCTION

In the post–9/11 years, the U.S. government with some frequency apprehended suspected terrorists outside of the United States and detained and interrogated them. Some continued to be detained for a period at so-called "black sites". Others were transferred to the Guantanamo Bay detention facility, and still others were reportedly transferred to other countries where they were imprisoned and further interrogated. We have little detailed information about these practices variously termed, extraordinary or irregular rendition, that is, the surreptitious transfer of individuals against their will, often without the official permission of the country in which the travel begins and without going through traditional legal process such as extradition or ordinary rendition where the first country cooperates with sending the individual to another country.

Because U.S. courts generally rule that in a criminal case, the court will not inquire into how the defendant was brought before the court, whether by unlawful or law means, in criminal cases questions of alleged irregularity of the rendition have not been litigated While some civil lawsuits have been filed by alleged victims of such activities seeking redress, the government has, through invocation of different legal doctrines, generally been able to avoid judicial consideration of the propriety of the government's actions. Generally, the courts have not reached the merits of the plaintiffs' cases.

One consequence of this situation is that our information regarding these practices is limited; most of what we "know" has come from the allegations of the "victims" and some unofficial investigations. We have, accordingly, included here material regarding some of the civil lawsuits that have been filed because they contain the best information available, limited as it is. In addition, in a couple of instances, a foreign government has brought a prosecution against U.S. officials located there, accusing them of participating in illegal rendition actions in their country, and we have included information about these cases, too. Finally, some efforts have been made to obtain information through freedom of information lawsuits and by committees of the Congress, but these have not been very successful.

When persons suspected of crimes violative of U.S. law, including terrorists, are apprehended abroad, and the government wishes to bring them to the United States for trial, interrogation or detention, there are a number of traditional, lawful ways in which such removal can be effected. In this chapter we review these traditional ways as background for our consideration of the practice of irregular or extraordinary rendition.

The normal way in which individuals who have been apprehended in a foreign country are brought to the United States to be prosecuted is through the legal procedure of extradition which is governed by treaties between various foreign countries and the United States.

A second possibility is that the individual waives extradition and is voluntarily transferred to the U.S. See, e.g., Hong Kong Terror Suspects Agree to Extradition to U.S., LA Times, January 6, 2002, at A4.

A third possibility is that police of the foreign jurisdiction turn the individual over to U.S. officials informally for transportation back to the U.S. For example, the individual might be put on an airliner and into the custody of U.S. agents who would then transport the person to the United States. Compare the handing over of Verdugo–Urquidez to U.S. agents, as described by Chief Justice Rehnquist, *supra*, p. 261.

A fourth possibility is reflected in a type of sting operation involving apprehension in international waters, such as that described below in an excerpt from United States v. Yunis, 924 F.2d 1086 (D.C.Cir.1991):

> An American investigation identified Yunis as the probable leader of the hijackers and prompted U.S. civilian and military agencies, led by the Federal Bureau of Investigation (FBI), to plan Yunis' arrest. After obtaining an arrest warrant, the FBI put "Operation Goldenrod" into effect in September 1987. Undercover FBI agents lured Yunis onto a yacht in the eastern Mediterranean Sea with promises of a drug deal, and arrested him once the vessel entered international waters. The agents transferred Yunis to a United States Navy munitions ship and interrogated him for several days as the vessel steamed toward a second rendezvous, this time with a Navy aircraft carrier. Yunis was flown to Andrews Air Force Base from the aircraft carrier, and taken from there to Washington, D.C.

A fifth possibility involves forcibly kidnapping the person in a foreign country, with or without, the cooperation or acquiescence of officials of the host country. This type of fact scenario led to the Supreme Court's decision in United States v. Alvarez–Machain, 504 U.S. 655 (1992). It also led to the criminal prosecution in Italy of CIA agents and other U.S. officials. See infra p. 392.

Closely related to the kidnapping of a person to bring him/her back to the U.S. for trial, as reflected in the Alvarez–Machain case, is the, previously-mentioned practice that has arisen in the context of present-day anti-terrorism enforcement—irregular rendition. An example of an early news report about the practice is Wash. Post, December 27, 2004, p. A01, reporting on a mysterious Gulfstream V turbojet that was purportedly being used by the CIA to carry out "renditions," transporting suspected terrorists to various countries, with one of the suspected purposes, "to transfer captives to countries that use harsh interrogation methods outlawed in the United States."

Among the early actions of the Obama administration was to close down CIA "black" sites in foreign countries where some prisoners were detained and interrogated. See the Executive Order issued on January 22, 2009, *supra*, p. 322. The Obama administration did not indicate that it would stop the practice of irregular rendition, and there have been indications that the practice continues. See, e.g., U.S. to Prosecute a Somali Suspect in Civilian Court, NY Times A1, July 6, 2011, reporting on a person seized abroad, interrogated on a U.S. ship and then transferred to New York for prosecution in a federal district court.

We begin treatment of this subject with the Supreme Court's decision in a kidnapping case where there was an extradition treaty between the two concerned countries.

2.   KIDNAPPING IN LIEU OF EXTRADITION; EXTRADITION TREATIES

UNITED STATES v. ALVAREZ–MACHAIN

504 U.S. 655 (1992)

[REHNQUIST, C.J., delivered the opinion of the Court, in which WHITE, SCALIA, KENNEDY, SOUTER, and THOMAS, JJ., joined. STEVENS, J., filed a dissenting opinion, in which BLACKMUN and O'CONNOR, JJ., joined]

CHIEF JUSTICE REHNQUIST delivered the opinion of the Court.

The issue in this case is whether a criminal defendant, abducted to the United States from a nation with which it has an extradition treaty, thereby acquires a defense to the jurisdiction of this country's courts. We hold that he does not, and that he may be tried in federal district court for violations of the criminal law of the United States.

Respondent, Humberto Alvarez–Machain, is a citizen and resident of Mexico. He was indicted for participating in the kidnap and murder of United States Drug Enforcement Administration (DEA) special agent Enrique Camarena–Salazar and a Mexican pilot working with Camarena, Alfredo Zavala–Avelar. The DEA believes that respondent, a medical doctor, participated in the murder by prolonging Agent Camarena's life so that others could further torture and interrogate him. On April 2, 1990, respondent was forcibly kidnaped from his medical office in Guadalajara, Mexico, to be flown by private plane to El Paso, Texas, where he was arrested by DEA officials. The District Court concluded that DEA agents were responsible for respondent's abduction, although they were not personally involved in it. *United States v. Caro–Quintero*, 745 F.Supp. 599, 602–604, 609 (C.D.Cal.1990).[15]

Respondent moved to dismiss the indictment, claiming that his abduction constituted outrageous governmental conduct, and that the District Court lacked jurisdiction to try him because he was abducted in violation of the extradition treaty between the United States and Mexico. Extradition Treaty, May 4, 1978, [1979] United States–United Mexican States, 31 U.S. T. 5059, T. I. A. S. No. 9656 (Extradition Treaty or Treaty). The District Court rejected the outrageous governmental conduct claim, but held that it lacked jurisdiction to try respondent because his abduction violated the Extradition Treaty. The District Court discharged respondent and ordered that he be repatriated to Mexico. 745 F.Supp. at 614.

The Court of Appeals affirmed the dismissal of the indictment and the repatriation of respondent, relying on its decision in *United States v. Verdugo–Urquidez*, 939 F.2d 1341 (C.A.9 1991), cert. pending, No. 91–670,

---

15. Apparently, DEA officials had attempted to gain respondent's presence in the United States through informal negotiations with Mexican officials, but were unsuccessful. DEA officials then, through a contact in Mexico, offered to pay a reward and expenses in return for the delivery of respondent to the United States. *United States v. Caro–Quintero*, 745 F.Supp. at 602–604.

946 F.2d 1466 (1991). In *Verdugo*, the Court of Appeals held that the forcible abduction of a Mexican national with the authorization or participation of the United States violated the Extradition Treaty between the United States and Mexico. Although the Treaty does not expressly prohibit such abductions, the Court of Appeals held that the "purpose" of the Treaty was violated by a forcible abduction, 939 F.2d at 1350, which, along with a formal protest by the offended nation, would give a defendant the right to invoke the Treaty violation to defeat jurisdiction of the District Court to try him. The Court of Appeals further held that the proper remedy for such a violation would be dismissal of the indictment and repatriation of the defendant to Mexico.

. . .

We granted certiorari, and now reverse.

Although we have never before addressed the precise issue raised in the present case, we have previously considered proceedings in claimed violation of an extradition treaty and proceedings against a defendant brought before a court by means of a forcible abduction. We addressed the former issue in *United States v. Rauscher*, 119 U.S. 407, 30 L.Ed. 425, 7 S.Ct. 234 (1886); more precisely, the issue whether the Webster–Ashburton Treaty of 1842, 8 Stat. 576, which governed extraditions between England and the United States, prohibited the prosecution of defendant Rauscher for a crime other than the crime for which he had been extradited. Whether this prohibition, known as the doctrine of specialty, was an intended part of the treaty had been disputed between the two nations for some time. *Rauscher*, 119 U.S. at 411. Justice Miller delivered the opinion of the Court, which carefully examined the terms and history of the treaty; the practice of nations in regards to extradition treaties; the case law from the States; and the writings of commentators, and reached the following conclusion:

> "[A] person who has been brought within the jurisdiction of the court *by virtue of proceedings under an extradition treaty*, can only be tried for one of the offences described in that treaty, and for the offence with which he is charged in the proceedings for his extradition, until a reasonable time and opportunity have been given him, after his release or trial upon such charge, to return to the country from whose asylum he had been forcibly taken under those proceedings." *Id.*, at 430 (emphasis added).

. . . Unlike the case before us today, the defendant in *Rauscher* had been brought to the United States by way of an extradition treaty; there was no issue of a forcible abduction.

In *Ker v. Illinois*, 119 U.S. 436, 30 L.Ed. 421, 7 S.Ct. 225 (1886), also written by Justice Miller and decided the same day as *Rauscher*, we addressed the issue of a defendant brought before the court by way of a forcible abduction. Frederick Ker had been tried and convicted in an Illinois court for larceny; his presence before the court was procured by means of forcible abduction from Peru. A messenger was sent to Lima with the proper warrant to demand Ker by virtue of the extradition treaty between Peru and the United States. The messenger, however, disdained reliance on the treaty processes, and instead forcibly kidnaped Ker and brought him to the United States. We distinguished Ker's case from *Rauscher*, on the basis that Ker was not brought into the United States by virtue of the extradition treaty between the United States and Peru, and rejected Ker's argument that he had a right under the extradition treaty to be returned to this country only in accordance with its terms. We rejected Ker's due process argument more broadly, holding in line with "the highest authorities" that "such forcible abduction is no sufficient reason why the party should not answer when brought within the jurisdiction of the court which has the right to try him for such an offence, and presents no valid objection to his trial in such court." *Ker, supra*, at 444.

. . .

In *Frisbie v. Collins*, 342 U.S. 519, 96 L.Ed. 541, 72 S.Ct. 509, rehearing denied, 343 U.S. 937, 96 L.Ed. 1344, 72 S.Ct. 768 (1952), we applied the rule in *Ker* to a case in which the defendant had been kidnaped in Chicago by Michigan officers and brought to trial in Michigan. We upheld the conviction over objections based on the Due Process Clause and the federal Kidnaping Act and stated:

> "This Court has never departed from the rule announced in *[Ker]* that the power of a court to try a person for crime is not impaired by the fact that he had been brought within the court's jurisdiction by reason of a 'forcible abduction.' No persuasive reasons are now presented to justify overruling this line of cases. They rest on the sound basis that due process of law is satisfied when one present in court is convicted of crime after having been fairly apprized of the charges against him and after a fair trial in accordance with constitutional procedural safeguards. There is nothing in the Constitution that requires a court to permit a guilty person rightfully convicted to escape justice because he was brought to trial against his will." *Frisbie, supra*, at 522.

The only differences between *Ker* and the present case are that *Ker* was decided on the premise that there was no governmental involvement in the abduction, 119 U.S. at 443; and Peru, from which Ker was abducted, did not object to his prosecution. Respondent finds these differences to be dispositive, as did the Court of Appeals in *Verdugo*, contending that they show that respondent's prosecution, like the prosecution of Rauscher, violates the implied terms of a valid extradition treaty. The Government, on the other hand, argues that *Rauscher* stands as an "exception" to the rule in *Ker* only when an extradition treaty is invoked, and the terms of the treaty provide that its breach will limit the jurisdiction of a court. Therefore, our first inquiry must be whether the abduction of respondent from Mexico violated the Extradition Treaty between the United States and Mexico. If we conclude that the Treaty does not prohibit respondent's abduction, the rule in *Ker* applies, and the court need not inquire as to how respondent came before it.

In construing a treaty, as in construing a statute, we first look to its terms to determine its meaning. The Treaty says nothing about the obligations of the United States and Mexico to refrain from forcible abductions of people from the territory of the other nation, or the consequences under the Treaty if such an abduction occurs. Respondent submits that Article 22(1) of the Treaty, which states that it "shall apply to offenses specified in Article 2 [including murder] committed before and after this Treaty enters into force," evidences an intent to make application of the Treaty mandatory for those offenses. However, the more natural conclusion is that Article 22 was included to ensure that the Treaty was applied to extraditions requested after the Treaty went into force, regardless of when the crime of extradition occurred.

More critical to respondent's argument is Article 9 of the Treaty, which provides:

> "1. Neither Contracting Party shall be bound to deliver up its own nationals, but the executive authority of the requested Party shall, if not prevented by the laws of that Party, have the power to deliver them up if, in its discretion, it be deemed proper to do so.

> "2. If extradition is not granted pursuant to paragraph 1 of this Article, the requested Party shall submit the case to its competent authorities for the purpose of prosecution, provided that Party has jurisdiction over the offense."

According to respondent, Article 9 embodies the terms of the bargain which the United States struck: If the United States wishes to prosecute a Mexican national, it may request that individual's extradition. Upon a request from the United States, Mexico may either extradite the individual or submit the case to the proper authorities for prosecution in Mexico. In this way, respondent reasons, each nation preserved its right to choose whether its nationals would be tried in its own courts or by the courts of the other nation. This preservation of rights would be frustrated if either nation were free to abduct nationals of the other nation for the purposes of prosecution. More broadly, respondent reasons, as did the Court of Appeals, that all the processes and restrictions on the obligation to extradite established by the Treaty would make no sense if either nation were free to resort to forcible kidnaping to gain the presence of an individual for prosecution in a manner not contemplated by the Treaty.

We do not read the Treaty in such a fashion. Article 9 does not purport to specify the only way in which one country may gain custody of a national of the other country for the purposes of prosecution. In the absence of an extradition treaty, nations are under no obligation to surrender those in their country to foreign authorities for prosecution.... Extradition treaties exist so as to impose mutual obligations to surrender individuals in certain defined sets of circumstances, following established procedures. See 1 J. Moore, A Treatise on Extradition and Interstate

Rendition § 72 (1891). The Treaty thus provides a mechanism which would not otherwise exist, requiring, under certain circumstances, the United States and Mexico to extradite individuals to the other country, and establishing the procedures to be followed when the Treaty is invoked.

The history of negotiation and practice under the Treaty also fails to show that abductions outside of the Treaty constitute a violation of the Treaty. As the Solicitor General notes, the Mexican Government was made aware, as early as 1906, of the *Ker* doctrine, and the United States' position that it applied to forcible abductions made outside of the terms of the United States–Mexico Extradition Treaty.[16] Nonetheless, the current version of the Treaty, signed in 1978, does not attempt to establish a rule that would in any way curtail the effect of *Ker*.[17] Moreover, although language which would grant individuals exactly the right sought by respondent had been considered and drafted as early as 1935 by a prominent group of legal scholars sponsored by the faculty of Harvard Law School, no such clause appears in the current Treaty.[18]

Thus, the language of the Treaty, in the context of its history, does not support the proposition that the Treaty prohibits abductions outside of its terms. The remaining question, therefore, is whether the Treaty should be interpreted so as to include an implied term prohibiting prosecution where the defendant's presence is obtained by means other than those established by the Treaty. . . .

Respondent contends that the Treaty must be interpreted against the backdrop of customary international law, and that international abductions are "so clearly prohibited in international law" that there was no reason to include such a clause in the Treaty itself. The international censure of international abductions is further evidenced, according to respondent, by the United Nations Charter and the Charter of the Organization of American States. Respondent does not argue that these

---

16. In correspondence between the United States and Mexico growing out of the 1905 Martinez incident, in which a Mexican national was abducted from Mexico and brought to the United States for trial, the Mexican Charge wrote to the Secretary of State protesting that as Martinez' arrest was made outside of the procedures established in the extradition treaty, "the action pending against the man can not rest [on] any legal foundation." Letter of Balbino Davalos to Secretary of State, reprinted in Papers Relating to the Foreign Relations of the United States, H. R. Doc. No. 1, 59th Cong., 2d Sess., pt. 2, p. 1121 (1906). The Secretary of State responded that the exact issue raised by the Martinez incident had been decided by *Ker*, and that the remedy open to the Mexican Government, namely, a request to the United States for extradition of Martinez' abductor, had been granted by the United States. Letter of Robert Bacon to Mexican Charge, reprinted in Papers Relating to the Foreign Relations of the United States, H. R. Doc. No. 1, *supra*, at 1121–1122.

17. The parties did expressly include the doctrine of specialty in Article 17 of the Treaty, notwithstanding the judicial recognition of it in *United States v. Rauscher*, 119 U.S. 407, 30 L.Ed. 425, 7 S.Ct. 234 (1886). 31 U.S. T., at 5071–5072.

18. In Article 16 of the Draft Convention on Jurisdiction with Respect to Crime, the Advisory Committee of the Research in International Law proposed:

"In exercising jurisdiction under this Convention, no State shall prosecute or punish any person who has been brought within its territory or a place subject to its authority by recourse to measures in violation of international law or international convention without first obtaining the consent of the State or States whose rights have been violated by such measures." Harvard Research in International Law, 29 Am. J. Int'l L. 442 (Supp. 1935).

sources of international law provide an independent basis for the right respondent asserts not to be tried in the United States, but rather that they should inform the interpretation of the Treaty terms.

The Court of Appeals deemed it essential, in order for the individual defendant to assert a right under the Treaty, that the affected foreign government had registered a protest. ("In the kidnapping case there must be a formal protest from the offended government after the kidnapping"). Respondent agrees that the right exercised by the individual is derivative of the nation's right under the Treaty, since nations are authorized, notwithstanding the terms of an extradition treaty, to voluntarily render an individual to the other country on terms completely outside of those provided in the treaty. The formal protest, therefore, ensures that the "offended" nation actually objects to the abduction and has not in some way voluntarily rendered the individual for prosecution. Thus the Extradition Treaty only prohibits gaining the defendant's presence by means other than those set forth in the Treaty when the nation from which the defendant was abducted objects.

This argument seems to us inconsistent with the remainder of respondent's argument. The Extradition Treaty has the force of law, and if, as respondent asserts, it is self-executing, it would appear that a court must enforce it on behalf of an individual regardless of the offensiveness of the practice of one nation to the other nation. In *Rauscher*, the Court noted that Great Britain had taken the position in other cases that the Webster–Ashburton Treaty included the doctrine of specialty, but no importance was attached to whether or not Great Britain had protested the prosecution of Rauscher for the crime of cruel and unusual punishment as opposed to murder. More fundamentally, the difficulty with the support respondent garners from international law is that none of it relates to the practice of nations in relation to extradition treaties. In *Rauscher*, we implied a term in the Webster–Ashburton Treaty because of the practice of nations with regard to extradition treaties. In the instant case, respondent would imply terms in the Extradition Treaty from the practice of nations with regards to international law more generally. Respondent would have us find that the Treaty acts as a prohibition against a violation of the general principle of international law that one government may not "exercise its police power in the territory of another state." There are many actions which could be taken by a nation that would violate this principle, including waging war, but it cannot seriously be contended that an invasion of the United States by Mexico would violate the terms of the Extradition Treaty between the two nations.

In sum, to infer from this Treaty and its terms that it prohibits all means of gaining the presence of an individual outside of its terms goes beyond established precedent and practice. In *Rauscher*, the implication of a doctrine of specialty into the terms of the Webster–Ashburton Treaty, which, by its terms, required the presentation of evidence establishing probable cause of the crime of extradition before extradition was required, was a small step to take. By contrast, to imply from the terms of this

Treaty that it prohibits obtaining the presence of an individual by means outside of the procedures the Treaty establishes requires a much larger inferential leap, with only the most general of international law principles to support it. The general principles cited by respondent simply fail to persuade us that we should imply in the United States–Mexico Extradition Treaty a term prohibiting international abductions.

Respondent and his *amici* may be correct that respondent's abduction was "shocking," and that it may be in violation of general international law principles. Mexico has protested the abduction of respondent through diplomatic notes, and the decision of whether respondent should be returned to Mexico, as a matter outside of the Treaty, is a matter for the Executive Branch.[19] We conclude, however, that respondent's abduction was not in violation of the Extradition Treaty between the United States and Mexico, and therefore the rule of *Ker v. Illinois* is fully applicable to this case. The fact of respondent's forcible abduction does not therefore prohibit his trial in a court in the United States for violations of the criminal laws of the United States.

The judgment of the Court of Appeals is therefore reversed, and the case is remanded for further proceedings consistent with this opinion.

So ordered.

QUESTIONS AND NOTES

1. Three years before the decision in the Alvarez–Machain case, the Office of Legal Counsel in the Department of Justice issued the following opinion, 13 U.S. Op. Off. Legal Counsel 163, 1989 WL 595835 (O.L.C.):

Office of Legal Counsel

U.S. Department of Justice

AUTHORITY OF THE FEDERAL BUREAU OF INVESTIGATION TO OVERRIDE INTERNATIONAL LAW IN EXTRATERRITORIAL LAW ENFORCEMENT ACTIVITIES

June 21, 1989

At the direction of the President or the Attorney General, the FBI may use its statutory authority to investigate and arrest individuals for violating United States law, even if the FBI's actions contravene customary international law. The President, acting through the Attorney General, has the inherent constitutional authority to deploy the FBI to investigate and arrest individuals for violating United States law, even if those actions contravene customary international law. Extraterritorial law enforcement activities that are authorized by domestic law are not barred even if they contravene unexecuted treaties or treaty provisions, such as

---

19. The Mexican Government has also requested from the United States the extradition of two individuals it suspects of having abducted respondent in Mexico, on charges of kidnapping. App. 39–66. . . .

Article 2(4) of the United Nations Charter. An arrest that is inconsistent with international or foreign law does not violate the Fourth Amendment.

This memorandum responds to the request of the Federal Bureau of Investigation ("FBI") that we reconsider our 1980 opinion that the FBI has no authority under 28 U.S.C. § 533(1) to apprehend and abduct a fugitive residing in a foreign state when those actions would be contrary to customary international law. Extraterritorial Apprehension by the Federal Bureau of Investigation, 4B Op. O.L.C. 543 (1980) (the "1980 Opinion" or "Opinion"). After undertaking a comprehensive review of the applicable law, we conclude that the 1980 Opinion erred in ruling that the FBI does not have legal authority to carry out extraterritorial law enforcement activities that contravene customary international law.

First, we conclude that, with appropriate direction, the FBI may use its broad statutory authority under 28 U.S.C. § 533(1) and 18 U.S.C. § 3052 to investigate and arrest individuals for violations of United States law even if those investigations and arrests are not consistent with international law. Second, we conclude that the President, acting through the Attorney General, has inherent constitutional authority to order the FBI to investigate and arrest individuals in a manner that departs from international law. The international law that may be abridged in this manner includes not only customary international law but also Article 2(4) of the U.N. Charter and other unexecuted treaties or treaty provisions that have not become part of the domestic law of the United States. Finally, we reaffirm the conclusion of the 1980 Opinion that an arrest departing from international law does not violate the Fourth Amendment, and we further conclude that an arrest in violation of foreign law does not abridge the Fourth Amendment.

We caution that this memorandum addresses only whether the FBI has the legal authority to carry out law enforcement operations that contravene international law. It does not address the serious policy considerations that may weigh against carrying out such operations.

The 1980 Opinion addressed the legal implications of a proposed operation in which FBI agents would forcibly apprehend a fugitive in a foreign country that would not consent to the apprehension. That Opinion acknowledges that 28 U.S.C. § 533(1), the statute authorizing FBI investigations, contains no explicit geographical restrictions. It also refers to a previous opinion issued by this Office that concluded that the statute's general authorization to detect and prosecute crimes against the United States appears broad enough to include such law enforcement activity no matter where it is undertaken. The 1980 Opinion asserts, however, that customary and other international law limits the reach of section 533(1). Under customary international law, as viewed by the 1980 Opinion, it is considered an invasion of sovereignty for one country to carry out law enforcement activities within another country without that country's consent. Thus, the Opinion concludes that section 533(1) authorizes extraterritorial apprehension of a fugitive only where the apprehension is approved by the asylum state.

The Opinion supports this conclusion with "two distinct but related lines of analysis." Id. at 552. First, citing The Schooner Exchange v. McFaddon, 11 U.S. (7 Cranch) 116, 136 (1812) (Marshall, C.J.), the Opinion concludes that the authority of the United States outside its territory is limited by the sovereignty of other nations. The Opinion does not explain the juridical source of this limitation on the authority of the United States. In The Schooner Exchange, however, Chief Justice Marshall relies on customary international law for many of his conclusions, and this part of the 1980 Opinion appears to suggest that customary international law imposes absolute jurisdictional limitations on the United States' lawmaking authority.

Second, the Opinion implicitly relies on the principle of statutory construction that statutes should be construed, when possible, so as to avoid conflict with international law. The Opinion notes that a statute imposing a duty ordinarily is construed to authorize all reasonable and necessary means of executing that duty. The Opinion concludes that although the law enforcement methods at issue may be necessary to carry out the FBI agents' duties under section 533(1), those methods are "unreasonable" and hence, unauthorized, if executed in violation of international law. Thus, the Opinion concludes that without asylum state consent, "the FBI is acting outside the bounds of its statutory authority when it makes an apprehension of the type proposed here—either because § 533 could not contemplate a violation of international law or because the powers of the FBI are delimited by those of the enabling sovereign." Id. at 553.

The 1980 Opinion's impact on the ability of the United States to execute necessary law enforcement operations may be significant. The reasoning of the 1980 Opinion would seem to apply to a broad range of law enforcement activities other than forcible apprehension. United States law enforcement agents frequently are required to travel to foreign countries to conduct investigative activities or to meet foreign informants. Formal consent cannot always be obtained from the foreign government, and indeed, in many cases to seek such consent would endanger both the agents and their investigation. Although such activities are less intrusive than forcible apprehension and removal of the fugitive, under the 1980 Opinion they nonetheless may be viewed as encroachments on the asylum state's sovereignty and hence, violations of international law, if not authorized by that state.... Thus, the 1980 Opinion has the potential to preclude the United States not only from apprehending fugitives in foreign countries, but also from engaging in a variety of more routine law enforcement activities. The United States is facing increasingly serious threats to its domestic security from both international terrorist groups and narcotics traffickers. While targeting the United States and United States citizens, these criminal organizations frequently operate from foreign sanctuaries. Unfortunately, some foreign governments have failed to take effective steps to protect the United States from these predations, and some foreign governments actually act in complicity with these groups. Accordingly, the extraterritorial enforcement of United States laws is becoming increasingly important to the nation's ability to protect its own vital national interests.

2.   To what extent might the OLC opinion in the previous note, as well as the majority opinion in the principal case have laid the foundation for the current practices of irregular rendition? Compare with the OLC opinion in the preceding note, footnote 21 from Justice Stevens' dissenting opinion in Alvarez–Machain:

> When Abraham Sofaer, Legal Adviser of the State Department, was questioned at a congressional hearing, he resisted the notion that such seizures were acceptable: " 'Can you imagine us going into Paris and seizing some person we regard as a terrorist . . .? [H]ow would we feel if some foreign nation—let us take the United Kingdom—came over here and seized some terrorist suspect in New York City, or Boston, or Philadelphia, . . . because we refused through the normal channels of international, legal communications, to extradite that individual?' " Bill To Authorize Prosecution of Terrorists and Others Who Attack U.S. Government Employees and Citizens Abroad: Hearing before the Subcommittee on Security and Terrorism of the Senate Committee on the Judiciary, 99th Cong., 1st Sess., 63 (1985).

3.   See Arar v. Ashcroft, 585 F.3d 559 (2d Cir. 2009):

> The United States Department of State records that, between 1993 and 2001, "rendition" provided the means for obtaining custody of ten suspected terrorists and "extradition" applied to another four suspects. *See* U.S. Dep't of State, *Patterns of Global Terrorism 2001,* App. D: Extraditions and Renditions of Terrorists to the United States. Accordingly, the rendition of suspected terrorists outside the mechanisms established by extradition treaties—so-called extraordinary rendition—had been employed as a means of combating terrorists for nearly a decade prior to the events giving rise to this litigation. *See* John B. Bellinger III, Legal Adviser, U.S. Dep't of State, Letter to the Editor, Wall St. J., July 5, 2006, at A25 (discussing the renditions of suspected terrorists Ramzi Yousef and Mir Aimal Kansi to the United States and the rendition of Illich Ramirez Sanchez, also known as "Carlos the Jackal," by French authorities from the Sudan to France, "which was subsequently upheld by the European Commission on Human Rights"), *reprinted in Digest of United States Practice in International Law* 162–63 (Sally J. Cummings ed., 2006); *see also* Remarks of Condoleezza Rice, U.S. Sec'y of State (Dec. 5, 2005) ("For decades, the United States and other countries have used 'renditions' to transport terrorist suspects from the country where they were captured to their home country or to other countries where they can be questioned, held, or brought to justice."), *in Digest of United States Practice in International Law* 100, 102 (Sally J. Cummings ed., 2005).

4.   United States v. Toscanino, 500 F.2d 267 (2d Cir.1974) is usually cited for the proposition that an abduction in which U.S. agents are involved and accompanying conduct that shocks the conscience are grounds for taking into account how the defendant came before the court and for dismissing the prosecution. The court in Toscanino described the defendant's claim and offer of proof as follows:

He alleged that he had been kidnapped from his home in Montevideo, Uruguay, and brought into the Eastern District only after he had been detained for three weeks of interrogation accompanied by physical torture in Brazil. He offered to prove the following:

"On or about January 6, 1973 Francisco Toscanino was lured from his home in Montevideo, Uruguay by a telephone call. This call had been placed by or at the direction of Hugo Campos Hermedia. Hermedia was at that time and still is a member of the police in Montevideo, Uruguay. In this effort, however, and those that will follow in this offer, Hermedia was acting *ultra vires* in that he was the paid agent of the United States government . . .

". . . The telephone call ruse succeeded in bringing Toscanino and his wife, seven months pregnant at the time, to an area near a deserted bowling alley in the City of Montevideo. Upon their arrival there Hermedia together with six associates abducted Toscanino. This was accomplished in full view of Toscanino's terrified wife by knocking him unconscious with a gun and throwing him into the rear seat of Hermedia's car. Thereupon Toscanino, bound and blindfolded, was driven to the Uruguayan–Brazilian border by a circuitous route . . .

"At one point during the long trip to the Brazilian border discussion was had among Toscanino's captors as to changing the license plates of the abductor's car in order to avoid detection by the Uruguayan authorities. At another point the abductor's car was abruptly brought to a halt, and Toscanino was ordered to get out. He was brought to an apparently secluded place and told to lie perfectly still or he would be shot then and there. Although his blindfold prevented him from seeing, Toscanino could feel the barrel of the gun against his head and could hear the rumbling noises of what appeared to be an Uruguayan military convoy. A short time after the noise of the convoy had died away, Toscanino was placed in another vehicle and whisked to the border. There by pre-arrangement and again at the connivance of the United States government, the car was met by a group of Brazilians who took custody of the body of Francisco Toscanino.

"At no time had there been any formal or informal request on the part of the United States of the government of Uruguay for the extradition of Francisco Toscanino nor was there any legal basis to justify this rank criminal enterprise. In fact, the Uruguayan government claims that it had no prior knowledge of the kidnapping nor did it consent thereto and had indeed condemned this kind of apprehension as alien to its laws.

"Once in the custody of Brazilians, Toscanino was brought to Porto Alegre where he was held incommunicado for eleven hours. His requests to consult with counsel, the Italian Consulate, and his family were all denied. During this time he was denied all food and water.

"Later that same day Toscanino was brought to Brasilia.... For seventeen days Toscanino was incessantly tortured and interrogated. Throughout this entire period the United States government and the United States Attorney for the Eastern District of New York prosecuting this case was aware of the interrogation and did in fact receive reports as to its progress. Furthermore, during this period of torture and interrogation a member of the United States Department of Justice, Bureau of Narcotics and Dangerous Drugs was present at one or more intervals and actually participated in portions of the interrogation.... [Toscanino's] captors denied him sleep and all forms of nourishment for days at a time. Nourishment was provided intravenously in a manner precisely equal to an amount necessary to keep him alive. Reminiscent of the horror stories told by our military men who returned from Korea and China, Toscanino was forced to walk up and down a hallway for seven or eight hours at a time. When he could no longer stand he was kicked and beaten but all in a manner contrived to punish without scarring. When he would not answer, his fingers were pinched with metal pliers. Alcohol was flushed into his eyes and nose and other fluids ... were forced up his anal passage. Incredibly, these agents of the United States government attached electrodes to Toscanino's earlobes, toes, and genitals. Jarring jolts of electricity were shot throughout his body, rendering him unconscious for indeterminate periods of time but again leaving no physical scars.

"Finally on or about January 25, 1973 Toscanino was brought to Rio de Janeiro where he was drugged by Brazilian–American agents and placed on Pan American Airways Flight #202 destined for the waiting arms of the United States government. On or about January 26, 1973 he woke in the United States, was arrested on the aircraft, and was brought immediately to Thomas Puccio, Assistant United States Attorney."

'...

The government prosecutor neither affirmed nor denied these allegations but claimed they were immaterial to the district court's power to proceed.

5.　Defendants in many subsequent cases of abduction have tried to invoke the so-called Toscanino "exception" to the Ker–Frisbie doctrine so as to divest the court of jurisdiction. Typically, these claims are rejected. See, e.g. United States v. Bridgewater, 175 F.Supp.2d 141 (D.Puerto Rico 2001): "There was no threat, no torture, no struggle, no violence, and no physical or verbal abuse."

6.　The United States has extradition treaties with approximately 100 different countries.

7.　Given the Ker–Frisbie doctrine and the apparent ease with which the United States in the past, acting through intermediaries or using its own agents, has been able through subterfuge or force been able to bring a suspect to the United States, one may wonder why extradition is still frequently used. In fact, in a significant number of cases, terrorism suspects have been extradited or brought to the United States through rendition, that is, the foreign country having surrendered the prisoner to United States agents.

8. What kinds of considerations might influence United States authorities not to go through standard legal channels and use extradition to bring a suspect to the United States? Does the Ker–Frisbie doctrine, in effect, encourage the use of kidnapping and sting operations to bring suspects to the United States? Should some mechanism be adopted to discourage such practices? What about the possible extradition of the kidnappers back to the country from which the suspect was taken? *See* footnotes 16 and 19 in the Alvarez–Machain case, supra, p. 360 and p. 362.

9. Some countries are reluctant to extradite individuals who may be subject to the death penalty in connection with the crime for which they are being extradited. In June, 2002, a related issue surfaced in connection with the prosecution of Zacarias Moussaoui. Both France and Germany indicated reluctance to provide information and evidence to the United States relating to Moussaoui as long as Moussaoui might be subject to the death penalty as an outcome of the prosecution. *See* Hugh Williamson, Schroeder Sees Way Out of Evidence Dispute, Financial Times, London, June 12, 2002, (reporting that Germany's Chancellor said that he expects Berlin and Washington to find a "common position" regarding the matter of Germany supplying the U.S. with evidence that could be used in the prosecution of Moussaoui).

10. Following the decision in United States v. Alvarez–Machain, the prosecution went to trial. At the close of the government's case, the district court granted the defendant's motion for a judgment of acquittal. Subsequently, Alvarez filed a civil action which ended up again in the Supreme Court. The issue before the Court was highly technical involving application of the Federal Tort Claims Act and the Alien Tort Statute which deals with civil actions by aliens for a tort committed in violation of the law of nations or a U.S. treaty. The Court concluded that he was not entitled to a remedy under either statute. Sosa v. Alvarez–Machain, 542 U.S. 692 (2004).

11. See Jacques Semmelman, Due Process, International Law, and Jurisdiction over Criminal Defendants Abducted Extraterritorially: The Ker–Frisbie Doctrine Reexamined, 30 Colum. J. Transnat'l L. 513 (1992); Malvina Halberstam, In Defense of the Supreme Court Decision in Alvarez–Machain, 86 Am. J. Int'l L. 736 (1992). For a fact situation similar to the principal case involving a forcible abduction in Pakistan by FBI agents of a person charged with the killing of CIA employees, see Kasi v. Angelone, 300 F.3d 487 (4th Cir.2002).

3. ACKNOWLEDGMENT BY THE U.S. GOVERNMENT OF TRANSFERS OF PERSONS, INTERROGATIONS AND "BLACK SITES"

September 6, 2006. THE PRESIDENT: Thank you. Thanks for the warm welcome. Welcome to the White House. . . .

. . .

After the 9/11 attacks, our coalition launched operations across the world to remove terrorist safe havens, and capture or kill terrorist operatives and leaders. Working with our allies, we've captured and detained thousands of terrorists and enemy fighters in Afghanistan, in Iraq, and other fronts of this war on terror. These enemy—these are enemy combatants, who were waging war on our nation. We have a right under the laws of war, and we have an obligation to the American people, to detain these enemies and stop them from rejoining the battle.

Most of the enemy combatants we capture are held in Afghanistan or in Iraq, where they're questioned by our military personnel. Many are released after questioning, or turned over to local authorities—if we determine that they do not pose a continuing threat and no longer have significant intelligence value. Others remain in American custody near the battlefield, to ensure that they don't return to the fight.

In some cases, we determine that individuals we have captured pose a significant threat, or may have intelligence that we and our allies need to have to prevent new attacks. Many are al Qaeda operatives or Taliban fighters trying to conceal their identities, and they withhold information that could save American lives. In these cases, it has been necessary to move these individuals to an environment where they can be held secretly [sic], questioned by experts, and—when appropriate—prosecuted for terrorist acts.

Some of these individuals are taken to the United States Naval Base at Guantanamo Bay, Cuba. It's important for Americans and others across the world to understand the kind of people held at Guantanamo. These aren't common criminals, or bystanders accidentally swept up on the battlefield—we have in place a rigorous process to ensure those held at Guantanamo Bay belong at Guantanamo. Those held at Guantanamo include suspected bomb makers, terrorist trainers, recruiters and facilitators, and potential suicide bombers. They are in our custody so they cannot murder our people. One detainee held at Guantanamo told a questioner questioning him—he said this: "I'll never forget your face. I will kill you, your brothers, your mother, and sisters."

In addition to the terrorists held at Guantanamo, a small number of suspected terrorist leaders and operatives captured during the war have been held and questioned outside the United States, in a separate program operated by the Central Intelligence Agency. This group includes individuals believed to be the key architects of the September the 11th attacks, and attacks on the USS Cole, an operative involved in the bombings of our embassies in Kenya and Tanzania, and individuals involved in other attacks that have taken the lives of innocent civilians across the world. These are dangerous men with unparalleled knowledge about terrorist networks and their plans for new attacks. The security of our nation and the lives of our citizens depend on our ability to learn what these terrorists know.

. . .

Information from the terrorists in this program has helped us to identify individuals that al Qaeda deemed suitable for Western operations, many of whom we had never heard about before. They include terrorists who were set to case targets inside the United States, including financial buildings in major cities on the East Coast. Information from terrorists in CIA custody has played a role in the capture or questioning of nearly every senior al Qaeda member or associate detained by the U.S. and its allies since this program began. By providing everything from initial leads to photo identifications, to precise locations of where terrorists were hiding, this program has helped us to take potential mass murderers off the streets before they were able to kill.

. . .

The information we get from these detainees is corroborated by intelligence, and we've received—that we've received from other sources—and together this intelligence has helped us connect the dots and stop attacks before they occur. Information from the terrorists questioned in this program helped unravel plots and terrorist cells in Europe and in other places. . . . By giving us information about terrorist plans we could not get anywhere else, this program has saved innocent lives.

This program has been subject to multiple legal reviews by the Department of Justice and CIA lawyers; they've determined it complied with our laws. This program has received strict oversight by the CIA's Inspector General. A small number of key leaders from both political parties on Capitol Hill were briefed about this program. All those involved in the questioning of the terrorists are carefully chosen and they're screened from a pool of experienced CIA officers. Those selected to conduct the most sensitive questioning had to complete more than 250 additional hours of specialized training before they are allowed to have contact with a captured terrorist.

. . . The CIA program has detained only a limited number of terrorists at any given time—and once we've determined that the terrorists held by the CIA have little or no additional intelligence value, many of them have been returned to their home countries for prosecution or detention by their governments. Others have been accused of terrible crimes against the American people, and we have a duty to bring those responsible for these crimes to justice. So we intend to prosecute these men, as appropriate, for their crimes.

. . .

4. LAWSUITS BROUGHT BY ALLEGED VICTIMS OF IRREGULAR RENDITION

ARAR v. ASHCROFT

585 F.3d 559 (2d Cir. 2009) (en banc), cert. denied 130 S.Ct. 3409 (2010)

[Before JACOBS, CHIEF JUDGE, MCLAUGHLIN, CALABRESI, CABRANES, POOLER, SACK, SOTOMAYOR,*** PARKER, RAGGI, WESLEY, HALL, and LIVINGSTON, CIRCUIT JUDGES. KATZMANN, CIRCUIT JUDGE, took no part in the consideration or decision of the case.

JACOBS, C.J., filed the majority opinion in which MCLAUGHLIN, CABRANES, RAGGI, WESLEY, HALL, and LIVINGSTON, JJ., joined.

SACK, J., filed a dissenting opinion in which CALABRESI, POOLER, and PARKER, JJ., joined. PARKER, J., filed a dissenting opinion in which CALABRESI, POOLER, and SACK, JJ., joined. POOLER, J., filed a dissenting opinion in which CALABRESI, SACK, and PARKER, JJ., joined.

CALABRESI, J., filed a dissenting opinion in which POOLER, SACK, and PARKER, JJ., joined.]

DENNIS JACOBS, CHIEF JUDGE:

Maher Arar appeals from a judgment of the United States District Court for the Eastern District of New York (Trager, J.) dismissing his complaint against the Attorney General of the United States, the Secretary of Homeland Security, the Director of the Federal Bureau of Investigation, and others, including senior immigration officials. Arar alleges that he was detained while changing planes at Kennedy Airport in New York (based on a warning from Canadian authorities that he was a member of Al Qaeda), mistreated for twelve days while in United States custody, and then removed to Syria via Jordan pursuant to an inter-governmental understanding that he would be detained and interrogated under torture by Syrian officials. The complaint alleges a violation of the Torture Victim Protection Act ("TVPA") and of his Fifth Amendment substantive due process rights arising from the conditions of his detention in the United States, the denial of his access to counsel and to the courts while in the United States, and his detention and torture in Syria.

The district court dismissed the complaint (with leave to re-plead only as to the conditions of detention in the United States and his access to counsel and the courts during that period) and Arar timely appealed (without undertaking to amend). Arar v. Ashcroft, 414 F.Supp.2d 250 (E.D.N.Y.2006). A three-judge panel of this Court unanimously held that: (1) the District Court had personal jurisdiction over Thompson, Ashcroft, and Mueller; (2) Arar failed to state a claim under the TVPA; and (3) Arar failed to establish subject matter jurisdiction over his request for a

---

*** The Honorable Sonia Sotomayor, who was originally a member of the in banc panel and who participated in oral argument, was elevated to the Supreme Court on August 8, 2009.

declaratory judgment. Arar v. Ashcroft, 532 F.3d 157 (2d Cir.2008). A majority of the panel also dismissed Arar's Bivens claims, with one member of the panel dissenting. Id. The Court voted to rehear the appeal in banc. We now affirm.

We have no trouble affirming the district court's conclusions that Arar sufficiently alleged personal jurisdiction over the defendants who challenged it, and that Arar lacks standing to seek declaratory relief. We do not reach issues of qualified immunity or the state secrets privilege. As to the TVPA, we agree with the unanimous position of the panel that Arar insufficiently pleaded that the alleged conduct of United States officials was done under color of foreign law. We agree with the district court that Arar insufficiently pleaded his claim regarding detention in the United States, a ruling that has been reinforced by the subsequent authority of Bell Atlantic Corp. v. Twombly, 550 U.S. 544, 570 (2007). Our attention is therefore focused on whether Arar's claims for detention and torture in Syria can be asserted under Bivens v. Six Unknown Named Agents of Federal Bureau of Narcotics, 403 U.S. 388, 91 S.Ct. 1999, 29 L.Ed.2d 619 (1971) ("Bivens").

To decide the Bivens issue, we must determine whether Arar's claims invoke Bivens in a new context; and, if so, whether an alternative remedial scheme was available to Arar, or whether (in the absence of affirmative action by Congress) 'special factors counsel[ ] hesitation.' This opinion holds that "extraordinary rendition" is a context new to Bivens claims, but avoids any categorical ruling on alternative remedies-because the dominant holding of this opinion is that, in the context of extraordinary rendition, hesitation is warranted by special factors. We therefore affirm.

. . .

Our ruling does not preclude judicial review and oversight in this context. But if a civil remedy in damages is to be created for harms suffered in the context of extraordinary rendition, it must be created by Congress, which alone has the institutional competence to set parameters, delineate safe harbors, and specify relief. If Congress chooses to legislate on this subject, then judicial review of such legislation would be available.

Applying our understanding of Supreme Court precedent, we decline to create, on our own, a new cause of action against officers and employees of the federal government. Rather, we conclude that, when a case presents the intractable "special factors" apparent here, it is for the Executive in the first instance to decide how to implement extraordinary rendition, and for the elected members of Congress—and not for us as judges—to decide whether an individual may seek compensation from government officers and employees directly, or from the government, for a constitutional violation. Administrations past and present have reserved the right to employ rendition, see David Johnston, U.S. Says Rendition to Continue, but with More Oversight, N.Y. Times, Aug. 24, 2009, and notwithstanding prolonged public debate, Congress has not prohibited the practice, imposed limits on its use, or created a cause of action for those who allege they have suffered constitutional injury as a consequence.

I

Arar's complaint sets forth the following factual allegations.

Arar is a dual citizen of Syria, where he was born and raised, and of Canada, to which his family immigrated when he was 17.

While on vacation in Tunisia in September 2002, Arar was called back to work in Montreal. His itinerary called for stops in Zurich and New York.

Arar landed at Kennedy Airport around noon on September 26. Between planes, Arar presented his Canadian passport to an immigration official who, after checking Arar's credentials, asked Arar to wait nearby. About two hours later, Arar was fingerprinted and his bags searched. Between 4 p.m. and 9 p.m., Arar was interviewed by an agent from the Federal Bureau of Investigation ("FBI"), who asked (*inter alia*) about his relationships with certain individuals who were suspected of terrorist ties. Arar admitted knowing at least one of them, but denied being a member of a terrorist group. Following the FBI interview, Arar was questioned by an official from the Immigration and Nationalization Service ("INS") for three more hours; he continued to deny terrorist affiliations.

Arar spent the night alone in a room at the airport. The next morning (September 27) he was questioned by FBI agents from approximately 9 a.m. until 2 p.m.; the agents asked him about Osama Bin Laden, Iraq, Palestine, and other things. That evening, Arar was given an opportunity to return voluntarily to Syria. He refused, citing a fear of torture, and asked instead to go to Canada or Switzerland. Later that evening, he was transferred to the Metropolitan Detention Center ("MDC") in Brooklyn, where he remained until October 8.

On October 1, the INS initiated removal proceedings, and served Arar with a document stating that he was inadmissible because he belonged to a terrorist organization. Later that day, he called his mother-in-law in Ottawa-his prior requests to place calls and speak to a lawyer having been denied or ignored. His family retained a lawyer to represent him and contacted the Canadian Consulate in New York.

A Canadian consular official visited Arar on October 3. The next day, immigration officers asked Arar to designate in writing the country to which he would want to be removed. He designated Canada. On the evening of October 5, Arar met with his attorney. The following evening, a Sunday, Arar was again questioned by INS officials. The INS District Director in New York left a voicemail message on the office phone of Arar's attorney that the interview would take place, but the attorney did not receive the message in time to attend. Arar was told that she chose not to attend. In days following, the attorney was given false information about Arar's whereabouts.

On October 8, 2002, Arar learned that the INS had: (1) ordered his removal to Syria, (2) made a (required) finding that such removal would be consistent with Article 3 of the Convention Against Torture ("CAT"), and (3) barred him from re-entering the United States for five years. He was found inadmissible to the United States on the basis of 8 U.S.C. § 1182(a)(3)(B)(i)(V), which provides that any alien who "is a member of a terrorist organization" is inadmissible to the United States. The finding was based on Arar's association with a suspected terrorist and other (classified) information. Thereafter, Defendant J. Scott Blackman, an INS Regional Director, made a determination that Arar was clearly and unequivocally a member of Al Qaeda and inadmissible to the United States. A "Final Notice of Inadmissibility," dated October 8, and signed by Defendant Deputy Attorney General Larry Thompson, stated that Arar's removal to Syria would be consistent with the CAT, notwithstanding Arar's articulated fear of torture.

Later that day, Arar was taken to New Jersey, whence he flew in a small jet to Washington, D.C., and then to Amman, Jordan. When he arrived in Amman on October 9, he was handed over to Jordanian authorities who treated him roughly and then delivered him to the custody of Syrian officials, who detained him at a Syrian Military Intelligence facility. Arar was in Syria for a year, the first ten months in an underground cell six feet by three, and seven feet high. He was interrogated for twelve days on his arrival in Syria, and in that period was beaten on his palms, hips, and lower back with a two-inch-thick electric cable and with bare hands. Arar alleges that United States officials conspired to send him to Syria for the purpose of interrogation under torture, and directed the interrogations from abroad by providing Syria with Arar's dossier, dictating questions for the Syrians to ask him, and receiving intelligence learned from the interviews.

On October 20, 2002, Canadian Embassy officials inquired of Syria as to Arar's whereabouts. The next day, Syria confirmed to Canada that Arar was in its custody; that same day, interrogation ceased. Arar remained in Syria, however, receiving visits from Canadian consular officials. On August 14, 2003, Arar defied his captors by telling the Canadians that he had been tortured and was confined to a small underground cell. Five days later, after signing a confession that he had trained as a terrorist in Afghanistan, Arar was moved to various locations. On October 5, 2003, Arar was released to the custody of a Canadian embassy official in Damascus, and was flown to Ottawa the next day.

    . . .

In Bivens v. Six Unknown Named Agents of Federal Bureau of Narcotics, 403 U.S. 388, 91 S.Ct. 1999, 29 L.Ed.2d 619 (1971), the Supreme Court "recognized for the first time an implied private action for damages against federal officers alleged to have violated a citizen's constitutional rights." The plaintiff in Bivens had been subjected to an unlawful, warrantless search which resulted in his arrest. The Supreme Court allowed him to state a cause of action for money damages directly under the Fourth Amendment, thereby giving rise to a judicially-created remedy stemming directly from the Constitution itself.

The purpose of the Bivens remedy "is to deter individual federal officers from committing constitutional violations." Malesko, 534 U.S. at 70, 122 S.Ct. 515. So a Bivens action is brought against individuals, and any damages are payable by the offending officers. Notwithstanding the potential breadth of claims that would serve that objective, the Supreme Court has warned that the Bivens remedy is an extraordinary thing that should rarely if ever be applied in "new contexts..."

This case requires us to examine whether allowing this Bivens action to proceed would extend Bivens to a new "context," and if so, whether such an extension is advisable.

"Context" is not defined in the case law. At a sufficiently high level of generality, any claim can be analogized to some other claim for which a Bivens action is afforded, just as at a sufficiently high level of particularity, every case has points of distinction. We construe the word "context" as it is commonly used in law: to reflect a potentially recurring scenario that has similar legal and factual components.

The context of this case is international rendition, specifically, "extraordinary rendition." Extraordinary rendition is treated as a distinct phenomenon in international law. See supra note 1. Indeed, law review articles that affirmatively advocate the creation of a remedy in cases like Arar's recognize "extraordinary rendition" as the context. See, e.g., Peter Johnston, Note, Leaving the Invisible Universe: Why All Victims of Extraordinary Rendition Need a Cause of Action Against the United States, 16 J.L. & Pol'y 357, 363 (2007). More particularly, the context of extraordinary rendition in Arar's case is the complicity or cooperation of United States government officials in the delivery of a non-citizen to a foreign country for torture (or with the expectation that torture will take place). This is a "new context": no court has previously afforded a Bivens remedy for extraordinary rendition.

Once we have identified the context as "new," we must decide whether to recognize a Bivens remedy in that environment of fact and law. The Supreme Court tells us that this is a two-part inquiry. In order to determine whether to recognize a Bivens remedy in a new context, we must consider: whether there is an alternative remedial scheme available to the plaintiff; and whether " 'special factors counsel[ ] hesitation' " in creating a Bivens remedy. Wilkie, 551 U.S. at 550, 127 S.Ct. 2588 (quoting Bush, 462 U.S. at 378, 103 S.Ct. 2404).

. . .

There are several possible alternative remedial schemes here.... In the end, we need not decide whether an alternative remedial scheme was available because, "even in the absence of an alternative [remedial scheme], a Bivens remedy is a subject of judgment ... [in which] courts must . . . pay particular heed . . . to any special factors counselling hesitation before authorizing a new kind of federal litigation." Such special factors are clearly present in the new context of this case, and they sternly counsel hesitation.

. . .

When the Bivens cause of action was created in 1971, the Supreme Court explained that such a remedy could be afforded because that "case involve[d] no special factors counselling hesitation in the absence of affirmative action by Congress." . . . Among the "special factors" that have "counsel[ed] hesitation" and thereby foreclosed a Bivens remedy are: military concerns,; separation of powers, the comprehensiveness of available statutory schemes, national security concerns, and foreign policy considerations, ... Two principles emerge from this review of case law:

• "Special factors" is an embracing category, not easily defined; but it is limited in terms to factors that provoke "hesitation." While special factors should be substantial enough to justify the absence of a damages remedy for a wrong, no account is taken of countervailing factors that might counsel alacrity or activism, and none has ever been cited by the Supreme Court as a reason for affording a Bivens remedy where it would not otherwise exist.

• The only relevant threshold-that a factor "counsels hesitation"-is remarkably low. It is at the opposite end of the continuum from the unflagging duty to exercise jurisdiction. . . .

. . .

Although this action is cast in terms of a claim for money damages against the defendants in their individual capacities, it operates as a constitutional challenge to policies promulgated by the executive. Our federal system of checks and balances provides means to consider allegedly unconstitutional executive policy, but a private action for money damages against individual policymakers is not one of them. . . . Here, we need not decide categorically whether a Bivens action can lie against policymakers because in the context of extraordinary rendition, such an action would have the natural tendency to affect diplomacy, foreign policy, and the security of the nation, and that fact counsels hesitation. Our holding need be no broader.

. . .

The Executive has practiced rendition since at least 1995. . . . A suit seeking a damages remedy against senior officials who implement such a policy is in critical respects a suit against the government as to which the government has not waived sovereign immunity. Such a suit unavoidably influences government policy, probes government secrets, invades government interests, enmeshes government lawyers, and thereby elicits government funds for settlement. (Canada has already paid Arar $10 million.)

It is a substantial understatement to say that one must hesitate before extending Bivens into such a context. A suit seeking a damages remedy against senior officials who implement an extraordinary rendition policy would enmesh the courts ineluctably in an assessment of the validity and rationale of that policy and its implementation in this particular case, matters that directly affect significant diplomatic and national security concerns. It is clear from the face of the complaint that Arar explicitly targets the "policy" of extraordinary rendition; he cites the policy twice in his complaint, and submits documents and media reports concerning the practice. His claim cannot proceed without inquiry into the perceived need for the policy, the threats to which it responds, the substance and sources of the intelligence used to formulate it, and the propriety of adopting specific responses to particular threats in light of apparent geopolitical circumstances and our relations with foreign countries.

The Supreme Court has expressly counseled that matters touching upon foreign policy and national security fall within "an area of executive action 'in which courts have long been hesitant to intrude'" absent congressional authorization.

. . .

Absent clear congressional authorization, the judicial review of extraordinary rendition would offend the separation of powers and inhibit this country's foreign policy. It does not matter for our purposes whether such consequences would flow from innocent interference or from deliberate manipulation. These concerns must counsel hesitation in creating a new damages remedy that Congress has not seen fit to authorize.

. . .

The extraordinary rendition context involves exchanges among the ministries and agencies of foreign countries on diplomatic, security, and intelligence issues. . . . Even the probing of these matters entails the risk that other countries will become less willing to cooperate with the United States in sharing intelligence resources to counter terrorism. "At its core," as the panel opinion observed, "this suit arises from the Executive Branch's alleged determination that (a) Arar was affiliated with Al Qaeda, and therefore a threat to national security, and (b) his removal to Syria was appropriate in light of U.S. diplomatic and national security interests." To determine the basis for Arar's alleged designation as an Al Qaeda member and his subsequent removal to Syria, the district court would have to consider what was done by the national security apparatus of at least three foreign countries, as well as that of the United States. Indeed, the Canadian government—which appears to have provided the intelligence that United States officials were acting upon when they detained Arar—paid Arar compensation for its role in the events surrounding this lawsuit, but has also asserted the need for Canada itself to maintain the confidentiality of certain classified materials related to Arar's claims.

. . .

Allegations of conspiracy among government agencies that must often work in secret inevitably implicate a lot of classified material that cannot be introduced into the public record. Allowing Arar's claims to proceed would very likely mean that some documents or information sought by Arar would be redacted, reviewed in camera, and otherwise concealed from the public. Concealment does not bespeak wrongdoing: in such matters, it is just as important to conceal what has not been done. Nevertheless, these measures would excite suspicion and speculation as to the true nature and depth of the supposed conspiracy, and as to the scope and depth of judicial oversight. Indeed, after an inquiry at oral argument as to whether classified materials relating to Arar's claims could be made available for review in camera, Arar objected to the supplementation of the record with material he could not see. See Letter from David Cole, Counsel for Maher Arar (Dec. 23, 2008). After pointing out that such materials are unnecessary to the adjudication of a motion on the pleadings (where the allegations of the complaint must be accepted as true), Arar protested that any materials submitted ex parte and in camera would not be subject to adversarial testing and that consideration of such documents would be "presumptively unconstitutional" since they would result in a decision "on the basis of secret information available to only one side of the dispute."

The court's reliance on information that cannot be introduced into the public record is likely to be a common feature of any Bivens actions arising in the context of alleged extraordinary rendition. This should provoke hesitation, given the strong preference in the Anglo–American legal tradition for open court proceedings, . . .

Granted, there are circumstances in which a court may close proceedings to which a public right of access presumptively attaches. . . . And the problems posed by the need to consider classified material are unavoidable in some criminal prosecutions and in other cases where we have a duty, imposed by Congress, to exercise jurisdiction. But this is not such a circumstance or such a case. The preference for open rather than clandestine court proceedings is a special factor that counsels hesitation in extending Bivens to the extraordinary rendition context.

     . . .

A government report states that this case involves assurances received from other governments in connection with the determination that Arar's removal to Syria would be consistent with Article 3 of the CAT. Office of Inspector General, Dep't of Homeland Sec., (Unclassified) The Removal of a Canadian Citizen to Syria 5, 22, 26–27 (2008). This case is not unique in that respect. Cases in the context of extraordinary rendition are very likely to present serious questions relating to private diplomatic assurances from foreign countries received by federal officials, and this feature of such claims opens the door to graymail.

     . . .

The regulations promulgated pursuant to the FARRA explicitly authorize the removal of an alien to a foreign country following receipt from that country of sufficiently reliable assurances that the alien will not be tortured. See 8 C.F.R. § 208.18(c). Should we decide to extend Bivens into the extraordinary rendition context, resolution of these actions will require us to determine whether any such assurances were received from the country of rendition and whether the relevant defendants relied upon them in good faith in removing the alien at issue.

Any analysis of these questions would necessarily involve us in an inquiry into the work of foreign governments and several federal agencies, the nature of certain classified information, and the extent of secret diplomatic relationships. An investigation into the existence and content of such assurances would potentially embarrass our government through inadvertent or deliberate disclosure of information harmful to our own and other states. Given the general allocation of authority over foreign relations to the political branches and the decidedly limited experience and knowledge of the federal judiciary regarding such matters, such an investigation would also implicate grave concerns about the separation of powers and our institutional competence. See, e.g., Kiyemba v. Obama, 561 F.3d 509, 515 (D.C.Cir.2009) ("[S]eparation of powers principles . . . preclude the courts from second-guessing the Executive's assessment of the likelihood a detainee will be tortured by a foreign sovereign."). These considerations strongly counsel hesitation in acknowledging a Bivens remedy in this context.

. . .

As emphasized above, Arar invokes Bivens to challenge policies promulgated and pursued by the executive branch, not simply isolated actions of individual federal employees. Such an extension of Bivens is without precedent and implicates questions of separation of powers as well as sovereign immunity. This, by itself, counsels hesitation; there is further reason to hesitate where, as in this case, the challenged government policies are the subject of classified communications: a possibility that such suits will make the government "vulnerable to 'graymail,' i.e., individual lawsuits brought to induce the [government] to settle a case (or prevent its filing) out of fear that any effort to litigate the action would reveal classified information that may undermine ongoing covert operations," or otherwise compromise foreign policy efforts. We cast no aspersions on Arar, or his lawyers; this dynamic inheres in any case where there is a risk that a defendant might "disclose classified information in the course of a trial." This is an endemic risk in cases (however few) which involve a claim like Arar's.

The risk of graymail is itself a special factor which counsels hesitation in creating a Bivens remedy. There would be hesitation enough in an ordinary graymail case, i.e., where the tactic is employed against the government, which can trade settlement cash (or the dismissal of criminal charges) for secrecy. But the graymail risk in a Bivens rendition case is uniquely troublesome. The interest in protecting military, diplomatic, and intelligence secrets is located (as always) in the government; yet a Bivens claim, by definition, is never pleaded against the government. So in a Bivens case, there is a dissociation between the holder of the non-disclosure interest (the government, which cannot be sued directly under Bivens) and the person with the incentive to disclose (the defendant, who cannot waive, but will be liable for any damages assessed). In a rendition case, the Bivens plaintiff could in effect pressure the individual defendants until the government cries uncle. Thus any Bivens action involving extraordinary rendition would inevitably suck the government into the case to protect its considerable interests, and—if disclosure is ordered—to appeal, or to suffer the disclosure, or to pay.

This pressure on the government to pay a settlement has (at least) two further perverse effects. First, a payment from the Treasury tends to obviate any payment or contribution by the individual defendants. Yet, "[Bivens] is concerned solely with deterring the unconstitutional acts of individual officers" by extracting payment from individual wrongdoers. When the government elects to settle a Bivens case which is susceptible to graymail, the individual wrongdoer pays nothing and the deterrent effect is lost. Second, the individual defendant in such a case has no incentive to resist discovery that imperils government interests; rather, discovery induces the government to settle. So in the extraordinary rendition context, there is a risk (or likelihood) that the government effectively becomes the real defendant in interest, and the named defendants become proxies that the government cannot control. . . .

In the end, a Bivens action based on rendition is—in all but name—a claim against the government. It is not for nothing that Canada (the government, not an individual officer of it) paid Arar $10 million dollars.

. . .

In the small number of contexts in which courts have implied a Bivens remedy, it has often been easy to identify both the line between constitutional and unconstitutional conduct, and the alternative course which officers should have pursued. The guard who beat a prisoner should not have beaten him; the agent who searched without a warrant should have gotten one; and the immigration officer who subjected an alien to multiple strip searches without cause should have left the alien in his clothes. This distinction may or may not amount to a special factor counseling hesitation in the implication of a Bivens remedy. But it is surely remarkable that the context of extraordinary rendition is so different, involving as it does a complex and rapidly changing legal framework beset with critical legal judgments that have not yet been made, as well as policy choices that are by no means easily reached.

Consider: should the officers here have let Arar go on his way and board his flight to Montreal? Canada was evidently unwilling to receive him; it was, after all, Canadian authorities who identified Arar as a terrorist (or did something that led their government to apologize publicly to Arar and pay him $10 million).

Should a person identified as a terrorist by his own country be allowed to board his plane and go on to his destination? Surely, that would raise questions as to what duty is owed to the other passengers and the crew.

Or should a suspected terrorist en route to Canada have been released on the Canadian border—over which he could re-enter the United States virtually at will? Or should he have been sent back whence his plane came, or to some third country? Should those governments be told that Canada thinks he is a terrorist? If so, what country would take him?

Or should the suspected terrorist have been sent to Guantanamo Bay or—if no other country would take him—kept in the United States with the prospect of release into the general population? See Zadvydas v. Davis, 533 U.S. 678, 699–700, 121 S.Ct. 2491, 150 L.Ed.2d 653 (2001).

None of this is to say that extraordinary rendition is or should be a favored policy choice. At the same time, the officials required to decide these vexed issues are "subject to the pull of competing obligations." Given the ample reasons for pause already discussed, we need not and do not rely on this consideration in concluding that it is inappropriate to extend Bivens to this context. Still, Congress is the appropriate branch of government to decide under what circumstances (if any) these kinds of policy decisions—which are directly related to the security of the population and the foreign affairs of the country—should be subjected to the influence of litigation brought by aliens.

. . .

All of these special factors notwithstanding, we cannot ignore that, as the panel dissent put it, "there is a long history of judicial review of Executive and Legislative decisions related to the conduct of foreign relations and national security." Where does that leave us? We recognize our limited competence, authority, and jurisdiction to make rules or set parameters to govern the practice called rendition. By the same token, we can easily locate that competence, expertise, and responsibility elsewhere: in Congress. Congress may be content for the Executive Branch to exercise these powers without judicial check. But if Congress wishes to create a remedy for individuals like Arar, it can enact legislation that includes enumerated eligibility parameters, delineated safe harbors, defined review processes, and specific relief to be afforded. Once Congress has performed this task, then the courts in a proper case will be able to review the statute and provide judicial oversight to the "Executive and Legislative decisions [which have been made with regard] to the conduct of foreign relations and national security."

. . .

For the reasons stated above, the judgment of the District Court is affirmed. The panel opinion is hereby vacated.

Questions and Notes

1. A case from the Fourth Circuit containing factual allegations similar to Arar and decided on state secret grounds is El–Masri v. United States, 479 F.3d 296 (4th Cir.2007), cert. denied 552 U.S. 947 (2007). A three-judge panel of the U.S. Court of Appeals affirmed the trial court's dismissal of the case, stating:

On December 6, 2005, El–Masri, a German citizen of Lebanese descent, filed his Complaint in this case, alleging, in substance, as follows: on December 31, 2003, while travelling in Macedonia, he was detained by Macedonian law enforcement officials; after twenty-three days in Macedonian custody, he was handed over to CIA operatives, who flew him to a CIA-operated detention facility near Kabul, Afghanistan; he was held in this CIA facility until May 28, 2004, when he was transported to Albania and released in a remote area; and Albanian officials then picked him up and took him to an airport in Tirana, Albania, from which he travelled to his home in Germany. The Complaint asserted that El–Masri had not only been held against his will, but had also been mistreated in a number of other ways during his detention, including being beaten, drugged, bound, and blindfolded during transport; confined in a small, unsanitary cell; interrogated several times; and consistently prevented from communicating with anyone outside the detention facility, including his family or the German government. El–Masri alleged that his detention and interrogation were carried out pursuant to an unlawful policy and practice devised and implemented by defendant Tenet known as "extraordinary rendition": the clandestine abduction and detention outside the United States of persons suspected of involvement in terrorist activities, and their subsequent interrogation using methods impermissible under U.S. and international laws.

According to the Complaint, the corporate defendants provided the CIA with an aircraft and crew to transport El–Masri to Afghanistan, pursuant to an agreement with Director Tenet, and they either knew or reasonably should have known that "Mr. El–Masri would be subjected to prolonged arbitrary detention, torture and cruel, inhuman, or degrading treatment in violation of federal and international laws during his transport to Afghanistan and while he was detained and interrogated there." El–Masri also alleges that CIA officials "believed early on that they had the wrong person," and that Director Tenet was notified in April 2004 that "the CIA had detained the wrong person" in El–Masri.

The Complaint alleged three separate causes of action. The first claim was against Director Tenet and the unknown CIA employees, pursuant to Bivens v. Six Unknown Named Agents of Federal Bureau of Narcotics, 403 U.S. 388, 91 S.Ct. 1999, 29 L.Ed.2d 619 (1971), for violations of El–Masri's Fifth Amendment right to due process. Specifically, El–Masri contends that Tenet and the defendant CIA employees contravened the Due Process Clause's prohibition against subjecting anyone held in United States custody to treatment that shocks the conscience or depriving a person of liberty in the absence of legal process.

El–Masri's second cause of action was initiated pursuant to the Alien Tort Statute (the "ATS"), and alleged that each of the defendants had contravened the international legal norm against prolonged arbitrary detention. The third cause of action was also asserted under the ATS, and maintained that each defendant had violated international legal norms prohibiting cruel, inhuman, or degrading treatment.

. . .

The effect of a successful interposition of the state secrets privilege by the United States will vary from case to case. If a proceeding involving state secrets can be fairly litigated without resort to the privileged information, it may continue. But if " 'the circumstances make clear that sensitive military secrets will be so central to the subject matter of the litigation that any attempt to proceed will threaten disclosure of the privileged matters,' dismissal is the proper remedy." The Supreme Court has recognized that some matters are so pervaded by state secrets as to be incapable of judicial resolution once the privilege has been invoked.

. . .

El–Masri also contends that, instead of dismissing his Complaint, the district court should have employed some procedure under which state secrets would have been revealed to him, his counsel, and the court, but withheld from the public. Specifically, he suggests that the court ought to have received all the state secrets evidence in camera and under seal, provided his counsel access to it pursuant to a nondisclosure agreement (after arranging for necessary security clearances), and then conducted an in camera trial. We need not dwell long on El–Masri's proposal in this regard, for it is expressly foreclosed by *Reynolds,* the Supreme Court decision that controls this entire field of inquiry. *Reynolds* plainly held that when "the occasion for the privilege is appropriate, . . . the court should not jeopardize the security which the privilege is meant to protect by insisting upon an examination of the evidence, even by the judge alone, in chambers." 345 U.S. at 10, 73 S.Ct. 528. El–Masri's assertion that the district court erred in not compelling the disclosure of state secrets to him and his lawyers is thus without merit.

In addition to his analysis under the controlling legal principles, El–Masri presents a sharp attack on what he views as the dire constitutional and policy consequences of dismissing his Complaint. He maintains that the district court's ruling, if affirmed, would enable the Executive to unilaterally avoid judicial scrutiny merely by asserting that state secrets are at stake in a given matter. More broadly, he questions the very application of the state secrets doctrine in matters where "egregious executive misconduct" is alleged, contending that, in such circumstances, the courts' "constitutional duty to review executive action" should trump the procedural protections traditionally accorded state secrets.

Contrary to El–Masri's assertion, the state secrets doctrine does not represent a surrender of judicial control over access to the courts. As we have explained, it is the court, not the Executive, that determines whether the state secrets privilege has been properly invoked. In order to successfully claim the state secrets privilege, the Executive must satisfy the court that disclosure of the information sought to be protected would expose matters that, in the interest of national security, ought to remain secret. Similarly, in order to win dismissal of an action on state secrets grounds, the Executive must persuade the court that state secrets are so central to the action that it cannot be fairly litigated without threatening their disclosure. The state secrets privilege cannot be successfully interposed, nor can it lead to dismissal of an action, based merely on the Executive's assertion that the pertinent standard has been met.

In this matter, the reasons for the United States' claim of the state secrets privilege and its motion to dismiss were explained largely in the Classified Declaration, which sets forth in detail the nature of the information that the Executive seeks to protect and explains why its disclosure would be detrimental to national security. We have reviewed the Classified Declaration, as did the district court, and the extensive information it contains is crucial to our decision in this matter. El–Masri's contention that his Complaint was dismissed based on the Executive's "unilateral assert[ion] of a need for secrecy" is entirely unfounded. It is no doubt frustrating to El–Masri that many of the specific reasons for the dismissal of his Complaint are classified. An inherent feature of the state secrets privilege, however, is that the party against whom it is asserted will often not be privy to the information that the Executive seeks to protect. That El–Masri is unfamiliar with the Classified Declaration's explanation for the privilege claim does not imply, as he would have it, that no such explanation was required, or that the district court's ruling was simply an unthinking ratification of a conclusory demand by the executive branch.

. . .

As we have observed in the past, the successful interposition of the state secrets privilege imposes a heavy burden on the party against whom the privilege is asserted. That party loses access to evidence that he needs to prosecute his action and, if privileged state secrets are sufficiently central to the matter, may lose his cause of action altogether. Moreover, a plaintiff suffers this reversal not through any fault of his own, but because his personal interest in pursuing his civil claim is subordinated to the collective interest in national security. *See id.* ("[T]here can be no doubt that, in limited circumstances like these, the fundamental principle of access to court must bow to the fact that a nation without sound intelligence is a nation at risk.").[7] In view of these considerations, we

---

7. It should be unnecessary for us to point out that the Executive's authority to protect confidential military and intelligence information is much broader in civil matters than in criminal prosecutions. The Supreme Court explained this principle in *Reynolds,* observing:

Respondents have cited us to those cases in the criminal field, where it has been held that the Government can invoke its evidentiary privileges only at the price of letting the defendant go free. The rationale of the criminal cases is that, since the Government which prosecutes an accused also has the duty to see that justice is done, it is unconscionable to allow it to undertake prosecution and then invoke its governmental privileges to deprive the accused of anything which might be material to his defense. Such rationale has no application in a civil forum where the Government is not the moving party, but is a defendant only on terms to which it has consented. 345 U.S. at 12, 73 S.Ct. 528.

recognize the gravity of our conclusion that El–Masri must be denied a judicial forum for his Complaint, and reiterate our past observations that dismissal on state secrets grounds is appropriate only in a narrow category of disputes. Nonetheless, we think it plain that the matter before us falls squarely within that narrow class, and we are unable to find merit in El–Masri's assertion to the contrary.

Pursuant to the foregoing, we affirm the Order of the district court.

2.   Another case, this time from the 9th circuit, where the court also based its decision on the state secrets doctrine is Mohamed v. Jeppesen Dataplan, Inc., 614 F.3d 1070 (9th Cir. 2010), cert. denied, 131 S.Ct. 2442 (2011) (like the Arar case, decided en banc):

> This case requires us to address the difficult balance the state secrets doctrine strikes between fundamental principles of our liberty, including justice, transparency, accountability and national security. Although as judges we strive to honor all of these principles, there are times when exceptional circumstances create an irreconcilable conflict between them. On those rare occasions, we are bound to follow the Supreme Court's admonition that "even the most compelling necessity cannot overcome the claim of privilege if the court is ultimately satisfied that [state] secrets are at stake." United States v. Reynolds, 345 U.S. 1, 11, 73 S.Ct. 528, 97 L.Ed. 727 (1953). After much deliberation, we reluctantly conclude this is such a case, and the plaintiffs' action must be dismissed. Accordingly, we affirm the judgment of the district court.

> I.   Background

> We begin with the factual ... history relevant to this appeal. In doing so, we largely draw upon the three-judge panel's language in Mohamed v. Jeppesen Dataplan, Inc., 579 F.3d 943, 949–52 (9th Cir.) (Jeppesen I), rehearing en banc granted, 586 F.3d 1108 (9th Cir.2009). We emphasize that this factual background is based only on the allegations of plaintiffs' complaint, which at this stage in the litigation we construe "in the light most favorable to the plaintiff[s], taking all [their] allegations as true and drawing all reasonable inferences from the complaint in [their] favor." Doe v. United States, 419 F.3d 1058, 1062 (9th Cir.2005). Whether plaintiffs' allegations are in fact true has not been decided in this litigation, and, given the sensitive nature of the allegations, nothing we say in this opinion should be understood otherwise.

> A.   Factual Background

> 1.   The Extraordinary Rendition Program

> Plaintiffs allege that the Central Intelligence Agency ("CIA"), working in concert with other government agencies and officials of foreign governments, operated an extraordinary rendition program to gather intelligence by apprehending foreign nationals suspected of involvement in terrorist activities and transferring them in secret to foreign countries for detention and interrogation by United States or foreign officials.

El–Masri's reliance on our decision in *United States v. Moussaoui*, 382 F.3d 453 (4th Cir.2004), in which we required the United States to grant a criminal defendant substantial access to enemy-combatant witnesses whose very identities were highly classified, is thus misplaced.

According to plaintiffs, this program has allowed agents of the U.S. government "to employ interrogation methods that would [otherwise have been] prohibited under federal or international law." Relying on documents in the public domain, plaintiffs, all foreign nationals, claim they were each processed through the extraordinary rendition program. They also make the following individual allegations.

Plaintiff Ahmed Agiza, an Egyptian national who had been seeking asylum in Sweden, was captured by Swedish authorities, allegedly transferred to American custody and flown to Egypt. In Egypt, he claims he was held for five weeks "in a squalid, windowless, and frigid cell," where he was "severely and repeatedly beaten" and subjected to electric shock through electrodes attached to his ear lobes, nipples and genitals. Agiza was held in detention for two and a half years, after which he was given a six-hour trial before a military court, convicted and sentenced to 15 years in Egyptian prison. According to plaintiffs, "[v]irtually every aspect of Agiza's rendition, including his torture in Egypt, has been publicly acknowledged by the Swedish government."

Plaintiff Abou Elkassim Britel, a 40–year–old Italian citizen of Moroccan origin, was arrested and detained in Pakistan on immigration charges. After several months in Pakistani detention, Britel was allegedly transferred to the custody of American officials. These officials dressed Britel in a diaper and a torn t-shirt and shackled and blindfolded him for a flight to Morocco. Once in Morocco, he says he was detained incommunicado by Moroccan security services at the Temara prison, where he was beaten, deprived of sleep and food and threatened with sexual torture, including sodomy with a bottle and castration. After being released and re-detained, Britel says he was coerced into signing a false confession, convicted of terrorism-related charges and sentenced to 15 years in a Moroccan prison.

Plaintiff Binyam Mohamed, a 28–year–old Ethiopian citizen and legal resident of the United Kingdom, was arrested in Pakistan on immigration charges. Mohamed was allegedly flown to Morocco under conditions similar to those described above, where he claims he was transferred to the custody of Moroccan security agents. These Moroccan authorities allegedly subjected Mohamed to "severe physical and psychological torture," including routinely beating him and breaking his bones. He says they cut him with a scalpel all over his body, including on his penis, and poured "hot stinging liquid" into the open wounds. He was blindfolded and handcuffed while being made "to listen to extremely loud music day and night." After 18 months in Moroccan custody, Mohamed was allegedly transferred back to American custody and flown to Afghanistan. He claims he was detained there in a CIA "dark prison" where he was kept in "near permanent darkness" and subjected to loud noise, such as the recorded screams of women and children, 24 hours a day. Mohamed was fed sparingly and irregularly and in four months he lost between 40 and 60 pounds. Eventually, Mohamed was transferred to the U.S. military prison at Guantanamo Bay, Cuba, where he remained for nearly five years. He was released and returned to the United Kingdom during the pendency of this appeal.

Plaintiff Bisher al-Rawi, a 39–year–old Iraqi citizen and legal resident of the United Kingdom, was arrested in Gambia while traveling on legitimate business. Like the other plaintiffs, al-Rawi claims he was put in a diaper and shackles and placed on an airplane, where he was flown to Afghanistan. He says he was detained in the same "dark prison" as Mohamed and loud noises were played 24 hours per day to deprive him of sleep. Al–Rawi alleges he was eventually transferred to Bagram Air Base, where he was "subjected to humiliation, degradation, and physical and psychological torture by U.S. officials," including being beaten, deprived of sleep and threatened with death. Al–Rawi was eventually transferred to Guantanamo; in preparation for the flight, he says he was "shackled and handcuffed in excruciating pain" as a result of his beatings. Al–Rawi was eventually released from Guantanamo and returned to the United Kingdom.

Plaintiff Farag Ahmad Bashmilah, a 38–year–old Yemeni citizen, says he was apprehended by agents of the Jordanian government while he was visiting Jordan to assist his ailing mother. After a brief detention during which he was "subject[ed] to severe physical and psychological abuse," Bashmilah claims he was given over to agents of the U.S. government, who flew him to Afghanistan in similar fashion as the other plaintiffs. Once in Afghanistan, Bashmilah says he was placed in solitary confinement, in 24–hour darkness, where he was deprived of sleep and shackled in painful positions. He was subsequently moved to another cell where he was subjected to 24–hour light and loud noise. Depressed by his conditions, Bashmilah attempted suicide three times. Later, Bashmilah claims he was transferred by airplane to an unknown CIA "black site" prison, where he "suffered sensory manipulation through constant exposure to white noise, alternating with deafeningly loud music" and 24–hour light. Bashmilah alleges he was transferred once more to Yemen, where he was tried and convicted of a trivial crime, sentenced to time served abroad and released.

2. Jeppesen's Alleged Involvement in the Rendition Program

Plaintiffs contend that publicly available information establishes that defendant Jeppesen Dataplan, Inc., a U.S. corporation, provided flight planning and logistical support services to the aircraft and crew on all of the flights transporting each of the five plaintiffs among the various locations where they were detained and allegedly subjected to torture. The complaint asserts "Jeppesen played an integral role in the forced" abductions and detentions and "provided direct and substantial services to the United States for its so-called 'extraordinary rendition' program," thereby "enabling the clandestine and forcible transportation of terrorism suspects to secret overseas detention facilities." It also alleges that Jeppesen provided this assistance with actual or constructive "knowledge of the objectives of the rendition program," including knowledge that the plaintiffs "would be subjected to forced disappearance, detention, and torture" by U.S. and foreign government officials.

. . .

While the appeal was pending Barack Obama succeeded George W. Bush as President of the United States. On September 23, 2009, the Obama administration announced new policies for invoking the state secrets privilege, effective October 1, 2009, in a memorandum from the Attorney General. See Memorandum from the Attorney Gen. to the Heads of Executive Dep'ts and Agencies on Policies and Procedures Governing Invocation of the State Secrets Privilege (Sept. 23, 2009) ("Holder Memo"), http://www. justice.gov/opa/documents/state-secret-privileges.pdf. The government certified both in its briefs and at oral argument before the en banc court that officials at the "highest levels of the Department of Justice" of the new administration had reviewed the assertion of privilege in this case and determined that it was appropriate under the newly announced policies. See Redacted, Unclassified Br. for U.S. on Reh'g En Banc ("U.S. Br.") 3.

. . .

Here, further litigation presents an unacceptable risk of disclosure of state secrets no matter what legal or factual theories Jeppesen would choose to advance during a defense. Whether or not Jeppesen provided logistical support in connection with the extraordinary rendition and interrogation programs, there is precious little Jeppesen could say about its relevant conduct and knowledge without revealing information about how the United States government does or does not conduct covert operations. Our conclusion holds no matter what protective procedures the district court might employ. Adversarial litigation, including pretrial discovery of documents and witnesses and the presentation of documents and testimony at trial, is inherently complex and unpredictable. Although district courts are well equipped to wall off isolated secrets from disclosure, the challenge is exponentially greater in exceptional cases like this one, where the relevant secrets are difficult or impossible to isolate and even efforts to define a boundary between privileged and unprivileged evidence would risk disclosure by implication. In these rare circumstances, the risk of disclosure that further proceedings would create cannot be averted through the use of devices such as protective orders or restrictions on testimony.

Dismissal at the pleading stage under Reynolds is a drastic result and should not be readily granted. We are not persuaded, however, by the dissent's views that the state secrets privilege can never be "asserted during the pleading stage to excise entire allegations," or that the government must be required "to make its claims of state secrets with regard to specific items of evidence or groups of such items as their use is sought in the lawsuit."

. . .

Although we are necessarily precluded from explaining precisely why this case cannot be litigated without risking disclosure of state secrets, or the nature of the harm to national security that we are convinced would result from further litigation, we are able to offer a few observations.

First, we recognize that plaintiffs have proffered hundreds of pages of publicly available documents, many catalogued in the dissent's Appendix, that they say corroborate some of their allegations concerning Jeppesen's alleged participation in aspects of the extraordinary rendition program. As the government has acknowledged, its claim of privilege does not extend to public documents. Accordingly, we do not hold that any of the documents plaintiffs have submitted are subject to the privilege; rather, we conclude that even assuming plaintiffs could establish their entire case solely through nonprivileged evidence-unlikely as that may be-any effort by Jeppesen to defend would unjustifiably risk disclosure of state secrets. . . .

Second, we do not hold that the existence of the extraordinary rendition program is itself a state secret. The program has been publicly acknowledged by numerous government officials including the President of the United States. Even if its mere existence may once have been a "matter[ ] which, in the interest of national security, should not be divulged," it is not a state secret now. Reynolds, 345 U.S. at 10, 73 S.Ct. 528; . . . Nonetheless, partial disclosure of the existence and even some aspects of the extraordinary rendition program does not preclude other details from remaining state secrets if their disclosure would risk grave harm to national security. . . .

Third, we acknowledge the government's certification at oral argument that its assertion of the state secrets privilege comports with the revised standards set forth in the current administration's September 23, 2009 memorandum, adopted several years after the government first invoked the privilege in this case. Those standards require the responsible agency to show that "assertion of the privilege is necessary to protect information the unauthorized disclosure of which reasonably could be expected to cause significant harm to the national defense or foreign relations." Holder Memo, supra, at 388. They also mandate that the Department of Justice "will not defend an invocation of the privilege in order to: (i) conceal violations of the law, inefficiency, or administrative error; (ii) prevent embarrassment to a person, organization, or agency of the United States government; (iii) restrain competition; or (iv) prevent or delay the release of information the release of which would not reasonably be expected to cause significant harm to national security." That certification here is consistent with our independent conclusion, having reviewed the government's public and classified declarations, that the government is not invoking the privilege to avoid embarrassment or to escape scrutiny of its recent controversial transfer and interrogation policies, rather than to protect legitimate national security concerns.

V. Other Remedies

Our holding today is not intended to foreclose—or to pre-judge— possible nonjudicial relief, should it be warranted for any of the plaintiffs. Denial of a judicial forum based on the state secrets doctrine poses concerns at both individual and structural levels. For the individual plaintiffs in this action, our decision forecloses at least one set of judicial remedies, and deprives them of the opportunity to prove their alleged mistreatment and obtain damages. At a structural level, terminating the case eliminates further judicial review in this civil litigation, one important check on alleged abuse by government officials and putative contractors. Other remedies may partially mitigate these concerns, however, although we recognize each of these options brings with it its own set of concerns and uncertainties.

First, that the judicial branch may have deferred to the executive branch's claim of privilege in the interest of national security does not preclude the government from honoring the fundamental principles of justice. The government, having access to the secret information, can determine whether plaintiffs' claims have merit and whether misjudgments or mistakes were made that violated plaintiffs' human rights. Should that be the case, the government may be able to find ways to remedy such alleged harms while still maintaining the secrecy national security demands. For instance, the government made reparations to Japanese Latin Americans abducted from Latin America for internment in the United States during World War II.

Second, Congress has the authority to investigate alleged wrongdoing and restrain excesses by the executive branch. . . .

Third, Congress also has the power to enact private bills. . . . Because as a general matter the federal courts are better equipped to handle claims, Congress can refer the case to the Court of Federal Claims to make a recommendation before deciding whether to enact a private bill, . . . although Congress alone will make the ultimate decision. When national security interests deny alleged victims of wrongful governmental action meaningful access to a judicial forum, private bills may be an appropriate alternative remedy. . .

Fourth, Congress has the authority to enact remedial legislation authorizing appropriate causes of action and procedures to address claims like those presented here. . . .

VI. Conclusion

We, like the dissent, emphasize that it should be a rare case when the state secrets doctrine leads to dismissal at the outset of a case. Nonetheless, there are such cases . . ., those where the mandate for dismissal is apparent even under the more searching examination required by Reynolds. This is one of those rare cases.

For all the reasons the dissent articulates-including the impact on human rights, the importance of constitutional protections and the constraints of a judge-made doctrine—we do not reach our decision lightly or without close and skeptical scrutiny of the record and the government's case for secrecy and dismissal. . . . We also acknowledge that this case presents a painful conflict between human rights and national security. As judges, we have tried our best to evaluate the competing claims of plaintiffs and the government and resolve that conflict according to the principles governing the state secrets doctrine set forth by the United States Supreme Court.

For the reasons stated, we hold that the government's valid assertion of the state secrets privilege warrants dismissal of the litigation, and affirm the judgment of the district court. The government shall bear all parties' costs on appeal.

3.   Footnote 8 in Jeppesen Dataplan, omitted in the excerpts from the case reproduced supra, states the following:

> ... [S]kepticism is all the more justified in cases that allege serious government wrongdoing. Such allegations heighten the risk that government officials may be motivated to invoke the state secrets doctrine not only by their obligation to protect national security but also by a desire to protect themselves or their associates from scrutiny.

4.   Note that the Supreme Court denied certiorari in all three of the cases presented above, Arar, El–Masri and Jeppesen Dataplan. Note also that these cases came from three different circuits, and in two, the circuit court decision was en banc. What significance do you attach to these facts?

5.   Following up on the Executive Order issued by President Obama on January 22, 2009, which, inter alia, appointed a Task Force to make recommendations about the United States' use of transfer (i.e. rendition), on August 24, 2009, Attorney General Holder reported on the recommendations of the Task Force:

> Transfers
>
> The Task Force also made policy recommendations with respect to scenarios in which the United States moves or facilitates the movement of a person from one country to another or from U.S. custody to the custody of another country to ensure that U.S. practices in such transfers comply with U.S. law, policy and international obligations and do not result in the transfer of individuals to face torture. In keeping with the broad language of the Executive Order, the Task Force considered seven types of transfers conducted by the U.S. government: extradition, transfers pursuant to immigration proceedings, transfers pursuant to the Geneva Conventions, transfers from Guantanamo Bay, military transfers within or from Afghanistan, military transfers within or from Iraq, and transfers pursuant to intelligence authorities.
>
> When the United States transfers individuals to other countries, it may rely on assurances from the receiving country. The Task Force made several recommendations aimed at clarifying and strengthening U.S. procedures for obtaining and evaluating those assurances. These included a recommendation that the State Department be involved in evaluating assurances in all cases and a recommendation that the Inspector Generals of the Departments of State, Defense, and Homeland Security prepare annually a coordinated report on transfers conducted by each of their agencies in reliance on assurances.
>
> The Task Force also made several recommendations aimed at improving the United States' ability to monitor the treatment of individuals transferred to other countries. These include a recommendation that agencies obtaining assurances from foreign countries insist on a monitoring mechanism, or otherwise establish a monitoring mechanism, to ensure consistent, private access to the individual who has been transferred, with minimal advance notice to the detaining government.

The Task Force also made a series of recommendations that are specific to immigration proceedings and military transfer scenarios. In addition, the Task Force made classified recommendations that are designed to ensure that, should the Intelligence Community participate in or otherwise support a transfer, any affected individuals are subjected to proper treatment.

Background Information

The Task Force on Interrogations and Transfer Policies is chaired by the Attorney General, with the Director of National Intelligence and the Secretary of Defense serving as Co–Vice–Chairs. Other members of the Task Force are the Secretaries of State and Homeland Security, the Director of the Central Intelligence Agency, and the Chairman of the Joint Chiefs of Staff. Each of these officials appointed senior-level representatives to serve on a working-level task force to complete the work of the Executive Order.

The Executive Order directed the Task Force to study and evaluate "whether the interrogation practices and techniques in Army Field Manual 2–22.3, when employed by departments and agencies outside the military, provide an appropriate means of acquiring the intelligence necessary to protect the Nation, and, if warranted, to recommend any additional or different guidance for other departments or agencies."

The Task Force was also directed to study and evaluate the practices of transferring individuals to other nations in order to ensure that such practices comply with the domestic laws, international obligations, and policies of the United States and do not result in the transfer of individuals to other nations to face torture or otherwise for the purpose, or with the effect, of undermining or circumventing the commitments or obligations of the United States to ensure the humane treatment of individuals in its custody and control.

5. CRIMINAL CHARGES BY FOREIGN GOVERNMENTS AGAINST U.S. AGENTS WHO ALLEGEDLY PERPETRATED IRREGULAR RENDITION TRANSFERS

In January, 2007, prosecutors in Munich, Germany issued arrest warrants against 10 CIA agents based on their alleged role in the kidnapping of Khaled El–Masri, a German national, and transporting him to Afghanistan for interrogation.

SPIEGEL ONLINE—June 25, 2007, 02:56 PM, in an article by John Goetz, Marcel Rosenbach and Holger Stark, URL:http://www.spiegel.de/international/germany/0,1518,490514,00.html, it was reported that the issuance of the arrest warrants was straining German–American relations; that the prosecutors in Munich were pushing to have the agents extradited to Germany so that they could stand trial; and that the German government has the authority by statute to stop any prosecution of the U.S. agents but realizes that to do so would cause a strong public reaction.

A similar scenario developed in Italy, where Italian prosecutors had charged 26 U.S. agents with kidnapping a radical imam known as Abu Omar on a Milan street in 2003 and taking him to Cairo, where he says he was tortured. In an article by Craig Whitlock, Washington Post Foreign Service, February 1, 2007, AO1, European law enforcement authorities were said to have acknowledged that it was high unlikely that any U.S. agents would be apprehended or extradited from the United States but that diplomatic relations between the concerned countries were being strained. Regarding the German–U.S. issue, a member of a parliamentary committee investigating the matter was quoted:

> This policy of rendition has to be stopped, "said Johannes Jung, a member of the Social Democratic Party." It's totally out of control, and the U.S. needs to rethink its policy in this regard. We couldn't imagine that this policy of rendition could really be true, but we have learned that it is true.

Italy authorizes prosecutions in absentia and none of the U.S. defendants were present when the trial of the 26 American defendants, some of whom were identified only by aliases and some Italian officials was begun in June, 2007. The U.S. government refused to cooperate with the prosecution. The trial was quickly interrupted when the Italian government tried to squelch the prosecution asserting that the prosecutor had violated state secrecy laws in gathering evidence. The issue of whether such secrecy laws were violated was then brought to the Italian Constitutional Court for resolution. See Ian Fisher and Elisabetta Povoledo, At issue in Italian trial: Are renditions a crime?, International Herald Tribune, June 8, 2007, p. 1, 2007 WLNR 10702717.

Subsequently, the Italian Constitutional Court's decision allowed the trial to proceed but with certain restrictions. On November 4, 2009, the Italian judge convicted 23 Americans, including the CIA base chief at the time. Three other Americans were not convicted based on their diplomatic immunity. Since the American defendants were tried in absentia, after the conviction, they became fugitives, which restricts their ability to travel, certainly to Italy and, possibly, to other countries. See NY Times, November 5, 2009, A14. The Times reported that most of the defendants have already left the CIA, with the exception of one of the defendants, the CIA's second-highest-ranking official.

6. AN UNOFFICIAL, NONGOVERNMENTAL REPORT ABOUT THE PRACTICE OF IRREGULAR RENDITION

Excerpts from a report by Amnesty International, USA, Report, United States of America, Below the Radar: Secret Flights to Torture and "Disappearance" (April 5, 2006)

Amnesty International uses the term "rendition" to describe the transfer of individuals from one country to another, by means that bypass all judicial and administrative due process. In the "war on terror" context, the practice is mainly—although not exclusively—initiated by the USA, and carried out with the collaboration, complicity or acquiescence of other governments. The most widely known manifestation of rendition is the secret transfer of terror suspects into the custody of other states—including Egypt, Jordan and Syria—where physical and psychological brutality feature prominently in interrogations. The rendition network's aim is to use whatever means necessary to gather intelligence, and to keep detainees away from any judicial oversight.

However, the rendition network also serves to transfer people into US custody, where they may end up in Guantánamo Bay in Cuba, detention centres in Iraq or Afghanistan, or in secret facilities known as "black sites" run by the USA's Central Intelligence Agency (CIA). In a number of cases, individuals have been transferred in and out of US custody several times. Muhammad Saad Iqbal Madni, for instance, was arrested by Indonesian intelligence agents in January 2002, allegedly on the instructions of the CIA, who flew him from Jakarta to Egypt, where he "disappeared" and was rumoured to have died under interrogation. In fact, he had been secretly returned to Afghanistan via Pakistan in April 2002 and held there for 11 months before being sent to Guantánamo Bay in March 2003. It was more than a year later that fellow detainees, who said he had been "driven mad" by his treatment, managed to get word of his existence to their lawyers.

Rendition is sometimes presented simply as an efficient means of transporting terror suspects from one place to another without red tape. Such benign characterizations conceal the truth about a system that puts the victim beyond the protection of the law, and sets the perpetrator above it.

Renditions involve multiple layers of human rights violations. Most victims of rendition were arrested and detained illegally in the first place: some were abducted; others were denied access to any legal process, including the ability to challenge the decision to transfer them because of the risk of torture. There is also a close link between renditions and enforced disappearances. Many of those who have been illegally detained in one country and illegally transported to another have subsequently "disappeared", including dozens who have "disappeared" in US custody. Every one of the victims of rendition interviewed by Amnesty International has described incidents of torture and other ill-treatment.

Because of the secrecy surrounding the practice of rendition, and because many of the victims have "disappeared", it is difficult to estimate the scope of the programme. In many countries, families are reluctant to report their relatives as missing, for fear that intelligence officials will turn their attention on them. Amnesty International has spoken to several people who have given credible accounts of rendition, but are unwilling to make their names or the circumstances of their arrests and transfers known. Some cases come to light when the victim is released or given access to a lawyer, although neither event is a common occurrence in the life of a rendition victim. The number of cases currently appears to be in the hundreds: Egypt's Prime Minister noted in 2005 that the USA had transferred some 60–70 detainees to Egypt alone, and a former CIA agent with experience in the region believes that hundreds of detainees have been sent by the USA to prisons in the Middle East. The USA has acknowledged the capture of about 30 "high value" detainees whose whereabouts remain unknown, and the CIA is reportedly investigating some three dozen additional cases of "erroneous rendition", in which people were detained based on flawed evidence or confusion over names.

However, this is a minimum estimate. Rendition, like "disappearance", is designed to evade public and judicial scrutiny, to hide the identity of the perpetrators and the fate of the victims.

. . .

Amnesty International makes the following recommendations as immediate and essential steps towards putting an end to the rendition programme and its associated practices, including enforced disappearance, torture and incommunicado and secret detention.

Recommendations to all governments:

No renditions

—Do not render or otherwise transfer to the custody of another state anyone suspected or accused of security offences unless the transfer is carried out under judicial supervision and in full observance of due legal process.

—Ensure that anyone subject to transfer has the right to challenge its legality before an independent tribunal, and that they have access to an independent lawyer and an effective right of appeal.

—Do not receive into custody anyone suspected or accused of security offences unless the transfer is carried out under judicial supervision and in full observance of due legal process.

—Information on the numbers, nationalities and current whereabouts of all terror suspects rendered, extradited or otherwise transferred into custody from abroad should be publicly available. Full personal details should be promptly supplied to the families and lawyers of the detainees, and to the International Committee of the Red Cross (ICRC).

—Bring all such detainees before a judicial authority within 24 hours of entry into custody.

—Ensure that detainees have prompt access to legal counsel and to family members, and that lawyers and family members are kept informed of the detainee's whereabouts.

—Ensure that detainees who are not nationals of the detaining country have access to diplomatic or other representatives of their country of nationality or former habitual residence.

No "disappearances", no secret detention

—End immediately the practices of incommunicado and secret detention wherever and under whatever agency it occurs.

—Hold detainees only in officially recognized places of detention with access to family, legal counsel and courts.

—Ensure that those responsible for "disappearances" are brought to justice, and that victims and families receive restitution, compensation and rehabilitation.

—Investigate any allegations that their territory hosts or has hosted secret detention facilities, and make public the results of such investigations.

No torture or other ill-treatment

—Ensure that interrogations are carried out in accordance with international standards, in particular without any use of torture or other cruel, inhuman or degrading treatment.

—Investigate all complaints and reports of torture or other ill-treatment promptly, impartially and effectively, using an agency independent of the alleged perpetrators, and ensure that anyone found responsible is brought to justice.

—Ensure that victims of torture obtain prompt reparation from the state including restitution, fair and adequate financial compensation and appropriate medical care and rehabilitation.

No diplomatic assurances

—Prohibit the return or transfer of people to places where they are at risk of torture or other ill-treatment.

—Do not require or accept "diplomatic assurances" or similar bilateral agreements to justify renditions or any other form of involuntary transfers of individuals to countries where there is a risk of torture or other ill-treatment.

No renditions flights

—Identify to the aviation authorities any plane or helicopter used to carry out the missions of the intelligence services as a state aircraft, even if the aircraft in question is chartered from a private company.

—Ensure that airports and airspace are not used to support and facilitate renditions or rendition flights.

—Maintain and update a register of aircraft operators whose planes have been implicated in rendition flights, and require them to provide detailed information before allowing them landing or flyover rights. Such information should include: the full flight plan of the aircraft, including onward stops and full itinerary, the full names and nationalities of all passengers on board, and the purposes of their travel.

—If any passengers are listed as prisoners or detainees, more detailed information about their status and the status of their flight should be required, including their destination and the legal basis for their transfer.

—Refuse access to airspace and airfields if requested information is not provided.

—If there are grounds to believe that an aircraft is being used in connection with renditions or other human rights violations, board the plane or require it to land for inspection.

—If such inspection indicates that the flight is being used for the unlawful transfer of people, or other human rights violations, the flight should be held until the lawfulness or otherwise of its purpose can be established, and appropriate law enforcement action taken.

Additional recommendations to the US government

—Ensure that anyone held in US custody in any part of the world can exercise the right to legal representation and to a fair and transparent legal process.

—Disclose the location and status of the detention centres where Muhammad Abdullah Salah al-Assad, Muhammad Faraj Ahmed Bashmilah and Salah Nasser Salim 'Ali Qaru were held between October 2003 and May 2005.

—Disclose the identities and whereabouts of all others held in secret locations and their legal status, and invite the ICRC to have full and regular access to all those detained.

—Release all detainees in US custody at undisclosed locations unless they are to be charged with internationally recognizable criminal offences and brought to trial promptly and fairly, in full accordance with relevant international standards, and without recourse to the death penalty.

—Promptly and thoroughly investigate all allegations of "disappearance", and bring those suspected of having committed, ordered or authorized a "disappearance" before the competent civil authorities for prosecution and trial.

Recommendations to private aircraft operators and leasing agents

—Ensure that the company is aware of the end use of any aircraft it is leasing or operating.

—Do not lease or otherwise allow the operation of any aircraft where there is reason to believe it might be used in human rights violations, including rendition or associated operations.

—Develop an explicit human rights policy, ensuring that it complies with the UN Norms on the Responsibilities of Transnational Corporations and Other Business Enterprises with Regard to Human Rights.

7.   IRREGULAR RENDITION LITERATURE

V. Noah Gimbel, Has the Rendition Program Disapppeared, FPIF June 16, 2011, http://www.fpif.org/articles/has_the_rendition_program_disappeared; Daniel L. Pines, Rendition Operations, Does U.S. Law Impose Any Restrictions, 42 Loy. U. Chi. L.J. 523 (2011); John Radsan, A More Regular Process for Irregular Rendition, 37 Seton Hall L.Rev. 1 (2006); Beth Henderson, From Justice to Torture: the Dramatic Evolution of U.S.-sponsored Renditions, Temple Int. and Comp. L.J. 189 (Spring 2006); Michael v. Sage, The Exploitation of Legal Loopholes in the Name of National Security: A Case Study on Extraordinary Rendition, Cal.Western Int'l L.J. (Fall 2006); Leila Nadya Sadat, Extraordinary Rendition, Torture, and other Nightmares from the War on Terror, Geo.Wash. L. Rev. 1200 (August 2007); John Yoo, Transferring Terrorists, 79 Notre Dame L. Rev. 1183, 1221–22 (2004) (discussing the President's authority and discretion over the liberty of captured enemy prisoners); David Weissbrodt and Amy Bergquist, Extraordinary Rendition and the Humanitarian Law of War and Occupation, Va.J. of Int.L.Assoc. 295 (2007); David Weissbrodt and Amy Bergquist, Extraordinary Rendition and the Torture Convention, Va.J. of Int'l L.Assoc. 585 (2006).

CHAPTER 8

MATERIAL WITNESS AND IMMIGRATION DETENTION

■ ■ ■

A. INTRODUCTION

Following on the previous four chapters, each of which explored investigatory tools used by the federal government in enforcement against terrorism, this chapter examines the use of the material witness statute and the power to detain aliens to ensure their availability for proceedings and in aid of investigation. But the power to detain an individual for an extended period is a potent weapon of enforcement that goes much beyond its use simply to ensure availability or for investigation. To be sure, a period of extended detention provides an opportunity to interrogate and obtain information—to be used against the person being detained or to assist in the apprehension and prosecution of others. Detention extended long enough, may also viewed as an effective means to take the person out of action and incapacitate and prevent the commission of crimes. Extended detention also serves as a kind of sanction, albeit without the sanctioned person having had a trial or having been convicted. The length of detention, the conditions under which a person is detained and what goes on during the detention have implications for the issue of whether the detention amounts to punishment.

The length, conditions and what goes on during incarceration are also relevant to the legality of any interrogation that takes place. Issues relating to the interrogation of detainees by U.S. agents or by surrogates were directly considered in chapter 7, but they remain highly relevant to the matters considered in this chapter.

The power to detain for an extended period without notifying relatives or providing access to the detainee and without providing a hearing before a judicial officer or charging the individual is one of the hallmarks of a totalitarian regime in which the people live in fear.

There are a number of different legal bases for detaining people in the United States, in addition to the detention imposed as the result of conviction of crime. Post-arrest, prior-to-charge detention that does not have any other basis is usually limited in length. Post-charge, pre-trial

399

detention can be quite lengthy if the accused is denied bail or cannot make the bail that is set. The use of preventive detention pending trial, on the ground that the accused is dangerous, is a relatively recent development in the federal system based on specific statutory authorization. See United States v. Salerno, 481 U.S. 739 (1987). Also see 18 U.S.C. § 3142(e) and (f), and section 6952 of the Intelligence Reform and Terrorism Prevention Act of 2004 (extending the presumption of preventive detention in certain category of cases to additional offenses).

There are special categories of persons subject to lawful extended detention, for example, under some circumstances, juveniles, sex offenders, and persons suffering from mental illness, but such instances are not directly relevant to the anti-terrorist enforcement effort, though in addressing legal issues in detention cases, the courts often look to such categories as either precedents or as cases to be distinguished. See, e.g., Zadvydas v. Davis, infra, p. 440.

Another basis for a detention that is not based on a criminal conviction that can last in certain circumstances up to one year, or possibly two, is the citing for contempt and detaining of a recalcitrant witness who refuses to testify before the grand jury, for the period during which the grand jury sits.

Following the traumatic events of September 11, 2001, federal agents, in aid of trying to prevent another terrorist act and investigating possible terrorist plots, arrested and detained over 1000 individuals, many of whom remained under detention for an extended period, in some cases for more than a year. Generally, either of two legal justifications was invoked for these detentions. One basis was that the individuals were being held as material witnesses. The second, more frequently cited basis, where it could be used, was that the individuals were aliens and had committed immigration law violations and could be held pending disposition of the alleged violations.

The focus in subsection B. below is on the first of these justifications for extended detention, namely, holding a person as a material witness, even though charges have not yet been filed against anyone. In subsection C., below, the detention of aliens based upon immigration law violations is addressed. In both subsections, the legality of using those legal justifications in aid of the investigation and prevention of terrorism is explored. Further, legislative provisions for detaining aliens on the ground that they are suspected terrorists are examined.

Issues relating to the widespread use of these two bases for extended detention have been litigated in a number of legal contexts. One of the initial legal efforts involved the attempt by a number of public interest groups to obtain detailed information about the detentions under both the material witness and immigration laws. The Department of Justice declined, however, to provide information about who was being detained, where these individuals were being detained and how many persons were being detained.

In response, lawsuits were filed under the Freedom of Information Act to obtain such information. The issues were eventually considered by the U.S. Court of Appeals for the District of Columbia, which generally ruled against requiring the government to release the information. Center for National Security Studies v. U.S. Department of Justice, 331 F.3d 918 (D.C.Cir. 2003), cert. denied 540 U.S. 1104 (2004).

B.　MATERIAL WITNESS DETENTION

1.　INTRODUCTION

The early litigation testing the government's use of the material witness statute post 9/11 involved direct challenges by the detained person to the legality and the incidents of the detention, see In re Material Witness Warrant, 213 F.Supp.2d 287 (S.D.N.Y.2002), or to a criminal prosecution that was argued to be the fruit of an illegal detention, see United States v. Awadallah, 349 F.3d 42 (2d Cir. 2003). The Awadallah case is reproduced infra, p. 403. Subsequently, the legal issues involved in these uses of the material witness statute were also litigated in civil lawsuits brought against government officials by a person who had been detained as a material witness alleging that the material witness statute, as it was being invoked under government policy, was being misused. See Ashcroft v. al-Kidd, infra, p. 416.

The federal material witness statute is 18 U.S.C. § 3144.

18 U.S.C.

§ 3144.　Release or detention of a material witness

If it appears from an affidavit filed by a party that the testimony of a person is material in a criminal proceeding, and if it is shown that it may become impracticable to secure the presence of the person by subpoena, a judicial officer may order the arrest of the person and treat the person in accordance with the provisions of section 3142 of this title. No material witness may be detained because of inability to comply with any condition of release if the testimony of such witness can adequately be secured by deposition, and if further detention is not necessary to prevent a failure of justice. Release of a material witness may be delayed for a reasonable period of time until the deposition of the witness can be taken pursuant to the Federal Rules of Criminal Procedure.

Also see Rule 46 of the Federal Rules of Criminal Procedure:

Rule 46.　Release from Custody; Supervising Detention

(a) Before Trial. The provisions of 18 U.S.C. §§ 3142 and 3144 govern pretrial release.

. . .

(h) Supervising Detention Pending Trial.

(1) *In General.* To eliminate unnecessary detention, the court must supervise the detention within the district of any defendants awaiting trial and of any persons held as material witnesses.

(2) *Reports.* An attorney for the government must report biweekly to the court, listing each material witness held in custody for more than 10 days pending indictment, arraignment, or trial. For each material witness listed in the report, an attorney for the government must state why the witness should not be released with or without a deposition being taken under Rule 15(a).

Questions and Notes

1. Under certain conditions, § 3144 authorizes the arrest and detention of a person whose testimony is material in a criminal proceeding:

a. An affidavit must be filed by the government alleging that the testimony of the person to be detained is "material in a criminal proceeding."

b. A showing must be made that it is impractical to secure the presence of the person by subpoena.

c. If the testimony of the material witness can be adequately secured by deposition and if detention is not necessary to prevent a failure of justice, he/she may not be detained.

2. The basic showing that needs to be made is that the testimony of the witness is material in a criminal proceeding. The government has taken the position that individuals can be held as material witnesses even if a relevant criminal prosecution has not been initiated, provided that the grand jury was sitting and investigating criminal matters. The government's theory is that the grand jury proceeding is a "criminal proceeding" within the meaning of § 3144.

Acceptance of the government's theory (see the Awadallah case below) seems to permit the government to hold the individual at least for the period in which the instant grand jury continues to sit. Compare the case of a witness called before the grand jury to testify who refuses to do so, is held in contempt and is subject to being detained for the duration of the period in which that grand jury sits.

3. The material witness provision, 18 U.S.C. § 3144 refers to § 3142, which deals with conditions of release and hearing requirements for defendants. § 3142 is discussed in Awadallah, infra.

4. Rule 46 of the Federal Rules of Criminal Procedure deals with material witness matters. An amendment of Rule 46 promulgated in 2002 is relevant to the issue of whether a grand jury proceeding is a criminal proceeding within the meaning of § 3144. See the discussion in Awadallah, infra.

2. DIRECT CHALLENGE TO MATERIAL WITNESS DETENTION

UNITED STATES v. AWADALLAH

349 F.3d 42 (2d Cir.2003), cert. denied, Awadallah
v. United States, 543 U.S. 1056 (2005)

Before: JACOBS and STRAUB, CIRCUIT JUDGES, and CARMAN, CHIEF JUDGE. JUDGE STRAUB has filed a separate concurrence.

JACOBS, CIRCUIT JUDGE.

This appeal, which arises from the government's investigation of the September 11, 2001 terrorist attacks, presents questions about the scope of the federal material witness statute and the government's powers of arrest and detention thereunder. *See* 18 U.S.C. § 3144. The district court (Scheindlin, J.) ruled that the statute cannot be applied constitutionally to a grand jury witness such as the defendant-appellee, Osama Awadallah, and dismissed the perjury indictment against him as fruit of an illegal detention.... We conclude that these rulings must be reversed and the indictment reinstated....

In the days immediately following September 11, 2001, the United States Attorney for the Southern District of New York initiated a grand jury investigation into the terrorist attacks. Investigators quickly identified Nawaf Al–Hazmi and Khalid Al–Mihdhar as two of the hijackers on American Airlines Flight 77, which crashed into the Pentagon. The Justice Department released the identities of all nineteen hijackers on Friday, September 14, 2001, and news media around the country publicized their names and photographs the following day. A search of the car Al–Hazmi abandoned at Dulles Airport in Virginia produced a piece of paper with the notation, "Osama 589–5316." Federal agents tracked this number to a San Diego address at which the defendant, Osama Awadallah, had lived approximately eighteen months earlier. Al–Hazmi and Al–Mihdhar also had lived in the San Diego vicinity around that time. The district court made extensive factual findings concerning the ensuing events of September 20 and 21, 2001. *See United States v. Awadallah*, 202 F.Supp.2d 82, 85–96 (S.D.N.Y.2002) (*"Awadallah IV"*). With two minor exceptions, the court credited Awadallah's testimony over that of the FBI agents.... However, the government "has elected not to appeal Judge Scheindlin's credibility findings and does not contest them here." For purposes of this appeal, then, the government accepts and relies on the facts found by the district court, as does Awadallah. Our recitation of the facts conforms to the district court's findings....

Throughout the questioning ..., the FBI agents in San Diego had been in contact with an Assistant United States Attorney ("AUSA") in New York. At approximately 2:00 p.m. Eastern time, the AUSA instructed the agents to arrest Awadallah as a material witness. The agents handcuffed Awadallah and took him to the San Diego correctional center for booking. Meanwhile, prosecutors and agents in New York prepared an application for a material witness warrant. In the supporting affidavit, FBI Special Agent Ryan Plunkett recounted how the FBI found the phone number in Al–Hazmi's car, Awadallah's admission that he knew Al–Hazmi, and the results of the agents' searches, including the "box-cutter" and the photographs of bin Laden. Agent Plunkett stated that it might become difficult to secure Awadallah's grand jury testimony because he had extensive family ties in Jordan and might be a flight risk. The affidavit did not say when Awadallah said he had last seen Al–Hazmi (over a year earlier); that Awadallah had moved eighteen months earlier from the address associated with the phone number; that Awadallah had used the "box-cutter" recently to install a new carpet in his apartment; that Awadallah had been (ostensibly) cooperative with the FBI agents in San Diego; or that Awadallah had three brothers who lived in San Diego, one of whom was an American citizen. Also, the affidavit stated that the "box-cutter" had been found in Awadallah's apartment when, in fact, it had been found in his inoperative second car. Shortly before 6:00 p.m. Eastern time, Agent Plunkett and an AUSA presented the material witness warrant application to Chief Judge Mukasey of the United States District Court for the Southern District of New York. Based solely on the contents of Agent Plunkett's affidavit, Chief Judge Mukasey issued a warrant to arrest Awadallah as a material witness pursuant to 18 U.S.C. § 3144. The court was unaware that Awadallah had already been arrested as a material witness three hours earlier.

On September 25, 2001, Awadallah appeared before a Magistrate Judge Ruben B. Brooks in the Southern District of California, who declined to release him on bail and ordered that he be removed to New York. On October 2, 2001, the day after he arrived in New York, Awadallah appeared before Chief Judge Mukasey for a second bail hearing. Chief Judge Mukasey also declined to release Awadallah on bail, finding his continued detention to be "reasonable under the circumstances."

During the period of his detention, Awadallah spent time in four prisons as he was transferred to the New York correctional center by way of Oklahoma City. He alleges that he received harsh and improper treatment during this period. Because these allegations of abuse and mistreatment were immaterial to the issues before the district court, Judge Scheindlin expressly declined to make "findings of fact on disputed issues regarding the conditions of confinement...." On October 10, 2001, twenty days after his arrest as a material witness, Awadallah testified before the grand jury in the Southern District of New York. The prosecutor questioned him for most of the day. In the course of his testimony, Awadallah denied knowing anyone named Khalid Al–Mihdhar or Khalid.... On October 15, 2001, when Awadallah again appeared before the grand jury, he stated that his recollection of Khalid's name had been refreshed by his October 10 testimony and that the disputed writing in the exam booklet was in fact his own. However, he did not admit to making false statements in his first grand jury appearance.

The United States Attorney for the Southern District of New York filed charges against Awadallah on two counts of making false statements to the grand jury in violation of 18 U.S.C. § 1623: falsely denying that he knew Khalid Al–Mihdhar (Count One); and falsely denying that the handwriting in the exam booklet was his own (Count Two).

On November 27, 2001, the district court (Scheindlin, J.) granted Awadallah's bail application. He satisfied the bail conditions and was released approximately two weeks later. In December 2001, Awadallah moved to dismiss the indictment. . . .

On April 30, 2002, after an evidentiary hearing and further briefing, the district court issued two orders dismissing the indictment against Awadallah. In *Awadallah III,* the court ruled that the federal material witness statute, 18 U.S.C. § 3144, did not apply to grand jury witnesses. 202 F.Supp.2d at 61–79. This ruling evidently was made without briefing or argument. The court held that Awadallah's arrest and detention were therefore unlawful. . . . Judge Scheindlin ruled that Awadallah's perjured grand jury testimony had to be suppressed as fruit of this illegal arrest and detention. . . .

The government filed a timely notice of appeal. . . . Awadallah remains free on bail at this time.

We consider the issues presented on appeal in the order in which the district court developed them: (1) whether the federal material witness statute, 18 U.S.C. § 3144, may be applied to grand jury witnesses like Awadallah; . . .

The first issue presented is whether the federal material witness statute, 18 U.S.C. § 3144, allows the arrest and detention of grand jury witnesses. In *Awadallah III,* the district court determined that it did not. Shortly thereafter, however, on July 11, 2002, Chief Judge Mukasey issued an opinion in an unrelated case that declined to follow the reasoning and holding of *Awadallah III.* Specifically, Judge Mukasey held that 18 U.S.C. § 3144 applies to grand jury witnesses. *See In re Material Witness Warrant,* 213 F.Supp.2d 287, 288 (S.D.N.Y.2002). Thus there is now a split of authority within the Circuit on this question.

. . . Both parties to this appeal, as well as the amici, persuasively urge us to decide whether § 3144 may properly be applied to grand jury witnesses. The issue is squarely presented, has been fully briefed, and will tend to evade review in future cases where the detention is brief or matters take a different procedural course.

18 U.S.C. § 3144 . . . is cast in terms of a material witness in "a criminal proceeding." The decisive question here is whether that term encompasses proceedings before a grand jury. Based on its study of the statutory wording, context, legislative history, and case law, the district court held that "Section 3144 only allows the detention of material

witnesses in the pretrial (as opposed to the grand jury) context." We have found no other decision that has arrived at this conclusion.

The only prior case that squarely considered the issue held that 18 U.S.C. § 3149, the precursor to today's material witness statute, allowed detention of grand jury witnesses. *See Bacon v. United States,* 449 F.2d 933, 936–41 (9th Cir.1971). The Ninth Circuit conceded that "[t]he term 'criminal proceeding,' absent a clear context, [was] ambiguous," but held that the relevant statutes and Federal Rules of Criminal Procedure, "[t]aken as a whole," were "clearly broad enough in scope to encompass grand jury investigations".

Other courts, including this one, have assumed that the material witness statute authorizes detention of grand jury witnesses. . . .

Two judges have also declined to follow the district court's ruling in this case. In *In re Material Witness Warrant,* 213 F.Supp.2d 287 (S.D.N.Y. 2002), Chief Judge Mukasey "decline[d] to follow the reasoning and holding in *Awadallah,"* holding instead:

> Given the broad language of the statute, its legislative history . . ., the substantial body of case law indicating that there is no constitutional impediment to detention of grand jury witnesses, and the unquestioned application of the statute to grand jury witnesses over a period of decades before *Awadallah,* to perceive a Congressional intention that grand jury witnesses be excluded from the reach of section 3144 is to perceive something that is not there.

[S]ee also In re Grand Jury Material Witness Detention, 271 F.Supp.2d 1266, 1268 (D.Or.2003) (concluding that "a grand jury proceeding constitutes a 'criminal proceeding,' as the term is used in § 3144"). Having the benefit of thorough opinions on both sides of the question, we conclude that the district court's ruling in this case must be reversed.

. . .

As noted above, § 3144 applies to witnesses whose testimony is material in "a criminal proceeding." 18 U.S.C. § 3144. "Criminal proceeding" is a broad and capacious term, and there is good reason to conclude that it includes a grand jury proceeding. First, it has long been recognized that "[t]he word 'proceeding' is not a technical one, and is aptly used by courts to designate an inquiry before a grand jury." Second, the term "criminal proceeding" has been construed in other statutes to encompass grand jury proceedings. . . .

Notwithstanding this support for the general view that "criminal proceedings" encompass grand jury proceedings, however, we cannot say that the statutory wording alone compels that conclusion. Black's Law Dictionary defines a "criminal proceeding" as "[a] proceeding instituted to determine a person's guilt or innocence or to set a convicted person's punishment; a criminal hearing or trial." *Black's Law Dictionary* 1221 (7th ed.1999). It defines a "grand jury" as "[a] body of . . . people . . . who, in ex parte proceedings, decide whether to issue indictments. If the grand jury decides that evidence is strong enough to hold a suspect for trial, it returns a bill of indictment . . . charging the suspect with a specific crime." Defined this way, a grand jury proceeding is not a "proceeding instituted to determine a person's guilt or innocence or to set a convicted person's punishment," but rather a proceeding to "decide whether to issue indictments." . . . A grand jury proceeding is certainly a stage of criminal justice; and it is certainly a proceeding. As a proceeding, it is certainly not civil, administrative, arbitral, commercial, social, or any type of proceeding other than (or as much as) criminal. Even so, the dictionary entries could suggest that grand jury proceedings lie outside the scope of § 3144.

. . .

The statutory context does not allay all uncertainty. Under § 3144, a judge "may order the arrest of the person and treat the person in accordance with the provisions of section 3142 of this title." 18 U.S.C. § 3144. Section 3142, which sets conditions for the "[r]elease or detention of a defendant pending trial," uses terms not normally associated with grand juries. It provides: Upon the appearance before a judicial officer of a person *charged with an offense,* the judicial officer shall issue an order that, *pending trial,* the person be—(1) released on personal recognizance or upon execution of an unsecured appearance bond . . . ; (2) released on a condition or combination of conditions . . . ; (3) temporarily detained to permit revocation of conditional release, deportation, or exclusion . . . ; or (4) detained. . . .

By its own terms, § 3142 applies during the post-indictment ("a person charged with an offense") and pretrial ("pending trial") phase of criminal prosecution. The section also goes on to identify factors to be considered "in determining whether there are conditions of release that will reasonably assure the appearance of the person as required and the safety of any other person and the community." 18 U.S.C. § 3142(g). Two of the four listed considerations have little bearing on the situation of an individual detained as a material witness in a grand jury proceeding. *See* 18 U.S.C. § 3142(g)(1) ("[t]he nature and circumstances of the offense charged"); *id.* § 3142(g)(2) ("the weight of the evidence against the person"). For these reasons, we must look beyond the text of § 3144 to discern the meaning of "criminal proceeding."

The legislative history of § 3144 makes clear Congress's intent to include grand jury proceedings within the definition of "criminal proceeding." Congress enacted § 3144 in its current form as part of the Bail Reform Act of 1984. *See* Pub.L. No. 98–473, 98 Stat. 1837, 1976–81 (1984). Its language is nearly identical to the text of its predecessor statute, 18 U.S.C. § 1349 (1966), which the Ninth Circuit construed to encompass grand juries. *See Bacon,* 449 F.2d at 939–41. . . .

The most telling piece of legislative history appears in the Senate Judiciary Committee Report that accompanied the 1984 enactment of § 3144. The Report stated that, "[i]f a person's testimony is material in any criminal proceeding, and if it is shown that it may become impracticable to secure his presence by subpoena, the government is authorized to take such person into custody." S.Rep. No. 98–225, at 28 (1983), *reprinted in* 1984 U.S.C.C.A.N. 3182, 3211. A footnote to this statement advised categorically that "[a] grand jury investigation is a 'criminal proceeding' within the meaning of this section. *Bacon v. United States,* 449 F.2d 933 (9th Cir.1971)." *Id.* at 25 n. 88, 1984 U.S.C.C.A.N. at 3208. The approving citation to *Bacon* by the Senate Committee with responsibility for this bill is as indicative as the text of the footnote....

In surveying legislative history we have repeatedly stated that the authoritative source for finding the Legislature's intent lies in the Committee Reports on the bill, which "represen[t] the considered and collective understanding of those Congressmen involved in drafting and studying proposed legislation."

Here, the Senate committee report states in so many words the intent to include grand jury proceedings within the ambit of the statute—an intent that is consistent with the statute's language, even if not compelled by it.

This statement of congressional intent is particularly telling, because the Bail Reform Act of 1984 reenacted the provisions of the former § 3149 in nearly identical language. "Congress is presumed to be aware of an administrative or judicial interpretation of a statute and to adopt that interpretation when it re-enacts a statute without change." ...

Awadallah and an amicus party supporting his position argue that this principle of ratification by reenactment is inapplicable because there was no "settled judicial interpretation" of the term "criminal proceeding" when § 3144 was enacted in 1984. We disagree. The Senate report stated that "[a] grand jury investigation is a 'criminal proceeding' *within the meaning of this section.*" S.Rep. No. 98–225, at 25 n. 88 (1983), 1984 U.S.C.C.A.N. at 3208 (emphasis added). As of 1984, a single court had expressly considered whether the term "criminal proceeding" within the meaning of the federal material witness statute included grand jury proceedings—and it had held that it did.... When Congress enacted § 3144—and until the district court ruled otherwise in this case—there was a settled view that a grand jury proceeding is a "criminal proceeding" for purposes of the material witness statute. We therefore conclude that a grand jury proceeding is a "criminal proceeding" for purposes of § 3144.

· · ·

As a threshold matter, the detention of material witnesses for the purpose of securing grand jury testimony has withstood constitutional challenge.

... [W]e see no serious constitutional problem that would warrant the exclusion of grand jury proceedings from the scope of § 3144.

· · ·

The essential purpose of the proscriptions in the Fourth Amendment is to impose a standard of "reasonableness" upon the exercise of discretion by government officials, including law enforcement agents, in order "to safeguard the privacy and security of individuals against arbitrary invasions. . . ." Thus, the permissibility of a particular law enforcement practice is judged by balancing its intrusion on the individual's Fourth Amendment interests against its promotion of legitimate governmental interests.

. . . Thus we must consider both "the nature and quality of the intrusion on the individual's Fourth Amendment interests" and "the importance of the governmental interests alleged to justify the intrusion." . . . In its balancing analysis, the district court found that "[t]he only legitimate reason to detain a grand jury witness is to aid in 'an ex parte investigation to determine whether a crime has been committed and whether criminal proceedings should be instituted against any person.' " . . . This is no small interest. . . . The district court noted (and we agree) that it would be improper for the government to use § 3144 for other ends, such as the detention of persons suspected of criminal activity for which probable cause has not yet been established. However, the district court made no finding (and we see no evidence to suggest) that the government arrested Awadallah for any purpose other than to secure information material to a grand jury investigation. Moreover, that grand jury was investigating the September 11 terrorist attacks. The particular governmental interests at stake therefore were the indictment and successful prosecution of terrorists whose attack, if committed by a sovereign, would have been tantamount to war, and the discovery of the conspirators' means, contacts, and operations in order to forestall future attacks.

On the other side of the balance, the district court found in essence that § 3144 was not calibrated to minimize the intrusion on the liberty of a grand jury witness. According to the district court, several procedural safeguards available to trial witnesses are not afforded in the grand jury context. We agree with the district court, of course, that arrest and detention are significant infringements on liberty, but we conclude that § 3144 sufficiently limits that infringement and reasonably balances it against the government's countervailing interests.

The first procedural safeguard to be considered is § 3144's provision that "[n]o material witness may be detained because of inability to comply with any condition of release *if the testimony of such witness can adequately be secured by deposition,* and if further detention is not necessary to prevent a failure of justice." 18 U.S.C. § 3144 (emphasis added). The district court agreed with the government that this deposition provision does not apply to grand jury witnesses. The government's altered position on appeal is that "Congress intended depositions to be available as a less restrictive alternative to detaining a grand jury witness." Such a pivot by the government on appeal is awkward, but we accept the government's explanation that it was persuaded by Chief Judge Mukasey's view in *In re Material Witness Warrant,* 213 F.Supp.2d at 296.

We conclude that the deposition mechanism is available for grand jury witnesses detained under § 3144. At the time of Awadallah's detention, the Federal Rule of Criminal Procedure that governs depositions provided:

If a witness is detained pursuant to [§ 3144], the court on written motion of the witness and upon notice to the parties may direct that the witness' deposition be taken. After the deposition has been subscribed the court may discharge the witness.

The district court is thereby authorized to order a deposition and to release the witness once it has been taken. Awadallah and the NYCDL argue that this provision cannot apply to grand jury witnesses because there can be no "party" or "trial" prior to indictment. The prosecutor and the witness may broadly be deemed parties, however, in the sense that each has interests to advance or protect before the grand jury. Thus, the rule governing the issuance of subpoenas—which indisputably applies during grand jury proceedings—refers to "the party requesting" a subpoena. Fed.R.Crim.P. 17(a).

The district court found the deposition provision inapplicable in the grand jury context in part because a conventional deposition is inconsistent with the procedural and evidentiary rules of a grand jury hearing. . . . [T]he district court may set additional conditions for the conduct of a deposition. Compare Fed.R.Crim.P. 15(d) (1987) ("[s]ubject to such additional conditions as the court shall provide"), *with* Fed.R.Crim.P. 15(e) (2003) ("[u]nless these rules or a court order provides otherwise"). The court thus can limit the deposition according to grand jury protocol, for example by limiting the witness's right to have counsel present during the deposition or by permitting the use of hearsay.

Rule 46 of the Federal Rules of Criminal Procedure, which governs detention and release, further supports the view that depositions are available to grand jury witnesses detained under § 3144. The version of Rule 46 in effect at the time of Awadallah's detention provided that "[t]he attorney for the government shall make a biweekly report to the court listing *each* defendant and *witness* who has been *held in custody pending indictment,* arraignment or trial for a period in excess of ten days," and as to "each witness so listed," state "the reasons why such witness should not be released with or without the taking of a *deposition* pursuant to Rule 15(a)." Fed.R.Crim.P. 46(g) (1993) (emphasis added). The new version of the rule, which omits the reference to defendants, is even more explicit:

An attorney for the government must report biweekly to the court, listing each material witness held in custody for more than 10 days pending indictment, arraignment, or trial. For each material witness listed in the report, an attorney for the government must state why the witness should not be released with or without a deposition being taken under Rule 15(a).

Fed. R. Crim. P. 46(h)(2) (2003).

Both versions of the rule expressly contemplate the deposition of a "witness held in custody ... pending indictment." It follows that the deposition mechanism of § 3144 is a safeguard available to grand jury witnesses.

The second procedural safeguard at issue is § 3144's express invocation of the bail and release provisions set forth in 18 U.S.C. § 3142. Section 3144 directs that "a judicial officer may ... treat the [detained] person in accordance with the provisions of section 3142 of this title." 18 U.S.C. § 3144. As noted above, § 3142 sets conditions for the "[r]elease or detention of a defendant pending trial," as follows:

Upon the appearance before a judicial officer of a person charged with an offense, the judicial officer shall issue an order that, pending trial, the person be—(1) released on personal recognizance or upon execution of an unsecured appearance bond ...; (2) released on a condition or combination of conditions ...; (3) temporarily detained to permit revocation of conditional release, deportation, or exclusion ...; or (4) detained.... 18 U.S.C. § 3142(a).

As the district court observed, some of the terms used in § 3142— namely, "a person charged with an offense" and "pending trial"—do not comport with the structure of grand jury proceedings. However, we do not deduce (as the district court did) that "it is plain that section 3142 cannot apply to grand jury proceedings." We agree with Chief Judge Mukasey that the provisions of § 3142 govern insofar as they are applicable in the grand jury setting:

[T]he common sense reading of section 3144 is that it refers to section 3142 only insofar as that section is applicable to witnesses, in making available such alternatives to incarceration as release on bail or on conditions, in suggesting standards such as risk of flight, likelihood that the person will appear, and danger to the community, and in providing for a detention hearing. Not every provision of section 3142 applies to witnesses, but some do, and those govern. *In re Material Witness Warrant*, 213 F.Supp.2d at 295.

Thus, a person detained as a material witness in a grand jury investigation may obtain a hearing on the propriety of his continued detention and the conditions, if any, which will allow his release.

The district court also observed that the closed nature of a grand jury investigation limits the court's ability to assess the materiality of a witness's testimony. This may be true at the margins, because the materiality of the testimony given by a trial witness can be assessed on the basis of the indictment, discovery materials, and trial evidence, whereas grand jury secrecy requires the judge to rely largely on the prosecutor's representations about the scope of the investigation and the materiality of the witness's testimony. However, as Chief Judge Mukasey observed, "courts make similar determinations all the time, based on sealed submissions, when deciding whether a subpoena calls for relevant information, whether such information is privileged, and the like." Moreover, "the hypothesized difficulty of the materiality decision can be just as great, or greater, when a court must determine if a trial witness must be detained, because the decision likely will have to be made before the trial begins and thus before it is possible to fit the witness's testimony into the grid of other evidence." The materiality determination called for by § 3144 lies within the district court's competence.

Finally, Awadallah and the NYCDL argue that § 3144 provides no limit on how long a grand jury witness may be detained, whereas the detention of a trial witness is implicitly limited (or speeded) by the time limits on prosecution contained in the Speedy Trial Act, 18 U.S.C. § 3161 *et seq.* However, the Speedy Trial Act permits delay for various reasons, *see* 18 U.S.C. § 3161(h), which may have the collateral effect of extending the detention of a material witness; and nothing in the Speedy Trial Act requires a court to consider the effect of a continuance or delay on a detained witness. The Act therefore provides cold comfort to a detained trial witness.

While § 3144 contains no express time limit, the statute and related rules require close institutional attention to the propriety and duration of detentions: "[n]o material witness may be detained because of inability to comply with any condition of release if the testimony of such witness can adequately be secured by deposition, and if further detention is not necessary to prevent a failure of justice." 18 U.S.C. § 3144. The court must "treat the person in accordance with the provisions of section 3142," which provides a mechanism for release. And release may be delayed only "for a reasonable period of time until the deposition of the witness can be taken pursuant to the Federal Rules of Criminal Procedure." Perhaps most important, Rule 46 requires the government to make a "biweekly report" to the court listing each material witness held in custody for more than ten days and justifying the continued detention of each witness. Fed.R.Crim.P. 46(g) (1993); *see also* Fed.R.Crim.P. 46(h)(2) (2003). These measures tend to ensure that material witnesses are detained no longer than necessary.

In light of the foregoing analysis, we must ask whether Awadallah was properly detained when he was held for several weeks without being allowed to give his deposition and obtain release. Such a detention constitutes a significant intrusion on liberty, since a material witness can be arrested with little or no notice, transported across the country, and detained for several days or weeks. Under the circumstances of this case, however, we are satisfied that Awadallah's detention was not unreasonably prolonged. . . .

As indicated above, the deposition mechanism invoked in § 3144 is available to grand jury witnesses, but it is not required in every instance. Section 3144 requires release after deposition only if "the testimony of such witness can *adequately* be secured by deposition" and "further detention is not necessary to prevent a failure of justice." 18 U.S.C. § 3144 (emphasis added). Similarly, § 3142 provides that a person may be detained if, "after a hearing . . . , the judicial officer finds that no condition or combination of conditions will reasonably assure the appearance of the person as required and the safety of any other person and the community." 18 U.S.C. § 3142(e).

The procedural history demonstrates that Awadallah received adequate process to ensure that the duration of his detention was reasonable. Awadallah was arrested on Friday, September 21, 2001. He first appeared before a magistrate judge in San Diego for a bail hearing on Monday, September 24. That hearing was adjourned until the following day in order for Awadallah's counsel to obtain a translator. When Awadallah appeared before the magistrate judge the next day, the court received testimony from his witnesses and heard argument from counsel. Awadallah's attorney argued, among other things, that a deposition should be taken pursuant to § 3144. The court found that, under § 3142, there were no conditions of release that would reasonably assure Awadallah's appearance before the grand jury. The court denied bail and ordered that Awadallah be removed to New York. The government transported Awadallah across the country, and he arrived in New York on Monday, October 1. The next day, he appeared for a second bail hearing before Chief Judge Mukasey in the Southern District of New York. Chief Judge Mukasey also declined to release Awadallah from detention, finding that, "given the facts alleged in the application[,] he may well have incentive to leave," and that "[t]here is no way to prevent him from leaving, no effective way, unless he is detained." The court found that his continued detention was "reasonable under the circumstances." During this hearing, the government informed the court that the grand jury met only on Mondays and Wednesdays, that the following Monday was a holiday, and that the next opportunity to present Awadallah to the grand jury would be Wednesday, October 10. The court therefore set October 11 as a control date for further hearings.

When Awadallah appeared before the grand jury on Wednesday, October 10, he made statements that resulted in perjury charges being filed against him. He testified before the grand jury a second time on Monday, October 15, and he was arrested on the perjury charges on Friday, October 19. All told, Awadallah spent 20 days in detention as a material witness before testifying before the grand jury and uttering the allegedly perjurious statements. The undisputed facts establish that he received two bail hearings pursuant to § 3142 within days of his arrest, and that the judges in both hearings found his continued detention to be both reasonable and necessary. Under these circumstances, Awadallah's detention as a material witness was a scrupulous and constitutional use of the federal material witness statute.

QUESTIONS AND NOTES

1. Note that the district court judge in Awadallah had ruled in favor of the detained person, but there was a contrary district court ruling in another

case that held that a grand jury proceeding was a criminal proceeding within the meaning of the material witness statute. In re Material Witness, 213 F.Supp.2d 287 (S.D.N.Y.2002). It is worth mentioning that the district judge in the latter case, Michael B. Mukasey, subsequently served, toward the end of the Bush administration, as Attorney General of the United States. The court of appeals in Awadallah relied heavily on Judge Mukasey's opinion in the unrelated case.

2. The issue of whether a grand jury proceeding is a criminal proceeding within the meaning of the material witness statute is addressed in some detail by the Awadallah court as an issue of statutory interpretation. Inter alia, the court relies on a judicial precedent and a legislative committee citation approval of that same precedent. The court also relies on the language of and an amendment of Rule 46 of the Federal Rules of Criminal Procedure. Can the language of Rule 46 that was in effect at the time of Awadallah's detention be read in a different way than the court's reading?

3. Note that the court of appeals in Awadallah, relying on Judge Mukasey's reasoning in his district court opinion in another case rejects arguments based on the awkward fit between applying the material witness statute at the grand jury stage and the language of 18 U.S.C. § 3142, which is made applicable to material witnesses by § 3144, the material witness statute.

4. Recall that arrest as a material witness is only authorized when a showing has been made that it is impractical to secure the presence of the witness by subpoena; and if the testimony can be secured by deposition, a person cannot be detained. How does the court of appeals treat these issues in the Awadallah case?

5. What are the practical implications of the use of the material witness statute even in the absence of a criminal charge having been filed against anyone? Does it mean that the material witness statute can be invoked in a much wider range of cases? Does it mean that there are increased risks of abuse of the statute, that is, that it can more easily be used for purposes other than those for which the statute was intended? Of course, that raises the question: What are the true purposes of the material witness statute?

6. The exact number of persons who were held as material witnesses in the immediate aftermath of the 9/11 attacks has not been made public. In 2002, the Washington Post reported that "at least 44 persons" have been detained under this heading since September 11, 2001. Washington Post, November 24, 2002, p. A01.

7. In the district court opinion in Center for National Security Studies v. U.S. DOJ, 215 F.Supp. 2d 94, 106 (D.D.C. 2002), Judge Kessler stated:

> The Government's reliance on grand jury secrecy rules to justify withholding the identities of material witnesses is fundamentally wrong as a matter of law. First, on its face, Fed. R. Crim. P. 6(e) does not bar disclosure of the identities of persons detained as material witnesses. Fed. R. Crim. P. 6(e) (2) prohibits disclosure of "matters occurring before the grand jury." Fed. R. Crim. P. 6(e) (6) provides that "records, orders and subpoenas relating to grand jury proceedings shall be kept under seal to

the extent and for such time as is necessary to prevent disclosure of matters occurring before a grand jury."

Compare, however, Judge Mukasey's view expressed in footnote 1 in In re Material Witness Warrant, 213 F.Supp. 2d 287, 288 (S.D.N.Y. 2002):

> The witness who has filed the current motion was taken into custody pursuant to a warrant issued in aid of a grand jury subpoena, and the docket and the record of all appearances in this matter have been sealed as proceedings ancillary to grand jury proceedings. See Fed. R. Crim. P. 6(e)(2), (5) and (6) (setting forth general rule of secrecy and rules for closing of hearings and sealing of records). Accordingly, neither the witness's name nor any identifying facts about him or this matter are set forth in this opinion, except to the extent necessary to treat the legal issues presented.

Judge Mukasey, however, was also reported to have given a talk at the Brooklyn Law School in which he mentioned the subject of secrecy surrounding the detention of a person as a material witness, indicating that the material witnesses were not being held "incommunicado," and that "[a]lthough the court proceedings were sealed ... the lawyers for the witnesses were free to talk about the cases or not, as they chose." Washington Post, November 24, 2002, p. AO1. The same article suggests that there is confusion among lawyers about what they can and cannot reveal. Ibid.

Can you reconcile the Kessler and Mukasey view (as he expressed it in In re Material Witness Warrant case) about the relevance of grand jury secrecy to material witness status in these matters? Is it an implication of the Mukasey view that government can keep secret the identities of any persons taken into custody as material witnesses on the theory that their testimony before a grand jury is needed?

8. It has also been suggested that a built-in safeguard in connection with the detaining of a person as a material witness is the fact that a judge always supervises the matter, although it has been reported that some former prosecutors do not believe that judges offer much supervision in such matters. Washington Post, November 24, 2002, p. AO1.

9. Awadallah was subsequently tried on the perjury charge that had been filed arising out of his grand jury testimony. He was acquitted in November, 2006. See NY Times online ed. November 17, 2006.

10. Sometimes arresting a person as a material witness is a temporizing action, while the prosecutor gathers enough evidence to charge the individual with a crime. See Laurie E. Levenson, 35 Loy. L.A. L.Rev. 1217, 1222 (2002). Some well-known defendants originally detained as material witnesses and then later charged with a crime include Zacarias Moussaoui and Jose Padilla. Padilla was originally detained as a material witness, and then the government switched his status to that of an "enemy combatant" in military custody, and still later, he was transferred back to civilian custody and indicted and prosecuted in a federal criminal trial. In this last-mentioned proceeding, he moved to suppress physical evidence on the ground that there had not been probable cause for his original detention as a material witness.

3. CIVIL LAWSUIT ALLEGING ILLEGAL DETENTION AS A MATERIAL WITNESS

ASHCROFT v. AL–KIDD

131 S.Ct. 2074 (2011)

[SCALIA, J., delivered the opinion of the Court, in which ROBERTS, C.J., and KENNEDY, THOMAS, and ALITO, JJ., joined. KENNEDY, J., filed a concurring opinion, in which GINSBURG, BREYER, and SOTOMAYOR, JJ., joined as to Part I. GINSBURG, J., filed an opinion concurring in the judgment, in which BREYER and SOTOMAYOR, JJ., joined. SOTOMAYOR, J., filed an opinion concurring in the judgment, in which GINSBURG and BREYER, JJ., joined. KAGAN, J., took no part in the consideration or decision of the case.]

JUSTICE SCALIA delivered the opinion of the Court.

We decide whether a former Attorney General enjoys immunity from suit for allegedly authorizing federal prosecutors to obtain valid material-witness warrants for detention of terrorism suspects whom they would otherwise lack probable cause to arrest.

I

The federal material-witness statute authorizes judges to "order the arrest of [a] person" whose testimony "is material in a criminal proceeding ... if it is shown that it may become impracticable to secure the presence of the person by subpoena." 18 U.S.C. § 3144. Material witnesses enjoy the same constitutional right to pretrial release as other federal detainees, and federal law requires release if their testimony "can adequately be secured by deposition, and if further detention is not necessary to prevent a failure of justice." *Ibid.*

Because this case arises from a motion to dismiss, we accept as true the factual allegations in Abdullah al-Kidd's complaint. The complaint alleges that, in the aftermath of the September 11th terrorist attacks, then-Attorney General John Ashcroft authorized federal prosecutors and law enforcement officials to use the material-witness statute to detain individuals with suspected ties to terrorist organizations. It is alleged that federal officials had no intention of calling most of these individuals as witnesses, and that they were detained, at Ashcroft's direction, because federal officials suspected them of supporting terrorism but lacked sufficient evidence to charge them with a crime.

It is alleged that this pretextual detention policy led to the material-witness arrest of al-Kidd, a native-born United States citizen. FBI agents apprehended him in March 2003 as he checked in for a flight to Saudi Arabia. Two days earlier, federal officials had informed a Magistrate Judge that, if al-Kidd boarded his flight, they believed information "crucial" to the prosecution of Sami Omar al-Hussayen would be lost. al-Kidd remained in federal custody for 16 days and on supervised release until al-Hussayen's trial concluded 14 months later. Prosecutors never called him as a witness.

In March 2005, al-Kidd filed this *Bivens* action, see *Bivens v. Six Unknown Fed. Narcotics Agents,* 403 U.S. 388, 91 S.Ct. 1999, 29 L.Ed.2d 619 (1971) to challenge the constitutionality of Ashcroft's alleged policy; he also asserted several other claims not relevant here against Ashcroft and others. Ashcroft filed a motion to dismiss based on absolute and qualified immunity, which the District Court denied. A divided panel of the United States Court of Appeals for the Ninth Circuit affirmed, holding that the Fourth Amendment prohibits pretextual arrests absent probable cause of criminal wrongdoing, and that Ashcroft could not claim qualified or absolute immunity.

Judge Bea dissented, 580 F.3d, at 981, and eight judges dissented from the denial of rehearing en banc, see 598 F.3d 1129, 1137, 1142 (C.A.9 2010). We granted certiorari.

II

Qualified immunity shields federal and state officials from money damages unless a plaintiff pleads facts showing (1) that the official violated a statutory or constitutional right, and (2) that the right was "clearly established" at the time of the challenged conduct....

... When ... a Court of Appeals does address both prongs of qualified-immunity analysis, we have discretion to correct its errors at each step. Although not necessary to reverse an erroneous judgment, doing so ensures that courts do not insulate constitutional decisions at the frontiers of the law from our review or inadvertently undermine the values qualified immunity seeks to promote. The former occurs when the constitutional-law question is wrongly decided; the latter when what is not clearly established is held to be so. In this case, the Court of Appeals' analysis at both steps of the qualified-immunity inquiry needs correction.

A

The Fourth Amendment protects "[t]he right of the people to be secure in their persons, houses, papers, and effects, against unreasonable searches and seizures." An arrest, of course, qualifies as a "seizure" of a "person" under this provision, *Dunaway v. New York,* 442 U.S. 200 (1979), and so must be reasonable under the circumstances. Al–Kidd does not assert that Government officials would have acted unreasonably if they had used a material-witness warrant to arrest him for the purpose of securing his testimony for trial. He contests, however (and the Court of Appeals here rejected), the reasonableness of using the warrant to detain him as a suspected criminal.

Fourth Amendment reasonableness "is predominantly an objective inquiry." *Edmond,* 121 S.Ct. 447. We ask whether "the circumstances, viewed objectively, justify [the challenged] action." If so, that action was reasonable *"whatever* the subjective intent" motivating the relevant officials. *Whren v. United States,* 517 U.S. 806, 814, 116 S.Ct. 1769, 135 L.Ed.2d 89 (1996). This approach recognizes that the Fourth Amendment regulates conduct rather than thoughts, and it promotes evenhanded, uniform enforcement of the law.

Two "limited exception[s]" to this rule are our special-needs and administrative-search cases, where "actual motivations" do matter. A judicial warrant and probable cause are not needed where the search or seizure is justified by "special needs, beyond the normal need for law enforcement," such as the need to deter drug use in public schools, or the need to assure that railroad employees engaged in train operations are not under the influence of drugs or alcohol; and where the search or seizure is in execution of an administrative warrant authorizing, for example, an inspection of fire-damaged premises to determine the cause, an inspection of residential premises to assure compliance with a housing code, *Camara v. Municipal Court of City and County of San Francisco,* 387 U.S. 523, 535–538, 87 S.Ct. 1727, 18 L.Ed.2d 930 (1967). But those exceptions do not apply where the officer's purpose is not to attend to the special needs or to the investigation for which the administrative inspection is justified. See *Whren, supra,* at 811–812, 116 S.Ct. 1769. The Government seeks to justify the present arrest on the basis of a properly issued judicial warrant—so that the special-needs and administrative-inspection cases cannot be the basis for a purpose inquiry here.

Apart from those cases, we have almost uniformly rejected invitations to probe subjective intent. There is one category of exception, upon which the Court of Appeals principally relied. In *Edmond,* 531 U.S. 32, 121 S.Ct. 447, 148 L.Ed.2d 333, we held that the Fourth Amendment could not condone suspicionless vehicle checkpoints set up for the purpose of detecting illegal narcotics. Although we had previously approved vehicle checkpoints set up for the purpose of keeping off the road unlicensed drivers, and for the purpose of interdicting those who illegally cross the border, we found the drug-detection purpose in *Edmond* invalidating because it was "ultimately indistinguishable from the general interest in crime control," 531 U.S., at 44, 121 S.Ct. 447. In the Court of Appeals' view, *Edmond* established that " 'programmatic purpose' is relevant to Fourth Amendment analysis of programs of seizures without probable cause." 580 F.3d, at 968.

That was mistaken. It was not the absence of probable cause that triggered the invalidating-purpose inquiry in *Edmond.* To the contrary, *Edmond* explicitly said that it would approve checkpoint stops for "general crime control purposes" that were based upon merely "some quantum of individualized suspicion." Purpose was relevant in *Edmond* because "programmatic purposes may be relevant to the validity of Fourth Amendment intrusions undertaken *pursuant to a general scheme without individualized suspicion,*"

Needless to say, warrantless, "suspicionless intrusions pursuant to a general scheme," are far removed from the facts of this case. A warrant issued by a neutral Magistrate Judge authorized al-Kidd's arrest. The affidavit accompanying the warrant application (as al-Kidd concedes) gave individualized reasons to believe that he was a material witness and that he would soon disappear. The existence of a judicial warrant based on individualized suspicion takes this case outside the domain of not only our special-needs and administrative-search cases, but of *Edmond* as well.

A warrant based on individualized suspicion in fact grants more protection against the malevolent and the incompetent than existed in most of our cases eschewing inquiries into intent. In *Whren,* 517 U.S., at 813, 116 S.Ct. 1769, we declined to probe the motives behind seizures supported by probable cause but lacking a warrant approved by a detached magistrate. We review even some suspicionless searches for objective reasonableness. If concerns about improper motives and pretext do not justify subjective inquiries in those less protective contexts, we see no reason to adopt that inquiry here.

Al–Kidd would read our cases more narrowly. He asserts that *Whren* establishes that we ignore subjective intent only when there exists "probable cause to believe that a violation of law has occurred,"—which was not the case here. That is a distortion of *Whren.* Our unanimous opinion held that we would not look behind an objectively reasonable traffic stop to determine whether racial profiling or a desire to investigate other potential crimes was the real motive. In the course of our analysis, we dismissed Whren's reliance on our inventory-search and administrative-inspection cases by explaining that those cases do not "endors[e] the principle that ulterior motives can invalidate police conduct that is justifiable on the basis of probable cause to believe that a violation of law has occurred," But to say that ulterior motives do *not* invalidate a search that is legitimate because of probable cause to believe a crime has occurred is not to say that it *does* invalidate all searches that are legitimate for other reasons.

"[O]nly an undiscerning reader," would think otherwise. . . .

Because al-Kidd concedes that individualized suspicion supported the issuance of the material-witness arrest warrant; and does not assert that his arrest would have been unconstitutional absent the alleged pretextual use of the warrant; we find no Fourth Amendment violation. Efficient[13] and evenhanded application of the law demands that we look to whether the arrest is objectively justified, rather than to the motive of the arresting officer.

---

13. [Renumbered.] We may note in passing that al-Kidd alleges that the Attorney General authorized the use of material-witness warrants for detention of suspected terrorists, but not that he forbade the use of those warrants to detain material witnesses. Which means that if al-Kidd's inquiry into actual motive is accepted, mere determination that the Attorney General promulgated the alleged policy would not alone decide the case. Al–Kidd would also have to prove that the officials who sought his material-arrest warrant were motivated by Ashcroft's policy, not by a desire to call al-Kidd as a witness.

B

A Government official's conduct violates clearly established law when, at the time of the challenged conduct, "[t]he contours of [a] right [are] sufficiently clear" that every "reasonable official would have understood that what he is doing violates that right." We do not require a case directly on point, but existing precedent must have placed the statutory or constitutional question beyond debate. The constitutional question in this case falls far short of that threshold.

At the time of al-Kidd's arrest, not a single judicial opinion had held that pretext could render an objectively reasonable arrest pursuant to a material-witness warrant unconstitutional. A district-court opinion had suggested, in a footnoted dictum devoid of supporting citation, that using such a warrant for preventive detention of suspects "is an illegitimate use of the statute"—implying (we accept for the sake of argument) that the detention would therefore be unconstitutional ... Even a district judge's *ipse dixit* of a holding is not "controlling authority" in any jurisdiction, much less in the entire United States; and his *ipse dixit* of a footnoted dictum falls far short of what is necessary absent controlling authority: a robust "consensus of cases of persuasive authority."

. . .

While featuring a District Court's footnoted dictum, the Court of Appeals made no mention of this Court's affirmation in *Edmond* of the "predominan[t]" rule that reasonableness is an objective inquiry. Nor did it mention *Whren*'s statements that subjective intent mattered in a very limited subset of our Fourth Amendment cases; . . . . The Court of Appeals seems to have cherry-picked the aspects of our opinions that gave colorable support to the proposition that the unconstitutionality of the action here was clearly established.

Qualified immunity gives government officials breathing room to make reasonable but mistaken judgments about open legal questions. When properly applied, it protects "all but the plainly incompetent or those who knowingly violate the law." Ashcroft deserves neither label, not least because eight Court of Appeals judges agreed with his judgment in a case of first impression. He deserves qualified immunity even assuming—contrafactually—that his alleged detention policy violated the Fourth Amendment.

* * *

We hold that an objectively reasonable arrest and detention of a material witness pursuant to a validly obtained warrant cannot be challenged as unconstitutional on the basis of allegations that the arresting authority had an improper motive. Because Ashcroft did not violate clearly established law, we need not address the more difficult question whether he enjoys absolute immunity. The judgment of the Court of Appeals is reversed, and the case is remanded for further proceedings consistent with this opinion.

It is so ordered.

JUSTICE KAGAN took no part in the consideration or decision of this case.

QUESTIONS AND NOTES

1.   In a companion case to the lower court decisions in the principal case, al-Kidd v. Gonzales, 2006 WL 5429570, an amicus brief was filed, excerpts from which are reproduced below:

AL–KIDD v. ASHCROFT

2007 WL 2786867

Brief of Amici Curiae Former Federal Prosecutors and Others in Support of Plaintiff–Appellee and in Support of Affirmance

. . .

STATEMENT OF INTEREST OF *AMICI CURIAE*

Amici curiae, identified in the Appendix, are former federal prosecutors and others who have worked prominently on issues related to the prosecution of federal crimes. We submit this *brief amici curiae*, with the consent of the parties, in support of Plaintiff–Appellee Abdullah al-Kidd's opposition to Defendant–Appellant John Ashcroft's appeal and affirmance of the District Court's denial of Appellant's motion to dismiss.

Collectively, *amici* have had decades of experience in federal criminal prosecution, including prosecution of domestic and international terrorism. All but four *amici* are former federal prosecutors, some of whom worked in the U.S. Department of Justice, and the other four *amici* are former presidents of the American Bar Association. *Amici* are therefore familiar with both the protocols and historical practices of the Department of Justice regarding the detention and treatment of material witnesses by federal prosecutors. *Amici* submit this brief to ensure a fair presentation of the practical issues presented by this matter.

INTRODUCTION

Based on personal experience, *amici* have a unique appreciation of the value of the federal material witness statute. If used properly, the statute is an indispensable law enforcement tool, permitting prosecutors to secure essential testimony when material witnesses are unwilling to testify. Yet *amici* are also aware of the dangers inherent in arresting and detaining individuals who are, in the eyes of the law, innocent. Great care must be taken to ensure that persons arrested and detained as material witnesses are treated throughout any arrest and detention as witnesses, unless and until probable cause exists to classify them otherwise.

Under the Department of Justice's explicit policy of using the federal material witness statute as a means of preventively arresting and detaining terrorism suspects, the critical distinction between material witnesses and criminal suspects has been blurred, and care has not been taken to ensure the protection of the particular constitutional rights of material witnesses. Because constitutional violations under this policy were foreseeable—if not expected—Appellant is not entitled to immunity, and the district court properly denied his motion to dismiss on immunity grounds.

SUMMARY OF THE ARGUMENT

While the language of the federal material witness statute is broad, federal prosecutors understand that constitutional limitations must guide the application of the statute. The arrest and detention of an individual as a material witness is no less an invasion of that individual's constitutional security and liberty interests than an arrest and detention on a criminal charge. Thus, the arrest of a material witness must be based on probable cause that the witness's testimony is material and that it would be impracticable to secure it by subpoena, and the conditions of a material witness's detention must be commensurate with his status as a witness.

In the case of Plaintiff–Appellee Abdullah al-Kidd, the material witness statute was not applied within these constitutional bounds: according to his complaint—the allegations of which are deemed to be true for this appeal—al-Kidd's arrest lacked probable cause because he was not an unwilling witness or a flight risk, and the harsh conditions of al-Kidd's detention amounted to punishment in violation of his due process rights.

Al–Kidd's legal action was properly allowed to proceed against Appellant, former Attorney General John Ashcroft, because the unconstitutional application of the statute in al-Kidd's case was not an aberrance, attributable to individual error by a federal prosecutor. Rather, it and the numerous other reported abuses of the federal material witness statute were the foreseeable consequences of an explicit policy regarding the application of the federal material witness statute, implemented by then-Attorney General Ashcroft. As part of a larger national security policy of preventively arresting and detaining terrorism suspects, Appellant instructed federal prosecutors, as well as the FBI and others, to use the federal material witness statute to arrest and detain persons purportedly connected to terrorism. This policy was expressly designed to secure indefinite detention of persons whom the government lacked probable cause to arrest and detain as criminal suspects, through "aggressive" application of the material witness statute. Fidelity to the specific legal requirements for detaining a person as a material witness were not addressed in these policy statements. Moreover, once detained, persons arrested as material witnesses in the anti-terrorism effort were treated not like witnesses, but like the most dangerous of criminal suspects.

Because the constitutional violations alleged by al-Kidd constituted foreseeable harm arising from Appellant's national security policy, Appellant is not immune from al-Kidd's suit. Appellant is not entitled to absolute prosecutorial immunity as his policy was implemented pursuant to his investigatory and national security functions, not pursuant to a pure prosecutorial function. Nor is Appellant entitled to qualified immunity, as his policy led to foreseeable violations of clearly established constitutional rights. *Amici* do not address the question of the district court's jurisdiction.

Amici therefore request that this Court affirm the decision of the district court denying Appellant's motion to dismiss on immunity grounds.

2.   Does Justice Scalia decide whether the alleged pretextual use of the material witness statute against al-Kidd is constitutional? Whether the material witness statute is consistent with the fourth amendment? Is his opinion premised on the notion that the material witness warrant was properly issued as far as the factual basis for its issuance. What specific issues did his opinion address and resolve?

3.   The amici brief, supra note 1, makes the following statement about the basis for issuance of a material witness warrant:

> Thus, the arrest of a material witness must be based on probable cause that the witness's testimony is material and that it would be impracticable to secure it by subpoena, and the conditions of a material witness's detention must be commensurate with his status as a witness.

Does Justice Scalia characterize the basis for issuance of a material witness warrant differently?

4.   a. Is it a misuse of the material witness statute to hold individuals because the government wants to be certain, that at least for the period of the detention, they are not free to engage in terrorist acts? Is this a proper basis on which to invoke the material witness statute? What does Awadallah say about that practice? What does al-Kidd say?

b.   Some have suggested that the use of statutes like the material witness law to detain individuals for extended periods can be used to coerce information. See, e.g., Christian Science Monitor, June 19, 2002, p. 1. Is this an improper reason to detain an individual under the material witness statute? Compare the use of a contempt citation and detention of a person who declines to answer questions before the grand jury. Is the use of the material witness statute for this purpose different?

5.   See Laurie E. Levenson, 35 Loy. L.A. L.Rev. 1217, 1222 (2002):

> When America adopted into its laws the power to detain material witnesses, the focus of the law was on having an individual available to testify in a criminal proceeding. Although they were being detained, material witnesses were conceptually different from defendants who were incarcerated. Material witnesses were to be held because they could assist

the criminal justice system in convicting those who pose a danger; they themselves were not considered a threat.

With the War on Terrorism, the legal seas have changed. The designation of material witness has often become a temporary moniker to identify an individual who will soon bear the status of defendant. Consider, for example, the initial designation of Terry Lynn Nichols as a material witness in the bombing of the Murrah Federal Building in Oklahoma City. When Nichols challenged the material witness warrant, the authorities simply substituted it with a criminal complaint charging malicious destruction of government property. Given the breadth of our conspiracy laws, it is not difficult to find a sufficient link to charge a person who has intimate knowledge regarding a crime as a co-conspirator to that crime.

Similarly, it has not been difficult for prosecutors in terrorism cases to convert material witnesses into defendants. One standard technique is to question the witness before the grand jury, knowing that the individual is unlikely to cooperate fully. When the detainee withholds information or lies to the grand jury, charges of perjury or obstruction of justice can be substituted for the material witness warrant.

Material witness laws provide the government with the perfect avenue to jail those it considers dangerous. It is preventive detention. . . . [T]he Attorney General has indicated he still considers material witness warrants as a viable investigative tool. The government uses these laws to round up people because of what it expects them to do, rather than what it can prove they have done.

6. Consider the characterization of the use of the material witness statute in the following excerpts from Heidee Stoller, Tahlia Townsend, Rashad Hussain, and Marcia Yablon, Developments in Law and Policy: The Costs of Post–9/11 National Security Strategy, 22 Yale L. & Pol'y Rev. 197, 199, 201–202, 205–206, 208–209 (2004).

Material witness detentions are controversial because they involve the extreme step of imprisoning individuals who have not been charged with committing any crime. The more usual procedure is to issue a subpoena to compel testimony, and only to imprison the witness once she has failed to comply with the subpoena.

. . . [I]t is often much easier to satisfy the probable cause requirement when arresting someone as a material witness for a grand jury proceeding than when taking her into custody as a criminal suspect. Whereas a suspected criminal may not be arrested until a judge has satisfied herself that the evidence of criminal activity is sufficient to establish probable cause, individuals who are suspected of having information material to a grand jury investigation and who may be deemed a flight risk (such as immigrants, those who cannot afford bail, and those with few ties to a community) can be subjected to arrest and detention solely on the basis of a statement from a law enforcement official.

. . . A recent report by the U.S. Department of Justice (DOJ) Office of the Inspector General has intensified concerns that the material witness warrant is being used in just such a pretextual manner to detain individuals for preventive or coercive purposes. According to the Inspector General's report, a DOJ official indicated that "the Department's official policy was to 'use whatever means legally available' to detain a person linked to the terrorists who might present a threat and to make sure that no one else was killed." A senior DOJ official, discussing the "hold until cleared" policy in a document entitled "Maintaining Custody of Terrorism Suspects," stated:

> The Department of Justice . . . is utilizing several tools to ensure that we maintain in custody all individuals suspected of being involved in the September 11 attacks without violating the rights of any person. If a person is legally present in this country, the person may be held only if federal or local law enforcement is pursuing criminal charges against him or pursuant to a material witness warrant.

These findings, along with statements by Attorney General Ashcroft and former Assistant Attorney General for the Office of Legal Policy Viet Dinh, raise the specter of a new DOJ policy under which, in the absence of evidence to sustain criminal or immigration charges, the material witness statute is to be used as a "tool" of preventive detention, allowing the DOJ to hold those suspected of connection with terrorist activity until their names have been cleared by the FBI. The fact that at least twenty of the individuals detained never testified before a grand jury prior to their release further supports the idea that these detentions may have diverged from their stated purpose of securing testimony.

The application of the law since September 11 has aroused controversy for at least three additional reasons, namely that all of the individuals arrested pursuant to these material witness warrants have been detained for appearance before a grand jury rather than as trial witnesses; more than fifty percent of the material witnesses detained in connection with the September 11 terrorist attacks were held for longer than a month, and several were detained longer than ninety days; and harsh conditions of confinement have been documented in a number of the cases.

. . .

The arrest and detention of a material witness to appear before the grand jury constitutes a seizure, and as such must conform to the requirements of the Fourth Amendment. Thus, for the detention of a material witness to be constitutional, the warrant for the witness' arrest must be based on probable cause, and the arrest and detention must also be reasonable.

. . .

In the context of a criminal arrest, probable cause means probable cause to believe that the suspect has committed a crime. In the case of a material witness, the question naturally arises: "Probable cause of what?" The Supreme Court has not addressed this issue, but in Bacon v. United States, the Ninth Circuit formulated a two-prong test for the satisfaction of the Fourth Amendment requirement of probable cause in the context of arrest and detention of a witness for appearance before a grand jury. . . . According to the Bacon court, "before a material witness arrest warrant may issue, the judicial officer must have probable cause to believe (1) 'that the testimony of a person is material' and (2) 'that it may become impracticable to secure his presence by subpoena.' " The flight risk aspect of the requirement means that the material witness warrant will primarily apply to people who have traditionally been considered flight risks, such as immigrants, those who cannot afford bail, and those who do not have significant ties to the community.

Although the Bacon court required a sufficient showing of the "underlying facts or circumstances" to determine flight risk, the Bacon standard for materiality is "a mere statement by a responsible official." While the court acknowledged that, in accordance with the Supreme Court's Fourth Amendment jurisprudence, normally "a judicial officer must be provided with information of sufficient specificity and apparent reliability to permit him to determine independently the existence vel non of probable cause," the Bacon court felt that this requirement could be waived in the light of the "special function of the grand jury" and the fact that "its proceedings are secret."

. . .

The asserted justification for determining materiality based solely on prosecutorial say-so, the need to protect grand jury secrecy, is also questionable, because the statute is already riddled with exceptions which allow disclosure.

7. If the material witness statute is only invoked where the express requirements of the statute are complied with, is there anything constitutionally suspect about the fact that (as the amici brief suggests, see note 2, supra) the Department of Justice has an explicit policy "of using the federal material witness statute as a means of preventively arresting and detaining terrorism suspects." In other words, does the motivation of the DOJ and its agents matter if the statutory material witness requirements are met? Of course, the detained person and the amici brief assert that the statutory requirements were not complied with. If that is true, does the DOJ policy matter? Why?

8. Assume, for purposes of discussion, that a court has concluded a) that the material witness statute requirements were complied with in the al-Kidd case, and b) therefore the fact that the Justice Department has the indicated policy about using the statute against terrorism suspects is not relevant to the disposition of the case. Assume that you work for a Senator who objects to this DOJ policy. What, if anything, can Congress do about this policy? Advise her.

9. Assume that you work for another Senator who believes that the DOJ policy is sound but also believes that the material witness statute should not be used as a vehicle for implementing the policy. He wishes to draft legislation that could be used to directly implement the aforementioned policy. What would be the key elements of such a statute? Would it be constitutional? In other words, is the problem in the indicated DOJ use of the material witness statute the government's goal, or in the use of the material witness statute to accomplish the goal? Could Congress constitutionally directly authorize what

the Attorney General was trying to accomplish? Would you vote for such legislation? Is it important for the Executive Branch to obtain the imprimatur of the Congress on such matters?

10.   See generally, David Cole, Out of the Shadows: Preventive Detention, Suspected Terrorists, and War, 97 Calif. L. Rev. 693 (2009); Donald Q. Cochran, Material Witness Detention in a Post–9/11 World: Mission Creep or Fresh Start?, 18 Geo. Mason L. Rev. 1 (2010); Ronald L. Carlson, Distorting Due Process for Noble Purposes: The Emasculation of America's Material Witness Laws, 42 Ga. L. Rev. 941 (2008); Carolyn B. Ramsey, In the Sweat Box: A Historical Perspective on the Detention of Material Witnesses, 6 Ohio St. J. Crim. L. 681 (2009); Bradley Parker, Abuse of the Material Witness: Suspects Detained as Witnesses in Violation of the Fourth Amendment, 36 Rutgers L. Rec. 22 (2009); Dianne Webber: Extreme Measures: Does the United States Need Preventive Detention to Combat Domestic Terrorism?, 14 Touro Int'l L. Rev. 128 (2010); James Mossimon, Al–Kidd v. Ashcroft: Clearly Established Confusion, 96 Iowa L. Rev. 331 (2010); Adam Klein, Benjamin Wittes, Preventive Detention in American Theory and Practice, 2 Harv. Nat'l Sec. J. 85 (2011); Joseph G. Cook, The Detention of Material Witnesses and the Fourth Amendment, 76 Miss. L.J. 585 (2006); Human Rights Watch, Witness to Abuse: Human Rights Abuses Under the Material Witness Law Since September 11 (2005) http://hrw.org/reports/2005/us0605/us0605.pdf.; Ricardo J. Bascuas, The Unconstitutionality of "Hold Until Cleared": Reexamining Material Witness Detentions in the Wake of the September 11th Dragnet, 58 Vand. L. Rev. 677 (2005); Roberto Iraola, Terrorism, Grand Juries, and the Federal Material Witness Statute, 34 St. Mary's L.J. 401 (2003); Stacey M. Studnicki & John P. Apol, Witness Detention and Intimidation: The History and Future of Material Witness Law, 76 St. John's L. Rev. 483 (2002).

11.   In the next section, C., we shall see how, in addition to the use of the material witness statute, in the aftermath of 9/11, the government also used the immigration laws to round up individuals.

C.   DETENTION OF ALIENS

1.   INTRODUCTION

The law regarding the detention and removal (i.e., deportation) of aliens is complex. In the immediate wake of the events of September 11, 2001, the government rounded up and detained over 1000 persons, most of whom were aliens of Middle Eastern or South Asian origin. (In addition, shortly after September 11, the government announced a plan to have the FBI interview approximately 5000 men between the ages of 18 and 33 who were from countries with "an al Qaeda terrorist presence." See Kenneth L. Wainstein, Final Report on Interview Project, Office of the Director, Executive Office for United States Attorneys, February 26, 2002 at 2.) A small number of those detained were held under the material witness statute. Most, however, were detained in connection with violations of the immigration laws. Subsection 2 examines the use of the immigration laws in aid of an anti-terrorism law enforcement purpose in the aftermath of 9/11. Subsection 3 presents recent decisions barring indefinite detention of persons slated for removal where a receiving country cannot be found, but noting a possible exception where terrorism is involved. Finally, in subsection 4, we focus on the provisions of the immigration laws that by their very terms are directed against terrorists and that establish special procedures for both their detention and their removal from the U.S. (including some provisions enacted in 2001 as part of the USA PATRIOT Act).

2. POST 9/11/01 DETENTIONS AND REMOVALS BASED ON IMMIGRATION LAW VIOLATIONS

a. The Use of Authority to Detain Aliens in Violation of the Immigration Laws as an Aid to Terrorism Investigation and as a Form of Preventive Detention

David Cole, The Priority of Morality, The Emergency Constitution's Blind Spot, 113 Yale L.J. 1753, 1777–1778 (2004):

> ... [T]he Attorney General ... has been able to subject over 5000 foreign nationals to preventive detention ... by ... using preexisting immigration and criminal law authorities. Many of those detainees were arrested and held without charges for much longer than seven days. And many were held for months on end without any judicial review. Under preexisting immigration law, the Attorney General has discretion to detain foreign nationals charged with immigration violations pending the outcome of their removal proceedings, although such detention generally requires proof that the individual poses either a risk of flight or a danger to the community. The Justice Department used that discretionary detention authority to deny bond to all immigration detainees deemed "of interest" to the September 11 investigation, without regard to whether it had any evidence whatsoever that they were dangerous, a flight risk, or in any way connected to terrorism. It interfered with their access to attorneys and sought delays and continuances in bond hearings to disguise the fact that it had no evidence justifying detention without bond. It promulgated a rule, subsequently declared unconstitutional by five federal judges, that permits immigration prosecutors to keep foreign nationals detained even after an immigration judge rules that there is no basis for denying bond. And it kept individuals in detention for months after their immigration charges were fully resolved, not because it had any affirmative evidence that they posed any danger, but simply because the FBI had not gotten around to "clearing" them.
>
> Where a person "of interest" could not be charged with an immigration violation, prosecutors searched for a criminal charge—

any charge. Individuals were charged with lying to FBI agents and the grand jury, credit card fraud, "trespassing" in a hotel room they were renting, and carrying a knife one-quarter inch longer than permitted under state law. Where neither a criminal nor an immigration charge was available, the Justice Department invoked the material witness statute. . . .

Through these tactics, all relying on preexisting immigration and criminal authority, the Attorney General was able to effectuate a mass preventive detention campaign. . . .

b. Must Deportation Hearings Be Open to the Public and the Press?

Following 9/11, the government took great pains to keep secret any information about the detainees who had been rounded up. Where the immigration laws were relied upon, in numerous instances, the government took steps to remove, that is, deport, individuals suspected of links to terrorism. In this connection, the Chief United States Immigration Judge issued a directive ordering that removal hearings involving such persons should be closed to the press and public. The closure order was challenged and two circuit court decisions applying the test developed in Richmond Newspapers, Inc. v. Virginia, 448 U.S. 555, 100 S. Ct. 2814, 65 L. Ed. 2d 973 (1980) reached opposite conclusions on the issue.

Richmond involved a murder case in which the trial judge had ordered that the courtroom be cleared of all persons except witnesses. The Supreme Court struck down the closure order, citing an "unbroken, uncontradicted history" of public access to criminal trials in Anglo American law, ruling that the right of the press and public to attend criminal trials was implicit in the First Amendment's guarantees.

The Third and Sixth Circuits addressed the question whether Richmond required that such removal proceedings be open to the press and public. North Jersey Media Group, Inc. v. Ashcroft, 308 F.3d 198 (3d Cir.2002), cert. denied, North Jersey Media Group v. Ashcroft, 538 U.S. 1056 (2003) ruled that deportation hearings did not have a strong history of openness and there were good national security reasons why they should not be generally open to the press and public. A few months prior to the North Jersey Media decision, the Sixth Circuit had rendered a contrary decision in Detroit Free Press v. Ashcroft, 303 F.3d 681 (6th Cir. 2002).

The court in New Jersey Media explained its conclusion:

For a First Amendment right of access to vest under Richmond Newspapers, we must consider whether "the place and process have historically been open to the press and general public," because such a "tradition of accessibility implies the favorable judgment of experience."

The strongest historical evidence of open deportation proceedings is that since the 1890s, when Congress first codified deportation procedures, "the governing statutes have always expressly closed exclusion hearings, but have never closed deportation hearings." . . . Congress codified the regulations governing deportation proceedings in 1904 and has reenacted them many times since, it has never authorized the general closure that has long existed in the exclusion context.

The Newspapers submit that under the rule of construction *expressio unius est exclusio alterius*, Congress's practice of closing exclusion proceedings while remaining silent on deportation proceedings creates a presumption that it intended deportation proceedings to be open. In support of this interpretation, they point out that the current Justice Department regulations provide explicitly that "all hearings, other than exclusion hearings, shall be open to the public except that . . . for the purpose of protecting . . . the public interest, the Immigration Judge may limit attendance or hold a closed hearing." 8 C.F.R. 3.27. From this they conclude that the regulations state explicitly what the statutes had long said implicitly, namely that deportation hearings are to be open unless an individualized case is made for closure.

But there is also evidence that, in practice, deportation hearings have frequently been closed to the general public. From the early 1900s, the government has often conducted deportation hearings in prisons, hospitals, or private homes, places where there is no general right of public access. Even in recent times, the government has continued to hold thousands of deportation hearings each year in federal and state prisons. Moreover, hearings involving abused alien children are closed by regulation no matter where they are held, and those involving abused alien spouses are closed presumptively. See 8 C.F.R. 3.27(c).

. . .

We ultimately do not believe that deportation hearings boast a tradition of openness sufficient to satisfy Richmond Newspapers. . . . The tradition of open deportation hearings is simply not comparable.

While the *expressio unius* distinction between exclusion and deportation proceedings is a tempting road to travel, we are unwilling effectively to craft a constitutional right from mere Congressional silence, especially when faced with evidence that some deportation proceedings were, and are, explicitly closed to the public or conducted in places unlikely to allow general public access.

. . .

The Government's security evidence is contained in the declaration of Dale Watson, the FBI's Executive Assistant Director for Counterterrorism and Counterintelligence. Watson presents a range of potential dangers, the most pressing of which we describe here.

First, public hearings would necessarily reveal sources and methods of investigation. That is information which, "when assimilated with other information the United States may or may not have in hand, allows a terrorist organization to build a picture of the investigation." Even minor pieces of evidence that might appear innocuous to us would provide valuable clues to a person within the terrorist network, clues that may allow them to thwart the government's efforts to investigate and prevent future acts of violence.

Second, "information about how any given individual entered the country (from where, when, and how) may not divulge significant information that would reveal sources and methods of investigation. However, putting entry information into the public realm regarding all 'special interest cases' would allow the terrorist organization to see patterns of entry, what works and what doesn't." That information would allow it to tailor future entries to exploit weaknesses in the United States immigration system.

Third, "information about what evidence the United States has against members of a particular cell collectively will inform the terrorist organization as to what cells to use and which not to use for further plots and attacks." A related concern is that open hearings would reveal what evidence the government lacks. For example, the United States may disclose in a public hearing certain evidence it possesses about a member of a terrorist organization. If that detainee is actually involved in planning an attack, opening the hearing might allow the organization to know that the United States is not yet aware of the attack based on the evidence it presents at the open hearing.

Fourth, if a terrorist organization discovers that a particular member is detained, or that information about a plot is known, it may accelerate the timing of a planned attack, thus reducing the amount of time the government has to detect and prevent it. If acceleration is impossible, it may still be able to shift the planned activity to a yet-undiscovered cell.

Fifth, a public hearing involving evidence about terrorist links could allow terrorist organizations to interfere with the pending proceedings by creating false or misleading evidence. Even more likely, a terrorist might destroy existing evidence or make it more difficult to obtain, such as by threatening or tampering with potential witnesses. Should potential informants not feel secure in coming forward, that would greatly impair the ongoing investigation.

Sixth, INS detainees have a substantial privacy interest in having their possible connection to the ongoing investigation kept undisclosed. "Although some particular detainees may choose to identify themselves, it is important to note that as to all INS detainees whose cases have been placed in the special interest category concerns remain about their connection to terrorism, and specifically to the worst attack ever committed on United States soil. Although they may eventually be found to have no connection to terrorist activity, discussion of the causes of their apprehension in open court would forever connect them to the September 11 attacks."

Finally, Watson represents that "the government cannot proceed to close hearings on a case-by-case basis, as the identification of certain cases for closure, and the introduction of evidence to support that closure, could itself expose critical information about which activities and patterns of behavior merit such closure." Moreover, he explains, given judges' relative lack of expertise regarding national security and their inability to see the mosaic, we should not entrust to them the decision whether an isolated fact is sensitive enough to warrant closure.

The Newspapers are undoubtedly correct that the representations of the Watson Declaration are to some degree speculative, at least insofar as there is no concrete evidence that closed deportation hearings have prevented, or will prevent, terrorist attacks. But the Richmond Newspapers logic prong is unavoidably speculative, for it is impossible to weigh objectively, for example, the community benefit of emotional catharsis against the security risk of disclosing the United States' methods of investigation and the extent of its knowledge. We are quite hesitant to conduct a judicial inquiry into the credibility of these security concerns, as national security is an area where courts have traditionally extended great deference to Executive expertise. . . . The assessments before us have been made by senior government officials responsible for investigating the events of September 11th and for preventing future attacks. These officials believe that closure of special interest hearings is necessary to advance these goals, and their concerns, as expressed in the Watson Declaration, have gone unrebutted. To the extent that the Attorney General's national security concerns seem credible, we will not lightly second-guess them.

We are keenly aware of the dangers presented by deference to the executive branch when constitutional liberties are at stake, especially in times of national crisis, when those liberties are likely in greatest jeopardy. On balance, however, we are unable to conclude that openness plays a positive role in special interest deportation hearings at a time when our nation is faced with threats of such profound and unknown dimension.

. . . Our judgment is confined to the extremely narrow class of deportation cases that are determined by the Attorney General to present significant national security concerns. In recognition of his experience (and our lack of experience) in this field, we will defer to his judgment. We note that although there may be no judicial remedy for these closures, there is, as always, the powerful check of political accountability on Executive discretion.

The importance of this case has not escaped us. As we approached it, we were acutely aware that the countervailing positions of the parties go to the heart of our institutions, our national values, and the republic itself. Commenting upon the great national dilemma in which this case ineluctably embroils us—the eternal struggle between liberty and security—a number of newspapers have editorialized favorably upon Judge Keith's eloquent language in the Detroit Free Press case:

> "Democracies die behind closed doors," . . . "When government begins closing doors, it selectively controls information rightfully belonging to the people. Selective information is misinformation."

Others have been less impressed. Michael Kelly has written in the Washington Post:

> "Democracies die behind closed doors. So they do, sometimes. But far more democracies have succumbed to open assaults of one sort or another—invasions from without, military coups and totalitarian revolutions from within—than from the usurpation-by-in-camera-incrementalism that Judge Keith fears.
>
> Democracy in America does at this moment face a serious threat. But it is not the threat the judge has in mind, at least not directly. It is true that last September's unprecedented mass-slaughter of American citizens on American soil inevitably forced the government to take security measures that infringed on some rights and privileges. But these do not in themselves represent any real threat to democracy. A real threat could arise, however, should the government fail in its mission to prevent another September 11. If that happens, the public will demand, and will get, immense restrictions on liberties."

In subsequent proceedings in the district court in the Detroit Free Press case, referred to above, the following opinions were handed down.

HADDAD v. ASHCROFT

221 F.Supp.2d 799 (E.D.Mich. 2002)

OPINION BY: NANCY G. EDMUNDS

This case arises from the Government's institution of removal proceedings against a number of non-citizens, primarily young men of Arab and Muslim background, following the horrific events of September 11, 2001, and the Government's decision to close those proceedings to the press and public. The plaintiff is Rabih Haddad ("Haddad"), one of the men arrested after September 11. The defendants are Attorney General John Ashcroft, Chief Immigration Judge Michael Creppy, and Immigration Judge Elizabeth Hacker (collectively "the Government"). Now before the Court is Haddad's motion for a preliminary injunction and the Government's corresponding motion to dismiss his complaint for failure to state a claim upon which relief can be granted.

Haddad, a native of Lebanon, resided in Ann Arbor, Michigan off-and-on since 1988. Haddad and his family most recently came to the United

States in 1998 on six-month tourist visas.[23] On December 14, 2001, the United States Immigration and Naturalization Service ("INS") took Haddad into custody for overstaying his visa and initiated removal proceedings in Detroit before Immigration Judge Elizabeth Hacker.

On September 21, 2001, prior to Haddad's arrest, Chief Immigration Judge Michael Creppy issued a directive (the "Creppy directive") to all United States Immigration Judges mandating that they close immigration proceedings to the press and public (including family members of the deportee) in certain "special interest" cases identified by the Office of the Chief Immigration Judge. Chief Immigration Judge Creppy issued this directive under United States Attorney General John Ashcroft's authorization.

On December 19, 2002, Immigration Judge Hacker conducted a bond hearing in Haddad's case. Haddad's family and members of the public and press sought to attend the hearing. Shortly before the hearing began, however, and without prior notice to Haddad or his counsel, courtroom security officers announced that the hearing was closed to the press and public. Haddad objected to the closure of his hearing. Immigration Judge Hacker stated that the decision to close the proceedings came from her supervisors and that she lacked the power to reverse the decision. Following the December 19 hearing, Judge Hacker denied bail and ordered Haddad detained.

Arguing that the closure of Haddad's hearings is unconstitutional, Haddad and members of the press and public (collectively the "Newspaper Plaintiffs") filed three separate cases seeking an injunction against such procedure in any future hearings. *See Detroit Free Press, Inc., et al. v. John Ashcroft, et al.,* Case No. 02–70339. Haddad claims that the Government's actions violate his rights under (1) the Administrative Procedures Act ("APA"), 5 U.S.C. § 551 *et seq.;* (2) the Immigration and Nationality Act ("INA"), as amended, 8 U.S.C. § 1229a, and the regulations promulgated thereunder, 8 C.F.R. §§ 3.27 & 240.10; and (3) the Due Process Clause of the Fifth Amendment of the United States Constitution. The Newspaper Plaintiffs claimed that they have a right of access to such immigration hearings in general and to Haddad's hearings in particular pursuant to the First Amendment of the United States Constitution, as well as statutory and regulatory law. Arguing that this Court lacks jurisdiction and that no constitutional rights are abridged by the exclusion of the press and public from the hearings, the Government filed motions asking that the cases be dismissed, or, in the alternative that the Court apply a deferential level of scrutiny to the Government's action.

On April 3, 2002, the Court issued an order denying the Government's motion to dismiss for lack of jurisdiction. On the same day, the Court issued an order granting the Newspaper Plaintiffs' motion for

---

23. Haddad and his family have applied with the Immigration and Naturalization Service (INS) for extensions of their visas. On April 30, 2001, Haddad also applied for alien labor certification, in order to adjust his status to permanent residency.

preliminary injunction. The Court held that the Government's blanket closure of removal hearings in "special interest" cases is unconstitutional because it infringes the press' and public's First Amendment right of access to removal proceedings and the Government was unable to demonstrate interests sufficient to justify its closure of Haddad's case. The Sixth Circuit Court of Appeals affirmed the Court's order on August 26, 2002. In the interim, pursuant to this Court's order, the Government opened Haddad's proceedings to the press and public. Haddad contends, however, that his continued detention violates his Due Process rights because the initial detention hearing over eight months ago was not open to the press and public. Haddad also argues that the Government's classification of his case as a "special interest" matter tainted the immigration judge presiding over his removal hearings. Thus Haddad seeks a new detention hearing, which is open to the press and public and which is conducted by a new immigration judge. For the same reason, Haddad requests that a different immigration judge preside over any other hearing in his case.

To determine whether to grant a motion for preliminary injunction, a court must analyze the following four factors:

> (1) whether the movant has a strong likelihood of success on the merits; (2) whether the movant would suffer irreparable injury without the injunction; (3) whether issuance of the injunction would cause substantial harm to others; and (4) whether the public interest would be served by issuance of the injunction.

Haddad argues that he is likely to succeed on the merits because the Government's closure of his deportation proceedings (1) violates the Due Process Clause of the Fifth Amendment; (2) violates INS regulations; and (3) violates the APA, to the extent that the Creppy directive is viewed as amending the governing regulations. The Court finds that Haddad does not have a strong likelihood of demonstrating that the Creppy directive violates INS regulations or the APA. The Court concludes, however, that Haddad has a strong likelihood of succeeding on his Due Process claim.

It is well established that aliens subject to deportation are entitled to the due process protections afforded by the Fifth Amendment of the United States Constitution. *See Zadvydas v. Davis,* 533 U.S. 678, 121 S. Ct. 2491, 2500–01, 150 L. Ed. 2d 653 (2001) As Justice Breyer wrote for the majority in *Zadvydas:* "the Due Process Clause applies to all 'persons' within the United States, including aliens, whether their presence here is unlawful, temporary, or permanent." In comparison, the Fifth Amendment's protections do not extend to aliens outside our geographic borders (even if they were once inside but have left).

While the Due Process Clause protects an alien subject to deportation, the nature of that protection may vary depending upon status and circumstance. Clearly an alien is entitled to notice and a "meaningful opportunity to be heard," as these are the basic requirements of due process.... To determine whether additional procedural protections are required, the Court must balance four factors: (1) the plaintiff's interest;

(2) the government's interest; (3) the probable value of additional or substitute procedures; and (4) the extent of the risk of erroneous deprivations of the plaintiff's interests.

Courts have found that an open hearing is fundamental to guarantee a fair hearing.... Thus long-standing INS regulations have required immigration judges to hold deportation hearings open to the public, except under certain circumstances. In finding that hearings at the administrative level should be open, the D.C. Circuit Court of Appeals stated,

> A fair trial in a fair tribunal is a basic requirement of due process. Fairness of course requires an absence of actual bias in the trial of cases. But our system of law has always endeavored to prevent even the probability of unfairness. That we regard an 'open and public hearing' to be a fundamental principle of fair play inherent in our judicial process cannot be seriously challenged. The Sixth Amendment requires a public trial in all criminal cases. Rule 77(b) of the Federal Rules of Civil Procedure requires that 'all trials upon the merits shall be conducted in open court ...' And in administrative hearings, the rule of the "open" forum is prevailing—if not by statutory mandate, then by regulation or practice.

Haddad's interest in a fair hearing before an impartial decision maker weighs heavily in favor of an open hearing in this case. As the issues to be addressed are whether Haddad should be detained in prison pending a final removal hearing and whether he ultimately should be removed from this country, there can be no doubt that the risks to Haddad of an erroneous decision based on fear or stereotype rather than the evidence presented are great. As the Sixth Circuit explained in the Newspaper Plaintiffs' case:

> A deportation proceeding, although administrative, is an adversarial, adjudicative process, designed to expel non-citizens from this country. "The ultimate individual stake in these proceedings is the same as or greater than in criminal or civil actions." ...

Adherence to the rule of the open forum is especially important in cases such as this one—where our nation's borders recently have been invaded and, as a result, our citizens feel threatened. Few could disagree that the events of September 11 altered the way we view our world and the safety of our nation. Since that dreadful day, we regard our own neighbors with suspicion and go about our day-to-day affairs wary of our own security.

Traditionally in such a climate, individuals (including some in government) are more willing to abridge the constitutional rights of people who are perceived to share something in common with the "enemy," either because of their race, ethnicity, or beliefs. It is highly likely in the climate of fear the events of 9/11 precipitated, that the Government's designation of Haddad's case as a matter of "special interest" tainted the immigration judge's decision whether to release Haddad into the general public. This classification inevitably suggested a link between Haddad and terrorists or terrorism or, more specifically, the attacks of September 11. Presence of the public and press at Haddad's detention and removal hearings, therefore, helps to assure that the immigration judge bases his or her opinion on the evidence presented, rather than on unsupported allegations or fears.

The Government has failed to make a particularized showing that its interests in fighting terrorism are implicated in Haddad's case.[24] As the Government recently admitted, there in fact has been no information disclosed in Haddad's case thus far that threatened "national security or the safety of the American people." (citing U.S. Dept. of Justice, *Statement of Associate Attorney General Jay Stephens Regarding the Sixth Circuit Decision in the Haddad Case,* (last modified 8/20/02)). Thus the Court concludes in this case that this second factor does not weigh against the application of additional procedures to protect Haddad's interest in fair detention and removal hearings.

It is important for the public, particularly individuals who feel that they are being targeted by the Government as a result of the terrorist attacks of September 11, to know that even during these sensitive times the Government is adhering to immigration procedures and respecting individuals' rights. Openness is necessary for the public to maintain confidence in the value and soundness of the Government's actions, as secrecy only breeds suspicion as to why the Government is proceeding against Haddad and aliens like him. And if in fact the Government determines that Haddad is connected to terrorist activity or organizations, a decision made openly concerning his deportation may assure the public that justice has been done.

As the Sixth Circuit cautioned, "democracies die behind closed doors." An open detention and removal hearing will assure the public that the Government itself is honoring the very democratic principles that the terrorists who committed the atrocities of 9/11 sought to destroy.

Accordingly, being fully advised in the premises, having read the pleadings, and for the reasons set forth above, the Court hereby orders as follows:

Haddad's motion for preliminary injunction is Granted;

Within ten days of this order, the Government must either release Haddad from detention or hold a new detention hearing that is open to the press and public, before a different immigration judge;

The Government's motion to dismiss complaint for failure to state a claim upon which relief can be granted is Denied.

/s/

Nancy G. Edmunds

---

24. Obviously the Government still may request that the immigration judge close the hearing if it wishes to introduce classified information or request that the information be sealed. And the immigration judge may do so after making a particularized determination that such closure is necessary to further a compelling interest. *See* 8 C.F.R. 3.27 240.10(b).

U.S. District Judge

After this decision by Judge Edmunds, another hearing in the same matter occurred, which resulted in the following opinion:

DETROIT FREE PRESS v. ASHCROFT

2002 WL 31317398 (E.D.Mich. 2002)

Pursuant to this Court's Order requiring the Government to conduct a new bond hearing for plaintiff Rabih Haddad ("Haddad"), before a new immigration judge, the immigration court began a bond redetermination hearing in Haddad's case on October 1, 2002, before Immigration Judge Robert Newberry. The October 1 hearing initially was open to the public; however, Judge Newberry closed a portion of the proceedings to the press and the public pursuant to agency regulations permitting closure to protect national security or law enforcement interests. *See* 8 C.F.R. § 3.46(a). Judge Newberry did not state on the record why the proceedings were being closed and denied the Newspaper Plaintiffs' counsel, who was present during the proceedings, the opportunity to object to the closure. According to the Government, the judge had reviewed the information the Government sought to introduce during a closed meeting earlier that morning and made particularized findings that closure was necessary.[25]

The Newspaper Plaintiffs and Haddad filed emergency motions with this Court, challenging Judge Newberry's closure of the proceedings. The Newspaper Plaintiffs ask the Court to require the immigration court to: (1) allow the Newspaper Plaintiffs' counsel to be heard; (2) make a particularized determination, on the record, that closure is necessary to further a compelling interest; (3) release transcripts of the closed proceedings; and (4) release a non-redacted copy of the Government's pre-hearing brief. Haddad essentially seeks the same relief, but additionally asks the immigration court to amend the Protective Order issued in Haddad's immigration case on October 1, 2002, to grant Haddad's counsel in this case access to the Declaration of FBI Agent Brent Potter ("Potter Declaration") in the form provided Haddad's immigration counsel.

The Court concludes that closure of Haddad's proceedings in order for the Government to introduce limited portions of the Potter Declaration was necessary to protect the source of the Government's information, and thus was necessary to protect the United States' national security or law enforcement interests. In accordance with this Court's earlier Order, however, Judge Newberry should have made particularized findings on the record as to why closure was necessary. Haddad's counsel in this case also should be given access to the evidence the Government introduced during the closed proceeding, under the terms set forth in the immigration court's October 1, 2002, Protective Order.

---

25. It is not clear from the parties' briefs whether the Government alone was present when Judge Newberry made his determination, or whether Haddad's immigration counsel also was present.

Being fully advised in the premises, having read the pleadings, and for the reasons stated on the record, the Court hereby orders as follows:

Plaintiffs' emergency motions are granted in part and denied in part;

In the future, the immigration court should make particularized findings on the record prior to closing Haddad's immigration proceedings to the press and the public.

The limited closure of Haddad's detention hearing on October 1, 2002, was necessary for the Government to introduce evidence which, if disclosed, could harm the national security or law enforcement interests of the United States; and, Haddad's counsel in this proceeding should have access to information provided to his counsel in his immigration proceeding, subject to the immigration court's October 1, 2002, Protective Order.

Nancy G. Edmunds

U.S. District Judge

Dated: Oct. 7, 2002.

The final legal chapter in the Haddad deportation proceeding was the following case:

HADDAD v. ASHCROFT

76 Fed. Appx. 672 (6th Cir. 2003)

JUDGES: Before: MERRITT, MOORE, and GILMAN, CIRCUIT JUDGES.

These appeals are from orders in a district court action that challenged the manner in which removal proceedings were being conducted in an immigration matter. In No. 02–2189, the defendants appeal an order directing that either a public hearing be conducted with respect to the plaintiff's detention or that he be released. In No. 03–1253, the plaintiff appeals a district court order that upheld the closure of a portion of the detention hearing. After these appeals were brought, the administrative proceedings were completed, and a final order of removal was entered. The plaintiff's direct petition for review of that order was dismissed as untimely. *Haddad v. Ashcroft,* Sixth Cir. No. 03–3852 (July 11, 2003) (order). Subsequently the plaintiff was deported from the United States. The government now moves to remand to the district court with instructions to vacate and dismiss the complaint as moot. There has been no response.

Because a final order of removal has been entered and effectuated, the conditions of the plaintiff's pre-removal detention are no longer at issue. . . . When a matter becomes moot on appeal, the proper course is to vacate the district court's decision and remand with instructions to dismiss the complaint.

Therefore, these appeals are REMANDED to the district court with instructions to vacate the orders of September 17 and October 7, 2002, and to dismiss the underlying complaint.

QUESTIONS AND NOTES

1. New Jersey Media ruled that across the board closure of special interest deportation hearings is not violative of the First Amendment. Detroit Free Press, on the other hand, requires open hearings but permits them to be closed when sensitive information or other national security concerns require it. How much different in their practical effects are the two contrary decisions?

2. How persuasive are the national security justifications for closing special interest deportation proceedings that are listed in the New Jersey Media case?

c. Is Indefinite, Open–Ended Detention Possible in Connection With Efforts to Remove an Individual From the United States?

In the following case, the Supreme Court addressed the question of how long an alien as to whom removal had been ordered could be detained if removal could not be effected, if, for example, the government could not find a country willing to accept the person. While not directly involving a terrorism-related matter, the case generally bears on preventive detention issues that have implications for terrorism enforcement. Also the majority opinion in the case contains dicta that directly touch upon the application of preventive detention to terrorists.

ZADVYDAS v. DAVIS

533 U.S. 678 (2001)

JUDGES: BREYER, J., delivered the opinion of the Court, in which STEVENS, O'CONNOR, SOUTER, and GINSBURG, JJ., joined. SCALIA, J., filed a dissenting opinion, in which THOMAS, J., joined. KENNEDY, J., filed a dissenting opinion, in which REHNQUIST, C.J., joined, and in which SCALIA and THOMAS, JJ., joined in part.

JUSTICE BREYER delivered the opinion of the Court.

When an alien has been found to be unlawfully present in the United States and a final order of removal has been entered, the Government ordinarily secures the alien's removal during a subsequent 90–day statutory "removal period," during which time the alien normally is held in custody.

A special statute authorizes further detention if the Government fails to remove the alien during those 90 days. It says:

> "An alien ordered removed [1] who is inadmissible ... [2] [or] removable [as a result of violations of status requirements or entry conditions, violations of criminal law, or reasons of security or foreign policy] or [3] who has been determined by the Attorney General to be a risk to the community or unlikely to comply with the order of removal, may be detained beyond the removal period and, if released,

shall be subject to [certain] terms of supervision...." 8 U.S.C. § 1231(a)(6) (1994 ed., Supp. V).

In these cases, we must decide whether this post-removal-period statute authorizes the Attorney General to detain a removable alien *indefinitely* beyond the removal period or only for a period *reasonably necessary* to secure the alien's removal. We deal here with aliens who were admitted to the United States but subsequently ordered removed. Aliens who have not yet gained initial admission to this country would present a very different question. Based on our conclusion that indefinite detention of aliens in the former category would raise serious constitutional concerns, we construe the statute to contain an implicit "reasonable time" limitation, the application of which is subject to federal court review.

The post-removal-period detention statute is one of a related set of statutes and regulations that govern detention during and after removal proceedings. While removal proceedings are in progress, most aliens may be released on bond or paroled. 66 Stat. 204, as added and amended, 110 Stat. 3009–585, 8 U.S.C. §§ 1226(a)(2), (c) (1994 ed., Supp. V). After entry of a final removal order and during the 90–day removal period, however, aliens must be held in custody. § 1231(a)(2). Subsequently, as the post-removal-period statute provides, the Government "may" continue to detain an alien who still remains here or release that alien under supervision. § 1231(a)(6).

.   .   .

We consider two separate instances of detention. The first concerns Kestutis Zadvydas, a resident alien who was born, apparently of Lithuanian parents, in a displaced persons camp in Germany in 1948. When he was eight years old, Zadvydas immigrated to the United States with his parents and other family members, and he has lived here ever since.

Zadvydas has a long criminal record, involving drug crimes, attempted robbery, attempted burglary, and theft. He has a history of flight, from both criminal and deportation proceedings. Most recently, he was convicted of possessing, with intent to distribute, cocaine; sentenced to 16 years' imprisonment; released on parole after two years; taken into INS custody; and, in 1994, ordered deported to Germany. See 8 U.S.C. § 1251(a)(2) (1988 ed., Supp. V) (delineating crimes that make alien deportable).

In 1994, Germany told the INS that it would not accept Zadvydas because he was not a German citizen. Shortly thereafter, Lithuania refused to accept Zadvydas because he was neither a Lithuanian citizen nor a permanent resident. In 1996, the INS asked the Dominican Republic (Zadvydas' wife's country) to accept him, but this effort proved unsuccessful. In 1998, Lithuania rejected, as inadequately documented, Zadvydas' effort to obtain Lithuanian citizenship based on his parents' citizenship; Zadvydas' reapplication is apparently still pending.

The INS kept Zadvydas in custody after expiration of the removal period. In September 1995, Zadvydas filed a petition for a writ of habeas corpus under 28 U.S.C. § 2241 challenging his continued detention. In October 1997, a Federal District Court granted that writ and ordered him released under supervision. In its view, the Government would never succeed in its efforts to remove Zadvydas from the United States, leading to his permanent confinement, contrary to the Constitution. The Fifth Circuit reversed this decision. *Zadvydas* v. *Underdown,* 185 F.3d 279 (1999). It concluded that Zadvydas' detention did not violate the Constitution because eventual deportation was not "impossible," good faith efforts to remove him from the United States continued, and his detention was subject to periodic administrative review. The Fifth Circuit stayed its mandate pending potential review in this Court.

The second case is that of Kim Ho Ma. Ma was born in Cambodia in 1977. When he was two, his family fled, taking him to refugee camps in Thailand and the Philippines and eventually to the United States, where he has lived as a resident alien since the age of seven. In 1995, at age 17, Ma was involved in a gang-related shooting, convicted of manslaughter, and sentenced to 38 months' imprisonment. He served two years, after which he was released into INS custody.

In light of his conviction of an "aggravated felony," Ma was ordered removed. See 8 U.S.C. §§ 1101(a)(43)(F) (defining certain violent crimes as aggravated felonies), 1227(a)(2)(A)(iii) (1994 ed., Supp. IV) (aliens convicted of aggravated felonies are deportable). The 90-day removal period expired in early 1999, but the INS continued to keep Ma in custody, because, in light of his former gang membership, the nature of his crime, and his planned participation in a prison hunger strike, it was "unable to conclude that Mr. Ma would remain nonviolent and not violate the conditions of release."

In 1999 Ma filed a petition for a writ of habeas corpus under 28 U.S.C. § 2241. A panel of five judges in the Federal District Court for the Western District of Washington, considering Ma's and about 100 similar cases together, issued a joint order holding that the Constitution forbids post-removal-period detention unless there is "a realistic chance that [the] alien will be deported" (thereby permitting classification of the detention as "in aid of deportation"). The District Court then held an evidentiary hearing, decided that there was no "realistic chance" that Cambodia (which has no repatriation treaty with the United States) would accept Ma, and ordered Ma released.

The Ninth Circuit affirmed Ma's release. *Kim Ho Ma* v. *Reno,* 208 F.3d 815 (2000). It concluded, based in part on constitutional concerns, that the statute did not authorize detention for more than a "reasonable time" beyond the 90-day period authorized for removal. And, given the lack of a repatriation agreement with Cambodia, that time had expired upon passage of the 90 days. Zadvydas asked us to review the decision of the Fifth Circuit authorizing his continued detention. The Government asked us to review the decision of the Ninth Circuit forbidding Ma's continued detention. We granted writs in both cases, agreeing to consider both statutory and related constitutional questions.

. . .

The post-removal-period detention statute applies to certain categories of aliens who have been ordered removed, namely inadmissible aliens, criminal aliens, aliens who have violated their nonimmigrant status conditions, and aliens removable for certain national security or foreign relations reasons, as well as any alien "who has been determined by the Attorney General to be a risk to the community or unlikely to comply with the order of removal." 8 U.S.C. § 1231(a)(6) (1994 ed., Supp. V). . . . It says that an alien who falls into one of these categories "may be detained beyond the removal period and, if released, shall be subject to [certain] terms of supervision."

The Government argues that the statute means what it literally says. It sets no "limit on the length of time beyond the removal period that an alien who falls within one of the Section 1231(a)(6) categories may be detained." Hence, "whether to continue to detain such an alien and, if so, in what circumstances and for how long" is up to the Attorney General, not up to the courts.

. . .

A statute permitting indefinite detention of an alien would raise a serious constitutional problem. The Fifth Amendment's Due Process Clause forbids the Government to "deprive" any "person . . . of . . . liberty . . . without due process of law." Freedom from imprisonment—from government custody, detention, or other forms of physical restraint—lies at the heart of the liberty that Clause protects, see *Foucha* v. *Louisiana*, 504 U.S. 71, 80, 112 S. Ct. 1780, 118 L. Ed. 2d 437 (1992). And this Court has said that government detention violates that Clause unless the detention is ordered in a *criminal* proceeding with adequate procedural protections, see *United States* v. *Salerno*, 481 U.S. 739, 107 S. Ct. 2095, 746, 95 L. Ed. 2d 697 (1987), or, in certain special and "narrow" nonpunitive "circumstances," *Foucha, supra*, at 80, where a special justification, such as harm-threatening mental illness, outweighs the "individual's constitutionally protected interest in avoiding physical restraint." *Kansas* v. *Hendricks*, 521 U.S. 346, 117 S. Ct. 2072, 356, 138 L. Ed. 2d 501 (1997).

The proceedings at issue here are civil, not criminal, and we assume that they are nonpunitive in purpose and effect. There is no sufficiently strong special justification here for indefinite civil detention—at least as administered under this statute. The statute, says the Government, has two regulatory goals: "ensuring the appearance of aliens at future immigration proceedings" and "preventing danger to the community." Brief for Respondents in No. 99–7791, p. 24. But by definition the first justification—preventing flight—is weak or nonexistent where removal seems a remote possibility at best. . . .

The second justification—protecting the community—does not necessarily diminish in force over time. But we have upheld preventive detention based on dangerousness only when limited to specially dangerous individuals and subject to strong procedural protections. Compare *Hendricks, supra*, at 368 (upholding scheme that imposes detention upon "a small segment of particularly dangerous individuals" and provides "strict procedural safeguards") and *Salerno, supra*, at 747, 750–752 (in upholding pretrial detention, stressing "stringent time limitations," the fact that detention is reserved for the "most serious of crimes," the requirement of proof of dangerousness by clear and convincing evidence, and the presence of judicial safeguards), with *Foucha, supra*, at 81–83 (striking down insanity-related detention system that placed burden on detainee to prove nondangerousness). In cases in which preventive detention is of potentially *indefinite* duration, we have also demanded that the dangerousness rationale be accompanied by some other special circumstance, such as mental illness, that helps to create the danger. See *Hendricks, supra*, at 358, 368.

The civil confinement here at issue is not limited, but potentially permanent. Cf. *Salerno, supra*, at 747 (noting that "maximum length of pretrial detention is limited" by "stringent" requirements).... The provision authorizing detention does not apply narrowly to "a small segment of particularly dangerous individuals," *Hendricks, supra*, at 368, say suspected terrorists, but broadly to aliens ordered removed for many and various reasons, including tourist visa violations cf. *Hendricks*, 521 U.S. at 357–358 (only individuals with "past sexually violent behavior and a present mental condition that creates a likelihood of such conduct in the future" may be detained). And, once the flight risk justification evaporates, the only special circumstance present is the alien's removable status itself, which bears no relation to a detainee's dangerousness.

Moreover, the sole procedural protections available to the alien are found in administrative proceedings, where the alien bears the burden of proving he is not dangerous, without (in the Government's view) significant later judicial review.... This Court has suggested, however, that the Constitution may well preclude granting "an administrative body the unreviewable authority to make determinations implicating fundamental rights." ... The serious constitutional problem arising out of a statute that, in these circumstances, permits an indefinite, perhaps permanent, deprivation of human liberty without any such protection is obvious.

The Government argues that, from a constitutional perspective, alien status itself can justify indefinite detention, and points to *Shaughnessy* v. *United States ex rel. Mezei*, 345 U.S. 206, 73 S. Ct. 625, 97 L. Ed. 956 (1953), as support. That case involved a once lawfully admitted alien who left the United States, returned after a trip abroad, was refused admission, and was left on Ellis Island, indefinitely detained there because the Government could not find another country to accept him. The Court held that Mezei's detention did not violate the Constitution. Id. at 215–216.

Although *Mezei*, like the present cases, involves indefinite detention, it differs from the present cases in a critical respect. As the Court emphasized, the alien's extended departure from the United States required him to seek entry into this country once again. His presence on Ellis Island did not count as entry into the United States. Hence, he was "treated," for constitutional purposes, "as if stopped at the border." And that made all the difference.

. . .

In light of this critical distinction between *Mezei* and the present cases, *Mezei* does not offer the Government significant support, and we need not consider the aliens' claim that subsequent developments have undermined *Mezei*'s legal authority.

The Government also looks for support to cases holding that Congress has "plenary power" to create immigration law, and that the judicial branch must defer to executive and legislative branch decisionmaking in that area. . . . But that power is subject to important constitutional limitations. . . . Rather, the issue we address is whether aliens that the Government finds itself unable to remove are to be condemned to an indefinite term of imprisonment within the United States.

. . .

Nor do the cases before us require us to consider the political branches' authority to control entry into the United States. Hence we leave no "unprotected spot in the Nation's armor. Neither do we consider terrorism or other special circumstances where special arguments might be made for forms of preventive detention and for heightened deference to the judgments of the political branches with respect to matters of national security. The sole foreign policy consideration the Government mentions here is the concern lest courts interfere with "sensitive" repatriation negotiations. But neither the Government nor the dissents explain how a habeas court's efforts to determine the likelihood of repatriation, if handled with appropriate sensitivity, could make a significant difference in this respect.

Finally, the Government argues that, whatever liberty interest the aliens possess, it is "greatly diminished" by their lack of a legal right to "live at large in this country." . . . The choice, however, is not between imprisonment and the alien "living at large." . . .

Despite this constitutional problem, if "Congress has made its intent" in the statute "clear, 'we must give effect to that intent.' " . . . We cannot find here, however, any clear indication of congressional intent to grant the Attorney General the power to hold indefinitely in confinement an alien ordered removed. And that is so whether protecting the community from dangerous aliens is a primary or (as we believe) secondary statutory purpose. After all, the provision is part of a statute that has as its basic purpose effectuating an alien's removal. Why should we assume that Congress saw the alien's dangerousness as unrelated to this purpose?

. . .

The Government points to similar related statutes that *require* detention of criminal aliens during removal proceedings and the removal period, and argues that these show that mandatory detention is the rule while discretionary release is the narrow exception. But the statute before us applies not only to terrorists and criminals, but also to ordinary visa violators, and, more importantly, post-removal-period detention, unlike detention pending a determination of removability or during the subsequent 90–day removal period, has no obvious termination point.

In early 1996, Congress explicitly expanded the group of aliens subject to mandatory detention, eliminating provisions that permitted release of criminal aliens who had at one time been lawfully admitted to the United States. Antiterrorism and Effective Death Penalty Act of 1996, § 439(c), 110 Stat. 1277. And later that year Congress enacted the present law, which liberalizes pre-existing law by shortening the removal period from six months to 90 days, mandates detention of certain criminal aliens during the removal proceedings and for the subsequent 90–day removal period, and adds the post-removal-period provision here at issue. Illegal Immigration Reform and Immigrant Responsibility Act of 1996, Div. C, §§ 303, 305, 110 Stat. 3009–585, 3009–598 to 3009–599; 8 U.S.C. §§ 1226(c), 1231(a) (1994 ed., Supp. V).

We have found nothing in the history of these statutes that clearly demonstrates a congressional intent to authorize indefinite, perhaps permanent, detention. Consequently, interpreting the statute to avoid a serious constitutional threat, we conclude that, once removal is no longer reasonably foreseeable, continued detention is no longer authorized by statute.

The Government seems to argue that, even under our interpretation of the statute, a federal habeas court would have to accept the Government's view about whether the implicit statutory limitation is satisfied in a particular case, conducting little or no independent review of the matter. In our view, that is not so.

In answering that basic question, the habeas court must ask whether the detention in question exceeds a period reasonably necessary to secure removal. It should measure reasonableness primarily in terms of the statute's basic purpose, namely assuring the alien's presence at the moment of removal. Thus, if removal is not reasonably foreseeable, the court should hold continued detention unreasonable and no longer authorized by statute. In that case, of course, the alien's release may and should be conditioned on any of the various forms of supervised release that are appropriate in the circumstances, and the alien may no doubt be returned to custody upon a violation of those conditions.... And if removal is reasonably foreseeable, the habeas court should consider the risk of the alien's committing further crimes as a factor potentially justifying confinement within that reasonable removal period.

We recognize, as the Government points out, that review must take appropriate account of the greater immigration-related expertise of the Executive Branch, of the serious administrative needs and concerns inherent in the necessarily extensive INS efforts to enforce this complex statute, and the Nation's need to "speak with one voice" in immigration matters. But we believe that courts can take appropriate account of such matters without abdicating their legal responsibility to review the lawfulness of an alien's continued detention.

. . .

We realize that recognizing this necessary Executive leeway will often call for difficult judgments. In order to limit the occasions when courts will need to make them, we think it practically necessary to recognize some presumptively reasonable period of detention.

. . .

While an argument can be made for confining any presumption to 90 days, we doubt that when Congress shortened the removal period to 90 days in 1996 it believed that all reasonably foreseeable removals could be accomplished in that time. We do have reason to believe, however, that Congress previously doubted the constitutionality of detention for more than six months. . . . Consequently, for the sake of uniform administration in the federal courts, we recognize that period. After this 6–month period, once the alien provides good reason to believe that there is no significant likelihood of removal in the reasonably foreseeable future, the Government must respond with evidence sufficient to rebut that showing. And for detention to remain reasonable, as the period of prior post-removal confinement grows, what counts as the "reasonably foreseeable future" conversely would have to shrink. This 6–month presumption, of course, does not mean that every alien not removed must be released after six months. To the contrary, an alien may be held in confinement until it has been determined that there is no significant likelihood of removal in the reasonably foreseeable future.

. . . [W]e vacate the decisions below and remand both cases for further proceedings consistent with this opinion.

It is so ordered.

QUESTIONS AND NOTES

1. On the one hand, Zadvydas provides some comfort for those who are concerned that the government is detaining people for too long based on too little evidence. The case establishes that indefinite, open-ended detention is impermissible for persons ordered to be removed from the U.S in circumstances where no country will accept them. Zadvydas thus is a strong statement against detention that extends too long, even for alien criminals.

2. On the other hand, Zadvydas several times seems to recognize that the detention of terrorists may be a possible exception to the restriction on

indefinite detention. How many times does Justice Breyer mention the matter of detaining terrorists? Does the court majority clearly opine on the question of extended detention of terrorists? What do you read into the majority's mention of terrorists in this context? Are the Court's statements mentioning terrorists restricted to alien terrorists?

3. In the wake of the Zadvydas decision, Congress enacted legislation as part of the USA PATRIOT Act that provided that aliens whose removal is unlikely in the reasonably foreseeable future and whose release "will threaten the security of the United States or the safety of the community or any person" may be detained subject to the detention being reviewed every six months. 8 U.S.C. § 1226a(a)(6). The full § 1226a is reproduced infra, p. 457.

4. Panel Discussion, Perversities and Prospects: Whither Immigration Enforcement and Detention in the Anti-terrorism Aftermath? 9 Geo. J. on Poverty L. & Pol'y 1, 17–18 (2002):

REMARKS OF PANELIST CHRISTINA DECONCINI

I've been asked to talk about a distinct group of people who are detained by the INS and referred to as "indefinite detainees" or "lifers."

I'll begin by defining an INS "indefinite detainee." Basically, it is someone who has received a final order to be removed from the United States, but whom the INS cannot remove, either because s/he is stateless, because the United States does not have a repatriation agreement with the home country (which is the case for Cubans, Laotians, Cambodians, Vietnamese, and others), or because the home country will not issue a travel document to allow that person to return. Prior to the Supreme Court's ruling in Zadvydas and subsequent release of some indefinite detainees, the INS estimated that there were nearly 4,000 people in this category. Indefinite detainees include individuals with no criminal background, people who have been found to be removable due to minor immigration violations, as well as non-citizens who have served time following criminal convictions here in the United States. All have been found to be removable from the United States but, through no fault of their own, the United States is unable to remove them. Instead of releasing these individuals, most remain incarcerated, often for years.

5. Following the decision in Zadvydas, the question of how to deal with aliens who had not yet been admitted into this country but ended up in U.S. custody and were otherwise in the same situation as Zadvydas came before the Supreme Court in Clark v. Martinez, 543 U.S. 371 (2005). Were aliens who had never been admitted to this country to be treated the same as the aliens in Zadvydas? Justice Scalia opined as follows:

The dissent's belief that *Zadvydas* compels this result rests primarily on that case's statement that "aliens who have not yet gained initial admission to this country would present a very different question." This mistakes the reservation of a question with its answer.... The opinion in that case considered whether § 1231(a)(6) permitted the Government to detain removable aliens indefinitely; relying on ambiguities in the statutory text and the canon that statutes should be interpreted to avoid constitutional doubts, the opinion held that it did not. Despite the dissent's repeated claims that § 1231(a)(6) could not be given a different reading for inadmissible aliens, the Court *refused to decide* that question—the question we answer today. It is indeed different from the question decided in *Zadvydas*, but because the statutory text provides for no distinction between admitted and nonadmitted aliens, we find that it results in the same answer.[26]

. . .

The *Zadvydas* dissent . . . concluded that the release of "Mariel Cubans and other illegal, inadmissible aliens . . . would seem *a necessary consequence of the majority's construction of the statute.*" Tellingly, the *Zadvydas* majority did not negate either charge.

The Government, joined by the dissent, argues that the statutory purpose and the constitutional concerns that influenced our statutory construction in *Zadvydas* are not present for aliens, such as Martinez and Benitez, who have not been admitted to the United States. Be that as it may, it cannot justify giving the *same* detention provision a different meaning when such aliens are involved.

. . .

The Government fears that the security of our borders will be compromised if it must release into the country inadmissible aliens who cannot be removed. If that is so, Congress can attend to it.[27] But for this Court to sanction indefinite detention in the face of *Zadvydas* would establish within our jurisprudence, beyond the power of Congress to remedy, the dangerous principle that judges can give the same statutory text different meanings in different cases.

Since the Government has suggested no reason why the period of time reasonably necessary to effect removal is longer for an inadmissible alien, the 6–month presumptive detention period we prescribed in *Zadvydas* applies. Both Martinez and Benitez were detained well beyond six months after their removal orders became final. The Government having brought forward nothing to indicate that a substantial likelihood of removal subsists despite the passage of six months (indeed, it concedes that it is no longer even involved in repatriation negotiations with Cuba); and the District Court in each case having determined that removal to Cuba is not reasonably foreseeable; the petitions for habeas corpus should have been granted. Accordingly, we affirm the judgment of the Ninth

---

26. The dissent is quite wrong in saying, . . . that the *Zadvydas* Court's belief that 1231(a)(6) did not apply to all aliens is evidenced by its statement that it did not consider terrorism or other special circumstances where special arrangements might be made for forms of preventive detention, The Court's interpretation of 1231(a)(6) did not affect the detention of alien terrorists for the simple reason that sustained detention of alien terrorists is a special arrangement authorized by a different statutory provision, 8 U.S.C. 1537(b)(2)(C).

27. That Congress has the capacity to do so is demonstrated by its reaction to our decision in *Zadvydas*. Less than four months after the release of our opinion, Congress enacted a statute which expressly authorized continued detention, for a period of six months beyond the removal period (and renewable indefinitely), of any alien (1) whose removal is not reasonably foreseeable and (2) who presents a national security threat or has been involved in terrorist activities. Uniting and Strengthening America by Providing Appropriate Tools Required to Intercept and Obstruct Terrorism Act of 2001 (USA PATRIOT Act, 412(a), 115 Stat. 350 (enacted Oct. 26, 2001) (codified at 8 U.S.C. 1226a(a)(6) (2000 ed., Supp. II)).

Circuit, reverse the judgment of the Eleventh Circuit, and remand both cases for proceedings consistent with this opinion.

d. Civil Suits by Aliens of Middle Eastern Origin Seeking Redress for Post–9/11 Detentions

ASHCROFT v. IQBAL

129 S.Ct. 1937 (2009)

JUSTICE KENNEDY delivered the opinion of the Court.

Respondent Javaid Iqbal is a citizen of Pakistan and a Muslim. In the wake of the September 11, 2001, terrorist attacks he was arrested in the United States on criminal charges and detained by federal officials. Respondent claims he was deprived of various constitutional protections while in federal custody. To redress the alleged deprivations, respondent filed a complaint against numerous federal officials, including John Ashcroft, the former Attorney General of the United States, and Robert Mueller, the Director of the Federal Bureau of Investigation (FBI). Ashcroft and Mueller are the petitioners in the case now before us. As to these two petitioners, the complaint alleges that they adopted an unconstitutional policy that subjected respondent to harsh conditions of confinement on account of his race, religion, or national origin.

In the District Court petitioners raised the defense of qualified immunity and moved to dismiss the suit, contending the complaint was not sufficient to state a claim against them. The District Court denied the motion to dismiss, concluding the complaint was sufficient to state a claim despite petitioners' official status at the times in question. . . .

Respondent's account of his prison ordeal could, if proved, demonstrate unconstitutional misconduct by some governmental actors. But the allegations and pleadings with respect to these actors are not before us here. This case instead turns on a narrower question: Did respondent, as the plaintiff in the District Court, plead factual matter that, if taken as true, states a claim that petitioners deprived him of his clearly established constitutional rights. We hold respondent's pleadings are insufficient.

Following the 2001 attacks, the FBI and other entities within the Department of Justice began an investigation of vast reach to identify the assailants and prevent them from attacking anew. The FBI dedicated more than 4,000 special agents and 3,000 support personnel to the endeavor. By September 18 "the FBI had received more than 96,000 tips or potential leads from the public." Dept. of Justice, Office of Inspector General, The September 11 Detainees: A Review of the Treatment of Aliens Held on Immigration Charges in Connection with the Investigation of the September 11 Attacks 1, 11–12 (Apr.2003) (hereinafter OIG Report), http://www.usdoj.gov/oig/special/0306/full.pdf?bcsi _scan _ 61073EC0F74759AD=0&bcsi _scan _filename=full.pdf (as visited May 14, 2009, and available in Clerk of Court's case file).

In the ensuing months the FBI questioned more than 1,000 people with suspected links to the attacks in particular or to terrorism in general. Of those individuals, some 762 were held on immigration charges; and a 184–member subset of that group was deemed to be "of 'high interest' " to the investigation. The high-interest detainees were held under restrictive conditions designed to prevent them from communicating with the general prison population or the outside world.

Respondent was one of the detainees. According to his complaint, in November 2001 agents of the FBI and Immigration and Naturalization Service arrested him on charges of fraud in relation to identification documents and conspiracy to defraud the United States. Iqbal v. Hasty, 490 F.3d 143, 147–148 (C.A.2 2007). Pending trial for those crimes, respondent was housed at the Metropolitan Detention Center (MDC) in Brooklyn, New York. Respondent was designated a person "of high interest" to the September 11 investigation and in January 2002 was placed in a section of the MDC known as the Administrative Maximum Special Housing Unit (ADMAX SHU). As the facility's name indicates, the ADMAX SHU incorporates the maximum security conditions allowable under Federal Bureau of Prison regulations. ADMAX SHU detainees were kept in lockdown 23 hours a day, spending the remaining hour outside their cells in handcuffs and leg irons accompanied by a four-officer escort.

Respondent pleaded guilty to the criminal charges, served a term of imprisonment, and was removed to his native Pakistan. He then filed a Bivens action in the United States District Court for the Eastern District of New York against 34 current and former federal officials and 19 "John Doe" federal corrections officers. See Bivens v. Six Unknown Fed. Narcotics Agents, 403 U.S. 388, 91 S.Ct. 1999, 29 L.Ed.2d 619 (1971). The defendants range from the correctional officers who had day-to-day contact with respondent during the term of his confinement, to the wardens of the MDC facility, all the way to petitioners-officials who were at the highest level of the federal law enforcement hierarchy.

The 21–cause–of–action complaint does not challenge respondent's arrest or his confinement in the MDC's general prison population. Rather, it concentrates on his treatment while confined to the ADMAX SHU. The complaint sets forth various claims against defendants who are not before us. For instance, the complaint alleges that respondent's jailors "kicked him in the stomach, punched him in the face, and dragged him across" his cell without justification, subjected him to serial strip and body-cavity searches when he posed no safety risk to himself or others, and refused to let him and other Muslims pray because there would be "[n]o prayers for terrorists,"

The allegations against petitioners are the only ones relevant here. The complaint contends that petitioners designated respondent a person of high interest on account of his race, religion, or national origin, in contravention of the First and Fifth Amendments to the Constitution. The complaint alleges that "the [FBI], under the direction of Defendant

Mueller, arrested and detained thousands of Arab Muslim men ... as part of its investigation of the events of September 11." It further alleges that "[t]he policy of holding post–September–11th detainees in highly restrictive conditions of confinement until they were 'cleared' by the FBI was approved by Defendants Ashcroft and Mueller in discussions in the weeks after September 11, 2001." Lastly, the complaint posits that petitioners "each knew of, condoned, and willfully and maliciously agreed to subject" respondent to harsh conditions of confinement "as a matter of policy, solely on account of [his] religion, race, and/or national origin and for no legitimate penological interest." The pleading names Ashcroft as the "principal architect" of the policy, and identifies Mueller as "instrumental in [its] adoption, promulgation, and implementation."

Petitioners moved to dismiss the complaint for failure to state sufficient allegations to show their own involvement in clearly established unconstitutional conduct. The District Court denied their motion. Accepting all of the allegations in respondent's complaint as true, the court held that "it cannot be said that there [is] no set of facts on which [respondent] would be entitled to relief as against" petitioners....

The Court of Appeals ... held respondent's pleading adequate to allege petitioners' personal involvement in discriminatory decisions which, if true, violated clearly established constitutional law.

Judge Cabranes concurred. He agreed that the majority's "discussion of the relevant pleading standards reflect[ed] the uneasy compromise ... between a qualified immunity privilege rooted in the need to preserve the effectiveness of government as contemplated by our constitutional structure and the pleading requirements of Rule 8(a) of the Federal Rules of Civil Procedure." Judge Cabranes nonetheless expressed concern at the prospect of subjecting high-ranking Government officials—entitled to assert the defense of qualified immunity and charged with responding to "a national and international security emergency unprecedented in the history of the American Republic"—to the burdens of discovery on the basis of a complaint as nonspecific as respondent's. Reluctant to vindicate that concern as a member of the Court of Appeals, Judge Cabranes urged this Court to address the appropriate pleading standard "at the earliest opportunity." We granted certiorari, 554 U.S. ___ (2008), and now reverse.

     . . .

... [W]e conclude that the Court of Appeals had jurisdiction to hear petitioners' appeal. The District Court's order denying petitioners' motion to dismiss turned on an issue of law and rejected the defense of qualified immunity. It was therefore a final decision "subject to immediate appeal." Respondent says that "a qualified immunity appeal based solely on the complaint's failure to state a claim, and not on the ultimate issues relevant to the qualified immunity defense itself, is not a proper subject of interlocutory jurisdiction."

In other words, respondent contends the Court of Appeals had jurisdiction to determine whether his complaint avers a clearly established constitutional violation but that it lacked jurisdiction to pass on the sufficiency of his pleadings. Our opinions, however, make clear that appellate jurisdiction is not so strictly confined.

. . .

. . . Here . . . we begin by taking note of the elements a plaintiff must plead to state a claim of unconstitutional discrimination against officials entitled to assert the defense of qualified immunity.

In Bivens—proceeding on the theory that a right suggests a remedy— this Court "recognized for the first time an implied private action for damages against federal officers alleged to have violated a citizen's constitutional rights." Because implied causes of action are disfavored, the Court has been reluctant to extend Bivens liability "to any new context or new category of defendants." That reluctance might well have disposed of respondent's First Amendment claim of religious discrimination. For while we have allowed a Bivens action to redress a violation of the equal protection component of the Due Process Clause of the Fifth Amendment, we have not found an implied damages remedy under the Free Exercise Clause. Indeed, we have declined to extend Bivens to a claim sounding in the First Amendment. Petitioners do not press this argument, however, so we assume, without deciding, that respondent's First Amendment claim is actionable under Bivens.

In the limited settings where Bivens does apply, the implied cause of action is the "federal analog to suits brought against state officials under Rev. Stat. § 1979, 42 U.S.C. § 1983." Based on the rules our precedents establish, respondent correctly concedes that Government officials may not be held liable for the unconstitutional conduct of their subordinates under a theory of respondeat superior. ("[I]t is undisputed that supervisory Bivens liability cannot be established solely on a theory of respondeat superior"). . . . Because vicarious liability is inapplicable to Bivens and § 1983 suits, a plaintiff must plead that each Government-official defendant, through the official's own individual actions, has violated the Constitution.

The factors necessary to establish a Bivens violation will vary with the constitutional provision at issue. Where the claim is invidious discrimination in contravention of the First and Fifth Amendments, our decisions make clear that the plaintiff must plead and prove that the defendant acted with discriminatory purpose. Church of Lukumi Babalu Aye, Inc. v. Hialeah, 508 U.S. 520, 540–541, 113 S.Ct. 2217, 124 L.Ed.2d 472 (1993) (First Amendment); Washington v. Davis, 426 U.S. 229, 240, 96 S.Ct. 2040, 48 L.Ed.2d 597 (1976) (Fifth Amendment). Under extant precedent purposeful discrimination requires more than "intent as volition or intent as awareness of consequences." Personnel Administrator of Mass. v. Feeney, 442 U.S. 256, 279, 99 S.Ct. 2282, 60 L.Ed.2d 870 (1979). It instead involves a decisionmaker's undertaking a course of action " 'because of,' not merely 'in spite of,' [the action's] adverse effects upon an identifiable group." It follows that, to state a claim based on a violation of a clearly established right, respondent must plead sufficient factual matter to show that petitioners adopted and implemented the detention policies at issue not for a neutral, investigative reason but for the purpose of discriminating on account of race, religion, or national origin.

Respondent disagrees. He argues that, under a theory of "supervisory liability," petitioners can be liable for "knowledge and acquiescence in their subordinates' use of discriminatory criteria to make classification decisions among detainees." That is to say, respondent believes a supervisor's mere knowledge of his subordinate's discriminatory purpose amounts to the supervisor's violating the Constitution. We reject this argument. Respondent's conception of "supervisory liability" is inconsistent with his accurate stipulation that petitioners may not be held accountable for the misdeeds of their agents. In a § 1983 suit or a Bivens action—where masters do not answer for the torts of their servants—the term "supervisory liability" is a misnomer. Absent vicarious liability, each Government official, his or her title notwithstanding, is only liable for his or her own misconduct. In the context of determining whether there is a violation of clearly established right to overcome qualified immunity, purpose rather than knowledge is required to impose Bivens liability on the subordinate for unconstitutional discrimination; the same holds true for an official charged with violations arising from his or her superintendent responsibilities.

We turn to respondent's complaint. . . .

. . .

We begin our analysis by identifying the allegations in the complaint that are not entitled to the assumption of truth. Respondent pleads that petitioners "knew of, condoned, and willfully and maliciously agreed to subject [him]" to harsh conditions of confinement "as a matter of policy, solely on account of [his] religion, race, and/or national origin and for no legitimate penological interest." The complaint alleges that Ashcroft was the "principal architect" of this invidious policy, and that Mueller was "instrumental" in adopting and executing it. These bare assertions, . . . amount to nothing more than a "formulaic recitation of the elements" of a constitutional discrimination claim, namely, that petitioners adopted a policy " 'because of,' not merely 'in spite of,' its adverse effects upon an identifiable group." As such, the allegations arc conclusory and not entitled to be assumed true. To be clear, we do not reject these bald allegations on the ground that they are unrealistic or nonsensical. . . . It is the conclusory nature of respondent's allegations, rather than their extravagantly fanciful nature, that disentitles them to the presumption of truth.

We next consider the factual allegations in respondent's complaint to determine if they plausibly suggest an entitlement to relief. The complaint alleges that "the [FBI], under the direction of Defendant MUELLER, arrested and detained thousands of Arab Muslim men . . . as part of its investigation of the events of September 11." It further claims that "[t]he policy of holding post–September–11th detainees in highly restrictive conditions of confinement until they were 'cleared' by the FBI was approved by Defendants ASHCROFT and MUELLER in discussions in the weeks after September 11, 2001." Taken as true, these allegations are consistent with petitioners' purposefully designating detainees "of high interest" because of their race, religion, or national origin. But given more likely explanations, they do not plausibly establish this purpose.

The September 11 attacks were perpetrated by 19 Arab Muslim hijackers who counted themselves members in good standing of al Qaeda, an Islamic fundamentalist group. Al Qaeda was headed by another Arab Muslim—Osama bin Laden—and composed in large part of his Arab Muslim disciples. It should come as no surprise that a legitimate policy directing law enforcement to arrest and detain individuals because of their suspected link to the attacks would produce a disparate, incidental impact on Arab Muslims, even though the purpose of the policy was to target neither Arabs nor Muslims. On the facts respondent alleges the arrests Mueller oversaw were likely lawful and justified by his nondiscriminatory intent to detain aliens who were illegally present in the United States and who had potential connections to those who committed terrorist acts. As between that "obvious alternative explanation" for the arrests, and the purposeful, invidious discrimination respondent asks us to infer, discrimination is not a plausible conclusion.

But even if the complaint's well-pleaded facts give rise to a plausible inference that respondent's arrest was the result of unconstitutional discrimination, that inference alone would not entitle respondent to relief. It is important to recall that respondent's complaint challenges neither the constitutionality of his arrest nor his initial detention in the MDC. Respondent's constitutional claims against petitioners rest solely on their ostensible "policy of holding post–September–11th detainees" in the AD-MAX SHU once they were categorized as "of high interest." To prevail on that theory, the complaint must contain facts plausibly showing that petitioners purposefully adopted a policy of classifying post–September–11 detainees as "of high interest" because of their race, religion, or national origin.

This the complaint fails to do. Though respondent alleges that various other defendants, who are not before us, may have labeled him a person of "of high interest" for impermissible reasons, his only factual allegation against petitioners accuses them of adopting a policy approving "restrictive conditions of confinement" for post–September–11 detainees until they were " 'cleared' by the FBI." Accepting the truth of that allegation, the complaint does not show, or even intimate, that petitioners purposefully housed detainees in the ADMAX SHU due to their race, religion, or national origin. All it plausibly suggests is that the Nation's top law enforcement officers, in the aftermath of a devastating terrorist attack, sought to keep suspected terrorists in the most secure conditions available until the suspects could be cleared of terrorist activity. Respondent does not argue, nor can he, that such a motive would violate petitioners' constitutional obligations. He would need to allege more by way of factual content to "nudg[e]" his claim of purposeful discrimination "across the line from conceivable to plausible."

... [R]espondent's complaint does not contain any factual allegation sufficient to plausibly suggest petitioners' discriminatory state of mind. His pleadings thus do not meet the standard necessary to comply with Rule 8.

It is important to note, however, that we express no opinion concerning the sufficiency of respondent's complaint against the defendants who are not before us. Respondent's account of his prison ordeal alleges serious official misconduct that we need not address here. Our decision is limited to the determination that respondent's complaint does not entitle him to relief from petitioners.

. . .

... The basic thrust of the qualified-immunity doctrine is to free officials from the concerns of litigation, including "avoidance of disruptive discovery." There are serious and legitimate reasons for this. If a Government official is to devote time to his or her duties, and to the formulation of sound and responsible policies, it is counterproductive to require the substantial diversion that is attendant to participating in litigation and making informed decisions as to how it should proceed. Litigation, though necessary to ensure that officials comply with the law, exacts heavy costs in terms of efficiency and expenditure of valuable time and resources that might otherwise be directed to the proper execution of the work of the Government. The costs of diversion are only magnified when Government officials are charged with responding to, as Judge Cabranes aptly put it, "a national and international security emergency unprecedented in the history of the American Republic."

It is no answer to these concerns to say that discovery for petitioners can be deferred while pretrial proceedings continue for other defendants. It is quite likely that, when discovery as to the other parties proceeds, it would prove necessary for petitioners and their counsel to participate in the process to ensure the case does not develop in a misleading or slanted way that causes prejudice to their position. Even if petitioners are not yet themselves subject to discovery orders, then, they would not be free from the burdens of discovery.

We decline respondent's invitation to relax the pleading requirements on the ground that the Court of Appeals promises petitioners minimally intrusive discovery. That promise provides especially cold comfort in this pleading context, where we are impelled to give real content to the concept of qualified immunity for high-level officials who must be neither deterred nor detracted from the vigorous performance of their duties. Because respondent's complaint is deficient under Rule 8, he is not entitled to discovery, cabined or otherwise.

We hold that respondent's complaint fails to plead sufficient facts to state a claim for purposeful and unlawful discrimination against petitioners. The Court of Appeals should decide in the first instance whether to remand to the District Court so that respondent can seek leave to amend his deficient complaint.

The judgment of the Court of Appeals is reversed, and the case is remanded for further proceedings consistent with this opinion.

[JUSTICE SOUTER, with whom JUSTICE STEVENS, JUSTICE GINSBURG, and JUSTICE BREYER joined, filed a dissenting opinion. JUSTICE BREYER also wrote a dissenting opinion.]

e. Statutory Detention and Removal Provisions Directed Specifically Toward Terrorists Under the USA PATRIOT Act and Other Immigration Law Provisions

The USA PATRIOT Act (P.L. 107–56, Oct. 26, 2001) added section 1226a to Title 8, United States Code, which contains the codified parts of the Immigration and Nationality Act of 1952. It added another tool to the array of immigration law provisions that could be used in alien terrorist cases. See footnote 27 in Clark v. Martinez, supra, p. 449, and reconsider the dicta in Zadvydas v. Davis, supra, p. 440.

§ 1226a. Mandatory detention of suspected terrorists; habeas corpus; judicial review

(a) Detention of terrorist aliens.

(1) Custody.—The Attorney General shall take into custody any alien who is certified under paragraph (3).

(2) Release.—Except as provided in paragraphs (5) and (6), the Attorney General shall maintain custody of such an alien until the alien is removed from the United States. Except as provided in paragraph (6), such custody shall be maintained irrespective of any relief from removal for which the alien may be eligible, or any relief from removal granted the alien, until the Attorney General determines that the alien is no longer an alien who may be certified under paragraph (3). If the alien is finally determined not to be removable, detention pursuant to this subsection shall terminate.

(3) Certification.—The Attorney General may certify an alien under this paragraph if the Attorney General has reasonable grounds to believe that the alien—

(A) is described in section 212(a)(3)(A)(i), 212(a)(3)(A)(iii), 212(a)(3)(B), 237(a)(4)(A)(i), 237(a)(4)(A)(iii), or 237(a)(4)(B) [8 USC §§ 1182(a)(3)(A)(i) 1182(a)(3)(A)(iii), 1182(a)(3)(B), 1227(a)(4)(A)(i), 1227(a)(4)(A)(iii), or 1227(a)(4)(B)]; or

(B) is engaged in any other activity that endangers the national security of the United States.

(4) Nondelegation.—The Attorney General may delegate the authority provided under paragraph (3) only to the Deputy Attorney General. The Deputy Attorney General may not delegate such authority.

(5) Commencement of proceedings.—The Attorney General shall place an alien detained under paragraph (1) in removal proceedings, or shall charge the alien with a criminal offense, not later than 7 days after the commencement of such detention. If the requirement of the preceding sentence is not satisfied, the Attorney General shall release the alien.

(6) Limitation on indefinite detention.—An alien detained solely under paragraph (1) who has not been removed under section 241(a)(1)(A) [8 USC § 1231(a)(1)(A)], and whose removal is unlikely in the reasonably foreseeable future, may be detained for additional periods of up to six months only if the release of the alien will threaten the national security of the United States or the safety of the community or any person.

(7) Review of certification.—The Attorney General shall review the certification made under paragraph (3) every 6 months. If the Attorney General determines, in the Attorney General's discretion, that the certification should be revoked, the alien may be released on such conditions as the Attorney General deems appropriate, unless such release is otherwise prohibited by law. The alien may request each 6 months in writing that the Attorney General reconsider the certification and may submit documents or other evidence in support of that request.

(b) Habeas corpus and judicial review.—

(1) In general.—Judicial review of any action or decision relating to this section (including judicial review of the merits of a determination made under subsection (a)(3) or (a)(6)) is available exclusively in habeas corpus proceedings consistent with this subsection. Except as provided in the preceding sentence, no court shall have jurisdiction to review, by habeas corpus petition or otherwise, any such action or decision.

(2) Application.—

(A) In general.—Notwithstanding any other provision of law, including section 2241(a) of title 28, United States Code, habeas corpus proceedings described in paragraph (1) may be initiated only by an application filed with—

(i) the Supreme Court;

(ii) any justice of the Supreme Court;

(iii) any circuit judge of the United States Court of Appeals for the District of Columbia Circuit; or

(iv) any district court otherwise having jurisdiction to entertain it.

(B) Application Transfer.—Section 2241(b) of title 28, United States Code, shall apply to an application for a writ of habeas corpus described in subparagraph (A).

(3) Appeals.—Notwithstanding any other provision of law, including section 2253 of title 28, in habeas corpus proceedings described in paragraph (1) before a circuit or district judge, the final order shall be subject to review, on appeal, by the United States Court of Appeals for the District of Columbia Circuit. There shall be no right of appeal in such proceedings to any other circuit court of appeals.

(4) Rule of decision.—The law applied by the Supreme Court and the United States Court of Appeals for the District of Columbia Circuit shall be regarded as the rule of decision in habeas corpus proceedings described in paragraph (1).

(c) Statutory construction.—The provisions of this section shall not be applicable to any other provision of this Act.

QUESTIONS AND NOTES

1. Provisions in the immigration laws dealing with persons suspected of being terrorists and providing for their removal (i.e. deportation) were on the books prior to September 11th. See below sections 1531–1537, 1227, Title 8, U.S.C. What does section 1226a add?

2. Subsection (a)(3) of section 1226a authorizes the Attorney General to certify an alien if he has reasonable grounds to believe that the alien has committed or will commit the crimes of espionage or sabotage, try to overthrow the government, commit terrorist acts, or engage in acts that threaten the national security. The consequences of the certification are discussed below. The reasonable belief standard is less than probable cause. It appears to be the same standard applied in Terry v. Ohio, 392 U.S. 1 (1968), authorizing police stopping and frisking of individuals based on "reason to believe that . . . [the officer] is dealing with an armed and dangerous individual."

3. The language of subsection (a)(2) in 1226a is upon a first reading somewhat confusing. Consider the following comments on this provision.

a) Panel Discussion, Perversities and Prospects, op. cit. supra, note 4, supra, p. 448, at 21:

Because we are in the post–September 11 climate and because an anti-terrorism bill was passed today, I do want to briefly touch on the topic of terrorism and the legislation as it relates to indefinite detention,. . . . The new legislation grants the Attorney General the power to detain immigrants, including long-time legal permanent residents, indefinitely without any meaningful judicial review. This new law must be read in light of the Zadvydas holding, and will likely be challenged based on this. While the Zadvydas decision did mention that terrorism or other special circumstances might justify preventative detention, it made clear that adequate procedural safeguards would be required in order to avoid running afoul of the Constitution, safeguards that are not present in the current review process. Under the anti-terrorist law passed today, a person could be indefinitely detained for an immigration related violation if he or she is "certified" as a terrorist. This certification requires the minimal "reasonable grounds to believe" standard, used in stop and frisk cases, and the government has no obligation to provide the detainee with a trial or a hearing in which the government must prove that he is, in fact, a terrorist. It seems doubtful that such a process would meet the constitutional requirements for indefinite detention as outlined by the court in Zadvydas.

b) Federalist Society, White Paper on the USA PATRIOT Act of 2001, Criminal Procedure Sections 13 (2001):

The final language [of 1226a] is confusing and possibly contradictory in subdivision (a)(2) regarding the effect of the outcome of the removal proceedings. The second sentence retains language from the original Senate bill that "custody should be maintained irrespective ... of any relief from removal granted the alien...." Yet the last sentence added in the final stages says, "If the alien is finally determined not to be removable, detention pursuant to this subsection shall terminate." If the basis of detention was also the ground for the removal and if the ground has been finally adjudicated to be false, continued detention would raise serious constitutional questions. It seems likely the courts would avoid the questions by relying on the last sentence.

c) Perhaps the apparently contradictory language in (a)(2) can be explained along the following lines. Under pre-September 11 statutes, if a person believed to be an alien terrorist was in custody and there was insufficient evidence to prosecute and convict him, the next best alternative was to deport him. Legislation reproduced below (see sections 1531–1534 enacted in 1996, and 1227, Title 8, U.S.C.) contains specific provisions dealing with this alternative. However, after 9/11, the administration may have seen the alien terrorist problem in a different light. In some cases, if the individual could not be convicted and incarcerated, the next best alternative might be seen as an extended detention rather than deportation. Why? Because the effect of the 9/11 attacks was to heighten concerns about freeing suspected terrorists who might have the capacity to inflict terrible devastating harm on U.S. people, property and other interests.

Under this reading of § 1226(a)(2), once the Attorney General has certified an alien as dangerous, that is subject to removal, he shall retain custody of him until he is removed irrespective of any *discretionary order* granting relief from the removal order, unless and until the Attorney General changes his mind about the dangerousness of the alien. If the Attorney General finally determines that the alien is not removable, that is, because he is no longer an alien who may be certified as dangerous under the specified criteria, the detention shall terminate. On this reading of 1226a, the legislative intention is that the judgment of the Attorney General that the individual falls into one of the dangerousness categories and is therefore removable trumps any other discretionary judgment made that there are circumstances that might provide extrinsic reasons for not deporting the individual.

Of course, section 1226a seems to authorize prolonged preventive detention of aliens who fall into specified categories of dangerousness subject to six month reviews. Do you think that such a provision is constitutional? Consider again the dicta in Zadvydas, supra, and reconsider the issue when in chapter 11, you come across, as you will, other expressions in opinions of individual justices of the Supreme court of some support for forms of preventive detention and express provisions promulgated by the Obama administration providing for extended detention for some detainees. Subsection (6) of § 1226a may be viewed as an attempt to temper the constitutional concerns somewhat by providing for regular review by the Attorney General of the status of the detained person, with the issue of his dangerousness to be regularly revisited.

4.   The special provisions providing for removal of persons believed to be terrorists, enacted in 1996 as part of the AEDPA, are reproduced below. They included provision for the establishment of a special court to deal with such cases where classified information is involved and some in camera proceedings are needed. General authority to remove persons because of terrorist activity is contained in other provisions of the immigration laws (see section 1227 below). As far as is known, the provisions dealing with the removal court have not yet been used. (Note that the same judges appointed to the special Foreign Intelligence Surveillance Court, see supra, Chapter 5, may be appointed to the removal court.)

Title 8, United States Code; Chapter 12, Immigration and Nationality; Subchapter V—Alien Terrorist Removal Procedures

§ 1531.   Definitions

As used in this subchapter—

(1) the term "alien terrorist" means any alien described in section 1227(a)(4)(B) of this title;

(2) the term "classified information" has the same meaning as in section 1(a) of the Classified Information Procedures Act (18 U.S.C. App.);

(3) the term "national security" has the same meaning as in section 1(b) of the Classified Information Procedures Act (18 U.S.C. App.);

(4) the term "removal court" means the court described in section 1532 of this title;

(5) the term "removal hearing" means the hearing described in section 1534 of this title;

(6) the term "removal proceeding" means a proceeding under this subchapter; and

(7) the term "special attorney" means an attorney who is on the panel established under section 1532(e) of this title.

§ 1532. Establishment of removal court

(a) Designation of judges

The Chief Justice of the United States shall publicly designate 5 district court judges from 5 of the United States judicial circuits who shall constitute a court that shall have jurisdiction to conduct all removal proceedings. The Chief Justice may, in the Chief Justice's discretion, designate the same judges under this section as are designated pursuant to section 103(a) of the Foreign Intelligence Surveillance Act of 1978 (50 U.S.C. 1803(a)).

(b) Terms

Each judge designated under subsection (a) of this section shall serve for a term of 5 years and shall be eligible for redesignation, except that of the members first designated—

(1) 1 member shall serve for a term of 1 year;

(2) 1 member shall serve for a term of 2 years;

(3) 1 member shall serve for a term of 3 years; and

(4) 1 member shall serve for a term of 4 years.

(c) Chief judge

(1) Designation

The Chief Justice shall publicly designate one of the judges of the removal court to be the chief judge of the removal court.

(2) Responsibilities

The chief judge shall—

(A) promulgate rules to facilitate the functioning of the removal court; and

(B) assign the consideration of cases to the various judges on the removal court.

(d) Expeditious and confidential nature of proceedings

The provisions of section 103(c) of the Foreign Intelligence Surveillance Act of 1978 (50 U.S.C. § 1803(c)) shall apply to removal proceedings in the same manner as they apply to proceedings under that Act (50 U.S.C. 1801 et seq.).

(e) Establishment of panel of special attorneys

The removal court shall provide for the designation of a panel of attorneys each of whom—

(1) has a security clearance which affords the attorney access to classified information, and

(2) has agreed to represent permanent resident aliens with respect to classified information under section 1534(e)(3) of this title in accordance with (and subject to the penalties under) this subchapter.

§ 1533. Removal court procedure

(a) Application

(1) In general

In any case in which the Attorney General has classified information that an alien is an alien terrorist, the Attorney General may seek removal of the alien under this subchapter by filing an application with the removal court that contains—

(A) the identity of the attorney in the Department of Justice making the application;

(B) a certification by the Attorney General or the Deputy Attorney General that the application satisfies the criteria and requirements of this section;

(C) the identity of the alien for whom authorization for the removal proceeding is sought; and

(D) a statement of the facts and circumstances relied on by the Department of Justice to establish probable cause that—

(i) the alien is an alien terrorist;

(ii) the alien is physically present in the United States; and

(iii) with respect to such alien, removal under subchapter II of this chapter would pose a risk to the national security of the United States.

(2) Filing

An application under this section shall be submitted ex parte and in camera, and shall be filed under seal with the removal court.

(b) Right to dismiss

The Attorney General may dismiss a removal action under this subchapter at any stage of the proceeding.

(c) Consideration of application

(1) Basis for decision

In determining whether to grant an application under this section, a single judge of the removal court may consider, ex parte and in camera, in addition to the information contained in the application—

(A) other information, including classified information, presented under oath or affirmation; and

(B) testimony received in any hearing on the application, of which a verbatim record shall be kept.

(2) Approval of order

The judge shall issue an order granting the application, if the judge finds that there is probable cause to believe that—

(A) the alien who is the subject of the application has been correctly identified and is an alien terrorist present in the United States; and

(B) removal under subchapter II of this chapter would pose a risk to the national security of the United States.

(3) Denial of order

If the judge denies the order requested in the application, the judge shall prepare a written statement of the reasons for the denial, taking all necessary precautions not to disclose any classified information contained in the Government's application.

(d) Exclusive provisions

If an order is issued under this section granting an application, the rights of the alien regarding removal and expulsion shall be governed solely by this subchapter, and except as they are specifically referenced in this subchapter, no other provisions of this chapter shall be applicable.

§ 1534. Removal hearing

(a) In general

(1) Expeditious hearing

In any case in which an application for an order is approved under section 1533(c)(2) of this title, a removal hearing shall be conducted under this section as expeditiously as practicable for the purpose of determining whether the alien to whom the order pertains should be removed from the United States on the grounds that the alien is an alien terrorist.

(2) Public hearing

The removal hearing shall be open to the public.

. . .

§ 1535. Appeals

. . .

(e) Appeal of detention order

. . .

(2) No review of continued detention. The determinations and actions of the Attorney General pursuant to section 507(b)(2)(C) [8 USCS § 1537(b)(2)(C)] shall not be subject to judicial review, including application for a writ of habeas corpus, except for a claim by the alien that continued detention violates the alien's rights under the Constitution. Jurisdiction over any such challenge shall lie exclusively in the United States Court of Appeals for the District of Columbia Circuit.

. . .

§ 1537. Custody and release after removal hearing

. . .

(b) Custody and removal

(1) Custody. If the judge decides that an alien shall be removed, the alien shall be detained pending the outcome of any appeal. After the conclusion of any judicial review thereof which affirms the

removal order, the Attorney General shall retain the alien in custody and remove the alien to a country specified under paragraph (2).

(2) Removal

(A) In general. The removal of an alien shall be to any country which the alien shall designate if such designation does not, in the judgment of the Attorney General, in consultation with the Secretary of State, impair the obligation of the United States under any treaty (including a treaty pertaining to extradition) or otherwise adversely affect the foreign policy of the United States.

(B) Alternate countries. If the alien refuses to designate a country to which the alien wishes to be removed or if the Attorney General, in consultation with the Secretary of State, determines that removal of the alien to the country so designated would impair a treaty obligation or adversely affect United States foreign policy, the Attorney General shall cause the alien to be removed to any country willing to receive such alien.

(C) Continued detention. If no country is willing to receive such an alien, the Attorney General may, notwithstanding any other provision of law, retain the alien in custody. The Attorney General, in coordination with the Secretary of State, shall make periodic efforts to reach agreement with other countries to accept such an alien and at least every 6 months shall provide to the attorney representing the alien at the removal hearing a written report on the Attorney General's efforts. Any alien in custody pursuant to this subparagraph shall be released from custody solely at the discretion of the Attorney General and subject to such conditions as the Attorney General shall deem appropriate.

§ 1227. General classes of deportable aliens

(a) Classes of deportable aliens

Any alien (including an alien crewman) in and admitted to the United States shall, upon the order of the Attorney General, be removed if the alien is within one or more of the following classes of deportable aliens:

. . .

(4) Security and related grounds

(A) In general

Any alien who has engaged, is engaged, or at any time after admission engages in—

(i) any activity to violate any law of the United States relating to espionage or sabotage or to violate or evade any law prohibiting the export from the United States of goods, technology, or sensitive information,

(ii) any other criminal activity which endangers public safety or national security, or

(iii) any activity a purpose of which is the opposition to, or the control or overthrow of, the Government of the United States by force, violence, or other unlawful means, is deportable.

(B) Terrorist activities

Any alien who has engaged, is engaged, or at any time after admission engages in any terrorist activity (as defined in section 1182(a)(3)(B)(iii) of this title) is deportable.

QUESTIONS AND NOTES

1. Neither § 1226a nor the special removal court provisions appear to have as yet been utilized by the administration against alien suspected terrorists.

2. See generally, Juliet P. Stumpf, The Implausible Alien: Iqbal and the influence of Immigration Law, 14 Lewis & Clark L. Rev. 231 (2010); Susan M. Akram & Maritza Karmely, *Immigration and Constitutional Consequences of Post–9/11 Policies Involving Arabs and Muslims in the United States: Is Alienage a Distinction without a Difference?*, 38 U.C. Davis L. Rev. 609 (2005).

3. In 2011, by Executive Order, the Obama administration adopted rules for reviewing the status of persons detained for extended periods. See infra, chapter 10, p. 607.

CHAPTER 9

CLASSIFIED INFORMATION IN CIVILIAN TERRORISM TRIALS

■ ■ ■

A. INTRODUCTION—THE CLASSIFIED INFORMATION PROCEDURES ACT

The Classified Information Procedures Act (CIPA) which addresses the handling of classified materials in federal criminal prosecutions is the main focus of this chapter. The five previous chapters have dealt primarily with pre-trial investigation and enforcement methods; this is the first time we have ventured into the processes of the trial itself. Moreover, we are not here addressing all of the many incidents of criminal trials in terrorism cases, such as the rules of evidence and procedure. (In previous chapters, we have touched upon issues that have evidentiary implications—e.g. rules governing the admissibility of interrogation statements.)

The subject of the handling of classified information has been singled out here because a) although they are not unique to terrorism prosecutions, classified information issues are likely to arise in almost every terrorism trial; b) students are unlikely to have encountered these issues in other courses in the curriculum; and c) it provides a foundation for comparing the handling of classified materials in civilian terrorism trials with how they are treated in military commission proceedings.

Why does classified information play such an important central role in U.S. district court terrorism cases? These prosecutions are often developed through intelligence information that the government is reluctant to reveal for fear of compromising sources or methods of obtaining the information, or where the information itself has a national security dimension. As the number of terrorism prosecutions has increased in the past decade, it has become important for lawyers and judges working in the terrorism enforcement process or those who wish to know something about the workings of that process to gain some familiarity with the CIPA and the handling of classified information in federal criminal trials. (During an earlier time, CIPA issues arose mainly in the prosecution of spies or cases involving leaks of information or the prosecution of federal employees for criminal behavior.)

The purpose of CIPA is to strike a balance between protecting the rights of a criminal defendant to know the evidence being used against him or her and the government's need to protect against disclosure of certain types of confidential information that the government is unwilling to disclose or have disclosed publicly.

Prior to the enactment of CIPA in 1980, the government often found itself in a dilemma—either disclose classified information that the government believed should not be disclosed, or face dismissal of the prosecution on the ground that the right of the defendant to access information needed for his/her defense was being denied. A defendant's putting the government in this kind of bind came to be known as the use of "graymail" (i.e. give me the information or else face dismissal of the prosecution, or, alternatively, I shall disclose the information if you prosecute me). The CIPA was intended to address and soften this tension in a way that adequately protected the rights of the criminal defendant while reducing the frequency with which the government is faced with the difficult choice whether to disclose the underlying information or give up the prosecution. An important question that you should consider in light of the materials in this chapter is the extent to which the CIPA resolved the underlying tension in this area.

We shall not delve here into all of the nooks and crannies of CIPA law, but rather shall only focus on several salient features that tend to arise in terrorism cases. We shall also take note of the extent to which practices have developed for dealing with classified information that are outside of the CIPA framework. This is a subject where developments and adjustments have occurred in practice for dealing with classified information issues that go beyond the written law.

Where classified information is relevant to issues in the case, CIPA makes provision for several possible alternative remedies, the most frequently utilized of which is providing a summary as a substitute for the information itself. Inter alia, we examine issues relating to the use of a summary as a means of resolving the recurring dilemma; the extent to which in camera, or in camera and ex parte, proceedings may be used under CIPA; and the use of security clearance of participants in the process as a means to resolve some of the dilemmas posed by the need to use classified information in a criminal case.

One view of CIPA is that it tracks Rule 16 of the Federal Rules of Criminal Procedure, which deals with criminal discovery by the defendant, and simply adds the use of a summary-as-a-substitute to the possible remedies in criminal discovery. To the extent that CIPA operates in a discovery context, this observation is essentially correct. However, CIPA issues can arise in contexts other than criminal discovery by the defendant. For example, CIPA issues can be raised when a criminal defendant proposes to disclose at trial classified information to which he already has access, although this scenario is not very likely in terrorism trials. CIPA issues can also arise at the instance of the government when the prosecutor anticipates that a discovery request for classified information will be made by the defendant. Similarly, the government itself may wish to use at trial information that is classified, and in order to do so, may propose to introduce a summary under the terms of CIPA. The context in which the CIPA issue is raised and who wishes to introduce the classified information or a substitute may affect the disposition of the matter.

B. THE CLASSIFIED INFORMATION PROCEDURES ACT

An excerpted text of CIPA (the full text of which can be found at 18 U.S.C. App. 3, §§ 1–16) is set forth below.

TITLE 18, UNITED STATES CODE (CRIMES AND CRIMINAL PROCEDURE)

APPENDIX 3.

CLASSIFIED INFORMATION PROCEDURES ACT

Public Law 96–456 (94 Stat. 2025), Oct. 15, 1980

§ 1. Definitions

(a) "Classified information", as used in this Act, means any information or material that has been determined by the United States Government pursuant to an Executive order, statute, or regulation, to require protection against unauthorized disclosure for reasons of national security and any restricted data, as defined in paragraph r. of section 11 of the Atomic Energy Act of 1954 (42 U.S.C. 2014(y)).

(b) "National security", as used in this Act, means the national defense and foreign relations of the United States.

§ 2. Pretrial Conference

At any time after the filing of the indictment or information, any party may move for a pretrial conference to consider matters relating to classified information that may arise in connection with the prosecution. Following such motion, or on its own motion, the court shall promptly hold a pretrial conference to establish the timing of requests for discovery, the provision of notice required by section 5 of this Act, and the initiation of the procedure established by section 6 of this Act. In addition, at the pretrial conference the court may consider any matters which relate to classified information or which may promote a fair and expeditious trial. No admission made by the defendant or by any attorney for the defendant at such a conference may be used against the defendant unless the admission is in writing and is signed by the defendant and by the attorney for the defendant.

§ 3. Protective Orders

Upon motion of the United States, the court shall issue an order to protect against the disclosure of any classified information disclosed by the United States to any defendant in any criminal case in a district court of the United States.

§ 4. Discovery of classified information by defendants

The court, upon a sufficient showing, may authorize the United States to delete specified items of classified information from documents to be made available to the defendant through discovery under the Federal Rules of Criminal Procedure, to substitute a summary of the information for such classified documents, or to substitute a statement admitting relevant facts that the classified information would tend to prove. The court may permit the United States to make a request for such authorization in the form of a written statement to be inspected by the court alone. If the court enters an order granting relief following such an ex parte showing, the entire text of the statement of the United States shall be sealed and preserved in the records of the court to be made available to the appellate court in the event of an appeal.

§ 5. Notice of defendant's intention to disclose classified information

(a) Notice by defendant

If a defendant reasonably expects to disclose or to cause the disclosure of classified information in any manner in connection with any trial or pretrial proceeding involving the criminal prosecution of such defendant, the defendant shall, within the time specified by the court or, where no time is specified, within thirty days prior to trial, notify the attorney for the United States and the court in writing. Such notice shall include a brief description of the classified information. Whenever a defendant learns of additional classified information he reasonably expects to disclose at any such proceeding, he shall notify the attorney for the United States and the court in writing as soon as possible thereafter and shall include a brief description of the classified information. No defendant shall disclose any information known or believed to be classified in connection with a trial or pretrial proceeding until notice has been given under this subsection and until the United States has been afforded a reasonable opportunity to seek a determination pursuant to the procedure set forth in section 6 of this Act, and until the time for the United States to appeal such determination under section 7 has expired or any appeal under section 7 by the United States is decided.

(b) Failure to comply

If the defendant fails to comply with the requirements of subsection (a) the court may preclude disclosure of any classified information not made the subject of notification and may prohibit the examination by the defendant of any witness with respect to any such information.

§ 6. Procedure for cases involving classified information

(a) Motion for hearing

Within the time specified by the court for the filing of a motion under this section, the United States may request the court to conduct a hearing to make all determinations concerning the use, relevance, or admissibility of classified information that would otherwise be made during the trial or pretrial proceeding. Upon such a request, the court shall conduct such a hearing. Any hearing held pursuant to this subsection (or any portion of such hearing specified in the request of the Attorney General) shall be held in camera if the Attorney General certifies to the court in such petition that a public proceeding may result in the disclosure of classified information. As to each item of classified information, the court shall set forth in writing the basis for its determination. Where the United States' motion under this subsection is filed prior to the trial or pretrial proceeding, the court shall rule prior to the commencement of the relevant proceeding.

(b) Notice

(1) Before any hearing is conducted pursuant to a request by the United States under subsection (a), the United States shall provide the defendant with notice of the classified information that is at issue. Such notice shall identify the specific classified information at issue whenever that information previously has been made available to the defendant by the United States. When the United States has not previously made the information available to the defendant in connection with the case, the information may be described by generic category, in such form as the court may approve, rather than by identification of the specific information of concern to the United States.

(2) Whenever the United States requests a hearing under subsection (a), the court, upon request of the defendant, may order the United States to provide the defendant, prior to trial, such details as to the portion of the indictment or information at issue in the hearing as are needed to give the defendant fair notice to prepare for the hearing.

(c) Alternative procedure for disclosure of classified information

(1) Upon any determination by the court authorizing the disclosure of specific classified information under the procedures established by this section, the United States may move that, in lieu of the disclosure of such specific classified information, the court order—

(A) the substitution for such classified information of a statement admitting relevant facts that the specific classified information would tend to prove; or

(B) the substitution for such classified information of a summary of the specific classified information.

The court shall grant such a motion of the United States if it finds that the statement or summary will provide the defendant with substantially the same ability to make his defense as would disclosure of the specific classified information. The court shall hold a hearing on any motion under this section. Any such hearing shall be held in camera at the request of the Attorney General.

(2) The United States may, in connection with a motion under paragraph (1), submit to the court an affidavit of the Attorney General certifying that disclosure of classified information would cause identifiable damage to the national security of the United States and explaining the basis for the classification of such information. If so requested by the United States, the court shall examine such affidavit in camera and ex parte.

(d) Sealing of records of in camera hearings

If at the close of an in camera hearing under this Act (or any portion of a hearing under this Act that is held in camera) the court determines that the classified information at issue may not be disclosed or elicited at the trial or pretrial proceeding, the record of such in camera hearing shall be sealed and preserved by the court for use in the event of an appeal. The defendant may seek reconsideration of the court's determination prior to or during trial.

(e) Prohibition on disclosure of classified information by defendant, relief for defendant when United States opposes disclosure

(1) Whenever the court denies a motion by the United States that it issue an order under subsection (c) and the United States files with the court an affidavit of the Attorney General objecting to disclosure of the classified information at issue, the court shall order that the defendant not disclose or cause the disclosure of such information.

(2) Whenever a defendant is prevented by an order under paragraph (1) from disclosing or causing the disclosure of classified information, the court shall dismiss the indictment or information; except that, when the court determines that the interests of justice would not be served by dismissal of the indictment or information, the court shall order such other action, in lieu of dismissing the indictment or information, as the court determines is appropriate. Such action may include, but need not be limited to—

(A) dismissing specified counts of the indictment or information;

(B) finding against the United States on any issue as to which the excluded classified information relates; or

(C) striking or precluding all or part of the testimony of a witness.

An order under this paragraph shall not take effect until the court has afforded the United States an opportunity to appeal such order under section 7, and thereafter to withdraw its objection to the disclosure of the classified information at issue.

(f) Reciprocity

Whenever the court determines pursuant to subsection (a) that classified information may be disclosed in connection with a trial or pretrial proceeding, the court shall, unless the interests of fairness do not so require, order the United States to provide the defendant with the information it expects to use to rebut the classified information. The court may place the United States under a continuing duty to disclose such rebuttal information. If the United States fails to comply with its obligation under this subsection, the court may exclude any evidence not made the subject of a required disclosure and may prohibit the examination by the United States of any witness with respect to such information.

§ 7. Interlocutory appeal

(a) An interlocutory appeal by the United States taken before or after the defendant has been placed in jeopardy shall lie to a court of appeals from a decision or order of a district court in a criminal case authorizing the disclosure of classified information, imposing sanctions for nondisclosure of classified information, or refusing a protective order sought by the United States to prevent the disclosure of classified information.

(b) An appeal taken pursuant to this section either before or during trial shall be expedited by the court of appeals. Prior to trial, an appeal shall be taken within ten days after the decision or order appealed from and the trial shall not commence until the appeal is resolved. . . .

§ 8. Introduction of classified information

(a) Classification status

Writings, recordings, and photographs containing classified information may be admitted into evidence without change in their classification status.

(b) Precautions by court

The court, in order to prevent unnecessary disclosure of classified information involved in any criminal proceeding, may order admission into evidence of only part of a writing, recording, or photograph, or may order admission into evidence of the whole writing, recording, or photograph with excision of some or all of the classified information contained therein, unless the whole ought in fairness be considered.

(c) Taking of testimony

During the examination of a witness in any criminal proceeding, the United States may object to any question or line of inquiry that may require the witness to disclose classified information not previously found to be admissible. Following such an objection, the court shall take such suitable action to determine whether the response is admissible as will safeguard against the compromise of any classified information. Such action may include requiring the United States to provide the court with a proffer of the witness' response to the question or line of inquiry and requiring the defendant to provide the court with a proffer of the nature of the information he seeks to elicit.

§ 9. Security procedures

(a) Within one hundred and twenty days of the date of the enactment of this Act, the Chief Justice of the United States, in consultation with the Attorney General, the Director of Central Intelligence, and the Secretary of Defense, shall prescribe rules establishing procedures for the protection against unauthorized disclosure of any classified information in the custody of the United States district courts, courts of appeal, or Supreme Court. Such rules, and any changes in such rules, shall be submitted to the appropriate committees of Congress and shall become effective forty-five days after such submission.

(b) Until such time as rules under subsection (a) first become effective, the Federal courts shall in each case involving classified information adopt procedures to protect against the unauthorized disclosure of such information.

§ 10. Identification of information related to national defense

In any prosecution in which the United States must establish that material relates to the national defense or constitutes classified information, the United States shall notify the defendant, within the time before trial specified by the court, of the portions of the material that it reasonably expects to rely upon to establish the national defense or classified information element of the offense.

. . .

§ 12. Attorney General guidelines

(a) Within one hundred and eighty days of enactment of this Act, the Attorney General shall issue guidelines specifying the factors to be used by the Department of Justice in rendering a decision whether to prosecute a violation of Federal law in which, in the judgment of the Attorney General, there is a possibility that classified information will be revealed. Such guidelines shall be transmitted to the appropriate committees of Congress.

(b) When the Department of Justice decides not to prosecute a violation of Federal law pursuant to subsection (a), an appropriate official of the Department of Justice shall prepare written findings detailing the reasons for the decision not to prosecute. The findings shall include—

>(1) the intelligence information which the Department of Justice officials believe might be disclosed,

>(2) the purpose for which the information might be disclosed,

>(3) the probability that the information would be disclosed, and

>(4) the possible consequences such disclosure would have on the national security.

. . .

C. ADJUDGING THE ADEQUACY OF SUBSTITUTIONS FOR CLASSIFIED INFORMATION

Under the terms of the CIPA, a summary may be substituted for the classified information when it provides "substantially the same ability to make [a] . . . defense" as the original information. If defense counsel is trying to introduce classified information in the hands of the government, which she has not ever had access to, she may have a difficult task in challenging the adequacy of the summary offered as a substitute, even given that standard. The inquiry regarding adequacy is conducted in camera. Query, is it also ex parte?

UNITED STATES v. REZAQ

134 F.3d 1121 (D.C.Cir. 1998)

Before WALD, SENTELLE and HENDERSON, CIRCUIT JUDGES.

WALD, CIRCUIT JUDGE:

Omar Mohammed Ali Rezaq appeals his conviction on one count of aircraft piracy under 49 U.S.C. App. § 1472(n) (1994). In 1985, Rezaq hijacked an Air Egypt flight shortly after takeoff from Athens, and ordered it to fly to Malta. On arrival, Rezaq shot a number of passengers, killing two of them, before he was apprehended. Rezaq pleaded guilty to murder charges in Malta, served seven years in prison, and was released in February 1993. Shortly afterwards, he was taken into custody in Nigeria by United States authorities and brought to the United States for trial . . .

I. Background

Rezaq did not deny committing the hijacking at trial, relying instead on the defenses of insanity and obedience to military orders. Thus, the following account of the hijacking was not contested at Rezaq's trial.

Rezaq is Palestinian, and was, at the time of the hijacking, a member of a Palestinian terrorist organization, which planned and ordered the hijacking. On the evening of November 23, 1985, Rezaq boarded Air Egypt Flight 648 in Athens. He was accompanied by two other hijackers; one of his confederates, named Salem, was the leader of the operation, and the name of the other is unknown. Shortly after the plane took off, the three produced weapons, announced that they were seizing the plane, and demanded that the captain fly it to Malta. A gun battle ensued between the hijackers and an Egyptian plainclothes sky marshal stationed on the plane, as a result of which Salem was killed and the sky marshal was wounded.

Rezaq then took charge of the hijacking. After the plane arrived in Malta, he separated the Israeli and American passengers from the others, and moved them to the front of the plane. He released a number of Egyptian and Filipino female passengers, as well as two wounded flight attendants. He then demanded that the aircraft be refueled; when the authorities refused, he announced that he would shoot a passenger every fifteen minutes until his demand was met.

Rezaq carried out his threat. He first shot Israeli national Tamar Artzi. Although he shot her twice, once in the head, she survived. Fifteen minutes later, he shot her companion, Nitzan Mendelson, also an Israeli; Ms. Mendelson died of her injuries nine days later. Rezaq then shot Patrick Baker, an American, but only succeeded in grazing his head. Two or three hours later, Rezaq shot Scarlett Rogenkamp—a United States citizen and an employee of the United States Air Force—in the head, killing her. Some time later, he shot Jackie Pflug, also an American, in the head, injuring her very seriously. Rezaq shot his victims near the front door of the plane, and either threw them or let them fall onto the tarmac; this may explain why three of the five were able to survive, either by escaping (Artzi and Baker), or by feigning death (Pflug).

In the evening of November 24th—about a day after the hijacking began—Egyptian commandos stormed the plane. The operation seems to have been a singularly incompetent one. The commandos fired indiscriminately, and set off an explosive device of some kind, as a result of which the aircraft burst into flames. Fifty-seven passengers were killed, as was the third hijacker. Rezaq was injured, and was taken, with a multitude of injured passengers, to a hospital. There, he was identified as the hijacker by passengers, members of the crew, and several of his victims.

The authorities in Malta charged Rezaq with murder, attempted murder, and hostage taking. He pled guilty, and was sentenced to 25 years' imprisonment. For reasons unclear, Maltese authorities released him some seven years later, in February 1993, and allowed him to board a plane to Ghana. Rezaq's itinerary was to carry him from there to Nigeria, and then to Ethiopia, and finally to Sudan. Ghanaian officials detained Rezaq for several months, but eventually allowed him to proceed to Nigeria. When Rezaq's plane landed in Nigeria, Nigerian authorities placed him in the custody of FBI agents, who transported him on a waiting aircraft to the United States.

Rezaq was indicted and tried for air piracy in the District Court for the District of Columbia. At trial, Rezaq invoked the defenses of insanity and obedience to military orders. In support of his insanity defense, Rezaq presented evidence that he suffered from post-traumatic stress disorder ("PTSD"). As witnesses, he called several members of his own family and three psychiatric experts; Rezaq himself also testified at length. Rezaq asserted that his PTSD sprang from numerous traumatic events he had experienced, first in the Jordanian refugee camp in which he spent much of his youth, and later in Lebanon, where he was active in Palestinian revolutionary organizations from 1978 to 1985. The Lebanese experiences he described included witnessing the killing of hundreds of refugees by Israeli forces in Beirut in 1982; witnessing the killings of the populations of entire villages; and nearly being killed in a car bombing. Rezaq's family testified that when he left Jordan he was normal, friendly, and extroverted, but that when he returned from Lebanon he was pale, inattentive, prone to nightmares, antisocial, and had lost his sense of humor. Rezaq's psychiatric experts said that these changes in behavior were symptomatic of PTSD, and, based on their examination of Rezaq and on the testimony of other witnesses, they concluded that Rezaq was suffering from PTSD when he committed the hijacking in November 1985. The United States presented two psychiatric experts of its own, who testified that Rezaq's symptoms were not as intense as those usually associated with PTSD, and that Rezaq was able to reason and make judgments normally at the time he hijacked the plane.

The jury did not credit Rezaq's defenses, and found him guilty of the one count with which he was charged, aircraft piracy in violation of 49 U.S.C. App. § 1472(n) (1994). At the time of Rezaq's prosecution, that section provided (it has since been amended):

> (1) Whoever aboard an aircraft in flight outside the special aircraft jurisdiction of the United States commits an "offense," as defined in the Convention for the Suppression of Unlawful Seizure of Aircraft, and is afterward found in the United States shall be punished—
>
> > (A) by imprisonment for not less than 20 years; or
> >
> > (B) if the death of another person results from the commission or attempted commission of the offense, by death or by imprisonment for life.
>
> (2) A person commits 'an offense,' as defined in the Convention for the Suppression of Unlawful Seizure of Aircraft, when, while aboard an aircraft in flight, he—
>
> > (A) unlawfully, by force or threat thereof, or by any other form of intimidation, seizes, or exercises control of, that aircraft, or attempts to perform any such act; or

49 U.S.C.App. § 1472(n) (1994). Because death resulted from Rezaq's commission of the offense, § 1472(n)(1)(B) applied, and the district court

sentenced Rezaq to life imprisonment. (The United States had not sought the death sentence.) The district court also ordered Rezaq to pay a total of $254,000 in restitution, an amount which it found to represent the financial cost to the victims of his crime.

. . .

When classified materials may be relevant to criminal proceedings, the Classified Information Procedures Act ("CIPA"), 18 U.S.C. App. III (1994), provides procedures designed to protect the rights of the defendant while minimizing the associated harm to national security. In the course of preparing for trial, the United States identified a number of arguably discoverable classified materials, and obtained permission from the district court to file an *ex parte, in camera* motion for a protective order. After reviewing this motion and the accompanying documents, the district court ordered the United States to prepare an index listing the contents of each document, whether it believed the document to be subject to discovery, and why. This document, too, was submitted *ex parte* and *in camera*; the district court subjected this document to detailed review, and prepared a list of the materials that it considered discoverable.

Under CIPA, the court may allow the United States to disclose "a statement admitting relevant facts that the classified information would tend to prove," in lieu of disclosing the information itself. 18 U.S.C. App. III § 4 (1994). The United States sought, and obtained, permission to substitute admissions for all of the documents that the district court had identified as discoverable. The district court reviewed the United States's proposed substitutions, and concluded that they fairly stated the relevant elements of the classified documents. The substitutions were then disclosed to Rezaq's attorney.

Rezaq's request on appeal is very limited. He does not ask us to review the district court's determination as to which documents were discoverable in the first instance. Instead, he asks only that we review the documents that the district court found to be discoverable, and decide whether the summaries that the court furnished to him were as helpful to his defense as the original documents would have been. He is particularly concerned that the summaries may have omitted important information, or that the process of transforming the documents into desiccated statements of material fact might have hampered the "evidentiary richness and narrative integrity" of the defense he was able to present.

We found in *Yunis* that a defendant seeking classified information is not entitled to receive it "on a mere showing of theoretical relevance," but "is entitled only to information that is at least 'helpful to the defense of the accused.'" 867 F.2d at 623 (quoting *Roviaro v. United States,* 353 U.S. 53, 60–61, 77 S.Ct. 623, 627–28, 1 L.Ed.2d 639 (1957)). This principle applies to sub-elements of individual documents; if some portion or aspect of a document is classified, a defendant is entitled to receive it only if it may be helpful to his defense. A court applying this rule should, of course, err on the side of protecting the interests of the defendant. In some cases, a court might legitimately conclude that it is necessary to place a fact in context in order to ensure that the jury is able to give it its full weight. For instance, it might be appropriate in some circumstances to attribute a statement to its source, or to phrase it as a quotation.

The district court's substitution decisions turned on the relevance of the facts contained in the discoverable documents, and are therefore reviewed, like other relevance decisions under CIPA, for abuse of discretion. *See United States v. Yunis,* 867 F.2d 617, 625 (D.C.Cir.1989). We are obliged to consider the district court's substitution decisions very carefully, as Rezaq's counsel is unable to consult the original documents, and so cannot present arguments on his client's behalf. We have accordingly conducted a detailed *in camera* comparison of the originals of the discoverable documents with the summaries approved by the district court. We find that the district court did a commendable job of discharging its obligations under CIPA, and in particular that its orders protected Rezaq's rights very effectively despite the fact that Rezaq's attorney was unable to participate in the CIPA proceedings. No information was omitted from the substitutions that might have been helpful to Rezaq's defense, and the discoverable documents had no unclassified features that might have been disclosed to Rezaq.

QUESTIONS AND NOTES

1. As mentioned in Rezaq, before reaching the question of whether the substituted summary is adequate, the court must determine whether the underlying classified information is admissible and therefore discoverable: the standard of admissibility is whether the evidence is relevant and helpful to the defense.

2. A case that should be compared with Rezaq is United States v. Fernandez, 913 F.2d 148 (4th Cir. 1990), a prosecution of a former CIA station chief for having made false statements to a body investigating the diversion of arms transfers, intended for Iran, to Nicaraguan resistance forces known as Contras (the Iran–Contra scandal). The summaries of classified documents prepared by the government were deemed not adequate to enable the defendant to make his defenses. The U.S. court of appeals affirmed the decision of the district court, dismissing the case with prejudice after the Attorney General filed an affidavit under § 6(e)(1) of CIPA prohibiting the disclosure of classified evidence that the district court had previously ruled to be relevant and admissible.

3. The Fernandez court's opinion addressing the adequacy of the substitutions is lengthy and very detailed. The flavor and amount of detail differs considerably from that of the Rezaq opinion. There are a number of things that might account for this difference. Might one of the factors be the fact that Rezaq involved an ex parte determination where the judge made his ruling essentially without any input from the defendant's counsel, while in Fernandez, the issues were addressed in an adversary proceeding? Why was the issue in Fernandez able to be addressed in an adversary hearing while Rezaq involved an ex parte proceeding? What accounts for this procedural

difference? Rezaq proceeded under section 4 of CIPA while Fernandez proceeded under section 6. Section 4 provides for an in camera ex parte proceeding while sec. 6 in subsec. (a) provides for an in camera hearing. (Compare, however, sec. 6(c)(2).)

4. Note, too, that Fernandez was a former CIA station chief who had earlier probably had full access to the documents involved and was generally familiar with them. Given that likelihood, why was the government so insistent on not permitting the introduction of the original documents into evidence? We must assume that this was an instance where it was not a concern about disclosing the information to the defendant, but rather disclosing it to the jury, and, ultimately, to the public.

5. Consider the differences between the ex parte in camera and the in camera proceedings in light of the following excerpt from Brian Z. Tamanaha, A Critical Review of the Classified Information Procedures Act, 13 Am. J.Crim.L. 277, 307–308 (1987):

> . . . [T]he creation of substitutions is the only feature unique to CIPA which effectively inhibits graymail. Substitutions are also powerful weapons for the prosecution with a high potential for abuse. They are used where the defendant's right to a fair trial most directly conflicts with the government's need to protect national security information. . . .

> The standard in section 6(c) that substitutions are not permissible unless substantially equivalent to the nondisclosed information, was included in fairness to the defendant. Likewise, to ensure that substitutions did not violate constitutional requirements, Congress provides in section 6 that substitutions may be approved only after a full adversary hearing in which the defendant has access to all the underlying documents.

> Not all substitutions, however, are created with the protection contained in section 6. Section 4 of CIPA allows the government to submit an ex parte request for the substitution of discoverable information in lieu of producing the actual documents. Since the substitution is formulated and approved ex parte, the defendant cannot oppose it and never has access to the underlying documents. The defendant has no way of knowing whether the substitution contains all the discoverable information, or whether it correctly states this information. . . .

> More troublesome, section 4 threatens to swallow the protections contained in section 6. To circumvent the adversary hearing in section 6, where the defendant has access to all the underlying information and is able to contest the adequacy of each substitution, the government may simply produce all or most of the discoverable information in the form of ex parte approved substitutions. Nothing in CIPA prohibits this approach and, indeed, a prosecutor would be remiss if this strategy were not adopted because it significantly reduces the amount of classified information that will be disclosed to the defendant. Following this strategy, the only substitutions subject to the adversary process will be those containing information already possessed by the defendant independent of discovery. Relevant classified information not possessed by the defendant may be substituted without input from the defense.

Congress was aware that substitutions are approved ex parte in section 4 and not in section 6. The rationale for this different treatment is that 'since the government is seeking to withhold classified information from the defendant, an adversary hearing with defense knowledge would defeat the very purpose of the discovery rules.'

D. CLASSIFIED INFORMATION AND THE RIGHT OF CONFRONTATION

UNITED STATES v. ABU ALI

528 F.3d 210 (4th Cir. 2008)

[For a detailed statement of the facts in this case, see the same case reproduced in the chapter on Interrogation and Irregular Rendition, supra, p. 344]

VI.

Abu Ali also challenges the district court's handling of certain classified information under the provisions of the Classified Information Procedures Act ("CIPA"), 18 U.S.C.App. 3, §§ 1–16 (West 2000 & Supp.2007).[1] Abu Ali's primary contention is that the district court violated his Sixth Amendment Confrontation Clause rights by admitting as evidence unredacted versions of two classified documents that Abu Ali had only been permitted to view in a redacted form, and by refusing to allow Abu Ali and his lead trial counsel to attend and participate in the hearings conducted under CIPA to discuss the classified evidence.

A.

The Sixth Amendment guarantees that "[i]n all criminal prosecutions, the accused shall enjoy ... the right to be confronted with the witnesses against him." U.S. Const. amend. VI. Its "main and essential purpose ... is to secure for the opponent the opportunity of cross-examination.".... Thus, while this is not the ordinary case, we think the criminal defendant's right to confront witnesses necessarily encompasses his right to also see any documentary evidence that such witnesses offer at trial as evidence to support a conviction....

A defendant's right to see the evidence that is tendered against him *during* trial, however, does not necessarily equate to a right to have classified information disclosed to him *prior* to trial. Evidentiary privileges may serve as valid bases to block the disclosure of certain types of evidence, and the validity of such privileges may be tested by in camera and ex parte proceedings before the court "for the limited purpose of determining whether the asserted privilege is genuinely applicable." As a general rule, "[i]f the court finds that the claimed privilege does not apply, then the other side must be given access to the information." If the court

---

1. [Renumbered] These issues were separately raised via classified briefs and argued in closed proceedings before this panel.

finds that the privilege does apply, then it may preclude access to the information. But neither scenario results in the conviction of a defendant "based upon evidence he was never permitted to see and to rebut."

In the area of national security and the government's privilege to protect classified information from public disclosure, we look to CIPA for appropriate procedures. . . .

. . . CIPA establishes procedures to protect classified information from public disclosure, including disclosure to a defendant and his counsel if they do not possess the requisite security clearance. Prior to CIPA, "the government had no method of evaluating such disclosure claims before trial actually began" and "[o]ftentimes . . . would abandon prosecution rather than risk possible disclosure of classified information." "CIPA establishes procedures for making decisions about the use of such information."

B.

Classified information, as defined by CIPA, includes "any information or material that has been determined by the United States Government pursuant to an Executive order, statute, or regulation, to require protection against unauthorized disclosure for reasons of national security." . . .

. . . CIPA vests district courts with wide latitude to deal with thorny problems of national security in the context of criminal proceedings. When evaluating the governmental privilege in classified information which CIPA serves to protect, however, district courts must ultimately balance this "public interest in protecting the information against the individual's right to prepare his defense." . . . Specifically, [t]he trial court is required to balance the public interest in nondisclosure against the defendant's right to prepare a defense. A decision on disclosure of such information must depend on the "particular circumstances of each case, taking into consideration the crime charged, the possible defenses, the possible significance of the [evidence,] and other relevant factors."

If the district court determines that the information "is helpful to the defense of an accused, or is essential to a fair determination of a cause," it must be admitted . . . ("There is no question that the Government cannot invoke national security concerns as a means of depriving [the defendant] of a fair trial.").

. . . Ultimately, as these cases make clear, the appropriate procedure is for the district court to order production of the evidence or witness and leave to the Government the choice of whether to comply with that order. If the Government refuses to produce the information at issue—as it may properly do—the result is ordinarily dismissal.

. . . The "district court may order disclosure only when the information is at least essential to the defense, necessary to [the] defense, and neither merely cumulative nor corroborative, nor speculative." But if the necessary showing is made and "no adequate substitution can be found, the government must decide whether it will [continue to] prohibit the disclosure of the classified information; if it does so, the district court must impose a sanction, which is presumptively dismissal of the indictment." In sum, CIPA "enjoins district courts to seek a solution that neither disadvantages the defendant nor penalizes the government (and the public) for protecting classified information that may be vital to national security."

C.

With these principles in mind, we turn first to Abu Ali's Confrontation Clause challenge to the government's introduction at trial of two unredacted, classified documents that memorialized communications between Sultan Jubran and Abu Ali in the days following the May 2003 safe house raids conducted by the Saudi officials in Medina, as well as to his exclusion from the CIPA proceedings in which these communications were discussed.

1.

We begin with some additional background facts. After Abu Ali was indicted, Attorney Khurrum Wahid and Attorney Ashraf Nubani appeared to represent him. However, because one failed to apply for security clearance and the other was not approved by the Department of Justice, neither attorney was authorized to view the classified documents. On September 8, 2005, the district court, informed that the case would involve national security interests and CIPA proceedings and anticipating Abu Ali's need for an attorney with the proper security clearance, appointed Attorney Nina J. Ginsberg to act as CIPA-cleared counsel for Abu Ali. On October 14, 2005, the government first produced unredacted copies of the classified documents to Ms. Ginsberg and informed her that it intended to introduce the documents as evidence at trial. However, the government advised Ms. Ginsberg that it would proceed under CIPA to seek "certain limitations on public disclosure that will be necessary to prevent the revelation of extremely sensitive national security information."

Three days later, the government provided Abu Ali's uncleared defense counsel with slightly redacted copies of the classified documents, which it described as "newly declassified communications between the defendant and Sultan Jubran Sultan al-Qahtani occurring on May 27, 2003, and June 6, 2003," in their Arabic versions and with English translations, and advised counsel of the government's "inten[t] to offer these communications into evidence at trial as proof that the defendant provided material support to al-Qaeda." The first declassified document was dated May 27, 2003, and read as follows:

> Peace, How are you and how is your family? I hope they are good. I heard the news about the children's sickness. I wish them a speedy recovery, God willing. Anyway, please keep in touch. Greetings to the group, Hani.

The government intended to demonstrate that "Hani" was a known alias of Abu Ali and that "news about the children's sickness" was a coded reference to the raids conducted by the Mabahith and the arrest of the Medina cell members. The second declassified document was dated June 6, 2003, and read as follows:

> To my brother, Peace to you with God's mercy and blessings. Thank God, I am fine. I was saved from the accident by a great miracle. I ask God that I would be thankful to Him. I have no idea about the others. However, according to what one doctor mentioned, 'Adil was not with them, thank God. The important thing is to get yourself ready for the medical checkup because you may have an appointment soon. Therefore, you must keep yourself ready by refraining from eating high fat meals and otherwise.

With regard to this communication, the government intended to demonstrate that the term "accident" was also a coded reference to the safe house raids. According to the government's theory, Sultan Jubran was advising Abu Ali that he did not know which cell members had escaped and which were captured, but that he and al-Faq'asi (a/k/a "Adil"), had escaped, and warning that Abu Ali might also be at risk.

A comparison of the classified and unclassified documents reveals that the declassified versions provided the dates, the opening salutations, the entire substance of the communications, and the closings, and had only been lightly redacted to omit certain identifying and forensic information.

On October 19, 2005, the government filed an in camera, ex parte motion pursuant to § 4 of CIPA, seeking a protective order prohibiting testimony and lines of questioning that would lead to the disclosure of the classified information during the trial. *See* 18 U.S.C.App. 3 § 4. The government advised that the classified portions of the communications could not be provided to Abu Ali and his uncleared counsel because they contained highly sensitive information which, if confirmed in a public setting, would divulge information detrimental to national security interests. The district court granted the government's motion by in camera, ex parte, sealed order. However, the district court ruled that the United States could use the "silent witness rule" to disclose the classified information to the jury at trial.[15]

Abu Ali immediately responded with a motion that the government declassify the documents in their entirety or be ordered to provide the dates on which the communications were obtained by the government and the manner in which they were obtained. The stated purpose of the

---

15. The "silent witness" rule was described in *United States v. Zettl,* 835 F.2d 1059, 1063 (4th Cir.1987), as follows.

[T]he witness would not disclose the information from the classified document in open court. Instead, the witness would have a copy of the classified document before him. The court, counsel and the jury would also have copies of the classified document. The witness would refer to specific places in the document in response to questioning. The jury would then refer to the particular part of the document as the witness answered. By this method, the classified information would not be made public at trial but the defense would be able to present that classified information to the jury.

request, however, was not to contest that Abu Ali was a party to the communications, but to enable Abu Ali to ascertain whether the government had discovered the existence of the communications prior to Abu Ali's arrest by the Saudi officials. If so, Abu Ali sought to rely upon this fact to demonstrate that each confession he made to the Saudi officials was the product of a joint venture with American law enforcement and, therefore, inadmissible.

On October 21, 2005, the district court conducted an in camera CIPA hearing to consider Abu Ali's motion. Abu Ali was not present at the hearing, but was represented by his CIPA-cleared counsel, who objected to the exclusion of her client and his other uncleared counsel, but did not specifically object to the use of the declassified version of the document or to the use of the "silent witness" procedure. With regard to the joint venture issue, the government advised the court that the communications were obtained prior to Abu Ali's arrest by the Saudi officials, but that they were obtained "based on intelligence collecting by the United States government with no involvement whatsoever of Saudi authorities." The district court found that the communications were discovered independently from the Saudi government's investigation and, therefore, were not the product of a joint venture. The district court also concluded that the declassified, redacted version of the documents provided to Abu Ali "me[t] the defense's need for access to the information."

After trial commenced, Abu Ali moved the court pursuant to § 5 of CIPA to allow uncleared counsel to question the two government witnesses slated to introduce the substance of the classified communications into evidence "about their role in extracting, sharing, transferring, and handling [the] communications." *See* 18 U.S.C.App. 3 § 5. The first witness was the compliance manager and custodian of records for the legal department of the communications carrier involved and the person tasked with the duty of responding to orders issued by the Foreign Intelligence Surveillance Act ("FISA") Court. The second was a Special Agent with the FBI, who received the information from the compliance manager. Because this line of questioning would lead to the disclosure of the classified information, the government opposed the motion. On November 9, 2005, the district court held another in camera hearing with CIPA-cleared defense counsel present but in the absence of Abu Ali and his uncleared counsel. 18 U.S.C.App. 3 § 6(a) (providing for such in camera proceedings to determine "the use, relevance, or admissibility of classified information that would otherwise be made during the trial or pretrial proceedings"). The district court denied Abu Ali's motion "because CIPA prohibits revealing such classified information to the public" and "uncleared defense counsel is barred under CIPA from receiving, or eliciting testimony that will likely reveal, classified information." In doing so, the district court also noted that "the defense's attempt to force the government to unnecessarily disclose the means and methods the government used to gather this classified information may amount to 'greymail,' which CIPA was intended to prevent." . . .

Nevertheless, the district court agreed to conduct an in camera hearing the next day, at which time CIPA-cleared counsel would be allowed to question the witnesses "to resolve any question that the defense might have about the reliability of the extraction process or the handling of it." Public cross-examination of the compliance manager about the substance of the communications, the fact that they were collected pursuant to a warrant, and the extent to which she could connect the communications to Abu Ali, and of the FBI Agent about how the information was received, managed, and kept in the chain of custody, by uncleared counsel was otherwise unrestricted.

In ruling upon the motion, the district court expressly considered Abu Ali's rights under the Confrontation Clause, but ruled that these rights were not infringed because Abu Ali and his uncleared counsel "know about and have been given the substantive contents of the communications" and would "have the opportunity to cross-examine the communications carrier representative and the FBI agent regarding the substance of those communications."; see also ACA 54 (noting that "the issue of the reliability of the collection of the database . . . [was] not of significant moment to have to reveal classified information" about how the communications were collected and extracted). Additionally, Abu Ali had CIPA-cleared counsel who would "be permitted to question these witnesses in a closed in camera hearing about the extraction, collection, storage, sharing, transfer, receipt, handling, or chain of custody relating to the . . . communications at issue."

At the in camera hearing held the following day, CIPA-cleared counsel conducted a thorough and unrestricted cross-examination of the compliance manager regarding the issues raised, but found it unnecessary to question the FBI agent. Abu Ali's uncleared counsel then returned to the courtroom and rather broadly objected "to this whole process with the IPA material." However, counsel focused the objection not on the fact that the jury would be receiving unredacted, classified versions of documents that had not been provided to Abu Ali personally, but rather on the fact that they were personally prohibited from appearing at the CIPA hearing and that the jury would be told that the evidence was secret. Counsel argued that this might "taint[ ] the jury with . . . the impression that there's something so important about this document that it's of national security value," and that his client "is a threat" when there was nothing within the documents "that in and of itself is . . . dangerous or in any way should be classified."

In support of this claim of alleged prejudice, uncleared counsel argued to the district court that "[i]t is very evident what the material is just by reading the evidence that has already been turned over to the defense," and that it "takes really, quite frankly, someone who is of less than regular intelligence to not figure out what the document is," In short, counsel was of the view that the classification designation was "a bit of a show that we're putting on" that "den[ied] my client his Sixth Amendment right to confront the evidence, his choice of attorney and to have his attorney conduct a proceeding in a manner that that attorney sees fit." In other words, uncleared counsel complained not that he and his client were in the dark about the redacted evidence, but rather that the government should declassify the documents because the redacted portions were not really a "secret" at all.

Noting that it was not at liberty under CIPA "to second guess the government's judgment to classify the information," the district court overruled the objection. The jury was instructed regarding the upcoming presentation of classified evidence, Ms. Ginsberg was introduced to the jury as "an attorney hired by Mr. Abu Ali to handle this aspect of the case," and the unredacted, classified versions of the documents were presented to the jury via the "silent witness" procedure.[16]

On appeal, Abu Ali challenges the district court's exclusion of him and his uncleared counsel from the CIPA proceedings and the district court's admission of the unredacted, classified documents into evidence for consideration by the jury, as violative of his rights under the Confrontation Clause. The government argues that the district court properly protected the redacted classified information from disclosure under CIPA and properly excluded Abu Ali and his uncleared counsel from the CIPA hearings because the matter involved highly sensitive intelligence information. The government also argues that Abu Ali's rights were not violated by the admission of the classified versions as evidence because Abu Ali was provided with virtually all of the text of the documents, including the substance of the communications, the dates of the communications, and the parties to the communications.

We review the trial court's rulings pursuant to CIPA under an abuse of discretion standard. In addition, "[o]ur role [on] appeal is circumscribed. We are not asked, and we have no authority, to consider judgments made by the Attorney General concerning the extent to which the information in issue here implicates national security. Similarly, neither the prosecutorial decisions in this case nor the possibility of graymail ... comes within our purview." Rather, "we are faced with a series of very narrow, fact-specific evidentiary determinations and with the question of

---

16. [Renumbered] Although uncleared defense counsel could have done so, Ms. Ginsberg also conducted the cross-examination of the two witnesses at trial. The compliance manager testified that she received an emergency authorization to provide the FBI with information relevant to the case on June 7, 2003. This was followed by a written order by the FISA court to conduct a physical search for historical communications. The compliance manager testified that she "searched [their] database for the name [provided] and confirmed ... information existed responsive" to the order. She testified that she had conducted similar searches "[t]housands of times" utilizing the same automated tool used here and that, based upon her experience, it "has always been reliable." She identified the unredacted, classified documents as those produced in response to the order, as well as the dates and times of the communications, and the parties to the communications. On cross-examination, she acknowledged that she had no knowledge as to when the search system was last tested, how many times the account was used or accessed after June 7, 2003, or whether the communications originated outside the United States. She testified that she was unable to personally vouch for the reliability of the date and time, had no knowledge of any of the persons alleged to be identified by the information, and had no way of knowing whether Abu Ali was a party to the communications. The FBI Agent followed with testimony regarding his receipt of the data provided pursuant to the FISA order and the steps taken to ensure that the data was properly maintained by the FBI.

whether the defendant could receive a fair trial without the aid of certain evidence." We review the constitutional claims de novo.

Having carefully considered the circumstances and evidence below, we conclude that the district court's determination that the redacted classified information need not be disclosed to the defendant, his uncleared counsel, and the public was not an abuse of discretion. Nor do we think that the district court's exclusion of Abu Ali and his uncleared counsel from the CIPA proceedings ran afoul of the Confrontation Clause. The district court's admission of the classified versions of the documents as evidence for consideration by the jury without disclosing the same versions to Abu Ali, however, was clearly contrary to the rights guaranteed to Abu Ali by the Confrontation Clause.

We begin with the district court's exclusion of Abu Ali and his uncleared counsel from the CIPA proceedings. The district court was presented with a § 4 motion by the government to protect the classified information and a § 5 motion, made at a later date, by Abu Ali that he be allowed to disclose that information. Initially, the district court found the redacted, unclassified version of the communications to be adequate to meet the defendant's need for information. CIPA expressly provides for such redactions of classified information from documents sought or required to be produced to the defendant, and the determination may be based upon an ex parte showing that the disclosure would jeopardize national security interests. The district court appropriately balanced the interests and made a reasonable determination that disclosure of the redacted information was not necessary to a fair trial.

There was likewise no abuse of discretion in the district court's decision to preclude Abu Ali's uncleared counsel from cross-examining the government's witnesses about the redacted information, which would have effectively disclosed the classified information that the court had already ruled need not be disclosed. A defendant and his counsel, if lacking in the requisite security clearance, must be excluded from hearings that determine what classified information is material and whether substitutions crafted by the government suffice to provide the defendant adequate means of presenting a defense and obtaining a fair trial. Thus, the mere exclusion of Abu Ali and his uncleared counsel from the CIPA hearings did not run afoul of CIPA or Abu Ali's Confrontation Clause rights.

We also conclude that the district court struck an appropriate balance between the government's national security interests and the defendant's right to explore the manner in which the communications were obtained and handled. Abu Ali and his uncleared counsel were provided with the substance of the communications, the dates, and the parties involved, and CIPA-cleared defense counsel was provided with the classified versions and afforded unfettered opportunity to cross-examine the government's witnesses concerning these matters. At the conclusion of the examinations, defense counsel pointed to no specific problem with the issues explored. The district court also expressly considered Abu Ali's rights under the Confrontation Clause and determined that public examination of these witnesses was not necessary to prevent infringement of them. Having fully considered the record and the classified information ourselves, we agree. Uncleared defense counsel were not entitled to disclose the classified information via their questioning of the witnesses about their roles in extracting, sharing, transferring, and handling the communications, and Abu Ali, who was ably represented by counsel at the hearing on this issue, was not deprived of his right to confrontation or to a fair trial merely because he and his uncleared counsel were not also allowed to attend.

The error in the case, which appears to have originated in the October 2005 CIPA proceeding, was that CIPA was taken one step too far. The district court did not abuse its discretion in protecting the classified information from disclosure to Abu Ali and his uncleared counsel, in approving a suitable substitute, or in determining that Abu Ali would receive a fair trial in the absence of such disclosure. But, for reasons that remain somewhat unclear to us, the district court granted the government's request that the complete, unredacted classified document could be presented to the jury via the "silent witness" procedure. The end result, therefore, was that the jury was privy to the information that was withheld from Abu Ali.[17]

As noted above, CIPA contemplates and authorizes district courts to prevent the disclosure of classified information, as was done in this case, so long as it does not deprive the defendant of a fair trial. *See* 18 U.S.C.App. 3 § 4, § 6(c), & § 8(b). CIPA also authorizes restrictions upon the questioning of the witnesses to ensure that classified information remains classified. *See* 18 U.S.C.App. 3, § 8(c). Indeed, even the "silent witness" procedure contemplates situations in which the jury is provided classified information that is withheld from the public, but not from the defendant. *See United States v. Zettl,* 835 F.2d 1059, 1063 (4th Cir.1987). In addition, CIPA provides district courts wide discretion to evaluate and approve suitable substitutions to be presented to the jury. CIPA does not, however, authorize courts to provide classified documents to the jury when only such substitutions are provided to the defendant. . . . Nor could it. There is a stark difference between ex parte submissions from prosecutors which protect the disclosure of irrelevant, nonexculpatory, or privileged information, and situations in which the government seeks to use *ex*

---

17. [Renumbered] We pause to note that while Abu Ali quite clearly argues on appeal that the district court violated his Confrontation Clause rights by allowing the government to introduce at trial evidence that the jury was allowed to see in its entirety while simultaneously providing him with only a redacted version of that evidence, his counsel was not so clear in stating this objection to the district court. As indicated above, Abu Ali's uncleared counsel repeatedly led the district court to believe that they were aware of what had been redacted and were much more concerned with the district court's refusal to allow *uncleared* counsel to publicly examine the government witnesses and disclose the redacted portions of the documents. In other words, they took issue with the government's decision to classify the information in the first instance which, as noted above, is not subject to question. When we view this matter in its entirety, we are more than a little troubled by this failure. However, we have chosen to consider the objections stated to the district court to be broad enough to encompass this ground for appeal and have considered the error under the harmless error standard as opposed to the plain error standard.

parte information in court as evidence to obtain a conviction. And, the notion that such "safeguards against wide-ranging discovery . . . would be sufficient to justify a conviction on secret evidence is patently absurd." *see also United States v. Innamorati,* 996 F.2d 456, 488 (1st Cir.1993) (finding no error in prosecutor's ex parte submission of information for consideration as to whether it must be disclosed to the defendant, but noting that "there [was] no question . . . of convictions based upon secret evidence furnished to the factfinder but withheld from the defendants").

The same can be said for the evidence here. If classified information is to be relied upon as evidence of guilt, the district court may consider steps to protect some or all of the information from unnecessary public disclosure in the interest of national security and in accordance with CIPA, which specifically contemplates such methods as redactions and substitutions so long as these alternatives do not deprive the defendant of a fair trial. However, the government must at a minimum provide the same version of the evidence to the defendant that is submitted to the jury. We do not balance a criminal defendant's right to see the evidence which will be used to convict him against the government's interest in protecting that evidence from public disclosure. If the government does not want the defendant to be privy to information that is classified, it may either declassify the document, seek approval of an effective substitute, or forego its use altogether. What the government cannot do is hide the evidence from the defendant, but give it to the jury. Such plainly violates the Confrontation Clause.

D.

Having determined that submission of the classified documents to the jury ran afoul of Abu Ali's Confrontation Clause rights, we turn now to consider whether that error was harmless. . . .

. . .

The harmless-error doctrine recognizes the principle that the central purpose of a criminal trial is to decide the factual question of the defendant's guilt or innocence, and promotes public respect for the criminal process by focusing on the underlying fairness of the trial rather than on the virtually inevitable presence of immaterial error.

When determining whether an error was harmless, "[t]he Court has the power to review the record *de novo.*" "In so doing, it must be determined whether the [government] has met its burden of demonstrating that the admission of [the evidence] did not contribute to [the] conviction." "[I]n order to find a district court's error harmless, we need only be able to say with fair assurance, after pondering all that happened without stripping the erroneous action from the whole, that the judgment was not substantially swayed by the error."

In this case, we are satisfied that the jury's decision to convict Abu Ali was not substantially swayed by the jury's access to the limited information redacted from the documents given to Abu Ali. Although Abu Ali was not privy to the redacted information, this is not a situation in which the jury was provided with substantive evidence that Abu Ali was prohibited from evaluating or responding to in an effective manner. Well in advance of trial, Abu Ali and his uncleared counsel were given copies of the declassified versions of the communications alleged to have taken place between Sultan Jubran and Abu Ali, which included the dates, opening salutations, unredacted substantive content, and closing signature of Abu Ali's alias "Hani." Thus, Abu Ali knew the precise dates that the alleged communications took place, the entire substantive content of the communications in which he allegedly participated, and the name of the other party to the communications. Abu Ali did not contest that he was a participant in the communications, nor was an argument advanced that disclosure of the redacted information was necessary for him to refute his involvement. On the contrary, Abu Ali had confessed to the Saudi Mabahith that he communicated with Sultan Jubran after the raids and his opposition to the government's motion to protect the information rested not upon a claim that the information provided was false, but upon his asserted right to disclosure of the dates on which the communications were *discovered* by the United States government in the singular hope of bolstering the claim that the United States was acting in joint venture with the Saudis when Abu Ali was interrogated and confessed to the crimes upon which he now stands convicted. With regard to the redaction of the forensic information, Abu Ali's CIPA-cleared counsel was provided with all classified information and afforded the unfettered opportunity to challenge the government witnesses regarding the information. Yet no showing was made then or now that disclosure of the redacted information was necessary to ensure that Abu Ali obtained a fair trial and no request was made to have that information evaluated by outside forensic experts with appropriate clearance.

Abu Ali's eleventh-hour argument that the government cannot demonstrate harmless error because he was prohibited from developing evidence of an alibi at the time of the communications or to otherwise contest that he was, in actuality, a party to them is unpersuasive for the same reasons. At no point prior to or during the trial did Abu Ali contest that he was a party to the declassified communications provided to him or attempt to formulate any such alibi, his CIPA-cleared counsel made no request that the identifying information be evaluated, and Abu Ali admitted that he had communicated with Sultan Jubran after the Medina safe houses were raided. Thus, the information that had been redacted from the declassified version was largely cumulative to Abu Ali's own confessions and the evidence discovered during the safe house raids, which were presented to the jury.

In sum, while the district court violated Abu Ali's Sixth Amendment right to confront the evidence against him by submitting the unredacted versions of the documents, instead of the redacted substitute versions, to the jury as evidence at trial, we are satisfied that the error was harmless beyond a reasonable doubt.

Questions and Notes

1. The CIPA issues in Abu Ali are somewhat unusual. First, there is the fact that one of his attorneys did not apply for security clearance and the other was not able to obtain security clearance and the fact that the court therefore appointed an attorney for him who had security clearance, who represented him in aspects of the case where clearance was necessary. These are not unheard-of circumstances, but probably not commonplace. Issues arising out of the need for security clearance for counsel are addressed in more detail infra, p. 511. Does the use of security cleared counsel in terrorism prosecution have the potential to generally resolve the dilemma posed by the use of classified information in such cases? Is there a problem where counsel for the defendant, or as in the principal case, one of defendant's counsel, has access to *relevant and material* classified information that the defendant himself is not able to see? See infra, notes 6–8, pp. 524–526.

2. Second, there is the use of the "silent witness" procedure. Normally, what is contemplated when this procedure is used? Who does not gain access to the classified information at issue? The court? Defense counsel? The defendant? The jury? The public including the press? Wherein did the trial court err in the use of the silent witness procedure in this case?

3. An important proposition comes out of the appellate court's conclusion that the right of confrontation was violated in this case. What is it?

4. What does Abu Ali tell us about the following issues? Would it violate the confrontation clause to have examination or cross-examination of a witness conducted in an in camera hearing (i.e. before the judge and outside of the hearing of the jury) by cleared counsel but not in the presence of the jury? Would it violate the confrontation clause to have evidence that the jury has seen available to defendant's cleared counsel but not to defendant himself?

5. The court was upset by the failure of uncleared counsel to object to the court's decision to allow the jury to see evidence that defendant was not given access to while objecting to the fact that they had been prevented from having access to the redacted, classified portions of the documents at issue and from being able to introduce them publicly at the trial. How serious was this failure?

E.　CLASSIFIED INFORMATION AND THE RIGHT TO COMPULSORY PROCESS OF WITNESSES

UNITED STATES v. MOUSSAOUI

382 F.3d 453 (4th Cir. 2004), cert. denied, Moussaoui
v. United States, 544 U.S. 931 (2005)

Before Wilkins, Chief Judge, and Williams and Gregory, Circuit Judges.

[Affirmed in part, vacated in part, and remanded by published opinion. Chief Judge Wilkins announced the judgment of the court and wrote an opinion, in which JUDGE WILLIAMS concurs, and in which JUDGE GREGORY concurs except as to Part V.C. JUDGE WILLIAMS wrote a concurring opinion. JUDGE GREGORY wrote an opinion concurring in part and dissenting in part.]

WILKINS, CHIEF JUDGE.

The Government appeals a series of rulings by the district court granting Appellee Zacarias Moussaoui access to certain individuals ("the enemy combatant witnesses" or "the witnesses") for the purpose of deposing them pursuant to Federal Rule of Criminal Procedure 15; rejecting the Government's proposed substitutions for the depositions; and imposing sanctions for the Government's refusal to produce the witnesses. We are presented with questions of grave significance—questions that test the commitment of this nation to an independent judiciary, to the constitutional guarantee of a fair trial even to one accused of the most heinous of crimes, and to the protection of our citizens against additional terrorist attacks. These questions do not admit of easy answers.

For the reasons set forth below, we reject the Government's claim that the district court exceeded its authority in granting Moussaoui access to the witnesses. We affirm the conclusion of the district court that the enemy combatant witnesses could provide material, favorable testimony on Moussaoui's behalf, and we agree with the district court that the Government's proposed substitutions for the witnesses' deposition testimony are inadequate. However, we reverse the district court insofar as it held that it is not possible to craft adequate substitutions, and we remand with instructions for the district court and the parties to craft substitutions under certain guidelines. Finally, we vacate the order imposing sanctions on the Government.

I.

A.   Background Information

. . .

Moussaoui was arrested for an immigration violation in mid-August 2001 and, in December of that year, was indicted on several charges of conspiracy related to the September 11 attacks. In July 2002, the Government filed a superseding indictment charging Moussaoui with six offenses: conspiracy to commit acts of terrorism transcending national boundaries, *see* 18 U.S.C.A. § 2332b(a)(2), (c) (West 2000); conspiracy to commit aircraft piracy, *see* 49 U.S.C.A. § 46502(a)(1)(A), (a)(2)(B) (West 1997); conspiracy to destroy aircraft, *see* 18 U.S.C.A. §§ 32(a)(7), 34 (West 2000); conspiracy to use weapons of mass destruction, *see* 18 U.S.C.A. § 2332a(a) (West 2000 & Supp.2003); conspiracy to murder United States employees, *see* 18 U.S.C.A. §§ 1114, 1117 (West 2000 & Supp.2003), and conspiracy to destroy property, *see* 18 U.S.C.A. § 844(f), (i), (n) (West 2000 & Supp. 2003). The Government seeks the death penalty on the first four of these charges.

According to the allegations of the indictment, Moussaoui was present at an al Qaeda training camp in April 1998. The indictment further alleges that Moussaoui arrived in the United States in late February 2001 and thereafter began flight lessons in Norman, Oklahoma. Other allegations in the indictment highlight similarities between Moussaoui's conduct and the conduct of the September 11 hijackers. Each of the four death-eligible counts of the indictment alleges that the actions of Moussaoui and his coconspirators "result[ed] in the deaths of thousands of persons on September 11, 2001."

. . .

Simultaneously with its prosecution of Moussaoui, the Executive Branch has been engaged in ongoing efforts to eradicate al Qaeda and to capture its leader, Usama bin Laden. These efforts have resulted in the capture of numerous members of al Qaeda, including the witnesses at issue here: [Redacted] ("Witness A"), [Redacted] ("Witness B"), [Redacted] and [Redacted] ("Witness C"), [Redacted]

Witness A was captured [Redacted]. Shortly thereafter, Moussaoui (who at that time was representing himself in the district court) moved for access to Witness A, asserting that the witness would be an important part of his defense. Moussaoui's motion was supported by then-standby counsel, who filed a motion seeking pretrial access to Witness A and a writ of habeas corpus *ad testificandum* to obtain Witness A's trial testimony. The Government opposed this request.

The district court conducted a hearing, after which it issued an oral ruling granting access to Witness A ("the January 30 order"). The court subsequently issued a memorandum opinion explaining its ruling in greater detail. The district court concluded that Witness A could offer material testimony in Moussaoui's defense; in particular, the court determined that Witness A had extensive knowledge of the September 11 plot and that his testimony would support Moussaoui's claim that he was not involved in the attacks. At a minimum, the court observed, Witness A's testimony could support an argument that Moussaoui should not receive the death penalty if convicted.

The district court acknowledged that Witness A is a national security asset and therefore denied standby counsel's request for unmonitored pretrial access and declined to order his production at trial. The court also determined, however, that the Government's national security interest must yield to Moussaoui's right to a fair trial. Accordingly, the court ordered that Witness A's testimony be preserved by means of a Rule 15 deposition. *See* Fed.R.Crim.P. 15(a)(1) (providing that court may order deposition of witness to preserve testimony for trial "because of exceptional circumstances and in the interest of justice"). In an attempt to minimize the effect of its order on national security, the district court ordered that certain precautions be taken. Specifically, the court directed that the deposition would be taken by remote video, with Witness A in an undisclosed location and Moussaoui, standby counsel, and counsel for the Government in the presence of the district court, [Redacted]

While the Government's appeal of the January 30 order was pending before this court, we remanded for the purpose of allowing the district court to determine whether any substitution existed that would place Moussaoui in substantially the same position as would a deposition. On remand, both the Government and standby counsel offered proposed substitutions for Witness A's deposition testimony.[5] The district court rejected the Government's proposed substitutions, reasoning that (a) the information in the [Redacted] reports was unreliable, and (b) the substitutions themselves were flawed in numerous respects. Believing itself bound to consider only the Government's proposed substitutions, the district court did not review the substitutions offered by standby counsel.

The proceedings on remand complete, we conducted oral argument on June 3, 2003. Upon receiving the mandate of this court, the district court entered an order directing the Government to inform the court whether it would comply with the January 30 order. On July 14, 2003, the Government filed a pleading indicating that it would refuse to provide access to Witness A for the purpose of conducting a deposition.

On August 29, the district court entered an order ("the August 29 order") granting access to Witnesses B and C for purposes of conducting Rule 15 depositions of those witnesses. The order imposed the same conditions as those applicable to Witness A.... Following the rejection of its proposed substitutions, the Government informed the court that it would not comply with the August 29 order.

The district court then directed the parties to submit briefs concerning the appropriate sanction to be imposed for the Government's refusal to comply with the January 30 and August 29 orders. Standby counsel sought dismissal but alternatively asked the district court to dismiss the death notice. The Government filed a responsive pleading stating that "[t]o present the issue most efficiently to the Court of Appeals, and because [the Classified Information Procedures Act] prescribes dismissal as the presumptive action a district court must take in these circumstances, we do not oppose standby counsel's suggestion that the appropriate action in this case is to dismiss the indictment." (asserting that "dismissal of the indictment ... is the surest route for ensuring that the questions at issue here can promptly be presented to the Fourth Circuit").

Noting that "[t]he unprecedented investment of both human and material resources in this case mandates the careful consideration of some

---

5. These substitutions were derived as follows. Those responsible [Redacted] have recorded the witnesses' answers to questions in [Redacted] reports. These highly classified reports are intended for use in the military and intelligence communities; they were not prepared with this litigation in mind. Portions of the [Redacted] reports concerning Moussaoui and the September 11 attacks have been excerpted and set forth in documents prepared for purposes of this litigation. These documents, deemed [Redacted] summaries by the parties and the district court, have been provided to defense counsel in conformance with the Government's obligations under *Brady v. Maryland,* 373 U.S. 83, 83 S.Ct. 1194, 10 L.Ed.2d 215 (1963). The proposed substitutions are based on the [Redacted] summaries.

sanction other than dismissal,'' the district court rejected the parties' claims that the indictment should be dismissed. Rather, the court dismissed the death notice, reasoning that Moussaoui had adequately demonstrated that the witnesses could provide testimony that, if believed, might preclude a jury from finding Moussaoui eligible for the death penalty. Further, because proof of Moussaoui's involvement in the September 11 attacks was not necessary to a conviction, and because the witnesses' testimony, if believed, could exonerate Moussaoui of involvement in those attacks, the district court prohibited the Government "from making any argument, or offering any evidence, suggesting that the defendant had any involvement in, or knowledge of, the September 11 attacks." In conjunction with this ruling, the district court denied the Government's motions to admit into evidence cockpit voice recordings made on September 11; video footage of the collapse of the World Trade Center towers; and photographs of the victims of the attacks.

The Government appealed, attacking multiple aspects of the rulings of the district court.

C. Events Leading to Issuance of this Amended Opinion

We issued our decision on April 22, 2004. *See United States v. Moussaoui*, 365 F.3d 292 (4th Cir.2004). Moussaoui thereafter timely filed a petition for rehearing and suggestion for rehearing en banc (the Petition). On May 12, the Government submitted a letter to the court purporting to "clarify certain factual matters." Letter to Deputy Clerk from United States Attorney at 1 (May 12, 2004) [hereinafter "Letter"]. In particular, the Government referred to pages 50–51 of the classified slip opinion, where the court stated:

[Redacted]

In response to the emphasized portion of the above quotation, the Government stated that members of the prosecution team, including FBI Special Agents assigned to the September 11 and other related investigations, [Redacted] have provided [Redacted] information [Redacted] consistent with the [Redacted] desire to maximize their own efforts to obtain actionable information [Redacted]

Letter at 2. The Government went on to note, however, that "[a]ny information or suggested areas of inquiry that have been shared [Redacted] have been used, like information from numerous other sources, at the sole discretion [Redacted]" *Id.* at 3. The Government asserted that [Redacted] *Id.*

Based in part on the revelations in the May 12 letter, we directed the Government to file a response to the Petition. In particular, we directed the Government to provide answers to the following questions:

(1) Why was the information in the May 12 Letter not provided to this court or the district court prior to May 12?

(2) [Redacted]

(3) [Redacted]

(4) [Redacted] provided inculpatory of exculpatory information regarding Moussaoui?

(5) In light of the information contained in the Letter and any other pertinent developments, would it now be appropriate to submit written questions to any of the enemy combatant witnesses?

(6) What restrictions would apply to such a process and how should it be conducted?

(7) If access is granted by written questions, is the Compulsory Process Clause satisfied?

(8) If access is granted by written questions, what effect, if any, would *Crawford v. Washington,* [541] U.S. [36], 124 S.Ct. 1354, 158 L.Ed.2d 177 (2004), have on such a process?

(9) If circumstances have changed such that submission of written questions is now possible, when did the circumstances change and why was neither this court nor the district court so informed at that time?

See United States v. Moussaoui, 365 F.3d 292 (4th Cir.2004) (order directing response to petition for rehearing and suggestion for rehearing en banc). Underlying this order were concerns among the panel members that members of the prosecution team may have [Redacted] rendered the witnesses' statements less reliable.

The Government filed its response (the Response), supplemented by a classified joint appendix and a classified ex parte appendix, on May 19. Moussaoui filed a reply on May 24, in which, *inter alia,* he raised concerns [Redacted].

We conducted a sealed oral argument regarding the petition for rehearing on June 3, 2004. During a discussion [Redacted] the panel asked the Government to provide documentation [Redacted]. On June 16, the Government filed an ex parte document responding to this request.

Additional Facts Contained in the Government's
Submissions in Response to the Petition

1. Agent Zebley and the PENTTBOM Team

The FBI team investigating the terrorist attacks of September 11, 2001 is known as "the PENTTBOM team." The Government considers these investigators to be part of the prosecution team. *See* Letter at 2.

. . .

The classified joint appendix submitted by the Government with the Response includes [Redacted]

2. Oral Communications

[Redacted]

3. Written Communications

[Redacted]

4. Intelligence Community Use of Information

[Redacted][12] [Redacted] the intelligence community is interested only in obtaining information that has foreign intelligence value; the intelligence community is not concerned with obtaining information to aid in the prosecution of Moussaoui. [Redacted] not create special [Redacted] reports for use by the prosecution, rather, the prosecution and the PESTTBOM team receive the same reports that are distributed to the intelligence community at large. Information is included in these reports only if [Redacted] the information to have foreign intelligence value.[14]

II.

. . .

III.

With respect to the merits, the Government first argues that the district court erred in ordering the production of the enemy combatant witnesses for the purpose of deposing them. Within the context of this argument, the Government makes two related claims. First, the Government asserts that because the witnesses are noncitizens outside the territorial boundaries of the United States, there is no means by which the district court can compel their appearance on Moussaoui's behalf. Second, the Government maintains that even if the district court has the power to reach the witnesses, its exercise of that power is curtailed by the reality that the witnesses are in military custody in time of war, and thus requiring them to be produced would violate constitutional principles of separation of powers. We address these arguments seriatim.

---

12. After the Petition was filed, news articles indicated that the National Commission on Terrorist Attacks Upon the United States ("the 9/11 Commission") had submitted questions to be asked of unidentified al Qaeda detainees. *See* Philip Shenon, "Accord Near for 9/11 Panel to Question Qaeda Leaders," *N.Y. Times*, May 12, 2004, at A20 (reporting a statement by the 9/11 Commission that it was "close to an agreement with the Bush administration that would allow the panel to submit questions to captured Qaeda leaders who are believed to have been involved in planning the attacks"); *see also* Associated Press, "Vice Chairman Expects Responses to Written Questions Soon" (May 13, 2004), *available at www.msnbc.msn.com/id/4972789* (stating that "[t]he Sept. 11 commission has submitted written questions about the 2001 attacks to al-Qaida detainees and expects to receive responses soon"). [Redacted] *see* Nat'l Comm'n on Terrorist Attacks upon the United States, *Staff Statement No. 16,* at 1 (released June 16, 2004) (stating that Commission had no "direct access" to al Qaeda members but rather relied on written materials).

14. The Government's submissions indicate that those responsible for [Redacted] the witnesses record and pass on only information [Redacted] to have foreign intelligence value. Consequently, it is at least possible, albeit unlikely, that one of the witnesses has imparted significant exculpatory information related to Moussaoui that has not been included [Redacted] If so, there may be a due process problem under *Brady v.* Maryland, 373 U.S. 83, 83 S.Ct. 1194, 10 L.Ed.2d 215 (1963). *See United States v. Perdomo,* 929 F.2d 967, 971 (3d Cir.1991) (stating that prosecution is obligated under *Brady* to disclose all exculpatory information "in the possession of some arm of the state"). We need not consider this question, however, as there is no evidence before us that the Government possesses exculpatory material that has not been disclosed to the defense.

. . .

The Government maintains that because the enemy combatant witnesses are foreign nationals outside the boundaries of the United States, they are beyond the process power of the district court and, hence, unavailable to Moussaoui.

The Government's argument rests primarily on the well established and undisputed principle that the process power of the district court does not extend to foreign nationals abroad. . . . This is not the controlling principle, however.

The Government's argument overlooks the critical fact that the enemy combatant witnesses are [Redacted] of the United States Government. Therefore, we are concerned not with the ability of the district court to issue a subpoena to the witnesses, but rather with its power to issue a writ of habeas corpus *ad testificandum* ("testimonial writ") to the witnesses' custodian.

In determining whether a district court possesses the power to serve a writ of habeas corpus, the critical principle is that the writ is served not upon the prisoner, but upon the custodian. . . . Therefore, the relevant question is not whether the district court can serve the *witnesses,* but rather whether the court can serve the *custodian.*[16]

. . .

The Government next argues that even if the district court would otherwise have the power to order the production of the witnesses, the January 30 and August 29 orders are improper because they infringe on the Executive's warmaking authority, in violation of separation of powers principles.

. . .

Stated in its simplest terms, the separation of powers doctrine prohibits each branch of the government from "intrud[ing] upon the central prerogatives of another." Such an intrusion occurs when one branch arrogates to itself powers constitutionally assigned to another branch or when the otherwise legitimate actions of one branch impair the functions of another.

---

16. At oral argument, the Government described the capture of the enemy combatant witnesses as "a windfall" from which Moussaoui should not be entitled to benefit. We agree with the Government's premise; there can be no doubt that, were it not for the capture of these witnesses, Moussaoui could have no hope of obtaining their testimony. It does not follow, however, that this fortuity should not inure to Moussaoui's benefit. Indeed, the Government acknowledged that if the witnesses were brought to the United States for reasons unrelated to Moussaoui's prosecution, the district court would have the power to order their production. We are unable to discern why Moussaoui should be entitled to the benefit of the second windfall but not the first.

We also think that the Government's "windfall" argument mistakenly focuses on the ability of the district court to serve process on the *witnesses,* rather than on the custodian. The district court has never had—and does not now have—the power to serve process on the witnesses. But, as explained in . . . [the text] the district court has always had the power to serve process on the custodian, [Redacted]

This is not a case involving arrogation of the powers or duties of another branch. The district court orders requiring production of the enemy combatant witnesses involved the resolution of questions properly—indeed, exclusively—reserved to the judiciary. Therefore, if there is a separation of powers problem at all, it arises only from the burden the actions of the district court place on the Executive's performance of its duties.The Supreme Court has explained on several occasions that determining whether a judicial act places impermissible burdens on another branch of government requires balancing the competing interests. *See, e.g., Nixon v. Admin'r of Gen. Servs.*, 433 U.S. 425, 443, 97 S.Ct. 2777, 53 L.Ed.2d 867 (1977). In a case concerning the extent of the President's executive immunity, the Supreme Court noted that "[c]ourts traditionally have recognized the President's constitutional responsibilities and status as factors counseling judicial deference and restraint." *Nixon v. Fitzgerald,* 457 U.S. 731, 753, 102 S.Ct. 2690, 73 L.Ed.2d 349 (1982). The Court continued,

It is settled law that the separation-of-powers doctrine does not bar every exercise of jurisdiction over the President of the United States. But our cases also have established that a court, before exercising jurisdiction, must balance the constitutional weight of the interest to be served against the dangers of intrusion on the authority and functions of the Executive Branch.

C. Balancing

1. The Burden on the Government

The Constitution charges the Congress and the Executive with the making and conduct of war. . . . It is not an exaggeration to state that the effective performance of these duties is essential to our continued existence as a sovereign nation. Indeed, "no governmental interest is more compelling than the security of the Nation." . . . Thus, [i]n accordance with [the] constitutional text, the Supreme Court has shown great deference to the political branches when called upon to decide cases implicating sensitive matters of foreign policy, national security, or military affairs.

The Government alleges—and we accept as true—that [Redacted] the enemy combatant witnesses is critical to the ongoing effort to combat terrorism by al Qaeda. The witnesses are [Redacted] al Qaeda operatives who have extensive knowledge concerning not just the September 11 attacks, but also other past attacks, future operations, and the structure, personnel, and tactics of al Qaeda. Their value as intelligence sources can hardly be overstated. And, we must defer to the Government's assertion that interruption [Redacted] of these witnesses will have devastating effects on the ability to gather information from them. *Cf. CIA v. Sims,* 471 U.S. 159, 176, 105 S.Ct. 1881, 85 L.Ed.2d 173 (1985) (noting that "whether an intelligence source will be harmed if his identity is revealed will often require complex political, historical, and psychological judgments" that courts are poorly equipped to make). [Redacted] it is not unreasonable to suppose that interruption [Redacted] could result in the loss of information that might prevent future terrorist attacks.

The Government also asserts that production of the witnesses would burden the Executive's ability to conduct foreign relations.... The Government claims that if the Executive's assurances of confidentiality can be abrogated by the judiciary, the vital ability to obtain the cooperation of other governments will be devastated. The Government also reminds us of the bolstering effect production of the witnesses might have on our enemies.

A basic consideration in *habeas corpus* practice is that the prisoner will be produced before the court.... To grant the writ to these prisoners might mean that our army must transport them across the seas for hearing. This would require allocation of shipping space, guarding personnel, billeting and rations.... The writ, since it is held to be a matter of right, would be equally available to enemies during active hostilities as in the present twilight between war and peace. Such trials would hamper the war effort and bring aid and comfort to the enemy. They would diminish the prestige of our commanders, not only with enemies but with wavering neutrals. It would be difficult to devise more effective fettering of a field commander than to allow the very enemies he is ordered to reduce to submission to call him to account in his own civil courts and divert his efforts and attention from the military offensive abroad to the legal defensive at home. Nor is it unlikely that the result of such enemy litigiousness would be a conflict between judicial and military opinion highly comforting to enemies of the United States.

In summary, the burdens that would arise from production of the enemy combatant witnesses are substantial.

2. Moussaoui's Interest

The importance of the Sixth Amendment right to compulsory process is not subject to question—it is integral to our adversarial criminal justice system:

The need to develop all relevant facts in the adversary system is both fundamental and comprehensive. The ends of criminal justice would be defeated if judgments were to be founded on a partial or speculative presentation of the facts. The very integrity of the judicial system and public confidence in the system depend on full disclosure of all the facts, within the framework of the rules of evidence. To ensure that justice is done, it is imperative to the function of the courts that compulsory process be available for the production of evidence needed either by the prosecution or by the defense.

To state the matter more succinctly, "[f]ew rights are more fundamental than that of an accused to present witnesses in his own defense."

The compulsory process right does not attach to any witness the defendant wishes to call, however. Rather, a defendant must demonstrate that the witness he desires to have produced would testify "in his favor,".

Thus, in order to assess Moussaoui's interest, we must determine whether the enemy combatant witnesses could provide testimony material to Moussaoui's defense.[20]

. . .

Because Moussaoui has not had—and will not receive—direct access to any of the witnesses, he cannot be required to show materiality with the degree of specificity that applies in the ordinary case. Rather, it is sufficient if Moussaoui can make a "plausible showing" of materiality. (noting that a defendant who has not interviewed a potential witness may demonstrate materiality by relating "the events to which a witness might testify[ ] and the relevance of those events to the crime charged"). However, in determining whether Moussaoui has made a plausible showing, we must bear in mind that Moussaoui *does* have access to the [Redacted] summaries.

Before considering whether Moussaoui has made the necessary showing with respect to each witness, we pause to consider some general arguments raised by the Government concerning materiality. First, the Government maintains that Moussaoui can demonstrate materiality only by relying on admissible evidence. We agree with the Government to a certain extent—Moussaoui should not be allowed to rely on obviously inadmissible statements (*e.g.,* statements resting on a witness' belief rather than his personal knowledge).... However, because many rulings on admissibility—particularly those relating to relevance—can only be decided in the context of a trial, most of the witnesses' statements cannot meaningfully be assessed for admissibility at this time. Moreover, statements that may not be admissible at the guilt phase may be admissible during the penalty phase, with its more relaxed evidentiary standards.

Second, the Government maintains that Moussaoui cannot establish materiality unless he can prove that the witnesses would not invoke their Fifth Amendment rights against self-incrimination. We have previously indicated, however, that a court should not assume that a potential witness will invoke the Fifth Amendment....

Additionally, the Government argues that even if the witnesses' testimony would tend to exonerate Moussaoui of involvement in the September 11 attacks, such testimony would not be material because the conspiracies with which Moussaoui is charged are broader than September 11. Thus, the Government argues, Moussaoui can be convicted even if he lacked any prior knowledge of September 11. This argument ignores the principle that the scope of an alleged conspiracy is a jury question, and the possibility that Moussaoui may assert that the conspiracy culminating in

---

20. We adhere to our prior ruling that CIPA does not apply because the January 30 and August 29 orders of the district court are not covered by either of the potentially relevant provisions of CIPA: § 4 (concerning deletion of classified information from *documents* to be turned over to the defendant during discovery) or § 6 (concerning the disclosure of classified information[ ] by the defense during pretrial or trial proceedings). *See Moussaoui I,* 333 F.3d at 514–15. Like the district court, however, we believe that CIPA provides a useful framework for considering the questions raised by Moussaoui's request for access to the enemy combatant witnesses.

the September 11 attacks was distinct from any conspiracy in which he was involved. Moreover, even if the jury accepts the Government's claims regarding the scope of the charged conspiracy, testimony regarding Moussaoui's non-involvement in September 11 is critical to the penalty phase. If Moussaoui had no involvement in or knowledge of September 11, it is entirely possible that he would not be found eligible for the death penalty.

We now consider the rulings of the district court regarding the ability of each witness to provide material testimony in Moussaoui's favor.

a.   Witness A

The district court did not err in concluding that Witness A could offer material evidence on Moussaoui's behalf. [Redacted] Several statements by Witness A tend to exculpate Moussaoui. [Redacted] to undermine the theory (which the Government may or may not intend to advance at trial) that Moussaoui was to pilot a fifth plane into the White House. [Redacted] This statement is significant in light of other evidence [Redacted]. This is consistent with Moussaoui's claim that he was to be part of a post-September 11 operation.

The Government argues that Witness A's statements are actually incriminatory of Moussaoui. It is true that Witness A has made some statements that arguably implicate Moussaoui in the September 11 attacks. [Redacted] On balance, however, Moussaoui has made a sufficient showing that evidence from Witness A would be more helpful than hurtful, or at least that we cannot have confidence in the outcome of the trial without Witness A's evidence.

b.   Witness B

There can be no question that Witness B could provide material evidence on behalf of Moussaoui. [Redacted] Witness B [Redacted] has indicated that Moussaoui's operational knowledge was limited, a fact that is clearly of exculpatory value as to both guilt and penalty. [Redacted] Thus, of all three witnesses, Witness B is of the greatest exculpatory value.

c.   Witness C

[Redacted]

The district court determined that Witness C could provide material evidence because he could support Moussaoui's contention that he was not involved in the September 11 attacks. We agree with the district court that a jury might reasonably infer, from Witness C [Redacted] that Moussaoui was not involved in September 11. We therefore conclude that Moussaoui has made a plausible showing that Witness C would, if available, be a favorable witness.

3.   Balancing

Having considered the burden alleged by the Government and the right claimed by Moussaoui, we now turn to the question of whether the district court should have refrained from acting in light of the national security interests asserted by the Government. The question is not unique; the Supreme Court has addressed similar matters on numerous occasions. In all cases of this type—cases falling into "what might loosely be called the area of constitutionally guaranteed access to evidence," . . . Ultimately, as these cases make clear, the appropriate procedure is for the district court to order production of the evidence or witness and leave to the Government the choice of whether to comply with that order. If the government refuses to produce the information at issue—as it may properly do—the result is ordinarily dismissal.

. . .

In addition to the pronouncements of the Supreme Court in this area, we are also mindful of Congress' judgment, expressed in CIPA, that the Executive's interest in protecting classified information does not overcome a defendant's right to present his case. Under CIPA, once the district court determines that an item of classified information is relevant and material, that item must be admitted unless the government provides an adequate substitution. . . . If no adequate substitution can be found, the government must decide whether it will prohibit the disclosure of the classified information; if it does so, the district court must impose a sanction, which is presumptively dismissal of the indictment.

In view of these authorities, it is clear that when an evidentiary privilege—even one that involves national security—is asserted by the Government in the context of its prosecution of a criminal offense, the "balancing" we must conduct is primarily, if not solely, an examination of whether the district court correctly determined that the information the Government seeks to withhold is material to the defense. We have determined that the enemy combatant witnesses can offer material testimony that is essential to Moussaoui's defense, and we therefore affirm the January 30 and August 29 orders, Thus, the choice is the Government's whether to comply with those orders or suffer a sanction.

V.

As noted previously, the Government has stated that it will not produce the enemy combatant witnesses for depositions (or, we presume, for any other purpose related to this litigation). We are thus left in the following situation: the district court has the power to order production of the enemy combatant witnesses and has properly determined that they could offer material testimony on Moussaoui's behalf, but the Government has refused to produce the witnesses. Under such circumstances, dismissal of the indictment is the usual course. Like the district court, however, we believe that a more measured approach is required. Additionally, we emphasize that no punitive sanction is warranted here because the Government has rightfully exercised its prerogative to protect national security interests by refusing to produce the witnesses.[26]

---

26. We emphasize that by all appearances, the Government's refusal to produce the witnesses is done in the utmost good faith. The Government is charged not only with the task of bringing

Although, as explained above, this is not a CIPA case, that act nevertheless provides useful guidance in determining the nature of the remedies that may be available. Under CIPA, dismissal of an indictment is authorized only if the government has failed to produce an adequate substitute for the classified information, and the interests of justice would not be served by imposition of a lesser sanction, CIPA thus enjoins district courts to seek a solution that neither disadvantages the defendant nor penalizes the government (and the public) for protecting classified information that may be vital to national security.

A similar approach is appropriate here. Under such an approach, the first question is whether there is any appropriate substitution for the witnesses' testimony. Because we conclude, for the reasons set forth below, that appropriate substitutions are available, we need not consider any other remedy.

A. Standard

CIPA provides that the government may avoid the disclosure of classified information by proposing a substitute for the information, which the district court must accept if it "will provide the defendant with substantially the same ability to make his defense as would disclosure of the specific classified information." . . .

B. Substitutions proposed by the Government

The Government proposed substitutions for the witnesses' deposition testimony in the form of a series of statements derived from the [Redacted] summaries.[27] The district court rejected all proposed substitutions as inadequate. The ruling of the district court was based on its conclusions regarding the inherent inadequacy of the substitutions and its findings regarding the specific failings of the Government's proposals. For the reasons set forth below, we reject the ruling of the district court that any substitution for the witnesses' testimony would be inadequate. We agree, however, with the assessment that the particular proposals submitted by the Government are inadequate in their current form.

First, the district court deemed the substitutions inherently inadequate because the [Redacted] reports, from which the substitutions were ultimately derived, were unreliable.[29] This was so, the court reasoned, because the witnesses' [Redacted]. The district court also complained that

---

wrongdoers to justice, but also with the grave responsibility of protecting the lives of the citizenry. The choice the Government has made is not without consequences, but those consequences are not punitive in nature.

27. In the case of Witness A, the proposed substitutions were submitted in narrative form rather than as excerpts from the [Redacted] summaries. The substitutions for Witnesses B and C more closely tracked the language of the [Redacted] summaries.

29. The court also deemed the substitutions inadequate because the use of substitutions would deprive Moussaoui of the ability to question the witnesses regarding matters that do not appear in the [Redacted] reports. In essence, the district court appears to have concluded that the substitutions are inadequate because they are not the same thing as a deposition. However, we have already determined that a proposed substitution need not provide Moussaoui with all the benefits of a deposition in order to be adequate.

it cannot be determined whether the [Redacted] reports accurately reflect the witnesses' statements [Redacted][30] The court further commented that the lack of quotation marks in the [Redacted] reports made it impossible to determine whether a given statement is a verbatim recording or [Redacted].

The conclusion of the district court that the proposed substitutions are inherently inadequate is tantamount to a declaration that there could be no adequate substitution for the witnesses' deposition testimony. We reject this conclusion. The answer to the concerns of the district court regarding the accuracy of the [Redacted] reports is that those who are [Redacted] the witnesses have a profound interest in obtaining accurate information from the witnesses and in reporting that information accurately to those who can use it to prevent acts of terrorism and to capture other al Qaeda operatives. These considerations provide sufficient indicia of reliability to alleviate the concerns of the district court.

Next, the district court noted that the substitutions do not indicate that they are summaries of statements made over the course of several months. We agree with the district court that in order to adequately protect Moussaoui's right to a fair trial, the jury must be made aware of certain information concerning the substitutions. The particular content of any instruction to the jury regarding the substitutions lies within the discretion of the district court. However, at the very least the jury should be informed that the substitutions are derived from reports [Redacted] of the witnesses. The instructions must account for the fact that members of the prosecution team have provided information and suggested [Redacted]. The jury should also be instructed that the statements were obtained under circumstances that support a conclusion that the statements are reliable.[31]

We reject the suggestion of the district court that the Government acted improperly in attempting to organize the information presented in the substitutions. Counsel rarely, if ever, present information to the jury in the order they received it during pretrial investigations. Indeed, organizing and distilling voluminous information for comprehensible presentation to a jury is a hallmark of effective advocacy. In short, while there may be problems with the *manner* in which the Government organized the substitutions, the fact that the Government has attempted such organization is not a mark against it.

---

30. The district court did not complain that the [Redacted] summaries do not accurately summarize the [Redacted] reports. At the hearing concerning the Government's proposed substitutions for Witness A's testimony, the court commented that it had been "impressed with the accuracy" of the [Redacted] summaries.

31. Nothing in the Government's submissions in connection with the Petition contradicts our conclusion that those [Redacted] the witnesses have a profound interest in obtaining truthful information. To the contrary, we are even more persuaded that the [Redacted] process is carefully designed to elicit truthful and accurate information from the witnesses.

We emphasize that we have never held, nor do we new hold, that the witnesses' statements are *in fact* truthful, and the jury should not be so instructed. Instead, the jury should be informed that the circumstances were designed to elicit truthful statements from the witnesses. We offer no opinion regarding whether this instruction may include information regarding [Redacted]

The district court identified particular problems with the proposed substitutions for Witness A's testimony. For example, the court noted that the proposed substitutions failed to include exculpatory information provided by Witness A and incorporated at least one incriminatory inference not supplied by Witness A's statements. [Redacted]. Our own review of the proposed substitutions for the testimony of Witnesses B and C reveals similar problems. [Redacted]. These problems, however, may be remedied as described below.

C. Instructions for the District Court

1. Submission of Questions by Moussaoui

The Government's submissions in response to the Petition make clear that members of the prosecution team, [Redacted] have had some input [Redacted] the enemy combatant witnesses. Our review of the circumstances of this access indicates that the input by the prosecution team into the [Redacted] process has worked no unfairness on Moussaoui. Nevertheless, in order to provide Moussaoui with the fullest possible range of information from the witnesses, we direct the district court to provide Moussaoui with an opportunity to [Redacted] for [Redacted] discretionary use [Redacted] of the witnesses.[34]

2. Substitutions

For the reasons set forth above, we conclude that the district court erred in ruling that any substitution for the witnesses' testimony is inherently inadequate to the extent it is derived from the [Redacted] reports. To the contrary, we hold that the [Redacted] summaries (which, as the district court determined, accurately recapitulate the [Redacted] reports) provide an adequate basis for the creation of written statements that may be submitted to the jury in lieu of the witnesses' deposition testimony.

The compiling of substitutions is a task best suited to the district court, given its greater familiarity with the facts of the case and its authority to manage the presentation of evidence.[35] Nevertheless, we think it is appropriate to provide some guidance to the court and the parties.

First, the circumstances of this case—most notably, the fact that the substitutions may very well support Moussaoui's defense—dictate that the

---

34. During the hearing regarding the Petition, defense counsel expressed concern over whether [Redacted] would result in the disclosure of trial strategy to the Government. The Government, in its June 16 filing, informs us that measures can be taken to avoid such disclosures. We leave the particulars of any such process to the discretion of the district court. At an absolute minimum, however, whatever process is adopted must ensure that the prosecution team is not privy to [Redacted] propounded by the defense, just as the defense was unaware or [Redacted] propounded by the prosecution team.

35. We note that the district court will not be drafting original language for submission to the jury. Instead, as we discuss further in the text, Moussaoui will designate portions of the [Redacted] summaries for submission; the Government will raise objections and cross-designate portions of the summaries it believes are required by the rule of completeness; and the district court will make rulings as necessary to compile an appropriate set of substitutions.

compiling of substitutions be an interactive process among the parties and the district court. Second, we think that accuracy and fairness are best achieved by compiling substitutions that use the exact language of the [Redacted] summaries to the greatest extent possible. We believe that the best means of achieving both of these objectives is for defense counsel to identify particular portions of the [Redacted] summaries that Moussaoui may want to admit into evidence at trial. The Government may then offer any objections and argue that additional portions must be included in the interest of completeness, as discussed below. If the substitutions are to be admitted at all (we leave open the possibility that Moussaoui may decide not to use the substitutions in his defense), they may be admitted only by Moussaoui. Based on defense counsel's submissions and the Government's objections, the district court could then compile an appropriate set of substitutions. We leave to the discretion of the district court the question of whether to rule on the admissibility of a particular substitution (*e.g.,* whether a substitution is relevant) at trial or during pre-trial proceedings.

As previously indicated, the jury must be provided with certain information regarding the substitutions. While we leave the particulars of the instructions to the district court, the jury must be informed, at a minimum, that the substitutions are what the witnesses would say if called to testify; that the substitutions are derived from statements obtained under conditions that provide circumstantial guarantees of reliability; that the substitutions contain statements obtained over the course of weeks or months; that members of the prosecution team have contributed to [Redacted] the witnesses; and, if applicable, that Moussaoui has [Redacted] to the witnesses.

. . .

b. CIPA

On rehearing, both parties acknowledged our holding that CIPA does not apply here but indicated their belief that once the district court has approved substitutions for the witnesses' testimony, CIPA comes into play, with the result that the Government may object to the disclosure of the classified information in the substitutions and request that the district court adopt an alternative form of evidence. We disagree.

It must be remembered that the substitution process we here order is a replacement for the testimony of the enemy combatant witnesses. Because the Government will not allow Moussaoui to have contact with the witnesses, we must provide a remedy adequate to protect Moussaoui's constitutional rights. Here, that remedy is substitutions. Once Moussaoui has selected the portions of the [Redacted] summaries he wishes to submit to the jury and the Government has been given an opportunity to be heard, the district court will compile the substitutions, using such additional language as may be necessary to aid the understanding of the jury. Once this process is complete, the matter is at an end—there are to be no additional or supplementary proceedings under CIPA regarding the substitutions.

VI.

In summary, the judgment of the court is as follows. The January 30 and August 29 orders are affirmed, as is the rejection of the Government's proposed substitutions by the district court. The order imposing sanctions on the Government is vacated, and the case is remanded for the compiling of substitutions for the deposition testimony of the enemy combatant witnesses.

QUESTIONS AND NOTES

1. Note how much material is redacted from the Moussaoui. At certain points, the redactions make portions of the opinion incomprehensible. Is there any solution to this problem? On the face of it, do some of the redactions also seem rather odd because they appear to redact material the content of which seems to be obvious. What concerns, if any, should we have about significant redactions in published appellate opinions?

2. In Abu Ali, supra, p. 481, in connection with the introduction of the substitutions, the court found a violation of the confrontation clause. Is there a confrontation issue in regard to the substitutions in the Moussaoui case? Is there a hearsay problem in Moussaoui?

3. For a characterization of the substitutions and a discussion of the legal implications of the *Moussaoui* opinion in the principal case, see Norman Abrams, Confrontation/Hearsay and Compulsory Process Issues in Post–Gitmo Federal Court Terrorism Prosecutions: Moussaoui and Paracha as Harbingers, 75 *Brooklyn L.Rev.* 1067 (2010):

> The substitutions approved in principal by the court had unique features. They were summaries, but of what? The witnesses were not subjected to depositions. Rather 1) detailed *statements* from the putative three witnesses [hereinafter declarants], labeled by the court as A, B and C, had been obtained, apparently through interrogation, by government agents seeking intelligence that could be used in preventing future terrorist actions and apprehending other terrorists. . . .

> The statements thus obtained from A, B, and C had then been "recorded" in "highly classified" 2) *reports* which had been prepared for "use in the military and intelligence communities; they were not prepared with this litigation in mind."

> Portions of the reports were then "excerpted and set forth in documents prepared for purposes of this litigation" which were labelled 3) *summaries*. The summaries were provided to defense counsel. 4) Finally, the *substitutions* to be offered into evidence were prepared from the summaries. These consisted of the summaries of statements that had been obtained over the course of several months but were not identical to the summaries since in preparing the substitutions, the government had reorganized the information.

> It is apparent from the foregoing that there are multiple levels of hearsay involved in the substitutions that were being considered by the court, with A, B, and C being the declarants at level 1), supra, and the

declarants involved in levels 2–4 being unknown government agents or employees.

4. On what grounds did the Moussaoui court conclude that the substitutions in the case were reliable? Are there any flaws in the court's reasoning?

5. As decided in the Moussaoui opinion, reproduced above, the Fourth Circuit remanded so that the district court, working with the parties, could revise the substitutions in lieu of requiring that the enemy combatant witnesses be produced. After the Supreme Court denied certiorari, Moussaoui pled guilty, apparently ending the case. Later, however, he moved to withdraw his plea of guilty. See United States v. Moussaoui, 591 F.3d 263 (4th Cir. 2010) where the fourth circuit reaffirmed the details of its earlier opinion. Further, the apparent effect of the earlier guilty plea had been to cut short the process of revising the substitutions. However, it turns out that the revision of the substitutions, in fact, took place. Thus in the 2010 Moussaoui circuit opinion, the court stated in footnote 18:

> 18 Finally, we note that the CIPA process actually continued after the guilty plea in preparation for the sentencing proceeding, and the exculpatory, classified information was made available for Moussaoui's use in an appropriate form. Moussaoui thereafter testified, confirmed his guilt to the offenses as charged, and *contradicted* the supposed exculpatory statements of the ECWs as they related to his intended participation in the 9/11 strikes. . . .

The adequacy of the substitutions thus prepared by the district court was not, however, subjected to any further appellate review (other than the appellate court's statement, "was made available for Moussaoui's use in an appropriate form," supra). The Fourth Circuit did not otherwise address the adequacy of the final version of the substitutions prepared by the district court, given Moussaoui's guilty plea, nor was further review of the case sought in the Supreme Court.

6. A district court in New York followed and used essentially Moussaoui-type instructions in a similar context as the approach in the principal case, See United States v. Paracha, 2006 WL 12768 (S.D.N.Y. 2006). The United States Court of Appeals for the Second Circuit then affirmed Paracha's conviction in an unpublished opinion, United States v. Paracha, 2008 WL 2477392, which contains the following paragraph:

> Paracha contends that his Sixth Amendment rights to compulsory process and confrontation of witnesses were violated by the government's discussion in summation of declassified summaries of interviews with witnesses not present at trial. We disagree. The government did not exceed the boundaries of the district court's limiting instructions—as the district court found, the government's reference to the summaries during its summation was not inculpatory but rather made for the purpose of trying to persuade the jury that, were the statements to be believed, they did not undermine the government's case—and Paracha waived any claim that his right to compulsory process was violated by the court's "compromise" solution of allowing the defense to introduce the summaries in lieu of live testimony.

F.   SECURITY CLEARANCE FOR COUNSEL

QUESTIONS AND NOTES

1. No express language in CIPA indicates that defense counsel are required to obtain security clearance, nor that if they wish to gain access to classified materials relating to the case at hand that they can request that they be permitted to go through security clearance. However, as the materials in this section indicate, the use of security clearance for counsel has become an almost ever-present occurrence in terrorism prosecutions.

2. What provisions of CIPA, if any, address the issue of security clearance? See section 9 of the Act, supra, pursuant to which the Chief Justice issued the following rules:

SECURITY PROCEDURES ESTABLISHED PURSUANT TO PUB.L. 96–456, 94 STAT. 2025, BY THE CHIEF JUSTICE OF THE UNITED STATES FOR THE PROTECTION OF CLASSIFIED INFORMATION

1. Purpose. The purpose of these procedures is to meet the requirements of Section 9(a) of the Classified Information Procedures Act of 1980, Pub.L. 96–456, 94 Stat. 2025, which in pertinent part provides that:

"... [T]he Chief Justice of the United States, in consultation with the Attorney General, the Director of Central Intelligence, and the Secretary of Defense, shall prescribe rules establishing procedures for the protection against unauthorized disclosure of any classified information in the custody of the United States district courts, courts of appeal, or Supreme Court...."

These procedures apply in all proceedings in criminal cases involving classified information, and appeals therefrom, before the United States district courts, the courts of appeal and the Supreme Court.

2. Court Security Officer. In any proceeding in a criminal case or appeal therefrom in which classified information is within, or reasonably expected to be within, the custody of the court, the court shall designate a court security officer. The Attorney General or the Department of Justice Security Officer, with the concurrence of the head of the agency or agencies from which the classified information originates, or their representatives, shall recommend to the court persons qualified to serve as court security officer. The court security officer shall be selected from among those persons so recommended.

The court security officer shall be an individual with demonstrated competence in security matters, and shall, prior to designation, have been certified to the court in writing by the Department of Justice Security Officer as cleared for the level and category of classified information that will be involved. The court security officer may be an employee of the Executive Branch of the Government detailed to the court for this purpose. One or more alternate court security officers, who have been recommended and cleared in the manner specified above, may be designated by the court as required. The court security officer shall be responsible to the court for document, physical, personnel and communications security, and shall take measures reasonably necessary to fulfill these responsibilities. The court security officer shall notify the court and the Department of Justice Security Officer of any actual, attempted, or potential violation of security procedures.

3. Secure Quarters. Any in camera proceeding—including a pretrial conference, motion hearing, or appellate hearing—concerning the use, relevance, or admissibility of classified information, shall be held in secure quarters recommended by the court security officer and approved by the court.

The secure quarters shall be located within the Federal courthouse, unless it is determined that none of the quarters available in the courthouse meets, or can reasonably be made equivalent to, security requirements of the Executive Branch applicable to the level and category of classified information involved. In that event, the court shall designate the facilities of another United States Government agency, recommended by the court security officer, which is located within the vicinity of the courthouse, as the site of the proceedings.

The court security officer shall make necessary arrangements to ensure that the applicable Executive Branch standards are met and shall conduct or arrange for such inspection of the quarters as may be necessary. The court security officer shall, in consultation with the United States Marshal, arrange for the installation of security devices and take such other measures as may be necessary to protect against any unauthorized access to classified information. All of the aforementioned activity shall be conducted in a manner which does not interfere with the orderly proceedings of the court. Prior to any hearing or other proceeding, the court security officer shall certify in writing to the court that the quarters are secure.

4. Personnel Security—Court Personnel. No person appointed by the court or designated for service therein shall be given access to any classified information in the custody of the court, unless such person has received a security clearance as provided herein and unless access to such information is necessary for the performance of an official function. A security clearance for justices and judges is not required, but such clearance shall be provided upon the request of any judicial officer who desires to be cleared.

The court shall inform the court security officer or the attorney for the government of the names of court personnel who may require access to classified information. That person shall then notify the Department of Justice Security Officer, who shall promptly make arrangements to obtain any necessary security clearances and shall approve such clearances under standards of the Executive Branch applicable to the level and category of classified information involved. The Department of Justice Security Officer shall advise the court in writing when the necessary security clearances have been obtained.

If security clearances cannot be obtained promptly, personnel in the Executive Branch having the necessary clearances may be temporarily assigned to assist the court. If a proceeding is required to be recorded and an official court reporter having the necessary security clearance is unavailable, the court may request the court security officer or the attorney for the government to have a cleared reporter from the Executive Branch designated to act as reporter in the proceedings. The reporter so designated shall take the oath of office as prescribed by 28 U.S.C. § 753(a).

Justices, judges and cleared court personnel shall not disclose classified information to anyone who does not have a security clearance and who does not require the information in the discharge of an official function. However, nothing contained in these procedures shall preclude a judge from discharging his official duties, including giving appropriate instructions to the jury. Any problem of security involving court personnel or persons acting for the court shall be referred to the court for appropriate action.

5. Persons Acting for the Defendant. The government may obtain information by any lawful means concerning the trustworthiness of persons associated with the defense and may bring such information to the attention of the court for the court's consideration in framing an appropriate protective order pursuant to Section 3 of the Act.

6. Jury. Nothing contained in these procedures shall be construed to require an investigation or security clearance of the members of the jury or interfere with the functions of a jury, including access to classified information introduced as evidence in the trial of a case.

After a verdict has been rendered by a jury, the trial judge should consider a government request for a cautionary instruction to jurors regarding the release or disclosure of classified information contained in documents they have reviewed during the trial.

UNITED STATES v. BIN LADEN

58 F.Supp.2d 113 (S.D.N.Y. 1999)

SAND, DISTRICT JUDGE.

The sixth superseding indictment in this case charges fifteen Defendants with numerous crimes arising from, among other things, the August 1998 bombings of the United States' embassies in Nairobi, Kenya, and Dar es Salaam, Tanzania, as well with subsequent attempts to hinder the investigation into those crimes. Five of the Defendants are presently in the custody of the Bureau of Prisons: Mamdouh Mahmud Salim, Ali Mohamed ("Mohamed"), Wadih El Hage ("El Hage"), Mohamed Sadeek Odeh ("Odeh"), and Mohamed Rashed Daoud Al–Owhali.

The Government has asked that the Court file a protective order containing the following language:

5. No defendant, counsel for a defendant, employee of counsel for a defendant, defense witness, or Courtroom personnel required by

the Court for its assistance, shall have access to any classified information involved in this case unless that person shall first have:

(a) received approval from either the Government or the Court for access to the particular classified information in question . . .; and

(b) . . . agree[d] to comply with the term[s] of this Order.

6. For the purpose of establishing security clearances necessary for access to classified information that may be involved in the pretrial preparation or trial or appeal of this case, Standard Form 86, "Questionnaire for National Security Positions," attached releases, and full fingerprints shall be completed and submitted to the CSO forthwith by all defense counsel, persons whose assistance the defense reasonably requires and by such [C]ourtroom personnel as the Court requires for its assistance.

The Department of Justice ("DOJ") regulations governing the clearance application process contain the following provisions:

(b) Eligibility for access to classified information is limited to United States citizens for whom an appropriate investigation of their personal and professional history affirmatively indicated loyalty to the United States, strength of character, trustworthiness, honesty, reliability, discretion, and sound judgment, as well as freedom from conflicting allegiances and potential for coercion, and willingness and ability to abide by regulations governing the use, handling, and protection of classified information. . . .

(c) The Department of Justice does not discriminate on the basis of race, color, religion, sex, national origin, disability, or sexual orientation in granting access to classified information. However, the Department may investigate and consider any matter that relates to the determination of whether access is clearly consistent with the interests of national security. No negative inferences concerning the standards for access may be raised solely on the basis of the sexual orientation of the employee or mental health counseling.

28 C.F.R. § 17.41 (1998).

The proposed security clearance procedure would be supervised by a Court-appointed Court Security Officer ("CSO") who (1) "would serve as an officer of this [C]ourt in implementing and enforcing the terms of the proposed protective order" and (2) would "not be a member of the prosecution team in this case."

The Government has also indicated that the CSO would be required to maintain the confidentiality of materials relating to any clearance application and that the DOJ's recommendation with respect to any such application would be furnished only to the Court and the particular applicant. The regulations governing the clearance procedures provide for appeal within DOJ, *see* Exec.Order No. 12968, 60 Fed.Reg. 40,245, at Part 5 (1995), and any applicant who received an adverse recommendation could ultimately raise *ex parte* objections with the Court, which would be the final arbiter of all clearance questions. *See generally United States v. Musa,* 833 F.Supp. 752, 755–57 (E.D.Mo.1993) (providing a detailed description of procedures used in a case involving classified information, albeit one in which the Government did not request clearance of counsel).

Defendant Odeh filed a motion objecting to the proposed protective order insofar as it requires his counsel to obtain clearance before viewing classified information. Defendants Mohamed and El Hage subsequently joined this motion at oral argument. The Moving Defendants argue that the Court lacks the authority to require clearance of counsel and that, even if the Court were to possess such authority, exercising it would violate their Sixth Amendment rights. At oral argument on June 22, 1999, counsel for Defendant Odeh moved to intervene in the proceedings for the limited purposes of asserting defense counsel's independent constitutional rights on this issue

We begin with three basic propositions. First, pursuant to Federal Rule of Criminal Procedure 16(d)(1), which governs the use of protective orders with respect to discovery in criminal cases, the Court "may at any time order that the discovery or inspection be denied, restricted, or deferred, or make such other order as is appropriate."

Second, pursuant to Section 3 of the Classified Information Procedures Act ("CIPA"), Pub.L. No. 96–456, 94 Stat. 2025 (1980), codified at 18 U.S.C. app. 3 § 3, the Court has the authority to "issue an order to protect against the disclosure of any classified information disclosed by the United States to any defendant in any criminal case in a district court of the United States."

Third, pursuant to Security Procedures Chief Justice Burger promulgated under Section 9 of CIPA, "[t]he government may obtain information by any lawful means concerning the trustworthiness of persons associated with the defense and may bring such information to the attention of the court for the court's consideration in framing an appropriate protective order pursuant to Section 3 of the Act."

The Court is therefore empowered to take information regarding the background of Defense counsel in this case, gleaned from an investigation conducted by the United States Attorney's Office, and consider that information in framing a protective order that attempts to prevent disclosure of confidential information. The Moving Defendants have argued, however, that the rules do not allow the Court to direct Defense counsel to participate in any clearance process and, in addition, that use of such a compulsory procedure would be both unconstitutional and undesirable.

We are therefore presented with three questions. (1) Do the rules governing cases involving classified information permit the Court to direct counsel to apply for security clearance? (2) Is it constitutional to require counsel to utilize a process in which DOJ makes an initial recommendation as to clearance applications but that leaves final authority to resolve all clearance matters with the Court? (3) If use of this procedure is in fact permissible, should the Court direct counsel for the Moving Defendants to submit to it or, in the alternative, should the Court allow counsel to "opt out" and therefore force the United States Attorney's Office to conduct its own investigation into each attorney's background and to furnish that background information to the Court, pursuant to Section 5 of the Chief Justice's Security Procedures? There is a remarkable paucity of case law addressing these questions and they certainly appear to be matters of first impression within this Circuit.

The Moving Defendants argue that the legislative history of CIPA and the circumstances surrounding Chief Justice Burger's promulgation of the Security Procedures create an inference that neither Congress nor the Chief Justice vested the Court with the authority to compel Defense counsel to undergo a DOJ-initiated security clearance procedure. We think the sounder reading of the available material indicates that although neither Congress nor the Chief Justice sought to impose a mandatory clearance requirement in all cases involving classified information, they did not attempt to foreclose resort to such a requirement in all circumstances.

CIPA and the accompanying Security Procedures create a system by which the trial court has wide latitude to impose reasonable restrictions likely to prevent the unauthorized disclosure of classified information. *See, e.g.,* S.Rep. 96–823 (1980), *reprint in* 1980 U.S.C.C.A.N. 4294 ("The details of each [protective] order are fashioned by the trial judge according to the circumstances of the particular case" ... and "under what conditions the materials may be reviewed")....

The text and structure of both CIPA and the Security Procedures therefore create a presumption that the Court possesses the authority to require Defense counsel to seek security clearance before the Court will provide them with access to classified materials. Even conceding that the history surrounding enactment of these provisions is at times murky, there is simply little to support the contention that Congress or the Chief Justice acted to *prohibit* the courts from utilizing a clearance requirement in every circumstance....

We recognize that this position may appear to be at odds with the result in *United States v. Jolliff,* 548 F.Supp. 232 (D.Md.1981), which stated that "Section 5 [of CIPA] does not provide the Court with authority to make submission to a security clearance requirement a prerequisite to representation of a defendant in a case involving classified information." *Id.* at 233....

The Government distinguishes ... [this case] on the ground that.... [this analysis is] limited to Section 5 of CIPA and make[s] no reference to Section 3. We find the Government's reading ... persuasive. We also note that the relevant clause from *Jolliff* may well be *obiter dictum* as the Government apparently did not request clearance in that case.

Even if we were to read *Jolliff* ... as holding that CIPA does not permit any clearance requirement, however, we would depart from their analyses. We simply see no indication that Congress or the Chief Justice aimed to preclude resort to compulsory clearance of counsel in all circumstances. To the contrary, both CIPA and the Security Procedures consistently leave the most sensitive questions surrounding classified information to be resolved in the sound discretion of the District Courts. We therefore conclude that our authority under the Federal Rules of Criminal Procedure, CIPA, and the Chief Justice's Security Procedures encompasses a power to require counsel to seek security clearance.

We must also evaluate whether it is consistent with the Federal Constitution to impose a clearance requirement on Defense counsel in this case. The Moving Defendants have asserted that imposition of a mandatory DOJ-initiated clearance procedure violates their rights under the Sixth Amendment. Our starting point must be the Supreme Court's conclusion that the Sixth Amendment does not promise a defendant his choice of counsel but rather aims to guarantee that each criminal defendant receives an effective advocate.

In essence, the Moving Defendants' argument boils down to the claim that any DOJ-initiated security clearance procedure necessarily vests the Government with veto power over the Moving Defendants' choice of counsel and that the philosophy behind such a system is fundamentally inimical to the adversarial process. Although we agree that it would be flatly unconstitutional to grant the Government an unfettered ability to remove any Defendant's counsel, the facts of this case are a great distance from the parade of horribles raised by the Moving Defendants.

First, the facts do not indicate that the Government unduly delayed before requesting this procedure, such as might allow for an inference that the Government's true motivation was to harass or otherwise interfere with the Moving Defendants' pretrial preparations. The Moving Defendants argue forcefully that the Government erred by failing to advise counsel prior to appointment, or immediately thereafter, of the likely need to seek clearance. We do not believe that the Government's conduct gives rise to a concern that the clearance requirement is designed to interfere with any counsel's ability to meaningfully represent his client.

On November 3, 1998, at the parties' first meeting, the Government advised Defense counsel "of the realistic probability that there would be classified information in the case, and that prudence dictated that they obtain security clearances to be permitted to receive such information." Two days later, the Government submitted a letter to the Court, which was also sent to counsel for each of the Defendants, summarizing the substance of this meeting. This letter contains the following passage:

> The Government advised defense counsel that it is anticipated that during the litigation and trial of this matter the Government and defense counsel will have to deal with classified material in some manner.... The Government also suggested that while it is too early to have a specific conversation about how classified information may become pertinent to the litigation of this case, defense counsel may

wish to apply (through the FBI) for security clearances which take some time to obtain.... [T]he Government will do whatever it can to assist in the expedited processing of security clearances for any defense counsel (or staff of the Court) seeking to obtain clearances. Given that past experience has shown that CIPA litigation can be time-consuming, it is respectfully suggested that any defense counsel who intend to seek a clearance do so promptly to avoid delay down the road when the issues crystallize.

. . .

We believe that the Government's notifications to counsel were sufficiently prompt to eliminate any inference of purposeful delay. The Moving Defendants assert that their counsel had already invested significant time in the case by the November 3 meeting, but the litigation was plainly in its infancy at that time and we see no reason to believe that the Government's request was aimed to disrupt established relationships between counsel and their clients.

In sum, the magnitude of the Government's investigation, the limited work Defense counsel had yet performed on behalf of their clients, and the fact that the Government advised Defense counsel about the need for clearance at the parties' first face-to-face meeting in early November, all serve to eliminate any inference that the Government purposefully delayed in requesting clearances to force a change of counsel mid-stream or for the purpose of harassment. We are simply not faced with a situation in which an eleventh hour request appears designed to disrupt counsels' preparations or to drive them from this litigation.

Second, we think the Moving Defendants overstate the danger that one of their attorneys might be arbitrarily dismissed at the behest of the prosecution. The CSO will be an officer of the Court, rather than a member of the prosecution, and will be prohibited from sharing *any* information regarding clearance applications, including their outcomes, with members of the prosecution.

Further, in the unlikely event that DOJ officials recommend that the Court deny any counsel's application for clearance, this result would be appealable both within the DOJ as well as directly to the Court. The Court will of course remain the ultimate arbiter of disputes surrounding the security clearance applications and will be available to insure both proper respect for counsels' confidentiality and that no applications are denied for improper reasons. *See, e.g., United States v. Musa,* 833 F.Supp. 752, 756–57 (E.D.Mo.1993) (stating that if "the CSO should determine that any person should not obtain a security clearance," the Court will "conduct an *ex parte* hearing to determine" that person's eligibility to see classified materials, that "[o]nly the CSO and defense counsel will be heard on this issue," and that "the prosecution will not be notified of the hearing or allowed to participate in it"). Although we recognize the Moving Defendants' concern that the Government not be given the unfettered power to disqualify their present counsel, we think the procedures governing the clearance process, when combined with the Court's vigilance in responding to questions of potential abuse in the application process, will be sufficient to protect the Moving Defendants' rights.

The exceptional facts of this case decidedly warrant some inquiry into counsels' backgrounds to minimize the risk of the unauthorized disclosure of classified information. Counsel for the Moving Defendants conceded as much at oral argument. We note that the exceptional facts alleged in the indictment also require clearance of Court personnel and members of the Government who will come into contact with classified information. The circumstances precipitating CIPA's enactment make it abundantly clear that it is easier and more effective to prevent the release of classified information in advance than to attempt to undo the damage of unauthorized disclosures after the fact.

. . .

The concerns are heightened in this case because the Government's investigation is ongoing, which increases the possibility that unauthorized disclosures might place additional lives in danger. In addition, the Government has alleged that the Defendants are part of a conspiracy whose members have previously gained access to unfiled court documents and forwarded those documents to other members of the conspiracy. The case therefore involves special circumstances warranting particular control over the flow of classified information, such as have already prompted the Court to impose restrictive conditions of confinement on the Defendants and which formed the basis of the protective order that the Court entered in December 1998.

Our insistence that every person who comes into contact with classified information in this litigation undergo some objective evaluation is, of course, no commentary on the reputations of the Defense counsel in this case. The fact remains that it is practically impossible to remedy the damage of an unauthorized disclosure *ex post* and we refuse to await the possibility of repairing what in this case might be a particularly disastrous security breach when reasonable measures could have prevented the disclosure altogether. We believe it is appropriate to require some form of clearance on the facts we have before us.

Having concluded that a clearance requirement is warranted, we must decide whether to utilize the DOJ-initiated clearance procedure or the alternative course discussed previously, by which the United States Attorney's Office would investigate counsel for the Moving Defendants and advise the Court of the results. The issue therefore is not "whether?" but "by whom?" the inquiry will be conducted. The Government suggests that it be done initially by the CSO, without involvement by the prosecution.[2]

---

2. The parties dispute the significance of the court's actions in another classified information case in the Eastern District of New York, *United States v. Pappas,* which are apparently unreported save for a Second Circuit decision that does not address the issues that presently concern us. *See* 94 F.3d 795 (2d Cir.1996). In *Pappas,* all defense counsel apparently sought clearance but the CSO expressed concern about one application. The Court thereafter entered a modified protective order granting that counsel access to at least some of the materials, albeit on

Counsel for one of the Moving Defendants has suggested that it be conducted by the United States Attorney's Office without counsels' cooperation and with a report to be made in the first instance to the Court.

Aside from the Moving Defendants' philosophical objection to the DOJ-initiated procedure on the ground that it requires their counsel to participate actively in certain phases of the review, we see not a single advantage to any investigation conducted by the United States Attorney's Office. Such an inquiry would certainly be more time-consuming and expensive than the DOJ-initiated procedure and would, in all likelihood, prove more intrusive and fundamentally inconsistent with the adversarial process.

Moreover, given that it presently takes DOJ more than two months to process clearance applications, we can only surmise how long it would take the United States Attorney's Office, which does not have the same expertise in that particular area, to conduct an equally probing investigation without the underlying individual's consent. It is inescapable that such a system would require a far lengthier investigation, during which time counsel for the Moving Defendants would of course be precluded from viewing classified information.

In addition, this approach would force the Court to make clearance determinations in the first instance without the reasoned judgment of the Department of Justice, the agency with the greatest expertise in this area. We find it entirely preferable to allow experts in clearance matters—who will be bound by strict rules of confidentiality—to consider each counsel's application initially rather than to resort to a system whereby the Court and the United States Attorney's Office are forced to act as amateur sleuths. In the likely event that counsels' clearance applications are unremarkable, the DOJ-initiated procedure offers the very real possibility that the fewest possible individuals will learn anything whatsoever about counsels' backgrounds.

Given the nature of the potential classified information and the special circumstances surrounding this case, we conclude that counsel must submit to the DOJ-initiated security clearance procedure should they wish to have access to classified information. Accordingly, the Moving Defendants' motion is denied.

The request to intervene by counsel for Defendant Odeh is sparsely briefed on both sides. Defendant Odeh's original brief only alluded to counsel's personal rights and counsel made no formal request to intervene until oral argument, after all briefs had been filed. Our research has not revealed any reported case, either from within this Circuit or elsewhere, in which a court entertained a request similar to that proffered by counsel to Defendant Odeh.

a restricted basis. In the event that similar circumstances arise here, the Court will consider entering an amended protective order. Until that time, however, Defense counsel who wish to have access to classified information must seek clearance.

Here, by contrast, counsel has asserted his own privacy rights. The Supreme Court has referred to two analytically distinct privacy interests: "[o]ne is the individual interest in avoiding disclosure of personal matters, and another is the interest in independence in making certain kinds of important decisions." *Whalen v. Roe,* 429 U.S. 589, 599–600, 97 S.Ct. 869, 51 L.Ed.2d 64 (1977) (footnote omitted). The former right, which the Second Circuit has characterized "as a right to 'confidentiality,' " *Doe v. City of New York,* 15 F.3d 264, 267 (2d Cir.1994), is implicated here because counsel objects to being required to disclose private information. We therefore do not quarrel with counsel's assertion that, if permitted to intervene, he could assert some valid interest in not being forced to reveal certain personal information.

The presence of a valid interest, however, does not terminate our inquiry. *See, e.g., Nixon v. Administrator of Gen. Servs.,* 433 U.S. 425, 458, 97 S.Ct. 2777, 53 L.Ed.2d 867 (1977). The Second Circuit has explained that claims for violation of a privacy right, such as that asserted by counsel, should be examined using intermediate scrutiny. *See Barry v. City of New York,* 712 F.2d 1554, 1559 (2d Cir.1983). Under this level of review, the Court balances the competing interests of counsel and the Government and must uphold the policy if it is "substantially related to an important governmental objective," *Clark v. Jeter,* 486 U.S. 456, 461, 108 S.Ct. 1910, 100 L.Ed.2d 465 (1988), or, in Second Circuit parlance, if the policy "is designed to further a substantial governmental interest and does not land very wide of any reasonable mark in making its classifications."

Here, there is plainly a substantial governmental objective in guarding against the unauthorized disclosure of classified information, this interest manifestly outweighs counsel's desire not to disclose personal information needed to conduct a thorough background check, and the clearance procedure presents a reasonable method for effecting the Government's legitimate goals.

Counsel has simply provided no authority, and we are aware of none, that would sustain his objections with respect to the clearance procedure. Any faithful balancing of the relevant interests must end with the conclusion that counsel's own privacy rights are outweighed by the Government's right to protect highly classified information, the unauthorized disclosure of which could cause irreparable harm to our national security. Accordingly, counsel's motion to intervene is denied.

QUESTIONS AND NOTES

1.   United States v. Al–Arian, 267 F. Supp.2d 1258 (M.D. Fla. 2003):

At the status conference, co-counsel for Al–Arian contended that this Court would violate their constitutional rights to privacy if it required them to submit forms and obtain a security clearance as part of their representation of Al–Arian. As an initial matter, this Court would note that the government has indicated in nearly every hearing since this case began that a majority of the telephone recordings were classified. Moreover, the government, the magistrate judge presiding over this case, and even this Court have repeatedly told defense counsel that they should go ahead and apply for security clearances to prevent delay of this case. Al–Arian's counsel never raised an objection nor a concern about obtaining a security clearance.[21] Now three months after their appointment, for the first time, they raise this issue.

This Court does not dispute that counsel will disclose personal matters as a result of completing the security clearance packet and the subsequent investigation.[22] This Court does not take issue with counsel's assertion that they have a privacy interest in avoiding disclosure of personal matters

The Eleventh Circuit and the former Fifth Circuit have held, however, that the fact that a privacy interest is implicated does not end the inquiry. Instead, these courts have held that the constitutional right to confidentiality is overcome if the government has a legitimate interest that outweighs the individual's privacy interest.

In this case, counsel's right to confidentiality is weighed against the United States' interest in protecting classified information. This Court cannot think of a more compelling or substantial interest that the United States possesses than protection of classified information. The Supreme Court of the United States has stated that without adequate procedures to protect classified information the United States will suffer irreparable harm without the ability to seek redress. See Snepp v. United States, 444 U.S. 507, 512–15, 100 S.Ct. 763, 62 L.Ed.2d 704 (1980) (per curiam). Requiring lawyers and their staffs to submit to a security clearance procedure to protect classified information outweighs an individual's privacy interest. Most recently, the Southern District of New York similarly concluded, applying a higher standard (intermediate scrutiny), that the government's interest in protecting classified information substantially outweighed a defense counsel's privacy interest. Bin Laden, 58 F. Supp. 2d at 123. Accordingly, this Court compels all defense counsel to submit security clearance packets to the appropriate authority within thirty (30) days.

2. United States v. Abdi, 498 F.Supp.2d 1048 (S.D.Ohio 2007):

Defendant moves to exclude all prejudicial discovery and motions filed pursuant to the Classified Information Procedure Act ("CIPA") or to compel discovery regarding these materials. . . .

Defendant objects to the "secretive procedures" under CIPA which allow the Government to file certain motions and evidence under seal, citing law review articles as the basis of his authority. The constitutional-

21. Indeed, if co-counsel felt so strongly about obtaining a security clearance, one has to wonder why they would accept the court appointment to this case. It should have been obvious to counsel that a security clearance was likely to be required and they should have refused appointment.

22. This Court would note for the record that it is requiring its whole staff to undergo this procedure also.

ity of CIPA has been upheld by every court that has considered the issue. *See, e.g., United States v. Wilson*, 750 F.2d 7, 9 (2d Cir. 1984); *United States v. Wilson*, 721 F.2d 967, 976 (4th Cir. 1983); *United States v. Collins*, 720 F.2d 1195, 1200 (11th Cir. 1983). The Government, however, is required to share the information and documents filed pursuant to CIPA with defense counsel, as long as he obtains the necessary security clearance. There is ample precedent supporting the position that defense counsel must obtain security clearance if he wishes to view classified CIPA materials. *See* 18 U.S.C. App. 3 Sec. 9., *United States v. Al–Arian*, 267 F. Supp. 2d 1258, 1266 (M.D. Fla. 2003); *United States v. Bin Laden*, 58 F. Supp. 2d 113, 118 (S.D.N.Y. 1999). Defense counsel retorts that the requirement that he undergo a security clearance in order to view CIPA-filed information violates his right to privacy. Several courts have held that a defense counsel's right to privacy is trumped by the Government's need to protect classified information for the safety of the country. *See, e.g., Al–Arian*, 267 F. Supp. 2d 1258, 1266 (M.D. Fla. 2003) In a case of this magnitude, the intrusion on defense counsel's private affairs is minimal in comparison to the national security issues implicated in this case. Thus, Defendant's Motions to Exclude CIPA material is DENIED. If defense counsel wishes to view the CIPA materials, he must submit to an FBI background check as required under CIPA.

3. See United States v. Oakley, 2007 WL 4118298 (E.D. Tenn. 2007): The court ruled that a proposed protective order agreed to by the parties neither adequately protected the government's interest in protecting classified information or the defendant's right to a fair trial. In order to give a defense counsel access to the classified information and rather than order defense counsel to seek security clearance, the court appointed a Federal Community Defender to act as cleared counsel for defendant.

4. Do the foregoing cases, Bin Laden, Al–Arian, Abdi, and Oakley indicate that CIPA has been effectively amended de facto by adding to the several alternatives provided in the statute for dealing with classified information (summaries, stipulations, etc.) the alternative of requiring counsel to obtain security clearance? See also United States v. Abujihaad, infra, where the district judge expressly presents the security clearance option as one of those to be considered alongside of the others expressly provided for in the CIPA statute. If security clearance is in fact just another option to be considered under the CIPA statute, what additional issues are raised as a result? Consider, for example, the implications of the material in the notes that follow.

5. Is there a potential for abuse in authorizing courts to require defense counsel to obtain security clearance? Compare the courts' treatment of the potential for abuse issue with the following excerpt from Brian Z. Tamanaha, op cit supra note 5, p. 480, at 288:

> Several defense counsel have balked at the security clearance requirement, contending that it is interfering with the Sixth Amendment right to counsel, the right to a fair trial and due process. The few defense counsel who have challenged this requirement by refusing to undergo a

clearance were either not provided with any classified information or were warned that other counsel might have to be retained.

The greatest danger of this de facto clearance requirement is that it gives the Department of Justice the ability to control who will work on classified matters for the defense. To eliminate a particularly troublesome opponent, the Justice Department may deny a security clearance to a specific attorney, investigator, or expert witness retained by the defendant, who needs access to classified information to be effective. The defendant must then either proceed to trial with incomplete access to the necessary information, or retain assistance more palatable to the Department of Justice and the intelligence agency involved.

The potential for abuse in this situation is troubling regardless of whether the prosecution does in fact deliberately use this power to its advantage. The appearance of impropriety created by giving the Justice Department veto power over who will aid its opponent is reason enough to halt this policy.

6.   Elllen C. Yaroshefsky, The Slow Erosion of the Adversary System: Article III Courts, FISA, CIPA and Ethical Dilemmas, 5 Cardozo Pub. L. Pol'y & Ethics J. 203, 216–217 (2006):

A second and critical ethical dilemma is that even in cases where classified information is disclosed to the defense counsel, it is prohibited from sharing the information with its client who does not have security clearance to review the materials.

As a prominent criminal defense lawyer said:

Instead, in this situation the client has no idea what the classified information is, but counsel cannot share it with him ... So how do you know what is relevant and what is not relevant? How do you know what is good to introduce into evidence and what is bad to introduce into evidence ...?

. . .

How do you prepare your client to testify when you have fifteen months of wire taps related to your client that are off limits to him?

Without the ability to utilize the information, counsel often cannot conduct an adequate investigation and prepare a defense. Significantly, the preparation of the defendant's potential testimony is severely hampered when counsel can only confront the evidence against him selectively. There is no simple resolution of this ethical dilemma. Perhaps, the only viable result of the appropriate balancing of the defendant's constitutional rights against the government's national security concerns may be to provide access to the information to a security-cleared defense counsel who is not permitted to share the information with his client. Most attorneys would rather have access to the information to defend the case and grapple with non-disclosure in lieu of not having the information.

The third significant problem is summary evidence. Even in cases where the defense lawyer has high-level security clearance, the lawyer may have to accept summaries or substituted statements with relevant facts in lieu of the actual information in the classified documents. Such substitutions not only deprive the defendant of the particulars of the documents in question but also prohibit the lawyers from utilizing the underlying facts to develop further exculpatory information. Second, summary evidence deprives the defendant of the right of confrontation, which guarantees not merely the formal opportunity to cross-examine but the opportunity for effective cross examination. It is " 'critical for ensuring the integrity of the fact-finding process' and 'is the principal means by which the believability of a witness and the truth of his testimony are tested.' " If we continue to believe that cross-examination is the engine that drives the trial, depriving a defendant of such a possibility must only occur in the most particularized circumstances of demonstrated need for secrecy where the defense lawyer has participated in the process of making that determination. While Congress urged judges to ensure that admissions and summaries were crafted so that the government obtained no unfair advantage, the practice of "substitutions and stipulations" can significantly alter the adversary process. They are "powerful weapons for the prosecution with a high potential for abuse."

7. The prosecution of Zacarias Moussaoui also presented a variant on the theme of defense counsel obtaining security clearance, being given access to classified information, but not being able to share it with the client-defendant. Moussaoui represented himself, with standby counsel to assist him. Should a defendant who represents himself be given access to classified information? In permitting Moussaoui to represent himself, the judge made clear to him that he would not be given access to classified information. See CNN report, Moussaoui Denied Access to Classified Papers, August 24, 2002, posted 2:48 p.m. EDT. Two kinds of problems are created by situations in which the defendant represents himself. The first is that the government in normal course will provide the defendant with numerous documents, and mistakes can be made. That is exactly what happened in the Moussaoui case. By accident, among the documents he was given were classified documents, which government agents then had to retrieve. See USA Today, Associate Press dispatch, Government Gives Moussaoui Classified Documents by Accident, September 24, 2002, updated 10:03 a.m. ET. The second is that while counsel might, if he or she obtains security clearance, be given access to classified documents relevant to the case, on condition that the documents not be shared with the defendant, a defendant representing himself will not be given such documents. This is a disadvantage built into the situation of a defendant representing himself where classified information is relevant to the case. To be distinguished are situations where a government employee who has security clearance is being prosecuted, let us say, for espionage, and the government employee already has had access to the classified information in question.

8. The foregoing excerpts above point out some concerns about 1) defense counsel having security clearance but being unable to share with her client the information in classified documents to which she has been given access, and 2) the use of summaries. Suppose the choice were between counsel being given access to the classified materials but not being able to share them

with the client, on the one hand, and, on the other hand, the use of summaries to which both counsel (whether or not she has security clearance) and the client have access? Which option would you choose if you were representing the defendant?

Would a still better option be to give counsel for the defendant, who has gone through security clearance, access to the original materials while at the same time giving summaries of the same material to the defendant?

PART 2

IN A MILITARY MODE

■ ■ ■

CHAPTER 10

DETENTION IN MILITARY CUSTODY

■ ■ ■

A. INTRODUCTION

The military detention approach which is the subject of this chapter involves us in addressing a wide range of issues relating to the military detention of terrorism suspects. Inter alia, it addresses a basis for detention that should be compared with the material witness and alien detention categories discussed in Chapter 8. Treating individuals as enemy combatants and detaining them in military custody is also closely tied to the question whether we are "at war," and if so, with whom?

The matters treated in the chapter include the right of Guantanamo detainees to habeas corpus review in U.S. courts as well as the administrative process developed in the military for determining the status of the detainees. The government also labeled as enemy combatants two persons arrested in the United States, and their cases are also discussed in this chapter. The Obama administration's new approach which seems, in some respects still to be evolving is also treated herein. Disposition of those still detained at Guantanamo and the closure of that facility are still very current issues.

B. LEGAL BASIS FOR EXTENDED MILITARY DETENTION; PROCESS DUE DETAINEES

1. THE AUMF

In the immediate aftermath of the attacks that occurred on September 11, 2001, at the behest of the administration, Congress passed the following Joint Resolution, S.J. Res. 23, 107th Cong., 115 Stat. 224 (2001), authorizing the use of military force which was signed by the President on September 18, 2001:

Public Law 107–40

107th Congress

Joint Resolution

To authorize the use of United States Armed Forces against those responsible for the recent attacks launched against the United States.

Whereas, on September 11, 2001, acts of treacherous violence were committed against the United States and its citizens; and

Whereas, such acts render it both necessary and appropriate that the United States exercise its rights to self-defense and to protect United States citizens both at home and abroad; and

Whereas, in light of the threat to the national security and foreign policy of the United States posed by these grave acts of violence; and

Whereas, such acts continue to pose an unusual and extraordinary threat to the national security and foreign policy of the United States; and

Whereas, the President has authority under the Constitution to take action to deter and prevent acts of international terrorism against the United States: Now, therefore, be it

Resolved by the Senate and House of Representatives of the United States of America in Congress assembled,

SECTION 1.   SHORT TITLE.

This joint resolution may be cited as the "Authorization for Use of Military Force."

SECTION 2. AUTHORIZATION FOR USE OF UNITED STATES ARMED FORCES.

(a) IN GENERAL.—That the President is authorized to use all necessary and appropriate force against those nations, organizations, or persons he determines planned, authorized, committed, or aided the terrorist attacks that occurred on September 11, 2001, or harbored such organizations or persons, in order to prevent any future acts of international terrorism against the United States by such nations, organizations or persons.

(b) WAR POWERS RESOLUTION REQUIREMENTS.—

(1) SPECIFIC STATUTORY AUTHORIZATION.—Consistent with section 8(a)(1) of the War Powers Resolution, the Congress declares that this section is intended to constitute specific statutory authorization within the meaning of section 5(b) of the War Powers Resolution.

(2) APPLICABILITY OF OTHER REQUIREMENTS.— Nothing in this resolution supersedes any requirement of the War Powers Resolution.

Approved September 18, 2001.

2.   THE MILITARY ORDER ISSUED BY THE PRESIDENT

On November 13, 2001, two months after September 11, 2001, President Bush issued a Military Order that provided for the detention of certain categories of persons involved in acts of international terrorism and prosecuting them before military commissions. In issuing the Order, the government expressly relied on the authority of the President, his authority as Commander in Chief of the Armed Forces, and the afore-mentioned congressional Authorization for Use of Military Force (AUMF) (Public Law 107–40, 115 Stat. 224), and also on two long-standing legislative provisions 10 U.S.C. §§ 821 and 836 which are reproduced in chapter 11, infra.

Notice

Detention, Treatment, and Trial of Certain Non–Citizens in the War Against Terrorism.

66 Fed. Reg. 57833.

By the authority vested in me as President and as Commander in Chief of the Armed Forces of the United States by the Constitution and the laws of the United States of America, including the Authorization for Use of Military Force Joint Resolution (Public Law 107–40, 115 Stat. 224) and sections 821 and 836 of title 10, United States Code, it is hereby ordered as follows:

Section 1.   Findings.

(a) International terrorists, including members of al Qaida, have carried out attacks on United States diplomatic and military personnel and facilities abroad and on citizens and property within the United States on a scale that has created a state of armed conflict that requires the use of the United States Armed Forces.

(b) In light of grave acts of terrorism and threats of terrorism, including the terrorist attacks on September 11, 2001, on the headquarters of the United States Department of Defense in the national capital region, on the World Trade Center in New York, and on civilian aircraft such as in Pennsylvania, I proclaimed a national emergency on September 14, 2001 (Proc. 7463, Declaration of National Emergency by Reason of Certain Terrorist Attacks).

(c) Individuals acting alone and in concert involved in international terrorism possess both the capability and the intention to undertake further terrorist attacks against the United States that, if not detected and prevented, will cause mass deaths, mass injuries, and massive destruction of property, and may place at risk the continuity of the operations of the United States Government.

(d) The ability of the United States to protect the United States and its citizens, and to help its allies and other cooperating nations protect their nations and their citizens, from such further terrorist attacks depends in significant part upon using the United States Armed Forces to identify terrorists and those who support them, to disrupt their activities, and to eliminate their ability to conduct or support such attacks.

(e) To protect the United States and its citizens, and for the effective conduct of military operations and prevention of terrorist attacks, it is necessary for individuals subject to this order pursuant to section 2 hereof to be detained, and, when tried, to be tried for violations of the laws of war and other applicable laws by military tribunals.

(f) Given the danger to the safety of the United States and the nature of international terrorism, and to the extent provided by and under this order, I find consistent with section 836 of title 10, United States Code, that it is not practicable to apply in military commissions under this order the principles of law and the rules of evidence generally recognized in the trial of criminal cases in the United States district courts.

(g) Having fully considered the magnitude of the potential deaths, injuries, and property destruction that would result from potential acts of terrorism against the United States, and the probability that such acts will occur, I have determined that an extraordinary emergency exists for national defense purposes, that this emergency constitutes an urgent and compelling government interest, and that issuance of this order is necessary to meet the emergency.

Sec. 2. Definition and Policy.

(a) The term "individual subject to this order" shall mean any individual who is not a United States citizen with respect to whom I determine from time to time in writing that:

(1) there is reason to believe that such individual, at the relevant times,

(i) is or was a member of the organization known as al Qaida;

(ii) has engaged in, aided or abetted, or conspired to commit, acts of international terrorism, or acts in preparation therefor, that have caused, threaten to cause, or have as their aim to cause, injury to or adverse effects on the United States, its citizens, national security, foreign policy, or economy; or

(iii) has knowingly harbored one or more individuals described in subparagraphs (i) or (ii) of subsection 2(a)(1) of this order; and

(2) it is in the interest of the United States that such individual be subject to this order.

(b) It is the policy of the United States that the Secretary of Defense shall take all necessary measures to ensure that any individual subject to this order is detained in accordance with section 3, and, if the individual is to be tried, that such individual is tried only in accordance with section 4.

(c) It is further the policy of the United States that any individual subject to this order who is not already under the control of the Secretary of Defense but who is under the control of any other officer or agent of the United States or any State shall, upon delivery of a copy of such written determination to such officer or agent, forthwith be placed under the control of the Secretary of Defense.

Sec. 3. Detention Authority of the Secretary of Defense. Any individual subject to this order shall be—

(a) detained at an appropriate location designated by the Secretary of Defense outside or within the United States;

(b) treated humanely, without any adverse distinction based on race, color, religion, gender, birth, wealth, or any similar criteria;

(c) afforded adequate food, drinking water, shelter, clothing, and medical treatment;

(d) allowed the free exercise of religion consistent with the requirements of such detention; and

(e) detained in accordance with such other conditions as the Secretary of Defense may prescribe.

Sec. 4. Authority of the Secretary of Defense Regarding Trials of Individuals Subject to this Order.

(a) Any individual subject to this order shall, when tried, be tried by military commission for any and all offenses triable by military commission that such individual is alleged to have committed, and may be punished in accordance with the penalties provided under applicable law, including life imprisonment or death.

(b) As a military function and in light of the findings in section 1, including subsection (f) thereof, the Secretary of Defense shall issue such orders and regulations, including orders for the appointment of one or more military commissions, as may be necessary to carry out subsection (a) of this section.

(c) Orders and regulations issued under subsection (b) of this section shall include, but not be limited to, rules for the conduct of the proceedings of military commissions, including pretrial, trial, and post-trial procedures, modes of proof, issuance of process, and qualifications of attorneys, which shall at a minimum provide for—

(1) military commissions to sit at any time and any place, consistent with such guidance regarding time and place as the Secretary of Defense may provide;

(2) a full and fair trial, with the military commission sitting as the triers of both fact and law;

(3) admission of such evidence as would, in the opinion of the presiding officer of the military commission (or instead, if any other member of the commission so requests at the time the presiding officer renders that opinion, the opinion of the commission rendered at that time by a majority of the commission), have probative value to a reasonable person;

(4) in a manner consistent with the protection of information classified or classifiable under Executive Order 12958 of April 17, 1995, as amended, or any successor Executive Order, protected by statute or rule from unauthorized disclosure, or otherwise protected by law, (A) the handling of, admission into evidence of, and access to materials and information, and (B) the conduct, closure of, and access to proceedings;

(5) conduct of the prosecution by one or more attorneys designated by the Secretary of Defense and conduct of the defense by attorneys for the individual subject to this order;

(6) conviction only upon the concurrence of two-thirds of the members of the commission present at the time of the vote, a majority being present;

(7) sentencing only upon the concurrence of two-thirds of the members of the commission present at the time of the vote, a majority being present; and

(8) submission of the record of the trial, including any conviction or sentence, for review and final decision by me or by the Secretary of Defense if so designated by me for that purpose.

Sec. 5. Obligation of Other Agencies to Assist the Secretary of Defense.

Departments, agencies, entities, and officers of the United States shall, to the maximum extent permitted by law, provide to the Secretary of Defense such assistance as he may request to implement this order.

Sec. 6. Additional Authorities of the Secretary of Defense.

(a) As a military function and in light of the findings in section 1, the Secretary of Defense shall issue such orders and regulations as may be necessary to carry out any of the provisions of this order.

(b) The Secretary of Defense may perform any of his functions or duties, and may exercise any of the powers provided to him under this order (other than under section 4(c)(8) hereof) in accordance with section 113(d) of title 10, United States Code.

Sec. 7. Relationship to Other Law and Forums.

(a) Nothing in this order shall be construed to—

(1) authorize the disclosure of state secrets to any person not otherwise authorized to have access to them;

(2) limit the authority of the President as Commander in Chief of the Armed Forces or the power of the President to grant reprieves and pardons; or

(3) limit the lawful authority of the Secretary of Defense, any military commander, or any other officer or agent of the United States or of any State to detain or try any person who is not an individual subject to this order.

(b) With respect to any individual subject to this order—

(1) military tribunals shall have exclusive jurisdiction with respect to offenses by the individual; and

(2) the individual shall not be privileged to seek any remedy or maintain any proceeding, directly or indirectly, or to have any such remedy or proceeding sought on the individual's behalf, in

(i) any court of the United States, or any State thereof,

(ii) any court of any foreign nation, or

(iii) any international tribunal.

(c) This order is not intended to and does not create any right, benefit, or privilege, substantive or procedural, enforceable at law or equity by any party, against the United States, its departments, agencies, or other entities, its officers or employees, or any other person.

(d) For purposes of this order, the term "State" includes any State, district, territory, or possession of the United States.

(e) I reserve the authority to direct the Secretary of Defense, at any time hereafter, to transfer to a governmental authority control of any individual subject to this order. Nothing in this order shall be construed to limit the authority of any such governmental authority to prosecute any individual for whom control is transferred.

Sec. 8. Publication.

This order shall be published in the Federal Register.

GEORGE W. BUSH

THE WHITE HOUSE,

November 13, 2001

QUESTIONS AND NOTES

1. The Bush administration interpreted the executive branch's authority very broadly and relied upon its expansive interpretation in support of many of the controversial actions that were undertaken by the administration, including the NSA electronic surveillance controversy, see supra, p. 205, and some of the measures taken in the process of interrogating detainees, see supra, pp. 309–313. In addition to relying on the President's authority as commander-in-chief, the notion of inherent presidential authority was part of

the justification offered. Note how in the preamble to the Military Order, supra, the phrasing is, "By the authority vested in me as President and as Commander-in-Chief . . ." Some of the views advanced by lawyers working in the Bush administration regarding presidential authority are controversial and have been rejected by many constitutional law scholars.

2. The Obama administration has not asserted as expansive a view as did the Bush administration of the President's inherent authority and his authority as Commander-in-Chief. The decisive moment may have been the filing of a memorandum on March 13, 2009 in the *In re Guantanamo Bay Detainee Litigation,* Misc. No. 08–442 (TFH), regarding the government's authority to detain the persons held at Guantanamo. In this memorandum, rather than relying, in part, on inherent and commander-in-chief authority (which had been relied upon in approving the Military Order, supra), the government relied exclusively on "the detention authority conferred by the AUMF" as informed by the laws of war.

3. What are the implications of the interpretative shift described in note 2? First, the new legal position became the basis for the government's legal arguments in litigating the habeas actions filed by Guantanamo detainees in the aftermath of the *Boumediene* decision. See infra. Since this claim of executive authority is based in a legislative act by the Congress, it means that it is limited by the terms of that act and can be withdrawn by an act of the Congress. Because it is founded in congressional action, it also avoids questions about whether the President might be asserting the authority to act contrary to congressional legislation, and the ultimate questions of constitutional authority that would pose. See Justice Jackson's concurring opinion in *Youngstown Sheet & Tube Co.* v. *Sawyer,* 343 U.S. 579 (1952).[18]

4. Had the Obama policy change been in effect, would it have changed the tone and tenor of the arguments made by the government in the NSA electronic surveillance controversy, or the arguments made in the legal memoranda prepared in support of the government's actions in interrogating detainees?

5. In May–June, 2011, the House of Representatives considered the National Defense Appropriations bill, HR 1540, which contained the following section:

Sec. 1034

Congress affirms that—

(1) the United States is engaged in an armed conflict with al-Qaeda, the Taliban, and associated forces and that those entities continue to pose a threat to the United States and its citizens, both domestically and abroad;

---

18. "When the President acts pursuant to an express or implied authorization of Congress, his authority is at its maximum, for it includes all that he possesses in his own right plus all that Congress can delegate." *Id.*, at 635. "When the President acts in absence of either a congressional grant or denial of authority, he can only rely upon his own independent powers, but there is a zone of twilight in which he and Congress may have concurrent authority, or in which its distribution is uncertain." *Id.*, at 637. And "[w]hen the President takes measures incompatible with the expressed or implied will of Congress, his power is at its lowest ebb." *Ibid.*

(2) the President has the authority to use all necessary and appropriate force during the current armed conflict with al-Qaeda, the Taliban, and associated forces pursuant to the Authorization for Use of Military Force (Public Law 107–40; 50 U.S.C. 1541 note);

(3) the current armed conflict includes nations, organization, and persons who—

(A) are part of, or are substantially supporting, al-Qaeda, the Taliban, or associated forces that are engaged in hostilities against the United States or its coalition partners; or

(B) have engaged in hostilities or have directly supported hostilities in aid of a nation, organization, or person described in subparagraph (A); and

(4) the President's authority pursuant to the Authorization for Use of Military Force (Public Law 107–40; 50 U.S.C. 1541 note) includes the authority to detain belligerents, including persons described in paragraph (3), until the termination of hostilities.

The House of Representatives rejected an amendment that would have stripped this section from the bill. The comparable Senate bill under consideration does not contain the exact equivalent of section 1034. Compare section 1031, S. 1253, 2012 National Defense Authorization Bill. See p. 615 infra. As of this writing, the legislation is pending.

5. The White House Office of Management and Budget issued its comments on HR 1540 that included the following:

The Administration strongly objects to section 1034 which, in purporting to affirm the conflict, would effectively recharacterize its scope and would risk creating confusion regarding applicable standards. At a minimum, this is an issue that merits more extensive consideration before possible inclusion.

6. Why did the Obama administration object to section 1034? How does it differ from the authority provided by the AUMF? How does it differ from the scope of authority provided in the President's Military Order, supra, insofar as that scope is reflected in the definition and policy applicable to the phrase, "individual subject to this order"? Compare § 948a(7) of the Military Commissions Act of 2009.

7. Is it likely that all of the individuals who have been detained at Guantanamo and other locations fall within the terms of the authority provided by the AUMF? Is the authority provided by the AUMF enhanced by the scope of authority defined under the Military Order or under the Military Commissions Act of 2009? If so, what is the basis for the exercise of authority claimed under the Military Order? Insofar as the exercise of authority under the Military Order or under the MCA may have gone beyond the authority provided by the AUMF, what are the implications of the Obama administration's exclusive reliance on the AUMF? Could it possibly mean that there might not be (or may not have been) a legal basis for detaining some of the Guantanamo detainees?

8. What is your view about the appropriateness of enacting section 1034? Is it desirable legislation?

3. HAMDI AND ITS AFTERMATH

HAMDI v. RUMSFELD

542 U.S. 507 (2004)

[O'CONNOR, J., announced the judgment of the Court and delivered an opinion, in which REHNQUIST, C.J., and KENNEDY and BREYER, JJ., joined. SOUTER, J., filed an opinion concurring in part, dissenting in part, and concurring in the judgment, in which GINSBURG, J., joined. SCALIA, J., filed a dissenting opinion, in which STEVENS, J., joined. THOMAS, J., filed a dissenting opinion.]

JUSTICE O'CONNOR announced the judgment of the Court and delivered an opinion, in which THE CHIEF JUSTICE, JUSTICE KENNEDY, and JUSTICE BREYER join.

At this difficult time in our Nation's history, we are called upon to consider the legality of the Government's detention of a United States citizen on United States soil as an "enemy combatant" and to address the process that is constitutionally owed to one who seeks to challenge his classification as such. The United States Court of Appeals for the Fourth Circuit held that petitioner's detention was legally authorized and that he was entitled to no further opportunity to challenge his enemy-combatant label. We now vacate and remand. We hold that although Congress authorized the detention of combatants in the narrow circumstances alleged here, due process demands that a citizen held in the United States as an enemy combatant be given a meaningful opportunity to contest the factual basis for that detention before a neutral decisionmaker.

I

On September 11, 2001, the al Qaeda terrorist network used hijacked commercial airliners to attack prominent targets in the United States. Approximately 3,000 people were killed in those attacks. One week later, in response to these "acts of treacherous violence," Congress passed a resolution authorizing the President to "use all necessary and appropriate force against those nations, organizations, or persons he determines planned, authorized, committed, or aided the terrorist attacks" or "harbored such organizations or persons, in order to prevent any future acts of international terrorism against the United States by such nations, organizations or persons." Authorization for Use of Military Force ("the AUMF"), 115 Stat. 224. Soon thereafter, the President ordered United States Armed Forces to Afghanistan, with a mission to subdue al Qaeda and quell the Taliban regime that was known to support it.

This case arises out of the detention of a man whom the Government alleges took up arms with the Taliban during this conflict. His name is Yaser Esam Hamdi. Born an American citizen in Louisiana in 1980,

Hamdi moved with his family to Saudi Arabia as a child. By 2001, the parties agree, he resided in Afghanistan. At some point that year, he was seized by members of the Northern Alliance, a coalition of military groups opposed to the Taliban government, and eventually was turned over to the United States military. The Government asserts that it initially detained and interrogated Hamdi in Afghanistan before transferring him to the United States Naval Base in Guantanamo Bay in January 2002. In April 2002, upon learning that Hamdi is an American citizen, authorities transferred him to a naval brig in Norfolk, Virginia, where he remained until a recent transfer to a brig in Charleston, South Carolina. The Government contends that Hamdi is an "enemy combatant," and that this status justifies holding him in the United States indefinitely—without formal charges or proceedings—unless and until it makes the determination that access to counsel or further process is warranted.

. . .

II

The threshold question before us is whether the Executive has the authority to detain citizens who qualify as "enemy combatants." There is some debate as to the proper scope of this term, and the Government has never provided any court with the full criteria that it uses in classifying individuals as such. It has made clear, however, that, for purposes of this case, the "enemy combatant" that it is seeking to detain is an individual who, it alleges, was " 'part of or supporting forces hostile to the United States or coalition partners' " in Afghanistan and who " 'engaged in an armed conflict against the United States' " there. We therefore answer only the narrow question before us: whether the detention of citizens falling within that definition is authorized.

The Government maintains that no explicit congressional authorization is required, because the Executive possesses plenary authority to detain pursuant to Article II of the Constitution. We do not reach the question whether Article II provides such authority, however, because we agree with the Government's alternative position, that Congress has in fact authorized Hamdi's detention, through the AUMF.

Our analysis on that point, set forth below, substantially overlaps with our analysis of Hamdi's principal argument for the illegality of his detention. He posits that his detention is forbidden by 18 U.S.C. § 4001(a). Section 4001(a) states that "[n]o citizen shall be imprisoned or otherwise detained by the United States except pursuant to an Act of Congress." Congress passed § 4001(a) in 1971 as part of a bill to repeal the Emergency Detention Act of 1950, 50 U.S.C. § 811 *et seq.,* which provided procedures for executive detention, during times of emergency, of individuals deemed likely to engage in espionage or sabotage. Congress was particularly concerned about the possibility that the Act could be used to reprise the Japanese internment camps of World War II. H.R.Rep. No. 92–116 (1971); *id.,* at 4, U.S.Code Cong. & Admin.News 1971, 1435, 1438 ("The concentration camp implications of the legislation render it abhorrent"). The Government again presses two alternative positions. First, it argues that § 4001(a), in light of its legislative history and its location in Title 18, applies only to "the control of civilian prisons and related detentions," not to military detentions. Second, it maintains that § 4001(a) is satisfied, because Hamdi is being detained "pursuant to an Act of Congress"—the AUMF. Again, because we conclude that the Government's second assertion is correct, we do not address the first. In other words, for the reasons that follow, we conclude that the AUMF is explicit congressional authorization for the detention of individuals in the narrow category we describe (assuming, without deciding, that such authorization is required), and that the AUMF satisfied § 4001(a)'s requirement that a detention be "pursuant to an Act of Congress" (assuming, without deciding, that § 4001(a) applies to military detentions).

The AUMF authorizes the President to use "all necessary and appropriate force" against "nations, organizations, or persons" associated with the September 11, 2001, terrorist attacks. 115 Stat. 224. There can be no doubt that individuals who fought against the United States in Afghanistan as part of the Taliban, an organization known to have supported the al Qaeda terrorist network responsible for those attacks, are individuals Congress sought to target in passing the AUMF. We conclude that detention of individuals falling into the limited category we are considering, for the duration of the particular conflict in which they were captured, is so fundamental and accepted an incident to war as to be an exercise of the "necessary and appropriate force" Congress has authorized the President to use.

The capture and detention of lawful combatants and the capture, detention, and trial of unlawful combatants, by "universal agreement and practice," are "important incident[s] of war." *Ex parte Quirin,* 317 U.S., at 28, 63 S.Ct. 2. The purpose of detention is to prevent captured individuals from returning to the field of battle and taking up arms once again.... Cf. *In re Territo,* 156 F.2d 142, 145 (C.A.9 1946) ("The object of capture is to prevent the captured individual from serving the enemy. He is disarmed and from then on must be removed as completely as practicable from the front, treated humanely, and in time exchanged, repatriated, or otherwise released".

There is no bar to this Nation's holding one of its own citizens as an enemy combatant. In *Quirin,* one of the detainees, Haupt, alleged that he was a naturalized United States citizen. 317 U.S., at 20, 63 S.Ct. 2. We held that "[c]itizens who associate themselves with the military arm of the enemy government, and with its aid, guidance and direction enter this country bent on hostile acts, are enemy belligerents within the meaning of ... the law of war...." A citizen, no less than an alien, can be "part of or supporting forces hostile to the United States or coalition partners" and "engaged in an armed conflict against the United States," ... such a citizen, if released, would pose the same threat of returning to the front during the ongoing conflict.

In light of these principles, it is of no moment that the AUMF does not use specific language of detention. Because detention to prevent a combatant's return to the battlefield is a fundamental incident of waging war, in permitting the use of "necessary and appropriate force," Congress has clearly and unmistakably authorized detention in the narrow circumstances considered here.

Hamdi objects, nevertheless, that Congress has not authorized the *indefinite* detention to which he is now subject. The Government responds that "the detention of enemy combatants during World War II was just as 'indefinite' while that war was being fought." We take Hamdi's objection to be not to the lack of certainty regarding the date on which the conflict will end, but to the substantial prospect of perpetual detention. We recognize that the national security underpinnings of the "war on terror," although crucially important, are broad and malleable. As the Government concedes, "given its unconventional nature, the current conflict is unlikely to end with a formal cease-fire agreement." The prospect Hamdi raises is therefore not far-fetched. If the Government does not consider this unconventional war won for two generations, and if it maintains during that time that Hamdi might, if released, rejoin forces fighting against the United States, then the position it has taken throughout the litigation of this case suggests that Hamdi's detention could last for the rest of his life.

It is a clearly established principle of the law of war that detention may last no longer than active hostilities. See Article 118 of the Geneva Convention (III) Relative to the Treatment of Prisoners of War, Aug. 12, 1949, [1955] 6 U.S.T. 3316, 3406, T.I.A.S. No. 3364 ("Prisoners of war shall be released and repatriated without delay after the cessation of active hostilities"). See also ... Paust, Judicial Power to Determine the Status and Rights of Persons Detained without Trial, 44 Harv. Int'l L.J. 503, 510–511 (2003) (prisoners of war "can be detained during an armed conflict, but the detaining country must release and repatriate them 'without delay after the cessation of active hostilities,' unless they are being lawfully prosecuted or have been lawfully convicted of crimes and are serving sentences".....

Hamdi contends that the AUMF does not authorize indefinite or perpetual detention. Certainly, we agree that indefinite detention for the purpose of interrogation is not authorized. Further, we understand Congress' grant of authority for the use of "necessary and appropriate force" to include the authority to detain for the duration of the relevant conflict, and our understanding is based on longstanding law-of-war principles. If the practical circumstances of a given conflict are entirely unlike those of the conflicts that informed the development of the law of war, that understanding may unravel. But that is not the situation we face as of this date. Active combat operations against Taliban fighters apparently are ongoing in Afghanistan.... The United States may detain, for the duration of these hostilities, individuals legitimately determined to be Taliban combatants who "engaged in an armed conflict against the United States." If the record establishes that United States troops are still involved in active combat in Afghanistan, those detentions are part of the exercise of "necessary and appropriate force," and therefore are authorized by the AUMF.

Ex parte Milligan, 4 Wall. 2, 125, 18 L.Ed. 281 (1866), does not undermine our holding about the Government's authority to seize enemy combatants, as we define that term today. In that case, the Court made repeated reference to the fact that its inquiry into whether the military tribunal had jurisdiction to try and punish Milligan turned in large part on the fact that Milligan was not a prisoner of war, but a resident of Indiana arrested while at home there. That fact was central to its conclusion. Had Milligan been captured while he was assisting Confederate soldiers by carrying a rifle against Union troops on a Confederate battlefield, the holding of the Court might well have been different. The Court's repeated explanations that Milligan was not a prisoner of war suggest that had these different circumstances been present he could have been detained under military authority for the duration of the conflict, whether or not he was a citizen.[28]

. . .

Quirin was a unanimous opinion. It both postdates and clarifies *Milligan,* providing us with the most apposite precedent that we have on the question of whether citizens may be detained in such circumstances. Brushing aside such precedent—particularly when doing so gives rise to a host of new questions never dealt with by this Court—is unjustified and unwise.

. . .

III

Even in cases in which the detention of enemy combatants is legally authorized, there remains the question of what process is constitutionally due to a citizen who disputes his enemy-combatant status. Hamdi argues that he is owed a meaningful and timely hearing and that "extra-judicial detention [that] begins and ends with the submission of an affidavit based on third-hand hearsay" does not comport with the Fifth and Fourteenth Amendments. The Government counters that any more process than was provided below would be both unworkable and "constitutionally intolerable." Our resolution of this dispute requires a careful examination both of the writ of habeas corpus, which Hamdi now seeks to employ as a mechanism of judicial review, and of the Due Process Clause, which informs the procedural contours of that mechanism in this instance.

A

Though they reach radically different conclusions on the process that ought to attend the present proceeding, the parties begin on common

---

28. Here the basis asserted for detention by the military is that Hamdi was carrying a weapon against American troops on a foreign battlefield; that is, that he was an enemy combatant. The legal category of enemy combatant has not been elaborated upon in great detail. The permissible bounds of the category will be defined by the lower courts as subsequent cases are presented to them.

ground. All agree that, absent suspension, the writ of habeas corpus remains available to every individual detained within the United States. U.S. Const., Art. I, § 9, cl. 2 ("The Privilege of the Writ of Habeas Corpus shall not be suspended, unless when in Cases of Rebellion or Invasion the public Safety may require it").... At all other times, it has remained a critical check on the Executive, ensuring that it does not detain individuals except in accordance with law.... All agree suspension of the writ has not occurred here. Thus, it is undisputed that Hamdi was properly before an Article III court to challenge his detention under 28 U.S.C. § 2241. Further, all agree that § 2241 and its companion provisions provide at least a skeletal outline of the procedures to be afforded a petitioner in federal habeas review. Most notably, § 2243 provides that "the person detained may, under oath, deny any of the facts set forth in the return or allege any other material facts," and § 2246 allows the taking of evidence in habeas proceedings by deposition, affidavit, or interrogatories.

The simple outline of § 2241 makes clear both that Congress envisioned that habeas petitioners would have some opportunity to present and rebut facts and that courts in cases like this retain some ability to vary the ways in which they do so as mandated by due process. The Government recognizes the basic procedural protections required by the habeas statute, but asks us to hold that, given both the flexibility of the habeas mechanism and the circumstances presented in this case, the presentation of the Mobbs Declaration to the habeas court completed the required factual development. It suggests two separate reasons for its position that no further process is due.

B

First, the Government urges the adoption of the Fourth Circuit's holding below—that because it is "undisputed" that Hamdi's seizure took place in a combat zone, the habeas determination can be made purely as a matter of law, with no further hearing or factfinding necessary. This argument is easily rejected. As the dissenters from the denial of rehearing en banc noted, the circumstances surrounding Hamdi's seizure cannot in any way be characterized as "undisputed," as "those circumstances are neither conceded in fact, nor susceptible to concession in law, because Hamdi has not been permitted to speak for himself or even through counsel as to those circumstances." Further, the "facts" that constitute the alleged concession are insufficient to support Hamdi's detention. Under the definition of enemy combatant that we accept today as falling within the scope of Congress' authorization, Hamdi would need to be "part of or supporting forces hostile to the United States or coalition partners" and "engaged in an armed conflict against the United States" to justify his detention in the United States for the duration of the relevant conflict. The habeas petition states only that "[w]hen seized by the United States Government, Mr. Hamdi resided in Afghanistan." An assertion that one *resided* in a country in which combat operations are taking place is not a concession that one was "*captured* in a zone of active combat operations in a foreign theater of war," and certainly is not a concession that one was "part of or supporting forces hostile to the United States or coalition partners" and "engaged in an armed conflict against the United States." Accordingly, we reject any argument that Hamdi has made concessions that eliminate any right to further process.

C

The Government's second argument requires closer consideration. This is the argument that further factual exploration is unwarranted and inappropriate in light of the extraordinary constitutional interests at stake. Under the Government's most extreme rendition of this argument, "[r]espect for separation of powers and the limited institutional capabilities of courts in matters of military decision-making in connection with an ongoing conflict" ought to eliminate entirely any individual process, restricting the courts to investigating only whether legal authorization exists for the broader detention scheme. At most, the Government argues, courts should review its determination that a citizen is an enemy combatant under a very deferential "some evidence" standard. *Id.,* at 34 ("Under the some evidence standard, the focus is exclusively on the factual basis supplied by the Executive to support its own determination") (citing *Superintendent, Mass. Correctional Institution at Walpole v. Hill,* 472 U.S. 445, 455–457, 105 S.Ct. 2768, 86 L.Ed.2d 356 (1985) (explaining that the some evidence standard "does not require" a "weighing of the evidence," but rather calls for assessing "whether there is any evidence in the record that could support the conclusion")). Under this review, a court would assume the accuracy of the Government's articulated basis for Hamdi's detention, as set forth in the Mobbs Declaration, and assess only whether that articulated basis was a legitimate one. . . .

In response, Hamdi emphasizes that this Court consistently has recognized that an individual challenging his detention may not be held at the will of the Executive without recourse to some proceeding before a neutral tribunal to determine whether the Executive's asserted justifications for that detention have basis in fact and warrant in law. . . . He argues that the Fourth Circuit inappropriately "ceded power to the Executive during wartime to define the conduct for which a citizen may be detained, judge whether that citizen has engaged in the proscribed conduct, and imprison that citizen indefinitely," and that due process demands that he receive a hearing in which he may challenge the Mobbs Declaration and adduce his own counter evidence. The District Court, agreeing with Hamdi, apparently believed that the appropriate process would approach the process that accompanies a criminal trial. It therefore disapproved of the hearsay nature of the Mobbs Declaration and anticipated quite extensive discovery of various military affairs. Anything less, it concluded, would not be "meaningful judicial review."

Both of these positions highlight legitimate concerns. And both emphasize the tension that often exists between the autonomy that the Government asserts is necessary in order to pursue effectively a particular goal and the process that a citizen contends he is due before he is deprived of a constitutional right. The ordinary mechanism that we use for balancing such serious competing interests, and for determining the procedures that are necessary to ensure that a citizen is not "deprived of life, liberty, or property, without due process of law," is the test that we articulated in *Mathews v. Eldridge,* 424 U.S. 319, 96 S.Ct. 893, 47 L.Ed.2d 18 (1976).... *Mathews* dictates that the process due in any given instance is determined by weighing "the private interest that will be affected by the official action" against the Government's asserted interest, "including the function involved" and the burdens the Government would face in providing greater process.... The *Mathews* calculus then contemplates a judicious balancing of these concerns, through an analysis of "the risk of an erroneous deprivation" of the private interest if the process were reduced and the "probable value, if any, of additional or substitute safeguards." We take each of these steps in turn.

It is beyond question that substantial interests lie on both sides of the scale in this case. Hamdi's "private interest ... affected by the official action," is the most elemental of liberty interests—the interest in being free from physical detention by one's own government....

Nor is the weight on this side of the *Mathews* scale offset by the circumstances of war or the accusation of treasonous behavior, for "[i]t is clear that commitment for *any* purpose constitutes a significant deprivation of liberty that requires due process protection,".... Moreover, as critical as the Government's interest may be in detaining those who actually pose an immediate threat to the national security of the United States during ongoing international conflict, history and common sense teach us that an unchecked system of detention carries the potential to become a means for oppression and abuse of others who do not present that sort of threat.... We reaffirm today the fundamental nature of a citizen's right to be free from involuntary confinement by his own government without due process of law, and we weigh the opposing governmental interests against the curtailment of liberty that such confinement entails.

On the other side of the scale are the weighty and sensitive governmental interests in ensuring that those who have in fact fought with the enemy during a war do not return to battle against the United States. As discussed above, ... the law of war and the realities of combat may render such detentions both necessary and appropriate, and our due process analysis need not blink at those realities. Without doubt, our Constitution recognizes that core strategic matters of warmaking belong in the hands of those who are best positioned and most politically accountable for making them. *Department of Navy v. Egan,* 484 U.S. 518, 530, 108 S.Ct. 818, 98 L.Ed.2d 918 (1988) (noting the reluctance of the courts "to intrude upon the authority of the Executive in military and national security affairs"); *Youngstown Sheet & Tube Co. v. Sawyer,* 343 U.S. 579, 587, 72 S.Ct. 863, 96 L.Ed. 1153 (1952) (acknowledging "broad powers in military commanders engaged in day-to-day fighting in a theater of war").

The Government also argues at some length that its interests in reducing the process available to alleged enemy combatants are heightened by the practical difficulties that would accompany a system of trial-like process. In its view, military officers who are engaged in the serious work of waging battle would be unnecessarily and dangerously distracted by litigation half a world away, and discovery into military operations would both intrude on the sensitive secrets of national defense and result in a futile search for evidence buried under the rubble of war. To the extent that these burdens are triggered by heightened procedures, they are properly taken into account in our due process analysis.

Striking the proper constitutional balance here is of great importance to the Nation during this period of ongoing combat. But it is equally vital that our calculus not give short shrift to the values that this country holds dear or to the privilege that is American citizenship. It is during our most challenging and uncertain moments that our Nation's commitment to due process is most severely tested; and it is in those times that we must preserve our commitment at home to the principles for which we fight abroad. . . .

With due recognition of these competing concerns, we believe that neither the process proposed by the Government nor the process apparently envisioned by the District Court below strikes the proper constitutional balance when a United States citizen is detained in the United States as an enemy combatant. That is, "the risk of erroneous deprivation" of a detainee's liberty interest is unacceptably high under the Government's proposed rule, while some of the "additional or substitute procedural safeguards" suggested by the District Court are unwarranted in light of their limited "probable value" and the burdens they may impose on the military in such cases.

We therefore hold that a citizen-detainee seeking to challenge his classification as an enemy combatant must receive notice of the factual basis for his classification, and a fair opportunity to rebut the Government's factual assertions before a neutral decisionmaker. . . . These essential constitutional promises may not be eroded.

At the same time, the exigencies of the circumstances may demand that, aside from these core elements, enemy combatant proceedings may be tailored to alleviate their uncommon potential to burden the Executive at a time of ongoing military conflict. Hearsay, for example, may need to be accepted as the most reliable available evidence from the Government in such a proceeding. Likewise, the Constitution would not be offended by a presumption in favor of the Government's evidence, so long as that presumption remained a rebuttable one and fair opportunity for rebuttal were provided. Thus, once the Government puts forth credible evidence that the habeas petitioner meets the enemy-combatant criteria, the onus could shift to the petitioner to rebut that evidence with more persuasive evidence that he falls outside the criteria. A burden-shifting scheme of this sort would meet the goal of ensuring that the errant tourist, embedded journalist, or local aid worker has a chance to prove military error while giving due regard to the Executive once it has put forth meaningful support for its conclusion that the detainee is in fact an enemy combatant.

We think it unlikely that this basic process will have the dire impact on the central functions of warmaking that the Government forecasts. The parties agree that initial captures on the battlefield need not receive the process we have discussed here; that process is due only when the determination is made to *continue* to hold those who have been seized. The Government has made clear in its briefing that documentation regarding battlefield detainees already is kept in the ordinary course of military affairs. Any factfinding imposition created by requiring a knowledgeable affiant to summarize these records to an independent tribunal is a minimal one. Likewise, arguments that military officers ought not have to wage war under the threat of litigation lose much of their steam when factual disputes at enemy-combatant hearings are limited to the alleged combatant's acts. This focus meddles little, if at all, in the strategy or conduct of war, inquiring only into the appropriateness of continuing to detain an individual claimed to have taken up arms against the United States. While we accord the greatest respect and consideration to the judgments of military authorities in matters relating to the actual prosecution of a war, and recognize that the scope of that discretion necessarily is wide, it does not infringe on the core role of the military for the courts to exercise their own time-honored and constitutionally mandated roles of reviewing and resolving claims like those presented here.

In sum, while the full protections that accompany challenges to detentions in other settings may prove unworkable and inappropriate in the enemy-combatant setting, the threats to military operations posed by a basic system of independent review are not so weighty as to trump a citizen's core rights to challenge meaningfully the Government's case and to be heard by an impartial adjudicator.

D

In so holding, we necessarily reject the Government's assertion that separation of powers principles mandate a heavily circumscribed role for the courts in such circumstances. Indeed, the position that the courts must forgo any examination of the individual case and focus exclusively on the legality of the broader detention scheme cannot be mandated by any reasonable view of separation of powers, as this approach serves only to *condense* power into a single branch of government. We have long since made clear that a state of war is not a blank check for the President when it comes to the rights of the Nation's citizens. *Youngstown Sheet & Tube,* 343 U.S., at 587, 72 S.Ct. 863. Whatever power the United States Constitution envisions for the Executive in its exchanges with other nations or with enemy organizations in times of conflict, it most assuredly envisions a role for all three branches when individual liberties are at stake. . . . Likewise, we have made clear that, unless Congress acts to suspend it, the Great Writ of habeas corpus allows the Judicial Branch to play a necessary role in maintaining this delicate balance of governance, serving as an important judicial check on the Executive's discretion in the realm of detentions.... Thus, while we do not question that our due process assessment must pay keen attention to the particular burdens faced by the Executive in the context of military action, it would turn our system of checks and balances on its head to suggest that a citizen could not make his way to court with a challenge to the factual basis for his detention by his government, simply because the Executive opposes making available such a challenge. Absent suspension of the writ by Congress, a citizen detained as an enemy combatant is entitled to this process.

Because we conclude that due process demands some system for a citizen detainee to refute his classification, the proposed "some evidence" standard is inadequate. Any process in which the Executive's factual assertions go wholly unchallenged or are simply presumed correct without any opportunity for the alleged combatant to demonstrate otherwise falls constitutionally short. As the Government itself has recognized, we have utilized the "some evidence" standard in the past as a standard of review, not as a standard of proof.... This standard therefore is ill suited to the situation in which a habeas petitioner has received no prior proceedings before any tribunal and had no prior opportunity to rebut the Executive's factual assertions before a neutral decisionmaker.

Today we are faced only with such a case. Aside from unspecified "screening" processes, and military interrogations in which the Government suggests Hamdi could have contested his classification, Hamdi has received no process. An interrogation by one's captor, however effective an intelligence-gathering tool, hardly constitutes a constitutionally adequate factfinding before a neutral decisionmaker.... Plainly, the "process" Hamdi has received is not that to which he is entitled under the Due Process Clause.

There remains the possibility that the standards we have articulated could be met by an appropriately authorized and properly constituted military tribunal. Indeed, it is notable that military regulations already provide for such process in related instances, dictating that tribunals be made available to determine the status of enemy detainees who assert prisoner-of-war status under the Geneva Convention. See Enemy Prisoners of War, Retained Personnel, Civilian Internees and Other Detainees, Army Regulation 190–8, § 1–6 (1997). In the absence of such process, however, a court that receives a petition for a writ of habeas corpus from an alleged enemy combatant must itself ensure that the minimum requirements of due process are achieved. Both courts below recognized as much, focusing their energies on the question of whether Hamdi was due an opportunity to rebut the Government's case against him. The Government, too, proceeded on this assumption, presenting its affidavit and then seeking that it be evaluated under a deferential standard of review based on burdens that it alleged would accompany any greater process. As we have discussed, a habeas court in a case such as this may accept affidavit evidence like that contained in the Mobbs Declaration, so long as it also permits the alleged combatant to present his own factual case to rebut the Government's return. We anticipate that a District Court would proceed with the caution that we have indicated is necessary in this setting, engaging in a factfinding process that is both prudent and incremental. We have no reason to doubt that courts faced with these sensitive matters will pay proper heed both to the matters of national security that might arise in an individual case and to the constitutional limitations safeguarding essential liberties that remain vibrant even in times of security concerns.

IV

Hamdi asks us to hold that the Fourth Circuit also erred by denying him immediate access to counsel upon his detention and by disposing of the case without permitting him to meet with an attorney. Since our grant of certiorari in this case, Hamdi has been appointed counsel, with whom he has met for consultation purposes on several occasions, and with whom he is now being granted unmonitored meetings. He unquestionably has the right to access to counsel in connection with the proceedings on remand. No further consideration of this issue is necessary at this stage of the case.

. . .

The judgment of the United States Court of Appeals for the Fourth Circuit is vacated, and the case is remanded for further proceedings.

It is so ordered.

Justice Souter, with whom Justice Ginsburg joins, concurring in part, dissenting in part, and concurring in the judgment.

. . .

IV

Because I find Hamdi's detention forbidden by § 4001(a) and unauthorized by the Force Resolution, I would not reach any questions of what process he may be due in litigating disputed issues in a proceeding under the habeas statute or prior to the habeas enquiry itself. For me, it suffices that the Government has failed to justify holding him in the absence of a further Act of Congress, criminal charges, a showing that the detention conforms to the laws of war, or a demonstration that § 4001(a) is unconstitutional. I would therefore vacate the judgment of the Court of Appeals and remand for proceedings consistent with this view.

Since this disposition does not command a majority of the Court, however, the need to give practical effect to the conclusions of eight members of the Court rejecting the Government's position calls for me to join with the plurality in ordering remand on terms closest to those I would impose. Although I think litigation of Hamdi's status as an enemy combatant is unnecessary, the terms of the plurality's remand will allow Hamdi to offer evidence that he is not an enemy combatant, and he should at the least have the benefit of that opportunity.

It should go without saying that in joining with the plurality to produce a judgment, I do not adopt the plurality's resolution of constitutional issues that I would not reach. It is not that I could disagree with the plurality's determinations (given the plurality's view of the Force Resolution) that someone in Hamdi's position is entitled at a minimum to notice of the Government's claimed factual basis for holding him, and to a fair chance to rebut it before a neutral decision maker ...; nor, of course, could I disagree with the plurality's affirmation of Hamdi's right to counsel, ... On the other hand, I do not mean to imply agreement that the Government could claim an evidentiary presumption casting the burden of rebuttal on Hamdi, or that an opportunity to litigate before a military tribunal might obviate or truncate enquiry by a court on habeas....

Subject to these qualifications, I join with the plurality in a judgment of the Court vacating the Fourth Circuit's judgment and remanding the case.

JUSTICE SCALIA, with whom JUSTICE STEVENS joins, dissenting.

... This case brings into conflict the competing demands of national security and our citizens' constitutional right to personal liberty. Although I share the Court's evident unease as it seeks to reconcile the two, I do not agree with its resolution.

Where the Government accuses a citizen of waging war against it, our constitutional tradition has been to prosecute him in federal court for treason or some other crime. Where the exigencies of war prevent that, the Constitution's Suspension Clause, Art. I, § 9, cl. 2, allows Congress to relax the usual protections temporarily. Absent suspension, however, the Executive's assertion of military exigency has not been thought sufficient to permit detention without charge. No one contends that the congressional Authorization for Use of Military Force, on which the Government relies to justify its actions here, is an implementation of the Suspension Clause. Accordingly, I would reverse the decision below.

. . .

Many think it not only inevitable but entirely proper that liberty give way to security in times of national crisis—that, at the extremes of military exigency, *inter arma silent leges*. Whatever the general merits of the view that war silences law or modulates its voice, that view has no place in the interpretation and application of a Constitution designed precisely to confront war and, in a manner that accords with democratic principles, to accommodate it. Because the Court has proceeded to meet the current emergency in a manner the Constitution does not envision, I respectfully dissent.

JUSTICE THOMAS, dissenting.

The Executive Branch, acting pursuant to the powers vested in the President by the Constitution and with explicit congressional approval, has determined that Yaser Hamdi is an enemy combatant and should be detained. This detention falls squarely within the Federal Government's war powers, and we lack the expertise and capacity to second-guess that decision. As such, petitioners' habeas challenge should fail, and there is no reason to remand the case. The plurality reaches a contrary conclusion by failing adequately to consider basic principles of the constitutional structure as it relates to national security and foreign affairs and by using the balancing scheme of *Mathews v. Eldridge,* 424 U.S. 319, 96 S.Ct. 893, 47 L.Ed.2d 18 (1976). I do not think that the Federal Government's war powers can be balanced away by this Court. Arguably, Congress could provide for additional procedural protections, but until it does, we have no right to insist upon them. But even if I were to agree with the general approach the plurality takes, I could not accept the particulars. The plurality utterly fails to account for the Government's compelling interests and for our own institutional inability to weigh competing concerns correctly. I respectfully dissent.

QUESTIONS AND NOTES

1. Writing for a plurality of the Court, what legal basis did Justice O'Connor articulate for the extended detention of Hamdi? To what extent were the legal grounds based on the AUMF? On the fact that Hamdi had been seized on the battlefield? On the fact that the war with the Taliban was still going on? On the fact that we were at war with al Qaeda? What will be the legal effect when the U.S. withdraws its forces from Afghanistan? Will the legal basis for detaining individuals seized in the war against the Taliban disappear? Are we at war with al Qaeda?

2. In the aftermath of the Supreme Court's decision in the Hamdi case, the government and Hamdi reached a negotiated settlement. (The Supreme Court opinion was handed down on June 28, 2004; the settlement was finalized on September 17, 2004.) Under the terms of the settlement, Hamdi was released and transported to Saudi Arabia; the U.S. agreed to make no request that he be detained by the Saudis; he agreed that he would not engage in any combat activities against the U.S. nor engage in terrorism or aid or affiliate with al Qaeda, the Taliban or any terrorist organization, and he would inform Saudi officials and the U.S. embassy if he were solicited to engage in such activities; he also agreed to renounce his U.S. nationality; he agreed not to travel outside of the Saudi Arabian kingdom for a period of five years, never to travel to Afghanistan, Iraq, Israel, Pakistan, Syria, the West Bank or the Gaza Strip, nor to travel to the United States for ten years and then only having obtained express permission from named high U.S. government officials, and for 15 years to notify the U.S. Embassy of any plans to travel outside of Saudi Arabia. Hamdi also agreed that if he failed to fulfill the conditions of the agreement, he was subject to being detained immediately "insofar as consistent with the law of armed conflict." Finally, the settlement provided for dismissal of the action, Hamdi v. Rumsfeld, with prejudice.

3. Consider the significance of the Hamdi settlement. Should the government have entered into the settlement prior to the Supreme Court decision in the case? Are there any terms that you consider inappropriate?

Any terms that might have been added? How easy or difficult is it likely to be to enforce the terms, if Hamdi does not abide by them?

4. Following announcement of the settlement in the Hamdi case, lawyers for John Walker Lindh filed a request for clemency. LA Times, Sept. 29, 2004, p.A1. Lindh had been wounded in the fighting in Afghanistan and pleaded guilty to supplying services to the Taliban and carrying firearms and destructive devices. He received a 20 year sentence. Both Lindh and Hamdi were seized in the same general area of Afghanistan. Both are American citizens. Does the Hamdi settlement warrant granting clemency to Lindh?

5. In Ex parte Quirin, 317 U.S. 1 (1942), the Supreme Court made the following statements distinguishing between lawful and unlawful combatants (the Quirin case is reproduced in Chapter 11, infra):

> By universal agreement and practice the law of war draws a distinction between the armed forces and the peaceful populations of belligerent nations and also between those who are lawful and unlawful combatants. Lawful combatants are subject to capture and detention as prisoners of war by opposing military forces. Unlawful combatants are likewise subject to capture and detention, but in addition they are subject to trial and punishment by military tribunals for acts which render their belligerency unlawful. The spy who secretly and without uniform passes the military lines of a belligerent in time of war, seeking to gather military information and communicate it to the enemy, or an enemy combatant who without uniform comes secretly through the lines for the purpose of waging war by destruction of life or property, are familiar examples of belligerents who are generally deemed not to be entitled to the status of prisoners of war, but to be offenders against the law of war subject to trial and punishment by military tribunals. . . .

> Our Government, by thus defining lawful belligerents entitled to be treated as prisoners of war, has recognized that there is a class of unlawful belligerents not entitled to that privilege, including those who though combatants do not wear 'fixed and distinctive emblems'.

>   . . .

> Citizenship in the United States of an enemy belligerent does not relieve him from the consequences of a belligerency which is unlawful because in violation of the law of war. Citizens who associate themselves with the military arm of the enemy government, and with its aid, guidance and direction enter this country bent on hostile acts are enemy belligerents within the meaning of the Hague Convention and the law of war. . . .

6. Review carefully the positions taken in each of the opinions in the Hamdi case and the lineup of the various justices in support of each position. How many justices supported the government's position in the case? How many justices would have released Hamdi? How many justices were of the view that the preferred outcome was that which actually occurred?

7. Does the Hamdi case authorize indefinite detention of terrorist detainees? Does it establish ground rules for the kind of process that needs to be

afforded in cases of extended or indefinite detention? For the Obama administration's policy statement on these issues, see p. 607, infra.

8.   Two other terrorism-related cases were decided the same day as Hamdi. In one, Rasul v. Bush, 542 U.S. 466 (2004), the court addressed whether the Guantanamo detainees had a statutory right to habeas corpus. The question of what are the habeas corpus rights of the Gitmo detainees, is treated infra.

The third case was Rumsfeld v. Padilla, 542 U.S. 426 (2004), in which the Supreme Court reversed the court of appeals decision, 352 F.3d 695 (2d Cir. 2003), which in turn had reversed the district court decision. Padilla was an American citizen arrested at Chicago's O'Hare Airport, originally as a material witness in connection with an alleged plot to detonate a dirty bomb (i.e. an explosive device sheathed in radioactive material). Subsequently, the President issued an order declaring Padilla an enemy combatant and he was transferred to military jurisdiction and detained in a military brig. From that point forward, he was denied access to counsel and had no contact with anyone on the outside. His attorney, retained earlier when he was still in material witness status, filed suit on his behalf in New York against the Secretary of Defense.

In the Supreme Court, a majority of the justices concluded that the Secretary of Defense was not the proper respondent in the case; the appropriate respondent was the commander of the naval brig where Padilla was detained. Further, the district court in the Southern District of New York did not have jurisdiction over the commander of the brig. Accordingly, the court of appeals decision was reversed, and the case was dismissed "without prejudice." The Court majority (Rehnquist, C.J. joined by Justices O'Connor, Scalia, Kennedy and Thomas) did not reach the merits of whether the President had authority to detain Padilla militarily. The four dissenting justices (Stevens J. joined by Justices Souter, Ginsburg and Breyer) voted to uphold the district court's jurisdiction and, reaching the merits, stated:

> Whether respondent is entitled to immediate release is a question that reasonable jurists may answer in different ways.[29] There is, however, only one possible answer to the question whether he is entitled to a hearing on the justification for his detention.[30]

At stake in this case is nothing less than the essence of a free society. Even more important than the method of selecting the people's rulers and their successors is the character of the constraints imposed on the Executive by the rule of law. Unconstrained Executive detention for the purpose of investigating and preventing subversive activity is the hall-

---

29.   Consistent with the judgment of the Court of Appeals, I believe that the Non–Detention Act, 18 U.S.C. § 4001(a), prohibits—and the Authorization for Use of Military Force Joint Resolution, 115 Stat. 224, adopted on September 18, 2001, does not authorize—the protracted, incommunicado detention of American citizens arrested in the United States.

30.   Respondent's custodian has been remarkably candid about the Government's motive in detaining respondent: " '[O]ur interest really in his case is not law enforcement, it is not punishment because he was a terrorist or working with the terrorists. Our interest at the moment is to try and find out everything he knows so that hopefully we can stop other terrorist acts.' " 233 F.Supp.2d 564, 573–574 (S.D.N.Y.2002) (quoting News Briefing, Dept. of Defense (June 12, 2002), 2002 WL 22026773).

mark of the Star Chamber.[31] Access to counsel for the purpose of protecting the citizen from official mistakes and mistreatment is the hallmark of due process.

Executive detention of subversive citizens, like detention of enemy soldiers to keep them off the battlefield, may sometimes be justified to prevent persons from launching or becoming missiles of destruction. It may not, however, be justified by the naked interest in using unlawful procedures to extract information. Incommunicado detention for months on end is such a procedure. Whether the information so procured is more or less reliable than that acquired by more extreme forms of torture is of no consequence. For if this Nation is to remain true to the ideals symbolized by its flag, it must not wield the tools of tyrants even to resist an assault by the forces of tyranny. . . .

9. Justice Stevens wrote for the four dissenters in Padilla, and he joined with Justice Scalia in dissent in Hamdi. Are those two votes and the supporting positions consistent? Justice Stevens also wrote in a footnote in his dissent in Padilla that the relevant statutes do not authorize protracted, incommunicado detention of an American citizen, but as quoted above, he also wrote in the text:

Executive detention of subversive citizens, like detention of enemy soldiers to keep them off the battlefield, may sometimes be justified to prevent persons from launching or becoming missiles of destruction.

Are the statements in the text and in the cited footnote reconcilable? Where would the authority to take the action described in the text come from? Might the government's protracted detention of Padilla possibly be justified on the ground that he was involved in plans to detonate a "dirty bomb"; that his detention was necessary to keep him from launching a "missile of destruction"?

10. Arguably, the issues that arise when an alleged terrorist is apprehended in the United States and is treated by the government as an unlawful enemy combatant diverge from those issues that are raised by the cases of the detainees who were captured on the battlefield in Afghanistan (or seized elsewhere in the world) and removed to the Guantanamo Bay prison facility. Of course, Hamdi was seized on the battlefield and initially detained at Guantanamo but later removed to a South Carolina naval brig when it was discovered that he was a U.S. citizen, while most of the Guantanamo detainees are aliens. And Padilla is the prototype case of a U.S. citizen arrested in the U.S. and then treated as an enemy combatant, while another case to be treated below, that of Ali Saleh Kahlah al-Marri, presents another variation— a person legally in the United States but not a U.S. citizen who was arrested and, like Padilla, then declared to be an enemy combatant and detained in military custody. For a detailed description and discussion of the Padilla and al-Marri cases, see infra, p. 622.

---

31. See *Watts v. Indiana*, 338 U.S. 49, 54, 69 S.Ct. 1347, 93 L.Ed. 1801 (1949) (opinion of Frankfurter, J.). "There is torture of mind as well as body; the will is as much affected by fear as by force. And there comes a point where this Court should not be ignorant as judges of what we know as men." *Id.*, at 52, 69 S.Ct. 1347.

11.   We first address below in section C various legal issues relating to the detainees at Guantanamo and then proceed in section D to consider the two "enemy combatant" cases involving individuals arrested in the United States, Padilla and al-Marri.

C. PROCESS DUE DETAINEES AT GUANTANAMO; DISPOSITION OF GUANTANAMO AND THE REMAINING DETAINEES

A substantial number of legal issues have arisen regarding the detainees at Guantanamo: whether they have a right to access to U.S. courts; what kinds of substantive rights, if any, are U.S. courts required to afford them, and the related question, what kind of procedural protections are they entitled to in administrative legal proceedings to determine their status; and ultimately, how long can their detention continue. These and related questions are addressed below.

1. DO THE DETAINEES HAVE HABEAS CORPUS RIGHTS IN U.S. COURTS?

Yaser Hamdi sought his freedom through a writ of habeas corpus in a U.S. court, but Hamdi at the time was a U.S. citizen detained in a naval brig in the United States. Do aliens detained at the Guantanamo Bay detention facility, a base leased by the U.S. from Cuba, or at other U.S. bases abroad, have a right to access U.S. courts seeking their freedom through a writ of habeas corpus.

The Supreme Court in Rasul v. Bush, 542 U.S. 466 (2004) initially ruled on that issue, holding that U.S. courts had jurisdiction to hear actions filed by foreign national detainees who had been captured abroad in connection with hostilities and housed at Guantanamo and who were challenging the legal basis for their detention. Subsequently, Congress passed legislation providing for limited review of certain administrative determinations concerning their status and withdrawing jurisdiction from the federal courts to hear their habeas actions. Subsequently, the detainees sought habeas relief in the federal courts challenging the constitutionality of the statutory withdrawal of habeas jurisdiction.

BOUMEDIENE v. BUSH
553 U.S. 723 (2008)

[Kennedy, J., delivered the opinion of the Court, in which Stevens, Souter, Ginsburg, and Breyer, JJ., joined. Souter, J., filed a concurring opinion, in which Ginsburg and Breyer, JJ., joined. Roberts, C. J., filed a dissenting opinion, in which Scalia, Thomas, and Alito, JJ., joined. Scalia, J., filed a dissenting opinion, in which Roberts, C. J., and Thomas and Alito, JJ., joined.]

Justice Kennedy delivered the opinion of the Court.

Petitioners are aliens designated as enemy combatants and detained at the United States Naval Station at Guantanamo Bay, Cuba. There are others detained there, also aliens, who are not parties to this suit.

Petitioners present a question not resolved by our earlier cases relating to the detention of aliens at Guantanamo: whether they have the constitutional privilege of habeas corpus, a privilege not to be withdrawn except in conformance with the Suspension Clause, Art. I, § 9, cl. 2. We hold these petitioners do have the habeas corpus privilege. Congress has enacted a statute, the Detainee Treatment Act of 2005 (DTA), 119 Stat. 2739, that provides certain procedures for review of the detainees' status. We hold that those procedures are not an adequate and effective substitute for habeas corpus. Therefore § 7 of the Military Commissions Act of 2006 (MCA), 28 U. S. C. A. § 2241(e) (Supp. 2007), operates as an unconstitutional suspension of the writ. We do not address whether the President has authority to detain these petitioners nor do we hold that the writ must issue. These and other questions regarding the legality of the detention are to be resolved in the first instance by the District Court.

I

Under the Authorization for Use of Military Force (AUMF), § 2(a), 115 Stat. 224, note following 50 U. S. C. § 1541 (2000 ed., Supp. V), the President is authorized "to use all necessary and appropriate force against those nations, organizations, or persons he determines planned, authorized, committed, or aided the terrorist attacks that occurred on September 11, 2001, or harbored such organizations or persons, in order to prevent any future acts of international terrorism against the United States by such nations, organizations or persons."

In Hamdi v. Rumsfeld, 542 U. S. 507 (2004), five Members of the Court recognized that detention of individuals who fought against the United States in Afghanistan "for the duration of the particular conflict in which they were captured, is so fundamental and accepted an incident to war as to be an exercise of the 'necessary and appropriate force' Congress has authorized the President to use." *Id.*, at 518 (plurality opinion of O'Connor, J.), *id.*, at 588–589 (Thomas, J., dissenting). After Hamdi, the Deputy Secretary of Defense established Combatant Status Review Tribunals (CSRTs) to determine whether individuals detained at Guantanamo were "enemy combatants," as the Department defines that term. A later memorandum established procedures to implement the CSRTs. The Government maintains these procedures were designed to comply with the due process requirements identified by the plurality in Hamdi.

Interpreting the AUMF, the Department of Defense ordered the detention of these petitioners, and they were transferred to Guantanamo. Some of these individuals were apprehended on the battlefield in Afghanistan, others in places as far away from there as Bosnia and Gambia. All are foreign nationals, but none is a citizen of a nation now at war with the United States. Each denies he is a member of the al Qaeda terrorist network that carried out the September 11 attacks or of the Taliban regime that provided sanctuary for al Qaeda. Each petitioner appeared before a separate CSRT; was determined to be an enemy combatant; and has sought a writ of habeas corpus in the United States District Court for the District of Columbia.

. . .

After Rasul, petitioners' cases were consolidated and entertained in two separate proceedings. In the first set of cases, Judge Richard J. Leon granted the Government's motion to dismiss, holding that the detainees had no rights that could be vindicated in a habeas corpus action. In the second set of cases Judge Joyce Hens Green reached the opposite conclusion, holding the detainees had rights under the Due Process Clause of the Fifth Amendment. See Khalid v. Bush, 355 F. Supp. 2d 311, 314 (DDC 2005); In re Guantanamo Detainee Cases, 355 F. Supp. 2d 443, 464 (DDC 2005).

While appeals were pending from the District Court decisions, Congress passed the DTA. Subsection (e) of § 1005 of the DTA amended 28 U. S. C. § 2241 to provide that "no court, justice, or judge shall have jurisdiction to hear or consider . . . an application for a writ of habeas corpus filed by or on behalf of an alien detained by the Department of Defense at Guantanamo Bay, Cuba." 119 Stat. 2742. Section 1005 further provides that the Court of Appeals for the District of Columbia Circuit shall have "exclusive" jurisdiction to review decisions of the CSRTs. Ibid.

. . .

Petitioners' cases were consolidated on appeal, and the parties filed supplemental briefs in light of our decision in Hamdan [v. Rumsfeld, 548 U.S. 557 (2006)] The Court of Appeals' ruling, 476 F. 3d 981 (CADC 2007), is the subject of our present review and today's decision.

The Court of Appeals concluded that MCA § 7 must be read to strip from it, and all federal courts, jurisdiction to consider petitioners' habeas corpus applications, id., at 987; that petitioners are not entitled to the privilege of the writ or the protections of the Suspension Clause, id., at 990–991; and, as a result, that it was unnecessary to consider whether Congress provided an adequate and effective substitute for habeas corpus in the DTA.

We granted certiorari.

II

As a threshold matter, we must decide whether MCA § 7 denies the federal courts jurisdiction to hear habeas corpus actions pending at the time of its enactment. We hold the statute does deny that jurisdiction, so that, if the statute is valid, petitioners' cases must be dismissed.

. . .

If this ongoing dialogue between and among the branches of Government is to be respected, we cannot ignore that the MCA was a direct response to Hamdan's holding that the DTA's jurisdiction-stripping provision had no application to pending cases. The Court of Appeals was correct to take note of the legislative history when construing the statute . . .; and we agree with its conclusion that the MCA deprives the federal courts of jurisdiction to entertain the habeas corpus actions now before us.

III

In deciding the constitutional questions now presented we must determine whether petitioners are barred from seeking the writ or invoking the protections of the Suspension Clause either because of their status, i.e., petitioners' designation by the Executive Branch as enemy combatants, or their physical location, i.e., their presence at Guantanamo Bay. The Government contends that noncitizens designated as enemy combatants and detained in territory located outside our Nation's borders have no constitutional rights and no privilege of habeas corpus. Petitioners contend they do have cognizable constitutional rights and that Congress, in seeking to eliminate recourse to habeas corpus as a means to assert those rights, acted in violation of the Suspension Clause.

We begin with a brief account of the history and origins of the writ. Our account proceeds from two propositions. First, protection for the privilege of habeas corpus was one of the few safeguards of liberty specified in a Constitution that, at the outset, had no Bill of Rights. In the system conceived by the Framers the writ had a centrality that must inform proper interpretation of the Suspension Clause. Second, to the extent there were settled precedents or legal commentaries in 1789 regarding the extraterritorial scope of the writ or its application to enemy aliens, those authorities can be instructive for the present cases.

A

The Framers viewed freedom from unlawful restraint as a fundamental precept of liberty, and they understood the writ of habeas corpus as a vital instrument to secure that freedom. Experience taught, however, that the common-law writ all too often had been insufficient to guard against the abuse of monarchial power. That history counseled the necessity for specific language in the Constitution to secure the writ and ensure its place in our legal system.

. . .

Post–1789 habeas developments in England, though not bearing upon the Framers' intent, do verify their foresight. Those later events would underscore the need for structural barriers against arbitrary suspensions of the writ. Just as the writ had been vulnerable to executive and parliamentary encroachment on both sides of the Atlantic before the American Revolution, despite the Habeas Corpus Act of 1679, the writ was suspended with frequency in England during times of political unrest after 1789. . . .

In our own system the Suspension Clause is designed to protect against these cyclical abuses. The Clause protects the rights of the detained by a means consistent with the essential design of the Constitution. It ensures that, except during periods of formal suspension, the Judiciary will have a time-tested device, the writ, to maintain the "delicate balance of governance" that is itself the surest safeguard of liberty. The Clause protects the rights of the detained by affirming the duty and authority of the Judiciary to call the jailer to account.... The separation-of-powers doctrine, and the history that influenced its design, therefore must inform the reach and purpose of the Suspension Clause.

B

The broad historical narrative of the writ and its function is central to our analysis, but we seek guidance as well from founding-era authorities addressing the specific question before us: whether foreign nationals, apprehended and detained in distant countries during a time of serious threats to our Nation's security, may assert the privilege of the writ and seek its protection. The Court has been careful not to foreclose the possibility that the protections of the Suspension Clause have expanded along with post–1789 developments that define the present scope of the writ.... But the analysis may begin with precedents as of 1789, for the Court has said that "at the absolute minimum" the Clause protects the writ as it existed when the Constitution was drafted and ratified.

. . .

We know that at common law a petitioner's status as an alien was not a categorical bar to habeas corpus relief.... We know as well that common-law courts entertained habeas petitions brought by enemy aliens detained in England-"entertained" at least in the sense that the courts held hearings to determine the threshold question of entitlement to the writ....

... To the extent these authorities suggest the common-law courts abstained altogether from matters involving prisoners of war, there was greater justification for doing so in the context of declared wars with other nation states. Judicial intervention might have complicated the military's ability to negotiate exchange of prisoners with the enemy, a wartime practice well known to the Framers....

We find the evidence as to the geographic scope of the writ at common law informative, but, again, not dispositive. Petitioners argue the site of their detention is analogous to two territories outside of England to which the writ did run: the so-called "exempt jurisdictions," like the Channel Islands; and (in former times) India. There are critical differences between these places and Guantanamo, however.

. . .

In the end a categorical or formal conception of sovereignty does not provide a comprehensive or altogether satisfactory explanation for the general understanding that prevailed when Lord Mansfield considered issuance of the writ outside England. In 1759 the writ did not run to Scotland but did run to Ireland, even though, at that point, Scotland and

England had merged under the rule of a single sovereign, whereas the Crowns of Great Britain and Ireland remained separate (at least in theory).... But there was at least one major difference between Scotland's and Ireland's relationship with England during this period that might explain why the writ ran to Ireland but not to Scotland. English law did not generally apply in Scotland (even after the Act of Union) but it did apply in Ireland.... This distinction, and not formal notions of sovereignty, may well explain why the writ did not run to Scotland (and Hanover) but would run to Ireland.

The prudential barriers that may have prevented the English courts from issuing the writ to Scotland and Hanover are not relevant here. We have no reason to believe an order from a federal court would be disobeyed at Guantanamo. No Cuban court has jurisdiction to hear these petitioners' claims, and no law other than the laws of the United States applies at the naval station. The modern-day relations between the United States and Guantanamo thus differ in important respects from the 18th–century relations between England and the kingdoms of Scotland and Hanover. This is reason enough for us to discount the relevance of the Government's analogy.

Each side in the present matter argues that the very lack of a precedent on point supports its position. The Government points out there is no evidence that a court sitting in England granted habeas relief to an enemy alien detained abroad; petitioners respond there is no evidence that a court refused to do so for lack of jurisdiction.

Both arguments are premised, however, upon the assumption that the historical record is complete and that the common law, if properly understood, yields a definite answer to the questions before us. There are reasons to doubt both assumptions. Recent scholarship points to the inherent shortcomings in the historical record.... And given the unique status of Guantanamo Bay and the particular dangers of terrorism in the modern age, the common-law courts simply may not have confronted cases with close parallels to this one. We decline, therefore, to infer too much, one way or the other, from the lack of historical evidence on point....

IV

Drawing from its position that at common law the writ ran only to territories over which the Crown was sovereign, the Government says the Suspension Clause affords petitioners no rights because the United States does not claim sovereignty over the place of detention.

Guantanamo Bay is not formally part of the United States. See DTA § 1005(g), 119 Stat. 2743. And under the terms of the lease between the United States and Cuba, Cuba retains "ultimate sovereignty" over the territory while the United States exercises "complete jurisdiction and control." See Lease of Lands for Coaling and Naval Stations, Feb. 23, 1903, U. S.–Cuba, Art. III, T. S. No. 418 (hereinafter 1903 Lease Agreement); Rasul, 542 U. S., at 471. Under the terms of the 1934 Treaty, however, Cuba effectively has no rights as a sovereign until the parties agree to modification of the 1903 Lease Agreement or the United States abandons the base. See Treaty Defining Relations with Cuba, May 29, 1934, U. S.–Cuba, Art. III, 48 Stat. 1683, T. S. No. 866.

The United States contends, nevertheless, that Guantanamo is not within its sovereign control. This was the Government's position well before the events of September 11, 2001. And in other contexts the Court has held that questions of sovereignty are for the political branches to decide.... Even if this were a treaty interpretation case that did not involve a political question, the President's construction of the lease agreement would be entitled to great respect....

We therefore do not question the Government's position that Cuba, not the United States, maintains sovereignty, in the legal and technical sense of the term, over Guantanamo Bay. But this does not end the analysis. Our cases do not hold it is improper for us to inquire into the objective degree of control the Nation asserts over foreign territory.... As we did in Rasul, however, we take notice of the obvious and uncontested fact that the United States, by virtue of its complete jurisdiction and control over the base, maintains de facto sovereignty over this territory.

Were we to hold that the present cases turn on the political question doctrine, we would be required first to accept the Government's premise that de jure sovereignty is the touchstone of habeas corpus jurisdiction. This premise, however, is unfounded. For the reasons indicated above, the history of common-law habeas corpus provides scant support for this proposition; and, for the reasons indicated below, that position would be inconsistent with our precedents and contrary to fundamental separation-of-powers principles.

A

The Court has discussed the issue of the Constitution's extraterritorial application on many occasions. These decisions undermine the Government's argument that, at least as applied to noncitizens, the Constitution necessarily stops where de jure sovereignty ends

. . .

Practical considerations weighed heavily as well in Johnson v. Eisentrager, 339 U. S. 763 (1950), where the Court addressed whether habeas corpus jurisdiction extended to enemy aliens who had been convicted of violating the laws of war. The prisoners were detained at Landsberg Prison in Germany during the Allied Powers' postwar occupation. The Court stressed the difficulties of ordering the Government to produce the prisoners in a habeas corpus proceeding. It "would require allocation of shipping space, guarding personnel, billeting and rations" and would damage the prestige of military commanders at a sensitive time. In considering these factors the Court sought to balance the constraints of military occupation with constitutional necessities. [S]ee Rasul, 542 U. S., at 475–476 (discussing the factors relevant to Eisentrager's constitutional holding); 542 U. S., at 486 (Kennedy, J., concurring in judgment) (same).

. . .

... [B]ecause the United States lacked both de jure sovereignty and plenary control over Landsberg Prison, it is far from clear that the Eisentrager Court used the term sovereignty only in the narrow technical sense and not to connote the degree of control the military asserted over the facility. The Justices who decided Eisentrager would have understood sovereignty as a multifaceted concept.... Even if we assume the Eisentrager Court considered the United States' lack of formal legal sovereignty over Landsberg Prison as the decisive factor in that case, its holding is not inconsistent with a functional approach to questions of extraterritoriality. The formal legal status of a given territory affects, at least to some extent, the political branches' control over that territory. De jure sovereignty is a factor that bears upon which constitutional guarantees apply there.

. . .

B

The Government's formal sovereignty-based test raises troubling separation-of-powers concerns as well. The political history of Guantanamo illustrates the deficiencies of this approach.... The necessary implication of the argument is that by surrendering formal sovereignty over any unincorporated territory to a third party, while at the same time entering into a lease that grants total control over the territory back to the United States, it would be possible for the political branches to govern without legal constraint.

Our basic charter cannot be contracted away like this. The Constitution grants Congress and the President the power to acquire, dispose of, and govern territory, not the power to decide when and where its terms apply.... Abstaining from questions involving formal sovereignty and territorial governance is one thing. To hold the political branches have the power to switch the Constitution on or off at will is quite another. The former position reflects this Court's recognition that certain matters requiring political judgments are best left to the political branches. The latter would permit a striking anomaly in our tripartite system of government, leading to a regime in which Congress and the President, not this Court, say "what the law is." Marbury v. Madison, 1 Cranch 137, 177 (1803).

These concerns have particular bearing upon the Suspension Clause question in the cases now before us, for the writ of habeas corpus is itself an indispensable mechanism for monitoring the separation of powers. The test for determining the scope of this provision must not be subject to manipulation by those whose power it is designed to restrain.

C

As we recognized in Rasul, 542 U. S., at 476; id., at 487 (Kennedy, J., concurring in judgment), the outlines of a framework for determining the reach of the Suspension Clause are suggested by the factors the Court relied upon in Eisentrager. In addition to the practical concerns discussed above, the Eisentrager Court found relevant that each petitioner:

"(a) is an enemy alien; (b) has never been or resided in the United States; (c) was captured outside of our territory and there held in military custody as a prisoner of war; (d) was tried and convicted by a Military Commission sitting outside the United States; (e) for offenses against laws of war committed outside the United States; (f) and is at all times imprisoned outside the United States." 339 U. S., at 777.

Based on this language from Eisentrager, and the reasoning in our other extraterritoriality opinions, we conclude that at least three factors are relevant in determining the reach of the Suspension Clause: (1) the citizenship and status of the detainee and the adequacy of the process through which that status determination was made; (2) the nature of the sites where apprehension and then detention took place; and (3) the practical obstacles inherent in resolving the prisoner's entitlement to the writ.

Applying this framework, we note at the onset that the status of these detainees is a matter of dispute. The petitioners, like those in Eisentrager, are not American citizens. But the petitioners in Eisentrager did not contest, it seems, the Court's assertion that they were "enemy alien[s]." In the instant cases, by contrast, the detainees deny they are enemy combatants. They have been afforded some process in CSRT proceedings to determine their status; but, unlike in Eisentrager, there has been no trial by military commission for violations of the laws of war. The difference is not trivial. The records from the Eisentrager trials suggest that, well before the petitioners brought their case to this Court, there had been a rigorous adversarial process to test the legality of their detention. . . .

In comparison the procedural protections afforded to the detainees in the CSRT hearings are far more limited, and, we conclude, fall well short of the procedures and adversarial mechanisms that would eliminate the need for habeas corpus review. Although the detainee is assigned a "Personal Representative" to assist him during CSRT proceedings, the Secretary of the Navy's memorandum makes clear that person is not the detainee's lawyer or even his "advocate." The Government's evidence is accorded a presumption of validity. The detainee is allowed to present "reasonably available" evidence, but his ability to rebut the Government's evidence against him is limited by the circumstances of his confinement and his lack of counsel at this stage. And although the detainee can seek review of his status determination in the Court of Appeals, that review process cannot cure all defects in the earlier proceedings. See Part V, infra.

As to the second factor relevant to this analysis, the detainees here are similarly situated to the Eisentrager petitioners in that the sites of their apprehension and detention are technically outside the sovereign territory of the United States. As noted earlier, this is a factor that weighs against finding they have rights under the Suspension Clause. But there are critical differences between Landsberg Prison, circa 1950, and the United States Naval Station at Guantanamo Bay in 2008. Unlike its present control over the naval station, the United States' control over the prison in Germany was neither absolute nor indefinite. Like all parts of occupied Germany, the prison was under the jurisdiction of the combined Allied Forces.... The Allies had not planned a long-term occupation of Germany, nor did they intend to displace all German institutions even during the period of occupation.... Guantanamo Bay, on the other hand, is no transient possession. In every practical sense Guantanamo is not abroad; it is within the constant jurisdiction of the United States

As to the third factor, we recognize, as the Court did in Eisentrager, that there are costs to holding the Suspension Clause applicable in a case of military detention abroad. Habeas corpus proceedings may require expenditure of funds by the Government and may divert the attention of military personnel from other pressing tasks. While we are sensitive to these concerns, we do not find them dispositive. Compliance with any judicial process requires some incremental expenditure of resources ... The Government presents no credible arguments that the military mission at Guantanamo would be compromised if habeas corpus courts had jurisdiction to hear the detainees' claims. And in light of the plenary control the United States asserts over the base, none are apparent to us.

The situation in Eisentrager was far different, given the historical context and nature of the military's mission in post-War Germany.... In addition to supervising massive reconstruction and aid efforts the American forces stationed in Germany faced potential security threats from a defeated enemy. In retrospect the post-War occupation may seem uneventful. But at the time Eisentrager was decided, the Court was right to be concerned about judicial interference with the military's efforts to contain "enemy elements, guerilla fighters, and 'were-wolves.' "

Similar threats are not apparent here; nor does the Government argue that they are. The United States Naval Station at Guantanamo Bay consists of 45 square miles of land and water. The base has been used, at various points, to house migrants and refugees temporarily. At present, however, other than the detainees themselves, the only long-term residents are American military personnel, their families, and a small number of workers. See History of Guantanamo Bay online at https://www.cnic. navy.mil/Guantanamo/AboutGTMO/gtmohistorygeneral/ gtmohistgeneral. The detainees have been deemed enemies of the United States. At present, dangerous as they may be if released, they are contained in a secure prison facility located on an isolated and heavily fortified military base.

There is no indication, furthermore, that adjudicating a habeas corpus petition would cause friction with the host government. No Cuban court has jurisdiction over American military personnel at Guantanamo or the enemy combatants detained there. While obligated to abide by the terms of the lease, the United States is, for all practical purposes, answerable to no other sovereign for its acts on the base. Were that not the case, or if the detention facility were located in an active theater of war, arguments that issuing the writ would be "impracticable or anomalous" would have more weight. Under the facts presented here, however, there are few practical barriers to the running of the writ. To the extent barriers arise, habeas corpus procedures likely can be modified to address them. See Part VI–B, infra.

It is true that before today the Court has never held that noncitizens detained by our Government in territory over which another country maintains de jure sovereignty have any rights under our Constitution. But the cases before us lack any precise historical parallel. They involve individuals detained by executive order for the duration of a conflict that, if measured from September 11, 2001, to the present, is already among the longest wars in American history. . . . The detainees, moreover, are held in a territory that, while technically not part of the United States, is under the complete and total control of our Government. Under these circumstances the lack of a precedent on point is no barrier to our holding.

We hold that Art. I, § 9, cl. 2, of the Constitution has full effect at Guantanamo Bay. If the privilege of habeas corpus is to be denied to the detainees now before us, Congress must act in accordance with the requirements of the Suspension Clause. Cf. Hamdi, 542 U. S., at 564 (Scalia, J., dissenting) ("[I]ndefinite imprisonment on reasonable suspicion is not an available option of treatment for those accused of aiding the enemy, absent a suspension of the writ"). This Court may not impose a de facto suspension by abstaining from these controversies. . . . The MCA does not purport to be a formal suspension of the writ; and the Government, in its submissions to us, has not argued that it is. Petitioners, therefore, are entitled to the privilege of habeas corpus to challenge the legality of their detention.

V

In light of this holding the question becomes whether the statute stripping jurisdiction to issue the writ avoids the Suspension Clause mandate because Congress has provided adequate substitute procedures for habeas corpus. The Government submits there has been compliance with the Suspension Clause because the DTA review process in the Court of Appeals, see DTA § 1005(e), provides an adequate substitute. Congress has granted that court jurisdiction to consider

"(i) whether the status determination of the [CSRT] . . . was consistent with the standards and procedures specified by the Secretary of Defense . . . and (ii) to the extent the Constitution and laws of the United States are applicable, whether the use of such standards and procedures to make the determination is consistent with the Constitution and laws of the United States." § 1005(e)(2)(C), 119 Stat. 2742.

The Court of Appeals, having decided that the writ does not run to the detainees in any event, found it unnecessary to consider whether an adequate substitute has been provided. In the ordinary course we would remand to the Court of Appeals to consider this question in the first instance ... Departure from the rule is appropriate in "exceptional" circumstances.

The gravity of the separation-of-powers issues raised by these cases and the fact that these detainees have been denied meaningful access to a judicial forum for a period of years render these cases exceptional. The parties before us have addressed the adequacy issue. While we would have found it informative to consider the reasoning of the Court of Appeals on this point, we must weigh that against the harms petitioners may endure from additional delay. And, given there are few precedents addressing what features an adequate substitute for habeas corpus must contain, in all likelihood a remand simply would delay ultimate resolution of the issue by this Court.

We do have the benefit of the Court of Appeals' construction of key provisions of the DTA. When we granted certiorari in these cases, we noted "it would be of material assistance to consult any decision" in the parallel DTA review proceedings pending in the Court of Appeals, specifically any rulings in the matter of Bismullah v. Gates. 551 U. S. ___ (2007). Although the Court of Appeals has yet to complete a DTA review proceeding, the three-judge panel in Bismullah has issued an interim order giving guidance as to what evidence can be made part of the record on review and what access the detainees can have to counsel and to classified information. See 501 F. 3d 178 (CADC) (Bismullah I), reh'g denied, 503 F. 3d 137 (CADC 2007) (Bismullah II). In that matter the full court denied the Government's motion for rehearing en banc, see Bismullah v. Gates, 514 F. 3d 1291 (CADC 2008) (Bismullah III). The order denying rehearing was accompanied by five separate statements from members of the court, which offer differing views as to scope of the judicial review Congress intended these detainees to have. Ibid.

Under the circumstances we believe the costs of further delay substantially outweigh any benefits of remanding to the Court of Appeals to consider the issue it did not address in these cases.

A

Our case law does not contain extensive discussion of standards defining suspension of the writ or of circumstances under which suspension has occurred. This simply confirms the care Congress has taken throughout our Nation's history to preserve the writ and its function. Indeed, most of the major legislative enactments pertaining to habeas corpus have acted not to contract the writ's protection but to expand it or to hasten resolution of prisoners' claims. . . .

There are exceptions, of course. . . .

... [H]ere we confront statutes, the DTA and the MCA, that were intended to circumscribe habeas review....

... [T]he DTA's jurisdictional grant is quite limited. The Court of Appeals has jurisdiction not to inquire into the legality of the detention generally but only to assess whether the CSRT complied with the "standards and procedures specified by the Secretary of Defense" and whether those standards and procedures are lawful. DTA § 1005(e)(2)(C), 119 Stat. 2742. If Congress had envisioned DTA review as coextensive with traditional habeas corpus, it would not have drafted the statute in this manner.... [M]oreover, there has been no effort to preserve habeas corpus review as an avenue of last resort. No saving clause exists in either the MCA or the DTA. And MCA § 7 eliminates habeas review for these petitioners.

The differences between the DTA and the habeas statute that would govern in MCA § 7's absence, 28 U. S. C. § 2241 (2000 ed. and Supp. V), are likewise telling. In § 2241 (2000 ed.) Congress confirmed the authority of "any justice" or "circuit judge" to issue the writ. That statute accommodates the necessity for factfinding that will arise in some cases by allowing the appellate judge or Justice to transfer the case to a district court of competent jurisdiction, whose institutional capacity for factfinding is superior to his or her own. See 28 U. S. C. § 2241(b). By granting the Court of Appeals "exclusive" jurisdiction over petitioners' cases, see DTA § 1005(e)(2)(A), 119 Stat. 2742, Congress has foreclosed that option. This choice indicates Congress intended the Court of Appeals to have a more limited role in enemy combatant status determinations than a district court has in habeas corpus proceedings. The DTA should be interpreted to accord some latitude to the Court of Appeals to fashion procedures necessary to make its review function a meaningful one, but, if congressional intent is to be respected, the procedures adopted cannot be as extensive or as protective of the rights of the detainees as they would be in a § 2241 proceeding. Otherwise there would have been no, or very little, purpose for enacting the DTA.

To the extent any doubt remains about Congress' intent, the legislative history confirms what the plain text strongly suggests: In passing the DTA Congress did not intend to create a process that differs from traditional habeas corpus process in name only. It intended to create a more limited procedure.... It is against this background that we must interpret the DTA and assess its adequacy as a substitute for habeas corpus....

B

We do not endeavor to offer a comprehensive summary of the requisites for an adequate substitute for habeas corpus. We do consider it uncontroversial, however, that the privilege of habeas corpus entitles the prisoner to a meaningful opportunity to demonstrate that he is being held pursuant to "the erroneous application or interpretation" of relevant law. St. Cyr, 533 U. S., at 302. And the habeas court must have the power to order the conditional release of an individual unlawfully detained-though release need not be the exclusive remedy and is not the appropriate one in every case in which the writ is granted. . . . These are the easily identified attributes of any constitutionally adequate habeas corpus proceeding. But, depending on the circumstances, more may be required.

Indeed, common-law habeas corpus was, above all, an adaptable remedy. Its precise application and scope changed depending upon the circumstances. . . . It appears the common-law habeas court's role was most extensive in cases of pretrial and noncriminal detention, where there had been little or no previous judicial review of the cause for detention. . . .

There is evidence from 19th–century American sources indicating that, even in States that accorded strong res judicata effect to prior adjudications, habeas courts in this country routinely allowed prisoners to introduce exculpatory evidence that was either unknown or previously unavailable to the prisoner. . . .

The idea that the necessary scope of habeas review in part depends upon the rigor of any earlier proceedings accords with our test for procedural adequacy in the due process context. . . . This principle has an established foundation in habeas corpus jurisprudence as well, ...

. . .

Where a person is detained by executive order, rather than, say, after being tried and convicted in a court, the need for collateral review is most pressing. A criminal conviction in the usual course occurs after a judicial hearing before a tribunal disinterested in the outcome and committed to procedures designed to ensure its own independence. These dynamics are not inherent in executive detention orders or executive review procedures. In this context the need for habeas corpus is more urgent. The intended duration of the detention and the reasons for it bear upon the precise scope of the inquiry. Habeas corpus proceedings need not resemble a criminal trial, even when the detention is by executive order. But the writ must be effective. The habeas court must have sufficient authority to conduct a meaningful review of both the cause for detention and the Executive's power to detain.

To determine the necessary scope of habeas corpus review, therefore, we must assess the CSRT process, the mechanism through which petitioners' designation as enemy combatants became final. Whether one characterizes the CSRT process as direct review of the Executive's battlefield determination that the detainee is an enemy combatant-as the parties have and as we do-or as the first step in the collateral review of a battlefield determination makes no difference in a proper analysis of whether the procedures Congress put in place are an adequate substitute for habeas corpus. What matters is the sum total of procedural protections afforded to the detainee at all stages, direct and collateral.

Petitioners identify what they see as myriad deficiencies in the CSRTs. The most relevant for our purposes are the constraints upon the detainee's ability to rebut the factual basis for the Government's assertion that he is an enemy combatant. As already noted, see Part IV–C, supra, at the CSRT stage the detainee has limited means to find or present evidence to challenge the Government's case against him. He does not have the assistance of counsel and may not be aware of the most critical allegations that the Government relied upon to order his detention. . . . [T]he detainee can access only the "unclassified portion of the Government Information". The detainee can confront witnesses that testify during the CSRT proceedings. But given that there are in effect no limits on the admission of hearsay evidence-the only requirement is that the tribunal deem the evidence "relevant and helpful,"-the detainee's opportunity to question witnesses is likely to be more theoretical than real.

The Government defends the CSRT process, arguing that it was designed to conform to the procedures suggested by the plurality in Hamdi. Setting aside the fact that the relevant language in Hamdi did not garner a majority of the Court, it does not control the matter at hand. None of the parties in Hamdi argued there had been a suspension of the writ. Nor could they. The § 2241 habeas corpus process remained in place, ... Accordingly, the plurality concentrated on whether the Executive had the authority to detain and, if so, what rights the detainee had under the Due Process Clause. True, there are places in the Hamdi plurality opinion where it is difficult to tell where its extrapolation of § 2241 ends and its analysis of the petitioner's Due Process rights begins. But the Court had no occasion to define the necessary scope of habeas review, for Suspension Clause purposes, in the context of enemy combatant detentions. The closest the plurality came to doing so was in discussing whether, in light of separation-of-powers concerns, § 2241 should be construed to forbid the District Court from inquiring beyond the affidavit Hamdi's custodian provided in answer to the detainee's habeas petition. The plurality answered this question with an emphatic "no."

Even if we were to assume that the CSRTs satisfy due process standards, it would not end our inquiry. Habeas corpus is a collateral process that exists, in Justice Holmes' words, to "cu[t] through all forms and g[o] to the very tissue of the structure. It comes in from the outside, not in subordination to the proceedings, and although every form may have been preserved opens the inquiry whether they have been more than an empty shell." Frank v. Mangum, 237 U. S. 309, 346 (1915) (dissenting opinion). Even when the procedures authorizing detention are structurally sound, the Suspension Clause remains applicable and the writ relevant . . .

Although we make no judgment as to whether the CSRTs, as currently constituted, satisfy due process standards, we agree with petitioners that, even when all the parties involved in this process act with diligence and in good faith, there is considerable risk of error in the tribunal's findings of fact. This is a risk inherent in any process that, in the words of the former Chief Judge of the Court of Appeals, is "closed and accusatorial." See Bismullah III, 514 F. 3d, at 1296 (Ginsburg, C. J., concurring in denial of rehearing en banc). And given that the consequence of error may be detention of persons for the duration of hostilities that may last a generation or more, this is a risk too significant to ignore.

For the writ of habeas corpus, or its substitute, to function as an effective and proper remedy in this context, the court that conducts the habeas proceeding must have the means to correct errors that occurred during the CSRT proceedings. This includes some authority to assess the sufficiency of the Government's evidence against the detainee. It also must have the authority to admit and consider relevant exculpatory evidence that was not introduced during the earlier proceeding. Federal habeas petitioners long have had the means to supplement the record on review, even in the postconviction habeas setting.... Here that opportunity is constitutionally required.

   . . .

The extent of the showing required of the Government in these cases is a matter to be determined. We need not explore it further at this stage. We do hold that when the judicial power to issue habeas corpus properly is invoked the judicial officer must have adequate authority to make a determination in light of the relevant law and facts and to formulate and issue appropriate orders for relief, including, if necessary, an order directing the prisoner's release.

C

We now consider whether the DTA allows the Court of Appeals to conduct a proceeding meeting these standards....

   . . .

By foreclosing consideration of evidence not presented or reasonably available to the detainee at the CSRT proceedings, the DTA disadvantages the detainee by limiting the scope of collateral review to a record that may not be accurate or complete. In other contexts, e.g., in post-trial habeas cases where the prisoner already has had a full and fair opportunity to develop the factual predicate of his claims, similar limitations on the scope of habeas review may be appropriate.... In this context, however, where the underlying detention proceedings lack the necessary adversarial character, the detainee cannot be held responsible for all deficiencies in the record.

The Government does not make the alternative argument that the DTA allows for the introduction of previously unavailable exculpatory evidence on appeal. It does point out, however, that if a detainee obtains such evidence, he can request that the Deputy Secretary of Defense convene a new CSRT. See Supp. Brief for Respondents 4. Whatever the merits of this procedure, it is an insufficient replacement for the factual review these detainees are entitled to receive through habeas corpus. The Deputy Secretary's determination whether to initiate new proceedings is wholly a discretionary one....

We do not imply DTA review would be a constitutionally sufficient replacement for habeas corpus but for these limitations on the detainee's ability to present exculpatory evidence. For even if it were possible, as a textual matter, to read into the statute each of the necessary procedures we have identified, we could not overlook the cumulative effect of our doing so. To hold that the detainees at Guantanamo may, under the DTA, challenge the President's legal authority to detain them, contest the CSRT's findings of fact, supplement the record on review with exculpatory evidence, and request an order of release would come close to reinstating the § 2241 habeas corpus process Congress sought to deny them. The language of the statute, read in light of Congress' reasons for enacting it, cannot bear this interpretation. Petitioners have met their burden of establishing that the DTA review process is, on its face, an inadequate substitute for habeas corpus.

. . .

VI

A

In light of our conclusion that there is no jurisdictional bar to the District Court's entertaining petitioners' claims the question remains whether there are prudential barriers to habeas corpus review under these circumstances.

The Government argues petitioners must seek review of their CSRT determinations in the Court of Appeals before they can proceed with their habeas corpus actions in the District Court. As noted earlier, in other contexts and for prudential reasons this Court has required exhaustion of alternative remedies before a prisoner can seek federal habeas relief. . . .

The real risks, the real threats, of terrorist attacks are constant and not likely soon to abate. The ways to disrupt our life and laws are so many and unforeseen that the Court should not attempt even some general catalogue of crises that might occur. Certain principles are apparent, however. Practical considerations and exigent circumstances inform the definition and reach of the law's writs, including habeas corpus. The cases and our tradition reflect this precept.

In cases involving foreign citizens detained abroad by the Executive, it likely would be both an impractical and unprecedented extension of judicial power to assume that habeas corpus would be available at the moment the prisoner is taken into custody. If and when habeas corpus jurisdiction applies, as it does in these cases, then proper deference can be accorded to reasonable procedures for screening and initial detention under lawful and proper conditions of confinement and treatment for a reasonable period of time. Domestic exigencies, furthermore, might also impose such onerous burdens on the Government that here, too, the Judicial Branch would be required to devise sensible rules for staying habeas corpus proceedings until the Government can comply with its requirements in a responsible way. Cf. Ex parte Milligan, 4 Wall., at 127

("If, in foreign invasion or civil war, the courts are actually closed, and it is impossible to administer criminal justice according to law, then, on the theatre of active military operations, where war really prevails, there is a necessity to furnish a substitute for the civil authority, thus overthrown, to preserve the safety of the army and society; and as no power is left but the military, it is allowed to govern by martial rule until the laws can have their free course"). Here, as is true with detainees apprehended abroad, a relevant consideration in determining the courts' role is whether there are suitable alternative processes in place to protect against the arbitrary exercise of governmental power.

The cases before us, however, do not involve detainees who have been held for a short period of time while awaiting their CSRT determinations. Were that the case, or were it probable that the Court of Appeals could complete a prompt review of their applications, the case for requiring temporary abstention or exhaustion of alternative remedies would be much stronger. These qualifications no longer pertain here. In some of these cases six years have elapsed without the judicial oversight that habeas corpus or an adequate substitute demands. And there has been no showing that the Executive faces such onerous burdens that it cannot respond to habeas corpus actions. To require these detainees to complete DTA review before proceeding with their habeas corpus actions would be to require additional months, if not years, of delay. The first DTA review applications were filed over a year ago, but no decisions on the merits have been issued. While some delay in fashioning new procedures is unavoidable, the costs of delay can no longer be borne by those who are held in custody. The detainees in these cases are entitled to a prompt habeas corpus hearing.

Our decision today holds only that the petitioners before us are entitled to seek the writ; that the DTA review procedures are an inadequate substitute for habeas corpus; and that the petitioners in these cases need not exhaust the review procedures in the Court of Appeals before proceeding with their habeas actions in the District Court. The only law we identify as unconstitutional is MCA § 7, 28 U. S. C. A. § 2241(e) (Supp. 2007). Accordingly, both the DTA and the CSRT process remain intact. Our holding with regard to exhaustion should not be read to imply that a habeas court should intervene the moment an enemy combatant steps foot in a territory where the writ runs. The Executive is entitled to a reasonable period of time to determine a detainee's status before a court entertains that detainee's habeas corpus petition. The CSRT process is the mechanism Congress and the President set up to deal with these issues. Except in cases of undue delay, federal courts should refrain from entertaining an enemy combatant's habeas corpus petition at least until after the Department, acting via the CSRT, has had a chance to review his status.

B

Although we hold that the DTA is not an adequate and effective substitute for habeas corpus, it does not follow that a habeas corpus court may disregard the dangers the detention in these cases was intended to prevent. . . . Certain accommodations can be made to reduce the burden habeas corpus proceedings will place on the military without impermissibly diluting the protections of the writ.

In the DTA Congress sought to consolidate review of petitioners' claims in the Court of Appeals. Channeling future cases to one district court would no doubt reduce administrative burdens on the Government. This is a legitimate objective that might be advanced even without an amendment to § 2241. If, in a future case, a detainee files a habeas petition in another judicial district in which a proper respondent can be served, see Rumsfeld v. Padilla, 542 U. S. 426, 435–436 (2004), the Government can move for change of venue to the court that will hear these petitioners' cases, . . .

Another of Congress' reasons for vesting exclusive jurisdiction in the Court of Appeals, perhaps, was to avoid the widespread dissemination of classified information. The Government has raised similar concerns here and elsewhere. See Brief for Respondents 55–56; Bismullah Pet. 30. We make no attempt to anticipate all of the evidentiary and access-to-counsel issues that will arise during the course of the detainees' habeas corpus proceedings. We recognize, however, that the Government has a legitimate interest in protecting sources and methods of intelligence gathering; and we expect that the District Court will use its discretion to accommodate this interest to the greatest extent possible. Cf. United States v. Reynolds, 345 U. S. 1, 10 (1953) (recognizing an evidentiary privilege in a civil damages case where "there is a reasonable danger that compulsion of the evidence will expose military matters which, in the interest of national security, should not be divulged").

These and the other remaining questions are within the expertise and competence of the District Court to address in the first instance.

* * *

. . .

Our opinion does not undermine the Executive's powers as Commander in Chief. On the contrary, the exercise of those powers is vindicated, not eroded, when confirmed by the Judicial Branch. Within the Constitution's separation-of-powers structure, few exercises of judicial power are as legitimate or as necessary as the responsibility to hear challenges to the authority of the Executive to imprison a person. Some of these petitioners have been in custody for six years with no definitive judicial determination as to the legality of their detention. Their access to the writ is a necessity to determine the lawfulness of their status, even if, in the end, they do not obtain the relief they seek.

Because our Nation's past military conflicts have been of limited duration, it has been possible to leave the outer boundaries of war powers undefined. If, as some fear, terrorism continues to pose dangerous threats to us for years to come, the Court might not have this luxury. This result is not inevitable, however. The political branches, consistent with their independent obligations to interpret and uphold the Constitution, can engage in a genuine debate about how best to preserve constitutional values while protecting the Nation from terrorism. Cf. Hamdan, 548 U. S., at 636 (Breyer, J., concurring) ("[J]udicial insistence upon that consultation does not weaken our Nation's ability to deal with danger. To the contrary, that insistence strengthens the Nation's ability to determine-through democratic means-how best to do so").

It bears repeating that our opinion does not address the content of the law that governs petitioners' detention. That is a matter yet to be determined. We hold that petitioners may invoke the fundamental procedural protections of habeas corpus. The laws and Constitution are designed to survive, and remain in force, in extraordinary times. Liberty and security can be reconciled; and in our system they are reconciled within the framework of the law. The Framers decided that habeas corpus, a right of first importance, must be a part of that framework, a part of that law.

The determination by the Court of Appeals that the Suspension Clause and its protections are inapplicable to petitioners was in error. The judgment of the Court of Appeals is reversed. The cases are remanded to the Court of Appeals with instructions that it remand the cases to the District Court for proceedings consistent with this opinion.

It is so ordered.

[JUSTICE SOUTER, with whom JUSTICE GINSBURG and JUSTICE BREYER joined wrote a separate concurring opinion.]

CHIEF JUSTICE ROBERTS, with whom JUSTICE SCALIA, JUSTICE THOMAS, and JUSTICE ALITO join, dissenting.

Today the Court strikes down as inadequate the most generous set of procedural protections ever afforded aliens detained by this country as enemy combatants. The political branches crafted these procedures amidst an ongoing military conflict, after much careful investigation and thorough debate. The Court rejects them today out of hand, without bothering to say what due process rights the detainees possess, without explaining how the statute fails to vindicate those rights, and before a single petitioner has even attempted to avail himself of the law's operation. And to what effect? The majority merely replaces a review system designed by the people's representatives with a set of shapeless procedures to be defined by federal courts at some future date. One cannot help but think, after surveying the modest practical results of the majority's ambitious opinion, that this decision is not really about the detainees at all, but about control of federal policy regarding enemy combatants.

. . .

If the CSRT procedures meet the minimal due process requirements outlined in Hamdi, and if an Article III court is available to ensure that these procedures are followed in future cases, . . . there is no need to reach the Suspension Clause question. Detainees will have received all the process the Constitution could possibly require, whether that process is called "habeas" or something else. The question of the writ's reach need not be addressed.

This is why the Court should have required petitioners to exhaust their remedies under the statute.... Because the majority refuses to assess whether the CSRTs comport with the Constitution, it ends up razing a system of collateral review that it admits may in fact satisfy the Due Process Clause and be "structurally sound." But if the collateral review procedures Congress has provided-CSRT review coupled with Article III scrutiny-are sound, interference by a federal habeas court may be entirely unnecessary.

The only way to know is to require petitioners to use the alternative procedures Congress designed. Mandating that the petitioners exhaust their statutory remedies "is in no sense a suspension of the writ of habeas corpus. It is merely a deferment of resort to the writ until other corrective procedures are shown to be futile."

. . .

II

The majority's overreaching is particularly egregious given the weakness of its objections to the DTA. Simply put, the Court's opinion fails on its own terms. The majority strikes down the statute because it is not an "adequate substitute" for habeas review, ... but fails to show what rights the detainees have that cannot be vindicated by the DTA system.

Because the central purpose of habeas corpus is to test the legality of executive detention, the writ requires most fundamentally an Article III court able to hear the prisoner's claims and, when necessary, order release.... The only issue in dispute is the process the Guantanamo prisoners are entitled to use to test the legality of their detention. Hamdi concluded that American citizens detained as enemy combatants are entitled to only limited process, and that much of that process could be supplied by a military tribunal, with review to follow in an Article III court. That is precisely the system we have here. It is adequate to vindicate whatever due process rights petitioners may have.

A

The Court reaches the opposite conclusion partly because it misreads the statute. The majority appears not to understand how the review system it invalidates actually works-specifically, how CSRT review and review by the D. C. Circuit fit together. After briefly acknowledging in its recitation of the facts that the Government designed the CSRTs "to comply with the due process requirements identified by the plurality in Hamdi," the Court proceeds to dismiss the tribunal proceedings as no more than a suspect method used by the Executive for determining the status of the detainees in the first instance. This leads the Court to treat the review the DTA provides in the D. C. Circuit as the only opportunity detainees have to challenge their status determination.

. . .

III

For all its eloquence about the detainees' right to the writ, the Court makes no effort to elaborate how exactly the remedy it prescribes will differ from the procedural protections detainees enjoy under the DTA. The Court objects to the detainees' limited access to witnesses and classified material, but proposes no alternatives of its own. Indeed, it simply ignores the many difficult questions its holding presents. What, for example, will become of the CSRT process? The majority says federal courts should generally refrain from entertaining detainee challenges until after the petitioner's CSRT proceeding has finished. (''[e]xcept in cases of undue delay''). But to what deference, if any, is that CSRT determination entitled?

. . .

The majority rests its decision on abstract and hypothetical concerns. Step back and consider what, in the real world, Congress and the Executive have actually granted aliens captured by our Armed Forces overseas and found to be enemy combatants:

The right to hear the bases of the charges against them, including a summary of any classified evidence.

The ability to challenge the bases of their detention before military tribunals modeled after Geneva Convention procedures. Some 38 detainees have been released as a result of this process.

The right, before the CSRT, to testify, introduce evidence, call witnesses, question those the Government calls, and secure release, if and when appropriate.

The right to the aid of a personal representative in arranging and presenting their cases before a CSRT.

Before the D. C. Circuit, the right to employ counsel, challenge the factual record, contest the lower tribunal's legal determinations, ensure compliance with the Constitution and laws, and secure release, if any errors below establish their entitlement to such relief.

In sum, the DTA satisfies the majority's own criteria for assessing adequacy. This statutory scheme provides the combatants held at Guantanamo greater procedural protections than have ever been afforded alleged enemy detainees-whether citizens or aliens-in our national history.

* * *

So who has won? Not the detainees. The Court's analysis leaves them with only the prospect of further litigation to determine the content of their new habeas right, followed by further litigation to resolve their particular cases, followed by further litigation before the D. C. Circuit-where they could have started had they invoked the DTA procedure. Not Congress, whose attempt to "determine-through democratic means-how best" to balance the security of the American people with the detainees' liberty interests, see Hamdan v. Rumsfeld, 548 U. S. 557, 636 (2006) (Breyer, J., concurring), has been unceremoniously brushed aside. Not the Great Writ, whose majesty is hardly enhanced by its extension to a jurisdictionally quirky outpost, with no tangible benefit to anyone. Not the rule of law, unless by that is meant the rule of lawyers, who will now arguably have a greater role than military and intelligence officials in shaping policy for alien enemy combatants. And certainly not the American people, who today lose a bit more control over the conduct of this Nation's foreign policy to unelected, politically unaccountable judges.

I respectfully dissent.

QUESTIONS AND NOTES

1. The original strategy of the Bush administration in establishing the detention facility at Guantanamo Bay in connection with its anti-terrorism efforts probably assumed that the fact that facility was offshore and not in territory *owned* by the United States would make it easier to argue: a) that U.S. civilian law and, specifically, most constitutional protections, were inapplicable to persons detained there; and b) persons detained there had no right to access U.S. courts. As we have seen in *Boumediene v. Bush*, supra, the Supreme Court ruled that the Guantanamo detainees had a constitutional right to obtain habeas corpus review of the legality of their detention. It remains to be seen whether the courts will apply other constitutional protections to the Guantanamo detainees, and if so, which ones.

2. As recounted by the majority opinion in the Boumediene case, in the wake of the Hamdi decision, the military authorities fashioned an administrative process, Combat Status Review Tribunals (CSRT'S), to determine in the first instance whether there was an adequate factual and legal basis for detaining the individual. (A system of annual reviews of the status of the individual following up after the CSRT process—to determine whether each detainee was still dangerous or still could provide intelligence, was also established, called Administrative Review Boards (ARB's)). Subsequently, a process for judicial review of the CSRT determinations was legislated in the Detainee Treatment Act (DTA). While in Boumediene the Court did not invalidate the CSRT process, it did seem to place greater weight on the habeas review by the federal courts. Accordingly, in order to give the reader a sense of how the habeas review has developed and how effective it is we present material on those topics in subsection 2, below. In subsection 3, below, additional material relating to status determinations through an administrative process is presented, including a new set of procedures for determining whether to continue to detain a person, promulgated by the Obama administration on March 7, 2011.

3. In the wake of the aforementioned decision, a further issue arose—whether an implication of Boumediene is that habeas corpus relief should be

available to individuals detained in a facility even further afield from the U.S. than Guantanamo Bay. The issue is addressed below.

AL–MAQALEH v. GATES

605 F.3d 84 (D.C. Cir. 2010)

SENTELLE, CHIEF JUDGE:

Three detainees at Bagram Air Force Base in Afghanistan petitioned the district court for habeas corpus relief from their confinement by the United States military. Appellants (collectively "the United States" or "the government") moved to dismiss for lack of jurisdiction based on § 7(a) of the Military Commissions Act of 2006, Pub.L. No. 109–366, 120 Stat. 2600 (2006) ("MCA"). The district court agreed with the United States that § 7(a) of the MCA purported to deprive the court of jurisdiction, but held that this section could not constitutionally be applied to deprive the court of jurisdiction under the Supreme Court's test articulated in *Boumediene v. Bush*, 553 U.S. 723, 128 S.Ct. 2229, 171 L.Ed.2d 41 (2008). The court therefore denied the motion to dismiss but certified the three habeas cases for interlocutory appeal under 28 U.S.C. § 1292(b). Pursuant to that certification, the government filed a petition to this court for interlocutory appeal. We granted the petition and now consider the jurisdictional question. Upon review, and applying the Supreme Court decision in *Boumediene,* we determine that the district court did not have jurisdiction to consider the petitions for habeas corpus. We therefore reverse the order of the district court and order that the petitions be dismissed.

. . .

All three petitioners are being held as unlawful enemy combatants at the Bagram Theater Internment Facility on the Bagram Airfield Military Base in Afghanistan. Petitioner Fadi Al–Maqaleh is a Yemeni citizen who alleges he was taken into custody in 2003. While Al–Maqaleh's petition asserts "on information and belief" that he was captured beyond Afghan borders, a sworn declaration from Colonel James W. Gray, Commander of Detention Operations, states that Al–Maqaleh was captured in Zabul, Afghanistan. Redha Al–Najar is a Tunisian citizen who alleges he was captured in Pakistan in 2002. Amin Al–Bakri is a Yemeni citizen who alleges he was captured in Thailand in 2002. Both Al–Najar and Al–Bakri allege they were first held in some other unknown location before being moved to Bagram.

. . .

Bagram Airfield Military Base is the largest military facility in Afghanistan occupied by United States and coalition forces. The United States entered into an "Accommodation Consignment Agreement for Lands and Facilities at Bagram Airfield" with the Islamic Republic of Afghanistan in 2006, which "consigns all facilities and land located at Bagram Airfield ... owned by [Afghanistan,] or Parwan Province, or private individuals, or others, for use by the United States and coalition forces for military purposes." (Accommodation and Consignment Agreement for Lands and Facilities at Bagram Airfield Between the Islamic Republic of Afghanistan and the United States of America). The Agreement refers to Afghanistan as the "host nation" and the United States "as the lessee." The leasehold created by the agreement is to continue "until the United States or its successors determine that the premises are no longer required for its use."

Afghanistan remains a theater of active military combat. The United States and coalition forces conduct "an ongoing military campaign against al Qaeda, the Taliban regime, and their affiliates and supporters in Afghanistan." These operations are conducted in part from Bagram Airfield. Bagram has been subject to repeated attacks from the Taliban and al Qaeda, including a March 2009 suicide bombing striking the gates of the facility, and Taliban rocket attacks in June of 2009 resulting in death and injury to United States service members and other personnel.

While the United States provides overall security to Bagram, numerous other nations have compounds on the base. Some of the other nations control access to their respective compounds. The troops of the other nations are present at Bagram both as part of the American-led military coalition in Afghanistan and as members of the International Security Assistance Force (ISAF) of the North Atlantic Treaty Organization. The mission of the ISAF is to support the Afghan government in the maintenance of security in Afghanistan.... According to the United States, as of February 1, 2010, approximately 38,000 non-United States troops were serving in Afghanistan as part of the ISAF, representing 42 other countries.

   . . .

Appellees in this action, three detainees at Bagram, filed habeas petitions against the President of the United States and the Secretary of Defense in the district court. The government moved to dismiss for lack of jurisdiction, relying principally upon § 7(a) of the Military Commissions Act of 2006. After the change in presidential administrations on January 22, 2009, the court invited the government to express any change in its position on the jurisdictional question. The government informed the district court that it "adheres to its previously articulated position."

The district court, recognizing that the issue of whether the court had jurisdiction presented a controlling question of law as to which there were substantial grounds for difference of opinion, certified the question for interlocutory appeal under 28 U.S.C. § 1292(b). We accepted the case for interlocutory review, bringing the jurisdictional issue before us in the present appeal.

   . . .

. . . [T]he Court [in *Boumediene]* concluded that "at least three factors are relevant in determining the reach of the Suspension Clause."

Those three factors, which we must apply today in answering the . . . question as to detainees at Bagram, are:

> (1) the citizenship and status of the detainee and the adequacy of the process through which that status determination was made; (2) the nature of the sites where apprehension and then detention took place; and (3) the practical obstacles inherent in resolving the prisoner's entitlement to the writ.

Applying these factors to the detainees at Guantanamo, the Court [in *Boumediene*] held that the petitioners had the protection of the Suspension Clause.

. . .

Our duty, as explained above, is to determine the reach of the right to habeas corpus and therefore of the Suspension Clause to the factual context underlying the petitions we consider in the present appeal. In doing so, we are controlled by the Supreme Court's interpretation of the Constitution in *Eisentrager* as construed and explained in the Court's more recent opinion in *Boumediene*. This is not an easy task, as illustrated by the thorough and careful opinion of the district court. While we are properly respectful of the district court's careful undertaking of this difficult task, as we review rulings on motions to dismiss . . . *de novo,* we reexamine the issue and ultimately reach a different conclusion.

At the outset, we note that each of the parties has asserted both an extreme understanding of the law after *Boumediene* and a more nuanced set of arguments upon which each relies in anticipation of the possible rejection of the bright-line arguments. The United States would like us to hold that the *Boumediene* analysis has no application beyond territories that are, like Guantanamo, outside the *de jure* sovereignty of the United States but are subject to its *de facto* sovereignty. As the government puts it in its reply brief, "[t]he real question before this Court, therefore, is whether Bagram may be considered effectively part of the United States in light of the nature and history of the U.S. presence there." We disagree.

Relying upon three independent reasons, the Court in *Boumediene* expressly repudiated the argument of the United States in that case to the effect "that the *Eisentrager* Court adopted a formalistic, sovereignty-based test for determining the reach of the Suspension Clause." . . . The *Boumediene* Court explicitly did "not accept the idea that . . . the [sovereignty discussion] from *Eisentrager* is the only authoritative language in the opinion and that all the rest is dicta. The Court's further determinations, based on practical considerations, were integral to Part II of its opinion and came before the decision announced its holding." Second, the Court rejected the Government's reading of *Eisentrager* because the meaning of the word "sovereignty" in the *Eisentrager* opinion was not limited to the "narrow technical sense" of the word and could be read "to connote the degree of control the military asserted over the facility." . . .

True, the second factor articulated in *Boumediene* for rejecting the government's reading of *Eisentrager* might apply differently in this case because of differences in the levels of control over the military facilities. But we must keep in mind that the second factor is only one of the three reasons offered by the *Boumediene* Court for the rejection of "a formalistic, sovereignty-based test for determining the reach of the Suspension Clause." Whatever the force of the second reason offered by the Court in *Boumediene,* the first and third reasons make it plain that the Court's understanding of *Eisentrager,* and therefore of the reach of the Suspension Clause, was based not on a formalistic attachment to sovereignty, but on a consideration of practical factors as well. We note that the very fact that the *Boumediene* Court set forth the three-factor test outlined above parallels the *Eisentrager* Court's further reasoning addressed by the *Boumediene* Court in its rejection of the bright-line *de jure* sovereignty argument before it. That is, had the *Boumediene* Court intended to limit its understanding of the reach of the Suspension Clause to territories over which the United States exercised *de facto* sovereignty, it would have had no need to outline the factors to be considered either generally or in the detail which it in fact adopted. We therefore reject the proposition that *Boumediene* adopted a bright-line test with the effect of substituting *de facto* for *de jure* in the otherwise rejected interpretation of *Eisentrager.*

For similar reasons, we reject the most extreme position offered by the petitioners. At various points, the petitioners seem to be arguing that the fact of United States control of Bagram under the lease of the military base is sufficient to trigger the extraterritorial application of the Suspension Clause, or at least satisfy the second factor of the three set forth in *Boumediene.* Again, we reject this extreme understanding. Such an interpretation would seem to create the potential for the extraterritorial extension of the Suspension Clause to noncitizens held in any United States military facility in the world, and perhaps to an undeterminable number of other United States-leased facilities as well. Significantly, the court engaged in an extended dialog with counsel for the petitioners in which we repeatedly sought some limiting principle that would distinguish Bagram from any other military installation. Counsel was able to produce no such distinction. Again, such an extended application is not a tenable interpretation of *Boumediene.* If it were the Supreme Court's intention to declare such a sweeping application, it would surely have said so. Just as we reject the extreme argument of the United States that would render most of the decision in *Boumediene* dicta, we reject the first line of argument offered by petitioners. Having rejected the bright-line arguments of both parties, we must proceed to their more nuanced arguments, and reach a conclusion based on the application of the Supreme Court's enumerated factors to the case before us.

The first of the enumerated factors is "the citizenship and status of the detainee and the adequacy of the process through which that status determination was made." Citizenship is, of course, an important factor in determining the constitutional rights of persons before the court. It is well established that there are "constitutional decisions of [the Supreme] Court expressly according differing protection to aliens than to citizens." *United States v. Verdugo–Urquidez,* 494 U.S. at 273, 110 S.Ct. 1056. However, clearly the alien citizenship of the petitioners in this case does not weigh against their claim to protection of the right of habeas corpus under the Suspension Clause. So far as citizenship is concerned, they differ in no material respect from the petitioners at Guantanamo who prevailed in *Boumediene.* As to status, the petitioners before us are held as enemy aliens. But so were the *Boumediene* petitioners. While the *Eisentrager* petitioners were in a weaker position by having the status of war criminals, that is immaterial to the question before us. This question is governed by *Boumediene* and the status of the petitioners before us again is the same as the Guantanamo detainees, so this factor supports their argument for the extension of the availability of the writ.

So far as the adequacy of the process through which that status determination was made, the petitioners are in a stronger position for the availability of the writ than were either the *Eisentrager* or *Boumediene* petitioners. As the Supreme Court noted, the *Boumediene* petitioners were in a very different posture than those in *Eisentrager* in that "there ha[d] been no trial by military commission for violations of the laws of war." Unlike the *Boumediene* petitioners or those before us, "[t]he *Eisentrager* petitioners were charged by a bill of particulars that made detailed factual allegations against them." The *Eisentrager* detainees were "entitled to representation by counsel, allowed to introduce evidence on their own behalf, and permitted to cross-examine the prosecution's witnesses" in an adversarial proceeding. The status of the *Boumediene* petitioners was determined by Combatant Status Review Tribunals (CSRTs) affording far less protection. Under the CSRT proceeding, the detainee, rather than being represented by an attorney, was advised by a "Personal Representative" who was "not the detainee's lawyer or even his 'advocate.'" The CSRT proceeding was less protective than the military tribunal procedures in *Eisentrager* in other particulars as well, and the Supreme Court clearly stated that "[t]he difference is not trivial."

The status of the Bagram detainees is determined not by a Combatant Status Review Tribunal but by an "Unlawful Enemy Combatant Review Board" (UECRB). As the district court correctly noted, proceedings before the UECRB afford even less protection to the rights of detainees in the determination of status than was the case with the CSRT.[4] Therefore, as the district court noted, "while the important adequacy of process factor strongly supported the extension of the Suspension Clause and habeas rights in *Boumediene,* it even more strongly favors petitioners here." Therefore, examining only the first of the Supreme Court's three enumerated factors, petitioners have made a strong argument that the right to

---

4. The Government argues that in our analysis of this first factor, we should consider new procedures that it has put into place at Bagram in the past few months for evaluating the continued detention of individuals. But we will decide this case based on the procedures that have been in place, not on the new procedures that are being implemented only now when the case is before the Court of Appeals.

habeas relief and the Suspension Clause apply in Bagram as in Guantanamo. However, we do not stop with the first factor.

The second factor, "the nature of the sites where apprehension and then detention took place," weighs heavily in favor of the United States. Like all petitioners in both *Eisentrager* and *Boumediene,* the petitioners here were apprehended abroad. While this in itself would appear to weigh against the extension of the writ, it obviously would not be sufficient, otherwise *Boumediene* would not have been decided as it was. However, the nature of the place where the detention takes place weighs more strongly in favor of the position argued by the United States and against the extension of habeas jurisdiction than was the case in either *Boumediene* or *Eisentrager.* In the first place, while *de facto* sovereignty is not determinative, for the reasons discussed above, the very fact that it was the subject of much discussion in *Boumediene* makes it obvious that it is not without relevance. As the Supreme Court set forth, Guantanamo Bay is "a territory that, while technically not part of the United States, is under the complete and total control of our Government." While it is true that the United States holds a leasehold interest in Bagram, and held a leasehold interest in Guantanamo, the surrounding circumstances are hardly the same. The United States has maintained its total control of Guantanamo Bay for over a century, even in the face of a hostile government maintaining *de jure* sovereignty over the property. In Bagram, while the United States has options as to duration of the lease agreement, there is no indication of any intent to occupy the base with permanence, nor is there hostility on the part of the "host" country. Therefore, the notion that *de facto* sovereignty extends to Bagram is no more real than would have been the same claim with respect to Landsberg in the *Eisentrager* case. While it is certainly realistic to assert that the United States has *de facto* sovereignty over Guantanamo, the same simply is not true with respect to Bagram. Though the site of detention analysis weighs in favor of the United States and against the petitioners, it is not determinative.

But we hold that the third factor, that is "the practical obstacles inherent in resolving the prisoner's entitlement to the writ," particularly when considered along with the second factor, weighs overwhelmingly in favor of the position of the United States. It is undisputed that Bagram, indeed the entire nation of Afghanistan, remains a theater of war. Not only does this suggest that the detention at Bagram is more like the detention at Landsberg than Guantanamo, the position of the United States is even stronger in this case than it was in *Eisentrager.* As the Supreme Court recognized in *Boumediene,* even though the active hostilities in the European theater had "c[o]me to an end," at the time of the *Eisentrager* decision, many of the problems of a theater of war remained:

> In addition to supervising massive reconstruction and aid efforts the American forces stationed in Germany faced potential security threats from a defeated enemy. In retrospect the post-War occupation may seem uneventful. But at the time *Eisentrager* was decided, the

Court was right to be concerned about judicial interference with the military's efforts to contain "enemy elements, guerilla fighters, and 'were-wolves.'" 128 S.Ct. at 2261 (quoting *Eisentrager,* 339 U.S. at 784, 70 S.Ct. 936).

In ruling for the extension of the writ to Guantanamo, the Supreme Court expressly noted that "[s]imilar threats are not apparent here." In the case before us, similar, if not greater, threats are indeed apparent. The United States asserts, and petitioners cannot credibly dispute, that all of the attributes of a facility exposed to the vagaries of war are present in Bagram. The Supreme Court expressly stated in *Boumediene* that at Guantanamo, "[w]hile obligated to abide by the terms of the lease, the United States is, for all practical purposes, answerable to no other sovereign for its acts on the base. Were that not the case, *or if the detention facility were located in an active theater of war,* arguments that issuing the writ would be 'impractical or anomalous' would have more weight." *Id.* at 2261–62 (emphasis added).... We therefore conclude that under both *Eisentrager* and *Boumediene,* the writ does not extend to the Bagram confinement in an active theater of war in a territory under neither the *de facto* nor *de jure* sovereignty of the United States and within the territory of another *de jure* sovereign.

We are supported in this conclusion by the rationale of *Eisentrager,* which was not only not overruled, but reinforced by the language and reasoning just referenced from *Boumediene.* As we referenced in the background discussion of this opinion, we set forth more fully now concerns expressed by the Supreme Court in reaching its decision in *Eisentrager:*

> Such trials would hamper the war effort and bring aid and comfort to the enemy. They would diminish the prestige of our commanders, not only with enemies but with wavering neutrals. It would be difficult to devise more effective fettering of a field commander than to allow the very enemies he is ordered to reduce to submission to call him to account in his own civil courts and divert his efforts and attention from the military offensive abroad to the legal defensive at home. Nor is it unlikely that the result of such enemy litigiousness would be a conflict between judicial and military opinion highly comforting to enemies of the United States. *Eisentrager,* 339 U.S. at 779, 70 S.Ct. 936.

Those factors are more relevant to the situation at Bagram than they were at Landsberg. While it is true, as the Supreme Court noted in *Boumediene,* that the United States forces in Germany in 1950 faced the possibility of unrest and guerilla warfare, operations in the European theater had ended with the surrender of Germany and Italy years earlier. Bagram remains in a theater of war. We cannot, consistent with *Eisentrager* as elucidated by *Boumediene,* hold that the right to the writ of habeas corpus and the constitutional protections of the Suspension Clause extend to Bagram detention facility in Afghanistan, and we therefore must reverse the decision of the district court denying the motion of the United States to dismiss the petitions.

We do not ignore the arguments of the detainees that the United States chose the place of detention and might be able "to evade judicial review of Executive detention decisions by transferring detainees into active conflict zones, thereby granting the Executive the power to switch the Constitution on or off at will." However, that is not what happened here. Indeed, without dismissing the legitimacy or sincerity of appellees' concerns, we doubt that this fact goes to either the second or third of the Supreme Court's enumerated factors. We need make no determination on the importance of this possibility, given that it remains only a possibility; its resolution can await a case in which the claim is a reality rather than a speculation. In so stating, we note that the Supreme Court did not dictate that the three enumerated factors are exhaustive. It only told us that "*at least* three factors" are relevant. Perhaps such manipulation by the Executive might constitute an additional factor in some case in which it is in fact present. However, the notion that the United States deliberately confined the detainees in the theater of war rather than at, for example, Guantanamo, is not only unsupported by the evidence, it is not supported by reason. To have made such a deliberate decision to "turn off the Constitution" would have required the military commanders or other Executive officials making the situs determination to anticipate the complex litigation history set forth above and predict the *Boumediene* decision long before it came down.

Also supportive of our decision that the third factor weighs heavily in favor of the United States, as the district court recognized, is the fact that the detention is within the sovereign territory of another nation, which itself creates practical difficulties. Indeed, it was on this factor that the district court relied in dismissing the fourth petition, which was filed by an Afghan citizen detainee. While that factor certainly weighed more heavily with respect to an Afghan citizen, it is not without force with respect to detainees who are alien to both the United States and Afghanistan. The United States holds the detainees pursuant to a cooperative arrangement with Afghanistan on territory as to which Afghanistan is sovereign. While we cannot say that extending our constitutional protections to the detainees would be in any way disruptive of that relationship, neither can we say with certainty what the reaction of the Afghan government would be.

In sum, taken together, the second and especially the third factors compel us to hold that the petitions should have been dismissed.

. . .

For the reasons set forth above, we hold that the jurisdiction of the courts to afford the right to habeas relief and the protection of the Suspension Clause does not extend to aliens held in Executive detention in the Bagram detention facility in the Afghan theater of war. We therefore reverse the order of the district court denying the motion for dismissal of the United States and order that the petitions be dismissed for lack of jurisdiction.

MAQALEH v. GATES

2011 WL 666883 (D.D.C.)

[Following the decision in Maqaleh, supra, the petitioners moved in the district court for rehearing based on a claim of new evidence. The court ruled as follows:]

Petitioners now seek to amend their habeas petitions with what they assert is newly discovered evidence that undercuts the basis of the D.C. Circuit's prior decision finding no jurisdiction over their petitions.

Generally, the additional evidence that petitioners now proffer is the following: operational and substantive changes to the U.S. detention system at Bagram Air Base, including the commencement of civilian criminal trials for Afghan nationals there; movement and retention of detainees in Afghanistan allegedly reflecting Executive Branch efforts to avoid judicial scrutiny of detention practices and policies; and current specifics of plans to continue to hold non-Afghan detainees in a new facility at Bagram in an attempt to evade any obligations before the courts. Petitioners claim that this purportedly new evidence warrants reexamination of the jurisdictional analysis undertaken in this case by this Court and then by the D.C. Circuit, applying Boumediene. . . .

. . . [U]ltimately the Court concludes that the examination respondents urge, and the assessment of petitioners' "new" evidence that the law (and arguably the D.C. Circuit's July 23, 2010 order) requires, is best undertaken by permitting the requested amendments and then addressing the petitions on their merits through the vehicle of a motion to dismiss filed by respondents. The proffered evidence is extensive (and arguably evolving) and, in some ways, its impact under the *Boumediene/Maqaleh* factors is subtle. While the Court has some doubts about the consequence of the additional evidence under that analytical framework, that issue is better explored through full consideration of the evidence and the parties' positions, rather than under the limited "futility" appraisal in which it is now presented. . . .

Therefore, the Court will grant petitioners' joint motion to amend their habeas corpus petitions. The Court expects, however, that granting the motion will enable more careful scrutiny of the amended petitions through a motion to dismiss filed by respondents, and through firm application of the analytical framework established by the Supreme Court in *Boumediene* and applied by the D.C. Circuit in *Maqaleh*. . . .

2. POST–BOUMEDIENE HABEAS CORPUS REVIEWS

Following the Supreme Court's decision in Boumediene v. Bush, a large number of habeas corpus actions were filed by individuals detained at Guantanamo. As of this writing, based on an unofficial score card, approximately 59 cases have been decided at least at the district court level. The statistics are complicated. Of the 59 cases, 17 involved Uighurs (an ethnic group from a western province in China and central Asia who are Muslims), and the government conceded or it was decided that their detention was unlawful. Approximately 18 additional cases were decided at the district court level in favor of the petitioning detainees. 14 of these have been finally resolved in favor of the detainee because the government did not appeal or the appeal was dismissed. In four cases decided in favor of the government at the district court level, the detainee did not appeal or the appeal was dismissed. 10 cases initially decided in favor of the government at the district court level are pending. Interestingly, of the cases which have been decided on the merits by the U.S. Court of Appeals, 10 cases were decided in favor of the government; thus far, none in favor of the detainee. The statistics are taken from Benjamin Wittes post on LawFare at 11:05 am on June 13, 2011.http://www.lawfareblog.com/category/guantanamo/litigation/dccircuit/. For a study of the Guantanamo habeas cases, see Benjamin Wittes, Robert M. Chesney, Larkin Reynolds, The Emerging Law of Detention 2.0 (Harvard Law School, Brookings, 2011).

BENSAYAH v. OBAMA

610 F.3d 718 (D.C. Cir. 2010)

Opinion for the Court filed by CIRCUIT JUDGE GINSBURG.

GINSBURG, CIRCUIT JUDGE:

Belkacem Bensayah petitioned the district court for a writ of habeas corpus in order to challenge his detention at the Naval Station at Guantanamo Bay, Cuba. The district court denied his petition, holding the Government had shown by a preponderance of the evidence that Bensayah was being held lawfully pursuant to the Authorization for Use of Military Force (AUMF), because he had provided "support" to al Qaeda. On appeal the Government has eschewed reliance upon certain evidence the district court had considered and has abandoned its position that Bensayah's detention is lawful because of the support he rendered to al Qaeda; instead it argues only that his detention is lawful because he was "part of" that organization-a contention the district court did not reach.

We agree with the Government that its authority under the AUMF extends to the detention of individuals who are functionally part of al Qaeda. The evidence upon which the district court relied in concluding Bensayah supported al Qaeda is insufficient, however, to show he was part of that organization. We therefore remand this case for the district court to determine whether, considering all reliable evidence, Bensayah was functionally part of al Qaeda.

   . . .

Bensayah, an Algerian citizen, was arrested by the Bosnian police on immigration charges in late 2001. He was later told that he and five other Algerian men arrested in Bosnia were suspected of plotting to attack the United States Embassy in Sarajevo. Because the ensuing three-month investigation failed to uncover evidence sufficient to continue the detention of the six men, the Supreme Court of the Federation of Bosnia and Herzogovina ordered that they be released. The men were then turned over to the United States Government and transported to the U.S. Naval Station at Guantanamo Bay, where they have been detained since January 2002.

   . . .

In August 2008 the district court entered a case management order (CMO) establishing the procedures that would govern this case. *See* CMO, *Boumediene v. Bush,* No. 04–1166 (RJL) (D.D.C. Aug. 27, 2008). The CMO placed upon the Government the burden of establishing, by a preponderance of the evidence, the lawfulness of the petitioner's detention. The Government was required to submit a return stating the factual and legal bases for detaining that prisoner, who was then required to file a traverse stating the relevant facts in support of his petition and a rebuttal of the Government's legal justification for his detention. The CMO allowed discovery only "by leave of the Court for good cause shown," and required that requests for discovery

> (1) be narrowly tailored; (2) specify why the request is likely to produce evidence both relevant and material to the petitioner's case; (3) specify the nature of the request . . .; and (4) explain why the burden on the Government to produce such evidence is neither unfairly disruptive nor unduly burdensome.

It also required the Government to provide to the petitioner any exculpatory evidence "contained in the material reviewed in developing the return for the petitioner [ ] and in preparation for the hearing for the petitioner."

The Government claimed authority to detain the six men pursuant both to the AUMF and to the President's inherent powers as Commander in Chief. It argued each of the six men was lawfully detained as an "enemy combatant," which the district court had in an earlier order defined as

> an individual who was part of or supporting Taliban or al Qaeda forces, or associated forces that are engaged in hostilities against the United States or its coalition partners. This includes any person who has committed a belligerent act or has directly supported hostilities in aid of enemy armed forces.

Boumediene v. Bush, 583 F.Supp.2d 133, 135 (2008). The Government contended all six men were lawfully detained because they had planned to travel to Afghanistan in late 2001 in order to take up arms against the United States and allied forces. It also contended Bensayah's detention was lawful because he was a member of and a travel facilitator for al Qaeda. The only direct evidence the Government offered in support of its contentions about Bensayah was contained in a classified document [redacted] from an unnamed source and in certain other pieces of evidence it claimed corroborated that document.

The district court granted habeas to each petitioner other than Bensayah, holding the Government had failed to show by a preponderance of the evidence that they had planned to travel to Afghanistan to fight against the United States. *Boumediene,* 579 F.Supp.2d at 197–98. Because the Government did not sufficiently establish the reliability of the allegations in the classified document about those petitioners, the court refused to credit those allegations.

The district court denied Bensayah's petition because it determined "the Government has met its burden by providing additional evidence that sufficiently corroborates its allegations from this unnamed source that Bensayah is an al-Qaida facilitator. The corroborative evidence provided by the Government is of three sorts: (1) evidence linking Bensayah to al Qaeda, and specifically to a "senior al-Qaida facilitator"; (2) evidence of Bensayah's history of travel "between and among countries using false passports in multiple names"; and (3) evidence creating "sufficient doubt as to Bensayah's credibility."

Having deemed the allegations about Bensayah in the classified document reliable, the district court held "the Government has established by a preponderance of the evidence that it is more likely than not . . . Bensayah not only planned to take up arms against the United States but also [planned to] facilitate the travel of unnamed others to do the same." The court further held such planning and facilitating "amounts to 'support' within the meaning of the 'enemy combatant' definition governing this case." Because it held Bensayah's detention was lawful based upon his support of al Qaeda, the court did not go on to consider whether he was a "member" of al Qaeda or whether his detention was lawful on the alternative ground that he was "part of" that organization.

There have been three developments since the district court's decision. First, the Government has eschewed reliance upon a portion of the evidence that the "senior al-Qaida facilitator" with whom Bensayah allegedly had contact was in fact a senior al Qaeda facilitator. Second, the Government has changed its position concerning the source and scope of its authority to detain Bensayah. Whereas the Government had previously claimed authority to detain Bensayah based upon both the AUMF and the President's constitutional authority as Commander in Chief, it now relies solely upon the AUMF. Third, the Government has abandoned its argument that Bensayah is being detained lawfully because of the support he rendered to al Qaeda—the sole basis upon which the district court denied Bensayah's petition. The Government now contends that Bensayah's detention is lawful only because he was "part of" al Qaeda.

. . .

Some but not all Bensayah's many arguments on appeal were mooted when the Government abandoned its theory that Bensayah's detention is lawful because he rendered support to al Qaeda. As for matters of procedure, Bensayah still challenges the district court's (1) reliance upon the preponderance of the evidence standard, (2) refusal to require the Government to search for reasonably available exculpatory evidence in its possession, (3) denial of his discovery requests, and (4) admission of the Government's "rebuttal" evidence. As for matters of substance, Bensayah still argues the district court erred in (1) adopting an overbroad definition of the Executive's detention authority, and (2) crediting "inadequately corroborated raw intelligence." Even if that evidence is credited, he argues (3) it is insufficient to establish his detention is lawful.

We review de novo the district court's conclusions of law, including its ultimate denial of a writ of habeas corpus. We review its factual determinations for clear error, and its evidentiary rulings for abuse of discretion, Whether a detainee was "part of" al Qaeda is a mixed question of law and fact. *Awad v. Obama,* No. 09–5351, slip op. at 17 (June 2, 2010). "That is, whether a detainee's alleged conduct . . . justifies his detention under the AUMF is a legal question. The question whether the [G]overnment has proven that conduct . . . is a factual question that we review for clear error." *Barhoumi v. Obama,* No. 09–5383, slip op. at 12–13 (June 11, 2010).

. . .

In *Boumediene* the Supreme Court held detainees at Guantanamo Bay are entitled to "the fundamental procedural protections of habeas corpus," but did not expand upon which procedural protections are "fundamental." It left open, for instance, the standard of proof the Government must meet in order to defeat a petition for habeas corpus. ("The extent of the showing required of the Government in these cases is a matter to be determined"). Bensayah argues that because he is liable to be held "for the duration of hostilities that may last a generation or more," requiring the Government to prove the lawfulness of his detention by a mere preponderance of the evidence is inappropriate. He contends the district court should have required the Government to prove its case beyond a reasonable doubt, or at least by clear and convincing evidence. This argument has been overtaken by events, for we have recently held a standard of proof higher than a preponderance of the evidence is not a "fundamental procedural protection" of habeas required by *Boumediene. Awad,* slip op. at 18 ("A preponderance of the evidence standard satisfies constitutional requirements in considering a habeas petition from a detainee held pursuant to the AUMF"); *Al–Bihani v. Obama,* 590 F.3d 866, 878 (2010) ("Our narrow charge is to determine whether a preponderance standard is unconstitutional. Absent more specific and relevant guidance, we find no indication that it is.").

The CMO requires the Government to

> provide on an ongoing basis any evidence contained in the material [it] reviewed in developing the return for the petitioner, and in preparation for the hearing for the petitioner, that tends materially to undermine the Government's theory as to the lawfulness of the petitioner's detention.

Bensayah argues the district court abused its discretion by imposing upon the Government an impermissibly narrow obligation to disclose exculpatory evidence. He maintains the Government must search all "reasonably available" information and disclose not only information that "tends materially to undermine the Government's theory as to the lawfulness of the petitioner's detention" but also information that "undermines the reliability of other purportedly inculpatory evidence" or "names potential witnesses capable of providing material evidence."

Bensayah does not contend the disclosure requirement imposed by the district court is in any way unconstitutional. Nor has he shown that broader disclosure is required by any opinion of the Supreme Court or of this court. He cites *Bismullah v. Gates,* 503 F.3d 137, 138–39 (D.C.Cir. 2007), for the proposition that the Government must search all "reasonably available" information, but that decision was compelled by the terms of a statutory scheme not at issue here. He cites *Al Odah,* 559 F.3d at 546, for the proposition that evidence may be material even if it is not directly exculpatory. The CMO is not, however, in tension with *Al Odah.* Information that undermines the reliability of other materials, *e.g.,* inculpatory evidence, also tends "materially to undermine the Government's theory as to the lawfulness of the petitioner's detention" and hence must be disclosed by the Government. We therefore agree with the Government that the standard for disclosure ordered by the district court, coupled with the opportunity to make specific discovery requests, is consistent with the Supreme Court's directive in *Boumediene* that a detainee be provided with the opportunity to challenge "the sufficiency of the Government's evidence" and to "supplement the record on review" with additional "exculpatory evidence."

Bensayah's primary concern seems to be that the disclosure requirement allows the Government to withhold exculpatory evidence because personnel from other agencies will pass only inculpatory evidence on to the attorneys actually "developing the return" and "preparing for the hearing." That practice is not permissible, however, under the current disclosure requirement. Any information that has been strategically filtered out of the record in order to withhold exculpatory evidence is plainly "material reviewed in developing the return"-and hence subject to the disclosure requirement-even if the individual doing the filtering works for a Government agency other than the Department of Justice.

Bensayah next argues that the district court erred by placing upon him the burden of explaining why each of his discovery requests would be neither "unfairly disruptive [nor] unduly burdensome to the Government." The district court did not abuse its discretion in structuring discovery this way. The Supreme Court specifically recognized the district court's discretion to accommodate the Government's legitimate interest in protecting sources and intelligence-gathering methods, acknowledging that "[c]ertain accommodations can be made to reduce the burden habeas corpus proceedings will place on the military without impermissibly diluting the protections of the writ." It is not necessary to address Bensayah's specific discovery requests relating to [redacted] because, as explained below, we hold this exhibit may not be relied upon by the district court on remand in the absence of additional corroborative evidence. Any discovery requests pertaining to new corroborative evidence should be decided by the district court in the first instance. Finally, we find no merit in Bensayah's claims the district court abused its discretion in denying his request for discovery into the treatment of [redacted] or in allowing the Government to present "rebuttal" evidence.

. . .

The Government asserts the authority to detain Bensayah pursuant to the AUMF, in which the Congress authorized the President

> to use all necessary and appropriate force against those nations, organizations, or persons he determines planned, authorized, committed, or aided the terrorist attacks that occurred on September 11, 2001, or harbored such organizations or persons, in order to prevent any future acts of international terrorism against the United States by such nations, organizations or persons.

As mentioned before, the Government contends it may lawfully detain an individual if he is "part of" al Qaeda. Bensayah objects to this formulation, but we have made clear elsewhere that the AUMF authorizes the Executive to detain, at the least, any individual who is functionally part of al Qaeda. *Barhoumi,* slip op. at 29 (detainee "was 'part of an al-Qaida-associated force and therefore properly detained pursuant to the AUMF'"); *Awad,* slip op. at 19 ("Once [a petitioner is shown to be] 'part of al Qaeda . . . the requirements of the AUMF [are] satisfied"); *Al–Bihani,* 590 F.3d at 872–74.

Although it is clear al Qaeda has, or at least at one time had, a particular organizational structure, *see* The 9/11 Commission Report: Final Report of the National Commission on Terrorist Attacks upon the United States 56 (2004) ("[Al Qaeda's] structure included as its operating arms an intelligence component, a military committee, a financial committee, a political committee, and a committee in charge of media affairs and propaganda"), the details of its structure are generally unknown, *see* Audrey Kurth Cronin, Congressional Research Service Report for Congress: Al Qaeda After the Iraq Conflict (2003) ("There is a great deal that remains unknown or debatable about the specific nature, size, structure and reach of [al Qaeda]"), but it is thought to be somewhat amorphous, Kenneth Katzman, Congressional Research Service Report for Congress: Al Qaeda: Profile and Threat Assessment (2005) ("Al Qaeda has always been more a coalition of different groups than a unified structure, many argue, and it has been this diversity that gives Al Qaeda global reach"). As a result, it is impossible to provide an exhaustive list of criteria for determining whether an individual is "part of" al Qaeda. That determination must be made on a case-by-case basis by using a functional rather than a formal approach and by focusing upon the actions of the individual in relation to the organization. That an individual operates within al Qaeda's formal command structure is surely sufficient but is not necessary to show he is "part of" the organization; there may be other indicia that a particular individual is sufficiently involved with the organization to be deemed part of it, *see Awad,* slip op. at 19 ("there are ways other than making a 'command structure' showing to prove that a detainee is 'part of' al Qaeda"), but the purely independent conduct of a freelancer is not enough.

As the district court noted, a [redacted] is the only evidence directly suggesting that Bensayah is an al Qaeda facilitator. That document, [redacted], contains the warning "INFORMATION REPORT, NOT FINALLY EVALUATED INTELLIGENCE." [redacted]

[redacted] contains a number of allegations about Bensayah. It states:

> [redacted]
>
> [redacted]
>
> [redacted]
>
> [redacted]

The district court, quoting *Parhat v. Gates,* 532 F.3d 834, 847 (D.C.Cir.2008), correctly stated that it must "evaluate the raw evidence, finding it to be sufficiently reliable and sufficiently probative to demonstrate the truth of the asserted proposition with the requisite degree of certainty." *See Barhoumi,* slip op. at 21 ("we agree ... *Parhat* sets the guideposts for our inquiry into the reliability of the ... evidence [in a detainee's habeas case]"). Although the district court found [redacted] contains some inherent indicia of reliability, *viz.,* [redacted] uncertainty about the source of the document and about how the information therein was gathered led the court to conclude [redacted] is not by itself reliable.

In *Parhat* we made clear that the reliability of evidence can be determined not only by looking at the evidence alone but, alternatively, by considering "sufficient additional information ... permit[ting the factfinder] to assess its reliability." Here the district court, after looking at additional information, concluded "there is sufficient corroborating evidence in the record to credit and rely upon the [ ] assertions made in [redacted] about Bensayah." The evidence in question is of three sorts: (1) evidence linking Bensayah to al Qaeda, and specifically to, [redacted], allegedly a "senior al-Qaida operative and facilitator"; (2) evidence of

Bensayah's travel plans and travel history; and (3) evidence raising "questions . . . about Bensayah's whereabouts in the early 1990s," which evidence created "sufficient doubt as to Bensayah's credibility."

Bensayah argues the district court clearly erred by finding [redacted] reliable. He contends the [redacted] upon which the district court relied were categorically insufficient to corroborate [redacted]. We disagree with Bensayah's broad contention that two pieces of evidence, each unreliable when viewed alone, cannot ever corroborate each other. . . . We agree, however, with his alternative argument that even if the additional evidence relied upon by the district court in this case is itself reliable, it is not sufficiently corroborative to support reliance upon the statements concerning Bensayah in [redacted].

. . .

The district court found [redacted] were corroborated by Bensayah's "connections" to al Qaeda, *viz.*, (1) Bensayah was directly linked to [redacted], allegedly a "senior al-Qaida operative and facilitator," and (2) [redacted].

Evidence linking Bensayah to [redacted] included [redacted]. The district court found the Government "has put forth more than sufficient credible evidence that [redacted] was a senior al-Qaida operative and facilitator." Since the district court's decision, however, the Government has eschewed reliance upon much of that evidence; it now maintains the other evidence upon which the district court relied is sufficient to link [redacted] to al Qaeda. In an order denying a Rule 60(b) motion filed by Bensayah, the district court indicated it would have concluded [redacted] was sufficiently corroborated to be relied upon, even "putting aside completely any evidence linking Bensayah to [redacted].

Assuming, as the Government contends, [redacted] was connected to al Qaeda, the evidence linking Bensayah to [redacted] and al Qaeda does not, by itself or together with the other evidence discussed below, corroborate [redacted] sufficiently so that it can be relied upon. The Government presented no direct evidence of actual communication between Bensayah and any al Qaeda member, much less evidence suggesting Bensayah communicated with [redacted] or anyone else in order to facilitate travel by an al Qaeda member. Indeed, the district court determined the record did not support the allegations in [redacted] concerning the only individuals named therein whose travel Bensayah allegedly planned to facilitate.

. . .

The district court found the assertions in [redacted] were corroborated by evidence that Bensayah (1) [redacted], and (2) had "experience in obtaining and traveling in and out of numerous countries on fraudulent passports." Bensayah admits to having used multiple travel documents, "some of which were in an assumed name," but maintains he traveled under fraudulent documents in order to avoid being sent back to Algeria, "where he reasonably feared persecution." He presented "unrebutted declarations" that "mere possession and use of false travel documents is neither proof of involvement with terrorism nor evidence of facilitation of travel by others." We agree. That Bensayah had experience with fraudulent travel documents [redacted] is not sufficiently corroborative of [redacted] that Bensayah was a travel facilitator for al Qaeda or anyone else. As noted in the prior paragraph, the district court determined the Government had failed to show that Bensayah's co-petitioners planned to travel to Afghanistan in order to engage U.S. forces. Therefore, Bensayah could not have been facilitating their travel for that purpose.

. . .

The district court found "serious questions [had] been raised about Bensayah's whereabouts in the early 1990s." This finding at most undermines Bensayah's own credibility; no account of his whereabouts ties him to al Qaeda or suggests he facilitated anyone's travel during that time. These "questions" in no way demonstrate that Bensayah had ties to and facilitated travel for al Qaeda in 2001.

* * *

Because the evidence, viewed in isolation or together, is insufficiently corroborative of [redacted], the district court on remand may not, in the absence of additional corroborative evidence not already considered, rely upon that exhibit in determining whether Bensayah was part of al Qaeda.

. . .

The Government argues it is authorized by the AUMF to detain Bensayah solely on the ground he was functionally a member or "part of" al Qaeda. The evidence upon which the district court relied in concluding Bensayah "supported" al Qaeda is insufficient, however, to show he was part of that organization. Accordingly, we reverse the judgment of the district court and remand the case for the district court to hear such evidence as the parties may submit and to decide in the first instance whether Bensayah was functionally part of al Qaeda.

QUESTIONS AND NOTES

1. A number of questions have surfaced in the Guantanamo detainee post-*Boumediene* habeas cases, including the following:

　　a. What is (are) the legal standard(s) applied in determining the legality of the detention?

　　b. What is (are) the source(s) of legal authority relied upon by the government as the basis for the detention?

　　c. What is the burden of proof applied in these cases?

　　d. Who has the burden of persuasion?

　　e. What is the detainee's right to discovery?

　　f. How is classified information handled?

g. What rule regarding the admissibility of hearsay is applied and how is it implemented?

h. What rule regarding the admissibility of confessions, allegedly coerced, is applied?

i. What is the scope of appellate review of a district court habeas decision?

2. The *Bensayah* case, supra, provides answers or information regarding the answers to questions 1.a–f, supra. Reread the case with attention to what the case tells us about each of these questions. Regarding questions 1.g, 1.h and 1.i., see the notes below.

3. Regarding reliance on hearsay evidence: Compare *Al–Bihani v. Obama,* 590 F.3d 866, 879 (D.C. Cir. 2010) ("[T]he question a habeas court must ask when presented with hearsay is not whether it is admissible-it is always admissible-but what probative weight to ascribe to whatever indicia of reliability it exhibits.") with *Awad v. Obama,* 608 F.3d 1, 7 (D.C. Cir. 2010) ("We have already held that hearsay evidence is admissible in this type of habeas proceeding if the hearsay is reliable," citing *Bihani*). For a habeas decision determining the reliability of a specific item of hearsay evidence, see *Barhoumi v. Obama,* 609 F.3d 416 (D.C. Cir. 2010).

4. Regarding the treatment of allegedly coerced statements in the habeas hearings, see, e.g., *Salahi v. Obama,* 710 F.Supp.2d 1 (D.D.C. 2010):

There is ample evidence in this record that Salahi was subjected to extensive and severe mistreatment at Guantanamo from mid-June 2003 to September 2003. Salahi's position is that every incriminating statement he made while in custody must therefore be disregarded. Salahi made most, if not all, of the statements that the government seeks to use against him during the mistreatment or during the 2 years following it.

The government acknowledges that Salahi's abusive treatment could diminish the reliability of some of his statements. But abuse and coercive interrogation methods do not throw a blanket over every statement, no matter when given, or to whom, or under what circumstances. Allegations of mistreatment certainly taint petitioner's statements, raising questions about their reliability. But at some point—after the passage of time and intervening events, and considering the circumstances—the taint of abuse and coercion may be attenuated enough for a witness's statements to be considered reliable—there must certainly be a "clean break" between the mistreatment and any such statement. Here, it is the government's burden to demonstrate that a particular statement was not the product of coercion, and that it has other indicia of reliability.

The government submits that the only statements of Salahi's on which it relies were made after a clean break, and after the passage of enough time to attenuate any taint, and that they are corroborated by documentary evidence and the statements of other persons (some of them detainees). Salahi attacks corroborating statements as unreliable hearsay, or subject to the same coercive tactics described above, or both. My approach here, ... has been to formally "receive" all the evidence offered by either side, and to give it the weight I believe it deserves....

The government had to adduce evidence—which is different from intelligence—showing that it was more likely than not that Salahi was "part of" al-Qaida. To do so, it had to show that the support Salahi undoubtedly did provide from time to time was provided within al-Qaida's command structure. The government has not done so. The government has shown that Salahi was an al-Qaida sympathizer—perhaps a "fellow traveler"; that he was in touch with al-Qaida members; and that from time to time, before his capture, he provided sporadic support to members of al-Qaida.

The government's problem is that its proof that Salahi gave material support to terrorists is so attenuated, or so tainted by coercion and mistreatment, or so classified, that it cannot support a successful criminal prosecution. Nevertheless, the government wants to hold Salahi indefinitely, because of its concern that he might renew his oath to al-Qaida and become a terrorist upon his release. That concern may indeed be well-founded. Salahi fought with al-Qaida in Afghanistan (twenty years ago), associated with at least a half-dozen known al-Qaida members and terrorists, and somehow found and lived among or with al-Qaida cell members in Montreal. But a habeas court may not permit a man to be held indefinitely upon suspicion, or because of the government's prediction that he may do unlawful acts in the future—any more than a habeas court may rely upon its prediction that a man will not be dangerous in the future and order his release if he was lawfully detained in the first place. The question, upon which the government had the burden of proof, was whether, at the time of his capture, Salahi was a "part of al-Qaida. On the record before me, I cannot find that he was.

5. For a description of torture and mistreatment used to obtain information and the government's efforts to persuade the court to rely on the statements, see *Abdah v. Obama,* 708 F.Supp.2d 9 (D.D.C. 2010):

Uthman has submitted to the Court a declaration of Kristin B. Wilhelm, an attorney who represents Hajj, summarizing Hajj's description to her of his treatment while in custody. The declaration states that while held in Jordan, Hajj "was regularly beaten and threatened with electrocution and molestation," and he eventually "manufactured facts" and confessed to his interrogators' allegations "in order to make the torture stop." After transfer to a secret CIA-run prison in Kabul, Afghanistan, Hajj was reportedly "kept in complete darkness and was subject to continuous loud music."

Uthman has also submitted a declaration of Martha Rayner, a Professor at Fordham University Law School who represents Kazimi, regarding Kazimi's description of his treatment in detention. Rayner reports that while Kazimi was detained outside the United States, his interrogators beat him; held him naked and shackled in a dark, cold cell; dropped him into cold water while his hands and legs were bound; and sexually abused him. Kazimi told Rayner that eventually "[h]e made up his mind to say 'Yes' to anything the interrogators said to avoid further torture." According to Rayner's declaration, Kazimi was relocated to a prison run by the CIA where he was always in darkness and where he was hooded, given injections, beaten, hit with electric cables, suspended from above, made to be naked, and subjected to continuous loud music. Kazimi reported trying to kill himself on three occasions. He told Rayner that he realized "he could mitigate the torture by telling the interrogators what they wanted to hear." Next, Kazimi was moved to a U.S. detention facility in Bagram, Afghanistan, where, he told Rayner, he was isolated, shackled, "psychologically tortured and traumatized by guards' desecration of the Koran" and interrogated "day and night, and very frequently." Kazimi told Rayner that he "tried very hard" to tell his interrogators at Bagram the same information he had told his previous interrogators "so they would not hurt him."

. . .

Respondents replied to these declarations by presenting as a witness a criminal investigator for CITF, but the testimony of the investigator fails to effectively rebut the evidence of abuse of Hajj and Kazimi. The investigator conducted interviews of Hajj and Kazimi in June 2004 at the Air Force Base in Bagram, Afghanistan at which both men were then held, as well as later that year in Guantanamo Bay. . . . The investigator's testimony added to the record persuasive evidence that the investigator herself did not mistreat Hajj or Kazimi and that the investigator did not observe any torture, or even any signs of abuse in the demeanor or physical state of either man, while the investigator was with them. But the investigator has no knowledge of the circumstances of either detainee's confinement before his arrival at Bagram and quite limited knowledge of his treatment there. The investigator testified to meeting with each man in an interrogation room on several days for approximately four hours at a time. The investigator did not see Hajj or Kazimi other than during those four-hour sessions and did not inquire of them, or anyone else, about their treatment in the various prisons in which they were held.

. . .

Uthman asserts that the proximity in time between the torture Hajj and Kamizi described and their interrogations by the CITF investigator, however cordial, renders their statements unreliable. In general, "resort to coercive tactics by an interrogator renders the information less likely to be true." To determine admissibility in analogous situations in criminal cases, courts assess the voluntariness of statements made after the application of coercive techniques based on a totality of the circumstances test. ("In determining whether a defendant's will was overborne in a particular case, the Court has assessed the totality of all the surrounding circumstances."). Judges of this Court have adopted this test in the cases of other Guantanamo Bay detainees seeking release. *See, e.g., Anam v. Obama*, F. Supp. 2d, 2010 WL 58965, at 4 (D.D.C. Jan. 6, 2010). The test calls for considering, *inter alia*, "the time that passes between confessions, the change in place of interrogations, and the change in identity of the interrogators."

Respondents do not argue that the alleged torture of Hajj and Kazimi is sufficiently attenuated from the interviews at which they gave the relevant statements to support a conclusion that despite the coercion, the statements are nonetheless reliable. The interviews occurred in Bagram, where torture of Hajj was ongoing and where Kazimi had arrived directly from the CIA prison, at which he was tortured, only about a month earlier. Therefore, the Court concludes that there has been no "break in the stream of events ... sufficient to insulate the statement from the effect of all that went before." Accordingly, the Court will not treat Hajj and Kazimi's statements as true.

6. Regarding the handling of classified information in the habeas hearings, note the significant number of redactions in the *Bensayah* opinion, which makes it difficult for the reader to determine the factual underpinnings for some of the court's rulings. This is a problem resulting from the government's reliance on classified information in the course of the hearing. See generally Chapter 9, supra, which deals mainly with the Classified Information Procedures Act (CIPA), which is applicable only in criminal proceedings, not habeas cases. The habeas courts have, however, tended to look to CIPA for general guidance

7. Counsel in *Bensayah* obtained security clearance, and they generally had access to the classified information in the case, but, of course, could not share this information with their detainee-clients. See *Odah v. United States,* 559 F. 3d 539 (D.C. Cir. 2009), holding that in a habeas action the government must provide classified information that is relevant and material to detainee's counsel who has obtained security clearance but may also consider the use of alternative means such as substitutions. Regarding the problems associated with this type of situation, see, generally, casebook, pp. 523–526, supra. Final arguments in *Bensayah* were held in closed sessions because of the need to refer to classified information; neither the detainee-petitioners nor members of the public were present at these sessions.

8. In *Bensayah*, the government also proposed to provide the court with additional material on an ex parte basis, so-called "black box" material that was sufficiently sensitive that it could not be shared with security-cleared counsel for the detainees who vigorously opposed the government's proposal.

9. One of the five detainees whose release was ordered by the district court was Lakhdar Boumediene, the lead petitioner in *Boumediene v. Bush.*

10. In January, 2010, the Guantanamo Review Task Force appointed by President Obama completed its review of the detainees at Guantanamo. The Executive Summary of the Report stated:

> The decisions reached on the 240 detainees subject to the review are as follows:
>
> – **126 detainees** were approved for transfer. To date, 44 of these detainees have been transferred from Guantanamo to countries outside the United States.
>
> – **44 detainees** over the course of the review were referred for prosecution either in federal court or a military commission, and **36 of these detainees** remain the subject of active cases or investigations. The Attorney General has announced that the government will pursue prose-

cutions against six of these detainees in federal court and will pursue prosecutions against six others in military commissions.

– **48 detainees** were determined to be too dangerous to transfer but not feasible for prosecution. They will remain in detention pursuant to the government's authority under the Authorization for Use of Military Force passed by Congress in response to the attacks of September 11, 2001. Detainees may challenge the legality of their detention in federal court and will periodically receive further review within the Executive Branch

3. MILITARY ADMINISTRATIVE PROCESS FOR DETERMINING THE STATUS OF DETAINEES

a. Evolution of the Military Administrative Process

QUESTIONS AND NOTES

1. Early in 2002, the issue of what status to accord to al Qaeda and Taliban captives was being debated in the Department of Justice and the Department of State. White House memos and letters from that period reveal the nature of the debate. On February 1, 2002, Attorney General Ashcroft sent a letter to the President describing "two basic theories" that supported the conclusion that Taliban combatants are not legally entitled to Geneva Convention protections as prisoners of war: a) Afghanistan was a failed state; as such the treaty's protections do not apply because it has lost its status as party to the treaty able to fulfill its obligations; b) if during the relevant times Afghanistan was a party to the treaty, Taliban combatants were not entitled to Geneva Convention III prisoner of war status because they were unlawful combatants. The letter went on to detail the advantages of adopting the one theory or the other, namely, under theory a) no court would subsequently entertain charges that U.S. officials had violated the War Crimes Act through a violation of the Geneva Convention, whereas theory b) would not "accord American officials the same protection from legal consequences."

2. A week before, on January 25, 2002, a draft memorandum for the President had been prepared by the Alberto Gonzales, then Counsel to the President (later Attorney General) noting that on January 18, 2002, he had advised the President that the Department of Justice had issued a formal legal opinion concluding that the Geneva Convention III on the Treatment of Prisoners (GPW) does not apply to the conflict with al Qaeda; also that there are reasonable grounds for concluding that the Convention does not apply to the Taliban; and noting that the President had decided that the Convention does not apply and that al Qaeda and Taliban detainees are not POWs under the Convention. This was a key early presidential decision made regarding the legal status of the Guantanamo detainees. The January 25 memorandum went on to relate that the Secretary of State had requested that the President reconsider that decision and that the Legal Adviser to the State Department had reached conclusions different from the Department of Justice. In this

memorandum, Mr. Gonzales presented arguments in support of reconsideration and reversal of the decision that the GPW does not apply to either al Qaeda or the Taliban as well as the arguments opposed. Some of the arguments presented for reversing the decision were as follows:

- The United States could not invoke the GPW if enemy forces threatened to mistreat ... U.S. or coalition forces captured during operations in Afghanistan, or if they denied Red Cross access or other POW privileges.

  . . .

- Our position would likely provoke widespread condemnation among our allies and in some domestic quarters, even if we make clear that we will comply with the core humanitarian principles of the treaty as a matter of policy.

  . . .

- Other countries may be less inclined to turn over terrorists or provide legal assistance to us if we do not recognize a legal obligation to comply with the GPW.

- A determination that GPW does not apply to al Qaeda and the Taliban could undermine U.S. military culture which emphasizes maintaining the highest standards of conduct in combat, and could introduce an element of uncertainty in the status of adversaries.

Mr. Gonzalez then stated his belief that "on balance" these arguments were unpersuasive and presented responses to them:

- ... [Y]our [i.e the President's] policy of providing humane treatment to enemy detainees gives us the credibility to insist on like treatment for our soldiers.

- ... [O]ur adversaries in several recent conflicts have not been deterred by GPW in their mistreatment of captured U.S. personnel, and terrorists will not follow GPW in any event.

  . . .

- The statement that other nations would criticize the U.S. because we have determined that GPW does not apply is undoubtedly true.... [W]e can facilitate cooperation with other nations by reassuring them that we fully support GPW where it is applicable and by acknowledging that in this conflict the U.S. continues to respect other recognized standards.

  . . .

- [T]he argument based on military culture fails to recognize that our military remain bound to apply the principles of GPW because that is what you [i.e the President] have directed them to do.

3. In July 2004, the Government adopted the following definition of enemy combatant, which was applied to foreign nationals held at Guantanamo:

[A]n individual who was part of or supporting Taliban or al Qaeda forces, or associated forces that are engaged in hostilities against the

United States or its coalition partners. This includes any person who has committed a belligerent act or has directly supported hostilities in aid of enemy armed forces.

See Deputy Secretary of Defense Paul Wolfowitz, Memorandum for the Secretary of the Navy, *Order Establishing Combatant Status Review Tribunal* (July 7, 2004) (hereinafter "CSRT Order"), cited in Khalid v. Bush, 355 F.Supp.2d 311 (D.D.C. 2005).

4. A primary element in the legal background against which the presidential decision, described in notes 1 and 2 above, was made is the Geneva Convention. Relevant provisions from the Geneva Convention that describe the factors that determine whether a captive is entitled to prisoner of war status and governing the treatment of prisoners of war are reproduced below:

Geneva Convention III Relative to the Treatment of Prisoners of War, 75 U.N.T.S. 135, *entered into force* Oct. 21, 1950.

General Provisions

Article 1

The High Contracting Parties undertake to respect and to ensure respect for the present Convention in all circumstances.

Article 2

In addition to the provisions which shall be implemented in peace time, the present Convention shall apply to all cases of declared war or of any other armed conflict which may arise between two or more of the High Contracting Parties, even if the state of war is not recognized by one of them.

The Convention shall also apply to all cases of partial or total occupation of the territory of a High Contracting Party, even if the said occupation meets with no armed resistance.

Although one of the Powers in conflict may not be a party to the present Convention, the Powers who are parties thereto shall remain bound by it in their mutual relations. They shall furthermore be bound by the Convention in relation to the said Power, if the latter accepts and applies the provisions thereof.

. . .

Article 4

A. Prisoners of war, in the sense of the present Convention, are persons belonging to one of the following categories, who have fallen into the power of the enemy:

1. Members of the armed forces of a Party to the conflict as well as members of militias or volunteer corps forming part of such armed forces.

2. Members of other militias and members of other volunteer corps, including those of organized resistance movements, belonging to a Party to the conflict and operating in or outside their own territory, even if this territory is occupied, provided that such militias

or volunteer corps, including such organized resistance movements, fulfill the following conditions:

(a) That of being commanded by a person responsible for his subordinates;

(b) That of having a fixed distinctive sign recognizable at a distance;

(c) That of carrying arms openly;

(d) That of conducting their operations in accordance with the laws and customs of war.

3. Members of regular armed forces who profess allegiance to a government or an authority not recognized by the Detaining Power.

. . .

6. Inhabitants of a non-occupied territory, who on the approach of the enemy spontaneously take up arms to resist the invading forces, without having had time to form themselves into regular armed units, provided they carry arms openly and respect the laws and customs of war.

. . .

Article 5

The present Convention shall apply to the persons referred to in Article 4 from the time they fall into the power of the enemy and until their final release and repatriation.

Should any doubt arise as to whether persons, having committed a belligerent act and having fallen into the hands of the enemy, belong to any of the categories enumerated in Article 4, such persons shall enjoy the protection of the present Convention until such time as their status has been determined by a competent tribunal.

. . .

Article 9

The provisions of the present Convention constitute no obstacle to the humanitarian activities which the International Committee of the Red Cross or any other impartial humanitarian organization may, subject to the consent of the Parties to the conflict concerned, undertake for the protection of prisoners of war and for their relief.

Article 10

. . .

When prisoners of war do not benefit or cease to benefit, no matter for what reason, by the activities of a Protecting Power or of an organization provided for in the first paragraph above, the Detaining Power shall request a neutral State, or such an organization, to undertake the functions performed under the present Convention by a Protecting Power designated by the Parties to a conflict.

If protection cannot be arranged accordingly, the Detaining Power shall request or shall accept, subject to the provisions of this Article, the offer of the services of a humanitarian organization, such as the International Committee of the Red Cross, to assume the humanitarian functions performed by Protecting Powers under the present Convention.

Any neutral Power or any organization invited by the Power concerned or offering itself for these purposes, shall be required to act with a sense of responsibility towards the Party to the conflict on which persons protected by the present Convention depend, and shall be required to furnish sufficient assurances that it is in a position to undertake the appropriate functions and to discharge them impartially.

Article 11

In cases where they deem it advisable in the interest of protected persons, particularly in cases of disagreement between the Parties to the conflict as to the application or interpretation of the provisions of the present Convention, the Protecting Powers shall lend their good offices with a view to settling the disagreement.

For this purpose, each of the Protecting Powers may, either at the invitation of one Party or on its own initiative, propose to the Parties to the conflict a meeting of their representatives, and in particular of the authorities responsible for prisoners of war, possibly on neutral territory suitably chosen. The Parties to the conflict shall be bound to give effect to the proposals made to them for this purpose. The Protecting Powers may, if necessary, propose for approval by the Parties to the conflict a person belonging to a neutral Power, or delegated by the International Committee of the Red Cross, who shall be invited to take part in such a meeting.

PART II

General Protection of Prisoners of War

. . .

Article 13

Prisoners of war must at all times be humanely treated. Any unlawful act or omission by the Detaining Power causing death or seriously endangering the health of a prisoner of war in its custody is prohibited, and will be regarded as a serious breach of the present Convention. In particular, no prisoner of war may be subjected to physical mutilation or to medical or scientific experiments of any kind which are not justified by the medical, dental or hospital treatment of the prisoner concerned and carried out in his interest.

Likewise, prisoners of war must at all times be protected, particularly against acts of violence or intimidation and against insults and public curiosity.

Measures of reprisal against prisoners of war are prohibited.

Article 14

Prisoners of war are entitled in all circumstances to respect for their persons and their honour.

Women shall be treated with all the regard due to their sex and shall in all cases benefit by treatment as favourable as that granted to men.

Prisoners of war shall retain the full civil capacity which they enjoyed at the time of their capture. The Detaining Power may not restrict the exercise, either within or without its own territory, of the rights such capacity confers except in so far as the captivity requires.

Article 15

The Power detaining prisoners of war shall be bound to provide free of charge for their maintenance and for the medical attention required by their state of health.

Article 16

Taking into consideration the provisions of the present Convention relating to rank and sex, and subject to any privileged treatment which may be accorded to them by reason of their state of health, age or professional qualifications, all prisoners of war shall be treated alike by the Detaining Power, without any adverse distinction based on race, nationality, religious belief or political opinions, or any other distinction founded on similar criteria.

Captivity

Section I

Beginning of Captivity

Article 17

Every prisoner of war, when questioned on the subject, is bound to give only his surname, first names and rank, date of birth, and army, regimental, personal or serial number, or failing this, equivalent information.

If he wilfully infringes this rule, he may render himself liable to a restriction of the privileges accorded to his rank or status.

Each Party to a conflict is required to furnish the persons under its jurisdiction who are liable to become prisoners of war, with an identity card showing the owner's surname, first names, rank, ...

No physical or mental torture, nor any other form of coercion, may be inflicted on prisoners of war to secure from them information of any kind whatever. Prisoners of war who refuse to answer may not be threatened, insulted, or exposed to any unpleasant or disadvantageous treatment of any kind.

. . .

5. Numerous questions are raised by the administration's position on the prisoner of war versus enemy combatant issue. Insofar as the provisions of the Geneva Convention, supra, are deemed relevant, the Bush administration apparently relied on the four-part test of Article 4A.2., supra. This test includes in the category of prisoners of war, those members of militia or organized resistance forces who have serve under a commander, with a "fixed distinctive sign recognizable at a distance", who carry "arms openly," and who observe the laws of war in their conduct. The administration argues, inter alia, that members of the al Qaeda and the Taliban do not wear uniforms or the equivalent; therefore they do not qualify for prisoner of war

status. Of course, the issue of whether prisoner of war status is warranted under the terms of the Convention may vary depending on which group of captives is being considered. For example, should members of the Taliban qualify under Article 4A.1. as, "Members of the armed forces of a Party to the conflict"? There appears to be no requirement for a distinctive insignia under that provision. Even if the Taliban do not qualify under the first clause of 4A.1, might they qualify under the second clause "as members of militias or volunteer corps forming part of such armed forces"? Further, might any members of al Qaeda captured on the Afghanistan battlefield qualify under that same second clause of Article 4A.1. ?

6. Consider what difference it would have made if Geneva Convention-prisoner of war status were given to the detainees? Among other things, it would have made it difficult for the government to interrogate and, possibly, obtain information from them, given the terms of Article 17 of the Convention. The Convention also contemplates repatriation at the end of hostilities. While both the Bush and Obama administrations have released a large majority of the detainees to their home countries or to another country, both the Bush administration and the Obama administration have contemplated extended, even indefinite, detention of some of them.

7. "However, even if the detainees were not covered by the Third Geneva Convention, a person may not be held forever without charges or trial. At some point, in some manner, ... the question of indefinite and possibly permanent detention without trial must eventually arise.... Moreover, one could argue—decisively, in my view—that as long as operations are carried out against Al Qaeda, the organization whose destruction is one of the war aims of the United States, the United States is perfectly entitled ... to detain fighters whom it determines to be a security risk.... It probably could not do so with respect to an endless and essentially metaphorical 'war on terrorism' dealing with targets wholly unrelated to Al Qaeda— a war which might indeed have no end—but it is certainly entitled to do so with fighters ... connected even loosely with Al Qaeda, wherever they may be." Kenneth Anderson, What To Do with Bin Laden and Al Qaeda Terrorists? A Qualified Defense of Military Commissions and United States Policy on Detainees at Guantanamo Bay Naval Base, 25 Harv. J.L. & Pub Pol'y 591, 625–626 (2002)

8. Prior to the decision in Hamdi, the government had been working on establishing a formal review procedure for all of the Guantanamo detainees, and, indeed, had informally reviewed and released a couple hundred detainees to their home countries.

Following the decision in Hamdi, the government quickly established two kinds of administrative reviews of detainees' status—Combatant Status Review Tribunals (CSRT's), as described in the Boumediene opinion and Administrative Review Boards (ARB's). Detailed information about these two types of reviews, their purposes, makeup, and information about the process in proceedings before them was provided by the government—see, e.g., Special Department of Defense Briefing by Gordon England, Secretary of the Navy, December 20, 2004, reported by Federal News Service.

9.   The issue in the CSRT review was whether or not the particular detainee is an enemy combatant. The issue in the ARB review was whether the individual (who has previously gone through a CSRT proceeding which determined him to an enemy combatant) continued to be a threat or had intelligence information which would be of value.

10.   The CSRT hearings were heard by three person boards of military officers. A military officer who acted as a representative, not as his attorney or advocate, was made available to each of the detainees whose case was reviewed by the CSRT. Some of the detainees were represented by counsel in connection with their habeas corpus actions and any related lawsuits. Each detainee was given a written document with those accusations that did not reveal classified information that bore on the question of the detainee's status as an enemy combatant. The CSRT, however, also considered classified information not contained in the document provided to the detainee. At the hearing, the detainee was allowed to testify, and his family and home nation were allowed to submit written testimony. Reportedly, almost half the detainees refused to participate in the proceedings.

11.   Following completion of the CSRT hearing, the hearing procedure was reviewed administratively to make sure that it was conducted properly and then sent to an Admiral who has been delegated authority to make the final decision in these cases. The recommendations of the ARB'S were reviewed by the Secretary of the Navy. Special Department of Defense Briefing conducted by Gordon England, Secretary of the Navy, Federal News Service, December 20, 2004. Subsequently, the Detainee Treatment Act of 2005 subjected the CSRT determinations to a limited form of judicial review in the U.S. Court of Appeals for the District of Columbia, as described in the Boumediene opinion.

12.   Determination in a CSRT hearing that a detainee was not an enemy combatant resulted in the release of the individual and arrangement by the State Department to return him to his home country. Determination that he was an enemy combatant resulted in continued detention and subsequent annual review in the ARB procedure. In the ARB proceeding, any of three dispositions was possible: release of the detainee and transportation to his home country; transfer of the detainee to his home country with conditions as negotiated with that country; or continued detention at Guantanamo. Ibid.

13.   The final CSRT hearing in the original series of cases was held on January 22, 2005. In all, the cases of 558 detainees were originally reviewed in the CSRT procedure. In 2007, the cases of 14 high value detainees who had been held abroad but were then transferred to Guantanamo were also reviewed in CSRT hearings. In all, the Office for the Administrative Review of the Detention of Enemy Combatants (OARDEC) held 572 tribunals between July 30, 2004 and June 15, 2007. The tribunals determined that 534 detainees were properly classified as enemy combatants and 38 detainees were found no longer to be classified as enemy combatants.

14.   In the April 26, 2006 report regarding Administrative Review Tribunal (ARB) hearings held annually, in the second round of such hearings, 330 hearings were held. The outcome was that 55 detainees were to be trans-

ferred; 273 were to continue to be detained. (As of that date, there had been no ruling in two cases.)

15.　In March, 2007, the Defense Department reported that in 2006, 111 detainees had been either released or transferred from Guantanamo resulting in a cumulative total of approximately 390 releases and transfers since 2002. The number of detainees at the time at Guantanamo was approximately 385, of which more than 80 had been designated for release or transfer, pending discussions with other nations or pending resolution of litigation in U.S. courts.

16.　Prior to the creation of the CSRT procedure, approximately 200 detainees had been released and the government believed that at least 12 of these returned to terrorist activity. Special Department of Defense Briefing conducted by Gordon England, Secretary of the Navy, Federal News Service, December 20, 2004.

17.　In Boumediene, the Supreme Court concluded that the CSRT process was not an adequate substitute for habeas corpus review in an Article III court, even when combined with the judicial review established under the DTA of 2005. What are the weaknesses of the CSRT process? How does the process afforded in habeas review differ? Consider the follow list of infirmities of the CSRT process? Does the habeas review process supply or strengthen these elements? Are there any other weaknesses of the CSRT process that you can add to the list?

In the CSRT process:

a.　the detainee was not represented by a lawyer

b.　the detainee did not have access to the classified information relied upon by the decisionmaker or a substitute that meets the standards of the Classified Information Procedures Act

c.　the process was not a true adversary process

d.　until December 2005, there was no appeal to an Article III court

e.　since December 2005, judicial review has been available but it is circumscribed.

b.　The Obama Administration Policy

QUESTIONS AND NOTES

1.　On March 7, 2011, the White House issued a press release reporting, inter alia, on the renewal of military commission prosecutions, again reporting on the fact that many of the detainees would be prosecuted in Article III courts and that an Executive Order was being issued providing for periodic review of detainees who continue to be held without prosecution. The press release appears immediately below. Excerpts from the Executive Order are reproduced in note 2, infra.

THE WHITE HOUSE

Office of the Press Secretary

For Immediate Release March 7, 2011

FACT SHEET: NEW ACTIONS ON GUANTANAMO AND DETAINEE POLICY

In a speech nearly two years ago at the National Archives, the President advanced a four-part approach to closing the detention facility at Guantanamo Bay, keeping our country safe, and upholding the law: (1) to bring detainees to justice in prosecutions in either federal civilian courts or in reformed military commissions, (2) to comply with court-ordered releases of detainees, (3) to transfer detainees from Guantanamo whenever it is possible to do so safely and humanely, and (4) when neither prosecution nor other legal options are available, to hold these individuals in lawful military detention. He affirmed that "whenever feasible, we will try those who have violated American criminal laws in federal courts."

The Administration remains committed to closing the detention facility at Guantanamo Bay, and to maintain a lawful, sustainable and principled regime for the handling of detainees there, consistent with the full range of U.S. national security interests. In keeping with the strategy we laid out, we are proceeding today with the following actions:

Resumption of Military Commissions

The Secretary of Defense will issue an order rescinding his prior suspension on the swearing and referring of new charges in the military commissions. New charges in military commissions have been suspended since the President announced his review of detainee policy, shortly after taking office.

The Administration, working on a bipartisan basis with members of Congress, has successfully enacted key reforms, such as a ban on the use of statements taken as a result of cruel, inhuman or degrading treatment, and a better system for handling classified information. With these and other reforms, military commissions, along with prosecutions of suspected terrorists in civilian courts, are an available and important tool in combating international terrorists that fall within their jurisdiction while upholding the rule of law.

Executive Order on Periodic Review

In the Archives speech, the President recognized there are certain Guantanamo detainees who have not been charged, convicted, or designated for transfer, but must continue to be detained because they "in effect, remain at war with the United States." For this category of detainees, the President stated: "We must have a thorough process of periodic review, so that any prolonged detention is carefully evaluated and justified."

Today, the President issued an Executive Order establishing such a process for these detainees. A copy of the order is attached.

The periodic review established by this order will help to ensure that individuals who we have determined will be subject to long-term detention continue to be detained only when lawful and necessary to protect against a significant threat to the security of the United States. If a final determination is made that a detainee no longer constitutes a significant threat to our security, the Executive Order provides that the Secretaries of State and Defense are to identify a suitable transfer location outside the United States, consistent with the national security and foreign policy interests of the United States and applicable law. As the President has stated before, no Guantanamo detainee will be released into the United States.

We are grateful to all of our allies and partners who have worked with the Administration to implement the transfers undertaken thus far in a secure and humane manner, especially those who have resettled detainees from third countries. Our friends and allies should know that we remain determined in our efforts and that, with their continued assistance, we intend to complete the difficult challenge of closing Guantanamo.

Continued Commitment to Article III Trials

Pursuant to the President's order to close Guantanamo, this Administration instituted the most thorough review process ever applied to the detainees held there. Among other things, for the first time, we consolidated all information available to the federal government about these individuals. That information was carefully examined by some of our government's most experienced prosecutors, a process that resulted in the referral of 36 individuals for potential prosecution. Since the time of those referrals, the Departments of Justice and Defense, with the advice of career military and civilian prosecutors, have been working to bring these defendants to justice, securing convictions in a number of cases and evaluating others to determine which system—military or civilian—is most appropriate based on the nature of the evidence and traditional principles of prosecution.

In recent months, some in Congress have sought to undermine this process. In December, Congress enacted restrictions on the prosecution of Guantanamo detainees in Federal courts. The Administration opposes these restrictions as a dangerous and unprecedented challenge to Executive authority to select the most effective means available to bring terrorists to justice and safeguard our security. The Executive Branch possesses the information and expertise necessary to make the best judgment about where a particular prosecution should proceed, and Congress's intrusion upon this function is inconsistent with the long-standing and appropriate allocation of authority between the Executive and Legislative branches.

Time and again, our Federal courts have delivered swift justice and severe punishment to those who seek to attack us. In the last two years alone, federal prosecutors have convicted numerous defendants charged with terrorism offenses, including those who plotted to bomb the New

York subway system; attempted to detonate a bomb in Times Square; and conspired in murderous attacks on our embassies abroad. These prosecutions have generated invaluable intelligence about our enemies, permitted us to incapacitate and detain dangerous terrorists, and vindicated the interests of victims—all while reaffirming our commitment to the rule of law. Spanning multiple administrations, Republican and Democratic, our Federal courts have proven to be one of our most effective counterterrorism tools, and should not be restricted in any circumstances.

Military commissions should proceed in cases where it has been determined appropriate to do so. Because there are situations, however, in which our federal courts are a more appropriate forum for trying particular individuals, we will seek repeal of the restrictions imposed by Congress, so that we can move forward in the forum that is, in our judgment, most in line with our national security interests and the interests of justice.

We will continue to vigorously defend the authority of the Executive to make these well-informed prosecution decisions, both with respect to those detainees in our custody at Guantanamo and those we may apprehend in the future. A one-size-fits-all policy for the prosecution of suspected terrorists, whether for past or future cases, undermines our Nation's counterterrorism efforts and harms our national security.

. . .

2. The Executive Order establishing periodic review of detainees who continue in detention without being prosecuted criminally appears below. Compare this process with the prior CSRT process and with the process provided in the post-Boumediene habeas actions.

THE WHITE HOUSE

Office of the Press Secretary

For Immediate Release March 7, 2011

EXECUTIVE ORDER

PERIODIC REVIEW OF INDIVIDUALS
DETAINED AT GUANTÁNAMO BAY NAVAL STATION PURSUANT TO THE AUTHORIZATION FOR USE OF MILITARY FORCE

By the authority vested in me as President by the Constitution and the laws of the United States of America, including the Authorization for Use of Military Force of September 2001 (AUMF), Public Law 107–40, and in order to ensure that military detention of individuals now held at the U.S. Naval Station, Guantánamo Bay, Cuba (Guantánamo), who were subject to the interagency review under section 4 of Executive Order 13492 of January 22, 2009, continues to be carefully evaluated and justified, consistent with the national security and foreign policy interests of the United States and the interests of justice, I hereby order as follows:

Section 1. Scope and Purpose. (a) The periodic review described in section 3 of this order applies only to those detainees held at Guantánamo on the date of this order, whom the interagency review established by Executive Order 13492 has (i) designated for continued law of war detention; or (ii) referred for prosecution, except for those detainees against whom charges are pending or a judgment of conviction has been entered.

(b) This order is intended solely to establish, as a discretionary matter, a process to review on a periodic basis the executive branch's continued, discretionary exercise of existing detention authority in individual cases. It does not create any additional or separate source of detention authority, and it does not affect the scope of detention authority under existing law. Detainees at Guantánamo have the constitutional privilege of the writ of habeas corpus, and nothing in this order is intended to affect the jurisdiction of Federal courts to determine the legality of their detention.

(c) In the event detainees covered by this order are transferred from Guantánamo to another U.S. detention facility where they remain in law of war detention, this order shall continue to apply to them.

Sec. 2. Standard for Continued Detention. Continued law of war detention is warranted for a detainee subject to the periodic review in section 3 of this order if it is necessary to protect against a significant threat to the security of the United States.

Sec. 3. Periodic Review. The Secretary of Defense shall coordinate a process of periodic review of continued law of war detention for each detainee described in section 1(a) of this order. In consultation with the Attorney General, the Secretary of Defense shall issue implementing guidelines governing the process, consistent with the following requirements:

(a) Initial Review. For each detainee, an initial review shall commence as soon as possible but no later than 1 year from the date of this order. The initial review will consist of a hearing before a Periodic Review Board (PRB). The review and hearing shall follow a process that includes the following requirements:

(1) Each detainee shall be provided, in writing and in a language the detainee understands, with advance notice of the PRB review and an unclassified summary of the factors and information the PRB will consider in evaluating whether the detainee meets the standard set forth in section 2 of this order. The written summary shall be sufficiently comprehensive to provide adequate notice to the detainee of the reasons for continued detention.

(2) The detainee shall be assisted in proceedings before the PRB by a Government-provided personal representative (representative) who possesses the security clearances necessary for access to the information described in subsection (a)(4) of this section. The representative shall advocate on behalf of the detainee before the PRB and shall be responsible for challenging the Government's information and introducing infor-

mation on behalf of the detainee. In addition to the representative, the detainee may be assisted in proceedings before the PRB by private counsel, at no expense to the Government.

(3) The detainee shall be permitted to (i) present to the PRB a written or oral statement; (ii) introduce relevant information, including written declarations; (iii) answer any questions posed by the PRB; and (iv) call witnesses who are reasonably available and willing to provide information that is relevant and material to the standard set forth in section 2 of this order.

(4) The Secretary of Defense, in coordination with other relevant Government agencies, shall compile and provide to the PRB all information in the detainee disposition recommendations produced by the Task Force established under Executive Order 13492 that is relevant to the determination whether the standard in section 2 of this order has been met and on which the Government seeks to rely for that determination. In addition, the Secretary of Defense, in coordination with other relevant Government agencies, shall compile any additional information relevant to that determination, and on which the Government seeks to rely for that determination, that has become available since the conclusion of the Executive Order 13492 review. All mitigating information relevant to that determination must be provided to the PRB.

(5) The information provided in subsection (a)(4) of this section shall be provided to the detainee's representative. In exceptional circumstances where it is necessary to protect national security, including intelligence sources and methods, the PRB may determine that the representative must receive a sufficient substitute or summary, rather than the underlying information. If the detainee is represented by private counsel, the information provided in subsection (a)(4) of this section shall be provided to such counsel unless the Government determines that the need to protect national security, including intelligence sources and methods, or law enforcement or privilege concerns, requires the Government to provide counsel with a sufficient substitute or summary of the information. A sufficient substitute or summary must provide a meaningful opportunity to assist the detainee during the review process.

(6) The PRB shall conduct a hearing to consider the information described in subsection (a)(4) of this section, and other relevant information provided by the detainee or the detainee's representative or counsel, to determine whether the standard in section 2 of this order is met. The PRB shall consider the reliability of any information provided to it in making its determination.

(7) The PRB shall make a prompt determination, by consensus and in writing, as to whether the detainee's continued detention is warranted under the standard in section 2 of this order. If the PRB determines that the standard is not met, the PRB shall also recommend any conditions that relate to the detainee's transfer. The PRB shall provide a written summary of any final determination in unclassified form to the detainee, in a language the detainee understands, within 30 days of the determination when practicable.

(8) The Secretary of Defense shall establish a secretariat to administer the PRB review and hearing process. The Director of National Intelligence shall assist in preparing the unclassified notice and the substitutes or summaries described above. Other executive departments and agencies shall assist in the process of providing the PRB with information required for the review processes detailed in this order.

(b) Subsequent Full Review. The continued detention of each detainee shall be subject to subsequent full reviews and hearings by the PRB on a triennial basis. Each subsequent review shall employ the procedures set forth in section 3(a) of this order.

(c) File Reviews. The continued detention of each detainee shall also be subject to a file review every 6 months in the intervening years between full reviews. This file review will be conducted by the PRB and shall consist of a review of any relevant new information related to the detainee compiled by the Secretary of Defense, in coordination with other relevant agencies, since the last review and, as appropriate, information considered during any prior PRB review. The detainee shall be permitted to make a written submission in connection with each file review. If, during the file review, a significant question is raised as to whether the detainee's continued detention is warranted under the standard in section 2 of this order, the PRB will promptly convene a full review pursuant to the standards in section 3(a) of this order.

(d) Review of PRB Determinations. The Review Committee (Committee), as defined in section 9(d) of this order, shall conduct a review if (i) a member of the Committee seeks review of a PRB determination within 30 days of that determination; or (ii) consensus within the PRB cannot be reached.

Sec. 4. Effect of Determination to Transfer. (a) If a final determination is made that a detainee does not meet the standard in section 2 of this order, the Secretaries of State and Defense shall be responsible for ensuring that vigorous efforts are undertaken to identify a suitable transfer location for any such detainee, outside of the United States, consistent with the national security and foreign policy interests of the United States and the commitment set forth in section 2242(a) of the Foreign Affairs Reform and Restructuring Act of 1998 (Public Law 105–277).

(b) The Secretary of State, in consultation with the Secretary of Defense, shall be responsible for obtaining appropriate security and humane treatment assurances regarding any detainee to be transferred to another country, and for determining, after consultation with members of the Committee, that it is appropriate to proceed with the transfer.

(c) The Secretary of State shall evaluate humane treatment assurances in all cases, consistent with the recommendations of the Special Task Force on Interrogation and Transfer Policies established by Executive Order 13491 of January 22, 2009.

Sec. 5. Annual Committee Review. (a) The Committee shall conduct an annual review of sufficiency and efficacy of transfer efforts, including:

(1) the status of transfer efforts for any detainee who has been subject to the periodic review under section 3 of this order, whose continued detention has been determined not to be warranted, and who has not been transferred more than 6 months after the date of such determination;

(2) the status of transfer efforts for any detainee whose petition for a writ of habeas corpus has been granted by a U.S. Federal court with no pending appeal and who has not been transferred;

(3) the status of transfer efforts for any detainee who has been designated for transfer or conditional detention by the Executive Order 13492 review and who has not been transferred; and

(4) the security and other conditions in the countries to which detainees might be transferred, including a review of any suspension of transfers to a particular country, in order to determine whether further steps to facilitate transfers are appropriate or to provide a recommendation to the President regarding whether continuation of any such suspension is warranted.

(b) After completion of the initial reviews under section 3(a) of this order, and at least once every 4 years thereafter, the Committee shall review whether a continued law of war detention policy remains consistent with the interests of the United States, including national security interests.

Sec. 6.   Continuing Obligation of the Departments of Justice and Defense to Assess Feasibility of Prosecution. As to each detainee whom the interagency review established by Executive Order 13492 has designated for continued law of war detention, the Attorney General and the Secretary of Defense shall continue to assess whether prosecution of the detainee is feasible and in the national security interests of the United States, and shall refer detainees for prosecution, as appropriate.

Sec. 7.   Obligation of Other Departments and Agencies to Assist the Secretary of Defense. All departments, agencies, entities, and officers of the United States, to the maximum extent permitted by law, shall provide the Secretary of Defense such assistance as may be requested to implement this order.

Sec. 8.   Legality of Detention. The process established under this order does not address the legality of any detainee's law of war detention. If, at any time during the periodic review process established in this order, material information calls into question the legality of detention, the matter will be referred immediately to the Secretary of Defense and the Attorney General for appropriate action.

Sec. 9.   Definitions. (a) "Law of War Detention" means: detention authorized by the Congress under the AUMF, as informed by the laws of war.

(b) "Periodic Review Board" means: a board composed of senior officials tasked with fulfilling the functions described in section 3 of this order, one appointed by each of the following departments and offices: the Departments of State, Defense, Justice, and Homeland Security, as well as the Offices of the Director of National Intelligence and the Chairman of the Joint Chiefs of Staff.

(c) "Conditional Detention" means: the status of those detainees designated by the Executive Order 13492 review as eligible for transfer if one of the following conditions is satisfied: (1) the security situation improves in Yemen; (2) an appropriate rehabilitation program becomes available; or (3) an appropriate third-country resettlement option becomes available.

(d) "Review Committee" means: a committee composed of the Secretary of State, the Secretary of Defense, the Attorney General, the Secretary of Homeland Security, the Director of National Intelligence, and the Chairman of the Joint Chiefs of Staff.

Sec. 10.   General Provisions. (a) Nothing in this order shall prejudice the authority of the Secretary of Defense or any other official to determine the disposition of any detainee not covered by this order.

(b) This order shall be implemented subject to the availability of necessary appropriations and consistent with applicable law including: the Convention Against Torture; Common Article 3 of the Geneva Conventions; the Detainee Treatment Act of 2005; and other laws relating to the transfer, treatment, and interrogation of individuals detained in an armed conflict.

(c) This order is not intended to, and does not, create any right or benefit, substantive or procedural, enforceable at law or in equity by any party against the United States, its departments, agencies, or entities, its officers, employees, or agents, or any other person.

(d) Nothing in this order, and no determination made under this order, shall be construed as grounds for release of detainees covered by this order into the United States.

BARACK OBAMA

THE WHITE HOUSE,

March 7, 2011.

3.   In late June, 2011, the Senate Armed Services Committee reported out its version of the 2012 National Defense Appropriations Bill, S. 1253, which contained the following provisions dealing with detainee matters.

2012 National Defense Appropriations Bill

S. 1253

Subtitle D—Detainee Matters

4 SEC. 1031.   AUTHORITY TO DETAIN UNPRIVILEGED ENEMY

5 BELLIGERENTS CAPTURED PURSUANT TO

6 THE AUTHORIZATION FOR USE OF MILITARY

7 FORCE.

8 (a) IN GENERAL.—The Armed Forces of the United

9 States are authorized to detain covered persons captured

10 in the course of hostilities authorized by the Authorization

11 for Use of Military Force (Public Law 107–40) as

12 unprivileged enemy belligerents pending disposition under

13 the law of war.

14 (b) COVERED PERSONS.—A covered person under

15 this section is any person, including but not limited to persons for whom detention is required under section 1032,

17 as follows:

18 (1) A person who planned, authorized, committed, or aided the terrorist attacks that occurred on September 11, 2001, or harbored those responsible for those attacks.

22 (2) A person who was a part of or substantially

23 supported al-Qaeda, the Taliban, or associated forces

24 that are engaged in hostilities against the United

25 States or its coalition partners, including any person

1 who has committed a belligerent act or has directly

2 supported such hostilities in aid of such enemy forces.

4 (c) DISPOSITION UNDER LAW OF WAR.—The disposition of a person under the law of war as described

6 in subsection (a) may include the following:

7 (1) Long-term detention under the law of war

8 without trial until the end of hostilities against the

9 nations, organizations, and persons subject to the

10 Authorization for Use of Military Force.

11 (2) Trial under chapter 47A of title 10, United

12 States Code (as amended by the Military Commissions Act of 2009 (title XVIII of Public Law 111–14 84)).

15 (3) Transfer for trial by an alternative court or

16 competent tribunal having lawful jurisdiction.

17 (4) Transfer to the custody or control of the

18 person's country of origin, any other foreign country, or any other foreign entity.

20 (d) CONSTITUTIONAL LIMITATION ON APPLICABILITY TO UNITED STATES PERSONS.—The authority to

22 detain a person under this section does not extend to the

23 detention of citizens or lawful resident aliens of the United

24 States on the basis of conduct taking place within the

1 United States except to the extent permitted by the Constitution of the United States.

3 SEC. 1032. REQUIRED MILITARY CUSTODY FOR MEMBERS

4 OF AL–QAEDA AND AFFILIATED ENTITIES.

5 (a) CUSTODY PENDING DISPOSITION UNDER LAW OF

6 WAR.—

7 (1) IN GENERAL.—Except as provided in paragraph (4), the Armed Forces of the United States shall hold a person described in paragraph (2) in 10 military custody as an unprivileged enemy belligerent pending disposition under the law of war.

12 (2) APPLICABILITY TO AL–QAEDA AND AFFILIATED ENTITIES.—The requirement in paragraph (1)

14 shall apply to any covered person under section 1031(b) who is determined to be—

16 (A) a member of, or part of, al-Qaeda or

17 an affiliated entity; and

18 (B) a participant in the course of planning

19 or carrying out an attack or attempted attack

20 against the United States or its coalition partners.

22 (3) DISPOSITION UNDER LAW OF WAR.—For

23 purposes of this subsection, the disposition of a person under the law of war has the meaning given in section 1031(c), except that no transfer otherwise

1 described in paragraph (4) of that section shall be

2 made unless consistent with the requirements of section 1033.

4 (4) WAIVER FOR NATIONAL SECURITY.—The

5 Secretary of Defense may, in consultation with the

6 Secretary of State and the Director of National Intelligence, waive the requirement of paragraph (1) if

8 the Secretary submits to Congress a certification in

9 writing that such a waiver is in the national security

10 interests of the United States.

11 (b) REQUIREMENT INAPPLICABLE TO UNITED

12 STATES CITIZENS.—The requirement to detain a person

13 in military custody under this section does not extend to

14 citizens of the United States.

15 (c) EFFECTIVE DATE.—This section shall take effect

16 on the date of the enactment of this Act, and shall apply

17 with respect to persons described in subsection (a)(2) who

18 are taken into the custody or brought under the control

19 of the United States on or after that date.

. . .

19 **SEC. 1036. PROCEDURES FOR STATUS DETERMINA-TION OF**

20 **UNPRIVILEGED ENEMY BELLIGERENTS.**

21 (a) IN GENERAL.—Not later than 90 days after the

22 date of the enactment of this Act, the Secretary of Defense

23 shall submit to the appropriate committees of Congress

24 a report setting forth the procedures for determining the

25 status of persons captured in the course of hostilities authorized by the Authorization for Use of Military Force

2 (Public Law 107–40) for purposes of section 1031.

3 (b) ELEMENTS OF PROCEDURES.—The procedures

4 required by this section shall provide for the following in

5 the case of any unprivileged enemy belligerent who will

6 be held in long-term detention under the law of war pursuant to the Authorization for Use of Military Force:

8 (1) A military judge shall preside at proceedings for the determination of status of an unprivileged enemy belligerent.

11 (2) An unprivileged enemy belligerent may, at

12 the election of the belligerent, be represented by

13 military counsel at proceedings for the determination

14 of status of the belligerent.

15 (c) REPORT ON MODIFICATION OF PROCEDURES.—

16 The Secretary of Defense shall submit to the appropriate

17 committees of Congress a report on any modification of

18 the procedures submitted under this section. The report

19 on any such modification shall be so submitted not later

20 than 60 days before the date on which such modification

21 goes into effect.

22 (d) APPROPRIATE COMMITTEES OF CONGRESS DE-FINED.—In this section, the term "appropriate committees of Congress" means—

1 (1) the Committee on Armed Services and the

2 Select Committee on Intelligence of the Senate; and

3 (2) the Committee on Armed Services and the

4 Permanent Select Committee on Intelligence of the

5 House of Representatives.

4. The foregoing provisions should be compared with the related provisions of the comparable House bill, HR 1540, which is discussed supra, p. 535 Of course, these are bills reported out by their respective committees and not enacted into law as of the date of this writing. They do, however, provide a window into some of the current thinking in the Congress regarding detainee matters and also pose important issues about how such legislative proposals would affect existing law.

5. Compare the scope of section 1034 in the House bill, p. 535, supra, and section 1031 in the Senate bill. What is the difference? Is the criticism warranted of the House bill that was triggered when section 1034 was made public?

6. Suppose the foregoing provisions had been in effect at the time of the apprehension of Jose Padilla or Ali Saleh Kahlah al-Marri, whose cases are described infra, p. 622. Would the government's actions in those cases have been affected by these enactments?

7. Compare these provisions in S. 1253 with the positions taken in the White House press release, supra. In what ways, if any, do they differ? Note that we have omitted in the S.1253 provisions reproduced here those which permanently barred the use of federal funds to transfer Guantanamo detainees to the mainland United States.

NOTE ON THE CONTROVERSY SURROUNDING THE PROPOSED CLOSURE OF THE GUANTANAMO BAY FACILITY AND WHERE TO PROSECUTE GITMO DETAINEES; WHERE TO DETAIN AND PROSECUTE NEW APPREHENDED DETAINEES

As recounted above, the decision in Boumediene opened the door to numerous habeas corpus actions filed by Guantanamo detainees. Meanwhile another complex scenario was occurring in relation to the Guantanamo Bay facility. President Obama had pledged to close Guantanamo within a year of his assuming office. As it turned out, there was strong opposition, mainly from Republicans in the Congress) a) to closing Guantanamo, and b) to transferring the remaining detainees to a prison in the mainland U.S. (After a search, the Obama administration reportedly planned to buy a currently unused state prison facility in Illinois for this purpose.) Congress, however, proceeded to block by legislative means the plan to transfer the remaining Guantanamo detainees to the mainland U.S. At the time of this writing, the plan to close Guantanamo remains in limbo. See White House Press Release, supra.

During this same general period, Attorney General Holder announced plans to prosecute five "high value" Guantanamo detainees in federal court, while also indicating that of the remaining detainees who were going to be prosecuted, some of the prosecutions would occur in a federal district court in the U.S., and some would be prosecuted before the military commissions. The plan to prosecute the five high value detainees (at least some of them were alleged to have been involved in the planning of the 9/11 attacks) also generated significant controversy, and after more than a year of delay, the Attorney General announced that the five would be prosecuted before military commissions. Thus far, it appears that one Guantanamo detainee has been prosecuted in New York, see United States v. Ghailani, 761 F.Supp.2d 167 (S.D.N.Y 2011).

Meanwhile, the Obama administration has been faced with a dilemma. While it has not been able to close Guantanamo, it appears that it does not want to send there any persons newly seized abroad. What options does it have? The strategy appears to be still evolving. See, for example, hearings before the Senate Armed Services Committee on June 28, 2011 relating to the nominations of Admiral McRaven as the new SOCOM commander and General Allen as the new commander in Afghanistan where the following testimony was given:

SENATOR GRAHAM: . . . If you caught someone tomorrow in Yemen, Somalia, you name the theater, outside of Afghanistan, where would you detain that person?

ADMIRAL MCRAVEN: Sir, right now, as you're well aware, that is always a difficult issue for us. When we conduct an operation outside the major theaters of war in Iraq or Afghanistan, we put forth—we— . . . No two cases seem to be alike. As you know, there are certain individuals that are under the AUMF, the use of military force, and those are easier to deal with than folks that may not have been under the authority for AUMF. In many cases, we will put them on a naval vessel and we will hold them until we can either get a case to prosecute them in U.S. court or . . .

. . .

SENATOR GRAHAM: What's the longest we can keep somebody on the ship?

ADMIRAL MCRAVEN: Sir, I think it depends on whether or not we think we can prosecute that individual in a U.S. court or we can return him to a third party country.

SENATOR GRAHAM: What if you can't do either one of those?

ADMIRAL MCRAVEN: Sir, it—again, if we can't do either one of those, then we'll release that individual and that becomes the—the unenviable option, but it is an option.

. . .

SENATOR LEVIN: Finally, Admiral . . . you made reference to a couple I think that are on a ship, something like that. Is there any legal prohibition against them being tried before an Article 3 court or before a military commission?

ADMIRAL MCRAVEN: Sir, again, it depends on the individual case, and I'd be more than happy to discuss the cases that we've dealt with.

SENATOR LEVIN: Well, no, not . . . specific cases so much as is there any legal prohibition, assuming it's planned . . . having those people tried either before an Article 3 court, if they've committed a crime against the United States, or if they've committed a crime of war, by being tried by a U.S. military commission?

ADMIRAL MCRAVEN: Sir, not to my knowledge, there is no prohibition.

. . .

SENATOR AYOTTE:. . . . I wanted to follow up, General Allen, on the question of detention. If we were to, for example, capture someone like Ayman al-Zawahri in Yemen, for example, outside of Afghanistan, could we detain him in Afghanistan at the detention facilities there?

GENERAL ALLEN: We would not recommend that.

SENATOR AYOTTE: And why is that?

GENERAL ALLEN: Because Afghanistan is a sovereign country.

SENATOR AYOTTE: So we're not going to use the detention facilities, for example, in Afghanistan to detain terrorists who are captured outside the territory of Afghanistan?

GENERAL ALLEN: It's not our intention.

SENATOR AYOTTE: And following up, Admiral, with respect to detention, if we, for example, were to capture al-Zawahiri and—capture and not kill him but hold him for purposes of gathering intelligence and detaining him long term, because we felt we needed to under the law of war, where would we hold him?

ADMIRAL MCRAVEN: Yes, ma'am, I think that is a policy question that I'm really not in a position to answer. From a practical military standpoint, obviously we can hold—hold Zawahiri or Anwar al-Awlaki or anybody else in a number of places, from a practical standpoint. It becomes a policy issue and a sovereignty issue for various countries. And as General Allen said, we have looked a number of times at whether or not we would do that in Afghanistan, but owing to the nature of the sovereignty of Afghanistan and the concern about the potential backlash from the Afghan government, we have recommended not to do that.

SENATOR AYOTTE: And, Admiral, would it not be helpful 10 years into the war on terror to have a long-term detention and interrogation facility that would be secure for individuals where we need to gather further intelligence?

ADMIRAL MCRAVEN: Ma'am, I believe it would be very helpful.

SENATOR AYOTTE: And as far as you understand it, is Guantanamo Bay still off the table in terms of being used for that type of facility?

ADMIRAL MCRAVEN: As far as I understand it, it is, yes, ma'am.

The question remains, however, suppose a person is apprehended abroad and then interrogated on shipboard. What should the government then do? See, for example, U.S. to Prosecute a Somali Suspect in Civilian Court, NY Times A1, July 6, 2011 reporting that the Obama administration had announced that after interrogating Ahmed Abdukadir Warsame for some months on shipboard, he was going to be prosecuted in civilian federal court in New York City.

Suppose it was not feasible to prosecute Warsame but he was considered dangerous and the government wished to continue to detain him. The question remains. Where would he be detained.? Is there any choice other than Guantanamo in light of the present stalemate between the President and the Congress? Suppose you were working in the White House on detainee matters. What advice would you give regarding these issues?

D.   MILITARY CUSTODY FOR PERSONS ARRESTED IN THE UNITED STATES— CITIZEN AND NON–CITIZEN: THE JOSE PADILLA AND ALI SALEH KAHLAH AL–MARRI CASES

Early in the post–9/11 period, on two different occasions, the government arrested two persons in the United States as material witnesses and thereafter declared them to be enemy combatants and shifted them into military custody. One, Jose Padilla, is a U.S. citizen, whose first foray to the Supreme Court is described supra, p. 552. Ali Saleh Kahlah al-Marri, the second, is not a U.S. citizen or permanent resident. The trail of litigation in both cases is treated below.

1.   THE SAGA OF JOSE PADILLA

As previously described, the import of the Supreme Court's decision in Rumsfeld v. Padilla was that Padilla had sued the wrong defendant in the wrong court. Soon thereafter, in July, 2004, Padilla filed a new habeas corpus action in the U.S. District Court for the District of South Carolina against the commander of the brig in which he was being detained. Padilla moved for summary judgment, and the district court ruled in favor of Padilla. That decision was reversed by the U.S. Court of Appeals for the Fourth Circuit in the following opinion:

PADILLA v. HANFT

423 F.3d 386 (4th Cir.2005)

Before LUTTIG, MICHAEL, and TRAXLER, CIRCUIT JUDGES.

JUDGE LUTTIG wrote the opinion for the Court, in which JUDGE MICHAEL and JUDGE TRAXLER joined.

LUTTIG, CIRCUIT JUDGE.

Appellee Jose Padilla, a United States citizen, associated with forces hostile to the United States in Afghanistan and took up arms against United States forces in that country in our war against al Qaeda. Upon his escape to Pakistan from the battlefield in Afghanistan, Padilla was recruited, trained, funded, and equipped by al Qaeda leaders to continue prosecution of the war in the United States by blowing up apartment buildings in this country. Padilla flew to the United States on May 8, 2002, to begin carrying out his assignment, but was arrested by civilian law enforcement authorities upon his arrival at O'Hare International Airport in Chicago.

Thereafter, in a letter to the Secretary of Defense, the President of the United States personally designated Padilla an "enemy combatant" against this country, stating that the United States is "at war" with al Qaeda, that "Mr. Padilla engaged in conduct that constituted hostile and war-like acts, including conduct in preparation for acts of international terrorism that had the aim to cause injury to or adverse effects on the United States," and that "Mr. Padilla represents a continuing, present and grave danger to the national security of the United States." Having determined that "detention of Mr. Padilla is necessary to prevent him from aiding al Qaeda in its efforts to attack the United States or its armed forces, other governmental personnel, or citizens," the President directed the Secretary of Defense to take Padilla into military custody, in which custody Padilla has remained ever since. The full text of the President's memorandum to the Secretary of Defense reads as follows:

THE WHITE HOUSE WASHINGTON

FOR OFFICIAL USE ONLY

TO THE SECRETARY OF DEFENSE:

Based on the information available to me from all sources,

REDACTED

In accordance with the Constitution and consistent with the laws of the United States, including the Authorization for Use of Military Force Joint Resolution (Public Law 107–40);

I, GEORGE W. BUSH, as President of the United States and Commander in Chief of the U.S. armed forces, hereby DETERMINE for the United States of America that:

(1) Jose Padilla, who is under the control of the Department of Justice and who is a U.S. citizen, is, and at the time he entered the United States in May 2002 was, an enemy combatant;

(2) Mr. Padilla is closely associated with al Qaeda, an international terrorist organization with which the United States is at war;

(3) Mr. Padilla engaged in conduct that constituted hostile and war-like acts, including conduct in preparation for acts of international terrorism that had the aim to cause injury to or adverse effects on the United States;

(4) Mr. Padilla possesses intelligence, including intelligence about personnel and activities of al Qaeda, that, if communicated

to the U.S., would aid U.S. efforts to prevent attacks by al Qaeda on the United States or its armed forces, other governmental personnel, or citizens;

(5) Mr. Padilla represents a continuing, present and grave danger to the national security of the United States, and detention of Mr. Padilla is necessary to prevent him from aiding al Qaeda in its efforts to attack the United States or its armed forces, other governmental personnel, or citizens;

(6) it is in the interest of the United States that the Secretary of Defense detain Mr. Padilla as an enemy combatant; and

(7) it is REDACTED consistent with U.S. law and the laws of war for the Secretary of Defense to detain Mr. Padilla as enemy combatant.

Accordingly, you are directed to receive Mr. Padilla from the Department of Justice and to detain him as an enemy combatant.

DATE: June 9, 2002

Signature

/George Bush/

The exceedingly important question before us is whether the President of the United States possesses the authority to detain militarily a citizen of this country who is closely associated with al Qaeda, an entity with which the United States is at war; who took up arms on behalf of that enemy and against our country in a foreign combat zone of that war; *and* who thereafter traveled to the United States for the avowed purpose of further prosecuting that war on American soil, against American citizens and targets.

We conclude that the President does possess such authority pursuant to the Authorization for Use of Military Force Joint Resolution enacted by Congress in the wake of the attacks on the United States of September 11, 2001. Accordingly, the judgment of the district court is reversed.

Al Qaeda operatives recruited Jose Padilla, a United States citizen, to train for jihad in Afghanistan in February 2000, while Padilla was on a religious pilgrimage to Saudi Arabia.[1] Subsequently, Padilla met with al Qaeda operatives in Afghanistan, received explosives training in an al Qaeda–affiliated camp, and served as an armed guard at what he understood to be a Taliban outpost. When United States military operations began in Afghanistan, Padilla and other al Qaeda operatives moved from safehouse to safehouse to evade bombing or capture. Padilla was, on the facts with which we are presented, "armed and present in a combat zone during armed conflict between al Qaeda/Taliban forces and the armed forces of the United States."

---

1. For purposes of Padilla's summary judgment motion, the parties have stipulated to the facts as set forth by the government. J.A. 30–31. It is only on these facts that we consider whether the President has the authority to detain Padilla.

Padilla eventually escaped to Pakistan, armed with an assault rifle. Once in Pakistan, Padilla met with Khalid Sheikh Mohammad, a senior al Qaeda operations planner, who directed Padilla to travel to the United States for the purpose of blowing up apartment buildings, in continued prosecution of al Qaeda's war of terror against the United States. After receiving further training, as well as cash, travel documents, and communication devices, Padilla flew to the United States in order to carry out his accepted assignment.

Upon arrival at Chicago's O'Hare International Airport on May 8, 2002, Padilla was detained by FBI agents, who interviewed and eventually arrested him pursuant to a material witness warrant issued by the district court for the Southern District of New York in conjunction with a grand jury investigation of the September 11 attacks. Padilla was transported to New York, where he was held at a civilian correctional facility until, on June 9, 2002, the President designated him an "enemy combatant" against the United States and directed the Secretary of Defense to take him into military custody. Since his delivery into the custody of military authorities, Padilla has been detained at a naval brig in South Carolina.

On June 11, 2002, Padilla filed a petition for a writ of habeas corpus in the Southern District of New York, claiming that his detention violated the Constitution. The Supreme Court of the United States ultimately ordered Padilla's petition dismissed without prejudice, holding that his petition was improperly filed in the Southern District of New York. *Rumsfeld v. Padilla,* 542 U.S. 426, 124 S.Ct. 2711, 2727, 159 L.Ed.2d 513 (2004). And on July 2, 2004, Padilla filed the present petition for a writ of habeas corpus in the District of South Carolina.

The district court subsequently held that the President lacks the authority to detain Padilla, that Padilla's detention is in violation of the Constitution and laws of the United States, and that Padilla therefore must either be criminally charged or released. This appeal followed. We expedited consideration of this appeal at the request of the parties, hearing argument in the case on July 19, 2005.

The Authorization for Use of Military Force Joint Resolution (AUMF), upon which the President explicitly relied in his order that Padilla be detained by the military and upon which the government chiefly relies in support of the President's authority to detain Padilla, was enacted by Congress in the immediate aftermath of the September 11, 2001, terrorist attacks on the United States. It provides as follows:

[T]he President is authorized to use all necessary and appropriate force against those nations, organizations, or persons he determines planned, authorized, committed, or aided the terrorist attacks that occurred on September 11, 2001, or harbored such organizations or persons, in order to prevent any future acts of international terrorism against the United States by such nations, organizations or persons.

Pub.L. No. 107–40, § 2(a), 115 Stat. 224 (September 18, 2001). The Supreme Court has already once interpreted this Joint Resolution in the context of a military detention by the President. In *Hamdi v. Rumsfeld,* the Supreme Court held, on the facts alleged by the government, that the AUMF authorized the military detention of Yaser Esam Hamdi, an American citizen who fought alongside Taliban forces in Afghanistan, was captured by United States allies on a battlefield there, and was detained in the United States by the military.[2] The narrow question, addressed by the Court in *Hamdi* was whether the Executive has the authority to detain citizens who qualify as enemy combatants, defined for purposes of that case as individual[s] who ... [were] part of or supporting forces hostile to the United States or coalition partners in Afghanistan and who engaged in an armed conflict against the United States there. The controlling plurality of the Court answered that narrow question in the affirmative, concluding, based upon longstanding law-of-war principles, that Hamdi's detention was necessary and appropriate within the meaning of the AUMF because [t]he capture and detention of lawful combatants and the capture, detention, and trial of unlawful combatants, by universal agreement and practice, are important incident[s] of war. The rationale for this law-of-war principle, Justice O'Connor explained for the plurality, is that detention to prevent a combatant's return to the battlefield is a fundamental incident of waging war.

As the AUMF authorized Hamdi's detention by the President, so also does it authorize Padilla's detention. Under the facts as presented here, Padilla unquestionably qualifies as an "enemy combatant" as that term was defined for purposes of the controlling opinion in *Hamdi.* Indeed, under the definition of "enemy combatant" employed in *Hamdi,* we can discern no difference in principle between Hamdi and Padilla. Like Hamdi, Padilla associated with forces hostile to the United States in Afghanistan. *Compare* J.A. 19–23 (detailing Padilla's association with al Qaeda in Afghanistan and Pakistan), *with Hamdi,* 124 S.Ct. at 2637 (describing Hamdi's affiliation with the Taliban in Afghanistan). And, like Hamdi, Padilla took up arms against United States forces in that country in the same way and to the same extent as did Hamdi. *Compare* J.A. 21 (averring that Padilla was "armed and present in a combat zone during armed conflict between al Qaeda/Taliban forces and the armed forces of the United States"), *and* (alleging that Padilla was "armed with an assault rifle" as he escaped to Pakistan), *with Hamdi,* 124 S.Ct. at 2642, n. 1 (noting that the asserted basis for detaining Hamdi was that he "carr[ied] a weapon against American troops on a foreign battlefield"), *and id.* at 2637 (quoting Mobbs Affidavit that Hamdi had " 'surrender[ed] his Kalishnikov assault rifle' " to Northern Alliance forces (alteration in original)). Because, like Hamdi, Padilla is an enemy combatant, and because his detention is no less necessary than was Hamdi's in order to prevent his return to the battlefield, the President is authorized by the AUMF to detain Padilla as a fundamental incident to the conduct of war.

---

2. Having concluded that detention was authorized on the facts alleged by the government, the Court in *Hamdi* remanded the case for a hearing to determine, pursuant to the due process requirements set forth in its opinion, whether those alleged facts were true.

Our conclusion that the AUMF as interpreted by the Supreme Court in *Hamdi* authorizes the President's detention of Padilla as an enemy combatant is reinforced by the Supreme Court's decision in *Ex parte Quirin,* on which the plurality in *Hamdi* itself heavily relied. In *Quirin,* the Court held that Congress had authorized the military trial of Haupt, a United States citizen who entered the country with orders from the Nazis to blow up domestic war facilities but was captured before he could execute those orders. The Court reasoned that Haupt's citizenship was no bar to his military trial as an unlawful enemy belligerent, concluding that "[c]itizens who associate themselves with the military arm of the enemy government, and with its aid, guidance and direction enter this country bent on hostile acts, are enemy belligerents within the meaning of ... the law of war."

Like Haupt, Padilla associated with the military arm of the enemy, and with its aid, guidance, and direction entered this country bent on committing hostile acts on American soil. J.A. 22–23. Padilla thus falls within *Quirin*'s definition of enemy belligerent, as well as within the definition of the equivalent term accepted by the plurality in *Hamdi. Compare Quirin,* 317 U.S. at 37–38, 63 S.Ct. 2 (holding that [c]itizens who associate themselves with the military arm of the enemy government, and with its aid, guidance and direction enter this country bent on hostile acts, are enemy belligerents within the meaning of ... the law of war), *with Hamdi,* 124 S.Ct. at 2639 (accepting for purposes of the case the government's definition of enemy combatants as those who were part of or supporting forces hostile to the United States or coalition partners' in Afghanistan and who engaged in an armed conflict against the United States' there).

We understand the plurality's *reasoning* in *Hamdi* to be that the AUMF authorizes the President to detain all those who qualify as enemy combatants within the meaning of the laws of war, such power being universally accepted under the laws of war as necessary in order to prevent the return of combatants to the battlefield during conflict. Given that Padilla qualifies as an enemy combatant under both the definition adopted by the Court in *Quirin* and the definition accepted by the controlling opinion in *Hamdi,* his military detention as an enemy combatant by the President is unquestionably authorized by the AUMF as a fundamental incident to the President's prosecution of the war against al Qaeda in Afghanistan.[3]

Padilla marshals essentially four arguments for the conclusion that his detention is unlawful. None of them ultimately is persuasive.

Recognizing the hurdle to his position represented by the Supreme Court's decision in *Hamdi,* Padilla principally argues that his case does not fall within the narrow circumstances considered by the Court in that

---

3. Under *Hamdi,* the power to detain that is authorized under the AUMF is not a power to detain indefinitely. Detention is limited to the duration of the hostilities as to which the detention is authorized. Because the United States remains engaged in the conflict with al Qaeda in Afghanistan, Padilla's detention has not exceeded in duration that authorized by the AUMF.

case because, although he too stood alongside Taliban forces in Afghanistan, he was seized on American soil, whereas Hamdi was captured on a foreign battlefield. In other words, Padilla maintains that capture on a foreign battlefield was one of the narrow circumstances to which the plurality in *Hamdi* confined its opinion. We disagree. When the plurality articulated the narrow question before it, it referred simply to the permissibility of detaining an individual who ... was part of or supporting forces hostile to the United States or coalition partners in Afghanistan and who engaged in an armed conflict against the United States' there. Nowhere in its framing of the narrow question presented did the plurality even mention the locus of capture.

The actual reasoning that the plurality thereafter employed is consistent with the question having been framed so as to render locus of capture irrelevant. That reasoning was that Hamdi's detention was an exercise of necessary and appropriate force within the meaning of the AUMF because detention to prevent a combatant's return to the battlefield is a fundamental incident of waging war. This reasoning simply does not admit of a distinction between an enemy combatant captured abroad and detained in the United States, such as Hamdi, and an enemy combatant who escaped capture abroad but was ultimately captured domestically and detained in the United States, such as Padilla. As we previously explained, Padilla poses the same threat of returning to the battlefield as Hamdi posed at the time of the Supreme Court's adjudication of Hamdi's petition. Padilla's detention is thus necessary and appropriate to the same extent as was Hamdi's.

Padilla directs us to a passage from the plurality's opinion in *Hamdi* in which, when responding to the dissent, the plurality charged that the dissent ignore[d] the context of th[e] case: a United States citizen captured in a *foreign* combat zone. Padilla argues that this passage proves that *capture on a foreign battlefield* was one of the factual circumstances by which the Court's opinion was limited. If this language stood alone, Padilla's argument as to the limitation of *Hamdi* at least would have more force, though to acknowledge that foreign battlefield capture was part of the *context* of the case still is not to say (at least not necessarily) that the locus of capture was essential to the Court's *reasoning*. However, this language simply cannot bear the weight that Padilla would have it bear when it is considered against the backdrop of both the quite different limitations that were expressly imposed by the Court through its framing of the question presented, and the actual reasoning that was employed by the Court in reaching its conclusion, which reasoning was consistent with the question having been framed so as to render an enemy combatant's point of capture irrelevant to the President's power to detain. In short, the plurality carefully limited its opinion, but not in a way that leaves room for argument that the President's power to detain one who has associated with the enemy and taken up arms against the United States in a foreign combat zone varies depending upon the geographic location where that enemy combatant happens to be captured.

Our conclusion that the reasoning in *Hamdi* does not support a distinction based on the locus of capture is buttressed by the plurality's analysis of *Quirin*. Although at issue in *Quirin* was the authority of the President to subject a United States citizen who was also an enemy combatant to military trial, the plurality in *Hamdi* went to lengths to observe that Haupt, *who had been captured domestically,* could instead have been permissibly *detained* for the duration of hostilities. That analysis strongly suggests, if it does not confirm, that the plurality did not regard the locus of capture (within or without the United States) as relevant to the President's authority to detain an enemy combatant who is also a citizen, and that it believed that the detention of such a combatant is not more or less a necessary incident of the President's power to wage war depending upon the locus of eventual capture.

Given the lack of any reference to locus of capture in the plurality's articulation of the narrow question before it, the absence of any basis in *Hamdi*'s reasoning for a distinction between foreign and domestic capture of one who has both associated with the enemy and taken up arms against the United States on behalf of that enemy in a foreign combat zone, and the plurality's understanding of and reliance upon *Quirin* as a precedent that would permit the detention of an enemy combatant who had been captured domestically, we simply cannot ascribe to the rejoinder to Justice Scalia the significance, much less the dispositive significance, that Padilla urges.[4]

Padilla also argues, and the district court held, that Padilla's military detention is neither necessary nor appropriate because he is amenable to criminal prosecution. Related to this argument, Padilla attempts to distinguish *Quirin* from his case on the grounds that he has simply been detained, unlike Haupt who was charged and tried in *Quirin*. Neither the argument nor the attempted distinction is convincing.

As to the fact that Padilla can be prosecuted, the availability of criminal process does not distinguish him from Hamdi. If the mere availability of criminal prosecution rendered detention unnecessary within the meaning of the AUMF, then Hamdi's detention would have been unnecessary and therefore unauthorized, since he too was detained in the United States and amenable to criminal prosecution. We are convinced, in any event, that the availability of criminal process cannot be determinative of the power to detain, if for no other reason than that criminal prosecution may well not achieve the very purpose for which detention is authorized in the first place—the prevention of return to the field of battle. Equally important, in many instances criminal prosecution would impede the Executive in its efforts to gather intelligence from the detainee

---

4. Padilla also argues that the locus of capture should be legally relevant to the scope of the AUMF's authorization because there is a higher probability of an erroneous determination that one is an enemy combatant when the seizure occurs on American soil. It is far from clear that this is actually the case. In any event, Padilla's argument confuses the scope of the President's *power* to detain enemy combatants under the AUMF with the *process* for establishing that a detainee is in fact an enemy combatant. *Hamdi* itself provides process to guard against the erroneous detention of non-enemy combatants.

and to restrict the detainee's communication with confederates so as to ensure that the detainee does not pose a continuing threat to national security even as he is confined—impediments that would render military detention not only an appropriate, but also the necessary, course of action to be taken in the interest of national security.

The district court acknowledged the need to defer to the President's determination that Padilla's detention is necessary and appropriate in the interest of national security. However, we believe that the district court ultimately accorded insufficient deference to that determination, effectively imposing upon the President the equivalent of a least-restrictive-means test. To subject to such exacting scrutiny the President's determination that criminal prosecution would not adequately protect the Nation's security at a very minimum fails to accord the President the deference that is his when he acts pursuant to a broad delegation of authority from Congress, such as the AUMF.

As for Padilla's attempted distinction of *Quirin* on the grounds that, unlike Haupt, he has never been charged and tried by the military, the plurality in *Hamdi* rejected as immaterial the distinction between detention and trial (apparently regarding the former as a lesser imposition than the latter), noting that "nothing in *Quirin* suggests that [Haupt's United States] citizenship would have precluded his *mere detention* for the duration of the relevant hostilities."

Padilla, citing *Ex parte Endo,* 323 U.S. 283, 65 S.Ct. 208, 89 L.Ed. 243 (1944), and relying upon *Quirin,* next argues that only a clear statement from Congress can authorize his detention, and that the AUMF is not itself, and does not contain, such a clear statement.

In *Endo,* the Court did state that, when asked to find implied powers in a wartime statute, it must assume that "the law makers intended to place no greater restraint on the citizen than was clearly and unmistakably indicated by the language [the law makers] used." The Court almost immediately thereafter observed, however, that the "fact that the Act" at issue was "silent on detention [did] not of course mean that any power to detain [was] lacking," an observation that proves that the Court did not adopt or even apply in that case a "clear statement" rule of the kind for which Padilla argues.

Padilla contends that *Quirin* also supports the existence of a clear statement rule. However, in no place in *Quirin* did the Court even purport to establish a clear statement rule. In its opinion, the Court did note that Congress had "explicitly" authorized Haupt's military trial.... In fact, to the extent that *Quirin* can be understood to have addressed the need for a clear statement of authority from Congress at all, the rule would appear the opposite:

[T]he detention and trial of petitioners—ordered by the President in the declared exercise of his powers as Commander in Chief of the Army in time of war and of grave public danger—are not to be set aside by the courts without the clear conviction that they are in conflict with the Constitution or laws of Congress constitutionally enacted.

Of course, even were a clear statement by Congress required, the AUMF constitutes such a clear statement according to the Supreme Court. In *Hamdi,* stating that "it [was] of no moment that the AUMF does not use specific language of detention," the plurality held that the AUMF "clearly and unmistakably authorized" Hamdi's detention. Nothing in the AUMF permits us to conclude that the Joint Resolution clearly and unmistakably authorized Hamdi's detention but not Padilla's. To the contrary, read in light of its purpose clause ("in order to prevent any future acts of international terrorism against the United States") and its preamble (stating that the acts of 9/11 "render it both necessary and appropriate ... to protect United States citizens both at home and abroad"), the AUMF applies even more clearly and unmistakably to Padilla than to Hamdi. Padilla, after all, in addition to supporting hostile forces in Afghanistan and taking up arms against our troops on a battlefield in that country like Hamdi, *also* came to the United States in order to commit future acts of terrorism against American citizens and targets.

These facts unquestionably establish that Padilla poses the requisite threat of return to battle in the ongoing armed conflict between the United States and al Qaeda in Afghanistan, and that his detention is authorized as a "fundamental incident of waging war," in order "to prevent a combatant's return to the battlefield," Congress "clearly and unmistakably," authorized such detention when, in the AUMF, it "permitt[ed] the use of 'necessary and appropriate force,'" to prevent other attacks like those of September 11, 2001.

. . .

The Congress of the United States, in the Authorization for Use of Military Force Joint Resolution, provided the President all powers necessary and appropriate to protect American citizens from terrorist acts by those who attacked the United States on September 11, 2001. As would be expected, and as the Supreme Court has held, those powers include the power to detain identified and committed enemies such as Padilla, who associated with al Qaeda and the Taliban regime, who took up arms against this Nation in its war against these enemies, *and* who entered the United States for the avowed purpose of further prosecuting that war by attacking American citizens and targets on our own soil—a power without which, Congress understood, the President could well be unable to protect American citizens from the very kind of savage attack that occurred four years ago almost to the day.

The detention of petitioner being fully authorized by Act of Congress, the judgment of the district court that the detention of petitioner by the President of the United States is without support in law is hereby reversed.

REVERSED.

Following the court of appeals decision, supra, the Padilla saga continued. He sought certiorari review in the Supreme Court. Justice Kennedy's opinion concurring in the denial of certiorari details what happened next.

PADILLA v. HANFT
547 U.S. 1062 (2006)

Case below, 423 F.3d 386.

Petition for writ of certiorari to the United States Court of Appeals for the Fourth Circuit denied.

The petition for a writ of certiorari is denied. JUSTICE SOUTER and JUSTICE BREYER would grant the petition for a writ of certiorari.

JUSTICE KENNEDY, with whom THE CHIEF JUSTICE and JUSTICE STEVENS join, concurring in the denial of certiorari.

The Court's decision to deny the petition for writ of certiorari is, in my view, a proper exercise of its discretion in light of the circumstances of the case. The history of petitioner Jose Padilla's detention, however, does require this brief explanatory statement.

Padilla is a United States citizen. Acting pursuant to a material witness warrant issued by the United States District Court for the Southern District of New York, federal agents apprehended Padilla at Chicago's O'Hare International Airport on May 8, 2002. He was transported to New York, and on May 22 he moved to vacate the warrant. On June 9, while that motion was pending, the President issued an order to the Secretary of Defense designating Padilla an enemy combatant and ordering his military detention. The District Court, notified of this action by the Government's *ex parte* motion, vacated the material witness warrant.

Padilla was taken to the Consolidated Naval Brig in Charleston, South Carolina. On June 11, Padilla's counsel filed a habeas corpus petition in the Southern District of New York challenging the military detention. The District Court denied the petition, but the Court of Appeals for the Second Circuit reversed and ordered the issuance of a writ directing Padilla's release. This Court granted certiorari and ordered dismissal of the habeas corpus petition without prejudice, holding that the District Court for the Southern District of New York was not the appropriate court to consider it. See *Rumsfeld v. Padilla,* 542 U.S. 426, 124 S.Ct. 2711, 159 L.Ed.2d 513 (2004).

The present case arises from Padilla's subsequent habeas corpus petition, filed in the United States District Court for the District of South Carolina on July 2, 2004. Padilla requested that he be released immediately or else charged with a crime. The District Court granted the petition on February 28, 2005, but the Court of Appeals for the Fourth Circuit reversed that judgment on September 9, 2005. Padilla then filed the instant petition for writ of certiorari.

After Padilla sought certiorari in this Court, the Government obtained an indictment charging him with various federal crimes. The President ordered that Padilla be released from military custody and transferred to the control of the Attorney General to face criminal charges. The Government filed a motion for approval of Padilla's transfer in the Court of Appeals for the Fourth Circuit. The Court of Appeals denied the motion, but this Court granted the Government's subsequent application respecting the transfer. *Hanft v. Padilla,* 546 U.S. 1084, 126 S.Ct. 978, 163 L.Ed.2d 721 (2006). The Government also filed a brief in opposition to certiorari, arguing, among other things, that Padilla's petition should be denied as moot.

The Government's mootness argument is based on the premise that Padilla, now having been charged with crimes and released from military custody, has received the principal relief he sought. Padilla responds that his case was not mooted by the Government's voluntary actions because there remains a possibility that he will be redesignated and redetained as an enemy combatant.

Whatever the ultimate merits of the parties' mootness arguments, there are strong prudential considerations disfavoring the exercise of the Court's certiorari power. Even if the Court were to rule in Padilla's favor, his present custody status would be unaffected. Padilla is scheduled to be tried on criminal charges. Any consideration of what rights he might be able to assert if he were returned to military custody would be hypothetical, and to no effect, at this stage of the proceedings.

In light of the previous changes in his custody status and the fact that nearly four years have passed since he first was detained, Padilla, it must be acknowledged, has a continuing concern that his status might be altered again. That concern, however, can be addressed if the necessity arises. Padilla is now being held pursuant to the control and supervision of the United States District Court for the Southern District of Florida, pending trial of the criminal case. In the course of its supervision over Padilla's custody and trial the District Court will be obliged to afford him the protection, including the right to a speedy trial, guaranteed to all federal criminal defendants. See, *e.g.,* U.S. Const., Amdt. 6; 18 U.S.C. § 3161. Were the Government to seek to change the status or conditions of Padilla's custody, that court would be in a position to rule quickly on any responsive filings submitted by Padilla. In such an event, the District Court, as well as other courts of competent jurisdiction, should act promptly to ensure that the office and purposes of the writ of habeas corpus are not compromised. Padilla, moreover, retains the option of seeking a writ of habeas corpus in this Court. See this Court's Rule 20; 28 U.S.C. §§ 1651(a), 2241.

That Padilla's claims raise fundamental issues respecting the separation of powers, including consideration of the role and function of the courts, also counsels against addressing those claims when the course of legal proceedings has made them, at least for now, hypothetical. This is especially true given that Padilla's current custody is part of the relief he sought, and that its lawfulness is uncontested.

These are the reasons for my vote to deny certiorari.

JUSTICE GINSBURG, dissenting from the denial of certiorari.

This case, here for the second time, raises a question "of profound importance to the Nation," *Rumsfeld v. Padilla,* 542 U.S. 426, 455, 124 S.Ct. 2711, 159 L.Ed.2d 513 (2004) (Stevens, J., dissenting): Does the President have authority to imprison indefinitely a United States citizen arrested on United States soil distant from a zone of combat, based on an Executive declaration that the citizen was, at the time of his arrest, an "enemy combatant"? It is a question the Court heard, and should have decided, two years ago. Nothing the Government has yet done purports to retract the assertion of Executive power Padilla protests.

Although the Government has recently lodged charges against Padilla in a civilian court, nothing prevents the Executive from returning to the road it earlier constructed and defended. A party's voluntary cessation does not make a case less capable of repetition or less evasive of review. See *Spencer v. Kemna,* 523 U.S. 1, 17, 118 S.Ct. 978, 140 L.Ed.2d 43 (1998) (the capable-of-repetition exception to mootness applies where "(1) the challenged action [is] in its duration too short to be fully litigated prior to *cessation* or expiration, and (2) there [is] a reasonable expectation that the same complaining party [will] be subject to the same action again" (emphasis added)) (citations and internal quotation marks omitted); cf. *United States v. Concentrated Phosphate Export Assn., Inc.,* 393 U.S. 199, 203, 89 S.Ct. 361, 21 L.Ed.2d 344 (1968) (party whose actions threaten to moot a case must make "absolutely clear that the allegedly wrongful behavior could not reasonably be expected to recur"); *United States v. W. T. Grant Co.,* 345 U.S. 629, 632–633, 73 S.Ct. 894, 97 L.Ed. 1303 (1953) (voluntary cessation of illegal activity will not render case moot unless there is "no reasonable expectation that the wrong will be repeated". See also *Lane v. Williams,* 455 U.S. 624, 633–634, 102 S.Ct. 1322, 71 L.Ed.2d 508 (1982) (applying "capable of repetition, yet evading review" in a habeas case. Satisfied that this case is not moot, I would grant the petition for certiorari.

NOTE ON STRATEGIC CONSIDERATIONS IN THE CIVILIAN CRIMINAL PROSECUTION OF JOSE PADILLA

Padilla was arrested in 2002 as a material witness, two months later labeled an enemy combatant, held in military custody for three years, then transferred back to civilian custody and indicted on terrorism charges based on evidence obtained before he was placed in military custody. From the perspective of Padilla's counsel in the civilian criminal case, Padilla had been seriously disadvantaged by the manner in which the government had proceeded in this case: originally arrested in 2002, detained for three years, allegedly abused during this incarceration and then only indicted and tried in 2005–

2006. The challenge for counsel was how to test in court the way in which the government had proceeded. How would you try to get the court to address the issues raised by the way the government had proceeded and the disadvantage to which Padilla had been subjected?

UNITED STATES v. PADILLA

2007 WL 1079090 (S.D.Fla. 2007)

MARCIA G. COOKE, UNITED STATES DISTRICT JUDGE.

This cause came before the Court upon defendant Jose Padilla's Motion to Dismiss for Outrageous Government Conduct filed on October 5, 2006. The government filed its Response on November 13, 2006 and defendant Padilla filed his Reply on December 1, 2006. This Court has reviewed these pleadings, and finds as follows:

. . .

Padilla filed the instant motion to dismiss the indictment for outrageous government conduct on October 5, 2006. In his motion, Mr. Padilla argues that the conditions of his military detention and interrogation while at the Naval Brig "shock[ ] the conscience" in violation of his due process rights. Padilla claims that the mistreatment he allegedly suffered while at the Naval Brig divests the government of its jurisdiction to prosecute him for the crimes charged in the indictment. Mr. Padilla's allegations with regard to his mistreatment stem exclusively from his time at the Naval Brig. Padilla makes no allegations regarding outrageous government conduct prior to his arrest, during the course of his arrest or during his civilian custodial detention in connection with the crimes charged in the indictment. Mr. Padilla also makes no claim of prosecutorial misconduct related to the government's efforts to try this case. For the reasons addressed in this Order, Defendant Padilla's Motion to Dismiss [the Indictment] for Outrageous Government Conduct is denied.

In *United States v. Russell,* 411 U.S. 423 (1973), the Court noted, in dicta, that it "may some day be presented with a situation in which the conduct of law enforcement agents is so outrageous that due process principles would absolutely bar the government from invoking judicial process to obtain a conviction." The *Russell* court ultimately found that the governmental conduct at issue did not rise to this level, and cited the defendant's predisposition to commit the crime charged as fatal to his entrapment claim.

. . .

Regardless of whether courts choose to recognize, yet not apply the doctrine, or reject the doctrine outright, the question comes up almost exclusively within the context of government involvement in the defendant's crime and entrapment. Since the doctrine has never been effectively applied in any context, courts have had difficulty ascertaining its precise contours, if any. Interpreting the austere dicta in *Russell,* courts have attempted to delineate precisely when governmental involvement in the crime charged is so substantial and objectionable, that it should be deemed "outrageous."

. . .

In its Response to Mr. Padilla's Motion to Dismiss [the Indictment] for Outrageous Government Conduct the government argues that the "motion fails as a matter of law." In order to assess whether Padilla's motion is legally insufficient, this Court must accept its allegations as true, and determine whether he has stated a cognizable claim. Thus, while this Court has not held a hearing, nor made any findings with regard to Padilla's claims of abuse and torture at the Naval Brig, for the sake of this Order, this Court will accept Padilla's allegations as true.

In his pleadings, Padilla fails to cite any cases where charges were dismissed for outrageous government conduct. While failure to provide evidence of the claim's application is by no means fatal to Padilla's motion, it bears testament to the claim's severely narrow scope. Furthermore, the case law that Padilla does cite is predominantly comprised of cases where the doctrine is considered in the context of governmental participation in the crime charged and entrapment. In fact, many cases that defendant cites expressly state that the *only* instance where the claim may be properly invoked is within this governmental participation context.[6]

. . .

In one of the few cases cited by defendant where the outrageous governmental conduct stems from something other than governmental participation in the charged crime, the court is careful to delineate the appropriate contours of the claim. In *United States v. Boone,* 437 F.3d 829, 841–42 (8th Cir.2006), the defendant argued that the attempted murder charge against her should have been dismissed due to the outrageous government conduct of an FBI agent. Defendant claimed that she was threatened, intimidated, verbally abused, and subjected to other inappropriate conduct by the FBI agent during the investigation of the crime and the subsequent arrest. The court held "the rule that outrageous government conduct can foreclose criminal charges has been applied by our court almost exclusively to situations involving entrapment, where law enforcement officers have sought to create crimes in order to lure a defendant into illegal activity that she was not otherwise ready and willing to

---

6. In Defendant's Reply, Mr. Padilla refutes the government's assertion that the circuits have not been willing to consider outrageous government conduct claims by citing to a litany of cases where the appellate courts have recognized the doctrine. However, Padilla fails to acknowledge that in the cited string of cases, the claim arises almost exclusively in the context of governmental participation in the crime charged and entrapment. This factor significantly distinguishes these cases from Padilla's case. In the cited cases, the allegedly objectionable governmental conduct occurred during the commission of the offense that the defendant was seeking to dismiss from the indictment. In Padilla's case, however, he is seeking to have criminal charges dismissed because of governmental actions perpetrated after the commission of the charged crimes. Furthermore, the objectionable governmental action did not occur during the course of his detainment for the criminal charges he is currently attempting to dismiss. Rather, the allegedly outrageous governmental conduct occurred during an independent military detainment in connection with his enemy combatant status.

commit." The court concluded that since defendant "has not even alleged that any government official had engaged in such conduct [in the case at bar, defendant] has not shown any due process bar to her attempted murder conviction."

Mr. Padilla's failure to cite case law where outrageous government conduct claims are premised upon post-arrest abuse of the defendant is of no small moment. In *Boone,* the Eighth Circuit echoed the holdings of its sister circuits by articulating that in order to invoke an outrageous government conduct claim, the government need first involve itself in the criminal scheme along with the defendant. This makes practical sense since the claim itself is borne out of due process concerns. Thus, a law enforcement officer may be behaving "outrageously" in certain instances where her over-involvement in a criminal enterprise "violates fundamental fairness" or is "shocking to the universal sense of justice." On these occasions, due process concerns could preclude prosecution of the very claim in which the governmental agent was overzealously embroiled. Thus, courts have noted, that in the rarest of circumstances, if it was impossible to extract the objectionable governmental conduct from the crime, the prosecution may need to be stymied.

Mr. Padilla's claim does not present this scenario. Padilla claims that his charges should be dismissed due to outrageous governmental conduct perpetrated after the commission of his alleged crimes. Padilla seeks this relief despite the fact that the objectionable conduct occurred during his military detention in connection with his enemy combatant status. Padilla's argument contains numerous legal infirmities.

First, the fact that the governmental conduct occurred at a time and place removed from the crimes charged makes the remedy Padilla is seeking considerably more attenuated and arbitrary. Short of resorting to a "two wrongs make a right" judicial process, it is difficult for this Court to ascertain how the remedy sought emanates from the infirmity defendant describes. This is considerably distinguishable from a government entrapment scenario, where the crime that the defendant is charged with is the crux of the outrageous government conduct claim.[7]

Second, the outrageous conduct occurred while Padilla was under military control at the Naval Brig in Charleston, South Carolina. At this time, Padilla was being held under Presidential orders in connection with his enemy combatant status and had not been charged with the crimes he is currently facing. This further attenuates Padilla's outrageous government conduct claim. Even if Padilla's due process rights were violated while being held at the Naval Brig as an enemy combatant, he fails to

---

7. An indictment may also be dismissed upon a sufficient showing of prejudice within the prosecutorial misconduct context. *See United States v. Accetturo,* 858 F.2d 679 (11th Cir.1988). Prosecutorial misconduct is analogous to claims of outrageous government conduct premised on entrapment or government participation in the defendant's crime. In both instances, government action has prejudiced defendant with respect to the charges he is attempting to dismiss. Conversely, Mr. Padilla's claim focuses on governmental conduct that is not necessarily related to the charges he is facing and does not prejudice him in this prosecution. Although the pleadings cite to cases covering prosecutorial misconduct, Mr. Padilla has made no claim to this effect.

explain how this violation should result in the dismissal of distinct crimes that he was not charged with at that point.[8]

Third, Mr. Padilla fails to explain why suppressing governmental use of any evidence obtained from him at the Naval Brig is insufficient for purposes of this trial. In his motion, Padilla acknowledges that the government has already averred not to seek introduction of any of the Naval Brig evidence at trial.[9] Despite summarily rejecting this remedy as "clearly inadequate," Padilla fails to support this contention or explain why his requested remedy is more appropriate.[10] In fact, in his motion, Padilla relies heavily on *United States v. Toscanino,* 500 F.2d 267 (2d Cir.1974), a case where the Second Circuit sanctions this very approach. Padilla's Motion concedes that "the court in *Toscanino* noted that many cases involving due process violations center on unlawful government acquisition of evidence and that, in those instances, the proper remedy would be the exclusion of the tainted evidence."

   . . .

For the reasons set forth above, it is hereby:

Ordered and adjudged that Defendant Padilla's Motion to Dismiss for Outrageous Government Conduct filed on October 5, 2006 is denied.

———

As detailed in Padilla v. Hanft, supra, p. 632, after being returned to the custody of civilian authorities, Padilla was indicted in Miami, Florida along with four other defendants on three counts: "Conspiracy to Murder, Kidnap, and Maim Persons in a Foreign Country"; "Conspiracy to Provide Material Support to Terrorists" and providing "Material Support to Terrorists". On August 15, 2007, he was convicted on all counts, the jury having taken little more than a day to reach its verdict. Padilla, age 37, was subsequently sentenced to 17 years and four months. The judge said that she took into consideration the harsh treatment he had undergone

---

8. Taken to its logical extreme, this rationale would effectively provide a defendant with amnesty for any uncharged crime so long as the government violated that defendant's due process rights at some prior point. This erroneous recitation clearly misconstrues the law regarding the outrageous government conduct doctrine as well as defendant's due process rights.

9. Counsel for the government has stated to this Court in a number of contexts that the Naval Brig events are irrelevant to this criminal prosecution. The government has even sought to exclude all references to events at the Naval Brig. *See* Government's Motion *In Limine* to Exclude Evidence and Argument Regarding the Circumstances of Defendant Padilla's Pre–Indictment Detention as an Unlawful Enemy Combatant. However, the government has not agreed to absolutely preclude referencing Naval Brig events at trial. The government has stated, that should Mr. Padilla testify at trial, Padilla's Naval Brig statements may be offered as impeachment evidence. The Court has yet to rule on the government's motion to exclude Naval Brig evidence at trial. However, should any Naval Brig statements be introduced at trial, for impeachment or otherwise, the circumstances surrounding the making of the statements may be relevant and hence admissible.

10. This Court's holding does not imply that this is Mr. Padilla's only remedy with regard to any alleged mistreatment at the Naval Brig, only that it is the most appropriate remedy within the framework of this prosecution. Mr. Padilla is free to institute a Bivens action, an action for monetary damages or any other form of redress that he is legally entitled to pursue.

while detained as an enemy combatant in military custody. The prosecutor had sought a life sentence. Washington Post, January 23, 2008, AO3. On September 19, 2011, the 11th Circuit United States Court of Appeals vacated Padilla's sentence on the ground that the trial court had relied on improper factors in reducing his sentence. The circuit court remanded the case for resentencing. United States v. Jayyousi, 2011 WL 4346322 (11th Cir. 2011).

2. ALI SALEH KAHLAH AL–MARRI

QUESTIONS AND NOTES

1. Another detainee, in a situation similar to Padilla's, was arrested in the United States by civilian authorities and then declared to be an enemy combatant and transferred to military custody, but in this instance he was a non-U.S. citizen. Ali Saleh Kahlah al-Marri, like Padilla, was originally arrested as a material witness, indicted on civilian criminal charges and subsequently, again like Padilla, declared by Presidential order to be an enemy combatant. *He* was detained for four years in military custody and sought habeas corpus review. The fourth circuit eventually decided his petition en banc in Al–Marri v. Pucciarelli, 534 F.3d 213 (4th Cir. 2008) where the court ruled as follows:

> The parties present two principal issues for our consideration: (1) assuming the Government's allegations about al-Marri are true, whether Congress has empowered the President to detain al-Marri as an enemy combatant; and (2) assuming Congress has empowered the President to detain al-Marri as an enemy combatant provided the Government's allegations against him are true, whether al-Marri has been afforded sufficient process to challenge his designation as an enemy combatant.

> Having considered the briefs and arguments of the parties, the *en banc* court now holds: (1) by a 5 to 4 vote (Chief Judge Williams and Judges Wilkinson, Niemeyer, Traxler, and Duncan voting in the affirmative; Judges Michael, Motz, King, and Gregory voting in the negative), that, if the Government's allegations about al-Marri are true, Congress has empowered the President to detain him as an enemy combatant; and (2) by a 5 to 4 vote (Judges Michael, Motz, Traxler, King, and Gregory voting in the affirmative; Chief Judge Williams and Judges Wilkinson, Niemeyer, and Duncan voting in the negative), that, assuming Congress has empowered the President to detain al-Marri as an enemy combatant provided the Government's allegations against him are true, al-Marri has not been afforded sufficient process to challenge his designation as an enemy combatant.

Al–Marri's subsequent petition for certiorari to the Supreme Court was granted. Before the Supreme Court could review the case on the merits, the Department of Justice moved to transfer al-Marri from military to civilian custody. The Supreme Court granted the application, vacated the decision in al-Marri v. Pucciarelli, supra, and ordered a dismissal of the appeal as moot. Al–Marri v. Spagone, 129 S.Ct. 1545 (2009).

2.   After he was transferred to civilian custody, al-Marri was indicted in the Central District of Illinois on two counts, conspiracy to provide material support to a foreign terrorist organization and providing material support to a foreign terrorist organization. On April 29, 2009, al-Marri pleaded guilty to one count of conspiring to provide material support to a foreign terrorist organization. He was subsequently sentenced to eight years in prison.

3.   Suppose that al-Marri had not pleaded guilty. What kind of issues might the government have encountered in seeking to obtain a conviction?

4.   For an excellent in depth treatment of the al-Marri case (as well as many of the other issues and decisions facing the Obama administration), see Jane Mayer, Reporter at Large, The Hard Cases, The New Yorker, Feb. 23, 2009.

5.   There are some parallels in the way that the government handled the cases of Jose Padilla and Ali Saleh Kahlah al-Marri. Are the cases similar? What are the differences, if any?

CHAPTER 11

MILITARY COMMISSIONS

■ ■ ■

A. LEGAL AUTHORITY

1. THE QUIRIN CASE

A foundational case for the establishment of military commissions for the trial of "unlawful enemy combatants" is Ex Parte Quirin, a case involving the trial and execution of Nazi saboteurs toward the beginning of World War II.

EX PARTE QUIRIN
317 U.S. 1 (1942)

MR. CHIEF JUSTICE STONE delivered the opinion of the Court.

These cases are brought here by petitioners' several applications for leave to file petitions for habeas corpus in this Court, and by their petitions for certiorari to review orders of the District Court for the District of Columbia, which denied their applications for leave to file petitions for habeas corpus in that court.

The question for decision is whether the detention of petitioners by respondent for trial by Military Commission, appointed by Order of the President of July 2, 1942, on charges preferred against them purporting to set out their violations of the law of war and of the Articles of War, is in conformity to the laws and Constitution of the United States.

After denial of their applications by the District Court, 47 F.Supp. 431, petitioners asked leave to file petitions for habeas corpus in this Court. In view of the public importance of the questions raised by their petitions and of the duty which rests on the courts, in time of war as well as in time of peace, to preserve unimpaired the constitutional safeguards of civil liberty, and because in our opinion the public interest required that we consider and decide those questions without any avoidable delay, we directed that petitioners' applications be set down for full oral argument at a special term of this Court, convened on July 29, 1942. The applications for leave to file the petitions were presented in open court on that day and were heard on the petitions, the answers to them of respondent, a stipulation of facts by counsel, and the record of the testimony given before the Commission.

While the argument was proceeding before us, petitioners perfected their appeals from the orders of the District Court to the United States Court of Appeals for the District of Columbia and thereupon filed with this Court petitions for certiorari to the Court of Appeals before judgment, pursuant to Section 240(a) of the Judicial Code, 28 U.S.C. § 347(a). We granted certiorari before judgment for the reasons which moved us to convene the special term of Court. In accordance with the stipulation of counsel we treat the record, briefs and arguments in the habeas corpus proceedings in this Court as the record, briefs and arguments upon the writs of certiorari.

On July 31, 1942, after hearing argument of counsel and after full consideration of all questions raised, this Court affirmed the orders of the District Court and denied petitioners' applications for leave to file petitions for habeas corpus. By per curiam opinion, . . . we announced the decision of the Court, and that the full opinion in the causes would be prepared and filed with the Clerk.

The following facts appear from the petitions or are stipulated. Except as noted they are undisputed.

All the petitioners were born in Germany; all have lived in the United States. All returned to Germany between 1933 and 1941. All except petitioner Haupt are admittedly citizens of the German Reich, with which the United States is at war. Haupt came to this country with his parents when he was five years old; it is contended that he became a citizen of the United States by virtue of the naturalization of his parents during his minority and that he has not since lost his citizenship. The Government, however, takes the position that on attaining his majority he elected to maintain German allegiance and citizenship or in any case that he has by his conduct renounced or abandoned his United States citizenship. See Perkins v. Elg, 307 U.S. 325, 334, 59 S.Ct. 884, 889, 83 L.Ed. 1320; United States ex rel. Rojak v. Marshall, D.C., 34 F.2d 219; United States ex rel. Scimeca v. Husband, 2 Cir., 6 F.2d 957, 958; 8 U.S.C. § 801, and compare 8 U.S.C. § 808. For reasons presently to be stated we do not find it necessary to resolve these contentions.

After the declaration of war between the United States and the German Reich, petitioners received training at a sabotage school near Berlin, Germany, where they were instructed in the use of explosives and in methods of secret writing. Thereafter petitioners, with a German citizen, Dasch, proceeded from Germany to a seaport in Occupied France, where petitioners Burger, Heinck and Quirin, together with Dasch, boarded a German submarine which proceeded across the Atlantic to Amagansett Beach on Long Island, New York. The four were there landed from the submarine in the hours of darkness, on or about June 13, 1942, carrying with them a supply of explosives, fuses and incendiary and timing devices. While landing they wore German Marine Infantry uniforms or parts of uniforms. Immediately after landing they buried their uniforms and the other articles mentioned and proceeded in civilian dress to New York City.

The remaining four petitioners at the same French port boarded another German submarine, which carried them across the Atlantic to Ponte Vedra Beach, Florida. On or about June 17, 1942, they came ashore during the hours of darkness wearing caps of the German Marine Infantry and carrying with them a supply of explosives, fuses, and incendiary and timing devices. They immediately buried their caps and the other articles mentioned and proceeded in civilian dress to Jacksonville, Florida, and thence to various points in the United States. All were taken into custody in New York or Chicago by agents of the Federal Bureau of Investigation. All had received instructions in Germany from an officer of the German High Command to destroy war industries and war facilities in the United States, for which they or their relatives in Germany were to receive salary payments from the German Government. They also had been paid by the German Government during their course of training at the sabotage school and had received substantial sums in United States currency, which were in their possession when arrested. The currency had been handed to them by an officer of the German High Command, who had instructed them to wear their German uniforms while landing in the United States.

The President, as President and Commander in Chief of the Army and Navy, by Order of July 2, 1942, appointed a Military Commission and directed it to try petitioners for offenses against the law of war and the Articles of War, and prescribed regulations for the procedure on the trial and for review of the record of the trial and of any judgment or sentence of the Commission. On the same day, by Proclamation, the President declared that 'all persons who are subjects, citizens or residents of any nation at war with the United States or who give obedience to or act under the direction of any such nation, and who during time of war enter or attempt to enter the United States ... through coastal or boundary defenses, and are charged with committing or attempting or preparing to commit sabotage, espionage, hostile or warlike acts, or violations of the law of war, shall be subject to the law of war and to the jurisdiction of military tribunals'.

The Proclamation also stated in terms that all such persons were denied access to the courts.

Pursuant to direction of the Attorney General, the Federal Bureau of Investigation surrendered custody of petitioners to respondent, Provost Marshal of the Military District of Washington, who was directed by the Secretary of War to receive and keep them in custody, and who thereafter held petitioners for trial before the Commission.

On July 3, 1942, the Judge Advocate General's Department of the Army prepared and lodged with the Commission the following charges against petitioners, supported by specifications:

    1.   Violation of the law of war.

2.   Violation of Article 81 of the Articles of War, defining the offense of relieving or attempting to relieve, or corresponding with or giving intelligence to, the enemy.

3.   Violation of Article 82, defining the offense of spying.

4.   Conspiracy to commit the offenses alleged in charges 1, 2 and 3.

The Commission met on July 8, 1942, and proceeded with the trial, which continued in progress while the causes were pending in this Court. On July 27th, before petitioners' applications to the District Court, all the evidence for the prosecution and the defense had been taken by the Commission and the case had been closed except for arguments of counsel. It is conceded that ever since petitioners' arrest the state and federal courts in Florida, New York, and the District of Columbia, and in the states in which each of the petitioners was arrested or detained, have been open and functioning normally.

. . .

Petitioners' main contention is that the President is without any statutory or constitutional authority to order the petitioners to be tried by military tribunal for offenses with which they are charged; that in consequence they are entitled to be tried in the civil courts with the safeguards, including trial by jury, which the Fifth and Sixth Amendments guarantee to all persons charged in such courts with criminal offenses. In any case it is urged that the President's Order, in prescribing the procedure of the Commission and the method for review of its findings and sentence, and the proceedings of the Commission under the Order, conflict with Articles of War adopted by Congress—particularly Articles 38, 43, 46, 50 1/2 and 70—and are illegal and void.

The Government challenges each of these propositions. But regardless of their merits, it also insists that petitioners must be denied access to the courts, both because they are enemy aliens or have entered our territory as enemy belligerents, and because the President's Proclamation undertakes in terms to deny such access to the class of persons defined by the Proclamation, which aptly describes the character and conduct of petitioners. It is urged that if they are enemy aliens or if the Proclamation has force no court may afford the petitioners a hearing. But there is certainly nothing in the Proclamation to preclude access to the courts for determining its applicability to the particular case. And neither the Proclamation nor the fact that they are enemy aliens forecloses consideration by the courts of petitioners' contentions that the Constitution and laws of the United States constitutionally enacted forbid their trial by military commission. As announced in our per curiam opinion we have resolved those questions by our conclusion that the Commission has jurisdiction to try the charge preferred against petitioners. There is therefore no occasion to decide contentions of the parties unrelated to this issue. We pass at once to the consideration of the basis of the Commission's authority.

We are not here concerned with any question of the guilt or innocence of petitioners. Constitutional safeguards for the protection of all who are charged with offenses are not to be disregarded in order to inflict merited punishment on some who are guilty. Ex parte Milligan, 4 Wall. 119, 132, 18 L.Ed. 281; Tumey v. Ohio, 273 U.S. 510, 535, 47 S.Ct. 437, 445, 71 L.Ed. 749, 50 A.L.R. 1243; Hill v. Texas, 316 U.S. 400, 62 S.Ct. 1159, 1161, 1162, 86 L.Ed. 1559. But the detention and trial of petitioners—ordered by the President in the declared exercise of his powers as Commander in Chief of the Army in time of war and of grave public danger—are not to be set aside by the courts without the clear conviction that they are in conflict with the Constitution or laws of Congress constitutionally enacted.

Congress and the President, like the courts, possess no power not derived from the Constitution. But one of the objects of the Constitution, as declared by its preamble, is to 'provide for the common defence'. As a means to that end the Constitution gives to Congress the power to 'provide for the common Defence', Art. I, § 8, cl. 1; 'To raise and support Armies', 'To provide and maintain a Navy', Art. I, § 8, cls. 12, 13; and 'To make Rules for the Government and Regulation of the land and naval Forces', Art. I, § 8, cl. 14. Congress is given authority 'To declare War, grant Letters of Marque and Reprisal, and make Rules concerning Captures on Land and Water', Art. I, § 8, cl. 11; and 'To define and punish Piracies and Felonies committed on the high Seas, and Offenses against the Law of Nations', Art. I, § 8, cl. 10. And finally the Constitution authorizes Congress 'To make all Laws which shall be necessary and proper for carrying into Execution the foregoing Powers, and all other Powers vested by this Constitution in the Government of the United States, or in any Department or Officer thereof.' Art. I, § 8, cl. 18.

The Constitution confers on the President the 'executive Power', Art II, § 1, cl. 1, and imposes on him the duty to 'take Care that the Laws be faithfully executed'. Art. II, § 3. It makes him the Commander in Chief of the Army and Navy, Art. II, § 2, cl. 1, and empowers him to appoint and commission officers of the United States. Art. II, § 3, cl. 1.

The Constitution thus invests the President as Commander in Chief with the power to wage war which Congress has declared, and to carry into effect all laws passed by Congress for the conduct of war and for the government and regulation of the Armed Forces, and all laws defining and punishing offences against the law of nations, including those which pertain to the conduct of war.

By the Articles of War, 10 U.S.C. §§ 1471–1593, Congress has provided rules for the government of the Army. It has provided for the trial and punishment, by courts martial, of violations of the Articles by members of the armed forces and by specified classes of persons associated or serving with the Army. Arts. 1, 2. But the Articles also recognize the 'military commission' appointed by military command as an appropriate tribunal for the trial and punishment of offenses against the law of war not ordinarily tried by court martial. See Arts. 12, 15. Articles 38 and 46 authorize the President, with certain limitations, to prescribe the procedure for military commissions. Articles 81 and 82 authorize trial, either by court martial or military commission, of those charged with relieving, harboring or corresponding with the enemy and those charged with spying. And Article 15 declares that 'the provisions of these articles conferring jurisdiction upon courts-martial shall not be construed as depriving military commissions ... or other military tribunals of concurrent jurisdiction in respect of offenders or offenses that by statute or by the law of war may be triable by such military commissions ... or other military tribunals'. Article 2 includes among those persons subject to military law the personnel of our own military establishment. But this, as Article 12 provides, does not exclude from that class 'any other person who by the law of war is subject to trial by military tribunals' and who under Article 12 may be tried by court martial or under Article 15 by military commission.

Similarly the Espionage Act of 1917, which authorizes trial in the district courts of certain offenses that tend to interfere with the prosecution of war, provides that nothing contained in the act 'shall be deemed to limit the jurisdiction of the general courts-martial, military commissions, or naval courts-martial'. 50 U.S.C. § 38.

From the very beginning of its history this Court has recognized and applied the law of war as including that part of the law of nations which prescribes, for the conduct of war, the status, rights and duties of enemy nations as well as of enemy individuals. By the Articles of War, and especially Article 15, Congress has explicitly provided, so far as it may constitutionally do so, that military tribunals shall have jurisdiction to try offenders or offenses against the law of war in appropriate cases. Congress, in addition to making rules for the government of our Armed Forces, has thus exercised its authority to define and punish offenses against the law of nations by sanctioning, within constitutional limitations, the jurisdiction of military commissions to try persons for offenses which, according to the rules and precepts of the law of nations, and more particularly the law of war, are cognizable by such tribunals. And the President, as Commander in Chief, by his Proclamation in time of war has invoked that law. By his Order creating the present Commission he has undertaken to exercise the authority conferred upon him by Congress, and also such authority as the Constitution itself gives the Commander in Chief, to direct the performance of those functions which may constitutionally be performed by the military arm of the nation in time of war.

An important incident to the conduct of war is the adoption of measures by the military command not only to repel and defeat the enemy, but to seize and subject to disciplinary measures those enemies who in their attempt to thwart or impede our military effort have violated the law of war. It is unnecessary for present purposes to determine to what extent the President as Commander in Chief has constitutional power to create military commissions without the support of Congressional legislation. For here Congress has authorized trial of offenses against the law of war before such commissions. We are concerned only with the question whether it is within the constitutional power of the national government to place petitioners upon trial before a military commission for the offenses with which they are charged. We must therefore first inquire whether any of the acts charged is an offense against the law of war cognizable before a military tribunal, and if so whether the Constitution prohibits the trial. We may assume that there are acts regarded in other countries, or by some writers on international law, as offenses against the law of war which would not be triable by military tribunal here, either because they are not recognized by our courts as violations of the law of war or because they are of that class of offenses constitutionally triable only by a jury. It was upon such grounds that the Court denied the right to proceed by military tribunal in Ex parte Milligan, supra. But as we shall show, these petitioners were charged with an offense against the law of war which the Constitution does not require to be tried by jury.

It is no objection that Congress in providing for the trial of such offenses has not itself undertaken to codify that branch of international law or to mark its precise boundaries, or to enumerate or define by statute all the acts which that law condemns. An Act of Congress punishing 'the crime of piracy as defined by the law of nations' is an appropriate exercise of its constitutional authority, Art. I, § 8, cl. 10, 'to define and punish' the offense since it has adopted by reference the sufficiently precise definition of international law. United States v. Smith, 5 Wheat. 153, 5 L.Ed. 57; see The Marianna Flora, 11 Wheat. 1, 40, 41, 6 L.Ed. 405; United States v. The Malek Adhel, 2 How. 210, 232, 11 L.Ed. 239; The Ambrose Light, D.C., 25 F. 408, 423, 428; 18 U.S.C. § 481. Similarly by the reference in the 15th Article of War to 'offenders or offenses that . . . by the law of war may be triable by such military commissions', Congress has incorporated by reference, as within the jurisdiction of military commissions, all offenses which are defined as such by the law of war (compare Dynes v. Hoover, 20 How. 65, 82, 15 L.Ed. 838), and which may constitutionally be included within that jurisdiction. Congress had the choice of crystallizing in permanent form and in minute detail every offense against the law of war, or of adopting the system of common law applied by military tribunals so far as it should be recognized and deemed applicable by the courts. It chose the latter course.

By universal agreement and practice the law of war draws a distinction between the armed forces and the peaceful populations of belligerent nations and also between those who are lawful and unlawful combatants. Lawful combatants are subject to capture and detention as prisoners of war by opposing military forces. Unlawful combatants are likewise subject to capture and detention, but in addition they are subject to trial and punishment by military tribunals for acts which render their belligerency unlawful. The spy who secretly and without uniform passes the military lines of a belligerent in time of war, seeking to gather military information and communicate it to the enemy, or an enemy combatant who without uniform comes secretly through the lines for the purpose of waging war by destruction of life or property, are familiar examples of belligerents who are generally deemed not to be entitled to the status of prisoners of war, but to be offenders against the law of war subject to trial and punishment by military tribunals. See Winthrop, Military Law, 2d Ed., pp. 1196–1197, 1219–1221; Instructions for the Government of Armies of the United States in the Field, approved by the President, General Order No. 100, April 24, 1863, sections IV and V.

Such was the practice of our own military authorities before the adoption of the Constitution, and during the Mexican and Civil Wars.

. . .

Our Government, by thus defining lawful belligerents entitled to be treated as prisoners of war, has recognized that there is a class of unlawful belligerents not entitled to that privilege, including those who though combatants do not wear 'fixed and distinctive emblems'. And by Article 15 of the Articles of War Congress has made provision for their trial and punishment by military commission, according to 'the law of war'.

By a long course of practical administrative construction by its military authorities, our Government has likewise recognized that those who during time of war pass surreptitiously from enemy territory into our own, discarding their uniforms upon entry, for the commission of hostile acts involving destruction of life or property, have the status of unlawful combatants punishable as such by military commission. This precept of the law of war has been so recognized in practice both here and abroad, and has so generally been accepted as valid by authorities on international law that we think it must be regarded as a rule or principle of the law of war recognized by this Government....

Specification 1 of the First charge is sufficient to charge all the petitioners with the offense of unlawful belligerency, trial of which is within the jurisdiction of the Commission, and the admitted facts affirmatively show that the charge is not merely colorable or without foundation.

Specification 1 states that petitioners 'being enemies of the United States and acting for ... the German Reich, a belligerent enemy nation, secretly and covertly passed, in civilian dress, contrary to the law of war, through the military and naval lines and defenses of the United States ... and went behind such lines, contrary to the law of war, in civilian dress ... for the purpose of committing ... hostile acts, and, in particular, to destroy certain war industries, war utilities and war materials within the United States'.

This specification so plainly alleges violation of the law of war as to require but brief discussion of petitioners' contentions. As we have seen, entry upon our territory in time of war by enemy belligerents, including those acting under the direction of the armed forces of the enemy, for the purpose of destroying property used or useful in prosecuting the war, is a hostile and war-like act. It subjects those who participate in it without uniform to the punishment prescribed by the law of war for unlawful belligerents. It is without significance that petitioners were not alleged to have borne conventional weapons or that their proposed hostile acts did not necessarily contemplate collision with the Armed Forces of the United States. Paragraphs 351 and 352 of the Rules of Land Warfare, already referred to, plainly contemplate that the hostile acts and purposes for which unlawful belligerents may be punished are not limited to assaults on the Armed Forces of the United States. Modern warfare is directed at the destruction of enemy war supplies and the implements of their production and transportation quite as much as at the armed forces. Every consideration which makes the unlawful belligerent punishable is equally applicable whether his objective is the one or the other. The law of war cannot rightly treat those agents of enemy armies who enter our territory, armed with explosives intended for the destruction of war industries and supplies, as any the less belligerent enemies than are agents similarly entering for the purpose of destroying fortified places or our Armed Forces. By passing our boundaries for such purposes without uniform or other emblem signifying their belligerent status, or by discarding that means of identification after entry, such enemies become unlawful belligerents subject to trial and punishment.

Citizenship in the United States of an enemy belligerent does not relieve him from the consequences of a belligerency which is unlawful because in violation of the law of war. Citizens who associate themselves with the military arm of the enemy government, and with its aid, guidance and direction enter this country bent on hostile acts are enemy belligerents within the meaning of the Hague Convention and the law of war. Cf. Gates v. Goodloe, 101 U.S. 612, 615, 617, 618, 25 L.Ed. 895. It is as an enemy belligerent that petitioner Haupt is charged with entering the United States, and unlawful belligerency is the gravamen of the offense of which he is accused.

Nor are petitioners any the less belligerents if, as they argue, they have not actually committed or attempted to commit any act of depredation or entered the theatre or zone of active military operations. The argument leaves out of account the nature of the offense which the Government charges and which the Act of Congress, by incorporating the law of war, punishes. It is that each petitioner, in circumstances which gave him the status of an enemy belligerent, passed our military and naval lines and defenses or went behind those lines, in civilian dress and with hostile purpose. The offense was complete when with that purpose they entered—or, having so entered, they remained upon—our territory in time of war without uniform or other appropriate means of identification. For that reason, even when committed by a citizen, the offense is distinct from the crime of treason defined in Article III, § 3 of the Constitution, since the absence of uniform essential to one is irrelevant to the other.

But petitioners insist that even if the offenses with which they are charged are offenses against the law of war, their trial is subject to the requirement of the Fifth Amendment that no person shall be held to answer for a capital or otherwise infamous crime unless on a presentment or indictment of a grand jury, and that such trials by Article III, § 2, and the Sixth Amendment must be by jury in a civil court. Before the Amendments, § 2 of Article III, the Judiciary Article, had provided: 'The Trial of all Crimes, except in Cases of Impeachment, shall be by Jury', and had directed that 'such Trial shall be held in the State where the said Crimes shall have been committed'.

Presentment by a grand jury and trial by a jury of the vicinage where the crime was committed were at the time of the adoption of the Constitution familiar parts of the machinery for criminal trials in the civil courts. But they were procedures unknown to military tribunals, which are not courts in the sense of the Judiciary Article, Ex parte Vallandigham, 1 Wall. 243, 17 L.Ed. 589; In re Vidal, 179 U.S. 126, 21 S.Ct. 48, 45 L.Ed. 118; cf. Williams v. United States, 289 U.S. 553, 53 S.Ct. 751, 77 L.Ed. 1372, and which in the natural course of events are usually called upon to function under conditions precluding resort to such procedures. As this Court has often recognized, it was not the purpose or effect of § 2 of Article III, read in the light of the common law, to enlarge the then existing right to a jury trial. The object was to preserve unimpaired trial by jury in all those cases in which it had been recognized by the common law and in all cases of a like nature as they might arise in the future, District of Columbia v. Colts, 282 U.S. 63, 51 S.Ct. 52, 75 L.Ed. 177, but not to bring within the sweep of the guaranty those cases in which it was then well understood that a jury trial could not be demanded as of right.

    . . .

In the light of this long-continued and consistent interpretation we must conclude that § 2 of Article III and the Fifth and Sixth Amendments cannot be taken to have extended the right to demand a jury to trials by military commission, or to have required that offenses against the law of war not triable by jury at common law be tried only in the civil courts.

    . . .

Section 2 of the Act of Congress of April 10, 1806, 2 Stat. 371, derived from the Resolution of the Continental Congress of August 21, 1776, imposed the death penalty on alien spies 'according to the law and usage of nations, by sentence of a general court martial'. This enactment must be regarded as a contemporary construction of both Article III, § 2, and the Amendments as not foreclosing trial by military tribunals, without a jury, of offenses against the law of war committed by enemies not in or associated with our Armed Forces. It is a construction of the Constitution which has been followed since the founding of our government, and is now continued in the 82nd Article of War. Such a construction is entitled to the greatest respect. Stuart v. Laird, 1 Cranch, 299, 309, 2 L.Ed. 115; Field v. Clark, 143 U.S. 649, 691, 12 S.Ct. 495, 504, 36 L.Ed. 294; United States v. Curtiss–Wright Corp., 299 U.S. 304, 328, 57 S.Ct. 216, 224, 81 L.Ed. 255. It has not hitherto been challenged, and so far as we are advised it has never been suggested in the very extensive literature of the subject that an alien spy, in time of war, could not be tried by military tribunal without a jury.

The exception from the Amendments of 'cases arising in the land or naval forces' was not aimed at trials by military tribunals, without a jury, of such offenses against the law of war. Its objective was quite different— to authorize the trial by court martial of the members of our Armed Forces for all that class of crimes which under the Fifth and Sixth Amendments might otherwise have been deemed triable in the civil courts. The cases mentioned in the exception are not restricted to those involving offenses against the law of war alone, but extend to trial of all offenses, including crimes which were of the class traditionally triable by jury at common law.

Since the Amendments, like § 2 of Article III, do not preclude all trials of offenses against the law of war by military commission without a jury when the offenders are aliens not members of our Armed Forces, it is plain that they present no greater obstacle to the trial in like manner of citizen enemies who have violated the law of war applicable to enemies. Under the original statute authorizing trial of alien spies by military tribunals, the offenders were outside the constitutional guaranty of trial by jury, not because they were aliens but only because they had violated the law of war by committing offenses constitutionally triable by military tribunal.

We cannot say that Congress in preparing the Fifth and Sixth Amendments intended to extend trial by jury to the cases of alien or citizen offenders against the law of war otherwise triable by military commission, while withholding it from members of our own armed forces charged with infractions of the Articles of War punishable by death. It is equally inadmissible to construe the Amendments—whose primary purpose was to continue unimpaired presentment by grand jury and trial by petit jury in all those cases in which they had been customary—as either abolishing all trials by military tribunals, save those of the personnel of our own armed forces, or what in effect comes to the same thing, as imposing on all such tribunals the necessity of proceeding against unlawful enemy belligerents only on presentment and trial by jury. We conclude that the Fifth and Sixth Amendments did not restrict whatever authority was conferred by the Constitution to try offenses against the law of war by military commission, and that petitioners, charged with such an offense not required to be tried by jury at common law, were lawfully placed on trial by the Commission without a jury.

Petitioners, and especially petitioner Haupt, stress the pronouncement of this Court in the Milligan case, 4 Wall. page 121, 18 L.Ed. 281, that the law of war 'can never be applied to citizens in states which have upheld the authority of the government, and where the courts are open and their process unobstructed'.

Elsewhere in its opinion, 4 Wall. at pages 118, 121, 122, and 131, 18 L.Ed. 281, the Court was at pains to point out that Milligan, a citizen twenty years resident in Indiana, who had never been a resident of any of the states in rebellion, was not an enemy belligerent either entitled to the status of a prisoner of war or subject to the penalties imposed upon unlawful belligerents. We construe the Court's statement as to the inapplicability of the law of war to Milligan's case as having particular reference to the facts before it. From them the Court concluded that Milligan, not being a part of or associated with the armed forces of the enemy, was a non-belligerent, not subject to the law of war save as—in circumstances found not there to be present and not involved here— martial law might be constitutionally established.

The Court's opinion is inapplicable to the case presented by the present record. We have no occasion now to define with meticulous care the ultimate boundaries of the jurisdiction of military tribunals to try persons according to the law of war. It is enough that petitioners here, upon the conceded facts, were plainly within those boundaries, and were held in good faith for trial by military commission, charged with being enemies who, with the purpose of destroying war materials and utilities, entered or after entry remained in our territory without uniform—an offense against the law of war. We hold only that those particular acts constitute an offense against the law of war which the Constitution authorizes to be tried by military commission.

. . .

Accordingly, we conclude that Charge I, on which petitioners were detained for trial by the Military Commission, alleged an offense which the President is authorized to order tried by military commission; that his Order convening the Commission was a lawful order and that the Commission was lawfully constituted; that the petitioners were held in lawful custody and did not show cause for their discharge. It follows that the orders of the District Court should be affirmed, and that leave to file petitions for habeas corpus in this Court should be denied.

MR. JUSTICE MURPHY took no part in the consideration or decision of these cases.

Orders of District Court affirmed and leave to file petitions for habeas corpus in the Supreme Court denied.

2. THE PRESIDENT'S MILITARY ORDER REDUX

In chapter 10, the Authorization to Use Military Force (AUMF) and the President's Military Order issued on November 13, 2001 were reproduced because they provide the legal basis for detaining individuals in military custody. The Military Order also provides presidential authority for the establishment of, and trial by "military commission" of certain categories of persons involved in acts of international terrorism. As reported in chapter 10, in issuing the Order, the government expressly relied on the President's authority as Commander in Chief of the Armed Forces; on the Joint Resolution of the Congress, (Authorization for Use of

Military Force Joint Resolution) (Public Law 107–40, 115 Stat. 224), and on two long-standing legislative provisions 10 U.S.C. §§ 821 and 836. Excerpts from the Military Order that deal with, or are relevant to military commissions matters are again reproduced here as well as the two relevant legislative provisions.

Notice: Detention, Treatment, and Trial of Certain Non–Citizens in the War Against Terrorism.

66 Fed. Reg. 57833.

By the authority vested in me as President and as Commander in Chief of the Armed Forces of the United States by the Constitution and the laws of the United States of America, including the Authorization for Use of Military Force Joint Resolution (Public Law 107–40, 115 Stat. 224) and sections 821 and 836 of title 10, United States Code, it is hereby ordered as follows:

Section 1.   Findings.

(a) International terrorists, including members of al Qaida, have carried out attacks on United States diplomatic and military personnel and facilities abroad and on citizens and property within the United States on a scale that has created a state of armed conflict that requires the use of the United States Armed Forces.

(b) In light of grave acts of terrorism and threats of terrorism, including the terrorist attacks on September 11, 2001, on the headquarters of the United States Department of Defense in the national capital region, on the World Trade Center in New York, and on civilian aircraft such as in Pennsylvania, I proclaimed a national emergency on September 14, 2001 (Proc. 7463, Declaration of National Emergency by Reason of Certain Terrorist Attacks).

(c) Individuals acting alone and in concert involved in international terrorism possess both the capability and the intention to undertake further terrorist attacks against the United States that, if not detected and prevented, will cause mass deaths, mass injuries, and massive destruction of property, and may place at risk the continuity of the operations of the United States Government.

(d) The ability of the United States to protect the United States and its citizens, and to help its allies and other cooperating nations protect their nations and their citizens, from such further terrorist attacks depends in significant part upon using the United States Armed Forces to identify terrorists and those who support them, to disrupt their activities, and to eliminate their ability to conduct or support such attacks.

(e) To protect the United States and its citizens, and for the effective conduct of military operations and prevention of terrorist attacks, it is necessary for individuals subject to this order pursuant to section 2 hereof to be detained, and, when tried, to be tried for violations of the laws of war and other applicable laws by military tribunals.

(f) Given the danger to the safety of the United States and the nature of international terrorism, and to the extent provided by and under this order, I find consistent with section 836 of title 10, United States Code, that it is not practicable to apply in military commissions under this order the principles of law and the rules of evidence generally recognized in the trial of criminal cases in the United States district courts.

(g) Having fully considered the magnitude of the potential deaths, injuries, and property destruction that would result from potential acts of terrorism against the United States, and the probability that such acts will occur, I have determined that an extraordinary emergency exists for national defense purposes, that this emergency constitutes an urgent and compelling government interest, and that issuance of this order is necessary to meet the emergency.

Sec. 2. Definition and Policy.

(a) The term "individual subject to this order" shall mean any individual who is not a United States citizen with respect to whom I determine from time to time in writing that:

(1) there is reason to believe that such individual, at the relevant times,

(i) is or was a member of the organization known as al Qaida;

(ii) has engaged in, aided or abetted, or conspired to commit, acts of international terrorism, or acts in preparation therefor, that have caused, threaten to cause, or have as their aim to cause, injury to or adverse effects on the United States, its citizens, national security, foreign policy, or economy; or

(iii) has knowingly harbored one or more individuals described in subparagraphs (i) or (ii) of subsection 2(a)(1) of this order; and

(2) it is in the interest of the United States that such individual be subject to this order.

(b) It is the policy of the United States that the Secretary of Defense shall take all necessary measures to ensure that any individual subject to this order ... if the individual is to be tried, that such individual is tried only in accordance with section 4.

. . .

Sec. 4. Authority of the Secretary of Defense Regarding Trials of Individuals Subject to this Order.

(a) Any individual subject to this order shall, when tried, be tried by military commission for any and all offenses triable by military commission that such individual is alleged to have committed, and may be punished in accordance with the penalties provided under applicable law, including life imprisonment or death.

(b) As a military function and in light of the findings in section 1, including subsection (f) thereof, the Secretary of Defense shall issue such orders and regulations, including orders for the appointment of one or more military commissions, as may be necessary to carry out subsection (a) of this section.

(c) Orders and regulations issued under subsection (b) of this section shall include, but not be limited to, rules for the conduct of the proceedings of military commissions, including pretrial, trial, and post-trial procedures, modes of proof, issuance of process, and qualifications of attorneys, which shall at a minimum provide for—

> (1) military commissions to sit at any time and any place, consistent with such guidance regarding time and place as the Secretary of Defense may provide;

> (2) a full and fair trial, with the military commission sitting as the triers of both fact and law;

> (3) admission of such evidence as would, in the opinion of the presiding officer of the military commission (or instead, if any other member of the commission so requests at the time the presiding officer renders that opinion, the opinion of the commission rendered at that time by a majority of the commission), have probative value to a reasonable person;

> (4) in a manner consistent with the protection of information classified or classifiable under Executive Order 12958 of April 17, 1995, as amended, or any successor Executive Order, protected by statute or rule from unauthorized disclosure, or otherwise protected by law, (A) the handling of, admission into evidence of, and access to materials and information, and (B) the conduct, closure of, and access to proceedings;

> (5) conduct of the prosecution by one or more attorneys designated by the Secretary of Defense and conduct of the defense by attorneys for the individual subject to this order;

(6) conviction only upon the concurrence of two-thirds of the members of the commission present at the time of the vote, a majority being present;

(7) sentencing only upon the concurrence of two-thirds of the members of the commission present at the time of the vote, a majority being present; and

(8) submission of the record of the trial, including any conviction or sentence, for review and final decision by me or by the Secretary of Defense if so designated by me for that purpose.

Sec. 6. Additional Authorities of the Secretary of Defense.

(a) As a military function and in light of the findings in section 1, the Secretary of Defense shall issue such orders and regulations as may be necessary to carry out any of the provisions of this order.

(b) The Secretary of Defense may perform any of his functions or duties, and may exercise any of the powers provided to him under this order (other than under section 4(c)(8) hereof) in accordance with section 113(d) of title 10, United States Code.

Sec. 7. Relationship to Other Law and Forums.

(a) Nothing in this order shall be construed to—

(1) authorize the disclosure of state secrets to any person not otherwise authorized to have access to them;

(2) limit the authority of the President as Commander in Chief of the Armed Forces or the power of the President to grant reprieves and pardons; or

(3) limit the lawful authority of the Secretary of Defense, any military commander, or any other officer or agent of the United States or of any State to detain or try any person who is not an individual subject to this order.

(b) With respect to any individual subject to this order—

(1) military tribunals shall have exclusive jurisdiction with respect to offenses by the individual; and

(2) the individual shall not be privileged to seek any remedy or maintain any proceeding, directly or indirectly, or to have any such remedy or proceeding sought on the individual's behalf, in

(i) any court of the United States, or any State thereof,

(ii) any court of any foreign nation, or

(iii) any international tribunal.

. . .

3. RELEVANT MILITARY JURISDICTION AND PROCEDURE STATUTES

TITLE 10—UNITED STATES CODE (ARMED FORCES) SUBTITLE A—GENERAL MILITARY LAW PART II—PERSONNEL CHAPTER 47—UNIFORM CODE OF MILITARY JUSTICE—SUBCHAPTER IV—COURT–MARTIAL JURISDICTION

Section 821. Art. 21.   Jurisdiction of courts-martial not exclusive

The provisions of this chapter conferring jurisdiction upon courts-martial do not deprive military commissions, provost courts, or other military tribunals of concurrent jurisdiction with respect to offenders or offenses that by statute or by the law of war may be tried by military commissions, provost courts, or other military tribunals.

Section 836. Art. 36.   President may prescribe rules

(a) Pretrial, trial, and post-trial procedures, including modes of proof, for cases arising under this chapter triable in courts-martial, military commissions and other military tribunals, and procedures for courts of inquiry, may be prescribed by the President by regulations which shall, so far as he considers practicable, apply the principles of law and the rules of evidence generally recognized in the trial of criminal cases in the United States district courts, but which may not be contrary to or inconsistent with this chapter.

(b) All rules and regulations made under this article shall be uniform insofar as practicable.

QUESTIONS AND NOTES

1. The issuance of the Presidential Military Order generated a great deal of commentary, both in law reviews and the general media. Much of the commentary attacked the Order as being either an unconstitutional or unwise assertion of authority by the President. The main constitutional argument made against the Order was that the President did not have the authority to issue the order without congressional authorization. The response of the administration and the administration's defenders was that the President had such authority as Commander in Chief. If further congressional authorization was needed, the post-Sept. 11 Joint Resolution (Public Law 107–40) and the two long-standing Title 10 sections, supra, provided such authority. The government also cited the decision of the Supreme Court in Ex parte Quirin, 317 U.S. 1 (1942).

2. Does Quirin provide adequate support for the issuance of the Military Order by the President? Following the issuance of the Military Order, the legal literature filled with scholarly debate about the question of presidential power to authorize the establishment of military commissions. See, e.g., Neal K. Katyal and Laurence H. Tribe, Waging War, Deciding Guilt: Trying the Military Tribunals, 111 Yale L.J. 1259, 1269–1270 (2002); Curtis A. Bradley

and Jack L. Goldsmith, The Constitutional Validity of Military Commissions, 5 Green Bag 2d 249, 252 (Spring 2002); Ruth Wedgwood, Agora: Military Commissions: Al Qaeda, Terrorism, and Military Commissions, 96 Am J. Int'l L. 328 (2002); Jonathan J. Paust, Antiterrorism Military Commissions: Courting Illegality, 23 Mich. J. Int'l L. 1, 5–9 (2001); Harold Hongju Koh, The Case against Military Commissions, 96 Am. Int'l L 337, 339–342 (2002).

3. Criticisms were also directed against the prospect of prosecution before military commissions, reflecting concerns about the lack of procedural protections. See, e.g., Koh, supra note 2, at 340:

> These specific legal deficiencies stand atop a much broader rule-of-law concern. International law permits the United States to redress the unprovoked killing of thousands on September 11, 2001, by itself engaging in an armed attack upon the Al Qaeda perpetrators. But should those culprits be captured, the United States must try, not lynch, them to promote four legal values higher than vengeance: holding them accountable for their crimes against humanity; telling the world the truth about those crimes; reaffirming that such acts violate all norms of civilized society; and demonstrating that law-abiding societies, unlike terrorists, respect human rights by channeling retribution into criminal punishment for even the most heinous outlaws.
>
> The Military Order undermines each of these values. . . .

See also George P. Fletcher, The Military Tribunal Order: On Justice and War: Contradictions in the Proposed Military Tribunals, 25 Harv. J.L. & Pub. Pol'y 635, 639 (2002).

4. Many of the criticisms and scholarly concerns (but certainly not all) were responded to when the Department of Defense in March, 2002, issued regulations under the authority of the Military Order, titled Military Commissions Order No. 1, as supplemented by subsequent amendments, that spelled out in some detail the procedures to be followed in hearings before the commissions. These original regulations were published at *http://www.defense link.mil/news/Mar2002/d20020321ord.pdf*.

4. AUTHORITY TO ESTABLISH MILITARY COMMISSIONS—THE HAMDAN CASE

HAMDAN v. RUMSFELD

548 U.S. 557 (2006)

[The opinion of the Court and the concurring opinions are reproduced here. The dissenting opinions have been omitted.]

ON WRIT OF CERTIORARI TO THE UNITED STATES COURT OF APPEALS FOR THE DISTRICT OF COLUMBIA CIRCUIT

JUSTICE STEVENS announced the judgment of the Court and delivered the opinion of the Court with respect to Parts I through IV, Parts VI through VI–D-iii, Part VI–D-v, and Part VII, and an opinion with respect to Parts V and VI–D-iv, in which JUSTICE SOUTER, JUSTICE GINSBURG, and JUSTICE BREYER join.

Petitioner Salim Ahmed Hamdan, a Yemeni national, is in custody at an American prison in Guantanamo Bay, Cuba. In November 2001, during hostilities between the United States and the Taliban (which then governed Afghanistan), Hamdan was captured by militia forces and turned over to the U.S. military. In June 2002, he was transported to Guantanamo Bay. Over a year later, the President deemed him eligible for trial by military commission for then-unspecified crimes. After another year had passed, Hamdan was charged with one count of conspiracy "to commit . . . offenses triable by military commission."

Hamdan filed petitions for writs of habeas corpus and mandamus to challenge the Executive Branch's intended means of prosecuting this charge. He concedes that a court-martial constituted in accordance with the Uniform Code of Military Justice (UCMJ), 10 U.S.C. § 801 *et seq.* (2000 ed. and Supp. III), would have authority to try him. His objection is that the military commission the President has convened lacks such authority, for two principal reasons: First, neither congressional Act nor the common law of war supports trial by this commission for the crime of conspiracy-an offense that, Hamdan says, is not a violation of the law of war. Second, Hamdan contends, the procedures that the President has adopted to try him violate the most basic tenets of military and international law, including the principle that a defendant must be permitted to see and hear the evidence against him.

The District Court granted Hamdan's request for a writ of habeas corpus. 344 F. Supp. 2d 152 (DC 2004). The Court of Appeals for the District of Columbia Circuit reversed. 415 F. 3d 33 (2005). Recognizing, as we did over a half-century ago, that trial by military commission is an extraordinary measure raising important questions about the balance of powers in our constitutional structure, *Ex parte Quirin,* 317 U.S. 1, 19 (1942), we granted certiorari.

For the reasons that follow, we conclude that the military commission convened to try Hamdan lacks power to proceed because its structure and procedures violate both the UCMJ and the Geneva Conventions. Four of us also conclude, see Part V, *infra,* that the offense with which Hamdan has been charged is not an "offens[e] that by . . . the law of war may be tried by military commissions." 10 U.S.C. § 821.

I

On September 11, 2001, agents of the al Qaeda terrorist organization hijacked commercial airplanes and attacked the World Trade Center in New York City and the national headquarters of the Department of Defense in Arlington, Virginia. Americans will never forget the devastation wrought by these acts. Nearly 3,000 civilians were killed.

Congress responded by adopting a Joint Resolution authorizing the President to "use all necessary and appropriate force against those nations, organizations, or persons he determines planned, authorized, committed, or aided the terrorist attacks . . . in order to prevent any future acts of international terrorism against the United States by such nations, organizations or persons." Authorization for Use of Military Force

(AUMF), 115 Stat. 224, note following 50 U.S.C. § 1541 (2000 ed., Supp. III). Acting pursuant to the AUMF, and having determined that the Taliban regime had supported al Qaeda, the President ordered the Armed Forces of the United States to invade Afghanistan. In the ensuing hostilities, hundreds of individuals, Hamdan among them, were captured and eventually detained at Guantanamo Bay.

On November 13, 2001, while the United States was still engaged in active combat with the Taliban, the President issued a comprehensive military order intended to govern the "Detention, Treatment, and Trial of Certain Non–Citizens in the War Against Terrorism," 66 Fed. Reg. 57833 (hereinafter November 13 Order or Order). Those subject to the November 13 Order include any noncitizen for whom the President determines "there is reason to believe" that he or she (1) "is or was" a member of al Qaeda or (2) has engaged or participated in terrorist activities aimed at or harmful to the United States. *Id.*, at 57834. Any such individual "shall, when tried, be tried by military commission for any and all offenses triable by military commission that such individual is alleged to have committed, and may be punished in accordance with the penalties provided under applicable law, including imprisonment or death." *Ibid.* The November 13 Order vested in the Secretary of Defense the power to appoint military commissions to try individuals subject to the Order, but that power has since been delegated to John D. Altenberg, Jr., a retired Army major general and longtime military lawyer who has been designated "Appointing Authority for Military Commissions."

On July 3, 2003, the President announced his determination that Hamdan and five other detainees at Guantanamo Bay were subject to the November 13 Order and thus triable by military commission. In December 2003, military counsel was appointed to represent Hamdan. Two months later, counsel filed demands for charges and for a speedy trial pursuant to Article 10 of the UCMJ, 10 U.S.C. § 810. On February 23, 2004, the legal adviser to the Appointing Authority denied the applications, ruling that Hamdan was not entitled to any of the protections of the UCMJ. Not until July 13, 2004, after Hamdan had commenced this action in the United States District Court for the Western District of Washington, did the Government finally charge him with the offense for which, a year earlier, he had been deemed eligible for trial by military commission.

The charging document, which is unsigned, contains 13 numbered paragraphs. The first two paragraphs recite the asserted bases for the military commission's jurisdiction-namely, the November 13 Order and the President's July 3, 2003, declaration that Hamdan is eligible for trial by military commission. The next nine paragraphs, collectively entitled "General Allegations," describe al Qaeda's activities from its inception in 1989 through 2001 and identify Osama bin Laden as the group's leader. Hamdan is not mentioned in these paragraphs.

Only the final two paragraphs, entitled "Charge: Conspiracy," contain allegations against Hamdan. Paragraph 12 charges that "from on or about

February 1996 to on or about November 24, 2001," Hamdan "willfully and knowingly joined an enterprise of persons who shared a common criminal purpose and conspired and agreed with [named members of al Qaeda] to commit the following offenses triable by military commission: attacking civilians; attacking civilian objects; murder by an unprivileged belligerent; and terrorism." App. to Pet. for Cert. 65a. There is no allegation that Hamdan had any command responsibilities, played a leadership role, or participated in the planning of any activity.

Paragraph 13 lists four "overt acts" that Hamdan is alleged to have committed sometime between 1996 and November 2001 in furtherance of the "enterprise and conspiracy": (1) he acted as Osama bin Laden's "bodyguard and personal driver," "believ[ing]" all the while that bin Laden "and his associates were involved in" terrorist acts prior to and including the attacks of September 11, 2001; (2) he arranged for transportation of, and actually transported, weapons used by al Qaeda members and by bin Laden's bodyguards (Hamdan among them); (3) he "drove or accompanied [O]sama bin Laden to various al Qaida-sponsored training camps, press conferences, or lectures," at which bin Laden encouraged attacks against Americans; and (4) he received weapons training at al Qaeda-sponsored camps. *Id.*, at 65a–67a.

．　．　．

On November 7, 2005, we granted certiorari to decide whether the military commission convened to try Hamdan has authority to do so, and whether Hamdan may rely on the Geneva Conventions in these proceedings.

．　．　．

As the Court of Appeals here recognized, *Quirin* "provides a compelling historical precedent for the power of civilian courts to entertain challenges that seek to interrupt the processes of military commissions." The circumstances of this case, like those in *Quirin*, simply do not implicate the "obligations of comity" that, under appropriate circumstances, justify abstention.

Finally, the Government has identified no other "important countervailing interest" that would permit federal courts to depart from their general "duty to exercise the jurisdiction that is conferred upon them by Congress." To the contrary, Hamdan and the Government both have a compelling interest in knowing in advance whether Hamdan may be tried by a military commission that arguably is without any basis in law and operates free from many of the procedural rules prescribed by Congress for courts-martial-rules intended to safeguard the accused and ensure the reliability of any conviction. While we certainly do not foreclose the possibility that abstention may be appropriate in some cases seeking review of ongoing military commission proceedings (such as military commissions convened on the battlefield), the foregoing discussion makes clear that, under our precedent, abstention is not justified here. We therefore proceed to consider the merits of Hamdan's challenge.

IV

The military commission, a tribunal neither mentioned in the Constitution nor created by statute, was born of military necessity. See W. Winthrop, Military Law and Precedents 831 (rev. 2d ed. 1920) (hereinafter Winthrop). Though foreshadowed in some respects by earlier tribunals like the Board of General Officers that General Washington convened to try British Major John André for spying during the Revolutionary War, the commission "as such" was inaugurated in 1847. *Id.*, at 832; G. Davis, A Treatise on the Military Law of the United States 308 (2d ed. 1909) (hereinafter Davis). As commander of occupied Mexican territory, and having available to him no other tribunal, General Winfield Scott that year ordered the establishment of both " *'military commissions'* " to try ordinary crimes committed in the occupied territory and a *"council of war"* to try offenses against the law of war. Winthrop 832 (emphases in original).

When the exigencies of war next gave rise to a need for use of military commissions, during the Civil War, the dual system favored by General Scott was not adopted. Instead, a single tribunal often took jurisdiction over ordinary crimes, war crimes, and breaches of military orders alike. As further discussed below, each aspect of that seemingly broad jurisdiction was in fact supported by a separate military exigency. Generally, though, the need for military commissions during this period-as during the Mexican War-was driven largely by the then very limited jurisdiction of courts-martial: "The *occasion* for the military commission arises principally from the fact that the jurisdiction of the court-martial proper, in our law, is restricted by statute almost exclusively to members of the military force and to certain specific offences defined in a written code." *Id.*, at 831 (emphasis in original).

Exigency alone, of course, will not justify the establishment and use of penal tribunals not contemplated by Article I, § 8 and Article III, § 1 of the Constitution unless some other part of that document authorizes a response to the felt need. See *Ex parte Milligan*, 4 Wall. 2, 121 (1866) ("Certainly no part of the judicial power of the country was conferred on [military commissions]"); . . . And that authority, if it exists, can derive only from the powers granted jointly to the President and Congress in time of war. See *id.*, at 26–29; *In re Yamashita*, 327 U.S. 1, 11 (1946).

The Constitution makes the President the "Commander in Chief" of the Armed Forces, Art. II, § 2, cl. 1, but vests in Congress the powers to "declare War ... and make Rules concerning Captures on Land and Water," Art. I, § 8, cl. 11, to "raise and support Armies," *id.*, cl. 12, to "define and punish ... Offences against the Law of Nations," *id.*, cl. 10, and "To make Rules for the Government and Regulation of the land and naval Forces," *id.*, cl. 14. The interplay between these powers was described by Chief Justice Chase in the seminal case of *Ex parte Milligan*:

"The power to make the necessary laws is in Congress; the power to execute in the President. Both powers imply many subordinate and auxiliary powers. Each includes all authorities essential to its due exercise. But neither can the President, in war more than in peace, intrude upon the proper authority of Congress, nor Congress upon the proper authority of the President.... Congress cannot direct the conduct of campaigns, nor can the President, or any commander under him, without the sanction of Congress, institute tribunals for the trial and punishment of offences, either of soldiers or civilians, unless in cases of a controlling necessity, which justifies what it compels, or at least insures acts of indemnity from the justice of the legislature." 4 Wall., at 139–140.

Whether Chief Justice Chase was correct in suggesting that the President may constitutionally convene military commissions "without the sanction of Congress" in cases of "controlling necessity" is a question this Court has not answered definitively, and need not answer today. For we held in *Quirin* that Congress had, through Article of War 15, sanctioned the use of military commissions in such circumstances. 317 U.S., at 28 ("By the Articles of War, and especially Article 15, Congress has explicitly provided, so far as it may constitutionally do so, that military tribunals shall have jurisdiction to try offenders or offenses against the law of war in appropriate cases"). Article 21 of the UCMJ, the language of which is substantially identical to the old Article 15 and was preserved by Congress after World War II, reads as follows:

> "Jurisdiction of courts-martial not exclusive.
>
> "The provisions of this code conferring jurisdiction upon courts-martial shall not be construed as depriving military commissions, provost courts, or other military tribunals of concurrent jurisdiction in respect of offenders or offenses that by statute or by the law of war may be tried by such military commissions, provost courts, or other military tribunals." 64 Stat. 115.

We have no occasion to revisit *Quirin*'s controversial characterization of Article of War 15 as congressional authorization for military commissions. Contrary to the Government's assertion, however, even *Quirin* did not view the authorization as a sweeping mandate for the President to "invoke military commissions when he deems them necessary." Rather, the *Quirin* Court recognized that Congress had simply preserved what power, under the Constitution and the common law of war, the President had had before 1916 to convene military commissions-with the express condition that the President and those under his command comply with the law of war. That much is evidenced by the Court's inquiry, *following* its conclusion that Congress had authorized military commissions, into whether the law of war had indeed been complied with in that case. See *ibid.*

The Government would have us dispense with the inquiry that the *Quirin* Court undertook and find in either the AUMF or the DTA specific, overriding authorization for the very commission that has been convened to try Hamdan. Neither of these congressional Acts, however, expands the President's authority to convene military commissions. First, while we assume that the AUMF activated the President's war powers, see *Hamdi v. Rumsfeld*, 542 U.S. 507 (2004) (plurality opinion), and that those powers include the authority to convene military commissions in appropriate circumstances, see *id.*, at 518; *Quirin*, 317 U.S., at 28–29; see also *Yamashita*, 327 U.S., at 11, there is nothing in the text or legislative history of the AUMF even hinting that Congress intended to expand or alter the authorization set forth in Article 21 of the UCMJ.

Likewise, the DTA cannot be read to authorize this commission. Although the DTA, unlike either Article 21 or the AUMF, was enacted after the President had convened Hamdan's commission, it contains no language authorizing that tribunal or any other at Guantanamo Bay. The DTA obviously "recognize[s]" the existence of the Guantanamo Bay commissions in the weakest sense, Brief for Respondents 15, because it references some of the military orders governing them and creates limited judicial review of their "final decision[s]," DTA § 1005(e)(3), 119 Stat. 2743. But the statute also pointedly reserves judgment on whether "the Constitution and laws of the United States are applicable" in reviewing such decisions and whether, if they are, the "standards and procedures" used to try Hamdan and other detainees actually violate the "Constitution and laws." *Ibid.*

Together, the UCMJ, the AUMF, and the DTA at most acknowledge a general Presidential authority to convene military commissions in circumstances where justified under the "Constitution and laws," including the law of war. Absent a more specific congressional authorization, the task of this Court is, as it was in *Quirin*, to decide whether Hamdan's military commission is so justified. It is to that inquiry we now turn.

V

The common law governing military commissions may be gleaned from past practice and what sparse legal precedent exists. Commissions historically have been used in three situations. See Bradley & Goldsmith, Congressional Authorization and the War on Terrorism, 118 Harv. L. Rev. 2048, 2132–2133 (2005); ... First, they have substituted for civilian courts at times and in places where martial law has been declared.... Second, commissions have been established to try civilians "as part of a temporary military government over occupied enemy territory or territory regained from an enemy where civilian government cannot and does not function." ... Illustrative of this second kind of commission is the one that was established, with jurisdiction to apply the German Criminal Code, in occupied Germany following the end of World War II.

The third type of commission, convened as an "incident to the conduct of war" when there is a need "to seize and subject to disciplinary measures those enemies who in their attempt to thwart or impede our military effort have violated the law of war," *Quirin*, 317 U.S., at 28–29, has been described as "utterly different" from the other two. Bickers, Military Commissions are Constitutionally Sound: A Response to Professors Katyal and Tribe, 34 Tex. Tech. L. Rev. 899, 902 (2002–2003). Not only is its jurisdiction limited to offenses cognizable during time of war, but its role is primarily a factfinding one-to determine, typically on the battlefield itself, whether the defendant has violated the law of war. The last time the U.S. Armed Forces used the law-of-war military commission was during World War II. In *Quirin*, this Court sanctioned President Roosevelt's use of such a tribunal to try Nazi saboteurs captured on American soil during the War. And in *Yamashita*, we held that a military commission had jurisdiction to try a Japanese commander for failing to prevent troops under his command from committing atrocities in the Philippines.

Quirin is the model the Government invokes most frequently to defend the commission convened to try Hamdan. That is both appropriate and unsurprising. Since Guantanamo Bay is neither enemy-occupied territory nor under martial law, the law-of-war commission is the only model available. At the same time, no more robust model of executive power exists; *Quirin* represents the high-water mark of military power to try enemy combatants for war crimes.

The classic treatise penned by Colonel William Winthrop, whom we have called "the 'Blackstone of Military Law,' " *Reid* v. *Covert,* 354 U.S. 1, 19, n. 38 (1957) (plurality opinion), describes at least four preconditions for exercise of jurisdiction by a tribunal of the type convened to try Hamdan. First, "[a] military commission, (except where otherwise authorized by statute), can legally assume jurisdiction only of offenses committed within the field of the command of the convening commander." Winthrop 836. The "field of command" in these circumstances means the "theatre of war." Second, the offense charged "must have been committed within the period of the war." No jurisdiction exists to try offenses "committed either before or after the war." Third, a military commission not established pursuant to martial law or an occupation may try only "[i]ndividuals of the enemy's army who have been guilty of illegitimate warfare or other offences in violation of the laws of war" and members of one's own army "who, in time of war, become chargeable with crimes or offences not cognizable, or triable, by the criminal courts or under the Articles of war." Finally, a law-of-war commission has jurisdiction to try only two kinds of offense: "Violations of the laws and usages of war cognizable by military tribunals only," and "[b]reaches of military orders or regulations for which offenders are not legally triable by court-martial under the Articles of war."

All parties agree that Colonel Winthrop's treatise accurately describes the common law governing military commissions, and that the jurisdictional limitations he identifies were incorporated in Article of War 15 and, later, Article 21 of the UCMJ. It also is undisputed that Hamdan's commission lacks jurisdiction to try him unless the charge "properly set[s] forth, not only the details of the act charged, but the circumstances conferring *jurisdiction*." *Id.*, at 842 (emphasis in original). The question is whether the preconditions designed to ensure that a military necessity exists to justify the use of this extraordinary tribunal have been satisfied here.

The charge against Hamdan, described in detail in Part I, *supra*, alleges a conspiracy extending over a number of years, from 1996 to November 2001. All but two months of that more than 5–year–long period preceded the attacks of September 11, 2001, and the enactment of the AUMF—the Act of Congress on which the Government relies for exercise of its war powers and thus for its authority to convene military commissions. Neither the purported agreement with Osama bin Laden and others to commit war crimes, nor a single overt act, is alleged to have occurred in a theater of war or on any specified date after September 11, 2001. None of the overt acts that Hamdan is alleged to have committed violates the law of war.

These facts alone cast doubt on the legality of the charge and, hence, the commission; as Winthrop makes plain, the offense alleged must have been committed both in a theater of war and *during*, not before, the relevant conflict. But the deficiencies in the time and place allegations also underscore-indeed are symptomatic of-the most serious defect of this charge: The offense it alleges is not triable by law-of-war military commission. See *Yamashita*, 327 U.S., at 13 ("Neither congressional action nor the military orders constituting the commission authorized it to place petitioner on trial unless the charge proffered against him is of a violation of the law of war").

There is no suggestion that Congress has, in exercise of its constitutional authority to "define and punish ... Offences against the Law of Nations," U.S. Const., Art. I, § 8, cl. 10, positively identified "conspiracy" as a war crime. As we explained in *Quirin*, that is not necessarily fatal to the Government's claim of authority to try the alleged offense by military commission; Congress, through Article 21 of the UCMJ, has "incorporated by reference" the common law of war, which may render triable by military commission certain offenses not defined by statute. When, however, neither the elements of the offense nor the range of permissible punishments is defined by statute or treaty, the precedent must be plain and unambiguous. To demand any less would be to risk concentrating in military hands a degree of adjudicative and punitive power in excess of that contemplated either by statute or by the Constitution. . . .

This high standard was met in *Quirin;* the violation there alleged was, by "universal agreement and practice" both in this country and internationally, recognized as an offense against the law of war. . . .

At a minimum, the Government must make a substantial showing that the crime for which it seeks to try a defendant by military commission is acknowledged to be an offense against the law of war. That burden is far from satisfied here. The crime of "conspiracy" has rarely if ever been tried as such in this country by any law-of-war military commission not exercising some other form of jurisdiction, and does not appear in either the Geneva Conventions or the Hague Conventions-the major treaties on the law of war. Winthrop explains that under the common law governing military commissions, it is not enough to intend to violate the law of war and commit overt acts in furtherance of that intention unless the overt acts either are themselves offenses against the law of war or constitute steps sufficiently substantial to qualify as an attempt. See Winthrop 841.

The Government cites three sources that it says show otherwise. First, it points out that the Nazi saboteurs in *Quirin* were charged with conspiracy. Second, it observes that Winthrop at one point in his treatise identifies conspiracy as an offense "prosecuted by military commissions." Finally, it notes that another military historian, Charles Roscoe Howland, lists conspiracy " 'to violate the laws of war by destroying life or property in aid of the enemy' " as an offense that was tried as a violation of the law of war during the Civil War. On close analysis, however, these sources at best lend little support to the Government's position and at worst undermine it. By any measure, they fail to satisfy the high standard of clarity required to justify the use of a military commission.

That the defendants in *Quirin* were charged with conspiracy is not persuasive, since the Court declined to address whether the offense actually qualified as a violation of the law of war-let alone one triable by military commission. The *Quirin* defendants were charged with the following offenses:

"[I.]   Violation of the law of war.

"[II.]   Violation of Article 81 of the Articles of War, defining the offense of relieving or attempting to relieve, or corresponding with or giving intelligence to, the enemy.

"[III.]   Violation of Article 82, defining the offense of spying.

"[IV.]   Conspiracy to commit the offenses alleged in charges [I, II, and III]." 317 U.S., at 23.

The Government, defending its charge, argued that the conspiracy alleged "constitute[d] an additional violation of the law of war." The saboteurs disagreed; they maintained that "[t]he charge of conspiracy can not stand if the other charges fall." The Court, however, declined to resolve the dispute. It concluded, first, that the specification supporting Charge I adequately alleged a "violation of the law of war" that was not "merely colorable or without foundation." The facts the Court deemed sufficient for this purpose were that the defendants, admitted enemy combatants, entered upon U.S. territory in time of war without uniform "for the purpose of destroying property used or useful in prosecuting the war." That act was "a hostile and warlike" one. The Court was careful in its decision to identify an overt, "complete" act. Responding to the argument that the saboteurs had "not actually committed or attempted to commit any act of depredation or entered the theatre or zone of active military operations" and therefore had not violated the law of war, the Court responded that they had actually "passed our military and naval lines and defenses or went behind those lines, in civilian dress and with hostile purpose." "The offense was complete when with that purpose they entered—or, having so entered, they remained upon—our territory in time of war without uniform or other appropriate means of identification."

Turning to the other charges alleged, the Court explained that "[s]ince the first specification of Charge I sets forth a violation of the law of war, we have no occasion to pass on the adequacy of the second specification of Charge I, or to construe the 81st and 82nd Articles of War for the purpose of ascertaining whether the specifications under Charges II and III allege violations of those Articles or whether if so construed they are constitutional." No mention was made at all of Charge IV-the conspiracy charge.

If anything, *Quirin* supports Hamdan's argument that conspiracy is not a violation of the law of war. Not only did the Court pointedly omit any discussion of the conspiracy charge, but its analysis of Charge I placed special emphasis on the *completion* of an offense; it took seriously the saboteurs' argument that there can be no violation of a law of war-at least not one triable by military commission-without the actual commission of or attempt to commit a "hostile and warlike act."

That limitation makes eminent sense when one considers the necessity from whence this kind of military commission grew: The need to dispense swift justice, often in the form of execution, to illegal belligerents captured on the battlefield.... The same urgency would not have been felt vis—vis enemies who had done little more than agree to violate the laws of war. Cf. 31 Op. Atty. Gen. 356, 357, 361 (1918) (opining that a German spy could not be tried by military commission because, having been apprehended before entering "any camp, fortification or other military premises of the United States," he had "committed [his offenses] outside of the field of military operations"). The *Quirin* Court acknowledged as much when it described the President's authority to use law-of-war military commissions as the power to "seize and subject to disciplinary measures those enemies *who in their attempt to thwart or impede our military effort* have violated the law of war."

Winthrop and Howland are only superficially more helpful to the Government. Howland, granted, lists "conspiracy by two or more to violate the laws of war by destroying life or property in aid of the enemy" as one of over 20 "offenses against the laws and usages of war" "passed upon and punished by military commissions." Howland 1071. But while the records of cases that Howland cites following his list of offenses against the law of war support inclusion of the other offenses mentioned, they provide no support for the inclusion of conspiracy as a violation of the law of war. Winthrop, apparently recognizing as much, excludes conspiracy of any kind from his own list of offenses against the law of war. See Winthrop 839–840 ...

Finally, international sources confirm that the crime charged here is not a recognized violation of the law of war.... The International Military

Tribunal at Nuremberg, over the prosecution's objections, pointedly refused to recognize as a violation of the law of war conspiracy to commit war crimes, ... and convicted only Hitler's most senior associates of conspiracy to wage aggressive war, see S. Pomorski, Conspiracy and Criminal Organization, in the Nuremberg Trial and International Law 213, 233–235 (G. Ginsburgs & V. Kudriavtsev eds. 1990). As one prominent figure from the Nuremberg trials has explained, members of the Tribunal objected to recognition of conspiracy as a violation of the law of war on the ground that "[t]he Anglo–American concept of conspiracy was not part of European legal systems and arguably not an element of the internationally recognized laws of war." T. Taylor, Anatomy of the Nuremberg Trials: A Personal Memoir 36 (1992); . . . .

In sum, the sources that the Government and Justice Thomas rely upon to show that conspiracy to violate the law of war is itself a violation of the law of war in fact demonstrate quite the opposite. Far from making the requisite substantial showing, the Government has failed even to offer a "merely colorable" case for inclusion of conspiracy among those offenses cognizable by law-of-war military commission. Because the charge does not support the commission's jurisdiction, the commission lacks authority to try Hamdan.

The charge's shortcomings are not merely formal, but are indicative of a broader inability on the Executive's part here to satisfy the most basic precondition-at least in the absence of specific congressional authorization-for establishment of military commissions: military necessity. Hamdan's tribunal was appointed not by a military commander in the field of battle, but by a retired major general stationed away from any active hostilities. Hamdan is charged not with an overt act for which he was caught redhanded in a theater of war and which military efficiency demands be tried expeditiously, but with an *agreement* the inception of which long predated the attacks of September 11, 2001 and the AUMF. That may well be a crime, but it is not an offense that "by the law of war may be tried by military commissio[n]." 10 U.S.C. § 821. None of the overt acts alleged to have been committed in furtherance of the agreement is itself a war crime, or even necessarily occurred during time of, or in a theater of, war. Any urgent need for imposition or execution of judgment is utterly belied by the record; Hamdan was arrested in November 2001 and he was not charged until mid–2004. These simply are not the circumstances in which, by any stretch of the historical evidence or this Court's precedents, a military commission established by Executive Order under the authority of Article 21 of the UCMJ may lawfully try a person and subject him to punishment.

VI

Whether or not the Government has charged Hamdan with an offense against the law of war cognizable by military commission, the commission lacks power to proceed. The UCMJ conditions the President's use of military commissions on compliance not only with the American common law of war, but also with the rest of the UCMJ itself, insofar as applicable, and with the "rules and precepts of the law of nations," *Quirin*, 317 U.S., at 28–including, *inter alia*, the four Geneva Conventions signed in 1949. See *Yamashita*, 327 U.S., at 20–21, 23–24. The procedures that the Government has decreed will govern Hamdan's trial by commission violate these laws.

A

The commission's procedures are set forth in Commission Order No. 1, which was amended most recently on August 31, 2005–after Hamdan's trial had already begun. Every commission established pursuant to Commission Order No. 1 must have a presiding officer and at least three other members, all of whom must be commissioned officers. § 4(A)(1). The presiding officer's job is to rule on questions of law and other evidentiary and interlocutory issues; the other members make findings and, if applicable, sentencing decisions. § 4(A)(5). The accused is entitled to appointed military counsel and may hire civilian counsel at his own expense so long as such counsel is a U.S. citizen with security clearance "at the level SECRET or higher." §§ 4(C)(2)–(3).

The accused also is entitled to a copy of the charge(s) against him, both in English and his own language (if different), to a presumption of innocence, and to certain other rights typically afforded criminal defendants in civilian courts and courts-martial. See §§ 5(A)–(P). These rights are subject, however, to one glaring condition: The accused and his civilian counsel may be excluded from, and precluded from ever learning what evidence was presented during, any part of the proceeding that either the Appointing Authority or the presiding officer decides to "close." Grounds for such closure "include the protection of information classified or classifiable . . .; information protected by law or rule from unauthorized disclosure; the physical safety of participants in Commission proceedings, including prospective witnesses; intelligence and law enforcement sources, methods, or activities; and other national security interests." § 6(B)(3). Appointed military defense counsel must be privy to these closed sessions, but may, at the presiding officer's discretion, be forbidden to reveal to his or her client what took place therein. *Ibid.*

Another striking feature of the rules governing Hamdan's commission is that they permit the admission of *any* evidence that, in the opinion of the presiding officer, "would have probative value to a reasonable person." § 6(D)(1). Under this test, not only is testimonial hearsay and evidence obtained through coercion fully admissible, but neither live testimony nor witnesses' written statements need be sworn. See §§ 6(D)(2)(b), (3). Moreover, the accused and his civilian counsel may be denied access to evidence in the form of "protected information" (which includes classified information as well as "information protected by law or rule from unauthorized disclosure" and "information concerning other national security interests," §§ 6(B)(3), 6(D)(5)(a)(v)), so long as the presiding officer concludes that the evidence is "probative" under

§ 6(D)(1) and that its admission without the accused's knowledge would not "result in the denial of a full and fair trial." § 6(D)(5)(b). Finally, a presiding officer's determination that evidence "would not have probative value to a reasonable person" may be overridden by a majority of the other commission members. § 6(D)(1).

Once all the evidence is in, the commission members (not including the presiding officer) must vote on the accused's guilt. A two-thirds vote will suffice for both a verdict of guilty and for imposition of any sentence not including death (the imposition of which requires a unanimous vote). § 6(F). Any appeal is taken to a three-member review panel composed of military officers and designated by the Secretary of Defense, only one member of which need have experience as a judge. § 6(H)(4). The review panel is directed to "disregard any variance from procedures specified in this Order or elsewhere that would not materially have affected the outcome of the trial before the Commission." *Ibid.* Once the panel makes its recommendation to the Secretary of Defense, the Secretary can either remand for further proceedings or forward the record to the President with his recommendation as to final disposition. § 6(H)(5). The President then, unless he has delegated the task to the Secretary, makes the "final decision." § 6(H)(6). He may change the commission's findings or sentence only in a manner favorable to the accused. *Ibid.*

B

Hamdan raises both general and particular objections to the procedures set forth in Commission Order No. 1. His general objection is that the procedures' admitted deviation from those governing courts-martial itself renders the commission illegal. Chief among his particular objections are that he may, under the Commission Order, be convicted based on evidence he has not seen or heard, and that any evidence admitted against him need not comply with the admissibility or relevance rules typically applicable in criminal trials and court-martial proceedings.

The Government objects to our consideration of any procedural challenge at this stage. . . .

First, because Hamdan apparently is not subject to the death penalty (at least as matters now stand) and may receive a sentence shorter than 10 years' imprisonment, he has no automatic right to review of the commission's "final decision" before a federal court under the DTA. See § 1005(e)(3), 119 Stat. 2743. Second, contrary to the Government's assertion, there *is* a "basis to presume" that the procedures employed during Hamdan's trial will violate the law: The procedures are described with particularity in Commission Order No. 1, and implementation of some of them has already occurred. One of Hamdan's complaints is that he will be, and *indeed already has been*, excluded from his own trial. See Reply Brief for Petitioner 12; App. to Pet. for Cert. 45a. Under these circumstances, review of the procedures in advance of a "final decision"—the timing of which is left entirely to the discretion of the President under the DTA—is appropriate. We turn, then, to consider the merits of Hamdan's procedural challenge.

C

In part because the difference between military commissions and courts-martial originally was a difference of jurisdiction alone, and in part to protect against abuse and ensure evenhandedness under the pressures of war, the procedures governing trials by military commission historically have been the same as those governing courts-martial. See, *e.g.*, 1 The War of the Rebellion 248 (2d series 1894) (General Order 1 issued during the Civil War required military commissions to "be constituted in a similar manner and their proceedings be conducted according to the same general rules as courts-martial in order to prevent abuses which might otherwise arise"). Accounts of commentators from Winthrop through General Crowder-who drafted Article of War 15 and whose views have been deemed "authoritative" by this Court, *Madsen*, 343 U.S., at 353–confirm as much. As recently as the Korean and Vietnam wars, during which use of military commissions was contemplated but never made, the principle of procedural parity was espoused as a background assumption. See Paust, Antiterrorism Military Commissions: Courting Illegality, 23 Mich. J. Int'l L. 1, 3–5 (2001–2002).

There is a glaring historical exception to this general rule. The procedures and evidentiary rules used to try General Yamashita near the end of World War II deviated in significant respects from those then governing courts-martial. See 327 U.S. 1. The force of that precedent, however, has been seriously undermined by post-World War II developments.

Yamashita, from late 1944 until September 1945, was Commanding General of the Fourteenth Army Group of the Imperial Japanese Army, which had exercised control over the Philippine Islands. On September 3, 1945, after American forces regained control of the Philippines, Yamashita surrendered. Three weeks later, he was charged with violations of the law of war. A few weeks after that, he was arraigned before a military commission convened in the Philippines. He pleaded not guilty, and his trial lasted for two months. On December 7, 1945, Yamashita was convicted and sentenced to hang. This Court upheld the denial of his petition for a writ of habeas corpus.

The procedures and rules of evidence employed during Yamashita's trial departed so far from those used in courts-martial that they generated an unusually long and vociferous critique from two Members of this Court. See *id.*, at 41–81 (Rutledge, J., joined by Murphy, J., dissenting). Among the dissenters' primary concerns was that the commission had free rein to consider all evidence "which in the commission's opinion 'would be of assistance in proving or disproving the charge,' without any of the usual modes of authentication."

The majority, however, did not pass on the merits of Yamashita's procedural challenges because it concluded that his status disentitled him to any protection under the Articles of War (specifically, those set forth in Article 38, which would become Article 36 of the UCMJ) or the Geneva Convention of 1929, 47 Stat. 2021 (1929 Geneva Convention). The Court explained that Yamashita was neither a "person made subject to the Articles of War by Article 2" thereof, 327 U.S., at 20, nor a protected prisoner of war being tried for crimes committed during his detention, *id.*, at 21.

At least partially in response to subsequent criticism of General Yamashita's trial, the UCMJ's codification of the Articles of War after World War II expanded the category of persons subject thereto to include defendants in Yamashita's (and Hamdan's) position, and the Third Geneva Convention of 1949 extended prisoner-of-war protections to individuals tried for crimes committed before their capture. See 3 Int'l Comm. of Red Cross, Commentary: Geneva Convention Relative to the Treatment of Prisoners of War 413 (1960) (hereinafter GCIII Commentary) (explaining that Article 85, which extends the Convention's protections to "[p]risoners of war prosecuted under the laws of the Detaining Power for acts committed prior to capture," was adopted in response to judicial interpretations of the 1929 Convention, including this Court's decision in *Yamashita*). The most notorious exception to the principle of uniformity, then, has been stripped of its precedential value.

The uniformity principle is not an inflexible one; it does not preclude all departures from the procedures dictated for use by courts-martial. But any departure must be tailored to the exigency that necessitates it. See Winthrop 835, n. 81. That understanding is reflected in Article 36 of the UCMJ, which provides:

> "(a) The procedure, including modes of proof, in cases before courts-martial, courts of inquiry, military commissions, and other military tribunals may be prescribed by the President by regulations which shall, so far as he considers practicable, apply the principles of law and the rules of evidence generally recognized in the trial of criminal cases in the United States district courts, but which may not be contrary to or inconsistent with this chapter.

> "(b) All rules and regulations made under this article shall be uniform insofar as practicable and shall be reported to Congress." 70A Stat. 50.

Article 36 places two restrictions on the President's power to promulgate rules of procedure for courts-martial and military commissions alike. First, no procedural rule he adopts may be "contrary to or inconsistent with" the UCMJ-however practical it may seem. Second, the rules adopted must be "uniform insofar as practicable." That is, the rules applied to military commissions must be the same as those applied to courts-martial unless such uniformity proves impracticable.

Hamdan argues that Commission Order No. 1 violates both of these restrictions; he maintains that the procedures described in the Commission Order are inconsistent with the UCMJ and that the Government has offered no explanation for their deviation from the procedures governing courts-martial, which are set forth in the Manual for Courts–Martial, United States (2005 ed.) (Manual for Courts–Martial). Among the inconsistencies Hamdan identifies is that between § 6 of the Commission Order, which permits exclusion of the accused from proceedings and denial of his access to evidence in certain circumstances, and the UCMJ's requirement that "[a]ll ... proceedings" other than votes and deliberations by courts-martial "shall be made a part of the record and shall be in the presence of the accused." 10 U.S.C.A. § 839(c) (Supp. 2006). Hamdan also observes that the Commission Order dispenses with virtually all evidentiary rules applicable in courts-martial.

The Government has three responses. First, it argues, only 9 of the UCMJ's 158 Articles-the ones that expressly mention "military commissions" actually apply to commissions, and Commission Order No. 1 sets forth no procedure that is "contrary to or inconsistent with" those 9 provisions. Second, the Government contends, military commissions would be of no use if the President were hamstrung by those provisions of the UCMJ that govern courts-martial. Finally, the President's determination that "the danger to the safety of the United States and the nature of international terrorism" renders it impracticable "to apply in military commissions ... the principles of law and rules of evidence generally recognized in the trial of criminal cases in the United States district courts," November 13 Order § 1(f), is, in the Government's view, explanation enough for any deviation from court-martial procedures. See Brief for Respondents 43–47, and n. 22.

Hamdan has the better of this argument. Without reaching the question whether any provision of Commission Order No. 1 is strictly "contrary to or inconsistent with" other provisions of the UCMJ, we conclude that the "practicability" determination the President has made is insufficient to justify variances from the procedures governing courts-martial. Subsection (b) of Article 36 was added after World War II, and requires a different showing of impracticability from the one required by subsection (a). Subsection (a) requires that the rules the President promulgates for courts-martial, provost courts, and military commissions alike conform to those that govern procedures in *Article III courts*, "so far as *he considers* practicable." 10 U.S.C. § 836(a) (emphasis added). Subsection (b), by contrast, demands that the rules applied in courts-martial, provost courts, and military commissions-whether or not they conform with the Federal Rules of Evidence-be "uniform *insofar as practicable*." § 836(b) (emphasis added). Under the latter provision, then, the rules set forth in the Manual for Courts–Martial must apply to military commissions unless impracticable.

The President here has determined, pursuant to subsection (a), that it is impracticable to apply the rules and principles of law that govern "the trial of criminal cases in the United States district courts," § 836(a), to Hamdan's commission. We assume that complete deference is owed that determination. The President has not, however, made a similar official determination that it is impracticable to apply the rules for courts-martial. And even if subsection (b)'s requirements may be satisfied without such an official determination, the requirements of that subsection are not satisfied here.

Nothing in the record before us demonstrates that it would be impracticable to apply court-martial rules in this case. There is no suggestion, for example, of any logistical difficulty in securing properly sworn and authenticated evidence or in applying the usual principles of relevance and admissibility. Assuming *arguendo* that the reasons articulated in the President's Article 36(a) determination ought to be considered in evaluating the impracticability of applying court-martial rules, the only reason offered in support of that determination is the danger posed by international terrorism. Without for one moment underestimating that danger, it is not evident to us why it should require, in the case of Hamdan's trial, any variance from the rules that govern courts-martial.

The absence of any showing of impracticability is particularly disturbing when considered in light of the clear and admitted failure to apply one of the most fundamental protections afforded not just by the Manual for Courts–Martial but also by the UCMJ itself: the right to be present. See 10 U.S.C.A. § 839(c) (Supp. 2006). Whether or not that departure technically is "contrary to or inconsistent with" the terms of the UCMJ, 10 U.S.C. § 836(a), the jettisoning of so basic a right cannot lightly be excused as "practicable."

Under the circumstances, then, the rules applicable in courts-martial must apply. Since it is undisputed that Commission Order No. 1 deviates in many significant respects from those rules, it necessarily violates Article 36(b).

The Government's objection that requiring compliance with the court-martial rules imposes an undue burden both ignores the plain meaning of Article 36(b) and misunderstands the purpose and the history of military commissions. The military commission was not born of a desire to dispense a more summary form of justice than is afforded by courts-martial; it developed, rather, as a tribunal of necessity to be employed when courts-martial lacked jurisdiction over either the accused or the subject matter. See Winthrop 831. Exigency lent the commission its legitimacy, but did not further justify the wholesale jettisoning of procedural protections. That history explains why the military commission's procedures typically have been the ones used by courts-martial. That the jurisdiction of the two tribunals today may sometimes overlap, see *Madsen*, 343 U.S., at 354, does not detract from the force of this history; Article 21 did not transform the military commission from a tribunal of true exigency into a more convenient adjudicatory tool. Article 36, confirming as much, strikes a careful balance between uniform procedure and the need to accommodate exigencies that may sometimes arise in a theater of war. That Article not having been complied with here, the rules specified for Hamdan's trial are illegal.

D

The procedures adopted to try Hamdan also violate the Geneva Conventions. . . .

i

The Court of Appeals relied on *Johnson* v. *Eisentrager,* 339 U.S. 763 (1950), to hold that Hamdan could not invoke the Geneva Conventions to challenge the Government's plan to prosecute him in accordance with Commission Order No. 1. *Eisentrager* involved a challenge by 21 German nationals to their 1945 convictions for war crimes by a military tribunal convened in Nanking, China, and to their subsequent imprisonment in occupied Germany. The petitioners argued, *inter alia*, that the 1929 Geneva Convention rendered illegal some of the procedures employed during their trials, which they said deviated impermissibly from the procedures used by courts-martial to try American soldiers. We rejected that claim on the merits because the petitioners (unlike Hamdan here) had failed to identify any prejudicial disparity "between the Commission that tried [them] and those that would try an offending soldier of the American forces of like rank," and in any event could claim no protection, under the 1929 Convention, during trials for crimes that occurred before their confinement as prisoners of war.

Buried in a footnote of the opinion, however, is this curious statement suggesting that the Court lacked power even to consider the merits of the Geneva Convention argument:

> "We are not holding that these prisoners have no right which the military authorities are bound to respect. The United States, by the Geneva Convention of July 27, 1929, 47 Stat. 2021, concluded with forty-six other countries, including the German Reich, an agreement upon the treatment to be accorded captives. These prisoners claim to be and are entitled to its protection. It is, however, the obvious scheme of the Agreement that responsibility for observance and enforcement of these rights is upon political and military authorities. Rights of alien enemies are vindicated under it only through protests and intervention of protecting powers as the rights of our citizens against foreign governments are vindicated only by Presidential intervention." *Id.*, at 789, n. 14.

The Court of Appeals, on the strength of this footnote, held that "the 1949 Geneva Convention does not confer upon Hamdan a right to enforce its provisions in court." 415 F. 3d, at 40.

Whatever else might be said about the *Eisentrager* footnote, it does not control this case. We may assume that "the obvious scheme" of the 1949 Conventions is identical in all relevant respects to that of the 1929

Convention, and even that that scheme would, absent some other provision of law, preclude Hamdan's invocation of the Convention's provisions as an independent source of law binding the Government's actions and furnishing petitioner with any enforceable right. For, regardless of the nature of the rights conferred on Hamdan, they are, as the Government does not dispute, part of the law of war. See *Hamdi*, 542 U.S., at 520–521 (plurality opinion). And compliance with the law of war is the condition upon which the authority set forth in Article 21 is granted.

ii

For the Court of Appeals, acknowledgment of that condition was no bar to Hamdan's trial by commission. As an alternative to its holding that Hamdan could not invoke the Geneva Conventions at all, the Court of Appeals concluded that the Conventions did not in any event apply to the armed conflict during which Hamdan was captured. The court accepted the Executive's assertions that Hamdan was captured in connection with the United States' war with al Qaeda and that that war is distinct from the war with the Taliban in Afghanistan. It further reasoned that the war with al Qaeda evades the reach of the Geneva Conventions. See 415 F. 3d, at 41–42. We, like Judge Williams, disagree with the latter conclusion.

The conflict with al Qaeda is not, according to the Government, a conflict to which the full protections afforded detainees under the 1949 Geneva Conventions apply because Article 2 of those Conventions (which appears in all four Conventions) renders the full protections applicable only to "all cases of declared war or of any other armed conflict which may arise between two or more of the High Contracting Parties." 6 U.S.T., at 3318. Since Hamdan was captured and detained incident to the conflict with al Qaeda and not the conflict with the Taliban, and since al Qaeda, unlike Afghanistan, is not a "High Contracting Party"—*i.e.*, a signatory of the Conventions, the protections of those Conventions are not, it is argued, applicable to Hamdan.

We need not decide the merits of this argument because there is at least one provision of the Geneva Conventions that applies here even if the relevant conflict is not one between signatories. Article 3, often referred to as Common Article 3 because, like Article 2, it appears in all four Geneva Conventions, provides that in a "conflict not of an international character occurring in the territory of one of the High Contracting Parties, each Party to the conflict shall be bound to apply, as a minimum," certain provisions protecting "[p]ersons taking no active part in the hostilities, including members of armed forces who have laid down their arms and those placed *hors de combat* by ... detention." One such provision prohibits "the passing of sentences and the carrying out of executions without previous judgment pronounced by a regularly constituted court affording all the judicial guarantees which are recognized as indispensable by civilized peoples." *Ibid*.

The Court of Appeals thought, and the Government asserts, that Common Article 3 does not apply to Hamdan because the conflict with al

Qaeda, being " 'international in scope,' " does not qualify as a " 'conflict not of an international character.' " 415 F. 3d, at 41. That reasoning is erroneous. The term "conflict not of an international character" is used here in contradistinction to a conflict between nations. So much is demonstrated by the "fundamental logic [of] the Convention's provisions on its application." *Id.*, at 44 (Williams, J., concurring). Common Article 2 provides that "the present Convention shall apply to all cases of declared war or of any other armed conflict which may arise between two or more of the High Contracting Parties." 6 U.S.T., at 3318 (Art. 2, ¶ 1). High Contracting Parties (signatories) also must abide by all terms of the Conventions vis—vis one another even if one party to the conflict is a nonsignatory "Power," and must so abide vis—vis the nonsignatory if "the latter accepts and applies" those terms. *Ibid.* (Art. 2, ¶ 3). Common Article 3, by contrast, affords some minimal protection, falling short of full protection under the Conventions, to individuals associated with neither a signatory nor even a nonsignatory "Power" who are involved in a conflict "in the territory of" a signatory. The latter kind of conflict is distinguishable from the conflict described in Common Article 2 chiefly because it does not involve a clash between nations (whether signatories or not). In context, then, the phrase "not of an international character" bears its literal meaning. See, *e.g.*, J. Bentham, Introduction to the Principles of Morals and Legislation 6, 296 (J. Burns & H. Hart eds. 1970) (using the term "international law" as a "new though not inexpressive appellation" meaning "betwixt nation and nation"; defining "international" to include "mutual transactions between sovereigns as such"); Commentary on the Additional Protocols to the Geneva Conventions of 12 August 1949, p. 1351 (1987) ("[A] non-international armed conflict is distinct from an international armed conflict because of the legal status of the entities opposing each other").

Although the official commentaries accompanying Common Article 3 indicate that an important purpose of the provision was to furnish minimal protection to rebels involved in one kind of "conflict not of an international character," *i.e.*, a civil war, see GCIII Commentary 36–37, the commentaries also make clear "that the scope of the Article must be as wide as possible," *id.*, at 36. In fact, limiting language that would have rendered Common Article 3 applicable "especially [to] cases of civil war, colonial conflicts, or wars of religion," was omitted from the final version of the Article, which coupled broader scope of application with a narrower range of rights than did earlier proposed iterations. See GCIII Commentary 42–43.

iii

Common Article 3, then, is applicable here and, as indicated above, requires that Hamdan be tried by a "regularly constituted court affording all the judicial guarantees which are recognized as indispensable by civilized peoples." 6 U.S.T., at 3320 (Art. 3, ¶ 1(d)). While the term "regularly constituted court" is not specifically defined in either Common

Article 3 or its accompanying commentary, other sources disclose its core meaning. The commentary accompanying a provision of the Fourth Geneva Convention, for example, defines " 'regularly constituted' " tribunals to include "ordinary military courts" and "definitely exclud[e] all special tribunals." GCIV Commentary 340 (defining the term "properly constituted" in Article 66, which the commentary treats as identical to "regularly constituted"); . . . .

The Government offers only a cursory defense of Hamdan's military commission in light of Common Article 3. See Brief for Respondents 49–50. As Justice Kennedy explains, that defense fails because "[t]he regular military courts in our system are the courts-martial established by congressional statutes." At a minimum, a military commission "can be 'regularly constituted' by the standards of our military justice system only if some practical need explains deviations from court-martial practice." As we have explained, see Part VI–C, *supra*, no such need has been demonstrated here.

iv

Inextricably intertwined with the question of regular constitution is the evaluation of the procedures governing the tribunal and whether they afford "all the judicial guarantees which are recognized as indispensable by civilized peoples." 6 U.S.T., at 3320 (Art. 3, ¶ 1(d)). Like the phrase "regularly constituted court," this phrase is not defined in the text of the Geneva Conventions. But it must be understood to incorporate at least the barest of those trial protections that have been recognized by customary international law. Many of these are described in Article 75 of Protocol I to the Geneva Conventions of 1949, adopted in 1977 (Protocol I). Although the United States declined to ratify Protocol I, its objections were not to Article 75 thereof. Indeed, it appears that the Government "regard[s] the provisions of Article 75 as an articulation of safeguards to which all persons in the hands of an enemy are entitled." Taft, The Law of Armed Conflict After 9/11: Some Salient Features, 28 Yale J. Int'l L. 319, 322 (2003). Among the rights set forth in Article 75 is the "right to be tried in [one's] presence." Protocol I, Art. 75(4)(e).

We agree with Justice Kennedy that the procedures adopted to try Hamdan deviate from those governing courts-martial in ways not justified by any "evident practical need," *post*, at 11, and for that reason, at least, fail to afford the requisite guarantees. We add only that, as noted in Part VI–A, *supra*, various provisions of Commission Order No. 1 dispense with the principles, articulated in Article 75 and indisputably part of the customary international law, that an accused must, absent disruptive conduct or consent, be present for his trial and must be privy to the evidence against him. See §§ 6(B)(3), (D). That the Government has a compelling interest in denying Hamdan access to certain sensitive information is not doubted. But, at least absent express statutory provision to the contrary, information used to convict a person of a crime must be disclosed to him.

V

Common Article 3 obviously tolerates a great degree of flexibility in trying individuals captured during armed conflict; its requirements are general ones, crafted to accommodate a wide variety of legal systems. But *requirements* they are nonetheless. The commission that the President has convened to try Hamdan does not meet those requirements.

VII

We have assumed, as we must, that the allegations made in the Government's charge against Hamdan are true. We have assumed, moreover, the truth of the message implicit in that charge—viz., that Hamdan is a dangerous individual whose beliefs, if acted upon, would cause great harm and even death to innocent civilians, and who would act upon those beliefs if given the opportunity. It bears emphasizing that Hamdan does not challenge, and we do not today address, the Government's power to detain him for the duration of active hostilities in order to prevent such harm. But in undertaking to try Hamdan and subject him to criminal punishment, the Executive is bound to comply with the Rule of Law that prevails in this jurisdiction.

The judgment of the Court of Appeals is reversed, and the case is remanded for further proceedings.

It is so ordered.

The Chief Justice took no part in the consideration or decision of this case.

JUSTICE BREYER, with whom JUSTICE KENNEDY, JUSTICE SOUTER, and JUSTICE GINSBURG join, concurring.

The dissenters say that today's decision would "sorely hamper the President's ability to confront and defeat a new and deadly enemy." (opinion of Thomas, J.). They suggest that it undermines our Nation's ability to "preven[t] future attacks" of the grievous sort that we have already suffered. That claim leads me to state briefly what I believe the majority sets forth both explicitly and implicitly at greater length. The Court's conclusion ultimately rests upon a single ground: Congress has not issued the Executive a "blank check." Cf. *Hamdi* v. *Rumsfeld,* 542 U.S. 507, 536 (2004) (plurality opinion). Indeed, Congress has denied the President the legislative authority to create military commissions of the kind at issue here. Nothing prevents the President from returning to Congress to seek the authority he believes necessary.

Where, as here, no emergency prevents consultation with Congress, judicial insistence upon that consultation does not weaken our Nation's ability to deal with danger. To the contrary, that insistence strengthens the Nation's ability to determine-through democratic means-how best to do so. The Constitution places its faith in those democratic means. Our Court today simply does the same.

JUSTICE KENNEDY, with whom JUSTICE SOUTER, JUSTICE GINSBURG, and JUSTICE BREYER join as to Parts I and II (Ed. Part II of the Opinion of the Court has not been reproduced here), concurring in part.

Military Commission Order No. 1, which governs the military commission established to try petitioner Salim Hamdan for war crimes, exceeds limits that certain statutes, duly enacted by Congress, have placed on the President's authority to convene military courts. This is not a case, then, where the Executive can assert some unilateral authority to fill a void left by congressional inaction. It is a case where Congress, in the proper exercise of its powers as an independent branch of government, and as part of a long tradition of legislative involvement in matters of military justice, has considered the subject of military tribunals and set limits on the President's authority. Where a statute provides the conditions for the exercise of governmental power, its requirements are the result of a deliberative and reflective process engaging both of the political branches. Respect for laws derived from the customary operation of the Executive and Legislative Branches gives some assurance of stability in time of crisis. The Constitution is best preserved by reliance on standards tested over time and insulated from the pressures of the moment.

These principles seem vindicated here, for a case that may be of extraordinary importance is resolved by ordinary rules. The rules of most relevance here are those pertaining to the authority of Congress and the interpretation of its enactments.

It seems appropriate to recite these rather fundamental points because the Court refers, as it should in its exposition of the case, to the requirement of the Geneva Conventions of 1949 that military tribunals be "regularly constituted"—a requirement that controls here, if for no other reason, because Congress requires that military commissions like the ones at issue conform to the "law of war," 10 U.S.C. § 821. Whatever the substance and content of the term "regularly constituted" as interpreted in this and any later cases, there seems little doubt that it relies upon the importance of standards deliberated upon and chosen in advance of crisis, under a system where the single power of the Executive is checked by other constitutional mechanisms. All of which returns us to the point of beginning-that domestic statutes control this case. If Congress, after due consideration, deems it appropriate to change the controlling statutes, in conformance with the Constitution and other laws, it has the power and prerogative to do so.

I join the Court's opinion, save Parts V and VI–D-iv. To state my reasons for this reservation, and to show my agreement with the remainder of the Court's analysis by identifying particular deficiencies in the military commissions at issue, this separate opinion seems appropriate.

I

Trial by military commission raises separation-of-powers concerns of the highest order. Located within a single branch, these courts carry the risk that offenses will be defined, prosecuted, and adjudicated by executive officials without independent review. Concentration of power puts personal liberty in peril of arbitrary action by officials, an incursion the Constitution's three-part system is designed to avoid. It is imperative, then, that when military tribunals are established, full and proper authority exists for the Presidential directive.

The proper framework for assessing whether Executive actions are authorized is the three-part scheme used by Justice Jackson in his opinion in *Youngstown Sheet & Tube Co.* v. *Sawyer,* 343 U.S. 579 (1952). "When the President acts pursuant to an express or implied authorization of Congress, his authority is at its maximum, for it includes all that he possesses in his own right plus all that Congress can delegate." *Id.*, at 635. "When the President acts in absence of either a congressional grant or denial of authority, he can only rely upon his own independent powers, but there is a zone of twilight in which he and Congress may have concurrent authority, or in which its distribution is uncertain." *Id.*, at 637. And "[w]hen the President takes measures incompatible with the expressed or implied will of Congress, his power is at its lowest ebb." *Ibid.*

In this case, as the Court observes, the President has acted in a field with a history of congressional participation and regulation. . . . While these laws provide authority for certain forms of military courts, they also impose limitations, at least two of which control this case. If the President has exceeded these limits, this becomes a case of conflict between Presidential and congressional action—a case within Justice Jackson's third category, not the second or first.

. . . Again, however, courts-martial provide the relevant benchmark. Subject to constitutional limitations, Congress has the power and responsibility to determine the necessity for military courts, and to provide the jurisdiction and procedures applicable to them. The guidance Congress has provided with respect to courts-martial indicates the level of independence and procedural rigor that Congress has deemed necessary, at least as a general matter, in the military context.

   . . .

At a minimum a military commission like the one at issue-a commission specially convened by the President to try specific persons without express congressional authorization—can be "regularly constituted" by the standards of our military justice system only if some practical need explains deviations from court-martial practice. In this regard the standard of Common Article 3, applied here in conformity with § 821, parallels the practicability standard of § 836(b). Section 836, however, is limited by its terms to matters properly characterized as procedural-that is, "[p]retrial, trial, and post-trial procedures"—while Common Article 3 permits broader consideration of matters of structure, organization, and mechanisms to promote the tribunal's insulation from command influence. Thus the combined effect of the two statutes discussed here-§§ 836 and 821—is that considerations of practicability must support departures from court-martial practice. Relevant concerns, as noted earlier, relate to logistical constraints, accommodation of witnesses, security of the proceedings, and the like, not mere expedience or convenience. This determination, of course, must be made with due regard for the constitutional principle that congressional statutes can be controlling, including the congressional direction that the law of war has a bearing on the determination.

These principles provide the framework for an analysis of the specific military commission at issue here.

II

In assessing the validity of Hamdan's military commission the precise circumstances of this case bear emphasis. The allegations against Hamdan are undoubtedly serious. Captured in Afghanistan during our Nation's armed conflict with the Taliban and al Qaeda—a conflict that continues as we speak—Hamdan stands accused of overt acts in furtherance of a conspiracy to commit terrorism: delivering weapons and ammunition to al Qaeda, acquiring trucks for use by Osama bin Laden's bodyguards, providing security services to bin Laden, and receiving weapons training at a terrorist camp. Nevertheless, the circumstances of Hamdan's trial present no exigency requiring special speed or precluding careful consideration of evidence. For roughly four years, Hamdan has been detained at a permanent United States military base in Guantanamo Bay, Cuba. And regardless of the outcome of the criminal proceedings at issue, the Government claims authority to continue to detain him based on his status as an enemy combatant.

Against this background, the Court is correct to conclude that the military commission the President has convened to try Hamdan is unauthorized. The following analysis, which expands on the Court's discussion, explains my reasons for reaching this conclusion.

To begin with, the structure and composition of the military commission deviate from conventional court-martial standards. Although these deviations raise questions about the fairness of the trial, no evident practical need explains them.

Under the UCMJ, courts-martial are organized by a "convening authority"—either a commanding officer, the Secretary of Defense, the Secretary concerned, or the President. 10 U.S.C. §§ 822–824 (2000 ed. and Supp. III). The convening authority refers charges for trial, Manual for Courts–Martial, United States, Rule for Courts–Martial 401 (2005 ed.) (hereinafter R. C. M.), and selects the court-martial members who vote on the guilt or innocence of the accused and determine the sentence, 10 U.S.C. §§ 825(d)(2), 851–852 (2000 ed.); R. C. M. 503(a). Paralleling this structure, under Military Commission Order No. 1 an " 'Appointing Authority' "—either the Secretary of Defense or the Secretary's "designee"—establishes commissions subject to the order, MCO No. 1, § 2, approves and refers charges to be tried by those commissions, § 4(B)(2)(a), and appoints commission members who vote on the conviction and sentence, §§ 4(A)(1–3). In addition the Appointing Authority determines the number of commission members (at least three), oversees the chief prose-cutor, provides "investigative or other resources" to the defense insofar as he or she "deems necessary for a full and fair trial," approves or rejects plea agreements, approves or disapproves communications with news media by prosecution or defense counsel (a function shared by the General Counsel of the Department of Defense), and issues supplementary com-mission regulations (subject to approval by the General Counsel of the Department of Defense, unless the Appointing Authority is the Secretary of Defense). See MCO No. 1, §§ 4(A)(2), 5(H), 6(A)(4), 7(A); Military Commission Instruction No. 3, § 5(C) (July 15, 2005) (hereinafter MCI), available at www.defenselink.mil/news/Aug2005/d20050811MC13.pdf; MCI No. 4, § 5(C) (Sept. 16, 2005), available at www.defenselink.mil/news/Oct 2005/d20051003MCI4.pdf; MCI No. 6, § 3(B)(3) (April 15, 2004), available at www.defenselink.mil/news/Apr2004/d20040420ins6.pdf (all Internet ma-terials as visited June 27, 2006, and available in Clerk of Court's case file).

Against the background of these significant powers for the Appointing Authority, which in certain respects at least conform to ordinary court-martial standards, the regulations governing the commissions at issue make several noteworthy departures. At a general court-martial—the only type authorized to impose penalties of more than one year's incarceration or to adjudicate offenses against the law of war, R. C. M. 201(f); 10 U.S.C. §§ 818–820 (2000 ed. and Supp. III)—the presiding officer who rules on legal issues must be a military judge. R. C. M. 501(a)(1), 801(a)(4)–(5); 10 U.S.C. § 816(1) (2000 ed., Supp. III); see also R. C. M. 201(f)(2)(B)(ii) (likewise requiring a military judge for certain other courts-martial); 10 U.S.C. § 819 (2000 ed. and Supp. III) (same). A military judge is an officer who is a member of a state or federal bar and has been specially certified for judicial duties by the Judge Advocate General for the officer's Armed Service. R. C. M. 502(c); 10 U.S.C. § 826(b). To protect their indepen-dence, military judges at general courts-martial are "assigned and directly responsible to the Judge Advocate General or the Judge Advocate Gener-al's designee." R. C. M. 502(c). They must be detailed to the court, in accordance with applicable regulations, "by a person assigned as a mili-tary judge and directly responsible to the Judge Advocate General or the Judge Advocate General's designee." R. C. M. 503(b); see also 10 U.S.C. § 826(c); see generally *Weiss* v. *United States,* 510 U.S. 163, 179–181 (1994) (discussing provisions that "insulat[e] military judges from the effects of command influence" and thus "preserve judicial impartiality"). Here, by contrast, the Appointing Authority selects the presiding officer, MCO No. 1, §§ 4(A)(1), (A)(4); and that officer need only be a judge advocate, that is, a military lawyer, § 4(A)(4).

The Appointing Authority, moreover, exercises supervisory powers that continue during trial. Any interlocutory question "the disposition of which would effect a termination of proceedings with respect to a charge" is subject to decision not by the presiding officer, but by the Appointing Authority. § 4(A)(5)(e) (stating that the presiding officer "shall certify" such questions to the Appointing Authority). Other interlocutory questions may be certified to the Appointing Authority as the presiding officer "deems appropriate." *Ibid.* While in some circumstances the Government may appeal certain rulings at a court-martial—including "an order or ruling that terminates the proceedings with respect to a charge or specification," R. C. M. 908(a); see also 10 U. S. C. § 862(a)—the appeals go to a body called the Court of Criminal Appeals, not to the convening authority. R. C. M. 908; 10 U.S.C. § 862(b); see also R. C. M. 1107 (requiring the convening authority to approve or disapprove the findings and sentence of a court-martial but providing for such action only after entry of sentence and restricting actions that increase penalties); 10 U.S.C. § 860 (same); cf. § 837(a) (barring command influence on court-martial actions). The Court of Criminal Appeals functions as the military's intermediate appeals court; it is established by the Judge Advocate General for each Armed Service and composed of appellate military judges. R. C. M. 1203; 10 U.S.C. § 866. This is another means in which, by structure and tradition, the court-martial process is insulated from those who have an interest in the outcome of the proceedings.

Finally, in addition to these powers with respect to the presiding officer, the Appointing Authority has greater flexibility in appointing commission members. While a general court-martial requires, absent a contrary election by the accused, at least five members, R. C. M. 501(a)(1); 10 U.S.C. § 816(1) (2000 ed. and Supp. III), the Appointing Authority here is free, as noted earlier, to select as few as three. MCO No. 1, § 4(A)(2). This difference may affect the deliberative process and the prosecution's burden of persuasion.

As compared to the role of the convening authority in a court-martial, the greater powers of the Appointing Authority here—including even the resolution of dispositive issues in the middle of the trial—raise concerns that the commission's decisionmaking may not be neutral. If the differences are supported by some practical need beyond the goal of constant and ongoing supervision, that need is neither apparent from the record nor established by the Government's submissions.

It is no answer that, at the end of the day, the Detainee Treatment Act of 2005 (DTA), 119 Stat. 2739, affords military-commission defendants the opportunity for judicial review in federal court. As the Court is correct to observe, the scope of that review is limited, DTA § 1005(e)(3)(D), *id.,* at 2743; and the review is not automatic if the defendant's sentence is under 10 years, § 1005(e)(3)(B), *ibid* . . . .

These structural differences between the military commissions and courts-martial—the concentration of functions, including legal decisionmaking, in a single executive official; the less rigorous standards for composition of the tribunal; and the creation of special review procedures in place of institutions created and regulated by Congress—remove safeguards that are important to the fairness of the proceedings and the independence of the court. Congress has prescribed these guarantees for courts-martial; and no evident practical need explains the departures here.

For these reasons the commission cannot be considered regularly constituted under United States law and thus does not satisfy Congress' requirement that military commissions conform to the law of war.

Apart from these structural issues, moreover, the basic procedures for the commissions deviate from procedures for courts-martial, in violation of § 836(b). As the Court explains, *ante*, the Military Commission Order abandons the detailed Military Rules of Evidence, which are modeled on the Federal Rules of Evidence in conformity with § 836(a)'s requirement of presumptive compliance with district-court rules.

Instead, the order imposes just one evidentiary rule: "Evidence shall be admitted if . . . the evidence would have probative value to a reasonable person," MCO No. 1, § 6(D)(1). Although it is true some military commissions applied an amorphous evidence standard in the past, see, *e.g.*, 1 Law Reports 117–118 (discussing World War II military commission orders); Exec. Order No. 9185, 7 Fed. Reg. 5103 (1942) (order convening military commission to try Nazi saboteurs), the evidentiary rules for those commissions were adopted before Congress enacted the uniformity requirement of 10 U.S.C. § 836(b) as part of the UCMJ, see Act of May 5, 1950, ch. 169, 64 Stat. 107, 120, 149. And while some flexibility may be necessary to permit trial of battlefield captives like Hamdan, military statutes and rules already provide for introduction of deposition testimony for absent witnesses, 10 U.S.C. § 849(d); R. C. M. 702, and use of classified information, Military Rule Evid. 505. Indeed, the deposition—testimony provision specifically mentions military commissions and thus is one of the provisions the Government concedes must be followed by the commission at issue. That provision authorizes admission of deposition testimony only if the witness is absent for specified reasons, § 849(d)-a requirement that makes no sense if military commissions may consider all probative evidence. Whether or not this conflict renders the rules at issue "contrary to or inconsistent with" the UCMJ under § 836(a), it creates a uniformity problem under § 836(b).

The rule here could permit admission of multiple hearsay and other forms of evidence generally prohibited on grounds of unreliability. Indeed, the commission regulations specifically contemplate admission of unsworn written statements, MCO No. 1, § 6(D)(3); and they make no provision for exclusion of coerced declarations save those "established to have been made as a result of torture," MCI No. 10, § 3(A) (Mar. 24, 2006), available at www.defenselink.mil/news/Mar2006/d20060327MCI10.pdf; cf. Military Rule Evid. 304(c)(3) (generally barring use of statements obtained "through the use of coercion, unlawful influence, or unlawful inducement"); 10 U.S.C. § 831(d) (same). Besides, even if evidence is deemed nonprobative by the presiding officer at Hamdan's trial, the military-commission members still may view it. In another departure from court-martial practice the military commission members may object to the presiding officer's evidence rulings and determine themselves, by majority vote, whether to admit the evidence. MCO No. 1, § 6(D)(1); cf. R. C. M.

801(a)(4), (e)(1) (providing that the military judge at a court-martial determines all questions of law).

As the Court explains, the Government has made no demonstration of practical need for these special rules and procedures, either in this particular case or as to the military commissions in general; nor is any such need self-evident. For all the Government's regulations and submissions reveal, it would be feasible for most, if not all, of the conventional military evidence rules and procedures to be followed.

In sum, as presently structured, Hamdan's military commission exceeds the bounds Congress has placed on the President's authority in §§ 836 and 821 of the UCMJ. Because Congress has prescribed these limits, Congress can change them, requiring a new analysis consistent with the Constitution and other governing laws. At this time, however, we must apply the standards Congress has provided. By those standards the military commission is deficient.

III

In light of the conclusion that the military commission here is unauthorized under the UCMJ, I see no need to consider several further issues addressed in the plurality opinion by Justice Stevens and the dissent by Justice Thomas.

First, I would not decide whether Common Article 3's standard—a "regularly constituted court affording all the judicial guarantees which are recognized as indispensable by civilized peoples," 6 U.S.T., at 3320 (¶ (1)(d))—necessarily requires that the accused have the right to be present at all stages of a criminal trial. As Justice Stevens explains, Military Commission Order No. 1 authorizes exclusion of the accused from the proceedings if the presiding officer determines that, among other things, protection of classified information so requires. See §§ 6(B)(3), (D)(5); Justice Stevens observes that these regulations create the possibility of a conviction and sentence based on evidence Hamdan has not seen or heard—a possibility the plurality is correct to consider troubling. . . .

As the dissent by Justice Thomas points out, however, the regulations bar the presiding officer from admitting secret evidence if doing so would deprive the accused of a "full and fair trial." MCO No. 1, § 6(D)(5)(b); [t]his fairness determination, moreover, is unambiguously subject to judicial review under the DTA. See § 1005(e)(3)(D)(i), 119 Stat. 2743 (allowing review of compliance with the "standards and procedures" in Military Commission Order No. 1). The evidentiary proceedings at Hamdan's trial have yet to commence, and it remains to be seen whether he will suffer any prejudicial exclusion.

There should be reluctance, furthermore, to reach unnecessarily the question whether, as the plurality seems to conclude, Article 75 of Protocol I to the Geneva Conventions is binding law notwithstanding the earlier decision by our Government not to accede to the Protocol. For all these reasons, and without detracting from the importance of the right of presence, I would rely on other deficiencies noted here and in the opinion by the Court—deficiencies that relate to the structure and procedure of the commission and that inevitably will affect the proceedings—as the basis for finding the military commissions lack authorization under 10 U.S.C. § 836 and fail to be regularly constituted under Common Article 3 and § 821.

I likewise see no need to address the validity of the conspiracy charge against Hamdan—an issue addressed at length in Part V of Justice Stevens' opinion and in Part II–C of Justice Thomas' dissent (Ed. not reproduced here). In light of the conclusion that the military commissions at issue are unauthorized Congress may choose to provide further guidance in this area. Congress, not the Court, is the branch in the better position to undertake the "sensitive task of establishing a principle not inconsistent with the national interest or international justice." *Banco Nacional de Cuba* v. *Sabbatino,* 376 U. S. 398, 428 (1964).

Finally, for the same reason, I express no view on the merits of other limitations on military commissions described as elements of the common law of war in Part V of Justice Stevens' opinion.

With these observations I join the Court's opinion with the exception of Parts V and VI–D–iv.

[ROBERTS, C.J. took no part in the consideration or decision of the case. JUSTICES SCALIA, THOMAS and ALITO each filed dissenting opinions joined variously by the other two dissenting justices.]

5. THE RESPONSE TO HAMDAN—CONGRESSION-AL ENACTMENT OF THE MILITARY COMMIS-SIONS ACT OF 2006, AND LATER, THE MILI-TARY COMMISSIONS ACT OF 2009

In Hamdan, a number of the Justices had indicated that in establishing the military commissions, the President had acted without legislative authority. Congress responded quickly by enacting the Military Commissions Act (MCA) in the early fall, 2006. The MCA of 2006 contained provisions authorizing the establishment of military commissions by the President and generally prescribed procedures and some rules of evidence, as well as related matters. The Act also listed and defined offenses that arc triable before the commissions. [The Act also withdrew habeas corpus jurisdiction and provided for an exclusive route for judicial review of decisions of the military commissions. These latter provisions were addressed by the Supreme Court in the Boumediene case supra, chapter 10.] Subsequently, in 2009, at the instance of the Obama administration, the Military Commissions Act of 2009 was enacted, which amended the 2006 Act in a number of important respects. The provisions below are from the MCA of 2009.

[Note: In 2010, a revised Manual for Military Commissions was issued; it, of course, tracks the statute, but also contains more detailed provisions, including, for example, a very detailed set of rules of evidence. The Manual is available at www.defense.gov/news/2010_Manual_for_Military_Commissions.pdf]

The portion of the provisions of the MCA of 2009 reproduced in subsection C are intended to provide an overall sense of the structure of the commissions and their operating ground rules These provisions, for example, provide a window into the composition of the military commissions; how representatives for the prosecution and defense are provided; decision-making processes; basic procedures; and certain important rules of evidence. The provisions in the 2009 MCA describing and defining the crimes that may be charged in commissions proceedings are also reproduced below.

Among the provisions of the 2009 Act, certain key provisions mainly dealing with issues of evidentiary admissibility are reproduced in bold type in subsection C. so that they can be easily located among the many provisions reproduced. The substance and impact of these particular provisions are addressed in subsection B., below. Separate consideration of these bolded provisions helps in making comparisons between the military commissions process and trials in civilian federal court. The bolded provisions deal with such subjects as the admissibility of evidence seized without a warrant, the applicability of the Miranda warnings, and rules regarding confessions, hearsay and classified information.

Because the Obama administration continues to indicate that some enemy combatant cases will be prosecuted in military commission trials and some in federal district courts, it is useful to understand the extent to which the two processes are similar and the ways in which they differ. But see NY Times, October 28, 2011, A4, reporting that congressional Republicans are pushing to ban civilian trials for al Qaeda suspects who are not U.S. citizens, even if they were arrested in the United States.

In connection with specific consideration of some of the selected items in subsection B. below, a brief review is presented about how the provisions dealing with the particular subject have been changed and evolved through the various amendments of Military Commissions Order No. 1 and through enactments of the MCA of 2006 and now the 2009 Act—that is, how the current rules are different from earlier versions of the military commission process. The differences between the military commissions process and federal district court trials are much less today than when these military commissions were first authorized in 2001. Each successive set of amendments and rule changes have moved the military commissions process closer to the rules applicable in ordinary federal criminal trials. But differences still remain. As you move through these materials, you should ask yourself: What are the remaining differences? How important are they?

B.   SELECTED MILITARY COMMISSION EVIDENTIARY RULES

In enacting the Military Commissions Act of 2009, supra, which amended the MCA of 2006, Congress, inter alia, enacted or amended provisions dealing with selected subjects such as search and seizure, coerced confessions, hearsay and classified information. Additionally, in the same legislative act containing the 2009 MCA, namely the 2010 National Defense Authorization Act, Congress also separately enacted provisions dealing with the applicability of the Miranda warning requirements. As mentioned, supra, we have highlighted the relevant provisions by reproducing them in bold typeface in the set of excerpts from the 2009 MCA reproduced in subsection C., below.

1. Search and Seizure–Exclusionary Rule

Sec. 949a (b)(3)(A), bolded in subsection C., below, contains the relevant provision which authorizes the Secretary of Defense to make the exclusionary rule inapplicable in military commission proceedings where the evidence was seized outside of the United States without a warrant or without authority. The 2009 MCA narrowed the 2006 MCA rule by restricting the inapplicability of the exclusionary rule that the Secretary could authorize to situations involving evidence seized outside of the United States.

2. Miranda Warnings

In the National Defense Authorization Act for 2010, separate from the Military Commissions Act amendments, which were in the same legislative package, Congress legislated the following prohibition on Department of Defense employees giving Miranda warnings to foreign nationals captured or detained outside the United States as enemy belligerents. The prohibition, by its terms, does not apply to persons in the custody of the Department of Justice or to employees of the Department of Justice, namely, the FBI.

SEC. 1040.　NO MIRANDA WARNINGS FOR AL QAEDA TERRORISTS.

(a) No Miranda Warnings—

(1) IN GENERAL—Absent a court order requiring the reading of such statements, no member of the Armed Forces and no official or employee of the Department of Defense or a component of the intelligence community (other than the Department of Justice) may read to a foreign national who is captured or detained outside the United States as an enemy belligerent and is in the custody or under the effective control of the Department of Defense or otherwise under detention in a Department of Defense facility the statement required by Miranda v. Arizona (384 U.S. 436 (1966)), or otherwise inform such an individual of any rights that the individual may or may not have to counsel or to remain silent consistent with Miranda v. Arizona (384 U.S. 436 (1966)).

(2) NONAPPLICABILITY TO DEPARTMENT OF JUSTICE—This subsection shall not apply to the Department of Justice.

(3) DEFINITIONS—In this subsection:

(A) The term 'foreign national' means an individual who is not a citizen or national of the United States.

(B) The term 'enemy belligerent' includes a privileged belligerent against the United States and an unprivileged enemy belligerent, as those terms are defined in section 948a of title 10, United States Code, as amended by section 1802 of this Act.

(b) Report Required on Notification of Detainees of Rights Under Miranda v. Arizona—Not later than 90 days after the date of the enactment of this Act, the Secretary of Defense shall submit to the congressional defense committees a report on how the reading of rights under Miranda v. Arizona (384 U.S. 436 (1966)) to individuals detained by the United States in Afghanistan may affect—

(1) the tactical questioning of detainees at the point of capture by United States Armed Forces deployed in support of Operation Enduring Freedom;

(2) post-capture theater-level interrogations and intelligence-gathering activities conducted as part of Operation Enduring Freedom;

(3) the overall counterinsurgency strategy and objectives of the United States for Operation Enduring Freedom;

(4) United States military operations and objectives in Afghanistan; and

(5) potential risks to members of the Armed Forces operating in Afghanistan.

Section 1040 deals with DOD employees and the inapplicability of Miranda warnings to foreign national prisoners abroad. This leaves open the question of whether FBI agents are required to give Miranda warnings abroad to foreign nationals. We have considered this issue and related questions in chapter 7, in connection with United States v. Odeh, supra, p. 326.

3. Confessions

The main set of provisions dealing with allegedly coerced confessions is found in section 948r of the 2009 MCA, reproduced in bold typeface below. Section 949a(b)(3)(B) also deals with the subject by referencing 948r.

Section 948r makes inadmissible statements obtained through torture or cruel, inhuman or degrading treatment (cidt), thereby amending the approach taken in the 2006 statute. The 2006 MCA had distinguished between those two categories of statements, ruling statements obtained by torture inadmissible under all circumstances and the cidt statements admissible if obtained prior to December 2005, but inadmissible if obtained after that date.

The justification for drawing that distinction was that the Detainee Treatment Act was enacted in December 2005, and the DTA for the first time expressly prohibited cruel, inhuman or degrading treatment of persons detained by U.S. agents. Distinguishing between statements obtained prior to December 2005 and those taken after that date can be viewed as part of a strategy on the part of the Bush administration to try to retain admissibility for interrogation statements obtained through the use of rather extreme interrogation methods in the early years following 9/11.

Recall that, as developed in chapter 7, supra, lawyers for the Bush administration had written memoranda concluding that certain extreme methods of interrogation, e.g., waterboarding, were not torture; under this approach, they were able to use the category of cruel, inhuman or degrading treatment as a safe harbor, at least until December 2005.

But the 2006 MCA did, for the first time, raise some significant barriers to the admissibility of confessions compared with the prior applicable law, namely the Military Commission Order No. 1 and its various amendments. Under those provisions, confessions were admissible if of sufficient reliability and probative value.

The 2009 statute also introduces the notion of voluntariness for determining the admissibility of confessions that are not barred by the torture or cidt barriers. The statute thus, for the first time begins to link up with constitutional law doctrine applicable to confessions in federal criminal prosecutions, but the linkage is not complete. The statute does not expressly incorporate by reference the Supreme Court's case law on this subject. Rather, it develops its own definitional terms, which, surely overlap somewhat with, but in the end, may or may not accord exactly with doctrine developed in the Supreme Court cases. § 948r incorporates considerations relating to military circumstances and seems to make a special point of including as relevant lapse of time between interrogation sessions and changes in who is doing the questioning as factors affecting admissibility.

One conclusion that can be drawn from the foregoing is that military commissions confessions law has evolved significantly so that it now is quite similar to, if not identical with the constitutional law applied to allegedly coerced confessions in federal district court proceedings. What remains to be seen is whether the courts, especially the Supreme Court will apply to military commission trials the same coerced confession doctrine applicable to ordinary federal criminal prosecutions, and if not, whether it will deem the standards enacted in section 948r to be consistent with the Constitution.

4. Hearsay

The provisions in the 2009 MCA dealing with hearsay are found in section 949a (b)(3)(D) et seq., in bold typeface below. Several things should be noted about these provisions. They are essentially procedural, requiring notice to the opposing party and what factors should be taken into account by the military judge in determining whether to admit the evidence. Note that not all hearsay is subject to these procedures, only hearsay that would not otherwise be admissible under the rules of evidence applicable in courtsmartial proceedings—that is, the traditional rules of evidence with all of the hearsay exceptions. The Manual for Military Commissions adopts a definition for hearsay in rule 801 borrowing the language from the Federal Rules of Evidence.

The principal change from the 2006 MCA provisions is that the 2006 statute puts the burden on the opponent of the hearsay evidence whereas the 2009 MCA puts the burden where it would be most appropriate to put it . . . on the proponent.

Under the pre–2006 applicable law, the President's Military Order and the Military Commissions Order No. 1 with its amendments, there were no special provisions or procedures for dealing with hearsay; it was admissible if deemed to have probative value to a reasonable person.

5. Classified Information

The provisions in the 2009 MCA dealing with classified information are found in sections 949p–1 through 949p–7; they are quite extensive, and, accordingly, only a few salient provisions have been highlighted by bolding the typeface. The provisions in the 2009 statute largely track the provisions of the Classified Information Procedures Act (CIPA), which were studied in chapter 9.

Perhaps, the largest degree of change in the applicable rules for military commissions has occurred in the odyssey and evolution of the provisions for dealing with classified information. Under the early approach taken in the Military Commissions Order No. 1, the accused was given detailed defense counsel, that is, an assigned officer, and might also have a civilian defense counsel. The presiding officer had broad powers to deal with classified information, with no applicable standard limiting his authority. His authority extended even to excluding the accused and the civilian counsel, but not detailed defense counsel from the courtroom. Classified evidence could be considered by the judges even though not available to the accused or civilian defense counsel but it could not be admitted into evidence for consideration by the Commission if not presented to detailed defense counsel.

The early approach thus relied upon drawing a distinction between civilian and detailed defense counsel and allowing for the exclusion of the accused from the courtroom (and also civilian defense counsel) for the classified portion of the proceedings. It was this aspect of the military commission process that a plurality of the Supreme Court criticized in their Hamdan opinion.

The 2006 MCA, responding to the Hamdan opinion, largely adopted the CIPA approach but without providing expressly for the possibility of dismissal of the proceeding or setting forth a standard that substituted evidence must meet. The 2009 provisions track CIPA in this respect: the test that substitutions must meet is to provide the accused with substantially the same ability to make his defense, and if that standard cannot be met, the possible remedies include dismissal of charges.

C. THE PROVISIONS OF THE MCA OF 2009

SUBCHAPTER I—GENERAL PROVISIONS

"Sec. 948a. Definitions

"In this chapter:

"(1) ALIEN.—The term "alien" means an individual who is not a citizen of the United States.

"(2) CLASSIFIED INFORMATION.—The term "classified information" means the following:

"(A) Any information or material that has been determined by the United States Government pursuant to statute, Executive order, or regulation to require protection against unauthorized disclosure for reasons of national security.

"(B) Any restricted data, as that term is defined in section 11 y. of the Atomic Energy Act of 1954 (42 U.S.C. 2014(y)).

"(3) COALITION PARTNER.—The term "coalition partner", with respect to hostilities engaged in by the United States, means any State or armed force directly engaged along with the United States in such hostilities or providing direct operational support to the United States in connection with such hostilities.

"(4) GENEVA CONVENTION RELATIVE TO THE TREATMENT OF PRISONERS OF WAR.—The term "Geneva Convention Relative to the Treatment of Prisoners of War" means the Convention Relative to the Treatment of Prisoners of War, done at Geneva August 12, 1949 (6 UST 3316).

"(5) GENEVA CONVENTIONS.—The term "Geneva Conventions" means the international conventions signed at Geneva on August 12, 1949.

"(6) PRIVILEGED BELLIGERENT.—The term "privileged belligerent" means an individual belonging to one of the eight categories enumerated in Article 4 of the Geneva Convention Relative to the Treatment of Prisoners of War.

"(7) UNPRIVILEGED ENEMY BELLIGERENT.—The term "unprivileged enemy belligerent" means an individual (other than a privileged belligerent) who—

"(A) has engaged in hostilities against the United States or its coalition partners;

"(B) has purposefully and materially supported hostilities against the United States or its coalition partners; or

"(C) was a part of al Qaeda at the time of the alleged offense under this chapter.

"(8) NATIONAL SECURITY.—The term "national security" means the national defense and foreign relations of the United States.

"(9) HOSTILITIES.—The term "hostilities" means any conflict subject to the laws of war.

"Sec. 948b.   Military commissions generally

"(a) Purpose.—This chapter establishes procedures governing the use of military commissions to try alien unprivileged enemy belligerents for violations of the law of war and other offenses triable by military commission.

"(b) Authority for Military Commissions Under This Chapter.—The President is authorized to establish military commissions under this chapter for offenses triable by military commission as provided in this chapter.

"(c) Construction of Provisions.—The procedures for military commissions set forth in this chapter are based upon the procedures for trial by general courts-martial under chapter 47 of this title (the Uniform Code of Military Justice). Chapter 47 of this title does not, by its terms, apply to trial by military commission except as specifically provided therein or in this chapter, and many of the provisions of chapter 47 of this title are by their terms inapplicable to military commissions. The judicial construction and application of chapter 47 of this title, while instructive, is therefore not of its own force binding on military commissions established under this chapter.

"(d) Inapplicability of Certain Provisions.—

"(1) The following provisions of this title shall not apply to trial by military commission under this chapter:

"(A) Section 810 (article 10 of the Uniform Code of Military Justice), relating to speedy trial, including any rule of courts-martial relating to speedy trial.

"(B) Sections 831(a), (b), and (d) (articles 31(a), (b), and (d) of the Uniform Code of Military Justice), relating to compulsory self-incrimination.

"(C) Section 832 (article 32 of the Uniform Code of Military Justice), relating to pretrial investigation.

"(2) Other provisions of chapter 47 of this title shall apply to trial by military commission under this chapter only to the extent provided by the terms of such provisions or by this chapter.

"(e) Geneva Conventions Not Establishing Private Right of Action.—No alien unprivileged enemy belligerent subject to trial by military commission under this chapter may invoke the Geneva Conventions as a basis for a private right of action.

"Sec. 948c.   Persons subject to military commissions

"Any alien unprivileged enemy belligerent is subject to trial by military commission as set forth in this chapter.

"Sec. 948d.   Jurisdiction of military commissions

"A military commission under this chapter shall have jurisdiction to try persons subject to this chapter for any offense made punishable by this chapter, sections 904 and 906 of this title (articles 104 and 106 of the Uniform Code of Military Justice), or the law of war, whether such offense was committed before, on, or after September 11, 2001, and may, under such limitations as the President may prescribe, adjudge any punishment not forbidden by this chapter, including the penalty of death when specifically authorized under this chapter. A military commission is a competent tribunal to make a finding sufficient for jurisdiction.

"SUBCHAPTER II—COMPOSITION OF MILITARY COMMISSIONS

. . .

Sec. 948i.   Who may serve on military commissions

"(a) In General.—Any commissioned officer of the armed forces on active duty is eligible to serve on a military commission under this chapter, including commissioned officers of the reserve components of the armed forces on active duty, commissioned officers of the National Guard on active duty in Federal service, or retired commissioned officers recalled to active duty.

"(b) Detail of Members.—When convening a military commission under this chapter, the convening authority shall detail as members thereof such members of the armed forces eligible under subsection (a) who, in the opinion of the convening authority, are best qualified for the duty by reason of age, education, training, experience, length of service, and judicial temperament. No member of an armed force is eligible to serve as a member of a military commission when such member is the accuser or a witness for the prosecution or has acted as an investigator or counsel in the same case.

"(c) Excuse of Members.—Before a military commission under this chapter is assembled for the trial of a case, the convening authority may excuse a member from participating in the case.

"Sec. 948j.   Military judge of a military commission

"(a) Detail of Military Judge.—A military judge shall be detailed to each military commission under this chapter. The Secretary of Defense shall prescribe regulations providing for the manner in which military judges are so detailed to military commissions. The military judge shall preside over each military commission to which such military judge has been detailed.

"(b) Eligibility.—A military judge shall be a commissioned officer of the armed forces who is a member of the bar of a Federal court, or a member of the bar of the highest court of a State, and who is certified to be qualified for duty under section 826 of this title (article 26 of the Uniform Code of Military Justice) as a military judge of general courts-martial by the Judge Advocate General of the armed force. . . .

"(f) Prohibition on Evaluation of Fitness by Convening Authority.—The convening authority of a military commission under this chapter may not prepare or review any report concerning the effectiveness, fitness, or efficiency of a military judge detailed to the military commission which relates to such judge's performance of duty as a military judge on the military commission.

"Sec. 948k.   Detail of trial counsel and defense counsel

"(a) Detail of Counsel Generally.—

"(1) Trial counsel and military defense counsel shall be detailed for each military commission under this chapter.

"(2) Assistant trial counsel and assistant and associate defense counsel may be detailed for a military commission under this chapter.

"(3) Military defense counsel for a military commission under this chapter shall be detailed as soon as practicable.

"(4) The Secretary of Defense shall prescribe regulations providing for the manner in which trial counsel and military defense counsel are detailed for military commissions under this chapter and for the persons who are authorized to detail such counsel for such military commissions.

"(b) Trial Counsel.—Subject to subsection (e), a trial counsel detailed for a military commission under this chapter shall be—

"(1) a judge advocate (as that term is defined in section 801 of this title (article 1 of the Uniform Code of Military Justice)) who is—

"(A) a graduate of an accredited law school or a member of the bar of a Federal court or of the highest court of a State; and

"(B) certified as competent to perform duties as trial counsel before general courts-martial by the Judge Advocate General of the armed force of which such judge advocate is a member; or

"(2) a civilian who is—

"(A) a member of the bar of a Federal court or of the highest court of a State; and

"(B) otherwise qualified to practice before the military commission pursuant to regulations prescribed by the Secretary of Defense.

"(c) Defense Counsel.—

"(1) Subject to subsection (e), a military defense counsel detailed for a military commission under this chapter shall be a judge advocate (as so defined) who is—

"(A) a graduate of an accredited law school or a member of the bar of a Federal court or of the highest court of a State; and

"(B) certified as competent to perform duties as defense counsel before general courts-martial by the Judge Advocate General of the armed force of which such judge advocate is a member.

"(2) The Secretary of Defense shall prescribe regulations for the appointment and performance of defense counsel in capital cases under this chapter.

"(d) Chief Prosecutor; Chief Defense Counsel.—

"(1) The Chief Prosecutor in a military commission under this chapter shall meet the requirements set forth in subsection (b)(1).

"(2) The Chief Defense Counsel in a military commission under this chapter shall meet the requirements set forth in subsection (c)(1).

. . .

"Sec. 948m. Number of members; excuse of members; absent and additional members

"(a) Number of Members.—

"(1) Except as provided in paragraph (2), a military commission under this chapter shall have at least five members.

"(2) In a case in which the accused before a military commission under this chapter may be sentenced to a penalty of death, the military commission shall have the number of members prescribed by section 949m(c) of this title.

"(b) Excuse of Members.—No member of a military commission under this chapter may be absent or excused after the military commission has been assembled for the trial of a case unless excused—

"(1) as a result of challenge;

"(2) by the military judge for physical disability or other good cause; or

"(3) by order of the convening authority for good cause.

"(c) Absent and Additional Members.—Whenever a military commission under this chapter is reduced below the number of members required by subsection (a), the trial may not proceed unless the convening authority details new members sufficient to provide not less than such number. The trial may proceed with the new members present after the recorded evidence previously introduced before the members has been read to the military commission in the presence of the military judge, the accused (except as provided in section 949d of this title), and counsel for both sides.

"SUBCHAPTER III—PRE–TRIAL PROCEDURE

. . .

"Sec. 948r. Exclusion of statements obtained by torture or cruel, inhuman, or degrading treatment; prohibition of self-incrimination; admission of other statements of the accused

"(a) Exclusion of Statements Obtain by Torture or Cruel, Inhuman, or Degrading Treatment.—No statement obtained by the use of torture or by cruel, inhuman, or degrading treatment (as defined by section 1003 of the Detainee Treatment Act of 2005 (42 U.S.C. 2000dd)), whether or not under color of law, shall be admissible in a military commission under this chapter, except against a person accused of torture or such treatment as evidence that the statement was made.

"(b) Self-incrimination Prohibited.—No person shall be required to testify against himself or herself at a proceeding of a military commission under this chapter.

"(c) Other Statements of the Accused.—A statement of the accused may be admitted in evidence in a military commission under this chapter only if the military judge finds—

"(1) that the totality of the circumstances renders the statement reliable and possessing sufficient probative value; and

"(2) that—

"(A) the statement was made incident to lawful conduct during military operations at the point of capture or during closely related active combat engagement, and the interests of justice would best be served by admission of the statement into evidence; or

"(B) the statement was voluntarily given.

"(d) Determination of Voluntariness.—In determining for purposes of subsection (c)(2)(B) whether a statement was voluntarily given, the military judge shall consider the totality of the circumstances, including, as appropriate, the following:

"(1) The details of the taking of the statement, accounting for the circumstances of the conduct of military and intelligence operations during hostilities.

"(2) The characteristics of the accused, such as military training, age, and education level.

"(3) The lapse of time, change of place, or change in identity of the questioners between the statement sought to be admitted and any prior questioning of the accused.

"SUBCHAPTER IV—TRIAL PROCEDURE

. . .

Sec. 949a.   Rules

"(a) Procedures and Rules of Evidence.—Pretrial, trial, and post-trial procedures, including elements and modes of proof, for cases triable by military commission under this chapter may be prescribed by the Secretary of Defense. Such procedures may not be contrary to or inconsistent with this chapter. Except as otherwise provided in this chapter or chapter 47 of this title, the procedures and rules of evidence applicable in trials by general courts-martial of the United States shall apply in trials by military commission under this chapter.

"(b) Exceptions.—

"(1) In trials by military commission under this chapter, the Secretary of Defense, in consultation with the Attorney General, may make such exceptions in the applicability of the procedures and rules of evidence otherwise applicable in general courts-martial as may be required by the unique circumstances of the conduct of military and intelligence operations during hostilities or by other practical need consistent with this chapter.

"(2) Notwithstanding any exceptions authorized by paragraph (1), the procedures and rules of evidence in trials by military commission under this chapter shall include, at a minimum, the following rights of the accused:

"(A) To present evidence in the accused's defense, to cross-examine the witnesses who testify against the accused, and to examine and respond to all evidence admitted against the accused on the issue of guilt or innocence and for sentencing, as provided for by this chapter.

"(B) To be present at all sessions of the military commission (other than those for deliberations or voting), except when excluded under section 949d of this title.

"(C)

"(i) When none of the charges preferred against the accused are capital, to be represented before a military commission by civilian counsel if provided at no expense to the Government, and by either the defense counsel detailed or the military counsel of the accused's own selection, if reasonably available.

"(ii) When any of the charges preferred against the accused are capital, to be represented before a military commission in accordance with clause (i) and, to the greatest extent practicable, by at least one additional counsel who is learned in applicable law relating to capital cases and who, if necessary, may be a civilian and compensated in accordance with regulations prescribed by the Secretary of Defense.

"(D) To self-representation, if the accused knowingly and competently waives the assistance of counsel, subject to the provisions of paragraph (4).

"(E) To the suppression of evidence that is not reliable or probative.

"(F) To the suppression of evidence the probative value of which is substantially outweighed by—

"(i) the danger of unfair prejudice, confusion of the issues, or misleading the members; or

"(ii) considerations of undue delay, waste of time, or needless presentation of cumulative evidence.

"(3) In making exceptions in the applicability in trials by military commission under this chapter from the procedures and rules otherwise applicable in general courts-martial, the Secretary of Defense may provide the following:

"(A) Evidence seized outside the United States shall not be excluded from trial by military commission on the grounds that the evidence was not seized pursuant to a search warrant or authorization.

"(B) A statement of the accused that is otherwise admissible shall not be excluded from trial by military commission on grounds of alleged coercion or compulsory self-incrimination so long as the evidence complies with the provisions of section 948r of this title.

"(C) Evidence shall be admitted as authentic so long as—

"(i) the military judge of the military commission determines that there is sufficient evidence that the evidence is what it is claimed to be; and "(ii) the military judge instructs the members that they may consider any issue as to authentication or identification of evidence in determining the weight, if any, to be given to the evidence.

"(D) Hearsay evidence not otherwise admissible under the rules of evidence applicable in trial by general courts-martial may be admitted in a trial by military commission only if—

"(i) the proponent of the evidence makes known to the adverse party, sufficiently in advance to provide the adverse party with a fair opportunity to meet the evidence, the proponent's intention to offer the evidence, and the particulars of the evidence (including information on the circumstances under which the evidence was obtained); and

"(ii) the military judge, after taking into account all of the circumstances surrounding the taking of the statement, including the degree to which the statement is corroborated, the indicia of reliability within the statement itself, and whether the will of the declarant was overborne, determines that—

"(I) the statement is offered as evidence of a material fact;

"(II) the statement is probative on the point for which it is offered;

"(III) direct testimony from the witness is not available as a practical matter, taking into consideration the physical location of the witness, the unique circumstances of military and intelligence operations during hostilities, and the adverse impacts on military or intelligence operations that would likely result from the production of the witness; and

"(IV) the general purposes of the rules of evidence and the interests of justice will best be served by admission of the statement into evidence.

"(4)

"(A) The accused in a military commission under this chapter who exercises the right to self-representation under paragraph (2)(D) shall conform the accused's deportment and the conduct of the defense to the rules of evidence, procedure, and decorum applicable to trials by military commission.

"(B) Failure of the accused to conform to the rules described in subparagraph (A) may result in a partial or total revocation by the military judge of the right of self-representation under paragraph (2)(D). In such case, the military counsel of the accused or an appropriately authorized civilian counsel shall perform the functions necessary for the defense.

"(c) Delegation of Authority To Prescribe Regulations.—The Secretary of Defense may delegate the authority of the Secretary to prescribe regulations under this chapter.

"(d) Notice to Congress of Modification of Rules.—Not later than 60 days before the date on which any proposed modification of the rules in effect for military commissions under this chapter goes into effect, the Secretary of Defense shall submit to the Committee on Armed Services of the Senate and the Committee on Armed Services of the House of Representatives a report describing the proposed modification.

. . .

"Sec. 949c.   Duties of trial counsel and defense counsel

"(a) Trial Counsel.—The trial counsel of a military commission under this chapter shall prosecute in the name of the United States.

"(b) Defense Counsel.—

"(1) The accused shall be represented in the accused's defense before a military commission under this chapter as provided in this subsection.

"(2) The accused may be represented by military counsel detailed under section 948k of this title or by military counsel of the accused's own selection, if reasonably available.

"*(3)* The accused may be represented by civilian counsel if retained by the accused, provided that such civilian counsel—

"(A) is a United States citizen;

"(B) is admitted to the practice of law in a State, district, or possession of the United States, or before a Federal court;

"(C) has not been the subject of any sanction of disciplinary action by any court, bar, or other competent governmental authority for relevant misconduct;

"(D) has been determined to be eligible for access to information classified at the level Secret or higher; and

"(E) has signed a written agreement to comply with all applicable regulations or instructions for counsel, including any rules of court for conduct during the proceedings.

"(4) If the accused is represented by civilian counsel, military counsel shall act as associate counsel.

"(5) The accused is not entitled to be represented by more than one military counsel. However, the person authorized under regulations prescribed under section 948k of this title to detail counsel, in such person's sole discretion, may detail additional military counsel to represent the accused.

"(6) Defense counsel may cross-examine each witness for the prosecution who testifies before a military commission under this chapter.

"(7) Civilian defense counsel shall protect any classified information received during the course of representation of the accused in accordance with all applicable law governing the protection of classified information, and may not divulge such information to any person not authorized to receive it.

"Sec. 949d. Sessions

"(a) Sessions Without Presence of Members.—

"(1) At any time after the service of charges which have been referred for trial by military commission under this chapter, the military judge may call the military commission into session without the presence of the members for the purpose of—

"(A) hearing and determining motions raising defenses or objections which are capable of determination without trial of the issues raised by a plea of not guilty;

"(B) hearing and ruling upon any matter which may be ruled upon by the military judge under this chapter, whether or not the matter is appropriate for later consideration or decision by the members;

"(C) if permitted by regulations prescribed by the Secretary of Defense, receiving the pleas of the accused; and

"(D) performing any other procedural function which may be performed by the military judge under this chapter or under rules prescribed pursuant to section 949a of this title and which does not require the presence of the members.

"(2) Except as provided in subsections (b), (c), and (d), any proceedings under paragraph (1) shall be conducted in the presence of the accused, defense counsel, and trial counsel, and shall be made part of the record.

"(b) Deliberation or Vote of Members.—When the members of a military commission under this chapter deliberate or vote, only the members may be present.

"(c) Closure of Proceedings.—

"(1) The military judge may close to the public all or part of the proceedings of a military commission under this chapter.

"(2) The military judge may close to the public all or a portion of the proceedings under paragraph (1) only upon making a specific finding that such closure is necessary to—

"(A) protect information the disclosure of which could reasonably be expected to cause damage to the national security, including intelligence or law enforcement sources, methods, or activities; or

"(B) ensure the physical safety of individuals.

"(3) A finding under paragraph (2) may be based upon a presentation, including a presentation ex parte or in camera, by either trial counsel or defense counsel.

"(d) Exclusion of Accused From Certain Proceedings.— The military judge may exclude the accused from any portion of a proceeding upon a determination that, after being warned by the military judge, the accused persists in conduct that justifies exclusion from the courtroom—

"(1) to ensure the physical safety of individuals; or

"(2) to prevent disruption of the proceedings by the accused.

" . . .

"Sec. 949j. Opportunity to obtain witnesses and other evidence

"(a) In General.—

"(1) Defense counsel in a military commission under this chapter shall have a reasonable opportunity to obtain witnesses and other evidence as provided in regulations prescribed by the Secretary of Defense. The opportunity to obtain witnesses and evidence shall be comparable to the opportunity available to a criminal defendant in a court of the United States under article III of the Constitution.

"(2) Process issued in military commissions under this chapter to compel witnesses to appear and testify and to compel the production of other evidence—

"(A) shall be similar to that which courts of the United States having criminal jurisdiction may lawfully issue; and

"(B) shall run to any place where the United States shall have jurisdiction thereof.

"(b) Disclosure of Exculpatory Evidence.—

"(1) As soon as practicable, trial counsel in a military commission under this chapter shall disclose to the defense the existence of any evidence that reasonably tends to—

    "(A) negate the guilt of the accused of an offense charged; or

    "(B) reduce the degree of guilt of the accused with respect to an offense charged.

"(2) The trial counsel shall, as soon as practicable, disclose to the defense the existence of evidence that reasonably tends to impeach the credibility of a witness whom the government intends to call at trial.

"(3) The trial counsel shall, as soon as practicable upon a finding of guilt, disclose to the defense the existence of evidence that is not subject to paragraph (1) or paragraph (2) but that reasonably may be viewed as mitigation evidence at sentencing.

"(4) The disclosure obligations under this subsection encompass evidence that is known or reasonably should be known to any government officials who participated in the investigation and prosecution of the case against the defendant.

"Sec. 949k.   Defense of lack of mental responsibility

"(a) Affirmative Defense.—It is an affirmative defense in a trial by military commission under this chapter that, at the time of the commission of the acts constituting the offense, the accused, as a result of a severe mental disease or defect, was unable to appreciate the nature and quality or the wrongfulness of the acts. Mental disease or defect does not otherwise constitute a defense.

"(b) Burden of Proof.—The accused in a military commission under this chapter has the burden of proving the defense of lack of mental responsibility by clear and convincing evidence.

"(c) Findings Following Assertion of Defense.—Whenever lack of mental responsibility of the accused with respect to an offense is properly at issue in a military commission under this chapter, the military judge shall instruct the members as to the defense of lack of mental responsibility under this section and shall charge the members to find the accused—

    "(1) guilty;

    "(2) not guilty; or

    "(3) subject to subsection (d), not guilty by reason of lack of mental responsibility.

"(d) Majority Vote Required for Finding.—The accused shall be found not guilty by reason of lack of mental responsibility under subsection (c)(3) only if a majority of the members present at the time the vote is taken determines that the defense of lack of mental responsibility has been established.

"Sec. 949l. Voting and rulings

"(a) Vote by Secret Written Ballot.—Voting by members of a military commission under this chapter on the findings and on the sentence shall be by secret written ballot.

"(b) Rulings.—

"(1) The military judge in a military commission under this chapter shall rule upon all questions of law, including the admissibility of evidence and all interlocutory questions arising during the proceedings.

"(2) Any ruling made by the military judge upon a question of law or an interlocutory question (other than the factual issue of mental responsibility of the accused) is conclusive and constitutes the ruling of the military commission. However, a military judge may change such a ruling at any time during the trial.

"(c) Instructions Prior to Vote.—Before a vote is taken of the findings of a military commission under this chapter, the military judge shall, in the presence of the accused and counsel, instruct the members as to the elements of the offense and charge the members—

"(1) that the accused must be presumed to be innocent until the accused's guilt is established by legal and competent evidence beyond a reasonable doubt;

"(2) that in the case being considered, if there is a reasonable doubt as to the guilt of the accused, the doubt must be resolved in favor of the accused and the accused must be acquitted;

"(3) that, if there is reasonable doubt as to the degree of guilt, the finding must be in a lower degree as to which there is no reasonable doubt; and

"(4) that the burden of proof to establish the guilt of the accused beyond a reasonable doubt is upon the United States.

"Sec. 949m. Number of votes required

"(a) Conviction.—No person may be convicted by a military commission under this chapter of any offense, except as provided in section 949i(b) of this title or by concurrence of two-thirds of the members present at the time the vote is taken.

"(b) Sentences.—

"(1) Except as provided in paragraphs (2) and (3), sentences shall be determined by a military commission by the concurrence of two-thirds of the members present at the time the vote is taken.

"(2) No person may be sentenced to death by a military commission, except insofar as—

"(A) the penalty of death has been expressly authorized under this chapter, chapter 47 of this title, or the law of war for an offense of which the accused has been found guilty;

"(B) trial counsel expressly sought the penalty of death by filing an appropriate notice in advance of trial;

"(C) the accused was convicted of the offense by the concurrence of all the members present at the time the vote is taken; and

"(D) all members present at the time the vote was taken concurred in the sentence of death.

"(3) No person may be sentenced to life imprisonment, or to confinement for more than 10 years, by a military commission under this chapter except by the concurrence of three-fourths of the members present at the time the vote is taken.

"(c) Number of Members Required for Penalty of Death.—

"(1) Except as provided in paragraph (2), in a case in which the penalty of death is sought, the number of members of the military commission under this chapter shall be not less than 12 members.

"(2) In any case described in paragraph (1) in which 12 members are not reasonably available for a military commission because of physical conditions or military exigencies, the convening authority shall specify a lesser number of members for the military commission (but not fewer than 9 members), and the military commission may be assembled, and the trial held, with not less than the number of members so specified. In any such case, the convening authority shall make a detailed written statement, to be appended to the record, stating why a greater number of members were not reasonably available.

. . .

"Sec. 949o.   Record of trial

. . .

"(b) Complete Record Required.—A complete record of the proceedings and testimony shall be prepared in every military commission under this chapter.

"(c) Provision of Copy to Accused.—A copy of the record of the proceedings of the military commission under this chapter shall be given the accused as soon as it is authenticated. If the record contains classified information, or a classified annex, the accused shall receive a redacted version of the record consistent with the requirements of subchapter V of this chapter. **Defense counsel shall have access to the unredacted record, as provided in regulations prescribed by the Secretary of Defense.**

"SUBCHAPTER V—CLASSIFIED INFORMATION PROCEDURES

. . .

"Sec. 949p–1. Protection of classified information: applicability of subchapter

"(a) Protection of Classified Information.—Classified information shall be protected and is privileged from disclosure if disclosure would be detrimental to the national security. Under no circumstances may a military judge order the release of classified information to any person not authorized to receive such information.

"(b) Access to Evidence.—Any information admitted into evidence pursuant to any rule, procedure, or order by the military judge shall be provided to the accused.

"(c) Declassification.—Trial counsel shall work with the original classification authorities for evidence that may be used at trial to ensure that such evidence is declassified to the maximum extent possible, consistent with the requirements of national security. A decision not to declassify evidence under this section shall not be subject to review by a military commission or upon appeal.

"(d) Construction of Provisions.—The judicial construction of the Classified Information Procedures Act (18 U.S.C. App.) shall be authoritative in the interpretation of this subchapter, except to the extent that such construction is inconsistent with the specific requirements of this chapter.

"Sec. 949p–2. Pretrial conference

"(a) Motion.—At any time after service of charges, any party may move for a pretrial conference to consider matters relating to classified information that may arise in connection with the prosecution.

"(b) Conference.—Following a motion under subsection (a), or sua sponte, the military judge shall promptly hold a pretrial conference. Upon request by either party, the court shall hold such conference ex parte to the extent necessary to protect classified information from disclosure, in accordance with the practice of the Federal courts under the Classified Information Procedures Act (18 U.S.C. App.).

"(c) Matters To Be Established at Pretrial Conference.—

"(1) TIMING OF SUBSEQUENT ACTIONS.—At the pretrial conference, the military judge shall establish the timing of—

"(A) requests for discovery;

"(B) the provision of notice required by section 949p–5 of this title; and

"(C) the initiation of the procedure established by section 949p–6 of this title.

"(2) OTHER MATTERS.—At the pretrial conference, the military judge may also consider any matter—

"(A) which relates to classified information; or

"(B) which may promote a fair and expeditious trial.

"(d) Effect of Admissions by Accused at Pretrial Conference.—No admission made by the accused or by any counsel for the accused at a pretrial conference under this section may be used against the accused unless the admission is in writing and is signed by the accused and by the counsel for the accused.

"Sec. 949p–3. Protective orders

"Upon motion of the trial counsel, the military judge shall issue an order to protect against the disclosure of any classified information that has been disclosed by the United States to any accused in any military commission under this chapter or that has otherwise been provided to, or obtained by, any such accused in any such military commission.

"Sec. 949p–4. Discovery of, and access to, classified information by the accused

"(a) Limitations on Discovery or Access by the Accused.—

"(1) DECLARATIONS BY THE UNITED STATES OF DAMAGE TO NATIONAL SECURITY.—In any case before a military commission in which the United States seeks to delete, withhold, or otherwise obtain other relief with respect to the discovery of or access to any classified information, the trial counsel shall submit a declaration invoking the United States' classified information privilege and setting forth the damage to the national security that the discovery of or access to such information reasonably could be expected to cause. The declaration shall be signed by a knowledgeable United States official possessing authority to classify information.

"(2) STANDARD FOR AUTHORIZATION OF DISCOVERY OR ACCESS.—Upon the submission of a declaration under paragraph (1), the military judge may not authorize the discovery of or access to such classified information unless the military judge determines that such classified information would be noncumulative, relevant, and helpful to a legally cognizable defense, rebuttal of the prosecution's case, or to sentencing, in accordance with standards generally applicable to discovery of or access to classified information in Federal criminal cases. If the discovery of or access to such classified information is authorized, it shall be addressed in accordance with the requirements of subsection (b).

"(b) Discovery of Classified Information.—

"(1) *SUBSTITUTIONS AND OTHER RELIEF.*— The military judge, in assessing the accused's discovery of or access to classified information under this section, may authorize the United States—

> **"(A) to delete or withhold specified items of classified information;**

> **"(B) to substitute a summary for classified information; or**

> **"(C) to substitute a statement admitting relevant facts that the classified information or material would tend to prove.**

"(2) EX PARTE PRESENTATIONS.—The military judge shall permit the trial counsel to make a request for an authorization under paragraph (1) in the form of an ex parte presentation to the extent necessary to protect classified information, in accordance with the practice of the Federal courts under the Classified Information Procedures Act (18 U.S.C. App.). If the military judge enters an order granting relief following such an ex parte showing, the entire presentation (including the text of any written submission, verbatim transcript of the ex parte oral conference or hearing, and any exhibits received by the court as part of the ex parte presentation) shall be sealed and preserved in the records of the military commission to be made available to the appellate court in the event of an appeal.

"(3) ACTION BY MILITARY JUDGE.—The military judge shall grant the request of the trial counsel to substitute a summary or to substitute a statement admitting relevant facts, or to provide other relief in accordance with paragraph (1), if the military judge finds that the summary, statement, or other relief would provide the accused with substantially the same ability to make a defense as would discovery of or access to the specific classified information.

"(c) Reconsideration.—An order of a military judge authorizing a request of the trial counsel to substitute, summarize, withhold, or prevent access to classified information under this section is not subject to a motion for reconsideration by the accused, if such order was entered pursuant to an ex parte showing under this section.

"...

"**Sec. 949p–6. Procedure for cases involving classified information**

"(a) Motion for Hearing.—

"(1) REQUEST FOR HEARING.—Within the time specified by the military judge for the filing of a motion under this section, either party may request the military judge to conduct a hearing to make all determinations concerning the use, relevance, or admissibility of classified information that would otherwise be made during the trial or pretrial proceeding.

"(2) CONDUCT OF HEARING.—Upon a request by either party under paragraph (1), the military judge shall conduct such a hearing and shall rule prior to conducting any further proceedings.

"**(3) IN CAMERA HEARING UPON DECLARATION TO COURT BY APPROPRIATE OFFICIAL OF RISK OF DISCLOSURE OF CLASSIFIED INFORMATION.—Any hearing held pursuant to this subsection (or any portion of such hearing specified in the request of a knowledgeable United States official) shall be held in camera if a knowledgeable United States official possessing authority to classify information submits to the military judge a declaration that a public proceeding may result in the disclosure of classified information. Classified information is not subject to disclosure under this section unless the information is relevant and necessary to an element of the offense or a legally cognizable defense and is otherwise admissible in evidence.**

"(4) MILITARY JUDGE TO MAKE DETERMINATIONS IN WRITING.—As to each item of classified information, the military judge shall set forth in writing the basis for the determination.

"(b) Notice and Use of Classified Information by the Government.—

"(1) NOTICE TO ACCUSED.—Before any hearing is conducted pursuant to a request by the trial counsel under subsection (a), trial counsel shall provide the accused with notice of the classified information that is at issue. Such notice shall identify the specific classified information at issue whenever that information previously has been made available to the accused by the United States. When the United States has not previously made the information available to the accused in connection with the case the information may be described by generic category, in such forms as the military judge may approve, rather than by identification of the specific information of concern to the United States.

"(2) ORDER BY MILITARY JUDGE UPON REQUEST OF ACCUSED.—Whenever the trial counsel requests a hearing under subsection (a), the military judge, upon request of the accused, may order the trial counsel to provide the accused, prior to trial, such details as to the portion of the charge or specification at issue in the hearing as are needed to give the accused fair notice to prepare for the hearing.

"(c) Substitutions.—

"**(1) IN CAMERA PRETRIAL HEARING.—Upon request of the trial counsel pursuant to the Military Commission Rules of Evidence, and in accordance with the security procedures established by the military judge, the military judge shall conduct a classified in camera pretrial hearing concerning the admissibility of classified information.**

"*(2) PROTECTION OF SOURCES, METHODS, AND ACTIVITIES BY WHICH EVIDENCE ACQUIRED.—***When trial counsel seeks to introduce evidence before a military commission under this chapter and the Executive branch has classified the sources, methods, or activities by which the United States acquired the evidence, the military judge shall permit trial counsel to introduce the evidence, including a substituted evidentiary foundation pursuant to the procedures described in subsection (d), while protecting from disclosure information identifying those sources, methods, or activities, if—**

"**(A) the evidence is otherwise admissible; and**

"**(B) the military judge finds that—**

"**(i) the evidence is reliable; and**

"**(ii) the redaction is consistent with affording the accused a fair trial.**

"**(d) Alternative Procedure for Disclosure of Classified Information.—**

"**(1) MOTION BY THE UNITED STATES.—Upon any determination by the military judge authorizing the disclosure of specific classified information under the procedures established by this section, the trial counsel may move that, in lieu of the disclosure of such specific classified information, the military judge order—**

"**(A) the substitution for such classified information of a statement admitting relevant facts that the specific classified information would tend to prove;**

"(B) the substitution for such classified information of a summary of the specific classified information; or

"(C) any other procedure or redaction limiting the disclosure of specific classified information.

"(2) ACTION ON MOTION.—The military judge shall grant such a motion of the trial counsel if the military judge finds that the statement, summary, or other procedure or redaction will provide the defendant with substantially the same ability to make his defense as would disclosure of the specific classified information.

"(3) HEARING ON MOTION.—The military judge shall hold a hearing on any motion under this subsection. Any such hearing shall be held in camera at the request of a knowledgeable United States official possessing authority to classify information.

"(4) SUBMISSION OF STATEMENT OF DAMAGE TO NATIONAL SECURITY IF DISCLOSURE ORDERED.—The trial counsel may, in connection with a motion under paragraph (1), submit to the military judge a declaration signed by a knowledgeable United States official possessing authority to classify information certifying that disclosure of classified information would cause identifiable damage to the national security of the United States and explaining the basis for the classification of such information. If so requested by the trial counsel, the military judge shall examine such declaration during an ex parte presentation.

"(e) Sealing of Records of in Camera Hearings.—If at the close of an in camera hearing under this section (or any portion of a hearing under this section that is held in camera), the military judge determines that the classified information at issue may not be disclosed or elicited at the trial or pretrial proceeding, the record of such in camera hearing shall be sealed and preserved for use in the event of an appeal. The accused may seek reconsideration of the military judge's determination prior to or during trial.

"(f) Prohibition on Disclosure of Classified Information by the Accused; Relief for Accused When the United States Opposes Disclosure.—

"(1) ORDER TO PREVENT DISCLOSURE BY ACCUSED.—Whenever the military judge denies a motion by the trial counsel that the judge issue an order under subsection (a), (c), or (d) and the trial counsel files with the military judge a declaration signed by a knowledgeable United States official possessing authority to classify information objecting to disclosure of the classified information at issue, the military judge shall order that the accused not disclose or cause the disclosure of such information.

"(2) RESULT OF ORDER UNDER PARAGRAPH (1).—Whenever an accused is prevented by an order under paragraph (1) from disclosing or causing the disclosure of classified information, the military judge shall dismiss the case, except that, when the military judge determines that the interests of justice would not be served by dismissal of the case, the military judge shall order such other action, in lieu of dismissing the charge or specification, as the military judge determines is appropriate. Such action may include, but need not be limited to, the following:

"(A) Dismissing specified charges or specifications.

"(B) Finding against the United States on any issue as to which the excluded classified information relates.

"(C) Striking or precluding all or part of the testimony of a witness.

"(3) TIME FOR THE UNITED STATES TO SEEK INTERLOCUTORY APPEAL.—An order under paragraph (2) shall not take effect until the military judge has afforded the United States—

"(A) an opportunity to appeal such order under section 950d of this title; and

"(B) an opportunity thereafter to withdraw its objection to the disclosure of the classified information at issue.

"(g) Reciprocity.—

"(1) DISCLOSURE OF REBUTTAL INFORMATION.—Whenever the military judge determines that classified information may be disclosed in connection with a trial or pretrial proceeding, the military judge shall, unless the interests of fairness do not so require, order the United States to provide the accused with the information it expects to use to rebut the classified information. The military judge may place the United States under a continuing duty to disclose such rebuttal information.

"(2) SANCTION FOR FAILURE TO COMPLY.—If the United States fails to comply with its obligation under this subsection, the military judge—

"(A) may exclude any evidence not made the subject of a required disclosure; and

"(B) may prohibit the examination by the United States of any witness with respect to such information.

"Sec. 949p–7.   Introduction of classified information into evidence

"(a) Preservation of Classification Status.—Writings, recordings, and photographs containing classified information may be admitted into evidence in proceedings of military commissions under this chapter without change in their classification status.

"(b) Precautions by Military Judges.—

"(1) PRECAUTIONS IN ADMITTING CLASSIFIED INFORMATION INTO EVIDENCE.—The military judge in a trial by military commission, in order to prevent unnecessary disclosure of classified information, may order admission into evidence of only part of a writing, recording, or photograph, or may order admission into evidence of the whole writing, recording, or photograph with excision of some or all of the classified information contained therein, unless the whole ought in fairness be considered.

"(2) CLASSIFIED INFORMATION KEPT UNDER SEAL.— The military judge shall allow classified information offered or accepted into evidence to remain under seal during the trial, even if such evidence is disclosed in the military commission, and may, upon motion by the United States, seal exhibits containing classified information for any period after trial as necessary to prevent a disclosure of classified information when a knowledgeable United States official possessing authority to classify information submits to the military judge a declaration setting forth the damage to the national security that the disclosure of such information reasonably could be expected to cause.

"(c) Taking of Testimony.—

"(1) OBJECTION BY TRIAL COUNSEL.—During the examination of a witness, trial counsel may object to any question or line of inquiry that may require the witness to disclose classified information not previously found to be admissible.

"(2) ACTION BY MILITARY JUDGE.—Following an objection under paragraph (1), the military judge shall take such suitable action to determine whether the response is admissible as will safeguard against the compromise of any classified information. Such action may include requiring trial counsel to provide the military judge with a proffer of the witness' response to the question or line of inquiry and requiring the accused to provide the military judge with a proffer of the nature of the information sought to be elicited by the accused. Upon request, the military judge may accept an ex parte proffer by trial counsel to the extent necessary to protect classified information from disclosure, in accordance with the practice of the Federal courts under the Classified Information Procedures Act (18 U.S.C. App.).

"(d) Disclosure at Trial of Certain Statements Previously Made by a Witness.—

"(1) MOTION FOR PRODUCTION OF STATEMENTS IN POSSESSION OF THE UNITED STATES.—After a witness called by the trial counsel has testified on direct examination, the military judge, on motion of the accused, may order production of statements of the witness in the possession of the United States which relate to the subject matter as to which the witness has testified. This paragraph does not preclude discovery or assertion of a privilege otherwise authorized.

"(2) INVOCATION OF PRIVILEGE BY THE UNITED STATES.—If the United States invokes a privilege, the trial counsel may provide the prior statements of the witness to the military judge during an ex parte presentation to the extent necessary to protect classified information from disclosure, in accordance with the practice of the Federal courts under the Classified Information Procedures Act (18 U.S.C. App.).

"(3) ACTION BY MILITARY JUDGE ON MOTION.—If the military judge finds that disclosure of any portion of the statement identified by the United States as classified would be detrimental to the national security in the degree to warrant classification under the applicable Executive Order, statute, or regulation, that such portion of the statement is consistent with the testimony of the witness, and that the disclosure of such portion is not necessary to afford the accused a fair trial, the military judge shall excise that portion from the statement. If the military judge finds that such portion of the statement is inconsistent with the testimony of the witness or that its disclosure is necessary to afford the accused a fair trial, the military judge, shall, upon the request of the trial counsel, review alternatives to disclosure in accordance with section 949p–6(d) of this title.

"§ 950f. Review by United States Court of Military Commission Review

"(a) ESTABLISHMENT.—There is a court of record to be known as the 'United States Court of Military Commission Review' (in this section referred to as the 'Court'). The Court shall consist of one or more panels, each composed of not less than three appellate military judges. For the purpose of reviewing decisions of military commissions under this chapter, the Court may sit in panels or as a whole, in accordance with rules prescribed by the Secretary of Defense.

"(b) JUDGES.—(1) Judges on the Court shall be assigned or appointed in a manner consistent with the provisions of this subsection. "(2) The Secretary of Defense may assign persons who are appellate military judges to be judges on the Court. Any judge so assigned shall be a commissioned officer of the armed forces, and shall meet the qualifications for military judges prescribed by section 948j(b) of this title.

"(3) The President may appoint, by and with the advice and consent of the Senate, additional judges to the United States Court of Military Commission Review.—The Court shall, in accordance with procedures prescribed"

(4) No person may serve as a judge on the Court in any case in which that person acted as a military judge, counsel, or reviewing official.

"(c) CASES TO BE REVIEWED.—The Court shall, in accordance with procedures prescribed under regulations of the Secretary, review the record in each case that is referred to the Court by the convening authority under section 950c of this title with respect to any matter properly raised by the accused.

"(d) STANDARD AND SCOPE OF REVIEW.—In a case reviewed by the Court under this section, the Court may act only with respect to the findings and sentence as approved by the convening authority. The Court may affirm only such findings of guilty, and the sentence or such part or amount of the sentence, as the Court finds correct in law and fact and determines, on the basis of the entire record, should be approved. In considering the record, the Court may weigh the evidence, judge the credibility of witnesses, and determine controverted questions of fact, recognizing that the military commission saw and heard the witnesses.

. . .

"§ 950g. Review by United States Court of Appeals for the District of Columbia Circuit; writ of certiorari to Supreme Court

"(a) EXCLUSIVE APPELLATE JURISDICTION.—Except as provided in subsection (b), the United States Court of Appeals for the District of Columbia Circuit shall have exclusive jurisdiction to determine the validity of a final judgment rendered by a military commission (as approved by the convening authority and, where applicable, the United States Court of Military Commission Review) under this chapter.

H. R. 2647—415

"(b) EXHAUSTION OF OTHER APPEALS.—The United States Court of Appeals for the District of Columbia Circuit may not review a final judgment described in subsection (a) until all other appeals under this chapter have been waived or exhausted.

. . .

"(d) SCOPE AND NATURE OF REVIEW.—The United States Court of Appeals for the District of Columbia Circuit may act under this section only with respect to the findings and sentence as approved by the convening authority and as affirmed or set aside as incorrect in law by the United States Court of Military Commission Review, and shall take action only with respect to matters of law, including the sufficiency of the evidence to support the verdict.

"(e) REVIEW BY SUPREME COURT.—The Supreme Court may review by writ of certiorari pursuant to section 1254 of title 28 the final judgment of the United States Court of Appeals for the District of Columbia Circuit under this section.

. . .

Sec. 950p. Definitions; construction of certain offenses; common circumstances

'(a) Definitions—In this subchapter:

'(1) The term 'military objective' means combatants and those objects during hostilities which, by their nature, location, purpose, or use, effectively contribute to the war-fighting or war-sustaining capability of an opposing force and whose total or partial destruction, capture, or neutralization would constitute a definite military advantage to the attacker under the circumstances at the time of an attack.

'(2) The term 'protected person' means any person entitled to protection under one or more of the Geneva Conventions, including civilians not taking an active part in hostilities, military personnel placed out of combat by sickness, wounds, or detention, and military medical or religious personnel.

'(3) The term 'protected property' means any property specifically protected by the law of war, including buildings dedicated to religion, education, art, science, or charitable purposes, historic monuments, hospitals, and places where the sick and wounded are collected, but only if and to the extent such property is not being used for military purposes or is not otherwise a military objective. The term includes objects properly identified by one of the distinctive emblems of the Geneva Conventions, but does not include civilian property that is a military objective.

'(b) Construction of Certain Offenses—The intent required for offenses under paragraphs (1), (2), (3), (4), and (12) of section 950t of this title precludes the applicability of such offenses with regard to collateral damage or to death, damage, or injury incident to a lawful attack.

'(c) Common Circumstances—An offense specified in this subchapter is triable by military commission under this chapter only if the offense is committed in the context of and associated with hostilities.

'(d) Effect—The provisions of this subchapter codify offenses that have traditionally been triable by military commission. This chapter does not establish new crimes that did not exist before the date of the enactment of this subchapter, as amended by the National Defense Authorization Act for Fiscal Year 2010, but rather codifies those crimes for trial by military commission. Because the provisions of this subchapter codify offenses that have traditionally been triable under the law of war or otherwise triable by military commission, this subchapter does not preclude trial for offenses that occurred before the date of the enactment of this subchapter, as so amended.

'Sec. 950q. Principals

'Any person punishable under this chapter who—

'(1) commits an offense punishable by this chapter, or aids, abets, counsels, commands, or procures its commission;

'(2) causes an act to be done which if directly performed by him would be punishable by this chapter; or

'(3) is a superior commander who, with regard to acts punishable by this chapter, knew, had reason to know, or should have known, that a subordinate was about to commit such acts or had done so and who failed to take the necessary and reasonable measures to prevent such acts or to punish the perpetrators thereof,

is a principal.

'Sec. 950r. Accessory after the fact

'Any person subject to this chapter who, knowing that an offense punishable by this chapter has been committed, receives, comforts, or assists the offender in order to hinder or prevent his apprehension, trial, or punishment shall be punished as a military commission under this chapter may direct.

'Sec. 950s. Conviction of lesser offenses

'An accused may be found guilty of an offense necessarily included in the offense charged or of an attempt to commit either the offense charged or an attempt to commit either the offense charged or an offense necessarily included therein.

'Sec. 950t. Crimes triable by military commission

'The following offenses shall be triable by military commission under this chapter at any time without limitation:

'(1) MURDER OF PROTECTED PERSONS—Any person subject to this chapter who intentionally kills one or more protected persons shall be punished by death or such other punishment as a military commission under this chapter may direct.

'(2) ATTACKING CIVILIANS—Any person subject to this chapter who intentionally engages in an attack upon a civilian population as such, or individual civilians not taking active part in hostilities, shall be punished, if death results to one or more of the victims, by death or such other punishment as a military commission under this chapter may direct, and, if death does not result to any of the victims, by such punishment, other than death, as a military commission under this chapter may direct.

'(3) ATTACKING CIVILIAN OBJECTS—Any person subject to this chapter who intentionally engages in an attack upon a civilian object that is not a military objective shall be punished as a military commission under this chapter may direct.

'(4) ATTACKING PROTECTED PROPERTY—Any person subject to this chapter who intentionally engages in an attack upon protected property shall be punished as a military commission under this chapter may direct.

'(5) PILLAGING—Any person subject to this chapter who intentionally and in the absence of military necessity appropriates or seizes property for private or personal use, without the consent of a person with authority to permit such appropriation or seizure, shall be punished as a military commission under this chapter may direct.

'(6) DENYING QUARTER—Any person subject to this chapter who, with effective command or control over subordinate groups, declares, orders, or otherwise indicates to those groups that there shall be no survivors or surrender accepted, with the intent to threaten an adversary or to conduct hostilities such that there would be no survivors or surrender accepted, shall be punished as a military commission under this chapter may direct.

'(7) TAKING HOSTAGES—Any person subject to this chapter who, having knowingly seized or detained one or more persons, threatens to kill, injure, or continue to detain such person or persons with the intent of compelling any nation, person other than the hostage, or group of persons to act or refrain from acting as an explicit or implicit condition for the safety or release of such person or persons, shall be punished, if death results to one or more of the victims, by death or such other punishment as a military commission under this chapter may direct, and, if death does not result to any of the victims, by such punishment, other than death, as a military commission under this chapter may direct.

'(8) EMPLOYING POISON OR SIMILAR WEAPONS—Any person subject to this chapter who intentionally, as a method of warfare, employs a substance or weapon that releases a substance that causes death or serious and lasting damage to health in the ordinary course of events, through its asphyxiating, bacteriological, or toxic properties, shall be punished, if death results to one or more of the victims, by death or such other punishment as a military commission under this chapter may direct, and, if death does not result to any of the victims, by such punishment, other than death, as a military commission under this chapter may direct.

'(9) USING PROTECTED PERSONS AS A SHIELD—Any person subject to this chapter who positions, or otherwise takes advantage of, a protected person with the intent to shield a military objective from attack. or to shield, favor, or impede military operations, shall be punished, if death results to one or more of the victims, by death or such other punishment as a military commission under this chapter may direct, and, if death does not result to any of the victims, by such punishment, other than death, as a military commission under this chapter may direct.

'(10) USING PROTECTED PROPERTY AS A SHIELD—Any person subject to this chapter who positions, or otherwise takes advantage of the location of, protected property with the intent to shield a military objective from attack, or to shield, favor, or impede military operations, shall be punished as a military commission under this chapter may direct.

'(11) TORTURE—

'(A) OFFENSE—Any person subject to this chapter who commits an act specifically intended to inflict severe physical or mental pain or suffering (other than pain or suffering incidental to lawful sanctions) upon another person within his custody or physical control for the purpose of obtaining information or a confession, punishment, intimidation, coercion, or any reason based on discrimination of any kind, shall be punished, if death results to one or more of the victims, by death or such other punishment as a military commission under this chapter may direct, and, if death does not result to any of the victims, by such punishment, other than death, as a military commission under this chapter may direct.

'(B) SEVERE MENTAL PAIN OR SUFFERING DEFINED—In this paragraph, the term 'severe mental pain or suffering' has the meaning given that term in section 2340(2) of title 18.

'(12) CRUEL OR INHUMAN TREATMENT—Any person subject to this chapter who subjects another person in their custody or under their physical control, regardless of nationality or physical location, to cruel or inhuman treatment that constitutes a grave breach of common Article 3 of the Geneva Conventions shall be punished, if death results to the victim, by death or such other punishment as a military commission under this chapter may direct, and, if death does not result to the victim, by such punishment, other than death, as a military commission under this chapter may direct.

'(13) INTENTIONALLY CAUSING SERIOUS BODILY INJURY—

'(A) OFFENSE—Any person subject to this chapter who intentionally causes serious bodily injury to one or more persons, including privileged belligerents, in violation of the law of war shall be punished, if death results to one or more of the victims, by death or such other punishment as a military commission under this chapter may direct, and, if death does not result to any of the victims, by such punishment, other than death, as a military commission under this chapter may direct.

'(B) SERIOUS BODILY INJURY DEFINED—In this paragraph, the term 'serious bodily injury' means bodily injury which involves—

'(i) a substantial risk of death;

'(ii) extreme physical pain;

'(iii) protracted and obvious disfigurement; or

'(iv) protracted loss or impairment of the function of a bodily member, organ, or mental faculty.

'(14) MUTILATING OR MAIMING—Any person subject to this chapter who intentionally injures one or more protected persons by disfiguring the person or persons by any mutilation of the person or persons, or by permanently disabling any member, limb, or organ of the body of the person or persons, without any legitimate medical or dental purpose, shall be punished, if death results to one or more of the victims, by death or such other punishment as a military commission under this chapter may direct, and, if death does not result to any of the victims, by such punishment, other than death, as a military commission under this chapter may direct.

'(15) MURDER IN VIOLATION OF THE LAW OF WAR—Any person subject to this chapter who intentionally kills one or more persons, including privileged belligerents, in violation of the law of war shall be punished by death or such other punishment as a military commission under this chapter may direct.

'(16) DESTRUCTION OF PROPERTY IN VIOLATION OF THE LAW OF WAR—Any person subject to this chapter who intentionally destroys property belonging to another person in violation of the law of war shall punished as a military commission under this chapter may direct.

'(17) USING TREACHERY OR PERFIDY—Any person subject to this chapter who, after inviting the confidence or belief of one or more persons that they were entitled to, or obliged to accord, protection under the law of war, intentionally makes use of that confidence or belief in killing, injuring, or capturing such person or persons shall be punished, if death results to one or more of the victims, by death or such other punishment as a military commission under this chapter may direct, and, if death does not result to any of the victims, by such punishment, other than death, as a military commission under this chapter may direct.

'(18) IMPROPERLY USING A FLAG OF TRUCE—Any person subject to this chapter who uses a flag of truce to feign an intention to negotiate, surrender, or otherwise suspend hostilities when there is no such intention shall be punished as a military commission under this chapter may direct.

'(19) IMPROPERLY USING A DISTINCTIVE EMBLEM—Any person subject to this chapter who intentionally uses a distinctive emblem recognized by the law of war for combatant purposes in a manner prohibited by the law of war shall be punished as a military commission under this chapter may direct.

'(20) INTENTIONALLY MISTREATING A DEAD BODY—Any person subject to this chapter who intentionally mistreats the body of a dead person, without justification by legitimate military necessary, shall be punished as a military commission under this chapter may direct.

'(21) RAPE—Any person subject to this chapter who forcibly or with coercion or threat of force wrongfully invades the body of a person by penetrating, however slightly, the anal or genital opening of the victim with any part of the body of the accused, or with any foreign object, shall be punished as a military commission under this chapter may direct.

'(22) SEXUAL ASSAULT OR ABUSE—Any person subject to this chapter who forcibly or with coercion or threat of force engages in sexual contact with one or more persons, or causes one or more persons to engage in sexual contact, shall be punished as a military commission under this chapter may direct

'(23) HIJACKING OR HAZARDING A VESSEL OR AIR-CRAFT—Any person subject to this chapter who intentionally seizes, exercises unauthorized control over, or endangers the safe navigation of a vessel or aircraft that is not a legitimate military objective shall be punished, if death results to one or more of the victims, by death or such other punishment as a military commission under this chapter may direct, and, if death does not result to any of the victims, by such punishment, other than death, as a military commission under this chapter may direct.

'(24) TERRORISM—Any person subject to this chapter who intentionally kills or inflicts great bodily harm on one or more protected persons, or intentionally engages in an act that evinces a wanton disregard for human life, in a manner calculated to influence or affect the conduct of government or civilian population by intimidation or coercion, or to retaliate against government conduct, shall be punished, if death results to one or more of the victims, by death or such other punishment as a military commission under this chapter may direct, and, if death does not result to any of the victims, by such punishment, other than death, as a military commission under this chapter may direct.

'(25) PROVIDING MATERIAL SUPPORT FOR TERRORISM—

'(A) OFFENSE—Any person subject to this chapter who provides material support or resources, knowing or intending that they are to be used in preparation for, or in carrying out, an act of terrorism (as set forth in paragraph (24) of this section), or who intentionally provides material support or resources to an international terrorist organization engaged in hostilities against the United States, knowing that such organization has engaged or engages in terrorism (as so set forth), shall be punished as a military commission under this chapter may direct.

'(B) MATERIAL SUPPORT OR RESOURCES DEFINED— In this paragraph, the term 'material support or resources' has the meaning given that term in section 2339A(b) of title 18.

'(26) WRONGFULLY AIDING THE ENEMY—Any person subject to this chapter who, in breach of an allegiance or duty to the United States, knowingly and intentionally aids an enemy of the United States, or one of the co-belligerents of the enemy, shall be punished as a military commission under this chapter may direct.

'(27) SPYING—Any person subject to this chapter who, in violation of the law of war and with intent or reason to believe that it is to be used to the injury of the United States or to the advantage of a foreign power, collects or attempts to collect information by clandestine means or while acting under false pretenses, for the purpose of conveying such information to an enemy of the United States, or one of the co-belligerents of the enemy, shall be punished by death or such other punishment as a military commission under this chapter may direct.

'(28) ATTEMPTS—

'(A) IN GENERAL—Any person subject to this chapter who attempts to commit any offense punishable by this chapter shall be punished as a military commission under this chapter may direct.

'(B) SCOPE OF OFFENSE—An act, done with specific intent to commit an offense under this chapter, amounting to more than mere preparation and tending, even though failing, to effect its commission, is an attempt to commit that offense.

'(C) EFFECT OF CONSUMMATION—Any person subject to this chapter may be convicted of an attempt to commit an offense although it appears on the trial that the offense was consummated.

'(29) CONSPIRACY—Any person subject to this chapter who conspires to commit one or more substantive offenses triable by military commission under this subchapter, and who knowingly does any overt act to effect the object of the conspiracy, shall be punished, if death results to one or more of the victims, by death or such other punishment as a military commission under this chapter may direct, and, if death does not result to any of the victims, by such punishment, other than death, as a military commission under this chapter may direct.

'(30) SOLICITATION—Any person subject to this chapter who solicits or advises another or others to commit one or more substantive offenses triable by military commission under this chapter shall, if the offense solicited or advised is attempted or committed, be punished with the punishment provided for the commission of the offense, but, if the offense solicited or advised is not committed or attempted, shall be punished as a military commission under this chapter may direct.

'(31) CONTEMPT—A military commission under this chapter may punish for contempt any person who uses any menacing word, sign, or gesture in its presence, or who disturbs its proceedings by any riot or disorder.

'(32) PERJURY AND OBSTRUCTION OF JUSTICE—A military commission under this chapter may try offenses and impose such punishment as the military commission may direct for perjury, false testimony, or obstruction of justice related to the military commission.'.

D. SUMMARY REVIEW OF THE HISTORY OF THE POST–9/11 MILITARY COMMISSIONS TRIALS

Prior to the decision of the Supreme Court in Hamdan v. Rumsfeld, supra p. 658, the military commissions operated under the terms of President Bush's post–9/11 Military Order authorizing establishment of the military commissions and also, inter alia, under the terms of Military Commissions Order No. 1, supplemented by amendments which contained detailed provisions regarding the procedures to be used in military commission hearings.

Prior to the Supreme Court's decision in Hamdan v. Rumsfeld, 10 individuals had been charged with offenses to be tried before the military commissions. The charges variously included conspiracy to commit various offenses including attacking civilians, murder by an unprivileged belligerent, and terrorism. Proceedings against some of those charged were conducted in the late summer and early fall, 2004. News reports regarding these proceedings reported that "officials acknowledge that the process is in turmoil." NY Times, Sept. 26, 2004, Pt. I, 26. Among other problems, some of the trial panel's members were successfully challenged for bias or conflict of interest, and the translation system was inadequate. Ibid.

The Supreme Court's decision in Hamdan v. Rumsfeld and the subsequent enactment of the Military Commissions Act changed the legal landscape and required the prosecution, in effect, to start again in charging individuals for trial before the military commissions.

In the immediate aftermath of the Hamdan decision, Congress enacted the Military Commissions Act of 2006 (MCA), in an effort to respond to the issues raised in Hamdan. It contained numerous procedural provisions, see supra, and it also authorized the adoption of more specific rules and procedures by the Secretary of Defense. Under this authorization, the Secretary issued a Manual for Military Commissions. Subsequently, at the instance of the Obama administration in 2009, Congress amended the 2006 Act in a number of important details but its basic approach remained intact. Similarly, in 2010, a revised version of the Manual for Military Commissions was issued.

In January, 2007, at a Department of Defense press briefing, it was reported that 10 cases had been initiated before the military commissions, that there were 14 cases in various stages of preparation, and that there were potentially viable charges for violations of law of war in 60 to 80 cases.

Prior to the inauguration of President Obama in January, 2009, only three commission trials initiated post-Hamdan and post 2006 MCA, had been completed. As one of his first official acts after the inauguration, President Obama requested that ongoing and impending military commission trials be suspended for 120 days. The three cases that had been completed prior to this suspension were:

David Hicks, who pleaded guilty. He had been charged with providing material support for terrorism and attempted murder in violation of the law of war. In March, 2007, he entered into a plea agreement, under the terms of which he effectively served an additional nine months in exchange for which he pleaded guilty. The plea agreement was accepted by the military commission and he was sentenced to seven years, suspended except for nine months, with that time to be served in Australia.

Salim Ahmed Hamdan. Hamdan was convicted in August, 2008 on a charge of providing material support to terrorism and acquitted on a charge of conspiracy. He was sentenced to five and a half years in prison which, given time already served, meant that he only had to serve four additional months. He was subsequently released and transferred to Yemen in November, 2008 where he served the remainder of his sentence. He was released from jail in Yemen in January, 2009. After his release, he filed an appeal aimed at setting aside his conviction. The appeal is described further, infra.

Ali Hamza al Bahlul. He was convicted on November 2, 2008 by a nine person jury of military officers for conspiracy, solicitation to commit murder and providing material support for terrorism. Bahlul refused to participate in the trial or to permit his counsel to participate. Bahlul had scripted videotaped wills of two of the September 11 hijackers and was charged with having made a two hour al Qaeda promotional video designed to recruit suicide bombers that included a portrayal and praise of the attack on the U.S.S. Cole. Bahlul was sentenced to life in prison. His appeal is also described infra.

A number of other cases were pending before the military commissions at the time President Obama suspended proceedings. Later the government requested an additional suspension of the proceedings, initially while the administration sought new legislation, which it eventually obtained in the form of the 2009 revision of the Military Commissions Act. In a few instances, the government moved to dismiss the charges before the commissions.

QUESTIONS AND NOTES

1.   Several of the offenses listed under the MCA are controversial in that context; the question is whether they are offenses under the law of war, and if not, whether applying them to persons who engaged in the proscribed conduct before the MCA was enacted can be punished thereunder. Among the controversial offenses are conspiracy and the crime of providing material support. Recall that Justice Stevens in Hamdan, speaking for a plurality of the Court, addressed the question of whether conspiracy was a crime under the law of war.

2.   Two cases mentioned above were appealed to the United States Court of Military Commission Review, that of Salim Ahmed Hamdan and Ali Hamza Ahmad Suliman Bahlul. The general issue described in note 1 supra, was before the reviewing court in both the Hamdan and Bahlul cases. The Hamdan conviction which involved reliance on the material support offense was affirmed in an opinion handed down on June 24, 2011, United States v. Hamden, CMCR 09–002, in which the court stated:

> Appellant contends that Congress exceeded its authority in violation of the Constitution's Define and Punish Clause, art. I, § 8, cl. 10, when Congress established providing material support for terrorism as an offense in the 2006 M.C.A. We disagree. Provided their actions are taken respecting the Constitution, the President and the Congress have broad discretion when acting during an ongoing conflict in the areas of war powers, foreign relations, and aliens. Nothing in the current appeal serves to challenge the outer limits of the Congress's authority under the Constitution's Define and Punish Clause.

3.   The Bahlul conviction was affirmed, United States v. al Bahlul, ___ F.Supp.2d ___, 2011 WL 4916373 (USCMCR, 2011). The case had been argued on March 17, 2011 respecting the following questions that had been specified by the court:

> I.   Assuming that Charges I, II, and III allege underlying conduct (e.g., murder of protected persons) that violates the law of armed conflict and that "joint criminal enterprise" is a theory of individual criminal liability under the law of armed conflict, what, if any, impact does the "joint criminal enterprise" theory of individual criminal liability have on this Court's determinations of whether Charges I through III constitute offenses triable by military commission and whether those charges violate the *Ex Post Facto clause of the Constitution?*

II. In numerous Civil War and Philippine Insurrection cases, military commissions convicted persons of aiding or providing support to the enemy. Is the offense of aiding the enemy limited to those who have betrayed an allegiance or duty to a sovereign nation?

4. An excerpt from the defendant's reply brief in the Bahlul appeal, supra, appears below:

Appellee does not appear to contest the fact that it did not charge Mr. al Bahlul with underlying war crimes on the basis of a joint criminal enterprise or any other theory of vicarious liability. Nor do they argue that the evidence would support charging Mr. al Bahlul for underlying substantive war crimes. Nor do they contend that they actually brought to trial someone who was involved in the USS Cole Attack or the atrocities committed on September 11th. Appellee implies, however, that this Court could find Mr. al Bahlul criminally culpable for the "execution of that common plan" to perpetrate them.

As stated in Appellant's initial brief, criminal complicity in the execution of war crimes was not what prosecutors charged, what the evidence showed, what the military judge instructed, nor what the members found. Appellee cannot now vary its theory of the case two and half years after trial.

5. In March, 2011, the Obama administration had indicated that trials before the military commissions would resume. On April 4, 2011, Attorney General Holder, reversing a previous decision to prosecute the cases in federal court in New York, announced that Sheik Mohammed and four others, accused of having planned the 9/11 attacks, would be prosecuted in military commission trials.

6. On July 7, 2010, Ibrahim Ahmed Mahmoud al-Qosi, a Guantanamo detainee, pled guilty to conspiring with al-Qaeda and to providing material support for terrorism. This was the first military commission proceeding brought to closure, during the Obama administration.

7. See George P. Fletcher, 5 J.Int.Crim.J. 39 (2007), commenting on the 2006 MCA; the issues he raises are not changed by the 2009 MCA:

Abstract

The Military Commissions Act 2006 seems to have a much broader application than the 2003 Military Commission Instruction Number 2, ... None of the 28 specific crimes listed in § 950v(b) of the 2006 Act mentions a nexus with armed conflict. This Act raises a number of questions. In particular three issues are relevant: (i) Congress intended to act under its constitutional power 'to define offenses against the law of nations.' In so far as some of these offences are not violations of the law of nations, they fall outside the field of legislative competence; (ii) the Military Commissions are given excessive discretion in the field of sentencing. There are no terms of imprisonment provided. In many cases the death penalty is allowed. Otherwise the Commissions may impose any sentence they wish. This degree of discretion arguably violates the Eighth Amendment against 'cruel and unusual punishment'; (iii) there might be a violation of the principle of equal protection: is it constitutional to impose a special regime on suspects simply because they are 'aliens'?

8. Regarding the offense of "terrorism," Professor Fletcher earlier commented regarding the provision for that offense under the pre-Hamdan legal regime, George P. Fletcher, War Crimes Proceedings in Iraq? The Bush Administration's Dilemma, posted on Findlaw.com on April 4, 2003. The crime of terror is contained in the 2009 MCA, as it was in the 2006 statute:

> Most of the crimes described ... come straight from the Geneva Conventions, and run parallel to the war crimes defined in the Rome Statute [that] established the International Criminal Court. These include the crimes of killing civilians, taking hostages, using poisonous weapons, and killing or injuring treacherously.

> But, significantly, the list includes some new offenses—crimes not now recognized under American law. For example, the term "terrorism" is used, much like the phrase "organized crime," to refer to a category of offenses, rather than a single offense. No crime by the name of "terrorism" is to be found in either the Rome Statute or U.S. federal law.

E. THE CHOICE BETWEEN MILITARY AND CIVILIAN CUSTODY AND MILITARY COMMISSION AND CIVILIAN PROSECUTION

The Military Commissions Act, like the President's November 13, 2001 Military Order, only authorizes trial of aliens before the military commissions. At the same time, the government has, in two instances thus far, the cases of Hamdi and Padilla, claimed the authority to hold U.S. citizens as unlawful enemy combatants. In the case of Hamdi, a settlement was reached and he was released to Saudi Arabia. In the case of Padilla, he was transferred back to civilian jurisdiction, prosecuted and convicted of, and sentenced for terrorism offenses. There is a disconnect between the assertion of the power to hold U.S. citizens as enemy combatants and the fact that the power to try them before a military commission is lacking. That disconnect may help to account for the government's decision to shift Padilla back to civilian custody.

The bases, too, on which the government early on was making the decision whether to treat some individuals as normal criminal arrestees and some as enemy combatants have not been publicly articulated. Examination of what is publicly known about the persons who have been treated in one category or the other does not entirely help to explicate the criteria that are being applied. One possible speculation is that the government was more likely to use the enemy combatant approach when it believed that the individual being detained had important information and wished to be able to interrogate at length, without being restricted by the procedural protections that attach in normal civilian criminal process. A second factor might be that the enemy combatant category was more likely to be used when the government considered the person to be guilty and too dangerous to release but did not have enough admissible evidence to convict.

Some of the cases that have been prosecuted have made the choices made seem puzzling. For example, John Walker Lindh was picked up on the battlefield, and prosecution was initiated in a United States district court in the Eastern District of Virginia. It is hard to see how his case differed from that of Hamdi, and on the face of things, the case for treating him as an enemy combatant seemed, if anything, stronger than the Padilla case. A possible explanation of the decision to prosecute Walker Lindh in a civilian forum is that it was the first one in this series, and at the time the government may not have yet sorted through how it was going to handle such cases.

Other cases, too, present similar conundrums as well. Zacarias Moussaoui, is a French citizen who was apprehended in the United States and was prosecuted in a U.S. District Court although at times there were statements made by government officials that seemed to indicate there was a possibility that his case would be transferred to military jurisdiction. Richard Reid, a British citizen, the so-called "shoe bomber," was apprehended on an airplane bound for the United States, and he, too, was criminally charged in a civilian court in Massachusetts where the plane was diverted. Recently, the Obama administration has been more frequently choosing to charge terrorists, in civilian courts, even if seized abroad.

Our criminal enforcement system, of course, is rife with choices that prosecutors make regarding the forum in which to prosecute. A frequent choice-of-forum issue is between a state or a federal prosecution, and many different kinds of considerations can affect that choice, including the legal advantages of prosecuting in one or the other forum. See generally, Norman Abrams, Sara Sun Beale and Susan Riva Klein, Federal Criminal Law and Its Enforcement, pp. 76–84 (5th ed. 2010). At an early stage and prior to the promulgation of any regulations establishing the procedures to be used before the military commissions, they appeared to have enormous legal and practical advantages for the government (and corresponding disadvantages for a defendant) in comparison with prosecution in a federal court. The gap between the two kinds of procedures has been narrowed at each successive stage of regulatory or legislative change. What comparative advantages and disadvantages remain between military and civilian prosecution under the procedures provided for in the MCA and the Manual for Military Commissions?

QUESTIONS AND NOTES

1. Numerous pragmatic justifications have been offered by the government as to why military commissions are needed. Of course, ultimately, the use of a military commission is premised on the fact that we are at war and that cases against enemy combatants can be adjudicated under the laws of war before military commissions.

2. How many of the following justifications are likely to be applicable to some cases and not to others? How many of them, if applicable in a particular

case, might be grounds for using a military commission instead of a federal district court?

    a.   Military handling of a matter permits more effective interrogation of the defendant and a lengthier period in which to gather evidence;

    b.   It is easier to maintain the confidentiality of classified information in a military commission (in this connection, compare the protection afforded to classified information in a civilian court under the Classified Information Procedures Act);

    c.   Military trials can be conducted more quickly—it is possible to avoid prolonged delays and lengthy proceedings;

    d.   It does not make sense to bring hundreds of persons captured in military encounters abroad to the United States to be tried in U.S. civil courts for being accessories to terrorism; there is even less justification for bringing such persons to the U.S. for trial when they are almost all foreign nationals;

    e.   It is easier to close a military commission proceeding to the press and public than to close a civilian trial. Non-public proceedings may be desirable and even necessary in some of these cases;

    f.   It is easier to keep the participants safe from retaliatory terrorist activity in a military setting;

    g.   Military commissions avoid the use of lay juries. Juries in these cases make for inefficiency, change the style of presentation of the evidence, and open up the possibility of the jurors' passions and prejudices affecting the proceeding.

    3.   Can you think of other pragmatic factors that might be taken into account in deciding whether to prosecute in a military commission a person who is subject to the terms of the MCA?

F.   LITERATURE REGARDING MILITARY COMMISSIONS

    A great deal has been written in the scholarly literature about the military commissions and enemy combatant status. A brief selection includes: Jennifer Elsea, Cong. Res. Service, CRS Rep. for Congress, The Military Commissions Act of 2006: Analysis of Procedural Rules and Comparison with Previous DOD Rules and the Uniform Code of Military Justice (Sep. 27, 2007), http://www.fas.org/sgp/crs/natsec/RL33688.pdf; Developments Regarding the Military Commissions Act and Detentions at Guantanamo Bay, 101 AM. J. INT'L L. 659 (2007); Richard H. Fallon, Jr. & Daniel J. Meltzer, Habeas Corpus Jurisdiction, Substantive Rights, and the War on Terror, 120 HARV. L. REV. 2029 (2007); Allison M. Danner, Defining Unlawful Enemy Combatants: a Centripetal Story, 43 TEX. INT'L L.J. 1 (2007); Carl Tobias, The Process Due Indefinitely Detained Citizens, 85 N.C. L. REV. 1687 (2007); Robert J. Pushaw, Jr., The "Enemy Combatant" Cases in Historical Context: the Inevitability of Pragmatic Judicial

Review, 82 NOTRE DAME L. REV. 1005 (2007); Christopher J. Schatz & Noah A. F. Horst, Will Justice Delayed be Justice Denied? Crisis Jurisprudence, the Guantanamo Detainees, and the Imperiled Role of Habeas Corpus in Curbing Abusive Government Detention, 11 LEWIS & CLARK L. REV. 539 (2007); Jennifer Van Bergen & Douglas Valentine, The Dangerous World of Indefinite Detentions: Vietnam to Abu Ghraib, 37 CASE W. RES. J. INT'L L. 449 (2006); Aya Gruber, Raising the Red Flag: the Continued Relevance of the Japanese Internment in the Post–Hamdi World, 54 U. KAN. L. REV. 307 (2006); John Ip, Comparative Perspective on the Detention of Terrorist Suspects, 16 TRANSNAT'L L. & CONTEMP. PROBS. 773 (2007); Jennifer Elsea, Cong. Res. Service, CRS Rep. for Congress, Detention of American Citizens as Enemy Combatants 2 (Mar. 31, 2005), http://www.fas.org/sgp/crs/natsec/RL317 24.pdf; Morris D. Davis, In Defense of Guantanamo Bay, 117 YALE L.J. Pocket Part 21 (2007); Stephen Vladeck, The Laws of War as a Constitutional Limit on Military Jurisdiction, 4 J. NAT'L SEC. L. & POL'Y 295 (2010).

CHAPTER 12

TARGETED KILLING

■ ■ ■

A. INTRODUCTION

The subject of targeted killing presents complexities and concerns different from any of the other topics addressed in this volume. Generally, there is difficulty in obtaining official information about it. Government policy is not available to be perused and evaluated. How the government makes decisions in individual cases is hidden from view. It is even less likely to be the subject of litigation, civil or criminal, than other matters treated in this book.

Nevertheless, some matters surface; others are leaked, though, of course, the reliability of leaked information is always in question. And, in an unusual confluence of circumstances, in one recent instance litigation was initiated challenging the alleged placing of an individual on a kill list. While the lawsuit was dismissed, it nevertheless presented an opportunity for a judicial airing, albeit limited, of some of the issues in this complex subject.

The topic, if anything, is recently more in the public eye. There are several reasons: The Al–Aulaqi litigation, mentioned above, initiated by his father along with others, engendered much media attention (which, of course, was part of its purpose). The U.S. policy to use drones extensively to target terrorists in the border regions of Afghanistan and Pakistan is a form of targeted killing, albeit in a clear-cut battle zone, and has contributed to keeping the general issue in the realm of public discussion. Finally, some of the ambiguity about the specific circumstances surrounding the killing of Osama Bin Laden raised the possibility of targeted killing. (Of course, in any close-encounter killing, the risk of danger to the attackers creates uncertainty about the question whether the killing was necessary in the circumstances.)

In subsection B, some presidential executive orders dealing with governmental policy regarding assassination are reproduced. Subsection C raises a series of issues and questions regarding targeted killing policy, and subsection D presents the Al–Aulaqi case.

B. EXECUTIVE ORDERS

Executive Order 11905 (United States Foreign Intelligence Activities)

February 18, 1976 [signed by President Gerald Ford].

41 FR 7703, 1976

Sec. 5. Restrictions on Intelligence Activities

. . .

(g) Prohibition of Assassination. No employee of the United States Government shall engage in, or conspire to engage in, political assassination.

. . .

Executive Order 12333 (United States Intelligence Activities)

December 4, 1981 [signed by President Ronald Reagan].

46 FR 59941, 1981 WL 76054.

Part 2

. . .

2.11 Prohibition on Assassination. No person employed by or acting on behalf of the United States Government shall engage in, or conspire to engage in, assassination.

2.12 Indirect Participation. No agency of the Intelligence Community shall participate in or request any person to undertake activities forbidden by this Order.

C. POLICY ISSUES

QUESTIONS AND NOTES

1. The Gerald Ford Executive Order prohibition on political assassination was reaffirmed by President Carter. Note that the Ford prohibition speaks of "political assassination" while the Reagan Order simply prohibits "assassination." Is this difference significant? How would you define "political assassination"? Note that during the Reagan administration the U.S. dropped bombs on the home of Libyan leader Colonel Muammar Gaddafi, the Libyan leader, in retaliation for a terrorist bombing in Germany directed against a place frequented by American soldiers. During the Clinton administration, the U.S. fired cruise missiles at suspected guerrilla camps in Afghanistan after the bombings of two U.S. embassies in Africa. *See* U.S. Policy on Assassination, CNN transcript, November 4, 2002, 6:38 p.m. Should these events be viewed as breaches of the policy or as a guide to how the assassination ban is being (should be?) interpreted?

2. It was reported by CNN, *supra* note 1, that after the September 11 attacks, the White House said that the prohibition against assassinations would not prevent the U.S from acting in self-defense. Other administration

sources have indicated that the ban on assassination does not apply in wartime. Then–Senate Joseph Biden was quoted as saying: "These are combatants of war. And I find no difficulty with it." *See* Senators Support CIA Anti–Terror Effort, Reuters, December 15, 2002, 4:18 p.m.

3. Apart from executive orders on the subject, there is no publicly available statement of policy in this area. News reports have indicated that after September 11, the President signed a secret finding that authorizes the CIA to covertly attack al Qaeda members anywhere in the world, contains no exemption for American citizens, and does not require that the President approve specific operations. Reportedly also, the administration has prepared a list of terrorist leaders the CIA is authorized to kill, but the CIA's authority to kill is not limited to those on the list. *See* James Risen and David Johnston, Threats and Responses: Hunt for al Qaeda: Bush Has Widened Authority of CIA To Kill Terrorists, NY Times, December 15, 2002.

4. On November 3, 2002, a missile fired by a U.S. unmanned aerial vehicle killed a carload of suspected operatives in Yemen. The principal target of the attack was a man named Qaed Salim Sinan al-Harethi, who was allegedly an al Qaeda operative in Yemen. He was suspected of having been involved in the terrorist attack on the U.S.S. Cole. Reportedly, an American citizen was also in the car which was totally destroyed. For a news story about a failed targeted killing that killed many bystanders and an indication that there were numerous such attacks early post-9/11, see Josh Meyer, CIA Expands Use of Drones in Terror War, LA Times, July 29, 2006. Also see articles cited in note 11, infra.

5. Immediately after the Yemen attack described in note 4, supra, many legal commentators criticized such targeting and killing of persons suspected of terrorist acts. *See* Laura K. Donohue, The "Good Guy" Turns Assassin, LA Times, Nov. 17, 2002, Sunday Opinion Section. Professor Donohue argues, *inter alia*: 1) how can we claim to be a protector of human rights when we engage in extrajudicial killings; 2) is it better to kill individuals whose guilt is unproved than for lives of Americans to be put at risk? 3) if we are at war, it should be a just war and we must be careful in the force that we use; 4) we need to provide immunity for innocents whenever possible; 5) assassination erodes national security by undermining our image and our moral authority before the world community. Also see Daniel B. Pickard, Legalizing Assassination? Terrorism, The Central Intelligence Agency and International Law, 39 Ga. J. Int'l & Comp.L. 1 (2001); Patricia Zengel, Assassination and the Law of Armed Conflict, 45 Mercer L. Rev. 615 (1992).

6. Is the argument that "we are at war and killing the enemy in wartime is acceptable" a sufficient answer to the kind of arguments articulated in the previous note? If you were in a position of authority in the administration, what position would you take on this issue?

7. Assume that in fact you are employed in the administration. Your superior asks you to prepare a set of policies and procedures governing the subject of target killings? Assume, too, that you have grave doubts about the morality and/or the efficacy of such a policy. What would you do?

8. Same case as note 7, *supra*, but assume that you do not have any qualms about developing policies and procedures on the subject of targeted

killings and therefore set to work on your assignment. What position would you recommend should be taken on the following issues?

a. At what level of government should the specific determination to target an individual suspected terrorist be made? Absent urgency, should the President be involved in each such case? Should the Secretary of Defense? Anyone else? Note: news reports have indicated that the President has issued a finding authorizing such killings, but is not consulted in the individual case.

b. What kind of terrorist involvement, al Qaeda membership, leadership role in al Qaeda, and/or specific terrorist acts should be required, before a targeting order is approved?

c. What kind of evidence of the involvements described in b. above should be required? Suppose all of the information is based on informants' reports? How would you formulate the standard of proof?

d. Should there be a kind of formal fact-finding process? What kinds of formalities, if any? Any process of review of the fact-finding determination? By whom? How many?

e. Under what circumstances should a targeted killing be considered an acceptable option? For example, should there be a specific determination that the option of capturing the suspect would be too dangerous or logistically impossible? Note that it is reported that Harethi was living in a remote area of Yemen that was a lawless region where the Yemeni government had little control. See NY Times, December 15, 2002, *supra*, note 3.

f. Targeted killings have occurred on the battlefield, that is, in Afghanistan and in Yemen. Should the policies distinguish between the kinds of settings?

g. Should the consent of the host country's government be required, before undertaking such an action? Note that news reports indicated that unofficially the Yemeni government actually assisted in the Harethi killing by providing intelligence. Suppose the host country is one that tacitly or actively supports the terrorist organizations?

h. Should the policies distinguish between the killing of leaders and those who are lower down in the terrorist organizational hierarchy?

i. Should the policies require input from U.S. law enforcement agencies involved in the anti-terrorism effort, before a determination to target an individual is made?

j. Should the policies prohibit targeted killings on U.S. soil?

k. What kind of assurance should be required in the policies that innocent bystanders will not be injured? What kind of "collateral damage" should be deemed acceptable?

9. A feature of this area is that the actual policy(ies) we are applying and any procedures connected thereto are not publicly available. Nor is this an area where it seems feasible to obtain judicial review that would inquire into the applications of the policy. See infra, Al–Aulaqi v. Obama. In other words, almost all of what we know is derived from the news media and the

occasional interview of government officials, or purported leaks. The policy and practice is essentially unknown and unreviewable outside of the Executive Branch. Would it be desirable to change these features of the situation?

10. The New York Times (David Johnston and David E. Sanger, Yemen Killing Based on Rules Set Out by Bush, NY Times, Nov. 6, 2002) reported that the CIA did not "seek input from or consult law enforcement officials" prior to the killing by missile of Mr. Harethi and his companions in Yemen, *supra* note 4. Law enforcement officials indicated they had wanted to question Harethi about the Cole attack, but they were not unhappy that he had been killed. This would appear to be an area where coordination between the law enforcement and intelligence-military operation is not occurring, even after post-September 11th congressional and administration efforts to improve communication and coordination between these governmental functions. Do you think efforts should be made also to introduce greater coordination into this arena of anti-terrorist activity?

11. For news reports and discussion of some targeted killing efforts, see:

(a) Dana Priest, Surveillance Operation in Pakistan Located and Killed Al Qaeda Official, WASH. POST, May 15, 2005, at A25, available at: http://www.washingtonpost.com/wp-dyn/content/article/2005/05/14/AR 2005051401121.html;

(b) Douglas Jehl & Mohammad Khan, Top Qaeda Aide is Called Target in U.S. Air Raid, N.Y. TIMES, Jan. 14, 2006, at A1, available at: http://www.nytimes.com/2006/01/14/politics/14afghan.html;

(c) Griff Witte & Kamran Khan, U.S. Strike On Al Qaeda Top Deputy Said to Fail: Thousands Protest After Attack In Pakistan Leaves 17 Dead, WASH. POST, Jan. 15, 2006, at A1, available at http://www.washingtonpost.com/wp-yn/content/article/2006/01/14/AR2006011400961_pf.html;

(d) Carlotta Gall & Douglas Jehl, Strike Aimed at Qaeda Figure Stirs More Pakistan Protests, N.Y. TIMES, Jan. 16, 2006, at A3, available at: http://www.nytimes.com/2006/01/16/international/asia/16pakistan.html;

(e) For correspondence between U.N. Special Rapporteur on Extrajudicial, Summary, or Arbitrary Executions and the U.S. government concerning the above incidents, see Project on Extrajudicial Executions, Center for Human Rights and Global Justice, N.Y.U. School of Law, http://www.extrajudicialexecutions.org/communications/united_states.html#2006.

12. For additional journal articles on the subject, see W. Jason Fisher, Targeted Killing, Norms and International Law, 45 COLUM. J. TRANSNAT'L L. 711 (2007); Saad Gul & Katherine M. Royal, Burning the Barn to Roast the Pig? Proportionality Concerns in the War on Terror and the Damadola Incident, 14 WILLAMETTE J. INT'L L. & DISP. RESOL. 49 (2006); David Kretzmer, Targeted Killing of Terrorists: Extra–Judicial Executions or Legitimate Means of Defence?, 16 EUR. J. INT'L L. 171 (2005); Daniel Statman, Targeted Killing, 5 THEORETICAL INQUIRIES IN L. 179 (2004).

D. THE AL–AULAQI CASE

NASSER AL–AULAQI v. OBAMA

727 F. Supp. 2d 1 (D.D.C 2010)

JUDGE: JOHN D. BATES

MEMORANDUM OPINION

On August 30, 2010, plaintiff Nasser Al–Aulaqi ("plaintiff") filed this action, claiming that the President, the Secretary of Defense, and the Director of the CIA (collectively, "defendants") have unlawfully authorized the targeted killing of plaintiff's son, Anwar Al–Aulaqi, a dual U.S.–Yemeni citizen currently hiding in Yemen who has alleged ties to al Qaeda in the Arabian Peninsula ("AQAP"). Plaintiff seeks an injunction prohibiting defendants from intentionally killing Anwar Al–Aulaqi "unless he presents a concrete, specific, and imminent threat to life or physical safety, and there are no means other than lethal force that could reasonably be employed to neutralize the threat." Defendants have responded with a motion to dismiss plaintiff's complaint on five threshold grounds: standing, the political question doctrine, the Court's exercise of its "equitable discretion," the absence of a cause of action under the Alien Tort Statute ("ATS"), and the state secrets privilege.

This is a unique and extraordinary case. Both the threshold and merits issues present fundamental questions of separation of powers involving the proper role of the courts in our constitutional structure.... Vital considerations of national security and of military and foreign affairs (and hence potentially of state secrets) are at play.

Stark, and perplexing, questions readily come to mind, including the following: How is it that judicial approval is required when the United States decides to target a U.S. citizen overseas for electronic surveillance, but that, according to defendants, judicial scrutiny is prohibited when the United States decides to target a U.S. citizen overseas for death? Can a U.S. citizen—himself or through another—use the U.S. judicial system to vindicate his constitutional rights while simultaneously evading U.S. law enforcement authorities, calling for "jihad against the West," and engaging in operational planning for an organization that has already carried out numerous terrorist attacks against the United States? Can the Executive order the assassination of a U.S. citizen without first affording him any form of judicial process whatsoever, based on the mere assertion that he is a dangerous member of a terrorist organization? How can the courts, as plaintiff proposes, make real-time assessments of the nature and severity of alleged threats to national security, determine the imminence of those threats, weigh the benefits and costs of possible diplomatic and military responses, and ultimately decide whether, and under what circumstances, the use of military force against such threats is justified? When would it ever make sense for the United States to disclose in advance to the "target" of contemplated military action the precise standards under which it will take that military action? And how does the evolving AQAP relate to core al Qaeda for purposes of assessing the legality of targeting AQAP (or its principals) under the September 18, 2001 Authorization for the Use of Military Force?

These and other legal and policy questions posed by this case are controversial and of great public interest. "Unfortunately, however, no matter how interesting and no matter how important this case may be ... we cannot address it unless we have jurisdiction." Before reaching the merits of plaintiff's claims, then, this Court must decide whether plaintiff is the proper person to bring the constitutional and statutory challenges he asserts, and whether plaintiff's challenges, as framed, state claims within the ambit of the Judiciary to resolve. These jurisdictional issues pose "distinct and separate limitation[s], so that either the absence of standing or the presence of a political question suffices to prevent the power of the federal judiciary from being invoked by the complaining party."

... Because these questions of justiciability require dismissal of this case at the outset, the serious issues regarding the merits of the alleged authorization of the targeted killing of a U.S. citizen overseas must await another day or another (non-judicial) forum.

BACKGROUND

This case arises from the United States's alleged policy of "authorizing, planning, and carrying out targeted killings, including of U.S. citizens, outside the context of armed conflict." Specifically, plaintiff, a Yemeni citizen, claims that the United States has authorized the targeted killing of plaintiff's son, Anwar Al–Aulaqi, in violation of the Constitution and international law. See id.

Anwar Al–Aulaqi is a Muslim cleric with dual U.S.–Yemeni citizenship, who is currently believed to be in hiding in Yemen.... Anwar Al–Aulaqi was born in New Mexico in 1971, and spent much of his early life in the United States, attending college at Colorado State University and receiving his master's degree from San Diego State University before moving to Yemen in 2004. On July 16, 2010, the U.S. Treasury Department's Office of Foreign Assets Control ("OFAC") designated Anwar Al–Aulaqi as a Specially Designated Global Terrorist ("SDGT") in light of evidence that he was "acting for or on behalf of al-Qa'ida in the Arabian Peninsula (AQAP)" and "providing financial, material or technological support for, or other services to or in support of, acts of terrorism[.]".... In its designation, OFAC explained that Anwar Al–Aulaqi had "taken on an increasingly operational role" in AQAP since late 2009, as he "facilitated training camps in Yemen in support of acts of terrorism" and provided "instructions" to Umar Farouk Abdulmutallab, the man accused of attempting to detonate a bomb aboard a Detroit-bound Northwest Airlines flight on Christmas Day 2009. Media sources have also reported ties between Anwar Al–Aulaqi and Nidal Malik Hasan, the U.S. Army Major suspected of killing 13 people in a November 2009 shooting at Fort Hood, Texas. According to a January 2010 Los Angeles Times article, unnamed "U.S. officials" have discovered that Anwar Al–Aulaqi and Hasan exchanged as many as eighteen e-mails prior to the Fort Hood shootings.

Recently, Anwar Al–Aulaqi has made numerous public statements calling for "jihad against the West," praising the actions of "his students" Abdulmutallab and Hasan, and asking others to "follow suit." Michael Leiter, Director of the National Counterterrorism Center, has explained that Anwar Al–Aulaqi's "familiarity with the West" is a "key concern[]" for the United States, and media sources have similarly cited Anwar Al–Aulaqi's ability to communicate with an English-speaking audience as a source of "particular concern" to U.S. officials.... But despite the United States's expressed "concern" regarding Anwar Al–Aulaqi's "familiarity with the West" and his "role in AQAP," United States has not yet publicly charged Anwar Al–Aulaqi with any crime. For his part, Anwar Al–Aulaqi has made clear that he has no intention of making himself available for criminal prosecution in U.S. courts, remarking in a May 2010 AQAP video interview that he "will never surrender" to the United States, and that "[i]f the Americans want me, [they can] come look for me." ... Plaintiff does not deny his son's affiliation with AQAP or his designation as a SDGT. Rather, plaintiff challenges his son's alleged unlawful inclusion on so-called "kill lists" that he contends are maintained by the CIA and the Joint Special Operations Command ("JSOC"). In support of his claim that the United States has placed Anwar Al–Aulaqi on "kill lists," plaintiff cites a number of media reports, which attribute their information to anonymous U.S. military and intelligence sources. For example, in January 2010, The Washington Post reported that, according to unnamed military officials, Anwar Al–Aulaqi was on "a shortlist of U.S. citizens" that JSOC was authorized to kill or capture. A few months later, The Washington Post cited an anonymous U.S. official as stating that Anwar Al–Aulaqi had become "the first U.S. citizen added to a list of suspected terrorists the CIA is authorized to kill." And in July 2010, National Public Radio announced—on the basis of unidentified "[i]ntelligence sources"—that the United States had already ordered "almost a dozen" unsuccessful drone and air-strikes targeting Anwar Al–Aulaqi in Yemen.

Based on these news reports, plaintiff claims that the United States has placed Anwar Al–Aulaqi on the CIA and JSOC "kill lists" without "charge, trial, or conviction." Plaintiff alleges that individuals like his son are placed on "kill lists" after a "closed executive process" in which defendants and other executive officials determine that "secret criteria" have been satisfied. Plaintiff further avers "[u]pon information and belief" that once an individual is placed on a "kill list," he remains there for "months at a time." (quoting unnamed U.S. officials as stating that "kill lists" are reviewed every six months and names are removed from the list if there is no longer intelligence linking the person to "known terrorists or [terrorist] plans"). Consequently, plaintiff argues, Anwar Al–Aulaqi is "now subject to a standing order that permits the CIA and JSOC to kill him ... without regard to whether, at the time lethal force will be used, he presents a concrete, specific, and imminent threat to life, or whether there are reasonable means short of lethal force that could be used to address any such threat."

The United States has neither confirmed nor denied the allegation that it has issued a "standing order" authorizing the CIA and JSOC to kill plaintiff's son. Additionally, the United States has neither confirmed nor denied whether—if it has, in fact, authorized the use of lethal force against plaintiff's son—the authorization was made with regard to whether Anwar Al–Aulaqi presents a concrete, specific, and imminent threat to life, or whether there were reasonable means short of lethal force that could be used to address any such threat. The United States has, however, repeatedly stated that if Anwar Al–Aulaqi "were to surrender or otherwise present himself to the proper authorities in a peaceful and appropriate manner, legal principles with which the United States has traditionally and uniformly complied would prohibit using lethal force or other violence against him in such circumstances."

Nevertheless, plaintiff alleges that due to his son's inclusion on the CIA and JSOC "kill lists," Anwar Al–Aulaqi is in "hiding under threat of death and cannot access counsel or the courts to assert his constitutional rights without disclosing his whereabouts and exposing himself to possible attack by Defendants."

Plaintiff therefore brings four claims—three constitutional, and one statutory—on his son's behalf. He asserts that the United States's alleged policy of authorizing the targeted killing of U.S. citizens, including plaintiff's son, outside of armed conflict, "in circumstances in which they do not present concrete, specific, and imminent threats to life or physical safety, and where there are means other than lethal force that could reasonably be employed to neutralize any such threat," violates (1) Anwar Al–Aulaqi's *Fourth Amendment* right to be free from unreasonable seizures and (2) his *Fifth Amendment* right not to be deprived of life without due process of law. Plaintiff further claims that (3) the United States's refusal to disclose the criteria by which it selects U.S. citizens like plaintiff's son for targeted killing independently violates the notice requirement of the *Fifth Amendment Due Process Clause*. Finally, plaintiff brings (4) a statutory claim under the Alien Tort Statute ("ATS"), *28 U.S.C. § 1350*, alleging that the United States's "policy of targeted killings violates treaty and customary international law."

Plaintiff seeks both declaratory and injunctive relief. First, he requests a declaration that, outside of armed conflict, the Constitution prohibits defendants "from carrying out the targeted killing of U.S. citizens," including Anwar Al–Aulaqi, "except in circumstances in which they present a concrete, specific, and imminent threat to life or physical safety, and there are no means other than lethal force that could reasonably be employed to neutralize the threat." Second, plaintiff requests a declaration that, outside of armed conflict, "treaty and customary international law" prohibit the targeted killing of all individuals—regardless of their citizenship—except in those same, limited circumstances. Third, plaintiff requests a preliminary injunction prohibiting defendants from intentionally killing Anwar Al–Aulaqi "unless he presents a concrete, specific, and imminent threat to life or physical safety, and there are no means other than lethal force that could reasonably be employed to neutralize the threat." Finally, plaintiff seeks an injunction ordering defendants to disclose the criteria that the United States uses to determine whether a U.S. citizen will be targeted for killing.

[The court proceeded in a lengthy opinion to dismiss the complaint on the grounds that the plaintiff lacks standing, there is no cause of action under the Alien Tort Statute and the issues raise a political question. The court declined to decide the defendants' state secret privilege argument. In addressing the political question issue, the court made the following comments:]

. . .

Judicial resolution of the "particular questions" posed by plaintiff in this case would require this Court to decide: (1) the precise nature and extent of Anwar Al-bAulaqi's affiliation with AQAP; (2) whether AQAP and al Qaeda are so closely linked that the defendants' targeted killing of Anwar Al–Aulaqi in Yemen would come within the United States's current armed conflict with al Qaeda; (3) whether (assuming plaintiff's proffered legal standard applies) Anwar Al–Aulaqi's alleged terrorist activity renders him a "concrete, specific, and imminent threat to life or physical safety," and (4) whether there are "means short of lethal force" that the United States could "reasonably" employ to address any threat that Anwar Al–Aulaqi poses to U.S. national security interests. Such determinations, in turn, would require this Court, in defendants' view, to understand and assess "the capabilities of the [alleged] terrorist operative to carry out a threatened attack, what response would be sufficient to address that threat, possible diplomatic considerations that may bear on such responses, the vulnerability of potential targets that the [alleged] terrorist[] may strike, the availability of military and non-military options, and the risks to military and nonmilitary personnel in attempting application of non-lethal force." Viewed through these prisms, it becomes clear that plaintiff's claims pose precisely the types of complex policy questions that the D.C. Circuit has historically held non-justiciable under the political question doctrine.

. . .

The type of relief that plaintiff seeks only underscores the impropriety of judicial review here. Plaintiff requests both a declaration setting forth the standard under which the United States can select individuals for targeted killing as well as an injunction prohibiting defendants from intentionally killing Anwar Al–Aulaqi unless he meets that standard—i.e., unless he "presents a concrete, specific, and imminent threat to life or physical safety, and there are no means other than lethal force that could reasonably be employed to neutralize the threat." Yet plaintiff concedes that the " 'imminence' requirement" of his proffered legal standard would render any "real-time judicial review" of targeting decisions "infeasible," and he therefore urges this Court to issue his requested preliminary injunction and then enforce the injunction "through an after-the-fact contempt motion or an after-the-fact damages action ... [T]here is a "textually demonstrable constitutional commitment" of the United States's decision to employ military force to coordinate political departments (Congress and the Executive), and any after-the-fact judicial review of the Executive's decision to employ military force abroad would reveal a "lack of respect due coordinate branches of government" and create "the potentiality of embarrassment of multifarious pronouncements by various departments on one question."

. . .

To be sure, this Court recognizes the somewhat unsettling nature of its conclusion—that there are circumstances in which the Executive's unilateral decision to kill a U.S. citizen overseas is "constitutionally committed to the political branches" and judicially unreviewable. But this case squarely presents such a circumstance. . . .

QUESTIONS AND NOTES

1. Anwar Al–Aulagi was killed by a U.S. drone strike on September 30, 2011. Does the court's discussion in Al–Aulaqi affect your views about any of the policy issues in this area of terrorism law? For example, about the possible feasibility or efficacy of judicial review of these issues?

2. The court in the Al–Aulaqi makes passing reference to one of the arguments raised by plaintiffs—why should governmental intrusions on privacy abroad through electronic surveillance be subject to legislative regulation (see ch. 5, supra) while governmental targeting killings abroad are not? Are these two areas of the law different?

3. The fact that Anwar Al–Aulaqi's name was put on a kill list was leaked (if it was a leak of accurate information). This may have been, like many leaks of confidential information, leaked against the wishes of government authorities, motivated by the private reasons of the leaker. There is, however, another possibility: the government may have wanted to disseminate the information. How many reasons might there be why the government would want to make this information unofficially public?

4. The Al–Aulaqi case quickly triggered a number of papers: See, e.g., Ryan Patrick Alford, The Rule of Law at the Crossroads: Consequences of Targeted Killings of Citizens, http://ssrn.com/abstract=1780584; Debate–Targeted Killing: The Case of Anwar Al–Aulaqi, 159 U. Penn. L. Rev. 175 (2011); Robert Chesney, Who May be Killed? Anwar Al–Awlaki as a Case Study in the International Legal Regulation of Lethal Force, Yearbook of International Humanitarian Law (forthcoming 2011).

CHAPTER 13

USING THE MILITARY IN DOMESTIC LAW ENFORCEMENT

■ ■ ■

A. INTRODUCTION

The attacks on September 11, 2001 posed many questions for this country never before asked. Among them is whether our existing law enforcement agencies are adequate to deal with the dangers that the terrorism poses to our security on the home front. A few leaders have raised the possibility of increasing the role of the military in helping to deal with the problem of terrorism in the United States.[1] Throughout our history, we have been reluctant, however, to expand the role of the military beyond its traditional confines. Justice Douglas dissenting in Laird v. Tatum, 408 U.S. 1, 19, 23–24 (1972), considered *supra* in Chapter 4, at p. 141, described our tradition very well:

> Our tradition reflects a desire for civilian supremacy and subordination of military power. The tradition of civilian control over the Armed Forces was stated by Chief Justice Warren:
>
>> "The military establishment is, of course, a necessary organ of government; but the reach of its power must be carefully limited lest the delicate balance between freedom and order be upset. The maintenance of the balance is made more difficult by the fact that while the military serves the vital function of preserving the existence of the nation, it is, at the same time, the one element of government that exercises a type of authority not easily assimilated in a free society....
>
> . . .
>
>> "In times of peace, the factors leading to an extraordinary deference to claims of military necessity have naturally not been as weighty. This has been true even in the all too imperfect peace that has been our lot for the past fifteen years—and quite rightly

---

1. *See* Eric Schmitt, Wider Military Role in U.S. Is Urged, NY Times, July 21, 2002, at A16 (reporting that the new commanding general of the U.S. military's North America command supported an expansion of military activities against terrorism.) *See also* Joyce Howard Price, Biden Backs Letting Soldiers Arrest Civilians, Wash. Times, July 22, 2002 at A1.

so, in my judgment. It is instructive to recall that our Nation at the time of the Constitutional Convention was also faced with formidable problems. The English, the French, the Spanish, and various tribes of hostile Indians were all ready and eager to subvert or occupy the fledgling Republic. Nevertheless, in that environment, our Founding Fathers conceived a Constitution and Bill of Rights replete with provisions indicating their determination to protect human rights. There was no call for a garrison state in those times of precarious peace. We should heed no such call now. If we were to fail in these days to enforce the freedom that until now has been the American citizen's birthright, we would be abandoning for the foreseeable future the constitutional balance of powers and rights in whose name we arm."

. . .

The action in turning the "armies" loose on surveillance of civilians was a gross repudiation of our traditions. The military, though important to us, is subservient and restricted purely to military missions.

. . .

The act of turning the military loose on civilians even if sanctioned by an Act of Congress, which it has not been, would raise serious and profound constitutional questions. Standing as it does only on brute power and Pentagon policy, it must be repudiated as a usurpation dangerous to the civil liberties on which free men are dependent. For, as Senator Sam Ervin has said, "this claim of an inherent executive branch power of investigation and surveillance on the basis of people's beliefs and attitudes may be more of a threat to our internal security than any enemies beyond our borders."

The challenge to the army surveillance program in Laird was framed in constitutional First Amendment terms, but it also arguably might have posed an issue[2] under the Posse Comitatus statute, 18 U.S.C. § 1385, which provides:

> Whoever, except in cases and under circumstances expressly authorized by the Constitution or Act of Congress, willfully uses any part of the Army or the Air Force as a posse comitatus or otherwise to execute the laws shall be fined under this title or imprisoned not more than two years, or both.

The Posse Comitatus Act was enacted after the Civil War to bar the use of federal troops in overseeing elections and in other ways in the former Confederate States once civilian authority had reestablished itself. The Act was later amended to include the Air Force. Although the Navy

---

2. The surveillance program challenged in Laird was begun by the U.S. Army in the wake of the urban riots in the summer of 1967 when it was thought that federal troops might be needed to quell the disturbances. That type of emergency role has traditionally been viewed as an exception to the Posse Comitatus prohibition, which is governed by other provisions in federal law. See, e.g., 10 U.S.C. § 331.

and Marines are not mentioned in the Act, those services have applied the prohibition expressed in the Act to themselves. The Coast Guard, which had been in the Department of Transportation but is now in the Department of Homeland Security, has traditionally had a domestic law enforcement role in policing our shores, and thus has not been affected by the Act. The federal army reserves have always been considered subject to the Act, but the states' National Guard units have not, for historic reasons related to Federalism.

The Posse Comitatus Act has served both symbolically and in practice as a major[3] legal restriction on the domestic use of the military for law enforcement purposes. Thus when proposals for using the military against terrorism have been broached, they have sometimes been framed in terms of amending the Act.[4]

Modifications of the prohibition also occur through the recognition of exceptions or through direct grants of authority under specific statutes. For example, Section 104 of the USA PATRIOT Act authorized the Attorney General to request the Secretary of Defense to provide assistance in support of Department of Justice activities relating to the enforcement of Federal criminal code provisions regarding the use of weapons of mass destruction during an emergency situation involving a weapon of mass destruction. This section broadened the authority of the President, Pentagon and Justice Department to use military assets for assisting law enforcement in situations involving the use of weapons of mass destruction in the United States.

In 2002, in enacting the provisions of the new Homeland Security Act, Congress addressed both the relationship between the new Department of Homeland Security and the Department of Defense, and the question of using the military in the fight against terrorism.

These provisions seemed to reflect the desire of Congress to separate the functions of the two largest departments in the government, and, at the same time, continued the policy of preventing the military from playing anything more than a supporting role in the domestic anti-terrorism effort. Section 876 of the Homeland Security Act explicitly precluded the new Department from engaging in any military activity. Section 886 expressed a "sense of Congress" that the new agency not undermine the existing Posse Comitatus doctrine by using the military in more than a supporting role against terrorism.

Homeland Security Act of 2002

PL 107–296 (HR 5005; 116 Stat. 2135).

November 25, 2002.

SEC. 876.   MILITARY ACTIVITIES.

Nothing in this Act shall confer upon the Secretary any authority to engage in warfighting, the military defense of the United States, or

---

3.   The Act is not the only restriction. See, e.g., *infra*, pp. 766–768.

4.   *See* note 34, *supra*. Senator Biden was quoted as saying that the Act "has to be amended."

other military activities, nor shall anything in this Act limit the existing authority of the Department of Defense or the Armed Forces to engage in warfighting, the military defense of the United States, or other military activities.

SEC. 886. SENSE OF CONGRESS REAFFIRMING THE CONTINUED IMPORTANCE AND APPLICABILITY OF THE POSSE COMITATUS ACT.

(a) FINDINGS—Congress finds the following

(1) Section 1385 of title 18, United States Code (commonly known as the 'Posse Comitatus Act'), prohibits the use of the Armed Forces as a posse comitatus to execute the laws except in cases and under circumstances expressly authorized by the Constitution or Act of Congress.

(2) Enacted in 1878, the Posse Comitatus Act was expressly intended to prevent United States Marshals, on their own initiative, from calling on the Army for assistance in enforcing Federal law.

(3) The Posse Comitatus Act has served the Nation well in limiting the use of the Armed Forces to enforce the law.

(4) Nevertheless, by its express terms, the Posse Comitatus Act is not a complete barrier to the use of the Armed Forces for a range of domestic purposes, including law enforcement functions, when the use of the Armed Forces is authorized by Act of Congress or the President determines that the use of the Armed Forces is required to fulfill the President's obligations under the Constitution to respond promptly in time of war, insurrection, or other serious emergency.

(5) Existing laws, including chapter 15 of title 10, United States Code (commonly known as the 'Insurrection Act'), and the Robert T. Stafford Disaster Relief and Emergency Assistance Act (42 U.S.C. 5121 et seq.), grant the President broad powers that may be invoked in the event of domestic emergencies, including an attack against the Nation using weapons of mass destruction, and these laws specifically authorize the President to use the Armed Forces to help restore public order.

(b) SENSE OF CONGRESS—Congress reaffirms the continued importance of section 1385 of title 18, United States Code, and it is the sense of Congress that nothing in this Act should be construed to alter the applicability of such section to any use of the Armed Forces as a posse comitatus to execute the laws.

Several years later, however, in 2006, the Insurrection Act, cited in section (a)(5) of section 886, supra, was significantly amended. The amended language is reproduced and addressed in section C. below, following consideration of the legal authorities interpreting the Posse Comitatus Act.

B. INTERPRETATION AND APPLICATION OF THE POSSE COMITATUS ACT

Over the years, violations of the Posse Comitatus Act have been alleged, but most of these have not come close to a broad-based use of the military in domestic law enforcement. Typically they have involved police actions by military against civilians close to a military base; a few military personnel assisting local law enforcement, typically, in drug cases; the military being called upon to assist law enforcement in hostage or long-term stand-off cases; or the use of the Navy on the high seas in aid of anti-drug enforcement.[5] As mentioned above, the army surveillance program challenged in Laird v. Tatum was perhaps the most comprehensive nation-wide military program that has surfaced that could be viewed as relating to domestic law enforcement, but that program began with a concern about civil disturbances that could justify military involvement as an exception to the Posse Comitatus Act.

The Act is framed as a criminal prohibition, but no one has ever been prosecuted for violating the Act. Questions of the interpretation of the Act, specifically, what it means "to execute the laws," have arisen, however, when persons charged with criminal violations claim, for example, that the military was involved in apprehending or interrogating them, and they argue that evidence obtained from them should be excluded because of violation of the Act. Typically, the courts reject the idea that a violation of the Act can result in the exclusion of evidence, but along the way, they discuss whether the Act has in fact been violated. The district court opinion in United States v. Yunis, reproduced below, is such a case. It provides a good summary of the various approaches taken in interpreting the Act.

UNITED STATES v. YUNIS

681 F.Supp. 891 (D.D.C.1988)

[The following statement of facts is taken from the Court of Appeals opinion in the same case, United States v. Yunis, 924 F.2d 1086 (D.C.Cir. 1991):

On June 11, 1985, appellant and four other men boarded Royal Jordanian Airlines Flight 402 ("Flight 402") shortly before its scheduled departure from Beirut, Lebanon. They wore civilian clothes and carried military assault rifles, ammunition bandoleers, and hand grenades. Appellant took control of the cockpit and forced the pilot to take off immediately. The remaining hijackers tied up Jordanian air marshals assigned to the flight and held the civilian passengers, including two American citizens, captive in their seats. The hijackers explained to the crew and passengers

---

5. The majority of statutory exceptions to the Posse Comitatus doctrine were enacted during the 1980s to support the "war on drugs" during the Reagan and Bush Administrations. See 10 U.S.C. §§ 371–382. *See also*, Major Craig T. Trebilcock, The Myth of Posse Comitatus, Journal of Homeland Security, October 2000.

that they wanted the plane to fly to Tunis, where a conference of the Arab League was under way. The hijackers further explained that they wanted a meeting with delegates to the conference and that their ultimate goal was removal of all Palestinians from Lebanon.

After a refueling stop in Cyprus, the airplane headed for Tunis but turned away when authorities blocked the airport runway. Following a refueling stop at Palermo, Sicily, another attempt to land in Tunis, and a second stop in Cyprus, the plane returned to Beirut, where more hijackers came aboard. These reinforcements included an official of Lebanon's Amal Militia, the group at whose direction Yunis claims he acted. The plane then took off for Syria, but was turned away and went back to Beirut. There, the hijackers released the passengers, held a press conference reiterating their demand that Palestinians leave Lebanon, blew up the plane, and fled from the airport.

An American investigation identified Yunis as the probable leader of the hijackers and prompted U.S. civilian and military agencies, led by the Federal Bureau of Investigation (FBI), to plan Yunis' arrest. After obtaining an arrest warrant, the FBI put "Operation Goldenrod" into effect in September 1987. Undercover FBI agents lured Yunis onto a yacht in the eastern Mediterranean Sea with promises of a drug deal, and arrested him once the vessel entered international waters. The agents transferred Yunis to a United States Navy munitions ship and interrogated him for several days as the vessel steamed toward a second rendezvous, this time with a Navy aircraft carrier. Yunis was flown to Andrews Air Force Base from the aircraft carrier, and taken from there to Washington, D.C. In Washington, Yunis was arraigned on an original indictment charging him with conspiracy, hostage taking, and aircraft damage. A grand jury subsequently returned a superseding indictment adding additional aircraft damage counts and a charge of air piracy.]

PRETRIAL MEMORANDUM ORDER NO. 3

(Denying Defendant's Motion to Dismiss for Violation of the Posse Comitatus Act)

BARRINGTON D. PARKER, UNITED STATES DISTRICT JUDGE:

The Posse Comitatus Act ("the Act"), 18 U.S.C. § 1385, prohibits the use of the nation's military forces as a posse comitatus[6] or otherwise to execute the laws of the United States. Counsel for Fawaz Yunis has moved to dismiss the indictment claiming that the involvement of the United States Navy in the apprehension and arrest of the defendant in the Mediterranean Sea and later, his transportation to the United States, violated the Act.

This Court concludes that the motion should be denied. The Navy's participation and involvement did not embrace nor did it extend to such

---

6. The phrase "posse comitatus" is literally translated from Latin as the "power of the county" and is defined at common law to refer to all those over the age of 15 upon whom a sheriff could call for assistance in preventing any type of civil disorder. *United States v. Hartley*, 796 F.2d 112, 114 (5th Cir.1986) (citing H.R. Rep. No. 97–71, Part II, 97th Cong., 1st Sess. 4 (1981)).

regulatory, proscriptive, or compulsory military powers as contemplated under the Act. The facts in this case show that the Navy played at most, a passive role which indirectly aided the execution of United States laws. By providing military materials, supplies and equipment to the Federal Bureau of Investigation ("FBI"), the Navy did not violate the Posse Comitatus Act. Moreover, that service branch was merely aiding law enforcement efforts of FBI agents in international waters, where no civil governmental authority existed.

The Act provides that:

> Whoever, except in cases and under circumstances expressly authorized by the Constitution or Act of Congress, willfully uses any part of the Army or the Air Force as a posse comitatus or otherwise to execute the laws shall be fined not more than $10,000 or imprisoned not more than two years, or both. 18 U.S.C. § 1385 (1979).

It was originally enacted in response to the use of military personnel to enforce laws in the South during the reconstruction period following the Civil War. Legislative history indicates that the immediate objective of the Act was to end the use of federal troops in former confederate states where civil power had been reestablished. Many southerners believed the troops altered the outcome of state elections by actively supporting reconstruction candidates in disputed elections.... Nearly 40 years ago, our Circuit Court noted that Congress intended to preclude the military from assisting local law enforcement officers in carrying out their duties. *Gillars v. United States*, 87 U.S. App. D.C. 16, 182 F.2d 962, 972 (D.C.Cir. 1950). As noted in a recent appellate ruling, the Act was designed to limit "the direct active use of federal troops by civil law enforcement officers" to enforce the laws of the nation. *United States v. Hartley*, 796 F.2d 112, 114 (5th Cir.1986) (quoting *United States v. Red Feather*, 392 F.Supp. 916, 922 (D.S.D.1975)). Limiting military involvement in civilian affairs is basic to our system of government and the protection of individual constitutional rights.

Because the proscriptions of the Act have been relied upon in various situations, several tests have been articulated to determine whether an individual's rights have been infringed upon through violations of the statute. In the litigation which arose out of the standoff between Native American Indians and federal law enforcement authorities at Wounded Knee, South Dakota, in 1973, United States Marshals, FBI agents, the National Guard, as well as Army and Air Force personnel were both visible and involved. The first test was whether civilian law enforcement agents made "direct active use" of military personnel to execute the laws. *Red Feather*, 392 F.Supp. at 921. (The statute prohibits the "direct active use of Army or Air Force personnel and does not mean the use of Army or Air Force equipment or materiel." *Id.*). The second, whether "use of any part of the Army or Air Force pervaded the activities" of the civilian law enforcement agents. *United States v. Jaramillo*, 380 F.Supp. 1375 (D.Neb. 1974), appeal dismissed, 510 F.2d 808 (8th Cir.1975) (No one questioned that substantial amounts of Army material and equipment were used. But "it is the use of military personnel, not materiel, which is proscribed by 18 U.S.C. § 1385." *Id.* at 1379. Since there was reasonable doubt whether military personnel were involved enough to render their actions unlawful, the defendants were acquitted. *Id.* at 1381). The third test is whether the military personnel subjected citizens to the exercise of military power which was regulatory, proscriptive, or compulsory in nature. *United States v. McArthur*, 419 F.Supp. 186 (D.N.D.1975), *aff'd sub nom. United States v. Casper*, 541 F.2d 1275 (8th Cir.1976), *cert. denied*, 430 U.S. 970, 52 L.Ed.2d 362, 97 S.Ct. 1654 (1977). (In *McArthur*, military personnel were used, but it was "not material enough to taint the presumption that the law enforcement officers were acting in performance of their duties." *Id.* at 195. "The borrowing of highly skilled personnel, like pilots and highly technical equipment like aircraft and cameras, for a specific, limited, temporary purpose is far preferable to the maintenance of such personnel and equipment by the United States Marshals' Service." *Id.* at 194).

It is not surprising that arguments similar to those relied upon by Yunis' counsel have been regularly advanced by a number of defendants charged with federal crimes, who resided abroad when the military was utilized to effect their arrest. In the late 1940's the First Circuit held when United States military forces arrested a defendant overseas in an area where no civil regime exists, that there was no violation of the Act. *Chandler v. United States*, 171 F.2d 921 (1st Cir.1948), *cert. denied*, 336 U.S. 918, 93 L.Ed. 1081, 69 S.Ct. 640 (1949) ("This is the type of criminal statute which is properly presumed to have no extraterritorial application in the absence of statutory language indicating a contrary intent," particularly in an enemy territory occupied by the United States military. *Id.* at 936). In another situation, when military authorities in an allegedly illegal and unlawful manner brought from Japan to San Francisco, a notorious American citizen—Tokyo Rose—suspected of treason, her counsel's claim that the Posse Comitatus Act had been violated, and that the federal court lacked jurisdiction, was of no avail. *Iva Ikuko Toguri D'Aquino v. United States*, 192 F.2d 338, 351 (9th Cir.1951). Relying upon *Chandler* and *Gillars,* the Ninth Circuit held that the defendant's claim was without merit. Both *Toguri D'Aquino* and *Chandler* involved situations where the United States military had a substantial presence in post-war enemy territory. More than two decades later, the Ninth Circuit in *United States v. Cotten*, 471 F.2d 744 (9th Cir.1973), again rejected the posse comitatus argument as applied to persons abducted overseas. Two Americans living in Viet Nam were forcibly returned to the United States and later charged with federal law violations. They claimed that the use of military personnel and equipment to remove them from Viet Nam and bring them to the United States violated the Act as well as their due process rights. The Ninth Circuit recognized that defendants had been treated severely (military handcuffs, leg irons and cargo chains were used and defendants were "physically subdued" with blows to the back of the head). The government acknowledged that the military's removal was in fact a kidnapping of the defendants. Nonetheless, the Circuit Court found no violations of the Act and denied challenges to federal court jurisdiction.

At the recent February 5, 1988 argument on this motion, government counsel took the position as it had done throughout their pleadings that the Act by its express terms does not apply to the Navy. Thus Navy participation did not provide a basis for the relief sought—dismissal of the indictment. Counsel for defendant however, has steadfastly maintained that the Act applies to the Navy even though only the Army and Air Force are the services mentioned in Title 18. A canvass and review of case law shows that there may be some merit to his position. In this connection Yunis' counsel relies upon 10 U.S.C. §§ 371–378. That statute was enacted in 1981, as a part of the Department of Defense Authorization for Appropriations for Fiscal Year 1982, Pub. L. No. 97–86, 95 Stat. 1099 (1981). Title IX, § 905 of the Act, "Military Cooperation with Civilian Law Enforcement Officials," is the pertinent section and is codified at 10 U.S.C. §§ 371–378. As a part of the 1982 Defense Appropriations Act, new provisions were enacted to "clarify and reaffirm the authority of the Secretary of Defense to provide indirect assistance to civilian law enforcement officials, consistent with the principles established in the Posse Comitatus Act." S. Rep. No. 58, 97th Cong., 1st Sess. 148 (1981). The Senate Armed Services Committee further explained the rationale behind the laws:

The Department of Defense historically has provided some forms of indirect assistance to civilian law enforcement officials within the framework of the Posse Comitatus Act.... The Department has also loaned military equipment for use by civilian law enforcement agencies. But due to the age of the Posse Comitatus Act and its rather vague legislative history on the subject of indirect aid, court decisions have failed to outline uniformly the precise limits of permissible indirect assistance. This diverse guidance has created some uncertainties as to the authority of the Department ... to provide such aid. *Id.*

Recognizing that the Department of Defense ("DoD") is primarily concerned with military preparedness, the committee stated that "where available, indirect assistance by the Department of Defense can help civilian law enforcement officials.... For example, the loan of equipment or access to base or research facilities, where it does not interfere with military preparedness, would avoid cost duplication in buying and maintaining such equipment and facilities." *Id.* The final version of the appropriations bill agreed upon by a joint conference committee contained the same provisions which "clarif[ied] the authority of the Secretary of Defense to make available certain military equipment and facilities." H.R. Conf. Rep. 311, 97th Cong., 1st Sess. 119, *reprinted in* 1981 U.S. Code Cong. & Admin. News 1860.

Very few cases have involved the military cooperation provisions of the Defense Authorization Act for 1982. A recent 1986 District Court opinion with facts similar to those presented here, held that the newly enacted sections 371–378, actually authorize the use of military aircraft to transport defendants when such defendants are under the direct control of civilian law enforcement officials. In *United States v. Gerena*, 649 F.Supp. 1179 (D.Conn.1986),[7] the use of naval helicopters and a military air base to transport civilian defendants from Puerto Rico to New York was upheld under the authority of §§ 372 and 375. Defendants were in the custody of United States Marshals at all times. The trial court in ruling that the military's involvement did not constitute a violation of either the Posse Comitatus Act or 10 U.S.C. §§ 371–378 noted:

> Among the legitimate governmental interests promoted by the use of military involvement in civilian affairs is the interest 'in improving the efficiency of civilian law enforcement by giving it the benefit of military technologies, equipment, information, and training personnel. 649 F.Supp. at 1182.

Section 372 actually empowers the Secretary of Defense to make available "any equipment, base facility, or research facility of the Army, *Navy*, Air Force, or Marine Corps to any Federal, State, or local civilian law enforcement purposes." 10 U.S.C. § 372 (emphasis added). This includes the assignment of military personnel, provided such assignment is done in accordance with adequate regulation and in compliance with applicable law. 10 U.S.C. § 375.

Regulations promulgated under the Appropriations Act, 32 C.F.R. §§ 213.1–213.11 (1987), also permit local DoD components to authorize the use of available military equipment for civilian law enforcement purposes. Section 210 of the federal regulations lays out the restrictions on DoD personnel participation: "The primary restriction on military participation in civilian law enforcement activities is the Posse Comitatus Act. . . ." In explanation of the connection between the DoD military cooperation statutes and the Posse Comitatus Act, the regulations provide:

> The following forms of *indirect assistance activities are not restricted by the Posse Comitatus Act* . . . :
>
> (ii) Such other actions, approved in accordance with procedures established by the head of the DoD Component concerned, that do not subject civilians to the exercise of military power that is regulatory, proscriptive, or compulsory in nature.

---

7. *Gerena* was decided in December 1986, nearly twelve months after *United States v. Roberts*, 779 F.2d 565 (9th Cir.1986), a Ninth Circuit opinion which held that the Posse Comitatus Act did not apply to the Navy. In *Roberts*, the Court recognized, however, that the Navy had adopted the Act as a matter of policy. *Id.* at 567. In its opinion the Court declined to "defy [the] plain language by extending it [the Act] to prohibit use of the Navy." *Id.* Instead, the Court chose to focus on the proscriptions of 10 U.S.C. §§ 371–378, finding those provisions to be more directly applicable to the Navy. In analyzing §§ 371–378, the Court stated that "the Posse Comitatus Act and sections 371–378 of Title 10 embody similar proscriptions against military involvement in civilian law enforcement." *Id.* at 568. The *Gerena* Court did not follow the Ninth Circuit's strict construction of the Act. It relied upon *United States v. Del Prado–Montero, 740 F.2d 113 (1st Cir.), cert. denied 469 U.S. 1021, 105 S.Ct. 441, 83 L.Ed.2d 366 (1984)* (the Act is "a proscription that has been extended by executive act to the Navy." *740 F.2d at 116)* and the regulations promulgated under 32 C.F.R. § 213 which specifically address the Act's applicability to the Navy.

32 C.F.R. § 213.10(a)(7). Under this regulation a court in reviewing the legality of the military involvement at issue, must decide whether the assistance in question subjected defendant Yunis "to the exercise of military power that is regulatory, proscriptive, or compulsory in nature."

In this proceeding, the Navy's activities in the apprehension of Yunis were not the type prohibited by the Posse Comitatus Act, nor were they prohibited by the DoD military cooperation laws. The FBI was in charge of the operation at all times. At most, the Navy merely provided necessary support services. Navy personnel never participated in the arrest or interrogation of the defendant. Their equipment and staff already stationed in the Mediterranean were at the disposal of the FBI for only limited purposes, involving a passive role. Their limited role included: advising the FBI crew aboard the yacht (used in the capture of the defendant) on its location in international waters; providing a launch to transport the defendant from the FBI yacht to the Navy vessel—the U.S.S. Butte, supplying the defendant with shelter, clothes, food, and toiletries while on board the Navy launch and providing required medical attention; arranging a rendezvous between the Butte and the aircraft carrier—the USS Saratoga; piloting the Navy plane with the defendant and his FBI custodians from the Saratoga to the United States.

It is clear from these facts that the Navy's activities did not constitute direct active involvement in the execution of the laws, nor did the use of military personnel pervade the activities of the civilian authorities. Rather, it was a civilian operation originating from within the FBI. By its very nature, the operation required the aid of military located in the area. Under the direction of the FBI, the Navy gave the necessary support in the form of equipment, supplies, and services. The furnishing of materials, work, and services, standing alone, is not a violation of the Posse Comitatus Act. *See, e.g., Hartley*, 796 F.2d at 114; *Bissonette v. Haig*, 776 F.2d 1384, 1390 (8th Cir.1985); *Caspar*, 541 F.2d at 1276, *aff'g McArthur*, 419 F.Supp. at 194–95; *United States v. Hartley*, 486 F.Supp. 1348, 1356–57 (M.D.Fla.1980); *Red Feather*, 392 F.Supp. at 923; *Jaramillo*, 380 F.Supp. at 1379.

There is further support for the position that Congress did not intend that the Posse Comitatus Act should prohibit the use of military material, supplies or equipment in the aid of executing the laws. More than fifty years ago, Congress established procedures that enable any government department (especially military departments) to furnish materials, work, and services to any other bureau or agency within the government. The Economy Act of 1932, 31 U.S.C. § 686.

Finally, the Navy personnel involved in the transportation of the defendant played passive roles. The Naval doctor gave Yunis a physical examination and later treated him for seasickness and pain to his wrist. The defendant's food was prepared by Navy personnel.

None of the Navy's activities constituted the exercise of regulatory, proscriptive, or compulsory military power. A power regulatory in nature is one which controls or directs. In this case defendant Yunis was under the exclusive control and authority (as well as the physical custody) of the FBI agents accompanying him. The military did not exercise any authority or control over the defendant, nor did the military threaten such control or authority.

Nor can it be said that the military's involvement was proscriptive. A power proscriptive in nature is one that prohibits or condemns. Again, the defendant was never confined by Navy personnel but at all times was in the custody of the FBI agents who arrested him. Yunis was in no real way ever subject to the proscriptive powers of the military or military law.

Finally, it cannot be said that the Navy's involvement was compulsory. A power compulsory in nature is one that exerts some coercive force. The military personnel involved exerted no such force over the defendant. In reality, the Navy's involvement in the operation was indifferent, passive, and subservient to the FBI's task.

Conclusion

For the above stated reasons, the Court concludes that the Navy's involvement in the apprehension, arrest and transportation of the defendant from international waters of the Mediterranean Sea, until he arrived at Andrews Air Force Base, Maryland, did not violate the Posse Comitatus Act or any other federal law.

QUESTIONS AND NOTES

1. The defendant in Yunis moved to dismiss based on an alleged violation of the Posse Comitatus Act. If the court had found a violation of the Act, would this have been grounds to grant the motion?

2. The court in Yunis describes three different tests that were articulated in three cases growing out of the events in 1973 at Wounded Knee, South Dakota. How do the tests differ from each other? Which do you think should be *the* test? Why?

3. One learns from Yunis that qualifications and exceptions to the Act have been adopted either by statute or in regulations, and the case cites and quotes some of them. Note that the DoD regulation contained in 32 C.F.R. § 213.10(a)(7) adopts the same test for determining the applicability of the Act's prohibition that was first formulated in United States v. McArthur, supra.

4. National Guard units trace their history back to state militias before the American Revolution. Today, National Guard officers work first for their state governor, and second for the President. This gives them a unique legal status as state officers who are not governed by the Posse Comitatus Act. This makes sense given the law's history—it was enacted to protect states' rights at the end of post-Civil War Reconstruction. In Gilbert v. United States, 165 F.3d 470 (6th Cir.1999), the 6th Circuit explained this doctrine:

> By its own terms, the [Posse Comitatus] Act applies to the Army and Air Force. *United States v. Yunis*, 288 U.S. App. D.C. 129, 924 F.2d 1086,

1093 (D.C.Cir.1991) (Act inapplicable to the Navy); *Schowengerdt v. General Dynamics Corp.*, 823 F.2d 1328, 1340 (9th Cir.1987) (same). See also *United States v. Roberts*, 779 F.2d 565, 567 (9th Cir.1986) (Act extended by Executive Order to include the Navy.) The Act does not apply to members of the National Guard unless they have been called into "federal service." Until called into such service, members of the National Guard remain state, rather than federal officers. *Perpich v. Department of Defense*, 496 U.S. 334, 345, 110 S.Ct. 2418, 110 L.Ed.2d 312 (1990) ("unless and until ordered to active duty in the Army, [Guardsmen] retained their status as members of a separate State Guard unit"). Thus, "except when employed in the service of the United States, officers of the National Guard continue to be officers of the state and not officers of the United States or of the Military Establishment of the United States." *United States v. Dern*, 74 F.2d 485, 487, 64 App. D.C. 81 (D.C.Cir.1934). "Guardsmen do not become part of the Army itself," as pointed out in *United States v. Hutchings*, 127 F.3d 1255, 1258 (10th Cir.1997), "until such time as they may be ordered into active federal duty by an official acting under a grant of statutory authority from Congress." Only when "that triggering event occurs [does] a Guardsman become[] a part of the Army and lose[] his status as a state serviceman." *Id. See generally*, Steven B. Rich, *The National Guard, Drug Interdiction and Counterdrug Activities and Posse Comitatus: The Meaning and Implications of "in Federal Service*," 1994 Army Law. 16.

The record in this case shows conclusively that the National Guardsmen who participated in appellants' arrests and ensuing searches and seizures were in state, rather than federal service when they did so. Aside from the complete absence of any proof that the Guardsmen had been called into active service with the Army, see *id.* at 18 (noting limited and specific ways in which Guardsmen may enter active duty), the record contains ample evidence that the Guardsmen were acting in response to directives issued by their Commander-in-Chief, the Governor of Kentucky.

The Governor issued an executive order creating a Marijuana Strike Force. The Strike Force's objective was "total eradication of marijuana in [the] Commonwealth." Command of the Strike Force was delegated to a ten member committee, one of whose members was an officer with the National Guard's Department of Military Affairs. Although federal officials were also members of the Strike Force and its governing committee, those officials were from civilian agencies, rather than the United States Army. The Guardsmen assigned to the Strike Force were unquestionably under state, rather than federal control.

Notwithstanding this proof of the Guardsmen's status, appellants contend that, because the Guardsmen were serving in a full-time capacity and were being compensated with federal, rather than state funds, they were "in federal service" and acting as members of the United States Army. These circumstances are immaterial: "the issue of status depends on command and control and not on whether: state or federal benefits apply; state or federal funds are being used; the authority for the duty lies in state or federal law; or any combination thereof." "Although

National Guard members receive federal pay and allowances ... while performing full-time National Guard Duty," they remain members of the state National Guard and not members on active duty in federal service with the United States Army. *Id.* Consequently, the Act, which applies only to members of the federal armed services, does not apply to the Guardsmen in this case.

Similarly, the fact that the Guardsmen looked and acted like soldiers, rather than law enforcement officers, is immaterial. "These indicia, however persuasive they may be to the eye," the court noted in *Hutchings*, 127 F.3d at 1258, "have never determined the character of a Guardsman's service.... That question depends solely on whether command of the Guardsman has been taken away from a state's governor by one authorized to do so by Congress." In this case, as in *Hutchings*, command remained with the state.

Alternatively, the circumstances under which the Guardsmen were acting in this case were, as permitted by the terms of the Act, authorized by an Act of Congress. Pursuant to 32 U.S.C. § 112(b), full-time National Guardsmen may be used for the "purpose of carrying out drug interdiction and counter-drug activities." Use by the Commonwealth of Kentucky of its Guardsmen in accordance with this federal statute provides another basis for exempting those officers from the Posse Comitatus Act.

We conclude, accordingly, that officers of the Kentucky National Guard did not violate the Posse Comitatus Act when they participated in the surveillance of appellants' marijuana cultivation and harvesting, arrested them for those unlawful activities, and searched them and the area in which they had been growing their contraband crop.[8]

5.　Note that while the Congress in 2002 in the Homeland Security Act reaffirmed the importance of maintaining the general thrust of the Posse Comitatus prohibition, it also expressly recognized the President's responsibility to deal with any domestic emergencies, including, in his capacity as Commander-in-Chief, the possible use of the military in such circumstances.

6.　Consider the following excerpt from Major Kirk L. Davies, The Imposition of Martial Law In The United States, 49 A.F. L. Rev. 67, 80–85 (2000) regarding the use of the military in domestic emergencies:

Determining when the military is in violation of the [Posse Comitatus] Act can be difficult. However, considering the Act's punitive provisions, commanders have an obvious interest in ensuring they do not disobey it. Over time, Congress has authorized relatively significant exceptions to the Act's sweeping prohibitions. None of the exceptions

---

8.　We need not reach the issue of whether, had we found the Act to have been violated, suppression should have occurred. We note, however, that every federal court to have considered the issue has held that suppression is not an appropriate remedy for a violation of the Act. United States v. Al–Talib, 55 F.3d 923, 930 (4th Cir.1995); Hayes v. Hawes, 921 F.2d 100, 103 (7th Cir.1990); United States v. Hartley, 796 F.2d 112, 115 (5th Cir.1986). Accord, United States v. Griley, 814 F.2d 967, 976 (4th Cir.1987); United States v. Wolffs, 594 F.2d 77, 85 (5th Cir.1979); United States v. Walden, 490 F.2d 372, 376–77 (4th Cir.1974). See also Note, The Posse Comitatus Act as an Exclusionary Rule: Is the Criminal to go Free Because the Soldier Has Blundered?, 61 N.D. L.Rev. 107, 129 (1985) ("There is no evidence Congress intended the Posse Comitatus Act to double as an exclusionary rule").

have specifically granted the military a domestic law enforcement role, but the recent pattern is to accord the military a greater role in civilian affairs than had been previously envisioned.

. . .

Congress has also granted the President specific statutory authority to use federal troops in a law enforcement role in the case of national emergency involving civil disturbances. This authority exists even though responsibility for quelling such rebellions lies primarily with State and local governments. These statutory exceptions to the Posse Comitatus Act include insurrections within a state (upon the Governor's request); rebellions which makes it impracticable to enforce federal laws; or any insurrection or violence which impedes the state's ability to protect citizens of their constitutional rights, and the state is unable or unwilling to protect those rights.

Perhaps the President already has the authority to act in situations involving maintenance of public order, even without congressional authorization. According to the Code of Federal Regulations (CFR), "the Constitution and Acts of Congress establish six exceptions,[9] generally applicable within the entire territory of the United States, to which the Posse Comitatus Act prohibition does not apply."[10] The CFR cites two constitutional exceptions. The first is an emergency authority to prevent loss of life or property during serious disturbances or calamities.[11] The second authority allows the use of military forces to protect Federal property and governmental functions.

Obviously, the Code of Federal Regulations is not the source of the President's emergency response authority.[12] However, when considering whether Congress has granted the President either "express or implied" authority to use military troops in a domestic crisis, evidence of a federal

---

9. Besides the two constitutional exceptions, the Code of Federal Regulations lists four statutory exceptions to the Posse Comitatus Act. They include the three statutory exceptions found in 10 U.S.C. §§ 331–33, and another exception for assisting the Secret Service in providing protection to governmental officials and political candidates. 32 C.F.R. § 215.4(c)(2)(i)(a-d).

10. Id. at § 215.4 (c)

11. *Id.* at § 215.4(c)(1)(i) states:

The emergency authority. Authorizes prompt and vigorous Federal action, including use of military forces to prevent loss of life or wanton destruction of property and to restore governmental functioning and public order when sudden and unexpected civil disturbances, disasters, or calamities seriously endanger life and property and disrupt normal governmental functions to such an extent that duly constituted local authorities are unable to control the situations.

12. Interestingly, the Code of Federal Regulations also defines martial law. *Id.* at § 501.4. Noting, in relevant part, that,

martial law depends for its justification upon public necessity. Necessity gives rise to its creation; necessity justifies its exercise; and necessity limits its duration . . . In most instances the decision to impose martial law is made by the President, who normally announces his decision by a proclamation, which usually contains his instructions concerning its exercise and any limitations thereon . . . When Federal Armed Forces have been committed in an objective area in a martial law situation, the population of the affected area will be informed of the rules of conduct and other restrictive measures the military is authorized to enforce . . . Federal Armed Forces ordinarily will exercise police powers previously inoperative in the affected area, restore and maintain order, insure the essential mechanics of distribution, transportation, and communication, and initiate necessary relief measures.

regulation that recognizes such a constitutional basis for authority is extremely relevant. This is especially true if Congress takes no action to modify or interpret the language of the Code.

. . .

In recent years, Department of Defense personnel have acted in civilian emergency situations without any specific statutory authorization. They have done so under a theory of "immediate response authority." An example of the military acting under this immediate response authority occurred in Oklahoma City after the bombing of the Alfred P. Murrah federal building. In that case, local authorities could be assisted by the military providing support to the investigation in the form of "medevac aircraft, ambulances, bomb detection dog teams, and various military personnel." Local commanders at Fort Sill and Tinker Air Force Base provided this support under the theory of the commander's immediate response authority.

This immediate response authority is mentioned in two Department of Defense Directives, one relating to disaster relief support to civil authorities, and the other relating to support for civilian agencies during civil disturbances. According to these regulations, commanders may act to prevent human suffering, save lives, or mitigate great property damage, even without prior authorization from the President. Commanders may act in these cases if there is an emergency that "overwhelms the capabilities of local authorities."

The "most commonly cited rationale to support Immediate Response actions is the common law principle of necessity." From a humanitarian, common sense perspective, it seems self-evident that a military commander should be able to use available resources to alleviate human suffering, without first requiring a bureaucratic permission slip. Arguably, that is why Department of Defense directives articulate this authority. Interestingly, even though Congress undoubtedly is aware of the military's actions under these Department of Defense directives, congressional leaders have not acted to limit or codify a commander's authority to act in these types of scenarios.

. . .

It appears that the traditional prejudice against military involvement in civil affairs may be on the decline. The evidence of that decline is manifest in congressional willingness to create exceptions to the Posse Comitatus rules allowing for military support during law enforcement activities, and the President's continued use of the armed forces in these roles. Whatever the reason, Congress has implicitly or explicitly given the military increased authority in the civilian domain, an authority Presidents have not hesitated to use. This trend has serious implications for the legality of a President's actions under a proclamation of martial law.

. . .

Ideally, the President will never have to declare martial law in response to a national crisis. The best scenario envisions the nation responding to such a crisis with civilian agencies in the forefront and the

Department of Defense in its traditional support role. However, should civilian agencies become overwhelmed in an environment of chaos and panic, one of the President's obvious options for restoring order would be to declare martial law. Such a response is an extreme option, well beyond what is contemplated under statutes relating to disaster response actions or limited military support to civilian law enforcement authorities.

7. In connection with the kind of terrorism-caused emergencies that might trigger military involvement on the domestic U.S. scene, consider the following excerpt from Davies, op. cit. supra, note 6 at footnote 19:

> As the country pays more attention these issues, the military will likely emerge as a central player in whatever course the nation ultimately takes. For example, the DoD is "stationing 10 Rapid Assessment and Detection Teams (RADT), each composed of 22 specially trained Air Force and Army National Guard personnel, in 10 states to respond to chemical and biological weapons attacks." Jim Landers, *U.S. Quietly Upgrading Homeland Defense Plan*, The Dallas Morning News, Feb. 9, 1999 at 1A. In addition, some factors indicate that FEMA is not prepared to properly execute its statutorily authorized role to control disasters. One author stated,
>
> > In practice, nobody knows who would do what if American city-dwellers faced a lethal cloud of anthrax or nerve gas. An exercise in March, designed to test the authorities' response to a genetically engineered virus spread by terrorists on the Mexican–American border, led to bitter squabbling among rival agencies. "There is no clear demarcation line between the FEMA, and knowledge about disease and hazardous materials is spread over a broad array of institutions," says Zachary Selden, a germ-warfare boffin. "Somebody is needed to sit on top of these operations."

8. Also see NY Times, Jan. 23, 2005, www.nytimes.com/2005/01/23/national/nationalspecial3/23code.html?pagewanted=2&_r=2 reporting that a small group of super-secret commandos, with state of the art weaponry, operating under a secret counterterrorism program code-named Power Geyser, was on standby ready to help protect the presidential inauguration; that the Command to which this unit belonged has in the past provided support to domestic law enforcement agencies for events such as the Olympics and political party conventions.

C. EXCEPTIONS TO THE POSSE COMITATUS RULE? MORE EXTENSIVE USE OF THE MILITARY IN EMERGENCIES AND FOR OTHER PURPOSES?

1. The following commentary was written four years before September 11, 2001, but after the Oklahoma City bombing and first World Trade Center bombing. Did September 11th change the situation?

Matthew Carlton Hammond, Note: The Posse Comitatus Act: A Principle in Need of Renewal, 75 Wash. U. L. Q. 953 (1997):

. . .

In the last fifteen years, Congress has deliberately eroded this principle by involving the military in drug interdiction at our borders. This erosion will continue unless Congress renews the PCA's (Posse Comitatus Act) principle to preserve the necessary and traditional separation of civilian and military authority.

The need for reaffirmation of the PCA's principle is increasing because in recent years, Congress and the public have seen the military as a panacea for domestic problems. Within one week of the bombing of the federal building in Oklahoma City, President Clinton proposed an exception to the PCA to allow the military to aid civilian authorities in investigations involving "weapons of mass destruction." In addition to this proposal Congress also considered legislation to directly involve federal troops in enforcing customs and immigration laws at the border. In the 1996 presidential campaign, candidate Bob Dole pledged to increase the role of the military in the drug war, and candidate Lamar Alexander even proposed replacing the Immigration and Naturalization Service and the Border Patrol with a new branch of the armed forces.

The growing haste and ease with which the military is considered a panacea for domestic problems will quickly undermine the PCA if it remains unchecked. Minor exceptions to the PCA can quickly expand to become major exceptions. For example in 1981, Congress created an exception to the PCA to allow military involvement in drug interdiction at our borders. Then in 1989, Congress designated the Department of Defense as the "single lead agency" in drug interdiction efforts.

. . .

Major and minor exceptions to the PCA, which allow the use of the military in law enforcement roles, blur the line between military and civilian roles, undermine civilian control of the military, damage military readiness, and inefficiently solve the problems that they supposedly address. Additionally, increasing the role of the military would strengthen the federal law enforcement apparatus that is currently under close scrutiny for overreaching its authority. Although it seems benign, such an increase in military authority revives fears of past overreaching during the late 1960s.

. . .

This dearth of judicial interpretation has left "the parameters of the [PCA] . . . substantially untested." Due to the resulting lack of clarity, the PCA does not actually prohibit all so-called "exceptions" to its application, and such exceptions-in-name have been enacted to clarify—or, depending upon your view, alter—its boundaries and to provide guidance to military commanders. The greatest uncertainties regarding the PCA concern what constitutes "any part of the Army or Air Force" and what actions "execute the laws."

. . .

The PCA explicitly recognizes constitutional and legislative exceptions to its application. The existence of any constitutional exceptions was contested at the time of the PCA's enactment. Some proponents of the PCA saw the exceptions as inherent in the executive powers of the President and in his position as Commander-in-Chief of the armed forces, thus making them beyond the reach of Congress to limit. Others who supported the PCA's passage recognized no such exceptions. The existence of constitutional exceptions to the PCA may only actually lie in the "twilight zone" where the President may act where Congress has not. . . .

Another "constitutional" exception to the PCA is described by the Department of Defense regulations based upon the "inherent right of the U.S. Government . . . to ensure the preservation of public order and to carry out governmental operations . . . by force, if necessary." The Office of Legal Counsel of the Department of Justice has promulgated a similar view in recognition of the U.S. government's power to protect federal functions. The power to protect federal functions has been so broadly interpreted, however, that if accepted it would become the exception that swallows the rule. Now–Chief Justice William Rehnquist interpreted this power to extend to any "uniquely federal responsibility" while he was an attorney in the Office of Legal Counsel. However, this exception has yet to be tested in the courts and would likely be interpreted as narrowly as the other exceptions to the PCA.

Congress itself has recognized several exceptions to the PCA, which this Note categorizes as exceptions-in-fact and exceptions-in-name. The exceptions-in-fact are true exceptions that exempt otherwise criminal actions under the PCA and alter its boundaries. Exceptions-in-name include exceptions that are described or perceived as exceptions to the PCA, but which authorize allowable acts under any of the court-created tests. Exceptions-in-name do not alter the accepted boundaries of the PCA and do not make previously criminal acts legal. They are sometimes simply termed "clarifications."

Exceptions-in-name allow the military to provide equipment and supplies, technical assistance, information, and training to law enforcement agencies. Such provisions constitute passive assistance to civilian law enforcement, which does not subject any civilian to the regulatory, proscriptive, or coercive power of the military.

. . .

Exceptions-in-fact . . . include the quelling of civil disturbances and labor strife that rises to the level of civil disorder. For example, Troops were used to put down the Whiskey Rebellion long before the

PCA was passed and to maintain order during school desegregation in the South after the Act's passage. Troops have . . . been used to quell riots in Detroit and other cities. More recently, they were deployed on the streets of Los Angeles in 1992 after the Rodney King verdict.

The courts have recognized another type of exception through the military purpose doctrine, which is not explicitly mentioned in the PCA. The doctrine allows the military to enforce civilian laws on military installations, to police themselves, and to perform their military functions even if there is an incidental benefit to civilian law enforcement.

. . .

There are many other uses of the military which seem to implicate the PCA, but are not within its scope because law is not being enforced. Since the passage of the PCA, the military has been used several times for domestic purposes that do not conform to its traditional role. The PCA proscribes use of the army in civilian law enforcement, but it has not prevented military assistance in what have been deemed national emergencies, such as strike replacements and disaster relief. However, these emergencies differ in character from other exceptions to the PCA by their very nature as emergencies and by the duration of the military involvement.

. . .

The PCA's exceptions-in-name and exceptions-in-fact endanger the military and the United States by blurring the traditional line between military and civilian roles, undermining civilian control of the military, damaging military readiness, and providing the wrong tool for the job.

. . .

The military's primary mission is national security, and the wisdom of all military decisions is ultimately weighed against whether national security is enhanced or damaged. Military readiness is a key to modern warfare and to the maintenance of national security. In recognition of this fact, the military can refuse a request for aid in drug interdiction and in the investigation of chemical and biological weapons if military readiness might be compromised. However, this power of refusal does not prevent injury to military readiness, because while the military still takes on these missions, their mere consideration injures readiness through the redirection of resources in the decisionmaking process by adding a nonmilitary factor to the decision.

The border duty, investigative support, and drug interdiction exceptions are double-edged swords with respect to military readiness. The military has embraced new missions like drug interdiction as a way to preserve force structure and budget levels and to improve public relations. In this respect, these new missions may aid readiness by preserving support for military strength and funding, but this benefit is outweighed by the shift of focus slightly away from the mission to fight a war. This change of focus lessens the fighting edge of the military and dampens the "warrior spirit." Additionally, these missions require equipment modifications and the reallocation of resources. For example, F–15 pilots do not hone their dogfighting skills by tracking a single-engine Cessna flying north from Mexico; in the Gulf War, there were stories of inadequately trained National Guard units that had participated more frequently in nontraditional missions, yet were incapable of fulfilling their military mission.

The three exceptions to the PCA affect military readiness in a variety of ways. Drug interdiction has injured military readiness as a result of expensive equipment modifications and the redirection of resources. The 1993 Department of Defense budget included more than $1.4 billion for drug interdiction missions. This budget allocation has resulted in a "drug command" of sorts which is entirely focussed on the domestic mission of drug interdiction. Border duty requires a different mindset and a different level of restraint than warfare, thus disrupting the optimum culture and mindset needed to maintain national security. Investigatory support by the military is also a mission differing from that which currently exists in the military. To redirect resources or to consider performing such nonmilitary missions involves considerations that lessen the importance of strictly improving military readiness, even when the only question is where to train.

Illegal immigration, drug interdiction, and investigative support relating to terrorism are all long-term problems requiring long-term solutions. These problems are not easily resolved, however, and no foreseeable end to the military's involvement appears forthcoming. Because of the significance of the problems and their continuing and chronic nature, using the military to combat these problems is like using a sledge hammer to open a locked trunk when all one needs is the key. It is better to fashion a key than to destroy the trunk.

All three exceptions to the PCA require using the wrong tool for the job. For example, border duty forces the military to alter its mindset and training. The border patrol and other law enforcement agencies already have the proper mindset and qualifications and are better able to do the job. Using an F–15 to track drug smugglers' slow planes is both excessive and expensive. A basic military soldier costs the government $82,000 a year in training and upkeep. A soldier's involvement in drug interdiction is much more expensive than a civilian counterpart's participation. Investigatory support for weapons of mass destruction to counter terrorism is more than a minor exception because terrorism is a continuing problem without end. We would best be served by developing these resources in civilian law enforcement.

The fundamental precept of maintaining the separation between the military and civilian spheres of action must be renewed, not eroded by exceptions. Both exceptions-in-name and exceptions-in-fact should be avoided because they injure that separation. To maintain the principle that animates the PCA, the PCA should be reaffirmed and strengthened. The need to fight "the war" on drugs, to combat terrorism, and to deter illegal immigration are long-term problems that are currently high on the public agenda and will not go away without long-term solutions. Tight budgets and the desire for a quick-fix do not create an emergency justifying the conversion of martial rhetoric to reality. Relegating these problems to a military solution poses dangers to our individual rights and to the history and underlying structure of the United States that should not be ignored.

. . .

Resources must be made available to create viable civilian law enforcement responses to these problems. If these resources must be redirected from the military, then Congress should do so. Declare "war," but let it be fought by civilian law enforcement with the right weapons for the job. The military should be the last resort, not the first solution. In the long run, the "war" will be more effectively fought with dedicated "soldiers" with an undivided focus.

2.   Hurricane Katrina placed enormous strains on the major exception to the Posse Comitatus Act that is carved out in the Insurrection Act, 10 U.S.C. § 333. For an excellent, detailed recounting of the dynamic that occurred at the time between the Bush administration and the governor of Louisiana, see Thaddeus Hoffmeister, "The Transformative Power of Law: An Insurrection Act for the Twenty–First Century," 39 Stetson L. Rev. 861 (2010). As a result of these strains and concerns about the ability to use the military to respond to major emergencies, 10 U.S.C. § 333 was substantially rewritten by the Congress, without significant public discussion, to read as follows:

10 U.S.C. § 333

§ 333. Major public emergencies; interference with State and Federal law

(a) Use of armed forces in major public emergencies.

(1) The President may employ the armed forces, including the National Guard in Federal service, to—

(A) restore public order and enforce the laws of the United States when, as a result of a natural disaster, epidemic, or other serious public health emergency, terrorist attack or incident, or other condition in any State or possession of the United States, the President determines that—

(i) domestic violence has occurred to such an extent that the constituted authorities of the State or possession are incapable of maintaining public order; and

(ii) such violence results in a condition described in paragraph (2); or

(B) suppress, in a State, any insurrection, domestic violence, unlawful combination, or conspiracy if such insurrection, violation, combination, or conspiracy results in a condition described in paragraph (2).

(2) A condition described in this paragraph is a condition that—

(A) so hinders the execution of the laws of a State or possession, as applicable, and of the United States within that State or possession, that any part or class of its people is deprived of a right, privilege, immunity, or protection named in the Constitution and secured by law, and the constituted authorities of that State or possession are unable, fail, or refuse to protect that right, privilege, or immunity, or to give that protection; or

(B) opposes or obstructs the execution of the laws of the United States or impedes the course of justice under those laws.

(3) In any situation covered by paragraph (1)(B), the State shall be considered to have denied the equal protection of the laws secured by the Constitution.

(b) Notice to Congress. The President shall notify Congress of the determination to exercise the authority in subsection (a)(1)(A) as soon as practicable after the determination and every 14 days thereafter during the duration of the exercise of that authority.

3.   This amended version of the statute caused concerns, mainly among state governors, and as result, the 2006 version of 10 U.S.C. § 333 was repealed in 2008, and the prior version reinstated. The earlier and current version reads as follows:

§ 333.   Interference with State and Federal law

The President, by using the militia or the armed forces, or both, or by any other means, shall take such measures as he considers necessary to suppress, in a State, any insurrection, domestic violence, unlawful combination, or conspiracy, if it—

(1) so hinders the execution of the laws of that State, and of the United States within the State, that any part or class of its people is deprived of a right, privilege, immunity, or protection named in the Constitution and secured by law, and the constituted authorities of that State are unable, fail, or refuse to protect that right, privilege, or immunity, or to give that protection; or

(2) opposes or obstructs the execution of the laws of the United States or impedes the course of justice under those laws.

In any situation covered by clause (1), the State shall be considered to have denied the equal protection of the laws secured by the Constitution.

4. The same concerns which had prompted the enactment of the 2006 statute persisted, however, and scholars have called for revision of the Insurrection Act. Thus, for example, Professor Hoffmeister, see note 2, supra, argues for a revised version of the 2006 Act. Also see Ashley J. Craw, A Call to Arms: Civil Disorder Following Hurricane Katrina Warrants Attack on the Posse Comitatus Act, 14 Geo. Mason L. Rev. 829, 850–851 (2007):

> Due to the . . . inadequacies of the law enforcement component of current natural disaster response systems, Congress should pass a statutory exception to the PCA allowing the military to keep the peace and prevent chaos immediately following a large-scale natural disaster.

5. How did the 2006 amendment of the Insurrection Act change the circumstances in which the President could order the military to act on the domestic front? Was this a significant inroad on the policy underlying the Posse Comitatus Act?

6. Were there adequate safeguards in the 2006 amended language? To protect against what/ Would you have added any more?

7. Suppose it is concluded that the FBI does not have adequate resources to handle the task of policing the entire country in regard to terrorism? What are our options for increasing the manpower to be thrown into the anti-terrorism effort? Should using the military be considered as one of the viable options?

8. Clearly there are exceptions even under existing law that permit the military to provide assistance to law enforcement agencies. Are there specific tasks which the military should be prohibited from performing domestically?

9. Can you imagine a scenario where the U.S. military might be used to help in the hunt for a criminal suspect, such as a serial killer? Could the statutory exceptions be employed to use military surveillance planes or intelligence assets to track down a criminal suspect without any clear nexus to terrorism? During the hunt in Oct. 2002 for the alleged "Washington DC Sniper," this is exactly what happened. Consider Phillip Carter, Why Can the Army Help Cops Catch the D.C. Sniper?, Slate, Oct. 17, 2002:

> The U.S. Army has sent aircraft to help Beltway police find the sniper who has murdered nine people. But a federal statute prohibits the military from enforcing domestic law. So, when, exactly, can soldiers help the cops?
>
> Almost always, so long as they don't *directly* engage in police work. The Army can offer intelligence, transportation, and logistical assistance to cops, but it can't conduct searches or make arrests.

. . .

No one has ever been prosecuted for violating the Posse Comitatus Act. That's partly because it has a number of exceptions—enough exceptions, it turns out, to virtually swallow the rule.

. . .

In the 1980s . . . [t]he main exceptions grew out of the "War on Drugs," allowing the military to do things like fly surveillance planes on the U.S. border with Mexico, train police officers in various military specialties, or provide radar data to the U.S. Border Patrol and Customs Service. A federal law also allows the military to share intelligence with local law enforcement officers, provided the intel is collected during normal military operations. Another major exception, created in 1996 after the Oklahoma City bombing, authorizes the military to provide support to local cops in the event of a chemical or biological attack.

The Army's current plan to fly reconnaissance planes in Maryland is covered by these exceptions: Army personnel will fly the planes and operate the equipment, but civilian police will ride along to analyze any evidence gathered while in flight.

10.   Are the core values that the Posse Comitatus Act is designed to serve threatened by permitting Army personnel to get involved in a domestic criminal or terrorism investigation by flying reconnaissance planes and operating the plane's surveillance equipment? Is this a slippery slope issue?

11.   See the lead editorial in the *New York Times,* July, 30, 2009, The Military Is Not the Police, A 24, expressing concerns about the use of the military in a police role, specifically reacting to a news story that President Bush had considered sending troops into Buffalo in 2002 to arrest a group of terrorist suspects.

Chapter 14

Epilogue

■ ■ ■

In the preceding chapters, we examined a series of new applications and extensions of the criminal law and enforcement methods that have been involved in the government's very active program of anti-terrorism. We first examined the civilian track—that is, using the federal criminal code, the FBI, and special investigatory rules and substantive law in civilian criminal terrorism investigations and prosecutions. Then, for purposes of comparison, we addressed how the military arm is being used in anti-terrorism enforcement through military custody, military commissions and, even, through targeted killing by the military. Having taken up these various subjects seriatim, it may be useful to take a step back and make some general observations about what appears to be going on in the U.S. legal system as a result of the anti-terrorist efforts of the government.

It is obvious, and perhaps not surprising, that the government in aid of its anti-terrorism activities has consistently opted for laws, process, procedures and investigatory methods that are designed to make its efforts more efficient, effective, and, the government hopes, more successful.

Thus, early in the post–9/11 period, invoking the general notion that "we are at war," the government mustered legal support and justification for the lengthy (and in some instances, indefinite) detention of individuals using material witness doctrine; immigration laws and status-as-aliens; and enemy combatant status. It also established a set of military commissions which, while the rules established for them have now moved in the general direction of the United States district courts, still provide somewhat less procedural protection for individuals than our regular civilian court system.

With the assistance of the Congress, it has largely eliminated the previously-existing separation between intelligence and law enforcement information gathering in foreign intelligence electronic surveillance. While that separation, when it was maintained, may not have bee particularly effective in protecting Fourth Amendment interests, it at least reflected an effort in that direction. Also with Congress' assistance, the government has broadened significantly its electronic surveillance authority, now having established a system of regulation even for eavesdropping which takes place abroad.

In the realm of privacy and First Amendment interests, the government, again with the assistance of new legislation, has received broadened authority to obtain information regarding individuals. Similarly, through a simple change in administrative policy, the government has regained authority it once exercised to have undercover informants attend meetings of organizations, churches, mosques and synagogues, seeking information that might be relevant to anti-terrorism enforcement.

Further, the government is actively using new kinds of anti-terrorist crimes as well as civil enforcement legislation against organizations and individuals in the United States. Abroad, the government is wielding a big stick: It, of course, has recently functioned in a military manner on the battlefield where at least some of the enemy were members of al Qaeda, but it is also using other methods that do not directly involve the battlefield. For a period, for example, it used extreme measures in interrogating suspected terrorists, whether directly or through surrogates, and it transferred suspected terrorists between countries without using legal process. It also appears to have engaged in targeted killing of suspected terrorists in certain foreign countries.

A number of the policies followed by the Bush administration were changed in certain, crucial respects when President Obama assumed office, but in the main, the change in administrations did not produce major changes in the U.S. government's anti-terrorism policies.

We appreciate the national security concerns that led the government to these various actions. We recount these various steps that have been taken, most of them in the wake of the attacks on September 11, not because we think any one of them necessarily lacks legal or sound policy justifications. Reasonable persons can disagree about the extent of the danger, whether we are truly at war, and whether specific actions of those listed are warranted by national security concerns.

Taking note of the impact of these various actions, however, as a totality is a rather startling experience. Each of the steps taken on the home front, in its own way, has decreased somewhat our liberties, privacy, and traditional procedural protections to some discernible degree. Taken in their totality, these domestic actions arguably have effected a substantial change in the relationship between the individual and the government of the United States. While these actions may not have been felt yet by most of us directly, they are affecting individual members of our society in specific instances. It behooves us to keep in mind that "There but for ... go I." These actions have surely also affected our moral image and status in the world.

What is also striking is the speed with which these changes have occurred and the relative lack of public outcry about them. The absence of much protest probably reflects the fact that the changes have not had a direct impact on much of the population at large, and, given the trauma that September 11 wreaked on the psyche of America, the general public is receptive to the notion of "doing what needs to be done" to deal with the threat.

Review of the materials in this volume reveals another striking pattern that warrants our attention:

> The picture that emerges ... is that in major areas of anti-terrorism enforcement activities there has been frequent use of both self-imposed and super-imposed techniques of deferring or avoiding decision on important questions of governmental authority. The Supreme Court itself has, on several occasions, utilized traditional legal techniques to avoid deciding particular cases or particular issues. The Congress, too, has engaged in temporizing action by its use of sunset clauses and has also by statute acted to take away from the courts some jurisdiction to decide. Even more frequently, the Executive Branch has taken a number of different approaches each of which has had the effect of avoiding decision of important constitutional issues by the Supreme Court. And when the Congress has sought to obtain information about controversial activities with a view to finding out whether legislation is needed, the Executive Branch has been less than forthcoming, invoking at every turn the need for protecting secrecy. In almost every instance where judicial or legislative action might have addressed the merits of important anti-terrorism actions by the Executive Branch, there has been deferral or avoidance of the issues, sometimes voluntarily by one of the other branches and sometimes because of "defensive" actions taken by the Executive.
>
>   . . .
>
> Insofar ... as the use of these techniques has the effect of postponing adequate consideration of important legislative matters or deferring judicial resolution of important constitutional issues, they inevitably interfere with the effective operation of the system of checks and balances. When this occurs only for a short time, either because the exigent circumstances that created the substantive issues end or because the Court eventually decides the significant questions on the merits, the undermining of the checks and balances system is a temporary phenomenon that can be tolerated. If, however, the weakening of the system is likely to continue into the indefinite future, the situation may begin to undermine the traditional structural balance of our constitutional system.
>
>   . . .
>
> Each of the deferral or avoidance actions that have been taken, viewed in isolation, may appear to be justified or warranted under the circumstances. It is not the individual deferral or avoidance that has been significant. Rather it is the pattern and, indeed, the omnipresence of the phenomenon among all the branches of government, that give cause for serious concern. This is what makes the use of deferral and avoidance techniques in the field of anti-terrorism law since 9/11

so unusual and, it can be argued, unique. When these deferral/avoidance actions are viewed collectively, it becomes clear that the overall effect has been to block consideration by any of the other major branches of government of the merits of almost every major anti-terrorism action undertaken by the Executive Branch.

There have been additional consequences. Because of the pattern of deferral/avoidance, the Administration's actions that have affected individuals have continued to have effect. Deciding not to decide is a decision with effects. It leaves in place the status quo ante....

Among the several branches of the government, the "war on terror" can be seen as the occasion when additional authority has flowed to our executive branch, thus far, without much effective restraint by the other branches of government.... Our checks and balances may still be working, but in these times of exigency they have not been working very well.

    . . .

There is another avenue to think about that we have not previously mentioned, a kind of check outside the normal legal-political equation, the check that a free press and an enlightened citizenry can impose on the instruments of government. The press has generally been fulfilling its responsibilities; it has been the source of many of the disclosures of otherwise secret governmental actions. The public, however, is another matter. Generally, when it comes to issues of enforcement against terrorism, public opinion polls have shown significant support for the Executive Branch's actions. Is it possible to educate the public on such matters so that it can begin to be a source of check on the accretion of power to the Executive Branch? It would be nice to be more sanguine about this possibility, but it seems much more likely that the public's fear of further catastrophic terrorist actions will trump any concerns that it may have about the erosion of civil liberties and the concentration of power in the Executive.

Norman Abrams, Developments in U.S. Anti-terrorism Law: Checks and Balances Undermined, 4 J.Int.Crim.J 1117, 1130–1132 (2006).

Since the foregoing was written, there have been some further developments but, thus far, no marked change in the pattern. The Supreme Court has begun to grant review in cases where it might pass on the merits of the executive actions being taken, but it is still not clear how far the Court will go. Meanwhile, Congress continues to show marked deference to the wishes of the executive branch in the legislation that has been enacted.

A final note. Many have observed on numerous occasions that if we are in a "war," it is a war that may not have an ending. This observation obviously has important implications for the changes in the relation between government and individual that are justified as "wartime measures." Are we witnessing legal changes in the essential nature of the U.S. society that are to be with us for the indefinite future? It is a sobering thought.

INDEX

References are to Pages

ABU GHRAIB INCIDENT
Generally, 307, 315

ACTUS REUS
Material support offenses, 59
Terrorism definitions, 9

ADMINISTRATIVE REVIEW BOARDS (ARB)
Enemy combatant detentions, 576, 605

ADMINISTRATIVE SUBPOENAS
See Subpoenas, this index

AFGHAN DETENTIONS
Habeas corpus jurisdiction, 577

AIRCRAFT
Anti-aircraft missile prohibitions, 52
Antihijacking Act, 13
Drone warfare, 734
Jurisdiction, aircraft-related crimes, 12

AL QAEDA
Generally, 455
Bin Laden execution, 3, 734
Interrogation of detainees, 312
Organizational structure, 591

ALIEN TORT STATUTE (ATS)
Irregular rendition claims, 383

ALIENS
9/11 attack, alien interviews and detentions following, 427, 450
Immigration Detentions, this index
Removal of Aliens, this index

ANTITERRORISM
Civilian Approach to Anti-Terrorism, this index
Military Approach to Anti-Terrorism, this index

ANTITERRORISM AND EFFECTIVE DEATH PENALTY ACT (AEDPA)
Anti-terrorist applications, 53
Classified information evidence, 113
Constitutionality, 121
Immigration detentions, 461
Material support offenses amendments, 95

ARAB CONVENTION ON THE SUPPRESSION OF TERRORISM
Generally, 16

ARMY FIELD MANUAL (AFM)
Generally, 306
Admissibility of coerced confessions, 344
Evidence admissibility issues, 325
Interrogation techniques, 321
Obama administration adopts, 319
Obama administration policy on interrogations, 392
Torture controversy and adoption of, 317
Waterboarding, 318

ARREST
See also Detentions, this index
Enemy combatant arrests in US, 622
Foreign country arrests on narcotics charges, 270
International waters, arrests on, 355
Mansfield Amendment, 269
Miranda warning requirements, 342
Operational terrorist arrest interrogations, 341
Pretextual arrests under material witness warrants, 420
US, arrests in of enemy combatants, 622

ARTICLES OF WAR
Military commissions and tribunals, 641, 645

ASHCROFT GUIDELINES
Proactive surveillance, 136

ASSASSINATION
See Targeted Killing, this index

ATTORNEY GENERAL
See Justice Department, this index

ATTORNEYS
CIPA clearances of counsel
Generally, 511 et seq.
See also Classified Information Procedures Act, this index
CIPA court security officer appointments, 511, 514
Material support offenses, advocacy-related, 69
Military Commissions Act of defense counsel
Generally, 698
Duties, 703
Right to Counsel, this index

AUTHORIZATION FOR USE OF MILITARY FORCE (AUMF)
Al-Marri detention and prosecution, 639
Combatant Status Review Tribunals, 555
Detainee Treatment Act of 2005, 555, 571
Duration of enemy combatant detentions, 536

**AUTHORIZATION FOR USE OF MILI-
TARY FORCE (AUMF)**—Cont'd
Enactment, 528
Enemy combatant detentions, 528
Guantanamo detainees, authority for deten-
tion, 536
Military commissions and tribunals, 652
Padilla detention and prosecution, 622
Terrorism Surveillance Program and, 206
Text, 528
US citizens, detentions as enemy combatants
Hamdi, 537
Lindh, 551
Padilla, 552
War Powers Resolution and, 529

BAIL
Material witness detentions, 406, 411

BIVENS ACTIONS
Generally, 372, 374, 453
See also Civil Damages Actions, this index;
Judicial Review, this index
Claims of violations of constitutional rights,
372
Classified information evidence problems, 378
Conditions of confinement, immigration deten-
tions, 450
Discriminatory purpose element, 453
Graymail risks, 379
Immigration detentions, 450
Immunity, this index
Implied nature of cause of action, 453
Material witness detentions, 416
Parties defendant, 379
Parties plaintiff, 263
Policy considerations, 380
Proactive surveillance, 127
Qualified immunity, 417
Religious rights violations, 453
Sovereign immunity, 376
Supervisory liability, 454
Vicarious and supervisory liability distin-
guished, 454

BLACK SITES
Generally, 354
See also Irregular Rendition, this index
Amnesty International report, 394
Bush administration policies, 368
Obama administration closing, 4

BUSH ADMINISTRATION
Black site policies, 368
Detention policies, 368
Electronic surveillance, 161
Enemy combatant detention policy, 534, 604
Guantanamo detention policies, 368, 576
Interrogation policies, 368
Irregular rendition policies, 368
Obama administration policy compared
Generally, 4
See also Obama Administration, this in-
dex
Enemy combatant detentions, 535
Epilogue, 771

BUSH ADMINISTRATION—Cont'd
Obama administration policy compared
—Cont'd
Interrogations, 306
Proactive surveillance, 128
Torture, 306
Torture policies, 306, 309, 313

BYBEE MEMORANDUM
Torture controversy, 309, 312, 314

**CENTRAL INTELLIGENCE AGENCY
(CIA)**
Black sites
Generally, 394
See also Black Sites, this index
Detention policies, 370
Irregular rendition activities
Generally, 355, 385
Erroneous rendition case investigations,
395
Foreign government criminal charges
against US agents, 392
Targeted killing instructions, 736

CHOICE OF FORUM
Generally, 730
See also Civilian vs Military Trial Controversy,
this index

CIVIL DAMAGES ACTIONS
See also Judicial Review, this index
Bivens Actions, this index
Immunity, this index
Irregular rendition, civil remedies of victims
Generally, 354, 371 et seq.
Nongovernmental parties, claims against,
385
State secrets privilege, 388
Material witness detentions, 416
Nongovernmental parties, irregular rendition
claims against, 385
Targeted killing claim, 739
Torture, civil remedies of victims
Generally, 371 et seq.
Nongovernmental parties, claims against,
385
State secrets privilege, 388
Torture Victim Protection Act, 371

CIVIL LIBERTIES PROTECTIONS
9/11 attack, liberty/security tensions following,
433
See also First Amendment Protections, this
index; Liberty/Security Conflict, this
index
Classified Information Procedure Act, liber-
ty/security tensions, 493
Epilogue, 771
Foreign Intelligence Surveillance Act protec-
tions, 174
Library provision, 278
Material witness detentions, 422
Military Use in Domestic Law Enforcement,
this index
Section 215 orders, 278
Terrorism Surveillance Program, 207

CIVILIAN APPROACH TO ANTI–TER-RORISM
Generally, 7 et seq.
Military countermeasures compared, 2

CIVILIAN VS MILITARY TRIAL CONTROVERSY
Generally, 344, 730, 732
See also Military Use in Domestic Law Enforcement, this index
Adaptability of criminal justice system to post-9/11 world, 345
Classified information evidence, 467
Conscience shocking law enforcement behavior, 362, 365
Interrogation restraints as factor, 730
Lindh prosecution, 731
Moussaoui prosecution, 731
Obama administration policies, 53, 325
Padilla prosecution, 730
US citizen prosecutions, 730

CLASSIFIED INFORMATION EVIDENCE
See also Classified Information Procedures Act, this index; Foreign Intelligence Surveillance Act, this index
Adequacy of CIPA summaries, 475
Antiterrorism and Effective Death Penalty Act, 113
Bivens litigation, 378
Compulsory process conflicts, 492 et seq.
Counsel, CIPA clearances
Generally, 511 et seq.
See also Classified Information Procedures Act, this index
Criminal prosecution use of FISA evidence
Generally, 191
Significant purpose formula, 185, 187
Defense evidence, 468
Definitions, 469, 482
Enemy combatant witnesses, 493
Foreign Terrorist Organization listings supported by, 113, 117
Government privilege, 116
Guantanamo detainees, habeas corpus applications, 598
Immigration detention hearings, 431
Military Commissions Act of 2009
Generally, 709
Evidentiary rules, 693
Military vs civilian proceedings, 467
Silent witness rule, 484, 492
State Secrets Privilege, this index
Substitutions, CIPA
Generally, 468, 495
Adequacy determinations, 475
Hearsay issues, 509
Watson Declaration, 430

CLASSIFIED INFORMATION PROCEDURES ACT (CIPA)
Generally, 467 et seq.
See also Classified Information Evidence, this index
Admissibility determinations, 479
Bin Laden prosecution, 513

CLASSIFIED INFORMATION PROCEDURES ACT (CIPA)—Cont'd
Confrontation rights conflicts, 481 et seq.
Counsel, CIPA clearances
Generally, 511 et seq.
Appointments, 483
Bin Laden prosecution, 513
Constitutionality challenge, 517
Liberty/security balancing, 522
Privacy rights of counsel, 521
Right to counsel conflicts, 513, 517
Rules for clearances, 511
Uncleared counsel participation, 486
Court security officer appointments, 511, 514
Defense evidence suppression, 468
Definitions, 469, 482
Discovery, 470
Enactment, 468
Enemy combatant witnesses, 493
Ex parte in camera proceedings, 480
Foreign Terrorist Organizations listing procedures applicability, 118
Graymail defense, 468
Hearings, 485
Helpfulness determinations, 478
In camera proceedings, 480
Juror qualifications in CIPA cases, 513
Liberty/security balancing
Generally, 493
Counsel clearance requirements, 522
Materiality determinations, 502
Military Commissions Act of 2009, 709
Protective orders, 469
Purpose of statute, 468, 478
Rules for clearances of counsel, 511
Silent witness rule, 484, 492
Substitutions
Generally, 468, 495
Adequacy determinations, 475
Hearsay issues, 509
Military Commissions Act of 2009, 711
Text, 469

CODE OF FEDERAL REGULATIONS
Terrorism definitions, 31

COERCION
See also Torture Controversy, this index
Army Field Manual, admissibility of coerced confessions, 344
Confessions, coerced
Admissibility, 343 et seq.
Evidentiary value, 595
Defining terrorism, coercion intent, 31, 48
Material witness detentions, coercive use of process, 423

COMBATANT STATUS REVIEW TRIBUNALS (CSRT)
Generally, 567, 605
Constitutionality, 555
Judicial review, 555, 571

COMMANDER–IN–CHIEF AUTHORITY
Generally, 2
See also Presidential Authority, this index

COMMANDER–IN–CHIEF AUTHORITY
—Cont'd
Enemy combatant detentions, 534
Military commissions and tribunals, 645, 652

COMPLICITY
Material support compared, 58, 81

CONFESSIONS
See also Interrogation, this index
Military Commissions Act of 2009 evidentiary
rules, 691, 699

CONSPIRACY
Law of war, 668
Material support offenses compared, 58
Military Commissions Act of 2009, 725

CONSTITUTIONAL LAW
Antiterrorism and Effective Death Penalty Act,
121
Bivens claims for violations of constitutional
rights
Generally, 372
See also Bivens Actions, this index
Civil Liberties Protections, this index
Classified Information Procedures Act
Confrontation rights conflicts, 481 et seq.
Counsel clearance requirements, 517
Combatant Status Review Panel, 555, 571
Detainee Treatment Act of 2005, 555, 571
Due Process, this index
Electronic surveillance
Generally, 161
See also Electronic Surveillance, this index
Extraterritorial habeas corpus rights, 4
First Amendment Protections, this index
Fourth Amendment, foreign searches, 260
Habeas Corpus, this index
Judicial review, Article III standards, 123
Liberty/Security Conflict, this index
Material support offenses, vagueness chal-
lenges, 69 et seq., 87 et seq.
Military commissions and tribunals, Bill of
Rights protections, applicability, 649
Military Use in Domestic Law Enforcement,
this index
Proactive surveillance
Generally, 127 et seq.
See also Proactive Surveillance, this in-
dex
Civil liberties tensions, 129, 139
Vagueness challenges, material support of-
fenses, 69 et seq., 87 et seq.

**CONVENTION AGAINST TORTURE AND
OTHER CRUEL, INHUMAN AND DE-
GRADING TREATMENT OR PUNISH-
MENT**
Generally, 307

CREPPY DIRECTIVE
Immigration detentions, special interest cases,
434

**CRUEL, INHUMAN OR DEGRADING
TREATMENT (CIDT)**
Definition, 318
Detainee Treatment Act of 2005, 317
Military Commissions Act of 2009, evidentiary
rules, 699
Torture distinguished, 313

CUSTOMARY INTERNATIONAL LAW
Generally, 11
Extraterritorial law enforcement activities, 362
Jurisdiction, universality principle, 11
Torture, 313

DATA MINING
Generally, 201
Judicial review of activities, 202

DEATH PENALTY
Antiterrorism and Effective Death Penalty Act,
this index
Extradition treaties and death penalty policies,
368
Military Commissions Act of 2009, 708
Targeted Killing, this index

DEFENSE DEPARTMENT
Enemy combatant detentions, Secretary of De-
fense authority, 533
Military use in domestic law enforcement, 753
Posse Comitatus Act, this index

DEFINING TERRORISM
8 USC Section 1182, 25
18 USC Section 956, 33
18 USC Section 2331, 25
18 USC Section 2332, 34
18 USC Section 2333, 53
18 USC Section 2332a, 38
18 USC Section 2339A, 60
18 USC Section 2332b, 41, 45
18 USC Section 2339B, 61
18 USC Section 2332d, 52
18 USC Section 2332(d), 36
18 USC Section 2332f, 48, 51
22 USC Section 2656f, 26
Action-based definitions, 16
Activity, terrorist, 26
Anti-aircraft missiles prohibitions, 52
Arab Convention on the Suppression of Terrorism, 16
Attorney General determinations creating
criminal elements, 35
Bodily injury risks, 19
Bomb-related offenses, 48
Borrowed statutory definitions, 23
Code of Federal Regulations, 31
Coercion intent, 31, 48
Conduct transcending national boundaries, 41,
44, 46
Conduct-related definitions, 23
Customary international law, 11
Differences and distinctions, 31
Domestic and international terrorism distin-
guished, 20
Domestic/international distinctions for law en-
forcement purposes, 31

DEFINING TERRORISM—Cont'd
Enemy combatant detentions, 531
European Convention on the Suppression of
    Terrorism, 16
Executive Order 13224 Terrorist Financing
    listings, 28
FBI listings, 30
Financing of terrorism, 28
Foreign Intelligence Surveillance Act, 32, 163,
    177
Foreign Terrorist Organization listings, 28
Freedom fighters or terrorists, 16, 96
    Generally, 8
Hoaxes involving threats of terrorist acts, 40
Immigration and Nationality Act, 24
Improvised explosive device activities, 41
Influence government conduct, intent to, 20
Intelligence Reform and Terrorism Prevention
    Act of 2004, 40, 52
Intent to affect government conduct, 20
Intent-based definitions, 31, 48
International terrorism prosecutions since
    9/11, 53
International/domestic distinctions for law en-
    forcement purposes, 31
Intimidation intent, 31, 48
Jurisdictional implications of definitions, 37,
    40, 51
Justice Department listings, 30
Military Commissions Act of 2006, 730
Military Commissions Act of 2009, 724
Motive-based definitions, 16
National Security Division statistics, 54
Patriot USA Act
    Domestic terrorism, 31
    Listings, 30
Piracy and terrorism distinguished, 17
Policy considerations, 31
Policy definitions, 27
Predicate definitions, 31
Property damage, acts limited to, 18
Prosecutorial discretion, 36
Purpose based definitions, 22
Purposes of terrorism determinations, 9
Radiological dispersal device prohibitions, 52
Retaliate against government conduct, intent
    to, 20, 48
Selected terrorism statutes, 33 et seq.
Self-determination motives, 16
Sentencing Guidelines, 17, 20
Simpliciter, terrorism, 23
Specific offenses as markers for terrorism, 22
State criminal laws, 33
State Department determinations
    Generally, 24, 26
    Listings, 27
State Sponsors of Terrorism listings, 28
State-sponsored terrorism, 15
Threats of terrorist acts, 40
Universality principle, customary international
    law, 11
Virus transmission prohibitions, 52
Weapon-based definitions, 16
Weapons of mass destruction offenses, 38

DEFINITIONS
    See also Defining Terrorism, this index
AEDPA, 88
AFM, 307
AOR, 326
ARB, 576
ATF, 21
ATS, 383
AUMf, 206
Black site, 4, 354
CAT, 313
CIA, 232
CIDT, 313
CIPA, 118
Classified information, 469, 482
Conduct transcending national boundaries, 44,
    46
Crimes against humanity, 15
Criminal proceeding, 406
Cruel, inhuman and degrading treatment, 318
CSO, 514
CSRT, 555
Customary international law, 11
DOJ, 201
EC, 303
Electronic surveillance
    Generally, 165, 210, 214
        Technology changes affecting definitions,
        233
Enemy combatant, 538, 587
Extraordinary rendition, 365, 375
FAA, 237
Facility of interstate or foreign commerce, 44
FISA, 160
Foreign Intelligence Surveillance Act defini-
    tions, 163, 177
Foreign Terrorist Organization, 28
FTO, 27
Graymail defense, 468
HIG, 323
IC, 232
ICRC, 319
IED, 41
IG, 204
Indefinite detainee, 448
Irregular rendition, 365, 375
IRTPA, 62
Law of war detention, 614
LHBSA, 341
Library, 279
Lifer, 448
Material support offenses, statutory definitions
    Generally, 61, 63
    Humanitarian Law Project decision, 88
MCA (2006), 688
MCA (2009), 689
Military Commissions Act of 2006 definitions,
    719
Military Commissions Act of 2009 definitions,
    694
MLAT, 269
National security letters, 246
NATO, 16
NSA, 160
NSP, 200

DEFINITIONS—Cont'd
OARDEC, 606
OIG, 295
OLC, 304
PCA, 762
Posse comitatus, 750
PRB, 611
Predicates, 31
Privileged and unprivileged enemy beligerents, 694
Proactive surveillance, 129
PSP, 203
Rendition, 365, 394
Reverse targeting, 236
SAM, 68
Silent witness, 484
State-sponsored terrorism, 15
TEL, 27
Torture, 308
TSP, 161
TVPA, 371
UCMJ, 659
UECRB, 581
USG, 27
Weapon of mass destruction, 39

DEPARTMENTS OF GOVERNMENT
Defense Department, this index
Justice Department, this index
State Department, this index

DEPORTATION
Aliens, this index
Immigration Detentions, this index
Removal of Aliens, this index

DETAINEE TREATMENT ACT OF 2005 (DTA)
Constitutionality, 555, 571
Cruel, inhuman and degrading treatment, 317
Habeas corpus, 555
Judicial review, 685
Military commissions authority, 664

DETENTIONS
Bases for, 399
Bush administration policies, 368
CIA policies, 370
Conditional detention, 615
Contempt detentions, 400
Emergency Detention Act of 1950, 538
Enemy Combatant Detentions, this index
Extended detention as terrorism countermeasure, 399
Freedom of Information Act use to determine reasons for detention, 401
Guantanamo Detainees, this index
Immigration Detentions, this index
Irregular Rendition, this index
Law of war detention, term defined, 614
Material Witness Detentions, this index
Preventive Detention, this index

DISCOVERY
Classified Information Procedures Act, 470
Military Commissions Act of 2009, 710

DOMESTIC INVESTIGATIONS AND OPERATIONS GUIDELINES
Generally, 130
History of guidelines, 137
Publication, 131

DOMESTIC TERRORISM
International terrorism distinguished, 20

DRONE WARFARE
Targeted killing, 734

DRUG LAWS
Administrative subpoenas in drug-related investigations, 284 et seq.
Military use in domestic law enforcement, 749, 757, 765

DUE PROCESS
Balancing inquiries, 115
Enemy combatant detentions
Generally, 537
Exigent circumstances considerations, 545
Exigent circumstances, 545
Foreign entities, due process rights of, 114, 118
Guantanamo detainees
Generally, 554 et seq.
See also Guantanamo Detainees, this index
Fundamental procedural protections, 589
Right to Counsel, this index
Suspension Clause, 549
Three factors, 115

ELECTRONIC COMMUNICATIONS PRIVACY ACT (ECPA)
Patriot Act amending, 301

ELECTRONIC SURVEILLANCE
Generally, 160 et seq.
See also Foreign Intelligence Surveillance Act, this index
Bush administration, 161
Criminal prosecutions using FISA-derived material, 191
Definitions
Generally, 165, 210, 214
Technology changes affecting, 233
Domestic vs foreign activities
Generally, 247
FISA Amendments Act, 237
Reverse targeting, 236
Emergency FISA orders, 174, 179
Federal preemption of state laws, 231
Foreign intelligence information, law enforcement use of, 182
Foreign/domestic intelligence distinctions, 181
Fourth Amendment requirements, 161
Law enforcement uses of FISA acquired information, 182
National Security Agency activities, 160
Omnibus Crime Control and Safe Streets Act, this index
Overview of anti-terrorism measures, 128
Post-Terrorism Surveillance Program legislation, 215 et seq.
President's inherent powers, 194

ELECTRONIC SURVEILLANCE—Cont'd
Primary purpose of FISA intercepts, 187
Probable cause determinations, FISA, 173
Reverse targeting, 236
Searches, domestic search authorizations compared, 247
Significant purpose of FISA intercepts, 185, 187, 190
Technology changes affecting, 233
TSP
    Generally, 128, 200 et seq.
    See also Terrorism Surveillance Program, this index
  Post-TSP legislation, 215 et seq.
Unidentified targets, 179, 198
Volume of FISA surveillance approvals, 179
Warrant requirements, 160

EMERGENCIES
  See also Exigent Circumstances, this index
Detentions, Emergency Detention Act of 1950, 538
Electronic surveillance, FISA emergency orders, 174, 179
Federal Emergency Management Agency, Posse Comitatus Act and, 761
Posse Comitatus Act exceptions in, 759, 761, 766

ENEMY COMBATANT DETENTIONS
  Generally, 528 et seq.
Administrative Review Boards, 576, 605
Alien vs US citizen detentions and prosecutions, 730
Al-Marri detention and prosecution, 639
Arrests in US, 622
Authorization for Use of Military Force as basis for, 528
Bush administration policy, 534, 604
Capture law, 539
Classified information evidence and enemy combatant witnesses, 493
Combat zone activities justifying, 542
Combatant Status Review Tribunals, this index
Commander-in-Chief authority of President, 534
Conditional detention, 615
Definitions, 531, 538, 587
Detainee Treatment Act of 2005, 555, 571
Due process requirements
    Generally, 537
  Exigent circumstances considerations, 545
Duration under AUMF, 536
Extended detentions, legal basis, 528 et seq.
Extraterritorial detentions, habeas corpus
    Generally, 554
  Afghan detentions, 577
Foreign Affairs Reform and Restructuring Act, relocations, 613
Geneva Convention protections, 599
Guantanamo detainees
    See also Guantanamo Detainees, this index
  Authority for detention, 536

ENEMY COMBATANT DETENTIONS—Cont'd
Habeas corpus
    Generally, 541
  Evidentiary standards, 595
  Extraterritorial detention
      Generally, 554
    Afghan detentions, 577
  Jurisdiction, 552
Hamdi habeas corpus application
    Generally, 537
  Settlement, 550
Immigration detentions compared, 528
Incommunicado detention, 552
Inherent authority of President, 534
Japanese internment camps of World War II, 538
Judicial review
    Generally, 537
  Combatant Status Review Panel, 555, 571
  Detainee Treatment Act of 2005, 555, 571
  Jurisdictional issues, 552
  Military administrative processes compared, 599 et seq.
Law of war detention, term defined, 614
Lawful and unlawful combatants, 539, 551
Legal basis, 528 et seq.
Liberty/security conflicts, 549
Material witness detentions compared, 528
Military administrative processes, 599 et seq.
Military Commissions Act of 2009, this index
Military Order, 529
Military tribunal reviews of status, 547
Mobbs Declaration, 542
National Defense Appropriations Bill provisions, 615
Obama administration policy, 4, 528, 535, 607
Padilla detention and prosecution, 622
Periodic review boards, 611
Prisoners of war
    See also Prisoners of War, this index
  Unlawful belligerents distinguished, 648
Privileged and unprivileged enemy belligerents, 694
Relocations, Foreign Affairs Reform and Restructuring Act, 613
Right to counsel
    Generally, 548
  Incommunicado detention, 552
Secretary of Defense authorities, 533
Torture claims, 596
Unlawful Enemy Combatant Review Board, 581
US, arrests in, 622
US citizens
  Hamdi, 537
  Lindh, 551
  Padilla, 552

EUROPEAN CONVENTION ON THE SUPPRESSION OF TERRORISM
Defining terrorism, 16

EVIDENCE
Army Field Manual interrogation rules, evidence admissibility issues, 325

EVIDENCE—Cont'd

Classified Information Evidence, this index

Coerced confessions
    Admissibility, 343 et seq.
    Evidentiary value, 595

Confessions
    Military Commissions Act of 2009 evidentiary rules, 691, 699

Confessions obtained abroad, admissibility, 325 et seq.

Criminal prosecution, use of FISA evidence
    Generally, 191
    Significant purpose formula, 185, 187

Criminal prosecutions using FISA-derived material, 191

Disclosure of exculpatory evidence, Military Commissions Act of 2009, 706

Exclusionary rule, Military Commissions Act of 2009, 690, 699

FBI interrogation guidelines, 339

Foreign government interrogations, admissibility issues, 344

Foreign Terrorist Organization listings supported by, 113

Guantanamo detainee habeas corpus applications, evidentiary standards, 595

Hearsay, Military Commissions Act of 2009, 692, 702

Interrogation evidence admissibility issues
    Generally, 325 et seq.
    Coerced confessions, 343 et seq.
    Confessions obtained abroad, 325 et seq.
    Foreign government interrogation practices, 344
    Joint venture interrogations with foreign governments, 352
    Miranda warnings, 326

Joint venture interrogations with foreign governments, interrogation admissibility issues, 352

Military Commissions Act of 2009 evidentiary rules, 689

Miranda rules
    See also Miranda Warnings, this index
    Military Commissions Act of 2009 evidentiary rules, 690
    Public safety exception, 306, 331, 339

Search and seizure, Military Commissions Act of 2009, 690

Uniform Code of Military Justice standards, 686

EXECUTIONS

See Targeted Killing, this index

EXECUTIVE ORDERS

12333
    Amendments of Order, 130
    Assassination, 735
    Undercover agents, 130

11905, assassination, 735

13492, conditional detention, 615

13440, revocation, 320

13491, Special Task Force on Interrogations and Transfer Policies, 322

13224, terrorist financing listings, 28

EXIGENT CIRCUMSTANCES

See also Emergencies, this index

Due process in, 545

Enemy combatant detentions, exigent circumstances considerations, 545

Miranda warnings in, 339

National Security Letters, exigent circumstances requests, 300

Surveillance, exigent circumstances triggering special powers, 128

EXIGENT LETTERS

See also Subpoenas, this index

National Security Letters distinguished, 301

EXTRADITION

See also Irregular Rendition, this index

Conscience shocking law enforcement behavior, 362, 365

Death penalty policies impeding formal extradition, 368

Rendition distinguished, 365

Traditional practices of, 354

EXTRAORDINARY RENDITION

Generally, 306

See also Irregular Rendition, this index

FEDERAL BUREAU OF INVESTIGATION (FBI)

9/11 attack, alien interviews and detentions following, 427, 450

Authority, National Security Letters, 278

Civil suit challenges, proactive surveillance, 147

Domestic Investigations and Operations Guidelines
    Generally, 130
    History of guidelines, 137
    Publication, 131

Extraterritorial law enforcement activities, 362

General principles of operations, proactive surveillance, 151

Guidelines for Extraterritorial FBI Operations, 131

Interrogation
    FBI guidelines, 339
    Legal Handbook for Special Agents, 341

National Security Letter issuances, 288

National Security Letters, authority, 278

Oklahoma City bombing, 138

PENTBOM investigation, 497

Proactive surveillance
    Attorney General Guidelines, 129
    Civil suit challenges, 147
    General principles of operations, 151
    Oklahoma City bombing, 138

Terrorism listings, 30

FEDERAL EMERGENCY MANAGEMENT AGENCY
Posse Comitatus Act and, 761

FIRST AMENDMENT PROTECTIONS
See also Liberty/Security Conflict, this index
Chilling effects of proactive surveillance, 129, 141, 144
Epilogue, 771
Material support prosecutions
Generally, 59
See also Material Support Offenses, this index
National Security Letters challenges, 293
Proactive surveillance conflicts
Chilling effects on rights exercises, 129, 141, 144
Civil liberties tensions, 129, 139

FOREIGN AFFAIRS REFORM AND RE-STRUCTURING ACT (FARRA)
Enemy combatant relocations, 613
Rendition, 379

FOREIGN INTELLIGENCE SURVEIL-LANCE ACT (FISA)
2008 amendments
Generally, 161
Domestic vs foreign activities, 237
Judicial review, 237
Terrorism Surveillance Program, 203
Generally, 215
Legislative history, 232
Attorney General reports to Congress, 181
Civil liberties protections, 174
Court, FISA
Generally, 162
Secrecy of proceedings, 199
Terrorism Surveillance Program approvals, 202
Court of Review, 190
Criminal prosecution use of FISA evidence
Generally, 191
Significant purpose formula, 185, 187, 190
Definitions, 163, 177
Domestic vs foreign activities
FISA Amendments Act, 237
Reverse targeting, 236
Duration of warrants, 179
Emergency orders, 174, 179
Federal preemption of state electronic surveillance laws, 231
FISA Amendments Act. 2008 amendments, above
Fourth Amendment rights balancing, 195
Generally, 160 et seq.
History and background, 162
Homeland Security Act amendments, 182
Intelligence Reform and Terrorism Prevention Act of 2004 amendments, 176, 178, 180
International terrorism subject to, 32
Judicial review
FISA Amendments Act, 237
Sealed Case, 185, 199

FOREIGN INTELLIGENCE SURVEIL-LANCE ACT (FISA)—Cont'd
Law enforcement uses of acquired information, 182
Omnibus Crime Control and Safe Streets Act standards compared, 176
Omnibus Crime Control and Safe Streets Act warrant standards compared, 161
Orders, 172
Patriot USA Act amendments, 182, 188
Physical searches, 246
Primary purpose of FISA intercepts, 187
Probable cause
Determinations, 173
Findings, 195
Requirements, 176
Standards, 185
Public disclosure of activities, 180
Sealed Case review of FISA court operations, 185, 199
Search warrants, 189
Searches, 246
Secrecy of FISA court proceedings, 199
Significant purpose of FISA intercepts, 185, 187, 190
Terrorism subject to, 32
Terrorism Surveillance Program and
Generally, 207, 208
See also Terrorism Surveillance Program, this index
FISA amendments addressing
Generally, 203, 215
Legislative history, 232
Unidentified targets of electronic surveillance, 179, 198
Volume of surveillance approvals, 179
Warrants
Generally, 189
Criminal investigation warrants compared, 246
Searches, 247

FOREIGN TERRORIST ENTITIES
Due process rights of, 114, 118
Knowledge of status, material support offenses, 83

FOREIGN TERRORIST ORGANIZA-TIONS (FTO)
See also Material Support Offenses, this index
Alter ego organizations, 119
Benign support, 97
Classified Information Procedures Act applicability to listing procedures, 118
Classified materials evidence supporting listings, 113, 117
Criminal appeals challenging designations, 120
Designations, procedural requirements, 102
Due process rights of foreign entities, 114, 118
Evidence supporting listings, 113
Intelligence Reform and Terrorism Protection Act amendments, 111

FOREIGN TERRORIST ORGANIZA-TIONS (FTO)—Cont'd
Judicial review of listings
    Generally, 107 et seq.
    Classified materials evidence supporting listings, 113
    Criminal appeals challenging designations, 120
    Jurisdictional limitation, 122
Jurisdictional limitation on judicial review of listings, 122
Knowledge of status, material support offenses, 83
Lawful activities of FTOs, support of, 87, 98
Notice of pending designations, 107, 116, 118
Procedural requirements
    Classified Information Procedures Act applicability, 118
    Designations, 102
    Renewals of designations, 107
Renewals of designations, 107
Revocation of listings, 107
State Department designations, 102
State Department listings, 27, 28
Statutory authority, 101
Substantial support for listing determinations, 112
Umbrella organizations, 119
What and when questions, 116

FOREIGN–STUDENT MONITORING PROGRAM
Proactive surveillance, 130

FORUM CHOICE
Generally, 730
See also Civilian vs Military Trial Controversy, this index

FREEDOM FIGHTERS
Terrorism offenses, definitional difficulties, 16, 96

FREEDOM OF INFORMATION ACT
Detention challenges, 401

GENEVA CONVENTIONS
Enemy combatant detentions, 599
Military commissions and tribunals as subject to, 659, 676
Prisoners of war protections, 601

GOVERNMENTAL POWER
Anti-terrorism expansions, 1

GRAND JURIES
Material witness detentions, 405, 414

GRAYMAIL DEFENSE
Generally, 468
Bivens remedies, graymail risks, 379

GUANTANAMO DETAINEES
Generally, 554 et seq.
Authority for detention
    Generally, 536
    See also Authorization for Use of Military Force, this index
Bush administration policy, 368, 576

GUANTANAMO DETAINEES—Cont'd
Closure, Obama administration policy, 619
Combatant Status Review Tribunals, 555
Due process
    Generally, 554 et seq.
    Fundamental procedural protections, 589
    Habeas corpus, below
Habeas corpus
    Generally, 554 et seq.
    Classified information evidence, 598
    Detainee Treatment Act of 2005 (DTA), 555
    Evidentiary standards, 595
    Fundamental procedural protections, 589
    Pending applications, 586
    Prudential barriers to relief, 570
    Separation of powers issues, 568
    Statutory limitations, 554
Obama administration policy
    Generally, 5, 598, 607 et seq.
    Closure, 619
Statutory limitations on habeas corpus, 554
Torture controversy, 314
US citizen detentions, 553

GUIDELINES FOR EXTRATERRITORIAL FBI OPERATIONS
Justice Department, 131

HABEAS CORPUS
Generally, 557
See also Judicial Review, this index
Classified information evidence, 598
Detainee Treatment Act of 2005 (DTA), 555
Enemy combatant detention challenges
    Generally, 541
    Jurisdiction, 552
Extraterritorial applications
    Generally, 554
    Afghan detentions, 577
    Constitutional protections, 4
Fundamental procedural protections, 589
Guantanamo detainees
    Generally, 554 et seq.
    See also Guantanamo Detainees, this index
Hamdi application
    Generally, 537
    Settlement, 550
Immigration detentions, 458
Jurisdiction
    See also Guantanamo Detainees, this index
    Afghan detentions, 577
    Enemy combatant detention, 552
    Extraterritorial detention, 554, 577
    Statutory limitations, 554
Military Commissions Act of 2006, 555, 688
Military commissions and tribunals, judicial review, 641
Prudential barriers to relief, 570
Scope of right and limitations, 546
Statutory limitations, Guantanamo detainees, 554
Suspension Clause as limitations, 557

HEARINGS
Classified Information Procedures Act, 485

HIGH–VALUE DETAINEE INTERROGA-TION GROUP (HIG)
Generally, 323

HOLDER MEMORANDUM
State secret privilege, 389

HOMELAND SECURITY ACT
Foreign Intelligence Surveillance Act amendments, 182
Military use in domestic law enforcement, 747
Posse Comitatus Act and, 758
Proactive security, 130
TIPS program, 130

HUMANITY, CRIMES AGAINST
Universal jurisdiction, 15

IMMIGRATION AND NATIONALITY ACT
Defining terrorism, 24

IMMIGRATION DETENTIONS
9/11 attack, alien interviews and detentions following, 427, 450
Alien terrorist removal procedures, 461
Antiterrorism and Effective Death Penalty Act, 461
Bivens claims, 450
Bond hearings, 428
Certifications, Patriot Act, 457
Classified information evidence use at hearings, 431
Conditions of confinement, Bivens claims, 450
Discretionary detention authority, 428
Enemy combatant detentions compared, 528
Extended detention as terrorism countermeasure, 399
Freedom of Information Act use to determine reasons for detention, 401
    Generally, 427 et seq.
Habeas corpus, 458
Hearings, public access, 429
Immigration law violations, 428
Inadmissible aliens, 448
Indefinite detention
    Generally, 440, 448, 458
    Patriot Act, 460
Judicial review
    Bivens claims, 450
    Habeas corpus, 458
    Hearings, public access, 429
    Indefinite detention, 440
Justice Department discretionary detention authority, 428
Lifers, 448
Material witness process, use of
    Generally, 429
    See also Material Witness Detentions, this index
6-month presumptive detention period, 447, 449
Obama administration policy, 466
Open-ended detention, 440
Patriot Act
    Generally, 428, 448, 457 et seq.
    Certifications, 457
    Indefinite detention, 460

IMMIGRATION DETENTIONS—Cont'd
Posse Comitatus Act and immigration law enforcement, 765
Preventive detention aspects, 429
Preventive detention uses, 428
Proof standards, 428
Special interest cases, Creppy Directive, 434
Special removal court, 461, 466
Term of detention, 440
Unremovable aliens, 440, 447

IMMUNITY
Bivens claims, qualified immunity, 417
Civil damages claims, material witness detentions, 416
Conditions of confinement, immigration detentions, 450
Immigration detentions, 450
Intent issues, qualified immunity, 418
Material witness detentions, civil damages claims, 416
Proactive surveillance, immunity defenses to civil claims, 127
Qualified immunity
    Generally, 420
    Bivens claims, 417
    Intent issues, 418

IMPROVISED EXPLOSIVE DEVICES (IED)
Terrorism definitions, 41

INHERENT AUTHORITY OF PRESIDENT
Enemy combatant detentions, 534

INTELLIGENCE REFORM AND TERRORISM PROTECTION ACT (IRTPA)
FISA amendments, 176, 178, 180
Foreign Terrorist Organizations listings, 111
Material support offense statutes, amendments, 62, 89
Preventive detention, 400
Threats, 40, 52

INTERNAL SECURITY ACT OF 1950
Proactive surveillance, 138

INTERNATIONAL LAW
Customary International Law, this index
Extraterritorial law enforcement activities, 362
Irregular rendition, 362
Protective or security principle, 16
State-sponsored terrorism, 15

INTERNET
Data mining
    Generally, 201
    Judicial review of activities, 202
Electronic Surveillance, this index

INTERROGATION
    Generally, 306 et seq.
    See also Torture Controversy, this index
Advice of Rights forms, 326
AFM
    Generally, 306
    See also Army Field Manual, this index

INTERROGATION—Cont'd
Al Qaeda detainees, 312
Bush administration policies, 368
Civilian vs military trial controversy, interrogation restraints as factor, 730
Coerced confessions
    Admissibility, 343 et seq.
    Evidentiary value, 595
Confessions obtained abroad, admissibility, 325 et seq.
Cruel, Inhuman or Degrading Treatment, this index
Evidence admissibility issues
    Generally, 325 et seq.
    Coerced confessions, 343 et seq.
    Confessions obtained abroad, 325 et seq.
    FBI guidelines, 339
    Foreign government interrogation practices, 344
    Joint venture interrogations with foreign governments, 352
    Miranda warnings, 326
    Public safety exception to Miranda rules, 306, 331, 339
Evidentiary value of coerced statements, 595
Extended detention interrogations, 399
FBI guidelines, 339
Foreign government criminal charges against US agents, 392
Foreign government interrogation practices, evidence admissibility issues, 344
Foreign interrogations, Miranda warnings, 306
High-Value Detainee Interrogation Group, 323
Joint venture interrogations with foreign governments, evidence admissibility issues, 352
Legal Handbook for Special Agents, 341
Miranda Warnings, this index
Obama administration policy, 4
Obama and Bush administration policies compared, 306
Operational terrorist arrests, 341
Overview of anti-terrorism measures, 128
Public safety exception to Miranda rules, 306, 331, 339
Special Task Force on Interrogations and Transfer Policies, 322, 392

IRREGULAR RENDITION
    Generally, 306, 353 et seq.
Alien Tort Statute claims, 383
Amnesty International report, 393
Black Sites, this index
Bush administration policies, 368
Central Intelligence Agency activities, 385
CIA activities, 355
Civil litigation claims based on, 354
Civil remedies of victims
    Generally, 371 et seq.
    Nongovernmental parties, claims against, 385
    State secrets privilege, 388

IRREGULAR RENDITION—Cont'd
Conscience shocking law enforcement behavior, 362, 365
Criminal procedure jurisdiction rules, 354
Death penalty policies impeding formal extradition, 368
Definitions, 365, 375
Erroneous rendition cases, CIA investigations, 395
Extradition
    Rendition distinguished, 365
    Traditional practices of, 354
Extraordinary rendition, 306, 354
Foreign government criminal charges against US agents, 392
International law, 362
Judicial review
    Civil claims, 371
    Separation of powers issues, 377, 379
    State secret defense, 382
Jurisdiction obtained by kidnapping
    Generally, 355, 356 et seq.
    Ker-Frisbie doctrine, 367
Ker-Frisbie doctrine, 367
Military countermeasures involving, 306
Monitoring mechanisms, 391
Nongovernmental parties, claims against, 385
Obama administration policy, 322, 355, 391
Policy considerations
    Generally, 381
    Amnesty International report, 393
Research references, 398
Right to counsel, 373
Secrecy of counter-terrorism activities, 354
Separation of powers issues, 377, 379
Special factors affecting civil remedies, 372
State Department role in rendition decisions, 391
Task Force on Interrogations and Transfer Policies, 392
Torture following
    Generally, 374
    See also Torture Controversy, this index
    Holder Memorandum, 391
US criminal procedure rules applicability, 354

JAPANESE INTERNMENT CAMPS OF WORLD WAR II
Generally, 538

JUDICIAL REVIEW
Administrative law determinations, statutory limitations, 125
Article III standards, 123
Bivens Actions, this index
Civil Damages Actions, this index
Data mining, 202
Detainee Treatment Act of 2005, 555, 571, 685
Domestic search authorizations, 250
Enemy combatant detentions
    Generally, 537
    Combatant Status Review Panel, 555, 571
    Jurisdictional issues, 552
    Military administrative processes compared, 599 et seq.

JUDICIAL REVIEW—Cont'd
FISA
    See also Foreign Intelligence Surveil-
        lance Act, this index
    FISA Amendments Act, 237
Foreign searches of US persons by non-US
    agents, 261
Foreign Terrorist Organization listings
    Generally, 107 et seq.
    Criminal appeals challenging designations,
        120
    Jurisdictional limitation, 122
Habeas Corpus, this index
Immigration detentions
    Bivens claims, 450
    Habeas corpus, 458
    Hearings, public access, 429
    Indefinite detention, 440
Irregular rendition
    Civil claims, 371
    Separation of powers issues, 377, 379
    State secret defense, 382
Jurisdiction
    Enemy combatant detentions, 552
    Limitation on reviews of Foreign Terrorist
        Organizations listings, 122
    Military Commissions Act of 2009, 718, 728
Material witness detentions
    Civil damages claims, 416
    Direct challenges, 403
Military Commissions Act of 2006, 555, 688
Military Commissions Act of 2009, 718, 728
Military commissions and tribunals
    Generally, 641
    Hamdan prosecution, 658 et seq.
Military countermeasures
    Proactive surveillance, 141
    Standing to challenge, 145
National Security Agency activities, 211
National Security Letters
    Generally, 280, 288
    Nondisclosure requirements, 288
Posse Comitatus Act, 749
Proactive surveillance
    Generally, 127
    Military countermeasures, 141
Searches
    Domestic searches, 250
    Foreign searches of US persons by non-US
        agents, 261
    US person searches by non-US agents, 261
Separation of powers issues, irregular rendi-
    tion, 377, 379
Standing
    FISA Amendments Act challenge, 237
    Injury in fact, 244
    Military countermeasures, 145
State secret defense
    Generally, 388
    Irregular rendition, 382
Strict scrutiny review, 295
Subpoenas, National Security Letters, 280
Targeted killing, 734, 739
Terrorism Surveillance Program, 202, 211, 214
US person searches by non-US agents, 261

JURISDICTION
    See also Civilian vs Military Trial Contro-
        versy, this index
Afghan detentions, habeas corpus, 577
Aircraft-related crimes, 12
Antihijacking Act, universal jurisdiction, 13
Conscience shocking law enforcement behav-
    ior, 362, 365
Criminal procedure jurisdiction rules, 354
Customary international law
    Extraterritorial law enforcement activities,
        362
    Universality principle, 11
Enemy combatant detentions, 552
Extradition, traditional practices of, 354
Extraterritorial assertions by US
    Generally, 11
    Interstate or foreign commerce require-
        ments compared, 40
    Law enforcement activities, customary in-
        ternational law, 362
    Material support offenses, 80
Extraterritorial detention
    Generally, 554
    See also Guantanamo Detainees, this in-
        dex
    Afghan detentions, 577
Foreign Terrorist Organization listings, juris-
    dictional limitation on judicial review,
    122
Habeas Corpus, this index
Humanity, universal jurisdiction over crimes
    against, 15
International waters, arrests on, 355
Interstate or foreign commerce requirements,
    extraterritorial requirements compared,
    40
Judicial review
    Enemy combatant detentions, 552
    Foreign Terrorist Organizations listings, ju-
        risdictional limitation, 122
    Military Commissions Act of 2009, 718, 728
Ker-Frisbie doctrine, 367
Kidnapping, criminal jurisdiction obtained by
    Generally, 355, 356 et seq.
    Ker-Frisbie doctrine, 367
Military commissions and tribunals
    Field of command jurisdiction, 665
    Hamdan prosecution, 658 et seq.
    Statutory authority, 657
Montreal Convention, 12
Persons found in US, 10
Piracy, universal jurisdiction, 15
Protective or security principle of international
    law, 16
Rendition, this index
Terrorism definitions, jurisdictional implica-
    tions, 37, 40, 51
Torture Victim Protection Act, 371
Universal jurisdiction
    Antihijacking Act, 13
    Customary international law, 11
    Humanity, crimes against, 15
    Piracy, 15
    Torture, 313
    War crimes, 14
War crimes, 14

JUSTICE DEPARTMENT
Attorney General determinations, creating terrorism criminal elements, 35
Attorney General Guidelines, proactive surveillance activities, 129
Discretionary detention authority
    Immigration detentions, 428
Domestic Investigations and Operations Guidelines
    Generally, 130
    History of guidelines, 137
    Publication, 131
Foreign Intelligence Surveillance Act reports to Congress, 181
Geneva Convention applicability to enemy combatants, 599
Guidelines for Extraterritorial FBI Operations, 131
Immigration detentions, discretionary detention authority, 428
International terrorism prosecutions since 9/11, 53
Proactive surveillance activities, Attorney General Guidelines, 129
Terrorism, Attorney General determinations creating criminal elements, 35
Terrorism listings, 30
Terrorism Surveillance Program memorandum, 201
Terrorism Surveillance Program White Paper, 205

KIDNAPPING
Criminal jurisdiction obtained by
    Generally, 355, 356 et seq.
    Ker-Frisbie doctrine, 367

KILLING
See Targeted Killing, this index

KNOWLEDGE
Foreign terrorist organization status, knowledge of, 83
Material support offenses
    See also Material Support Offenses, this index
    Purpose and knowledge distinguished, 82

LAW OF WAR
Conspiracy, 668
Detention, 614
Lawful and unlawful combatants, 539, 551
Military Commissions Act of 2009 offenses, 723, 728
Prisoner of war status, 551
Privileged and unprivileged enemy beligerents, 694
Targeted killing, 736

LEVIN MEMORANDUM
Torture controversy, 315

LIBERTY/SECURITY CONFLICT
9/11 attack responses, 433
    See also Privacy Protections, this index

Civil Liberties Protections, this index
Classified Information Procedure Act
    Generally, 493
    Counsel, CIPA clearances, 522
Enemy combatant detentions, 549
First Amendment Protections, this index
Military Use in Domestic Law Enforcement, this index

LIBRARY PROVISION
Generally, 281
Actual exercises of provision, 286
Civil liberties issues, 278
Congressional reaction, 286
Criticism, 285
Definition of library, 279
National Security Letters compared, 287
Policy considerations, 287
Section 215 orders, 277

LINDH PROSECUTION
Civilian vs military trial controversy, 731
Section 2332b, 48

LOCAL POLICE ACTIVITIES
Proactive surveillance, Vietnam war era, 149

MANSFIELD AMENDMENT
Foreign searches, 269

MATERIAL SUPPORT OFFENSES
2339A
    Antiterrorism and Effective Death Penalty Act amendments, 95
    Knowledge-or-intent formulation, 77, 81
    Personal activities as statutory provision of personnel, 63
    Statutory text, 60
    Vagueness, 69 et seq.
Actus reus, 59
Adaptability, 59
Advocacy for prosecuted terrorist
    First Amendment issues, 68, 69
Afghanistan training activities, 2339B, 79
Aiding and abetting compared, 58
Antiterrorism and Effective Death Penalty Act amendments, 95
Attempt offenses compared, 58
2339B
    Afghanistan training activities, 79
    Expert advice or assistance, provision of, 87 et seq.
    Findings and purpose, 88
    First Amendment issues, 87 et seq.
    Personnel, provision of, 87 et seq.
    Service, provision of, 87 et seq.
    Specific intent, 83
    Specific intent, provision of, 87 et seq.
    Statutory text, 61
    Training, provision of, 87 et seq.
    Vagueness, 87 et seq.
Benign support, 97
Channeling support through third parties, 86
Complicity crimes compared, 58, 81

MATERIAL SUPPORT OFFENSES
—Cont'd
Conspiracy compared, 58
Criminal appeals challenging Foreign Terrorist
    Organizations listings, 120
2339D, 79
Definitions
    Generally, 61, 63
    Humanitarian Law Project decision, 88
Expert advice or assistance, provision of,
    2339B, 87 et seq.
Extraterritorial jurisdiction, 80
First Amendment issues
    Advocacy for prosecuted terrorist, 68, 69
    2339B, 87 et seq.
    Generally, 59
FTO designations
        Generally, 101 et seq.
        See also Foreign Terrorist Organiza-
            tions, this index
        Criminal appeals challenging Foreign Ter-
            rorist Organizations listings, 120
        Knowledge of status, 83
Funneling support through third parties, 86
    Generally, 57
Humanitarian Law Project decision, 87 et seq.
Inchoateness of, 57
Intelligence Reform and Terrorism Protection
    Act amendments, 62, 89
Interpretation, 62
Jurisdiction, 80
Knowledge element, 59, 83
Knowledge-or-intent formulation, 2339A vs
    2339B, 77, 81
Lawful activities of Foreign Terrorist Organi-
    zations, support of, 87, 98
Listed categories of material support, 59, 81
Mens rea, 59, 81
Military Commissions Act of 2006, 728
Military Commissions Act of 2009, 725
Overview, 60
Personal activities as statutory provision of
    personnel, 63
Personnel, provision of, 87 et seq.
Personnel, term defined, 63
Policy considerations, 58
Preparatory or precursor conduct, 57
Punishments, 58
Purpose and knowledge distinguished, 82
Service, provision of, 87 et seq.
Specific intent, 83, 87 et seq.
Third parties, support channeled through, 85
Training, provision of, 87 et seq.
Triggers, listed, 59, 81
Unique nature of, 2
Vagueness challenge to 2339A, 69 et seq.
Vagueness challenge to 2339B, 87 et seq.

MATERIAL WITNESS DETENTIONS
9/11 attack, practices following, 425
    See also Immigration Detentions, this index
Affidavit requirements, 401
Aliens, 429
Bail, 406, 411
Bivens claims, 416

MATERIAL WITNESS DETENTIONS
—Cont'd
Civil damages claims, 416
Civil rights conflicts, 422
Coercive use of process, 423
Contempt detentions of witnesses distin-
    guished, 400, 423
Criminal proceeding determinations, 406
Deposition alternative, 401, 410
Direct challenges, 403
Enemy combatant detentions compared, 528
Extended detention as terrorism countermeas-
    ure, 399
Freedom of Information Act use to determine
    reasons for detention, 401
Grand jury witnesses, 405, 414
Historical practice, 421
Judicial review
    Civil damages claims, 416
    Direct challenges, 403
Materiality showings, 402
Overview of anti-terrorism measures, 128
Policy considerations, 421
Post-9/11, 401
Pretextual arrests, 420
Preventive detention and, 420, 426
Preventive detention uses, 425
Probable cause standards, 422
Purpose, relevance to immunity issues, 418
Reports to court, 402, 410
Statutory authority, 401
Temporizing use of procedure, 415
Warrants
        Generally, 404
    Pretextual arrests, 420

MENS REA
Material support offenses, 59, 81
Terrorism definitions, 9

**MILITARY APPROACH TO ANTI–TER-
RORISM**
        Generally, 527 et seq.
Civilian approach compared, 2
Irregular rendition, 306
Proactive surveillance
    Civil suits challenging, 141
    Judicial review, 141
    Standing to challenge, 145
    Vietnam war era, 141

MILITARY COMMISSIONS ACT OF 2006
        Generally, 688
        See also Military Commissions and Tribu-
            nals, this index
Habeas corpus, 555, 688
Judicial review, 555, 688
Material support offenses, 728
Terrorism, term defined, 730

**MILITARY COMMISSIONS ACT OF 2009
(MCA)**
        Generally, 694 et seq.
        See also Military Commissions and Tribu-
            nals, this index
Burden of proof, 706, 707

References are to Pages

MILITARY COMMISSIONS ACT OF 2009 (MCA)—Cont'd

Civilian vs Military Trial Controversy, this index

Classified information procedures, 709

Classified Information Procedures Act applicability, 709

Closure of proceedings, 705

Composition of commissions, 696

Confessions, 699

Conspiracy, 725

Crimes triable, 720

Death penalty, 708

Defense counsel
    Generally, 698
    Duties, 703

Defenses, 706

Definitions, 694, 719

Disclosure of exculpatory evidence, 706

Discovery, 710

Duties of counsel, 703

Evidentiary rules, 689

Exclusionary rule, 699

Hearsay evidence, 702

History of post 9/11 military commissions trials, 726

Judicial review, 718, 728

Law of war offenses, 723, 728

Manual for Military Commissions, 688, 727

Material support offenses, 725

Obama administration policy, 689

Obama administration proposal of, 727

Pleas, 706

Presumption of innocence, 707

Pretrial conferences, 709

Pre-trial procedure, 699

Privileged and unprivileged enemy belligerents, 694

Privileges, 717

Protection of evidence sources, 713

Record of trial, 708

Right to counsel, 698, 703

Sentences, 707

Standard and scope of review, 718, 728

Substitutions for classified evidence, 711

Terrorism, term defined, 724

Trial counsel
    Generally, 697
    Duties, 703

Trial procedure, 700

Voting by commission members, 707

Witnesses, 705

MILITARY COMMISSIONS AND TRIBUNALS

    Generally, 641 et seq.
    See also Civilian vs Military Trial Controversy, this index; Military Commissions Act of 2006, this index; Military Commissions Act of 2009, this index

Articles of War, 641, 645

Authority to establish, 658 et seq.

Authorization to Use Military Force and, 652

Bill of Rights protections, applicability, 649

MILITARY COMMISSIONS AND TRIBUNALS—Cont'd

Combatant Status Review Tribunals, this index

Commander in Chief authority of President, 645, 652

Courts-martial, 646, 663

Detainee Treatment Act of 2005, 664

Enemy combatant detentions, military tribunal reviews of status, 547

Geneva Convention applicability, 659, 676

Habeas corpus judicial review, 641

Hamdan prosecution, 658 et seq.

Historical practices, 662

History of post 9/11 military commissions trials, 726

Judicial review
    Generally, 641
    Habeas corpus, 641
    Hamdan prosecution, 658 et seq.

Jurisdiction
    Field of command jurisdiction, 665
    Hamdan prosecution, 658 et seq.
    Statutory authority, 657

Manual for Military Commissions, 688, 727

Obama administration policy, 607 et seq., 689

Obama administration suspension, 4

Policy considerations, 658

Posse Comitatus Act, this index

Presidential Military Order, 653, 657

Separation of powers issues, 681

Statutory authority, 657

Uniform Code of Military Justice authority, 659, 669

World War II tribunals, 672

MILITARY USE IN DOMESTIC LAW ENFORCEMENT

    Generally, 745 et seq.
    See also Civilian vs Military Trial Controversy, this index

Defense Department actions, 753

Drug law enforcement, 749, 757, 765

Homeland Security Act, 747

Immediate response authority of military commanders, 760

Immigration law enforcement, 765

Martial law, definition of term, 759

Patriot USA Act, 747

Posse Comitatus Act, this index

Transportation for detained persons, 754

MIRANDA WARNINGS

Advice of Rights forms, 326

Arrest requirements, 342

Coerced confessions, admissibility, 343 et seq.

Exigent circumstances, 339

Foreign government interrogation practices, evidence admissibility issues, 344

Foreign interrogations, 306

Interrogation evidence admissibility issues, 326

Military Commissions Act of 2009 evidentiary rules, 690

Public safety exception, 306, 331, 339

MOBBS DECLARATION
Enemy combatant detentions, 542

MONTREAL CONVENTION
Jurisdiction, 12

MOUSSAOUI PROSECUTION
Civilian vs military trial controversy, 731
Section 2332b, 48

MUKASEY GUIDELINES
Proactive surveillance, 131, 135, 153

MUTUAL LEGAL ASSISTANCE TREA-TIES (MLAT)
Foreign searches, 269

NATIONAL DEFENSE APPROPRIA-TIONS BILL
Enemy combatant detention provisions, 615

NATIONAL DISASTERS
See Emergencies, this index

NATIONAL SECURITY
Liberty/Security Conflict, this index

NATIONAL SECURITY AGENCY (NSA)
Generally, 200 et seq.
See also Terrorism Surveillance Program, this index
Authorization for Use of Military Force and, 206
Data mining, 201
Electronic surveillance, 160
Judicial review of Terrorism Surveillance Program activities, 211
Library provision, Section 215 orders, 277
Post-Terrorism Surveillance Program legislation, 215 et seq.
Report on President's Surveillance Program, 203

NATIONAL SECURITY DIVISION
Terrorism prosecution statistics, 54

NATIONAL SECURITY LETTERS (NSL)
Generally, 246
See also Subpoenas, this index
Blanket NSLs, 302
Congressional report, 301
Corrective NSLs, 300
Exigent circumstances requests, 300
Exigent letters distinguished, 301
FBI issuance, 288
First Amendment challenges, 293
Journalists' records, 303
Judicial review, nondisclosure requirements, 288
Library provision compared, 287
Nondisclosure requirements, 288
Volume of requests, 300

9/11 ATTACKS
Alien interviews and detentions after, 427, 450
Assassination policy after, 735
Authorization for Use of Military Force enactment, 528, 537

9/11 ATTACKS—Cont'd
Criminal justice system in post-9/11 world, 3, 345
Liberty/security tensions following, 433
Material witness detentions following, 401, 425
Military commission use following, 726
Moussaoui prosecution, 493
PENTBOM investigation, 497
Targeted killing policy after, 735
Terrorism prosecutions after, 53

OBAMA ADMINISTRATION
Generally, 3
Army Field Manual adopted, 319
Army Field Manual use in interrogations, 392
Article III prosecutions of enemy combatants, 607
Black sites closing, 4
Bush administration policy compared
Generally, 4
See also Bush Administration, this index
Civilian vs military trial controversy, 53, 325
Enemy combatant detention policy
Generally, 4, 528, 535
Article III prosecutions of, 607
Guantanamo detainees policy
Generally, 5, 598, 607 et seq.
Closure of facility, 619
Immigration detention policy, 466
Interrogation policy, 4, 392
Irregular rendition policy, 322, 355
Military commission suspensions, 4
Military Commissions Act of 2009, 727
Military commissions and tribunals policy, 607 et seq., 689
Presidential authority policy, 5
State secrets privilege policies, 388
Torture controversy, 4, 312
War on terror terminology, 4
Waterboarding policy, 4

OKLAHOMA CITY BOMBING
Proactive surveillance responses, 138

OMNIBUS CRIME CONTROL AND SAFE STREETS ACT
FISA standards compared, 176
Terrorism Surveillance Program and, 211
Warrants, FISA authorization standards compared, 161

PATRIOT USA ACT
Certifications, immigration detentions, 457
Domestic terrorism, 31
Electronic Communications Privacy Act amended, 301
FISA amendments, 182, 188
Immigration detentions
Generally, 428, 448, 457 et seq.
Certifications, 457
Indefinite detention, 460
Library orders
See also Library Provision, this index
National security letters compared, 246
Military use in domestic law enforcement, 747
Proactive surveillance authority, 130

PATRIOT USA ACT—Cont'd
Removal of aliens, 457 et seq.
Terrorist Exclusion List, 30

PENTAGON ATTACK
See 9/11 Attacks, this index

PIRACY
Terrorism distinguished, 17
Universal jurisdiction, 15

POLICE ACTIVITIES
Proactive surveillance, civil suit challenges, 147

POLICY CONSIDERATIONS
9/11 attacks, targeted killing policy after, 735
Bivens actions, 380
Bush Administration, this index
Civilian vs military trial controversy, 344, 732
Defining terrorism, 27, 31
Enemy Combatant Detentions, this index
Guantanamo Detainees, this index
Immigration detentions, 466
Interrogation, 4, 392
Irregular rendition
 Generally, 381
  Amnesty International report, 393
  Obama administration policy, 322, 391
Library provision, 287
Material support offenses, 58
Material witness detentions, 421
Military Commissions Act of 2009, 689
Military commissions and tribunals, 607 et seq., 658
Obama Administration, this index
Posse Comitatus Act, 761
Targeted killing, 735
Torture controversy, 4, 316

POSSE COMITATUS ACT
Application, 749
Congressional intent, 748
Drug law enforcement, 749, 757, 765
Emergencies, exceptions in, 759, 761, 766
Enactment, 746
Exceptions, 761
Federal Emergency Management Agency and, 761
Homeland Security Act and, 758
Immediate response authority of military commanders, 760
Immigration law enforcement, 765
Indirect assistance activities permitted, 754
Interpretation, 749
Judicial review, 749
Martial law, definition of term, 759
National Guard activities, 756
Navy, applicability of Act to, 754
Policy considerations, 761
Renditions, 752
Scope of indirect assistance activities permitted, 754
Transportation for detained persons, 754

PRESIDENTIAL AUTHORITY
Anti-terrorism expansions, 1
Civilian and military exercises distinguished, 2
Commander-in-chief status as source
 Generally, 2
 See also Commander-in-Chief Authority, this index
Congressionally delegated, 535
Inherent
 Generally, 1
 Electronic surveillance, 194
 Enemy combatant detentions, 534
Military and civilian exercises distinguished, 2
National security as source of, 1
Obama administration policy, 5

PRESIDENT'S SURVEILLANCE PROGRAM (PSP)
 See also Terrorism Surveillance Program, this index
Public report of activities, 203

PREVENTIVE DETENTION
Immigration detentions used as, 428
Intelligence Reform and Terrorism Prevention Act, 400
Material witness detentions and, 420, 426
Statutory authorizations, 400

PRISONERS
Special Administrative Measures restraining communications, 68, 71

PRISONERS OF WAR
 Generally, 551
 See also Enemy Combatant Detentions, this index
Geneva Convention protections, 601
Unlawful belligerents distinguished, 648

PRIVACY PROTECTIONS
Classified Information Procedures Act counsel clearances, 521
Electronic Communications Privacy Act, Patriot Act amendments, 301
Epilogue, 771

PRIVILEGES
Law enforcement privilege, 158
Military Commissions Act of 2009, 717
State Secrets Privilege, this index

PROACTIVE SURVEILLANCE
 Generally, 127 et seq.
 See also Electronic Surveillance, this index
Ashcroft Guidelines, 136
Bivens claims, 127
Civil liberties tensions, 129, 139
Civil suit challenges
 Generally, 127
 FBI activities, 147
 Military activities, 141
 Police activities, 147
Definition, 129
Documentation requirements, 135

PROACTIVE SURVEILLANCE—Cont'd
Domestic Investigations and Operations Guidelines
    Generally, 130
  History of guidelines, 137
  Publication, 131
Executive Order 12333, 130
FBI
  Attorney General Guidelines, 129
  Civil suit challenges, 147
  General principles of operations, 151
  Martin Luther King investigation, 155
First Amendment protection conflicts, 129, 141, 144
Foreign-student monitoring program, 130
Guidelines for Extraterritorial FBI Operations, 131
History of domestic operations, 137
Homeland Security Act, 130
Immunity defenses to civil claims, 127
Internal Security Act of 1950, 138
Judicial review
    Generally, 127
  Military countermeasures, 141
Law enforcement privilege, 158
Local police activities, Vietnam war era, 149
Military activities
  Judicial review, 141
  Standing to challenge, 145
  Vietnam war era, 141
Mukasey Guidelines, 131, 135, 153
Obama and Bush administration policies compared, 128
Oklahoma City bombing responses, 138
Overview of anti-terrorism measures, 128
Patriot USA Act authority, 130
Police activities, civil suit challenges, 147
Probable cause issues, 129
Recordkeeping requirements, 135
Religious groups, 136
Standing to challenge military activities, 145
State secrets doctrine justifying activities, 127
Subversive activities era, 138
Threat assessments, 136
TIPS program, 130
Undercover agents use
    Generally, 129
  See also Undercover Activities, this index
Vietnam war era
  Local police activities, 149
  Military countermeasures, 141

PROBABLE CAUSE
Electronic surveillance determinations, 173
FISA standards
  Determinations, 173
  Findings, 195
  Requirements, 176
  Standards, 185
Material witness detention standards, 422, 425
Proactive surveillance, 129

PROSECUTIONS
9/11 attacks, terrorism prosecutions after, 53
  See also Civilian vs Military Trial Controversy, this index

PROSECUTIONS—Cont'd
Al-Marri, 639
Article III prosecutions of enemy combatants, 607
Bin Laden, 513
Discretion, prosecutorial and separation of powers delegations, 36
Hamdan, 658 et seq.
Lindh
  Civilian vs military trial controversy, 731
  Section 2332b, 48
Material support prosecutions
    Generally, 59
  See also Material Support Offenses, this index
Moussaoui
  Civilian vs military trial controversy, 731
  Section 2332b, 48
National Security Division statistics, 54
Obama administration policy, 607
Padilla, 622, 730

PROSECUTORIAL DISCRETION
Separation of powers delegations, 36

PROTECT AMERICA ACT
Terrorism Surveillance Program amendments, 203, 215

PUBLIC INTERNATIONAL LAW
State-sponsored terrorism, 15

PURPOSE
Material support offenses, purpose and knowledge distinguished, 82

RECORDINGS
Electronic Surveillance, this index

RELIGIOUS GROUPS
Proactive surveillance, 136

REMOVAL OF ALIENS
    Generally, 429 et seq.
  See also Immigration Detentions, this index
Patriot Act, 457 et seq.
Special removal court, 461, 466
Terrorist removal procedures, 461
Unremovable aliens, detention standards, 440, 447

RENDITION
  See Irregular Rendition, this index
Obama administration policy, 391
Overview of anti-terrorism measures, 128
Posse Comitatus Act challenges, 752

RICO
Anti-terrorist applications, 53

RIGHT TO COUNSEL
CIPA clearances of counsel in classified information cases
    Generally, 511 et seq.
  See also Classified Information Procedures Act, this index

RIGHT TO COUNSEL—Cont'd
Enemy combatant detentions
    Generally, 548
    Incommunicado detention, 552
Irregular rendition, 373
Material support offenses, advocacy-related, 69
Military Commissions Act of 2009, 698, 703

SEARCHES
    See also Surveillance, this index
Domestic searches
    Generally, 247 et seq.
    Additional grounds for issuing warrants, 258
    Electronic surveillance authorizations compared, 247
    Federal Rules of Criminal Procedure, 255
    Foreign Intelligence Surveillance Act warrants, 247
    Judicial review of authorizations, 250
    Presidential authorizations, 249
    Secrecy of warrant procedures, 247
Federal Rules of Criminal Procedure, 255
Foreign Intelligence Surveillance Act search warrants, 189
Foreign Intelligence Surveillance Act warrants, 247
Foreign searches
    Generally, 260 et seq.
    Fourth Amendment applicability, 260
    Joint ventures of US and foreign agents, 266, 269
    Mansfield Amendment, 269
    Mutual legal assistance treaties, 269
    Premises of US person searches by US agents, 270
    Totality of the circumstances standard, 274
    US person searches by non-US agents, 260
Fourth Amendment applicability, 260
Joint ventures of US and foreign agents, 266, 269
Judicial review, US person searches by non-US agents, 261
Library Provision, this index
Mansfield Amendment, 269
Military Commissions Act of 2009 evidentiary rules, 690
Mutual legal assistance treaties, 269
Overview of anti-terrorism measures, 128
Premises, foreign, of US person searches by US agents, 270
Presidential authorizations, 249
Records vs tangible things as subjects of, 285
Secrecy of warrant procedures, 247
Secret subpoenas, 285, 288
Tangible things vs records as subjects of, 285
Totality of the circumstances standard, 274
US person searches by non-US agents, 260
Warrants, subpoenas compared, 247

SEARCHES AND ADMINISTRATIVE SUBPOENAS
    Generally, 246 et seq.
Foreign Intelligence Surveillance Act, this index

SEARCHES AND ADMINISTRATIVE SUBPOENAS—Cont'd
Searches, this index
Subpoenas, this index
Warrants, this index

SECRECY
Classified Information Evidence, this index
Classified Information Procedures Act, this index

SECRETARY OF DEFENSE
See Defense Department, this index

SECTION 215 ORDERS
    See also National Security Letters, this index
Secrecy, 288

SENTENCES
Death Penalty, this index
Military Commissions Act of 2009, 707
Sentencing Guidelines, terrorism enhancements, 17, 20

SEPARATION OF POWERS
Anti-terrorism expansions, presidential authority, 1
Delegations, prosecutorial discretion, 36
Guantanamo detainee habeas corpus applications, 568
Judicial review, Article III standards, 123
Military commissions and tribunals, 681
Military Use in Domestic Law Enforcement, this index
Posse Comitatus Act, this index
Presidential authority, anti-terrorism expansions, 1
Prosecutorial discretion delegations, 36

SILENT WITNESS RULE
Classified Information Procedures Act, 484, 492

SOVEREIGN IMMUNITY
Bivens remedies, 376

SPECIAL ADMINISTRATIVE MEASURES (SAM)
Prisoners, restraints on communications of, 68, 71

SPECIAL TASK FORCE ON INTERROGATIONS AND TRANSFER POLICIES
Executive Order 13491, 322

STATE DEPARTMENT
Foreign Terrorist Organization designations, 102
Geneva Convention applicability to enemy combatants, 599
Judicial review of Foreign Terrorist Organization listings
    Generally, 107 et seq.
    Criminal appeals challenging designations, 120
    Jurisdictional limitation, 122

STATE DEPARTMENT—Cont'd
Notice requirements as to pending Foreign Terrorist Organization designations, 107, 116, 118
Rendition determinations, 391
Terrorism determinations
Generally, 24, 26
Listings, 27

STATE SECRETS PRIVILEGE
See also Classified Information Evidence, this index
Civil remedies of victims, 388
Disclosure risks inherent in litigation, 389
Fundamental principles litigation seeking to protect, 385
Holder Memorandum, 389
Irregular rendition litigation, 382
Judicial review, 388
Obama administration policies, 388

STATE–SPONSORED TERRORISM
Definition, 15

SUBPOENAS
Generally, 277, 277 et seq.
Administrative, 278
Authority
Administrative subpoenas in drug-related investigations, 284 et seq.
National Security Letters, 278
Civil liberties issues, Section 215 orders, 278
Drug-related investigation subpoenas, authority to issue, 284 et seq.
Exigent letters, National Security Letters distinguished, 301
Journalists' records, 303
Judicial review, National Security Letters, 280
Library provision
See also Library Provision, this index
Section 215 orders, 277, 278
National Security Letters
Authority, 278
Exigent letters distinguished, 301
FBI authority, 278
Judicial review, 280
Patriot Act library orders compared, 246
Overview of anti-terrorism measures, 128
Search warrants compared, 247
Secret subpoenas, 285, 288
Section 215 orders, 277
Sneak peeks, 303

SUBVERSIVE ACTIVITIES
Proactive surveillance policies during subversive activities era, 138

SURVEILLANCE
Domestic vs offshore activities, 128
Electronic Surveillance, this index
Exigent circumstances triggering special powers, 128

SURVEILLANCE—Cont'd
Foreign Intelligence Surveillance Act, this index
President's Surveillance Program, 203
Proactive Surveillance, this index
Terrorism Surveillance Program, this index

SUSPENSION CLAUSE
Habeas corpus rights, limitations on, 557

TARGETED KILLING
9/11 attacks, effect on US policy, 735
Generally, 734
Al-Aulagi killing, 744
Bin Laden execution, 734
CIA instructions, 736
Civil litigation involving, 739
Drone warfare, 734
Executive Order 11905, 735
Executive Order 12333, 735
Judicial review, 734, 739
Law of war, 736
Policy considerations, 735
Retaliatory actions, 735

TERRORISM SURVEILLANCE PROGRAM (TSP)
Generally, 200 et seq.
See also National Security Agency, this index
Authorization for Use of Military Force and, 206
Civil liberties issues, 207
Congressional hearings, 201
Data mining, 201
Domestic vs foreign intercepts, 202
Electronic surveillance, 128
FISA and
Generally, 207, 208
Amendments Act of 2008
Generally, 203, 215
Legislative history, 232
Court approvals, 202
Inspectors General, report of, 204
Judicial review, 202, 211, 214
Justice Department memorandum, 201
Justice Department White Paper, 205
Legality issues, 205
Omnibus Crime Control and Safe Streets Act and, 211
Post-TSP legislation, 215 et seq.
Presidential authorization, 161, 200
Presidential public statement, 201
Protect America Act amendments, 203, 215
Report on President's Surveillance Program, 203
Telephone company involvement
Generally, 201
Liability issues, 203
Termination of program, 214

TERRORIST EXCLUSION LIST (TEL)
Generally, 27

THREATS
Assessments, proactive surveillance, 136
Weapons of mass destruction, threats involving, 40

TIPS PROGRAM
Proactive surveillance, 130

TORTURE CONTROVERSY
    Generally, 307 et seq.
Abu Ghraib incident, 307, 315
Abuse of prisoners distinguished, 315
Army Field Manual standards
        Generally, 317
    See also Army Field Manual, this index
Bush administration policies, 309, 313
Bybee memorandum, 309, 312, 314
Civil remedies of victims
        Generally, 371 et seq.
    Nongovernmental parties, claims against, 385
    State secrets privilege, 388
Coerced statements
    Admissibility, 343 et seq.
    Evidentiary value, 595
Convention against Torture and Other Cruel, Inhuman and Degrading Treatment or Punishment, 307
Cruel, inhuman or degrading treatment distinguished, 313
Customary international law, 313
Definitions, 308
Enemy combatant detentions, torture claims, 596
Evidentiary value of coerced statements, 595
Foreign Affairs Reform and Restructuring Act rendition regulations, 379
Foreign government criminal charges against US agents, 392
Guantanamo, 314
Interrogation, 306
Irregular rendition leading to torture
        Generally, 374
    Holder Memorandum, 391
Levin Memorandum, 315
Military Commissions Act of 2009 evidentiary rules, 699
Nongovernmental parties, claims against, 385
Obama administration policies, 4, 312
Obama and Bush administration policies compared, 306
Policy considerations, 316
Special Task Force on Interrogations and Transfer Policies, 322
Torture Victim Protection Act civil remedies, 371
Universal criminal jurisdiction, 313
Warrant proposal, 316
Waterboarding, this index

TORTURE VICTIM PROTECTION ACT (TVPA)
Civil litigation, 371

UNDERCOVER ACTIVITIES
    See also Proactive Surveillance, this index
Ashcroft Guidelines, 136
Executive Order 12333, 130
Law enforcement privilege, 158
Mukasey Guidelines, 131, 135, 153
Proactive surveillance activities, 129

UNIFORM CODE OF MILITARY JUSTICE (UCMJ)
Evidentiary standards, 686
Military commissions and tribunals, 659, 669

UNIVERSAL JURISDICTION
See Jurisdiction, this index

UNLAWFUL ENEMY COMBATANT REVIEW BOARD (UECRB)
Enemy combatant detentions, 581

USA PATRIOT ACT
See Patriot USA Act, this index

VIETNAM WAR ERA
Local police activities, 149
Military surveillance, 141

WAR CRIMES
    See also Law of War, this index
Universal jurisdiction, 14

WAR ON TERRORISM
    See also 9/11 Attacks, this index
Epilogue, 773
Terminology, Obama administration policy, 4

WAR POWERS RESOLUTION
AUMF and, 529

WARRANTS
Additional grounds for issuing warrants, 258
Domestic searches, 247 et seq.
Duration of FISA warrants, 179
Electronic surveillance, 160
Federal Rules of Criminal Procedure, 255
FISA authorizations
        See also Foreign Intelligence Surveillance Act, this index
    Criminal investigation warrants compared, 246
    Duration of warrants, 179
    Omnibus Crime Control and Safe Streets Act standards compared, 161, 176
    Probable cause findings, 195
Material witness detentions
        Generally, 404
    Pretextual arrests, 420
Multiple purposes for issuance, 190
Omnibus Crime Control and Safe Streets Act, FISA standards compared, 161, 176
Probable Cause, this index
Secrecy of warrant procedures, 247
Terrorism vs criminal investigation standards, 160
Torture controversy, warrant proposal, 316

WATERBOARDING
Army Field Manual, 318
Obama administration policy, 4
Torture controversy, 312

WATSON DECLARATION
Classified information evidence, 430

WEAPONS OF MASS DESTRUCTION
Definition, 39
Terrorism definitions involving, 38
Threats involving, 40

WIRETAPS
Electronic Surveillance, this index

WITNESSES
Classified information evidence
    Enemy combatant witnesses, 493
    Silent witness rule, 484, 492
Contempt detentions, 400
Material Witness Detentions, this index

WORLD TRADE CENTER ATTACK
See 9/11 Attacks, this index

†